A POPULATION HISTORY OF NORTH AMERICA

Professors Haines and Steckel bring together leading scholars to present an expansive population history of North America from pre-Columbian times to the present. Covering the populations of Canada, the United States, Mexico, and the Caribbean, including two essays on the Amerindian population, this volume takes advantage of considerable recent progress in demographic history to offer timely, knowledgeable information in a nontechnical format. A statistical appendix summarizes basic demographic measures over time for the United States, Canada, and Mexico.

Michael R. Haines is the Banfi Vintners Distinguished Professor of Economics at Colgate University. He also works as a consultant to the National Institutes of Health and the World Bank. Professor Haines is the author of *Fertility and Occupation: Population Patterns in Industrialization, Economic-Demographic Interrelations in Developing Agricultural Regions: A Case Study of Prussian Upper Silesia, 1810–1914,* and *Fatal Years: Child Mortality in Late Nineteenth-Century America* (with Samuel H. Preston). His articles have appeared in the *Journal of Economic History, Demography, Population Studies, Research in Economic History,* and numerous other publications.

Richard H. Steckel is Professor of Economics and Anthropology at Ohio State University and a Research Associate at the National Bureau of Economic Research. Professor Steckel is the author of *The Economics of U.S. Slave and Southern White Fertility.* His articles have appeared in *Annals of Human Biology, Social Science History,* the *Journal of Family History,* and numerous other publications.

A POPULATION HISTORY OF
NORTH AMERICA

Edited by

MICHAEL R. HAINES

Colgate University

RICHARD H. STECKEL

Ohio State University

CAMBRIDGE
UNIVERSITY PRESS

PUBLISHED BY THE PRESS SYNDICATE OF THE UNIVERSITY OF CAMBRIDGE
The Pitt Building, Trumpington Street, Cambridge, United Kingdom

CAMBRIDGE UNIVERSITY PRESS
The Edinburgh Building, Cambridge CB2 2RU, UK   http://www.cup.cam.ac.uk
40 West 20th Street, New York, NY 10011-4211, USA   http://www.cup.org
10 Stamford Road, Oakleigh, Melbourne 3166, Australia
Ruiz de Alarcón 13, 28014 Madrid, Spain

First published 2000

Printed in the United States of America

Typeface Garamond 11/13 pt.   *System* QuarkXPress [BTS]

A catalog record for this book is available from the British Library.

Library of Congress Cataloging in Publication Data
Haines, Michael R.
A population history of North America / Michael R. Haines, Richard
H. Steckel.
p.   cm.
Includes index.
ISBN 0-521-49666-7 (hb)
1. North America – Population – History.   I. Steckel, Richard H.
(Richard Hall), 1944– .   II. Title.
HB3503. A3H35   2000
304.6'097 – dc21   99–23284
CIP

ISBN 0 521 49666 7 hardback

CONTENTS

List of Illustrations   *page* vii
List of Tables   x
List of Contributors   xvii
Acknowledgments   xix
Maps of North America   xxi

1 Introduction   1
   MICHAEL R. HAINES AND RICHARD H. STECKEL

2 Population History of Native North Americans   9
   RUSSELL THORNTON

3 Patterns of Disease in Early North American
   Populations   51
   DOUGLAS H. UBELAKER

4 The Population of the St. Lawrence Valley, 1608–1760   99
   HUBERT CHARBONNEAU, BERTRAND DESJARDINS,
   JACQUES LÉGARÉ, AND HUBERT DENIS

5 The White Population of the Colonial United States,
   1607–1790   143
   HENRY A. GEMERY

6 The African American Population of the
   Colonial United States   191
   LORENA S. WALSH

7 The Peopling of Mexico from Origins to Revolution   241
   ROBERT MCCAA

8   The White Population of the United States, 1790–1920   305
    MICHAEL R. HAINES
9   The Population of Canada in the Nineteenth Century   371
    MARVIN MCINNIS
10 The African American Population of the United States,
    1790–1920   433
    RICHARD H. STECKEL
11 A Population History of the Caribbean   483
    STANLEY L. ENGERMAN
12 Canada's Population in the Twentieth Century   529
    MARVIN MCINNIS
13 Mexico's Demographic Transformation: From 1920 to 1990   601
    ZADIA M. FELICIANO
14 Growth and Composition of the American Population
    in the Twentieth Century   631
    RICHARD A. EASTERLIN
15 Concluding Remarks   677
    MICHAEL R. HAINES AND RICHARD H. STECKEL

    Appendix   685
        Measurement and Estimation   685
        Basic Data   693
    Index   705

ILLUSTRATIONS

MAPS

	Canada	*page* xxi
	Mexico	xxii
	United States of America	xxiii
2.1	Native Americans at time of European contact	10
2.2	Major trade routes	16
2.3	Contemporary federal and state reservations	36
7.1	Physiographic map of ancient Mexico identifying places mentioned in text	243
7.2	States and territories of Mexico, showing population, in-migrants, and out-migrants, 1900	282
11.1	The Caribbean region	484

FIGURES

4.1	Crude birth, death, and marriage rates and population estimates, 1630–1800	105
4.2	Observed and pioneer immigration according to period of arrival, 1608–1759	107
4.3	Seasonality of first marriages according to period of marriage	112
4.4	Age at first marriage of Canadian-born spouses according to sex and period of marriage, 1660–1755	114

4.5 Proportion of individuals who remarried according to period of first marriage and age at widowhood — 115

4.6 Seasonality of conceptions according to birth order — 118

4.7 Age-specific fertility rates (at all ages at marriage) for selected categories of women — 119

4.8 Distribution of families according to size and type, five parishes of New France, 1640–1762 — 120

4.9 Age-specific fertility rates (at all ages at marriage) according to social class — 122

4.10 Ratio of five-year death probabilities of males and females according to age — 125

4.11 Seasonality of deaths according to age at death — 127

4.12 Variation in time of the contribution of the pioneers to the genetic endowment of the French-speaking population of Quebec, 1680–1930 — 129

4.13 Distribution of pioneers according to the total number of descendants present on January 1, 1730 — 130

7.1 Population of the Basin of Mexico across the millennia — 245

7.2 Aguirre-Beltrán's ethno-races of New Spain — 263

7.3 Region and race in a long century of epidemics — 267

7.4 The decorated hemline of this 13-year-old girl shows that she is becoming a "grown maiden of marriageable age" — 272

7.5 Population of Mexico, 1790–1910 — 280

7.6 Speakers of native languages, Mexico, 1900 — 286

7.7 Disasters checked population growth of Mexico City — 287

8.1 Immigrants to the United States, 1820–1920 — 345

9.1 Immigration to British North America, 1829–1860 — 385

9.2 Indices of fertility, Canada and Europe, ca. 1861 — 392

9.3 Indices of fertility, Canada and Europe, ca. 1891 — 410

9.4 Immigration to Canada, overseas arrivals less departures to the United States, 1861–1900 — 423

11.1 Caribbean populations, 1700–1900: Total and slave — 500

11.2 Caribbean populations, 1900–1990 — 514

12.1 Immigration to Canada and emigration to the United States, 1900–1931 — 534

12.2 Age-specific fertility rates, Canada, 1931 and 1941 — 565

12.3 Total fertility rates, Canada and the United States, 1936–1981   572

12.4 Actual and trend total fertility rates, Canada, 1901–1981   574

12.5 Age-specific birth rates, Canada, 1936–1981   579

12.6 Total period and cohort fertility rates, Canada, 1936–1981   581

12.7 Immigration to Canada, 1945–1981   583

13.1 Crude mortality rate in Mexico, 1900–1990   605

13.2 Infant mortality rate in Mexico, 1901–1990   606

13.3 Crude birth rate in Mexico, 1900–1990   609

13.4 Crude birth and mortality rates in Mexico, 1900–1990   612

13.5 Morality rate by region, 1930–1990   618

13.6 General fertility rate by region, 1930–1990   620

13.7 Percentage of the population that speaks an Indian language, 1930 and 1990   622

TABLES

2.1 Twentieth-century estimates of the aboriginal
population of North American Indians   *page* 13

2.2 Age-specific case-fatality rates of smallpox
(*Variola major*) in unvaccinated populations   20

2.3 North American aboriginal population estimates and
yearly rates of decline   22

2.4 American Indian population in the United States
(minus Alaska and Hawaii), 1800–1890   24

2.5 Decline of the aboriginal American Indian population
of California, to 1900   25

2.6 California indentured Indians   29

2.7 Recovery of the Native American population of the
United States, 1900–1990   32

2.8 Blood quantum requirement of American Indian tribes
by reservation basis and size   34

2.9 Percentage urban of American Indian population of the
United States, 1900–1990   38

2.10 Recovery of the American Indian population of
California, 1900–1990   39

3.1 Estimates of North American population size prior to
European contact   53

3.2 Parasites identified from North American
archaeological contexts   74

4.1 Immigrants who experienced a family life in Quebec
according to country of origin and period of arrival,
1608–1765   108

4.2   Immigrants according to category and period of arrival,
1608–1759   110

4.3   Summary of nuptiality   116

4.4   Summary of fertility   123

4.5   Summary of mortality   126

5.1   White population in the mainland British colonies and
early Republic, 1610–1790   150

5.2   Mean age at first marriage, family size, and fertility,
1652–1799   153

5.3   Age structure of the white population of New York,
1703–1790   155

5.4   Comparison of white crude birth rate estimates,
1760–1810   157

5.5   Comparative crude death rates for Andover,
Boston, and Philadelphia, 1720–1724 to
1770–1774   159

5.6   Life expectancy and inferred crude death rates for
American mainland populations, seventeenth and
eighteenth centuries   163

5.7   Alternative rates of natural increase and implicit crude
birth and death rates   167

5.8   Inferred migration given assumed rates of natural
increase and seasoning and passage mortality for
regions, 1610–1620 to 1780–1790   171

5.9   Colony persistence and out-migration, American
Revolution: Proportion of recruits born in colony by
place of residence at enlistment   174

5.10   Probable components of white population growth in
the mainland British colonies and the early Republic,
1610–1790   178

6.1   Percentage of African Americans in the total population
of the British colonies, 1660–1790   193

6.2   Age at first conception of native-born southern slave
women in the eighteenth century   203

6.3   The U.S. African American population in 1790   220

7.1   Mean age at death, selected ages: Mesoamerican
precontact populations and others at various
economic-technological levels   249

7.2 Demographic disaster in Mexico, 1519–1595:
Authoritative estimates of total population and
implied rates of decrease   253

7.3 Life expectancy at age 15 in colonial Mexico   275

7.4 Two series of population estimates: Mexico, 1790–1910   279

7.5 Life expectancy in Mexico (both sexes combined),
1800–1950   285

8.1 Population by race, residence, nativity, age, and sex,
United States, 1800–1990   306

8.2 Fertility and mortality, white population,
United States, 1800–1990   308

8.3 Components of population growth, United States,
1790–1990   315

8.4 White population by region, United States,
1790–1920   318

8.5 Recorded immigration to the United States by origin,
1819–1920   346

9.1 Population of Canada and its regions, 1761–1901,
European population only   373

9.2 Emigration from the United Kingdom to Canada and
immigration to Canada, 1815–1860   380

9.3 A conjectural accounting of Canada's population
change, 1821–1861   387

9.4 Indexes of fertility, British North America, 1861   394

9.5 Infant mortality in Canadian cities, provinces, and
counties, 1891   403

9.6 Fertility and change in fertility, Canadian cities and
provinces, 1861–1891   407

9.7 Fertility and change in fertility, selected counties of
Quebec and Ontario, 1861–1891   408

9.8 Accounting for Canadian population change,
intercensal decades, 1861–1891   422

10.1 Growth of the black population in the United States,
1790–1920   435

10.2 Slave population by state, 1790–1860   438

10.3 Child/woman ratios for slaves and whites, 1820–1860   442

10.4 Demographic characteristics by plantation size   444

10.5 Free black population by state, 1790–1860   454

10.6 Child/woman ratios: Free blacks by region, 1820–1860   457

10.7	Black population by state and percentage urban, 1870–1920	462
10.8	Percentage black population by state, 1870–1920	465
10.9	Child/woman ratios: Blacks by region, 1870–1920	467
11.1	Estimated net slave imports by Caribbean areas of settlement, 1500–1800	489
11.2	Estimated migration of Europeans to the Caribbean, by European nation of origin, 1500–1800	491
11.3	Caribbean populations, 1750	494
11.4	Caribbean populations, 1830	496
11.5	Caribbean populations, 1880	498
11.6	Shares of Caribbean populations, by European settling area, 1750, 1880, 1990	501
11.7	Estimates of flows of contract labor to the Caribbean and return flow, nineteenth and twentieth centuries	502
11.8	Slave birth rates and death rates by British West Indian colony, ca. 1820s	506
11.9	Estimates of crude birth and death rates in Trinidad, Jamaica, and the United States	508
11.10	Total fertility rates of slaves in the United States (ca. 1830) and in Trinidad (ca. 1813), with an explanation for the difference in these rates	509
11.11	Caribbean populations, 1900, 1950, 1990	512
11.12	Crude birth and death rates, Caribbean, 1900, 1950, 1990	513
11.13	Five largest areas based on population, Caribbean, selected years	515
11.14	Caribbean immigrants (legal) into United States by country of birth, 1951–1990	517
12.1	Canada's population at census dates and intercensal growth rate	530
12.2	Immigrant population at census dates by period of arrival, Canada and regions, 1911–1931	538
12.3	Total and immigrant populations of larger Canadian cities, 1921	541
12.4	Foreign-born workers in major occupations, Canada, 1921	542
12.5	Canadian immigrant population by country of birth and period of arrival	544

12.6   Canada's immigrants by region of residence and area of
       origin, 1900–1921   545
12.7   Estimated fertility rates, Canada, 1891–1931   547
12.8   Indexes of fertility and nuptiality, Canadian cities and
       provinces, 1891, 1921, 1931   549
12.9   Average number of children ever born to
       Canadian-born 45- to 54-year-old women   554
12.10 Components of Canada's population growth,
       intercensal decades, 1901–1931   556
12.11 Comparative cause-specific death rates, Canada,
       1901–1981   570
12.12 Variations in 1941–1961 change in gross reproduction
       rates by geographic districts   576
12.13 Summary of 1981 immigrant population by period of
       arrival   585
12.14 Migrant population of selected metropolitan areas as a
       percentage of total population, 1976–1981 migrants
       and total post-1945 immigrants   592
12.15 Components of decadal population change, Canada,
       1951–1981   595
12A.1 Principal indicators of Canada's demographic record   596
12A.2 Urban and metropolitan Canada   597
12A.3 Canadian fertility rates and related measures, 1946–1981   598
13.1   Basic demographic indicators for Mexico, 1900–1990   604
13.2   Life expectancy, 1900–1990   607
13.3   Percentage of deaths by cause, 1930–1990   608
13.4   Fertility statistics, 1900–1990   611
13.5   Demographic balancing equation, 1900–1990   612
13.6   Socioeconomic indicators, 1900–1990   613
13.7   Regression of crude death rate on socioeconomic
       conditions   615
13.8   Mortality and fertility by region, 1930–1990   618
13.9   Regressions of mortality rate and general fertility rate
       on socioeconomic conditions   619
13.10 Urbanization and the growth of Mexico City,
       1890–1990   624
13.11 Emigration from Mexico to the United States,
       1890–1990   626

14.1 Race-nativity distribution of U.S. population, 1900 and 1950 — 633

14.2 Occupational distribution of native white stock, foreign white stock, and nonwhites, 1910 — 634

14.3 Urban-rural distribution of native white stock, foreign white stock, and nonwhites, 1910 — 635

14.4 Occupational distribution of females and males, 1900 and 1950 — 638

14.5 Occupational distribution of whites and blacks, 1950 — 644

14.6 Race-ethnicity distribution of U.S. population, 1970 and 1990 — 663

14.7 Occupational distribution of race-ethnicity groups by sex, 1990 — 664

A.1 Estimated population of North America, 1650–1990 — 694

A.2 Fertility and mortality in North America, 1800–1991 — 696

A.3 Components of population growth, United States (1800–1990), Canada (1851–1991), and Mexico (1900–1990) — 700

A.4 Population by race, residence, nativity, age, and sex, United States (1800–1990), Canada (1851–1991), and Mexico (1900–1990) — 702

CONTRIBUTORS

Hubert Charbonneau
Departement de demographie
Université de Montréal
C.P. 6128 Succ. A
Montreal, Quebec H3J 3J7
Canada

Bertrand Desjardins
Departement de demographie
Université de Montréal
C.P. 6128 Succ. A
Montreal, Quebec H3J 3J7
Canada

Hubert Denis
Departement de demographie
Université de Montréal
C.P. 6128 Succ. A.
Montreal, Quebec H3J 3J7
Canada

Richard A. Easterlin
Department of Economics
University of Southern California
Los Angeles, CA 90089-0152

Stanley L. Engerman
Department of Economics
University of Rochester
Rochester, NY 14627

Zadia M. Feliciano
Department of Economics
Queen's College
65-30 Kissena Blvd.
Flushing, NY 11367-1597

Henry A. Gemery
Department of Economics
Colby College
Waterville, ME 04901

Michael R. Haines
Department of Economics
Colgate University
Hamilton, NY 13346

Jacques Légaré
Departement de demographie
Université de Montréal
C.P. 6128 Succ. A
Montreal, Quebec H3J 3J7
Canada

Robert McCaa
Department of History
Social Sciences 614
University of Minnesota
Minneapolis, MN 55455

Marvin McInnis
Department of Economics
Queen's University
Kingston, Ontario K7L 3N6
Canada

Richard H. Steckel
Department of Economics
Ohio State University
Columbus, OH 43210-1367

Russell Thornton
Department of Anthropology
University of California, Los Angeles
Los Angeles, CA 90024

Douglas H. Ubelaker
Department of Anthropology
Smithsonian Institution
Museum of Natural History
Washington, DC 20560

Lorena S. Walsh
40 Holly Rd.
Severna Park, MD 21146

ACKNOWLEDGMENTS

The authors appreciate the considerable help we received from the staff at Cambridge University Press. Our editor, Frank Smith, nurtured the project from its inception several years ago, and Cathy Felgar, Janis Bolster, Vicky Macintyre, and Glorieux Dougherty followed with numerous valuable contributions on organization, content, and indexing. One of our students, William White, provided excellent research and editorial assistance. We also thank Colgate University and Ohio State University for financial support.

Canada (*Source*: Graphic image created using ArcView® GIS software. Source data: ESRI.)

Mexico. Key to state codes:

Code	State	Code	State
AGU	Aguascalientes	MOR	Morelos
BCN	Baja California Norte	NAY	Nayarit
BCS	Baja California Sur	NL	Nuevo Leon
CAM	Campeche	OAX	Oaxaca
CHIA	Chiapas	PUE	Puebla
CHIH	Chihuahua	QR	Quintana Roo
COA	Coahuila	QUE	Queretaro
COL	Colima	SIN	Sinaloa
DF	Distrito Federal	SLP	San Luis Potosi
DUR	Durango	SON	Sonora
GUA	Guanajuato	TAB	Tabasco
GUE	Guerrero	TAM	Tamaulipas
HID	Hidalgo	TLA	Tlaxcala
JAL	Jalisco	VER	Vera Cruz
MEX	Mexico (State)	YUC	Yucatan
MICH	Michoacan	ZAC	Zacatecas

(*Source*: Graphic image created using ArcView® GIS software. Source data: ESRI.)

United States of America. Key to state codes:

Code	State	Code	State
AL	Alabama	MT	Montana
AK	Alaska	NE	Nebraska
AZ	Arizona	NV	Nevada
AR	Arkansas	NH	New Hampshire
CA	California	NJ	New Jersey
CO	Colorado	NM	New Mexico
CT	Connecticut	NY	New York
DE	Delaware	NC	North Carolina
DC	District of Columbia	ND	North Dakota
FL	Florida	OH	Ohio
GA	Georgia	OK	Oklahoma
HI	Hawaii	OR	Oregon
ID	Idaho	PA	Pennsylvania
IL	Illinois	RI	Rhode Island
IN	Indiana	SC	South Carolina
IA	Iowa	SD	South Dakota
KS	Kansas	TN	Tennessee
KY	Kentucky	TX	Texas
LA	Louisiana	UT	Utah
ME	Maine	VT	Vermont
MD	Maryland	VA	Virginia
MA	Massachusetts	WA	Washington
MI	Michigan	WV	West Virginia
MN	Minnesota	WI	Wisconsin
MS	Mississippi	WY	Wyoming
MO	Missouri		

(*Source*: Graphic image created using ArcView® GIS software. Source data: ESRI.)

*To Richard Easterlin and
Robert Fogel, our graduate school
mentors in population history*

1

INTRODUCTION

MICHAEL R. HAINES AND RICHARD H. STECKEL

The population of North America has undergone enormous changes in size, geographic distribution, and ethnic composition over the past several centuries. It has grown from a few million, largely rural inhabitants on the eve of Columbus's arrival to approximately 420 million, substantially urban residents at the end of the twentieth century.[1] Once composed entirely of Native Americans, the population now includes most ethnic groups from around the globe.

These changes were instigated by substantial immigration from Europe, Africa, and Asia, and by significant shifts in fertility and mortality. Whereas families of 6 to 10 children were common in the eighteenth century, the average today in most countries of North America is two to three births per woman. Life expectancy at birth now exceeds 70 years in all but the very poorest regions, an increase of roughly 100% over the past 150 years.

Population growth and redistribution have had numerous implications for economic, political, and social history. For example, the aboriginal population was decimated by disease and warfare following the arrival of Europeans and their colonial empires in the sixteenth and seventeenth centuries. Conflict within the United States and between the United States and other countries accompanied westward expansion in the nineteenth century. And women took on new roles inside and outside the home during the transition from a high-fertility rural way of life in the nineteenth century to low-fertility urban living in the twentieth century.

---

[1] For the purposes of this discussion, North America includes the United States, Canada, Mexico, and the Caribbean.

The story of population change in the United States was surveyed two decades ago by Richard Easterlin, in a single article, but since then research on the United States, and on North America more broadly, has mushroomed.[2] Bolstered by the declining costs of collecting evidence, particularly at the individual or household level, and by newly mined data sources and new demographic techniques, the current state of information in the field could hardly be summarized in a single chapter. Important research has been published not only by economists, demographers, and historians, but also by anthropologists, geographers, and political scientists. Hence, there is broad interest in the history of population, and the proliferation of literature has challenged specialists in the area of historical demography, not to mention those in related fields, to remain informed. This geographic expansion and the current impetus for North American economic cooperation suggest that a survey volume on North America would be useful and timely.

Census manuscript schedules of population illustrate the growth in data availability. In recent years, the costs of collection have declined to the point where massive samples can now be processed and analyzed. Large public-use samples and numerous specialty samples from this source have been studied in recent years for insights into fertility and migration. Similarly, population or parish records in Quebec and Mexico have yielded a wealth of information. Heights, which give considerable information on health and nutrition, have emerged as a valuable data source since the mid-1970s, and bioarcheological evidence, important for the era before written records are available, has also accumulated. In addition, economic historians have examined genealogical records to shed light on trends in fertility, mortality, and migration.

Several new techniques have emerged to enrich the analysis of existing or new data. Own-children methods, for example, are being used to assign children to mothers from sources such as the manuscript schedules of population. The results make it possible to construct fertility measures for various subgroups of the population on the basis of nativity, occupation, literacy, geographic location, or wealth. Data on children ever born and children surviving can be used to estimate childhood mortality with the aid of systems of model life tables. These systems use the proportion of children who are dead for various groups of women, whose experience is

[2] Richard Easterlin, "Population Issues in American Economic History: A Survey and Critique," in *Recent Developments in the Study of Business and Economic History: Essays in Honor of Herman E. Kroos* (Greenwich, Conn.: JAI Press, 1977).

adjusted for fertility patterns, to estimate model life tables. New computer resources have made it possible to match various data sources, such as households in different census years or census manuscript schedules and immigrant lists, to study geographic mobility.

This volume brings together 13 essays by population specialists summarizing the state of knowledge in this rapidly expanding field. The appendix presents basic data series that are helpful in making comparisons. Each essay discusses a basic set of topics including materials and sources; methods of analysis; trends and patterns of fertility, mortality, and internal and international migration; possible explanations of trends and patterns; implications; and research opportunities. The balance of these topics may vary from essay to essay, depending on the availability of data and research output. Each chapter includes a brief bibliographical essay.

The volume is organized in loose chronological order, beginning with Native American populations. Chapter 2 by Russell Thornton draws on archeological evidence to discuss pre-Columbian patterns of health, life expectancy, and population growth. Thornton evaluates the considerable research devoted to questions of aboriginal population size and distribution. He also examines the effects of European expansion into North America on population size and the consequent adaptations to depopulation such as migration and attempted revitalizations. Removals and relocations, the development of the reservation system, and allotments are his major focus for the nineteenth century. The twentieth-century portion of the essay considers patterns of recovery and change, intermarrriage, changing definitions and self-identifications, tribal membership requirements, and urbanization. The concluding section discusses population projections, fullblood/mixed-blood differences, and the possible decline of tribalism.

In Chapter 3, Douglas Ubelaker examines disease in pre-Columbian America. He notes the antiquity of specific disorders, temporal changes in the pattern of disease, and geographic variability in this pattern throughout the Americas. He also discusses factors contributing to disease, including population size, settlement pattern, diet, and cultural variables. The author looks at temporal changes in the pattern of disease not only in the pre-Columbian period but also in the early historic period. He surveys the general impact of European-introduced diseases and their relationship to preexisting disease conditions. Since the impact of disease on specific historic populations or on population numbers is covered in other essays,

Ubelaker concentrates on the relationship between disease, environment, and culture in early North American populations.

Hubert Charbonneau, Bertrand Desjardins, Jacques Légaré, and Hubert Denis begin Chapter 4 by reminding us that conditions are excellent for the study of the historical population of Quebec: substantially complete records exist from the outset of European settlement, immigration was fairly low (preventing the population from growing to incommensurable numbers quickly), and emigration did not become significant before the nineteenth century. Researchers at the University of Montreal have created a computerized data file covering demographic events of the entire population of European descent who lived in the present territory of the Province of Quebec. The authors' analysis of these data includes new estimates of population growth, taking into account the elusive male immigrants who remained single (an important segment of the population in the earlier period). They discuss measures of fertility, nuptiality, and mortality, as well as internal migration. They compare the first wave of French settlers and their descendants, making special note of settlement patterns and the importance of fur trading to demographic behavior.

In Chapter 5, Henry Gemery examines white population change in the pre-census period of the colonial United States. In the absence of any systematic and regularized census data, population totals as well as mortality, fertility, and migration figures must be estimated from militia, tax, and emigration records and from individual colonial censuses that appeared sporadically. Beginning with a survey of these sources and the feasibility of deriving a demographic record from them, Gemery outlines the problems in analyzing trends and patterns from imperfect and fragmentary data and reviews what is known of patterns and trends based on the research undertaken to date regarding total population change; trends in sex ratios, fertility, and mortality; and patterns of immigration and internal migration. He then turns to the causal mechanisms at work in defining the observed demographic patterns and proposes directions for further research.

Colonial African American demography is the subject of Chapter 6, by Lorena Walsh, who observes that the literature in this area relies to a great degree on inference and ingenuity owing to the lack of evidence. Nevertheless, a relatively consistent overview of basic demographic patterns among early African Americans is beginning to emerge. Until roughly the mid–eighteenth century the majority of the colonial black population was both immigrant and enslaved. Walsh reviews Philip Curtin's migration estimates and subsequent refinements and additions to those estimates. Next she examines the geographic distribution over time of the African and African American populations in the continental United States. Estimates of fertility and mortality are generally derived from analyses of sex ratios, child/woman ratios, and age structures of groups of slaves in various geographic subregions. Population densities, size and sex distribution of slaveholdings, and immigrant/Creole differences are employed to explain differing patterns. Most disputes, Walsh notes, revolve around the nature and severity of constraints on reproductive unions in the context of particular population densities and the distribution of slaves among holdings of various sizes. Other topics covered include the influence of African social behaviors retained in the New World, the likely effects of cultural alienation on fertility and morbidity, and differing experiences of immigrant and Creole slaves (paralleling the white population with a time lag). Walsh also considers similarities and differences in basic demographic rates between slaves and free blacks; urban/rural differentials; the influence of climate, staple crop regimes, and differing labor systems on demographic behavior; distinctive seasonal patterns of births and deaths among blacks and the differing susceptibility or resistance of blacks to particular New World disease environments; and sex-related mortality differentials.

Robert McCaa begins his discussion of Mexico in Chapter 7 with the peopling of ancient Mesoamerica. The greatest demographic success was attained in the Central Mexican Basin, where the population probably exceeded one million as long as two millennia ago. Despite the success suggested by the numbers alone, the population experienced very high mortality rates and suffered from numerous degenerative diseases. McCaa then discusses colonial Mexico and what is known about population size at the time of the European invasion in 1519. He considers the size of the ensuing demographic disaster, its principal causes, and the effects of the Spanish conquest and colonization. The nineteenth century was disappointing for many Mexicans, in part because numerous wars and conflicts followed independence in 1821. Population growth slowed in the mid-1800s but rebounded to an annual rate of 1.5% in the last quarter of the century.

Michael Haines organizes his essay on the white population of the United States in Chapter 8 around the topics of data sources, techniques of population analysis, and results on fertility, mortality, migration, and emigration. The federal censuses beginning in 1790 were the major sources for the study of population growth, structure, redistribution, and fertility prior to the twentieth century. Unfortunately, the system of vital registration (conducted by states) was not well under way until the turn of the twentieth century, but official emigration statistics were maintained from 1819 on. The United States clearly ranked high among nations in total population growth. Haines discusses various estimation techniques and results for crude birth and death rates, child-woman ratios, total fertility, rates of total and natural increase, and rates of net migration. Possible explanations for the fertility transition, which began in the early nineteenth century, and cycles in health as depicted by life expectancy and stature occupy the central portion of the essay. The influence of geographic patterns, such as rural-urban areas, on demographic behavior are carefully articulated. Theories of migration are brought to bear on the westward movement, urbanization, and international migration flows.

Chapter 9 by Marvin McInnis is about nineteenth-century Canada. The author concentrates on the second half of the period, when data resources were fairly abundant. McInnis sketches early immigration and settlement, providing population totals for several years prior to the comprehensive census of 1851. He shows that declines in marital fertility must have begun earlier in some districts of Canada. Birth rates were already lower in cities and towns than in rural areas, and the characteristic North American pattern of a relationship between fertility rates and duration of settlement was already evident in Ontario and the anglophone districts of Quebec. Francophone fertility rates were almost uniformly high – close to Hutterite levels. The remainder of the chapter focuses on two topics: (a) the early stages of the fertility transition and the extent of reduction achieved by the end of the century, and (b) Canada's transition to a country of emigration. Although little information is available on change in mortality, McInnis attempts to establish the likely level of mortality rates; he finds little evidence of significant change before the very end of the century.

Richard Steckel's essay on the African American population in Chapter 10 covers slavery, the experience of free blacks up to 1860, and the postemancipation black population. The federal population census furnishes much of the evidence for Steckel's study, but important sources such as plantation records, slave manifests (which contain stature), and probate records are important sources on the demographic behavior of slaves. Central questions addressed for slaves include the decision-making environment for fertility and mortality (the relationship between planters and slaves); the decline of birth rates before 1860; and the unusual age pattern of slave health (children were remarkably unhealthy, but adults were in reasonably good health). Since relatively little research has been done on the demographic behavior of free blacks before 1860, the author assembles evidence readily at hand to describe and analyze fertility, mortality, migration, and emancipations. Demographic behavior after the Civil War is compared with that under slavery, and overall patterns are discussed in relation to those of whites. The essay concludes by discussing the dimensions and determinants of population redistribution from the South to northern cities that began in the early part of the twentieth century.

In Chapter 11 Stanley Engerman documents several phases of demographic change in the Caribbean. Although techniques, data sources, and results vary, scholars estimate that the population of Amerindians, which includes the Ciboney, the Arawak, and the Carib, may have been 750,000 when Columbus arrived in the late 1400s. During the years of colonization and slavery, immigration was high and the West Indies became predominantly black. After slavery was abolished in the 1800s, immigrant contract workers replaced forced labor. During the twentieth century, the Caribbean, much like the rest of the developing world, experienced a demographic transition characterized by mortality decline followed by falling fertility. After World War II, these was substantial outmigration to North America and Western Europe.

Marvin McInnis divides his discussion of Canada's population in the twentieth century in Chapter 12 into two main parts beginning with the period up to 1931, which marks the completion of the fertility transition and resumption of large-scale immigration into the country. The settlement of the Canadian West and the great urban growth in eastern Canada that accompanied it involved very large inflows of immigrants. The composition of immigration also changed, with the United States and Central and Eastern Europe emerging as large sources of inflow. Interestingly, Canada also sent large numbers of emigrants to the United States during this period. By 1931 the fertility decline had bottomed out among the anglophone population. Although births remained high in the francophone population, the rates were coming down and there was considerable geographic diversity. Turning to the period after 1931, McInnis first discusses population change during the period of the Great Depression, assessing the fertility and mortality regimes attained at that time. He then moves on to the changes in immigration and fertility during the post–World War II years. The baby boom was essentially an urban phenomenon and the subsequent fertility decline was shorter, sharper, and deeper in Canada than in the United States. After the war immigration resumed on a large scale, primarily from countries of the Third World. The chapter concludes with a short examination of the recent, relatively stable situation in a regime of below-replacement natural population change, modified by continuing immigration at a moderately high level.

Unlike the population of Canada or the United States, that of Mexico continued to grow rapidly up to the 1970s by an excess of births over deaths, as Zadia Feliciano notes in Chapter 13, which sketches the major components of Mexico's population change from the late nineteenth century to the present. Until the recent promotion of family planning, birth rates generally exceeded 5% in an environment in which mortality rates had been trending downward since the early twentieth century, a phenomenon assisted by economic growth and improved availability of health services such as vaccinations. The crude death rate declined from 34.4 per thousand in 1895–1899 to 15.1 per thousand in 1950–1954. The resulting rapid population growth and its consequences form the core of the remainder of the essay. Accelerating population growth led to rapid urbanization, and Mexico City emerged as one of the largest and fastest-growing cities in the world. The share of Mexico's total population living in that city increased from 12% in 1900 to more than 23% in 1970. Emigration to the United States also accelerated, increasing from 0.2% of the population in 1900 to 2.2% in 1980. Immigration was a minor factor in overall population growth of Mexico, which differed in this respect from Canada and the United States.

As Richard Easterlin shows in Chapter 14, the U.S. experience in the twentieth century featured striking new developments in all the traditional areas of demographic study: fertility, mortality, internal migration, and international migration. In fertility, after seemingly reaching the final stage of the fertility transition in the 1930s, the country had a post–World War II baby boom followed by an equally surprising baby bust. Mortality decline, which some thought had reached an unbreachable low in the late 1950s, resumed in the 1960s as new breakthroughs in heart disease led to unprecedented improvements in life at older ages. The historic pattern of rural-to-urban internal migration slowed and reversed, as a new movement emerged into nonmetropolitan areas not linked to major population centers. Here, Easterlin notes, the composition of immigration shifted from traditional European to non-European sources.

2

POPULATION HISTORY OF
NATIVE NORTH AMERICANS

RUSSELL THORNTON

It is generally recognized that humans first came to North America from Asia and that their descendants share common ancestors with contemporary Asian mongoloids. How and when humans first arrived here is more controversial. Most scholars agree that they came across Beringia, a land mass sometimes connecting what is present-day Alaska with Siberia, and moved into the interior of North America across present-day Alaska and Canada, along the eastern edge of the Rocky Mountains. Some argue, however, that the first humans came by boat and perhaps moved along the northwest coast of North America before settling the interior regions. Dates of first arrival(s) are even more in dispute. They range from a mere 9,000 to 10,000 years ago to beyond 40,000 years ago. Many scholars now maintain that there were three separate migrations from Asia: the first took place perhaps 40,000 years ago, the second perhaps 12,000 years ago, and the third around 9,000 to 10,000 years ago. Each of these migrations produced distinct peoples: the first, the Paleo-Indians; the second, the Na-Dine; and the third, the Inuit (Eskimo)-Aleut (Aleutian Islanders), who themselves separated into distinct populations 3,000 years ago.[1]

Descendants of these first humans subsequently spread throughout the hemisphere, perhaps in only 1,000 years, though many scholars think it took much longer.[2] Eventually these first humans became the Native Americans – the American Indians, the Inuit (Eskimo), and the Aleuts – encountered by Scandinavian Norsemen some 1,000 years ago in their brief explorations of this hemisphere, and by Christopher Columbus in

---

This chapter draws freely on various recent publications of the author.
[1] Thornton, *American Indian Holocaust*, pp. 5–9.   [2] Ibid., p. 10.

Map 2.1. Native Americans at time of European contact (*Source*: Map from *Encyclopedia of North American Indians*, edited by Frederick E. Hoxie. Copyright © 1996 by Houghton Mifflin Company. Map reprinted by permission of Houghton Mifflin Company. All rights reserved.)

1492 upon his opening of this hemisphere to European colonization. Map 2.1 shows the distribution of Native American groups around 1600 for present-day North America.

The Western Hemisphere was not the only area colonized by Europeans both before and after 1492. European populations moved into different areas of the world, with varying effects on the indigenous populations. Many places experienced, indigenous population growth, often quickly, though sometimes with an initial population decline. According to Carr-

Saunders,[3] this occurred in India, Java, Madura in the Netherlands Indies, Egypt, Formosa, Algeria, and the Philippines. Of course, ascertaining indigenous population growth in these countries requires some informtion on pre-European population sizes. Estimates of these are typically tenuous and vary widely. For example, there is not much information on the population of the Netherlands Indies before the nineteenth century; the same may be said for Algeria.[4] European expansion also produced other patterns of indigenous population change. Some populations were destroyed or greatly reduced. Examples here include the peoples of Tasmania,[5] the Maori of New Zealand,[6] the Australian Aborigines,[7] and Native Hawaiians.[8] (Of course, indigenous populations are difficult to define and enumerate because of intermarriage between indigenous and immigrant populations and also because social and cultural changes obscure the nature of native populations.)

The Native American population of the total Western Hemisphere experienced a drastic population decline following European contact and colonialism. Some population recovery occurred; how much is open to debate, as estimates of aboriginal population size for the hemisphere vary enormously: they range from 8.4 million (as estimated by the anthropologist Alfred. L. Kroeber) to more than 100 million (as estimated by Henry Dobyns). As discussed in my book *American Indian Holocaust and Survival,* I consider 75 million a reasonable estimate.[9] Population recovery also depends on how historic and contemporary indigenous populations are defined. Such definitions are also open to debate and vary from country to country. Thus, no reliable figures exist as to the size of the total current Native American population of the Western Hemisphere. Certainly, it is much smaller than the estimated 75 million circa 1492. All that can be said with certainty is that specific Western Hemispheric populations were destroyed, almost "permanently reduced," or declined sharply and then experienced subsequent population growth, with the result that some specific populations are even far larger today than they were in 1492 (depending on how these populations are currently defined).

[3] Carr-Saunders, *World Population,* pp. 260–94.   [4] Palmer, "Culture Contacts," p. 262.
[5] Carr-Saunders, *World Population,* p. 295.   [6] Pool, *The Maori Population.*
[7] Butlin, *Our Original Aggression.*
[8] Nordyke, *The Peopling of Hawai'i*; Schmitt, *Demographic Statistics*; Stannard, *Before the Horror.*
[9] Thornton, *American Indian Holocaust,* pp. 22–25.

ABORIGINAL POPULATION SIZE OF NORTH AMERICA

Scholars disagree as to the size of the aboriginal Native American population north of present-day Mexico and the magnitude of the population decline there beginning sometime after A.D. 1500 and continuing to about 1900. Until recently, the standard authority on aboriginal population size was James Mooney. Early in the twentieth century, he estimated individual Native American tribal population sizes, summed them by regions, then totaled them to arrive at an estimate of 1,152,950 for North America north of the Rio Grande at first European contact.[10]

For a time, Mooney's estimate was generally accepted, although one noted scholar – Alfred L. Kroeber – suggested that it was excessive and lowered it accordingly (see the section "California as a Case Study" later in the chapter). In 1966, however, Henry Dobyns concluded from depopulation ratios that the aboriginal population size for this area was between 9 million and 12 million.[11] In 1983, Dobyns used depopulation ratios from epidemics along with possible carrying capacities to arrive at a figure of some 18 million Native Americans for the area north of Mesoamerica (which includes northern Mexico as well as the present-day United States, Canada, and Greenland).[12]

Most scholars now agree that Mooney's population estimate significantly underestimated aboriginal population size for the area north of the Rio Grande and thus also the baseline from which the area's aboriginal population decline may be assessed.[13] Most scholars also consider Dobyns's estimates to be excessive.[14] Yet there is little consensus as to a higher pop-

---

[10] Mooney, "Aboriginal Population"; see also Mooney, "Population."

[11] Dobyns, "Estimating Aboriginal American Population."

[12] Dobyns, *Their Number Become Thinned.*

[13] Dates for Mooney's regional estimates, from which his overall estimate was derived, varied widely: from A.D. 1600 to A.D. 1845, depending on the region in question. A reason for his underestimate of aboriginal population size, scholars now realize, was Mooney's assumption that little population decline had occurred prior to his dates for the beginning of an extended European presence in a region. Seemingly, prior depopulation had occurred in most if not all regions.

[14] There have been various criticisms of Dobyns's methodologies, particularly those in his 1983 book, but also those in his 1966 paper. Criticisms of his earlier paper may be found in Driver, "On the Population Nadir"; and Thornton and Marsh-Thornton, "Estimating Prehistoric American Indian Population Size." Criticisms of his book may be found in Fawcett and Swedlund, "Thinning Populations"; Henige, "Primary Source by Primary Source?"; Henige, "Their Number Become Thick"; Snow and Lanphear, "European Contact"; Thornton, "But How Thick Were They?"

Table 2.1. *Twentieth-century estimates of the aboriginal population of North American Indians*

North America	United States	Scholar (date)
1,148,000	846,000	Mooney (1910)
1,148,000	—	Rivet (1924)
2,000,000–3,000,000	—	Sapper (1924)
1,153,000	849,000	Mooney (1928)
1,002,000	—	Wilcox (1931)
900,000	720,000	Kroeber (1939)
1,000,000	—	Rosenblat (1945)
1,000,000	—	Steward (1945)
2,000,000–2,500,000	—	Ashburn (1947)
1,001,000	—	Steward (1949)
2,240,000	—	Aschmann (1959)
1–2,000,000	—	Driver (1961)
9,800,000–12,250,000	—	Dobyns (1966)
3,500,000	2,500,000	Driver (1969)
2,171,000	—	Ubelaker (1976)
4,400,000	—	Denevan (1976)
—	1,845,000	Thornton (1981)
18,000,000[a]	—	Dobyns (1983)
5,000,000–10,000,000	—	Hughes (1983)
12,000,000	—	Ramenofsky (1987)
7,000,000	5,000,000	Thornton (1987)
1,894,000	—	Ubelaker (1988)
2,000,000–8,000,000	—	Zambardino (1989)

[a] North of Mesoamerica.

ulation figure than Mooney's. Other recent estimates range from about 2 million to somewhat over 7 million, an estimate I developed and continue to use.[15] My 7+ million estimate for the area north of present-day Mexico includes somewhat over 5 million people for the conterminous United States and somewhat over 2 million for present-day Canada, Alaska, and Greenland combined. Some of these estimates are shown in Table 2.1. Whatever the original size, there is no question that substantial depopulation did eventually occur after European arrival. The Native American population of the United States, Canada, and Greenland reached a nadir

[15] Thornton, *American Indian Holocaust*, pp. 25–32; see also Daniels, "The Indian Population."

of perhaps only 375,000 at 1900,[16] although a somewhat larger nadir has also been posited.[17]

A "DISEASE-FREE" AMERICA?

The effects of Old World diseases on aboriginal populations have been an important issue in the debate on aboriginal population size and decline, and their role has been extensively discussed. The Old World diseases that affected native populations here were smallpox, measles, bubonic plague, cholera, typhoid, diphtheria, scarlet fever, whooping cough, pneumonia, malaria and yellow fever, and various venereal diseases.

None of these diseases were present in North America in 1492, though the continent was not disease-free, as Ubelaker discusses in Chapter 3.[18] Merbs states in this regard that "the picture of infectious disease in the New World differed from that in the Old World in many ways, but probably most dramatically in the absence or near absence of crowd infections capable of causing severe epidemics."[19] Reasons for the presence of fewer serious diseases here are not yet fully understood but apparently include the smaller number of domesticated animals (to which many human diseases may be traced), perhaps the lack of large centers of population concentration (which foster many diseases), and possibly low overall population density (a condition hindering the survival of many diseases). Scholars have also argued that migrations across cold, barren Beringia thousands of years ago served as a filter, which restricted pathogens from entering this hemisphere. They note that many such organisms are unable to survive in extremely cold temperatures.[20]

Native Americans lacked acquired immunity to new diseases from Europe and Africa. With no previous exposure to specific diseases, they had not developed the lifelong immunity recovery provides. It has been argued that they were also genetically homogeneous and because of this, viral infections were preadapted to successive hosts rather than encountering many new immune responses.[21] Native Americans had (and have), as a young Passamaquoddy immunologist expressed it to me, "a lack of

---

[16] Thornton, *American Indian Holocaust*, pp. 42–43; Thornton and Marsh-Thornton, "Estimating Prehistoric American Indian Population Size."
[17] Ubelaker, North American Indian Population Size."
[18] See also Merbs, "Infectious Disease."   [19] Ibid., p. 3.
[20] Thornton, *American Indian Holocaust*, pp. 40–1, also Merbs "Infections Disease." p. 5.
[21] Black, "Why Did They Die?"

genetic polymorphism in the MHC (major histocompatibility complex) alleles." New diseases introduced to North America often resulted in "virgin soil epidemics"; that is, conditions were such that a new disease could spread to virtually all members of a population (and become particularly virulent).[22]

Some serious diseases were present in the Western Hemisphere, however. These included tuberculosis and treponemal infections in some populations. Scholars have also shown that the life expectancies of Native Americans did not differ much from those of their European counterparts with various infectious diseases. Life expectancies for Native Americans – generally in the 20s to early 30s – were kept relatively low by famine, nutritional deficiency diseases (e.g., pellagra), warfare, parasites, dysentery, influenza, fevers, and other ailments, besides tuberculosis and treponemal infections.[23]

THE DECLINE: TIMING, MAGNITUDE, AND REASONS

The timing and magnitude of Old World disease episodes in North America and subsequent depopulation is another question still being debated. Soon after Europeans arrived in the Western Hemisphere, these diseases devastated American Indian populations in areas of present-day Mexico, the Caribbean, and Central and South America. However, it also has been argued that the diseases moved northward early in the sixteenth century from European settlements in the Caribbean and Mesoamerica and spread to North America through early European explorations, the establishment of colonies, slave raids, shipwrecks, and other native contacts (see Map 2.2).

EARLY, MASSIVE DEPOPULATION IN NORTH AMERICA?

Scholars have arrived at exceedingly high aboriginal population estimates by "working backward" from the assumption that sixteenth-century epidemics caused massive depopulation in the Southeast. Dobyns, for

---

[22] Crosby, "Virgin Soil Epidemics."
[23] Thornton, *American Indian Holocaust*, pp. 37–41; Newman, "Aboriginal New World Epidemiology"; Reinhard, "Archaeoparasitology."

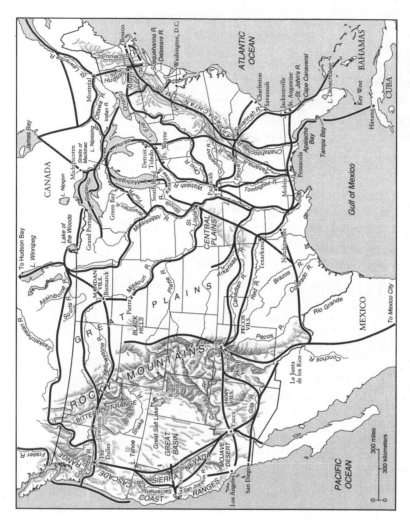

Map 2.2. Major trade routes (*Source*: Map from *Encyclopedia of North American Indians*, edited by Frederick E. Hoxie. Copyright © 1996 by Houghton Mifflin Company. Map reprinted by permission of Houghton Mifflin Company. All rights reserved.)

example, estimated that the Timucuan-speaking population of what is now Florida was 722,000 in 1517 by working backward from a population base of 36,450 in 1613–17 and supposing that nine possible intervening epidemics of disease produced 5 to 50% mortality. He calculated that the 1613–17 population base increased by the magnitude of mortality for each prior supposed epidemic.[24] Dobyns assumed no population recovery or further decline between the epidemics, however; in his view, the population levels remained constant. As I have demonstrated elsewhere, this may have been incorrect.[25]

According to various scholars, diseases infected many native populations in both the Southeast and the Southwest during the initial decades of the sixteenth century. Such outbreaks, some say, frequently culminated in epidemics and pandemics, which over the sixteenth and seventeenth centuries devastated aboriginal populations throughout North America. These populations were once large and dense, it is argued, and in all regions, not just the Southeast, their size was substantially reduced by disease during these two centuries.

The prevailing view, however, is that there were no continent-wide or pan-regional epidemics during the sixteenth century, and not even a great many localized disease episodes in the Southeast. Smith, for one, examined mass and multiple burials, population curves, site size, and population movements, but found little archaeological evidence to suggest the sixteenth-century population collapsed because of European disease. He did find evidence for the disintegration of the Southeastern Indians by the early seventeenth century, which he attributed to epidemic disease.[26] Following an analysis of Iroquois population history, Snow concluded that the Iroquois did not experience rapid depopulation until the seventeenth century.[27] And according to Milanich, the Calusa of Florida survived for more than 150 years after European contact: "We have more than 600 printed pages of documents about Jesuit mission efforts in the 1560s in La Florida, and there are no references to epidemics among the Calusa."[28]

At the same time, some research does support the presence of very early epidemic disease in the Southeast. In an analysis of settlements, Ramenofsky found archaeological evidence of population collapse during the

---

[24] Dobyns, *Their Number Become Thinned*, pp. 291–5.
[25] Thornton, Miller, and Warren, "American Indian Population Recovery."
[26] Smith, *Archaeology of Aboriginal Cultural Change*, pp. 54–85.
[27] Snow and Lanphear, "European Contact."   [28] Milanich, "The European Entrada," p. 8.

sixteenth century in the lower Mississippi Valley (although she did not find evidence for this in the middle Missouri Valley or central New York until the seventeenth century, which supports Snow's findings).[29] Upham argues that smallpox was present early in the sixteenth century in the Southwest.[30]

It is still not clear whether sixteenth-century diseases in the Southeast (and by implication, the Southwest) occurred as region-wide epidemics or as more isolated disease episodes. Diseases may have "burned themselves out" before spreading. The southeastern settlement pattern consisted of centers of population concentration, typically chiefdoms, surrounded by unoccupied or sparsely occupied buffer zones or deserts. Some areas (e.g., the pine barrens of north Florida and Georgia) were simply not suitable for habitation; of those that were suitable, many were chosen because of conflicts between chiefdoms. The zones served to isolate one chiefdom from another, though contact did occur through both war and trade.

Computer simulations of smallpox epidemics suggest that they did not last long in dense populations such as chiefdoms, particularly under virgin soil conditions, which meant virtually 100% infection rates. In other words, all individuals were quickly exposed to the virus and either recovered – and thus acquired immunity – or died, quickly leaving no more people to be infected. So, the epidemics may not have had time to spread from one area of population concentration to another. Conversely, sparsely populated buffer zones or deserts could have been reservoirs of smallpox for extended periods as the smallpox virus could be slowly transmitted from individual to individual, as long it was able to find enough hosts.[31]

All that seems certain is that epidemic disease was important in the overall decline of the Native American population north of Mexico, that disease had an impact on Native American populations in all areas of North America, and that population decline in the Southeast, and perhaps in the Southwest, began *sometime* during the sixteenth century. It cannot be concluded that significant depopulation occurred early in the sixteenth century or that it reached pan-regional proportions during the sixteenth century. Early, massive aboriginal depopulation from epidemic diseases cannot be used, therefore, to argue for exceedingly large aboriginal population sizes for North America.

[29] Ramenofsky, *Vectors of Death.*   [30] Upham, "Smallpox and Climate."
[31] Thornton, Warren, and Miller, "Depopulation in the Southeast."

THE EPIDEMIC DISEASE MYTH AND REASONS FOR POPULATION DECLINE

Many factors, both internal and external to populations, and both demographic and nondemographic in nature, determined the fate of various Native American populations following disease episodes of whatever nature. Regarding the effects of smallpox on American Indian populations, Duffy noted: "Certain tribes were literally wiped out, yet others survived many attacks, and were even, in the intervals between outbreaks, able to recoup their losses through natural increase."[32] This is attested to by research on the Cherokee. The Cherokee likely experienced three high-mortality smallpox epidemics during the eighteenth century, at least one of which had 50% mortality, as well as other depopulations through wars, but the total size of the Cherokee population decreased by less than 25% from 1700 to 1800.[33]

Similarly, Johansson observed that "premodern European village populations were regularly swept by devastating epidemics . . . without subsequently disappearing" and that "most populations have a surprising ability to recover from severe high mortality disease-related shocks if left to themselves."[34] According to historian William McNeill, "The period required for medieval European populations to absorb the shock of renewed exposure to plague seems to have been between 100 and 133 years, i.e., about five to six human generations."[35] Thus, although the Black Death plague of 1347–51 in Europe caused large population losses, it was the cyclic recurrence of the plague and the typhus, influenza, and measles epidemics that produced the long-term demographic effects from which European populations were not able to recover until the late fifteenth century.[36]

I have shown this phenomenon for American Indian populations through simulations of smallpox epidemics and stable population theory.[37] According to this theory, a population that does not migrate and is subject to constant age-specific birth and death rates over a considerable period will assume a particular stable age distribution; that is, proportions of the population in each age group will remain constant, and it will have a constant growth rate, either positive, negative, or zero. Shocks from a temporary change in birth and/or death rates – as might occur in a smallpox

[32] Duffy, "Smallpox and the Indians," p. 341.   [33] Thornton, *The Cherokees*.
[34] Johansson, "The Demographic History," p. 140.   [35] McNeill, *Plagues and Peoples*, p. 150.
[36] Gottfried, *The Black Death*, pp. xv–xvi, 129–35, 156–59.
[37] Thornton, Miller, and Warren, "American Indian Depopulation"; see also Herring, "There Were Young People."

epidemic – will disturb this stability, but the population will eventually return to its particular stable age distribution and constant growth rate. Given the U-shaped curve of mortality in smallpox epidemics, whereby the young and the old die disproportionately, populations may even experience a period of accelerated growth following the epidemic, before returning to normal patterns of growth, stability, or decline (see Table 2.2). This is due to the fact that the surviving segment of the population is concentrated in age groups with higher fertility and lower mortality rates.

All Native American populations had undoubtedly experienced exogenous biological shocks before 1492. Such shocks were so commonplace elsewhere in the world that it is hard to imagine the Western Hemisphere being free of them. Whether the shocks were from disease, war, or natural disaster, the Native Americans in 1492 had dealt with them and survived them. The arrival of Europeans with their diseases was yet another shock to the Native American populations, albeit one of a magnitude they probably never experienced before.

Some Native American populations were virtually exterminated following extremely severe epidemics of smallpox or other diseases. Likewise, some Native American populations experienced extended declines owing to the cycles of different European and African diseases infecting them,

Table 2.2. *Age-specific case-fatality rates of smallpox (*Variola major*) in unvaccinated populations*

Age	Mortality rate (%)
0–4 years	40
5–9 years	25
10–14 years	20
15–19 years	25
20–29 years	35
30–40 years	40
40–50 years	50
>50 years	60

Source: This table is reprinted from Thornton, Miller, and Warren, "American Indian Depopulation," p. 34. It is adapted from Dixon, *Smallpox*, p. 326.

which hindered or prevented recovery. However, this does not seem to account for all Native American population decline, or to explain the differential survival of various populations. The indirect effects of disease epidemics, other causes of depopulation following European colonialism (such as wars, removals, and destruction of tribal economic bases), the interaction of disease with colonialism, and other effects on the populations of Native American societies were involved, as were differences in Native American societies, cultures, and demographic regimes.

Indirect effects of epidemic disease may have been more devastating than direct ones, and the relevant question may be why they were so severe as to prevent recovery. Indirect effects encompass both decreased postepidemic fertility and increased postepidemic mortality resulting from the epidemic. Each may have produced further population decline following an epidemic. Decreased fertility could have resulted from reduced fecundity due to the disease in question, from marriage disruption (e.g., the loss of a spouse), or even from broader patterns of "social disorganization" that entailed the loss of crucial individuals. Increased mortality could have resulted from food shortages if the epidemic occurred during the critical agricultural period of planting or harvesting, or from the inability of mothers to care for their children.

Also, it could be argued that disease had a differential impact in different Native American societies. For example, larger societies may have experienced more "social disorganization" from population losses than did smaller societies; agriculturally based societies may have suffered more severely from population losses than did hunting and gathering ones.

As shown in Table 2.1, twentieth-century estimates of aboriginal North American population size vary greatly. Using an estimated nadir population size of 375,000 around A.D. 1900, I have calculated corresponding yearly rates of decline for roughly the preceding 400-year period.[38] Several rates of decline suggested for this period are presented in Table 2.3. The largest estimate shown, 18 million, would require an annual decline of slightly less than 1% to reach 375,000 by 1900, whereas more moderate estimates require significantly lower rates of decline. Thus changes in Native American populations whereby populations declined modestly over a long period *could have* produced dramatic depopulations. Moreover,

---

[38] Thornton, "Aboriginal North American Population."

Table 2.3. *North American aboriginal population estimates and yearly rates of decline*

Estimate	Yearly rate of decline (%) to 375,000 in 400 years
1,153,000 (Mooney [1928])	−0.28
1,894,280 (Ubelaker [1988])	−0.40
7,000,000 (Thornton [1987])	−0.73
9,800,000 (Dobyns [1966])	−0.82
18,000,000 (Dobyns [1983])[a]	−0.97

[a] North of Mesoamerica.

these rates of decline could have been produced by relatively modest changes in birth and death rates over the extended period. As I have shown using model life tables, even a 1% annual rate of decline could have been produced by only about a 16% decline in birth rates along with an 8 or 9% increase in mortality rates.

Native American populations were probably reduced not only by the direct and indirect effects of disease but also by direct and indirect effects of wars and genocide, enslavements, removals and relocations, and changes in American Indian societies, cultures, and subsistence patterns accompanying European colonialism. Larsen argues that the emphasis on disease "has overshadowed a host of other important consequences of contact such as population relocation, forced labor, dietary change, and other areas."[39] These were destructive in and of themselves in complex ways and often operated with disease to reduce American Indian populations. For example, Meister notes that "later population decline resulting from disease was made possible because Indians had been driven from their land and robbed of their other resources."[40]

Colonialism caused populations to decline through reduced fertility as well as increased mortality. For example, the Cherokee "Trail of Tears" from the Southeast to Indian Territory produced substantial population losses, partly through mortality due to diseases such as cholera, but also through reduced fertility and increased mortality due to malnutrition and starvation.[41] Plains Indians saw their social and cultural life and their eco-

[39] Larsen, "Wake of Columbus," p. 110. [40] Meister, "Demographic Consequences," p. 165.
[41] Thornton, "Cherokee Population Losses."

nomic base disappear when the large herds of buffalo in the West were destroyed in the nineteenth century.[42] As shown in the next section, Southern California Indians were missionized and confined in new disease environments that lowered fertility and raised mortality.[43] Many were eventually displaced, and this action resulted in selective out-migration and fertility reduction as well as assimilation.[44] Northern California Indians were subjected to outright genocide and had their patterns of subsistence destroyed.[45]

This may explain why Native American demographic regimes were unable to respond to European and African diseases. This may also explain how more subtle changes in Native American societies produced long-term population growth. It is this lack of response and probably other reasons for long-term population decline that underlie the myth that epidemic disease by itself was the cause of depopulation.

POPULATION ESTIMATES AND PATTERN OF DECLINE
FROM CIRCA 1492 TO 1900

Native American population estimates and the pattern of population decline from circa 1492 until nadir is a matter of conjecture. It was not until the beginning of the nineteenth century that reasonable population estimates for the native population were available. The Native American population of the United States then was perhaps some 600,000. Adding a still substantial number of Canadian natives at that time brings the figure to more than 750,000, although how much more may be debated. (Douglas Ubelaker has argued for a figure of about 1 million for 1800.) Through the nineteenth century, reasonable – though certainly not entirely accurate – population figures at certain dates until the nadir population may be obtained, as shown in Table 2.4. These figures show that the pattern of population decline from some 750,000 plus to 375,000 was linear.

It was surely not the case, however, that the pattern from circa 1492 until 1800 was linear. Dobyns, as mentioned, has argued for a very early, massive depopulation of North America from European diseases, which may have been particularly severe in the sixteenth century. Following this,

---

[42] Thornton, *American Indian Holocaust*, pp. 51–53.
[43] See also Walker and Johnson, "Decline of the Chumash."
[44] Harvey, "Population of the Cahuilla."
[45] Thornton, "Social Organization"; Thornton, "History, Structure and Survival"; Walker and Thornton, "Health, Nutrition, and Demographic Change."

Table 2.4. *American Indian population in*
the United States (minus Alaska and
Hawaii), 1800–1890

Date	Population
1800	600,000
1820	471,000
1847	383,000
1857	313,000
1870	278,000
1880	244,000
1890	228,000

Source: Thornton and Marsh-Thornton, "Estimating Prehistoric American Indian Population Size," p. 49.

there would have been some decrease in the rate of population decline.
Others, disputing Dobyns, view the sixteenth century as more benign:
Ubelaker's population estimates from 1500 until 1900, for example, depict
a fairly small rate of decline from 1500 to 1600, a steady rate of decline of
−.25 to −.30% from 1600 to 1800, and a large rate of decline from 1800
to 1900, with the overall rate of decline from 1500 to 1900 averaging
−.32%.

Naturally, the total Native American population of North America is a
mere composite of individual tribal populations, each of which exhibited
its own pattern of decline. There were also dramatic regional differences
in the pattern of decline, depending of such factors as original aboriginal
population size, the nature of Native American societies in question, and
the timing of extensive contact with Europeans, their diseases, and forms
of colonialism.

CALIFORNIA AS A CASE STUDY

The complex ways in which the factors of depopulation mentioned above
interacted and their importance in comparison with disease may be seen
by focusing on the California area. The consensus is that California had
a fairly large, dense aboriginal population, as shown in Table 2.5. Estimates
of its aboriginal population vary widely, however. Powers, who traveled
extensively in the area in the latter 1800s, estimated the pre-European pop-

Table 2.5. *Decline of the aboriginal American Indian population of California, to 1900*

Date	Population
Total	310,000–705,000
1800	260,000
1834	210,000
1849	100,000
1852	85,000
1856	50,000
1860	35,000
1870	30,000
1880	20,500
1890	18,000
1900	>15,377

ulation at approximately 750,000.[46] Most subsequent scholars concluded such a number was excessive and reduced it substantially. In Mooney's estimate, the population was 260,000, a figure obtained from Merriam;[47] Kroeber considered even this excessive and reduced it to a mere 133,000.[48] Recently, Cook settled on a figure of 310,000.[49] Other estimates have generally supported Cook's figure, though some are lower and some higher.[50] As we have seen, recent research has greatly influenced scholarly thinking regarding the size of the *total* North American aboriginal population (north of Mexico), and estimates of this size have been revised upward. As such, Cook's figure may be low: the range of from 310,000 to 705,000 may be the best acceptable estimate.

The Indian population of California may have been reduced only slightly by the beginning of the nineteenth century – depending, of course, on which aboriginal population size one accepts – owing to its isolation. Between the first and latter decades of the nineteenth century, however, the Indian population declined rapidly. It reached its nadir around 1900, totaling slightly more than 15,000 then.

The first direct European contact with the native peoples of the

[46] Powers, *Tribes of California*, p. 416.
[47] Mooney, "The Aboriginal Population of America"; see also Merriam, "The Indian Population of California."
[48] Kroeber, *Handbook*, p. 883; see also Kroeber, "Cultural and Natural Areas."
[49] Cook, "Historical Demography," p. 91.   [50] See, for example, Thornton, "Recent Estimates."

California area may have occurred as early as 1540, during the expeditions of Hernando de Alarcón and Melchor Díaz. It is possible, however, that Juan Rodriguez Cabrillo was the first European to arrive; he explored the southern coast in 1542. Little contact occurred in the following two centuries. The principal European visitors consisted of such explorers as Sir Francis Drake (1579), Sebastian Vizcaino (1602), and Juan de Oñate (1604), as well as European sailors who occasionally stopped along the coast to obtain fresh provisions.

In 1769, José Gálvez, the visitor-general of New Spain, organized a "sacred expedition" to establish both a presidio and a mission at what is now San Diego.[51] It was to serve as a way station between Baja California and a soon-to-be-established colony at Monterey in Alta California. The two men charged with this task were Gaspar de Portolá and Fray Junípero Serra. The mission at San Diego de Alcala was founded on 16 July 1769 by Serra, while Portolá searched for Monterey Bay. It was the first of 21 missions to be established in Alta California, many by Serra, many others by Fermin Lasuen. The final mission, San Francisco Solano, was established at Sonoma in 1823. A few decades later the entire mission system collapsed.

Many California Indians were brought into mission confines, sometimes forcibly, and most such individuals were prevented from leaving and punished for attempted escapes, no matter how they arrived. The Indian population of individual missions averaged perhaps 500 to 600, though some reached 1,000 to 2,000.[52] Overall, the 21 missions drew an estimated 54,000 California Indians into their confines during their history, with the total number of baptisms exceeding perhaps 80,000.[53] Not only did the Spanish padres baptize Indians and attempt to convert them to Catholicism, they also forced them to tend fields; herd cattle, sheep, and horses; and do other types of labor required in the microeconomic system of the mission.

Despite its short duration, the mission system profoundly affected Indian peoples of southern and central coastal California. Several of these tribes in southern California are known today as "Mission Indians." Demographically, the missions produced a population decline because of high mortality rates from newly encountered diseases, poor health condi-

---

[51] A mission system had been established ealier in Baja California; the system itself, as well as recurrent epidemics, reduced the native population there, as has been examined in Aschman, *The Central Desert.*

[52] Cook, *The Conflict,* p. 86.   [53] Ibid., pp. 58–59.

tions, and inadequate nutrition. Birth rates dropped also, because of high female death rates, effects of diseases (venereal and otherwise) on fertility and fecundity apart from female mortality, and other conditions imposed on the Indians. (Also, among some Indians, "infanticide was practiced upon children born out of the forced concubinage of Indian women by priests and soldiers.")[54]

New diseases became both epidemic and endemic in California Indian populations, mission and otherwise. This perhaps began with an epidemic (of an unknown disease) around Santa Clara in 1777, but diseases could have been present earlier, moving into Alta California from the coast with occasional landings by explorers, or via land, through expeditions from Baja California or "slave raids" in eastern California. Smallpox definitely dates from the late 1820s, with the most serious epidemic probably in 1838–39 and another serious epidemic in 1844.[55] Pneumonia, diphtheria, and measles may be dated from the early nineteenth century.[56] (It is *possible* that measles was present from the first half of the eighteenth century.) Malaria was also present in California, with probably a particularly destructive epidemic occurring in 1830–33.[57] Other diseases such as syphilis, tuberculosis, cholera, typhus, influenza, cholera, scarlet fever, and dysentery also took their toll. (Alcohol, if not actually alcoholism, may also be added to the list.) Syphilis, in particular, devastated California Indians, perhaps from 1777, or even 1769 with the Portolá expedition. It apparently spread quickly and extensively because of the widespread sexual relations between Indian women and Spanish soldiers, often through rape.[58]

Nowhere in the United States was there such a blatant, systematic destruction of American Indian peoples by Euro-Americans as in California. There was widespread conflict between the interior tribes to the south and Mexican colonists during the first half of the eighteenth century, and tribes there were subjected to brutality, violence, and genocide.[59] An even more glaring destruction occurred in northern California during the mid- to late nineteenth century. Following the discovery of gold in 1848 and the subsequent influx of miners and settlers, conflicts between American Indians and Euro-Americans developed as they competed for existing resources. As subsidiary activities of farming and livestock-raising arose

---

[54] Castillo, "The Impact of Euro-American Exploration," p. 104.
[55] Cook, "Smallpox in Spanish and Mexican California."   [56] Cook, *The Conflict*, p. 19.
[57] Cook, "The Epidemic of 1830–1833."   [58] Cook, "Historical Demography."
[59] Castillo, "The Impact of Euro-American Exploration," pp. 105–6.

to supply miners, Euro-Americans changed the local environments and displaced native plants and animals on which the Indians depended. Many California Indians were faced with starvation. The conflicts quickly escalated as the Indians raided white settlements for subsistence items and whites "disciplined" them; these incidents eventually culminated in atrocities, particularly against Indian women, and a determined, widespread massacre and destruction of northern California Indians. The famous Ishi, who ended his days at the University of California and whose story was popularized by Theodora Kroeber, was the last known survivor of the Yahi Yana Indians, victims of a series of such massacres.

As the record attests, "it was not uncommon for small groups or villages of Indians to be attacked by the immigrants, sometimes in the name of a particular war, and be virtually wiped out overnight."[60] In *Indian Wars of the Northwest*, Bledsoe described the effect on a northern California county in 1865: "Trinity County was cleared of all Indians who lived in rancherias and tribal relations. . . . The hostile tribes had been killed or captured, had been flooded by storms and driven by man, had been starved and beaten into absolute and final subjection."[61] In part because of such events, the California Indian population declined by two-thirds in slightly more than a decade, from 100,000 in 1849 to 35,000 in 1860 (see Table 2.3).

According to Sherburne Cook, the implications for surviving Indians were somewhat different in California than they were elsewhere in the United States.[62] He states that the typical U.S. pattern was to segregate Indians on reservations. (This happened in many areas of the United States but not all.) In California, however, "Indians were never reservationized but were left to merge as best they might with the American civilization which surrounded them."[63] In part, this was because of the way California was "settled" by Euro-Americans: "From 1848 to 1860 the entire coastal region was suddenly overrun by whites who, to be sure, killed and starved large numbers of the natives but who left the survivors to persist in their ancestral habitat."[64]

In the aftermath of this population destruction, most surviving California Indians were simply left "on their own." As a result, many became integrated as "wage laborers" at the lowest level of California's economic structure in the late nineteenth-century. Also, a pattern after the gold rush and during the early years of statehood was a system of virtual Indian

[60] Thornton, *American Indian Holocaust*, p. 107.   [61] Bledsoe, *Indian Wars*, pp. 260–61.
[62] Cook, "Migration and Urbanization," pp. 33–34.   [63] Ibid., p. 33.   [64] Ibid., p. 34.

Table 2.6. *California indentured Indians*

Name	Age	Age bound until	Name	Age	Age bound until
Simon	17	30	Little Sam	12	25
Big Jack	20	30	Job	12	25
Jackass	20	30	Billy	12	25
Jack White	16	30	Nancy	15	30
Joe	15	30	Susan	15	30
Elijah	18	30	Mary	18	30
Judas	18	30	Laura	10	25
Ben	17	30	Betsey	15	30
Tebalth	19	30	Julliet	17	30
Doc	18	30	Myra	18	30
Peter	19	30	Maggie	18	30
Big Sam	18	30	Venus	16	30
Number Two	17	30	Sally	17	30
Big Abe	19	30	Long Betsey	15	30
Darly	18	30	Dido	15	30
Tony	18	30	Big Sally	15	30
Ambrose	16	30	Fanny	12	25
Bob	18	30	Eliza	15	30
Bony	15	30	Van's Billy	17	30
Henry	17	30	Trowbridge	12	25
Jordan	18	30	Cooney	19	30
Prince	16	30	George	18	30
Yolo Boley	15	30			

Source: List obtained from Rawls, *Indians of California*, pp. 92–92.

slavery, meant to serve the California economy. It was established under Chapter 133, enacted by the first California state legislature, supposedly, "an act for the government and protection of the Indians." However, it actually "provided for the indenture of loitering and orphaned Indians, regulated their employment, and defined a special class of crimes and punishments for them."[65] Table 2.6 shows a list of years of indentured servitude for some Indian individuals, along with their ages.

Therefore, much of the California Indian decline occurred relatively late – during the nineteenth century; this was a result of the relative isolation of the area until the late 1700s and early 1800s. Epidemic diseases from Europe and Africa, while important in California, were perhaps

[65] Hurtado, *Indian Survival*, p. 5.

somewhat less important than in many other regions of the United States; however, venereal diseases, especially syphilis, were probably somewhat more important in California than most other regions. The mission system – introduced to control, colonize, and (theoretically) convert inhabitants – produced a significant population decline (often in interaction with diseases, venereal and otherwise) for reasons not found elsewhere, except perhaps in Texas and other areas of the Southwest and in areas of the Southeast where Spanish missions were established. Starvation among California Indians was likely more widespread than in many other areas, as traditional subsistence patterns were quickly destroyed. Vigilante raids and blatant genocide were instrumental in reducing native populations in California. In fact, California is the one place in the United States where few would dispute that a genocide of Native Americans occurred.

SURVIVAL, ADAPTATION, AND TWENTIETH-CENTURY POPULATION RECOVERY

Although many Native American peoples were subjected to similar forces of depopulation following Euro-American contact, the results were not always similar. As stated elsewhere, the *"differential survival of American Indian tribes does not seem to have been a straightforward result of depopulation experience*. Consequently, tribal social and cultural factors may have influenced survival."[66] Native American populations exhibited a wide range of responses to the shock and aftermath of European contact. Many attempted to adapt to the Euro-American presence and its implications. In this sense, some Native Americans were actively attempting to shape, if not actually shaping, their own destinies: they were victims, but not mere victims.

Many remnant American Indian groups in the eastern part of the United States joined with the Iroquois and were adopted by them, as were the Tuscarora who fled northward from the Carolinas to escape the slave trade. Similarly, various tribes migrated into the Mississippi River Valley and were amalgamated there. As Brain has noted, the Natchez changed their marriage rules to adopt other Indians as relatives.[67] My study of the Tolowa and Yuki Indians of northern California shows that depopulation

[66] Thornton, "Social Organization," p. 188; see also Decker, "Depopulation of the Northern Plains."
[67] Brain, "The Natchez."

by itself was not the only factor determining tribal survival. Reservation experiences played a role as well. In the case of the Yuki, they were placed on a reservation with other tribes and intermarried with them and thereby became merged with other tribes of the Covelo Indian Community of Confederated Tribes of the Round Valley Indian Reservation. Preexisting patterns of social organization were another significant factor. Tolowa kinship patterns, for example, allowed the easy incorporation of outsiders into the tribe through marriage, but with offspring defined as Tolowa since Tolowa society is both patrilocal and patrilineal.[68]

Various new "Native American" groups were created in response to the demographic events of Euro-American contact. The Métis of Canada and the U.S.-Canadian border region are the best-known such group: this Indian–white "racially mixed" group was created, they say, "nine months after the first white man set foot in Canada." New peoples also include the Lumbee, historically prominent tribes such as the Catawba, and various triracial groups throughout the Atlantic, southeastern, and southern states. James Mooney of the Smithsonian Institution surveyed many of these peoples in the early 1900s and found a strong sense of Indian identity along with a fear of being absorbed into the African American population.[69] William Harlen Gilbert, Jr., of the Library of Congress, surveyed such communities in the mid-1940s, and found "little evidence for the supposition that they are being absorbed to any great extent into either the white or the Negro groups."[70] (In fact, he found they were increasing in size.)[71]

POPULATION RECOVERY

At the beginning of the twentieth century, the Native American population of the United States and Canada began to increase. Census enumerations suggest an almost continuous increase since 1900 for the United States. (See Table 2.7 for the increase in the total Native American population.) This has been a result of both decreases in mortality rates and increases in fertility rates, because of which fertility has remained higher for Native Americans than for the total U.S. population.[72] This increase can also be traced to changes in individuals' self-identification as "Indian,"

[68] Thornton, "History, Structure and Survival."   [69] Mooney, "The Powhatan Confederacy."
[70] Gilbert, "Memorandum," p. 438.
[71] The total population of these groups in 1960 was estimated at 100,000 by Berry in *Almost White*, p. 57.
[72] Thornton, Sandefur, and Snipp, "American Indian Fertility."

Table 2.7. *Recovery of the Native American
population of the United States, 1900–1990*

Date	Population
1900	237,000
1910	291,000
1920	261,000
1930	362,000
1940	366,000
1950	377,000
1960	552,000
1970	827,000
1980	1,420,000
1990	1,959,000

Note: The population referred to is American Indian, Inuit,
and Aleut.

as reflected in recent censuses. Since the 1960 census, the U.S. system of enumeration has relied on self-identification to ascertain an individual's race. Studies show that much of the increase in the number of American Indians (not including Inuit and Aleuts) from 524,000 in 1960 to 793,000 in 1970, 1.4 million in 1980, and over 1.8 million in 1990 was a result of changing racial definitions from one census to another. About 25% of the change from 1960 to 1970, about 60% of the change from 1970 to 1980, and about 35% of the change from 1980 to 1990 has been attributed to these changing identifications.[73] In turn, these changing self-identifications are generally considered a result of the racial and ethnic consciousness of the 1960s and 1970s, as well as Native American political mobilization during the period.[74]

When Inuit and Aleuts are added to 1.8 million American Indians enumerated in the 1990 census, the total number of Native Americans in the United States in 1990 comes to more than 1.9 million.[75] To this figure may

[73] Passel, "Provisional Evaluation"; Passel and Berman, "Quality"; Harris, "The 1990 Census"; see also Thornton, "Tribal Membership Requirements."
[74] Changing self-identifications were perhaps a result of individuals of mixed ancestry who formerly did not identify as Native American because of the stigma attached to such an identity by larger society. However, some individuals with minimal (or no) Native American ancestry may have identified as Native American because of the desire to affirm a marginal (or establish a nonexistent) ethnic identity.
[75] Bureau of the Census, *Characteristics of American Indians by Tribe and Language*, Table 1.

be added some 740,000 Native Americans in Canada in the mid-1980s (575,000 American Indians, 35,000 Inuit, and 130,000 Métis and perhaps some 30,000 Native Americans in Greenland. Assuming some increase in natives in Canada to 1990, the total then comes to around 2.75 million Native Americans in 1990. This is obviously a very significant increase over the fewer than 400,000 around 1990; however, it is still far less than the estimated 7 million or more in 1492. (It is also only a very small fraction of the total populations of the United States [over 250 million in 1990] and Canada [over 25 million in 1990].)

U.S. census enumerations also provide self-reported tribal affiliations and ancestries. According to the 1990 census, the 10 largest tribal affiliations in the United States are Cherokee (308,000), Navajo (219,000), Chippewa (Ojibwa) (104,000), Sioux (103,000), Choctaw (82,000), Pueblo (53,000), Apache (50,000), Iroquois (49,000), Lumbee (48,000), and Creek (44,000).[76]

TRIBAL ENROLLMENT

There are 317 American Indian tribes in the United States "recognized" by the federal government and receiving services from the U.S. Bureau of Indian Affairs. There are also some 217 Alaska Native Village Areas identified in the 1990 census (containing a total of 9,807 American Indians, 32,502 Inuit, and 4,935 Aleut),[77] some 125–50 tribes seeking federal recognition, and dozens of other groups that might do so in future years. The Bureau of Indian Affairs has generally required a one-fourth degree of American Indian "ancestry" (blood quantum) and/or tribal membership to recognize an individual as American Indian. However, each tribe has a set of requirements, generally including a blood quantum requirement, for membership (enrollment) of individuals. Membership requirements are typically set forth in tribal constitutions approved by the U.S. Bureau of Indian Affairs. Requirements vary widely from tribe to tribe: some (such as the Walker River Paiute) require at least a one-half Indian (or tribal) blood quantum; others (e.g., the Navajo), require a one-fourth blood quantum; still others, generally in Oklahoma or California, require a one-eighth or one-sixteenth or one-thirty-second blood quantum; and some tribes have no minimum blood quantum requirement, but only require

---

[76] Bureau of the Census, *We*, Figure 2. It should be noted that about 11% of those individuals identifying as Native American in the 1990 census did not report a tribal affiliation.

[77] Bureau of the Census, *American Indian and Alaska Native Areas*, Table 2.

Table 2.8. *Blood quantum requirement of American Indian tribes by reservation basis and size*

Basis and size	Blood quantum requirement		
	More than 1/4	1/4 or less	No minimum requirement
Number of tribes	21	183	98
Reservation based (%)	85.7	83.1	63.9
Median size	1,022	1,096	1,185

Note: Information not available on 15 tribes. Based on unpublished tribal constitutions and tribal enrollment data obtained by the author from the U.S. Bureau of Indian Affairs.

some degree of American Indian lineage.[78] A summary of the blood quantum requirements for federally recognized tribes is presented in Table 2.8.

In 1990, some 437,079 American Indians (and 182 Inuit [Eskimo] and 97 Aleuts) lived on 314 reservations and trust lands. Half of these (218,290 American Indians, 25 Inuit, and 5 Aleuts) lived on the 10 largest reservations and trust lands: Navajo Reservation and trust lands (143,405), Pine Ridge Reservation and trust lands (11,182), Fort Apache Reservation (9,825), Gila River Reservation (9,116), Papago Reservation (8,480), Rosebud Reservation and trust lands (8,043), San Carlos Reservation (7,110), Zuni Pueblo (7,073), Hopi Pueblo and trust lands (7,061), and Blackfeet Reservation (7,025).[79] American Indian tribes on reservations tend to have higher blood quantum requirements for membership than those not on reservations, as indicated in Table 2.8. More than 85 percent of the tribes requiring more than a one-quarter blood quantum for membership are reservation based; less than 64 percent of tribes having no minimum requirement are reservation based. Also shown in Table 2.8, those tribes with higher blood quantum requirements tend to be slightly smaller than those tribes with lower blood quantum requirements.

The total membership of the more than 300 federally recognized tribes in the United States in the late 1980s was only slightly over 1 million; hence, only about 60 percent of the more than 1.8 million individuals self-identified as Indian in the 1990 census were actually enrolled in a

---

[78] Thornton, "Tribal Membership Requirements," p. 9.
[79] Bureau of the Census, *We*, p. 1 and Figure 12.

federally recognized tribe.[80] Differences in self-identification and tribal enrollment varied considerably from tribe to tribe. For example, most of the 219,000 or more Navajo in the 1990 census were enrolled in the Navajo Nation; only about one-third of the 300,000 or more Cherokee in the 1990 census were enrolled in one of the three Cherokee tribes: Cherokee Nation of Oklahoma, Eastern Band of Cherokee Indians; and United Keetoowah Band of Cherokee Indians.[81]

The situation in Canada is somewhat different. In Canada one must be registered under the Indian Act of Canada to be an "official" Indian. Categories of Canadian Indians include: (1) status (or registered) Indians, that is, those recognized under the act; and (2) nonstatus (or nonregistered) Indians, that is, those never registered under the act or those who gave up their registration (and became "enfranchised"). Depending on whether the group has ever entered into a treaty relationship with the Canadian government, status Indians are subdivided into treaty and nontreaty Indians. (The Métis, individuals of Indian and white ancestry, are not legally recognized as Indians.) Some 500,000 of the 575,000 Canadian Indians in the mid-1980s were registered.[82] About 70% of Canadian Indians live on one of 2,272 reserves. There were 578 bands of Canadian Indians in the early 1980s, most containing fewer than 500 members. Only three bands had more than 5,000 members: Six Nations of the Grand River (11,172), Blood (6,083), and Kahnawake (5,226).[83]

REDISTRIBUTION AND URBANIZATION

By the beginning of the twentieth century, the surviving Native American groups shown in Map 2.1 had been redistributed, as shown in Map 2.3. Much of this occurred during the nineteenth century with Native American removals, the establishment of the reservation system, and the subsequent elimination and allotment of some reservations. According to the 1990 census, the 10 states with the largest Native American populations were Oklahoma (252,000), California (242,000), Arizona (204,000), New Mexico (134,000), Alaska (86,000), Washington (81,000), North Carolina (80,000), Texas (66,000), New York (63,000), and Michigan (56,000).[84]

---

[80] Thornton, "Tribal Membership Requirements," p. 11.   [81] Ibid.
[82] Thornton, "Population," p. 463.
[83] Ibid. The largest Canadian "group" in terms of language and culture is the Chippewa-Ojibwa.
[84] Bureau of the Census, *We*, Figure 3.

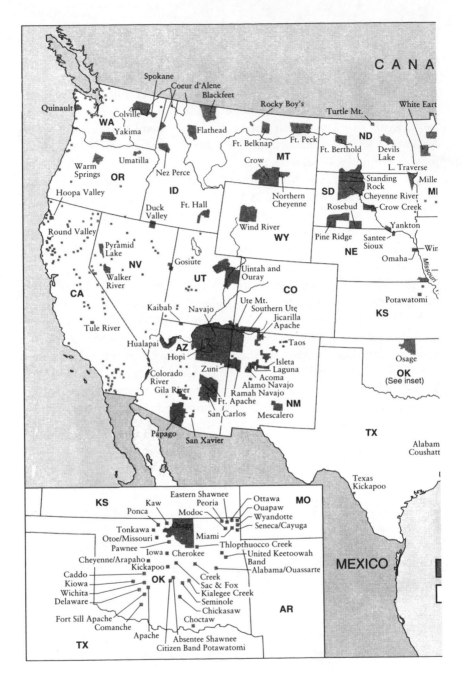

Map 2.3. Contemporary federal and state reservations (*Source*: Map from *Encyclopedia of North American Indians*, edited by Frederick E. Hoxie. Copyright © 1996 by Houghton Mifflin Company. Map reprinted by permission of Houghton Mifflin Company. All rights reserved.)

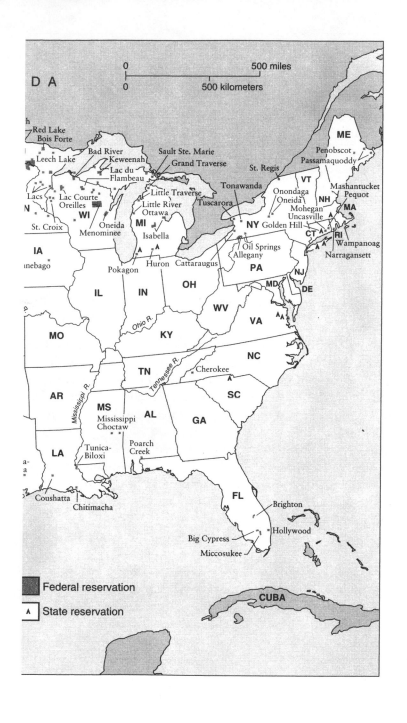

Table 2.9. *Percentage urban of American Indian population of the United States, 1900–1990*

Year	Percentage urban
1900	0.4
1910	4.5
1920	6.1
1930	9.9
1940	7.2
1950	13.4
1960	27.9
1970	44.5
1980	49.0
1990	56.2

A redistribution of Native Americans has also occurred through urbanization in the United States and Canada. As shown in Table 2.9, only 0.4% of the American Indians in the United States lived in urban areas in 1900. By 1950, this figure had increased to 13.4%, and in 1990 to 56.2%.[85] Thus the rate of increase from 1900 to 1950 was greater than that from 1950 to 1990.

Important in this urbanization was the migration to cities and towns, some of which occurred under the Bureau of Indian Affairs relocation program, which began in 1950 to assist American Indians in moving from reservation (and rural) areas to selected urban areas.[86] U.S. cities with the largest Native American populations are New York City, Oklahoma City, Phoenix, Tulsa, Los Angeles, Minneapolis–St. Paul, Anchorage, and Albuquerque.[87]

Canadian provinces with the largest number of Native Americans are Ontario, British Columbia, Saskatchewan, and Manitoba. About 40% of Canadian Native Americans lived in cities in the mid-1980s, primarily Vancouver, Edmonton, Regina, Winnipeg, Toronto, and Montreal. This was an increase from 30% in the early 1970s and a mere 13% in 1961. However, only about 20% of Canadian Inuit live in cities, and only about 30% of the status Indians do so.[88]

[85] Bureau of the Census, *American Indian and Alaskan Native Areas*; Thornton, "Tribal Membership Requirements," p. 12.
[86] Thornton, "Urbanization," pp. 670–1.   [87] Ibid.   [88] Ibid.

Table 2.10. *Recovery of the American Indian population of California, 1900–1990*

Date	Population
1900	>15,377
1910	16,371
1920	17,360
1930	19,212
1940	18,675
1950	19,947
1960	39,014[a]
1970	91,018[a]
1980	198,275[a]
1990	242,000

[a] Includes significant numbers of migrant Indians to California. One estimate is that only about 40,000 of the almost 200,000 American Indians in California in 1980 represented individuals from tribes indigenous to the state (Larry Meyers, personal communication, 1990); however, another estimate is that the figure is around 100,000; that is, about one-half of the 1980 population were descendants of indigenous tribes (see Heizer and Elsasser, *The Natural World*, p. 235).

Source: These data were derived from U.S. census enumerations and reflect changing procedures for defining and enumerating American Indians. They may also reflect some "underenumerations" of California Indians. California tribal roles (of descendants) in 1928, 1950, and 1970 list "descendant populations" of 23,585, 36,094, and 69,911, respectively (see Cook, *Population of California Indians*, p. 73).

POPULATION RECOVERY IN CALIFORNIA

The California Indian population also started to increase around the turn of this century, as mortality and fertility conditions became more favorable (see Table 2.10). Today, California has the second largest Native American population, just behind Oklahoma, as already mentioned. However, a large portion of the American Indian population of California consists of migrants to the state, or the descendants of migrants. For example, the California Native American Heritage Commission estimates that considerably less than 50% of the Native Americans in California are descendants of native tribes of California.[89] However, it has also been estimated that about one-half of the 200,000 California Native Americans in the 1980 census were descendants of non-California tribes[90] (and about one-fourth – over 50,000 individuals – were self-identified as Cherokee).[91] Sherburne Cook estimated that about two-thirds of the some 90,000 California Indians in 1970 were descendants of aboriginal California tribes;[92] he also estimated that about 10,000 descendants of aboriginal California tribes were living outside the state in 1970:[93] state rolls of California Indians undertaken in 1928, 1950, and 1970 give "descendant populations" of 23,585, 36,094, and 69,911, respectively.[94]

California has the largest number of federally recognized American Indian tribes in the United States (excluding Alaskan communities): over 100 (plus several dozen tribes seeking federal recognition). This represents one-third of all American Indian tribes recognized by the federal government. However, the tribes tend to be small: in the early 1980s, there were only 31,517 individuals enrolled in the federally recognized tribes of California.

ISSUES IN THE TWENTY-FIRST CENTURY

Native Americans will face new demographic threats in the twenty-first century because of urbanization and its partner, intermarriage. With the decline in numbers of Native Americans, increased contact with whites, blacks, and others, more and more Native Americans have married non-Indians. This pattern has accelerated with the recent increase in urbanization. In the United States today, almost 60% of all Native Americans (as defined in the census) are married to non-Indians.[95] It has also been argued that those "Native Americans" who changed their census definitions of themselves – individuals who could be called "new" Native Americans[96] – are more likely to be intermarried.[97]

---

[89] Larry Myers, personal communication, 1990.   [90] Heizer and Elsasser, *The Natural World*, p. 235.
[91] Thornton, *The Cherokees*, p. 147.   [92] Cook, *The Population of the California Indians*, p. 200.
[93] Ibid., p. 196.   [94] Ibid., p. 73.
[95] Sandefur and McKinnell, "American Indian Intermarriage," p. 348; Eschbach, "The Enduring and Vanishing American Indian," p. 95 and Table 1.
[96] Thornton, "Tribal Membership Requirements."
[97] Eschbach, "The Enduring and Vanishing American Indian"; Nagel, "Politics and the Resurgence," p. 953.

Urbanization has also reduced the sense of tribal identity. In the 1970 census, about 20% of American Indians overall reported no tribal affiliation; however, only about 10% of those on reservations reported no affiliation, whereas 30% of those in urban areas reported no affiliation.[98] The 1980 and 1990 censuses report no comparable data; however, 25% of the Native Americans in the 1980 census and 15% of those in the 1990 census reported no tribal affiliation.[99] The 1990 census also indicates that only about one-fourth of all Native Americans speak an Indian language at home.[100] Census enumerations indicate also that urban residents are far less likely than reservation residents to speak an Indian language or participate in cultural activities.[101]

I have summarized the implications of these developments elsewhere:

If these trends continue, both the genetic and tribal distinctiveness of the total Native American population will be greatly lessened. A Native American population comprised primarily of "old" Native Americans strongly attached to their tribes will change to a population with a predominance of "new" Native Americans who may or may not have tribal attachments or even tribal identities. It may even make sense at some point in the future to speak mainly of Native American ancestry or ethnicity.[102]

BIBLIOGRAPHIC ESSAY

I. NATIVE AMERICAN HISTORICAL DEMOGRAPHY

A general bibliography of the historical demography of Native Americans north of Mexico has been published under the auspices of the Newberry Library by Henry F. Dobyns, *Native American Historical Demography: A Critical Bibliography* (Bloomington: Indiana University Press, 1979); an update is Henry F. Dobyns, "Native American Population Collapse and Recovery," in *Scholars and the Indian Experience*, ed. William R. Swagerty (Bloomington: Indiana University Press, 1984), 17–35. S. Ryan Johansson also provides a bibliographic overview in "The Demographic History of the Native Peoples of North America: A Selective Bibliography," *Yearbook of Physical Anthropology*, 25 (1982), 133–52.

---

[98] Thornton, *American Indian Holocaust*, pp. 237–8.
[99] Thornton, "Tribal History," p. 238; Bureau of the Census, *Characteristics of American Indians by Tribe and Language*, Table 1.
[100] Bureau of the Census, *American Indian and Alaskan Native Areas, 1990*, p. 66.
[101] Thornton, *American Indian Holocaust*, p. 238.
[102] Thornton, "Tribal Membership Requirements," p. 14.

A general population history of Native Americans is Russell Thornton, *American Indian Holocaust and Survival: A Population History since 1492* (Norman: University of Oklahoma Press, 1987). It provides discussions of aboriginal population size, population reductions and reasons for them, including the differential experiences of Native American groups, and of the twentieth-century population recovery and urbanization. Russell Thornton also provides a brief overview of population history in "Population," in *Encyclopedia of Native Americans in the Twentieth Century*, ed. Mary B. Davis (New York: Garland, 1994), 461–63. An examination of changes in population size is Douglas H. Ubelaker, "North American Population Size, A.D. 1500 to 1985," *American Journal of Physical Anthropology*, 77 (1988), 189–94.

A population history of the California area may be found in Sherburne F. Cook, *The Population of the California Indians, 1769–1970* (Berkeley: University of California Press, 1976). Russell Thornton, *The Cherokees: A Population History* (Lincoln: University of Nebraska Press, 1991) is a book-length treatment of the population history of a specific American Indian tribe; John H. Moore, *The Cheyenne Nation* (Lincoln: University of Nebraska Press, 1987), is a social and demographic history of a particular tribe. Russell Thornton, "History, Structure and Survival: A Comparison of the Yuki (*Unkomno'n*) and Tolowa (*Hush*) Indians of Northern California," *Ethnology*, 25 (1986), 119–30, considers different patterns of survival between two Native American groups; D. Ann Herring, "There Were Young People and Old People and Babies Dying Every Week: The 1918–1919 Influenza Pandemic at Norway House," *Ethnohistory*, 41 (1994), 73–105, examines population recovery among a group of Canadian Indians following an influenza epidemic; and Jody F. Decker, "Depopulation of the Northern Plains Natives, *Social Science Medicine*, 33 (1991), 381–93 considers the differential impact of infectious disease on the population histories of several different tribes in Canada. Other population histories are Emily J. Blasingham, "The Depopulation of the Illinois Indians," *Ethnohistory*, 3 (1956), 193–224 and 361–412; M. R. Harvey, "Population of the Cahuilla Indians: Decline and Its Causes," *Eugenics Quarterly*, 14 (1967), 185–98; and Anita L. Alvarado, "Cultural Determinants of Population Stability in the Havasupai Indians," *American Journal of Physical Anthropology*, 33 (1970), 9–14.

Henry F. Dobyns, "Disease Transfer at Contact," *Annual Review of Anthropology*, 22 (1993), 273–91, reviews studies of the impact of "Old World" diseases on native populations of this hemisphere from contact through this century. Clarke Spencer Larsen discusses biological aspects of Native Americans following Columbus in "In the Wake of Columbus: Native Population Biology in the Postcontact Americans," *Yearbook of Physical Anthropology*, 37 (1994), 109–54; and Charles F. Merbs examines the impact of infectious disease on Native American populations in "A New World of Infectious Disease," *Yearbook of Physical Anthropology*, 35 (1992), 3–42.

2. ABORIGINAL POPULATION SIZE

The population size of the Western Hemisphere at the first arrival of Columbus is examined in the second edition of William M. Denevan, ed., *The Native Population of the Americas in 1492* (Madison: University of Wisconsin Press, 1992 [1976]). (It contains a slightly lower population estimate for the hemisphere than the original edition: 53.9 million as opposed to 57.3 million.) Other hemispheric estimates may be found in Alfred L. Kroeber, "Cultural and Natural Areas of Native North America," *Publications in American Archaeology and Ethnology*, 38 (Berkeley: University of California Press, 1939); and Henry F. Dobyns, "Estimating Aboriginal American Population: An Appraisal of Techniques with a New Hemispheric Estimate," *Current Anthropology*, 7 (1966), 395–416. All three of these works also contain estimates for the area north of present-day Mexico. (Denevan's estimate of 3.79 million is reduced from his earlier estimate of 4.4 million; Kroeber's estimate of 900,000 is the lowest I am aware of; and Dobyns's estimate of 9.8 million to 12.25 million is exceeded only by his more recent estimate of 18 million for north of Mesoamerica.)

The classic estimate of the aboriginal population size of America north of Mexico is found in James Mooney's, "Population," in *Handbook of American Indians North of Mexico*, ed. F. W. Hodge, II (Washington: U.S. Government Printing Office, 1910), 286–87, and "The Aboriginal Population of America North of Mexico," *Smithsonian Miscellaneous Collections*, 80 (Washington, D.C., 1928), 1–40. (His 1928 estimate of 1.153 million was revised slightly upward from his earlier estimate.) Mooney first estimated the sizes of individual tribes at "first extensive European contact" with particular regions (the dates of which varied), totaled them by region, and then summed to arrive at a total population figure. As Douglas H. Ubelaker has examined in "The Sources and Methodology for Mooney's Eestimates of North American Indian Populations," in *The Native Population of the Americas*, 243–88, Mooney relied on early historical sources. Russell Thornton, "Implications of Catlin's American Indian Population Estimates for Revision of Mooney's Estimate," *American Journal of Physical Anthropology*, 49 (1978), 11–14, also examines Mooney's work.

Henry Dobyns's "Estimating Aboriginal American Population Size" and *Their Number Become Thinned: Native Population Dynamics in Eastern North America* (Knoxville: University of Tennessee Press, 1983) both contain exceedingly high aboriginal population estimates, as a number of scholars have argued. Criticisms of Dobyn's earlier publication may be found in Harold E. Driver, "On the Population Nadir of Indians in the United States," *Current Anthropology*, 9 (1968), 330; and Russell Thornton and Joan Marsh-Thornton, "Estimating Prehistoric American Indian Population Size for the United States Area: Implications of the Nineteenth Century Population Decline," *American Journal of Physical Anthropology*, 55 (1981), 47–53. Criticisms of his book may be found in William B. Fawcett, Jr., and Alan C. Swedlund, "Thinning Populations and Population Thinners: The Historical Demography of Native Americans," *Reviews in Anthropology*, 11 (1984), 264–69; and David Henige, "Primary Source by Primary Source? On the Role of Epidemics in New World Depopulation," *Ethnohistory*, 33 (1986), 293–312.

A more moderate population estimate is provided by Russell Thornton in *American Indian Holocaust and Survival: A Population History since 1492* (Norman: University of Oklahoma Press, 1987), 25–32. (The estimate is 7+ million for all of North America north of present-day Mexico.) Other, recent discussion of aboriginal population size are Douglas H. Ubelaker's "North American Population Size, A.D. 1500 to 1985," *American Journal of Physical Anthropology*, 77 (1988), 289–294, and "North American Indian Population Size: Changing Perspectives," in *Disease and Demography in the Americas*, ed. John W. Verano and Douglas H. Ubelaker (Washington, D.C.: Smithsonian Institution Press, 1992), 169–76.

In "The Indian Population of North America in 1492," *William and Mary Quarterly*, 49 (1992), 298–320, John D. Daniels provides a detailed summary and discussion of various aboriginal population estimates along with the various methodologies used and estimates used in history textbooks. Special attention is given to the large number of population estimates for the California area, a result, Daniels asserts, of the records kept by Spanish colonists. Two such population estimates may be found in Sherburne F. Cook, "Historical Demography," in *Handbook of North American Indians: California*, ed. Robert F. Heizer (Washington, D.C.: Smithsonian Institution Press, 1978); and Russell Thornton, "Recent Estimates of the Prehistoric California Indian Population," *Current Anthropology*, 21 (1980), 702–04. Sherburne F. Cook, *The Indian Population of New England in the Seventh Century* (Berkeley: University California Press, 1976), discusses some methodological issues in estimating early Native American population sizes and provides tribe-by-tribe estimates for one region of North America.

3. NATIVE AMERICAN POPULATIONS TODAY

American Indians: The First of This Land (New York: Russell Sage, 1989), by C. Matthew Snipp, is a detailed social and demographic description of American Indians in the United States based on 1980 census data. Also using U.S. census data, Russell Thornton, Gary D. Sandefur, and C. Matthew Snipp examine twentieth-century American Indian fertility patterns in their "American Indian Fertility Patterns, 1910 and 1940 to 1980," *American Indian Quarterly*, 15 (1991), 359–97. Stephen J. Kunitz, *Disease Change and the Role of Medicine: The Navajo Experience* (Berkeley: University of California Press, 1983) considers recent demographic and epidemiological change on the Navajo Reservation.

Issues involved in the 1990 U.S. census count of Native Americans are discussed in David Harris, "The 1990 Census Count of American Indians: What Do the Numbers Really Mean?" *Social Science Quarterly*, 75 (1994), 580–93. Native American intermarriage is examined both in Gary D. Sandefur and Trudy McKinnell, "American Indian Intermarriage," *Social Science Research*, 15 (1986), 347–71; and Karl Eschbach, "The Enduring and Vanishing American Indian: American Indian Population Growth and Intermarriage in 1990," *Ethnic and Racial Studies*, 18 (1995), 89–108.

An examination of the scholarship on the urbanization of Native Americans may be found in Russell Thornton, Gary D. Sandefur, and Harold G. Grasmick, *The Urbanization of American Indians: A Critical Bibliography* (Bloomington: Indiana University Press, 1982). Russell Thornton, "Tribal Membership Requirements and the Demography of 'Old' and 'New' Native Americans," in *Changing Numbers, Changing Needs: American Indian Demography and Public Health*, ed. Gary D. Sandefur, Ronald R. Rindfuss, and Barney Cohen (Washington, D.C.: National Academy Press, 1996), 103–12, discusses the implications of urbanization and other phenomena for the future of the Native American population as reflected in both census and tribal enrollment populations. A general overview of urbanization is Russell Thornton's "Urbanization," in *Encyclopedia of*

Native Americans in the Twentieth Century, Mary B. Davis, ed. (New York: Garland, 1994), 670–71.

REFERENCES

Aschman, Homer. *The Central Desert of Baja California: Demography and Ecology. Ibero-Americana*, vol. 42. Berkeley: University of California Press, 1959.

Berry, Brewton. *Almost White: A Study of Certain Racial Hybrids in the Eastern United States.* New York: Macmillian, 1963.

Black, Francis L. "Why Did They Die?" *Science* 258 (December 11, 1992): 1739–40.

Bledsoe, Anthony J. *Indian Wars of the Northwest.* San Francisco: Bacon, 1885.

Brain, Jeffrey P. "The Natchez 'Paradox.'" *Ethnology* 10 (1971): 215–22.

Butlin, Noel. *Our Original Aggression.* Sydney: George Allen and Unwin, 1983.

Carr-Saunders, A. M. *World Population.* Oxford: Clarendon Press, 1936.

Castillo, Edward D. "The Impact of Euro-American Exploration and Settlement." In *California*, edited by Robert F. Heizer, 99–127. Vol. 8 of *Handbook of North American Indians*, William C. Sturtevant, general editor. Washington, D.C.: Smithsonian Institution, 1978.

Cook, Sherburne F. "Smallpox in Spanish and Mexican California." *Bulletin of the History of Medicine* 7 (1939): 153–91.

———. "Migration and Urbanization of the Indians in California." *Human Biology* 15 (1943): 33–45.

———. "The Epidemic of 1830–1833 in California and Oregon." *University of California Publications in American Archaeology and Ethnology* 43 (1955): 303–26.

———. *The Conflict between the California Indian and White Civilization.* Berkeley: University of California Press, 1976.

———. *The Population of the California Indians, 1969–1970.* Berkeley: University of California Press, 1976.

———. "Historical Demography." In *California*, edited by Robert F. Heizer, 91–98. Vol. 8 of *Handbook of North American Indians*, William L. Sturtevant, general editor. Washington, D.C.: Smithsonian Institution, 1978.

Crosby, Alfred W., Jr. "Virgin Soil Epidemics as a Factor in the Aboriginal Depopulation in America." *William and Mary Quarterly* 33 (1976): 289–99.

Decker, Jody F. "Depopulation of the Northern Plains Natives." *Social Science Medicine* 33 (1991): 381–93.

Daniels, John D. "The Indian Population of North America in 1492." *William and Mary Quarterly* 49 (1992): 298–320.

Denevan, William M., ed. *The Native Population of the Americas in 1492.* Madison: University of Wisconsin Press, 1992 [1976].

Dixon, C. W. "Smallpox in Tripolitania, 1946: An Epidemiological and Clinical Study of 500 Cases, Including Trials of Penicillin Treatment." *Journal of Hygiene* 46 (1948): 351–77.

———. *Smallpox.* London: J. A. Churchill, 1962.

Dobyns, Henry F. "Estimating Aboriginal American Population: An Appraisal of

Techniques with a New Hemispheric Estimate." *Current Anthropology* 7 (1966): 395–416.

———. *Their Number Become Thinned: Native American Population Dynamics in Eastern North America*. Knoxville: University of Tennessee Press, 1983.

Driver, Harold E. "On the Population Nadir of Indians in the United States." *Current Anthropology* 9 (1968): 330.

Duffy, John. "Smallpox and the Indians in the American Colonies." *Bulletin of the History of Medicine* 25 (1951): 324–41.

Eschbach, Karl. "The Enduring and Vanishing American Indian: American Indian Population Growth and Intermarriage in 1990." *Ethnic and Racial Studies* 18 (1995): 89–108.

Fawcett, William B., Jr., and Alan C. Swedlund. "Thinning Populations and Population Thinners: The Historical Demography of Native Americans, Review of *Their Number Become Thinned*, by Henry F. Dobyns." *Reviews in Anthropology* 11 (1984): 264–269.

Gilbert, William H., Jr. "Memorandum Concerning the Characteristics of the Larger Mixed-Blood Racial Islands of the Eastern United States." *Social Forces* 25 (1946): 438–47.

Gottfried, Robert S. *The Black Death*. New York: Free Press. 1983.

Harris, David. "The 1990 Census Count of American Indians: What Do the Numbers Really Mean?" *Social Science Quarterly* 75 (1994): 580–93.

Harvey, M. R. "Population of the Cahuilla Indians: Decline and Its Causes." *Eugenics Quarterly* 14 (1967): 185–98.

Heizer, Robert F., and Albert B. Elsasser. *The Natural World of the California Indians*. Berkeley: University of California Press, 1980.

Henige, David. "Primary Source by Primary Source? On the Role of Epidemics in New World Depopulation." *Ethnohistory* 33 (1986): 293–312.

———. "Their Number Become Thick: Native American Historical Demography as Expiation." In *The Invented Indian: Cultural Fictions and Government Policies*, edited by James Clifton, 169–91. Princeton, N.J.: Transaction Books, 1990.

Herring, D. Ann. "There Were Young People and Old People and Babies Dying Every Week": The 1918–1919 Influenza Pandemic at Norway House." *Ethnohistory* 41 (1994): 73–105.

Hoxie, Frederick E., ed. *Encyclopedia of North American Indians*. Boston: Houghton Mifflin, 1996.

Hurtado, Albert L. *Indian Survival on the California Frontier*. New Haven: Yale University Press, 1988.

Johansson, S. Ryan. "The Demographic History of the Native Peoples of North America: A Selective Bibliography." *Yearbook of Physical Anthropology* 25 (1982): 133–52.

Kroeber, Alfred L. *Handbook of the Indians of California*. Washington, D.C.: U.S. Government Printing Office, 1925.

———. "Cultural and Natural Areas of Native North America." *University of California Publications in American Archaeology and Ethnology* 38 (1939): 1–242.

Larsen, Clark Spencer. "In the Wake of Columbus: Native Population Biology in the Postcontact Americas." *Yearbook of Physical Anthropology* 37 (1994): 109–54.

McNeill, William H. *Plagues and Peoples*. Garden City, N.Y.: Anchor Doubleday, 1976.

Meister, Cary W. "Demographic Consequences of Euro-American Contact on Selected

American Indian Populations and Their Relationship to the Demographic Transistion." *Ethnohistory* 23 (1976): 161–72.

Merbs, Charles F. "A New World of Infectious Disease." *Yearbook of Physical Anthropology* 35 (1992): 3–42.

Merriam, C. Hart. "The Indian Population of California." *American Anthropologist* 7 (1905): 594–606.

Milanich, Jerald T. "The European Entrada into La Florida." In *Columbian Consequences*, vol. 2 of *Archaeological and Historical Perspectives on the Spanish Borderlands East*, edited by David Hurst Thomas, 3–26. Washington, D.C.: Smithsonian Institution Press, 1990.

Mooney, James. "The Powhatan Confederacy, Past and Present." *American Anthropologist* 9 (1907): 129–52.

———. "Population." In *Handbook of American Indians North of Mexico*, vol. 2, edited by Frederick W. Hodge, 286–87. Smithsonian Institution, Bureau of American Ethnology Bulletin 30. Washington, D.C.: U.S. Government Printing Office, 1910.

———. "The Aboriginal Population of America North of Mexico." In *Smithsonian Miscellaneous Collections*, vol. 80 (1928), edited by John R. Swanton, 1–40.

Nagel, Joane. "Politics and the Resurgence of American Indian Ethnic Identity." *American Sociological Review* 60 (1995): 947–65.

Newman, Marshall T. "Aboriginal New World Epidemiology and Medical Care, and The Impact of Old World Disease Imports." *American Journal of Physical Anthropology* 45 (1976): 667–72.

Nordyke, Eleanor C. *The Peopling of Hawai'i*, 2d ed. Honolulu: University of Hawaii Press, 1989 [1977].

Palmer, Edward Nelson. "Culture Contacts and Population Growth." *American Journal of Sociology* 53 (1948): 258–62.

Passel, Jeffery S. "Provisional Evaluation of the 1970 Census Count of American Indians." *Demography* 13 (1976): 397–409.

Passel, Jeffery S., and Patricia A. Berman, "Quality of 1980 Census Data for American Indians," *Social Biology* 33 (1986): 163–82.

Pool, D. Ian. *The Maori Population of New Zealand*, 1769–1971. Auckland: Auckland University Press, 1977.

Powers, Stephen. *Tribes of California. Contributions to North American Ethnology*, vol. 3. Reprint. Washington, D.C.: U.S. Government Printing Office, 1987.

Ramenofsky, Ann F. *Vectors of Death*: The Archaeology of European Contact. Albuquerque: University of New Mexico Press, 1987.

Rawls, James J. *Indians of California*: *The Changing Image*. Norman: University of Oklahoma Press, 1984.

Reff, Daniel T. "The Introduction of Smallpox in the Greater Southwest." *American Anthropologist* 89 (1987): 704–8.

Reinhard, Karl J. "Archaeoparasitology in North America." *American Journal of Physical Anthropology* 82 (1990): 145–63.

Sandefur, Gary D., and Trudy McKinnell. "American Indian Intermarriage." *Social Science Research* 15 (1986): 347–71.

Schmitt, Robert C. *Demographic Statistics of Hawaii: 1778–1965.* Honolulu: University of Hawaii Press, 1968.

Smith, Marvin T. *Archaeology of Aboriginal Cultural Change in the Interior Southeast.* Gainesville: University of Florida Press, 1987.

Snow, Dean, and Kim M. Lanphear. "European Contact and Indian Depopulation in the Northeast: The Timing of the First Epidemics." *Ethnohistory* 35 (1988): 15–33.

Stannard, David E. *Before the Horror.* Honolulu: University of Hawaii Press, 1989.

Thornton, Russell. "Recent Estimates of the Prehistoric California Indian Population. *Current Anthropology* 21 (1980): 702–4.

———. "But How Thick Were They? Review Essay of *Their Number Become Thinned,* by Henry F. Dobyns." *Contemporary Sociology* 13 (1984): 145–50.

———. "Cherokee Population Losses during the 'Trail of Tears': A New Perspective and a New Estimate." *Ethnohistory* 31 (1984): 289–300.

———. "Social Organization and the Demographic Survival of the Tolowa." *Ethnohistory* 31 (1984): 187–96.

———. "History, Structure and Survival: A Comparison of the Yuki (Unkomno'n) and Tolowa (Hush) Indians of Northern California." *Ethnology* 25 (1986): 119–30.

———. *American Indian Holocaust and Survival: A Population History since 1492.* Norman: University of Oklahoma Press, 1987.

———. *Tribal History, Tribal Population, and Tribal Membership Requirements: The Case of the Cherokees."* Occasional Papers Series no. 8. D'Arcy McNickle Center for the History of the American Indian, Newberry Library.

———. *The Cherokees: A Population History.* Lincoln: University of Nebraska Press, 1991.

———. "Population." In *Native Americans in the 20th Century: An Encyclopedia,* edited by Mary B. Davis, 461–64. New York: Garland, 1994.

———. "Urbanization." In *Native Americans in the 20th Century: An Encyclopedia,* edited by Mary B. Davis, 670–72. New York: Garland, 1994.

———. "Tribal Membership Requirements and the Demography of 'Old' and 'New' Native Americans. In *Changing Numbers, Changing Needs: American Indian Demography and Public Health,* edited by Gary D. Sandefur, Ronald R. Rindfuss, and Barney Cohen, 103–12. Washington, D.C.: National Academy Press, 1996.

———. "Aboriginal North American Population and Rates of Decline, ca. A.D. 1500–1900." *Current Anthropology,* in press.

Thornton, Russell, and Joan Marsh-Thornton. "Estimating Prehistoric American Indian Population Size for United States Area: Implications of the Nineteenth Century Population Decline and Nadir." *American Journal of Physical Anthropology* 55 (1981): 47–53.

Thornton, Russell, Tim Miller, and Jonathan Warren. "American Indian Population Recovery following Smallpox Epidemics." *American Anthropologist* 93 (1991): 20–38.

Thornton, Russell, Gary D. Sandefur, and C. Matthew Snipp. "American Indian Fertility Patterns: 1910 and 1940 to 1980." *American Indian Quarterly* 15 (1991): 359–67.

Thornton, Russell, Jonathan Warren, and Tim Miller. "Depopulation in the Southeast after 1492." In *Disease and Demography in the Americas,* edited by John W. Verano and Douglas H. Ubelaker, 187–95. Washington, D.C.: Smithsonian Institution Press, 1992.

Ubelaker, Douglas H. "North American Indian Population Size, 49A.D. 1500 to 1985." *American Journal of Physical Anthropology* 77 (1988): 289–94.

U.S. Bureau of the Census. *1990 Census of Population. General Population Characteristics. American Indian and Alaska Native Areas.* Washington, D.C.: U.S. Government Printing Office, September 1992.

———. *1990 Census of Population. Characteristics of American Indians by Tribe and Language, 1990 CP-3-7.* Washington, D.C.: U.S. Government Printing Office, July 1994.

———. *We the . . . First Americans.* Washington, D.C.: U.S. Government Printing Office, September 1993.

Upham, Steadman. "Smallpox and Climate in the American Southwest." *American Anthropologist* 88 (1986): 115–28.

Walker, Phillip L., and John R. Johnson. "The Decline of the Chumash Indian Population." In *In the Wake of Contact: Biological Responses to Conquest*, edited by C. S. Larsen and G. R. Milner, 109–20. New York: Wiley-Liss, 1994.

Walker, Phillip L., and Russell Thornton. "Health, Nutrition, and Demographic Change in Native California." Paper presented at the Second Conference on a History of Health and Nutrition in the Western Hemisphere, Columbus, Ohio, 1996.

3

PATTERNS OF DISEASE IN EARLY NORTH AMERICAN POPULATIONS

DOUGLAS H. UBELAKER

Few issues relating to the history of the American Indian have involved more academic controversy than the size of the North American population in 1492. Low numbers imply that population growth prior to 1492 was limited by fertility, food resources, and/or disease. Low numbers also suggest that post-1492 mortality was less severe and that the present Indian population has stronger links to the past. High estimates of population size suggest that few checks operated on pre-1492 population growth and that historic mortality was devastating, reducing the North American Indian population to a small fraction of the original number. Debate on these issues focuses on interpretation of data from a variety of sources (including early historic accounts), information on the impact of infectious diseases in other regions, ethnohistorical and archaeological evidence for diet and social complexity, and study of the skeletal remains of the ancient peoples themselves.

POPULATION ESTIMATES FOR 1492

Given the inexact nature of these sources, it should come as no surprise that scholars cannot agree on the numbers. Most attempts to estimate 1492 population size rely heavily upon the earliest written accounts. Such sources were European explorers, settlers, military and religious leaders, or others who were not trained census takers. Their contact with the groups in question may have been limited, and some may have exaggerated the counts to fit their own political needs or assumptions. In many cases, their estimates of population size or descriptions of the people they encountered may have come too late to contribute to our knowledge of precontact population size. The introduction of disease pathogens into Native American communities, spread through Indian networks, may have preceded actual contact by Europeans.

Archaeological sources offer information directly relevant to the time periods in question. Theoretically, the size of occupation areas, coupled with accurate dating and some sound reasoning from ethnohistoric analogy, should generate estimates of population size. Frequently, researchers utilizing such approaches have difficulty controlling for variables such as the number of structures within the site occupied contemporaneously, the duration of occupation for each structure, and the number of individuals living within each structure. In many cases, erosion or incomplete excavation may limit the extent of the occupation area studied.

Analysis of human remains recovered from archaeological sites offers direct information on numbers of individuals. Estimates of age at death, assembled to reconstruct life tables and other demographic statistics, not only provide useful indicators of mortality and survivorship, but allow the calculation of the crude mortality rate. This statistic, used with knowledge of the length of time represented by the skeletal sample, can generate population estimates.[1] Although promising, these data also have limitations. In many cases, skeletal age (especially in the elderly) cannot be estimated accurately, especially from fragmentary remains. The archaeologically recovered skeletal sample may not adequately represent deaths in the population because of incomplete excavation, curation factors, complex mortuary procedures, or preservation. The fragile skeletons of the very young and very old are especially susceptible to postmortem decomposition. Although the distribution of ages at death clearly reflects population mortality, the statistics generated from such samples can be influenced by population growth and fertility.

Instability in this database has led scholars to quite varied estimates of the size of the North American population in 1492 (Table 3.1). Low estimates of 900,000 to just over one million were reported by a number of scholars working prior to 1962. The most comprehensive approach of the period was that of James Mooney, a Smithsonian Institution ethnologist who attempted to estimate the size of each tribe using a variety of data. His data and total of 1,148,000 were published posthumously by John R. Swanton in 1928 and formed most of the basis of A. L. Kroeber's work in

---

[1] Ubelaker, *Reconstruction of Demographic Profiles.*

Table 3.1. *Estimates of North American population size prior to European contact*

Author	Estimate
Mooney 1910	1,148,000
Sapper 1924	2,500,000–3,500,000
Rivet 1924	1,148,000
Mooney 1928	1,153,000
Willcox 1931	1,002,000
Kroeber 1939	900,000
Rosenblat 1945	1,000,000
Steward 1945	1,000,000
Ashburn 1947	2,000,000–2,500,000
Steward 1949	1,000,880
Rivet, Stresser, and Loukotka 1952	1,000,000
Driver 1961	1,000,000–2,000,000
Dobyns 1966	9,800,000
Ubelaker 1976	2,171,125
Denevan 1976	4,400,000
Dobyns 1983	18,000,000
Thornton 1987	7,000,000
Ubelaker 1988	1,894,350

Source: Modified from Ubelaker, "North American Indian population size," p. 171.

1939. Kroeber adopted all of Mooney's estimates except those for California, where he substituted his own and studied the relationship between population density and ecological factors. The Mooney–Kroeber estimates influenced scholars for decades and were for the most part derived from Mooney's careful reading of the early ethnohistorical sources.[2]

Archival study of Mooney's unpublished notes on this project revealed that his estimates generally reflected the earliest reliable figures available and not necessarily the estimate for the condition in 1492.[3] In many instances, his notes indicate that the 1492 number likely was greater than the figure presented, since the population may have already declined in size prior to the date of the population figures available. This point was elaborated in a 1966 publication by Henry Dobyns, which has greatly influenced subsequent estimates. Dobyns argued that epidemic disease,

[2] Ubelaker, "The sources and methodology," pp. 243–88.
[3] Ubelaker, "The sources and methodology."

introduced by European contact, spread rapidly ahead of actual European contact and greatly reduced American Indian population size. Using broad projections of the expected ratio between aboriginal numbers and the number at nadir (point of maximum population decline), Dobyns estimated the North American population size at 9.8 million, a figure nearly 11 times greater than Kroeber had estimated back in 1939. In effect, Dobyns argued that previous estimates greatly underestimated population size, because their primary sources were dated too late to recognize major early population declines due to epidemic disease. Later, Dobyns increased his North American estimate to 18 million.[4]

Although the large Dobyns estimates have been criticized for incorporating unsupported interpretations of primary sources, they have greatly influenced many scholars who generally recognize greater population size than suggested by Mooney and Kroeber.[5] Even then, estimates of individual tribal groups, utilizing all the data available, generally exceed earlier estimates, but fall significantly short of the figure predicted by Dobyns. A 1988 survey of estimates of individual tribal population size by specialists on those groups calculated that the total North American population in 1492 was 1,894,350.[6]

All scholars agree that during early historic times, the American Indian population declined. Elsewhere I have suggested that the North American population reached a low point of about 530,000 around 1900.[7] This figure suggests a population decline of 97% using the high Dobyns figure, but only 72% using my figure of 1,894,350, and only 41% using the low Kroeber figure of 900,000. Obviously, a 97% reduction implies a more catastrophic impact of disease than 41% and greatly affects one's perception of the American Indian experience in the early historic period.

In generating his high estimates, Dobyns assumes high fertility and low mortality on the part of the pre-1492 American Indian population. Dobyns employs a Malthusian logic that population increased rapidly with an abundant food supply and in the absence of significant disease. In a chapter subtitled "Paradise Lost" in his 1983 book, Dobyns argues that the American Indian population increased rapidly because it was in a "relatively disease free environment."[8] Dobyns's review of the early

---

[4] Dobyns, *Their Number Become Thinned.*
[5] Henige, "Their number become thick," pp. 169–91; Ubelaker, "The sources and methodology."
[6] Ubelaker, "North American Indian population size," pp. 289–94.
[7] Ubelaker, "North American census, 1492," pp. 32–35.
[8] Dobyns, *Their Number Become Thinned*, p. 34.

ethnohistorical literature and other sources suggested the pre-European contact presence of *verruga*, some form of treponemal disease, and intestinal parasites. He argued that *verruga* was transmitted by a *verruga* sand fly and was confined in the Americas to Andean highland valleys. In his view, the "near-absence of lethal pathogens in the aboriginal New World allowed the native peoples to live in almost a paradise of well-being [and] people simply did not very often die from illnesses prior to the Columbian Exchange."[9] Dobyns and others who estimate a very large pre-Columbian North American Indian population assume that the lack of disease allowed North American populations to increase to the limits of their food resources.

In a general survey of human infectious disease around the world, Van Blerkom also argues for the "relative lack of disease in the Americas."[10] This view of comparative good health in the Americas is echoed by prominent physical anthropologist T. D. Stewart, who in 1973 described the precontact American population as comparatively healthy.[11] Stewart attributed their good health to their original migration route through Beringia, with cold temperatures unfavorable to the transmission of disease. This "cold filter" hypothesis has been used by others to explain Old World–New World differences in disease patterns. How realistic is this interpretation? This essay explores the evidence for morbidity in pre-European-contact North America. This evidence suggests that a variety of disease conditions were present, and that they were increasing in frequency through time prior to European contact. Such problems may have constrained population growth.

PALEOPATHOLOGY

Although some evidence for precontact disease in North America originates from early ethnohistorical sources and art, the most reliable data are derived from the study of precontact human remains through the science of paleopathology and human skeletal biology. In many cases, human remains offer direct evidence of the disease experience of the individual. Interpretation is complicated by the fact that not all diseases affect bone and many disease processes can affect bone in similar ways.

---

[9] Dobyns, *Their Number Become Thinned*, p. 35.   [10] Van Blerkom, *The Evolution*.
[11] Stewart, *The People of America*.

The science of paleopathology began back in 1774 when Johann Friedrich Esper published his analysis of the diseased femur of a fossil cave bear found in France. Since then, the field has grown dramatically into an interdisciplinary science that involves interpretation of diverse evidence. In the early history of the field, discussion of unusual conditions found on North American samples was largely limited to interpreting cranial deformation, caused by practices employed to alter the shape of the skull during growth.[12]

The first major analysis of disease in North American Indian remains was conducted by Joseph Jones in 1876, concentrating on human remains recovered archaeologically from the eastern United States. Various publications throughout the remainder of the nineteenth century presented growing evidence for considerable trauma in pre-Columbian times and debated the evidence for syphilis. From 1900 to 1930, Aleš Hrdlička, R. L. Moodie, H. U. Williams, and others expanded the research to infectious disease and presented further evidence of diversity of disease in pre-Columbian America.[13]

The period following 1930 witnessed a surge of professional interest in paleopathology and a shift in emphasis to a more population-oriented, epidemiological approach. Early pioneers of this research, such as E. A. Hooton and J. L. Angel, demonstrated that analysis of skeletal disease linked with archaeological information regarding population density and cultural factors allowed significant interpretation at the population level.[14] The epidemiological approach focuses less on tracing the history of individual diseases (the prior emphasis) and more on the frequency of disease expression in the population and how it relates to cultural factors. To a large extent, this approach was only possible after 1930, when large, carefully excavated samples of well-documented human remains became available for study.

The arrival of the modern period of epidemiological/population

---

[12] Ubelaker, "The development," pp. 337–56; Warren, "Account," pp. 129–44; Warren, "North American antiquities," pp. 47–49.

[13] Hrdlička, "Description"; Hrdlička, "Report," pp. 103–319; Hrdlička, "Physical anthropology"; Hrdlička, "Anthropology and medicine," pp. 1–9; Moodie, "Studies in paleopathology," pp. 374–93; Moodie, *The Antiquity of Disease*; Moodie, *Paleopathology*; Williams, "Human paleopathology," pp. 839–902.

[14] Hooton, *The Indians*; Angel, "Health and the course of civilization," pp. 15–17 and 45–48; Angel, "Human biological changes," pp. 266–70; Angel, "Physical anthropology and medicine," pp. 107–16; Angel, "Osteoporosis," pp. 369–74; Angel, "Porotic hyperostosis, anemias, malarias, and marshes," pp. 760–63; Angel, *Early Skeletons*; Angel, "Porotic hyperostosis or osteoporosis symmetrica," pp. 378–89; Angel, *The People of Lerna*; Angel, "Early Neolithic people," pp. 103–12; Angel, "Patterns of fractures," pp. 9–18; Angel, "Paleoecology," pp. 167–90.

approaches within paleopathology is coupled with technological and methodological advances in researchers' ability to diagnose individual disease. Traditional observational approaches to diagnosis now can be supplemented with radiographic, microscopic, and chemical techniques, including new molecular DNA technology.[15] Diagnosis has also been improved by more thoughtful analysis of bone response to specific disease and how various diseases produce similar bone reaction.[16] The role of pseudopathology, or postmortem change mimicking pathology, also has been recognized.[17]

TUBERCULOSIS

Human tuberculosis is caused by the acid-fast bacillus *Mycobacterium tuberculosis*. The organism is usually introduced through the respiratory tract but also can enter through the digestive system. The more common respiratory involvement leads to a primary focus in the lungs, with secondary involvement in the lymphatic system. In modern times, the primary focus heals without further involvement of the system. If this focus does not heal, the organism may be distributed by the circulatory system to other areas of the body. This process may take years and be precipitated by other body stress. The skeleton is involved in 3 to 7% of individuals with the disease.[18]

Skeletal tuberculosis usually is apparent in the vertebral column, especially the lower thoracic and upper lumbar region. Other areas of involvement include the hip, knee, ankle, fingers and toes, sacroiliac joint, femur, shoulder, elbow, ribs, and skull. In the vertebrae, it is known as Pott's disease and produces extensive destruction of bone, primarily on the centra. The result is structurally weakened bone that can collapse under mechanical stress. Collapsed bone with minimal bone regeneration leads to marked curvature (kyphosis) of the spine. Since the spine is the most frequent site of skeletal tuberculosis, it usually provides the evidence for paleopathological diagnosis. Other diseases that can show skeletal effects similar to those produced by tuberculosis are osteomyelitis (bone infection) and trauma.

[15] Morell, "Mummy," pp. 1686–7; Salo et al., pp. 2091–4.
[16] Ortner and Putschar, *Identification*; Steinbock, *Paleopathological Diagnosis and Interpretation*; Buikstra, ed., *Prehistoric Tuberculosis*.
[17] Minear and Rhine, "Increased radiographic density," pp. 1–8.
[18] Steinbock, *Paleopathological Diagnosis and Interpretation*; Kastert and Uehlinger, "Skelettuberkulose."

H. Jean Shadomy notes that several diseases caused by fungi, especially *Coccidioides immitis, Blastomyces dermatitides*, and *Cryptococcus neoformans*, can produce skeletal changes similar to those of tuberculosis.[19]

Historically, tuberculosis has been a significant disease among North American Indians. Hrdlička's 1909 survey of the disease among tribes revealed much higher frequencies than found among other North American populations.[20] Hrdlička felt the high frequency of the disease was caused by their living conditions and customs but also suggested they may have lacked immunological ability to resist because the disease was relatively new. Hrdlička felt the disease was rare (if it existed at all) in precontact times. His evidence for this was (1) the lack of ethnohistorical reference to the disease, (2) the lack of Indian knowledge of treatment, (3) Indian oral history indicating that it was a new disease, (4) the lack of evidence of prior exposure among the elderly, (5) ethnohistorical references to increased frequency in the recent past, (6) the lack of skeletal evidence from precontact contexts, (7) greater vulnerability to the disease among Indians than among others, and (8) the assumption that pre-reservation life was less conducive to the disease.

Since Hrdlička's time, academic interpretations of the likelihood of pre-Columbian tuberculosis have changed dramatically. Scholars note that early ethnohistorical descriptions of nearly all diseases are difficult to interpret because the language of the times lacked descriptive medical precision. Lack of evidence among the elderly only indicates lack of exposure in the previous few decades, whereas precontact disease and even early episodes of disease introduced at contact would have predated Hrdlička by more than one generation. Jane E. Buikstra argues that Hrdlička's point 8 is the key conjecture; that is, reservation conditions and the change in lifestyle associated with acculturation greatly increased Indian vulnerability to the disease.[21]

Even more important, paleopathological analysis of precontact human remains from the Americas clearly demonstrates that Hrdlička's point 6 was erroneous. The disease was in the Americas prior to 1492. The strongest evidence for this recently comes from a 40- to 45-year-old mummified woman of the 900-year-old Chiribaya culture of the south coast of Peru. Scientists examined lung and lymph node samples using

---

[19] Shadomy, "The differential diagnosis," pp. 25–34.
[20] Hrdlička, *Tuberculosis*.   [21] Buikstra, "Introduction," pp. 1–23.

molecular PCR techniques, and DNA amplification produced a sequence matching modern *Mycobacterium tuberculosis.*[22]

The DNA-based diagnosis follows the discovery of acid-fast bacilli in a South American mummy, otherwise exhibiting evidence of skeletal and soft-tissue tuberculosis.[23] The mummy from southern Peru was reported to be of Nazca culture, dating to about A.D. 700. Autopsy revealed tuberculosis of the lung, pleura, liver, and right kidney, as well as Pott's disease with a psoas abscess. According to Buikstra, the precontact date for this mummy is not entirely secure.[24] Marvin J. Allison, Daniel Mendoza, and Alejandro Pezzia further report that subsequent analysis of 330 mummies dating back to the eighth century A.D. revealed two pulmonary cases with acid-fast bacilli and nine more presenting evidence for tuberculosis, but not for bacilli.[25]

Skeletal evidence for tuberculosis in precontact North America is now abundant. Examples of skeletal lesions consistent with tuberculosis have been reported from precontact archaeological contexts in the American Southwest.[26] M. Anne Katzenberg and Lee Widmer and Anthony J. Perzigian describe various examples from Ohio and Tennessee, all dating to before A.D. 1275.[27] Perzigian et al. report tuberculosis from a Fort Ancient sample (Mississippian) from the Ohio River Valley.[28] John A. Williams found five cases of skeletal tuberculosis in samples of Archaic and Woodland populations in the Northern Plains.[29] John B. Gregg and Pauline S. Gregg and Ann M. Palkovich report examples from the Plains, although Palkovich's Arikara sample was protohistoric and thus in the period of possible European introduction of disease.[30] Buikstra and Della C. Cook suggest that tuberculosis has not been detected during Woodland times in Illinois but is found in Mississippian period (last millennium) peoples.[31] The Illinois presence is further dis-

---

[22] Morell, "Mummy"; Salo et al., "Identification."

[23] Allison, Mendoza, and Pezzia, "Documentation," pp. 985–91.

[24] Buikstra, "Introduction."   [25] Allison, Gerszten, et al., "Tuberculosis," pp. 49–61.

[26] Stodder and Martin, "Health and disease," pp. 55–73; Merbs, "Patterns of health and sickness," pp. 41–55; Fink, "Tuberculosis and anemia," pp. 359–79; Micozzi and Kelley, "Evidence for precolumbian tuberculosis," pp. 347–58.

[27] Katzenberg, "An investigation of spinal disease," pp. 349–55; Widmer and Perzigian, "The ecology and etiology," pp. 99–113.

[28] Perzigian, Tench, and Braun, "Prehistoric health," pp. 347–66.

[29] Williams, "Disease profiles," pp. 91–108.

[30] Gregg and Gregg, *Dry Bones*; Palkovich, "Tuberculosis epidemiology," pp. 161–75.

[31] Buikstra and Cook, "Pre-Columbian tuberculosis," pp. 115–39.

cussed by George R. Milner and Milner et al.[32] Norman C. Sullivan describes resorptive spinal disease suggestive of tuberculosis in a subadult male from the Raisbeck Mounds, Grant County, Wisconsin, dating to the Middle Effigy Mound phase, A.D. 700 to 1100.[33] Clark Spencer Larsen et al. report evidence for tuberculosis from the Irene Mound site on the Georgia coast, dating from A.D. 1200 to 1450.[34] Patricia Miller-Shaivitz and Mehmet Yasar Iscan include tuberculosis among diseases detected in their prehistoric sample from Fort Center, Florida.[35] Precontact Canadian samples are reported by Jerome S. Cybulski from Hesquiat Harbour, British Columbia; by Patrick C. Hartney from the Glen Williams site, an Iroquoian ossuary in southern Ontario; and by Susan Pfeiffer and Scott I. Fairgrieve from various Ontario ossuaries predating A.D. 1400.[36]

Mary Lucas Powell reports likely tuberculosis in a young adult male from the Mississippian site of Moundville, Alabama, dating to between A.D. 1050 and 1550.[37] In a review of these and other cases, Powell found examples of precontact tuberculosis in specimens from Chile, Peru, Ontario, New York, Ohio, Illinois, Arizona, New Mexico, Arkansas, Tennessee, Alabama, and Georgia.[38] The numerous examples led Mahmoud Y. El-Najjar to conclude that the disease was endemic in the pre-Columbian New World.[39] R. Ted Steinbock considers tuberculosis to have been present in both the New and Old Worlds prior to 1492.[40]

TREPONEMAL DISEASE

Most researchers recognize four closely related types of treponemal disease: venereal syphilis, nonvenereal syphilis (bejel), yaws, and pinta. The skeleton can be involved in all but pinta. Venereal syphilis is acquired through sexual intercourse and may be transmitted to a fetus through an infected mother (hence the name congenital syphilis). According to Steinbock, only 10 to 20% of patients with acquired venereal syphilis have skeletal

---

[32] Milner, "Health and cultural change," pp. 52–69; Milner, Anderson, and Smith, "Warfare," pp. 581–603.
[33] Sullivan, "Tuberculosis," pp. 71–76.
[34] Larsen, Ruff, Schoeninger, and Hutchinson, "Population decline," pp. 25–39.
[35] Miller-Shaivitz and Iscan, "The prehistoric people," pp. 131–47.
[36] Cybulski, *An Earlier Population*; Hartney." Tuberculosis lesions," pp. 141–60; Pfeiffer and Fairgrieve, "Evidence from ossuaries," pp. 47–61.
[37] Powell, "Ranked status and health," pp. 22–51.   [38] Powell, "Health and disease," pp. 41–53.
[39] El-Najjar, "Human treponematosis and tuberculosis," pp. 599–618.
[40] Steinbock, *Paleopathological Diagnosis and Interpretation*.

symptoms.[41] The bones most often involved are the tibia, fibula, nasal, parietal, frontal, palatine, clavicle, radius, and ulna, although many others may also be involved. Usually, the outer layer of the bone is involved, producing thickening and increased density. As a result, the entire bone is abnormally thick, with irregular surfaces.

Early congenital syphilis can involve different types of bone infection, namely osteochondritis, periostitis, and diaphyseal osteomyelitis, usually in the long bones. According to Steinbock, the skull is involved in only 5 to 10% of the cases.[42] If the disease remains latent in the early childhood years and becomes skeletally involved in ages 5 to 15, then the skeletal manifestation resembles acquired syphilis. The "classic" expressions are substantial bone deposits on the anterior surface of the tibiae, producing "saber-shin tibiae," and bony destruction around the nasal area. Dental alterations also can result from congenital syphilis, usually affecting the maxillary teeth. Specific dental changes include Hutchinson's teeth (deformed incisors) and mulberry molars (irregular first molar).

Nonvenereal syphilis, or bejel, occurs in warm, arid climates and usually is transmitted during childhood. Skeletal involvement is unusual and, unlike venereal syphilis, the disease rarely involves the cranial vault. Other skeletal manifestations closely resemble those of venereal syphilis, especially characteristic changes of the nasal/palatal area and bone deposits on the tibia.

Yaws is found in hot, humid climates and is primarily a childhood disease. Yaws produces skin ulcers, which allow disease transmission among scantily clad children in tropical areas. Bony involvement is uncommon (1 to 5%) but when present is similar to that of congenital syphilis, except that greater involvement of the hand bones occurs in the late stages of yaws.

Researchers have long debated the relationship of these treponemal diseases. Some have argued that they represent distinct diseases, others that they are different expressions of the same disease or are caused by different strains of the organism *Treponema pallidum*. Clearly, syphilis and yaws can produce similar skeletal alterations.

In 1973, Stewart noted the difficulties in recognizing individual treponemal disease.[43] He believed that pinta or yaws had to have been present in the Americas, but he remained unconvinced by the evidence for syphilis

[41] Steinbock, *Paleopathological Diagnosis and Interpretation*, p. 109.
[42] Steinbock, *Paleopathological Diagnosis and Interpretation*, p. 99.
[43] Stewart, *The People of America*.

in all early skeletons, both in the New and Old Worlds. Stewart suggested that the different forms of treponemal disease known today might be different environmental expressions of the same disease and questioned whether syphilis might be a relatively new disease.

Paleopathological research has gradually accumulated strong evidence of treponemal-like lesions from pre-Columbian skeletons. Harold N. Cole et al. report two adult skeletons "pathognomonic of syphilis" from an Arizona cave dating to between A.D. 1233 and A.D. 1306.[44] Charles F. Merbs and Ann L. W. Stodder and Debra L. Martin summarize additional evidence from the Southwest.[45] Phillip L. Walker and Patricia Lambert report evidence for endemic syphilis in prehistoric California populations.[46] Dan Morse found likely treponemal disease in a sample from Dickson Mound, Illinois (A.D. 1200–1400).[47] Milner adds evidence of possible treponemal disease from the prehistoric Cahokia site in Illinois.[48] Gregg and Gregg report treponemal disease from the prehistoric Plains Crow Creek site.[49] James J. Elting and William A. Starna add a possible case from the Palatine Bridge site dating to 500 B.C.[50] S. J. Schermer et al. report evidence of treponemal disease from the Iowa sites Pooler, Haven, and the Council Bluffs Ossuary dating from the Late Archaic to Woodland.[51]

In the Southeast, Miller-Shaivitz and Iscan report treponemal disease from the prehistoric site of Fort Center, Florida.[52] Larsen et al. found evidence for the disease at the Irene Mound site (A.D. 1200–1450).[53] Kathleen J. Reichs describes a possible case of treponemal disease in a 35- to 50-year-old female from the late prehistoric Hardin site in the North Carolina Piedmont region.[54] Barbara Lewis describes evidence for endemic syphilis in a southeastern Tchefuncte burial dating to 500 B.C. to A.D. 300.[55] Powell found evidence for endemic treponematosis at the Mississippian site of Moundville, Alabama.[56] Adelaide K. Bullen summarizes evidence for the disease in precontact Florida.[57] Georgieann Bogdan and

---

[44] Cole, Harlein, et al., "Pre-Columbian osseous syphilis," pp. 231–38.
[45] Merbs, "Patterns of health and sickness"; Stodder and Martin, "Health and disease."
[46] Walker and Lambert, "Skeletal evidence"; Walker and Lambert, "Paleopathological evidence."
[47] Morse, "Two cases," pp. 48–60.   [48] Milner, "Health and cultural change."
[49] Gregg and Gregg, *Dry Bones.*   [50] Elting and Starna, "A possible case," pp. 267–73.
[51] Schermer, Fisher, and Hodges, "Endemic treponematosis," pp. 109–21.
[52] Miller-Shaivitz and Iscan, "The prehistoric people."
[53] Larsen, Ruff, Schoeninger, and Hutchinson, "Population decline."
[54] Reichs, "Treponematosis," pp. 289–303.
[55] Lewis, "Treponematosis and Lyme Borreliosis connections," pp. 455–75.
[56] Powell, "Ranked status and health."   [57] Bullen, "Paleoepidemiology," pp. 133–71.

David S. Weaver provide additional discussion of examples from North Carolina.[58]

In a review of these examples (and others), Powell and B. J. Baker and G. J. Armelagos report that evidence for precontact treponemal disease in the New World is available for many states and countries, including Alabama, Arizona, Arkansas, California, Canada, Colorado, Florida, Georgia, Illinois, Iowa, Kentucky, Missouri, New Mexico, New York, North Carolina, Ohio, Oklahoma, Tennessee, Virginia, Argentina, Colombia, Guatemala, Mexico, and Peru.[59] Such evidence led El-Najjar to suggest that syphilis survived the cold Arctic early human migration route to produce a new, virulent strain of the disease.[60] Following others, Merbs includes syphilis and pinta among precontact New World diseases.[61]

OTHER DISEASE CONDITIONS

Although evidence for tuberculosis and treponemal disease has attracted considerable scholarly attention, many other abnormal conditions are thought to have been present in pre-Columbian North America. As early as 1923, Moodie recorded many examples of trauma for the period, including simple fractures and congenital hip abnormalities, ear exostoses, periostitis, arthritis, dental problems (especially dental caries), and evidence of violence such as embedded arrow points.[62] He also mentioned ankylosing spondylitis and osteomyelitis.

In a thoughtful overview of the pre-1492 New World disease presence, Merbs lists hepatitis, leishmaniasis (uta), oroya fever, *verruga peruana*, staphylococcal and streptococcal infections, gastroenteritis, fungal infections, gastrointestinal illnesses, respiratory infections, and a variety of parasites.[63] He also notes more speculative evidence for leptospirosis, paratyphoid fever, shigellosis, tularemia, Rocky Mountain spotted fever, paracoccidioidomycosis, coccidioidomycosis, and rheumatoid arthritis.

Additional literature suggests that pre-1492 North American health problems included multiple myeloma, microcephaly, congenital radioulnar synostosis, achondroplasia, spondylolisthesis, possibly Paget's disease, degenerative bone disease, amputation, penetrating wounds, scalping,

---

[58] Bogdan and Weaver, "Pre-Columbian treponematosis," pp. 155–63.
[59] Powell, "Health and disease"; Baker and Armelagos, "The origin and antiquity," pp. 703–37.
[60] El-Najjar, "Human treponematosis and tuberculosis."   [61] Merbs, "A new world," pp. 3–24.
[62] Moodie, *Paleopathology*.   [63] Merbs, "A new world."

cysts, calcified subperiosteal hematoma, nasal septal deformities, osteomas, myositis ossificans, torus palatinus, stafne defect, hemangioma, probable osteochondroma, fibrous dysplasia, enchondroma, Histiocytosis X (eosinophilic granuloma), cortical bone loss with age, cribra orbitalia, lines of arrested growth, iron deficiency anemia, scurvy, hip dislocation, pseudoarthrosis, osteochondritis dissecans, osteoporosis, macrocephaly, cleft palate, mandible asymmetry, sinus maldevelopment, various forms of dental disease, and intentional modifications of the body, especially dental mutilation and cranial deformation.[64] The evidence suggesting these pathological conditions can be gleaned from scores of studies of individual well-documented skeletal samples from ancient times.

DENTAL CARIES

Likely the most common affliction in precontact North America was dental caries, a disease that breaks down the tooth surface through substances produced by colonizing bacteria. Although the frequency of dental caries varies, there is at least some evidence of the disease among all North American populations.[65]

Throughout North America, the frequency of dental caries increased over time, largely because of shifts in subsistence. Caries-generating bacteria thrive on the plaque produced by high-carbohydrate diets. Food preparation techniques also are important. Merbs notes that the practice of many American Indian groups of grinding maize to form fine flour and making tortilla-like bread produced a sticky material ideal for caries production.[66] The sugar in wild honey also may have been a factor. The dietary correlation is strong enough that some have proposed that two carious lesions per person could be regarded as the dividing point between high- and low-carbohydrate diets.[67]

[64] Morse, *Ancient Disease*; Gregg and Gregg, *Dry Bones*; Brooks and Melbye, "Skeletal lesions," pp. 23–29; Stewart, *The People of America*.

[65] Berry, "Aspects of paleodemography," pp. 43–64; Berry, "Dental paleopathology," pp. 253–74; Cybulski, "Culture change," pp. 75–85; Merbs, "Patterns of health and sickness"; Merbs and Vestergaard, "The paleopathology of Sundown," pp. 85–103; Perzigian, Tench, and Braun, "Prehistoric health"; Pfeiffer and Fairgrieve, "Evidence from ossuaries"; Rose, Marks, and Tieszen, "Bioarchaeology and subsistence," pp. 7–21; Stodder and Martin, "Health and disease."

[66] Merbs, "Patterns of health and sickness."

[67] Rose, Burnett, et al., "Paleopathology and the origins," pp. 393–424; Rose, Marks, and Tieszen, "Bioarchaeology and subsistence"; Turner, "Dental anthropological indications," pp. 619–36.

OTHER DENTAL DISEASE

Other forms of dental disease commonly present include dental abscesses, dental attrition, periodontal disease, and tooth loss. Abscesses occur when tooth pulp cavities are exposed to bacteria because of caries or rapid dental attrition. Periodontal disease usually accompanies dental caries, since it also is produced by concentrations of mouth bacteria. Dental attrition can be regarded as a cultural factor to some extent, since it represents the loss of tooth surface due to the mechanical process of chewing. Attrition was especially rapid in North American groups with considerable grit and rough materials in their diet. Such materials can originate from the method of food preparation (e.g., grit from grinding stones) or bits of broken bone, shell, nuts, or other coarse dietary items.[68]

POROTIC HYPEROSTOSIS

Porotic hyperostosis refers to bony changes on the cranial vault and within the upper orbits. This condition consists of increased porosity on the bone surface and abnormal thickening of the bone. In extreme cases, the lesions resemble honeycombs and can involve both the vault and orbits. Although a variety of conditions can cause bony changes of this type, most researchers regard the condition in pre-1492 North American skeletons as a bony response to extreme anemia.[69]

Various examples of porotic hyperostosis have been reported throughout North America. A partial survey of these reports documents its presence in a Southern Sinagua population from Oak Creek Pueblo, Arizona; the Sundown site near Prescott, Arizona; the Black Mesa Anasazi; an Anasazi child from New Mexico; and various other Southwestern sites.[70]

In the Plains and Great Basin, porotic hyperostosis is reported from the American Bottom, Illinois, and west-central Illinois; the McCutchan-McLaughlin site in Oklahoma; the central and lower portions of the

---

[68] Hartnady and Rose, "Abnormal tooth-loss patterns."

[69] El-Najjar, Lozoff, and Ryan, "The paleoepidemiology of porotic hyperostosis," pp. 918–24.

[70] Taylor, "The paleopathology," pp. 115–18; Merbs and Vestergaard, "The paleopathology of Sundown"; Martin, Piacentini, and Armelagos, "Paleopathology of the Black Mesa Anasazi," pp. 104–14; Martin, Goodman, et al., *Black Mesa Anasazi Health*; Fink, "Tuberculosis and anemia; Merbs, "Patterns of health and sickness"; Stodder and Martin, "Health and disease."

Mississippi Valley; the Ohio River Valley; the Crow Creek site, central South Dakota; and the Nevada Great Basin.[71]

In the Southeast, Powell reports porotic hyperostosis is rare at Moundville, Alabama.[72] The condition is present in the Fort Center, Florida, sample and in the Averbuch site in Middle Tennessee.[73]

Pfeiffer and Fairgrieve report porotic hyperostosis from Iroquoian ossuaries, and Cybulski found the condition in 13 to 14% of Northwest Coast populations he studied.[74]

Although many researchers believe that the condition reflects severe anemia, opinion is divided on the cause of the anemia. Some researchers, especially those studying samples from the American Southwest, have argued that excessive maize consumption can lead to iron deficiency anemia. Thus subsistence may be a causal factor. More recently, researchers have considered the possible role of other factors, especially malnutrition, prolonged breast feeding, poor living conditions, dysentery, and parasitism.[75] Karl J. Reinhard relates that diarrhea is a likely cause of anemia, the probable culprit organisms being *Entamoeba hystolitica*, Salmonella, *Escherichia coli*, and Shigella.[76]

TRAUMA

As already noted, fractures and other evidence of trauma are relatively common throughout pre-1492 North American population samples.[77]

---

[71] Milner, "Health and cultural change"; Powell and Rogers, *Bioarchaeology of the McCutchan-McLaughlin Site*; Rose, Marks, and Tieszen, "Bioarchaeology and subsistence"; Perzigian, Tench, and Braun, "Prehistoric health"; Willey, *Prehistoric Warfare*; Stark and Brooks, "A survey of prehistoric paleopathology," pp. 65–78.

[72] Powell, "Ranked status and health."

[73] Miller-Shaivitz and Iscan, "The Prehistoric People"; Eisenberg, "Mississippian cultural terminations," pp. 70–88.

[74] Pfeiffer and Fairgrieve, "Evidence from ossuaries"; Cybulski, "Culture change."

[75] Walker, "Anemia among prehistoric Indians," pp. 139–64; Weaver, "Subsistence and settlement patterns," pp. 119–27; Merbs, "Patterns of health and sickness."

[76] Reinhard, "Patterns of diet, parasitism, and anemia," pp. 219–58.

[77] Bovee and Owsley, "Evidence of warfare," pp. 355–62; Bridges, "Spondylolysis," pp. 321–9; Cybulski, "Culture change"; Cybulski, *An Earlier Population*; Hollimon and Owsley, "Osteology of the Fay Tolton Site," pp. 345–53; Merbs, "Patterns of health and sickness; Merbs and Vestergaard, "The paleopathology of Sundown"; Miller-Shaivitz and Iscan, "The prehistoric people"; Moodie, *Paleopathology*; Owsley, "Warfare in coalescent tradition populations," pp. 333–43; Pfeiffer and Fairgrieve, "Evidence from ossuaries"; Powell, "Ranked status and health"; Powell and Rogers, *Bioarchaeology of the McCutchan-McLaughlin Site*; Stark and Brooks, "A survey of prehistoric paleopathology"; Walker and Lambert, "Paleopathological evidence"; Walker and Lambert, "Skeletal evidence"; Wheeler, "Pathology in late thirteenth century Zuni," pp. 79–84; Williams, "Disease profiles."

This evidence ranges from fractures from simple falls (e.g., Colles fractures) and dislocations to signs of interpersonal or intergroup violence. Fractures occur as a result of direct force on normal bone, or as a result of normal mechanical stress on bone weakened by other disease conditions (pathological fractures).

Behavioral and cultural factors also can lead to fracture-related developmental defects, such as the condition known as spondylolysis. This condition consists of a fracture within the vertebral arch, frequently in the lumbar or other lower vertebrae. Initially, its high frequency among Eskimo and Aleut skeletons suggested a population difference in those groups. Merbs suggests the condition results from physical stress in that area of the back.[78] He notes higher frequencies of the condition among Asian groups than in European or African groups and more occurrences in contemporary athletes than in the rest of the population. Patricia S. Bridges reports frequencies of spondylolysis of 17% in males and 20% in females among Archaic period Indians in northwest Alabama.[79] The condition tends to occur at an early age in males, likely induced by activity, but after age 40 in females, perhaps stimulated by osteoporosis.

C. Owen Lovejoy and Kingsbury G. Heiple present a detailed analysis of the pattern of fractures within a Late Woodland sample from the Libben site, Ottowa County, Ohio.[80] They found that most fractures in this sample probably resulted from accidents. Statistical analysis revealed a relatively high (45%) risk for a single individual. Risk was greatest for these aged 10 to 25 and those older than 45.

Most regional studies reveal a temporal increase in the frequency of fractures. The likely explanation is that throughout North America, as population size and density increased, so did competition and conflict among groups. For example, Walker found depressed cranial fractures (likely produced by blows to the head) in 18.6% of individuals on the northern coast of California but noted that they were uncommon on the southern coast.[81] He found that the frequency of fractures increased through time and thought this was due to an increasing pattern of violence associated with population growth.

Indications of scalping also suggest increasing violence through time among North American Indians. For example, Wilma H. Allen et al. found abundant evidence of scalping on four female and six male crania

[78] Merbs, "Spondylolysis," pp. 163–69. [79] Bridges, "Spondylolysis," pp. 321–29.
[80] Lovejoy and Heiple, "The analysis of fractures," pp. 529–41.
[81] Walker, "Cranial injuries," pp. 313–23.

from two prehistoric Arizona sites.[82] Clusters of cut marks on the crania were interpreted as indicative of stone-knife scalping. Elsewhere in the American Southwest, Stodder and Martin's analysis of human remains from the Gallina site revealed evidence of traumatic injury, defense wounds, massacre, and possibly cannibalism.[83]

The evidence of violent death in Milner et al.'s study of 264 burials from west-central Illinois suggests chronic warfare in one-third of the adults.[84] This evidence included not only cut marks, but also chert fragments lodged within the bone. Fourteen individuals showed evidence of scalping and 11 had been decapitated.

As Douglas W. Owsley notes, small-scale warfare was common throughout the Plains from prehistoric to historic times.[85] Williams's survey of Archaic and Woodland period skeletal samples from the Northern Plains detected evidence for trauma and violence but found it more uncommon than in later periods.[86] In addition to finding accidental-type fractures concentrated in the arms, he reports three early cases of violence: evidence of scalping from the Bahm and Blasky Mound sites and a projectile point embedded in the spine of a 17-year-old female from Jamestown Mounds.

Probably the most dramatic skeletal example of prehistoric violence in North America comes from the Crow Creek site in central South Dakota. Archaeological excavations revealed about 486 skeletons within a fortification ditch on the periphery of the habitation area. The site represents the Initial Coalescent period and dates to about 1325 A.D. P. Willey's analysis revealed that 90% of the individuals had cut marks characteristic of scalping.[87] Also common were depressed fractures and decapitation. Three examples of facial mutilation were also present. Clearly, the individuals buried at Crow Creek were victims of a massacre with abundant evidence of body mutilation. Willey's survey of the comparative literature in the area revealed that evidence of perimortem trauma was relatively common at the earlier Middle Missouri sites as well as at those of the Coalescent tradition.

Sandra E. Hollimon and Owsley describe evidence for a smaller and earlier massacre at the Fay Tolton site.[88] This Plains Village site dates from the Initial Middle Missouri period, A.D. 950–1250. Five individuals were

[82] Allen, Merbs, and Birkby, "Evidence for prehistoric scalping," pp. 23–42.
[83] Stodder and Martin, "Health and disease," p. 61.
[84] Milner, Anderson, and Smith, "Warfare."
[85] Owsley, "Warfare in coalescent tradition populations."   [86] Williams, "Disease profiles."
[87] Willey, *Prehistoric Warfare.*   [88] Hollimon and Owsley, "Osteology of the Fay Tolton Site."

recovered within house refuse. Two were partially burned, two showed evidence of perimortem body alteration, two displayed antemortem healed trauma, and one had perimortem injury. A five- to seven-year-old child showed evidence of a healed depressed fracture and also evidence of scalping.

Dana L. Bovee and Owsley present evidence for warfare from the southern Plains.[89] Analysis of an adult female burial from the Heerwald site in Oklahoma (A.D. 1377–1535) revealed a cutmark on the left second rib, a fractured left scapula, cranial evidence of scalping, and a projectile point embedded within a vertebra, with another found nearby. Bovee and Owsley's summary of the literature of that area reveals similar evidence of prehistoric violence from 14 other sites.

NONSPECIFIC EVIDENCE OF INFECTION

Much of the skeletal evidence for infection consists of abnormal bone deposits on the normal outer (periosteal) surface of the bone. Such lesions indicate that something stimulated the periosteum to deposit bone in an abnormal manner. Usually the stimulus is infection, although trauma and other problems may be factors as well. Interpretation is complicated since different types of infection can produce similar effects. For this reason, many researchers do not attempt a differential diagnosis of such evidence but simply classify it as "periostitis" or "periosteal lesions." When initially formed, the lesions show fine bone structure with porosity. Later, these become remodeled and appear as rough, thickened areas of the bone. Thus, analysis can differentiate recently formed lesions that may be associated with conditions leading to death from those sustained earlier in life. Although nonspecific, periosteal lesions provide a valuable marker of morbidity in the population. They document an episode of morbidity, even though it may not have been lethal.

Such evidence of morbidity has been found throughout North America at all time periods.[90] Relatively high frequencies of periosteal lesions are

---

[89] Bovee and Owsley, "Evidence of warfare."

[90] Cybulski, "Culture change"; Cybulski, *An Earlier Population*; Eisenberg, "Mississippian cultural terminations"; Martin, Goodman, et al., *Black Mesa Anasazi Health*; Miller-Shaivitz and Iscan, "The prehistoric people"; Milner, "Health and cultural change"; Moodie, *Paleopathology*; Palkovich, "Interpreting prehistoric morbidity and mortality risk," pp. 128–38; Palkovich, "Agriculture," pp. 425–38; Perzigian, Tench, and Braun, "Prehistoric health"; Pfeiffer and Fairgrieve, "Evidence from

reported from the Libben Late Woodland site in Ohio (A.D. 800–1100) by Robert P. Mensforth and from the Black Mesa site in Arizona by Martin et al.[91] Samples from Black Mesa revealed lesions on the tibia in about 67% of subadults and 32% of adults. Martin et al. attribute this high frequency to harsh ecological conditions and cultural factors; they point out that their study contrasts with other studies of Southwestern samples that generally reveal relatively low levels of lesions.

Various investigators have suggested a general increase in periosteal lesions through time in prehistoric North America.[92] For example, Perzigian et al. report a temporal increase in the frequency of periosteal lesions through time in their study of human remains from the Ohio River Valley.[93] Larsen found a sharp increase in periosteal lesions in prehistoric agricultural populations from the Georgia coast in comparison with preagricultural samples.[94]

Interpretation is complicated by the nonspecific nature of periosteal lesions, however clearly they reflect morbidity and most likely serious, but usually not fatal, local infection. The temporal increase presumably reflects the greater opportunity for the spread of infection with increased population density and a more sedentary lifestyle.

DENTAL HYPOPLASIA

Many recent researchers have turned to dental hypoplasia as an indicator of generalized childhood stress. Dental hypoplasia represents a defect in the dental enamel caused by a disruption in the growth process. In most cases, such a disruption is presumed to be caused by morbidity. The location of the defect in the tooth reveals information about the age of formation of the defect. Some have suggested that the size of the defect may be correlated with the duration or the severity of the problem.[95]

Dental hypoplasia commonly occurs in prehistoric North American

---

ossuaries"; Powell, "Ranked Status and Health"; Powell and Rogers, *Bioarchaeology of the McCutchan-McLaughlin Site*; Stark and Brooks, "A survey of prehistoric paleopathology"; Wheeler, "Pathology in late thirteenth century Zuni"; Willey, *Prehistoric Warfare*.

[91] Mensforth et al., "The role of constitutional factors," pp. 1–59; Martin, Goodman, et al., *Black Mesa Anasazi Health*.

[92] Cohen and Armelagos, "Paleopathology at the origins of agriculture." pp. 585–601.

[93] Perzigian, Tench, and Braun, "Prehistoric health."

[94] Larsen, "Health and disease," pp. 367–92.

[95] Hutchinson and Larsen, "Determination of stress episode duration," pp. 93–110.

dentitions.[96] Although different forms of hypoplasia exist and criteria for scoring varies among investigators, the lesions seem to correlate well with high levels of stress and population morbidity.[97] For example, Walker and Lambert report high frequencies of hypoplasia in prehistoric California populations during periods of documented cultural change and likely stress.[98] In their Southwestern study, Martin et al. found the greatest severity of enamel defects, as well as other measures of stress, at the time of abandonment of the area.[99]

Alan H. Goodman and Jerome C. Rose report that hypoplasia is common in Third World countries.[100] Frequencies as high as 90% are reported among Chinese children. In a literature survey, Goodman et al. found frequencies as high as 66% of all adults from Dickson Mounds, Illinois (A.D. 950–1300) with at least one hypoplastic tooth.[101] Thomas K. Black III found 94% of canines from a Mississippian cemetery in Missouri were hypoplastic.[102] Dale L. Hutchinson and Larsen report a 70% frequency from the prehistoric Georgia coast.[103]

John W. Lallo and Rose and Goodman et al. found that the frequency of dental defects increases through time in their study of two chronologically distinct samples from Dickson Mounds, Illinois (A.D. 1050–1200 and A.D. 1200–1300).[104] Similar trends are reported by David N. Dickel et al. from central California, by Cook from the lower Illinois Valley, and by Claire Monod Cassidy for the Ohio River Valley.[105]

Most researchers suggest the temporal increase in dental hypoplasia among prehistoric North American Indians is due to a general increase in morbidity related to increasing population density and changes in settlement pattern and subsistence.

[96] Cassidy, "Skeletal evidence," pp. 307–45; Cook, "Subsistence and health," pp. 235–69; Dickel, Schulz, and McHenry, "Central California," pp. 439–61; Goodman, Lallo, et al., "Health changes," pp. 271–305; Goodman and Rose, "Dental enamel hypoplasias," pp. 279–93; Hutchinson and Larsen, "Determination of stress episode duration"; Hutchinson and Larsen, "Stress and lifeway change," pp. 50–65; Lallo and Rose, "Patterns of stress," pp. 323–35; Martin, Piacentini, and Armelagos, "Paleopathology of the Black Mesa Anasazi"; Walker and Lambert, "Paleopathological evidence"; Walker and Lambert, "Skeletal evidence."

[97] Buikstra and Ubelaker, *Standards for Data Collection.*

[98] Walker and Lambert, "Skeletal evidence."

[99] Martin, Piacentini, and Armelagos, "Paleopathology of the Black Mesa Anasazi."

[100] Goodman and Rose, "Dental enamel hypoplasias."

[101] Goodman, Armelagos, and Rose, "Enamel hypoplasias," pp. 515–28.

[102] Black, *The Biological and Social Analysis*, p. 82.

[103] Hutchinson and Larsen, "Determination of stress episode duration."

[104] Lallo and Rose, "Patterns of stress"; Goodman, Lallo, et al., "Health changes."

[105] Dickel, Schulz, and McHenry, "Central California"; Cook, "Subsistence and health"; Cassidy, "Skeletal evidence."

LINES OF INCREASED DENSITY

Often termed "Harris lines," lines of increased density offer additional data on morbidity. Like enamel hypoplasia, they are thought to be caused by temporary disruptions in normal growth. They consist of lines or bands of increased bone density visible in radiography within long bone diaphyses. They likely are produced when longitudinal bone growth is slowed by disease, poor nutrition, or some other factor. To the extent they can be correlated with disease and nutritional events, the lines offer additional data on morbidity. Unlike enamel hypoplasia, lines of increased density can be removed or altered later in life by normal bone remodeling. Thus the frequency of lines present when growth terminates in the teenage years will probably decline later in life.

Although present in prehistoric skeletal samples throughout North America, the lines provide mixed signals on temporal trends of morbidity. Although measures of population morbidity increased through time, lines of increased density actually declined in the Ohio River Valley, the lower Illinois Valley, and central California.[106] Martin et al. found frequencies of lines of increased density along with other measures of morbidity to be high at the Black Mesa Anasazi site.[107]

INTESTINAL PARASITES

Growing evidence suggests that pre-Columbian populations in North America suffered from a large variety of intestinal parasites. Most of this evidence comes from studies of coprolites, human feces that have been preserved in dry environments. Because of the environmental factors involved in preservation, the bulk of the data originate from arid areas of North America, especially the Southwest, Northern Mexico, and the Great Basin. Although limited in North America, some evidence also comes from mummified human remains and soil analysis of latrines.

In one such study, Reinhard examined preserved coprolites of Basketmaker and Pueblo people at Antelope House, a Puebloan village in Canyon de Chelley, Arizona.[108] He found evidence of the cestode *Hymenolepis* and

---

[106] Perzigian, Tench, and Braun, "Prehistoric health"; Cassidy, "Skeletal evidence"; Cook, "Subsistence and health"; Dickel, Schulz, and McHenry, "Central California."
[107] Martin, Piacentini, and Armelagos, "Paleopathology of the Black Mesa Anasazi."
[108] Reinhard, "Parasitism at Antelope House," pp. 220–33.

the nematode pinworms *Enterobius vermicularis, Trichostrongylus,* and *Strongyloides.* In a separate study at Antelope House dated to A.D. 1125 to 1250, Reinhard discovered larvae of the roundworm *Strongyloides stercoralis* in dog feces. Knowledge of the life cycle and behavior of this parasite suggests that humans were likely infected as well.

Reinhard provides an overview of the evidence for parasitism in North America.[109] In the northern areas, most evidence is equivocal. In the northern Plains, Williams describes an intact hydatid cyst associated with a female skeleton from North Dakota dating to about A.D. 600.[110] The cyst suggested the presence of *Echinococcus granulosus,* a disease currently endemic in the area.

Andrew McClary reported eggs probably from *Diphyllobothrium* from prehistoric coprolites from the Schultz site, Michigan.[111] This organism causes the disease diphyllobothriasis and is linked to consumption of raw fish. Eggs likely from *Echinococcus* or *Taenia* were also recovered.

Evidence for parasitism in other, mostly drier areas of North America, is extensive. Table 3.2 reproduces Reinhard's partial listing of the parasites that have been identified, their dates, and geographic area of discovery.[112] Note that this listing includes some examples from postcontact dates as well, also that lice and nits have been recovered from mummified hair as well as from coprolites, all from prehistoric contexts. Reinhard suggests that lice were likely consumed after being removed from the hair as a prehistoric grooming practice.

Although hookworm traditionally has been regarded as a historic period introduction to the New World, some evidence from South Carolina and South America suggests that hookworm (Ancylostmidae) may have been present as well.[113]

Clearly, human parasitism has great antiquity in North America. Eggs of *Enterobius vermicularis* and *ancanthocephalans* were recovered from Hogup and Danger caves in Utah, dating to around 8,000 B.C. Our interpretation of both the variety and the biogeographical distribution of parasites in ancient North America is limited by preservation factors. In Reinhard's view, limited evidence suggests that parasites were more common in later agricultural groups than in earlier hunter-gatherers.[114]

---

[109] Reinhard, "Archaeoparisitology," pp. 145–63.
[110] Williams, "Evidence of hydatid disease," pp. 25–28.
[111] McClary, "Notes," pp. 131–36. [112] Reinhard, "Archaeoparisitology."
[113] Rathbun, Sexton, and Michie, "Disease patterns," pp. 52–74; Reinhard, "Archaeoparisitology."
[114] Reinhard, "Archaeoparisitology."

Table 3.2. *Parasites identified from North American archaeological contexts*

Taxon	Date	Locality
Nematodes		
Adult, species unknown	A.D. 700–1200	Granado Cave, Texas*
Eggs, species unknown	A.D. 500–1200	Clyde's Cavern, Utah
Enterobius vermicularis	ca. 8000 B.C.	Danger Cave, Utah
	4800–4300 B.C.	Dirty Shame Shelter, Oregon
	4010 B.C.	Hogup Cave, Utah
	2100–600 B.C.	Hinds Cave, Utah
	1250 B.C.	Hogup Cave, Utah
	650 B.C.	Hogup Cave, Utah
	A.D. 400	Turkey Pen Cave, Utah
	A.D. 600	Antelope House, Arizona*
	A.D. 600	Rio Zape, Durango
	A.D. 500–1200	Clyde's Cavern, Utah
	A.D. 920–1020	Pueblo Bonito, New Mexico
	A.D. 1080–1130	Pueblo Bonito, New Mexico
	A.D. 1000–1200	Mesa Verde, Colorado
	A.D. 1075–1140	Antelope House, Arizona
	A.D. 1100–1250	Elden Pueblo, Arizona
	A.D. 1100–1250	Salmon Ruin, New Mexico
	A.D. 1250–1300	Inscription House, Arizona
Trichuris trichiura	A.D. 1100–1250	Elden Pueblo, Arizona
	A.D. 1720	Colonial Williamsburg, Virginia
	A.D. 1760–1776	Newport, Rhode Island
	ca. A.D. 1806	Newport, Rhode Island
	A.D. 1830–1850	Greenwich Village, New York
Ascaris lumbricoides	570–290 B.C.	Upper Salts Cave, Kentucky
	A.D. 1100–1250	Elden Pueblo, Arizona
	A.D. 1720	Colonial Williamsburg, Virginia
	A.D. 1760–1776	Newport, Rhode Island
	ca. A.D. 1806	Newport, Rhode Island
Strongyloides sp.	A.D. 500–1200	Clyde's Cavern, Utah
	A.D. 1075–1140	Antelope House, Arizona
Trichostrongylus sp.	A.D. 1075–1140	Antelope House, Arizona
Possible ancyostomidae	1300–1700 B.C.	Daws Island, South Carolina
Trichinella spiralis	A.D. 1550	Point Barrow, Alaska
Trematodes		
Cryptocotyle lingus	A.D. 400	St. Lawrence Island, Alaska*
Unidentified egg	A.D. 1250–1300	Glen Canyon, Utah
Unidentified egg	500 B.C.–A.D. 1150	Lovelock Cave, Nevada

Table 3.2. *(cont.)*

Taxon	Date	Locality
Cestodes		
Diphyllobothrium latum	300 B.C.–A.D. 200	Schultz Site, Michigan
Hymenolepididae	A.D. 1075–1140	Antelope House, Arizona
	A.D. 1100–1250	Elden Pueblo, Arizona
Taeniidae	ca. 4500 B.C.	Hogup Cave, Utah
	ca. 4200 B.C.	Hogup Cave, Utah
	ca. 2000 B.C.	Hogup Cave, Utah
	300 B.C.–A.D. 200	Schultz Site, Michigan
	ca. 20 A.D.	Danger Cave, Utah
	A.D. 1100–1250	Elden Pueblo, Arizona
	A.D. 1250–1300	Glen Canyon, Utah
Echinococcus sp.	Pre-Contact	Kodiak Island, Alaska*
	A.D. 600	North Dakota*
Acanthocephalans		
Unidentifiable eggs	A.D. 460–1500	Clyde's Cavern, Utah
	A.D. 900–1100	Black Mesa, Arizona
	A.D. 900–1100	Glen Canyon, Utah
Moniliformis clarki	10,000–8500 B.C.	Danger Cave, Utah
	ca. 8000 B.C.	Danger Cave, Utah
	6400–4856 B.C.	Hogup Cave, Utah
	4800–4300 B.C.	Dirty Shame Shelter, Oregon
	4300–5900 B.C.	Dirty Shame Shelter, Oregon
	ca. 2000 B.C.	Hogup Cave, Utah
	1869 B.C.	Danger Cave, Utah
	ca. 20 A.D.	Danger Cave, Utah
	A.D. 600–900	Dirty Shame Shelter, Oregon

*Asterisks indicate finds in mummies or skeleton. All other finds are from coprolites or latrine remains.

Source: Reinhard, Karl J., "Archaeoparasitology in North America," *American Journal of Physical Anthropology*, 82:145–163, Copyright © 1990, Wiley-Liss. Reprinted by permission of Wiley-Liss, Inc., a subsidiary of John Wiley & Sons, Inc.

He notes that 357 coprolites were recovered from seven Archaic period hunter-gatherer sites, with only 14 yielding helminth remains. In contrast, nine later agricultural sites from the Colorado area yielded 513 coprolites, with 89 containing evidence for helminths. The increase in parasite infection with time is logical, since the later agricultural period brought more dense populations and less mobility, hence greater opportunity for parasites to complete their life cycles.

ARTHRITIS

Inflammation of the joints can be caused by many diseases.[115] The most common expression of arthritis seen in precontact North American skeletons is degenerative joint disease, especially osteoarthritis. An expected development with aging, osteoarthritis has been found with all skeletal samples containing older adults.[116] In the vertebrae, osteoarthritis usually involves osteophyte formation on the borders of the centra. In extreme cases, many or all vertebrae may become fused. Such fusion describes the condition "ankylosing spondylitis" that has been found in North American samples.[117]

Unusual distribution of degenerative joint change can provide clues to occupation or behavioral problems. A case in point from precontact North America is Robert J. Miller's study of a skeletal sample from Nuvakwewtaqa (Chavez Pass), Arizona.[118] The sample dated from between A.D. 1000 and 1400 and displayed evidence of degeneration of the elbow joint likely related to maize grinding.

Bruce M. Rothschild et al. proposed a method to detect rheumatoid arthritis in archaeologically recovered human remains.[119] Although differentiating such a disorder from postmortem change and from other related diseases can be troublesome, they claim to have detected the disease in pre-1492 North American human remains concentrated in the American Southeast. Their research also has suggested evidence of calcium pyrophosphate deposition disease, and spondyloarthropathy, two other forms of arthritis.[120]

CONGENITAL DISORDERS

Although congenital disorders are found in precontact North American samples, they do not represent conditions that contributed to morbidity

---

[115] Ubelaker, *Human Skeletal Remains*.
[116] Cybulski, *An Earlier Population*; Merbs and Vestergaard, "The paleopathology of Sundown"; Moodie, *Paleopathology*; Reinhard, Tieszen, et al., "Trade, contact, and female health," pp. 63–74; Wheeler, "Pathology in late thirteenth century Zuni"; Willey, *Prehistoric Warfare*.
[117] Merbs and Vestergaard, "The paleopathology of Sundown"; Moodie, *Paleopathology*, p. 153.
[118] Miller, "Lateral epicondylitis," pp. 391–400.
[119] Rothschild, Woods, et al., "Geographic distribution," pp. 181–87.
[120] Rothschild and Woods, "Geographic distribution," pp. 315–18; Rothschild and Woods, "Character," pp. 1229–35.

or mortality. Such disorders usually take the form of osteomas, small bony projections on the cranial vault or such abnormal conditions as fused ribs or fusion of the bones of the forearm (radius and ulna).[121]

KIDNEY AND BLADDER STONE DISEASE

Some evidence suggests precontact North Americans suffered from renal or bladder stones. Stones were recovered in association with three individuals from the Indian Knoll site in Kentucky. Most of this site is thought to be Archaic, dating to as early as 3500 to 3000 B.C.[122] Steinbock also discusses renal stones from a late Archaic site (about 1500 B.C.) from Fulton County, Illinois, and from a Late Woodland site in Marion County, Indiana, dating to about A.D. 1500. Bladder stones were found in association with Arizona mummies dating to between 100 B.C. and A.D. 750.

DEMOGRAPHY

Demographic reconstruction from human skeletal remains requires large representative samples that can be adequately dated and are sufficiently well preserved to allow accurate estimates of sex and age at death. Often, representation is a factor in such studies since ancient mortuary practices, museum curation policies, excavation techniques, skeletal preservation, and other factors can exclude some individuals from the samples under study. Obviously, the human remains provide direct evidence of mortality. Even though cause of death can rarely be determined, the age distribution of the dead can provide evidence of the impact of disease and may even suggest the type of diseases involved. Demographic data must be interpreted with caution since inaccurate methods of age determination and population dynamics in fertility and related factors can affect interpretation.

In spite of some methodological complications surrounding demographic reconstruction from ancient bone samples, considerable research with precontact North American samples suggests that infant mortality was generally high and life expectancy low in comparison with

---

[121] Cybulski, *An Earlier Population*; Gregg and Gregg, *Dry Bones*; Miler-Shaivitz and Iscan, "The prehistoric people"; Morse, *Ancient Disease*; Powell and Rogers, *Bioarchaeology of the McCutchan-McLaughlin Site*; Willey, *Prehistoric Warfare*.
[122] Steinbock, "The history, epidemiology, and paleopathology," pp. 177–97.

contemporary North American populations, but that both were similar to levels in Europe at about that time.

The Crow Creek site from central South Dakota, dating to about A.D. 1325, offers an unusually accurate look at the demographic structure of a precontact North American sample. Archaeological evidence suggests the remains recovered at this site represent a massacre of the Arikara. Since all individuals present died at once, the sample provides a unique view of the demographic structure of a population. This sample contrasts with most mortuary site samples, which represent a gradual accumulation of the deceased. Willey's analysis of the sample suggested that some young adult females (possible captives) and some old males may be missing from the sample.[123] Demographic reconstruction suggested that 41% were below the age of 15, with some individuals nearly 60.

Owsley has summarized the available demographic evidence for mortality among early Northern and Northeastern Plains populations.[124] This research involves estimation of age at death from skeletons recovered from mortuary site excavations. Presumably, they represent a gradual accumulation of the deceased, as opposed to the massacre site sample of Crow Creek. In his Northern Plains Woodland sample, dating between A.D. 1 and A.D. 600, Owsley found preadult mortality to be about 44% from the Northeastern Plains and 46% in a related group termed Sonota Complex. The figures increased in later samples to 60% in Coalescent Tradition remains, 65% among Central Plains, and 66% for Southern Plains samples.

Comparative data from the American Southwest are provided by Martin et al.'s study of the Black Mesa remains.[125] Their total sample ranged chronologically from 200 B.C. to A.D. 1150. Demographic reconstruction revealed that 44% of their sample was below the age of 15. Approximate percentages of mortality for successive age intervals are as follows:

Age interval	Percentage	Age interval	Percentage
<1	10	25–30	5
1–5	18	30–35	6
5–10	6	35–40	5
10–15	9	40–45	3
15–20	5	45–50	5
20–25	5	50–60	22

[123] Willey, *Prehistoric Warfare*.   [124] Owsley, "Demography," pp. 75–86.
[125] Martin, Goodman, et al., *Black Mesa Anasazi Health*.

These data suggest a life expectancy at birth of about 25 years, and a mean adult age at death of about 41 years (life expectancy at age 15 of about 26 years).

Elsewhere in the Southwest, at Grasshopper Pueblo, Arizona, David R. Berry describes 55% mortality during the first five years of life and reduced adult life expectancy.[126] Mark G. Taylor found high infant mortality in a Southern Sinagua population from Oak Creek Pueblo, Arizona.[127] Palkovich describes high infant mortality at Arroyo Hondo Pueblo, New Mexico, dating to between A.D. 1300 and 1345.[128] Merbs attributes the high infant death rate to "congenital malformation, trauma, malnutrition (including weaning stress), and infection."[129]

Lallo et al. present demographic data gleaned from their analysis of Illinois Dickson Mound material consisting of Late Woodland and Mississippian Acculturated Late Woodland (A.D. 950–1200) samples, as well as Middle Mississippian samples (A.D. 1200).[130] Life table reconstruction suggests that about 36% of the earlier population died before the age of 15. The figure was about 50% for the later Middle Mississippian group. In the earlier sample, life expectancy at birth was about 26 years, and 23 years at age 15. For the later sample, life expectancy at birth was about 19 years and about 18 years at age 15.

In Tennessee, Hugh E. Berryman documented low life expectancy at the prehistoric Averbuch site.[131] His analysis suggested life expectancy at birth for females of 14.6 years and 17.4 years for males.

Elsewhere in the Southeast, Robert L. Blakely studied remains from Etowah, Georgia, from the Mississippian period, dating to just after A.D. 1040.[132] He calculated the average age at death to be 23 years, with 32% mortality prior to age 10, and 91% by age 50.

Douglas H. Ubelaker provides the following summary of life expectancy drawn from the literature: population at Indian Knoll, Kentucky, 3000 B.C., 18.9 years; population of Nubia, Egypt, A.D. 1050–1600, 19.2 years; Ancient Greeks, 670 B.C.–A.D. 600, 23.0 years; Texas Indians, A.D. 850–1700, 30.5 years; European ruling families, A.D. 1480–1579, 33.7 years; U.S. Caucasian, A.D. 1800, 30–35 years; females from England and Wales, A.D. 1965–1967, 74.9 years.[133]

---

[126] Berry, "Aspects of paleodemography."   [127] Taylor, "The paleopathology."
[128] Palkovich, "Interpreting prehistoric morbidity and mortality risk."
[129] Merbs, "Patterns of health and sickness," p. 45.
[130] Lallo, Armelagos, and Rose, "Paleoepidemiology of infectious disease," pp. 17–23.
[131] Berryman, *The Averbuch Skeletal Series.*   [132] Blakely, *Biocultural Adaptation.*
[133] Ubelaker, *Reconstruction.*

A. J. Jaffe's review of the literature suggests a precontact North American average life span of less than 20 years.[134] He suggests the high death rate likely was due to warfare, hunting accidents, childbirth in women, childhood diseases, diarrhea, enteritis, congenital malformations, low birth weight, and food shortages. His reading of the literature suggested only 1 to 2% of the population survived beyond age 50.

TEMPORAL TRENDS

As early as 1971, T. Aiden Cockburn postulated a correlation between agriculture and disease in ancient populations.[135] He argued that the dietary shift associated with the adoption of agriculture may have created some negative health results, but the major contributor to morbidity associated with this change was the loss of mobility. He reasoned that as populations shifted their subsistence from foraging to agriculture, they changed their settlement pattern from one of mobility to increased sedentism. The lack of population mobility eventually led to sanitation problems, which, coupled with increased population density, produced greater opportunity for the spread of infectious disease.

Since 1971, researchers have studied many pre-1492 skeletal samples from throughout North America, all suggesting that Cockburn's interpretations were likely correct. With some minor variation, regional studies indicate that, prior to 1492, morbidity and mortality were increasing through time. The following is a region-by-region summary of the evidence, utilizing traits, terminology, and, in most cases, references discussed earlier in the chapter.

In the North American Southeast, most evidence for temporal trends, and perhaps the most comprehensive data for all of North America, originates from the work of Larsen and his colleagues.[136] Working with large samples, primarily from the Georgia coast, they document that as populations shifted their subsistence to agriculture, morbidity increased. Comparisons between earlier preagricultural and later agricultural samples indicate a decrease through time in degenerative joint disease, bone size,

---

[134] Jaffe, *The First Immigrants.*   [135] Cockburn, "Infectious disease," pp. 45–62.

[136] Hutchinson and Larsen, "Determination of stress episode duration"; Hutchinson and Larsen, "Stress and lifeway change"; Larsen, "Health and disease"; Larsen and Ruff, "Biomechanical adaptation"; Larsen and Ruff, "The stresses of conquest," pp. 21–34; Larsen, Ruff, Schoeninger, and Hutchinson, "Population decline"; Larsen, Shavit, and Griffin, "Dental caries evidence," pp. 179–202.

bone robusticity, living stature, bone mechanical strength, dental hypoplasia, and the general quality of life. Sharp increases are seen in periosteal lesions and dental caries. The caries increase was related to elevated consumption of maize, containing cariogenic substances. The increase in periosteal lesions presumably resulted from enhanced population density and the increase in sedentism associated with a subsistence economy based on agriculture. A decrease in mechanical demand on the skeleton in the latter period likely produced a reduction in degenerative bone disease. This decrease, coupled with poorer nutrition, likely led to diminished stature and other reductions in bone size and strength.

In a somewhat complementary study comparing Archaic period hunter-gatherers with Mississippian period agriculturalists in northwestern Alabama, Bridges found bone strength to increase.[137] She attributed this change to greater workload in the populations represented by the sample.

Central California samples showed comparatively little pathology but a late increase in dental hypoplasia, a decrease in lines of arrested growth, and little change in stature.[138]

Lambert found that skeletal pathology increased with time among prehistoric samples from the Santa Barbara Channel Islands.[139] She reports increased evidence of infection and of a decline in stature, also increased food production due to increased fishing. Disease, likely resulting from increased population density, explains the higher rate of morbidity.

Walker's analysis of coastal California samples shows that violence increased through time.[140] This conclusion is based on depressed fractures on crania, which likely reflect a temporal increase in violence, associated with population growth and increased density.

In the Plains area of the United States, Owsley found that preadult mortality increased from about 45% among Woodland hunter-gatherers to over 60% among the more sedentary horticulturists.[141] As in the Southeast, increased sedentism and the spread of infectious disease likely was an important factor.

In the Central Ohio River Valley, Cassidy's study of prehistoric remains ranging temporally from late Archaic to Mississippian suggests a temporal decrease in life expectancy, infant death rate, cortical thickness, Harris lines, and dental abscess, and no change in arthritic conditions.[142] The

[137] Bridges, "Skeletal evidence," pp. 89–101.
[138] Dickel, Schulz, and McHenry, "Central California."
[139] Lambert, "Health in prehistoric population," pp. 509–22.   [140] Walker, "Cranial injuries."
[141] Owsley, "Demography."   [142] Cassidy, "Skeletal evidence."

frequency of dental hypoplasia increased slightly, with a great increase in
the death rate of toddlers, periosteal reactive bone disease (likely evidence
of infection), porotic hyperostosis, and dental caries.

Working in the Lower Illinois Valley, Cook studied population change
from the Middle Archaic (6,000 to 3,000 B.C.) through the early
Mississippian period (before A.D. 1200).[143] She found that stature, sexual
dimorphism, and cortical bone loss varied little. Temporal increases were
detected in the frequency of dental caries, dental hypoplasia, porotic
hyperostosis, and skeletal evidence of violence. Lesions suggestive of tuberculosis appeared in the latest period. Previously, Buikstra and Cook had
noted that pre-Columbian tuberculosis in west-central Illinois was not
found in Woodland peoples but appeared in Mississippian populations
during the last 1,000 years.[144]

In their study of remains from Dickson Mounds, Illinois, Goodman
et al. found no temporal change in sexual dimorphism or frequencies
of lines of increased density.[145] Moderate increases were noted in the
growth rates of the long bones, enamel hypoplasia, and evidence for
trauma. Substantial increases were found with porotic hyperostosis,
skeletal evidence for infection and general mortality. In an earlier study
of the Dickson Mound samples, Lallo et al. found that porotic
hyperostosis and the general incidence of pathology increased in the
Late Woodland to the Middle Mississippian samples.[146] In 1979, Lallo
and Rose argued that differences between the two samples in maize
consumption, population density, sedentism, and other social factors
correlated with an increase in levels of infectious disease, dental defects,
and mortality.[147]

In a temporal study of Ohio River Valley samples, Perzigian et al. found
a decrease in sexual dimorphism and the frequency of lines of arrested
growth, while stature did not change.[148] Frequencies of periosteal lesions
showed some increase, while the greatest increase occurred with linear
hypoplasia of the teeth, dental caries, and porotic hyperostosis. As in
Illinois, evidence for tuberculosis was confined to the relatively late
Fort Ancient sample, of Mississippian times.

Rose et al. studied a temporal series from the Lower Mississippi Valley

---

[143] Cook, "Subsistence and health."   [144] Buikstra and Cook, "Pre-Columbian tuberculosis."
[145] Goodman, Lallo, et al., "Health changes."
[146] Lallo, Armelagos, and Rose, "Paleoepidemiology of infectious disease."
[147] Lallo and Rose, "Patterns of stress."   [148] Perzigian, Tench, and Braun, "Prehistoric health."

dating back to an Archaic sample as early as 400 B.C.[149] Evidence of arthritis and sexual dimorphism decreased through time. Trauma frequencies showed no change. A moderate increase was recorded for periosteal lesions, porotic hyperostosis, and evidence of infection. Sharp increases were found in dental caries.

Merbs's general survey of disease in the American Southwest notes a temporal increase in dental caries.[150] Frequency is especially high in groups practicing agriculture. Like others, he attributed the elevated frequency to a high carbohydrate diet (maize) and methods of food preparation, and, as noted earlier, possibly to the consumption of wild honey (high in sugar).

As also mentioned earlier, Reinhard's survey of the evidence of parasitism revealed a probably temporal trend within prehistoric North America.[151] Among the Anasazi, he noted that periosteal lesions increased from 15% at A.D. 850–975 to 45% between A.D. 1100 and 1150.[152]

CONCLUSIONS

Clearly, North American populations prior to 1492 experienced significant disease morbidity and mortality. Although the range of diseases was likely not as great as that in the Old World, many health problems were present. Furthermore, abundant data now suggest that the levels of morbidity and mortality increased through time. The data throughout North America indicate that as many North American populations increased in density, changed their diet, and became more sedentary, exposure to disease increased. The evidence for increased morbidity and mortality through time is strong. The large populations engaged in horticultural activities allowed such crowd-type diseases as tuberculosis and treponemal disease to become endemic. Toward the end of the prehistoric period, levels of morbidity were high, and mortality, especially infant mortality, climbed to levels similar to those experienced in Europe. The disease experience was, of course, greatly exacerbated at European contact, when new lethal diseases were introduced with devastating demographic impact. The concept of disease and early death was certainly not new to the pre-1492 inhabitants of North America.

[149] Rose, Burnett, et al., "Paleopathology and the origins."
[150] Merbs, "Patterns of health and sickness."   [151] Reinhard, "Archaeoparisitology."
[152] Reinhard, "Patterns of diet, parasitism, and anemia."

BIBLIOGRAPHICAL ESSAY

I. ESTIMATES OF PRECONTACT NORTH AMERICAN INDIAN POPULATION SIZE

John D. Daniels, in his "The Indian Population of North America in 1492," provides a recent summary of the varied attempts to estimate North American 1492 population size. Daniels's survey of the field includes estimates utilized by current textbooks and those made by individual research efforts, as well as a summary of the variable methodological approaches employed.

The original, and still most-detailed estimate of individual tribal population size is provided by James Mooney in "Population," and "The aboriginal population of America north of Mexico." Mooney used a tribe-by-tribe systematic inventory approach, relying heavily on early ethnohistorical sources. His estimates became the main basis for A. L. Kroeber's "Cultural and natural Areas of native North America." This publication presents Mooney's estimates (except for California) in a broad cultural and ecological perspective. Douglas H. Ubelaker, in "The sources and methodology for Mooney's estimates of North American Indian populations," provides archival perspective on Mooney's sources and methodology for this work.

The primary sources for most estimates of high population numbers for North America are two works by Henry Dobyns: "Estimating aboriginal American population: An appraisal of techniques with a new hemispheric estimate," and *Their Number Become Thinned: Native Population Dynamics in Eastern North America*. In both publications, Dobyns utilizes a variety of evidence to suggest relatively high numbers. For a critical review of the Dobyns approach, see Henige, "On the current devaluation of the notion of evidence: A Rejoinder to Dobyns," and "Their number become thick: Native American historical demography as expiation."

Additional historical perspective and more recent evaluation of the tribe-by-tribe approach are provided by Douglas H. Ubelaker, in "North American population size, A.D. 1500 to 1985" and "North American Indian population size: Changing perspectives." The first of these articles also presents data and interpretation on North American Indian population size from 1492 until recent times (1985). Such modern perspective is also provided by R. Thornton in *American Indian Holocaust and Survival: A Population History since 1492*.

2. PALEOPATHOLOGY

The interpretation of the evidence for disease in archaeologically recovered human remains is a difficult process frequently requiring multidisciplinary expertise. For historical perspective on the development of the field of paleopathology, see Douglas H. Ubelaker's synthesis, "The development of American paleopathology."

Several texts are available focusing specifically on diagnosis within paleopathology. The most comprehensive of these are *Identification of Pathological Conditions in Human Skeletal Remains*, by Donald J. Ortner and Walter G. J. Putschar and *The Cambridge Encyclopedia of Human Paleopathology* by Arthur C. Aufderheide and Conrado Rodríguez-Martin. These texts combine the perspective of an experienced anthropologist and pathologists to present the skeletal manifestations of disease. The volumes not only provide diagnostic criteria but are also well illustrated with skeletal examples from museum collections. The Cambridge volume also contains information on disease inpretation from mummified soft tissue.

Other texts include R. Ted Steinbock's *Paleopathological Diagnosis and Interpretation, Bone Diseases in Ancient Human Populations*, and Michael R. Zimmerman and Marc A. Kelley's *Atlas of Human Paleopathology*. These texts are well illustrated and present both a medical and an anthropological perspective.

3. DISEASE IN ANCIENT NORTH AMERICA

An early and historically important synthesis of the evidence for disease in ancient human bone is Roy L. Moodie's *Paleopathology, an Introduction to the Study of Ancient Evidences of Disease*. This text provides worldwide examples of disease in ancient bone, but includes a detailed discussion of North American examples.

Another important early work is Aleš Hrdlička's *Tuberculosis among Certain Indian Tribes of the United States*. This volume summarized the evidence available for pre-1492 tuberculosis in the Americas and provided the perspective of the pioneer of American physical anthropology. A modern reevaluation of this problem is presented by a volume edited by Jane E. Buikstra, *Prehistoric Tuberculosis in the Americas*. This volume includes articles by specialists focusing on diagnostic criteria as well as the evidence from archaeological samples.

A regional synthesis from the U.S. Southwest is provided in *Health and*

Disease in the Prehistoric Southwest, edited by Charles F. Merbs and Robert J. Miller. Merbs also provides a thorough review of the evidence for disease in all of North America in the publication "A new world of infectious disease."

The Midwest area of the United States has proven to be an important source of paleopathological evidence owing to the excellent bone preservation in the area and the extent of archaeological and physical anthropological investigation. An early synthesis of work in the area is provided by Dan Morse, *Ancient Disease in the Midwest, Reports of Investigations*. The volume presents extensive discussion and illustrations of the evidence for ancient disease in the area. Additional regional perspective with a similar approach is John B. Gregg and Pauline S. Gregg's volume, *Dry Bones, Dakota Territory Reflected*. A broader anthropological context for disease in the area is provided by Douglas W. Owsley and Richard L. Jantz in *Skeletal Biology in the Great Plains: Migration, Warfare, Health, and Subsistence*.

Much of the evidence regarding correlations of disease and subsistence and related cultural factors can be found in *Paleopathology at the Origins of Agriculture*, edited by Mark Nathan Cohen and George J. Armelagos. This volume is worldwide in scope but includes important North American regional syntheses on the temporal trends in patterns of disease and their correlations with cultural factors.

An overview of demographic issues is provided by A. J. Jaffe's *The First Immigrants from Asia: A Population History of the North American Indians*. This volume brings together diverse data on population history and attempts a synthesis of demographic trends.

Disease and Demography in the Americas, edited by John W. Verano and Douglas H. Ubelaker includes 27 scholarly essays exploring the evidence for disease in the Americas prior to 1492, the size of the population through time, and the impact of disease after European contact.

Two recent works offer synthesis on the post-1492 disease experience in the Americas but also include a pre-1492 perspective: "In the wake of Columbus: Native population biology in the postcontact Americas," by Clark Spencer Larsen, and *In the Wake of Contact, Biological Responses to Conquest*, edited by Clark Spencer Larsen and George R. Milner.

REFERENCES

Allen, Wilma H., Charles F. Merbs, and Walter H. Birkby. "Evidence for prehistoric scalping at Nuvakwewtaqa (Chavez Pass) and Grasshopper Ruin, Arizona." In *Health and*

Disease in the Prehistoric Southwest, Charles F. Merbs and Robert J. Miller, eds. Tempe: Arizona State University, 1985, pp. 23–42.

Allison, Marvin J., Enrique Gerszten, Juan Munizaga, Calogero Santoro, and Daniel Mendoza. "Tuberculosis in pre-Columbian Andean populations." In *Prehistoric Tuberculosis in the Americas,* Jane E. Buikstra, ed. Evanston: Northwestern University Archeological Program, 1981, pp. 49–61.

Allison, Marvin J., Daniel Mendoza, and Alejandro Pezzia. "Documentation of a case of tuberculosis in Pre-Columbian America." *Annual Review of Respiratory Disease,* 107 (1973), pp. 985–91.

Angel, J. L. "Health and the course of civilization as seen in ancient Greece, Part 1." *The Interne,* January (1948), pp. 15–17, and 45–48.

———. "Human biological changes in ancient Greece, with special reference to Lerna." *Yearbook of the American Philosophical Society* (1957), pp. 266–70.

———. "Physical anthropology and medicine." *Journal of the National Medical Association,* 55 (1963), pp. 107–16.

———. "Osteoporosis: Thalassemia?" *American Journal of Physical Anthropology,* 22 (1964), pp. 369–74.

———. "Porotic hyperostosis, anemias, malarias, and marshes in the prehistoric Eastern Mediterranean." *Science,* 153 (1966), pp. 760–63.

———. *Early Skeletons from Tranquillity, California.* Smithsonian Contributions to Anthropology, vol. 2. Washington, D.C.: Smithsonian Institution Press, 1966.

———. "Porotic hyperostosis or osteoporosis symmetrica." In *Diseases in Antiquity,* Don Brothwell and A. T. Sandison, eds. Springfield, Ill.: C. C. Thomas, 1967, pp. 378–89.

———. *The People of Lerna.* Princeton, N.J.: American School of Classical Studies at Athens, 1971.

———. "Early Neolithic people of Nea Nikomedeia." *Fundamenta Monographien zur Urgeschichte, B,* 3 (1973), pp. 103–12.

———. "Patterns of fractures from Neolithic to modern times." *Anthropological Közlemények,* 18 (1974), pp. 9–18.

———. "Paleoecology, paleodemography, and health." In *Ninth International Congress of Anthropological and Ethnological Sciences,* S. Polgar, ed. The Hague, 1975, pp. 167–90.

Aufderheide, Arthur C., and Conrado Rodríguez-martín. *The Cambridge Encyclopedia of Human Paleopathology.* Cambridge: Cambridge University Press, 1998.

Baker, B. J., and G. J. Armelagos. "The origin and antiquity of syphilis: Paleopathological diagnosis and interpretation." *Current Anthropology,* 29 (1988), pp. 703–37.

Berry, David R. "Aspects of paleodemography at Grasshopper Pueblo, Arizona." In *Health and Disease in the Prehistoric Southwest,* Charles F. Merbs and Robert J. Miller, eds. Tempe: Arizona State University, 1985, pp. 43–64.

———. "Dental paleopathology of Grasshopper Pueblo, Arizona." In *Health and Disease in the Prehistoric Southwest,* Charles F. Merbs and Robert J. Miller, eds. Tempe: Arizona State University, 1985, pp. 253–74.

Berryman, Hugh E. *The Averbuch Skeletal Series: A Study of Biological and Social Stress at a Late Mississippian Period Site from Middle Tennessee.* Ph.D. dissertation, University of Tennessee, 1981.

Black, Thomas K. III. *The Biological and Social Analysis of a Mississippian Cemetery from Southeast Missouri: The Turner Site, 23BU21A.* University of Michigan Museum of

Anthropology Papers 26. Ann Arbor: Museum of Anthropology, University of Michigan, 1979.

Blakely, Robert L., ed. *Biocultural Adaptation in Prehistoric America*. Athens, Georgia: University of Georgia Press, 1977.

Bogdan, Georgieann, and David S. Weaver. "Pre-Columbian treponematosis in coastal North Carolina." In *Disease and Demography in the Americas*, John W. Verano and Douglas H. Ubelaker, eds. Washington, D.C.: Smithsonian Institution Press, 1992, pp. 155–63.

Bovee, Dana L., and Douglas W. Owsley. "Evidence of warfare at the Heerwald Site." In *Skeletal Biology in the Great Plains: Migration, Warfare, Health, and Subsistence*, Douglas W. Owsley and Richard L. Jantz, eds. Washington: Smithsonian Institution Press, 1994, pp. 355–62.

Bridges, Patricia S. "Spondylolysis and its relationship to degenerative joint disease in the prehistoric southeastern United States." *American Journal of Physical Anthropology*, 79 (1989), pp. 321–29.

———. "Skeletal evidence of changes in subsistence activities between the Archaic and Mississippian time periods in Northwestern Alabama." In *What Mean These Bones?: Studies in Southeastern Bioarcheology*, Mary Lucas Powell, Patricia S. Bridges, and Ann Marie Wagner Mires, eds. Tuscaloosa: University of Alabama Press, 1991, pp. 89–101.

Brooks, Sheilagh T., and Jerome Melbye. "Skeletal lesions suggestive of pre-Columbian multiple myeloma in a burial from the Kane Mounds, near St. Louis, Missouri." In *Miscellaneous Papers in Paleopathology* 1, William D. Wade, ed. Flagstaff: Northern Arizona Society of Science and Art, 1967, pp. 23–29.

Buikstra, Jane E. "Introduction." In *Prehistoric Tuberculosis in the Americas*, Jane E. Buikstra, ed. Evanston: Northwestern University Archeological Program, 1981, pp. 1–23.

———, ed. *Prehistoric Tuberculosis in the Americas*. Evanston: Northwestern University Archeological Program, 1981.

———, and Della C. Cook. "Pre-Columbian tuberculosis in west-central Illinois: Prehistoric disease in biocultural perspective." In *Prehistoric Tuberculosis in the Americas*, Jane E. Buikstra, ed. Evanston: Northwestern University Archeological Program, 1981, pp. 115–39.

———, and Douglas H. Ubelaker, eds. *Standards for Data Collection from Human Skeletal Remains*. Arkansas Archeological Survey Research Series 44. Fayetteville, Ark.: Arkansas Archeological Survey, 1994.

Bullen, Adelaide K. "Paleoepidemiology and distribution of prehistoric treponemiasis (syphilis) in Florida." *Florida Anthropologist*, 25 (1972), pp. 133–71.

Cassidy, Claire Monod. "Skeletal evidence for prehistoric subsistence adaptation in the central Ohio River Valley." In *Paleopathology at the Origins of Agriculture*, Mark Nathan Cohen and George J. Armelagos, eds. New York: Academic Press, 1984, pp. 307–45.

Cockburn, T. Aiden. "Infectious disease in ancient populations." *Current Anthropology*, 12 (1971), pp. 45–62.

Cohen, Mark Nathan, and George J. Armelagos. "Paleopathology at the origins of agriculture: Editors' summation." In *Paleopathology at the Origins of Agriculture*, Mark Nathan Cohen and George J. Armelagos, eds. New York: Academic Press, 1984, pp. 585–601.

Cole, Harold N., James C. Harkin, Bertram S. Kraus, and Alan R. Moritz. "Pre-Columbian osseous syphilis: Skeletal remains found at Kinishba and Vandal Cave, Arizona with some comments on pertinent literature." *Archives of Dermatology and Syphilogy*, 71 (1955), pp. 231–38.

Cook, Della Collins. "Subsistence and health in the lower Illinois Valley: Osteological evidence." In *Paleopathology at the Origins of Agriculture*, Mark Nathan Cohen and George J. Armelagos, eds. New York: Academic Press, 1984, pp. 235–69.

Cybulski, Jerome S. *An Earlier Population of Hesquiat Harbour, British Columbia: A Contribution of Nootkan Osteology and Physical Anthropology*. Victoria: British Columbia Provincial Museum, 1978.

———. "Culture change, demographic history, and health and disease on the Northwest Coast." In *In the Wake of Contact: Biological Responses to Conquest*, Clark Spencer Larsen and George R. Milner, eds. New York: Wiley-Liss, 1994, pp. 75–85.

Daniels, John D. "The Indian Population of North America in 1492." *William and Mary Quarterly*, 49 (April, 1992), pp. 298–320.

Dickel, David N., Peter D. Schulz, and Henry M. McHenry. "Central California: Pre-historic subsistence changes and health." In *Paleopathology at the Origins of Agriculture*, Mark Nathan Cohen and George J. Armelagos, eds. New York: Academic Press, 1984, pp. 439–61.

Dobyns, Henry F. "Estimating aboriginal American population: An appraisal of techniques with a new hemispheric estimate." *Current Anthropology*, 7 (1966), pp. 395–416.

———. *Their Number Become Thinned: Native American Population Dynamics in Eastern North America*. Knoxville: University of Tennessee Press, 1983.

Eisenberg, Leslie E. "Mississippian cultural terminations in middle Tennessee: What the bioarchaeological evidence can tell us." In *What Mean These Bones?: Studies in Southeastern Bioarcheology*, Mary Lucas Powell, Patricia S. Bridges, and Ann Marie Wagner Mires, eds. Tuscaloosa: University of Alabama Press, 1991, pp. 70–88.

El-Najjar, Mahmoud Y. "Human treponematosis and tuberculosis: Evidence from the New World." *American Journal of Physical Anthropology*, 51 (1979), pp. 599–618.

El-Najjar, Mahmoud Y., Betsy Lozoff, and Dennis J. Ryan. "The paleoepidemiology of porotic hyperostosis in the American Southwest: Radiological and ecological considerations." *American Journal of Roentgenology*, 125 (1975), pp. 918–24.

Elting, James J., and William A. Starna. "A possible case of Pre-Columbian treponematosis from New York state." *American Journal of Physical Anthropology*, 65 (1984), pp. 267–73.

Fink, T. Michael. "Tuberculosis and anemia in a Pueblo III (ca. A.D. 900–1300) Anasazi child from New Mexico." In *Health and Disease in the Prehistoric Southwest*, Charles F. Merbs and Robert J. Miller, eds. Tempe: Arizona State University, 1985, pp. 359–79.

Goodman, Alan H., George J. Armelagos, and Jerome C. Rose. "Enamel hypoplasias as indicators of stress in three historic populations from Illinois." *Human Biology*, 52 (1980), pp. 515–28.

———, John Lallo, George J. Armelagos, and Jerome C. Rose. "Health changes at Dickson Mounds, Illinois (A.D. 950–1300)." In *Paleopathology at the Origins of Agriculture*, Mark Nathan Cohen and George J. Armelagos, eds. New York: Academic Press, 1984, pp. 271–305.

————, and Jerome C. Rose. "Dental enamel hypoplasias as indicators of nutritional status." In *Advances in Dental Anthropology*, Marc A. Kelley and Clark Spencer Larsen, eds. New York: Wiley-Liss, 1991, pp. 279–93.

Gregg, John B., and Pauline S. Gregg. *Dry Bones: Dakota Territory Reflected*. Sioux Falls: J. B. and P. S. Gregg, 1987.

Hartnady, Philip, and Jerome C. Rose. "Abnormal tooth-loss patterns among Archaic-period inhabitants of the lower Pecos region, Texas." In *Advances in Dental Anthropology*, Marc A. Kelley and Clark Spencer Larsen, eds. New York: Wiley-Liss, 1991, pp. 267–78.

Hartney, Patrick C. "Tuberculosis lesions in a prehistoric population sample from southern Ontario." In *Prehistoric Tuberculosis in the Americas*, Jane E. Buikstra, ed. Evanston: Northwestern University Archeological Program, 1981, pp. 141–60.

Henige, David. "On the current devaluation of the notion of evidence: A rejoinder to Dobyns." *Ethnohistory* 36 (1989), pp. 304–7.

————. "Their number become thick: Native American historical demography as expiation." In *The Invented Indian: Cultural Fictions and Government Policies*, James A. Clifton, ed. New Brunswick, N.J.: Transaction Publishers, 1990, p. 169–91.

Hollimon, Sandra E., and Douglas W. Owsley. "Osteology of the Fay Tolton Site: Implications for warfare during the Initial Middle Missouri Variant." In *Skeletal Biology in the Great Plains: Migration, Warfare, Health, and Subsistence*, Douglas W. Owsley and Richard L. Jantz, eds. Washington, D.C.: Smithsonian Institution Press, 1994, pp. 345–53.

Hooton, Earnest Albert. *The Indians of Pecos Pueblo, A Study of Their Skeletal Remains*. Papers of the Southwestern Expedition 4. New Haven, Conn.: Yale University Press, 1930.

Hrdlička, Aleš. "Description de un antiquo esqueleto humano anormal del Valle de Mexico." *Anales del Museo Nacional*, 7 (Mexico, 1900).

————. *Tuberculosis among Certain Indian Tribes of the United States*. Bureau of American Ethnology, Bulletin 42. Washington: Government Printing Office, 1909.

————. "Report on skeletal material form Missouri mounds, collected in 1906–1907 by Mr. Gerand Fowke." *Smithsonian Institution Bureau of American Ethnology Bulletin*, 37 (1910), pp. 103–319.

————. "Physical anthropology of the Lenape or Delawares, and of the eastern Indians in general." *Smithsonian Institution Bureau of American Ethnology Bulletin*, 62 (1916).

————. "Anthropology and medicine." *American Journal of Physical Anthropology*, 10 (1927), pp. 1–9.

Hutchinson, Dale L., and Clark Spencer Larsen. "Determination of stress episode duration from linear enamel hypoplasias: A case study from St. Catherines Island, Georgia." *Human Biology*, 60 (1988), pp. 93–110.

————. "Stress and lifeway change: The evidence from enamel hypoplasias." In *The Archaeology of Mission Santa Catalina de Guale, 2. Biocultural Interpretations of a Population in Transition*, Clark Spencer Larsen, ed. New York: American Museum of Natural History, 1990, pp. 50–65.

Jaffe, A. J. *The First Immigrants from Asia: A Population History of the North American Indians*. New York: Plenum Press, 1992.

Kastert, J., and E. Uehlinger. "Skelettuberkulose: Mit einen Beitrag über Allgemeine Pathologie und Pathologische Anatomie der Skelettuberkulose." In *Handbuch der Tuberkulose*, J. Hein, H. Kleinschmidt, and E. Uehlinger, eds. Stuttgart: Thieme, 1958–64.

Katzenberg, M. Anne. "An investigation of spinal disease in a Midwest aboriginal population." *Yearbook of Physical Anthropology*, 20 (1976), pp. 349–55.

Kroeber, A. L. "Cultural and natural Areas of native North America." *Publications in American Archaeology and Ethnology*, 38. Berkeley: University of California, 1939.

Lallo, John, George J. Armelagos, and Jerome C. Rose. "Paleoepidemiology of infectious disease in the Dickson Mound population." *MCV Quarterly*, 14 (1978), pp. 17–23.

Lallo, John W., and Jerome C. Rose. "Patterns of stress, disease, and mortality in two prehistoric populations from North America." *Journal of Human Evolution* 8 (1979), pp. 323–35.

Lambert, Patricia M. "Health in prehistoric population of the Santa Barbar Channel Islands." *American Antiquity*, 58 (1992), pp. 509–22.

Larsen, Clark Spencer. "Health and disease in prehistoric Georgia: The transition to agriculture." In *Paleopathology at the Origins of Agriculture*, Mark Nathan Cohen and George J. Armelagos, eds. New York: Academic Press, 1984, pp. 367–92.

Larsen, Clark Spencer, and Christopher B. Ruff. "Biomechanical adaptation and behavior on the prehistoric Georgia coast." In *What Mean These Bones?: Studies in Southeastern Bioarcheology*, Mary Lucas Powell, Patricia S. Bridges, and Ann Marie Wagner Mires, eds. Tuscaloosa: University of Alabama Press, 1991, pp. 102–13.

———. "The stresses of conquest in Spanish Florida: Structural adaptation and change before and after contact." In *In the Wake of Contact: Biological Responses to Conquest*, Clark Spencer Larsen and George R. Milner, eds. New York: Wiley-Liss, 1994, pp. 21–34.

Larsen, Clark Spencer, Christopher B. Ruff, Margaret J. Schoeninger, and Dale L. Hutchinson. "Population decline and extinction in La Florida." in *Disease and Demography in the Americas*, John W. Verano and Douglas H. Ubelaker, eds. Washington, D.C.: Smithsonian Institution Press, 1992, pp. 25–39.

Larsen, Clark Spencer, Rebecca Shavit, and Mark C. Griffin. "Dental caries evidence for dietary change: An archaeological context." In *Advances in Dental Anthropology*, Marc A. Kelley and Clark Spencer Larsen, eds. New York: Wiley-Liss, 1991, pp. 179–202.

Lewis, Barbara. "Treponematosis and Lyme Borreliosis connections: Explanation for Tchefuncte disease syndromes?" *American Journal of Physical Anthropology*, 93 (1994), pp. 455–75.

Lovejoy, C. Owen, and Kingsbury G. Heiple. "The analysis of fractures in skeletal populations with an example from the Libben site, Ottawa County, Ohio." *American Journal of Physical Anthropology*, 55 (1981), pp. 529–41.

McClary, Andrew. "Notes on some Late Middle Woodland coprolites." In *The Schultz Site at Green Point: A Stratified Occupation Area in the Saginaw Valley of Michigan*. University of Michigan Memoirs of the Museum of Anthropology 4, James E. Fitting, ed. Ann Arbor: Museum of Anthropology, University of Michigan, 1972, pp. 131–36.

Martin, Debra L., Alan H. Goodman, George J. Armelagos, and Ann L. Magennis. *Black Mesa Anasazi Health: Reconstructing Life from Patterns of Death and Disease.* Southern Illinois University at Carbondale Center for Archaeological Investigations Occasional Paper No. 14. 1991.

Martin, Debra L., Carol Piacentini, and George J. Armelagos. "Paleopathology of the Black Mesa Anasazi: A biocultural approach." In *Health and Disease in the Prehistoric Southwest*, Charles F. Merbs and Robert J. Miller, eds. Tempe: Arizona State University, 1985, pp. 104–14.

Mensforth, Robert P., C. Owen Lovejoy, John W. Lallo, and George J. Armelagos. "The role of constitutional factors, diet, and infectious disease in the etiology of porotic hyperostosis and periosteal reactions in prehistoric infants and children." *Medical Anthropology*, 2 (1978), pp. 1–59.

Merbs, Charles F. "Patterns of health and sickness in the precontact Southwest." In *Columbian Consequences: Archeological and Historical Perspectives on the Spanish Borderlands West*, David Hurst Thomas, ed. Washington, D.C.: Smithsonian Institution Press, 1989, pp. 41–55.

———. "Spondylolysis: Its nature and anthropological significance." *International Journal of Anthropology*, 4 (1989), pp. 163–69.

———. "A new world of infectious disease." *Yearbook of Physical Anthropology*, 35 (1992), pp. 3–24.

Merbs, Charles F., and Ellen M. Vestergaard. "The paleopathology of Sundown, a prehistoric site near Prescott, Arizona." In *Health and Disease in the Prehistoric Southwest*, Charles F. Merbs and Robert J. Miller, eds. Tempe: Arizona State University, 1985, pp. 85–103.

Micozzi, Marc S., and Marc A. Kelley. "Evidence for precolumbian tuberculosis at the Point of Pines Site, Arizona: Skeletal pathology in the sacro-iliac region." In *Health and Disease in the Prehistoric Southwest*, Charles F. Merbs and Robert J. Miller, eds. Tempe: Arizona State University, 1985, pp. 347–58.

Miller, Robert J. "Lateral epicondylitis in the prehistoric Indian population from Nuvak-wewtaqa (Chavez Pass), Arizona." In *Health and Disease in the Prehistoric Southwest*, Charles F. Merbs and Robert J. Miller, eds. Tempe: Arizona State University, 1985, pp. 391–400.

Miller-Shaivitz, Patricia, and Mehmet Yasar Iscan. "The prehistoric people of Fort Center: Physical and health characteristics." In *What Mean These Bones?: Studies in Southeastern Bioarcheology*, Mary Lucas Powell, Patricia S. Bridges, and Ann Marie Wagner Mires, eds. Tuscaloosa: University of Alabama Press, 1991, pp. 131–47.

Milner, George R. "Health and cultural change in the late prehistoric American Bottom, Illinois." In *What Mean These Bones?: Studies in Southeastern Bioarcheology*, Mary Lucas Powell, Patricia S. Bridges, and Ann Marie Wagner Mires, eds. Tuscaloosa: University of Alabama Press, 1991, pp. 52–69.

Milner, George R., Eve Anderson, and Virginia G. Smith. "Warfare in late prehistoric West-Central Illinois." *American Antiquity*, 56 (1991), pp. 581–603.

Minear, William L., and Stanley Rhine. "Increased radiographic density in lumbar vertebrae from prehistoric New Mexico." In *Health and Disease in the Prehistoric Southwest*, Charles F. Merbs and Robert J. Miller, eds. Tempe: Arizona State University, 1985.

Moodie, Roy Lee. "Studies in paleopathology. 1, General consideration of the evidences of pathological conditions found among fossil remains." *Annals of Medical History*, 1 (1917), pp. 374–93.

———. *The Antiquity of Disease*. Chicago: University of Chicago Press, 1923.

———. *Paleopathology: An Introduction to the Study of Ancient Evidences of Disease*. Urbana: University of Illinois Press, 1923.

Mooney, James. "Population." *Handbook of American Indians North of Mexico*, Bureau of American Ethnology Bulletin 30, F. W. Hodge II, ed. Washington, D.C.: Government Printing Office, 1910, pp. 286–87.

———. "The aboriginal population of America north of Mexico." *Smithsonian Miscellaneous Collections* 80. Washington, D.C.: Smithsonian Institution, 1928, pp. 1–40.

Morell, Virginia. "Mummy settles TB antiquity debate." *Science*, 263 (1994), pp. 1686–87.

Morse, Dan. "Two cases of possible treponema infection in prehistoric America." *Miscellaneous Papers in Paleopathology, Technical Series* 7, W. Wade, ed. Flagstaff: Northern Arizona Society of Science and Art, 1967, pp. 48–60.

———. *Ancient Disease in the Midwest*, 2d ed. Springfield: Illinois State Museum, 1978.

Ortner, Donald J., and Walter G. Putschar. *Identification of Pathological Conditions in Human Skeletal Remains*. Smithsonian Contributions to Anthropology 28. Washington, D.C.: Smithsonian Institution Press, 1981.

Owsley, Douglas W. "Demography of prehistoric and early historic Northern Plains populations." In *Disease and Demography in the Americas*, John W. Verano and Douglas H. Ubelaker, eds. Washington, D.C.: Smithsonian Institution Press, 1992, pp. 75–86.

———. "Warfare in coalescent tradition populations of the Northern Plains." In *Skeletal Biology in the Great Plains: Migration, Warfare, Health, and Subsistence*, Douglas W. Owsley and Richard L. Jantz, eds. Washington, D.C.: Smithsonian Institution Press, 1994, pp. 333–43.

Palkovich, Ann M. "Tuberculosis epidemiology in two Arikara skeletal samples: A study of disease impact." In *Prehistoric Tuberculosis in the Americas*, Jane E. Buikstra, ed. Evanston, Ill.: Northwestern University Archeological Program, 1981, pp. 161–75.

———. "Agriculture, marginal environments, and nutritional stress in the prehistoric Southwest." In *Paleopathology at the Origins of Agriculture*, Mark Nathan Cohen and George J. Armelagos, eds. New York: Academic Press, 1984, pp. 425–38.

———. "Interpreting prehistoric morbidity and mortality risk: Nutritional stress at Arroyo Hondo Pueblo, New Mexico." In *Health and Disease in the Prehistoric Southwest*, Charles F. Merbs and Robert J. Miller, eds. Tempe: Arizona State University, 1985, pp. 128–38.

Perzigian, Anthony J., Patricia A. Tench, and Donna J. Braun. "Prehistoric health in the Ohio River Valley." In *Paleopathology at the Origins of Agriculture*, Mark Nathan Cohen and George J. Armelagos, eds. New York: Academic Press, 1984, pp. 347–66.

Pfeiffer, Susan, and Scott I. Fairgrieve. "Evidence from ossuaries: The effect of contact on the health of Iroquoians." In *In the Wake of Contact: Biological Responses to Conquest*, Clark Spencer Larsen and George R. Milner, eds. New York: Wiley-Liss, 1994, pp. 47–61.

Powell, Mary Lucas. "Ranked status and health in the Mississippian chiefdom at Moundville." In *What Mean These Bones?: Studies in Southeastern Bioarcheology*, Mary Lucas Powell, Patricia S. Bridges, and Ann Marie Wagner Mires, eds. Tuscaloosa: University of Alabama Press, 1991, pp. 22–51.

————. "Health and disease in the late prehistoric Southeast." In *Disease and Demography in the Americas*, John W. Verano and Douglas H. Ubelaker, eds. Washington, D.C.: Smithsonian Institution Press, 1992, pp. 41–53.

Powell, Mary Lucas, and J. Daniel Rogers. *Bioarchaeology of the McCutchan-McLaughlin Site (34Lt-11): Biophysical and Mortuary Variability in Eastern Oklahoma.* Norman: Oklahoma Archeological Survey, 1980.

Rathbun, Ted A., Jim Sexton, and James Michie. "Disease patterns in a Formative Period South Carolina coastal population." *Tennessce Anthropological Association Miscellaneous Paper*, 5 (1980), pp. 52–74.

Reichs, Kathleen J. "Treponematosis: A possible case from the late prehistoric of North Carolina." *American Journal of Physical Anthropology*, 79 (1989), pp. 289–303.

Reinhard, Karl J. "Parasitism at Antelope House, a Puebloan village in Canyon de Chelley, Arizona." In *Health and Disease in the Prehistoric Southwest*, Charles F. Merbs and Robert J. Miller, eds. Tempe: Arizona State University, 1985, pp. 220–33.

————. "Archaeoparisitology in North America." *American Journal of Physical Anthropology*, 82 (1990), pp. 145–63.

————. "Patterns of diet, parasitism, and anemia in prehistoric west North America." In *Diet, Demography, and Disease: Changing Perspectives in Anemia*, Patricia Stuart McAdam and Susan Kent, eds. New York: Aldine de Gruyter, 1992, pp. 219–58.

Reinhard, Karl J., Larry Tieszen, Karin L. Sandness, Lynae M. Beiningen, Elizabeth Miller, A. Mohammad Ghazi, Christiana E. Miewald, and Sandra B. Barnum. "Trade, contact, and female health in northeast Nebraska." In *In the Wake of Contact: Biological Responses to Conquest*, Clark Spencer Larsen and George R. Milner, eds. New York: Wiley-Liss, 1994, pp. 63–74.

Rothschild, Bruce M., and Robert J. Woods. "Character of Precolumbian North American spondyloarthropathy." *Journal of Rheumatology*, 19 (1992), pp. 1229–35.

————. "Geographic distribution of calcium pyrophosphate (CPPD) deposition disease in pre-Columbian North America: Independent validation of CPPD criteria." *Clinical and Experimental Rheumatology*, 11 (1993), pp. 315–18.

Rothschild, Bruce M., Robert J. Woods, Christine Rothschild, and Jeno I. Sebes. "Geographic distribution of rheumatoid arthritis in ancient North America: Implications for pathogenesis." *Seminars in Arthritis and Rheumatism*, 22 (1992), pp. 181–87.

Rose, Jerome C., Barbara A. Burnett, Michael S. Nassaney, and Mark W. Blaeuer. "Paleopathology and the origins of maize agriculture in the lower Mississippi Valley and Caddoan area." In *Paleopathology at the Origins of Agriculture*, Mark Nathan Cohen and George J. Armelagos, eds. New York: Academic Press, 1984, pp. 393–424.

Rose, Jerome C., Murray K. Marks, and Larry L. Tieszen. "Bioarchaeology and subsistence in the central and lower portions of the Mississippi Valley." In *What Mean These Bones?: Studies in Southeastern Bioarcheology*, Mary Lucas Powell, Patricia S. Bridges, and Ann Marie Wagner Mires, eds. Tuscaloosa: University of Alabama Press, 1991, pp. 7–21.

Salo, W. L., A. C. Aufderheide, J. Buikstra, and T. A. Holcomb. "Identification of *Mycobacterium tuberculosis* DNA in a pre-Columbian Peruvian mummy." *Proceedings of the National Academy of Sciences of the United States of America*, 91 (1994), pp. 2091–94.

Schermer, S. J., A. K. Fisher, and D. C. Hodges. "Endemic treponematosis in prehistoric western Iowa." In *Skeletal Biology in the Great Plains: Migration, Warfare, Health, and Subsistence*, Douglas W. Owsley and Richard L. Jantz, eds. Washington, D.C.: Smithsonian Institution Press, 1994, pp. 109–21.

Shadomy, H. Jean. "The differential diagnosis of various fungal pathogens and tuberculosis in the prehistoric Indians." In *Prehistoric Tuberculosis in the Americas*, Jane E. Buikstra, ed. Evanston, Ill.: Northwestern University Archeological Program, 1981.

Stark, Carolyn, and Sheilagh T. Brooks. "A survey of prehistoric paleopathology in the Nevada Great Basin." In *Health and Disease in the Prehistoric Southwest*, Charles F. Merbs and Robert J. Miller, eds. Tempe: Arizona State University, 1985, pp. 65–78.

Steinbock, R. Ted. *Paleopathological Diagnosis and Interpretation.* Springfield, Ill.: Thomas, 1976.

———. "The history, epidemiology, and paleopathology of kidney and bladder stone disease." In *Health and Disease in the Prehistoric Southwest*, Charles F. Merbs and Robert J. Miller, eds. Tempe: Arizona State University, 1985, pp. 177–97.

Stewart, T. D. *The People of America.* New York: Scribner's, 1973.

Stodder, Ann L. W., and Debra L. Martin. "Health and disease in the Southwest before and after Spanish contact." In *Disease and Demography in the Americas*, John W. Verano and Douglas H. Ubelaker, eds. Washington, D.C.: Smithsonian Institution Press, 1992, pp. 55–73.

Sullivan, Norman C. "Tuberculosis in a Late Woodland Effigy Mound population." *Wisconsin Archeologist*, 66 (1985), pp. 71–76.

Taylor, Mark G. "The paleopathology of a southern Sinagua population from Oak Creek Pueblo, Arizona." In *Health and Disease in the Prehistoric Southwest*, Charles F. Merbs and Robert J. Miller, eds. Tempe: Arizona State University, 1985, pp. 115–18.

Thornton, Russell. *American Indian Holocaust and Survival: A Population History since 1492.* Norman: University of Oklahoma Press, 1987.

Turner, C. G. II. "Dental anthropological indications of agriculture among the Jomon people of central Japan." *American Journal of Physical Anthropology*, 51 (1979), pp. 619–36.

Ubelaker, Douglas H. *Reconstruction of Demographic Profiles from Ossuary Skeletal Samples: A Case Study from the Tidewater Potomac.* Smithsonian Contributions to Anthropology 18. Washington, D.C.: Smithsonian Institution Press, 1974.

———. "The sources and methodology for Mooney's estimates of North American Indian populations." In *The Native Population of the Americas in 1492*, William M. Denevan, ed. Madison: University of Wisconsin Press, 1976.

———. "The development of American paleopathology." In *A History of American Physical Anthropology 1930–1980*, Frank Spencer, ed. New York: Academic Press, 1982, pp. 337–56.

————. "North American Indian population size, A.D. 1500 to 1985." *American Journal of Physical Anthropology*, 77 (1988), pp. 289–94.

————. *Human Skeletal Remains: Excavation, Analysis, Interpretation*, 2d ed. Washington: Taraxacum, 1989.

————. "North American Indian population size: Changing perspectives." In *Disease and Demography in the Americas*, J. W. Verano and D. H. Ubelaker, eds. Washington, D.C.: Smithsonian Institution Press, 1992, pp. 169–76.

————. "North American census, 1492." *Pacific Discovery*, Winter (1992), pp. 32–35.

Van Blerkom, Linda Miller. *The Evolution of Human Infectious Disease in the Eastern and Western Hemispheres*. Ph.D. dissertation, University of Colorado, 1985. Ann Arbor: U.M.I. Dissertation Information Service, 1990.

Verano, J. W., and D. H. Ubelaker, eds. *Disease and Demography in the Americas*. Washington, D.C.: Smithsonian Institution Press.

Walker, Phillip L. "Anemia among prehistoric Indians of the American Southwest." In *Health and Disease in the Prehistoric Southwest*, Charles F. Merbs and Robert J. Miller, eds. Tempe: Arizona State University, 1985, pp. 139–64.

————. "Cranial injuries as evidence of violence in prehistoric southern California." *American Journal of Physical Anthropology*, 80 (1989), pp. 313–23.

Walker, Phillip L., and Patricia Lambert. "Skeletal evidence for stress during a period of cultural change in prehistoric California." In *Advances in Paleopathology*. Journal of Paleopathology Monographic Publication 1, Luigi Capasso, ed. Chieti, Italy: M. Solfanelli, 1989.

————. "Paleopathological evidence for stress in a prehistoric northern California Indian population" (abstract). Paper presented at the Paleopathology Association, Barcelona, 1992.

Warren, John Collins. "Account of the crania of some of the aborigines of the United States." In *A Comparative View of the Sensorial and Nervous Systems in Men and Animals*. Boston: J. W. Ingraham, 1822.

————. "North American antiquities." *American Journal of Science and Arts*, 34 (1838), pp. 47–49.

Weaver, David S. "Subsistence and settlement patterns at Casas Grandes, Chihuahua, Mexico." In *Health and Disease in the Prehistoric Southwest*, Charles F. Merbs and Robert J. Miller, eds. Tempe: Arizona State University, 1985, pp. 119–27.

Wheeler, R. Linda. "Pathology in late thirteenth century Zuni from the El Morro Valley, New Mexico." In *Health and Disease in the Prehistoric Southwest*, Charles F. Merbs and Robert J. Miller, eds. Tempe: Arizona State University, 1985, pp. 79–84.

Widmer, Lee, and Anthony J. Perzigian. "The ecology and etiology of skeletal lesions in late prehistoric populations from eastern North America." In *Prehistoric Tuberculosis in the Americas*, Jane E. Buikstra, ed. Evanston, Ill.: Northwestern University Archeological Program, 1981, pp. 99–113.

Willey, Patrick S. *Prehistoric Warfare on the Great Plains: Skeletal Analysis of the Crow Creek Massacre Victims*. New York: Garland, 1990.

Williams, H. U. "Human paleopathology, with some original observations on symmetrical osteoporosis of the skull." *Archives of Pathology*, 7 (1929), pp. 839–902.

Williams, John A. "Evidence of hydatid disease in a Plains Woodland burial." *Plains Anthropol.*, 30 (1985), pp. 25–28.

————. "Disease profiles of Archaic and Woodland populations in the Northern Plains." In *Skeletal Biology in the Great Plains: Migration, Warfare, Health, and Subsistence*, Douglas W. Owsley and Richard L. Jantz, eds. Washington, D.C.: Smithsonian Institution Press, 1994, pp. 91–108.

Zimmerman, Michael R., and Marc A. Kelley. *Atlas of Human Paleopathology*. New York: Praeger, 1982.

4

THE POPULATION OF THE ST. LAWRENCE VALLEY, 1608–1760

HUBERT CHARBONNEAU, BERTRAND DESJARDINS, JACQUES LÉGARÉ, AND HUBERT DENIS

When Samuel de Champlain founded the first permanent French settlement in North America at Quebec in 1608, the St. Lawrence Valley had no sedentary population. It was used for fishing and hunting, however, by a few thousand Algonquians. The St. Lawrence, providing access to the heart of North America, was the core of an empire known as New France for over 150 years. New France stretched from the mouth of the St. Lawrence to Louisiana and included the area around the Great Lakes as well as the Mississippi Valley. At the turn of the seventeenth century, three-quarters of North America was owned by France.

At that time, the colony called Canada, made up of the Laurentian lowlands, was entirely within the boundaries of what is now the province of Quebec. The colony had a surface area of 35,000 square kilometers and measured over 500 kilometers in length. Although the landscape around Montreal is relatively flat, the St. Lawrence narrows from Trois-Rivières, and the lowlands remain constricted from there on. The river proved to be an excellent means of communication, with good farmland on both sides. True, the winter was long and hard, but the environment was far from hostile. The abundant rain combined with the warm summer weather allowed for the growth of dense forest vegetation and a diversified fauna, rich with game and fish.

Populating the colony proved to be difficult. Regardless of the agricultural potential, French interest in the valley rested primarily in the fur trade, since furs were used to fabricate felt hats, a popular style in Europe at the time. The French authorities were not ready to defray the costs of colonization, having just emerged from 40 years of war. Hence, they passed this on to private interests who, in exchange for the monopoly over the fur trade, were required to recruit, transport, and establish colonists.

Since it was the natives who collected and transported the furs, the fur industry required very little European labor. As a result, merchants were hardly motivated to populate the colony, and it remained little more than a trading post for the first 50 years of its existence. The native wars which took place during the mid–seventeenth century changed the context because, once their Huron allies were driven away from the lake which had become their namesake, the French were obliged to handle all aspects of the trade by themselves. This prompted great expeditions toward the West and the development of a class of laborers known as the *coureurs de bois* (literally, someone who roams the forest). This new situation required an increase in agricultural production, since supplies were necessary to provide for a population which was occupied with activities other than agriculture. These supplies were also necessary as barter with the native peoples of the West, whose contribution was indispensable for the continued growth of the fur trade and who traditionally obtained their corn provisions from the now-departed Hurons.

It was around this period, in 1663, that Louis XIV took over the administration of the colony. He, together with Jean-Baptiste Colbert, his minister of finance, put together Canada's first true colonization policy. Like his contemporaries, Colbert felt that the population of France was declining; and, true to his mercantilist principles, which stated that the best part of both economic and human resources should be reserved for the mother country, held to the idea that the colony should grow mainly on its own. Accordingly, measures targeting natural increase were given more importance than the promotion of immigration. Over the long run, the policy must be considered a failure, since despite a very high rate of natural increase, the French population of North America did not achieve levels that would allow it to master its own destiny.

Based on the European feudal system, territorial management was delegated to seigneurs, who drew revenues by distributing land to tenants free of charge in exchange for a percentage of their income. The usual plot of land was 150 meters wide and 1,600 meters long, fronting on the St. Lawrence or one of its tributaries. The organization of Quebec's territory still bears the marks of this model of land concession. Although the Coutume de Paris, the legal system of the colony, dictated that family wealth be divided among the children, in practice the original plot was rarely subdivided. Since those children who did not end up with the family farm could easily find a piece of land elsewhere, the rural community could be seen as equalitarian under the French regime. Hierarchical stratification only became an issue once new plots of land became scarce.

The colonial government was absolute and dominated by officials from France. If at first they sought to re-create their Old Regime society, the colonial context led to the development of an original society which was less closed than its parent, though still far from open in nature. In contrast to the situation in France, the colonial nobility could not live solely on their rental income. As a result, they were much less isolated from the rest of the population as they involved themselves in business activities and were barely distinguishable from the bourgeois within the elite.

Right from the beginning, the church was omnipresent, and the religious orders took charge of the schools and hospitals. To maintain these institutions, the orders were forced to become landowners, earning revenue from their tenants' labor. The clergy were recruited from the heart of the elite, and the bishop was one of the most influential men in the colony.

Nevertheless, the existence in the northeastern part of the North American continent of two colonies, whose home countries were more often than not at war, would change the course of history for the population. The French-Canadian presence in the Mississippi Valley hindered the development of the already booming New England. Furthermore, the two colonies were in competition for the trading territories. It was inevitable, therefore, that the two would be constantly in conflict, the fight ending only in 1763, when the Treaty of Versailles sanctioned the British conquest of New France which had taken place three years earlier. As immense as New France was, its low demographic density proved to be its weakness, and thus the empire was unable to defend itself against the strength of New England. Numbers would inevitably conquer.

SOURCES: ABUNDANT AND OF GOOD QUALITY

Knowledge of an ancient population requires reliable sources. In this respect, Quebec is privileged. Owing to the diligence of the clergy and authorities of the period, we now have at our disposal numerous sources of good data. Many years of exhaustive research combined with the fact that the population was relatively small and isolated have led to the development of a computerized population register known as the Registre de la Population du Québec Ancien (RPQA).

SOURCES

From its origin, the colony adopted the custom of keeping birth, marriage, and burial registers, a practice which had started in France during the sixteenth century. From its beginnings to 1800, the colony registered and recorded approximately 700,000 baptisms, marriages, and burials, creating by far the most fundamental source for the study of the demography of the Laurentian Valley during the French regime. The registers consist of information relating strictly to the Catholic population. Thus, although Indians were numerous during the early years of the colony, only those who converted to the Catholic faith, a very small fraction of the whole, found any mention in the registers.

The registers were also well kept. On the one hand, the relative calm of the period combined with the observation of the 1678 regulation, which stipulated that all registers be kept in duplicate, meant that few losses took place. In the period from 1608 to 1765, only about 7% of parish-years of registration were lost, and even this number is exaggerated since the larger and more populous parishes were better able to keep records than those parishes just starting to grow. Most losses occurred in the first decades, with the seventeenth century, which only held a tenth of all register entries, making up a full third of all those that were lost. The high level of education of the keepers of the registers also ensured a high quality of registered information.

The information obtained from three nominative censuses (1666, 1667, and 1681) can also be used in the demographic study of the population of Quebec. These censuses were administered around the major immigrant wave, and they benefited from the fact that they recorded the age of the immigrants during a time when most were still young. These censuses also provide information concerning the professions of most of the immigrants. Two censuses for Quebec City are also available, one in 1716 and the other in 1744. The 1765 census was done at the beginning of the British regime and provides a view of the colony at the time of the conquest. In addition, during the period from 1685 to 1739, 26 anonymous enumerations took place, establishing, by seigneuries, the condition of the population and agricultural production.

Marriage contracts are also of great use, because they allow us to compensate for gaps in the church registers, particularly since the period between the signing of the contract and the actual ceremony was often short. Among other sources which may be used in the study of the colonial population are judicial archives and hospital registers. Other documents, at our disposal included lists for the military, religious, and fur trade employees. Finally, our study benefited from several histories, as well as from works on genealogy, which have proven to be numerous in Quebec.

A COMPUTERIZED POPULATION REGISTER OF THE QUEBEC POPULATION

The idea of a computerized Quebec population register was developed at the Université de Montréal during the second half of the 1960s. This project become possible because of a series of circumstances: the abundance and quality of the sources, the reduced size and semiclosed character of the population, and developments in computerization.

The primary objective of this register was to reconstitute the population of Quebec from its origin to the end of the eighteenth century. An essential tool in gaining knowledge of the history of the Canadian population, the RPQA is also a true population laboratory built to serve the interests of researchers in a number of disciplines.

Most of the data in the RPQA come from Quebec's parish registers. These registers provide a solid database because of their high quality; and the integration of alternative sources (censuses, notarial acts, genealogical studies) make it quasi-perfect: the study of the Laurentian Valley is defined with rare precision. Some small uncertainties still exist, but they are of little consequence in our population study.

To demonstrate the quality of the register, we know the exact date of birth of 95% of the 20,000 people who were born in the colony during the seventeenth century. We also have access, through church or notarial registration, to 97% of the dates of marriages which were celebrated within the colony. Finally, excluding some cases of emigration, less than 25% of all deaths escaped us. In two out of three of these cases, we are able to determine within a small margin when the death took place. On the whole, the demographic biographies of more than 90% of the 20,000 colonists are precisely known. For the remaining 10%, it is possible to determine the missing information through simple assumption. Few population historians have the benefit of working with such data.

FROM A DIFFICULT BEGINNING TO A STRONG AND CONTINUED GROWTH

The beginnings of the European presence in the St. Lawrence Valley were very difficult. Although the first permanent settlers arrived in Quebec in 1608, the process of populating the colony really began after the period from 1629 to 1632, when it was under British rule. Before 1632 there were only three marriages and eight births in the colony, with the white population reaching only 60 inhabitants.

The French created new permanent settlements, at Trois-Rivières in 1634 and at Montreal in 1642. These two locations and Quebec City became the colony's administrative centers, with parishes growing around them; the oldest ones were located around Quebec City. The establishment of new parishes marked out the development of the population upstream along the banks of the St-Lawrence. By 1681, there were over 40 parishes, a little more than half within the jurisdiction of the city of Quebec. By 1722, their numbers had doubled, with Quebec's importance slowly waning in favor of Montreal. According to the last count made under the French regime (1739), the population was spread over 500 kilometers on both sides of the St. Lawrence.

The population had grown to over 70,000 by the time of the British conquest in 1760 (Figure 4.1), a number which could have been higher but for emigration. Out of the 20,000 Canadians born in the Laurentian Valley during the seventeenth century, more than 7% left the colony. The majority were single men, with only 2% of women, usually married, emigrating elsewhere.

Only a total of 10,000 immigrants established themselves in the colony over the span of a century and a half. After the immigration years 1663–73, the excess of births over deaths became the main factor of growth. The population thus began to quickly become "Canadian": whereas in 1663, 6 out of 10 inhabitants were immigrants, by 1700, more than 80% of the population was of Canadian origin. From 1660 to 1670, the population grew at a rate of a little more than 3% per annum and, as net migration eased, the average growth rate diminished and stabilized at 2.5%. Within the next one or two five-year periods, growth settled at a constant high rate, solely as a result of natural increase.

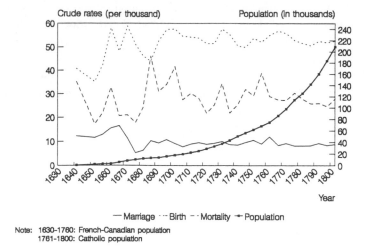

Figure 4.1. Crude birth, death, and marriage rates and population estimates, 1630–1800

There was also a transient population within the colony, which was much less observable as it consisted primarily of soldiers stationed within the colony temporarily and of French merchants who, because of their business, arrived in the summer and left before winter's arrival. This population was sometimes of considerable importance during the seventeenth century, but it declined to only 5% of the total population by 1700. This proportion probably remained constant thereafter until the colony experienced an influx of 4,500 French soldiers in the 1755–59 period, a number corresponding to 6 or 7% of the local population.

The evolution of the crude marriage, birth, and death rates is indicative of the trends which took place within the population (Figure 4.1). Before 1675, the marriage rate was very high owing to the constant influx of immigrants. Between 1675 and 1685, this rate dropped tremendously, owing to immigration's decline, but it increased again during the 1685–1689 period, to remain steady until the end of the French regime, as the first Canadian-born generations began to marry.[1]

During the seventeenth century, the birth rate reflected trends in the marriage rate. A disproportion between the sexes kept the rate low during the colony's first years. After the migration wave of the 1660s, the rate quickly increased. The decline which took place from 1680 to 1690

[1] By comparison, the gross marriage rate in France during the 1740–59 period was about 9 per thousand. See Henry and Blayo, "La population de la France", p. 109.

was due in part to the decrease in marriages but was also due to the high mortality rate of the 1685–89 period. From 1690 on, the birth rate remained consistently high, with fluctuations due primarily to the mortality rate.[2]

The five-year average mortality rate fluctuated greatly owing to epidemics. Although some of these proved to be brutal, such as the smallpox epidemics of 1703 and 1733, only the typhoid epidemic of 1687 caused, over a five-year period, a small excess in deaths over births. At a level of 30 per 1,000, the colony's mortality rate during the eighteenth century could be described as favorable.[3]

The immigration wave which took place during the 1660s was the turning point in the evolution of Canada's population. Before this time, the population struggled and had difficulty in growing. Then, mostly as a result of natural increase, the colonial population's growth strengthened. During the eighteenth century, the population grew at an annual rate of about 2.5% and did so without any significant migration. This rate was equivalent to a doubling of the population every thirty years. Within the span of 150 years, Canada had grown from a simple fur-trading post to a society worthy of its name. As Figure 4.1 also indicates, the conquest did not disrupt the growth of the French-Canadian population so that by the end of the eighteenth century, it had reached 180,000 people.

A WEAK AND HOMOGENEOUS IMMIGRATION

The estimated number of immigrants who spent at least one winter in the St. Lawrence Valley before 1760 was at least 25,000. From this group, 14,000 settled permanently, with 10,000 of them marrying within the colony. Compared with the support given New England, which received hundreds of thousands of immigrants during the same period, France's support seems rather paltry. This is not only because the French migrated very little, but the Laurentian Valley received only about 7 to 8% of the total French migrants, most of whom preferred the southern colonies of the Antilles and Guyana. Thus, the French contribution each year to the

---

[2] The birth rate in France was much lower, at around 40 per thousand for the period from 1740 to 1759. See Henry and Blayo, "La population de la France," p. 109.

[3] It was less than that of the home country, which dropped from 40 per thousand to 35 per thousand during the 1740s and 1750s. See Henry and Blayo, "La population de la France," p. 109.

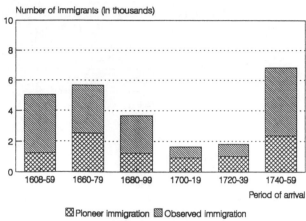

Figure 4.2. Observed and pioneer immigration according to period of arrival, 1608–1759

development of New France represented only about 8 out of every million persons living in France at that time.

A DISCONTINUOUS MOVEMENT

The arrival of immigrants was not a regular event (see Figure 4.2). Boom periods were followed by lean ones. Immigration was weak before 1663, even during the 1632–63 period, when colonization was a responsibility of the companies which were given a mandate to settle a certain number of people within the colony in exchange for a monopoly on exploitation of the colony's resources. During this period, only 400 colonists were brought in, which was one-tenth of the number the companies had agreed to achieve.

The royal government took back the administration of the colony in 1663, marking the only period of relatively high French immigration. From 1663 to 1673, the Crown sent 800 women, called Filles du Roi, to the colony, and provided them with dowries in an attempt to make them more attractive for marriage. The Crown also brought 450 soldiers and officers from the Carignan regiment to the colony, providing them with generous bonuses and pieces of land. Following this, there were two other peaks in military immigration: the first was the arrival of the marine troops from

Table 4.1. *Immigrants who experienced a family life in Quebec according to country of origin and period of arrival, 1608–1765*

Country of origin	Period of arrival				
	1608–79	1680–99	1700–29	1730–65	Total
France	98.8	92.4	76.1	85.7	90.1
Brittany	2.5	6.0	7.7	36.4	4.8
Normandy	22.4	8.9	5.1	9.7	13.6
Paris	17.5	11.1	15.9	10.0	13.3
Loire	8.4	5.6	7.0	5.2	6.5
North	2.6	1.5	2.6	4.9	3.2
East	3.3	2.9	6.3	13.7	7.2
Poitou-Charentes	29.1	28.1	26.1	11.0	21.3
Center	2.1	5.6	4.1	3.9	3.3
South	3.4	13.0	14.4	20.4	11.6
Undetermined	7.7	9.7	10.9	0.3	5.4
Acadia	0.1	2.2	5.8	6.5	3.4
Hinterland posts		0.2	5.9	0.5	1.1
English colonies		2.0	5.2	0.3	1.1
Europe (except France)	0.8	2.7	4.6	5.3	3.1
Native Americans[a]	0.3	0.5	2.1	1.0	0.9
Others			0.3	0.7	0.3
Total	100.0	100.0	100.0	100.0	100.0
	(N = 3,808)	(N = 1,205)	(N = 1,437)	(N = 3,496)	(N = 9,946)

[a] Only those Native Americans who became intergrated into the European population were counted. They are considered to have "immigrated" into the colonial population.

1683 to 1693, and the second was the arrival of the troops who were stationed to defend the colony from 1755 through 1759, during the Seven Years' War. These two periods, combined with that from 1663 to 1673, made up half of the immigration which took place before 1760.

A CONCENTRATED GEOGRAPHIC ORIGIN

Of the 10,000 immigrants who settled and experienced a family life in the Laurentian Valley, 9,000 came directly from France, while most of the others were Acadians and Europeans originating from the countries bordering France (Table 4.1). All the regions of France participated in the development of Canada, but to differing degrees. If we were to draw a line from Bordeaux to Soissons, which is about 100 kilometers northeast of Paris, we would notice that about three-quarters of all departures took place north of this line. Specifically, the Charentes and the Poitou regions dominated, each making up one-quarter of immigrants, while Normandy and the Ile-de-France, including Paris, provided 15% each. In proportion to their populations, the provinces of Aunis and Perche provided the most, while the ports of call dwindled in importance compared with the peripheral areas from which the troops were recruited.

About 4 of every 10 immigrants came from urban areas; this figure rises to two-thirds in the case of women. This proportion may seem high for a country that was 85% rural, considering that the colonial economy was based on agriculture and the fur trade. However, one must bear in mind that even when they were in the cities, the French were never far from their rural roots.

AT FIRST FAMILY IMMIGRATION, AND THEN ESSENTIALLY INDIVIDUAL

Of the immigrants who arrived before 1700, 3 out of every 10 were either married or with family members. Most of these arrived before 1663, since families were actively recruited. While half of immigrants at that point moved as a family, only a fifth did later on. Women migrated in a family setting more often than men. Excluding the Filles du Roi, 4 out of every 10 women came alone, and, after 1663, 85% of men did the same. The nuclear family was privileged since it encompassed 75% of all immigrants who came as a family.

A YOUNG, MALE, AND PREDOMINANTLY UNMARRIED IMMIGRATION

On the whole, about 13 to 14 times more men than women landed in the Laurentian Valley. If we examine those immigrants established by marriage, we find four men to every woman, with the proportion varying over time. During the period of high family immigration which took place before 1663, the proportion was four women to six men. After 1663, following the halt in female immigration, the male immigration became predominant, with seven men for every woman arriving. This surplus in the male population created an imbalance in the marriage market which affected nuptial behavior, particularly for the first generations of Canadians. This effect lingered on until natural growth normalized the male–female ratio, near the end of the seventeenth century.

Table 4.2. *Immigrants according to category and period*
of arrival, 1608–1759

Period of arrival	Category of immigrants						
	Miletary	Indentured	Women arriving above	Prisoners	Religious	Others[a]	Total
1608–59	170	1,890	450		139	2,394	5,043
1660–79	2,034	520	1,176		131	1,816	5,677
1680–99	3,192	190	146		145	141	3,814
1700–19	949	380	187		122	54	1,692
1720–39	554	558	75	481	115	31	1,814
1740–59	6,177	362	71	113	122	390	6,884
Total	13,076	3,900	2,105	594	774	4,475	24,924

[a] Wives and children, members of the colonial administration, merchants, etc.

The immigrants who arrived in Quebec were fairly young, the average age being 25 for men and 22 for women. Three times out of four, the immigrant was between 15 and 25 years of age. Immigrants aged 45 and older were rare, and whereas children made up 15% of all immigrants before 1663, their arrival was reduced to a minimum afterward. Most of the immigrants were also unmarried, with married and widowed immigrants making up less than a twentieth of the total who came to Quebec during the French regime.

PEOPLE FROM ALL BACKGROUNDS, AND YET A HOMOGENEOUS GROUP

While the immigrants came from diverse backgrounds, they were on the whole homogeneous in nature and were in no way representative of the overall French population. On the male side, the military accounted for half of both the total and the pioneer immigration, with indentured servants forming the next most important group (see Table 4.2). As for women, the Filles du Roi and the mothers and daughters who arrived as members of a family combined equally to make up two-thirds of the total female population.

Save for those who arrived during the pre-1663 period, the immigrants were poorly qualified. It should be noted that the colonial economic status, which was based primarily upon agriculture and the fur trade, did not attract tradespeople. Finally, the immigrants from urban areas had a higher rate of illiteracy than their counterparts who remained in France.

INDIVIDUALS SELECTED THREEFOLD

Civil and military recruits alike were required to meet certain physical standards: those who were physically not up to standards were ineligible for recruitment. In addition candidates had to be able to endure the voyage, which often took as long as three months. Living conditions during this period were horrendous; the lack of personal hygiene combined with the inevitable crowding were perfect conditions for disease, most commonly typhoid. Therefore, it is not surprising that during the French regime, the death rate on the boats making the voyage to the colony ranged from 7 to 10%. Finally, contrary to the will of the authorities, many immigrants returned to Europe. Those who chose to remain, especially before 1700, were faced with a barrage of ordeals, including hostile Indians, the cold, and geographic isolation. Without doubt, their persistence can be attributed to the fact that their chances of success were better in North America than in their homeland.

Of the 27,000 immigrants who left for Quebec, only 25,000 actually made it to their destination. Of this group, little more than half opted for permanent settlement, and only 4 out of 10 actually began having families. It was these individuals who were the link between the two continents. Derived primarily from the French mosaic, they quickly developed into a homogeneous society. Thus, from a small group of 10,000 immigrants who settled down and took advantage of the healthy colonial environment, the society grew at a rate seldom equaled anytime anywhere. From this society descended an entire people.

NUPTIALITY: THE DICTATES OF THE MARRIAGE MARKET

In early populations, particularly those of an agrarian nature, marriage depended on possibilities for establishment. In the newly developed colony, with its open territory and lack of women, the situation was the reverse: settlement became a function of the possibility of marriage.

The peculiar evolution of the numerical relation between the sexes created the two successive matrimonial regimes. The first occurred during

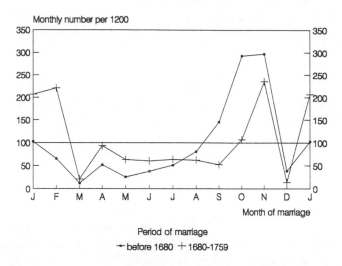

Figure 4.3. Seasonality of first marriages according to period of marriage

almost the entire seventeenth century and was the result of an essentially male immigration, which caused a surplus of men available for marriage. In 1663, for example, there were six to seven men available for each woman. This had an influence on all aspects of nuptiality, particularly for women. Afterward, with the slowdown in immigration and the strong natural growth, the male–female ratio quickly leveled. The Canadian matrimonial model was modified to resemble that found in France, albeit while still preserving differences linked to socioeconomic factors.

SEASONAL VARIATIONS

On the whole, the timing of first marriages within the colony resembled that found in most rural regions of the past, with marriages taking place primarily during the slack farming period, that is, between the autumn harvest and the spring planting (see Figure 4.3). Prior to 1680, the imbalance in the marriage market had a direct influence on the monthly movement of first marriages; since the arrival of eligible female immigrants took place only during the summer months, marriages during the fall months were numerous, with September and October holding an importance which they would later lose.

It is also interesting to note that notwithstanding church prescriptions, 1 of every 20 marriages took place during prohibited periods; although shorter than Lent, Advent accounted for 60% of the marriages that occurred during the prohibited periods. As we will later see, most of these marriages were within the elite.

PROPORTIONS NEVER MARRIED

As in France, it does not appear that the proportion remaining single was very high in the Laurentian Valley.[4] Throughout the entire period, only about 6.5 to 10% of those people aged 50 and over had never been married. For both men and women, the proportion of never-married individuals dropped as time progressed. This went hand in hand with the leveling off of the marriage market at about 7.5% for both sexes during the seventeenth century, and falling to 5% during the next.

Although this pattern might be expected as far as the men are concerned, the same cannot be said for the women; the explanation lies in the decline in religious celibacy. While religious recruitment of men remained stable during the period, with 0.9% of men born before 1730 and having reached the age of 20 deciding to join a religious order, that of women lost its intensity and developed contrary to what the marriage market would have indicated. Thus, whereas 6% of all Canadian women who were born before 1680 and reached the age of 20 joined a religious order, this proportion dropped to 1.3% for those born during the first part of the eighteenth century. Religious communities developed from scratch in the seventeenth century and required vigorous recruitment. Since the female congregations were recruited among the Canadian-born, a practice unlike that for male congregations, it is not surprising that religious celibacy was quite high during the first years of the colony, particularly since the population had not yet grown in size.

AGE AT FIRST MARRIAGE AND AGE DIFFERENCE BETWEEN SPOUSES

The evolution of the marriage market influenced women's behavior in particular. Whereas the age at marriage varied little for men, the same was not true for women. Women who married for the first time before 1680 were in general seven years younger than those in the same group at the

[4] The proportion of people who reached the age of 50 and had never been married never exceeded 9% for France under the Old Regime. See Henry and Houdaille, "Célibat et âge au mariage au XVIIIe et XIXe siècles en France."

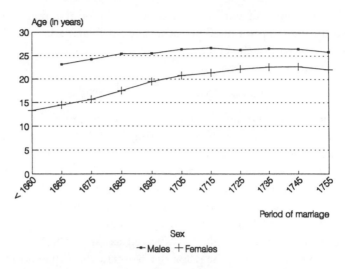

Figure 4.4. Age at first marriage of Canadian-born spouses according to sex and period of marriage, 1660–1755

end of the French regime (see Figure 4.4). It follows that during the colony's first decades, the age difference between husbands and wives was greater, thus having a direct effect on widowhood and remarriage. As the imbalance in the marriage market diminished over time, the age difference between spouses also diminished: it reached more than nine years for those marriages which took place before 1680 but dropped to fewer than five years during the last decade of the French regime. Regardless of the normalization of the male–female ratio, the age difference between spouses still remained slightly higher than that in France, owing to the earlier marriage of the women within the colony.

WIDOWHOOD AND REMARRIAGE

Widowhood and remarriage were also affected by the evolution of the marriage market. Given the large age difference between spouses during the first decades of the colony's existence, young women who were married to older men were widowed in two out of every three marriages. This proportion dropped and stabilized at about 55% during the eighteenth century.

Since the number of female spouses was limited, marriages between

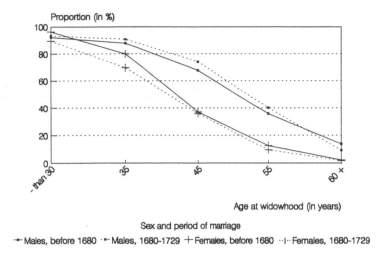

Sex and period of marriage

—•— Males, before 1680   ·—•·· Males, 1680-1729   + Females, before 1680   ··|·· Females, 1680-1729

Figure 4.5. Proportion of individuals who remarried according to period of first marriage and age at widowhood

single men and widowed women, usually quite rare, became more frequent, making up a seventh of all marriages which took place during the seventeenth century. The importance of this type of union was to drop by about half during the next century, to the benefit of marriages between widowed men and single women, which doubled in number to make up an eighth of all marriages at the end of the French regime.

Since women were fewer in number, they had more opportunities to remarry, whereas men were less able to do so. For those individuals who married before 1680, the tendency to remarry was about 40% for both sexes. More than one man out of every two would remarry during the next century while the proportion of women who remarried would fall to a third (see Figure 4.5).

The change in the interval between widowhood and remarriage also demonstrates this pressure. Thus, whereas widows during the seventeenth century waited on average 35 months before remarrying, this waiting period was extended by another 6 months during the next century. In the case of men, the interval remained stable at 26 months. Once the male–female ratio stabilized, the characteristics of widowhood and remarriage shifted to resemble those found in France, while still maintaining some particularities (see Table 4.3).

Finally, throughout the entire French regime, age constituted an impor-

Table 4.3. *Summary of nuptiality*

Nuptiality characteristics	Seventeenth-century marriages		Eighteenth-century marriages		France[b] Seventeenth–Eighteenth centuries
	Whole	Elite[a]	Whole	Elite[a]	
Age at first marriage					
Males	28.1	28.4	27.0	30.7	27.0
Females	18.9	19.4	22.2	23.5	24.0
Proportion of marriages between a single man and a widow (%)	13.0	13.4	7.9	9.2	7.5
Average age at widowhood (years)					
Males	50.8		50.0		
Females	47.3		49.8		
Proportion of marriages broken by the death of the husband (%)	61.8	59.6	54.8	47.9	57.5
Proportion who remarried (%)					
Males	50.0		53.7	55.5[c]	50.0
Females	36.2		31.7	23.6[c]	33.0
Proportion of widowhood-remarriage intervals <1 year					
Males	43.8		36.9	8.3[c]	50.0
Females	28.7		17.2	1.5[c]	25.0

[a] The elite's figures were based upon specific studies concerning the colonial nobility and bourgeoisie (see the bibliographical essay).
[b] Broad averages hiding, of course, regional and time variations.
[c] Seventeenth- and eighteenth-century marriages combined.

tant factor in remarriage and varied according to sex. Remarriage for women was extremely frequent for those under the age of 40, with the frequency quickly diminishing after this age. For men, the decrease was less marked (see Figure 4.5). And, although age may barely affect the period of widowhood in the case of men, it is evident that there is a definite effect for widows who tended to remarry faster if they were younger and had dependent children.

A DIFFERENT NUPTIALITY FOR THE ELITE

As in France, nobles and the bourgeoisie differed from the rest of the population in their marital behavior. The proportion remaining single was very high, with almost 1 out of every 5 men and 3 out of every 10 women never having been married by the age of 50. This can be explained to a large extent by the fact that a number entered religious orders: 1 of every 6 women who reached the age of 15, and 1 of every 14 men who reached the age of 20. Although the elite made up only a tenth of the population, they provided almost half of the colony's clergy, with certain families, it seems, specializing in service to the church.

Whereas during the seventeenth century the age at which the elite and the masses married was similar, things changed during the next century, particularly in the case of men. Further, men of the elite remarried in proportions similar to the rest of the population, but women did so less frequently, particularly in the case of the younger ones. Since the elite's widowed members could afford to wait before choosing a new spouse, the interval between widowhood and remarriage within this group was also much longer.

Finally, the monthly movement in marriages among the elite, much less subject to the agricultural seasons, shows no autumn low or winter high. The forbidden periods were also less respected, with members of the elite marrying five times more often during these periods than the rest of the population, which demonstrates both a greater freedom of morals and the influence that the class had on the church.

The evolution of the male–female ratio marked the matrimonial regime of the colony. As long as the imbalance existed, women continued to marry at much younger ages, creating a great difference in ages between the spouses that shaped the characteristics of widowhood and remarriage. Once an equilibrium was reestablished, the colony's marital characteristics became more similar to those of the mother country, while still maintaining some particularities which were demonstrative of the socioeconomic differences which existed between the old and the new world.

A HIGH-FERTILITY REGIME

Since migration ultimately was of little importance, the colony's population grew essentially from the excess of births over deaths. As the high birth rates indicate, women demonstrated a remarkable fertility, which was accentuated by the healthiness of the Laurentian Valley's environment.

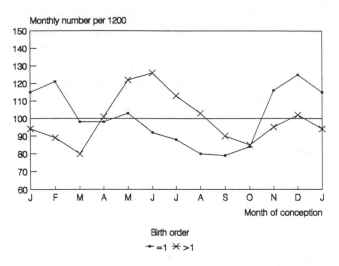

Figure 4.6. Seasonality of conceptions according to birth order

MONTHLY VARIATIONS OF BIRTHS

When analyzing the monthly variations in births, first births must be separated from the others because of the influence of the seasonal movement of marriages (see Figure 4.6). This is particularly true for births which took place during the seventeenth century, since there was a high concentration of fall weddings by immigrants who married within the months just after their arrival to the colony. As with other premodern populations, births of other ranks followed the rhythm of the farm work and often were the result of spring and summer conceptions, as opposed to the fall harvest period and winter months.

HIGH FERTILITY

Regardless of whether they were born in France or in the colony, women were extremely fertile, more so than their French counterparts (see Figure 4.7). When marrying before the age of 20 and surviving until the end of their fertile period, the women of the Laurentian Valley had on average two children more than the women of France. This difference can be explained by the colonial context, which favored a rise of fecundity and a fall in intrauterine mortality, so that women of the colony had pregnan-

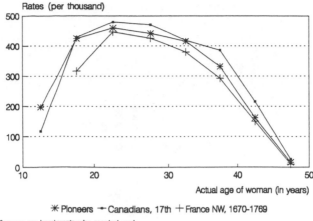

Figure 4.7. Age-specific fertility rates (at all ages at marriage) for selected categories of women

cies closer together in time and were less inclined to become prematurely sterile.[5]

Couples did not practice any form of birth control, as evidenced by an average age of women at last birth of 40 years, which is similar to the results found in France; they can thus be said to have lived in natural fertility conditions. The average family had between 7 and 8 children, taking into consideration that mortality often disrupted marriages prematurely. This average covers a diversity of families, even within families which had remained intact until the woman reached the end of her fertile period: within these families, 6.5% had no children while 40% had at least 10 children (see Figure 4.8).

ENVIRONMENT AND FERTILITY

The colonial situation combined immigrants with Canadian-born women and thus provides for easy comparison of the two groups, as well as indicating the effect of a change of surroundings on the fertility behavior of the immigrants. The fertility of pioneers, that is, the immigrant women

---

[5] The interval between births for the women of the Laurentian Valley could have been influenced by a shorter breast-feeding period. However, it has been estimated that breast-feeding lasted on average between 14 and 15 months (see Yves Landry, "Orphelines en France, Pionnières au Canada: Les Filles du Roi au XVIIe siècle"). This duration is quite similar to that in France (see Rollet, "L'allaitement artificiel des nourrissons avant Pasteur").

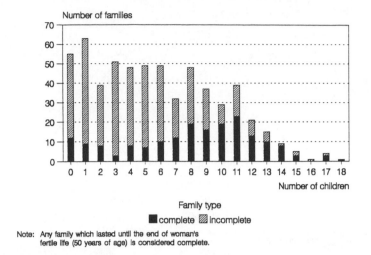

Figure 4.8. Distribution of families according to size and type, five parishes of New France, 1640–1762

who married and settled in the colony before 1680, was midway between that of women born in the colony and that of the French (see Figure 4.7). Since the average interval between births for immigrant women is similar to that of Canadian-born women, it seems as though this difference in fertility is due to a more rapid onset of sterility among the former. Indeed, immigrant women had their last birth at 39.4 years on average, compared with 41 years for Canadian-born women. This tendency toward sterility appears to be a result of the difficult conditions in which pioneer women lived while in France, which the favorable environment of the colony was not sufficient to counterbalance.

PREMARITAL CONCEPTIONS AND ILLEGITIMATE BIRTHS

In Quebec, 1 woman out of 16 who was married before 1725 was already pregnant at the time of marriage, a figure which is no different from that found in France during the same period.[6] This proportion rose with time

---

[6] It has been estimated that for France from 1670 to 1739, 6.7% of the first births were the result of a premarital conception. See Dupâquier, "La population française au XVIIe et XVIIIe siècles," p. 59.

since, given the sex imbalance of the colony's first decades, women were pressed to marry early and remarry quickly, effectively preventing pre-marital relations. Thus only 4.6% of first births during the seventeenth century were conceived before marriage, as opposed to 7.2% for those births which occurred during the first quarter of the following century.

Widows conceived more often before marriage than did single people, particularly when the latter were very young. Unmarried women whose father had passed away also had a higher frequency of premarital concep-tion. Finally, we note that 60% of these births entailed an anticipated mar-riage, possibly meaning that sexual freedom existed in the context of an eventual marriage.

Illegitimate births were also rare, since they represented only 1.25% of all of births which took place before 1730, a rate similar to that found in France during the same period.[7] Like premarital conceptions, the phe-nomenon grew in time, as the sex ratio stabilized.

The infant mortality rate of illegitimate children was extremely high, with 6 out of every 10 of them not reaching 1 year of age and only a fifth reaching the age of 15. The mothers of illegitimate children were 25 years old on average and were proportionately more often widows; 8 out of 10 eventually married, and almost a third did so with the father of the child.

DIFFERENTIAL FERTILITY OF THE ELITE

During the seventeenth century, the fertility of the elite population was in line with that of the rest of the population, but the same is not true for the following century (see Figure 4.9).[8] The rise in fertility of the elite at younger ages can be explained by the adoption of wet-nursing. This phenomenon influenced the entire fertility history of women among the elite since, through a shortening of the intervals between births, it raised their propensity to become prematurely sterile, thus lowering the age of the women at the time of last birth and increasing the rate of maternal mortality.

---

[7] During the period from 1670 to 1739, the proportion of illegitimate births in rural France was esti-mated at 1.0%. See Dupaquier, "La population française au XVIIe et XVIIIe siècles," p. 59.

[8] At first, the higher fecundity of the bourgeoisie over the nobility appears evident. However, as members of the military, nobles were generally more mobile; part of the gap could thus be linked to the nonobservation of some births occuring outside the Laurentian Valley. It is also possible that a trend toward birth control had begun within the nobility, but this point needs to be further researched.

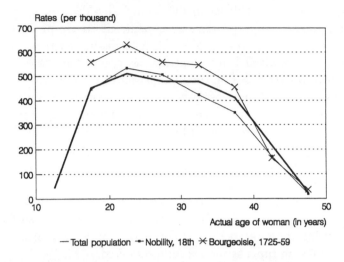

Figure 4.9. Age-specific fertility rates (at all ages at marriage) according to social class

On the whole, the elite fell within the norms of premarital conceptions. The sons of the elite, however, may have conceived before marriage at a rate higher than average, whereas their sisters did so at a rate below average. And as could be expected, the monthly fluctuations in conceptions for this group indicates that they were not influenced by the demands of a farming life: contrary to the rest of the population, they conceived more often during the fall and early winter months. Further, the summer departure of military officers is underscored by the rarity of conceptions during this time of year for the noble families.

Women, under conditions of natural fertility, benefited from the favorable environment of colonial life. Marrying young and enjoying low mortality for the time, they had large families on average (see Table 4.4). Women of the elite, however, set themselves apart; because they used wet nurses, they experienced pregnancies in quick succession, most probably to the detriment of their health.

A RELATIVELY LOW MORTALITY

Since in the past mortality was clearly related to the healthiness of one's surroundings, the Canadian environment had an important effect on the

Table 4.4. *Summary of fertility*

Fertility characteristics	Whole population, 1608–1760	Elite, 1608–1760	France, Northwest region, 1670–1769
Fertility rate at age 30 (per thousand, all ages at marriage)	479	470[a]/509[b]	403
Fertility rate at age 30, subsequently fertile women (per thousand, women married at ages 20–24)	543	644[c]	429
Average interval between births at age 30 (years, women married at ages 20–24)	1.84	1.55[c]	2.33
Proportion of permanently sterile couples at age 30 (per thousand, all ages at marriage)	70[a]/104[b]	144	90
Duration of the interval between marriage and first birth (months, women married at ages 20–24)			
Average	14.3	13.2	12.7
Median	11.6	10.0	
Average age at birth of last child (years, women married before age 20)	40.1	39.0	38.7
Complete fertility (women married before age 20)	11.8	11.4	9.5
Average number of children per family (all ages at marriage)	7.3	6.1	4.7[d]
Proportion of premarital conceptions (%, all ages at marriage)	6.1	6.6	6.7[d]
Proportion of illegitimate births (%, all ages at marriage)	1.3	1.3	1.0[d]

[a] Seventeenth-century marriages.
[b] Eighteenth-century marriages.
[c] Bourgeoisie only.
[d] Paris Basin, 1670–1739.

mortality rate of its inhabitants. It is true that the Canadian climate was rigorous, the growing season was short, and clearing the land was arduous work. The water, however, was clean, fauna were abundant, and the Laurentian land was fertile. A comparison of the Canadian and European mortality rates may help to ascertain if the positive aspects of the Canadian environment compensated for the negative ones.

INFANT AND CHILD MORTALITY

Quebec's children were favored compared with their French counterparts: for all children born before 1730, the infant mortality rate was 225 per 1,000.[9] An indication of the favorable conditions in which these children grew up is that the endogenous causes of mortality – those which are linked to genetic constitution, congenital malformations, or injuries from birth – had a larger impact than did the exogenous ones, such as infectious diseases or injuries not related to birth.[10] This analysis of the situation as a whole, however, conceals an increase over time; if the rate was 171 per 1,000 for those children born before 1680, it was 242 per 1,000 for those born during the first three decades of the eighteenth century.

Because of the increased density and the probable deterioration in the healthiness of the urban habitat, the impact of the exogenous component of mortality rose, going from a third during the seventeenth century to a half during the first three decades of the eighteenth century. Once a child had survived the first few months of life, the mortality rate was much lower. Therefore, two-thirds of Canadians born before 1730 survived to their fifteenth birthday, an achievement which was far superior to that of France during the same period.[11]

ADULT MORTALITY

Similarly, adult mortality was lower than that found in France during the same period (see Figure 4.10). However, because of a selection process, it seems that immigrants could expect to live a few years longer than their children born in the colony. Life expectation at age 20 (both sexes) for those immigrants who arrived before 1680 was 38.8 years, which was 5 years more than for those Canadians born before 1730 and a little more than 3 years more than for the French born between 1740 and 1759. This selection did not, however, extend throughout the entire life span because

---

[9] In France about 226 children out of 1,000 born between 1740 and 1759 would die before having reached their first birthday. Given the tendencies observed, it seems apparent that the mortality rate must have been even higher for the previous generations. See Blayo, "La mortalité en France en 1740 à 1829."

[10] There is a distinction between the two components of infant mortality: endogenous mortality, which is linked to the constitution of the child and the circumstances of its delivery, while exogenous mortality is due to the environment in which the child develops after his birth. See Bourgeois-Pichat, "La mesure et la mortalité infantile."

[11] For the French generations born between 1740 and 1759, less than one child out of every two reached this age. See Blayo, "La mortalité en France de 1740 à 1829."

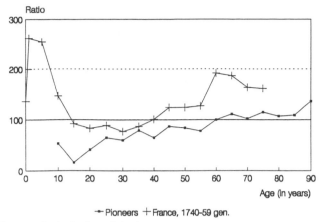

Note: Pioneers are immigrants who married and
settled in the St. Lawrence Valley before 1680.

Figure 4.10. Ratio of five-year death probabilities of males and females according to age (100 = probabilities of Canadians born before 1730)

by the time immigrants reached 60 years of age, their mortality rate was slightly higher than that of Canadians.

Contrary to infant mortality, adult mortality appears to have been relatively stable over time. The life expectancy for men during their earlier years rose slightly, whereas that for women dropped a small amount, no doubt because of the smallpox epidemics (1702–3, 1733), which were particularly hard on pregnant women. For those individuals aged 50 and older, mortality remained rather stable for both sexes throughout the French regime.

DIFFERENTIAL MORTALITY BETWEEN SOCIAL CLASSES

Although the situation before 1700 may have been beneficial for children of the nobility and of the bourgeoisie, it rapidly deteriorated to the point where, by the beginning of the next century, their children were dying younger than the others were. Since the exogenous infant mortality of the elite more than quadrupled during the eighteenth century, it must be assumed that the context of life after birth deteriorated with time. Part of this phenomenon may be explained by the adoption of wet nurses,[12] but

---

[12] Placing a child with a wet nurse exposes the child to several dangers, including the living conditions into which the child is brought, negligence on the part of the nurse, etc.

Table 4.5. *Summary of mortality*

Mortality characteristics	Whole population, 1608–1760	Elite, 1608–1760[a]	Clergy, 1608–1760	France, 1740–59[b]
Infant mortality (per thousand)	225[c]	351		287
Importance of the exogenous component of infant mortality (%)	45.4	55.3		
Life expectancy at birth (years)				
Males				25.5
Females				27.2
Both sexes	35.5			
Proportion of survivors at age 20 (%)				
Males				43.2
Females				45.8
Both sexes	63.4	48.2		
Life expectancy at age 20 (in years)				
Males			44.9	35.0
Females			41.4	35.8
Both sexes	33.9	36.4		
Proportion of survivors at age 50 among those who were living at age 20 (%)				
Males			72.2	60.5
Females			58.4	62.0
Both sexes	57.6	64.7		
Life expectancy at age 50 (years)				
Males			18.6	
Female			18.6	
Both sexes	17.9	17.5		

[a] The elite's figures were based upon specific studies concerning the colonial nobility and bourgeoisie (see the bibliographical essay).
[b] Broad averages hiding, of course, regional and time variations.
[c] Births before 1730.

it must be noted that this was done in the context of an overall rise in mortality rates, since the same phenomenon occurred in families that did not take up wet-nursing. Once they reached adulthood, the nobles and bourgeois were favored, as were members of the clergy, for whom studies indicate a favorable standard of living (see Table 4.5).

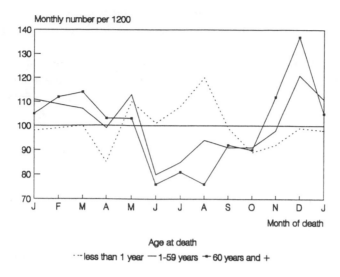

Figure 4.11. Seasonality of deaths according to age at death

CAUSES OF DEATH

The cause of death was rarely indicated in the registers; and, when it was, it was often done in a vague fashion if death was due to illness. The yearly distribution of the number of deaths demonstrates, however, that the colony suffered periodic mortality crises. The first major episode was the typhoid epidemic of 1687, which increased the number of deaths by a factor of 2.5 compared with adjacent years. From the beginning of the eighteenth century, contagious diseases appeared regularly. Notable among these were the smallpox epidemic of 1703, which resulted in a death rate five times the norm, and the smallpox epidemic of 1733.

The monthly fluctuation in burials also gives an indication of the causes of death (see Figure 4.11) and demonstrates that mortality factors varied according to the individual's age. On the one hand, it is probable that the high summer infant mortality rate was linked to heat-related illnesses of the digestive system. On the other hand, winter was a time of high mortality rates for the elderly. Finally, we can also attribute the high mortality rate of the autumn months to the contagious diseases transported by the boatloads of new arrivals.

In the case of maternal mortality, 1.5% of births led to the death of the mother. These women were more likely to have been multiparous and between 35 and 40 years of age, but a fifth of them were in their first pregnancy. Such deaths usually occurred quickly, with a third taking place the same day as the birth, and another third occurring within the first week.

Finally, if in traditional writings the Iroquois were generally depicted negatively, it is more because they posed a constant threat rather than because they actually killed many Europeans. Indeed, we estimate that only some 2% of all immigrant deaths which occurred before 1680 were due to Indian attacks.

There is little doubt that the Canadian environment was favorable to the colonists. Contrary to what might be presumed, they fared well in the cold and harsh conditions of the new land. The relatively low mortality rates, for the period, of the first immigrants in particular show that they formed a select group of exceptional vitality. However, they did not escape the hazards of contagious illnesses, which struck the population with intensity once the demographic density of the area had increased.

REPRODUCTION AND THE DEMOGRAPHIC SYSTEM

Although analyzed separately here, fertility, mortality, nuptiality, and migration of course interacted to yield a specific pattern of development for the population. One of the basic characteristics that emerged and has endured to this day is the homogeneity of the population. According to the ancestry of the some 70,000 inhabitants of the colony at the time of the British takeover, about 97% of their origins can be traced to France, a proportion that still held well into the twentieth century. French-Canadians living in Quebec have always tended to marry within their ethnic group. Although the early authorities wished for the colonists to mix with the Indian population, the indigenous populations had no liking for sedentary life, and thus mixed unions occurred only outside the settled areas. Not all French immigrants participated equally in reproduction, however.

THE IMPORTANCE OF THE FIRST IMMIGRANTS

Making up only 5 to 10% of the heads of lineages having arrived in Quebec before the second half of the twentieth century, the 1,500 men and 1,100 women who immigrated before 1680 can be said to be responsible for two-

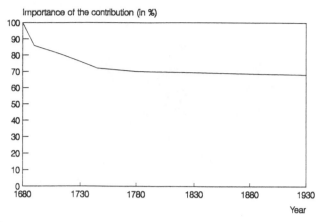

Figure 4.12. Variation in time of the contribution of the pioneers to the genetic endowment of the French-speaking population of Quebec, 1680–1930

thirds of the genetic makeup of today's Quebecers (see Figure 4.12). These people truly merited the name of pioneers as they founded the family roots which would descend throughout almost all of Quebec's French-speaking families. While other immigrants did found families after them, it is the seniority of the early pioneers that gave them an importance they would never relinquish.

DIFFERENTIAL REPRODUCTION

Within the group of pioneers, importance was again not shared equally. On January 1, 1730, each pioneer had on average 58 descendants in the colony, but the distribution surrounding this average is rather skewed: whereas 1 pioneer out of 5 had no descendants, almost a third had at least 50, and a seventh had at least 100 descendants (see Figure 4.13).

Besides randomness, there are several reasons for this difference. The primary factor is the date at which the individuals initiated their reproduction. Those marriages which took place before 1650 had a much higher chance of having a great number of descendants by 1730 than did those which took place after 1670. Yet if we examine marriages by period, we still find demographic variables which, because of biological and socioeconomic variables, created some heterogeneity. For example, infant mor-

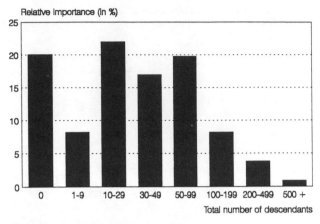

Note: Pioneers are immigrants who married and
settled in the St. Lawrence Valley before 1680.

Figure 4.13. Distribution of pioneers according to the total number of descendants present on January 1, 1730

tality has been shown to have a familial component even within the same homogenous surroundings. Added to this are marital and migratory behaviors, which varied greatly between families. In fact, among the demographic variables, only adult mortality, which was relatively homogenous in Quebec, seems to have been only a contingent factor in differential reproduction.

In this sense, membership in a socioprofessional group, because of group specific demographic behavior, entailed differential reproduction. It should not be surprising that during the eighteenth century the elite reproduced at a lesser rate than the rest of the population. Men married later, more daughters were sent to religious communities, and a greater proportion of children died prematurely. In addition, although this differentiation was true for the colony as a whole, it was also present on a subregional scale. Therefore, the elite of Quebec City participated little in the reproduction of the city's population, since the city was involved in issues which took its members outside its walls, with many settling elsewhere. However, craftsmen actively participated in the renewal of the population since it was generally here that their children established themselves.[13]

[13] Gauvreau, "Québec: Une ville et sa population au temps de la Nouvelle-France," p. 200.

THE DEMOGRAPHIC SITUATION AT
THE TIME OF THE CONQUEST OF 1760

Although the British conquest of 1760 may have meant the end of an empire, it did not mean the end of a French presence in North America. On the whole, the change in sovereign did not seem to greatly change the demographics within the colony (see Figure 4.1). The crude marriage, mortality, and natality rates remained relatively constant. In fact, the only group which appeared to be affected by the situation was the elite. Seeing its economic situation placed in danger, many of its members decided to leave the colony. In all, more than 2,000 people emigrated. About a third of the nobility, in particular, left immediately following the conquest.

In 1760, 70,000 people lived along the St. Lawrence. Three-quarters of them lived on farms; Quebec City, with its 8,000 residents, was the only true city. Montreal, now Quebec's largest city, was still but a frontier town, with 4,000 citizens.

Regardless of the definite halt in French immigration, the strong natural growth guaranteed the predominance of French peasants within the new British colony. The Laurentian Valley was still not fully cleared, and it was only during the first half of the nineteenth century that land began to grow scarce. This pushed people toward the colonization of regions farther away from the St. Lawrence, as well as toward the United States.

CONCLUSION

The population of New England far outnumbered the 70,000 residents of the St. Lawrence Valley of 1760. The difference is explained solely by a differential migration, since the 10,000 immigrants of the French regime, as well as their descendants, reproduced at the remarkable rate of 2.5% per annum.

What were the causes of this rapid growth? First, the birth rate was strong, owing to conditions of natural fertility. It was made even stronger by the fact that the women married early, particularly at the colony's start. In effect, during the seventeenth century the imbalance in the matrimonial market encouraged the marriage of women while limiting the possibilities for men. Once the male contribution to the eligible population was reestablished, the colony's marriage rate resembled that of France, altough it kept certain peculiarities, such as the lower age of women at the time of first marriage. The mortality of the adult population was relatively low, whereas that of the children continually rose, although at a lesser rate than it did in France.

The clean Laurentian environment appears to have played a fundamental role in the explanation of this growth. The fecundity of the land and the fauna as well as the clean water favored large and healthy families. Further, the low population density limited the spread of illnesses. Although infectious diseases would be more difficult to control during the eighteenth century, violent outbreaks were rare. This growth would be maintained until the middle of the nineteenth century. By then, the French-Canadian territory was saturated, and the young began heading toward peripheral regions, particularly New England.

BIBLIOGRAPHICAL ESSAY

Scientific interest in the French-Canadian population only began to develop during the second half of the nineteenth century. This interest was spearheaded by C. Tanguay who, with the help of J.-C. Taché, compiled the first figures on Quebec's demographic growth in the *Recensement de 1871* (vols. 4 and 5, Ottawa, 1876–78). Later, the first birth and death rates were presented by H. Bunle in the *Annuaire Statistique de la Province de Québec* (Quebec, 1914). But the first real demographic synthesis on the French-Canadian population was put forth in the 1930s by G. Langlois in his *Histoire de la population canadienne-française* (Montreal, 1934). Twenty years later, J. Henripin published *La population canadienne au début du XVIIIe siècle* (Paris, 1954), a study based upon families which had been reconstituted by C. Tanguay in his *Dictionnaire généalogique des familles canadiennes* (Montreal, 1871–90) and on a new methodology developed by L. Henry (see, among others, *Anciennes familles genevoises: Etude démographique, XVIIe–XXe siècle*, 1956).

Since the mid-1960s, the Programme de recherche en démographie historique (PRDH) at the Université de Montréal has been the leader in the study of the population of New France. For a survey of the group's activities, one may refer to "Le Programme de recherche en démographie historique de l'Université de Montréal: Fondements, méthodes, moyens et résultats" (*Etudes Canadiennes/Canadian Studies*, 1981) by J. Légaré.

This group's major work is the elaboration of the *Registre de la Population du Québec ancien*, a data bank based essentially on parish registers and aiming at the computerized reconstruction of the entire colonial population of the St. Lawrence Valley from its origin to 1800. The conceptual and methodological aspects of this register are synthesized in "Le registre de la population du Québec ancien: Genèse, fonctionnement et applications," the doctoral dissertation of B. Desjardins (Lyon, 1991), as well as in "A Population Register for Canada under the French Regime: Context, Scope, Content and Applications" (*Canadian Studies in Population*, 1988), by J. Légaré.

The members of the PRDH produced two important books on the overall demography of the colony: *Vie et mort de nos ancêtres* by H. Charbonneau (Montreal, 1975), based on a sample of marriages during the seventeenth century; and *The First French Canadians: Pioneers in the St. Lawrence Valley* (Newark, Del., 1993), by H. Charbonneau, B. Desjardins, A. Guillemette, Y. Landry, J. Légaré, and F. Nault, which studies the immigrants established in the Laurentian Valley before 1680. Before embarking on a transversal and chronological history of the colonial population, the PRDH is concentrating on a study of the demographic behavior of Canadians born in the seventeenth century. The demographics of the colony are also discussed in the following specialized works.

MORTALITY, FERTILITY, NUPTIALITY, AND MOBILITY

Demographic phenomena have been addressed both in general works and in several specific studies. In the area of infant mortality, the doctoral dissertation of R. Lalou entitled "Des enfants pour le paradis: La mortalité des nouveaux-nés en Nouvelle-France" (Montreal, 1990) is of particular note. Two articles were written on mortality at high ages: "La mortalité aux âges avancés des immigrants fondateurs de la Nouvelle-France" (*Annales de démographie historique*, 1985), by B. Desjardins; and "Vivre cent ans dans la Vallée du Saint-Laurent avant 1800" (*Annales de démographie historique*, 1990), by H. Charbonneau and B. Desjardins. Causes of death are investigated by Y. Landry and R. Lessard in "Causes of Death in Seventeenth and Eighteenth Century Quebec as Recorded in the Parish Registers" (*History of Registration of Causes of Death*, 1993).

Fertility studies are abundant. "Jeunes femmes et vieux maris: La fécondité des mariages précoces" (*Population*, 1980), by H. Charbonneau, discusses the fertility of young women. The same author, in "Remariage et fécondité en Nouvelle-France" (*Mariages et remariages dans les populations du passé*, 1981), shows the importance of remarriage in the reproduction of the population. In an article entitled "Fertility in France and New France: The Distinguishing Characteristics of Canadian Behavior in the Seventeenth and Eighteenth Centuries" (*Social Science History*, 1993), Y. Landry suggests explanations for the high fertility of Canadian women.

Marriage is the subject of R. Roy's and H. Charbonneau's article, "La nuptialité en situation de déséquilibre des sexes: le Canada du XVIIe siècle" (*Annales de démographie historique*, 1978), as well as S. Paillé's master's thesis, "Nuptialité selon le rang dans la famille en Nouvelle-France" (Montreal, 1992). On spatial mobility, one can refer to J. Lavigne's master's thesis, "Mesure des migrations internes au Canada sous le Régime français" (Montreal, 1974); the master's thesis of H. Périers entitled "Étude de la mobilité à partir de recensements rétrospectifs: Trois Rivières au 18e siècle" (Paris, 1993); and H. Denis's "Réflexions méthodologiques concernant l'étude longitudinale de la mobilité spatiale des Unions à partir du Registre de la population du Québec ancien" (*Les chemins de la migration*, 1995).

Several works also discuss the interrelationship between the various demographic phenomena. "The Life Course of Seventeenth-Century Immigrants to Canada" (*Journal of Family History*, 1987), by Y. Landry and J. Légaré, describes the expansion and contraction phases of families. Single parenthood is examined from the point of view of parents in "La monoparentalité: Un concept moderne, une réalité ancienne" (*Population*, 1991), by J. Légaré and B. Desjardins, while the point of view of the children is examined in "Les enfants de la monoparentalité, hier et aujourd'hui" (*Cahiers québécois de démographie*, 1995), by H. Denis, B. Desjardins, and J. Légaré. In "Effects of Reproductive Behaviour on Infant Mortality of French-Canadians during the Seventeenth and Eighteenth Centuries" (*Population Studies*, 1990), F. Nault, B. Desjardins, and J. Légaré analyze the link between infant mortality and fertility.

IMMIGRATION AND IMMIGRANTS

Most of the available information on the intensity and characteristics of immigration in the Laurentian Valley can be found in M. Boleda's doctoral dissertation, "Les migrations au Canada sous le Régime français (1608–1760)" (Montreal, 1983). H. Charbonneau's "Migrations et migrants de France en Canada avant 1760" (*La Contribution du Haut-Poitou au peuplement de la Nouvelle-France,* 1994) also includes a synthesis of existing information on the characteristics of immigration. In his *Catalogue des immigrants* (Montreal, 1983), M. Trudel attempts to date the arrival of the immigrants between 1632 and 1662. The importance of family network is demonstrated in "The Influence of Kinship on Seventeenth-Century Immigration to Canada" (*Continuity and Change,* 1989), by A. Guillemette and J. Légaré. In "Reluctant Exiles: Emigrants from France in Canada before 1760" (*William and Mary Quarterly,* 1989), P. Moogk analyzes the factors of attraction and repulsion experienced by the immigrants to Canada. Finally, H. Charbonneau's "Le caractère français des pionniers de la vallée laurentienne" (*Cahiers québécois de démographie,* 1990) and B. Desjardins's "Homogénéité ethnique de la population québécoise sous le Régime français" (*Cahiers québécois de démographie,* 1990) measure the ethnic composition of the population under the French regime.

PEOPLING THE COLONY

How the colony was peopled has been closely examined. A number of works have described and evaluated the various censuses and enumerations from a methodological point of view. "La population du Canada aux recensements de 1666 et 1667" (*Population,* 1967) by H. Charbonneau and J. Légaré and "Le recensement nominatif de 1681" (*Histoire sociale/Social History,* 1971) by H. Charbonneau, Y. Lavoie, and J. Légaré criticize and correct the three censuses of the seventeenth century, while "Une source en friche: Les dénombrements sous le Régime français" (*Revue d'histoire de l'Amèrique française,* 1988), by R. Lalou and M. Boleda, discusses the validity of the 39 censuses which took place between 1685 and 1739. *Le Canada français* (Paris, 1960), by R. Blanchard, proposes a history of the colonization of French Canada. In the first volume of the *Historical Atlas of Canada* (Toronto, 1987), H. Charbonneau and C. Harris proposes a series of demographic rates and an evolutionary curve of the population, both of which are the most accurate to date. H. Charbonneau and Y. Lavoie illustrate the extension of the peopling of the colony in relation to the opening of new parishes in their work entitled "Cartographie du premier découpage territorial des paroisses du Québec" (*La revue de Géographie de Montréal,* 1973). Finally, M. Trudel develops a portrait of the colonial population in *La population du Canada en 1663* (Montreal, 1973).

DIFFERENTIAL DEMOGRAPHY

The demographic behavior of the colonial elite is the subject of two major studies: *La Noblesse en Nouvelle-France: Familles et alliances* (Montreal, 1991), by L. Gadoury, and *Le comportement démographique de la Nouvelle-France* (Montreal, 1994), the doctoral dissertation of C. Simo-Noguera. Both male and female members of the clergy are the subject of a study by L. Pelletier entitled *Le clergé en Nouvelle-France* (Montreal, 1993). In *Les Filles du roi en Nouvelle-France: Étude de démographie historique* (Montreal, 1992), Y. Landry looks at a specific group of female immigrants who arrived between 1663 and 1673 and who were given dowries by the king in order to speed up their marriage. In "Le comportement démographique des voyageurs sous le Régime français" (*Histoire sociale/Social History*, 1978), H. Charbonneau, B. Desjardins, and P. Beauchamp describe the effect of the fur trade on the colonial demographics. In *Économie et Société en Nouvelle-France* (Presses de l'Université Laval, 1956), J. Hamelin examines tradespeople in particular. The situation of the military group is discussed in Y. Landry's "Mortalité, nuptialité et canadianisation des troupes françaises de la guerre de Sept ans" (*Histoire sociale/Social History*, 1979). Urban demography is discussed in *Québec: Une ville et sa population au temps de la Nouvelle-France* (Sillery, 1991), by D. Gauvreau; in chapters of L. Dechêne's *Habitants et marchands de Montréal au XVIIe siècle* (1974); and in the master's thesis of H. Périers entitled *Une ville à la campagne: Trois-Rivières sous le Régime français* (Montreal, 1992).

Several articles compare the demographics of various groups. "Démographie différentielle en Nouvelle-France: Villes et campagnes" (*Revue d'histoire de l'Amérique française*, 1985), by L. Gadoury, Y. Landry and H. Charbonneau, and "Démographie différentielle et catégories sociales en Nouvelle-France" (*XVe Congrès des sciences historiques*, Bucarest, 1982), by Y. Landry and H. Charbonneau, deal with this theme. J.-P. Bardet and H. Charbonneau compare colonial demographics with those of the metropolis in "Cultures et milieux en France et en Nouvelle-France: Différenciation des comportements démographiques" (*Évolution et éclatement du monde rural: Structures, fonctionnement et évolution différentielle des sociétés rurales françaises et québécoises, XVIIe–XX siècles*, 1986).

DIFFERENTIAL REPRODUCTION

The reproductive mechanisms of the population has recently become a more popular field. Looking at the population as a whole is the article by

H. Charbonneau and B. Desjardins entitled "Mesure de la descendance différentielle des fondateurs de la souche canadienne-française à partir du registre de population du Québec ancien" (*Revue, Informatique et Statistique dans les Sciences humaines*, 1987), which demonstrates the differential importance of the first immigrants in the genetic makeup of today's French-Canadian population. Reproduction within social groups and the resulting strategies within given boundaries are studied in D. Gauvreau's work on the city of Quebec mentioned in the preceding section.

INHERITABILITY OF DEMOGRAPHIC BEHAVIOR

It is only within recent years that genealogical data have been used to study genetic information. Such work includes Y. Pépin's master's thesis, "Hérédité de la gémellité en Nouvelle-France: Étude démographique" (Montreal, 1987); a study by E. Le Bourg et al., "Reproductive Life of French-Canadians in Seventeenth-Eighteenth Centuries: A Search for a Trade-off Between Early Fecundity and Longevity" (*Experimental Gerontology*, 1993); and B. Desjardins and H. Charbonneau's "L'héritabilité de la longévité (*Population*, 1990); B. Desjardins et al.'s "Intervals between Marriage and First Birth in Mothers and Daughters" (*Journal of Biosocial Science*, 1991), and their "Age of Mother at Last Birth in Two Historic Populations (*Journal of Biosocial Science*, 1994). In addition, the thesis of H. Vézina, entitled "Aspects démographiques et généalogiques de la maladie d'Alzheimer" (Montreal, 1997), looks at the genetic aspects of this illness.

A VARIETY OF STUDIES

Studies related to the population of Quebec in the seventeenth and eighteenth centuries cover a wide range of subjects. Among others, the metropolitan effort to populate the colony is analyzed in "La politique démographique en Nouvelle-France" (*Annales de démographie historique*, 1979), by H. Charbonneau and Y. Landry. The morals of the colony's residents are described in "Les conceptions prénuptiales dans la vallée du Saint-Laurent avant 1725" (*Revue d'histoire de l'Amérique française*, 1986), by R. Bates, and in "Les naissances illégitimes sur les rives du Saint-Laurent avant 1730" (*Revue d'histoire de l'Amérique française*, 1986), by L. Paquette and R. Bates.

The educational level of the population is examined in M. Chouinard's master's thesis, "Instruction et comportement démographique en Nouvelle-

France au XVIIe siècle" (Montreal, 1988). The importance of given names is discussed by G. Ribordy in *Au pays de la Sainte-Famille: Influences religieuses, familiales et sociales de la prénomination en Nouvelle-France* (Montreal, 1996), and by R. Bates in "Stock, caractéristiques et mode de transmission des prénoms dans une population traditionnelle: L'exemple du Quebec sous le Régime français" (*XVIe Congrès international des sciences onomastiques*, Quebec, 1987). The factors explaining the number of male births is analyzed in the master's thesis of G. Lassus, "Le rapport de masculinité à la naissance au Québec" (des origines à 1800) (Montreal, 1995). The households of Quebec City are discussed by G. Olivier-Lacamp and J. Légaré in "Quelques caractéristiques des ménages de la ville de Québec entre 1666 et 1716" (*Histoire sociale/Social History*, 1979).

REFERENCES

Bardet, Jean-Pierre, and Hubert Charbonneau. "Cultures et milieux en France et en Nouvelle-France: Différenciation des comportements démographiques." In *Évolution et éclatement du monde rural: Structures, fonctionnement et évolution différentielle des société rurales françaises et québécoises, XVIIᵉ–XXᵉ siècles*, edited by Joseph Goy and Jean-Pierre Wallot, 75–88. Paris et Montreal: Editions de l'Ecole des Hautes Etudes en Sciences Sociales et Presses de l'Université de Montréal, 1986.

Bates, Réal. "Les conceptions prénuptiales dans la vallée du Saint-Laurent avant 1725." *Revue d'histoire de l'Amérique française* 40, no. 2 (1986): 253–72.

———. "Stock, caractéristiques et mode de transmission des prénoms dans une population traditionnelle: L'exemple du Québec sous le Régime français." In *Actes du XVIe Congrès international des sciences onomastiques*, edited by Jean-Claude Boulanger, 163–75. Quebec, 1987.

Blanchard, Raoul. *Le Canada français*. Paris: Presses Universitaires de France, 1960.

Blayo, Yves. "La mortalité en France en 1740 à 1829." *Population* 30, special number (1975): 123–42.

Boleda, Mario. "Les migrations au Canada sous le régime français (1608–1760)." *Cahiers québécois de démographie* 13, no. 1 (1984): 23–39.

Bourgeois-Pichat, Jean. "La mesure et la mortalité infantile." *Population* 6, no. 2 (1951): 233–48.

Bunle, Henri. *Annuaire statistique de la Province de Québec* (1914): 180–90.

Charbonneau, Hubert. *Vie et mort de nos ancêtres*. Montréal: Les Presses de l'Université de Montréal, 1975.

———. "Les régimes de fécondité naturelle en Amérique du Nord: Bilan et analyse des observations." In *Fécondité naturelle: niveaux et déterminants de la fécondité naturelle*, edited by Henri Léridon and Jane Menken, 441–91. Liège: Ordina Éditions, 1979.

———. "Jeunes femmes et vieux maris: La fécondité des mariages précoces." *Population* 35, no. 6 (1980): 1101–22.

————. "Remariage et fécondité en Nouvelle-France." In *Mariages et remariages dans les populations du passé*, edited by Jacques Dupâquier, Etienne Hélin, Peter Laslett, Massimo Livi-Bacci, and Solvi Sogner, 561–71. London: Academic Press, 1981.

————. "Essai sur l'évolution démographique du Québec de 1534 à 2034." *Cahiers québécois de démographie* 13, no. 1 (1984): 5–21.

————. "Le caractère français des pionniers de la vallée laurentienne." *Cahiers québécois de démographie* 19, no. 1 (1990): 49–62.

————. "L'immigration au Canada avant 1900. Rapport de synthèse." In *Long Distance Migrations (1500–1900), Actes d'un colloque du XVIIe Congrès international des Sciences historiques*, edited by A. E. Roel, 153–68. Madrid: Commission internationale de démographie historique, 1990.

————. "Du bassin parisien à la vallée laurentienne au XVIIe siècle." In *Mesurer et comprendre: Mélanges offerts à Jacques Dupâquier*, 125–36. Paris: Presses Universitaires de France, 1993.

————. "Migrations et migrants de France en Canada avant 1760." In *La contribution du Haut-Poitou au peuplement de la Nouvelle-France*, edited by Robert Larin, 31–48. Moncton, N.B.: Les Editions d'Acadie, 1994.

Charbonneau, Hubert, and Bertrand Desjardins. "Mesure de la descendance différentielle des fondateurs de la souche canadienne-française à partir du registre de population du Québec ancien." *Revue, Informatique et Statistique dans les Sciences humaines* 23, no. 1–4 (1987): 9–20.

————. "Vivre cent ans dans la vallée du Saint-Laurent avant 1800." *Annales de démographie historique* (1990): 217–26.

Charbonneau, Hubert, Bertrand Desjardins, and Pierre Beauchamp. "Le comportement démographique des voyageurs sous le Régime français." *Histoire sociale/Social History* 11, no. 21 (1978): 120–33.

Charbonneau, Hubert, Bertrand Desjardins, André Guillemette, et al. *The First French Canadians: Pioneers in the St. Lawrence Valley.* Newark: University of Delaware Press, 1993.

Charbonneau, Hubert, and R. Cole Harris. "Resettling the St. Lawrence Valley." In *Historical Atlas of Canada*, vol. 1: *From the beginning to 1800*, edited by R. C. Harris, plate 46. Toronto: University of Toronto Press, 1987.

Charbonneau, Hubert, and Yves Landry. "La politique démographique en Nouvelle-France," *Annales de démographie historique* (1979): 29–57.

Charbonneau, Hubert, and Yolande Lavoie. "Cartographie du premier découpage territorial des paroisses du Québec." *La revue de Géographie de Montréal* 27, no. 1 (1973): 81–87.

Charbonneau, Hubert, Yolande Lavoie, and Jacques Légaré. "Le recensement nominatif de 1681." *Histoire sociale/Social History* no. 7 (1971): 77–98.

Charbonneau, Hubert, and Jacques Légaré. "La population du Canada aux recensements de 1666 et 1667." *Population* 22, no. 6 (1967): 1031–54.

Charbonneau, Hubert, and Normand Robert. "The French Origins of the Canadian Population, 1608–1759." In *Historical Atlas of Canada*, vol. 1: *From the beginning to 1800*, edited by R. C. Harris, plate 45. Toronto: University of Toronto Press, 1987.

Chouinard, Michel. "Instruction et comportement démographique en Nouvelle-France au XVIIe siècle." Mémoire de maîtrise présenté au département de démographie de l'Université de Montreal, 1988.

Dechêne, Louise. *Habitants et marchands de Montréal au XVIIe siècle.* Paris and Montreal: Plon, 1974.

Denis, Hubert. "Réflexions méthodologiques concernant l'étude longitudinale de la mobilité spatiale des unions à partir du Registre de la population du Québec ancien." In *Les chemins de la migration en Belgique et au Québec du XVIIe siècle au XXe siècle,* edited by Yves Landry, John A. Dickinson, Suzy Pasleau, and Claude Desama, 33–42. Louvain-la-Neuve and Beauport: Éditions Academia and Publications MNH, 1995.

Denis, Hubert, Bertrand Desjardins, and Jacques Légaré. "Les enfants de la monoparentalité, hier et aujourd'hui." *Cahiers québécois de démographie* 23, no. 1 (1995): 53–74.

Desjardins, Bertrand. "La mortalité aux âges avancés des immigrants fondateurs de la Nouvelle-France." *Annales de démographie historique* (1985): 71–83.

———. "Homogénéité ethnique de la population québécoise sous le Régime français." *Cahiers québécois de démographie* 19, no. 1 (1990): 63–76.

———. "Le registre de la population du Québec ancien: Genèse, fonctionnement et applications." Ph.D. diss., Université Lumière-Lyon 2, 1991.

———. "Demographic Aspects of the 1702–03 Smallpox Epidemic in the St. Lawrence Valley." *Canadian Studies in Population* 23, no. 1 (1996): 49–67.

Desjardins, Bertrand, Alain Bideau, and Guy Brunet. "Age of Mother at Last Birth in Two Historical Populations." *Journal of Biosocial Science* 26, no. 4 (1994): 509–16.

Desjardins, Bertrand, Alain Bideau, Évelyne Heyer, et al. "Intervals between Marriage and First Birth in Mothers and Daughters." *Journal of Biosocial Science* 23, no. 1 (1991): 49–54.

Desjardins, Bertrand, and Hubert Charbonneau. "L'héritabilité de la longévité." *Population* 45, no. 3 (1990): 603–16.

Dickinson, John A. "Les Amérindiens et les débuts de la Nouvelle-France." In *Canada ieri et oggi, Actes du 6e congrès international des Études Canadiennes,* edited by Selva di Fasano, 87–108. Bari: Schena Editore, 1986.

Dupaquier, Jacques. *La population française aux XVIIe et XVIIIe siècles.* Paris: Presses Universitaires de France, 1979.

Gadoury, Lorraine. *La Noblesse en Nouvelle-France: Familles et alliances.* Montreal: Editions HMH, 1991.

Gadoury, Lorraine, Yves Landry, and Hubert Charbonneau. "Démographie différentielle en Nouvelle-France: Villes et campagnes." *Revue d'histoire de l'Amérique française* 38, no. 3 (1985): 423–36.

Gauvreau, Danielle. *Québec: Une ville et sa population au temps de la Nouvelle-France.* Sillery: Les Presses de l'Université du Québec, 1991.

Guillemette, André, and Jacques Légaré. "The Influence of Kinship on Seventeenth-Century Immigration to Canada." *Continuity and Change* 4, no. 1 (1989): 79–102.

Hamelin, Jean. *Economie et Société en Nouvelle-France.* Quebec: Presses de l'Université Laval, 1956.

Henripin, Jacques. *La population canadienne au début du XVIIIe siècle: Nuptialité-fécondité-mortalité infantile.* Paris: Presses Universitaires de France, 1954.

Henripin, Jacques, and Yves Péron. "La transition démographique de la province de Québec." In *La population du Québec: Etudes rétrospectives,* edited by Hubert Charbonneau, 23–44. Trois-Rivières: Éditions du Boréal Express, 1973.

Henry, Louis. *Anciennes familles genevoises: Étude démographique: XVIe–XXe siècle.* Paris: Presses Universitaires de France, 1956.

Henry, Louis, and Yves Blayo. "La population de la France." *Population* 30 (November 1975): 109.

Henry, Louis, and Jacques Houdaille. "Célibat et âge au mariage au XVIIIe et XIXe siècles en France. I. Célibat definitif." *Population* 1 (1978): 43–84.

Lalou, Richard. "Des enfants pour le paradis: La mortalité des nouveaux-nés en Nouvelle-France." Ph.D. diss., Université de Montréal, 1990.

Lalou, Richard, and Mario Boleda. "Une source en friche: Les dénombrements sous le Régime français." *Revue d'histoire de l'Amérique française* 42, no. 1 (1988): 47–72.

Landry, Yves. "Mortalité, nuptialité et canadianisation des troupes françaises de la guerre de Sept ans." *Histoire Sociale/Social History* 12, no. 24 (1979): 298–315.

———. "Fécondité et habitat des immigrantes françaises en Nouvelle-France." *Annales de démographie historique* (1988): 259–76.

———. *Orphelines en France, pionnières au Canada: Les Filles du roi en Nouvelle-France.* Montreal: Leméac 1992.

———. "Fertility in France and New France: The Distinguishing Characteristics of Canadian Behavior in the Seventeenth and Eighteenth Centuries." *Social Science History* 17, no. 4 (1993): 577–92.

Landry, Yves, and Hubert Charbonneau. "Démographie différentielle et catégories sociales en Nouvelle-France." In *Actes du XVe Congrès international des sciences historiques,* 1150–63. Bucarest: Editura Academiei Republicii Socialiste Românîa 4, 1982.

Landry, Yves, and Jacques Légaré. "The Life Course of Seventeenth-Century Immigrants to Canada." *Journal of Family History* 12, no. 1–3 (1987): 201–12.

Landry, Yves, and Rénald Lessard. "Causes of Death in Seventeenth and Eighteenth Century Quebec as Recorded in the Parish Registers." In *Actes de la conférence History of Registration of Causes of Death.* Bloomington: Indiana University, 1993.

Langlois, Georges. *Histoire de la population Canadienne-Française.* Montreal: Lévêque, 1934.

Lassus, Géraud. "Le rapport de masculinité à la naissance au Québec (des origines à 1800)." M.sc. thesis, Université de Montréal, 1995.

Lavigne, Jacques. "Mesure des migrations internes au Canada sous le Régime français." Mémoire de maîtrise présenté au département de démographie de l'Université de Montréal, 1974.

Le Bourg, Éric, Bernard Thon, Bertrand Desjardins, et al. "Reproductive Life of French-Canadians in Seventeenth-Eighteenth Centuries: A Search for a Trade-off between Early Fecundity and Longevity." *Experimental Gerontology* 28 (1993): 217–32.

Légaré, Jacques. "Le programme de recherche en démographie historique de l'Université de Montréal: Fondements, méthodes, moyens et résultats." *Etudes Canadiennes/Canadian Studies* no. 10 (1981): 149–82.

———. "A Population Register for Canada under the French Regime: Context, Scope, Content and Applications." *Canadian Studies in Population* 15, no. 1 (1988): 1–16.

Légaré, Jacques, and Bertrand Desjardins. "La monoparentalité: Un concept moderne, une réalité ancienne." *Population* 46, no. 6 (1991): 1677–88.

Moogk, Peter. "Reluctant Exiles: Emigrants from France in Canada before 1760." *William and Mary Quarterly* 46 (1989): 463–505.

Nault, François, Bertrand Desjardins, and Jacques Légaré. "Effects of Reproductive Behaviour on Infant Mortality of French-Canadians during the Seventeenth and Eighteenth Centuries." *Population Studies* 44, no. 2 (1990): 273–85.

Olivier-Lacamp, Gael, and Jacques Légaré. "Quelques caractéristiques des ménages de la ville de Québec entre 1666 et 1716." *Histoire sociale/Social History* 12, no. 23 (1979): 66–78.

Paillé, Sylvain. "Nuptialité selon le rang dans la famille en Nouvelle-France." M.sc. thesis, Université de Montréal, 1992.

Paquette, Lyne, and Réal Bates. "Les naissances illégitimes sur les rives du Saint-Laurent avant 1730." *Revue d'histoire de l'Amérique française* 40, no. 2 (1986): 239–52.

Pelletier, Louis. *Le clergé en Nouvelle-France: Etude de démographie historique et répertoire bibliographique.* Montreal: Les Presses de l'Université de Montréal, 1993.

Pépin, Yves. "Hérédité de la gémellité en Nouvelle-France: Etude démographique." M.sc. thesis, Université de Montréal, 1987.

Périers, Hélène. "Une ville à la campagne: Trois-Rivières sous le Régime français." M.sc. thesis, Université de Montréal, 1992.

———. "Etude de la mobilité à partir de recensements rétrospectifs: Trois-Rivières au 18e siècle." M.sc. thesis, Université de la Sorbonne (Paris), 1993.

Programme de Recherche en Démographie Historique. *Répertoire des actes de baptême, mariage, sépulture et des recensements du Québec,* 47 volumes, edited by Hubert Charbonneau and Jacques Légaré. Montreal: Les Presses de l'Université de Montréal, 1980–91.

Ribordy, Geneviève. "Au pays de la Sainte-Famille: Influences religieuses, familiales et sociales de la prénomination en Nouvelle-France." Ph.d. diss., Université de Montréal, 1996.

Rollet, Catherine. "L'aillaitement artificiel des nourissons avant Pasteur." *Annales de Démographique Historique,* 1983: 81–92.

Roy, Raymond, and Hubert Charbonneau. "La nuptialité en situation de déséquilibre des sexes: Le Canada du XVIIe siècle." *Annales de démographie historique* (1978): 285–94.

Roy, Raymond, Yves Landry, and Hubert Charbonneau. "Quelques comportements des Canadiens au XVIIe siècle d'après les registres paroissiaux." *Revue d'histoire de l'Amérique française* 31, no. 1 (1977): 49–73.

Simo-Noguera, Carlès Javier. "Le comportement démographique de la Nouvelle-France." Ph.D. diss., Université de Montreal, 1994.

Tanguay, Cyprien. *Recensement du Canada,* vol. 5. Ottawa, 1878.

Trudel, Marcel. *Catalogue des immigrants.* Montreal: Hurtubise HMH, 1983.

———. *La population du Canada en 1663.* Montreal: Fides, 1973.

Vezina, H. "Aspects demographiques et généalogiques de la maladie d'Alzheimer." Ph.D. diss., Université de Montréal, 1997.

5

THE WHITE POPULATION OF THE COLONIAL UNITED STATES, 1607–1790

HENRY A. GEMERY

The growth of the white population of the British North American colonies, and subsequently the early Republic, is known in broad outline, though the components of that growth cannot be given with precision. Broadly, there was a remarkably rapid growth in population that, in Rossiter's words, began "with the population of Virginia in 1610 – the first population in a decennial year forming part of a continuous series – consisting of 210 souls maintaining a precarious foothold on a unexplored continent; [and ends] after the lapse of approximately two centuries, with an aggregate population of 3,929,625 inhabitants, possessing more than 800,000 square miles of territory, as shown by the Federal census of 1790."[1] However, the portion of that growth deriving from natural increase and that from immigration – and the changing contribution of those sources – can only be approximated, despite significant research in colonial demography undertaken in recent decades. In the absence of inclusive censuses of the colonies before 1790, the determination of total population numbers, vital rates, racial composition, and immigrant numbers must be made from reconstructed data. Those reconstructions draw on individual colony censuses that the British Privy Council and (after 1696) the Board of Trade periodically required from colonial governors, on tax rolls, on militia lists, baptism or other birth records, and on some (few) bills of mortality. Assembling a demographic record from sources as sporadic and incomplete as these challenged then-

This chapter has benefited from the comments of colleagues. I am indebted to David Galenson, Farley Grubb, James Horn, and Roger Schofield, as well as the editors of this volume. Andrew A. Weber provided capable research assistance. The deficiencies of the paper, however, remain with me.
[1] Rossiter, *A Century of Population Growth*, p. 10.

contemporary writers such as Benjamin Franklin, Ezra Stiles, Edward Wigglesworth, and Thomas Malthus, and later historians as well.[2] The question of the pace of colonial population growth is illustrative of that challenge. Franklin, and subsequently Malthus, supposed that the American population doubled every 25 years – the basis for Malthus's famous contention that unchecked population growth proceeds at a geometric rate. Although that doubling rate proved to be close to the actual case, Malthus did not know the relative roles of natural increase and immigration in that doubling. In assuming that the former was nearly wholly responsible, he left himself open to critics who attacked the "superfecundity" thesis implicit in his work.[3] Subsequent scholarship, largely in the twentieth century, has given considerably more definition to demographic patterns that Franklin and Malthus could only speculate on; nonetheless, areas of uncertainty remain.

COLONIAL POPULATION DATA: MEASUREMENT AND ESTIMATION

The discussion begins with a brief review of the problems in deriving population statistics from a pre-census period. The purpose is to make clear the reasons why a degree of uncertainty still attaches to colonial population data and why rather straightforward descriptive statistics are generally called for: rates of total increase, crude birth and death rates, child/woman ratios, and rates of net migration. There is a risk in using crude measures since they can be impaired by age and sex structure changes in the population. However, such changes are simply not known in sufficient detail for the colonial period. More refined demographic measures are possible with some data samples, so expectation-of-life data and fertility rates, for example, will be included when the underlying data warrant.

POPULATION TOTALS

Any population count not taken as a direct enumeration has to be extrapolated from "population proxies," such as militia lists, numbers of taxables, polls, families, and houses. Specifying the appropriate multiple to

---

[2] For discussion and references on these early authors, see McCusker and Menard, *The Economy of British America*, pp. 212–14.
[3] A notable critic of superfecundity is Michael Thomas Sadler; see his *The Law of Population*.

expand from these proxies to an aggregate population figure is a judgment based on corollary historical evidence. Further, the multiplier must be varied to account for differential regional patterns and/or changes occurring over time. Evarts B. Greene and Virginia D. Harrington's 1932 study, *American Population before the Federal Census of 1790* – still the basic reference series for the colonial period – calculated its population estimates with these multiples: militia, – 5 to 1; polls, taxables, and tax lists – 4 to 1; families – average size, 5.7 to 6; houses – 7 to 1.[4] Differing population densities, sex ratios, racial proportions, and family patterns across the colonies make the assignment of multipliers like these additionally complex.

Even when direct censuses – head counts – were taken in the colonies, incomplete coverage resulting from the difficulties of counting mobile and widely dispersed populations could occur, and consistency in the content of censuses from colonial governor to colonial governor was clearly unlikely. The combination of a resistant population who recognized that enumerations could, and probably would, result in military requisitions or tax assessments, together with local officials who were frequently ambivalent about their tasks as enumerators, adds further to the question of completeness of colonial censuses.[5]

The population series used in this chapter is largely that of Greene and Harrington, and of Stella H. Sutherland, appearing as Series Z 1–19 in *Historical Statistics of the United States, Colonial Times to 1970*. Portions of that series, particularly estimates for southern population levels in the early eighteenth century, have been revised by John J. McCusker and Russell R. Menard. Thus the Greene/Harrington/Sutherland series, as amended by McCusker and Menard, comprises the set of population estimates that will be employed here.[6]

VITAL RATES

Absent any systematic birth and mortality registration procedures, the determination of birth and death rates for the colonies necessarily draws on

[4] Greene and Harrington, *American Population before the Federal Census of 1790*. For a critical assessment of such population series and the minimal advance in our knowledge of colonial population numbers since the writings of the 1930s, see McCusker and Menard, *The Economy of British North America*, chap. 10.

[5] For an inventory, analysis, and discussion of possible errors in colonial censuses, see Wells, *The Population of the British Colonies in America before 1776*.

[6] U.S. Dept. of Commerce, Bureau of the Census, *Historical Statistics of the United States, Colonial Times to 1970*, Part 2, Series Z1–19, 1168. McCusker and Russell Menard, *The Economy of British North America*, Tables 6.4, 8.1, and 9.4.

partial census data, inferences from child/woman ratios, and fragmentary local records of vital events. The colonies also lacked the widely available parish records of baptisms and deaths that have given English historical demographers a base from which to reconstruct English population movements from the sixteenth through the nineteenth centuries.[7] Yet intensive work on local records by historians and demographers, particularly in New England and the Chesapeake regions, together with back projections of fertility rates in particular, and on vital rates reconstructed from genealogical samples, has produced a clearer picture of mortality and fertility patterns. As with population totals, however, these rates require an inferred extension from the local records or genealogical samples to the colony-wide or regional patterns – a step that cannot be taken with full confidence.

The calculation of vital rates is further complicated by the mobility characterizing colonial populations. Discriminating between a death and an out-migrant from a region under study can be an intractable problem created by internal migration. But internal migration is not the only, or perhaps even the major, form of mobility clouding the demographic scene. Immigration, a major element in colonial demographic history, had a significant impact on sex ratios, age structures, and had epidemiological effects – all factors which bear on the fertility and mortality experience of populations.

IMMIGRATION

Though immigration played a crucial role in the growth of American colonial populations, it is the least well-defined component of that growth. Immigration numbers for whites are known less well than for blacks, a tragic irony born of a market for unfree black labor that has left recorded market transactions of purchases, sales, and taxes. Such records provided Philip Curtin and other researchers with the historical materials for estimating transatlantic flows of blacks.[8] The movement of free white labor left fewer traces, though sporadic records of indentured and convict labor appeared, as did emigrant registers, headright records, and ship passenger lists. The surviving indenture lists have been studied intensively by A. E. Smith in the 1930s and by David Galenson, David Souden, James Horn, and Farley Grubb in recent decades.[9] Emigration registers were kept on

[7] Wrigley and Schofield, *The Population History of England*.
[8] Curtin, *The Atlantic Slave Trade*.
[9] Smith, *Colonists in Bondage*; Galenson, *White Servitude*; Souden, "Rogues, Whores"; Horn, "To Parts beyond the Seas"; Grubb, "The Incidence of Servitude", and "Immigrant Servant Labor."

occasion and have provided historians with considerable detail on the nature and composition of emigration in given periods. A notable example is Bernard Bailyn's use of the emigration registers for 1773–76.[10] Headright (land grant) records and ship passenger lists offer some further indications of immigrant numbers, but they, too, are sporadic in appearance, limited in coverage, and contain inherent biases that limit their usefulness. Surname analysis, probably the most speculative form of migration study, has also been undertaken by historians in an attempt to identify immigrants and their country origins.

None of these forms of historical evidence, or all in combination, can give more than a glimpse of the scale and timing of white immigration to the colonies. Full knowledge of immigration is beyond reach if it is to be derived from any direct measures.[11] A recourse to indirect measurement, as with population numbers, can provide estimates of immigration. Net migrant flow is definitionally that portion of the change in population stock that is not accounted for by natural increase or decrease, that is, births less deaths.[12] Calculated in this residual fashion, immigration series for the period 1630–1790 appear by generation in Fogel et al. and by decade in Gemery.[13] The methodology of the latter author can be summarized in formula terms.

$$M = (P_1 - P_0) - (B - D) \qquad (5.1)$$

where M = net total decennial migration, P_0 = total population at beginning of decade; P_1 = total population at end of decade; B = total decennial births; and D = total decennial deaths. The formula requires

[10] Bailyn, *Voyagers to the West*, chap. 3.

[11] A full knowledge of the growth of the American population in the colonial era would demand not only accurate immigrant numbers, but far more demographic detail than the historical record provides. Potter, "Growth of Population," p. 364, has summarized the requirements for such a full knowledge:

> One therefore needs to know, for each colony or state at any point of time, not merely the aggregate populations, but also the figures of native-born and foreign-born; migrant and non-migrant native-born; white and coloured; rural and urban. Such complete information would be essential for an accurate interpretation of the growth of the American population in the eighteenth and nineteenth centuries. Until the middle of the nineteenth century, however, much of the detail is lacking and one has to be content with much less than these basic requirements.

[12] Expressed in terms of rates, the demographic balancing equation is: the decennial rate of population change (RTI) equals the birth rate (CBR) minus the death rate (CDR) plus the rate of net migration (RNM).

[13] Fogel et al., "The Economics of Mortality," Table B.2; Gemery, "Emigration from the British Isles," Table A.5, p. 215, and "European Emigration to North America," Table 3, p. 303.

modification if significant mortality occurred in passage and/or on arrival in destination regions, and if births and deaths are not known as totals but can only be estimated as rates. Migrants dying in passage or in "seasoning" would appear in neither the decade population counts or, in the absence of a complete death registration system, in the total of decennial deaths. To estimate migration, then, some account must be taken of the proportion of migrants who died in passage or in the years immediately following their arrival. This can be done by rewriting equation (5.1) to recognize the impact of such deaths:

$$M = P_1 - P_0 - (P_0 R) + (MS) - \left[\frac{M(1-S)}{2} R \right] \qquad (5.2)$$

where R = average decennial rate of natural increase or decrease; and S = proportion of migrants dying in passage and seasoning. The MS term now explicitly recognizes the "gate mortality" experienced by migrants. The surviving migrants, $M(1 - S)$, are assumed to have increased at a rate, R, that is the same as that applicable to the native population, P_0. Two separate R variables would be more appropriate – one applicable to the native population and a second to the surviving migrants – but the vital rate data necessary to discriminate that finely do not exist. The calculations can, however, be "tailored" to regions of the destination country if differing demographic regimes can be identified.[14]

Since these migration calculations are residuals that depend on population totals and vital rates that themselves are approximate in some degree, the migration series are necessarily approximate, "quasi numbers" in Gemery's terminology. They are in addition approximate where seasoning mortality is significant. Seasoning mortality was the contemporary term for the mortality that accompanied adjustment to new lands, what is now recognized as a morbidity/mortality effect stemming from contact with a new epidemiological environment. The heavy death toll on newly arrived migrants meant that a portion of the migrants never appeared in any population count. The phenomenon is particularly at issue for the southern mainland colonies, where seasoning mortalities extended well into the eighteenth century.[15]

---

[14] The formula summary is exerpted from Gemery, "European Emigration to North America," pp. 283–342.

[15] The methodology followed in Gemery attempts to account for both seasoning and passage mortality in estimating net emigration from Europe to the New World.

POPULATION GROWTH, 1607–1790

The population estimates of Table 5.1 indicate the magnitude of growth occurring by decade over the colonial and early national periods. The movement from an initial population of some 1,000 in 1620 to 240,000 in 1700 required an average annual growth rate of 7.1%. Growth rates of that magnitude reflected the settlement process of mainly British labor, the majority of whom were indentured laborers transferred to the New World colonies. The reverse side of that population transfer can be seen in the negative and zero annual rates of population growth in England from 1651 to 1691.[16] From the "settlement growth rates" of that century, the eighteenth century's growth rate dropped to an average of 2.9% per annum, the rate Malthus observed and judged to be largely a product of natural fecundity. These growth rates gave the British indisputable leadership in populating the New World. One component of that growth, the indentured labor flows from England, was perhaps 50 to 100 times the size of such flows originating in any other European nation in the 1630–1780 period.[17] In 1790 the now-independent British colonies had a white population that was two-fifths of that of England and an eighth of that of France.

In large part, the spatial distribution of the colonies' growth in the seventeenth century reflected the changing areas of settlement. The southern colonies and New England were the prime destinations of English emigrants, as indicated by the shares of those regions in population and population change. By the late decades of the seventeenth century, the rise of Pennsylvania and other middle colonies is evident, as their share of population growth rose to 36–40%. By the eighteenth century, both population distribution and population growth were more evenly balanced across the regions. As natural increase and internal migration increasingly dominated the regional population changes from midcentury, the South became a prime contributor to the white population growth, accounting for some 40% of that growth in the last half of the eighteenth century. In all regions, the rate of total increase progressively decreased from the original settlement rates to rates that come closer to those of natural increase. The anomaly in that pattern is the 1780–90 decade, when the rates of total

[16] Wrigley and Schofield, *Population History of England*, Table 7.14, Col. 3.
[17] Gemery, "Markets for Migrants," p. 33.

Table 5.1. White population in the mainland British colonies and early Republic, 1610–1790

Decade	Total			New England				Middle colonies				South			
	beginning decade population (thousands) (1)	Population Δ over decade (%) (2)	RTI (3)	Population (thousands) (4)	Population share (%) (5)	Share of population change (%) (6)	RTI (7)	Population (thousands) (8)	Population share (%) (9)	Share of population change (%) (10)	RTI (11)	Population (thousands) (12)	Population share (%) (13)	Share of population change (%) (14)	RTI (15)
1610–20	0.3	0.7	127.9	0.0	0.0	14.3	—	0.0	0.0	0.0	—	0.3	100.0	85.7	116.1
1620–30	1.0	3.6	164.9	0.1	10.0	47.2	335.1	0.0	0.0	11.1	—	0.9	90.0	41.7	103.1
1630–40	4.6	18.6	175.6	1.8	39.1	62.9	223.2	0.4	8.7	7.0	155.7	2.4	52.2	30.1	127.9
1640–50	23.2	15.5	52.5	13.5	58.2	58.1	52.4	1.7	7.3	13.5	83.8	8.0	34.5	28.4	44.8
1650–60	38.7	23.7	48.9	22.5	58.1	42.6	37.8	3.8	9.8	4.2	23.6	12.4	32.0	53.2	72.6
1660–70	62.4	38.1	48.8	32.6	52.2	49.6	46.8	4.8	7.7	5.0	33.9	25.0	40.1	45.4	54.0
1670–80	100.5	42.7	36.0	51.5	51.2	38.6	28.2	6.7	6.7	15.7	71.8	42.3	42.1	45.7	38.6
1680–90	143.2	53.1	32.0	68.0	47.5	33.9	23.8	13.4	9.4	35.8	92.3	61.8	43.2	30.3	23.4
1690–1700	196.3	43.5	20.2	86.0	43.8	11.7	5.8	32.4	16.5	40.2	44.1	77.9	39.7	48.0	24.1
1700–10	239.8	56.2	21.3	91.1	38.0	38.1	21.3	49.9	20.8	24.0	24.2	98.8	41.2	37.9	19.7
1710–20	296.0	116.0	33.6	112.5	38.0	46.9	40.2	63.4	21.4	24.9	38.3	120.1	40.6	28.2	24.4
1720–30	412.0	139.9	29.7	166.9	40.5	31.7	23.8	92.3	22.4	30.7	39.0	152.8	37.1	37.6	30.0
1730–40	551.9	203.7	31.9	211.2	38.3	34.4	29.0	135.3	24.5	33.8	42.0	205.4	37.2	31.9	27.8
1740–50	755.6	178.7	21.5	281.2	37.2	37.9	21.8	204.1	27.0	40.1	30.5	270.3	35.8	22.0	13.7
1750–60	934.3	333.5	31.0	349.0	37.4	26.4	22.7	275.7	29.5	36.9	37.6	309.6	33.1	36.7	33.9
1760–70	1,267.8	406.5	28.2	436.9	34.5	31.7	26.2	398.9	31.5	30.0	27.1	432.0	34.1	38.3	31.2
1770–80	1,674.3	484.4	25.7	565.7	33.8	27.4	21.3	521.0	31.1	32.9	27.1	587.6	35.1	39.7	28.7
1780–90	2,158.7	1,014.3	39.3	698.4	32.4	29.1	35.9	680.5	31.5	27.0	34.4	779.8	36.1	43.9	46.2
1790–	3,173.0	—	—	994.0	31.3	—	—	954.0	30.1	—	—	1,225.0	38.6	—	—

Notes: Total population and changes by decade and region in shares and rates of total increase. RTI = rate of total increase, expressed per thousand beginning period population per year.

Sources: Columns 1, 4, 8, and 12: calculated from *Historical Statistics of the United States, Part 2* (Washington, D.C., 1975) Series Z1–19, with revisions by McCusker and Menard, *The Economy of British America*, Tables 6.4, 8.1, and 9.4. Remaining columns are calculated.

increase were so high as to signal (a) an immigrant inrush after the Revolutionary War, (b) a post–Revolutionary War "baby boom," (c) a mortality decline, and/or (d) suspect population data generated by the movement from population estimates to the first population census of 1790.[18] Although population growth in the colonies clearly shifted from an immigration base in the early decades to a natural increase in the later decades, the trend and timing of that transition differed significantly by region. New England and the southern colonies occupied the end points on that spectrum of demographic change. New England experienced both higher fertility and lower mortality earlier than did the southern colonies, and it received fewer immigrants. There were two major reasons for that pattern. (1) Because it did not rely on indentured labor – at the beginning of its settlement or later – New England never experienced the unbalanced sex ratios that characterized immigration in the South. The sex ratios of the indentured immigrants were severely skewed: 76.7% were male in the 1654–99 period and 90.2% male in 1700–75.[19] (2) The mortality levels of New England never reached the magnitude of those in the South. The less virulent disease environment of the North made seasoning mortality far less severe and infant mortality lower. The mortality differential between New England and the South lasted into the nineteenth century.

The position of the middle colonies along this spectrum of demographic regimes was probably closest to the New England model, though the large in-migration in the region and the greater mortality effects of two major cities may suggest otherwise. The detailed data to support this description of differing regimes of population change are presented in the following discussions of nuptiality and fertility, mortality, and migration.

NUPTIALITY AND FERTILITY

With us in N. America, Marriages are generally in the Morning of Life, – our Children are therefore educated, and settled in the World by Noon, and thus our Business being done, we have an Afternoon and Evening of chearful leisure to ourselves, – . . . By these early Marriages, we are blest with more Children, and, from the Mode among us – founded in Nature – of every Mother suckling and nursing her own Child,

[18] The anomaly is apparent in an earlier study. See Gemery, "European Emigration to North America." For an examination of the possible reasons for the anomaly, see pp. 312–17. For a lower estimate of immigration in this period, see Grabbe, "European Immigration," pp. 190–214. Significant immigration may well have been occurring. For a facinating look at the political impact of such immigration, see Carter, "A 'Wild Irishman,'" pp. 178–89.

[19] Galenson, *White Servitude in Colonial America*, Table 2.2.

more of them are raised. Thence the swift Progress of Population, among us, –
unparallel'd in Europe.

— Benjamin Franklin to John Alleyne, 1768[20]

As early as 1751, Benjamin Franklin hypothesized that a major reason for
the populousness of the mainland American colonies lay in the ready availability of land, which meant that "marriages in America are more general,
and more generally early, than in Europe."[21] Franklin speculated that as a
result of the early marriages, the number of births occurring to a marriage
might be eight, as opposed to the four characteristic of patterns in Europe,
where restricted land availability led to less economic opportunity and
thus later marriages. The data of Table 5.2, showing mean age at first
marriage, mean completed family size, and total fertility, indicate how
close to the mark Franklin came. The average age at first marriage for
males was 25 to 26, approximately two years younger than for their English
counterparts at similar time periods. Women, too, married earlier, the
average age being 22–23, whereas English women married later by some
two years. The first marriage age for females was lowest in those colonies
that had the greatest skewness in sex ratios. Maryland is the clearest illus-
tration. All three of the Maryland samples show an average marriage age
of 18 to 19 in the early part of the eighteenth century. The sex ratio for
that colony in 1704, that is the ratio of white adult males to white adult
females was 1.54.[22] The female age of first marriage in general rose from
the seventeenth to the eighteenth century, a circumstance that probably
reflected the progressively more limited availability of land in the northern colonies and, with time, a more evenly balanced sex ratio in the southern colonies.

The fertility result of earlier marriages was as postulated by Franklin.
Mean completed family size, the number of births occurring over a
woman's childbearing years, ranged from six to eight, and reached nine in
some samples. The total fertility rate, a sum of age-specific birth rates
across the childbearing years of women, (15–44 in these samples), shows
a similar range. These fertility levels were indeed higher than those in
England, where the completed family size was closer to five. Over time,
however, the trend in completed family size in the colonies moved toward

---

[20] Quoted in Klepp, *Swift Progress of Population*, p. 1.
[21] *Franklin, Papers of Benjamin Franklin*, p. 228. For a discussion of Franklin's writing on the topic,
see Wells, "The Population of England's Colonies in America," pp. 85–102.
[22] For sex-ratio data in the colonies, see Wells, *Population of the British Colonies*, Table VII-4, p.
272.

Table 5.2. *Mean age at first marriage, family size, and fertility, 1652–1799*

Place and time	Mean age first marriage		Mean family size (completed) (3)	Total fertility (4)
	Males (1)	Females (2)		
Ipswich, Mass.				
1652–1700	27.2	21.1	—	—
1701–25	26.5	23.6	—	—
1726–50	24.0	23.3	—	—
18th century	—	—	6.4	7.0
Sturbridge, Mass.				
1730–59	24.8	19.5	—	9.2
1760–79	25.5	21.6	—	8.4
1780–99	25.6	23.6	—	8.7
Northampton, Mass.				
Before 1700	26.1	20.6	8.2	10.1
1700–49	27.6	23.9	6.9	9.4
1750–99	28.5	25.5	5.7	9.5
Nantucket, Mass.				
1680–1739	24.1	20.0	—	—
1740–79	23.1	20.9	—	—
1780–1839	25.0	22.6	—	—
1660–1724	—	—	8.8	8.8
1725–49	—	—	9.2	8.4
1750–74	—	—	6.7	7.5
1775–1850	—	—	6.8	6.0
Deerfield, Mass.				
1721–40	—	19.9	7.2	6.6
1741–60	—	21.1	7.8	7.5
1761–80	—	23.1	5.6	5.8
1781–1800	—	23.9	5.0	4.9
Hingham, Mass.				
1701–20	27.8	24.3	—	—
1721–40	26.3	23.3	—	—
1716–40	—	—	6.7	—
1741–60	25.7	22.5	7.2	—
1761–80	24.9	23.2	6.4	—
1781–1800	26.3	24.5	6.2	—
Quakers				
Born by 1730	26.5	22.0	7.5	8.8
1731–55	25.8	22.8	6.2	7.7
1756–85	26.8	23.4	5.1	6.4
Philadelphia gentry				
1700–75	—	—	9.2	9.9
1776–1825	—	—	9.1	9.3

Table 5.2. *(cont.)*

Place and time	Mean age first marriage		Mean family size (completed) (3)	Total fertility (4)
	Males (1)	Females (2)		
Maryland				
1650–1700	—	16.8	9.4	7.5
1700–50	—	18.6	9.0	8.8
1750–1800	—	22.2	6.9	8.0
Virginia gentry				
1710–59	—	20.9	8.4	—
1760–99	—	20.3	8.3	—
Chesapeake immigrants				
Born by 1700	30.2	—	—	—
Maryland Immigrants				
Eastern Shore, 1610–58	29.2	24.7	—	—
Charles County, MD				
Immigrants, 1610–59	30.3	25.0	—	—
Natives, 1640–93	24.1	17.8	—	—
Somerset County, Md. (natives)				
1648–69	23.1	16.5	—	—
1670–1711	22.8	17.0	—	—
1700–40	24.1	19.0	—	—
Middlesex County, Va.				
Natives born by 1700	24.7	20.6	—	—
Maryland, Western Shore natives				
1680–99	23.1	18.2	—	—
1700–19	23.7	18.5	—	—
1720–49	25.9	21.4	—	—
New England[a]				
1650–99	—	—	8.6	8.7
1700–49	—	—	7.4	8.4
1750–99	—	—	6.7	7.8
Mid-Atlantic region[a]				
1650–99	—	—	7.3	7.9
1700–49	—	—	6.7	8.3
1750–99	—	—	6.8	9.0
Southern region[a]				
1750–99	—	—	9.6	7.9

[a] U.S., genealogical sample, birth cohorts.
Sources: Wells "The Population of England's Colonies in America," Tables 1 and 2. The genealogical sample of U.S. birth cohorts is from Wahl, "New Results on the Decline in Household Fertility," Sample B, Table 8.7.

Table 5.3. *Age structure of the white population of New York, 1703–1790*

Sex	1703	1723	1746	1749	1756	1771	1786	1790
Males under 16	25.8	24.8	24.7	24.6	24.8	23.5	24.9	24.9
Females under 16	26.9	23.4	24.4	23.3	22.8	22.6	23.5	—[b]
Total under 16	52.7	48.2	49.1	47.9	47.6	46.1	48.4	
Males above 16	24.5	26.4	26.5	26.9	27.2	28.1	26.3	26.6
Females above 16	22.8	25.4	24.4	25.2	25.2	25.8	25.3	—[b]
Total above 16	47.3	51.8	50.9	52.1	52.4	53.9	51.6	
Males above 60	—[a]	—[b]	2.6	2.5	3.3	2.9	2.2	—[b]
Total males	50.3	51.1	51.1	51.5	51.9	51.6	51.1	51.5

[a] 125 persons (out of 20,000) are shown as "over 60," sex and color not being distinguished.
[b] Not shown.
Source: Potter, "The Growth of Population in America," p. 653.

that of the English case, as the figures for Northampton, Nantucket, and Deerfield, Massachusetts, indicate.

Another indicator of fertility is crude birth rate. Because crude rates are not standardized for the age and sex composition of the populations they describe, they are less accurate measures. However, they remain useful, particularly for the New England and middle colonies in the eighteenth century, when age structures and sex ratios there were not changing. The clearest evidence on age and sex structures in the eighteenth century appears in censuses for New York and New Jersey. Table 5.3 shows rather wide-bracket age information from a continuous series of eight censuses for New York dating from 1703 to 1790. There was little change in age structure or in the percentage of males over the period. A set of four censuses for New Jersey gives similar results. In that case, the percentage under 16 changed slightly, from 48.5% in 1726 to 50.0% in 1771–72, while the percentage of males held relatively constant – at 52.7% in the earlier period and 52.2% in the later one.[23] Though the New York and New Jersey data are probably representative of much of New England and the middle colonies, they are not apt to be broadly representative of the South, particularly for those colonies that received large infusions of indentured labor. Maryland, the one southern colony with eighteenth-century time

[23] For the New Jersey data, see Potter, "Growth of Population in America," Table 6, pp. 656–57.

series data on age composition and sex ratios, shows a rise in the percentage of whites under 16 from 40.2% in 1704 to a "New York" level of 49.3% in 1755. Over the same period, the white adult sex ratio dropped from 1.54 to 1.13.[24] Crude rates, then, are likely to be satisfactory measures for New England and the middle colonies, but less satisfactory for the South, where age structure and sex composition changed, as the Maryland figures show.

An adequate sampling of crude birth rates is in itself something of a problem. A patchwork of rates can be assembled from a variety of demographic studies. Jim Potter's crude birth rate figure for New Jersey for 1771–72, as calculated from the Downshire Papers, is 30.5. D. S. Smith's estimates of mean size for completed families in Hingham, Massachusetts, from before 1691 to 1800 range from 7.59 before 1691 to 4.61 in 1691–1715. From 1716 to 1800, the mean size moved to about 6.6, a level that implies crude birth rates in the middle forties. Such results are consistent with those of Greven Andover, who calculated birth rates in the 48–35 range, high at the beginning of the eighteenth century and then moving to the lower figure. A random sample of Massachusetts towns in the seventeenth century taken by Thomas and Anderson found an average size of completed family of 7.13, a figure associated in their data "with a range of birth rates between 48.4 and 49.2." Higgs and Stettler's estimates of crude birth rates for nine Connecticut and Massachusetts towns "whose records appear particularly good" show only one town with a rate higher than 50 in 1765. The rate for the nine towns as a whole was somewhat under 40. The authors comment: "Even allowing for substantial amounts of underreporting, it is quite unlikely that a rate exceeding fifty was reached."[25]

Birth rate levels as high as 50 are occasionally encountered in other samples in the eighteenth century. New France in the period 1700–30 had a completed family size of 8.39 and a birth rate of 55.8.[26] Gragg reports an average size of completed family of 9.6 and 8.4 among Quaker meetings in the South during 1731–55 and 1756–85, respectively. Quakers in the Middle Atlantic meetings, however, show the more typical completed

---

[24] Wells, *Population of the British Colonies*, Table V-2, p. 152, and Table VII-4, p. 272.

[25] See, respectively, Potter, "Growth of Population in America," p. 658; Smith, "Demographic History of Colonial New England," p. 177; Greven, *Four Generations.* pp. 184–85; Thomas and Anderson, "White Population, Labor Force, and Extensive Growth," p. 647; Higgs and Stettler, "Colonial New England Demography," pp. 288, 289.

[26] Henripin, *La Population canadienne au début du XVII siècle nuptialité-fecondité-mortalité infantile*, pp. 39, 40.

Table 5.4. *Comparison of white crude birth rate estimates, 1760–1810*

Years	Total United States				Rural: Colonies/States[a] Fertility model (5)
	Lotka (1)	Blodget (2)	Thompson and Whelpton (3)	Yasuba (4)	
1760–70					58.6
1770–80					57.0
1780–90					56.5
1790–1800	50.8				54.1
1790–1805		52–53			
1800			55.0	47.6–52.9	
1800–10					52.4

[a] Eleven colonies to 1790; 13 colonies/states in 1790–1800; 15 states in 1800–10.
Source: Schapiro, "Land Availability and Fertility in the United States," p. 595, table 4.

family sizes of 7.5, 6.2, and 5.1 in the period 1756–85.[27] The figures for the
South could easily give rise to crude birth rate levels of 60+, but it is
difficult to envision that these colonies were still receiving substantial
numbers of indentured servants with fertility levels approaching the
Quaker case. A fertility model published by Morton Schapiro has
extended crude birth rate estimates back through the last four decades of
the eighteenth century for a sample of 11 colonies/states in the New
England and Middle Atlantic region, but covering only rural areas.
Schapiro's crude birth rate estimates run from 58.6 in 1760–70 to 54.1 in
1790–1800; however, these estimates exclude urban areas and are probably biased upward, to an unknown degree, since urban rates were lower
than rural rates.[28]

Table 5.4 summarizes the few crude birth rate estimates in the literature that cover more than local samples. There are no such estimates for
the seventeenth century. Most of the evidence from local studies is in the
neighborhood of Yasuba's estimate of 47.6 to 53 for 1800. Schapiro's estimates define an upper bound series, while some local studies find levels
well below 47. There appears to be no trend in New England and Middle
Atlantic rates, though the southern colonies undoubtedly experienced
a fertility rise as a result of the increasingly balanced sex ratios that

[27] Gragg, *Migration in Early America*, p. 100.
[28] Schapiro, "Land Availability and Fertility in the United States," pp. 577–600.

likely developed from the seventeenth through the eighteenth centuries. Maryland, apparently the one southern colony in which adult sex ratios can be calculated for two dates in the eighteenth century, shows a drop in the sex ratio from 1.54 in 1704 to 1.09 in 1755, as the population of white women tripled between those years.[29] If the Maryland data are taken as a benchmark, they suggest that in the southern colonies the sexes approached a balance by the mid–eighteenth century, so southern fertility levels probably rose to match, or perhaps exceed, the New England and Middle Atlantic levels by that date.

MORTALITY

Mortality data are as fragmentary as those on fertility. Massachusetts has received the most intensive study because of its relatively more complete vital records and bills of mortality, but even there, Vinovskis comments, "the determination of death rates in Massachusetts before 1860 is seriously hampered by especially incomplete registration of deaths during the seventeenth and eighteenth centuries."[30] Imperfect though the data are, they suggest general levels of crude death rates in the range of 15–25 and in the 30s and 40s for cities (see Table 5.5). Did that pattern change over the course of the eighteenth and into the nineteenth century? Vinovskis has ventured two conclusions that, to this point, have not been challenged:

The eighteenth century witnessed the convergence of death rates of rural and urban areas as some of the smaller towns such as Andover and Ipswich experienced an increase in mortality rates while life expectancy rose in Salem, particularly for females. Boston continued to remain relatively unhealthy throughout most of the eighteenth century.... The surprising finding in this preliminary investigation of mortality rates is that death rates remained relatively constant throughout the entire period, especially for the smaller agricultural towns. Most of the significant declines in mortality occurred in the larger towns such as Salem and Boston which contained only a fraction of the population of the state as a whole. Furthermore, though rural-urban differences were pronounced in the

---

[29] See Wells, *Population of the British Colonies*, Table VII-4, p. 273.

[30] Vinovskis, "Mortality Rates and Trends," p. 185. Also see Cassedy's discussion of colonial bills of mortality where he notes that no such bills were published in the seventeenth century. He attributes their absence to printing priorites (only five printing presses were in the colonies in 1688) and an absence of legislative requirements. When publication began, some deaths were omitted from the lists. "The first regularly published colonial newspaper was *The Boston News Letter*. In its eleventh number, the issue for June 26–July 3, 1704, the paper printed a simple chart of the numbers of whites buried in Boston each month of 1701, 1702, and 1703. The printer-editor, John Campbell, explained that the chart did not include the many deaths at sea of Boston's large seafaring population." Cassedy, *Demography in Early America*, pp. 119, 120, and chap. 6.

Table 5.5. *Comparative crude death rates
for Andover, Boston, and Philadelphia,
1720–1724 to 1770–1774*

Years	Andover[a] (1)	Boston (2)	Philadelphia (3)
1720–24	11.1	46.8	—
1725–29	16.9	35.0	—
1730–34	9.6	38.8	—
1735–39	29.7	34.0	—
1740–44	11.7	34.6	39.9
1745–49	21.5	44.2	47.5
1750–54	15.1	40.2	47.2
1755–59	8.3	33.4	47.0
1760–64	13.5	32.2	45.3
1765–69	5.6	32.8	38.5
1770–74	3.8	34.2	36.3

[a] Significant underregistration, perhaps on the order of 40% to as high as 60%, may well make these figures artificially low. See discussion in Vinovskis, "Mortality Rates," pp. 196, 197.
Source: Smith, "Death and Life in a Colonial Immigrant City," p. 888, Table 9.

seventeenth and eighteenth centuries, they were much less important during the first half of the nineteenth century.[31]

The absence of a trend in the Massachusetts mortality experience is a likely circumstance for the remainder of New England and for the middle colonies as well, but again the South is a case apart. For that region, Fogel has suggested that mortality rates for whites declined sharply from levels of approximately 50 per thousand ca. 1700 to a figure perhaps below 25 by 1850–60.[32] Thus the region appears to have approached Massachusetts

---

[31] Vinovskis, "Mortality Rates and Trends," p. 212.

[32] Fogel et al., "The Economics of Mortality in North America," pp. 76, 77. Fogel's work on a sample of genealogies generated data on life expectancy in the United States since 1700 that suggests that an overall decline in mortality occurred among native-born white males over the course of the eighteenth century. The results remain provisional since the sample used contains, to date, potential biases, including an underrepresentation of the South. The preliminary results are reported in Fogel, "Nutrition and the Decline in Mortality," Table 9.1, p. 44; Figure 9.1, p. 465.

How sharp the decline in the Southern rate was – or indeed whether a decline occurred in some areas – remains an open issue. See Rutman and Rutman's discussion of mortality in *A Place in*

mortality levels over the course of the eighteenth century, though with a greater variance in decade-to-decade rates. As late as the 1820s and 1830s, however, the rates were not equalized, if one can infer population-wide rates from one limited study of comparative mortality done in 1840. Conducted from military personnel records on postings in the North and the South for the years 1819–39 and purposely attempting to test for "climatic differences" in mortality, the report notes:

The difference between the ratio of mortality of the Northern and Southern division, is quite striking, the average of the latter being according to the medical returns, nearly four-fold greater, and according to the Post returns nearly three times higher than that of the former. This disparity is equally manifest in the statistics of the first part, as shown by the results of four years, terminating with 1825. In 1822, this inequality, according to the Post returns, is very remarkable, the annual ratio of mortality in the Southern division being thirteen and five-tenths percent, and in the Northern no more than one and nine-tenths percent. A distinguishing feature between those two divisions is, that the Northern exhibits little variation in the annual mortality, whilst the Southern, in consequence of more fatal epidemic visitations, shows greater extremes.[33]

Though the military experience may accentuate the regional mortality difference because troops recruited in the North were posted to the South where they had no acquired immunities, it is still true that whether seasoning to the more virulent disease environment in the South occurred early or late, the mortality penalty remained. Using data in the 1860 census, Fogel and Engerman found that very early acclimatization was costly as well; the infant death rate of whites in the South was 21 percent higher than that of whites in the North.[34] The subsequent mortality experience through childhood in the South could hardly have redressed and quite probably worsened such a differential. Thus, while the trend of mortality in the South was downward toward the Massachusetts level, the data indicate that a "mortality gap" persisted to the mid–nineteenth century. Fogel et al. estimate that gap for 1850–60 at 4 to 8 points; that is, crude

Time, 2, *Explicatus*. On failing to find a declining mortality pattern, they comment: "These table values emerge from the data as something of a surprise inasmuch as Chesapeake scholars have been assuming (although in the absence of firm evidence) that the fearful mortality of the seventeenth century mitigated in the eighteenth as the native-born came to predominate in the population. At least in Middlesex, wracked as it was by devastating epidemics in the later century, this was not the case." *Explicatus*, 53–55. The Rutmans' earlier work on malaria leads them to suspect that the continuing high mortality was not simply a phenomenon of Middlesex County but may well prove to be true of the South more generally. Letter to the author, July 18, 1983.

[33] Lawson, "Statistical Report on the Sickness and Mortality," p. 375.

[34] Fogel and Engerman, *Time on the Cross*, p. 101.

death rates for the South were 24 to 28 if the rates for the North were at 20.[35]

These various fragments of mortality data can perhaps best be compared for regional trends if organized in a life expectancy table. Survival years beyond some given age can be estimated by the construction of a life table and a number of the studies of Northern and Chesapeake region towns, counties, and other populations have been presented in an "expectation-of-life" format. Most are adult age tables since the historical materials on the populations being analyzed rarely offer good information on infant and child mortality. Yet those early ages are the very ages most susceptible to virulent disease environments and thus were the likely – and sadly – prime ages contributing to overall mortality. Estimates of life expectancy from birth thus become quite conjectural if, indeed, most unrecorded deaths occur in infancy (year 0–1) or in childhood (years 1–14). Some of the New England studies have estimated infant and childhood mortality levels directly with reasonable confidence, but, where underreporting is probable, adjustments to the data can be made. For example, in his analysis of seventeenth-century mortality in Charles Parish, Virginia, Daniel Blake Smith utilized a technique developed by Louis Henry to estimate unrecorded infant deaths. For that parish, Smith followed Henry's method of examining birth intervals to estimate that 50% of infant deaths went unrecorded. Most infants probably died in their first few weeks of life and likely received a private burial that was unnoted in the parish death register. Adjusted for these omissions, Smith found infant death rates of 132.2 for males and 184.6 for females. In contrast, infant mortality rates in Andover and Ipswich, Massachusetts, were 115 and 112, respectively.[36] Smith regarded even the adjusted infant mortality rates as probably too low to reflect the impact of the severe malarial environment that seventeenth-century inhabitants of the Chesapeake experienced.

To circumvent the problems posed in estimating infant and child mortality, most life tables drawn from studies for the seventeenth and eighteenth centuries plot adult life expectancy only, those from ages 20, 30, or later. Robert V. Wells, in a 1992 study, assembled the available American mortality studies for the colonial period in a useful format for purposes of comparison.[37] For studies that showed only adult life expectancies, he extrapolated back to life expectancy at birth (e_0) by utilizing Princeton

[35] Fogel et al., "The Economics of Mortality," p. 77.
[36] Smith, "Mortality and Family in the Colonial Chesapeake," pp. 403–27.
[37] Wells, "Population of England's Colonies in America," pp. 85–102.

Model West life tables. The technique is approximate, as Wells cautions, since many of the studies have incomplete evidence on adult mortality and many are for males only. However, recognizing the approximate nature of the data and disregarding extreme numbers, such as those for life expectancy in the Plymouth colony, Wells's table provides the best comparative summary of our fragmented knowledge of colonial mortality. Table 5.6 reproduces Wells's life expectancy data for the American colonies in the left panel. Added here is a column of crude death rates that are implied by Wells's e_0 figures. The inferred crude death rates are included in the table in part as a check on the reasonableness of the e_0 figure and in part to array the northern and middle mortality rates against those of the southern colonies.' The derivation of the crude rates is a further approximation as e_0, already an approximation, is transformed into a crude death rate utilizing a formula developed by Fogel et al. in their research on the economics of mortality.[38]

Outcomes from these collected life table samples are consistent enough to point to:

(1) New England experienced a relatively benign demographic regime with life expectancies at birth ranging from 36 to 55, being greatest in inland towns such as Andover. Port towns like Salem, more densely settled and with more mobile components to their populations, had a greater exposure to disease and thus had lower life expectancies of 35–37 years. In crude death rate terms, the New England range was from the mid and upper teens to mid and upper 20s. There is little discernible evidence of trend, as Vinovskis has noted. Early settlement in the region appears to have been as favorable demographically as later. Whereas Andover's figures give some hint of life expectancy dropping from the seventeenth to the eighteenth centuries, Salem's show virtually no change. Crude death rates in the low to the mid-20s and even as low as 15 to 18 were experienced in both centuries; however significant underregistration in the Andover case make the very low ranges suspect.[39]

(2) Southern mortality levels contrast dramatically with those of New England, reinforcing the data discussed earlier. Crude death rates approaching the catastrophic appear in the seventeenth century data for areas such as Charles County, Maryland, and Charles Parish,

---

[38] Fogel et al., "The Economics of Mortality," pp. 103–4.
[39] See the discussion in Vinovskis, "Mortality Rates," pp. 196–97.

Table 5.6. *Life expectancy and inferred crude death rates for American mainland populations, seventeenth and eighteenth centuries*

| Place and time | Life expectancy at | | | | Inferred crude death rate[a] (4) |
	Birth (1)	Age 20 (2)	Age 30 (3) Male	Age 30 (3) Female	
Ipswich, Mass.					
18th century	(55)	45	—		14.7
Hingham, Mass.					
1721–1800	45[b]	(42)	38.4	38.6	19.5
Salem, Mass.					
17th century	(36–35)	36.1	29.2		26.7–27.7
18th century	(35–37)	35.5	30.3		27.7–25.7
Andover, Mass.					
1670–99	(54–59)	44.8	38.7		15.1–13.3
1730–59	(47–54)	41.6	36.3		18.3–15.1
Plymouth Colony					
17th century	(61–64)	48.2	40.0		12.7–11.9
East Haven, Ctonn.					
1773–1822	(45–50)	41.4	36.4		19.5–16.8
Harvard graduates					
18th century	35–40[c]	(37–39)	(30–32)		27.7–23.0
Yale graduates					
1701–74	49.5[c]	(43)	(36)		17.1
Quakers (middle colony)					
18th century	40–46[d]	(39–42)	(32–34)		23.0–18.9
Philadelphia gentry					
Males 1700–1800	40.9	38.2	31.2		22.3
Females 1700–1800	43.8	40.9	33.7		20.2
Maryland					
1650–1700	35[b]	(37)	(30)		27.8
1700–50	40[b]	(39)	(32)		23.0
1750–1800	40[b]	(39)	(32)		23.0
Maryland legislators					
Native 1618–99	(15)	—	19.5		91.0
Native 1700–67	(30)	(33)	27.0		34.4

Table 5.6. *(cont.)*

Place and time	Life expectancy at				Inferred crude death rate[a] (4)
	Birth (1)	Age 20 (2)	Age 30 (3) Male	Female	
Immigrant 1600–99	(15)	—	19.3		91.0
Immigrant 1700–58	(29)	(32)	26.6		36.1
Charles County, Md.					
Immigrant 17th century	(10.8–9)	22.7	17.4		144.3–142.4
Native 1652–99	(18–15)	26.0	20.4		70.5–91.0
Charles Parish, Va.					
Native 1665–1699	(7–8)	20.8	16.4		265.0–219.7
Middlesex County, Va.					
1650–1710	(22–15)	28.8	19.4		53.2–91.0
Perquimans County, N.C.					
17th century	(25)	30.5	24.4		44.5
18th century	(24–23)	30.2	23.1		47.1–50.0

Note: Figures in parentheses are life expectancies in model life tables associated with the life expectancies reported in the other columns. In extreme cases, figures have been extrapolated from the lowest model life table.
[a] Crude death rates are estimated from life expectancy at birth.
[b] Estimated from survival rates to age 20.
[c] Estimated from survival rates after 20.
[d] Estimated from infant mortality and mortality over age 5.
Sources: Columns 1, 2, and 3 from Wells "Population of England's Colonies in America," pp. 94–95, Table 3; column 4 calculated utilizing Fogel et al. formula:

$$374d^{-0.713} = e_0$$

where e_0 is life expectancy at birth, and d is the crude death rate. See Fogel et al., "The Economics of Mortality," pp. 103–4. The equation is transformed to:

$$d = \text{Exp}\left[-ln\left(\frac{e_0}{266.662}\right)\right].$$

Virginia, which experienced rates reaching the 140s and possibly even the 200s. The corresponding low life-expectancies were one-half or less of those found in New England. While some areas of Maryland had seventeenth-century life expectancies that approximated those of

New England port towns, the high death rates implicit in the majority of the life tables for the South reflect the combined impact of the virulent disease environment and the significant numbers of new arrivals to the region who carried no immunities to malaria, yellow fever, and other diseases. The clearest example of the impact of seasoning mortality can be found in the Menard and Walsh study of Charles County, Maryland, where the life expectancies of seventeenth-century immigrants were half those of natives. In a broader sampling of birth cohorts of legislators drawn from throughout Maryland, Levy found no immigrant/native differential in life expectancy but did find life expectancy low for both groups, with crude death rates approximating 91, a rate similar to that of natives in Charles County, Maryland.

The trend in mortality in the South is downward from such high seventeenth-century levels, as Fogel et al. have observed.[40] Eighteenth-century death rates dropped to levels ranging from a low of 23 in Maryland to 47–50 in Perquimans County, North Carolina. Apparently the movement inland, away from tidal lowlands, served to moderate the effects of malaria on the populace.

(3) Only two life tables for the middle colonies appear in Wells's data, one for the Quakers and another for the Philadelphia gentry. Neither covers the seventeenth century. The eighteenth-century life expectancy and mortality rates shown in the two studies are closely comparable to those of the New England colonies. Life expectancies at birth ranged in the low 40s with associated death rates in the low 20s. That century's pattern was likely an improvement over the seventeenth-century experience, judging by what scant evidence is available for the earlier century. The crude death rates for Bucks County Quakers and for urban Philadelphia in 1682–1702 ranged from 40 to 73, considerably higher than the eighteenth-century mortality rates.[41] As in New England, and for the same reasons, port cities experienced higher mortalities. Looking beyond the gentry case to Philadelphia's overall crude death rates, Smith found that they averaged 42.9 for 1722–50 and 42.4 from 1751 to the eve of the Revolution. For comparison, Boston's crude death rate averaged 36.9 for the 1720–74 period.[42]

[40] Fogel et al., "The Economics of Mortality," pp. 76, 77.
[41] Klepp, *The Swift Progress of Population*, Table 3.
[42] See Smith, "Death and Life in a Colonial Immigrant City," Tables 3 and 9.

MIGRATION: INTERNATIONAL
AND INTERNAL

Estimates of aggregate immigration to the colonies in the early Republic can be inferred by first postulating rates of natural increase and then deriving immigration flows as a residual. Fogel et al. first undertook this approach in a study of sampling design for a research project on mortality. To simulate the generational development of the white population, the authors made a judgment on the life table mortality level together with the net reproduction and gross reproduction rates appropriate to each generation. One product of that simulation exercise was the number of "new additions," that is, net immigrants, in the first generation across 30-year intervals from 1640 to 1910.[43] Gemery took a somewhat different approach, discussed earlier, that attempted to account for the interdependence between immigration and mortality levels, as well as for the differing demographic patterns appearing in the northern and southern colonies. As with the Fogel et al. simulation, the methodology requires a judgment on natural increase rates and trends and, in addition, estimates of the proportions of intending migrants dying in passage and seasoning.[44]

A rate of natural increase appropriate to the New England and middle colonies is perhaps best selected by recognizing the range within which those rates could have occurred. Table 5.7 summarizes alternative rates that were possible for both the New England and middle colonies and the southern tree. The upper bound is postulated on the basis of the maximum rate of increase observed for identical enumeration areas in the census years extending from 1790 to 1860. Adjusting all population figures to remove that portion of growth stemming from an extension of an enumeration area, Willcox found that the maximum observed rates of increase – from all sources – were 3.01 percent in 1800–10 and 3.03 percent in 1850–60.[45] Natural increase rates in the seventeenth and eighteenth centuries were unlikely to have been higher than these, particularly since these nineteenth-century growth rates were derived from all sources and not from natural increase alone. Thus the upper bound is set at an annual rate

---

[43] Fogel et al., "The Economics of Mortality," Table B.2. See also the discussion of simulation modeling and sampling design that defines the parameters used in the table.

[44] Gemery, "Emigration from the British Isles," pp. 179–231, and "European Emigration to North America," pp. 283–348.

[45] Willcox, *International Migrations*, Table 22, p. 98.

Table 5.7. *Alternative rates of natural increase and implicit crude birth and death rates (percentages)*

Area	Rates of natural increase		Implicit crude rate range	
	Annual[a] (1)	Decennial (2)	CBR[b] (3)	CDR[b] (4)
New England and middle colonies				
Lower bound	2.26	25.0	44.5–46.5	22–24
Intermediate	2.60	29.2	46–48	20–22
Upper bound	3.01	34.5	50–52	20–22
South				
Lower bound	−2.26	−25.0	15	40
Intermediate	1.41	15.0	40–48	25–27
Upper bound	2.26	25.0	46–48	21–23

[a] The annual rate of natural increase is the compounded rate giving rise to the decennial rate.

[b] Crude birth rate and crude death rate figures are in persons per thousand per year.

of 3.0 percent, with a decennial change of 34.5%. A probable lower bound for the New England and middle colonies is set by assuming crude birth rates in the middle 40s and crude death rates in 22–24 range. The intermediate rate chosen is a midpoint, but other judgments suggest that figure as well. Potter concluded that "the balance of probability seems to suggest . . . a birth rate of 45–50 . . . and a moderate death of 20–25 per thousand."[46] Thomas and Anderson employed a stable population model for New England to infer rates of natural increase between 2.64 and 2.72 annually.[47]

The rates of natural increase in the South appear to be bounded across a much greater range. The initial settlement decades were likely ones of negative natural increase with crude death rates in the 40 range and crude birth rates low, at perhaps 15. An intermediate rate of natural increase occurred as increasingly balanced sex ratios raised crude birth rates to perhaps to the 40 level, while the movement of populations to the interior dropped mortality rates to the mid and upper 20s. The upper bound for the South probably approximates the lower bound for the New

[46] Potter, "Growth of Population," p. 646.
[47] Thomas and Anderson, "White Population, Labor Force, and Intensive Growth," pp. 647–48.

England case. It is likely that the southern colonies passed through all of these stages of rates of natural increase as settlement progressed from the seventeenth to the eighteenth century.[48]

The evidence on passage and seasoning mortality is more intermittent and fragmentary than that for vital rates.[49] No samples of seventeenth-century passage mortality are broad enough to warrant use; however, four samples exist for eighteenth-century migrants undertaking the Atlantic crossing. The first is for 2,814 Palatine migrants who experienced a passage mortality rate of 15.8% in a convoy passage from England to New York in 1710.[50] Because this group spent an extended waiting time in port prior to departure, typhus broke out among them, and thus this passage mortality rate may well represent a high range. A second sample consists of English convicts transported to the New World from 1719 to 1772. A. E. Smith estimated that these convicts had a 10–15% voyage mortality.[51] A third sample consists of 8,400 British troops sent to the West Indies between 1775 and 1782 who experienced an average passage mortality of 11%.[52] The relevance of the data from these three samples can be questioned on the grounds that none represented the more typical passenger traffic across the Atlantic. Perhaps the most representative sample of passage mortality in more regular passenger traffic appears in Farley Grubb's study of immigration to Pennsylvania. That study identified 1,566 passengers sailing in nine voyages over the period 1727–1805 who experienced a passage mortality of 3.83%. That figure is somewhat difficult to interpret because the construction of the sample excluded voyages free of mortality, those in which mortality went unreported, and the disaster cases of shipwreck. Adjusting for the latter circumstance, Grubb suggests that the passage mortality rate could have been as high as 5.6%.[53] By the nineteenth century, enough data exist to confirm the Fogel et al. judgment

---

[48] For historians' judgments that Virginia and Maryland achieved a balance of birth and death rates only in the last decade of the seventeenth century or the beginning decade of the eighteenth, see Morgan, *American Slavery*, p. 409; and Menard, "Immigration into the Chesapeake Colonies," p. 326.

[49] Potter has noted that the concept of "migrant contribution" requires a clarification in the definition of a migrant. Should those dying in passage be counted or only those arriving? Should only permanent, surviving settlers be counted, and seasoning deaths be disregarded? The most inclusive definition is adopted in these calculations, but they can be modified, if desired, to remove the passage mortality. Removing seasoning mortalities is equally possible, but that would necessitate the use of the narrowest of migrant definitions. See Potter, "Demographic Development and Family Structure," p. 131.

[50] Knittle, *Early Eighteenth-Century Palatine Emigration*, p. 147.

[51] Smith, *Colonists in Bondage*, pp. 118, 327.

[52] House of Lords, December 14, 1792, *An Account of the Number of Troops*.

[53] Grubb, *Immigration and Servitude*, p. 70 and Table 12.

that passage mortality rates fell substantially from 1700 to 1860, probably to "the neighborhood of 2%" in the second quarter of the nineteenth century.[54] Reviewing this evidence, a passage mortality rate of 5% will be hypothesized for the seventeenth century and one of 3% for the eighteenth.

Seasoning mortality is a particular issue for the southern colonies, though some question as to its applicability for the middle colonies can be raised as well. Contemporaries who observed the early settling process had no question as to its lethal impact in the South. Governor Sir William Berkeley of Virginia, responding to a query about deaths made by the lords commissioners on foreign plantations, wrote in 1671:

All new plantations are, for an age or two, unhealthy, 'till they are thoroughly cleared of wood; but unless we had a particular register office, for the denoting of all that died, I cannot give a particular answer to this query, only this I can say, that there is not often unseasoned hands (as we term them) that die now whereas heretofore not one of five escaped the first year.[55]

Later historians made similar judgments. Stella Sutherland estimated that a "possible third" of seventeenth-century newcomers to Virginia and Maryland died before they had lived there a year.[56] Analyzing a sample of 275 indentured servants who arrived in Maryland before the end of 1642, Menard concluded that a mortality rate of over 40% may have characterized this group if an absence in subsequent records of free men could be interpreted as a death.[57] Since that mortality would have accumulated over the course of four to five years, the 40% figure could reflect a first-year death toll as high as 30–40% or as low as 10–20%. The trend in seasoning mortality was clearly downward as Governor Berkeley's observations suggest, and, as earlier noted, population dispersion away from the tidewater lowlands had the effect of reducing the incidence of malaria and the susceptibility to other diseases that followed in malaria's train.[58] Seasoning deaths as a percentage of migrant arrivals had probably declined to 5% by the 1660s and likely fell as low as 2% in the eighteenth century. There is some evidence of seasoning mortalities extending further north into the middle colonies, as, for example, in Grubb's finding of a post-voyage mortality rate of 4.95% in the first few months after the arrivals of

---

[54] Fogel et al., "The Economics of Mortality," p. 77.
[55] Hening, *The Statutes at Large*, p. 515.
[56] Sutherland, *Population Distribution in Colonial America*, p. 193.
[57] Menard, "From Servant to Freeholder, pp. 39–40.
[58] See Rutman and Rutman, "Of Agues and Fevers," pp. 31–60.

servants' in Philadelphia.[59] However, without additional data in hand, no seasoning mortality will be assigned to the middle colonies in the following calculations.

The estimated migrant flow for the seventeenth and eighteenth centuries in Table 5.8 is based on the assumptions discussed. Rates of natural increase are set at a decennial rate of 29% for both the New England and middle colonies, and both regions are given the same passage mortalities: 5% in the seventeenth century and 3% in the eighteenth. The South's rate of natural increase is assumed to have moved from a negative decennial rate of 25% in the first two decades, to a balance by the last decade of the seventeenth century, and then to natural increase levels that progressively rose to a decennial rate of 25% by the second decade of the eighteenth century. Seasoning mortalities for the South are estimated at 20% for 1620–40 and thence diminishing to 5% by the decade of the 1660s, when Governor Berkeley wrote of the recent mortality experience. A 2% seasoning mortality rate is retained for the South in the eighteenth century. Passage mortalities for migrants destined to southern ports are assumed to have been the same as those for the New England and middle colonies, that is, 5% in the seventeenth century and 3% in the eighteenth. With those assumptions in place, the numbers of migrants can be calculated as residuals for the three regions and for all.[60]

The aggregate number of migrants to the colonies and new Republic totaled an estimated 160,000 in the seventeenth century and 615,000 in the eighteenth, totals that are similar to those found in the Fogel et al. generational simulation that shows "new additions" of 159,000 and 663,000, respectively.[61] That similarity appears though a revised

---

[59] Grubb, *Immigration and Servitude*, pp. 72–73.

[60] Only the intermediate rates of natural increase for the New England and Middle Colonies are used in these calculations. "Bracket" estimates of migration can be made by using both the lower bound and upper bound assumptions. For such a use of bracketed estimates and a discussion of the implausibility of the upper bound case, see Gemery, "European Emigration to North America," pp. 307–20.

[61] A comparison of the Fogel et al. estimates of net migration and those of Table 5.8 is shown below.

Period	Fogel et al. "New Additions"	Table 5.8 Total M
1610–40	26	27.2
1640–70	71	61.7
1670–1700	62	70.9
Total	159	159.8
1700–30	143	56.5
1730–60	85	89.5
1760–90	435	469.1
Total	663	615.1

For the Fogel et al. "New Additions," see Fogel et al., "The Economics of Mortality," Table B.2, Generation 1.

Table 5.8. *Inferred migration (M) given assumed rates of natural increase (R) and seasoning and passage mortality (S) for regions, 1610–1620 to 1780–1790*

Decade	New England (1)	R (2)	S (3)	M (4)	Middle colonies (5)	R (6)	S (7)	M (8)	South (9)	R (10)	S (11)	M (12)	Total (13)	R^a (14)	S^a (15)	Total M (16)
1610–20	0.0	—	—	—	0.0	—	—	—	0.3	—	—	—	0.3	—	—	—
1620–30	0.1	0.29	0.05	1.54	0.0	0.29	0.05	0.37	0.9	−0.25	0.25	2.63	1.0	−0.20	0.23	5.48
1630–40	1.8	0.29	0.05	10.28	0.4	0.29	0.05	1.09	2.4	−0.25	0.25	9.45	4.6	0.01	0.15	21.72
1640–50	13.5	0.29	0.05	4.67	1.7	0.29	0.05	1.48	8.0	−0.20	0.20	8.33	23.2	0.12	0.10	13.33
1650–60	22.5	0.29	0.05	3.29	3.8	0.29	0.05	−0.09	12.4	−0.15	0.15	18.39	38.7	0.15	0.08	18.09
1660–70	32.6	0.29	0.05	8.68	4.8	0.29	0.05	0.47	25.0	−0.10	0.10	23.16	62.4	0.13	0.07	30.28
1670–80	51.5	0.29	0.05	1.44	6.7	0.29	0.05	4.37	42.3	−0.05	0.10	24.63	100.5	0.15	0.07	27.63
1680–90	68.0	0.29	0.05	−1.58	13.4	0.29	0.05	13.89	61.8	−0.05	0.10	21.87	143.2	0.14	0.07	33.21
1690–1700	86.0	0.29	0.05	−18.24	32.4	0.29	0.05	7.45	77.9	0.00	0.10	23.22	196.3	0.17	0.07	10.04
1700–10	91.1	0.29	0.03	−4.52	49.9	0.29	0.03	−0.87	98.8	0.15	0.05	6.35	239.8	0.23	0.04	0.98
1710–20	112.5	0.29	0.03	19.61	63.4	0.29	0.03	9.47	120.1	0.25	0.05	2.50	296.0	0.27	0.04	33.11
1720–30	166.9	0.29	0.03	−3.69	92.3	0.29	0.03	14.62	152.8	0.25	0.05	13.47	412.0	0.28	0.04	22.42
1730–40	211.2	0.29	0.03	7.88	135.3	0.29	0.03	26.62	205.4	0.25	0.05	12.68	551.9	0.28	0.04	44.93
1740–50	281.2	0.29	0.03	−12.38	204.1	0.29	0.03	11.17	270.3	0.26	0.05	−28.86	755.6	0.28	0.04	−30.03
1750–60	349.0	0.29	0.03	−11.98	275.7	0.29	0.03	38.94	309.6	0.24	0.05	45.2	934.3	0.27	0.04	74.56
1760–70	436.9	0.29	0.03	1.89	398.9	0.29	0.03	5.78	432.0	0.24	0.05	48.8	1,267.8	0.27	0.04	58.92
1770–80	565.7	0.29	0.03	−29.23	521.0	0.29	0.03	7.57	587.6	0.25	0.05	42.39	1,674.3	0.28	0.04	14.25
1780–90	698.4	0.29	0.03	83.79	680.5	0.29	0.03	68.57	779.8	0.24	0.05	242.53	2,158.7	0.27	0.04	395.97
1790–	994.0	—	—	—	954.0	—	—	—	1,225.0	—	—	—	3,173.0	—	—	—

Notes: All population figures are beginning decade populations expressed in thousands. M figures also in thousands.

^{a}Aggregate R and S figures are calculated as a population-weighted average of the R and S figures for the specific regions.

Sources: Populations, Table 5.1. R and S by assumption, see Table 5.7 and text.

population series is used here and somewhat different methodological approaches are followed in the two studies. Both also show the anomalously large migrant numbers noted earlier for the latter part of the colonial period and the beginning decade of independence. Fogel et al. find 435,000 "new additions" for the generation 1760–90, while this study estimates a total of 469,000 for that same generation, with by far the bulk of migrants, 396,000, appearing in the 1780–90 decade. That decade total is so large as to suggest a problem in the transition from population estimates to the population numbers generated by the first census. Studies of emigrant flows by nationality have not produced numbers of that magnitude. James Horn, for example, in estimating the possible number of European emigrants, arrives at a total some 200,000 lower for the 1780–90 decade but with greater migrant numbers than those of Table 5.8 for the 1700–80 period.[62] Horn's figures imply that the population estimate for 1780 in particular is too low; a higher population total for that date would leave a smaller population increase for the 1780–90 decade than the 39.3% growth given in Table 5.1. If the Greene/Harrington/Sutherland population estimate for 1780 is left in place, the large immigrant numbers generated by the residual calculation could only be reduced by a ballooning natural increase of the population in that decade. That, in turn, would have had to result from a baby boom and/or a precipitous drop in mortality. Neither appears likely, to judge from the (admittedly) scant demographic evidence. The likelihood, then, of an underestimated population total for 1780 is high.[63] Current demographic knowledge cannot resolve the question. A further anomaly shows up in the migrant total for the 1740–50 decade. The aggregate out-migration indicated for the decade is improbable on the basis of other historical evidence and thus raises a question about the accuracy of the population estimates and/or the vital rates assumed for those dates.

Regional out-migration is less problematical. The out-migration shown for New England reflects internal migration toward the greater land availability to the West, largely in upper New York State. Six of the seven decades of out-migration shown for New England probably reflect internal migration of this form. The exception is the 1770–80 decade, when Loyalist emigration to Canada is intermixed with internal migation. Unfortunately, the residual methodology cannot discriminate between an

---

[62] Horn, communication to the author, July 2, 1996.
[63] For a discussion of the possibilities of a "baby boom," a drop in mortality rates, or a misestimated population total, see Gemery, "European Emigration," pp. 305–7.

internal migrant moving across regions and an international one newly arrived (or departed), so the regional migration totals for the middle colonies and the South are inflated in some degree by internal migrant numbers.

An internal migration, westward across the Appalachians, can be inferred from population totals of newly settled regions such as Kentucky and Tennessee, where the 1790 census showed white population totals of 61,000 and 32,000, respectively; however, direct information on internal mobility in the colonies is nearly nonexistent.[64] The one, broad study that is available stems from a sampling of militia rolls from the French and Indian and Revolutionary wars that was undertaken by Villaflor and Sokoloff.[65] That study affords a remarkably detailed look at the internal migration patterns of colonial males of militia age. Several of those patterns are notable:

(1) Five colonies – Massachusetts, Connecticut, Pennsylvania, Maryland, and Virginia – experienced net out-migration of American-born men of militia age. Three of those – Massachusetts, Connecticut, and Virginia – probably incurred net losses even with foreign immigration. Pennsylvania and Maryland, however, experienced net gains because of the counterbalancing foreign inflows.

(2) The colonies with the greatest in-migration of the native-born were the Carolinas and New York.

(3) Migration across regions occurred in two distinct patterns. Internal migration from the New England region was to the middle colonies, but New York and Pennsylvania defined the outer limits of New Englanders' movement. The second pattern was from the middle colonies to the south. Table 5.9 illustrates the distinctiveness of these internal migration streams. Virtually no New Englanders moved to the South and, New York aside, few middle colony or Southern males of militia age moved North.

(4) Mobility was greater in the South, and the distances moved were greater as well.

(5) Internal migration was uniformly out of the cities, to rural areas. As Villaflor and Sokoloff comment: "Migration between rural and urban areas in the late eighteenth century seems mostly to have been a matter

---

[64] *Historical Statistics*, Series A, pp. 195–209.
[65] Villaflor and Sokoloff, "Migration in Colonial America," pp. 539–70.

Table 5.9. *Colony persistence and out-migration, American Revolution: Proportion of recruits born in colony by place of residence at enlistment*

Birthplace	Residence										
	ME	NH	MA	CT	NY	PA	DE	MD	VA	NC	SC
Maine	.90	0	.10	0	0	0	0	0	0	0	0
New Hampshire	.02	.85	.12	0	.02	0	0	0	0	0	0
Massachusetts	.02	.13	.78	.04	.02	—	0	0	—	0	0
Connecticut	—	.01	.07	.79	.12	.01	0	0	0	0	0
New York	0	.01	.02	.03	.91	.01	0	0	.01	0	—
Pennsylvania	0	0	.01	0	0	.51	.04	.09	.20	.04	.12
Delaware	0	0	0	0	0	.06	.85	0	.02	.07	0
Maryland	0	0	—	0	.01	.06	.02	.69	.13	.02	.08
Virginia	0	0	—	0	0	0	—	—	.72	.14	.14
North Carolina	—	0	—	0	0	—	0	0	.01	.88	.10
South Carolina	0	0	0	0	0	0	0	.03	.03	.04	.90

Notes: Entries are proportions of total number of recruits born in the colony, weighted by sample size and population. Proportions sum horizontally. A dash represents a proportion greater than zero but less than .01.
Source: Villaflor and Sokoloff, "Migration in Colonial America," pp. 539–70, Table 2.

of dispersing the multitudes of European immigrants and their American-born offspring who collected in the port cities."[66]

Whether these patterns of internal migration had an impact on vital rate levels and trends remains an open subject.

SOCIOECONOMIC DIMENSIONS OF THE COLONIAL DEMOGRAPHIC EXPERIENCE

Advertisement,

To all Trades-men, Husbandmen, Servants and others who are willing to Transport themselves unto the Province of New-East-Jersy in America, a great part of which belongs to Scots-men, Proprietors thereof.

... The Woods and Plains are stored with infinite quantities of Deer and Rae, Elcks, Beaver, Hares, Cunnies, wild Swine, and Horses, &c. and Wild-honey in great abundance:

[66] Villaflor and Sokoloff, "Migration in Colonial America," pp. 549–50.

The Trees abound with several sorts of Wine-grapes, Peaches, Apricots, Chestnuts, Walnuts, Plumbs, Mulberries, &c. The Sea and Rivers with Fishes, the Banks with Oysters, Clams, &c. Yea, the Soil is so excellent and fertile, that the Meadows naturally produce plenty of Strawberries, Purpy, and many more tender Plants, which will hardly grow here in Gardens: Wheat, Ry, Barley, Oats, Peas and Beans, &c. when sown yields ordinarly 20. and sometimes 30. fold Increase, and Indian-Corn, which is a Grain both wholesome and pleasant, yields ordinarly 150. and sometimes 200. fold: Sheep never miss to have two Lambs at a time, and for the most part three, and these Lambs have generally as many the next year: The Winter lasts not ordinarily above two months; and one Mans ordinary Labour will with ease and plenty, maintain a Family of ten or twelve persons.[67]

For all of the hyperbole of the seventeenth-century broadside, it made a significant point. The colonial diet was not likely to be a constrained one. Once colonists made the adjustment from the English grains of wheat and rye to the Indian corn of the New World and developed as well cattle and hog stocks, the nutritional levels derived from cultivated and wild food sources were high.[68] Dearth, after the initial settlement decades of the seventeenth century, was not a characteristic problem facing white colonists in any of the North American regions. One effect of nutritional sufficiency is an increase in stature, an effect observed in both modern and historical populations.[69] That research has demonstrated that the native-born, male populations of the colonial era (1) nearly matched modern height levels, at only 3 centimeters less than the levels of Americans born in the 1930s; (2) experienced relatively little fluctuation in nutritional levels since their range in average stature was less than 2 centimeters, compared with a 4-centimeter range in the nineteenth century and 6 in the twentieth; and (3) were taller than genetically similar populations of the same period (for example, American men in the mid–eighteenth century were on average 7 centimeters taller than British and Norwegian males, 6 centimeters taller than the Austrians, and 5 centimeters taller than the Swedes).[70] Further, the colonial society, even with its large indentured servant component, was relatively egalitarian, so stature differences between socioeconomic groups (occupations, ethnic background) were largely absent among the soldiers serving in the American Revolution.[71] That absence of socioeconomic effects on stature contrasts dramatically with that of Europe, where

---

[67] Excerpted from a printed broadside for ships intending departure from Leith, Montross, Aberdeen, and Glasgow, Scotland, to New-East-Jersy in May, June, and July of 1684.

[68] For a discussion of diet and an estimate of caloric levels for the Chesapeake, see Carr, "Emigration and the Standard of Living," pp. 273–80. See also Miller, "An Archeological Perspective," pp. 176–99.

[69] For a survey of that research, see Steckel, "Stature and the Standard of Living," pp. 1903–40.

[70] Steckel, "Nutritional Status," p. 215.   [71] Steckel, Nutritional Status," p. 218.

height differences ranging from 8 to 15 centimeters are observed between children drawn from the upper and lower classes.[72] Adequate nutrition is no defense against some diseases, and the seasoning mortalities evident in the South reflected the impact of many such diseases. Malaria, smallpox, yellow fever, and encephalitis demonstrated few or no links to nutritional status.[73] However, a number of diseases were sensitive to that status: measles, diarrhea, tuberculosis, most respiratory infections, whooping cough, most intestinal parasites, cholera, leprosy, and herpes.[74] Thus the favorable net nutritional status experienced by the colonists could, and did, have a moderating impact on morbidity and mortality deriving from some diseases. Lower population density and, outside of port cities, a relatively low mixing of populations with different aquired immunities, limited the scope and intensity of epidemics.[75] The favorable colonial nutritional status, then, was one among several factors that moderated the effects of disease and ill health. Thus the time series and comparative evidence on stature, reflective of net nutritional status, testifies to the fact that the 1684 broadside was not wholly puffery.[76]

SUMMARY

There was no "colonial demographic regime" but rather several regimes, each with a unique combination of vital rates and a unique outcome.[77]

---

[72] Steckel, "Nutritional Status," p. 219.

[73] A number of writers have written of the mortality impact of these diseases on family patterns and wealth transfer and accumulation in the South. See for example, Edmund S. Morgan's chapter, "Living with Death," in his *American Slavery American Freedom* (1975), as well as Carr and Walsh, "The Planter's Wife"; Rutman and Rutman, "'New-wives and Sons-in-Law'"; and Walsh, "'Till Death Do Us Part.'"

[74] Steckel, "Stature and the Standard of Living," p. 221.

[75] See Kunitz, "Mortality Change in America," pp. 559–82.

[76] Another, less direct, measure of well-being in the colonial era is found in wealthholding patterns derived from probate inventories. Alice Hanson Jones, concluding a study of wealthholding patterns on the eve of the American Revolution, comments: "I conclude that the level of living attained on the eve of the American Revolution by typical free colonists, even the 'poor' ones, was substantial. It included sufficient food and drink, including meat, cider, and often strong liquors." Jones, "Wealth and Growth of the Thirteen Colonies," p. 340.

[77] McCusker and Menard, *Economy of British North America*, p. 235. McCusker and Menard expressed considerable doubt about the prospect of attempting "all inclusive estimates of the sources of (population) growth in British America." However, they go on to observe: "While the range of vital rates argues against the notion of a single demographic *regime*, it is not incompatible with the more elastic concept of a population *system* that can be studied profitably as a unit. The diversity was regular rather than random, and it should prove capable of systematic explanation" (p. 235).

This survey has provided ample evidence in support of McCusker and Menard's point, though the variety of demographic experience treated in this essay has been collapsed into two major patterns, that for New England and the middle colonies and that for the South. Merging the experience of the middle colonies' with that of New England appears appropriate, though there are relatively few demographic studies available for the middle colonies on which to base that judgment. Further historical work in the region may permit some differentiation of the two regions.[78] However, there is no question that the South represented a clearly distinct demographic regime. Can the diversity of these two regimes be encompassed by any aggregate measures? One venturesome way to summarize the demographic experience of the colonies and the early Republic is to attempt estimates of the components of population growth across those decades. The diversity of demographic patterns from north to south and our tenuous estimates of the levels and trends of fertility, mortality, and migration are presented in Table 5.10, an exercise in the *probable* patterns of population change. Beginning with estimates of population levels by decade and rates of total increase, the table then hypothesizes rates of natural increase that are the weighted averages of the natural increase rates assumed for the major regions, as shown in Table 5.8. The weights are the regional population shares as they change across the two centuries. As in Table 5.8, migration is treated as the residual that allows natural increase and net migration to add up to total increase.

Total population growth over the entire period was rapid, averaging 5% per year. That average is made up of disparate components, however: the high settlement growth rates of the seventeenth century (7.2% per year), and the more "normal" eighteenth-century rates of later development (2.8% per year). Natural increase began at a negative rate in the initial decade of settlement traced here and then moved to a 2.1% average annual rate by the beginning decade of the eighteenth century. The remaining decades of the eighteenth century show an average rate of natural increase of 2.5%, which compares with an average of 2.6% that Haines finds for

---

[78] Menard has expressed strong doubts on this possibility, including the utility of using vital rates to discriminate between regions. "For one thing, even if research should establish a fairly uniform set of vital rates these will need to carry the qualifier, 'except for Philadelphia, New York, and perhaps a handful of other smaller towns.' A vital rates approach to the problem of a demographic regime simply lacks the elasticity to comprehend urban-rural differences in early modern America." See Menard, "Was There a 'Middle Colonies Demographic Regime'?" p. 217.

Table 5.10. *Probable components of white population growth in the mainland British colonies and the early Republic, 1610–1790*

Decade	Beginning Pop (000's) (1)	Pop Δ (2)	RTI (3)	RNI (4)	RNM (5)	RNM as % of RTI (6)
1610–20	0.3	0.7	—	—	—	—
1620–30	1.0	3.6	164.9	−18.1	183.0	111.0
1630–40	4.6	18.6	175.6	0.8	174.8	99.5
1640–50	23.2	15.5	52.5	11.5	41.0	78.1
1650–60	38.7	23.7	48.9	14.0	34.9	71.4
1660–70	62.4	38.1	48.8	12.6	36.2	74.2
1670–80	100.5	42.7	36.0	13.8	22.2	61.7
1680–90	143.2	53.1	32.0	13.5	18.5	57.9
1690–00	196.3	43.5	20.2	16.3	3.9	19.4
1700–10	239.8	56.2	21.3	21.1	0.2	0.8
1710–20	296.0	116.0	33.6	24.5	9.1	27.1
1720–30	412.0	139.9	29.7	24.6	5.1	17.1
1730–40	551.9	203.7	31.9	24.6	7.3	22.9
1740–50	755.6	178.7	21.5	24.6	−3.1	−14.7
1750–60	934.3	333.5	31.0	24.7	6.3	20.3
1760–70	1,267.8	406.5	28.2	24.7	3.5	12.4
1770–80	1,674.3	484.4	25.7	24.7	1.0	4.0
1780–90	2,158.7	1,014.3	39.3	24.6	14.7	37.4
1790–	3,173.0	—	—	—	—	—

Notes: RNI hypothesized, RNM residual. Rates per 1,000 beginning decade population per year. RTI = rate of total increase; RNI = rate of natural increase (a population weighted average of the R figures presented in Table 5.8); RNM = rate of net international migration calculated as a residual (RNM = RTI − RNI). The rates of net migration in this table are lower-bound estimates since they are derived using rates of natural increase that are the weighted averages of the R's in Table 5.8. Such weighted averages do not take account of the interaction between seasoning and passage mortalities, and migrant numbers; that is, the S in the migration equation. Rates of net migration cannot be directly calculated from the M series of Table 5.8 without introducing a circularity into the calculations, i.e., first assuming rates of natural increase to derive residual M's in Table 5.8, then using those inferred M's to derive residual RNI's in Table 5.9. To avoid that circularity, this table treats RNM as a residual, but it should be noted that the effect is to generate an M series lower than that in Table 8.9 – lower by an average of some 16%.

Sources: Column 1, 2, and 3 are from Table 5.1; column 4 calculated from Table 5.8 as regional RNI's weighted by population shares.

the immediately following decades, 1790–1820.[79] In comparison, England over those same decades had a rate of natural increase averaging 1.33 percent.[80]

As the settlement process would suggest, the rate of net migration fell from the high levels of the early settlement decades to relatively low levels of the eighteenth century. During the first nine decades of settlement, migration accounted for nearly three-quarters of the rate of population increase, though that figure is biased upward by the very high proportions arising from the small bases of the first three decades. By the eighteenth century, net migration accounted for an average of only 14.2% of the rate of total increase in population. While that aggregate figure points to the dominance of natural increase in accounting for eighteenth-century population growth, it also obscures the wide regional differences that existed. The average rates of net migration to the middle colonies and the South in the eighteenth century were nearly seven times larger than the rate for New England. New England actually experienced a net out-migration – largely to New York State – in five of the nine decades from 1700 to 1790. Not surprisingly, then, net migration accounted for little, 0.7%, of New England's rate of total increase. For the middle colonies and the South, however, net migration accounted for, respectively, 20% and 17% of the rates of total increase in the regions.

Thus the sources of population growth changed over time and differed significantly by region. Despite the high mortalities of the South, natural increase did predominate as the prime cause of growth in the eighteenth century for all regions. The causes of the rapid natural increase experienced first in New England and then in the middle and southern colonies were several: one was the early marriage patterns that Franklin postulated. Despite the delayed marriages resulting from the strictures of indentured servant contracts, the average age at marriage was lower than in England for both males and females, though the latter's marriage opportunities were considerably greater, given the male surpluses characterizing the colonies, particularly those in which indentured servant flows were heavy. The result of earlier marriages was the relatively high fertility rates reflected in the mean completed family sizes that ranged from six to eight, as compared with the five in England. Higher fertility, though, was not the only

---

[79] Haines, "Population of the United States," Table I. The comparison is not a precise one since Haines calculates his rates on the midperiod population figures, whereas beginning-period populations are used in Table 5.10.

[80] Wrigley and Schofield, *Population History of England*, calculated from Table A 3.3.

cause of higher natural increase. As noted earlier, the unbalanced sex ratios in the colonial population structures meant that the proportion of women who never married was quite low.[81] As with early marriage, the higher proportion of the population married added to fertility. A further factor boosted natural increase rates. Mortality levels – outside the South and outside urban areas – were relatively low and thus directly raised natural increase levels. The growth of the white population is thus the summed effects of substantial immigration in the early years followed by substantial natural increase in the second century of development.

BIBLIOGRAPHICAL ESSAY

Two surveys of colonial population change and economic change are prime sources of data and bibliographic material on the white population. John J. McCusker and Russell R. Menard's, *The Economy of British North America, 1607–1789* (Chapel Hill and London, 1985) devotes one chapter to the growth of population, white and black, and also includes chapters on regional patterns with the most recently revised population figures for colonial populations. The second major survey is David W. Galenson, "The settlement and growth of the colonies: Population, labor and economic development," in Stanley L. Engerman and Robert Gallman (eds.), *The Cambridge Economic History of North America* (forthcoming). Galenson's work is particularly valuable for its treatment of the labor force and wealth aspects of population change in the period. An older but still valuable survey of eighteenth-century population change is J. Potter, "The growth of population in America, 1700–1860," in D. V. Glass and D. E. C. Eversley (eds.) *Population in History* (London, 1965). See also Potter's subsequent survey of colonial demographic history, "Demographic development and family structure," in Jack P. Greene and J. R. Pole (eds.), *Colonial British America* (Baltimore, 1983) 123–56.

Estimates of colonial population totals appear in a series of three works that have provided the basis for the population statistics in *Historical Statistics of the United States, Colonial Times to 1970, Part II* (Washington, D.C., 1975). The first is W. S. Rossiter, *A Century of Population Growth* (Washington, D.C., 1909). Rossiter's work was followed by that of Evarts B. Greene and Virginia D. Harrington, *American Population before the*

---

[81] For data on the never-married proportions, see Wells, "Population of England's Colonies," p. 91.

Federal Census of 1790 (New York, 1932), whose population series benefited from the work of Stella H. Sutherland. Sutherland's own work is *Population Distribution in Colonial America* (New York, 1936). The Greene-Harrington-Sutherland series has been revised in portions, by McCusker and Menard most recently, but much of the original series continues in place. Though not offering a comprehensive population series of his own, Robert V. Wells has inventoried the extant colonial censuses and provided considerable additional demographic data in *The Population of the British Colonies in America before 1776* (Princeton, 1975).

Vital rate data are available largely in local studies. The one exception to that is the genealogical sampling that draws on a wider population base. Prime local studies begin with those done for New England towns and regions. They include John Demos, *A Little Commonwealth: Family Life in Plymouth Colony* (New York, 1970); Philip Greven, Jr., *Four Generations: Population, Land and Family in Colonial Andover, Massachusetts* (Ithaca, N.Y., 1970); Kenneth A. Lockridge, "The population of Dedham Massachusetts, 1636–1736," *Economic History Review* 19 (1966), 318–44; Edward Byers, "Fertility Transition in a New England Commerical Center: Nantucket, Massachusetts, 1680–1840," *Journal of Interdisciplinary History* 13 (1982), 17–40; Susan Norton, "Population growth in Colonial America: A study of Ipswich, Massachusetts," *Population Studies* 25 (1971), 433–52; Nancy Osterud and John Fulton, "Family limitation and age at marriage: Fertility decline in Sturbridge, Massachusetts 1730–1850," *Population Studies 30 (1976)*, 481–94; Daniel Scott Smith, "Population, family and society in Hingham, Massachusetts, 1635–1880" (unpublished Ph.D. dissertation, University of California, Berkeley, 1973); H. Temkin-Greener and A. C. Swedlund, "Fertility transition in the Connecticut Valley: 1740–1850," *Population Studies* 32 (1978), 27–41; Robert Paul Thomas and Terry L. Anderson, "White population, labor force, and extensive growth of the New England economy in the seventeenth century," *Journal of Economic History* 33 (September 1973), 634–61; and R. Higgs and H. L. Stettler, "Colonial New England demography: A sampling approach," *William and Mary Quarterly* 27 (1970), 282–94. For the latter part of the eighteenth century, see Maris A. Vinovskis, *Fertility in Massachusetts from the Revolution to the Civil War* (New York, 1981). See also Vinovskis, "Mortality rates and trends in Massachusetts before 1860," *Journal of Economic History* 32 (1972), 184–213. For a survey of the New England region, see Daniel Scott Smith, "The demographic history of Colonial New England," *Journal of Economic History* 32 (1972), 165–83.

Our knowledge of the demographic history of the Chesapeake region has improved dramatically with notable studies in the past two decades. See Lorena S. Walsh and Russell R. Menard, "Death in the Chesapeake: Two life tables for men in Early Colonial Maryland," *Maryland Historical Magazine* (1974), 211–27; Russell R. Menard, "Immigrants and their increase: The process of population growth in Early Colonial Maryland," in Aubrey Land, Lois Carr, and Edward Papenfuse (eds.), *Law, Society, and Politics in Early Maryland* (Baltimore, 1977), 88–110; Darrett B. Rutman and Anita H. Rutman, "Of agues and fevers: Malaria in the Early Chesapeake," *William and Mary Quarterly* 33 (1976), 31–60; and "More true and perfect lists: The reconstruction of the census for Middlesex County, Virginia, 1668–1704," *Virginia Magazine of History and Biography* 88 (1980), 37–74; and *A Place in Time: Middlesex County, Virginia, 1650–1750* (New York, 1984); Daniel S. Levy, "The life expectancies of Colonial Maryland legislators," *Historical Methods* 20 (1987), 17–28 and "The economic demography of the Colonial South" (unpublished Ph.D. dissertation, University of Chicago, 1991); Carville D. Earle, "Environment, disease, and mortality in Early Virginia," in Thad W. Tate and David L. Ammerman (eds.), *The Chesapeake in the Seventeenth Century* (Chapel Hill, N.C., 1979); Daniel Blake Smith, "Mortality and family in the Colonial Chesapeake," *Journal of Interdisciplinary History* 8 (1978), 403–27.

Vital rate data on the middle colonies are relatively sparse. What there is tends to center on Philadelphia and the Quaker experience. For an excellent bibliography, see Susan E. Klepp, *The Swift Progress of Population: A Documentary and Bibliographic Study of Philadelphia's Growth, 1642–1859* (Philadelphia, 1991). See also Klepp's Ph.D. dissertation, "Philadelphia in transition: A demographic history of the city and its occupational groups, 1720–1830" (University of Pennsylvania, 1980). For eighteenth-century vital rates, population totals, and natural increase for Philadelphia, see Billy G. Smith, "Death and life in a colonial immigrant city: A demographic analysis of Philadelphia," *Journal of Economic History* 37 (1977), 863–89. Other articles include Gary B. Nash and Billy G. Smith, "The population of eighteenth-century Philadelphia," *Pennsylvania Magazine of History and Biography* 99 (1975), 362–68; Sharon W. Salinger and Charles Wetherell, "A note on the population of Pre-Revolutionary Philadelphia," *Pennsylvania Magazine of History and Biography* 109 (1985), 369–86; Robert V. Wells, "Demographic change and the life cycle of American families," *Journal of Interdisciplinary History* 11 (1971), 273–82, his "Family size and fertility control in eighteenth century America: A study of Quaker families," *Population Studies* 25 (1971), 73–83, and "Quaker marriage patterns in a colonial perspective," *William and Mary Quarterly* 29 (1972), 415–42; Louise Kantrow, "The demographic history of colonial aristocracy: A Philadelphia case study" (Ph.D. dissertation, University of Pennsylvania, 1976), and "Philadelphia gentry: fertility and family limitation among an American aristocracy," *Population Studies* 34 (1980), 21–30.

The movement beyond intensive, localized demographic studies requires a broader data base. The Genealogical Library of the Church of Jesus Christ of Latter-day Saints in Salt Lake City has provided just that prospect. Large-scale sampling of these genealogical records and a linking of those samples with other data – probate records, military and maritime records, and census materials – has given researchers a further way to analyze white population mortality and fertility. The starting point for examining this research is Robert W. Fogel et al., "The economics of mortality in North America, 1650–1910: A description of a research project," *Historical Methods* 11 (1978), 75–108. For a subsequent report on the outcome of the mortality study, see Robert W. Fogel, "Nutrition and the decline in mortality since 1700: Some preliminary findings," in Stanley L. Engerman and Robert E. Gallman (eds.), *Long-term Factors in American Economic Growth* (Chicago, 1986), 439–555. For a report on fertility patterns deriving from that project, see Jenny Borne Wahl, "New results on the decline in household fertility in the United States from 1750 to 1900," in Engerman and Gallman, 391–437. A further report on late-eighteenth-century mortality, also stemming from the project, is Clayne L. Pope, "Adult mortality in America before 1900: A view from family histories," in Claudia Goldin and Hugh Rockoff (eds.), *Strategic Factors in Nineteenth-Century Economic History* (Chicago, 1992), 267–96.

There have been few attempts to model fertility patterns. The major example is one that focuses on the nineteenth century but also extends its estimates back through the last four decades of the eighteenth century. See Morton O. Schapiro, "Land availability and fertility in the United States, 1760–1870," *Journal of Economic History* 42 (1982), 577–600.

Migration studies, like those of vital rates, necessarily draw on the historical materials available and thus are specific in time, in labor form, and/or by nationality. There are a sizable number of excellent studies, of which the following sampling is far from inclusive: Abbot Emerson Smith, *Colonists in Bondage: White Servitude and Convict Labor in America, 1607–1776* (Chapel Hill, N.C., 1947); R. J. Dickson, *Ulster Emigration to Colonial America 1718–1775* (London, 1966); Mildred Campbell, "English emigration on the eve of the American Revolution," *American Historical Review* 61 (1955), 1–20; David Galenson, *White Servitude in Colonial America* (Cambridge, England, 1981); David Souden, "'Rogues, whores and vagabonds'? Indentured servant emigrants to North America, and the case of mid-seventeenth-century Bristol," *Social History* 3 (1978), 23–41; Russell R. Menard, "British Migration to the Chesapeake Colonies in the seventeenth century," in Lois Green Carr, Philip D. Morgan, and Jean B. Russo, (eds.), *Colonial Chesapeake Society* (Chapel Hill, 1988), 99–132; James Horn, "To parts beyond the seas: Free emigration to the Chesapeake in the seventeenth century," in Ida Altman and James Horn (eds.), *To Make America* (Berkeley, 1991); Bernard Bailyn, *The Peopling of British North America* (New York, 1986) and *Voyagers to the West: A Passage in the Peopling of America on the Eve of the Revolution* (New York, 1986); Marianne Wokeck, "The flow and the composition of German immigration to Philadelphia, 1727–1775," *Pennsylvania Magazine of History and Biography* 105 (1981), 249–78; Farley Grubb, "The incidence of servitude in trans-Atlantic migration, 1771–1804," *Explorations in Economic History* 22 (July 1985), 249–75, "Immigrant servant labor: Their occupational and geographic distribution in the late eighteenth-century Mid-Atlantic economy," *Social Science History* 9 (Summer 1985) 249–75, and "Redemptioner immigration to Pennsylvania: Evidence on contract choice and profitability," *Journal of Economic History* 46 (June 1986), 407–18; Hans-Jürgen Grabbe, "European immigration to the United States in the Early National period, 1793–1820," *Proceedings of the American Philosophical Society* 133, 2 (1989), 190–214; Aaron Fogleman, "Migrations to the thirteen British North American colonies, 1700–1775: New estimates," *Journal of Interdisciplinary History* 22, 4 (Spring 1992), 691–709; Henry A. Gemery, "Markets for migrants: English indentured servitude and emigration in the seventeenth and eighteenth centuries," in *Colonialism and Migration: Indentured Labour before and after Slavery* (1986).

As the text notes, assembling this mosaic of migration studies into a comprehensible picture of aggregate immigration into the colonies is an impossibility. Inferred numbers of immigrants can be derived from other demographic data. Such series are estimated in Robert W. Fogel et al., "The economics of mortality in North America, 1650–1910: A description of a research project," *Historical Methods* 11 (1978). Note Table B.2 and associated discussion. See also Henry A. Gemery, "Emigration from the British Isles to the New World, 1630–1700: Inferences from colonial populations," *Research in Economic History* 5 (1980), 179–231, and "European emigration to North America, 1700–1820: Numbers and quasi-numbers," *Perspectives in American History, New Series* 1 (1984), 283–342; David Galenson, *White Servitude in Colonial America* (Cambridge, England, 1981), Appendix H.

Studies of internal migration for the colonial period are rare. The Villaflor and Sokoloff sampling of militia records offers the most extensive data on internal migration for the period. See Gloria C. Villaflor and Kenneth L. Sokoloff, "Migration in Colonial America: Evidence from the militia muster rolls," *Social Science History* 6 (1982), 539–70. See also John W. Adams and Alice B. Kasakoff, "Migration of the family in Colonial New England: The view from genealogies," *Journal of Family History* 9 (1984), 24–43, and "Wealth and migration in Massachusetts and Maine," *Journal of Economic History* 45 (1985), 363–68.

Few studies specifically address the passage and seasoning mortalities experienced by colonial immigrants. Such data as there are (see the text), are incidental pieces of other historical work. For an example, see Edmund S. Morgan, *American Slavery, American Freedom* (New York, 1975), Chapter 8. One recent study that does specifically address passage mortality is Farley Grubb, "Morbidity and mortality on the North Atlantic passage: Eighteenth-century German immigration to Pennsylvania," *Journal of Interdisciplinary History* 17 (1987), 565–85. A major quantitative study focusing on the "relocation costs" encountered by Europeans moving overseas covers only the nineteenth century and only military personnel posted to the tropics. See Philip D. Curtin, *Death by Migration* (Cambridge, England, 1989).

REFERENCES

Adams, John W., and Alice B. Kasakoff. "Migration of the Family in Colonial New England: The View from Genealogies." *Journal of Family History* 9 (1984): 24–43.
———. "Wealth and Migration in Massachusetts and Maine." *Journal of Economic History* 45 (1985): 363–6.
Bailyn, Bernard. *The Peopling of British North America: An Introduction.* New York, 1986.
———. *Voyagers to the West: A Passage in the Peopling of America on the Eve of the Revolution.* New York, 1986.
Campbell, Mildred. "English Emigration on the Eve of the American Revolution." *American Historical Review* 61 (1955): 1–20.
Carr, Lois Green. "Emigration and the Standard of Living: the Seventeenth Century Chesapeake." *Journal of Economic History* 52 (1992): 271–91.
Carr, Louis, Green, and Lorena S. Walsh. "The Planter's Wife, The Experience of White

Women in Seventeenth-Century Maryland." *William and Mary Quarterly* 34 (1977): 542–71.

Carter, Edward C. II. "A 'Wild Irishman' under Every Federalist's Bed: Naturalization in Philadelphia, 1789–1806." *Proceedings of the American Philosophical Society*, 133, 2 (1989): 178–89.

Cassedy, John H. *Demography in Early America.* Cambridge, Mass. 1969.

Curtin, Philip D. *The Atlantic Slave Trade: A Census.* Madison, Wisc., 1969.

Demos, John. *A Little Commonwealth: Family Life in Plymouth Colony.* New York, 1970.

Dickson, R. J. *Ulster Emigration to Colonial America, 1718–1775.* London, 1966.

Duffy, J. *Epidemics in Colonial America.* Port Washington, N.Y., 1953.

Earle, Carville V. "Environment, Disease, and Mortality in Early Virginia." In *The Chesapeake in the Seventeenth Century,* edited by Thad W. Tate and David L. Ammerman. Chapel Hill, N.C., 1979.

Fogel, Robert W. "Nutrition and the Decline in Mortality since 1700: Some Preliminary Findings." In *Long-term Factors in American Economic Growth.* Chicago, 1986.

Fogel, Robert W., and Stanley L. Engerman. *Time on the Cross: The Economics of American Negro Slavery.* Boston, 1974.

———. *Time on the Cross: Evidence and Methods – A Supplement.* Boston, 1974.

Fogel, Robert W., Stanley L. Engerman, James Trussell, et al. "The Economics of Mortality in North America, 1650–1910: A Description of a Research Project." *Historical Methods* 11 (1978): 75–108.

Fogleman, Aaron. "Migrations to the Thirteen British North American Colonies, 1700–1775: New Estimates." *Journal of Interdisciplinary History* 225 (Spring 1992): 691–709.

Franklin, Benjamin. *The Papers of Benjamin Franklin.* Vol. 4, edited by Leonard W. Larabee. New Haven: 1961. Vol. 15, edited by William B. Willcox. New Haven, 1972.

Galenson, David. *White Servitude in Colonial America.* Cambridge, England, 1981.

———. "The Settlement and Growth of the Colonies: Population, Labor, and Economic Development." In *The Cambridge Economic History of the United States.* Vol. 1: *The Colonial Era,* edited by Stanley L. Engerman and Robert E. Gallman. Cambridge, England, 1996.

Gemery, Henry A. "Emigration from the British Isles to the New World, 1630–1700: Inferences from Colonial Populations." *Research in Economic History* 5 (1980): 179–231.

———. "European Emigration to North America, 1700–1820: Numbers and Quasi-numbers." *Perspectives in American History,* N.S. 1 (1984): 283–342.

———. "Markets for Migrants: English Indentured Servitude and Emigration in the Seventeenth and Eighteenth Centuries." In *Colonialism and Migration: Indentured Labour before and after Slavery,* edited by P. C. Emmer. Dordrecht, Netherlands, 1986.

Grabbe, Hans-Jürgen. "European Immigration to the United States in the Early National Period, 1783–1820." *Proceedings of the American Philosophical Society* 133, 2 (1989): 190–214.

Greene, Evarts B., and Virginia D. Harrington. *American Population before the Federal Census of 1790.* New York, 1932.

Gragg, Larry Dale. *Migration in Early America: The Virginia Quaker Experience.* Ann Arbor, 1980.

Greven, Philip J., Jr. *Four Generations: Population, Land and Family in Colonial Andover, Massachusetts.* Ithaca, N.Y., 1970.

Grubb, Farley W. Immigration and Servitude in the Colony and Commonwealth of Pennsylvania: A Quantitative and Economic Analysis." Ph.D. diss., University of Chicago, 1984.

———. "Immigrant Servant Labor: Their Occupational and Geographic Distribution in the Late Eighteenth-Century Mid-Atlantic Economy." *Social Science History* 9 (Summer 1985): 249–75.

———. "The Incidence of Servitude in Trans-Atlantic Migration, 1771–1804." *Explorations in Economic History* 22 (July 1985): 249–75.

———. "The Market for Indentured Immigrants: Evidence on the Efficiency of Forward-Labor Contracting in Philadelphia 1745–1773." *Journal of Economic History* 45 (1985): 855–68.

———. "Redemptioner Immigration to Pennsylvania: Evidence on Contract Choice and Profitability." *Journal of Economic History* 46 (June 1986): 407–18.

———. "Morbidity and Mortality on the North Atlantic Passage: Eighteenth-Century German Immigration to Pennsylvania." *Journal of Interdisciplinary History* 17 (Winter 1987): 565–85.

Haines, Michael R. "The Population of the United States, 1790–1920." In *The Long Nineteenth Century: Cambridge Economic History of The United States*. Vol. 2, edited by Stanley L. Engerman and Robert E. Gallman. Forthcoming.

Hansen, Marcus Lee. *The Atlantic Migration, 1607–1860*. Cambridge, Mass., 1951.

Hening, W. W., ed. *The Statutes at Large: Being a Collection of All the Laws of Virginia*. Vol. 2. Charlottesville, Va., 1823; repr., 1969.

Henripin, J. *La Population canadienne au début du XVIII siècle nuptialité-fecondité-mortalité infantile*. Paris, 1954.

Henry, Louis. *Manuel de Demographic Historique*. Paris, 1970.

Higgs, R., and H. L. Stettler. "Colonial New England Demography: A Sampling Approach." *William and Mary Quarterly* 27 (1970): 282–94.

Horn, James. "To Parts beyond the Seas: Free Emigration to the Chesapeake in the Seventeenth Century." In *"To Make America," European Emigration in the Early Modern Period*, edited by Ida Altman and James Horn. Berkeley, 1991.

———. *Adapting to a New World: English Society in the Seventeenth Century Chesapeake*. Chapel Hill, 1994.

House of Lords, Record Office Paper. *An Account of the Number of Troops Sent to the West Indies from 1775 to the Year 1782*. December 14, 1792.

Jones, Alice Hanson. *Wealth of a Nation to Be: The American Colonies on the Eve of the Revolution*. New York, 1980.

———. "Wealth and Growth of the Thirteen Colonies: Some Implications." *Journal of Economic History* 44 (1984): 239–54.

Kantrow, Louise. "The Demographic History of Colonial Aristocracy: A Philadelphia Case Study." Ph.D. diss., University of Pennsylvania, 1976.

———. "Philadelphia Gentry: Fertility and Family Limitation among an American Aristocracy." *Population Studies* 34 (1980): 21–30.

Klepp, Susan E. *The Swift Progress of Population, A Documentary and Bibliographic Study of Philadelphia's Growth, 1642–1859*. Philadelphia, 1991.

———. "Zachariah Poulson's Bills of Mortality, 1788–1801." In *Life in Early Philadelphia*, edited by Billy G. Smith. University Park, Pa., 1995.

Knittle, W. A. *Early Eighteenth-Century Palatine Emigration*. Philadelphia, 1937.

Kunitz, Stephen J. "Mortality Change in America, 1620–1920." *Human Biology* 56 (1984): 559–82.

Lawson, Thomas. "Statistical Report on the Sickness and Mortality in the Army of the United States." Washington, 1840. In *Essays on the Progress of Nations*, edited by Ezra C. Seaman. New York, 1852.

Levy, Daniel S. "The Life Expectancies of Colonial Maryland Legislators." *Historical Methods* 20 (1987): 17–27.

Lockridge, Kenneth A. "The Population of Dedham Massachusetts, 1636–1736." *Economic History Review* 19 (1966): 318–44.

McCusker, John J., and Russel R. Menard. *The Economy of British North America, 1607–1789* Chapel Hill, N.C., 1985.

Malthus, T. R. *An Essay on the Principle of Population.* London, 1798. Reprint for the Royal Economic Society London, 1926.

Menard, Russell R. "From Servant to Freeholder: Status Mobility and Property Accumulation in Seventeenth-Century Maryland." *William and Mary Quarterly* 30 (1973): 37–68.

———. "Immigration into the Chesapeake Colonies in the Seventeenth Century: A Review Essay." *Maryland History Magazine* 68 (1973).

———. "Immigrants and Their Increase: The Process of Population Growth in Early Colonial Maryland." In *Law, Society, and Politics in Early Maryland*, edited by Aubrey Land, Lois Carr, and Edward Papenfuse, pp. 88–110. Baltimore, 1977.

———. "British Migration to the Chesapeake Colonies in the Seventeenth Century." In *Colonial Chesapeake Society*, edited by Lois Green Carr, Philip D. Morgan, and Jean B. Russo, pp. 99–132. Chapel Hill, 1988.

———. "Was There a 'Middle Colonies Demographic Regime'?" *Proceedings of the American Philosophical Society* 133, 2 (1989).

Menard, Russell R., and Lorena Walsh. "Death in the Chesapeake: Two Life Tables for Men in Early Colonial Maryland." *Maryland Historical Magazine* 69 (1974): 211–27.

Miller, Henry, M. "An Archeological Perspective on the Evolution of Diet in the Colonial Chesapeake, 1620–1745." In *Colonial Chesapeake Society*, edited by Louis Green Carr, Philip D. Morgan, and Gene D. Russo, pp. 176–99. Chapel Hill, N.C., 1988.

Morgan, Edmund S. *American Slavery American Freedom.* New York, 1975.

Nash, Gray B., and Billy G. Smith. "The Population of Eighteenth-Century Philadelphia." *Pennsylvania Magazine of History and Biography* 99 (1975): 362–8.

Norton, Susan. "Population Growth in Colonial America: A Study of Ipswich Massachusetts." *Population Studies* 25: (1971): 433–52.

Osterud, Nancy, and John Fulton. "Family Limitation and Age at Marriage: Fertility Decline in Sturbridge, Massachusetts 1730–1850." *Population Studies* 30 (1976): 481–94.

Pope, Clayne L. "Adult Mortality in America before 1900: A View from Family Histories." In *Strategic Factors in Nineteenth Century Economic History* edited by Claudia Goldin and Hugh Rockoff, pp. 267–96. Chicago, 1992.

Potter J. "The Growth of Population in America, 1700–1860." In *Population in History*, edited by D. V. Glass and D. E. C. Eversley. London, 1965.

———. "Demographic Development and Family Structure." In *Colonial British America*, edited by Jack P. Greene and J. R. Pole. Baltimore, 1984.

Rossiter, W. S. *A Century of Population Growth.* Washington, 1909.

Rutman, Darrett B., and Anita H. Rutman. "Of Agues and Fevers: Malaria in the Early Chesapeake." *William and Mary Quarterly* 33 (1976): 31–60.

———. " 'New-wives and Sons-in-law': Parental Death in Seventeenth-Century Virginia County." In *The Chesapeake in the Seventeenth Century: Essays on Anglo-American Society and Politics,* edited by Thad W. Tate and David L. Ammerman, pp. 153–82. Chapel Hill, 1979.

———. "More True and Perfect Lists: The Reconstruction of the Census for Middlesex County, Virginia, 1668–1704." *Virginia Magazine of History and Biography* 88 (1980): 37–74.

———. *A Place in Time: Middlesex County, Virginia, 1650–1750.* New York, 1984.

Sadler, Michael Thomas. *The Law of Population, A Treatise in Six Books in Disproof of the Superfecundity of Human Beings and Developing the Real Principle of Their Increase.* London, 1830.

Salinger, Sharon W., and Charles Wetherell. "A Note on the Population of Pre-Revolutionary Philadephia." *Pennsylvania Magazine of History and Biography* 109 (1985): 369–86.

Schapiro, Morton O. "Land Availability and Fertility in the United States, 1760–1870." *Journal of Economic History* 42 (1982): 577–600.

———. "Economic Development and Population Growth: Implications from a Model of U.S. Demographic History." *Development Economics Research Memorandum* 98. Williams College, Mass., 1985.

———. "A General Dynamic Model of Nineteenth Century U.S. Population Change." *Economic Modeling* 2 (1985): 347–56.

Smith, Abbot Emerson. *Colonists in Bondage: White Servitude and Convict Labor in America, 1607–1776.* Chapel Hill, N.C., 1947.

Smith, Billy G. "Death and Life in a Colonial Immigrant City: A Demographic Analysis of Philadelphia." *Journal of Economic History* 37 (1977): 863–89.

Smith, Billy G., ed. *Life in Early Philadelphia: Documents from the Revolutionary and Early National Periods.* University Park, Pa., 1995.

Smith, Daniel Blake. "Mortality and Family in the Colonial Chesapeake." *Journal of Interdisciplinary History* 8, 3 (1978): 403–27.

Smith, Daniel Scott. "The Demographic History of Colonial New England." *Journal of Economic History* 32 (1972): 165–83.

Souden, David. " 'Rogues, Whores and Vagabonds'? Indentured Servant Emigrants to North America, and the Case of Mid-Seventeenth-Century Bristol." *Social History* 3 (1978): 23–41.

Steckel, Richard, H. "Nutritional Status in the Colonial American Economy," *William and Mary Quarterly* 56 (1999): 31–52.

———. "Stature and the Standard of Living." *Journal of Economic Literature* 33 (December 1995): 1903–40.

Stiles, Ezra. *Discourse on the Christian Union.* 1761.

Sutherland, Stella H. *Population Distribution in Colonial America.* New York, 1936.

Swedlund, A. C. "Fertility Transition in the Connecticut Valley: 1740–1850." *Population Studies* 32 (1978): 27–41.

Thomas, R., and T. L. Anderson. "White Population, Labor Force and Extensive Growth of the New England Economy in the Seventeenth Century." *Journal of Economic History* 33 (1973): 634–61.

U.S. Department of Commerce, Bureau of the Census. *Historical Statistics of the United States, Colonial Times to Present*, Parts 1 and 2. Washington, D.C.: Government Printing Office, 1975.

Villaflor, G. C., and K. L. Sokoloff. "Migration in Colonial America: Evidence from the Militia Muster Rolls." *Social Science History* 6 (1982): 539–70.

Vinovskis, Maris A. "Mortality Rates and Trends in Massachusetts before 1860." *Journal of Economic History* 32 (1972): 184–213.

———. *Fertility in Massachusetts from the Revolution to the Civil War*. New York, 1981.

Wahl, Jenny Bourne. "New Results on the Decline in Household Fertility in the United States from 1750 to 1900." In *Long Term Factors in American Economic Growth*, edited by Stanley L. Engerman and Robert E. Gallman. Chicago, 1986.

Walsh, Lorena, S. " 'Till Death Do Us Part': Marriage and Family in Seventeenth Century Maryland." In *The Chesapeake in the Seventeenth Century: Essays on Anglo-American Society and Politics*, edited by Thad W. Tate and David L. Ammerman, pp. 126–52. Chapel Hill, N.C., 1979.

Wells, Robert V. "Demographic Change and the Life Cycle of American Families." *Journal of Interdisciplinary History* 11 (1971): 273–82.

———. "Family Size and Fertility Control in Eighteenth Century America: A Study of Quaker Families." *Population Studies* 25 (1971): 73–83.

———. "Quaker Marriage Patterns in a Colonial Perspective." *William and Mary Quarterly* 29 (1972): 415–42.

———. *The Population of the British Colonies in America before 1776*. Cambridge, England, 1975.

———. "The Population of England's Colonies in America: Old English or New Americans?" *Population Studies* 46 (1992): 85–102.

Wigglesworth, Edward the Younger. *Calculations on the American Population*. 1775.

Willcox, Walter F. *International Migrations*. Vol. 2: *Interpretations*. New York, 1931.

Wokeck, Marianne. "The Flow and the Composition of German Immigration to Philadelphia, 1727–1775." *Pennsylvania Magazine of History and Biography* 105 (1981): 249–78.

———. "Irish Immigration to the Delaware Valley before the American Revolution." *Proceedings of the Royal Irish Academy*, 96, C, no. 5 (1996): 103–35.

Wrigley, E. A., and R. S. Schofield. *The Population History of England, 1541–1871: A Reconstruction*. London, 1981.

Yasuba, Y. *Birth Rates of the White Population in the United States, 1800–1860: An Economic Study*. Baltimore, 1962.

6

THE AFRICAN AMERICAN POPULATION OF THE COLONIAL UNITED STATES

LORENA S. WALSH

Current understanding of the population history of African Americans in the colonial United States is decidedly, if predictably, uneven. All but a tiny minority of the several million Africans who moved from the Old World to North America before 1790 did so involuntarily. Intensive study of the slave trade has yielded what two recent scholars have assessed as better documentation of the flow of Africans to the British American colonies (and also to French and later Spanish Louisiana) across this period than is available for comparable trans-Atlantic migrants of European origin.[1] On the other hand, we know much less about the collective demographic fortunes of men, women, and children of African origin, or of their American-born descendants, than we do about the contemporary colonial white population. To the extent that the population history of African Americans in the various colonial regions of the present United States can be derived from information about migrant flows across two centuries, we are on relatively firm ground, comparatively speaking. That is to say, rough generalizations are possible.

Conversely, our understanding of the subsequent demographic experience of Africans and African Americans in early America is decidedly limited. This bifurcation of information is a direct result of the economic and social relations of slavery. In the surviving historical record, African Americans, when and where they figured as commodities, are comparatively well documented. Estimating the size and composition of the black

---

[1] McCusker and Menard, *The Economy of British America, 1607–1789*, p. 224. Publication of *The Trans-Atlantic Slave Trade: A Database on CD-ROM* will assuredly promote further studies of the trade. Preliminary descriptions of the database are in Eltis and Richardson, eds., *Routes to Slavery*; Eltis and Richardson, "Productivity in the Transatlantic Slave Trade"; and in Eltis, Richardson, and Behrendt, "The Structure of the Transatlantic Slave Trade, 1595–1867."

population in various localities over time poses many of the same problems encountered for other groups. There are few true colony-wide censuses, and some of these are far from reliable. The more numerous partial counts of taxables that survive for various civil divisions of the mainland colonies require the use of multiples to arrive at total population, an error-prone procedure, and further interpolation to produce colony-wide estimates.[2] But since all adult slaves, both men and women, and from time to time youngsters between the ages of 12 and 15 as well, were subject to a head tax, counts of taxables indeed provide more comprehensive information about the size and composition of the slave population than they do about the free.

Otherwise, evidence is sparse, often intractable, and frequently nonexistent. Some understanding of the individual life courses of African Americans, for example, can only in exceptional circumstances be recovered from surviving documentary sources. Often individuals are not identified by name, and when they are, only by a single given name; thus the possibilities of family reconstitution, which have yielded rich information about colonial whites, can almost never be employed to reconstruct the life experiences of blacks. As a result, most scholars interested in sharply focused demographic questions have restricted their work to the antebellum years for which adequate evidence is more readily available. Consequently, most investigations of early African American population history have remained the province of social historians who usually have scant training in demographic techniques, and whose primary interests have turned to other topics for which population history is, at best, only part of the overall background.

POPULATION DISTRIBUTION AND GROWTH

The distribution of African American peoples in the mainland colonies can be accounted for in large part by the differing labor requirements of the various regional economies that elicited quite differing migration flows. Slave labor (and other forms of bound labor, including European indentured servants, transported convicts, and prisoners of European wars) were essential to the production of various staple export crops –

[2] McCusker and Menard, *The Economy of British America*, pp. 214–15.

Table 6.1. *Percentage of African Americans in the total population of the British colonies, 1660–1790*

Year	New England	Middle Colonies	Upper South	Lower South
1660	1.7	11.5	3.6	2.0
1700	1.8	6.8	13.1	17.6
1740	2.9	7.5	28.3	46.5
1780	2.0	5.9	38.6	41.2
1790	1.7	6.2	37.6	32.6

Sources: McCusker and Menard, *The Economy of British America*, p. 222; *Return of the Whole Number of Persons within the Several Districts of the United States* (Washington, D.C., 1802).

tobacco, naval stores, indigo, and rice – that at first enabled the more southerly continental North American settlements to become established and eventually to expand. By the last quarter of the eighteenth century, slaves were also involved in the production for export of wheat, iron, and timber products in the Upper and Lower South, and were employed in large-scale mixed agriculture in New York, New Jersey, and Rhode Island.

In contrast, bound labor was seldom used on the smaller farms or in the fisheries and other extractive industries of New England.

Marked differences in the number of bound laborers imported into the various regions initially determined whether the proportion of Africans in the total population was large or small. Subsequently, differences in the absolute size of the local black population, in the patterns of geographic and residential concentration, and in living and working conditions among those enslaved either facilitated or discouraged the growth of regional black populations through natural increase.[3]

Blacks made up less than 3% of New England's people across the colonial era, as shown in Table 6.1, and under 8% of the population of the middle colonies in the eighteenth century. The majority of these blacks lived and worked in a countryside where they were usually in a distinct minority. However a substantial percentage also lived in the major port cities, where they might constitute as much as one-third of the total urban population and perhaps one-half of the workforce.[4] By 1790, three-

---

[3] Overall population patterns are summarized in McCusker and Menard, *The Economy of British America*, chap. 10; specific regional patterns are discussed in chaps. 5 through 9. See also Berlin, "Time, Space, and the Evolution of Afro-American Society," and Berlin, *Many Thousands Gone*.

[4] Nash, "Forging Freedom"; Piersen, *Black Yankees*, chap. 2.

quarters of New England blacks were free. In the former middle colonies, nearly three-quarters of black residents were still enslaved, although their offspring who survived to adult years were eventually freed through gradual manumission in the 1800s through the 1840s.[5]

In contrast to the more northerly colonies, blacks became an important part of the South's population by the early eighteenth century, and by 1790 made up one-third of the total, almost all permanently enslaved. By then, both the Upper and Lower South included some areas where blacks were in the majority. In the most extreme case, the rice-growing districts of the Lower South, the racial composition of the local population approached that of the overwhelmingly black West Indian sugar islands. In 1790, for example, the population of all but two lowland South Carolina parishes was more than 70% black.[6] On the other hand, in parts of the upland South most recently taken up by Europeans, blacks formed only a small percentage of the resident population of Old World origin.

During the colonial era, free persons of color accounted for no more than 5% of the black population. The founders of most of these families were free immigrants or former slaves who had established free status in the 1600s. Many were of mixed ancestry; some were the children of free white men and slave women, but the majority were probably the descendants of free white mothers and slave fathers. Around the turn of the eighteenth century, the main slave colonies established stringent prohibitions against further manumissions. Consequently in the South the number of free blacks remained relatively small. During or shortly after the American Revolution, the New England and mid-Atlantic states (Delaware excepted) enacted either immediate or gradual emancipation, and the states of the Upper South for a time relaxed restrictions on manumissions. Between the 1770s and 1790s the free black population grew rapidly in all but the Lower South. Free black communities soon included both growing numbers of recently emancipated slaves and families with a long history of freedom. The majority continued to live in the countryside, but a disproportionate number relative to the size of the group remained in or moved into coastal cities, where they found greater opportunities for employment than in rural areas and better chances for establishing private lives freer of white interference.

[5] Nash and Soderlund, *Freedom by Degrees*; and Fogel and Engerman, "Philanthropy at Bargain Prices."

[6] Morgan, "The Development of Slave Culture," chap. 1.

IMMIGRATION

Scholars of the international slave trade have estimated migration indirectly, calculating the numbers of involuntary African migrants from data on the volume of trade between various European nations and Africa, from varying rates of mortality calculated over time for the trans-Atlantic voyage, from data on the numbers of slaves imported into the various Western Hemisphere colonies, and from estimates of the size and vital rates of African and African American populations in these colonies at various points in time.

Philip Curtin estimated 399,000 African slaves were brought to British North America between 1620 and 1810, and an additional 28,000 to Louisiana. This constituted only 4.5% of the total number of Africans forcibly transported to the Western Hemisphere in the era of the trans-Atlantic slave trade.[7] Robert Fogel and Stanley Engerman subsequently raised the estimated total brought to British North America to 596,000. Other recent estimates range from a low of 376,500 for the British colonies (523,000 if Louisiana is included), up to 623,000 (or 653,000 including Louisiana). Thus the basic "numbers game" is far from resolved.[8] Since the mainland received such a small fraction of the total number involved in the trade overall, most studies treat North America as a single destination. The migration flow into individual colonies is often not addressed.

District naval office records that report the number of slaves arriving on ships coming from other colonies or nations are the main source for the numbers of Africans imported into the various colonies. Additional information comes from the records of the Royal African Company (for the seventeenth century), and from newspaper notices and other scattered estimates in official reports and private papers. Although the surviving documents supply reasonable guides to the timing and to the overall volume of forced African migration into the various jurisdictions, the reported numbers of incoming slaves usually fall short of those estimated to have left Africa and survived the Middle Passage to arrive somewhere on the mainland. Documentation of any sort is particularly sparse for the

---

[7] Curtin, *The Atlantic Slave Trade*, pp. 88, 136–46.

[8] Fogel and Engerman, *Time on the Cross*, chap. 1, and *Time on the Cross: Evidence and Methods*, pp. 27–37. Fogel has subsequently revised estimates extrapolated from population growth rates upward (Fogel, "Revised Estimates of the U.S. Slave Trade"). Chambers, "'He Gwine Sing He Country,'" pp. 203–9, summarizes the recent estimates for North America.

seventeenth century; naval office records are much more complete for the eighteenth century, but there are still numerous gaps. Works dealing with the slave trade into individual colonies are cited in the bibliographical essay at the end of the chapter.

For many years, scholars judged the African origins of North American slaves too heterogeneous and too poorly documented to warrant close investigation. Highly unbalanced sex ratios are often adopted as the main indicator for a substantial African presence, and more equal proportions of males and females, of a primarily native-born population. Recently, however, analyses of the various African ports of departure contained in the trans-Atlantic slave trade data set, and, for individual colonies, in naval office records have yielded unexpectedly concrete information on the probable origins of many of the forcibly transported Africans. Large influxes of new African slaves usually arrived in a given colony over a relatively short time span, and often these migrants came primarily from just two or three areas in West Africa.[9]

Moreover, by the early eighteenth century, individual planters usually purchased the majority of the Africans in their workforce over an even shorter span of years. Correlating purchase records with shipping data often narrows probable regions of origin considerably. And more often than we have supposed, family papers provide evidence that can be pieced together to identify the places from which slaves on particular large plantations embarked, and the groups to which they belonged. Although the African population of a given colony as a whole was often composed of a bewildering variety of ethnic and linguistic groups, the origins of those living in particular localities may have been much more homogeneous than previously supposed.[10] Such information is particularly valuable for investigations of retained or constructed ethnicities and of African cultural carryovers and of African American cultural adjustments.

Immigration patterns are especially crucial to understanding the population history of African Americans throughout the New World. In all the plantation districts of the Americas, "demographic history tended to fall into a regular pattern over time."[11] This pattern reflects pronounced dif-

---

[9] Eltis and Richardson, "Productivity in the Transatlantic Slave Trade"; and Eltis, Richardson, and Behrendt, "The Structure of the Transatlantic Slave Trade, 1595–1867."

[10] Thornton, *Africa and Africans in the Making of the Atlantic World*, chap. 7; Gomez, *Exchanging Our Country Marks*; Chambers, "'He Gwine Sing He Country'"; Littlefield, *Rice and Slaves*; Hall, *Africans in Colonial Louisiana*; Kulikoff, "The Origins of Afro-American Society in Tidewater Maryland and Virginia"; Cody, "Slave Demography and Family Formation," chap. 1; Morgan, "Black Society in the Lowcountry"; Wax, "Preferences for Slaves in Colonial America"; and Walsh, *From Calabar to Carter's Grove*.

[11] Curtin, *Atlantic Slave Trade*, p. 29.

ferences between the reproductive performance of Africans and of their colonial-born offspring, with the proportion of Africans and creoles in a given local population largely determining the reproductive growth rate – ranging from net population loss without large and continued immigration, to, in exceptional cases, an end to further in-migration and rapid population growth from natural increase.[12]

In all the staple plantation colonies, the majority of African immigrants were male, and they suffered high rates of chronic sickness and early death in a new colonial disease environment where they were frequently subjected to exceptionally heavy labor and harsh discipline. Almost all male migrants from the Old World to the New, voluntary or involuntary, paid a high price for migrating in terms of possibilities for marrying, engendering and nurturing offspring, and living out a normal life. Slaves suffered disproportionately, given the initial emotional and physical trauma of capture in Africa and forced trans-Atlantic migration. After they arrived in the New World, they faced unhealthy work environments, harsh discipline, and severely restricted possibilities for movement, finding mates, and establishing and maintaining relatively stable families.

The less numerous women among the immigrants were often well advanced in their childbearing years when forced into slavery; afterward, frequent illness, prolonged periods of nursing, and perhaps reluctance to bear children into captivity lowered their potential fertility. The limited number of children they bore were too few to counter the overall effects of a surplus of males and of exceptionally high mortality among both children and adults. Among locally born slaves, in contrast, sex ratios were evenly balanced and adult life expectancies somewhat higher. In addition, native-born women began bearing children at earlier ages, and likely at more closely spaced intervals.

Early in the history of all staple crop regimes, planters relied on new African laborers to expand their output of export crops. In a population composed primarily of immigrants, deaths exceeded births, thus generating continued demand for additional migrants to make up the population deficit and to further expand production. Eventually, as older areas approached full production, the need for new workers diminished, the proportion of locally born blacks rose, the shortfall between deaths and births diminished, and the slave population began to grow largely through natural increase rather than through continued immigration. The length of time required for this demographic transition varied greatly from one place to

---

[12] McCusker and Menard, *The Economy of British America*, chap. 10.

another. In the tidewater Chesapeake, the transition occurred in the 1720s, and in South Carolina in the 1770s. In contrast, a reproducing creole majority did not emerge in Barbados until 1810, and in Jamaica, only in 1840.[13]

What differentiates mainland British North American colonies from the other slave colonies in the Western Hemisphere is the high rate of natural increase that began in some places early in the eighteenth century, a reproductive outcome that stands in marked contrast to that of slaves in British (and other European) West Indian colonies. Although the total number of Africans forcibly transported to the British islands before the American Revolution outnumbered those brought to the mainland colonies by about five to one, the African American population on the continent edged ahead of that of the British West Indies by the 1770s, ultimately including a substantial share of the total black population of the New World. Also in contrast to the islands, where men and women born in Africa remained in the majority into the early nineteenth century, by the 1770s about two-thirds of mainland slaves were native-born.[14] This extraordinary reproductive success is central to early African American history. And, although scholars have yet to pay it much attention, implications of the North American demographic transition may be one key to a more nuanced understanding of evolving African American culture.[15]

Several explanations have emerged to account for the differing rates of increase. One is that the exceptionally harsh tropical disease environment prevailing in the islands (and to a lesser extent in the lower mainland South) was responsible for much of the reproductive failure. A second sees slaveowners as the main cause, especially their calculating reliance on continued imports, lack of concern with reproduction, hard-driving manner, and scant maintenance. Other scholars put great weight on variations in optimum unit size, work conditions, and seasonal routines and intensity of labor entailed in producing the major plantation crops, all of which in turn affected reproduction. Yet another argument emphasizes the differing choices the slaves themselves made about marriage, living arrangements, and fertility.[16]

---

[13] Ibid.
[14] These arguments are most recently summarized in ibid. See also Fogel and Engerman, *Time on the Cross*: The Economics, chap. 1; Engerman, "Comments on the Study of Race and Slavery"; Engerman, "Some Economic and Demographic Comparisons of Slavery"; and Littlefield, "Plantations, Paternalism, and Profitability."
[15] Sensbach, "Charting a Course in Early African-American History"; Walsh, *From Calabar to Carter's Grove*.
[16] Menard and McCusker, *Economy of British America*, pp. 233–34; Engerman, "Some Economic and Demographic Comparisons."

NUPTIALITY AND FERTILITY

The laws of most colonies (and subsequently of the slave states) did not recognize slave marriages, and slaveowners documented de facto slave unions only when it suited their convenience.[17] Although some enumerations of residential groupings – probate inventories and periodic listings of slaves in other kinds of plantation records – often identify the mothers of infants and young children up to the ages of 10 or 12, they almost never identify husbands and fathers. More commonly, even basic information on individual mother/child relationships is unavailable.

Consequently many studies of African American marriage and child-bearing patterns in early America begin – and end – with tabulations of adult sex ratios and of proportions of slaves living on units of varying size. These indirect measures are so widely used because often no others are available. Adult sex ratios serve to establish the proportion of slaves who could conceivably find mates in a given locality. Because men usually outnumbered women, their marriage possibilities were circumscribed by the number of women living nearby. In addition, since slaves often had limited freedom of travel, chances for finding a spouse and especially for forming a stable family were greater for those living on large plantations than for those on small farms where there were few other bondspeople. The proportion of blacks in the total population also affected marital chances, as did their geographic density or dispersion. Wherever the black population was numerous and densely settled, the possibility increased for both co- and cross-residential and cross-owner unions.

Sex ratios and the size of residential units are, of course, exceedingly crude indicators of the possibilities for family formation, and ones that often overstate slaves' opportunities for marriage. Estimates of scale derived from probate inventories are likely to overemphasize the proportion of slaves living on larger holdings, since decedents in such cases were in general older and wealthier than the average householder.[18] Adult sex ratios aggregated across a given region are likely to obscure pronounced sex imbalances prevailing on individual plantations.[19] The link between

---

[17] New England was the exception. There marriages among blacks were solemnized and recorded in the same manner as those among whites. Slaves were usually compelled to marry in the manner prescribed for the general population and subsequently were expected to refrain from adultery (Greene, *The Negro in Colonial New England*, chap. 8).

[18] See, for example, Morgan and Nicholls, "Slaves in Piedmont Virginia," p. 228.

[19] Lee, "The Problem of Slave Culture in the Eighteenth-Century Chesapeake."

population densities and possible patterns of interaction could also vary greatly when topography and settlement patterns were dissimilar. Moreover, marital possibilities calculated from sex ratios and the size of residential units do not take into account the proportion of slaves who could not marry one another because of taboos against incest.[20] In addition, some slaveholders actively discouraged off-plantation unions. Even when courtships were successful, slave couples were at constant risk of separation by sale, estate divisions, or forced migration.

Despite these formidable obstacles, the proportion of slaves who entered into some form of marriage rose in the Upper and Lower South after 1740. Population densities increased, and the percentage of slaves living on large plantations increased even more. In the tidewater Chesapeake, for example, the proportions living on plantations with 20 or more black residents rose from roughly a quarter in the 1730s to one-third to two-thirds (depending on area) by the 1780s. Over the same period, the proportions living on units of fewer than 6 dropped from more than 20 to less than 10. By the 1760s three-quarters of slaves in both the Carolinas lived on units of 20 or more. More slaves were able to find mates and more often managed to maintain some semblance of a more settled family life. Plantation listings that include information on slave households demonstrate that the proportion living in nuclear households in the southern colonies rose in the second half of the century, especially on larger plantations. In addition, women living apart from their mates more often bore several children rather than remaining childless or having only one or two.[21]

In contrast, almost all blacks in the northern colonies continued to live with few others of their race. Their chances for finding mates and for establishing stable unions were fewer. Urban slaveowners often regarded infants as "an encumbrance only" and actively discouraged reproduction.[22] A study of eighteenth-century Philadelphia, for example, concludes that "disrupted families, relatively low fertility, high infant mortality, and the forced outmigration of children produced a population dominated by

[20] Kay and Cary, *Slavery in North Carolina, 1748–1775*, chap. 7; Stevenson, "Black Family Structure."
[21] Kay and Cary, *Slavery in North Carolina, 1748–1775*, chap. 7; Kulikoff, *Tobacco and Slaves*, chaps. 8–9; Morgan, "The Development of Slave Culture," chap. 4. For an account that argues the prevalence in Virginia of matrifocal families, abroad spouses, and extended family forms over monogamous marriages and nuclear slave families, see Stevenson, "Black Family Structure."
[22] [William Bradford?], "Another LETTER to a Clergyman in the country on the question, Whether the Children of slaves ought to be held in bondage," *Pennsylvania Packet*, Jan. 1, 1780, quoted in Klepp, "Seasoning and Society," p. 477.

adolescents and young adults, most born elsewhere." The situation in New York City was evidently similar.[23]

The ratio of children to women, another widely available measure readily calculated from probate inventories and other plantation listings, provides a better guide to actual reproductive outcomes. Again the measure is crude, since it can include only children alive and still resident with their mothers at the time the enumeration was made. The bias is overwhelmingly downward, since children who died early or who were sold or moved elsewhere are omitted; on the other hand, the presence of imported African children occasionally inflates the ratio. Some scholars prefer the ratio of girls to women, an alternative measure that minimizes the count of imported African children among whom boys predominated. In addition, the ratio is sensitive to variations in the proportions of Africans and the native-born, and to changes in the age structure of adult women, changes for which there is often little or no direct information.[24]

Variations in child/woman ratios do help us to sort out the relative importance of such factors as the balance between men and women, varying proportions of Africans and native-born, overall population densities, and unit size in encouraging or discouraging reproduction. In southern Maryland in the later seventeenth and early eighteenth centuries, for example, there was usually only about one child under the age of 16 for every adult female of childbearing age. The ratio increased to 2.0 by the 1730s, signaling the beginning of natural increase well before the proportions of men and women approached rough equality.[25] In South Carolina, adult sex ratios remained unbalanced across the eighteenth century, and although the surplus of men was less in the 1770s than in the 1740s, the child/woman ratio was lower in the 1770s than it had been in the 1740s – 1.25 in contrast to about 1.40, hardly an indicator of a naturally growing population.[26] In the newer Virginia piedmont, natural increase began soon after new areas were peopled; adult sex ratios rapidly approached rough

[23] Klepp, "Seasoning and Society," p. 477. Compare Davis, "These Enemies of Their Own Household."

[24] Other sources of error include inferring ages (often not specified) from price alone or from a combination of price, imprecise terms such as "girl," "boy," or "old," and from the internal structure of individual lists. Sometimes sex must be inferred from names that are occasionally ambiguous as to gender. On the various biases see Menard, "The Maryland Slave Population, 1658 to 1730"; and Kulikoff, "A 'Prolifick' People."

[25] Menard, "The Maryland Slave Population."

[26] Morgan, "The Development of Slave Culture," chap. 4.

equality within a decade or so of settlement, and child/woman ratios rose in tandem to about 2.0.[27] In the city of Philadelphia the numbers of adult men and women were roughly equal across the eighteenth century, but the girl/woman ratio remained below 1.0 through the 1780s.[28]

Adult sex ratios, in and of themselves, seem to have been less important than some have supposed. The effect of large influxes of new Africans on family formation needs further study, with particular attention to the proportions of African and native-born women in given populations. On the other hand, plantation size does emerge as one of the most significant circumstances facilitating natural increase. For example, higher child/woman ratios appear more consistently in parishes where larger farms predominated than in adjacent parishes with more small farms.[29]

Scholars have posited marked differences between the childbearing experiences of immigrant and native-born women, but almost no concrete measures exist for African-born women since their exact age is almost never known. For the native-born, there are a few measurements of the proportion of women who ever bore a child, age at first conception, the size of completed families, and the length of intervals between births.

Most enslaved African women were probably in their early 20s when they arrived.[30] In Virginia in the early eighteenth century, even African women living on large plantations rarely conceived a child until at least their third year in the colony, and many remained childless for several years more. In contrast, many native-born Virginia women began to bear children at an early age, and almost all had a child by their mid-20s. On South Carolina rice plantations, more than 85 percent of women born in the colonies near the end of the eighteenth century had at least one child by age 30.[31]

The mean age at which native Southern slave women first conceived a child was similar across the eighteenth century, and consistently two to

[27] Morgan and Nicholls, "Slaves in Piedmont Virginia."

[28] Nash and Soderlund, *Freedom by Degrees*, chap. 1.

[29] Kay and Cary, *Slavery in North Carolina*, chap. 7. Similar parish-by-parish differences also appear in South Carolina and in Maryland. See also Menard, "Slave Demography in the Low Country."

[30] Menard, "Maryland Slave Population," p. 46; Kulikoff, "A 'Prolifick' People," pp. 398–99. African girls and boys under 16 were usually no more than one-sixth of a typical slave ship cargo (Morgan and Nicholls, "Slaves in Piedmont Virginia," pp. 218–22, 247–51). Menard ("Maryland Slave Population," P. 46) concluded that "an average age at arrival of somewhat more than 20 years fits well with what little is known about the ages of slaves purchased by traders in Africa."

[31] Kulikoff, "A 'Prolifick' People"; Cody, "Slave Demography and Family Formation," chap. 3.

Table 6.2. *Age at first conception of native-born southern slave women in the eighteenth century*

Decade of birth of mother	Place	Mean age at estimated conception of first child	Median age at conception of first child	Total number of women
1710s	Southern Maryland	17.8[a]		5
1720s	Southern Maryland	17.5[a]		8
1730s	Southern Maryland	18.1[a]		17
1740s	Southern Maryland	18.5[a]		71
1750s	Southern Maryland	17.6[a]		79
1750s	Tidewater Virginia	17.6[b]		7
1760s	Piedmont Virginia	17.5[b]		15
1726–41	North Carolina	17.3[a]	17.9[a]	6
1766–80	North Carolina	16.3[a]	16.4[a]	15
1781–92	North Carolina	18.2[a]	17.7[a]	19
1710s–20s	South Carolina	19.7[b]		7
1730s–40s	South Carolina	19.3[b]		25
1750s–60s	South Carolina	18.8[b]		26
1770s–80s	South Carolina	17.9[b]		7
1720–49	South Carolina	19.3[c]	18.7[c]	10
1750–79	South Carolina	19.6[c]	18.3[c]	32
1780–1809	South Carolina	20.1[c]	19.4[c]	113

[a] Allowing for the estimated impact of infant mortality.
[b] Mean age of women at conception of eldest child living with her.
[c] Mean/median age at first birth.
Sources: Southern Maryland: Kulikoff, "A 'Prolifick' People," p. 407; Virginia: Morgan, "Development of Slave Cultures," p. 305, and *Slave Counterpoint*, p. 92; North Carolina: Kay and Cary, *Slavery in North Carolina*, pp. 293–94; South Carolina: 1710s through 1780s, Morgan, *Slave Counterpoint*, p. 92; 1720–1809: Cody, "Slave Demography and Family Formation," p. 161.

four years beyond the age – estimated at no later than 15 – at which they were physically capable of childbearing.[32] Table 6.2 shows a range of 16.3 to 19.7. Small numbers preclude firm generalizations about the distribution of maternal ages at first birth. The strongest evidence is from South Carolina. There, the proportion of women who bore their first child between 15 and 19 dropped from nearly 60% for those born in the third

[32] Trussell and Steckel, "The Estimation of the Mean Age of Female Slaves at the Time of Menarche and Their First Birth."

quarter of the eighteenth century to 50% among women born after 1780, with the proportions having a first child in their early 20s rising. More balanced sex ratios later in the century apparently reduced the pressure for women to begin sexual relations at exceptionally early ages.[33] The median age at last birth – 40 years – is available only for the South Carolina group.[34]

Mean completed family size across the South was also quite similar in the later eighteenth century, and relatively large, consistent with high rates of natural increase. The estimate for the Chesapeake in the second half of eighteenth century is about 8.0; for North Carolina women born between 1725 and 1825, 8.4; and for South Carolina low country women born at the end of the century, 8.5.[35] By the turn of the nineteenth century, the size of completed families in some parts of Virginia may have declined by about one child. The forced out-migration of a disproportionate number of young women is the most likely explanation.[36]

Age-specific marital fertility rates for immigrants are unknown, and there is evidence for only 32 native-born South Carolina women. There, fertility rates were similar to those of seventeenth-century French peasants, with the highest level of fertility occurring between the ages of 25 and 29. Rates for the 15 to 19 and 35 to 44 age groups were somewhat higher than the European rates, further contributing to large family size.[37]

Given the lack of data for immigrants, the question of whether African women had fewer children simply because they began childbearing later than natives or because of differences in childspacing remains a subject for debate. Comparison with the West Indies suggests that retention of customary African practices of breast-feeding children for at least two and sometimes three years and of abstaining from intercourse while nursing may be a major reason (in addition to poor diet, excessive work requirements, and infertility caused by disease) for the long intervals between births common in the Caribbean. Native-born blacks in North America, it has been argued, adopted contemporaneous European patterns of breastfeeding for only about one year, which should have contributed to more closely spaced births about every two years.[38]

---

[33] Cody, "Slave Demography and Family Formation," chap. 3.
[34] Cody, "Slave Demography and Family Formation," pp. 196–98.
[35] Kulikoff, "A 'Prolifick' People"; Kay and Cary, *Slavery in North Carolina*, chap. 7; Cody, "Slave Demography and Family Formation," chap. 6.
[36] Kulikoff, "A 'Prolifick People"; Morgan, "The Development of Slave Culture," chap. 4.
[37] Cody, "Slave Demography and Family Formation," chap. 3.
[38] Klein and Engerman, "Fertility Differentials between Slaves in the United States and the British West Indies."

Intervals between births of 25 to 29 months are found for Maryland women born between 1710 and 1750, and 28 months in a Virginia parish from the 1720s through the 1740s that included both immigrant and native-born blacks.[39] Both are consistent with the argument that the black women adopted European childspacing patterns. Although Virginia records yield similar mean birth intervals for both black and white women, many more of the black women had long gaps in their childbearing histories. A secondary cluster of birth intervals at three to four years is thought to suggest a continuation of African customs of longer nursing among immigrants. Frequent midlife gaps in childbearing (also found on other tidewater plantations) may have resulted from the death of a partner or forced separation.[40]

Birth intervals were longer in the Lower South. The median in North Carolina was 34 to 36 months (mean 33 to 36), and in the South Carolina low country, about 31 months. In South Carolina labor demands and epidemiological factors appear to have been the main reasons for these higher intervals, whereas in North Carolina African nursing practices seemingly played a greater role.[41]

Anglican parish registers from Virginia and plantation birth records from South Carolina reflect quite different seasonal patterns of conception and birth among African Americans than those prevailing among neighboring whites. In the Chesapeake, successful conceptions (births lagged by nine months to approximate a 280-day period of gestation) were most likely to occur from May through October, with a disproportionate number of births following in February through July, and relatively few births from August through January.[42] In South Carolina, conceptions were concentrated between October and January. There the resulting birth heap came in June through October, with a deficit between November and April. The argument that in South Carolina conceptions often occurred after the rice harvest – when work requirements were less rigor-

---

[39] Kulikoff, "A 'Prolifick' People"; Gundersen, "The Double Bonds of Race and Sex."

[40] Gundersen, "The Double Bonds of Race and Sex."

[41] Kay and Cary, *Slavery in North Carolina*, chap. 7; Cody, "Slave Demography and Family Formation," chap. 3; and Cody, "A Note on Changing Patterns of Slave Fertility in the South Carolina Rice District." Cody calculated shorter birth intervals for a handful of well-documented women. For mothers whose child died within the first nine months after birth, the interval was 23.5, and for those who bore a child that survived for nine months or longer, the figure was 29.5. The numbers, however, were very small, and intervals for less well-documented women were similar to those found in North Carolina. Morgan also found a shorter interval of 27.4 months for women under the age of 35 ("Development of Slave Culture," pp. 303–4).

[42] Rutman, Wetherell, and Rutman, "Rhythms of Life: Black and White Seasonality in the Early Chesapeake"; Gundersen, "The Double Bonds of Race and Sex."

ous, malarial attacks ending, and food abundant – seems plausible.[43] In the Chesapeake, however, conception most often took place during the malarial season and also encompassed the season of heavy summer hoeing and weeding and the early fall tobacco harvest. Consequently additional factors may have been at work here.[44]

These seasonal patterns clearly had an adverse effect on the health of both mothers and their newborn infants. The timing of conception in both places meant that women were often in the final stages of their pregnancies or gave birth in the very months when work requirements were heaviest and leisure for child care least.

MORTALITY

Mortality among colonial North American blacks is assumed to have been high in relation to the white population, but lower than the death rates prevailing in the West Indies. Here "lower" is indeed a relative term, one that describes something less than complete demographic catastrophe, but that tends to obscure exceedingly foreshortened life chances throughout much of coastal North America. Indeed, African American death rates in the lowland Carolina rice-growing districts may have approached the disastrously high rates found in the sugar islands. In the Chesapeake, for lack of better evidence, historians have assumed life expectancies for acclimated blacks equivalent to the markedly abridged life spans calculated for European migrants. Among colonial whites, life expectancy improved in more northerly latitudes. However, given their greater susceptibility to respiratory diseases, blacks living north of the Mason-Dixon line – at least those in cities – did not experience the same enhanced life chances as did whites. More precise measures are almost nonexistent.

Deaths among newly arrived immigrants due to "seasoning," that is, acclimation to a new disease environment, were especially high. The traditional belief was that one-third of all black immigrants died during their first three years in the New World. The only extant North American quantitative study found that between 1710 and 1718, 5.4% of the African slaves landed in Virginia died before they could be sold, and that 31% of 32 Africans purchased by a Stafford County, Virginia, planter between

[43] Cody, "Slave Demography and Family Formation," chap. 2.
[44] For a discussion of other possible explanations, see Rutman, Wetherell, and Rutman, "Rhythms of Life."

1733 and 1742 died within 3 years of arrival. Less than half were alive at the end of 10 years. This mortality experience probably provides an upper-bound estimate for the Chesapeake, since the Stafford plantation was located in a notoriously unhealthy micro-zone. The author of this study further concluded that life chances among those who survived for at least a decade improved, but his use of life tables for European immigrants to estimate death dates for slaves, where not known, is perhaps problematic.[45]

Analogy with the better-documented contemporary white population suggests that native-born black men should have suffered less from chronic ill-health and lived somewhat, but not markedly, longer than their parents. The probable, and likely different, life expectancies black women have not yet been seriously considered. We know nothing of the level of excess mortality they may experienced during their childbearing years. Since many enslaved African women bore few children, the risk of dying in childbirth, as in the ease of most European immigrant women, was somewhat diminished. Almost all native-born African American women, in contrast, faced greater risks. To what extent did endemic malaria heighten maternal mortality rates among black women? What of the interaction of this and other diseases with heavy forced physical labor during pregnancy and nursing?[46] The frequent surplus of women among Chesapeake slaves classified as "old" (nearly two to one in Maryland probate inventories between 1658 and 1710, for example, and often equally high in several Virginia counties across the eighteenth century), when contrasted with a predominance of males in other adult age groups, hints at a higher expectation of life for women who survived their childbearing years than for men of comparable age.[47]

But overall, the age distributions obtained from the various kinds of listings of slave holdings imply dismally limited life chances for most adults. Proportionally few survivors appear in the older age groups. Men and women in their early 40s were often described as "old," and those in their early 50s as "very old." Most slaves who survived into the mid-50s were judged too sick or infirm to perform any significant labor, and individuals living into their 60s were rare indeed. The impression of

[45] Kulikoff, "A 'Prolifick' People."

[46] For the general model, see ibid. For a discussion of elevated maternal mortality in areas with endemic malaria, see Rutman and Rutman, "Of Agues and Fevers: Malaria in the Early Chesapeake"; however, the authors presented no evidence for West Africa or for African Americans. For archaeological evidence, see the discussion later in the chapter.

[47] Menard, "The Maryland Slave Population"; Morgan, "Development of Slave Culture," chap. 4.

poor health and abridged life spans that such listings provide are, more-over, reinforced by analysis of human skeletons discussed later in this chapter.

A recent study of differential mortality in eighteenth-century Philadel-phia reveals that middle colony African Americans faced a substantially higher risk of death than did comparable free or dependent whites. The effects of an unfamiliar climate and disease environment were com-pounded by day-to-day decisions among slaveowners involving diet, medical care, and sleeping arrangements that produced much more unfa-vorable outcomes for slaves. Despite common wisdom to the contrary, both immigrant and locally born blacks died at much higher rates than immigrant and native whites.

Crude death rates for African Americans in Philadelphia averaged 67 per thousand between 1722 and 1775, in contrast to a rate of 46 per thou-sand for Europeans, this despite an underlying age structure (fewer infants or young children and almost no elderly persons) that should have reduced black death rates. Greater susceptibility to respiratory diseases in the winter months, and inadequate food, clothing, shelter, and medial care are advanced as the major causes for this excess mortality. Postemancipa-tion statistics underscore the fact that many of these deaths were pre-ventable even by contemporary standards. Freedom brought, for a brief time at the end of the century, substantial improvements in life chances; the crude death rate among blacks dropped to 42 per thousand, and births began to exceed deaths for the first time in Philadelphia's history.[48] Crude mortality rates among Boston blacks – from 54 to 67 per thousand between 1742 and 1760 – were nearly as high. Moreover, in years when mortality was high among both blacks and whites, the black death rate in Boston was twice that for whites.[49]

Monthly variations in the distribution of deaths have been used pri-marily as a tool for diagnosing ex post facto differential causes of death. In the Chesapeake, the winter and early spring months were the most haz-ardous for both blacks and whites. Tests have been inconclusive as to whether blacks were more susceptible than whites to the hazards of Chesa-peake winters. However, a secondary death peak among whites in Sep-tember and October, absent among blacks, confirms the latter's greater

---

[48] Klepp, "Seasoning and Society."
[49] Nash, "Slaves and Slaveowners in Colonial Philadelphia," p. 241; Levesque, *Black Boston*, chap. 12.

genetic protection against malaria.[50] In more northerly Philadelphia, white mortality was highest in the summer and fall owing to malaria and diarrheal diseases; black death rates were lowest across these months. Late fall and winter were exceptionally deadly to African Americans, and they suffered disproportionately compared with whites when winters were colder than average. Respiratory diseases were the most likely cause, thought to be more hazardous for blacks because of their lesser genetic ability to produce Vitamin D from available sunlight.[51]

This brief survey underscores how little is actually known about the mortality experience of African migrants who survived initial enslavement and transportation to North America in the colonial era, as well as about the experience of their immediate descendants. Mortality differences have been posited between immigrants and natives, between regions, and between blacks and whites. Further differences between men and women and between enslaved and free persons are also likely. High mortality continually appears as at least a partial explanation for the adoption of slavery, for the geographic distribution of African Americans in the colonies, for fragmented slave family life, and so forth. However, the general absence of concrete measures dilutes the explanatory potential of such factors.

In the absence of reliable age-specific measures of life chances for colonial African American males and females, no firmer conclusions can at present be drawn. The somewhat better evidence available for the nineteenth century, outlined in Chapter 10, demonstrates higher differential mortality among African Americans of all ages, and especially high mortality among enslaved children, in later years. There is no reason to suppose that some of the circumstances that contributed to excessive mortality – such as inadequate diet and housing, poor sanitation, and strenuous work requirements – were more favorable before 1790 than after; thus there is no reason to suppose that mortality levels were significantly lower in the colonial period. Moreover, in earlier years, a greater proportion of the African American population was concentrated in notoriously unhealthy parts of the eastern seaboard, where endemic malaria and gastrointestinal diseases likely left survivors of these ailments especially susceptible to other, more immediately lethal diseases.

---

[50] Rutman, Wetherell, and Rutman, "Rhythms of Life."

[51] Klepp, "Seasoning and Society." Warren, "Northern Chills, Southern Fevers," reports a similar seasonal pattern for Newport, Rhode Island, in the 1760s.

INTERNAL AND POSTWAR
INTERNATIONAL MIGRATION

Until the middle of the eighteenth century, most forced African migrants and their descendants continued to live in the seaboard areas of the mainland British colonies. Beginning in the 1740s, Virginia planters developed many new tobacco plantations in the interior piedmont region. By 1755 black men and women over the age of 16 accounted for 40% of the 103,318 taxables working in the piedmont and the Shenandoah Valley. On the eve of the Revolution, the proportion had increased to 50%. Many of the blacks residing in the inland areas were trans-Atlantic migrants. Piedmont planters likely purchased just under half of the 59,000 Africans imported into Virginia between 1725 and 1755, and almost all of the approximately 15,000 newcomers who arrived after 1755. In addition, about 17,000 largely native-born tidewater Virginia slaves were also forced to move to the piedmont between 1755 and 1782. Some went west to develop new tobacco farms on absentee-owned quarters, while others moved with migrating owners. The focus of tobacco agriculture shifted westward, and by the end of the Revolutionary War more Virginia slaves lived in the piedmont than in the tidewater.[52]

This internal migration apparently had less devastating demographic results for the black population than had the earlier trans-Atlantic migration. In the Virginia piedmont prior to the Revolution, among newly imported Africans, proportions of women and children were unusually high. Moreover, migrating planters took substantial numbers of native-born tidewater slave women and children with them. As a consequence, sex ratios among slaves in the new settlements became relatively balanced within a short time, with high rates of reproduction soon following.[53] Those slaves who were moved from the tidewater to higher, drier inland farms likely benefited from more favorable local disease environments. In addition, more fertile soils in the newer areas permitted, at least for a time, higher crop yields from less labor than could be obtained in many parts of the older seaboard.

After the war, many South Carolina and Georgia slaves were also forced to move into the back country. In South Carolina, for example, over 90%

---

[52] Morgan, "Slave Life in Piedmont Virginia"; Morgan and Nicholls, "Slaves in Piedmont Virginia"; and Dunn, "Black Society in the Chesapeake."
[53] Morgan and Nicholls, "Slaves in Piedmont Virginia."

of that colony's slaves were located in the low country in 1760. By 1810 almost half lived further up country. Similarly, in 1775, two-thirds of Georgia's slaves lived within 20 miles of the coast, but by 1790 more than half resided in the back country.[54] The demographic results for these Lower South African American migrants have yet to be examined.

The events accompanying and following the American Revolution not only afforded some opportunities for voluntary migration but also greatly accelerated involuntary moves. War-related disruptions and postwar migrations affected the lives of most blacks living in North America. Voluntary migration was of several sorts. During the war, southern blacks hoping to escape slavery ran away in large numbers to join British forces or to find refuge in the Carolina back country and British-held Florida. Estimates of the number of wartime runaways vary widely. The most conservative estimate is roughly 20,000; others range from 80,000 to 100,000. At the war's end, over 3,000 blacks left with the British forces evacuating New York City. Some few went to England, but most initially migrated to Nova Scotia; subsequently many of these refugees established expatriate African American settlements in West Africa.[55]

Also, in the first two decades after the war, many newly freed blacks in the former northern and middle colonies moved from the countryside to coastal towns in a search for economic sustenance. Freedmen and freedwomen from the Upper South moved to the now rapidly growing towns within the Chesapeake and into southeastern Pennsylvania, especially to Philadelphia.[56]

The number of involuntary migrants was much greater. In order to prevent large-scale slave desertions during the war, many coastal Southern masters forcibly moved their slaves from the vulnerable lowlands to more remote up-country districts. At the war's end, thousands of Southern blacks who were the property of loyalist slaveowners were forced to leave the country with their owners; the majority were transported to the West Indies, especially to Jamaica and the Bahamas. Others who had escaped to, or been taken up by, British forces were resold into slavery somewhere in the islands. This mass exodus of slaves from the Lower South created a severe labor shortage that Georgia and South Carolina planters sought to overcome by resuming the African slave trade as soon as peace was

[54] Morgan, "Black Society in the Lowcountry," pp. 83–85; Frey, *Water from the Rock*, pp. 241–15.
[55] Kulikoff, "Uprooted Peoples"; Frey, *Water from the Rock*, chaps. 6 and 7; Morgan, "Black Society in the Lowcountry," pp. 109–13.
[56] Soderlund, "Black Importation and Migration into Southeastern Pennsylvania"; Nash, "Forging Freedom."

declared. Nearly 20,000 newly enslaved Africans were landed in South Carolina, for example, between 1782 and 1790.[57]

Even before the peace treaty was signed, white planters and small farmers resumed further expansion into the southern back country. Prefiguring more substantial out-migration across the next three decades, during the 1780s migrating lowland planters took family-owned slaves into back-country Carolina and Georgia, across the Allegheny Mountains into Kentucky and Tennessee, and into Spanish Louisiana. Some cash-strapped resident tidewater slaveowners also began selling surplus slaves to professional slave traders for eventual resale in the West. The demographic consequences – not to mention the emotional toll for both movers and stayers – of the forced removal of a disproportionate number of older children and young adults were already evident in tidewater Virginia in the 1770s.[58]

Over the next two decades, few southern slaves escaped either forced moves or forced separations from neighbors and more distant kin, if not from immediate family members. This does not deny that most slaveowners did try to avoid separating husbands from wives and mothers from young children when they sold slaves, sent some slaves west to settle distant quarters, or else themselves pulled up stakes and moved most or all of their operations west. On the other hand, adolescent girls and boys were routinely separated from parents and other kin, cross-plantation marriages between slaves of different owners often broken up, and old people not infrequently left behind in the east when planters decided to try their fortunes in the west. Moreover, instrumental African American cross-plantation kin, social, and economic networks, some of which had developed relatively undisturbed over three or more generations in slavery, were irrevocably destroyed.[59]

BIOMEDICAL STUDIES, ANTHROPOMETRIC MEASURES, AND ARCHAEOLOGY

Given our frequent inability to construct the most basic of standard demographic measures for African American peoples in early North America,

[57] Kulikoff, "Uprooted Peoples"; Frey, *Water from the Rock*, chaps. 6 and 7.
[58] Morgan, "The Development of Slave Culture," chap. 4.
[59] For the conventional view that only a small proportion of slave families were destroyed by westward migration, see Fogel and Engerman, *Time on the Cross*, pp. 44–52. For opposing views, see Kulikoff, "Uprooted Peoples"; and Walsh, *From Calabar to Carters Grove*, chap. 7.

the contributions and new insights that alternative disciplines can provide are especially relevant. Biomedical studies that trace the transatlantic flow, incidence, and interaction of pathogens – as well as of people – over time and place have shed considerable light on observed demographic outcomes and suggested new questions and strategies for research. Curtin's 1967 essay on epidemiology and the slave trade, as well as his subsequent investigations of differential morbidity and mortality in West Africa and in the West Indies, for example, permit comparisons of the susceptibilities and immunities of people of African ancestry in both Old and New World disease environments.[60] Kiple and King's study of the interactions of inherited and acquired immunities, differential susceptibilities to disease, nutrition, and work requirements among North Americans of African heritage helps to explain, among other things, why slave infants and children were particularly subject to malnutrition, and consequently to a higher death rate than white children.[61]

Although most of the evidence underlying these ambitious interdisciplinary investigations comes from the first half of the nineteenth century, the implications for earlier periods are numerous. To date, Peter Wood's exploration of Africans' resistance to malaria as an important rationale for the adoption of slave labor in lowland South Carolina, Rutman and Rutman's study of the consequences of the introduction of falciparum malaria into the Chesapeake, and Klepp's investigation of the impact of differential susceptibilities to disease and of differential nutrition on the mortality experience of blacks and whites in early Philadelphia stand virtually alone.[62] They clearly demonstrate the exciting potential for further comparative biohistorical research.

Anthropometrics – the study of the physical stature of different groups within a given population – has recently emerged as an alternative way of measuring comparative standards of living and well-being. Average adult heights reflect the cumulative impact of nutrition, hygiene, disease, and stress, most especially during childhood. Information is often widely available (at least for adult men), for groups for whom other measures of well-being are lacking. Most studies of the stature of African Americans in North America are confined to the nineteenth century and are described in more detail in Chapter 10 of this volume. Limited evidence from the eighteenth century confirms that systematic differences in stature both

---

[60] Curtin, "Epidemiology and the Slave Trade"; Curtin, *Death by Migration.*
[61] Kiple and King, *Another Dimension to the Black Diaspora.*
[62] Wood, *Black Majority*; Rutman and Rutman, "Of Agues and Fevers"; Klepp, "Seasoning and Society."

between African and native-born slaves, and between contemporary native-born blacks and native-born whites had already emerged. Adult slaves born in the colonies were taller than adults transported from Africa, but shorter than contemporary native-born whites. This implies that from the outset slaves shared to some extent the nutritional advantages that usually arose when moving from the Old World to the New, but they also suffered higher levels of malnutrition, a direct result of the constraints of slavery, than did the free population.[63]

Variations in height among colonial blacks point to further issues needing research. A study drawn from newspaper advertisements for runaway slaves in all the colonies, for example, suggests a possible decline in stature during the second half of the eighteenth century.[64] Across this half century, the focus of the West African slave trade shifted from north to south. Within West Africa, peoples living in more southerly regions were – and still are – on average shorter than residents of northern West Africa. Thus the posited decline in stature among African American slaves may reflect in part the changing origins of the enslaved migrants. The impact of wartime disruptions during the American Revolution – severe local shortages of food and clothing, coupled with frequent forced internal migration and heightened exposure to disease – may also have affected adversely, and disproportionately, the subsequent well-being and life chances of young native African Americans growing up in the 1770s and 1780s.[65]

Archaeological evidence contributes to our understanding of early African American population history in two ways. First, it does so indirectly, through evidence on the composition of slave and free black diets that supplements and is often superior to period documentary sources. For the Chesapeake, plantation records consistently document that the customary owner-supplied ration was a peck of shelled corn per adult per week and half a peck for old people and for children between the ages of weaning and 16 years. This allotment had become the rule of thumb for all Chesapeake residents, bound or free, by the mid–seventeenth century. The slave ration was close to the standard ration for white indentured servants. One peck per week comes to 13 bushels a year; 3 barrels (15 bushels) of maize was the norm for servants and freedmen and was considered suf-

[63] Margo and Steckel, "The Height of American Slaves"; Steckel, "Heights and Health in the United States"; and Komlos, "The Height of Runaway Slaves in Colonial America."

[64] Komlos, "The Height of Runaway Slaves in Colonial America."

[65] Komlos, "The Height of Runaway Slaves in Colonial America"; and Steckel, "Heights and Health in the United States."

ficient to supply food for a year plus seed and a small reserve to feed poultry or to fatten a hog. By the later eighteenth century, planters generally had the grain ground at a plantation or other local mill and the allotment was delivered in the form of meal.[66] The maize ration was, as Richard Sutch concluded, "neither excessive nor generous," but was "adequate to provide sufficient energy to enable one to work like a slave."[67] Other grains might be temporarily substituted only when corn supplies ran out before the new crop was harvested.

In the Lower South, long-staple cotton and rice planters were notoriously stingy with meat rations, and the slaves here had to catch small wild mammals, turtles, and fish in order to enjoy any regular source of protein. In the Chesapeake, planters more often supplemented the maize ration with irregular distributions of salt pork or salt fish, and, less frequently, salt, fat, and molasses. Until about the 1770s Chesapeake slaveowners gave out meat rations only sporadically; as one leading planter put it, it was thought sufficient to issue meat "a bit now and then as they deserved it by their work and diligence".[68] Fresh meat – usually in the form of an old or sick steer or inferior sheep – was most often provided in times of exceptionally heavy labor such as the wheat harvest. On some plantations it was also customary to give the slaves a part of the butchery offal – intestines or heads – whenever animals were slaughtered for the planters' tables. By the last quarter of the eighteenth century, large Chesapeake planters more often issued regular rations of preserved meat, although the amount seems to have differed from plantation to plantation. The minimum ration appears to have been one-half pound of salt meat or fish per adult per week, and some plantation accounts suggest a weekly ration of one to two pounds of meat per adult. It is less clear whether planters usually supplied proportionate meat rations for children, or allotted meat only to workers; again, practices seem to have varied. What is clear is that any regular meat rations were considerably less than the amounts customarily consumed by poor whites.[69]

Although studies of food remains in trash pits cannot reveal per capita consumption of different kinds of foods, the contents of such pits on early African American sites do demonstrate a more diverse diet than the written evidence suggests. A consistent finding from estimates of the

---

[66] Walsh, "Work and Resistance in the New Republic," pp. 98–105; Moore, " 'Established and Well Cultivated' "; Morgan, *Slave Counterpoint*, pp. 134–45.
[67] Sutch, "The Care and Feeding of Slaves," p. 268.   [68] Carter, *Diary*, p. 871.
[69] Walsh, "Work and Resistance in the New Republic," pp. 98–105.

weights of meat represented by recovered bones on archaeological sites dating from the later seventeenth, eighteenth, and early nineteenth century is that slaves consumed relatively equal proportions of beef and pork. Most beef was eaten fresh in the late fall and early winter, and such distributions of fresh beef often go unmentioned in regular ration records. Thus the archaeological evidence counters the impression drawn from documentary records that colonial slaveowners allowed their bondspeople little or no meat whatsoever. But trash pit evidence also proves that slaves tried mightily to supplement allotted rations by hunting wild game, fishing, raising poultry, and gardening. Clearly, they found the amount of proteins that the owners doled out inadequate.

Counterbalancing the evidence from food remains for a more varied diet, obtained in part from extensive use of wild food resources, is other evidence that suggests continued overall scarcity and limited quality and variety. Slaves had access to few food storage or cooking vessels; meals had to be simply prepared, primarily by boiling. Long initial cooking or reheating of cooked foods may have destroyed much of its vitamin content. Archaeologists have found as well that the cuts of domestic livestock that slaveowners provided were usually of low quality. Available meat was hacked into small pieces for cooking, and the bones thoroughly scraped or pulverized to extract marrow.[70] Finely chopped or pulverized bone taken from parts of animals considered inferior by later colonial Anglo-Americans has been generally interpreted primarily as evidence of slave-owner's parsimony in supplying any meat. However, it may equally reflect the continuance of customary African methods of meat preparation, in which finely chopped pieces of flesh and bone are simmered in a liquid base. If so, slaves may have considered differing ratios of flesh to bone or differences in tenderness between various parts of larger animal carcasses irrelevant.

New perspectives on slave diet will likely emerge as more attention is paid to the interrelationships between all the various aspects of slave food-ways – not just what was eaten, but also how it was procured, processed, consumed, and the remains disposed of.

Archaeology also shows that diets of free blacks varied widely, depending both on urban or rural residence and on family income. Free blacks

---

[70] Walsh, "Consumer Behavior, Diet, and the Standard of Living in Late Colonial and Early Antebellum America," pp. 240–45, summarizes some recent findings from archaeology regarding African American diets. For other surveys, see Gibbs, Cargill, Lieberman, et al., "Nutrition in a Slave Population"; and Reitz, Gibbs, and Rathbun, "Archaeological Evidence for Subsistence on Coastal Plantations."

chose to consume some foods that were generally unavailable in slave quarters and perhaps prepared and served meals in different ways. Because they were forced to work long hours for their wages, however, they had little time for harvesting wild foods and bought whatever meat they ate from others.

The second important contribution of archaeology to population history is that it provides direct evidence of that history through the study of human skeletons. So far, the number of individuals who died prior to 1800 is too small, and the possibility that the burials are not representative of the overall decedent population is too great, to permit the broad generalizations about longevity that historians seek. The average age at death for most eighteenth-century adults, as indicated by skeletal data, was in the 40s; calculation of age-specific mortality patterns awaits the completion of ongoing studies of other skeletal assemblages. "Cemetery demography," so far reported for blacks born in the eighteenth century who died in such diverse places as New Orleans, the tidewater Chesapeake, western Maryland, and Philadelphia, leaves the question of differential mortality for males and females unresolved. In most eighteenth-century Chesapeake burials, for example, longevity for adult males was lower than that for females (a pattern also found in an early-nineteenth-century South Carolina cemetery). In both the New Orleans and Philadelphia cemeteries, in contrast, deaths during adolescence and early adulthood were more frequent among females than among male. Contemporary death records for both cities reveal a similar pattern of excess mortality among women of childbearing age.[71]

Skeletons also testify to what physical anthropologists have termed "life stresses of slavery." Nutritional stress is revealed by tooth decay and periodontal disease, and by lines on the teeth and in the long bones of the skeleton resulting from illness or inadequate diet, or both, during childhood. Other indicators of stress are short stature achieved by a given age, bowing of the leg bones (a possible indicator of rickets or chronic intestinal disease), and skull abnormalities caused by either sickle-cell anemia or anemias brought on by malnutrition.

[71] Owsley, Orser, Mann, et al., "Demography and Pathology of an Urban Slave Population from New Orleans"; Kelley and Angel, "Life Stresses of Slavery"; Angel, Kelley, Parrington, et al., "Life Stresses of the Free Black Community as Represented by the First African Baptist Church, Philadelphia"; and Reitz, Gibbs, and Rathbun, "Archaeological Evidence for Subsistence on Coastal Plantations," pp. 178–83. An ongoing study of 390 seventeenth- and eighteenth-century burials from New York City's African Burial Ground holds particular promise (African Burial Ground Office, "Questions and Answers on the African Burial Ground").

The preliminary results underscore stresses resulting from a poor diet. Tooth decay and periodontal disease, for example, were greater among urban than among rural blacks, a likely outcome given rural slaves' limited access to sugar and other sweeteners, and the short and unbalanced food supplies that we have reason to suspect were common among many city-dwellers.[72] On the other hand, North American blacks, unlike their white owners, were less likely to ingest harmful levels of lead, since they did not prepare foods in, or eat or drink from, vessels with a high content of lead.[73] Various measures of physical stature derived from skeletons are consistent with the anthropometric studies in that most individuals born in the later eighteenth century reached final adult heights comparable to twentieth-century African Americans. This indicates that colonial diets were usually adequate in calories. At the same time, various bone pathologies confirm generally inadequate overall nutritional levels, especially during infancy and childhood. Moderate levels of malnutrition were nearly universal.[74]

Skeletal evidence for work-related stress is also pronounced. Almost every one of the individuals that have been examined had encountered hard and sustained levels of physical labor beginning in adolescence. Degenerative skeletal changes associated with continued heavy manual labor appear in almost all older individuals. Sites on arm and leg bones where the major muscles and tendons are attached were particularly affected in many cases. Overall, few African Americans escaped the cumulative deleterious effects of hard manual labor.[75]

In addition, the archaeological record serves as a partial and poignant corrective to the bias toward men prevailing both in the surviving documentary record and in the research strategies of twentieth-century population historians. This is a result, first, of the fact that males predominated among forced African migrants; from numbers alone, one would expect to find more information. Second, it reflects the much better evidence usually surviving for men. Slaveowners, for example, took greater pains to record more detailed information about their primary short-term income

---

[72] Owsley et al., "Demography and Pathology of an Urban Slave Population from New Orleans"; Kelley and Angel, "Life Stresses of Slavery"; Angel et al., "Life Stresses of the Free Black Community"; and Ted A. Rathbun, "Health and Disease at a South Carolina Plantation."

[73] Aufderheide, Neiman, Wittmers, et al., "Lead in Bone II."

[74] Kelley and Angel, "Life Stresses of Slavery"; Angel et al., Life Stresses of the Free Black Community"; and Angel, "Colonial to Modern Skeletal Change in the U.S.A."

[75] Owsley et al., "Demography and Pathology of an Urban Slave Population from New Orleans"; Kelley and Angel, "Life Stresses of Slavery"; Angel et al., "Life Stresses of the Free Black Community."

producers than about their less highly valued female chattels. Men were also more likely to run away than women, and hence to be described in advertisements. Third, the quantity and quality of available data tend to determine the questions population historians ask.

Burials, in contrast, yield equivalent information for both sexes and remind us that life chances in early America were far from gender-neutral. The skeletal evidence suggests that the childhood diet of females was less adequate than that of contemporary males. Many of the women experienced degenerative changes in muscle attachment sites similar to those found in men. These charges suggest similar levels of hard physical labor, especially in the countryside. During their adult years, their dental health was almost surely worse, probably owing to a drain of calcium and other nutrients during pregnancy and nursing. The women among the dead analyzed so far bore on average just over two children each.[76] Given what we know about infant and childhood mortality, this level of reproduction was probably insufficient to sustain natural increase. But even this low level of childbearing, in combination with hard labor and poor diet, imposed a heavy burden.

SUMMARY

In 1790, as Table 6.3 shows, 90% of the 757,000 African Americans living in the new republic were concentrated in the Upper (56.7%) and Lower (32.7%) South. Of these nearly 677,000 individuals, 96% were enslaved, and most had scant hopes for ever attaining freedom. In contrast, almost half of African Americans in New England and the former middle colonies were already free, and most of the rest would eventually be freed through gradual emancipation. However, the 80,000 blacks residing north of the Mason-Dixon line were only 10% of the total African American population. The absolute numbers of free blacks were nearly evenly divided between North and South. But freedom surely had very different meanings in places where there were many blacks, almost all held as slaves, than it had in areas where free status was becoming increasingly common but blacks were a distinct minority in the total population.

No attempts have yet been made to estimate the proportion of Africans in the total black population in 1790. Still it is likely that by then the great

---

[76] Kelley and Angel, "Life Stresses of Slavery."

Table 6.3. *The U.S. African American population in 1790*

State or region	N free	N slave	Total black	Percentage slave	Total population	Pecentage of total population
Vermont	255	16	271	5.9		
New Hampshire	630	158	788	20.1		
Maine	538	0	538	0		
Massachusetts	5,463	0	5,463	0		
Rhode Island	3,407	948	4,355	21.8		
Connecticut	2,808	2,764	5,572	49.6		
New England	13,101	3,886	16,987	22.9	1,009,522	1.7
New York	4,654	21,324	25,978	82.1		
New Jersey	2,762	11,423	14,185	80.5		
Philadelphia	6,537	3,737	10,274	36.4		
Delaware	3,899	8,887	12,786	69.5		
Middle states	17,852	45,371	63,223	71.8	1,017,726	6.2
Maryland	8,043	103,036	111,079	92.8		
Virginia	12,866	292,627	305,493	95.8		
Kentucky	114	12,430	12,544	99.1		
Upper South	21,023	408,093	429,116	95.1	1,141,015	37.6
North Carolina	4,975	100,572	105,547	95.3		
South Carolina	1,801	107,094	108,895	98.3		
Georgia	398	29,264	29,662	98.7		
Southwest Teritory	361	3,417	3,778	90.4		
Lower South	7,535	240,347	247,882	97.0	761,063	32.6
Total	59,511	697,697	757,208	92.1	3,929,326	19.2

Source: *Return of the Whole Number of Persons within the Several Districts of the United States* (Washington, D.C., 1802).

majority had been born in the colonies rather than in Africa. Reliable projections are difficult to make, since they must rest on a combination of estimates of the number of slave imports by region and on highly conjectural survival rates for African immigrants. The proportion of native-born blacks was almost certainly 90% or more in older areas such as the tidewater Chesapeake, where few new African slaves were brought in after the middle of the eighteenth century, and was highest in the Lower South, where planters resumed the international trade in slaves after the Revolution.[77] Morgan's estimate of 26.8% African-born among

[77] Walsh, *From Calabar to Carter's Grove*, chap. 5, employs Rutman and Rutman's successive age structures flowing from a single hypothetical slave cargo entering the Chesapeake (*A Place in Time: Explicatus*, chap. 12) to explore the proportions of African and native-born slaves in the tidewater Chesapeake after the Revolution. Kulikoff ("A 'Prolifick' People," p. 423) estimated that the

adult slaves in South Carolina in 1790 provides an upper bound.[78] Thus in most parts of the new republic, the demographic characteristics of African Americans were those of a native-born rather than of an immigrant population.

In the 1960s and 1970s, a burst of scholarship on African Americans coincided with a renewed interest in colonial social history in general. Population history issues played a central role in much of this work. Demographic questions and methods focusing on interactions between migration, mortality, and fertility appeared to offer particular promise for broadening our understanding of early African American history. New methods were developed for teasing out "the demographic facts of everyday life" from previously unexploited sources. These in turn provided the building blocks for modeling the idea of an early American demographic regime that encompassed the life experiences of everyone who migrated from the Old World to the New, and of their immediate descendants. Subsequently, however, historians of the period have turned their attention to other issues, and African American demographic history, like colonial demographic history overall, has receded to the margin.[79]

This brief survey of early African American population history underscores the substantial gap that exists between our knowledge of transAtlantic migration patterns and of the later life experiences of African and native-born blacks in early North America. Economists and epidemiologists, through their continued comparisons of different regions of the New World, are providing new information on who moved from the Old World to the New, where, when, and why, and with what initial outcome. In contrast, the volume, composition, and consequences of internal and international migrations during the last quarter of the eighteenth century have been neglected.[80]

Meanwhile, historians of the early African Americans in North American have been absorbed in other issues – "resistance or accommodation to slavery, African cultural annihilation or creative adaptation, weakness or strength in black community and social life."[81] Anthropologists – archaeologists especially – have concentrated on power relation-

---

proportion of African adults in the total black population of the Chesapeake in 1755 was between 23 and 28%. Morgan and Nicholls ("Slaves in Piedmont Virginia," p. 220) offer estimates of the proportion of Africans among adult slaves in two piedmont Virginia counties in the eighteenth century but acknowledge that their calculations "are little more than educated guesses."

[78] Morgan, "Black Society in the Lowcountry," pp. 88–93.
[79] Menard, "Whatever Happened to Early American Population History?"
[80] Sensbach, "Charting a Course in Early African-American History."
[81] Sensbach, "Charting a Course in Early African-American History," p. 401.

Lorena S. Walsh

ships, a concern shared with feminist scholars investigating the social construction of gender.[82] In most instances, population history enters, if at
all, only as uncritically examined background. Attempting to study cultural change without taking into account changes in the composition of
the populations under study and of the differing life experiences of successive generations, for example, contributes to the "persistent vagueness"
that perplexes many recent investigations of African American cultural formation and change.[83]

In other cases, the problem is not so much that available demographic
insights are neglected, but that, without the stimulus of new work in the
field, thinking about them has ossified. Models and methods developed
some 20 years ago still dominate. Mainstream historians do acknowledge
that basic demographic "facts" mattered. The adverse impact of relatively
high mortality rates for family and community formation, for example,
are almost universally accepted, even if not further explored. The varying
local circumstances that the survivors encountered – balanced or unbalanced sex ratios among adults, size of residential units, population density,
and the like – are similarly accepted as important circumstances encouraging or discouraging marriage and reproduction. Almost all recent studies
of local African American communities address these issues to one degree
or another. But most rely only on the most basic and readily obtained
quantitative measures. The presupposition that nothing else can be devised
from the existing sources may indeed turn out to be correct. Simply
assuming this a priori, however, discourages critical examination and creative use of the evidence at hand.

Finally, population historians often fail to formulate unsolved demographic issues in ways that make explicit the relevance of their concerns
to others. In a recent summary of early American population growth, for
example, McCusker and Menard state that "accounting for the extraordinary reproductive success of blacks in North America is a central concern
of colonial economic history."[84] But why just economic history, and not also
cultural, material, religious, family, women's, and, especially, African
American history? The failure of the question, as stated, to take into
account the human considerations necessarily involved in procreation, or
to consider the nature of the communities in which the "extraordinary
reproductive success" took place, is telling.

[82] Kathleen M. Brown, "Brave New Worlds."
[83] Sensbach, "Charting a Course in Early African-American History," pp. 402–3.
[84] McCusker and Menard, *The Economy of British America*, p. 231.

BIBLIOGRAPHIC ESSAY

The most widely used estimates of the total colonial African American population appear in *Historical Statistics of the United States: Colonial Times to 1970, Part II* (Washington, D.C., 1975), 1168. Many of the colony-level counts on which this summary is based are reproduced in Evarts B. Greene and Virginia D. Harrington, *American Population before the Federal Census of 1790* (New York, 1932). Robert V. Wells, *The Population of the British Colonies in America before 1776: A Survey of Census Data* (Princeton, 1975) inventories extant colonial censuses and provides analyses of these materials broken down by race. John J. McCusker and Russell R. Menard, *The Economy of British America, 1607–1789* (Chapel Hill, N.C., 1985), summarize colonial black and white population growth in chapter 10, and include chapters on regional population patterns, incorporating most recently revised population figures.

Most data on the distribution of the early African American population and most vital rates are presented in local studies. A few works attempt wider synthesis. The comparative demographic well-being of slaves in the American South constituted a major focus in Robert William Fogel and Stanley L. Engerman, *Time on the Cross: The Economics of American Negro Slavery* (Boston, 1974). Subsequent essays that provide useful introductions to the issues raised by comparisons of African American population history between regions include Stanley L. Engerman, "Comments on the Study of Race and Slavery," in Stanley L. Engerman and Eugene D. Genovese, eds., *Race and Slavery in the Western Hemisphere: Quantitative Studies*, 495–530 (Princeton, 1975); Engerman, "Some Economic and Demographic Comparisons of Slavery in the United States and British West Indies," *Economic History Review*, 2d ser., 29 (1976), 258–75; Robert W. Fogel and Stanley L. Engerman, "Recent Findings in the Study of Slave Demography and Family Structure," *Sociology and Social Research* 63 (1979), 566–89; and Daniel C. Littlefield, "Plantations, Paternalism, and Profitability: Factors Affecting African Demography in the Old British Empire," *Journal of Southern History* 67 (1981), 167–82. Herbert S. Klein and Stanley L. Engerman, "Fertility Differentials between Slaves in the United States and the British West Indies: A Note on Lactation Practices," *William and Mary Quarterly*, 3d ser., 35 (1978), 357–74, discusses the reasons for differences in child-spacing patterns between the two regions.

A useful review of trends in early American demographic studies from the 1970s to the early 1990s is Russell R. Menard, "Whatever Happened to Early American Population History?" *William and Mary Quarterly*, 3d ser., 50 (1993), 356–66. Ira Berlin, "Time, Space, and the Evolution of Afro-American Society on British Mainland North America," *American Historical Review* 85 (1980), 44–78, provides an overview of population densities, family life, and labor conditions within the mainland colonies across the colonial era.

The seminal work on the international slave trade is Philip D. Curtin, *The Atlantic Slave Trade: A Census* (Madison, Wisc., 1969). Many of the relevant primary sources are reproduced in Elizabeth Donnan, ed., *Documents Illustrative of the History of the Slave Trade in America* (4 vols.; Washington, D.C., 1930–35). For overviews of the North American trade, see Ira Berlin, "The Slave Trade and the Development of Afro-American Society in English Mainland North America, 1619–1775," *Southern Studies* 20 (1981), 122–36; Steven Deyle, "'By farr the most profitable trade': Slave Trading in British Colonial America," *Slavery and Abolition* 10 (1989), 107–25; and Philip D. Morgan, "African Migration," in Mary Kupiec Cayton, Elliott J. Gorn, and Peter W. Williams, eds., *Encyclopedia of American Social History*, vol. 2 795–809 (3 vols.; New York, 1993). Other useful general studies include Kenneth Winslow Stetson, "A Quantitative Approach to Britain's American Slave Trade, 1700–1773," (master's thesis, University of Wisconsin, 1967); K. G. Davies, *The Royal African Company* (London, 1957); James A. Rawley, *The Transatlantic Slave Trade: A History* (New York, 1981); W. E. Minchinton, "The Slave Trade of Bristol with the British Mainland Colonies in North America, 1699–1770," in Roger Anstey and P. E. H. Hair, eds., *Liverpool, the African Slave Trade, and Abolition: Essays to Illustrate Current Knowledge and Research*, 39–59 (Liverpool, 1976); and Herbert S. Klein, *The Atlantic Slave Trade* (Cambridge, England, 1999).

Since mainland North America received a relatively small share of the total African migration to the Americas, most subsequent revisions to Curtin's initial estimates of the volume and pace of the trade have concentrated on other areas. Recent discussions relevant to the North American trade in the seventeenth and eighteenth centuries include Philip D. Curtin, "Measuring the Atlantic Slave Trade," in Engerman and Genovese, eds., *Race and Slavery in the Western Hemisphere*, 107–28; Roger Anstey, "The Volume and Profitability of the British Slave Trade, 1761–1807," in the same volume, 3–31; Jay Coughtrey, *The Notorious Tri-*

angle: Rhode Island and the African Slave Trade, 1700–1807 (Philadelphia, 1981); David Eltis and Stanley L. Engerman, "Was the Slave Trade Dominated by Men?" *Journal of Interdisciplinary History* 23 (1992), 237–57; Eltis and Engerman, "Fluctuations in Sex and Age Ratios in the Transatlantic Slave Trade, 1663–1864," *Economic History Review* 46 (1993), 308–23; David Geggus, "Sex Ratio, Age and Ethnicity in the Atlantic Slave Trade: Data from French Shipping and Plantation Records," *Journal of African History* 30 (1989), 23–44; Joseph E. Inikori and Stanley L. Engerman, "Introduction: Gainers and Losers in the Atlantic Slave Trade," in Joseph E. Inikori and Stanley L. Engerman, eds., *The Atlantic Slave Trade: Effects on Economies, Societies, and Peoples in Africa, the Americas, and Europe* 1–21 (Durham, 1992); Paul S. Lovejoy, "The Impact of the Atlantic Slave Trade on Africa: A Review of the Literature," *Journal of African History* 30, (1989), 365–94; David Richardson, "The Eighteenth-Century British Slave Trade: Estimates of Its Volume and Coastal Distribution in Africa," *Research in Economic History* 12 (1989), 151–95; and Richardson, "Slave Exports from West and West-Central Africa, 1700–1810: New Estimates of Volume and Distribution," *Journal of African History* 30 (1989), 1–22. Works on the trade to particular colonies are cited in the regional studies discussed next.

Among the recent studies that have made a strong case for the dominance of one or two African nations in most New World settings, and have posited a central role for ethnicity or nationality in the development of lives lived within slavery are John Thornton, *African and Africans in the Making of the Atlantic World, 1400–1680* (Cambridge, England, 1992); Gwendolyn Midlo Hall, *Africans in Colonial Louisiana: The Development of Afro-Creole Culture in the Eighteenth Century* (Baton Rouge, La., 1992); Douglas Brent Chambers, "'He Gwine Sing He Country': Africans, Afro-Virginians, and the Development of Slave Culture in Virginia, 1690–1820," (unpublished Ph.D. dissertation, University of Virginia, 1996); and Michael A. Gomez, *Exchanging Our Country Marks: The Transformation of African Identities in the Colonial and Antebellum South* (Chapel Hill, N.C., 1998). For an opposing view, see Philip D. Morgan, "The Cultural Implications of the Atlantic Slave Trade: African Regional Origins, American Destinations and New World Developments," in David Eltis and David Richardson, eds., *Routes to Slavery: Direction, Ethnicity and Mortality in the Atlantic Slave Trade* (London, 1997), pp. 122–45.

The best source for basic population information on African-Americans in New England remains Lorenzo Johnston Greene, *The Negro in Colonial New England* (1942; 2d ed., New York, 1968). William D. Piersen, *Black Yankees: The Development of an Afro-American Subculture in the Eighteenth Century* (Amherst, Mass., 1988), also provides information on population size and distribution and on New England slave families, as do James Oliver Horton and Lois C. Horton, *In Hope of Liberty: Culture, Community, and Protest among Northern Free Blacks, 1700–1860* (Oxford, 1997). For Massachusetts, see also George A. Levesque, *Black Boston: African American Life and Culture in Urban America, 1750–1860* (New York, 1994). Two studies on Rhode Island are Rhett S. Jones, "Plantation Slavery in the Narraganset Country of Rhode Island, 1640–1790: A Preliminary Study," *Plantation Society* 2 (1986), 157–70; and Louis P. Masur, "Slavery in Eighteenth-Century Rhode Island: Evidence from the Census of 1774," *Slavery and Abolition* 6 (1985), 139–50. Gary B. Nash, "Forging Freedom: The Emancipation Experience in the Northern Seaport Cities, 1775–1820," in Ira Berlin and Ronald Hoffman, eds., *Slavery and Freedom in the Age of the American Revolution* (Charlottesville, 1983), 3–48, explores the eighteenth-century African-American populations of the cities of Boston, New York, and Philadelphia.

Blacks in the middle colonies are the subject of numerous recent studies; population history issues inform them to varying degrees. For New York, see Thomas J. Davis, "These Enemies of Their Own Household," *Journal of the Afro-American Historical and Genealogical Society* 5 (1984), 133–47; Thelma Wills Foote, "Black Life in Colonial Manhattan, 1664–1786" (unpublished Ph.D. dissertation, Harvard University, 1991); Joyce D. Goodfriend, "Burghers and Blacks: The Evolution of a Slave Society at New Amsterdam," *New York History* 59 (1978), 125–44; Goodfriend, *Before the Melting Pot: Society and Culture in Colonial New York City, 1664–1730* (Princeton, 1992); Vivienne L. Kruger, "Born to Run: The Slave Family in Early New York, 1626–1827" (unpublished Ph.D. dissertation, Columbia University, 1985); James G. Lydon, "New York and the Slave Trade, 1700 to 1774," *William and Mary Quarterly* 35 (1978), 381–94; Richard Shannon Moss, *Slavery on Long Island: A Study in Local Instiitutional and Early African-Ameriican Communal Life* (New York, 1993); Johannes Menne Postma, *The Dutch in the Atlantic Slave Trade, 1600–1815* (Cambridge, England, 1990), 25; Shane White, *Somewhat More Independent: The End of Slavery in New York City, 1700–1810* (Athens, Ga., 1991); and A. J. Williams-Myers, "Hands That Picked No Cotton: An Exploratory Examination of African Slave Labor in the Colonial Economy of the Hudson River Valley to 1800," *Afro-Americans in New York Life and History,* 11 (1987), 25–52.

For the Pennsylvania slave trade, see Darold D. Wax, "Negro Imports into Pennsylvania, 1720–1766," *Pennsylvania History* 32 (1965), 254–87; Wax, "Africans on the Delaware: The Pennsylvania Slave Trade, 1759–1765," *Pennsylvania History* 50 (1983), 38–49; and Jean R. Soderlund, "Black Importation and Migration into Southeastern Pennsylvania, 1682–1810," *Proceedings of the American Philosophical Society* 133 (1989), 144–53. Other works on African Americans in the Quaker state include Jean R. Soderlund, *Quakers and Slavery: A Divided Spirit* (Princeton, N.J., 1985); Soderlund, "Black Women in Colonial Pennsylvania," *Pennsylvania Magazine of History and Biography* 107 (1983), 49–68; and Gary B. Nash and Jean R. Soderlund, *Freedom by Degrees: Emancipation in Pennsylvania and Its Aftermath* (New York, 1991).

A wealth of surviving documentary evidence has supported several especially detailed studies of blacks in the city of Philadelphia. Susan E. Klepp's groundbreaking study of differential mortality rates is particularly noteworthy ("Seasoning and Society: Racial Differences in Mortality in Eighteenth-Century Philadelphia," *William and Mary Quarterly,* 3d ser., 51 (1994), 473–506). Klepp, *"The Swift Progress of Population": A Documentary and Bibliographic Study of Philadelphia's Growth, 1642–1859* (Philadelphia, 1991), reproduces the original documents. Other works include Gary B. Nash, "Slaves and Slaveowners in Colonial Philadelphia," *William and Mary Quarterly,* 3d ser. 30 (1973), 223–56; and Billy G. Smith, *The "Lower Sort": Philadelphia's Laboring People, 1750–1800* (Ithaca, N.Y., 1990).

For New Jersey, see Soderlund, *Quakers and Slavery*; Peter O. Wacker and Paul G. E. Clemens, *Land Use in Early New Jersey: A Historical Geography* (Newark, N.J., 1995); and Graham and Russell Hodges, *Slavery and Freedom in the Rural North: African Americans in Monmouth County, New Jersey, 1665–1865* (Madison, Wis., 1997). Patience Essah, *A House Divided: Slavery and Emancipation in Delaware, 1638–1865* (Charlottesville, Va., 1996), and William H. Williams, *Slavery and Freedom in Delaware, 1639–1865* (Wilmington, Del., 1996), provide information for Delaware.

Scholars of the Chesapeake region have been intensely interested in understanding the population history of Africans and African Americans in the Chesapeake region. Data on the Virginia and Maryland slave trades is found in Chambers, "'He Gwine Sing He Country,'" chaps. 4 and 5; Herbert S. Klein, *The Middle Passage: Comparative Studies in the Atlantic*

Slave Trade (Princeton, 1978), chap. 6; Klein, "New Evidence on the Virginia Slave Trade," *Journal of Interdisciplinary History* 17 (1987), 871–77; Walter F. Minchinton, Celia King, and Peter Waite, eds., *Virginia Slave Trade Statistics, 1698–1771* (Richmond, Va., 1984); Donald M. Sweig, "The Importation of African Slaves to the Potomac River, 1732–1772," *William and Mary Quarterly*, 3d ser., 42 (1985), 507–24; Susan Westbury, "Slaves of Colonial Virginia: Where They Came From," *William and Mary Quarterly*, 3d ser., 42 (1985), 228–37; Westbury, "Analyzing a Regional Slave Trade: The West Indies and Virginia, 1698–1775," *Slavery and Abolition* 7 (1986), 241–57; and Darold D. Wax, "Black Immigrants: The Slave Trade in Colonial Maryland," *Maryland Historical Magazine* 73 (1978), 30–45.

Russell R. Menard's seminal study of the early Maryland slave population outlined methods for deriving demographic measures from slave listings in probate records, and outlined the demographic processes involved in the transition from an immigrant population that could not reproduce itself to a native-born population capable of growing by natural increase ("The Maryland Slave Population, 1658 to 1730: A Demographic Profile of Blacks in Four Counties," *William and Mary Quarterly*, 3d ser., 32 (1975), 29–54). Subsequently Menard investigated the transition from white indentured servant to slave labor in both colonies in "From Servants to Slaves: The Transformation of the Chesapeake Labor System, *Southern Studies* 16 (1977), 355–90. On this topic, see also David W. Galenson, "Economic Aspects of the Growth of Slavery in the Seventeenth-Century Chesapeake," in Barbara L. Solow, ed., *Slavery and the Rise of the Atlantic System*, 265–92 (Cambridge, England, 1991).

Allan Kulikoff's work on Chesapeake African American population history and society is especially comprehensive. In "The Origins of Afro-American Society in Tidewater Maryland and Virginia, 1700–1790," *William and Mary Quarterly*, 3d ser., 35 (1978), 226–59, Kulikoff developed his basic arguments linking demographic processes with social evolution. *Tobacco and Slaves: The Development of Southern Cultures in the Chesapeake, 1680–1800* (Chapel Hill, 1986) presents a more comprehensive survey of these topics. In "A 'Prolifick' People: Black Population Growth in the Chesapeake Colonies, 1700–1790," *Southern Studies* 16 (1977), 391–428, Kulikoff attempted to measure all the basic demographic variables – the volume and timing of immigration, population growth rates, fertility, and mortality.

Darrett B. Rutman and Anita H. Rutman traced the social and economic consequences of the introduction of slaves into a tidewater Virginia county in *A Place in Time: Middlesex County, Virginia, 1650–1750* (New York, 1984). In the accompanying *Explicatus* volume, chaps. 3 and 12, they attempt to reconstruct demographic trends in the county's population over time from exceptionally detailed local records, as well as model the successive population statistics resulting from the importation of a single hypothetical slave cargo over time. In addition, their exploration of the demographic consequences of the introduction of falciparum malaria into the Chesapeake, an unforeseen consequence of the forced migration of West Africans to the region, is a major contribution to biomedical history (Darrett B. Rutman and Anita H. Rutman, "Of Agues and Fevers: Malaria in the Early Chesapeake," *William and Mary Quarterly*, 3d ser., 33 (1976), 31–60). Their subsequent study of differential seasonal patterns of births and deaths by race (Darrett B. Rutman, Charles Wetherell, and Anita H. Rutman, "Rhythms of Life: Black and White Seasonality in the Early Chesapeake," *Journal of Interdisciplinary History* 11 [1980], 29–53) has set the standard for further investigations.

Philip David Morgan is also engaged in a wide-ranging comparative study of colonial Virginia and South Carolina slaves. His dissertation includes a wealth of information on subregional population distributions and sex ratios, family size and structure, and growth rates ("The Development of Slave Culture in Eighteenth-Century Plantation America," unpublished Ph. D. dissertation, University College, London, 1977). Some of this material is summarized in *Slave Counterpoint: Black Culture in the Eighteenth-Century Chesapeake and Lowcountry* (Chapel Hill, N.C., 1998). Alone and in collaboration with Michael L. Nicholls, Morgan has published studies of slaves in the Virginia piedmont that reveal the different and comparatively less destructive demographic outcomes accompanying the inland settlement of a mixture of forced trans-Atlantic and local migrants. See Morgan, "Slave Life in Piedmont Virginia, 1720–1800," in Lois Green Carr, Philip D. Morgan, and Jean B. Russo, eds., *Colonial Chesapeake Society*, 433–84 (Chapel Hill, 1988); and Philip D. Morgan and Michael L. Nicholls, "Slaves in Piedmont Virginia, 1720–1790," *William and Mary Quarterly*, 3d ser., 46 (1989), 211–51.

Other contributions to our understanding of eighteenth-century demographic patterns include John Randolph Barden, "Flushed with Notions of Freedom: The Growth and Emancipation of a Virginia Slave Community, 1732–1812" (unpublished Ph.D. dissertation, Duke University, 1993); and Joan Rezner Gundersen, "The Double Bonds of Race and Sex: Black and White Women in a Colonial Virginia Parish," *Journal of Southern History* 52 (1986), 407–18, which presents data on differential black and white fertility. Sarah S. Hughes, "Slaves for Hire: The Allocation of Black Labor in Elizabeth City County, Virginia, 1782 to 1810," *William and Mary Quarterly*, 3d ser., 35 (1978), 260–86, draws attention to the increasing frequency of slave hiring in the region and to the hardships this caused. On urban slave hiring, see also Midori Takagi, "Slavery in Richmond, Virginia, 1782–1865," (unpublished Ph.D. dissertation, Columbia University, 1994). Jean Butenhoff Lee, "The Problem of Slave Culture in the Eighteenth-Century Chesapeake," *William and Mary Quarterly*, 3d ser., 43 (1986), 333–61, challenges Kulikoff's more optimistic assessment of the chances most slaves had to establish a relatively stable family and community life in older tidewater areas. And Donald M. Sweig, "Northern Virginia Slavery: A Statistical and Demographic Investigation" (unpublished Ph.D. dissertation, College of William and Mary, 1982), supplies information on the composition of the black population in a later-settled part of Virginia.

For the late eighteenth century, Richard S. Dunn, "Black Society in the Chesapeake, 1776–1810," in Ira Berlin and Ronald Hoffman, eds., *Slavery and Freedom in the Age of the American Revolution*, 49–82 (Charlottesville, 1983), provides a comprehensive overview of population growth and migration patterns before and after the American Revolution. In the same volume, Mary Beth Norton, Herbert G. Gutman, and Ira Berlin describe the increasingly complex family networks emerging on large plantations. ("The Afro-American Family in the Age of Revolution," in *Slavery and Freedom*, 175–91.) Peter J. Albert, "The Protean Institution: The Geography, Economy, and Ideology of Slavery in Post-Revolutionary Virginia," (unpublished Ph.D. dissertation, University of Maryland, 1976) supplies information on post-Revolutionary residential patterns and on the composition of the growing free black population in the state.

Studies of the population history of African Americans in the Lower South are beginning to approach those for the Upper South in sheer number. For the regional slave trade, see W. Robert Higgins, "The Geographical Origins of Negro Slaves in Colonial South Carolina," *South Atlantic Quarterly* 70 (1971), 34–47; Daniel C. Littlefield, "The Slave Trade to Colonial South Carolina: A Profile," *South Carolina Historical Magazine* 90 (1990), 68–99; David Richardson, "The British Slave Trade to Colonial South Carolina," *Slavery and Abolition* 12 (1991), 125–72; and Darold D. Wax, "'New Negroes Are Always in Demand': The Slave Trade in Eighteenth-Century Georgia," *Georgia Historical Quarterly* 68 (1984), 193–220.

Peter H. Wood's pioneering work on South Carolina's African American population (*Black Majority: Negroes in Colonial South Carolina from 1670 through the Stono Rebellion* [New York, 1974], especially chap. 5) has set the standard for later investigations. Wood's recent estimates of the southern population by race and region from 1685 to 1790 ("The Changing Population of the Colonial South: An Overview by Race and Region, 1685–1790," in Peter H. Wood, Gregory A. Waselkov, and M. Thomas Hatley, eds., *Powhatan's Mantle: Indians in the Colonial Southeast*, 35–103 (Lincoln, Nebr., 1989), are especially valuable, and bring forcefully to attention the numerical predominance of Native Americans in the region in the seventeenth century.

Daniel C. Littlefield's study of the various West African origins of slaves transported to South Carolina (*Rice and Slaves: Ethnicity and the Slave Trade in Colonial South Carolina* (Baton Rouge, La., 1981), proved that the issue of ethnic backgrounds could indeed be pursued, especially in the Lower South, where the African origins of many slaves are well documented.

Philip David Morgan further plumbs the interrelationships between population size and densities, the organization of work, and family and community life in "The Development of Slave Culture in Eighteenth Century Plantation America," in "Black Life in Eighteenth-Century Charleston," *Perspectives in American History* New Series, I (1984), 187–232; in "Black Society in the Lowcountry, 1760–1810," in Berlin and Hoffman, eds., *Slavery and Freedom*, 83–142; and in *Slave Counterpoint*.

Additional information on early South Carolina African Americans is found in Peter A. Coclanis, *The Shadow of a Dream: Economic Life and Death in the South Carolina Low Country, 1670–1920* (New York, 1989), chap. 2; in Russell R. Menard, "The Africanization of the Lowcountry Labor Force, 1760–1730," in Winthrop D. Jordan and Sheila L. Skemp, eds., *Race and Family in the Colonial South*, 81–103 (Jackson, Miss., 1987); and in Menard, "Slave Demography in the Low Country, 1670–1740: From Frontier Society to Plantation Regime," *South Carolina Historical Magazine* 96 (1995): 280–303. Cheryll Ann Cody's work on the fertility and mortality of low-country slaves on large rice plantations supplies scarce evidence on fertility rates for the late eighteenth century: Ale "Slave Demography and Family Formation: A Community Study of the Ball Family Plantations, 1720–1896" (unpublished Ph.D. dissertation, University of Minnesota, 1982); and "A Note on Changing Patterns of Slave Fertility in the South Carolina Rice District, 1735–1865," *Southern Studies* 16 (1977), 457–63.

Marvin L. Michael Kay and Lorin Lee Cary, *Slavery in North Carolina, 1748–1775* (Chapel Hill, N.C., 1995), provide detailed information on the subregional distribution of North Carolina's African American population across the eighteenth century. Appendixes present useful summaries of various measures of fertility and family size for this and other southern colonies. See also their earlier essay, "A Demographic Analysis of Colonial North Carolina with Special Emphasis upon the Slave and Black Populations," in Jeffrey J. Crow and Flora J. Hatley, eds., *Black Americans in North Carolina*, 71–121 (Chapel Hill, N.C., 1984). The North Carolina slave trade has not yet been systematically analyzed; brief discussions appear in Kay and Cary, Chap. 1, and in Arna Alexander Bontemps, "A Social History of Black Culture in Colonial North Carolina" (Ph.D. dissertation, University of Illinois at Urbana-Champaign, 1989), chap. 3.

For Georgia, see Betty Wood, *Slavery in Colonial Georgia, 1730–1775* (Athens, Ga., 1984); and Julia Floyd Smith, *Slavery and Rice Culture in Low Country Georgia, 1750–1860* (Knoxville, Tenn., 1985).

Gwendolyn Midlo Hall's, *Africans in Colonial Louisiana: The Development of Afro-Creole Culture in the Eighteenth Century* (Baton Rouge, La., 1992), combines a detailed study of the Louisiana slave trade with a provocative analysis of the continuing influence of the slaves' West African origins in their adaptations to life in North America. On geographic and ethnic origins of Louisiana slaves, see also Peter Caron, "'Of a Nation Which the Others Do Not Understand': Bambara Slaves and African Ethnicity in Colonial Louisiana, 1718–60," in David Eltis and David Richardson, eds., *Routes to Slavery: Direction, Ethnicity and Mortality in the Atlantic Slave Trade* (London, 1997), 98–121; Thomas N. Ingersoll, "The Slave Trade and the Ethnic Diversity of Louisiana's Slave Community," *Louisiana History* 37 (1996), 133–61; and Daniel Usner, Jr., "From African Captivity to American Slavery: The Introduction of Black Laborers to Colonial Louisiana," *Louisiana History* 20 (1979), 25–48.

For Florida, see Jane L. Landers, "Traditions of African American Freedom and Community in Spanish Colonial Florida"; and Daniel L. Schafer, "Yellow Silk Ferret Tied Round Their Wrists: African Americans in British East Florida, 1763–1784," in David R. Colburn and Jane L. Landers, eds., *The African American Heritage of Florida* (Gainesville, Fla., 1995), 17–41, 71–103.

Works dealing with internal migration within the colonies include Morgan and Nicholls, "Slaves in Piedmont Virginia, 1720–1790." For the movements precipitated by the American Revolution and by westward expansion after the war, see Sylvia R. Frey, *Water from the Rock: Black Resistance in a Revolutionary Age* (Princeton, N.J., 1991), chaps. 6 and 7; and Allan Kulikoff, "Uprooted Peoples: Black Migrants in the Age of the American Revolution, 1790–1820," in Berlin and Hoffman, eds., *Slavery and Freedom in the Age of the American Revolution*, 143–71. For postwar urban migration, see Nash, "Forging Freedom"; and Soderlund, "Black Importation and Migration into Southeastern Pennsylvania."

The postwar international migrations of blacks who sided with the British during the conflict are discussed in James W. St. G. Walker, *The Black Loyalists: The Search for a Promised Land in Nova Scotia and Sierra Leone, 1783–1870* (1976; 2d ed., Toronto, 1992); Ellen Gibson Wilson, *The Loyal Blacks* (New York, 1976); Mary Beth Norton, "The Fate of Some Black Loyalists of the American Revolution," *Journal of Negro History* 58 (1973), 402–26; and Graham Russell Hodges, ed. *The Black Loyalist Directory: African Americans in Exile after the American Revolution* (New York, 1996).

Philip D. Curtin's "Epidemiology and the Slave Trade," *Political Science Quarterly* 83 (1967), 190–216, first brought issues of comparative epidemiology and of significantly different experiences with disease among blacks and whites to the forefront of comparative studies of slavery. The major work on the subject is Kenneth F. Kiple and Virginia Himmelsteib King, *Another Dimension to the Black Diaspora: Diet, Disease, and Racism* (Cambridge, England, 1981). Kenneth F. Kiple, "A Survey of Recent Literature on the Biological Past," *Social Science History* 10 (1986), 339–67, provides a useful introduction to the relevant literature and a summary of the issues. Some comparative colonial and early national period urban death rates are presented in Christian Warren, "Northern Chills, Southern Fevers: Race – Specific Mortality in American Cities, 1730–1900," *Journal of Southern History* 63 (1997), 23–56.

For a layman's introduction to the contributions and methodologies of anthropometrics, see John Komlos, ed. *Stature, Living Standards, and Economic Development: Essays in Anthropometric History* (Chicago, 1994). Studies of stature that deal with African Americans born in the eighteenth century include John Komlos, "The Height of Runaway Slaves in Colonial America, 1720–1770," in the preceding volume, 93–116; Richard H. Steckel, "Slave Height Profiles from Coastwise Manifests," *Explorations in*

Economic History 16 (1979), 363–80; Robert A. Margo and Richard H. Steckel, "The Height of American Slaves: New Evidence on Slave Nutrition and Health," *Social Science History* 6 (1982), 516–38; and Richard H. Steckel, "A Peculiar Population: The Nutrition, Health, and Mortality of American Slaves from Childhood to Maturity," *Journal of Economic History* 46 (1986), 721–41. These materials are conveniently summarized in Richard H. Steckel, "Heights and Health in the United States, 1710–1950," in Komlos, ed., *Stature, Living Standards, and Economic Development*, 153–70.

Most archaeological findings are available only in unpublished research reports with a limited circulation. Here I have not attempted a systematic review and listing of all relevant reports. Published studies that discuss the wider implications of findings on the colonial African-American diet include Tyson Gibbs, Cathleen Cargill, Leslie Sue Lieberman, and Elizabeth Reitz, "Nutrition in a Slave Population: An Anthropological Examination," *Medical Anthropology* 4 (1980), 175–262; and Elizabeth J. Reitz, Tyson Gibbs, and Ted A. Rathbun, "Archaeological Evidence for Subsistence on Coastal Plantations," in Theresa A. Singleton, ed., *The Archaeology of Slavery and Plantation Life*, 163–91 (Orlando, Fla., 1985). More recent archaeological investigations of Chesapeake and Lower South slave sites have produced a wealth of new information on slave diet, but this evidence has yet to be summarized. Lorena S. Walsh, "Consumer Behavior, Diet, and the Standard of Living in Late Colonial and Early Antebellum America, 1770–1840," in Robert E. Gallman and John Joseph Wallis, eds., *American Economic Growth and Standards of Living before the Civil War*, 240–45 (Chicago, 1992), summarizes some of the main findings about diet and references additional literature, as does Morgan, *Slave Counterpoint*, pp. 134–45.

Generally available articles on skeletal analysis for this period include Lawrence J. Angel, "Colonial to Modern Skeletal Change in the U.S.A.," *American Journal of Physical Anthropology* 45 (1976), 723–35; Arthur C. Aufderheide, Fraser D. Neiman, Lorentz E. Wittmers, Jr., and George Rapp, "Lead in Bone II: Skeletal-Lead Content as an Indicator of Lifetime Lead Ingestion and the Social Correlates in an Archaeological Population," *American Journal of Physical Anthropology* 55 (1981), 285–91; Douglas W. Owsley, Charles E. Orser, Jr., Robert W. Mann, Peer H. Moore-Jamsen, and Robert L. Montgomery, "Demography and Pathology of an Urban Slave Population from New Orleans," *American Journal of Physical Anthropology* 74 (1987), 185–97; Jennifer Olsen Kelley and J.

Lawrence Angel, "Life Stresses of Slavery," *American Journal of Physical Anthropology* 74 (1987), 199–211; and J. Lawrence Angel, Jennifer Olsen Kelley, Michael Parrington, and Stephanie Pinter, "Life Stresses of the Free Black Community as Represented by the First African Baptist Church, Philadelphia, 1823–1841," *American Journal of Physical Anthropology* 74 (1987), 213–29. See also Amy Friedlander, "Establishing Historical Probabilities for Archaeological Interpretations: Slave Demography of Two Plantations in the South Carolina Low Country, 1740–1820," in Singleton, ed., *The Archaeology of Slavery and Plantation Life*, 215–38; and Douglas H. Ubelaker and Philip D. Curtin, "Human Biology of Populations in the Chesapeake Watershed," in Philip D. Curtin, ed., *History of the Chesapeake Ecosystem*, forthcoming.

REFERENCES

African Burial Ground Office of Public Education and Interpretation. "Questions and Answers on the African Burial Ground & Five Points Archaeological Project." Mimeo, New York, 1993.

Angel, Lawrence J. "Colonial to Modern Skeletal Change in the U.S.A." *American Journal of Physical Anthropology* 45 (1976): 723–35.

Angel, Lawrence J., Jennifer Olsen Kelley, Michael Parrington, et al. "Life Stresses of the Free Black Community as Represented by the First African Baptist Church, Philadelphia, 1823–1841." *American Journal of Physical Anthropogy* 74 (1987): 312–29.

Aufderheide, Arthur C., Fraser D. Neiman, Lorentz E. Wittmers, Jr., et al. "Lead in Bone II: Skeletal-Lead Content as an Indicator of Lifetime Lead Ingestion and the Social Correlates in an Archaeological Population." *American Journal of Physical Anthropology* 55 (1981): 285–91.

Berlin, Ira. "Time, Space, and the Evolution of Afro-American Society on British Mainland North America." *American Historical Review* 85 (1980): 44–78.

———. *Many Thousands Gone: The First Two Centuries of Slavery in North America.* Cambridge, Mass.: Harvard University Press, 1998.

Brown, Kathleen M. "Brave New Worlds: Women's and Gender History." *William and Mary Quarterly*, 3d ser., 50 (1993): 311–28.

Carter, Landon. *The Diary of Col. Landon Carter of Sabine Hall, 1752–1778.* 2 vols. Edited by Jack P. Greene. Charlottesville: University Press of Virginia, 1965.

Chambers, Douglas Brent. "'He Gwine Sing He Country': Africans, Afro-Virginians, and the Development of Slave Culture in Virginia, 1690–1810." Ph.D. diss., University of Virginia, 1996.

Cody, Cheryll Ann. "A Note on Changing Patterns of Slave Fertility in the South Carolina Rice District, 1735–1865." *Southern Studies*, 16 (1977): 457–63.

———. "Slave Demography and Family Formation: A Community Study of the Ball Family Plantations, 1720–1896." Ph.D. diss., University of Minnesota, 1982.

Curtin, Philip D. "Epidemiology and the Slave Trade." *Political Science Quarterly* 83 (1967): 190–216.

———. *The Atlantic Slave Trade: A Census*. Madison, Wisc.: University of Wisconsin Press, 1969.

———. *Death by Migration: Europe's Encounter with the Tropical World in the Nineteenth Century*. Cambridge, England: Cambridge University Press, 1989.

Davis, Thomas J. "These Enemies of Their Own Household." *Journal of the Afro-American Historical and Genealogical Society* 5 (1984): 133–47.

Dunn, Richard S. "Black Society in the Chesapeake, 1776–1810." In *Slavery and Freedom in the Age of the American Revolution*, edited by Ira Berlin and Ronald Hoffman, 49–82. Charlottesville: University Press of Virginia, 1983.

Eltis, David, and David Richardson, eds. *Routes to Slavery: Direction, Ethnicity and Mortality in the Atlantic Slave Trade*. London: Frank Cass, 1997.

———. "Productivity in the Transatlantic Slave Trade." *Explorations in Economic History* 32 (1995): 465–84.

Eltis, David, David Richardson, and Stephen D. Behrendt. "The Structure of the Transatlantic Slave Trade, 1595–1867." In *Transatlantic Passages*, edited by Henry Louis Gates, Jr., Carl Pederson, and Maria Diedrich. Forthcoming.

Eltis, David, David Richardson, Stephen D. Behrendt, and Herbert S. Klein, eds. *The Trans-Atlantic Slave Trade: A Database on CD-ROM*. Cambridge, England: Cambridge University Press, 1998.

Engerman, Stanley L. "Comments on the Study of Race and Slavery." In *Race and Slavery in the Western Hemisphere: Quantitative Studies*, edited by Stanley L. Engerman and Eugene D. Genovese, 495–530. Princeton, N.J.: Princeton University Press, 1975.

———. "Some Economic and Demographic Comparisons of Slavery in the United States and the British West Indies." *Economic History Review*, 2d ser., 29 (1976): 258–75.

Fogel, Robert William and Engerman, Stanley L. "Philanthropy at Bargain Prices: Notes on the Economics of Gradual Emancipation." *Journal of Legal Studies* 3 (1974): 377–401.

———. *Time on the Cross: The Economics of American Negro Slavery*. Boston: Little, Brown, 1974.

———. "Revised Estimates of the U.S. Slave Trade and of the Native-Born Share of the Black Population." In *Without Consent or Contract: The Rise and Fall of American Slavery: Evidence and Methods*, edited by Robert W. Fogel, Ralph A. Galantine, and Richard L. Manning. New York: W. W. Norton, 1992.

Frey, Sylvia R. *Water from the Rock: Black Resistance in a Revolutionary Age*. Princeton, N.J.: Princeton University Press, 1991.

Gibbs, Tyson, Cathleen Cargill, Leslie Sue Liberman, et al. "Nutrition in a Slave Population: An Anthropological Examination." *Medical Anthropology* 4 (1980): 175–262.

Gomez, Michael A. *Exchanging Our Country Marks: The Transformation of African Identities in the Colonial and Antebellum South*. Chapel Hill: University of North Carolina Press, 1998.

Greéne, Lorenzo Johnston. *The Negro in Colonial New England*. 2d ed. New York: Athenaeum, 1968.

Gundersen, Joan Rezner. "The Double Bonds of Race and Sex: Black and White Women in a Colonial Virginia Parish." *Journal of Southern History* 52 (1986): 351–72.

Hall, Gwendolyn Midlo. *Africans in Colonial Louisiana: The Development of Afro-Creole Culture in the Eighteenth Century*. Baton Rouge: Louisiana State University Press, 1992.

Kay, Marvin L., and Lorin Lee Cary. *Slavery in North Carolina, 1748–1775*. Chapel Hill: University of North Carolina Press, 1995.

Kelley, Jennifer Olsen, and Lawrence J. Angel. "Life Stresses of Slavery." *American Journal of Physical Anthropology* 74 (1987): 199–211.

Kiple, Kenneth F., and Virginia Himmelsteib King. *Another Dimension to the Black Diaspora: Diet, Disease, and Racism*. Cambridge, England: Cambridge University Press, 1981.

Klein, Herbert S., and Stanley L. Engerman. "Fertility Differentials between Slaves in the United States and the British West Indies: A Note on Lactation Practices." *William and Mary Quarterly*, 3d ser., 35 (1978): 357–74.

Klepp, Susan E. "Seasoning and Society: Racial Differences in Mortality in Eighteenth-Century Philadelphia." *William and Mary Quarterly*, 3d ser., 51 (1994): 473–506.

Komlos, John. "The Height of Runaway Slaves in Colonial America, 1720–1770. "In *Stature, Living Standards, and Economic Development: Essays in Anthropometric History*, edited by John Komlos, 93–116. Chicago: University of Chicago Press, 1994.

Kulikoff, Allan. "A 'Prolifick' People: Black Population Growth in the Chesapeake Colonies, 1700–1790." *Southern Studies* 16 (1977): 391–428.

———. "The Origins of Afro-American Society in Tidewater Maryland and Virginia 1700–1790." *William and Mary Quarterly*, 3d ser., 35 (1978): 226–59.

———. "Uprooted Peoples: Black Migrants in the Age of the American Revolution, 1790–1820." In *Slavery and Freedom in the Age of the American Revolution*, edited by Ira Berlin and Ronald Hoffman, 143–71. Charlottesville: University Press of Virginia, 1983.

———. *Tobacco and Slaves: The Development of Southern Cultures in the Chesapeake, 1680–1800*. Chapel Hill: University of North Carolina Press, 1986.

Lee, Jean Butenhoff. "The Problem of Slave Culture in the Eighteenth-Century Chesapeake." *William and Mary Quarterly*, 3d ser., 43 (1984): 333–61.

Levesque, George A. *Black Boston: African American Life and Culture in Urban America, 1750–1860*. New York, 1994.

Littlefield, Daniel C. "Plantations, Paternalism, and Profitability: Factors Affecting African Demography in the Old British Empire." *Journal of Southern History* 47 (1981): 167–82.

———. *Rice and Slaves: Ethnicity and the Slave Trade in Colonial South Carolina*. Baton Rouge: Louisiana State University Press, 1981.

McCusker, John J., and Russell R. Menard. *The Economy of British America, 1607–1789*. Chapel Hill: University of North Carolina Press, 1985.

Margo, Robert A., and Richard H. Steckel. "The Heights of American Slaves: New Evidence on Slave Nutrition and Health." *Social Science History* 6 (1982): 516–38.

Menard, Russell R. "The Maryland Slave Population, 1658 to 1730: A Demographic Profile of Blacks in Four Counties." *William and Mary Quarterly*, 3d ser., 32 (1975): 29–54.

———. "Whatever Happened to Early American Population History?" *William and Mary Quarterly*, 3d ser., 50 (1993): 356–66.

————. "Slave Demography in the Low Country, 1670–1740: From Frontier Society to Plantation Regime." *South Carolina Historical Magazine* 96 (1995): 280–303.

Moore, Stacy Gibbons. "'Established and Well Cultivated': Afro-American Foodways in Early Virginia". *Virginia Cavalcade* 39 (2) (1989): 70–83.

Morgan, Philip David. "The Development of Slave Culture in Eighteenth-Century Plantation America." Ph. D. diss., University College, London, 1977.

————. "Black Society in the Lowcountry, 1760–1810." In *Slavery and Freedom in the Age of the American Revolution*, edited by Ira Berlin and Ronald Hoffman, 83–141. Charlottesville: University Press of Virginia, 1983.

————. *Slave Counterpoint: Black Culture in the Eighteenth-Century Chesapeake and Lowcountry*. Chapel Hill: University of North Carolina Press, 1998.

————. "Slave Life in Piedmont Virginia, 1720–1800." In *Colonial Chesapeake Society*, edited Lois Green Carr, Philip D. Morgan, and Jean B. Russo, 433–84. Chapel Hill: University of North Carolina Press, 1988.

Morgan, Philip D., and Michael L. Nicholls. "Slaves in Piedmont Virginia, 1720–1790." *William and Mary Quarterly*, 3d ser., 46 (1989): 211–51.

Nash, Gary B. "Slaves and Slaveowners in Colonial Philadelphia." *William and Mary Quarterly*, 3d ser., 30 (1973): 223–56.

————. "Forging Freedom: The Emancipation Experience in the Northern Seaport Cities, 1775–1820." In *Slavery and Freedom in the Age of the American Revolution*, edited by Ira Berlin and Ronald Hoffman, 3–48. Charlottesville: University Press of Virginia, 1983.

Nash, Gary B., and Jean R. Soderlund. *Freedom by Degrees: Emancipation in Pennsylvania and Its Aftermath*. New York: Oxford University Press, 1991.

Owsley, Douglas W., Charles E. Orser, Jr., Robert W. Mann, et al. "Demography and Pathology of an Urban Slave Population from New Orleans." *American Journal of Physical Anthropology* 74 (1987): 185–97.

Rathbun, Ted A. "Health and Disease at a South Carolina Plantation: 1840–1870." *American Journal of Physical Anthropology* 74 (1987): 239–53.

Reitz, Elizabeth J., Tyson Gibbs, and Ted A. Rathbun. "Archaeological Evidence for Subsistence on Coastal Plantations." In *The Archaeology of Slavery and Plantation Life*, edited by Theresa A. Singleton, 163–91. Orlando, Fla.: Academic Press, 1985.

Rutman, Darrett B., and Anita H. Rutman. "Of Agues and Fevers: Malaria in the Early Chesapeake." *William and Mary Quarterly*, 3d ser., 33 (1976): 31–60.

————. *A Place in Time: Explicatus*. New York: W. W. Norton, 1984.

Rutman, Darrett B., Charles Wetherell, and Anita H. Rutman. "Rhythms of Life: Black and White Seasonality in the Early Chesapeake." *Journal of Interdisciplinary History* 11 (1980): 29–53.

Sensbach, Jon F. "Charting a Course in Early African-American History." *William and Mary Quarterly*, 3d ser., 50 (1993): 394–405.

Soderlund, Jean R. "Black Importation and Migration into Southeastern Pennsylvania, 1682–1810." *Proceedings of the American Philosophical Society* 133 (1989): 144–53.

Steckel, Richard H. "Heights and Health in the United States, 1710–1950." In *Stature, Living Standards, and Economic Development*, edited by John Komlos, 153–70. Chicago: University of Chicago Press, 1994.

Stevenson, Brenda E. "Black Family Structure in Colonial and Antebellum Virginia: Amending the Revisionist Perspective." In *The Decline in Marriage among African Americans: Causes, Consequences, and Policy Implications*, edited by M. Belinda Tucker and Claudia Mitchell-Kernan, 27–56. New York: Russell Sage Foundation, 1995.

Sutch, Richard. "The Care and Feeding of Slaves." In *Reckoning with Slavery*, edited by Paul A. David, Herbert G. Gutman, Richard Sutch, et al., 123–301. New York: Oxford University Press, 1976.

Thornton, John. *Africa and Africans in the Making of the Atlantic World, 1400–1680.* Cambridge, England: Cambridge University Press, 1992.

Trussell, James, and Richard Steckel. "The Estimation of the Mean Age of Female slaves at the Time of Menarche and Their First Birth." *Journal of Interdisciplinary History* 8 (1978): 477–505.

Walsh, Lorena S. "Consumer Behavior, Diet, and the Standard of Living in Late Colonial and Early Antebellum America, 1770–1840." In *American Economic Growth and Standards Living before the Civil War*, edited by Robert E. Gallman and John Joseph Wallis, 217–61. Chicago: University of Chicago Press, 1992.

———. "Work and Resistance in the New Republic: The Case of the Chesapeake, 1770–1820." In *From Chattel Slaves to Wage Slaves: The Dynamics of Labour Bargaining in the Americas*, edited by Mary Turner, 97–122. Bloomington: Indiana University Press, 1995.

———. *From Calabar to Carter's Grove: The History of a Tidewater Virginia African-American Slave Community.* Charlottesville: University Press of Virginia, forthcoming, 1997.

Warren, Christian. "Northern Chills, Southern Fevers: Race-Specific Mortality in American Cities, 1730–1900." *Journal of Southern History* 63 (1997): 23–56.

Wax, Darold D. "Preferences for Slaves in Colonial America. *Journal of Negro History* 58 (1973): 371–401.

Wood, Peter H. *Black Majority: Negroes in Colonial South Carolina from 1670 through the Stono Rebellion.* New York: W. W. Norton, 1974.

7

THE PEOPLING OF MEXICO FROM ORIGINS TO REVOLUTION

ROBERT MCCAA

Great triumphs and terrible tragedies mark the population history of Mexico over the millennia. The first great swell of population growth in the Mexican subcontinent began almost ten thousand years ago with the domestication of gourds, squash, corn, and beans. The last started less than three-quarters of a century ago, thanks to advances in public health, food production, and mass education. The demographic dynamics of the region that we know today as the Republic of Mexico can be conveniently divided into four great epochs: ancient (A.D. −1519), colonial (1519–1821), national (1821–1910), and modern (1910–present). These political turning points in the history of this vast region had great demographic significance and therefore should not be discarded or ignored simply because they are political.[1] Each provoked demographic catastrophe to a greater or lesser degree, but each radically transformed basic conditions of life and death in Mexico. The first three periods – ancient, colonial, and national – are discussed in this essay.

ANCIENT MESOAMERICA

The peopling of ancient Mesoamerica is one of the most complex phenomena in Mexican prehistory. Perhaps because of this it is also one of the most prolifically studied and controversial. When did humans first appear on the Mexican subcontinent? Did the emergence of agriculture

---

[1] Kuznesof ("Gender Ideology") argues against the conventional colonial-national periodization based on politics to emphasize continuities in the history of gender and race relations in Mexico for the years 1750–1850.

spark a demographic revolution? What was the role of demographic pressure in the decay and collapse of many of the great cultural centers, such as La Venta, El Tajín, Cuicuilco, Tula, Teotihuacán, Palenque, Chichén Itzá, and elsewhere? At first contact with Europeans, were Amerindians under a Malthusian threat for exceeding the limits of the carrying capacity of the land, or had they achieved instead a harmonious balance with the environment? Answers to these questions are fundamental for understanding the evolution of ancient Mexican culture, politics, society, and economy.

Most archaeologists and geneticists accept the Asian origins of the first humans in the Americas, but considerable disagreement persists over the date of those origins, (estimates range from 20,000 to 70,000 years ago), as well as the number of migration "waves" from Asia (whether there was one, two, three, or even more). Recent, still tentative, mitochondrial DNA research suggests only two: the first some 34,000 years ago, followed by a second as recently as 15,000 years ago.[2] The dating of ancient habitational sites is also highly speculative. Human habitation at El Cedral in San Luis Potosí (Map 7.1) has been placed at 30,000 B.P. (before the present). Sites at Valsequillo and Tlapacoya are dated to 22,000 B.P. An intensive study of the Tehuacán Valley reveals continuous human occupation from 12,000 B.P..[3]

The Tehuacán Valley site offers a fascinating, if conjectural, sequence of habitational densities from remote antiquity to the moment of European contact.[4] From 9,000 to 7,000 years ago, demographic densities in the valley barely averaged two inhabitants per 100 square kilometers (2.2 inh./100 km²). Later, first gourd, then squash and, after several thousand years, tiny corn cobs appeared in the archaeological record – two millennia after the presence of corn pollen in the Valley of Oaxaca. Over several thousand years population densities drifted upward, increasing sixfold, to 14 inh./100 km² (5400–4300 B.P.). Millennia passed, and the agricultural "revolution" continued, but at a pace thousands of years slower than in the Middle East. Diffusion was a multimillennial process in Mesoamerica, slowed by the fact that expansion was along the more challenging south–north axis rather than east–west. Mesoamerican corn and other cultigens ultimately adapted both to varying day length as well as climate necessitated for longitudinal diffusion, but this required many centuries of experience and experiment.[5]

[2] Wallace, "Mitochondrial DNA," 46.   [3] Serrano Sánchez, "Orígen del hombre."
[4] MacNeish, *Prehistory*; MacNeish, "Social Implications."   [5] Diamond, *Guns*, pp. 178–91.

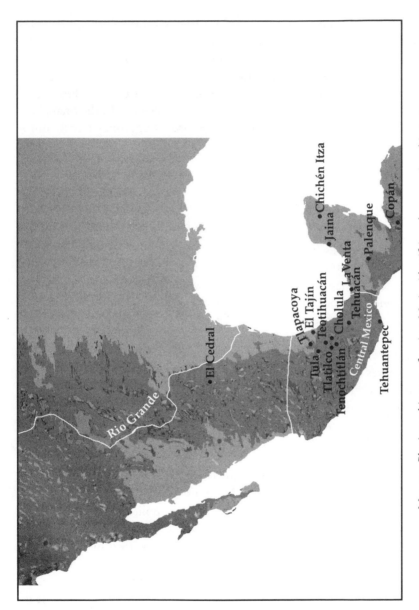

Map 7.1. Physiographic map of ancient Mexico identifying places mentioned in text

Demographic conditions scarcely improved with the agricultural revolution. In Tehuacán, it took 20 centuries for a 25-fold increase in population. Change occurred in "jumps and spurts" and with many false starts. As irrigation technique and practice evolved (2900–2100 B.P.) population growth slowly accelerated and densities expanded, from 43 inh./100 km^2 (3000 B.P.) to 165 (2500 B.P.) and 1,100 (2100–1300 B.P.). In the final phase (1,300–500 years ago), in the 8 centuries preceding contact with Europeans, population densities multiplied 3-fold, to some 3,600 inh./100 km^2, fortified towns developed, and "despotic primitive states" took root.[6]

POPULATION IN THE CENTRAL MEXICAN BASIN OVER THREE MILLENNIA

The greatest success in Mesoamerica in terms of demographic density is found in the Central Mexican Basin. From a study of more than 3,600 habitation sites, William T. Sanders and his co-workers pieced together an astonishing series of population estimates stretching over three millennia.[7] Figure 7.1 depicts the long-term evolution of population sizes in the basin. To take into account error and uncertainties, smoothed curves at 50% and 150% bracket their point estimates. The figure is scaled logarithmically – as are most figures in this essay – to suggest relative growth and decline for each period. The graph in Figure 7.1 shows the population of the Valley of Mexico expanding from fewer than 5,000 inhabitants 3,500 years ago to some 1–1.2 million in 1519. Three long cycles of growth stand out (3500–2100 B.P., 1850–1250 B.P., and 850–500 B.P.), punctuated by two periods of decay (2100–1850 B.P. and 1250–850 B.P.). Region-wide decline is explained sometimes by exogenous factors, a cooling climate or severe seismic activity, and at others by endogenous developments or lack thereof, such as population pressure, economic decay, or political disintegration.

To place colonial and postcolonial figures in perspective, I extend Sanders's archaeologically derived estimates, first, with a historical series he constructed from written sources for population decline in the Central Mexican Basin from 1520 to 1568, and, second, with my own estimates from a nadir in 1610, followed by recovery to 1793, 1900, and 1995. If we discount the most recent and as yet incomplete phase, the graph exhibits three growth cycles at intervals of roughly one thousand years, occurring 2,500, 1,500, and 500 years ago.

---

[6] MacNeish, "Social Implications."   [7] Sanders, Parsons, and Santley, *Basin of Mexico.*

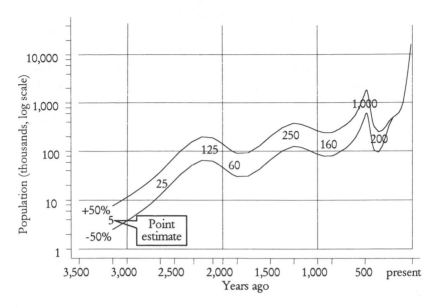

Figure 7.1. Population of the Basin of Mexico across the millennia: cycles of growth and decline (3,000–500 B.P.), disaster (A.D. 1519–1650), and recovery (1650 to present)

The graph also shows how tiny rates of change, averaging less than ±0.4% per year over many centuries, yield substantial shifts in population size and density. Thus, the agricultural revolution, a multimillennial process that began 4,000–8,000 years ago, led to a quickening of growth in Tehuacán, Teotihuacán, Oaxaca, Patzcuaro, and elsewhere, but not to a demographic revolution, although some archaeologists interpret the same data to mean a "demographic explosion."[8] Even when prehistoric growth rates reached their peak in the Central Mexican Basin, just 750 years ago, the annual average scarcely attained three-quarters of 1%. Figure 7.1 shows that this region has had only one demographic revolution, and it occurred in the twentieth century, when the annual baby crop topped 2 million and growth peaked at almost 3%. This revolution is already winding down. By the middle of the next millennium, twentieth-century growth may come to resemble one of the demographic swells of the paleolithic past.

Regional trends summarize myriad local experiences, fruitfully documented in the Teotihuacán Valley study. Regional variations show how

[8] McClung and Serra Puche, "La revolución agrícola," p. 155.

difficult it was to win the demographic lottery in ancient Mesoamerica.
The many "disappearances" of ancient civilizations have provoked much
speculation about causes. The pioneering bioarchaeologist Frank Saul suggests that we may be asking the wrong question about the decline of
Mesoamerican cities, cultures or peoples. Saul argues that the question
should be "not *why* they declined, but rather, *how* they managed to survive
for so long."[9] The bioarchaeological record reveals that Mesoamerican
populations (indeed, most ancient peoples) were fragile, weakened by
stress, poor nutrition, and ill health.[10] The old notion of strong, robust,
healthy populations in Mesoamerica – a pre-Columbian paradise – is
poorly supported by settlement patterns and the skeletal evidence.[11] Ethnohistorical interpretations highlight success stories,[12] but ethnohistorical
sources still await skeptical, demographically informed scrutiny.

STRESS, CONDITIONS OF LIFE, AND PALEODEMOGRAPHY

Physical and physiological stress seems ubiquitous in Mesoamerica,
although somewhat less so than among most peoples in northern North
America. Osteoarthritis (degenerative bone disease), likely due to extreme
physical exertion, is present in adult skeletal remains from 5,000 years
ago in the Tehuacán Valley. High rates of healed fractures, severe dental
wear, and advanced osteophytosis are common in the earliest extant
skeletal material. Tuberculosis and treponemal infection (forms of syphilis
and yaws) date from 3000 B.P. Also common are coral-like lesions on the
crania (porotic hyperostosis and cribra orbitalia), severe physiological
responses to acute or chronic anemia resulting from nutritional deficiencies, extreme parasitic infestation, debilitating infection, blood loss, or
some combination of these.[13] The architectural riches of Chichén Itzá
contrast starkly with the physiological poverty of its population, which
suffered from hard labor, illness, infection, and severe malnutrition.[14]
A tally of 752 adult Mesoamerican skeletons from the Health and Nutrition in the Americas database reveals women with higher rates of
facial fractures than men (gender abuse?) and more joint disease of the

[9] Saul, *Human Skeletal Remains*, p. 73.
[10] Serrano Sánchez, "Orígen del hombre," pp. 112–14; Cohen, "Does Paleopathology Measure." Cook
cites the lament of the Chilam Balam Chumayel that "Then all was well" (*Born to Die*, p. 215).
[11] Viesca, "Epidemiología," pp. 175–76, 180.
[12] Ortiz de Montellano, *Aztec Medicine.*   [13] Viesca, "Hambruna y epidemia," pp. 178–80.
[14] Márquez Morfín, Peraza, Gamboa, and Miranda, *Playa del Carmen.*

wrists (repetitive stress from the arduous labor of grinding corn for tortillas?). Spines of adults of both sexes show severe degenerative wear, averaging 40% or more at Jaina, Tlatilco, Cholula, and Copán (Honduras). The lesson learned from these skeletons is that where the human body was the principal mechanism for growing food, constructing buildings, and moving heavy burdens, the biological price was great. Hard, repetitive work exacted severe wear on Mesoamerican bodies of both sexes, particularly joints required for mobility, manipulation of objects, or bearing loads.

From Black Mesa pueblo in the arid northwest to Copán in the humid southeast, the emergence of agriculture reduced dental degeneration caused by the wear and tear of consuming foraged foods, but life-threatening caries, abscesses, and tooth loss became more pronounced in response to high-carbohydrate corn-based diets. As populations became more sedentary, diarrhea, typhus, and region-wide famine probably became more common.[15] With the spread of a monotonous diet of squash, corn, and beans, stature declined, at least for males. Shortening stature was an adaptive response to malnutrition, undernutrition, and concomitant disease levels, resulting from the adoption of a settled, neolithic way of life. These were the primary causes of regional and temporal differentials in stature. Males in the north, subsisting from hunting and gathering, averaged 165 cm, with little decline over time. In the center, the average stature for men in the classic period fell to 160 cm. Southward from Oaxaca, the average adult male stood at 155 cm, although along the coasts heights were greater. Female stature, averaging 145–155 cm, is more perplexing because there was little systematic variation in space or time.[16]

Paleodemography corroborates the findings of paleopathology. Extraordinarily low life expectancy was the rule for Mesoamerican populations. Paleodemographers favor life expectancy at birth as the measure of choice, but this indicator should be discounted because only extraordinary burial practices and exceptionally thorough archaeological recovery techniques yield representative samples. At most sites, too few skeletons of infants and children are recovered to be credible (Teotihuacán is an important exception), and paleodemographers' estimates of life expectancy at birth (e_0) are thereby greatly inflated. The ethnohistorian Ortiz de Montellano puts life expectancy at birth for the Aztec at 37 years, but the cited source

---

[15] Bustamante, "Aspectos históricos," pp. 37–47, reviews evidence on pre-Columbian hunger.
[16] McCaa and Márquez Morfín, "Paleodemography."

does not, in fact, support this figure.[17] A decidedly somber picture emerges when we examine life expectancies at older ages (see Table 7.1). At age 15 (e_{15}), Mesoamerican life expectancies were extremely low, ranging from 13 to 29 additional years of life. In other words, for those surviving to age 15, death came around age 28 through 44 on average. Even the most optimistic estimates are almost one-third worse than national figures for Mexico in 1940 (when e_{15} = 43 additional years, bringing life expectancy to 58; in 1980, e_{15} = 56, bringing it to 71). Indeed, the figures for prehistoric populations fall well below the worst conditions in model life tables, such as Coale and Demeny's Region South level 1, where e_{15} = 34 (bringing expectancy to age 49) and life expectancy at birth (e_0) is only 20 years.[18]

Nonquantitative sources support the interpretation that mortality was extremely high in Mesoamerica. The Nahua (Aztec) sculpted high morbidity in stone and structured high mortality in their language. Consider the vast Nahua pantheon constructed to beg for divine succor from a great diversity of afflictions and illnesses. Nahuatl grammar is obsessed, indeed burdened, with mortality. Why encumber the language with a grammatical suffix indicating whether kin are dead or alive unless mortality is an ever-present concern?

Extrapolating paleodemographic estimates for Mesoamerican populations points to life expectancies at birth of 15–20 years, or annual crude birth rates as high as 67 or as low as 50.[19] Since on the whole these paleopopulations were growing, the upper bound of the crude birth rate should be set a few points higher, at, say, 55–70 births per thousand population. Students of modern populations would dismiss the upper range as impossible. Nevertheless, a simple experiment reveals that a stable population with a crude birth rate of 70 and a growth rate of 0.5% per annum corresponds to a total fertility rate of 8.8 children. This is an astonishingly high figure, yet as recently as 1990, Mexican women with no schooling who survived to menopause averaged 7.5 children. This 1990 average was

---

[17] Ortiz de Montellano (*Aztec Medicine*, p. 126) incorrectly extrapolates life expectancy of the Aztecs from a figure for Tlatico recited third-hand. The Mexican bioarchaeologist Faulhaber, author of the original study, reports that for a collection of 155 skeletons dated to 2600–3100 B.P., 84% of male subjects probably died before age 35 ("La población de Tlatilco"), two years younger than what Ortiz de Montellano cites as average life expectancy at birth.

[18] Coale and Demeny, *Regional Model Life Tables*, p. 384; Camposortega Cruz, *Análisis*, p. 321.

[19] Demography teaches that the crude birth rate is simply the reciprocal of life expectancy at birth (e_0) – when the population growth rate (r) is zero; thus, an e_0 of 20 becomes 1/20 = .05, or a crude birth rate of 50 per thousand population. A crude birth rate of 67 is equivalent to an e_0 of 15 (1/15 = .067, or 67 births per thousand), when r = 0. See also note to Table 7.1.

Table 7.1. *Mean age at death, selected ages: Mesoamerican precontact populations and others at various economic-technological levels*

Population	Mean age at death from selected ages (years)		
	0	15	50
Tlatico, 2930–3250 B.P.[a]	32	37	54
La Ventanilla, 350–950[a]	36	40	54
Cholula, 850–1560[a]	29	35	54
Copán rural, 700–1000[a]	25	44	60
Copán urban, 700–1000[a]	36	41	57
Teotihuacán, early classic[b]	24	42	58
Teotihuacán, late classic[b]	16	34	66
Teotihuacán, 1580–1620[b]	13	28	52
Cholula, 1325–1520[c]	25	34	51
North American Indians[d]	22	35	55
Hunter-gatherers[d]	22	37	63
Primitive agriculturalists[d]	26	45	68
Model life table, South level 1[e]	20	49	65
Mexico, 1939–41[f]	40	58	70

Note: Calculations are based on conventional paleodemographic assumptions: skeletal remains are a random sample of deaths for the population studied; the population is closed (migration is nil) and static (crude birth and death rates are equal; therefore the rate of population change is zero). Under these conditions, the mean age at death from age x is equivalent to life expectancy at that age. Recently, paleodemographers have begun to accept the fact that fertility, not mortality, is the principal determinant of the age structure of a population, and hence, of the age structure of deaths (Johansson and Horowitz, "Estimating Motality"). The practical significance of this change in thinking is nil. As long as the assumption of a static system is retained, whether one first computes fertility and then derives mortality or does the reverse has no practical effect. Both approaches yield the same answer. Problems of bias remain (see also note 19).

Sources: [a] Health and Nutrition in the Western Hemisphere Database, October 12, 1995.
[b] Storey, *Life and Death*, pp. 184–5.
[c] Hayward, *Demographic Study*, pp. 221–22, Table 7.5.
[d] Johansson, "Demographic History," p. 136.
[e] Coale and Demeny, *Regional Model Life Tables*, p. 384.
[f] Camposortega Cruz, *Análisis*, p. 321.

attained even though marriage was delayed to around age 20 and not all women formed stable unions. If we look back into the nineteenth century we find women attaining this record, or nearly so: 8.5 was the average total fertility rate reported in carefully documented studies of Tzeltal-speakers of Amatenango (Chiapas) and the Euromestizo elite of Mexico City.[20]

HIGH-PRESSURE DEMOGRAPHIC SYSTEMS

Even with life expectancy at birth (e_0) as low as 16 years, a high-fertility paleopopulation could sustain a growth rate of 0.5% per year. The age structure would be young, with 40% of the population under 15 years of age and 90% under 50. Storey's paleodemographic reconstruction of a barrio in the Teotihuacán urban complex is close to the high-pressure demographic scenario envisioned here. To reach an 8.8 total fertility rate (Storey places the figure at 6 for Teotihuacán)[21] would have required 26.4 years of childbearing, with the first birth occurring three years after women became sexually active and birth intervals averaging 36 months. Since menopause sets in at around age 40 or 45, girls would have had to marry close to the age of puberty, at, say, 15 years. This is exactly what we find in the earliest extant documentary evidence for the Aztecs. Child marriage, involving cohabitation, was common in ancient Mexico. A high-pressure demographic regime is consistent with the bioarchaeological and ethnohistorical evidence for central Mexico before the invasion by Hernán Cortes and his Christian comrades in 1519.

Child marriage among the indigenes surprised Europeans, for as Viceroy Martin Enriquez observed in 1577, it was "the custom in the time of their paganism to marry almost at birth because no girl reached the age of twelve without marrying."[22] Pictorial life histories in the Codex Mendoza depict marriage occurring at age 15 and babies being weaned at age 3 (rationed to one-half tortilla [per meal?], rising to one whole tortilla at age 4, and two from age 13). In "natural fertility" populations, weaning facilitates ovulation and conception – when not actually precipitated by the birth of a second baby to be suckled. In the 1530s and 1540s, for rural Nahuas in Huitzillan and Quauhchichinollan (located in the modern state of Morelos), the average age at marriage (defined as co-residing couples) is estimated at 12.7 years for females and 19.4 for males. Data for this pop-

[20] Arrom, *Women*, p. 126–7; Klein, "Familia y Fertilidad," p. 119.
[21] Storey, *Life and Death*, pp. 259–65. [22] Quoted in McCaa, "Matrimonio infantil," pp. 13–14.

ulation of 2,500 ordinary folk reflect authentically indigenous practices because the Christian spiritual conquest had scarcely begun, according to the earliest surviving censuses from this region. Only one Catholic marriage versus almost 800 native unions appears in these remarkable listings, written on fig-bark "paper" in Nahuatl by native scribes. These documents display an obsession with fertility, or, better, infertility, with scribes noting not only the indigeneous names and ages of offspring but also, for each childless couple, the number of years of marriage.[23] The ancient Nahuas were passionate pronatalists. Sterility was a truly deadly sin, leading to the sacrifice of infecund couples, who "served only to occupy the world and not increase it."[24]

Nahua civilization, the most successful in Mesoamerica, survived, indeed thrived, by means of a high-pressure demographic system: high mortality and higher fertility with growth rates triple those of most paleopopulations, but less than one-third postrevolutionary Mexico's pace of 2 or 3% per annum maintained since the 1930s. The Nahua demographic logic can be seen as the triumph of many unconscious population experiments leading to a system of reproduction which worked over the long run. The fate of most small paleopopulations was extinction or migration, which in the archaeological record look much the same.[25] The loss of a reliable water supply, an outbreak of botulism, hemorrhagic fever or life-threatening diarrhea, a lengthy period of sterility or sub-fecundity, an unbalanced sex ratio, the exhaustion of food resources – paleodemographic roulette was unforgiving.

Agriculture improved the odds of winning, allowed for greater demographic densities, and led to the emergence of towns, cities, and city-states. Urban growth meant higher mortality and greater migration to replenish urban demographic sumps (such as in Teotihuacán, as noted earlier),[26] but in towns or cities opportunities for coupling also increased, thanks to a greater pool of potential mates. The Malthusian threat was not the inevitable outcome. Although by 1500, demographic densities around Lake Patzcuaro probably exceeded the long-term carrying capacity of the area, in the Central Basin technological innovations, the expansion of highly productive, raised-bed (*chinampa*) agriculture, improved grain transport and storage, and even warfare provided relief from the Malthusian menace. From 1519, with the intrusion of European aliens, catastro-

---

[23] McCaa, "Matrimonio infantil," pp. 27–28.   [24] Quoted in McCaa, "Marriageways," p. 14.
[25] See the nuanced discussion in Sugiura, "El ocaso."   [26] Storey, *Life and Death*, p. 258.

phe ensued with the death of millions from disease, exploitation, environmental degradation, and, to a much lesser extent, warfare.

COLONIAL MEXICO

How many people lived in "Mexico" (central and northern Mesoamerica) when Europeans first invaded in 1519? How large was the ensuing demographic disaster, and what were its principal causes? What were the effects of Spanish conquest and colonization on Mesoamericans, on the quality of life, family, and settlement patterns? What was the demographic legacy of European colonialism? With independence, did demographic decay set in, or was the nineteenth century a period of accelerated growth? Answers to these questions remain contentious, notwithstanding decades of research, writing, and debate. Now there are signs that a consensus is emerging on some of these questions, which in turn is stimulating new insight and dialogue.

THE DEMOGRAPHIC DISASTER OF CONQUEST
AND COLONIZATION

There is a consensus that the sixteenth century was a demographic disaster for Mesoamericans. Table 7.2 displays 10 authoritative estimates of population decline for the native population of Mexico (or diverse parts thereof) during the first century of Spanish conquest and colonization. Estimates of the magnitude of the disaster range from less than 25% to more than 90%. Three schools or interpretations cluster along this broad band of figures: catastrophists, moderates, and minimalists (Table 7.2). Catastrophists place the scale of demographic disaster at 90% or more and descry a large native population at contact, exceeding 10, 20, or even 30 million. Moderates detect decreases of "only" 50–85%, disasters nonetheless. They favor smaller populations at contact (5–10 million) but agree with catastrophists on population totals at nadir (1–1.5 million between 1600 and 1650). Minimalists perceive the scale of the disaster as much smaller, on the order of 25%. The principal proponent of the minimalist position, the Argentine linguist Angel Rosenblat, is the catastrophists' most determined critic. Rosenblat sees a decline of the native population from 4.5 to 3.4 million inhabitants, or 24%, and stabilization beginning within a half-million century of initial contact with Europeans. It seems

Table 7.2. *Demographic disaster in Mexico, 1519–1595: Authoritative estimates of total population and implied rates of decrease*

	Population (millions)		
	1519	1595	Percentage decrease
"Mexico"			
Rosenblat	4.5	3.5	22
Aguirre-Beltrán	4.5	2.0	56
Zambardino	5–10	1.1–1.7	64–89
Mendizabal	8.2	2.4	71
Cook and Simpson	10.5	2.1–3.0	71–80
Cook and Borah	18–30	1.4	78–95
Central Mexican symbiotic region			
Sanders	2.6–3.1	0.4	85–87
Valley of Mexico			
Whitmore	1.3–2.7	0.1–0.4	69–96
Gibson	1.5	0.2	87
Sanders	1.0–1.2	0.1	90
128 towns			
Kubler	0.2	0.1	50

Note: The nadir of the demographic disaster is usually placed in the seventeenth century. I chose 1595 for an end-point, not because I think this to be the nadir of the native population, but because it enabled me to interpolate, rather than extrapolate, comparable figures for the largest number of authors. Nevertheless, Sanders's figure for the Valley of Mexico is extrapolated from 1568.

Sources: Rosenblat, *Población indígena*, vol. 1, pp. 57–122; Aguirre-Beltrán, *Población negra*, pp. 200–201, 212; Zambardino, "Mexico's Population," pp. 21–22; Mendizábal, "Demografía Mexicana," vol. 3, p. 320; Cook and Simpson, *Population*, pp. 38, 43, 45; Borah and Cook, *Aborginal Population*, p. 88; Cook and Borah, *Indian Population*, pp. 46–47 (as corrected); Sanders, "Population of Central Mexican Symbiotic Region," p. 120; "Ecological Adaptation," p. 194; Whitmore, *Disease*, p. 154; Gibson, *Aztecs*, pp. 137–38; Kubler, "Population Movements," p. 621.

to me that the population of central Mexico at contact must have been no less than the minimalist estimate of 4 or 5 million and was likely double and possibly even triple that figure.[27]

The "war over numbers" continues because population estimates prior

---

[27] See citations in Table 7.1. Henige argues that the quest for a number, any number, is futile because the quantitative data are simply too frail ("Native American Population," p. 22).

to 1895, when the first national census was conducted, are unavoidably crude for any large region of the Mexican subcontinent. For the sixteenth century, the data are dreadfully crude: often derived from gross tax allotments, not actual receipts; or from numbers of taxpayers, not total population. Methods for working these data are more numerical than demographic, and at best the results point to orders of magnitude. The fact remains that most places extant in 1519 were never enumerated by either native or colonial authorities. Yet today there survives a surprisingly large corpus of population-like numbers for an exceedingly diverse array of administrative units: hamlets, barrios, subject boroughs, towns, district capitals (*cabeceras*), and provinces. Some places ceased to exist within decades of first contact, others changed names, and not a few were relocated through the Spanish policy of *congregación*. Most native capital "cities," with populations ranging from 10,000 to a disputed 350,000 for the Mexica capital Tenochtitlan, survived the conquest and subsequent demographic catastrophe.

Most natives resided in a dispersed pattern of settlement, to be near cornfields (*milpas*), following the rules of ecology or agronomy, rather than political geography. After conquest, successive *congregaciones* attempted to reduce natives to settlements conducive to Spanish political, economic, and religious control. By 1650, wherever these efforts were successful, milpa dwellers, formerly clustered near cornfields, were forced into Spanish-style hamlets, villages, and towns. Then, when authorities relaxed their grip, many natives drifted back to the fields. Nevertheless, village settlements in twentieth-century Mexico, with housing clustered around a central plaza, generally reflect colonial rather than pre-Hispanic origins.[28]

Sporadic censuses – and a few remarkably detailed enumerations from the sixteenth century still survive[29] – or tax surveys of small areas capture only a fraction of this movement and are simply inadequate for estimating population totals for large areas. Baptism and burial registers, which might fill the gap, do not become available in quantity until the late seventeenth century. The paucity of evidence has spawned much research and controversy.

The catastrophist position is best represented by Sherburne F. Cook and Woodrow Borah, the most tenacious researchers and prolific writers in the field of Mexican population history. Their point estimate of 25.2 million

---

[28] Gerhard, "Evolución."   [29] Cline, *Book*, pp. 5–16.

inhabitants in 1519 has become a talisman for many historians, while their more prudent range estimate of 18–30 million goes largely ignored. This range takes into account just two of the many sources of variation on which their estimates depend: a spectrum of average family sizes, from 3.6 to 5.0 individuals per family: and alternative frequencies of tribute collection, 4 or 4.5 times per year.[30] Cook and Borah scoured libraries and archives in Mexico, Spain, and the United States to develop the largest database of colonial population figures extant for "central Mexico," a region of one-half million square kilometers bounded in the north and west by a line connecting Tampico and Tepic and in the south and east by the Isthmus of Tehuantepec. Relentlessly quantitative, Cook and Borah standardized and converted taxes from such diverse units as corn, cotton, turkeys, blankets, and the like into taxpayers (*tributarios, casados*), then into total population, with whopping adjustments for tax-exempt classes, tax-free towns, omissions, errors, and lost records. They concluded that their research documented a demographic catastrophe, "one of the worst in the history of humanity."[31] Their point estimates show the native population imploding from 25.2 million in 1519 to 6.3 million by 1545, 2.5 million in 1570, and bottoming out at 1.2 million in 1620. Their reconstruction is widely accepted; indeed, it has become a paradigm to describe the devastation of European conquests elsewhere in the Americas and Oceania. Cook and Borah's depopulation ratios of 10–25:1 (suggesting population losses of 90–96%) are in general agreement with independent estimates by Charles Gibson, Peter Gerhard, Thomas Whitmore, and others using different data and methods for the Valley of Mexico or varying subregions of Mexico, or indeed, of Mesoamerica.[32]

As Cook and Borah revised their estimates sharply upward over the years, a great dispute ensued, particularly with specialists closest to field. Prior, more moderate reconstructions by Miguel Othón de Mendizábal and George Kubler received support from independent analyses by a younger generation of scholars. Sanders and co-workers developed a formidable challenge to catastrophist methodology and conclusions. Their systematic sample of more than 3,600 archaeological sites in the Valley of Mexico point to contact populations half the size of those proposed by Cook and Borah for the same region, yet it must be noted that the archaeological reconstruction (projected to 1595 in Table 7.2) sustains the thesis

---

[30] Cook and Borah, *Essays*, vol. 1, p. 115.   [31] Borah and Cook, "Despoblación," p. 6.
[32] Gibson, *Aztecs*, pp. 136–46; Gerhard, *Geografía histórica*, pp. 22–28; Whitmore, *Disease*, pp. 195–97.

of enormous demographic disaster for the native population.[33] The statistician Rudolph Zambardino questioned Cook and Borah's numbers and methods on quantitative grounds, urging researchers to apply ranges for each conversion factor rather than relying on point estimates alone. Zambardino favors figures of 5 million to 10 million at the beginning of the sixteenth century and one million at the end, a demographic collapse of 80–90%.[34]

A third position is staked out by Angel Rosenblat, who proclaims himself a "moderate" but by my reckoning is a minimalist. He defends his text-centered reconstruction as follows:

> If in fact I did derive moderate and even low figures for the 1492 population, it was not because I had intended to do so. The data I had about the Conquest allowed no other choice, unless one were to assume vast and horrible killing, which requires a macabre imagination and which I found unacceptable given the known extermination techniques of the sixteenth-century.[35]

Unfortunately, according to Rosenblat himself, in more than three decades of writing on this subject he rarely revised a figure or an interpretation – perhaps in part because, at least in the case of Mexico, no scholar critically scrutinized Rosenblat's reading of the sources.[36] After a comprehensive review of Mexican population figures from historians writing in any of five European languages, the Argentine linguist developed his own series using numbers for 1570 compiled by the royal Spanish cosmographer Juan López de Velasco. Rosenblat settled on 4.5 million as a "reasonable probability" for the native population of Mexico at contact, and 3.5 million for 1570, settling on 3.4 million around 1650 (then, slowly rising to 3.7 million by 1825).[37] Unfortunately, the pattern traced by Rosenblat's numbers is contradicted by the narrative on which he relies. López de Velasco concludes his own assessment of population change in sixteenth-century Mexico with the following words: "in the beginning the natives were many more in number than there were afterward, because in many provinces, where there used to be a great multitude of them, they have reached almost the point of extinction."[38] Rosenblat, writing after

---

[33] Sanders's series for the Basin of Mexico alone places the population in 1519 at 1 million, declining to 400,000 by 1568, 180,000 in 1585, and 100,000 in 1650 (a 90% decline). Almost four centuries later, perfect symmetry is achieved with the population of the Basin regaining the 1 million figure in 1900 (Sanders, "Ecological Adaptation," p. 194), surging to 16 million in 1995.

[34] See works cited in Table 7.2.   [35] Rosenblat, "Population," p. 45.

[36] McCaa, "Siglo XVI," pp. 128–30.   [37] Rosenblat, *Población indígena*, vol. 1, pp. 102, 88, 58, 36.

[38] López de Velasco, *Geografía*, p. 15; cited in McCaa, "Siglo XVI," p. 129.

historians almost unanimously espoused the thesis that epidemic disease was the principal cause of the decline in native populations, insisted on directing his attack against the Black Legend, arguing that the "extermination" of Indians was principally due to "vast and horrible killing."[39]

Gonzalo Aguirre-Beltrán, seemingly a champion of the minimalist camp because he embraces Rosenblat's figures for 1519 and 1570, is in my view a moderate. Although the Mexican scholar's figures imply "only" a 33% decline by 1595, in fact, his complete series places the nadir at 1645, with a total decrease of 70% (to 1.3 million natives), well within the moderate camp's 50–85% range of decline.[40]

The greatest contribution of the catastrophists' critics' is their detailed assessment of quantitative sources and methods, which emphasizes the difficulties – even the impossibility – of obtaining satisfactory estimates from tax records alone. Case studies of specific villages, such as Tomás Calvo's history of Acatzingo, point to contact populations as little as one-fifth Cook and Borah's estimates. Then, too, population densities implied by their figures – at more than 300 inh./km^2 for the Central Mexican Symbiotic Region (20,811 km^2), and exceeding 1,000 inh./km^2 for Mexico City and environs – are difficult to accept. The Federal District did not attain the latter until 1940, nor the state of Mexico the former until the late 1970s.[41] The catatrophist position is further weakened by a studied refusal to reply to challenges posed by its critics. Anyone tempted to join this debate must carefully examine the works of Cook and Borah, Rosenblat, Sanders, Aguirre-Beltrán, Whitmore, and others, as well as a weighty bookshelf of published primary sources. In the meantime, it is clear that before the Spanish conquest the population of the Mexican subcontinent was large, certainly 5 million, probably 10, and perhaps 15 million, if not 20 or 25 million.[42]

Nor does the thesis of demographic disaster rest solely on numbers. The many extant narratives provide a sound foundation for a qualitative view of the scale and causes of the calamity.[43] That the coastal and tropical regions suffered the greatest losses is widely accepted, as is the thesis that

---

[39] Rosenblat, "Population," p. 45. In drafting these lines, Rosenblat seems to have forgotten his own earlier discussion of the importance of disease in *Población indígena*, vol. 1, p. 74.

[40] Aguirre-Beltrán, *Población negra*, pp. 197–213.

[41] Sanders, "Central Mexican Symbiotic Region," pp. 120, 130–31; México, INEGI, *Estadísticas Históricas*, Table 1.13.

[42] McCaa, "Siglo XVI," pp. 131–34; Calvo, *Acatzingo*, p. 80.

[43] Prem, "Disease Outbreaks," pp. 20–48 offers a succinct account of the sixteenth-century narrative evidence; see also McCaa, "Siglo XVI."

the highlands had fewer fatalities. Colony-wide losses over the course of the sixteenth century reached at least one-half, and perhaps as much as nine-tenths over wide areas. War mortality was of decidedly secondary importance, limited primarily to a few towns in the central basin (Tlaxcala, Cholula, and Tenochtitlan (Mexico City)), Western Jalisco (during the Mixtón War of the 1540s), and the sparsely settled northern frontier, where fighting continued into the nineteenth century. Overwork, disruption of the native economy, ecological distress, and forced relocation were much more significant than war in causing the demographic disaster, but disease remains the principal explanation for most historians, just as it was four centuries ago for the first chroniclers.[44]

DISEASE AND RECOVERY

There is a consensus among historians that smallpox struck central Mexico in 1520, the first of a series of devastating, multiyear epidemics that erupted in the sixteenth century. A few months before January 1, 1521, when Hernán Cortes began his third trek to Tenochtitlan, now intent on subduing the Aztec capital by siege and sword, smallpox erupted in the heartland of the most powerful empire in Mesoamerica, killing the emperor Cuitlahuatzin, many caciques and warriors, and many women and children. The epidemic was particularly severe because, unlike in Europe, where the virus was a childhood disease, in Mexico it found "virgin soil," striking entire households, adults as well as children, in one massive blow. With almost everyone ill at once, there was no one to provide food, water, or care so that many who fell ill died, not of smallpox, but of hunger, dehydration, and despair.[45] The Franciscan Toribio de Benavente (Motolinía) in his *Memoriales* recounts the lethal effects of this horror: "Because they all fell ill at a stroke, [the Indians] could not nurse one another, nor was there anyone to make bread [tortillas], and in many parts it happened that all the residents of a house died and in others almost no one was left."[46] Native historians writing in Nahuatl are more descriptive, and less analytical or synthetic. Their eye-witness accounts privilege the unadorned facts, without editorial:

Cuitlauac . . . ruled eighty days after the Spaniards reached Mexico. In the time of this one, it happened that a great plague came, and then many died of it everywhere in the

---

[44] McCaa, "Spanish and Nahuatl Views," pp. 400–401; "Siglo XVI," p. 130.
[45] McCaa, "Spanish and Nahuatl Views," pp. 420–21. [46] Motolinía, *Memoriales*, p. 21.

cities. It was said that it was the smallpox, the great raising of blisters. Never once had this been seen; never had it been suffered in Mexico. Indeed, it smote the faces of everyone, so that pits and roughnesses were formed. No longer were the dead buried; they could only cast them all into the water – for in those times there was much water everywhere in Mexico. And there was a great, foul odor; the smell issued forth from the dead.[47]

Measles hit for the first time in 1531. When smallpox returned in 1532 and 1538, mortality was reduced because many adults, now immune from having survived an earlier attack, were available to provide care to those who fell ill. A second great multiyear epidemic struck in 1545 (*cocoliztli*, typhus? hemorrhagic fever? – the identification of sixteenth-century epidemics is almost as contentious as the dispute over the number of natives at contact) and a third in 1576 (*matlazahuatl*, perhaps typhus carried by human lice). Although a lively debate continues over which was most severe (the German scholar Hans Prem favors the first, that of 1520–21), it is clear that the effects of each were catastrophic.[48] The founder of New World ethnohistory, Father Bernardino de Sahagún, writing in November 1576 while the third great epidemic of the century was under way, recalled that because of the epidemic of 1545,

when the entire population wasted away, large pueblos were left depopulated, which afterwards were never resettled. Thirty years later the pestilence which now reigns appeared, and many pueblos were depopulated, and if this business continues, and if it lasts for three or four months, as it now is, no one will remain.[49]

Some catastrophists project these epidemics willy-nilly to encompass the length and breadth of the Americas, but the evidence for such so-called pandemics is thin. For example, the smallpox epidemic of 1520 is alleged to have raged north to the Great Plains, east to the Atlantic seaboard, west to the Columbia River Basin, and south through Central America down the Andes (where the Inca Huayna Capac died, it is claimed, of smallpox in 1525) and beyond. Daniel Reff judiciously reviewed much of the evidence for northern Mexico and concluded that there is no sign of the first smallpox epidemic sweeping beyond the Tarascan-speaking peoples of north-central Mexico (the modern states of Michoacán and Jalisco).[50]

Lesser crises of mumps, influenza, and others vaguely described as "plague" or "sickness" also occurred, often in tandem with famine. The eighteenth-century chronicler Cayetano Cabrera y Quintero blames higher

---

[47] Sagahún, *Florentine Codex*, vol. 8, p. 4.   [48] Prem, "Disease Outbreaks," pp. 47–48.
[49] Sagahún, *Historia general*, vol. 3, p. 355.
[50] Reff, *Disease*, pp. 102–3; Prem, "Disease Outbreaks," pp. 26–27; Cook, *Born to Die*, pp. 79–83.

mortality among the Indians on their poverty – bad nutrition, hunger, cold, and a lack of clothing – excessive drinking of the native intoxicant *pulque*, and an intense fatalism in the face of death. He chronicles seventeen major epidemics from 1544 to 1737, in addition to the smallpox epidemic of 1520–21.[51] The twentieth-century geographer Peter Gerhard offers an even longer list, noting 14 outbreaks for the "short" sixteenth century, 11 for the seventeenth, and 9 for the eighteenth.[52] The Mexican archaeologist-historian Lourdes Márquez Morfín extends Gerhard's roster, particularly for later centuries, and adds primary source citations. She logs three small-pox epidemics in the seventeenth century and six in the eighteenth (1711, 1734, 1748, 1761/62, 1779/80, and 1797).[53] In the last century of colonial rule, smallpox epidemics erupted every 15 to 20 years, with enormous loss of life. Then on November 30, 1798, Charles IV ordered a massive vacci-nation campaign for all the Spanish possessions. The ensuing unprece-dented philanthropic odyssey commanded by Francisco Xavier de Balmis carried the vaccine throughout Spanish America and on to the Philippines. With independence, intermittent vaccination campaigns greatly reduced mortality, although the disease was not extinguished on Mexican soil for another century and a half.

Most historians explain demographic recovery of the native population by means of natural selection or crude Darwinian evolutionism, confus-ing lifetime immunity with inherited genetic resistance, but there is little evidence to support this claim and much science that negates it. Small-pox mortality was much too low to play a role in human evolution, either after 1500 in the Americas or before in Europe, Africa, the Middle East, or even Asia, where it is presumed to have originated. There is no evi-dence that humans ever developed genetic resistance to smallpox. Indeed, smallpox has been called the "perfect weapon" of biological terrorism. Since humans are no longer vaccinated against smallpox and the last case of natural pox occurred decades ago, we are now all virgin soil for the virus. Should it be broadcast from the remaining, carefully guarded stocks, the disease would spread quickly. Secondary transmission would go unno-ticed for days. Draconian quarantine and mass vaccination would be required to prervent epidemiological disaster. Genes would offer little, if any, protection to anyone.[54] For example, in the city of London, after

---

[51] Cabrera y Quintero, *Escudo*, pp. 67–71.   [52] Gerhard, *Geografía histórica*, p. 23.
[53] Márquez Morfín, "Evolución cuantitativa," pp. 50–60.
[54] Gerhard, *Geografía histórica*, p. 26. See also Sánchez-Albornoz, *Población*, p. 83; and a recent text by Burkholder and Johnson, *Colonial Latin America*, p. 110. Jared Diamond (*Guns*, pp. 195–214)

probably half a millennium of experience with the virus, more than 2,000 smallpox deaths were recorded annually from 1710 to 1800, which accounted for no less than 7% of total burials in one of the most populous cities of Europe. Indeed, Europeans, confronting the horrors of the disease, were driven to extraordinary efforts, such as quarantine, inoculation with live virus, and ultimately vaccination, to staunch the spread. Genetic diversity characteristic of Old World populations may have provided an advantage, but this thesis remains controversial.[55]

Humans did learn how to provide care to smallpox victims – water to prevent dehydration, food to relieve hunger, blankets to alleviate chill, and soothing words to offer hope – instead of fleeing in horror and abandoning the ill to die untended. In the viceroyalty of New Spain, Native Americans quickly learned how to care for smallpox victims, as is attested in pictures drawn by native artists as early as 1575.[56] Mexicans were fortunate because here the disease remained epidemic, recurring at intervals of 15–20 years, instead of endemic as in London. When smallpox did strike in Mexico, 1 in 10 or 20 might die from it, as happened with the epidemic of 1779–80, which in Mexico City alone caused 12,345 deaths. What is remarkable is that four times that number fell ill, received public charity, and recovered. With the succeeding outbreak in 1797, smallpox mortality in the city was halved thanks to timely, systematic, block-by-block, person-to-person care for more than 75,000 of its residents.[57] Meanwhile in Guanajuato, authorities pursued preventive, yet more dangerous measures, hurriedly inoculating some four-fifths of the city's children with pus from live smallpox virus. Only one in a hundred of the inoculated died. In contrast, 28% of the some 3,000 who went untreated succumbed to the disease, many probably infected unintentionally by the inoculated.[58] In both cities, the smallpox mortality rate was reduced to around 6%. Care was the key in the capital, and prevention in the province.

Matlazahuatl (typhus?), another of the big killers of the sixteenth

endorses the genetic explanation (and the highest numbers for Native Americans at first encounter) without considering dissenting arguments. Bianchine and Russo ("Role of Epidemic Infectious Disease," p. 13) survey epidemiological evidence and conclude that "these findings dispute the theory that native Indians had a greater [genetic] susceptibility to these illnesses than Caucasians." Osterholm interview, "Plague War."

[55] Hopkins, *Princes*, pp. 37–55; for a brief discussion of genetic diversity, see McCaa, "Spanish and Nahuatl Views," pp. 419–20.

[56] McCaa, "Spanish and Nahuatl Views," pp. 423–24, n. 42.

[57] Biblioteca Nacional Madrid, *Raros*, tomo 13244, "Ephémeris astronómica al meridiano de México para el año de 1775 (hasta 31 de diciembre de 1786)," pp. 139–42; AGN, *Epidemias*, vol. 1, expedientes 1–7 (1797).

[58] Thompson, "To Save the Children," p. 440.

century but in this case probably of pre-Hispanic origin, did not recur with the same intensity as in 1576 until 1736–39, when it decimated much of Mexico. In the archbishopric of Puebla, for example, almost one-third of the inhabitants died from the disease, according to parish reports. A recurrence in 1761–62 was preceded by an outbreak of smallpox, and although less severe, this crisis still ranked as one of the great terrors of the eighteenth century. A half century later, in June 1813, while the war for independence raged in central Mexico, the last great typhus epidemic in Mexican history erupted. Within two months, one-tenth of the population of Mexico City died from the disease. By 1815, the epidemic had spread as far north as the Parral mining district in Nueva Viscaya and as far south as Teopisca in Chiapas.[59]

Recovery of the native population began, nonetheless, by the middle of the seventeenth century, according to most accounts. Rosenblat places the nadir at 3.4 million Indians around 1650, but, as noted earlier, Aguirre-Beltrán reckons the figure at only 1.3 million (plus 400,000 non-Indians). It is surprising that the Argentine linguist's figures are more than double those of the Mexican anthropologist-historian even though both cite the same source, Juan Diez de la Calle.[60]

RACE, ETHNICITY, AND SOCIAL TRANSFORMATION

Recovery was accompanied by a great mixing of peoples of different ethno-racial backgrounds. The only comprehensive figures on the subject for the entire colonial period were crafted by Aguirre-Beltrán. Figure 7.2 roughs out the evolution of the three principal ethnic stocks – Indian, African, and European – and their intermixtures from conquest to the last decade of colonial rule. Indians always made up the overwhelming majority of the population of colonial Mexico, and people of solely African or European origin were always only minor fractions. The second largest group by the end of the sixteenth century was the "Euromestizos," that is,

---

[59] Cook reasoned that it was unlikely that *matlazahuatl* was present in pre-Hispanic Mexico, but that if it was its impact was not as grave as in 1576 ("The incidence and significance of disease," pp. 321–2). Malvido and Viesca favor plague ("La epidemia"). Prem favors typhus ("Disease Outbreaks," pp. 38–42). For Mexico City in the late colonial period, see Cooper, *Epidemic Disease*; AGN, *Epidemias* tomo 13, exped. 2; Rabell, *Población novohispana*, 75–89; GSU, *Teopisca* film no. 725850 (Defunciones, libros 12–14, 1690–1859); APSJP, *Libros de Defunciones*.

[60] Rosenblat, *Población indígena*, vol. 1, pp. 79–82, 215–16; Aguirre-Beltran, *Población negra*, pp. 212–13. Rosenblat dismisses Borah's proportions for 1650 (1.2 million Indians and 0.3 non-Indians), asserting that "if these proportions had been true, Indians would no longer exist today in Mexico, only Mestizos and Whites" (vol. 1, p. 216).

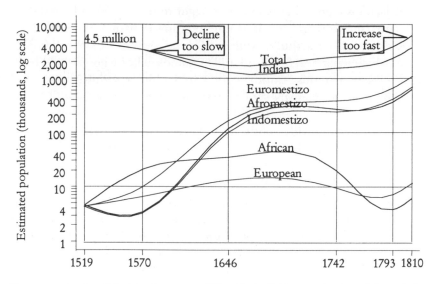

Figure 7.2. Aguirre-Beltrán's ethno-races of New Spain. Indians predominated through the end of the colonial period; mestizos proliferated from the late sixteenth century. (*Sources:* Rosenblat, Diez de la Calle, Villaseñor, Humboldt, and Navarro y Noriega)

Spanish-speakers of mixed Indian and European stock. Within a century of conquest, Indo-mestizos (mixed stock Indian-speakers) and Afromestizos (Spanish-speaking mixed groups with an African component) also made up a sizable fraction of the population.

The numbers underlying this graph always add up, but they suggest no more than orders of magnitude.[61] It seems likely that the scale of population disaster was less before 1570, for example, than after, contrary to what the series implies.[62] Likewise, the notion that the growth of the mixed groups was six times greater before 1650 than after seems improbable. Then in the late eighteenth century, the apparent ever-accelerating increase of all ethno-racial groups may be more mechanical than demographic, owing to improvements in census taking (and corrections) rather than to increased growth rates. The Villaseñor "census" of 1742 produced valuable reports for many parishes and towns but failed to cover the entire colony. For many places this document reports numbers of families – often crudely eyeballed – rather than inhabitants. For example, the town of

[61] To be fair, Aguirre-Beltrán characterizes his figures as "simple hypotheses" (*Población negra*, pp. 220, 234); see Cook and Borah's critique in *Essays*, vol. i, pp. 180–87.
[62] Prem, "Disease Outbreaks," pp. 20–21, 48.

Guadalajara is reported as containing "eight to nine thousand families of Spaniards, mestizos and mulatos, not counting Indians." More common is the degree of inexactitude expressed for the town of Actopan (Hidalgo state), which reports 50 Spanish families (almost all of whom would be in Aguirre-Beltrán's terms "euromestizos"), 2,750 Indian families, and 20 of other *castas* ("indomestizos," "afromestizos," and perhaps an African or two).[63]

The best colony-wide census was the last, that ordered by Viceroy Conde de Revillagigedo (1789–93) and the first to use a standard format for listing individuals by name, age, sex, occupation, race, and marital status. Nevertheless, this effort missed large expanses of New Spain. From his sojourn in the colony, the German savant Alexander von Humboldt prepared a four-volume *Essai* which revised the Revillagigedo figures to produce a comprehensive set of estimates, adjusted for growth to 1803. A decade later Francisco Navarro y Noriega increased the Revillagigedo numbers by 20% for underenumeration (Humboldt favored 10%), obtained figures for districts which had not reported earlier, and estimated growth to 1810 at 25% (1.5% per annum for 17 years, using arithmetic rather than geometric cumulation).[64]

For almost two centuries now, Navarro y Noriega's results remain the most widely cited,[65] yet they surely exaggerate the true population in 1810 by perhaps as much as one-fifth. This is evident in Figure 7.2 in the identical, steeply sloped curves for all ethno-racial groups from 1793. The graph shows that the totals for each group in 1810 were computed mechanically. Unfortunately, the royal accountant followed the method favored by Humboldt, estimating growth from parish records by subtracting burials from baptisms. Neither Navarro y Noriega nor Humboldt paid much heed to the fact that in Mexico baptisms were always more faithfully recorded than burials (until the latter decades of the nineteenth century, when civil registration undermined the religious system).[66] Faulty logic convinced Navarro y Noriega that annual growth was 1.5% per year – probably double the actual figure, although only half what Humboldt settled upon. Thus, 5 million to 5.5 million seems a more likely estimate for the population of Mexico in 1810 than Navarro y Noriega's 6,122,354 or Humboldt's 5.8 million for 1803 (and 6.5 million for 1808).[67] If his-

---

[63] Villaseñor y Sánchez, *Theatro*, pp. 408, 147.   [64] Navarro y Noriega, *Memoria*, p. 8.
[65] Lerner, "Consideraciones."   [66] Morin, "Los libros parroquiales."
[67] Rabell also rejects Humboldt's speculative figures (*Población novohispana*, pp. 66–67). Navarro y Noriega, *Memoria*, pp. 68–69. Humboldt claimed that the population of New Spain doubled every

torians insist on using these figures, then estimates for earlier and later years would have to be similarly corrected for errors and omissions, a forbidding challenge.

In any case, population growth in the closing decades of Spanish rule was much less than Navarro y Noriega, Humboldt, or other "triumphalists" of the era surmised.[68] There were regions of rapid growth in eighteenth-century Mexico. One of the fastest was the archbishopric of Michoacán, northwest of Mexico City. Here, population increased fivefold during the eighteenth century, but part of this growth was due to migration into the region. Then, too, there was a noticeable slowing in the final decades of the century, owing to successive waves of pestilence and famine.[69] Just when population increase was accelerating elsewhere in America and Western Europe, successive calamities condemned Bourbon Mexico to slow demographic growth.

There is a consensus that demographic recovery, in addition to growth, meant transformation. Infusions of European and African stocks were slight (and predominantly male), as Figure 7.2 shows. If the Aguirre-Beltrán series is sound, foreign stocks peaked around 1650 with 35,000 Africans (2% of total population), mostly slaves, and 10,000 Europeans, mainly Spanish-speakers. The most dramatic change was the growth of mestizos, or people of mixed stock, who, according to Aguirre-Beltrán, constituted almost 25% of the population as early as 1650, rising to 40% in 1810.[70] Historians agree that in colonial Mexico racial categorizations were fluid (documents usually speak of *calidad* instead of *raza*, character or reputation, instead of race), and that passing was common.[71] Thus, the rapid growth of the mixed population was a matter of economics, culture, and sociology, but demography was also important. Among Europeans and Africans the shortage of females ensured much interbreeding, if not intermarriage, with Amerindians. Then, too, social identities had their advantages, for undermining as well as upholding the colonial order. The

---

19 years (that is, 3.7% per annum! – see *Essai politique*, vol. 1, p. 339). Although his figures from parish baptism and burial registers (birth-minus-death equation) implied "only" a 2.7% increase per annum (vol. 1, pp. 330–37 and vol. 5, pp. 95–97), even this was a flagrant exaggeration because it did not consider the large fraction of deaths which went unrecorded. Regarding the 5.8 figure, Humboldt concludes, "Je m'arrête à un nombre qui, bien loin d'être exagéré, est probablement *au-dessous de la population existant*," emphasis in original (*Essai politique*, vol. 1, pp. 341–42).

[68] Brading, *Haciendas*, pp. 58–60.

[69] Morin, *Michoacán*, pp. 50–60 (cites 130,000 deaths for 1786, p. 57). See also Ouweneel, "Growth." On colonial migrations, see Swann, *Migrants*.

[70] Aguirre-Beltrán, *Población negra*, p. 234.

[71] Aguirre-Beltrán, *Población negra*, pp. 265–71; Morin, "Démographie"; McCaa, "Calidad," pp. 493–99; Cope, *Limits*, pp. 54–55, 76–78.

onerous head tax levied solely on Indians encouraged some to abandon the village of birth (particularly where land was scarce or made scarce by land-grabbing Spanish-speakers) for nearby haciendas or towns and to adapt to a non-Indian *calidad*.[72] In Michoacán, for example, the population as a whole increased fivefold over the eighteenth century, but the native population only tripled, in part because Indians abandoned village life to escape the head tax.[73]

For people of African roots – perhaps 200,000 slaves were imported into Mexico over three centuries – slavery gradually withered away. By the beginning of the eighteenth century, free labor was too abundant – that is too cheap – for slavery to compete. Then, too, slaves helped destroy slavery, by fleeing, extracting concessions, demanding freedom, taking advantage of civil and church law, and forming communities of free people called mulatos or pardos. Afro-Mexicans with conscious identities based on kinship and community numbered more than half a million by 1810 and "constituted the largest group of free blacks in the Western hemisphere."[74]

Recovery of the native population may be estimated from trends of baptismal series, once parish registers achieve a degree of consistent coverage in the late seventeenth century. Cecilia Rabell's regression analysis of baptism trends for nine parishes shows rapid growth in the north (as high as 1.5% per year in León and 1 percent in San Luis de la Paz, Valladolid, Charcas, and Marfil), but decelerating growth in the center. Rabell places the point of inflection, where rates of population change turn negative, at 1693 for parishes in the center, and at 1737 or 1763 elsewhere.[75]

Burial series for 10 parishes from Chihuahua to Chiapas illustrate the vast regional and ethnic volatility of year-to-year population change in eighteenth-century Mexico (Figure 7.3). Burial registers offer a somber view of the "long" eighteenth century (1690–1820), with deaths in crisis years mushrooming 4- to 14-fold above the norm, as in 1692, 1737, 1762, 1779, 1797, and 1813. The series depicts the classic workings of *ancien*

---

[72] Gerhard, "Evolución," p. 575. Aguirre-Beltrán's theses (*Población negra*, pp. 265–66) that the early colonial social structure was a "hermetic system of castes" and that rapid demographic growth from 1793 to 1810 signals the demise of the caste system and its replacement by one based on classes are not supported by recent scholarship, although the debate over meanings, fluidity, and significance of ethno-racial constructs continues. Bennett, *Lovers*, pp. 11–14; Carroll, "Mexicanos negros," pp. 432–37.

[73] Morin, *Michoacán*, pp. 74–83.

[74] Aguirre-Beltrán, *Población negra*, pp. 271–75; Carroll, *Blacks*, pp. 93–129; Bennett, *Lovers*, pp. 9, 164–75.

[75] Rabell, *Población novohispana*, pp. 69–72.

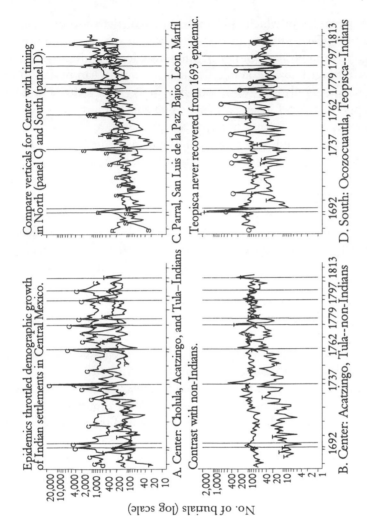

Figure 7.3. Region and race in a long century of epidemics. Crisis years are marked by first letter of parish name; vertical lines indicate crisis years in Central Mexico

Epidemics throttled demographic growth of Indian settlements in Central Mexico.

Compare verticals for Center with timing in North (panel C) and South (panel D).

No. of burials (log scale)

A. Center: Cholula, Acatzingo, and Tula–Indians Contrast with non-Indians.

B. Center: Acatzingo, Tula–non-Indians

C. Parral, San Luis de la Paz, Bajío, León, Marfil Teopisca never recovered from 1693 epidemic.

D. South: Ocozocuautla, Teopisca–Indians

1692   1737   1762 1779 1797 1813

regime demography, in which epidemics undercut the enormous growth potential of high-fertility populations.[76] Cholula, the site of one of the first, large-scale published studies in modern Mexican historical demography, is our best-known example. In normal years Indian burials in the Cholula region numbered 750–1,000, but in 1737 they skyrocketed to 16,926 (upper-left panel in Figure 7.3).[77] The authorities responded with the ancient Spanish refrain, "huir presto, irse lexos, volver tarde" (flee swiftly, go far away, and return belatedly), and sponsored public processions to call upon the saints for salvation.[78] Note, however, that non-Indians were not as affected by epidemics and famine (lower-left panel). The vast majority of deaths were Native Americans. The disaster raged through the heartland of New Spain (causing over 40,000 deaths in Mexico City alone), but only faint ripples reached the north (San José de Parral, upper-right panel) or the south (lower right) such as the Chiapan community of Teopisca (1739), and went completely unnoticed in nearby Ocozocuautla.[79]

The south had its crises as well (Figure 7.3, lower-right panel). Consider the epidemic of 1693. Before it struck, the parish of Teopisca numbered some 2,000 souls. Then, in 1693, 1,510 burials were recorded, a 14-fold increase over the average. The vicar reported that scarcely 350 people survived the devastation. A century later Teopisca still had not recovered, numbering fewer than a thousand souls. Nearby Ocozocuautla escaped much of the destruction of 1693 with "only" a 4-fold increase in burials, but in 1769–70 almost half the population of the parish died, and recovery remained elusive a half century later. These stories from individual parishes challenge the uniformitarian thesis that around the middle of the seventeenth century widespread growth of the native population resumed.[80]

LATE COLONIAL DEMOGRAPHIC DYNAMICS

Demography is a science of rates – of numerators and denominators, that is, of demographic events, such as deaths, and populations at risk of experiencing such events. Because we lack the makings of good rates for

[76] Rabell, *Población novohispana*, pp. 75–89; Brading, *Haciendas*, pp. 52–58; Pescador, *Bautizados*, pp. 98–105; APSJP, *Libros de Defunciones*.
[77] Malvido, "Factores," pp. 102, 106.   [78] Capello, *Remedios*, p. 12.
[79] Cabrera y Quintero, *Escudo*, p. 511. For a critique of these figures, see Pescador, *Bautizados*, p. 96. Also APSJP, *Libros de Defunciones*; GSU *Ocozocuautla* film no. 738960 (Defunciones 1671–1857).
[80] GSU, *Ocozocuautla*, film no. 738960 (Defunciones 1671–1857).

colonial Mexico, primarily denominators, much of its demographic history remains unknown and unknowable. Only where registration is relatively accurate, and reliable population censuses are available, can series of baptisms and burials be converted into birth and death rates. Everywhere in colonial Mexico many deaths went unrecorded.[81] High fees encouraged surreptitious burial, as did the widespread belief that final rites were not required for *angelitos*, innocent infants and children unsullied by sin. In high-pressure demographic systems babies and young children often account for one-half or more of deaths – but not according to colonial Mexican parish registers, which yield wholly implausible infant and child mortality rates.[82]

Baptisms were more faithfully performed, but even then, not necessarily recorded. Catholic priests in the New World were often responsible for 5 or 10 times as many souls as in the Old, and here parishioners procreated and died with what must have seemed demonic haste, in much higher proportions than in western Europe. Here, to expedite recordkeeping, priests often jotted the bare details of baptisms, burials, and other sacraments on scraps of paper. Then, as time permitted, perhaps weeks, months, or even years later – if at all – notes were transcribed in sacramental registries. A vicar's sudden death could result in the omission of days, months, or years of entries in a parish's books, or, if the successor found his predecessor's notes, in page-after-page of hastily transcribed entries written at several long sittings over a period of days, or even months.[83]

Consequently, the "royal road to historical demography," as Rabell calls the French "family reconstitution" method, proved to be a dead end in Mexico. The family reconstitution method is a rigorous procedure for constructing and analyzing demographically valid family genealogies of ordinary people. The five conditions required for a successful journey on the royal road – stable family names, a small parish, vital events faithfully recorded week-by-week for a century or longer, low illegitimacy, and little migration – do not seem to characterize even one of the more than one thousand parishes of colonial Mexico.[84]

---

[81] Brading, *Haciendas*, pp. 53, 58; Morin, "Los libros parroquiales."
[82] Rabell, *Población novohispana*, pp. 27–30.
[83] Cook and Borah, *Essays*, vol. 2, pp. 286–321; Morin, "Los libros parroquiales."
[84] Rabell, *Población novohispana*, pp. 8–9. Nothwithstanding Morin's timely warning about the inapplicability of the method to Mexican parish registers ("Libros parroquiales," pp. 400–401), the siren song of family reconstitution lured the unwary to their destruction while the prudent were frightened away. Robinson's *Research Inventory* provides a valuable catalogue to Mexican parish books.

Only two Mexican family reconstitution studies have been published since the method was invented over four decades ago.[85] Both offer intriguing insights into colonial demography, but neither is entirely faithful to the method. Lacunae in the records make for truncated studies and, in the case of Thomas Calvo's genealogies for Guadalajara, worrisome error rates. Herbert Klein's insightful demographic history of Amatenango, Chiapas (1785–1816), reveals a high-pressure demographic system persisting through the waning years of colonial rule. In Amatenango, Tzeltal women married at very young ages, averaging 16.1 years at first union (rising to 18.6 years in 1930, and in 1990, for non-Spanish-speaking women in Chiapas, 19.7 years), and nearly all married by age 20. Frequent widowhood was quickly repaired by rapid remarriage for women as well as men. Fertility was high. Birth intervals averaged 36 months, and the total fertility rate was 8.5 children. Klein concludes that early marriage and high fertility were demographic responses to an environment rich in resources which permitted unrestricted expansion, but he may have uncovered, instead, the tenacious persistence of time-tested prehispanic patterns which facilitated survival even under the most adverse circumstances.[86]

Family reconstitution provides valuable clues about legitimate fertility, but methodological limitations do not permit measurement of extramarital fertility. Where nonmarital fertility is common but variable, as in Mexico, other methods are required.[87] The handful of parishes in central Mexico for which crude birth rates have been computed average 52 baptisms (births) per thousand population,[88] which is remarkably close to Cook and Borah's figure of 51 for several dozen Oaxacan parishes from the same period.[89] Child/woman ratios also point to high fertility, averaging 750 children under 5 years of age per thousand women aged 15–44 (data are for 91 Oaxacan parishes in 1777),[90] compared with 500–600 in late eighteenth-century England.[91] The total fertility rate in early

---

[85] Calvo, "Familles mexicaines," p. 44, where error is placed at 32%, but this only applies to individuals who survived to adulthood. See also Klein, "Familia."

[86] Klein, "Familia," pp. 114, 117, 119. My computations, including all forms of unions, are based on the following sources: for 1930, AGN, *Gobernación, Fomento y Obras Publicas*, Ramo de Censo y Estadística, caja 49 leg. 1 fol. 27–40 ("Amatenango de Las Casas, pueblo"); for 1990, INEGI, *Población*; for early sixteenth-century patterns, McCaa, "Matrimonio infantil," p. 44.

[87] Morin, "libros parroquiales," pp. 408–9; Calvo, *Guadalajara*, vol. 1, pp. 90–107.

[88] Rabell, *Población novohispana*, p. 16.

[89] Cook and Borah, *Essays*, vol. 2, pp. 290–91.   [90] Cook and Borah, *Essays*, vol. 2, pp. 324–26.

[91] Wrigley and Schofield, *Population History*, pp. 228–36. For more than half a century the English total fertility rate rose steadily, from 4.6 children in 1756 to 6.1 in 1816, and then began a sustained, century-long descent. My computations of the English child/woman ratios are from the data developed by Wrigley and Schofield.

seventeenth-century Tacuba (1623–30) was eight children, just as it was 150 years later in San Luis de la Paz.[92] Reliable fertility data are too sparse to construct time series or compare social or ethnic groups. Error is likely to exceed measured differences. "Natural" fertility, without the slightest hint of birth control, characterize all reliably measured populations of colonial Mexico, although Calvo claims that he finds implicit evidence of birth control among the 256 Guadalajaran families "reconstituted" for the years 1666–1730. It seems more likely that this analysis does not adequately take into account children lost to the church registry.[93]

While natural fertility was the rule in colonial Mexico, in practice, attained fertility fell far short of biological limits. Marriage made the difference. "Marriageways," access to stable unions including those un-sanctioned by church or state, were socially constructed and differed over time and by ethnic or socioracial group.[94] Stable coupling was the key to regulating fertility and reproduction in New Spain.

For rural Indians, three features of the *feria nupcial* (nuptial fair or mar-riage market) stand out from the small number of studies completed to date. Marriage occurred at an early age and was nearly universal. Most births (85–95%) occurred in stable conjugal unions. The extreme may be two rural communities in the present-day state of Morelos, Huitzillan and Quauhchichinollan, where the average age for initiating cohabitation for females in the 1530s was less than 13 years. By age 25 all women were in unions or widowed. Illegitimacy was well below 5%.[95] Narrative sources also point to extremely youthful marriage among the indigenes. The Codex Mendoza tells the life cycle of the Mexica (Aztec) people from birth through old age (folios 57–71). The pictographs show females ready for marriage from age 13 (Figure 7.4). The informed exegesis of this scene by Frances Berdan and Patricia Anawalt reads:

The daughter now has taken on another of the household's daily domestic tasks. The gloss states that the thirteen-year-old girl is grinding [maize for] tortillas and preparing food. She kneels before the grinding stone, pulverizing the limewater-soaked maize kernels with the stone roller. . . . The girl, whose skirt now has a decorated hemline, is becoming a "grown maiden of marriageable age," whom Sahagún defines as one who grinds corn and makes *atole*.[96]

---

[92] These estimates are from my tabulations of the age distribution of deaths for Tacuba (GSU micro-film no. 0038301, *Defunciones* vol. 2, September 1623–October 1630, unpublished data discovered and compiled by Steven R. Alderson) and from Rabell, *Población novohispana*, p. 54, using her female data for normal mortality years.

[93] Calvo, "Familles mexicaines," pp. 48–49.   [94] McCaa, "Marriageways," pp. 21–31.

[95] McCaa, "Matrimonio infantil," pp. 25–31.

[96] Berdan and Anawalt, *Codex Mendoza*, vol. 2, p. 162; the pictographs are produced in vol. 3, p. 127.

/ Mother of the
children in this row

Two *tortillas*

A 13 year-old girl who is grinding [maize for]
tortillas and preparing food

Little bowl

Griddle

Tortillas

Pot with prepared food

Figure 7.4. The decorated hemline of this 13-year-old girl shows that she is becoming a "grown maiden of marriageable age" (Codex Mendoza, fol. 60r). (*Source*: Berdan and Anawalt, *Codex Mendoza*, vol. 4, p. 125, reprinted by permission of the authors)

A study of Acatzingo village in the archbishopric of Puebla shows female marriage age rising from an average of 14 or 15 years in the seventeenth century to 17 or 18 by the end of the colonial era. Elderly spinsters were rare.[97] The age gap between spouses also narrowed over time from five or six years in the sixteenth century to only two or three years in the eighteenth. For the last century of Spanish rule, a slow, sustained rise in marriage age has been documented in Oaxaca, Guadalajara, and elsewhere.[98]

Early marriage of Indian women left little time for prenuptial couplings. In rural areas, bastards, including *hijos naturales*, *hijos de la iglesia*, or *hijos de padres noconocidos*, typically amounted to 10 percent or less of Indian baptisms, with a surprising tendency to decline as marriage age rose toward the end of the colonial period. These patterns did not hold in the city, but only a small fraction of Indians resided in urban settlements. In the

[97] Calvo's (*Acatzingo*, p. 55) cautious hypothesis was confirmed by subsequent research.
[98] Cook and Borah, *Essays*, vol. 2, p. 285. Calvo's thesis that marriage ages fell at the end of the eighteenth century ("Familles mexicaines," p. 55) has received little support from recent research (McCaa, "Marriageways," pp. 27–28).

handful of colonial towns – only 10 numbered 10,000 or more inhabitants in 1750 – urban Indians married much later than in the countryside, probably because of the delay occasioned by migration itself. Bastardy was also more common in urban areas, particularly in the demographic black-hole that was Mexico City, where migration necessarily compensated for losses due to appalling mortality.[99]

For peninsular-born Spaniards, whose nuptial proclivities stood at the opposite extreme from rural Indians, migration certainly delayed marriage. Male *peninsulares* (there were few female immigrants) married very late, often in their 30s or 40s. Many never married at all, although this was no obstacle to siring more than their share of children.

Españoles, or Mexican-born Spaniards, evolved cultural patterns that by the end of the eighteenth century were akin to the practices of rural Andalucía in southern Spain, where women typically married in their early 20s but as many as 20% never married at all. The age gap between spouses was substantial, with husbands often four or more years older than their wives. In New Spain, bastardy rates are typically placed at 10% for *españoles* (several points greater than in Andalucía), but racial labels are particularly problematic for bastards, many of whom are listed as orphans of unknown parentage.

Intermediate between *españoles* and *indios* in terms of marriage age were mestizos and *castas*, who were also distinguished by unique marriage patterns. Bastardy sets these groups apart. In San Luis de la Paz at the beginning of the eighteenth century, for example, 20% of mestizo births were not legitimate, compared with 33% for castas, but only 13% for Indians and 10% for Spaniards. Nevertheless, these differences wore thin by the end of the colonial period.[100]

Fertility in colonial Mexico was constrained by remarriage as well. Widows are perplexing to historians, who do not understand why there were so many in the Latin American past. They insist that most must be fictive widows, that is, single mothers in disguise. For population historians, widows were the escape valve for the Malthusian pressure cooker of colonial demography, a socially accepted, and religiously sanctioned, means of restraining fertility. Consider that within 15 or 20 years of first marriage most conjugal unions were disrupted by the death of a spouse, usually the male. Widowed males readily remarried, regardless of social or ethnic origins, but this was not the case for females, particularly non-

[99] Arrom, *Women*, pp. 69–70, 122–23; Klein, "Demographic Structure," p. 85.
[100] Rabell, *Población novohispana*, p. 23.

Indians. *Españolas* who became widowed faced poor prospects in the nuptial fair, especially as they neared or surpassed their thirtieth "April." The full reproductive potential of Indians was least likely to be curtailed by widowhood, because Indian widows remarried in greater proportions.[101] (Were differences in remarriage prospects for widowed *españolas* and *indias* a matter of wheat bread versus corn tortillas, that is, a function of time necessary for preparing the daily bread?)[102] Over the eighteenth century, marriage and remarriage patterns converged in mixed ethnic communities throughout New Spain, but large contrasts in nuptial practices remained between Hispanicized settlements and Indian villages and between town and countryside. The cultural and material conditioning of remarriage and marriage, family and household implied by ethno-racial differences is yet to be fully mapped for colonial Mexico.[103]

The history of life expectancy also remains largely unwritten, but not for a lack of effort. The task is complicated by the poor quality of burial registers. The classic technique of computing mortality rates from recorded ages at death in a parish (numerator) coupled with a corresponding population census (denominator) yields implausibly low figures for colonial Mexico. At best, clues emerge from the inventive analysis of odd pieces of data: proportions orphaned or age distributions of skeletons, burials, or populations (Table 7.3). These straws in the wind all point to the brevity of life in New Spain, near or even below the worst levels recorded for early modern Europe.[104]

Life expectancy estimates for New Spain approach, but rarely attain, model life-table level-1 proportions (Table 7.3). An exceptionally detailed census from the 1530s written in the Nahuatl reveals that one in seven children aged 5–9 no longer had a surviving father. Of 261 children at that age, 15.6% were paternal orphans. This figure is three percentage points worse than level-one mortality (20%), suggesting a life expectancy at birth of 16 years or less.[105] A half century later in Teotihuacán, mortality con-

---

[101] Arrom, *Women*, pp. 116–19; McCaa, "La viuda viva"; Klein, "Familia," p. 120, and "Demographic Structure," p. 72.

[102] Bauer, "Millers and Grinders," pp. 4–5.

[103] Cook and Borah, *Essays*, vol. 1, pp. 119–299, vol. 2, pp. 270–85; Doenges, "Patterns," p. 19.

[104] Livi-Bacci, *Concise History*, p. 22.

[105] McCaa, "Matrimonio infantil," pp. 33–36. The early date of this census and the lack of evidence of epidemics suggest that these were normal mortality levels in the Mexica countryside. This hypothesis may be tested by the demographic analysis of other surviving Nahuatl censuses. The fraction of maternal orphans cannot be calculated because widows readily remarried and the census does not consistently distinguish step-children from others.

Table 7.3. *Life expectancy at age 15 (e₁₅) in colonial Mexico*

Place, period	e_{15} (years)	Author, method, data
Mexico, 1939–41	43	Camposortega, deaths, census
Model West, level 1 ($e_0 = 20$)	31	Coale and Demeny, stable populations
Morelos, 1530s	<30	McCaa, orphanhood, children
Teotihuacán, 1580–1620	13	Storey, mean age at death, skeletal remains
Cholula, 1642–90	29	Hayward, age at burial
San Luis de la Paz, 1745–94	33	Rabell, mean age at death, burial
Males	35	(Level 5)
Females	31	(Level 1)
Oaxaca, (1700–1777)	33	Cook and Borah, population age structure, census
Parral, 1808	<30	McCaa, orphanhood, newlyweds

Note: In 1939–41, Mexicans aged 15 years could expect to live 43 additional years on average, to age 58, given the mortality experience of that period.

Sources: Camposortega Cruz, *Análisis*, p. 321; Coale and Demeny, *Regional Model Life Tables*, p. 384; Cook and Borah, *Essays*, vol. 1, pp. 201–99; Hayward, "Demographic Study," pp. 221–22; McCaa, "Peopling," pp. 617–18; "Matrimonio infantil," pp. 32–34; Rabell, *Población novohispana*, p. 32; Storey, *Life and Death*, pp. 184–85.

ditions were so terrible as to imply extinction (e_{15} = 13 years!) – if we accept results obtained by conventional paleodemographic methods.[106] Written records and better methods suggest sustainable conditions but little variation over time or space (e_{15} = 29–33 years). There is evidence from the eighteenth century that men (e_{15} = 35) lived longer than women (e_{15} = 31), at least in the north-central, predominantly Indian parish of San Luis de la Paz.[107] On the northern frontier at the beginning of the nineteenth century, only 46% of fathers of grooms were alive when sons aged 25 or younger married. To attain level-one conditions (e_0 = 20), the figure should be bumped up five percentage points, or, to reach national levels of 1940, when life expectancy at birth was 40 years, it should be increased by exactly one-half to 70%.[108]

When independence was finally won in 1821, the result was a political

---

[106] Storey, *Life*, pp. 184–85.   [107] Rabell, *Población novohispana*, pp. 31–32.

[108] McCaa, "Peopling," pp. 617–19. Statistics on orphanhood at marriage of minors seem to be robust, notwithstanding the tedium required to collect the data nor the quantitative contortions necessary for their computation.

victory, not a social or demographic one. The demographic legacy of the Paleolithic past and three centuries of colonial rule remained. The ancien regime's high-pressure system – high fertility checked by high mortality – left a small, yet significant, margin for population increase.[109] Indeed, Malthusianists see demographic growth, heightened poverty, inequality, and discontent spawned by an inflexible colonial order as the roots of rebellion and the struggle for independence.[110] Enrique Florescano's evidence of price increases for corn and wheat preceding epidemics suggests Malthus's "positive check" at work,[111] but other historians find colonial grain price series less persuasive and favor epidemics as the autochthonous regulator of demographic change in Bourbon Mexico.[112] Questions of whether population growth led to misery and social crisis,[113] to agricultural innovation and expansion, or to social and cultural transformation, even protoindustrialization, call for further research.[114]

Demographic revolution incipient in late colonial Mexico would not erupt full blown until the 1930s. In Europe, the transformation was already well under way a century earlier.[115] By 1780, England's death rate was probably half that of Mexico's and its population growth rate likely twice as great. Epidemics in Bourbon Mexico were at least twice as devastating as in western Europe at the same time. Grain price fluctuations no longer governed the European mortality regime, unlike that in Mexico, where in 1786, the "year of hunger," 15% of the population of Michoacán died of starvation and related causes.[116] Indian mothers combated starvation by selling their children for a few coins (*reales*), the daily wage of an unskilled laborer in normal times. The first steps toward demographic revolution were taken under Spanish colonial rule: banning the use of corpses by beggars seeking alms, barring elaborate public burial for victims of epidemics, prohibiting the sale or rental of epidemic victims' clothing, imposing quarantine to contain the spread of infectious disease, mobilizing large-scale relief in times of crisis, vaccinating the mass of the population against smallpox, and so on. With independence greater strides would be made; at the same time, even greater ones were expected.

---

[109] Brading, *Haciendas*, pp. 59–60; Morin, *Michoacán*, p. 82.
[110] Morin, "Des terres," *Michoacán*, pp. 296–301; Reher, "Malthus," pp. 648–50.
[111] Florescano, *Precios*, pp. 159–63.   [112] Brading, *Haciendas*, p. 60.
[113] Pescador, *Bautizados*, pp. 141–44, 378.
[114] Van Young, *Hacienda and Market*, p. 356; Ouweneel, *Shadows*, pp. 253–331.
[115] Walter and Schofield, "Famine," pp. 49–55.
[116] Morin, *Michoacán*, p. 57; Florescano, *Precios*, p. 196.

INDEPENDENT MEXICO'S
CENSURED CENTURY

The nineteenth century was a disappointment for many Mexicans. Independence in 1821 followed a dozen years of war, an enormous loss of life, and widespread economic destruction. Then, over the ensuing half century of nation building, Mexicans fought innumerable insurrections and civil wars, lost Texas to English-speaking immigrants, found themselves at war with the United States, signed away the vast northern territories for a trifle, suffered the humiliation of invasion by a European army, and, before the chaos ended, were ruled by a Hapsburg princeling under the patronage of Napoleon III and a French imperial army! Grand dreams of making independent Mexico into a prosperous, populous nation were confounded by decades of political turmoil, civil war, and invasion.[117]

Education and immigration were supposed to transform independent Mexico, but almost a century after Father Hidalgo's "Grito" in 1810, this republic of 13.6 million people claimed barely 2 million citizens who could read. The literacy rate for females scarcely reached 20%, nine points less than for males, and both fell far short of expectations.

Immigration was an even greater disappointment. In 1900, after decades of promoting European immigration, 99.5% of the resident population of Mexico was also born in Mexico. Resident foreigners totaled only 57,491 and came mainly from three countries – Spain, the United States, and Guatemala – hardly what the proponents of immigration had in mind. Then, too, most immigrants to Mexico were male. According to the 1900 census, only 16,000 foreign-born females resided in the entire country, a rather meager base for remaking a race. The peopling of Mexico has always been a matter of natural increase with little immigration, and the nineteenth century was no exception.[118]

From the founding of the nation, Mexican political leaders equated population growth with economic prosperity and political power. As early as 1830 Salvador Piñeyro, the governor of the republic's most remote and poorest state, Chiapas, declared the debate regarding what constituted good or bad government as resolved. For Piñeyro, population figures

---

[117] These conclusions as well as much of the following discussion are based on data and interpretations in my longer essay entitled "The Peopling of Nineteenth-Century Mexico: Critical Scrutiny of a Censured Century" (McCaa, "Peopling," 603–33).

[118] México, INEGI, *Estadísticas Históricas*, table 1.11.1; México, DGE, *Resumen general ... de 1900*, p. 44; Gonzalez Navarro, *Extranjeros en Mexico*, vol. 2, p. 271.

settled the matter.[119] His simple rule would categorize most nineteenth-century governments as "bad," because until 1895 none managed to conduct even a national census, notwithstanding a constitutional requirement that the population be enumerated regularly for purposes of political representation.

AN ALTERNATIVE SCENARIO OF DEMOGRAPHIC CHANGE FOR NINETEENTH-CENTURY MEXICO

Among historians, the conventional view of the nineteenth century is a gloomy one, that demographic growth was slow well into the second half of the century, at less than 0.5% per year. Then from 1876, growth accelerated to 1.5% per annum and continued at this pace for the ensuing quarter century, when, after the passage of almost one hundred years, the supposedly high growth rates of the last decades of Spanish rule were finally regained.[120] If the symmetry of this scenario is seductive, the evidence supporting it is not persuasive. As I have argued, population figures for 1800–13 were inflated because the authors of the most commonly cited numbers – Alexander von Humboldt and Francisco Navarro y Noriega – greatly exaggerated the true rates of growth in late colonial times and corrected their figures in an entirely mechanical way.[121]

Table 7.4 (and Figure 7.5) contrasts the conventional scenario for the nineteenth century with a series constructed for this essay. The pattern suggested here would halve the commonly accepted growth rate for late colonial times, double that for the early republic, and retain the high rates of the late nineteenth century. I am persuaded that during the last decades of colonial rule mortality conditions were worse than during the early republic. Before discussing the mortality evidence consider the overall pattern of growth and spatial distribution of Mexico's population in the nineteenth century derived from these alternative figures.[122]

---

[119] "En el día ya han cesado las teorías sobre los gobiernos buenos o males, y la cuestión se decide por los padrones" (Piñeyro, *Memoria*, p. 10).

[120] México, INEGI, *Estadísticas Históricas*, Table 1.2; Brachet and Nettel, *La población*; Kicza, "Mexican Demographic History"; Urías Hermosillo and San Juan Victoria, "Población y desarrollo."

[121] Humboldt, *Essai politique*, vol. 1, pp. 325–42, and vol. 5, pp. 95–97; Navarro y Noriega, *Memoria*, p. 7; Tribunal del Consulado, "Noticias de Nueva España," p. 3; Mexico, INEGI, *Primer censo*.

[122] McCaa, "Peopling," 604–11. In this essay Navarro y Noriega's figures for 1811 are adjusted downward. Van Young (*Hacienda and Market*, p. 273) also thinks that population growth slowed in the late eighteenth century.

Table 7.4. *Two series of population estimates:*
Mexico, 1790–1910

Year	New Series[a]	Conventional Series	Author
1790	4.8		
1793		4.5	Revillagigedo[b]
1800	5.1		
1803		5.8	Humboldt[b]
1810	5.6	6.1	Navarro y Noriega[c]
1820	5.9	6.2	
1830	6.4	8.0	Burkhardt[c]
1836		7.8	
1840	7.2	8.1	
1850	7.6		
1854		7.9	Orozco y Berra[c]
1860	8.3		
1870	8.7	8.8	Hermosa[c]
1880	9.9		
1885		10.9	Fomento[c]
1890	11.5		
1895		12.6	I Censo[c]
1990	13.6	13.6	II Censo[c]
1910	15.2	15.2	III Censo[c]

[a] From McCaa, "Peopling," pp. 604–8 and as revised in this essay.
[b] Humboldt, *Essai politique*, vol. 1. pp. 325, 341.
[c] México, INEGI, *Estadísticas Históricas*, Table 1.2.

From some 5 million inhabitants in 1800, Mexico grew to 8 million by 1855, and to over 15 million in 1910. This tripling of the population over barely one hundred years probably equaled or exceeded the record for any other period in Mexican history prior to the great demographic revolution of the twentieth century. After 1910 the population of Mexico increased more than fivefold in nine decades, surpassing 80 million in 1990. Growth in the nineteenth century was well below the record of the twentieth, but was substantial nonetheless.

Figure 7.5 compares total population figures compiled by the National Statistical Institute (INEGI) with my totals constructed from state-level data. Because of the notorious deficiencies in baptism and burial registers,

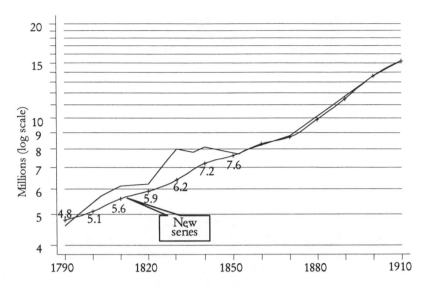

Figure 7.5. Population of Mexico, 1790–1910. New series increases figure for 1790, decreases figures for 1800–50. (*Sources*: Mexico, INEGI, *Estadísticas Históricas*; McCaa, "The Peopling," Table 1, as adjusted here)

the new series discards any figures derived from Humboldt's widely used, but wrong-headed, birth-minus-death equation. Now, the 1790s appear as years of noticeably slower growth than the first decade of the nineteenth century. The worst decades of that century were those of war: 1810, 1840, and 1860, with 1850 perhaps slightly better (a civil war erupted in 1857). The 1820s and 1830s were periods of higher-than-average growth, but these years did not attain the levels of the closing decades of the century.

In the early years of the twentieth century, population growth tapered off owing to a slight decline in birth rates, but largely because of Mexican emigration to the United States. The number of Mexicans enumerated north of the Río Bravo grew slowly, from 68,000 in 1880 to 78,000 in 1890 and 103,000 in 1900. In 1910, the U.S. Census Bureau enumerated 221,915 Mexican-born nationals but estimated the total "Mexican race" population at 367,510, including citizens of Mexican parents born in the United States. As the economies of the southwestern United States boomed, Mexicans flocked into the region, nearly half of them to Texas and more than one-fourth to California. When revolution erupted in

Mexico on November 25, 1910, almost 2.5 percent of native-born Mexicans already resided in the United States. This was double the figure of just 10 years before, but it was only one-third of what it would become following a decade of revolution, civil war, banditry, famine, and epidemics.[123]

REGIONAL CHANGE, MIGRATION, URBANIZATION, AND THE PERSISTENCE OF INDIAN LANGUAGE SPEAKERS

The Mexican republic's states and regions show great diversity in patterns of demographic change over the nineteenth century. The slowest-growing regions were the south and east, encompassing Oaxaca, Chiapas, Tabasco, Campeche, and the Yucatán. This region shrank from one-fifth of Mexico's total population at the beginning of the nineteenth century to one-seventh at the end. In contrast, the north doubled its demographic weight from 8% to 16%, notwithstanding the midcentury amputation of Texas, New Mexico, and Upper California. In the center, political chaos, beginning with the "Grito" on September 16, 1810, and ending with the execution of Austrian Archduke Ferdinand Maximilian on June 19, 1867, provoked nearly one million war deaths and displacements. Consequently, the Federal District and nine neighboring states shrank in relative size, from 49% in 1810 to 40% in 1870, and then recovered to 43% by 1910. The center north, on the other hand, (Jalisco, including Nayarit, Colima, Guanajuato, Aguascalientes, Zacatecas, San Luis Potosí, and Querétaro) was a place of refuge, gaining population during the early decades of the century when political unrest was greatest, and losing it in later decades when economic growth was more vigorous elsewhere.[124]

Notwithstanding these disparate regional growth patterns, migration between states seems to have been relatively modest over much of the nineteenth century. When reliable nation-wide migration data finally become available with the census of 1900, only 6.6% of males – and 6.1% of females – lived outside the "state" of birth ("federal entity" in Mexican statistical parlance). Almost one-third of all interstate migrants resided in the national capital, Mexico City (Map 7.2). Three entities accounted for almost half of all migrants: the capital, Veracruz, and Coahuila. Twenty-six federal entities attracted fewer than 50,000 migrants each; eighteen

[123] Gerhard, "Whose Frontier"; U.S. Bureau of the Census, *Fifteenth Census*, vol. 2, p. 41.
[124] McCaa, "Peopling," pp. 612–14.

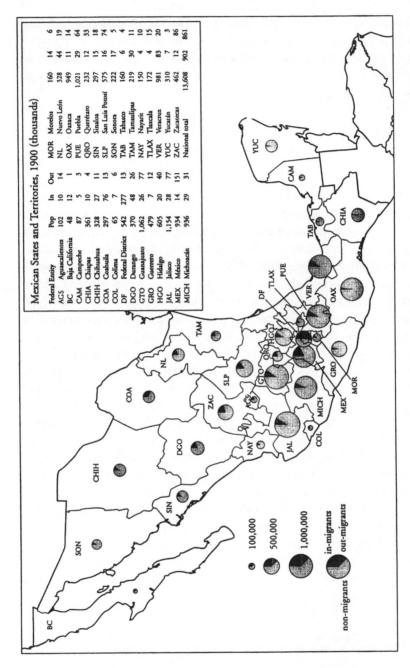

Mexican States and Territories, 1900 (thousands)

Federal Entity		Pop	In	Out
AGS	Aguascalientes	102	10	14
BC	Baja California	48	12	1
CAM	Campeche	87	5	3
CHIA	Chiapas	361	10	4
CHIH	Chihuahua	328	27	11
COA	Coahuila	297	76	13
COL	Colima	65	7	6
DF	Federal District	542	277	13
DGO	Durango	370	48	26
GTO	Guanajuato	1,062	26	77
GRO	Guerrero	479	7	12
HGO	Hidalgo	605	20	40
JAL	Jalisco	1,154	28	77
MEX	México	934	14	151
MICH	Michoacán	936	29	31
MOR	Morelos	160	14	6
NL	Nuevo León	328	44	19
OAX	Oaxaca	949	11	14
PUE	Puebla	1,021	29	64
QRO	Querétaro	232	12	33
SIN	Sinaloa	297	15	18
SLP	San Luis Potosí	575	16	74
SON	Sonora	222	17	5
TAB	Tabasco	160	6	4
TAM	Tamaulipas	219	30	11
NAY	Nayarit	150	4	10
TLAX	Tlaxcala	172	4	15
VER	Veracruz	981	83	20
YUC	Yucatán	310	7	3
ZAC	Zacatecas	462	12	86
	National total	13,608	902	861

100,000
500,000
1,000,000

in-migrants
out-migrants
non-migrants

Map 7.2. States and territories of Mexico, showing population, in-migrants, and out-migrants, 1900 (*Source:* Mexico, DGE, *Resumen general del censo*)

drew fewer than 25,000, accounting for 21% of all migrants. Neither sending nor receiving many migrants were four hermit states: Chiapas, Oaxaca, Yucatán and Guerrero. Fewer than 3% of their native sons and daughters lived outside the state of birth and a like proportion of current residents were in-migrants.

In half of all states migrants made up less than 4% of the population, and in only seven did they account for as much as 10 percent of the total population (in Aguascalientes, Coahuila, Colima, Durango, Morelos, Nuevo León, and Tamaulipas). The fact that Morelos, a seedbed for revolution in 1910, was a magnet for migrants – and the only central state whose residents withstood the seductions of the Federal District – suggests that material conditions may not have been as bad in the land of Emiliano Zapata as historians of the Mexican Revolution would have us believe.

In the Federal District itself, migrants constituted over one-half of its 541,516 inhabitants in 1900. It should be noted, too, that almost a century earlier fully 43% of the capital's residents were also born outside the city, and of these almost two-thirds were from neighboring districts.[125] Assisted in part by its small geographical size, Mexico City was the strongest migratory magnet in the Mexican nation at the beginning of the twentieth century, just as it had been one hundred years earlier for the viceroyalty of New Spain, and perhaps as long ago as half a millennium, as the center of the Mexica (Aztec) empire. This millennial-long process of urbanization at the core finally ended with the earthquake of 1985, after which the Federal District began to implode, expelling more migrants than it received.[126]

Rapid urbanization in Mexico is a phenomenon of the twentieth century.[127] In 1900, only four cities, in addition to the Federal District, numbered as many as 50,000 inhabitants: Guadalajara (101,208), Puebla (93,521), Monterrey (62,266), and San Luis Potosí (61,019). For much of the nineteenth century, to the extent that migration was important for urban growth, in-migrants were easily obtained from within the state. In the case of Guadalajara, during the period 1875 to 1905, 80% of the city's migrants came from within the state, according to data from city marriage

[125] Klein, "Demographic Structure," pp. 72–73, 84.
[126] México, DGE, *Resumen general . . . 1900*, pp. 1–17; McCaa, "Peopling," pp. 626–27; Arrom, *Women*, pp. 105–10; Klein, "Demographic Structure," pp. 72–75; Chavez Galindo and Savenberg, "Le Centre du Mexique," pp. 758–65.
[127] Moreno Toscano, "Cambios en los patrones"; Davies, "Tendencias demográficas."

registers. On the other hand, migrants were scarcely missed from the countryside because as late as 1900, 72% of all Mexicans still lived in communities of fewer than 2,500 inhabitants (down from 92% a century earlier). Over three-fourths of the working class continued to depend upon agriculture for a livelihood, while three-fourths of the middle class lived in towns and cities, which despite their small size offered migrants remunerative labor, schools, and a more open, egalitarian social structure.[128]

Indian villages languished while haciendas, ranchos, and towns with predominantly Spanish-speaking populations grew ever more rapidly. The declining number of Indian language speakers was due more to the spread of Spanish-based education (*castillanización*), changing identities, and mestizaje than to lower reproduction rates. With the universal repudiation of racial distinctions after independence, the emergence of what the noted Mexican educator José Vasconcelos felicitously termed "the cosmic race" can be examined only through extant, but inexact statistics compiled at the beginning and end of the century. Thus, Afro-Mexicans, who numbered one-half million in 1810, more or less "vanished," thoroughly intermingled and unidentifiable by 1895 if the official discourse is accepted at face value.[129] Indians, according to the ill-defined 1793 count, numbered 2.5 million in central Mexico. A century later only 2.1 million Mexicans spoke Indian languages in the entire republic, a decline from at least 50 to a scant 15% of the population.[130]

If speakers of Indian languages had grown at the national average of 1% per annum over the century, they would have numbered 6.5 million in 1900. Since death rates in Indian regions were higher than the national average (Table 7.5), perhaps half of the 4 million loss could be attributed to higher mortality. The other half should be assigned to mestizaje and transformed identities, sometimes forced by gun-toting land-grabbers who found it convenient to make native villages disappear. The spread of public education, market economies, and liberal politics in the nineteenth century proved nearly as perilous to the survival of Native Americans, their cultures, and communities as virgin soil epidemics in the sixteenth.

---

[128] México, DGE, *Resumen general . . . 1900*, vol. 34, pp. 1–17; Cook, "Migration as a Factor"; Anderson, "Cambios sociales."

[129] Aguirre-Beltrán (*Población negra*, p. 237) places the figures at 168,000 and concludes the story with the destruction of the "society of castes" in 1821 (pp. 287–92). On castillianization, see Kanter, "Hijos del Pueblo," pp. 329–30.

[130] Aguirre-Beltrán (*Población negra*, p. 237) indicates only 1.1 million in 1790. México, DGE, *Resumen general . . . 1900*, vol. 34, p. 71. Whether differences between 1895 and 1900 were real, the result of changing definitions, or undercounting is not clear.

Table 7.5. *Life expectancy in Mexico (both sexes combined), 1800–1950*

Place	1800	1830	1880	1900	1930	1950
At age 5 (e₅)						
Oaxaca (rural)	—	—	29	33	—	40
Jalisco (rural)	—	—	34	37	—	47
Guadalajara (urban)	—	—	37	39	—	47
Republic of Mexico	—	—	—	39	—	55
	1808	1828	1878		1930	
At age 0 (e₀)						
Parral	<20	27	37	—	<20	—

Sources: Cook and Borah, *Essays*, vol. 2, p. 398, figure 7.7; Mier y Terán, "Evolution," vol. 2, p. 196; McCaa, "Peopling," pp. 617–19.

In 1900, only six states reported one-fourth or more of total population, as accounted for by native language speakers – Oaxaca, Chiapas, Guerrero, Campeche, Yucatán, and Puebla. By 1910, the group was halved to three. In absolute terms, 80% of all native language speakers in 1900 lived in seven states, 50% in only three: Oaxaca, Puebla, and Yucatán (Figure 7.6). From 1900 to 1910, Indian language speakers increased their demographic weight in only three "states": Chihuahua, Nayarit, and San Luis Potosí. By 1950, according to official figures, speakers of Indian languages numbered 2.4 million, of whom one-third were monolinguals. In recent decades a significant resurgence has taken place, reaching 5.2 million in 1980, owing in part to the fact that acknowledging indigenous roots is increasingly a matter of pride rather than of shame, as in earlier times. Nevertheless, by 1980 the fraction of native language speakers dropped below 8%, barely half the figure at the beginning of the twentieth century.[131]

LIFE EXPECTANCY, DISEASE, AND THE DECLINE
OF EPIDEMICS

The slow acceleration of urbanization, migration, and emigration in nineteenth-century Mexico was probably accompanied by modest gains

[131] México, INEGI, *Estadísticas Históricas*, vol. 1, pp. 109–11.

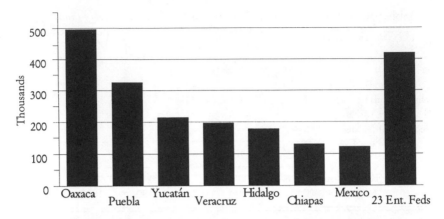

Figure 7.6. Speakers of native languages, Mexico, 1900. Eighty percent of 2,078,924 native language-speakers lived in seven states; 50% lived in three: Oaxaca, 495,000; Puebla, 325,000; Yucatán, 214,000.

in mortality. The nineteenth century has long been written off as a loss in terms of mortality, a period in which life chances were poor and remained so over much of the century.[132] Unfortunately, neither parish books nor civil registers are adequate for studying the course of life expectancy in Mexico until the twentieth century. When sufficient information to hazard national estimates becomes available, life expectancy at birth is estimated at less than 30 years for both males and females.[133] One might imagine that conditions could hardly have been worse at the beginning of the nineteenth century. Nonetheless, the thesis that mortality improved following independence is supported by four pieces of evidence: (1) growth rates implicit in national estimates of total population, (2) year-to-year fluctuations in mortality, (3) shifts in the mix of causes of death, and (4) estimates of life expectancy for various times and places.[134]

Turning now to the second factor, the settling down of annual fluctuations in burials over the century suggests accelerating demographic growth rates. Great crises provoked in earlier times by typhus, smallpox,

[132] Cosío Villegas, *Historia Moderna*, vol. 4, p. 43; the Mexican demographer Francisco Alba ("Population and the Crisis," p. 206) concurs that mortality probably improved during the last decades of the century.

[133] Arriaga, *New Life Tables*, pp. 172–73 places life expectancy at birth at 25.0 years for males and 25.6 for females in 1900. Mier y Terán estimates 29.5 and 30.2, respectively, for the period 1895–1910; see her "Evolución demográfica," pp. 82–83, and "Evolution de la population mexicaine," vol. 1, p. 252, and vol. 2, p. 196.

[134] For a contrary view, see Bustamante, "Situación epidemiológica."

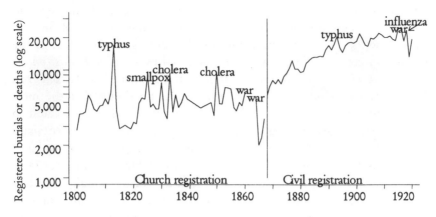

Figure 7.7. Disasters checked population growth of Mexico City. Severe crises were more frequent before 1850. (*Sources*: Maldonado 1800–67; AHSS 1868–1900; Greer 1901–20)

and famine gradually tapered off. Mexico City serves as an example, although its series is confounded by a lack of true rates and the reality of demographic growth through migration (Figure 7.7).[135] The last great crisis of colonial Mexico City was the typhus epidemic of 1813, when deaths more than tripled, rising from a greatly underrecorded annual average of 5,000 to 17,021. When the biggest subsequent epidemic of typhus erupted 80 years later, the population of the capital had probably doubled, but typhus deaths rose to "only" 2,653, scarcely 10% of total burials and a great public health victory by early modern standards.[136] Although mortality remained high in Mexico City until the 1920s, annual fluctuations lost much of the volatility characteristic of the colonial regimen. Similar developments characterize burial series for Chiapas and Oaxaca in the south and Chihuahua in the north.

Third, consider changes in the causes of death over the century: the decline in mortality due to famine, smallpox, and other big killers of the colonial era. Hunger was certainly not absent from Mexico in the

[135] The parish burial series for Mexico City is from Maldonado, *Estadísticas vitales*, pp. 24, 36, 48, 60, 72, 84, 96, 108, 120, 132, 144, 156, and 168 (I computed annual burials from her parish totals). The civil registration series attains a degree of reliability in 1867; my series for 1868–1920 is from AACM, *Estadística*, vol. 1032, exp. 68 "Mortalidad menusal y anual habida en al Municipalidad de México, durante el periodo de treinta años seis meses, de 1 de julio de 1867 a 31 de diciembre de 1897"; AHSS, *Fondo Salubridad Pública* Ramo Estadística, caja 11, exp. 1–2 "Mortalidad en la Ciudad de México, 1895–1920"; and for 1901–1920, Greer, "Demographic Impact," p. 92. The construction of a series for the capital of New Spain is virtually impossible because of numerous lacunae in the parish books.
[136] AHSS, *Fondo Salubridad Publica*, caja 3, exped. 4, "Estadísticas de enfermos durante 1893."

nineteenth century (or in the twentieth either), but the frequency and intensity of famine seem to have lessened following the end of Spanish colonialism. Corn output probably doubled during the first half of the nineteenth century while population increased by 50%. *A Treatise on the Cultivation of Maize in Mexico* written by the Mexican intellectual Don Luis de la Rosa and published in 1846 leaves no doubt that the most devastating hunger in Mexican history was that of 1786 (the greatest in Mexican *pre*-history ravaged central Mexico in 1450).[137] De La Rosa also expressed surprise and satisfaction at the great expanse of new lands brought under cultivation and sown in corn following the hunger of 1786. With independence, local, state, and federal authorities sought to anticipate shortages, increase production by early harvests brought from the tropical lowlands, and ensure that supplies were transported to areas of scarcity as needed – even during war years. Mexican intellectuals were pleased by this progress but were displeased that most women continued to spend a large portion of their time at the *metate*, because no means had been discovered for making fresh corn tortillas with the economies of baking wheat bread. Day-old tortillas acquired the texture of parchment, whereas day-old bread remained palatable.[138]

In times of dearth, grain could be purchased from abroad, particularly from the United States, as in 1845 and 1909.[139] During such times there was rarely a doubling, much less quadrupling, of grain prices in the Republic of Mexico, as was common in colonial Mexico.[140] Historians have long thought that in the decades prior to the revolution of 1910 food production did not keep pace with accelerating population growth, but John Coatsworth's meticulous critique of the evidence reveals this to be a myth. When reliable quantitative data become available, trends in per capita production of basic foodstuffs – corn, wheat, beans, and even

---

[137] Hassig, "Famine of One Rabbit," pp. 172–80; Viesca, "Hambruna y epidemia," pp. 157–65. Tutino ("Revolution in Mexican Independence") marshaling new archival evidence from the Bajío, argues that independence wrought a revolution in the countryside. The colonial logic of restraining production to profit from scarcity and famine was replaced by a new calculus, with tenant farmers and sharecroppers using their enhanced power to extract better tenancy arrangements, which led to greater returns from increased production. In Michoacan, Chowning finds that agrarian recovery came quickly after war ended as the old colonial land-holding elite was replaced by new owners seeking profits through increased production and diversification ("Reassessing the Prospects for Profits").

[138] De la Rosa, *Memoria*; Azcarate, *Noticias estadísticas*, p. 8: "pocas manos abastecerían a muchas."

[139] AGN, *Gobernación*, caja 303 exped. 13, 1845; 1.909(4)3.

[140] For colonial Mexico, see Florescano, *Precios*, pp. 140–93; and Van Young, *Hacienda and Market*, pp. 81–88. For the nineteenth century, see AGN, *Gobernación* caja 214 exp. 12, 1835 Yucatán; caja 303 exp. 13, 1845 Mexico; caja 383 exp. 21.1, 1850 Zacatecas; caja 495 exp. 5, 1863 Toluca; caja 498 exped. 13, 1863 Federal District; caja 558 exp. 1.1, 1870 Distrito Federal; etc.

pulque (a native beverage, mildly intoxicating but rich in calories and vitamins) – were positive from 1877 to 1907, and increases were greatest when
export agriculture was expanding most rapidly.[141] The killing frosts of 1907
created shortages that were overcome by massive imports from the United
States.[142] Some historians cite this crisis as evidence of the failure of
Mexican agrarian policies, which supposedly favored exports over domestic consumption.[143] The fact that foodstuffs were readily obtained from
the United States at reasonable prices prevented the recurrence of another
devastating famine such as that of 1786.

Mortality due to smallpox was greatly reduced following the introduction of vaccination in 1804. Thanks to royal patronage and enthusiastic
endorsement by both clerical and secular elites, vaccination was extended
quickly throughout the viceroyalty of New Spain.[144] If smallpox was not
eradicated in Mexico until 1951 (a decade prior to the last case in Great
Britain), its virulence was substantially attenuated over the course of the
nineteenth century. In the epidemic which erupted in Mexico City in
November 1829, for example, deaths increased "only" by three or four
thousand (the surge was due in part to simultaneous outbreaks of measles,
scarlet fever, and dysentery) instead of ten or twelve thousand, as was
common in the previous century (see Figure 7.7). The monetary costs of
stemming the tide of this epidemic, by hurriedly vaccinating the populace, was a fraction of the expense for care and hospitalization incurred
during the epidemics of 1779 and 1797. Again in 1840 and 1844, mortality was greatly reduced by vaccination campaigns.[145]

Historians looking back on the failure of Mexican authorities to erad-
icate smallpox by universal vaccination cite administrative chaos, in-
competence, negligence, and lack of foresight as causes. Likewise, the
transformation of smallpox into an endemic disease is interpreted as one
of the great failures in Mexican public health. Not until 1917 was a national
public health authority created. Then, too, until 1917 Mexican doctors
uniformly practiced the dangerous arm-to-arm method of vaccination,
which demanded professional supervision (and fees) to reduce the risks of
transmitting other communicable diseases such as syphilis.[146] While a
comprehensive history of smallpox will clear up many of the uncertain-

---

[141] Coatsworth, *Orígenes del atraso*, pp. 175–77.   [142] AGN, *Gobernación*, 1.909(4)3.
[143] Cosío Villegas, *Historia Moderna*, v. 3, pp. 125, 133.   [144] Fernandez del Castillo, *Viajes*.
[145] Erosa-Barbachano, "La viruela," pp. 545–47; Mexico, Secretaría de Estado, *Memoria*, 288–90;
Ciudad de México, *Manifiesto al publico*, p. 7.
[146] Bustamante, "La viruela en México."

ties about the demographic, social, and health significance of the disease, my reading of the evidence is that smallpox mortality declined sharply with the introduction of vaccination in 1804. Indeed, the rapid growth of Mexico City in the late nineteenth century was due in part to an unrelenting vaccination campaign, in which twenty to fifty thousand children were treated annually, and smallpox deaths were reduced to a few hundred. When epidemic threatened, authorities in Mexico City rushed vials of vaccine (of human origin) to the hinterland to curtail the eruption. According to official statistics for the years 1894 to 1903, more than 3.5 million Mexicans were vaccinated against smallpox, yet 215,578 died from the disease in those same years. Thus at the end of the century smallpox accounted annually for 3 or 4% of all deaths.[147] Measles and other big killers from colonial times were also tamed in the nineteenth century, although the causes remain unclear.

On the other hand, war and cholera were new to Mexico in the nineteenth century. The demographic costs of the former were substantial (and have been little studied), but the impact of cholera was relatively minor (and has been widely researched). Following conquest and during three centuries of colonial rule, there were few deaths from war, insurrection, or riot. The demographic catastrophe of the sixteenth century was mainly due to disease and exploitation, not war. On the northern frontier, in the *provincias internas* north from Durango, fighting continued into the nineteenth century and the destruction of native settlements was widespread, yet the demographic costs for the colony as a whole were minor. In the nineteenth century, struggles for independence, civil wars, and invasions (first by the United States in 1846 and then France in 1863) cost perhaps a half million lives, and another half million displacements as people permanently fled the war zones. The deadliest war of all was the decade of revolution and civil struggle that began in 1910. The assassination of President Francisco Madero in February 1913 and the ensuing confrontations of a score of regional bands inflicted massive destruction on the country.[148]

Cholera found virgin soil in Mexico in 1833, following outbreaks in Western Europe and North America. The disease flared again in 1850 and 1882, yet Mexican authorities anticipating the epidemic's appearance always sought the latest (at times, ineffective) methods from Europe to

[147] México, DGE, *Boletín demográfico, 1903*, pp. 787–88.   [148] McCaa, "Peopling," pp. 608–14.

attempt to contain the spread and reduce mortality (Figure 7.7). Cholera provoked great horror in the populace, afflicting adults as well as children, with excruciatingly painful symptoms, but the overall demographic impact was relatively minor. In Mexico City the number of deaths increased ten thousand in 1833 and by somewhat fewer in 1850, but these epidemics failed to penetrate sparsely populated rural areas or much of the hinterland.[149]

Life expectancy in nineteenth-century Mexico is difficult to estimate, but the few figures that we have point to significant improvements over the course of the century. A series for a parish with no war mortality during the nineteenth century, Hidalgo del Parral in Chihuahua state, suggests an increase in life expectancy at birth from less than 20 years during the last decades of colonial rule to almost 30 years for the first decades of the republic and nearly 40 years after midcentury, but falling below 20 again during the decade of revolution and the Spanish influenza epidemic of 1918–19 (Table 7.5).[150]

In rural Jalisco, life expectancy at age 5 (e_5) rose from 29 years in 1845–54 to 34 years in 1880 and 37 by 1900 (and 47 by 1950). The city of Guadalajara seems to have enjoyed an advantage of perhaps a year or two over its hinterland, while rural Oaxaca lagged behind Jalisco by four or five years.[151] National estimates of life expectancy at birth for 1900 range between 25 and 30 years.[152] One might imagine that the colonial record could not have been worse, but the life expectancy figures for Parral and the few annual burial series that we have for central Mexico convince me that during the last century there were substantial improvements in life chances, perhaps by as much as 5 or 10 years. If true, this signaled a prolongation of the average life span by at least one-fifth and perhaps as much as one-half above colonial levels.[153]

FERTILITY AND MARRIAGEWAYS

Birth rates for early modern Mexico are even more difficult to plot than death rates, because of the notorious shortcomings of parish and civil reg-

---

[149] Hutchinson, "Asiatic Cholera," pp. 3–23. Márquez Morfín, *La desigualdad*, offers an insightful study of the effects of epidemics in Mexico City. For Guadalajara, see Oliver Sánchez, *Un verano mortal.*

[150] McCaa, "Peopling," pp. 617–19.   [151] Cook and Borah, *Essays*, vol. 2, p. 398.

[152] Mier y Terán, "Evolution de la population mexicaine," p. 196; Arriaga, *New Life Tables*, pp. 172–73.

[153] McCaa, "Peopling," 616–20.

istration systems. In the Mixteca Alta of Oaxaca, a series developed by Cook and Borah reveals a century-long seesawing between 45 births per thousand population in 1770 and 52 for the first decades of the republic.[154] For 1900 demographers settle on 50 as a plausible crude birth rate for the nation as a whole. This corresponds to a total fertility rate of 6.8 children for women who survived to the end of their childbearing years. In other words, fertility was high in nineteenth-century Mexico, but trends and fluctuations remain obscure.[155]

Fertility probably declined over the century, not because of any conscious effort to limit births but rather from, on the one hand, a delay in the age at marriage (including all "marriageways" – religious, civil and consensual), and, on the other, from a decrease in the proportion of women who entered unions of any sort.[156] In late colonial Mexico, marriage was nearly universal. A church census for the archbishopric of Mexico covering more than one million people reveals that in 1779, 89% of females of marriageable age were married or widowed.[157] A century and a half later, according to the 1930 census (the first enumeration to consider all forms of unions), the figure had fallen twenty points to 69% (compared with 73% in the United States in the same year).[158] Concurrently, marriage age rose over the century. A study of Oaxaca's northern districts documents a sustained increase in average female age at marriage from 16.2 years in 1700 to 18.9 years in 1905.[159] In Mexico's grain belt, the Bajío, the median age rose from 17.0 years in 1782–85 to 18.6 in the 1850s.[160] In 1930, the national mean age at first union for females was 21.9 years and the proportion of women ultimately entering unions (by age 50) was 87% – surprisingly high in comparison to Europe or the United States, but low when compared to Mexico's own historical record. (After 1930, the first figure would remain stable over the ensuing half-century, while the proportion of females entering unions would actually rise to 93%, and the already

---

[154] Cook and Borah, *Essays*, vol. 2, p. 296.
[155] Mier y Terán, "Evolución demográfica," pp. 83–84; Zavala de Cosío, *Cambios de fecundidad*, pp. 25–26, 31–32.
[156] Cook and Borah, *Essays*, vol. 2, pp. 270–85; McCaa, "Women's Position."
[157] AGI, *Fondo Varios*, exp. 38, "Padrón exacto del Arzobispado de México con distinción de Clases, Estados, . . ."
[158] México, DEN, *Censo de población . . . 1930*. The apparently higher nuptiality rate in the United States is due mainly to an "older" age structure caused by lower fertility, higher life expectancy, and massive waves of mostly adult immigrants.
[159] Cook and Borah, *Essays*, vol. 2, pp. 270–85.
[160] Brading (*Haciendas and Ranchos*, p. 49) reports figures of 16 and 18 years, respectively. A recomputation of the medians following arithmetic convention which requires the calculation of decimals yields 17.0 and 18.6, respectively.

high birth rate would surge by several points before plummeting in the 1970s.)[161]

In the waning years of Spanish rule, the position of women in the marriage market was undermined by a royal edict which decreed that only written pledges of marriage were legally binding. Unfortunately for women, this restriction, issued in 1803, was carried over into republican civil codes. According to colonial custom among the popular classes, a spoken promise to marry by the male was followed by the female "losing her virginity to him" (from the male's viewpoint, "[I] took her virginity"). After a reasonable interval, marriage usually followed.[162] Church and civil courts stood ready to guarantee that a dallying suitor either fulfilled his promise or compensated the deflowered maiden. Court records show that notarized pledges were rarely obtained. After the edict of 1803, verbal seductions continued, but women were now stripped of the right to demand redress in the courts. In 1857, the institution of marriage was further weakened when civil marriage became the only form of legal wedlock in Mexico. Almost a century passed before the civil act became widely accepted.[163]

REFLECTIONS

For Mexico, the nineteenth century came to an end on November 20, 1910, with the outbreak of revolution. Demographic disaster, probably the worst since the sixteenth century, ensued with a decade of destruction – civil war, guerrilla fighting, and banditry. Mexico's population declined by almost 1 million instead of growing by 2 million, because the demographic pace of the last years of Porfirian rule had faltered. The loss is often explained away as being due to emigration to the United States or enumeration errors in the 1921 census, but these are easily exaggerated. Civilian deaths from war-induced famine, plague, and even influenza probably exceeded 1 million, while battlefield casualties numbered substantially less than 100,000. Fertility losses were more than one-half million.[164] The

---

[161] Quilodrán Salgado, "Le Mariage au Mexique," pp. 126–31, 286–90. From 1960 to 1990 average marriage age for Mexican females was between 20.7 and 22.0 years and the percentage ultimately marrying was 91 to 93%.

[162] Stern, *Secret History of Gender*, p. 273.

[163] Cook and Borah, *Essays*, vol. 2, pp. 270–85; Arrom, "Changes in Mexican Family Law," pp. 305–7.

[164] Ordorica and Lezama, "Consecuencias demográficas," pp. 51–53; U.S. Bureau of the Census, *Fifteenth Census*, vol. 2, pp. 27–41.

number of refugees was uncountable, because, on the one hand, they were indistinguishable from economic migrants drawn to the booming Southwest, and, on the other, many did not settle permanently in the United States. While the pace of Mexican emigration accelerated over the decade, the net outflow as measured in U.S. censuses was a mere 246,000. This loss was a minor fraction of those due to excess mortality or reduced fertility. It was also a minor fraction of the total Mexican "race" population in the United States. From 732,000 in 1920, the number of Mexicans doubled over the next decade, reaching 1,489,000 in 1930. Finally, the destinations of those who settled were not those of political refugees (towns along the border), but the fields, mines, and factories of Texas, California, Arizona, Colorado, and the entire Midwest.

Taken as a whole, Mexico's demographic recovery from revolution was slow. Total growth from 1910 to 1930 amounted to 1.4 million, less than the increase for 1900–10, when the social crisis of the old regime was supposedly at its worse.

Mexico's high-pressure system in 1910, notwithstanding the demographic changes occurring over the previous century, was more akin to what had existed when Mexicans fought for independence from Spain – indeed, closer to what they experienced before Christians invaded almost 400 years earlier – than to conditions of the late twentieth century. Spanish colonization during the sixteenth century, as well as liberal reforms in the nineteenth, destabilized, but did not destroy, the fundamental population dynamics of agrarian societies of ancient Mexico. This would be accomplished only after 1930, by the greatest demographic transformation to occur in Mesoamerica since first settlement 10,000–70,000 years ago.

The millennial model of vital rates hypothesized in this essay is one of high but slowly easing pressure. Birth rates drifted downward from perhaps 60–70 per thousand population per annum in the fifteenth century to 55–65 in the eighteenth and 50–55 in the nineteenth (and 20–25 by the end of the twentieth). In normal years – of which there were few – death rates moved in tandem with births but lagged a few points below. Beginning in the seventeenth century the gap slowly widened, and by the late nineteenth spread to 10 or 15 points, as death rates continued their downward drift, finally bottoming out at less than 7 deaths per thousand population by the year 2000. Birth rates declined too, although not as fast or as far. The decrease was due, at least prior to the twentieth-century fertility transition, to changing marriageways, not to birth control within marriage. With women marrying "later" (although still relatively early in comparison with rural folk of Western Europe or colonial British America) and widows confined to a secondary marriage market, sexual activity languished for a measurable fraction of the female population. Birth rates declined accordingly, although they remained much higher than anything seen in Western Europe since the Middle Ages.

Malthusian crises are often perceived as the underlying causes of great Mesoamerican political cataclysms – conquest, independence wars, and revolution – over the past half millennium. Demographic determinism for even one of these upheavals is not convincing. Each was a piece of a general process that impacted peoples throughout the Americas. Population growth provided fodder for political catastrophe, but in each instance hemispheric forces were at work, so that sparsely populated regions, as well as densely settled ones, suffered the consequences of conquest, war, and rebellion. What is astonishing is that once each catastrophe subsided, whether in Mesoamerica or the Southern Cone of South America, population expansion resumed, invariably attaining greater densities and greater social complexity, which, in turn, established the foundation for further demographic growth without the menace of Malthusian collapse. Demographic pressure over the millennia was important and interrelated with environmental, political, and even cultural change, but it was rarely the sole determinant, just as it is unlikely to be in the next millennium.

REFERENCES

Aguirre-Beltrán, Gonzalo. *La población negra de México: Estudio etnohistórico.* México, D.F.: Fondo de Cultura Ecónomica, 1972 (1st ed. 1946).

Alaman, Lucas. *Historia de Méjico.* México, D.F.: Editorial Jus, 1942.

Alba, Francisco. "Population and the Crisis of the Socio-Political System: The Case of Pre-revolutionary Mexico." In Eric Vilquin, ed., *Revolution et Population: Aspects démographiques des grandes révolutions politiques*, pp. 203–18. Louvain-la-Neuve: Academia, 1990.

Anderson, Rodney. "Cambios sociales y económicos en el 6° cuartel de Guadalajara: 1842–1888." *Encuentro El Colegio de Jalisco* 1, no. 4 (July–September 1984): pp. 17–37.

Archivo del Ayuntamiento de la Ciudad de México (AACM), *Estadística.*

Archivo General de Indias (AGI). *Fondo Varios.*

Archivo General de la Nación (AGN). *Ramo de Gobernación.*

Archivo Histórico de la Secretaría de la Salubridad (AHSS). *Fondo Salubridad Pública.*

Archivo Parroquial de San José de Parral (APSJP), *Libros de Defunciones.*

Arriaga, Eduardo A. *New Life Tables for Latin American Populations in the Nineteenth and Twentieth Centuries.* Berkeley: University of California Institute of International Studies, 1968.

Arrom, Silvia M. "Changes in Mexican Family Law in the Nineteenth Century: The Civil Codes of 1870 and 1884." *Journal of Family History* 7, no. 3 (Fall 1985): pp. 305–17.

———. *The Women of Mexico City, 1790–1857.* Stanford, Calif.: Stanford University Press, 1985.

Azcarate, Miguel Maria del. *Noticias Estadísticas que sobre los efectos de consumo introducidos en esta capital en el quinquenio de 1834 a 1838. . . .* Mexico, 1839.

Bauer, Arnold J. "Millers and Grinders: Technology and Household Economy in Meso-America." *Agricultural History* 64, no. 1 (Winter 1990): pp. 1–17.

Bennett, Herman Lee. *Lovers, Family and Friends: The Formation of Afro-Mexico, 1580–1810.* Unpub. Ph.D. diss., Duke University, 1993.

Berdan, Frances F., and Patricia Anawalt, eds. *The Codex Mendoza.* Berkeley: University of California Press, 1992.

Bianchine, Peter J., and Thomas A. Russo, "The Role of Epidemic Infectious Diseases in the Discovery of America." In Guy A. Settipane, ed., *Columbus and the New World: Medical Implications,* pp. 11–18. Providence, R.I.: Oceanside Publications, 1995.

Borah, Woodrow, and Sherburne F. Cook. "La despoblación del México central en el siglo XVI." *Historia Mexicana* 12, no. 1 (July–September 1962): pp. 1–12.

———. *The Aboriginal Population of Central Mexico on the Eve of the Spanish Conquest.* Berkeley: University of California Press, 1963.

———. "Marriage and Legitimacy in Mexican Culture: Mexico and California." *California Law Review* 54, no. 2, (1966): pp. 946–1008.

Brachet de Márquez, Viviane, and M. Nettel. *La población de los estados mexicanos en el siglo XIX, 1824–1895.* México, D.F.: Instituto Nacional de Antropología e Historia, 1976.

Brading, David A. *Haciendas and Ranchos in the Mexican Bajío: León, 1700–1860.* Cambridge, England: Cambridge University Press, 1978.

Burkholder, Mark A., and Lyman L. Johnson. *Colonial Latin America.* 3d ed. Oxford: Oxford University Press, 1998.

Bustamante, Miguel E. "Aspectos históricos y epidemiológicos del hambre en México." In Enrique Florescano and Elsa Malvido, eds., *Ensayos sobre la historia de las epidemias en México,* vol. 1, pp. 37–66. México, D.F.: Instituto Mexicano del Seguro Social, 1982.

———. "La situación epidemiológica de México en el siglo XIX." In Enrique Florescano and Elsa Malvido, eds., *Ensayos sobre la historia de las epidemias en México.* vol. 2, pp. 425–76. México, D.F.: Instituto Mexicano del Seguro Social, 1982.

———. "La viruela en México, desde su orígen hasta su erradicación." In Enrique Florescano and Elsa Malvido, eds., *Ensayos sobre la historia de las epidemias en México.* vol. 1, pp. 67–92. México, D.F.: Instituto Mexicano del Seguro Social, 1982.

Cabrera y Quintero, Cayetano. *Escudo de Armas de Mexico: Celestial proteccion de esta nobilissima ciudad de la Nueva España, y de casi todo el nuevo Mundo, Maria Santissima, en su portentosa imagen del Mexicano Guadalupe, milagrosamente apparecida en el Palacio Arzobispal el año de 1531, y jurada su principal patrona el passado de 1737 en la angustia que ocasiono la pestilencia, que cebada con mayor rigor en los Indios, mitigo sus ardores al abrigo de tanta sembra.* Mexico, 1746.

Calvo, Tomás. *Acatzingo: demografía de una parroquia mexicana*. México, D.F.: INAH-SEP Colección Científica (Historia), 1973.

————. "Familles mexicaines au XVIIe siècle: une tentative de reconstitution." *Annales de démographie historique* 1984, pp. 149–74.

————. *La Nueva Galicia en los siglos XVI y XVII*. Guadalajara: El Colegio de Jalisco and Centro de Estudios Mexicanos y Centroamericanos, 1989.

————. *Guadalajara y su región en el siglo XVII: población y economía*. Guadalajara: Centro de Estudios Mexicanos y Centroamericanos and H. Ayuntamiento de Guadalajara, 1992.

Camposortega Cruz, Sergio. *Análisis demográfico de la mortalidad en México, 1940–1980*. México, D.F.: El Colegio de México, 1992.

Capello, Juan Francisco. *Remedios contra la peste*. Mexico, 1737.

Carroll, Patrick J. *Blacks in Colonial Veracruz: Race, Ethnicity, and Regional Development*. Austin: University of Texas Press, 1991.

————. "Los mexicanos negros, el mestizaje y los fundamentos olvidados de la 'Raza Cósmica': Una perspectiva regional." *Historia Mexicana* 44 (January–March 1995): pp. 403–38.

Chavez Galindo, Ana Maria, and Sandra Savenberg. "Le Centre du Mexique: De la Suburbanisation vers la Mégalopolisation." *Population* 51, no. 3 (May–June 1996): pp. 756–66.

Chowning, Margaret. "Reassessing the Prospects for Profit in Nineteenth-Century Mexican Agriculture from a Regional Perspective: Michoacán, 1810–60." In Stephen Haber, ed., *How Latin American Fell Behind: Essays on the Economic Histories of Brazil and Mexico, 1800–1914*. Santford, Calif.: Stanford University Press, 1997, pp. 179–215.

Ciudad de México. *Manifiesto al publico que hace el ayuntamiento de 1840 acerca de la conducta que ha observado en los negocios municipales y del estado en que quedan los ramos de su cargo*. México, D.F.: Impreso por Ignacio Cumplido, 1840.

Cline, Sarah L. *The Book of Tributes. Early Sixteenth-Century Nahuatl Censuses from Morelos*. Los Angeles: University of California Press, 1993.

Coale, Ansley, and Paul Demeny. *Regional Model Life Tables and Stable Populations*. New York: Academic Press, 1983.

Coatsworth, John H. *Los orígenes del atraso: Nueve ensayos de historia económica de México en los siglos XVIII y XIX*. Mexico City: Alianza Editorial Mexicana, 1990.

Cohen, Mark Nathan. "Does Paleopathology Measure Community Health? A Rebuttal of 'The Osteological Paradox' and Its Implication for World History." In Richard R. Paine, ed., *Integrating Archaeological Demography: Multidisciplinary Approaches to Prehistoric Population*. Carbondale: Southern Illinois University, 1997, pp. 242–60.

Cook, Noble David. *Born to Die: Disease and New World Conquest, 1492–1650*. New York: Cambridge University Press, 1998.

Cook, Sherburne F. "The Incidence and Significance of Disease among the Aztecs and Related Tribes." *Hispanic American Historical Reviews* 21, no. 3 (August 1946): pp. 320–35.

————. "Migration as a Factor in the History of Mexican Population: Sample Data from West Central Mexico, 1793–1950." In Paul Deprez, ed., *Population and Economics*, pp. 279–302. Winnipeg: University of Manitoba Press, 1970.

Cook, Sherburne F., and Woodrow Borah. *Essays in Population History: Mexico and the Caribbean*. 3 vols. Berkeley: University of California Press, 1971–79.

————. *The Indian Population of Central Mexico 1531–1610*. Berkeley: University of California Press, 1960.

Cook, Sherburne F., and Lesley Bird Simpson. *The Population of Central Mexico in the Sixteenth Century*. Berkeley: University of California Press, 1948.

Cooper, D. B. *Epidemic Disease in Mexico City, 1761–1813: An Administrative, Social and Medical Study*. Austin: University of Texas Press, 1965.

Cope, Robert Douglas. *The Limits of Racial Domination: Plebeian Society in Colonial Mexico City, 1660–1720*. Madison: University of Wisconsin Press, 1994.

Cosío Villegas, Daniel, ed. *Historia Moderna de México*. 9 vols. México, D.F.: Editorial Hermes, 1955–72.

Davies, Keith A. "Tendencias demográficas urbanas durante el siglo XIX en México." *Historia Mexicana* 21, no. 3 (January–March 1972): pp. 481–524.

De la Rosa, Luis. *Memoria sobre el Cultivo del Maiz en Mexico*. Mexico, 1846.

Denevan, William M., ed. *The Native Population of the Americas in 1492*. Madison: University of Wisconsin Press, 1976 (rev. ed. 1992).

Diamond, Jared. *Guns, Germs, and Steel: The Fates of Human Societies*. New York: W. W. Norton, 1997.

Diez de la Calle, Juan. *Memorial, y noticias sacras, y reales del imperio de las Indias Occidentales*. Madrid, 1646.

Doenges, Catherine E. "Patterns of Domestic Life in Colonial Mexico: Views from the Household." *Latin American Population History Bulletin* no. 19 (Spring 1991): pp. 14–21.

Erosa-Barbachano, Arturo. "La viruela, desde la Independencia (1821) hasta la erradicación." In Enrique Florescano and Elsa Malvido, eds., *Ensayos sobre la historia de las epidemias en México*, vol. 2, pp. 545–50. México, D.F.: Instituto Mexicano del Seguro Social, 1982.

Faulhaber, Johanna. "La población de Tlatilco, México, caracterizada por sus entierros." In *Homenaje a Juan Comas en su 65° aniversario*, vol. 2, pp. 83–122. México, D.F.: Instituto Indigenista Interamericano, 1965.

Fernandez del Castillo, Francisco. *Los viajes de Don Francisco Xavier de Balmis: Notas para la historia de la expedición vacunal de España a América y Filipinas (1803–1806)*. México, D.F.: Galas de México, 1960.

Florescano, Enrique. *Precios del maíz y crisis agrícolas en México (1708–1810): Ensayo sobre el movimiento de los precios y sus consecuencias económicas y sociales*. México, D.F.: El Colegio de México, 1969.

Genealogical Society of Utah (GSU). Salt Lake City: Microfilm Collection of Parish Registers.

Gerhard, Peter. "La evolución del pueblo rural mexicano, 1519–1975." *Historia Mexicana* 24, no. 4 (April–June 1975): pp. 566–78.

————. *Geografía Histórica de la Nueva España 1519–1821*. México, D.F.: Universidad Nacional Autónoma de México, 1986 (1st English ed. 1972).

————. "Whose Frontier? The Mexican-United States Border in Perspective." *Geopolitics and International Boundaries* 2, no. 2 (Autumn 1997): pp. 57–69.

Gibson, Charles. *The Aztecs under Spanish Rule: A History of the Indians of the Valley of Mexico, 1519–1810*. Stanford, Calif.: Stanford University Press, 1964.

Gonzalez Navarro, Moisés. *Los extranjeros en México y los mexicanos en el extranjero,*

1821–1970, 3 vols. México, D.F.: Colegio de México and Centro de Estudios Históricos, 1993–94.

Greer, Robert Gordon. "The Demographic Impact of the Mexican Revolution." Unpub. Master's thesis, University of Texas at Austin, 1966.

Hassig, Ross. "The Famine of One Rabbit: Ecological Causes and Social Consequences of a Pre-Columbian Calamity." *Journal of Anthropological Research* 37 (1981): pp. 171–81.

Hayward, Michel H. "A Demographic Study of Cholula, México, from the late Postclassic and the Colonial Period of 1642–1738." Unpub. Ph.D. diss., State University of Pennsylvania, 1986.

Henige, David. "Native American Population at Contact: Standards of Proof and Styles of Discourse in the Debate." *Latin American Population History Bulletin*, no. 22 (1992): pp. 2–23.

Hopkins, Donald R. *Princes and Peasants: Smallpox and History*. Chicago: University of Chicago Press, 1983.

Hutchinson, Charles S. "The Asiatic Cholera Epidemic of 1833 in Mexico." *Bulletin of the History of Medicine* 32, no. 1 (January–February 1958): pp. 1–23 and 152–63.

Humboldt, Alexander von. *Essai politique sur le royaume de la Nouvelle-Espagne*. Paris: F. Schoell, 1811.

Johansson, S. Ryan. "The Demographic History of the Native Peoples of North America: A Selective Bibliography." *Yearbook of Physical Anthropology* 25 (1982): pp. 133–52.

Johansson, S. Ryan, and S. Horowitz. "Estimating Mortality in Skeletal Populations: Influence of the Growth Rate on the Interpretation of Levels and Trends during the Transition to Agriculture." *American Journal of Physical Anthropology* 71 (1986): pp. 233–50.

Kanter, Deborah E. "Hijos del Pueblo: Family, Community, and Gender in Rural Mexico, The Toluca Region, 1730–1830." Unpub. Ph.D. diss., University of Virginia, 1993.

Kicza, John E. "Mexican Demographic History of the Nineteenth Century: Evidence and Approaches." In James W. Wilkie and Stephen Haber, eds., *Statistical Abstract of Latin America*, vol. 21, pp. 592–609. Los Angeles: University of California Press, 1981.

Klein, Herbert S. "Familia y fertilidad en Amatenango, Chiapas (1785–1816)." In Elsa Malvido and Miguel Angel Cuenya, comp., *Demografía Histórica de México: siglos XVI–XIX*, pp. 112–22. México, D.F.: Universidad Autónoma Metropolitana and Instituto Mora, 1993.

———. "The Demographic Structure of Mexico City in 1811." *Journal of Urban History* 23, no. 1 (November 1996): pp. 66–93.

Kubler, George. "Population Movements in Mexico, 1520–1600." *Hispanic American Historical Review* 22, no. 4 (November 1942) pp. 606–43.

Kuznesof, Elizabeth Anne. "Gender Ideology, Race and Female Headed Households in Urban Mexico, 1750–1850." In Victor M. Uribe, ed., *State and Society in Spanish America During the 'Age of Revolution': New Research on Historical Continuities and Changes ca 1750s–1850s*. Durham, N.C.: Duke University Press, forthcoming.

Lerner, Victoria. "Consideraciones sobre la población de la Nueva España (1793–1810) Según Humboldt y Navarro y Noriega." *Historia Mexicana* 17, no. 3 (January–March 1968): pp. 327–48.

Livi-Bacci, Massimo. *A Concise History of World Population.* Cambridge, Mass: Blackwell, 1993.

López de Velasco, Juan. *Geografía y descripción universal de las Indias,* edited by Marcos Jimenez de la Espada. Madrid: Atlas, 1971.

McCaa, Robert. "*Calidad, Clase,* and Endogamy in Colonial Mexico: The Case of Parral, 1788–1790." *Hispanic American Historical Review* 64, no. 3 (August 1984): pp. 477–502.

———. "Women's Position, Family and Fertility Decline in Parral (Mexico) 1777–1930." *Annales de Démographie Historique* (1989): pp. 233–43.

———. "La viuda viva del México borbónico: Sus voces, variedades y vejaciones." In Pilar Gonzalbo, Aizpuru, ed., *Familias novohispanas Siglos XVI al XIX,* pp. 299–324. México, D.F.: El Colegio de México, 1991.

———. "The Peopling of Nineteenth-Century Mexico: Critical Scrutiny of a Censured Century." In James W. Wilkie, Carlos Alberto Contreras, and Christof Anders Weber, eds., *Statistical Abstract of Latin America,* vol. 30, part 1, pp. 603–33. Los Angeles: University of California at Los Angeles Latin American Studies Center, 1993.

———. "Marriageways in Mexico and Spain, 1500–1900." *Continuity and Change* 9, no. 1 (1994): pp. 11–44.

———. "¿Fue el siglo XVI una catástrofe demográfica para México? Una respuesta basada en la demografía histórica no cuantitativa." *Cuadernos de Historia* 15 (December 1995): pp. 123–36.

———. "Spanish and Nahuatl Views on Smallpox and Demographic Catastrophe in the Conquest of Mexico." *Journal of Interdisciplinary History* 25, no. 3 (Winter 1995): pp. 397–431.

———. "Descenso de la fecundidad y modos de uniones matrimoniales en México: casos de Chihuahua y Puebla." In *Actas de la VII Jornada Nacional de Historia Regional de Chile 1996,* pp. 59–78. Santiago: Universidad de Chile, Departamento de Ciencias Históricas, 1996.

———. "Matrimonio infantil, cemithualtin (familias complejas), y el antiguo pueblo nahua." *Historia Mexicana* 46, no. 1 (July–September 1996): pp. 3–70.

McCaa, Robert, and Márquez Morfín, Lourdes. "Paleodemography, Nutrition and Health in Ancient Mexico." Unpublished paper presented at the Social Science History Association annual meeting, Chicago, Ill., November 16, 1995.

McClung, E., and M. C. Serra Puche. "La revolución agrícola y las primeras poblaciones aldeanas." In *El Poblamiento de México,* vol. 1, pp. 138–63. México, D.F.: Consejo Nacional de la Población, 1993.

MacNeish, R. S. *The Prehistory of the Tehuacan Valley.* Austin: University of Texas Press, 1967.

———. "Social Implications of Changes in Population and Settlement Patterns of 12,000 Years of Prehistory in the Tehuacan Valley of Mexico." In P. Deprez, ed., *Population and Economics,* pp. 215–50. Winnipeg: University of Manitoba Press, 1970.

Maldonado, Celia L. *Estadísticas vitales de la ciudad de México. Siglo XIX.* México, D.F.: Instituto Nacional de Antropología e Historia, 1976.

Malvido, Elsa. "Factores de despoblación y de reposición de la población de Cholula (1641–1810)." *Historia Mexicana* 23, no. 1 (July–September 1973): pp. 52–110.

Malvido, Elsa, and Carlos Viesca. "La epidemia de cocoliztli de 1576." *Historia*, no. 11 (1985): pp. 27–33.

Márquez Morfín, Lourdes. "La evolución cuantitativa de la población novohispana: siglos XVI, XVII y XVIII." In *El Poblamiento de México*, vol. 2, pp. 36–63. México, D.F.: Consejo Nacional de la Población, 1993.

———. *La desigualdad ante la muerte en la Ciudad de México: el tifo y el cólera (1813–1833)*. México D.F.: Siglo XXI, 1994.

Marquéz Morfín, Lourdes, M. E. Peraza, J. Gamboa, and T. Miranda. *Playa del Carmen: Una población de la costa oriental en el postclásico (un estudio osteológico)*. Colección científica 119. México, D.F.: Instituto Nacional de Antropología e Historia, 1982.

Mendizábal, Miguel Othén de. "Demografía mexicana. Epoca colonial 1519–1810: Demografía del siglo XVI, 1519–1599." In *Obras Completas*, vol. 3, pp. 309–38. Mexico, D.F.: Talleres Gráficos de la Nación, 1946 (first published 1939).

México. Secretaría de Estado. *Memoria de la Secretaría de Estado y del Despacho de Relaciones Exteriores e Interiores, correspondiente al año de 1831*. México, D.F.: 1831.

———. Dirección General de Estadística (DGE). *Resumen general del censo de de la República Mexicana verificado el 28 de octubre de 1900*. México, D.F.: Secretaría de Fomento, 1905.

———. Dirección General de Estadística (DGE). *Boletín demográfico de la República Mexicana, 1903*. México, D.F.: Oficina Tip. de la Secretaría de Fomento, 1908.

———. Departamento de la Estadística Nacional (DEN). *Censo de población. 15 de mayo de 1930*. México, D.F.: Talleres gráficos de la nación, 1932.

———. Instituto Nacional de Estadística, Geografía e Informática (INEGI). *Primer censo de población de la Nueva España 1790. Censo de Revillagigedo, un censo condenado*. México, D.F.: INEGI, 1977.

———. Instituto Nacional de Estadística, Geografía e Informática (INEGI). *Estadísticas Históricas Mexicanas*. México, D.F.: INEGI, 1986, 2v.

———. Instituto Nacional de Estádística, Geografía e Informática (INEGI). *Población y vivienda. Muestra estadística del censo de 1990*. Aguascalientes: INEGI, 1994.

Mier y Terán, Marta. "Evolution de la population mexicaine à partir des données des recensements, 1895–1970." Unpub. Master's thesis, Université de Montréal, Département de Démographie, 1982.

———. "Evolución demográfica de México en el siglo XX." In Sérgio Odilon Nadalin, Maria Luiza Marcílio, and Altiva Pillati Balhana, eds., *História e População: Estudos sobre a América Latina*, pp. 81–87. São Paulo: Fundação Sistema Estadual de Análise de Dados, 1990.

Moreno Toscano, Alejandra. "Cambios en los patrones de urbanización en México, 1810–1910." *Historia Mexicana* 22, no. 2 (1972): pp. 160–87.

Morin, Claude. "Los libros parroquiales como fuente para la historia demográfica y social novohispana." *Historia Mexicana* 21, no. 3 (January–March 1972): pp. 389–418.

———. *Santa Inés Zacatelco (1646–1812): Contribución a la demografía histórica del México colonial*. México, D.F.: Instituto Nacional de Antropología e Historia, 1973.

———. "Démographie et différences ethniques en Amérique latine coloniale." *Annales de démographie historique* (1977): pp. 301–12.

————. *Michoacán en la Nueva España del siglo XVIII: Crecimiento y desigualdad en una economía colonial.* México, D.F.: Fondo de Cultura Económica, 1979.

————. "Des terres sans hommes aux hommes sans terres: Les paramètres agraires de l'évolution démographique dans l'Indoamérique (Mexique-Pérou)." In Antoinette Fauve-Chamoux, ed., *Evolution agraire et croissance démographique*, pp. 75–87. Liège: Ordina Editions, 1987.

Motolinía, Fray Toribio de Benavente. *Memoriales: libro de oro (MS JGI 31)*, edited by Nancy Joe Dyer. México, D.F.: El Colegio de México and Centro de Estudios Lingüísticos y Literarios, 1996.

Navarro y Noriega, Fernando. *Memoria sobre la población del reino de Nueva España.* México: en la Oficina de D. Juan Bautista de Arizpe, 1820.

Oliver Sánchez, Lilia V. *Un verano mortal. Análisis demográfico y social de una epidemia de cólera, Guadalajara 1833.* Guadalajara, Jalisco: Unidad Editorial del Gobierno del Estado, 1986.

Ortiz de Montellano, B. R. *Aztec Medicine, Health and Nutrition.* New Brunswick, N.J.: Rutgers University Press, 1990.

Osterholm, Michael. Interview, "Plague War." *PBS Frontline.* http://www.pbs.org/wgbh/pages/frontline/shows/plague/interviews/osterholm.html, 1998.

Ouweneel, Arij. "Growth, Stagnation, and Migration: An Explorative Analysis of the *Tributario* series of Anáhuac (1720–1800)." *Hispanic American Historical Review* 71, no. 3 (August 1991): pp. 531–77.

————. *Shadows over Anáhuac: An Ecological Interpretation of Crisis and Development in Central Mexico 1730–1800.* Albuquerque: University of New Mexico Press, 1996.

Ordorica, Manuel, and José Luis Lezama. "Consecuencias demográficas de la revolución mexicana." In *El poblamiento de México: Una visión histórico demográfica*, v. 4, pp. 32–53. México, D.F.: Consejo Nacional de Población, 1993.

Pescador, Juan J. *De Bautizados a fieles difuntos.* México, D.F.: El Colegio de México, 1992.

Piñeyro, Salvador. *Memoria del Estado . . . de las Chiapas.* San Cristoval, Chiapas, 1830.

Prem, Hanns J. "Disease Outbreaks in Central Mexico during the Sixteenth Century." In Noble David Cook and W. G. Lovell, eds., *Secret Judgments of God." Old World Disease in Colonial Spanish America*, pp. 20–48. Norman: University of Oklahoma Press, 1991.

Quilodrán Salgado, Julieta. "Le Mariage au Mexique: Evolution nationale et typologie régionale." Unpub. Ph.D. diss., Université Catholique de Louvain, 1996.

Rabell Romero, Cecilia A. *La población novohispana a la luz de los registros parroquiales.* México, D.F.: Universidad Autónoma Nacional de México, 1990.

Rabell Romero, Cecilia A., and N. Necochea. "La mortalidad adulta en una parroquia rural novohispana durante el siglo XVIII." *Historia Mexicana* 36, no. 3 (January–March 1987): pp. 405–42.

Ramos Escandón, Carmen. "Mujeres trabajadoras en el México porfiriano: Genero e ideología del trabajo femenino 1876–1911." *Revista Europea de Estudios Latinoamericanos y del Caribe* 48 (June 1990): pp. 27–45.

Reff, Daniel T. *Disease, Depopulation, and Culture Change in Northwestern New Spain, 1518–1764.* Salt Lake City: University of Utah Press, 1991.

Reher, David H. "¿Malthus de nuevo? Población y economía en México durante el siglo XVIII." *Historia Mexicana* 41, no. 4 (April–June 1992): pp. 615–64.

Robinson, David J. *Research Inventory of the Mexican Collection of Colonial Parish Registers*. Salt Lake City: University of Utah Press, 1980.

Rosenblat, Angel. *La población indígena y el mestizaje en América*. 2 vols. Buenos Aires: Editorial Nova, 1954.

———. "The Population of Hispaniola at the Time of Columbus." In William Denevan, ed., *The Native Population of the Americas in 1492*, pp. 43–66. Madison: University of Wisconsin Press, 1976 (rev. ed. 1992).

Sahagún, Fray Bernardino de. *Florentine Codex General History of the Things of New Spain*, translated by Arthur J. O. Anderson and Charles E. Dibble. 13 vols. Salt Lake City: University of Utah Press, 1950–82.

———. *Historia general de las cosas de Nueva España*. 4 vols. Angel Maria Garibay Kintana, ed. México, D.F.: Porrua, 1956.

Sánchez-Albornoz, Nicolás. *La población de América Latina: Desde los tiempos precolombinos al año 2025*. Madrid: Alianza Editorial, 1994.

Sanders, William T. "The Population of the Central Mexican Symbiotic Region, the Basin of Mexico, and the Teotihuacan Valley in the Sixteenth Century." In William Denevan, ed., *The Native Population of the Americas in 1492*, pp. 85–150. Madison: University of Wisconsin Press, 1976 (rev. ed. 1992).

———. "Ecological Adaptation in the Basin of Mexico 23,000 B.C. to the Present." In Ronald Spores, ed., *Supplement to the Handbook of Middle American Indians*, vol. 4, pp. 147–97. Austin: University of Texas Press, 1986.

Sanders, William T., Jeffrey R. Parsons, and R. S. Santley. *The Basin of Mexico: Ecological Processes in the Evolution of a Civilization*. New York: Academic Press, 1979.

Saul, F. *The Human Skeletal Remains of Altar de Sacrificios: An Osteobiographic Analysis*. Papers of the Peabody Museum, vol. 63, no. 2. Cambridge, Mass., 1972.

Serrano Sánchez, C. "Orígen del hombre americano y perfil biológico de la población prehispánica de México." In *El Poblamiento de México*, vol. 1, pp. 96–115. México, D.F.: Consejo Nacional de la Población, 1993.

Stern, Steven J. *The Secret History of Gender: Women, Men, and Power in Late Colonial Mexico*. Chapel Hill: University of North Carolina Press, 1995.

Storey, Rebecca. *Life and Death in the Ancient City of Teotihuacan. A Modern Paleodemographic Synthesis*. Tuscaloosa: University of Alabama Press, 1992.

Sugiura Yamamoto, Y. "El ocaso de las ciudades y los movimientos poblacionales en el Altiplano Central." In *El Poblamiento de México*, vol. 1, pp. 190–213. México, D.F.: Consejo Nacional de la Población, 1993.

Swann, Michael M. *Migrants in the Mexican North: Mobility, Economy, and Society in a Colonial World*. Boulder Colo.: Westview Press, 1989.

Thompson, Angela. "To Save the Children: Smallpox Inoculation, Vaccination, and Public Health in Guanajuato, Mexico, 1797–1840." *The Americas* 49, no. 4 (April 1993): pp. 431–55.

Tribunal del Consulado. "Noticias de Nueva España en 1805." *Boletín de la Sociedad Mexicana de Geografía y Estadística* 2 (1850): pp. 5–13.

Tutino, John. "The Revolution in Mexican Independence: Insurgency and the Renegotiation of Property, Production, and Patriarchy in the Bajío, 1800–1855." *Hispanic American Historical Review* 78, no. 3 (August 1998): pp. 367–418.

United States. Bureau of the Census. *Fifteenth Census of the United States, 1930: Population. General Reports, Statistics by Subjects.* Vol. 2. Washington, D.C.: Government Printing Office, 1933.

Urías Hermosillo, Miguel, and Carmen San Juan Victoria. "Población y desarrollo en el México del siglo XIX." *Investigación Económica* 162 (October–December 1982): pp. 129–77.

Van Young, Eric. *Hacienda and Market in Eighteenth-Century Mexico: The Rural Economy of the Guadalajara Region, 1675–1820.* Berkeley: University of California Press, 1981.

Viesca T., Carlos. "Hambruna y epidemia en Anáhuac (1540–1544) en la época de Moctezuma Ilhuicamina." In Enrique Florescano and Elsa Malvido, eds., *Ensayos sobre la historia de las epidemias en México*, vol. 1, pp. 157–68. México, D.F.: Instituto Mexicano del Seguro Social, 1982.

———. "Epidemiologia entre los mexicas." In Fernando Martínez Cortés, ed., *Historia General de la medicina en Mexico*, vol. 1, pp. 171–88. México, D.F.: Universidad Nacional Autónoma de México, 1984.

Villaseñor y Sánchez, José Antonio. *Theatro Americano: Descripción general de los reynos y provincianos de la Nueva España y sus jurisdicciones.* México, D.F.: Editorial Trillas, 1992.

Wallace, Douglas C. "Mitochondrial DNA in Aging and Disease." *Scientific American* 277, no. 2 (August 1997): pp. 40–47.

Walter, John, and Roger Schofield. "Famine, Disease and Crisis Mortality in Early Modern Society." In Walter and Schofield, eds., *Famine, Disease and the Social Order in Early Modern Society*, pp. 1–74. Cambridge, England: Cambridge University Press, 1989.

Whitmore, Thomas M. *Disease and Death in Early Colonial Mexico: Simulating Amerindian Depopulation.* Boulder, Colo.: Westview Press, 1992.

Wrigley, E. A., and Roger S. Schofield. *The Population History of England, 1541–1871: A Reconstruction.* London: Edward Arnold, 1981.

Zambardino, Rudolph A. "Mexico's Population in the Sixteenth Century: Demographic Anomaly or Mathematical Illusion." *Journal of Interdisciplinary History* 11, no. 1 (Summer 1980): pp. 1–27.

Zavala de Cosío, María Eugenia. *Cambios de fecundidad en México y políticas de población.* México D.F.: El Colegio de México y Fondo de Cultura Económica, 1992.

8

THE WHITE POPULATION OF THE UNITED STATES, 1790–1920

MICHAEL R. HAINES

In the late eighteenth century, Benjamin Franklin commented on the remarkably high fertility and large family size in what was British North America, which he attributed to the ease of acquiring good farmland. His comments were reiterated by Thomas Robert Malthus in his famous *Essay on the Principle of Population*:

> But the English North American colonies, now the powerful people of the United States of America, made by far the most rapid progress. To the plenty of good land which they possessed in common with the Spanish and Portuguese settlements, they added a greater degree of liberty and equality. . . . The political institutions that prevailed were favorable to the alienation and division of property. . . . There were no tithes in any of the States and scarcely any taxes. And on account of the extreme cheapness of good land a capital could not be more advantageously employed than in agriculture, which at the same time that it supplies the greatest quantity of healthy work affords the most valuable produce of society.
>
> The consequence of these favorable circumstances united was a rapidity of increase probably without parallel in history. Throughout all of the northern colonies, the population was found to double in twenty-five years.[1]

Although Malthus guessed at the rate of natural increase (implying a 2.8% per year rate of growth), he was not far off. During the period 1790 to 1810, population growth in the new nation (including migration) exceeded 3% per annum (see Table 8.1). In addition to notably high fertility, areas of North America, especially the New England and northern Middle Atlantic regions, also had a reputation as having more benign mortality conditions than those prevailing in much of Europe. These factors, combined with significant net in-migration in the early

---

[1] Malthus, *An Essay*, p. 105.

Table 8.1. Population by race, residence, nativity, age, and sex, United States, 1800–1990 (population in thousands)

Census date	Total	Growth (% p.a.)	White	Percentage White	Black	Other	Urban white[a]	%	Foreign-born white	%	Median age white	Sex ratio[b]
1790	3,929	—	3,172	80.7	757	n.a.	202	5.1	n.a.	—	n.a.	103.8
1800	5,308	3.01	4,306	81.1	1,002	n.a.	322	6.1	n.a.	—	16.0	104.0
1810	7,240	3.10	5,862	81.0	1,378	n.a.	525	7.3	n.a.	—	16.0	104.0
1820	9,639	2.86	7,867	81.6	1,772	n.a.	693	7.2	n.a.	—	16.6	103.2
1830	12,866	2.89	10,537	81.9	2,329	n.a.	1,127	8.8	n.a.	—	17.3	103.8
1840	17,070	2.83	14,196	83.2	2,874	n.a.	1,845	10.8	n.a.	—	17.9	104.5
1850	23,192	3.06	19,553	84.3	3,639	n.a.	3,544	15.3	2,241	11.5	19.2	105.2
1860	31,443	3.04	26,923	85.6	4,442	79	6,217	19.8	4,096	15.2	19.7	105.3
1870	39,819	2.36	33,589	84.4	4,880	89	9,902	24.9	5,494	16.4	20.4	102.8
1880	50,156	2.31	43,403	86.5	6,581	172	12,298	28.3	6,560	15.1	21.4	104.0
1890	62,948	2.27	55,101	87.5	7,489	358	19,318	35.1	9,122	16.6	22.5	105.4
1900	75,994	1.88	66,809	87.9	8,834	351	26,494	39.7	10,214	15.3	23.4	104.9
1910	91,972	1.91	81,732	88.9	9,828	413	39,832	48.7	13,346	16.3	24.5	106.6
1920	106,711	1.49	94,821	88.9	10,463	427	50,620	53.4	13,713	14.5	25.6	104.4
1930	122,755	1.40	110,287	89.8	11,891	597	63,560	57.6	13,983	12.7	26.9	102.9
1940	131,669	0.70	118,215	89.8	12,866	589	67,973	57.5	11,419	9.7	29.5	101.2
1950	150,697	1.35	134,942	89.5	15,042	713	86,756	64.3	10,095	7.5	30.8	99.0
1960	179,823	1.77	158,832	88.3	18,872	1,620	110,428	69.5	9,294	5.9	30.3	97.4
1970	203,302	1.23	178,098	87.6	22,580	2,883	128,773	72.3	8,734	4.9	28.9	95.3
1980	226,546	1.08	188,372	83.1	26,683	5,150	134,322	71.3	9,324	4.9	30.9	94.8
1990	248,710	0.93	208,704	83.9	30,483	9,523	187,053	75.2	10,023	4.8	36.9	95.4

n.a. Not available.

[a] Overall population 1790–1870. Current urban definition 1880–1990.

[b] Males per hundred females.

Sources: U.S. Bureau of the Census, Historical Statistics of the United States, and Statistical Abstract of the United States, 1992.

seventeenth century and after about 1720, led to the relatively high rates of population increase.[2]

Every modern, economically developed nation has undergone a demographic transition from high to low levels of fertility and mortality.[3] This was certainly true for the United States, which experienced a sustained fertility decline from at least about 1800. Around that time, the typical white American woman had about seven or eight live births during her reproductive years, and the average person probably lived about 35–40 years. But the American pattern was distinctive. First, the American fertility transition was under way from at least the beginning of the nineteenth century, and some evidence indicates that family size was declining in older settled areas from the late eighteenth century (see Table 8.2). All other Western developed nations, with the exception of France, began their sustained, irreversible decline in birth rates only in the late nineteenth or early twentieth centuries.[4] It is perhaps not coincidental that both France and the United States experienced important political revolutions in the late eighteenth century and were then characterized by small-scale, owner-occupier agriculture. Second, it appears that fertility in the white population in America was in sustained decline long before mortality. This is in contrast to the stylized view of the demographic transition, in which the mortality decline precedes or occurs simultaneously with the fertility decline. Mortality in the United States did not stabilize and begin a consistent decline until about the 1870s. Third, these demographic processes were influenced both by the large volume of international net in-migration and by the significant internal population redistribution to frontier areas and to cities, towns, and (later) suburbs.

Although the American case may be, in many respects, sui generis, it furnishes a long-term view of a completed demographic transition with accompanying urbanization. The new United States was a demographic laboratory in which natives and migrants, different racial and ethnic groups, and varying occupational and socioeconomic strata experienced these significant behavioral changes in a fertile, land-abundant, resource-rich land. This chapter deals with the white population over the "long"

---

[2] See Chapters 5 and 6 in this volume for a treatment of the demography of colonial British North America in the seventeenth and eighteenth centuries.

[3] The demographic transition is discussed in the introduction. For a survey of various theories of the fertility transition, see Alter, "Theories of Fertility Decline." For the mortality transition, see Easterlin, "The Nature and Causes of the Mortality Revolution," pp. 69–82.

[4] See Coale and Watkins, *The Decline of Fertility in Europe.*

Table 8.2. *Fertility and mortality, white population,*
United States, 1800–1990

Date	Birth-rate[a]	Child/woman ratio[b]	Total fertility Rate[c]	Expectation of life[d]	Infantiy mortal rate[e]
1800	55.0	1,342	7.04		
1810	54.3	1,358	6.92		
1820	52.8	1,295	6.73		
1830	51.4	1,145	6.55		
1840	48.3	1,085	6.14		
1850	43.3	892	5.42	39.5	216.8
1860	41.4	905	5.21	43.6	181.3
1870	38.3	814	4.55	45.2	175.5
1880	35.2	780	4.24	40.5	214.8
1890	31.5	685	3.87	46.8	150.7
1900	30.1	666	3.56	51.8[f]	110.8[f]
1910	29.2	631	3.42	54.6[g]	96.5[g]
1920	26.9	604	3.17	57.4	82.1
1930	20.6	506	2.45	60.9	60.1
1940	18.6	419	2.22	64.9	43.2
1950	23.0	580	2.98	69.0	26.8
1960	22.7	717	3.53	70.7	22.9
1970	17.4	507	2.39	71.6	17.8
1980	14.9	300	1.75	74.5	10.9
1990	15.5	298	1.89	76.1	7.6

[a] Births per thousand population per annum.

[b] Children aged 0–4 per thousand women aged 15–44. Taken from U.S. Bureau of the Census, *Historical Statistics of the United States,* Series 67–68 for 1800–1970.

[c] Total number of births per woman if she experienced the current period age-specific fertility rates throughout her life.

[d] Expectation of life at birth.

[e] Infant deaths per thousand live births per annum.

[f] Approximately 1895.

[g] Approximately 1903.

Sources: U.S. Bureau of the Census, *Historical Statistics of the United States*; U.S. Bureau of the Census, *Statistical Abstract of the United States, 1986*; *Statistical Abstract of the United States, 1993*; Coale and Zelnik, *New Estimates of Fertility and Population in the United States*; Preston and Haines, *Fatal Years*; Haines, "Estimated Life Tables for the United States. 1850–1910."

nineteenth century (i.e., 1790–1920). The black population for this period is described in Chapter 10 in this volume.

BACKGROUND AND SOURCES

A difficulty for the study of the historical demography of the United States is the lack of some types of data for the calculation of standard demographic measures. For the colonial period, regular census enumerations or vital registration were not in effect. A number of scholars have, nonetheless, conducted family reconstitutions and other demographic reconstructions using a variety of sources, including parish registers, genealogies, biographical data, wills and probates, and other local records.[5]

For the period prior to the first federal census in 1790, we have some ideas about vital rates and population characteristics. We know more about population size than other matters, especially because British colonial authorities carried out some enumerations.[6] By 1780 the non-Amerindian population of British North America had increased to about 2.5 million (with about 2 million whites and about half a million blacks). As just mentioned, white birth rates were high, with crude rates ranging from over 40 live births per thousand population per annum to well over 50.[7] The crude birth rate for the United States as a whole has been estimated at over 50 per thousand around 1800 (see Table 8.2). It is unlikely that there had been a substantial rise in fertility in the late eighteenth century. In general, data by age and sex in censuses in the eighteenth century imply crude birth rates in the range of 45 to 60 per thousand and total fertility rates between 6 and 7 per woman.[8]

---

[5] See examples in Vinovskis, *Studies in American Historical Demography*. See also Wells, *Uncle Sam's Family*.

[6] Wells, *Population of the British Colonies*. For the colonial period in British North America, see chapters 5 and 6 in this volume.

[7] An explanation of demographic terminology, basic demographic data, and technical demographic measurement may be found in the appendix to this volume.

[8] For the early nineteenth century, the relationship between the proportion of children aged 0–15 in the total population and a crude child/woman ratio (children aged 0–15 per thousand women aged 16 and older) was calculated for the white population of the United States for 1800, 1810, and 1820. The average relationship to crude birth rates and total fertility rates in Table 8.2 was calculated and applied to proportions of children and the child/woman ratios in the available colonial censuses from the U.S. Bureau of the Census, *Historical Statistics of the United States from Colonial Times to 1970*, pp. 1169–71. The resulting crude birth rates were in the range of 45–60 and the total fertility rates in the range of 6–7.

Mortality had been moderate prior to the nineteenth century. White crude death rates varied from about 20 per thousand population per year to over 40 (and even higher in crisis periods). Lower mortality was found, as a rule, in the colonies and states from Pennsylvania and New Jersey northward, and high mortality characterized the South. In the North, expectations of life at birth ranged all the way from the mid to early 20s to about 40 years. For the early nineteenth century, for example, the expectation of life at age 20 for males in Salem, Massachusetts, was reported as about 33 years in 1818–22 (as calculated from registered deaths), indicating a moderate worsening of mortality since the eighteenth century. Overall, both infant and adult mortality was equal to or better than that for Europe in the same era. Further south, New Jersey is believed to have had a crude death rate of at least 15–20 per thousand and likely higher in the early 1770s. The colonies still further south, in the Chesapeake region, had considerably higher mortality. Expectation of life at birth in Maryland and Virginia covered the range from about 20 to about 31 years, implying probable crude death rates above 30 and possibly as high as 40.[9] Available records and analysis done to date provide a good deal of information about New England, somewhat less about the middle colonies and states, and least about the South (with the notable exception of the Chesapeake area).

A milestone in American demographic history was the institution of the federal decennial census in 1790.[10] Originally intended to provide the basis for allocating seats in the U.S. House of Representatives, the published census grew from a modest one-volume compilation of spare aggregated statistics in 1790 to multiple-volume descriptions of the population, economy, and society by the late nineteenth and early twentieth centuries. Original manuscript returns exist for all dates except 1890, opening great analytical opportunities.[11] The census has been *the* major source for the

---

[9] See Vinovskis, *Studies in American Historical Demography*, pp. 185–202; Wells, *Population of the British Colonies*, pp. 141–2; Carr, "Emigration and the Standard of Living," Table 1.

[10] For a recent history of the American census, see Anderson, *The American Census*.

[11] The original enumerators' manuscripts exist for all the population censuses except 1890 and for many of the states for the censuses of manufacturing and agriculture for 1850–80. The 1890 census returns were destroyed in a fire in 1921. The population schedules are available on microfilm from the National Archives now up through 1920. Some of the manufacturing and agriculture schedules have been microfilmed for the 1850–80 period, but only a few escaped destruction for the period 1900–50. This has made it possible to construct machine-readable public use micro-data samples for 1850–60, 1900, 1910, 1920, and 1940–80. Integrated national public use microsamples have been (or are in process of being) constructed for 1850–80, 1900–20, and 1940–90 by Steven Ruggles and his colleagues involved in the IPUMS Project at the University of Minnesota. National samples of the agriculture schedules matched to population schedules have been done for

study of population growth, structure, and redistribution, as well as fertility prior to the twentieth century. Some states also took censuses, usually in years between the federal censuses. A number have been published and some also exist in manuscript form.[12]

Vital registration was left, however, to state and local governments and, in consequence, it was instituted unevenly. A variety of churches kept parish records of baptisms, burials, and marriages, and these have been used to construct demographic estimates for the colonial period, especially for New England and the Middle Atlantic regions.[13] Although some cities (e.g., New York, New Orleans, Baltimore, Philadelphia) began vital registration earlier in the nineteenth century, the first state to do so was Massachusetts in 1842. An official Death Registration Area consisting of 10 states and the District of Columbia was only successfully established in 1900, and data collection from all states was not completed until 1933. A parallel Birth Registration Area was instituted in 1915, and all-state collection was also achieved in 1933.[14] The federal census did collect mortality information with the censuses of 1850 to 1900, but there were significant problems with completeness. The data do improve over time, and, after 1880, census information was merged with state registration data.[15] Unfortunately nothing similar, was undertaken for birth data. As a consequence of the lack of vital registration data before the early twentieth century, scholars have resorted to special estimation techniques and indirect measures of fertility and mortality to gain insight into the demographic transition of the nineteenth century.

International migration statistics are better than the vital data, although they, too, have serious shortcomings. No official statistics exist prior to 1819, return migration was not counted until 1908, only immigrants through major ports were enumerated, and those crossing land borders were counted only for the period 1855–85 and again after 1904. Some of

---

1860. See Atack and Bateman, *To Their Own Soil;* Parker and Gallman, "Southern Farms Study, 1860," p. 116. National samples of the manufacturing schedules have been made for 1850–80. See Bateman and Weiss, *A Deplorable Scarcity,* Atack, "Returns to Scale" Bateman and Atack, "Did the United States Industrialize Too Slowly?"

[12] Dubester, *State Censuses.*

[13] See Wells, *Uncle Sam's Family;* Vinovskis, *Studies in American Historical Demography,* pp. 2–11.

[14] The 10 states in the Death Registration Area of 1900 were Maine, New Hampshire, Vermont, Massachusetts, Rhode Island, Connecticut, New York, New Jersey, Michigan, and Indiana, as well as the District of Columbia. The original states in the Birth Registration Area of 1915 were Maine, New Hampshire, Vermont, Massachusetts, Rhode Island, Connecticut, New York, Pennsylvania, Michigan, and Minnesota, and also the District of Columbia.

[15] Condran and Crimmins, "A Description and Evaluation of Mortality Data."

these deficiencies have been remedied by new estimates.[16] Despite their deficiencies, these enumerations provide a reasonable overview of this important source of population growth over the period 1790–1920.

The census also provides, from 1850, information on a person's place of birth and, after 1870, on the nativity of each person's parents. This was either state of birth for the native-born or country of birth for the foreign-born. These data permit one to study international migration (e.g., the geographic distribution of the foreign born) and also to analyze internal migration through cross-classification of the native-born by birth and current residence (from 1850 onward). Internal migration is a rather difficult issue to tackle because of the lack of evidence on date of change of residence between birth and current residence. For the foreign-born, questions on duration of residence in the United States were asked in the censuses of 1890 to 1930, but not all inhabitants were asked about duration of current residence until 1940 (when individuals were specifically asked to identify their place of residence five years prior to the census).

The census cannot be assumed to have been entirely accurate. A number of studies have been done on the federal census and on various systems which collected vital data in the nineteenth and twentieth centuries.[17] Overall, it seems that censuses in the mid–twentieth century missed anywhere from 5% to 25% of the population. A careful analysis of the white population from 1880 to 1960 indicates overall underenumeration of 6.1% in 1880, declining to 5.7% by 1920 and 2.1% by 1960.[18] Results varied by age and sex, with the very young and the elderly being least well enumerated. Blacks were more likely to be missed than whites. A summary of recent work on the mid-nineteenth-century federal census notes that those more likely to be counted were older, native-born, heads of more complex households, with moderate wealth and better-paying occupations, in the political mainstream, and living in smaller communities or rural areas having slow economic and population growth. Those less likely to be enumerated were younger, male, native-born sons or foreign-born boarders, living in smaller households, working in low-wage occupations

---

[16] Gemery, "European Emigration to North America, 1700–1820"; McClelland and Zeckhauser, *Demographic Dimensions of the New Republic;* Kuznets, "Long Swings in the Growth of Population.

[17] Coale and Zelnik, *New Estimates of Fertility and Population;* Condran and Crimmins, "A Description and Evaluation of Mortality"; Parkerson, "Comments on the Underenumeration of the U.S. Census"; Steckel, "The Quality of Census Data."

[18] Shryock, Siegel, and associates, *Methods and Materials of Demography*, based in part on the estimates of Coale and Zelnik, *New Estimates*.

in large, rapidly growing urban areas, and not in the political mainstream.[19]

Similarly, collection of vital data also had deficiencies. A criterion for
admission to the official federal Death Registration Area after 1900 and
the Birth Registration Area after 1915 was only that registration be 90%
complete. As late as 1935, it was estimated that birth registration was about
91% complete and only 80% complete for the non-white population.[20]
No comprehensive study of death registration completeness has been
done, but it appears to have been less than fully complete even in the best
states of the Death Registration Area in 1900.[21]

Nonetheless, many of these deficiencies do not affect overall results too
dramatically. Calculation of rates involves canceling errors. The extent of
the errors usually did not change too much from census to census or year
to year. In addition, demographic estimates often involve some corrections
to the data. Many of the tabular results presented here use uncorrected
data, but some of the estimates do make adjustments.

A number of other sources can be used to provide basic demographic
measures and some sophisticated analyses. Genealogies have been utilized
to provide estimates of fertility, mortality, and migration for particular
populations in the nineteenth century[22] Parish registers, tax rolls, military
muster rolls, pension records, wills, probates, and hospital and other institutional records are examples of other sources employed to reconstruct
American demographic history.[23]

POPULATION GROWTH IN THE
UNITED STATES, 1790–1920

The United States began its demographic transition from high to low
levels of fertility and mortality from at least the beginning of the nine-

[19] Parkerson, "Comments on the Underenumeration of the U.S. Census," p. 514.
[20] Shryock, Siegel, and associates, *Methods and Materials of Demography*, p. 404.
[21] Condran and Crimmins, "A Description and Evaluation of Mortality Data"; Crimmins, "The
Completeness of 1900 Mortality Data"; Shryock, Siegel, and associates, *Methods and Materials of
Demography*, chaps. 14 and 16.
[22] Examples include Bean, Mineau, and Anderton, *Fertility Change on the American Frontier;* Wahl,
"New Results"; Pope, "Adult Mortality in America before 1900"; A Adams and Kasakoff, "Migration and the Family in Colonial New England".
[23] For examples, see Wells, *Uncle Sam's Family*; Willigan and Lynch, *Sources and Methods of Historical Demography*; (Haines, "Economic History and Historical Demography." Hainesand Anderson,
"New Demographic History."

teenth century, if not earlier. Table 8.3 provides summary measures of population growth and its components by decades from 1790 to 1990. These results are for the total population (both black and white), since it is difficult to separate the subpopulations before the twentieth century. The results are dominated by the white population, however. Table 8.3 is organized around the demographic balancing equation, which states that the decade rate of population growth (RTI) equals the birth rate (CBR) minus the death rate (CDR) plus the rate of net migration (RNM). The difference between the birth rate and the death rate is the rate of natural increase (RNI).[24] For the period 1790 to 1870, the crude birth and death rates are not given because independent estimates of the crude death rate are too uncertain (see Table 8.1). For 1790–1870, the rate of natural increase is calculated as the difference between the rate of total increase and the rate of net migration. The rate of net migration is based on new direct calculations of white net migration supplemented by estimates of slave importation (smuggling after 1808, when slave imports were made illegal). For the decade of the 1860s, official estimates of gross in-migration were used. After 1870, estimates of births and deaths are available from the work of Simon Kuznets for the period 1870–1940. Official vital statistics are used thereafter to 1980. In addition, after 1870 the rate of net migration is calculated as the difference between the rates of total increase and natural increase (i.e., a residual).[25]

Several features of the American demographic transition can be discerned from Table 8.3. The United States experienced a truly remarkable population increase during its transition in the "long" nineteenth century (1790–1920). From a modest 4.5 million inhabitants in 1790, the population grew to over 114 million persons in 1920, an average annual growth rate of 2.5% per year. In the early years of the Republic, population growth rates were even higher, in excess of 3% per annum for the period 1790–1810 and again in the 1840s and 1850s. Such rapid growth is historically rather unusual and is comparable to the recent experience of some developing nations. Growth rates of that magnitude would lead to a doubling of the population in slightly more than two decades (approximately 23 years). The surge of growth in the 1840s and 1850s was particularly large owing to a significant increase in migration from abroad – the now familiar story of Irish, Germans, and others from Western and Northern Europe fleeing the great potato famine, the "Hungry Forties," and political

---

[24] That is, RTI = CBR − CDR + RNM, and CBR − CDR = RNI.   [25] See sources to Table 8.3.

Table 8.3. *Components of population growth, United States, 1790–1990*
(rates per thousand midperiod population per year

Period	Average population (thousands)	RTI	CBR	CDR	RNI[a]	RNM[a]	RNM as % of RTI
1790–1800	4,520	30.08			26.49	3.59	11.9
1800–10	6,132	31.04			26.85	4.19	13.5
1810–20	8,276	28.62			24.70	3.92	13.7
1820–30	11,031	28.88			26.93	1.95	6.8
1830–40	14,685	28.27			23.67	4.60	16.3
1840–50	19,686	30.65			22.88	7.77	25.3
1850–60	26,721	30.44			20.35	10.09	33.2
1860–70	35,156	23.62			17.64	5.98	25.3
1870–80	44,414	23.08	41.16	23.66	17.50	5.58	24.2
1880–90	55,853	22.72	37.03	21.34	15.69	7.03	30.9
1890–1900	68,876	18.83	32.22	19.44	12.78	6.06	32.2
1900–10	83,245	19.08	30.10	17.27	12.83	6.25	32.8
1910–20	98,807	14.86	27.15	15.70	11.45	3.41	23.0
1920–30	114,184	14.01	23.40	11.08	12.32	1.68	12.0
1930–40	127,058	7.01	18.39	11.18	7.21	−0.20	−2.9
1940–50	140,555	13.50	22.48	10.39	12.09	1.41	10.4
1950–60	164,011	17.67	24.81	9.47	15.34	2.33	13.2
1960–70	190,857	12.27	20.26	9.55	10.71	1.56	12.7
1970–80	214,306	10.83	15.49	9.00	6.49	4.34	40.1
1980–90	238,466	9.34	15.91	8.70	7.21	2.13	22.8

Note: RTI = rate of total increase; CBR = crude birth rate (live births per thousand population per year); CDR = crude death rate (deaths per thousand population per year); RNI = rate of natural increase (= CBR − CDR); RNM = rate of net international migration.

[a]Rate of net migration calculated directly from net migrants 1790–1860. Gross migrants used for 1860–70. For 1870–1980, RNM = RTI − RNI and thus is a residual. Prior to 1870, RNI is calculated as a residual (= RTI − RNM).

Sources: Unadjusted populations, and births and deaths, 1870–1980: U.S. Bureau of the Census, *Historical Statistics of the United States*; *Statistical Abstract of the United States, 1993*; Kuznets, "Long Swings in the Growth of Population and Related Economic Variables." Net migrants, 1790–1820: Gemery, "European Emigration to North America," Supplemented by estimates of slave imports from Curtin, *The Atlantic Slave Trade*. Net migrants, 1820–1860: McClelland and Zeckhauser, *Demographic Dimensions of the New Republic*, supplemented by estimates of slave imports from Curtin, *The Atlantic Slave Trade*.

upheaval and seeking better farming, business, and employment opportunities in the New World. Natural increase had been declining from the early 1800s, largely because of a decline in birth rates, especially for the white population. Some of the decline in natural increase in the 1840s and 1850s was also likely due to *rising* mortality in those decades. Table 8.3 indicates, however, that mortality did decline steadily from the 1870s onward.

Another feature notable in Table 8.3 is the dominant role played by natural increase in overall population growth. In the decades before 1840, less than a sixth or a seventh of total growth originated in net migration. With the surge in overseas migration after 1840, however, the share of net migration in total increase rose to a quarter or a third. (This would have been larger for the white population alone, since in-migration of blacks was very limited.) Notably, the share of *labor force* growth accounted for by migration was higher, since migration was selective of persons in the labor force ages. Despite declining birth rates, the American population grew rapidly in the nineteenth century, principally from an excess of births over deaths, although it must be recognized that the births to the foreign-born and their descendants contributed importantly. If it could be assumed that no immigration occurred after 1790 and that the natural increase of the colonial stock population had been what it actually was (with no effect of immigration on the natural increase of the native-born), then the white population would have been about 52 million in 1920, or about 55% of what it actually was.[26] The surge in migration after 1840 can also be recognized in Table 8.1 in the rise in the proportion of the white foreign-born population, from 11.5% in 1850 (as indicated by the first census for which such data were available) to over 16% in 1890 and 1910.

Although beyond the temporal scope of the present essay, a few comments on the post-1920 demographic evolution are in order. The effects of immigration restriction after World War I may be seen in the reduced rate of net migration after 1920. The Great Depression had a dramatic dampening effect on both fertility and migration from abroad. The post–World War II "baby boom" is apparent in the higher crude birth rates in the 1940s and 1950s. More recent changes in immigration regulations clearly affected the surge in net in-migrants in the 1970s, when over 40% of population growth was due to this source. This was unprecedented

---

[26] Easterlin, "Population Issues in American Economic History," p. 149.

in our history, even considering the decades preceding both the Civil War and World War I.

The effects of regional differences in population growth are apparent in the population distribution figures in Table 8.4. The 3.2 million white inhabitants in 1790 were clustered along the Atlantic coast, with slightly more in the New England and Middle Atlantic regions than in the original South (the South Atlantic region). By 1860 only 51% of the 27 million white Americans were still in these regions, and this fell to 41% in 1920. Regions of early settlement grew at an average rate of 1.9% per annum over the whole period, while the white population overall was growing at 2.6%. This regional disparity was driven, of course, by the relentless westward movement of population, agriculture, and industry. Much of the growth that did occur on the Atlantic coast was in yet another "frontier" – urban areas. In the regions of original European settlement, cities and towns grew from just 5% of the population in 1790 to 28% in 1860 to 61% in 1920, an annual growth rate of 3.8% per annum, whereas that of the rural population was merely 1.2% per annum. This led to an increase in the share of national urban population over the century from 5% in 1790 to over half of the population in 1920.[27]

FERTILITY AND NUPTIALITY

The young republic was notable for its large families and early marriages. The total fertility rate in Table 8.2 indicates an average number of births per white woman of approximately seven in 1800, and the TFR was still over five on the eve of the Civil War. While we know relatively little about marriage in the early nineteenth century, female age at first marriage was probably rather young, perhaps below 20. Males on average married when they were several years older, and all but a relatively small proportion of both sexes eventually married. The federal census did not ask about marital status until 1880 and did not begin reporting results on this until 1890. However, several state censuses did ask these questions earlier. A sample of seven New York state counties from the manuscripts of the census of 1865, for example, reveals an estimated age at first marriage of 23.7 years for females and 26.5 years for males. The levels for those never married by

[27] Urban areas are defined by the U.S. Bureau of the Census as places (incorporated or not) of 2,500 or more inhabitants. See its *Historical Statistics of the United States*, pp. 2–3.

Table 8.4. *White population by region, United States, 1790–1920 (thousands)*

Region	1790	%	1830	%	1860	%	1890	%	1920	%
New England	992	31.3	1,933	18.4	3,110	11.6	4,653	8.5	7,316	7.7
Middle Atlantic	908	28.6	3,478	33.0	7,328	27.2	12,469	22.7	21,642	22.8
East North Central	—	—	1,454	13.8	6,856	25.5	13,253	24.1	20,939	22.1
West North Central	—	—	115	1.1	2,044	7.6	8,659	15.7	12,225	12.9
South Atlantic	1,179	37.2	2,116	20.1	3,305	12.3	5,592	10.2	9,649	10.2
East South Central	93	2.9	1,314	12.5	2,626	9.8	4,306	7.8	6,368	6.7
West South Central	—	—	115	1.1	1,102	4.1	3,182	5.8	8,116	8.6
Mountain	—	—	—	—	164	0.6	1,116	2.0	3,213	3.4
Pacific	—	—	—	—	386	1.4	1,754	3.2	5,354	5.6
Total	3,172	100.0	10,526	100.0	26,923	100.0	54,984	100.0	94,821	100.0

Source: Tabulations from original published census data in ICPSR 0003.

the ages 45–54 were 7.7% for females and 6.3% for males, which were quite low.[28] Although marriage age was probably higher in New York than in the nation as a whole and although marriage age had very likely risen by 1865, nuptiality was still rather extensive by European standards. The average age at first marriage for females was 25.4 years in England and Wales in 1861 and 26.3 years in Germany in 1871 (with German males having had an average age at marriage as late as 28.8 years).[29]

In 1880, when the U.S. census first asked about marital status, the average white female was 23.3 years old at first marriage while males were 27.0 years old. The proportions never marrying by middle age were still relatively low, 8.1% for males and 7.0% for females. Age at marriage rose a bit up until 1890 and 1900 and thereafter began a longer-term decline up to the 1950s. By 1920, age at marriage had fallen to 22.7 years for white women and 26.1 years for white men, although this was now accompanied by a gradual increase in the proportion of those never marrying.[30]

Overall, marriage in the United States was pervasive and early compared with that in the western and northern European countries in which many of the migrants to North America originated. This was more so early in the nineteenth century, as the marriage age rose in the United States until roughly 1900. Americans were also very unlikely *not* to have been married at some time during their adult lives.

Similarly, in 1800 the United States was a nation of high fertility, but it then experienced a sustained decline in birth rates up until the 1940s when the Baby Boom interrupted this pattern. The unusual aspect of

[28] The counties are Allegany, Dutchess, Montgomery, Rensselaer, Steuben, Tompkins, and Warren. See Haines, "Long Term Marriage Patterns."

[29] Data for England and Wales are from Teitelbaum, *The British Fertility Decline*, p. 100. For Germany, see Knodel, *The Decline of Fertility in Germany*, p. 70.

[30] Calculations of the singulate mean age at marriage (SMAM) and of the proportion never marrying for the period 1890 to 1910 are based on published federal census data. SMAM is calculated by Hajnal's method (see Shryock, Siegel, and associates, *Methods and Materials*, pp. 294–95). The results for 1880 are based on a preliminary sample of the 1880 census made available by Steven Ruggles of the University of Minnesota. See Haines, "Long-Term Marriage Patterns in the United States." Table 2. Overall results for this period are as follows:

	SMAM		% Single at 45–54	
	Male	Female	Male	Female
1880	27.0	23.3	8.1	7.0
1890	27.7	23.8	9.2	7.3
1900	27.6	23.8	10.4	8.1
1910	26.9	23.4	11.4	8.9
1920	26.1	22.7	12.4	10.0

the American experience is that the reduction (at least for the white population) began before the nation was substantially urban or industrial.
Both rural *and* urban birth rates declined in parallel, although rural fertility remained higher throughout the period considered here. Fertility
decreased across regions, but the South lagged behind the Northeast and
Midwest in the timing and speed of the reduction. A decomposition of
the fertility transition into the contributions of nuptiality and marital fertility found that, up to approximately 1850, half of the decline could be
attributed to adjustments in marriage age and marriage incidence. Thereafter most of the decline originated in reductions of fertility within marriage.[31] Even the fertility of the antebellum slave population showed signs
of decline just prior to 1860, though family sizes for blacks were, on
average, significantly larger than those for whites.[32]

Such evidence as we have concerning fertility differentials by nativity
(native-versus foreign-born) points to relatively small differences at midcentury but generally higher fertility for the foreign-born thereafter. The
fertility of native white women continued to decline, while large families
continued among the successive cohorts of incoming migrants. Birth rates
of native-born women of foreign-born parentage were intermediate
between those of native white women of native parentage and foreign-
born white women, suggesting a form of assimilation to native white
demographic patterns. Data on children ever born (parity) from a sample
of seven New York counties in 1865 revealed few differences between
native- and foreign-born women born near the beginning of the nineteenth century. But published data from the Massachusetts census of 1885
showed substantially more births per ever-married foreign-born woman
in comparism with the native-born for those born between 1826 and 1855.
Such differentials also appeared in the parity data from the federal censuses of 1900 and 1910. Much of the difference was due to the lower age
at marriage and smaller percentages remaining single among the foreign-
born. But fertility within marriage was also greater for foreign-born
women in the late nineteenth and early twentieth centuries. Relatively few
of them, for instance, remained permanently childless. Published results
from the federal census of 1910 reported that native white women aged
55–64 (i.e., born in the years 1846–55) had an average number of children

---

[31] Sanderson, "Quantitative Aspects of Marriage, Fertility and Family Limitation." Sanderson treats
all fertility as marital fertility. Illegitimate fertility was not too important in nineteenth-century
America, and it was, in any event, difficult to measure. Sanderson uses an application of both the
Coale–McNeil marriage models and the Coale–Trussell model fertility schedules to estimate the
extent of fertility control within marriage.
[32] See Steckel, "The Fertility of American Slaves"; and Chapter 10 in this volume.

ever born of 4.4 (4.8 for ever-married women). Over 17% of all native white women (and 9% of those who married) remained childless. Among the foreign-born enumerated during the same census, the average number of children was 5.5 for all women and 5.8 for ever-married women, with only 12% of all women and 7% of ever-married women remaining childless. Such differentials between native- and foreign-born women had largely disappeared for those born at the end of the nineteenth century and enumerated in 1940.[33]

The inexorable decline in white American birth rates continued apace after the Civil War. By then most of the decline originated in adjustments in fertility within marriage. Recent work with parity data from the 1900, 1910, and 1940 federal censuses shows rapid reductions in marital fertility, especially among white urban women. In 1910, for example, over half of native white urban women aged 45–49 were estimated to have been effectively controlling fertility within marriage, and about a quarter of the rural farm and nonfarm women were doing the same. Among younger women (aged 15–34), the proportions were much higher, rising to over 70% for native white urban women and over half for native white farm women. It could certainly be said that the "two-child norm" was being established in the United States in this era. Some fascinating supporting evidence is furnished by the Mosher survey of several dozen wives of professional and white-collar men over the period 1892 to 1920. Mosher found extensive use of a wide variety of contraceptives and contraceptive practices and very active strategies of family limitation. This was a preview of the rapid adoption of such behaviors in the twentieth century.[34]

One of the conclusions from this detailed study of fertility has been

---

[33] A problem for the analysis of the fertility of the native-born versus the foreign-born is that most of the children of the foreign-born were native-born. Hence census tabulations by age, sex, race, and nativity cannot provide the appropriate child/woman ratios. One solution is reported in the text, namely that censuses could ask women to summarize their fertility history. This was first done in New York in 1865, in Massachusetts in 1885, and in the federal censuses of 1890–1910 and again from 1940 onward. No results were published for the federal censuses of 1890 and 1900, although the public use sample of the 1,900 manuscripts (as well as those of 1910) permits analysis. Another solution is to use the micro-data from the census manuscripts to estimate own-children birth rates by nativity of mother. For examples, see Hareven and Vinovskis, "Marital Fertility, Ethnicity, and Occupation in Urban Families"; Haines, *Fertility and Occupation,* chap. 4, and "American Fertility in Transition." Finally, there are some nineteenth- and early-twentieth-century birth registration data reported by mother's nativity. These reveal substantially higher birth rates for the foreign-born for Massachusetts and other states from the late nineteenth century. Much was due to higher marriage incidence for foreign women. See J.J. Spengler, "The Fecundity."

[34] See David and Sanderson, "Rudimentary Contraceptive Methods," and "The Emergence of a Two-Child Norm." Their results derive from a new technique known as cohort-parity analysis, which compares actual parity distributions for age or marriage-duration cohorts of women to a known "natural fertility" distribution. The survey referred to was conducted by Clelia Mosher.

that the spacing of births from early in childbearing was, by the late nineteenth century, as important as the more conventional behavior of stopping before the biological end of the female reproductive span. Results from a different source, the genealogical data base of the Mormon Historical Demography Project, have shown the importance of spacing behavior, which had formerly been considered a relatively modern development, prevalent only in populations with very low fertility. New estimates of age-specific fertility rates for the United States around the turn of the century point to low marital fertility at young ages, quite unlike the rates in Europe at the time and further suggesting spacing early in childbearing in American families. The one exception was France, which shared with the United States an early fertility decline preceding significant urbanization and industrialization.[35]

The period after 1865 was further marked by reductions in fertility by residence and by race. For the rural and urban populations, relative differences in child/woman ratios did not disappear. Rural fertility remained above urban fertility, but absolute differences diminished as both types of residents progressively limited family size. The rural child/woman ratio was 56% higher than the urban ratio in 1800, 62% higher in 1840, and 58% greater in 1920. But the absolute gap had dropped from 474 more children aged 0–4 per thousand women of childbearing age in rural areas in 1800 to 273 in 1920. A standardization and decomposition of the rural–urban differential and its connection to the fertility transition found that over 50% of the overall decline in child/woman ratios from 1800 to 1940 originated in the decline in rural birth rates, with over one quarter due to urban fertility decline, and only about 20% stemming from the shift from higher fertility in rural areas to lower fertility in urban areas.[36]

Birth rates also varied across regions after the Civil War, with the South and West experiencing higher fertility than the Northeast and Midwest. Variation across space narrowed from 1800 onward, but the convergence was not smooth. The coefficient of variation (the standard deviation divided by the mean) of child/woman ratios across the nine census regions was .57 in 1810 but declined to .16 in 1860.[37] It rose thereafter to .22, before

---

[35] See Bean, Mineau, and Anderton, *Fertility Change on the American Frontier*, chap. 7; Haines, "Western Fertility in Mid-Transition."

[36] Grabill, Kiser, and Whelpton, *The Fertility of American Women*, pp. 16–19.

[37] The nine census regions are New England, Middle Atlantic, East North Central, West North Central, South Atlantic, East South Central, West South Central, Mountain, and Pacific.

falling again to .15 in 1920. In 1810 the South had fertility ratios over 30% higher than in New England (the lowest fertility region). This differential increased to about 60% in 1860, and the relative difference was nearly the same in 1910, before modern convergence began. The Midwest moved from being a region of quite large families to, by 1920, one with fertility close to the "leaders" in the transition, New England and the Middle Atlantic states.

Finally, although we know rather less about the fertility of different socioeconomic status groups, the evidence points to smaller families among higher socioeconomic status groups, such as professionals, proprietors, clerks, and other white-collar workers. This was true, at least, from the middle of the nineteenth century onward. Among proprietors, however, an exception was owner-occupier farmers, who, throughout the century, typically had larger families than other groups. Unskilled workers (often characterized simply as laborers or farm laborers) tended to have fertility closer to that of farmers, while skilled and semiskilled manual workers and craftsmen occupied an intermediate position. These socioeconomic fertility differences may have widened over the course of the nineteenth century before they eventually narrowed.[38]

One consequence of declining fertility has been an aging of the population. As Table 8.1 shows, the median age of the American people rose from 16 years in 1800 to over 20 in 1870 and over 25 in 1920. Today it stands at 37. The reason is that the age structure of the population, particularly the proportion of children, is most affected by fertility, which adds only to the base of the age pyramid. Mortality, in contrast, affects all ages. As fertility declines, so does the proportion of children and teenagers. The population ages. The implications of this are great, changing the society from one oriented toward children to one centered on adults and eventually the elderly. This process was under way at the end of our period (1920), but its effects are more dramatic today.

THEORIES OF FERTILITY DECLINE

The American demographic transition raises a number of difficult issues. Conventional demographic transition theory has placed great reliance on

---

[38] For a summary of evidence on this, see Haines, "Occupation and Social Class during Fertility Decline."

the changes in child costs and benefits associated with structural changes accompanying modern economic growth, such as urbanization, industrialization, the rise in literacy and education, and increased employment of women outside the home. A classic statement of the theory was made by Frank Notestein in 1953:

The new ideal of the small family arose typically in the urban industrial society. It is impossible to be precise about the various causal factors, but apparently many were important. Urban life stripped the family of many functions in production, consumption, recreation, and education. In factory employment the individual stood on his own accomplishments. The new mobility of young people and the anonymity of city life reduced the pressure toward traditional behavior exerted by the family and community. In a period of rapidly developing technology, new skills were needed, and new opportunities for individual advancement arose. Education and a rational point of view became increasingly important. As a consequence the cost of child-rearing grew and the possibilities for economic contributions by children declined. Falling death-rates at once increased the size of the family to be supported and lowered the inducements to have many births. Women, moreover, found new independence from household obligations and new economic roles less compatible with childbearing.[39]

But, of course, the fertility transition began in the United States well before many of these structural changes became important.

The leading theory of the American fertility decline for the antebellum period has been the land availability hypothesis. It is a special case of a child cost theory and was first proposed by Yasuba in 1962, when he discovered, for the period 1800–60, a strong inverse relationship between population density and child/woman ratios. He interpreted density as measuring the availability of cheap potential agricultural land. High population density would raise the price of land and increase the cost to farm families of endowing their children with adequate farmsteads, that is, with a suitable means of earning a living. This is, in reality, a rather sophisticated concept involving bequest motives and intergenerational transfers. More refined fertility and land availability measures and statistical analysis were subsequently employed by Forster and Tucker, but, if anything, the results were strengthened. Research on colonial New England suggests that this kind of transfer was taking place there prior to 1800. Further tests using county-level data within states, micro-data from the 1860 census, and data for the analogous case of Canada have provided support.[40]

---

[39] Notestein, "The Economics of Population and Food Supplies."
[40] Yasuba, *Birth Rates of the White Population of the United States*, 1962; Forster and Tucker, *Economic Opportunity and Whiter American Fertility Ratios*. A county-level analysis of Ohio has been provided by Leet, "The Determinants of Fertility Transition in Antebellum Ohio," pp. 359–78; and

The decline in American fertility did not take place evenly across regions. Much of the interest in the historical fertility patterns arose because of spatial differences in the timing and pace of the fertility transition. A prominent feature of regional fertility differentials of whites in the nineteenth century has been a consistent east-west gradient, with higher fertility in the Midwest and the South Central regions than in the Northeast and South Atlantic areas. The gradient was prominent up to about 1900 but had largely disappeared by 1920. To a lesser extent there was a north-south gradient, with higher fertility among Southern whites. This became more prominent over the nineteenth century.[41]

Others look to more conventional economic and demographic variables to explain the phenomenon. One possibility is that sex ratios were biased toward males on the frontier because of sex-selective migration. Since the child/woman ratios measure total and not marital fertility, the observed differences might have been largely due to more complete and earlier marriage for the frontier female population. This was true, but data from census micro-samples still reveal strong differences in marital child/woman ratios by density and settlement date. In another study, Vinovskis found much stronger associations of state-level fertility ratios for 1850 and 1860 with the extent of urbanization, industrialization, and literacy. Yasuba had seen the weakening of the density effect on fertility for censuses closer to the Civil War, but Vinovskis also noted that urban child/woman ratios fell in parallel with rural ones. This is unlikely to be explained by land availability. Finally, after 1860 such structural variables as urbanization, industrialization, labor force composition, literacy, and so on dominated the statistical relationship.[42]

An intriguing alternative to the land availability–child bequest hypothesis has been proposed by Sundstrom and David, who suggest a model of life cycle fertility, savings, parental demand for old age support, and bargaining within the family. They argue that the development of nearby nonagricultural labor market opportunities had much more to do with

the 1860 census micro-data for the North have been used by Easterlin, Alter, and Condran, in "Farms and Farm Families in Old and New Areas." Easterlin, "Population Change and Farm Settlement." McInnis, "Childbearing and Land Availability" provides results for Canada. For the colonial period, see McCusker and Menard, *The Economy of British America*, chap. 5.

[41] Taeuber and Taeuber, *Changing Population of the United States* p. 250–253.

[42] Maris A. Vinovskis, "Socioeconomic Determinants of Interstate Fertility Differentials"; "Recent Trends in American Historical Demography." The post-1870 situation was analyzed by Okun, *Trends in Birth Rates*. The urban/industrial explanations were found to dominate in 1900 by Guest, "Social Structure and U.S. Inter-state Fertility Differentials."

smaller families than the march of the frontier and the disappearance of inexpensive bequests. Larger material inducements were then necessary to keep children "down on the farm" once jobs were readily available within easy distance. Urban growth and increased education behind the frontier would have been part of this process. This hypothesis can also explain the decline in rural birth rates after the Civil War and is relevant to the urban fertility transition. A related model, that of Ransom and Sutch, emphasizes the westward migration of children, who then "defaulted" on their implicit contracts to care for their parents in old age. In response, parents began accumulating real and financial assets as a substitute for offspring as retirement insurance, leading to smaller families.[43]

Still other hypotheses, or at least provocative findings, have appeared in the search for explanations for the unusual American fertility transition. Steckel, using micro-data from the 1850 and 1860 federal censuses, ran some tests on competing hypotheses. While finding some modest support for the land availability view, he reports the strongest predictors of marital fertility differentials just prior to the Civil War to be the presence of financial intermediaries (banks) and labor force structure (i.e., the ratio of the nonagricultural to agricultural labor force). This is more supportive of the bargaining and/or old age/savings theories. A more theoretical inquiry by Wahl finds that parents progressively traded off quantity (number of children) for quality (education, health care, etc. per child) as the nineteenth century progressed. As the price (cost) of quality declined (via public education, more effective public health, and medicine), parents opted for greater human capital per child.[44]

Wahl's study draws on the extensive and rich Mormon genealogical database, which was also used by Bean, Mineau, and Anderton to study fertility decline in Utah from the mid–nineteenth century to the early twentieth century. In the latter work, the emphasis is on distinguishing between family limitation as an adaptation to changing environmental, economic, and social circumstances versus a behavioral innovation which simply spread across groups. These distinctions are related to Ansley Coale's statement of the three preconditions for family limitation: (1) fertility control must be within the calculus of conscious choice; (2) an effective means of regulating fertility must be available at a reasonable cost; and (3) it must be economically and socially advantageous to limit family

[43] Sundstrom and David, "Old-Age Security Motives, Labor Markets, and Farm Family Fertility"; Ransom and Sutch, "Two Strategies for a More Secure Old Age."

[44] Steckel, "Fertility Transition in the United States"; Wahl, "Trading Quantity for Quality."

size. These preconditions are more likely true with adaptive behavior, that is, when family limitation is understood and accepted and occurs when socioeconomic conditions favor it. The Utah study of the Mormon Historical Demography Project looks in detail at age-specific cohort and period fertility data and concludes that adaptive behavior is the most consistent explanation. It provides some support for a number of the hypotheses attempting to explain fertility decline, since the changing circumstances to which behavior adapted included not just land costs and availability but also improved socioeconomic opportunities in nonagrarian sectors (e.g., higher urban wages), as well as changes in the institutional and cultural environment. While not entirely satisfactory on grounds of parsimonious explanation, the case is made for a rather more complex explanatory framework.[45]

Most of the hypotheses about the American fertility transition can also be fit into the more general model offered by Caldwell.[46] He proposes that family limitation sets in when the net flow of resources over the life course shifts from children to parents over to parents to children. This signifies a rise in the net cost of children (i.e., benefits minus costs) and is accelerated by such things as the introduction of mass education (implying more years in school and greater enrollment rates), child labor laws, compulsory education laws, and more pervasive views on the positive value of transmitting improved human capital across generations. This intergenerational wealth transfer view is consistent with both the land availability and the socioeconomic and cultural structural adjustment hypotheses. It can also fit the quantity-quality trade-off explanation.

In sum, the fertility transition of the white population of the United States was unusual. It began in a largely rural and agrarian nation long before most of the developed nations of today began their fertility transitions in the late nineteenth century. Prior to 1860 it seems that the disappearance of good, cheap land for bequests to offspring provides a reasonable model for declining family size across states, at least for rural areas. As the nineteenth century progressed, however, the more conventional socioeconomic variables seem have had more explanatory power. These variables would include rising literacy and education, increased urbanization (with more expensive housing and crowding), more work by women and children outside the home, the spread of institutional

[45] Bean, Mineau, and Anderton, *Fertility Change on the American Frontier*; Coale, "The Demographic Transition."
[46] Caldwell, *Theory of Fertility Decline.*

restrictions such as child labor laws and compulsory education statutes, the rising value of time as real wages and incomes increased, less reliance on children for support in old age, and less available familial child care as smaller, urban nuclear families became dominant. There is also likely a role for declining infant and child mortality, at least after about 1880, which reduced the number of births necessary to achieve a desired number of children surviving to adulthood (see Table 8.2 and the next section). The land availability hypothesis contributes little to explaining the nineteenth-century urban fertility decline. Several other models have been discussed, many of which emphasize a rise in net child costs and an increased desire of parents to trade off numbers of children for greater human capital per child. It is not unreasonable to conclude that a range of changing circumstances – including increased scarcity of resources (especially land), the rise of mass education, greater accessibility to urban labor markets, rising real incomes, and value of time – all contributed to the transition. But the fact remains that the United States was unusual, although similar to France. As noted earlier, it is perhaps not coinciden- tal that both nations had democratic political revolutions late in the eigh- teenth century and were characterized, in the nineteenth century, mostly by smallholder agriculture.

MORTALITY

We know less about the American mortality transition of the nineteenth century than we do about the fertility transition. There are no ready census-based mortality measures such as the child/woman ratio, and vital statistics were unavailable or incomplete for most areas up until the early twentieth century. We know the most about Massachusetts, which began statewide civil vital registration in 1842, but Massachusetts was not typical of the nation in the nineteenth century. It was more urban and industrial, had more immigrants, and had lower fertility.[47] The federal census col- lected mortality information from 1850 to 1900, but the data were incom- plete, biased, and uneven in their coverage. In consequence, there has been disagreement about trends, levels, and differentials in American mortality over the nineteenth century.

---

[47] For example, in 1880 Massachusetts was 75% urban, 25% of the population was foreign-born, and the crude birth rate was 24.8. For the United States as a whole, the proportions were 28% urban and 13% foreign-born, with an estimated crude birth rate of 39.8.

As mentioned, the official Death Registration Area was not formed until 1900, although there had been earlier attempts to do so. In 1900, the Death Registration Area comprised 10 states and the District of Columbia, covering 26% of the population. It was significantly more urban (63%) than the nation as a whole (40%) and had a higher fraction of foreign-born (22% versus 14%). Since we know that mortality rates differed according to rural-urban residence and size of place of residence, these are significant considerations. By 1920 the Death Registration Area covered 34 states and the District of Columbia, or 81% of the population. It encompassed the entire United States from 1933 onward.

For years prior to 1900, official mortality data are limited to figures from selected states and cities and from the imperfect census. Massachusetts is a widely cited source for nineteenth-century mortality information. Its data were of reasonable quality by about 1860, but evidence on earlier times must be culled from other sources, such as genealogies, family reconstitutions, and bills of mortality. Some analysts, such as Coale and Zelnik, have assumed that Massachusetts mortality was typical of the nation, but questions have been raised about its representativeness, particularly as depicted in Jacobson's Massachusetts-Maryland life table for 1850. Studies of earlier periods, including the colonial years, also concentrate on local evidence, and find reasonable levels of expectation of life in New England but few signs of improvement in the eighteenth century. Research on the Chesapeake does point to some improvement from very unfavorable mortality levels in the seventeenth century. But we know discouragingly little about mortality in colonial America.[48]

Some previous work has involved strong assumptions and considerable a priori reasoning. Thompson and Whelpton assumed a decline in mortality throughout the nineteenth century with an acceleration after about 1880. Taeuber and Taeuber posited little improvement prior to about 1850, but considerable gains in expectation of life thereafter. Coale and Zelnik assumed a linear trend in improvement from 1850 to 1900 and used the Jacobson Massachusetts-Maryland life table of 1850 to anchor their estimates, as well as a model life table system based on the experience of six European nations. Easterlin, assuming an inverse association between

---

[48] Coale and Zelnik, *New Estimates of Fertility and Population*. The representativeness of the Massachusetts data, especially the 1850 Massachusetts-Maryland life table, has been questioned by Vinovskis, "The Jacobson Life Table of 1850." On the colonial period, see Wells, *Uncle Sam's Family*, chap. 3; McCusker and Menard, *The Economy of British America*, sec. 2; Vinovskis, *Studies in American Historical Demography*, pp. 1–46, 181–254.

mortality and income per capita and between mortality and public health and a positive association between mortality and urbanization, suggested that rising income per capita after about 1840 dominated these effects and outweighed the negative effect of urban growth, with public health playing only a small role in the nineteenth century. This led him to believe that expectation of life was rising from about 1840. Vinovskis, on the other hand, believes that little change in Massachusetts mortality levels took place between the 1790s and 1860.

More recent work based on the Mormon genealogical data by Fogel and Pope suggests that adult mortality (on a period basis) was relatively stable after about 1800, rose in the 1840s and 1850s, and then improved after the Civil War. This finding is unusual, since we have evidence of rising real income per capita and of significant economic growth during the 1840–60 period. But income distribution may have worsened and urbanization and immigration may have had more deleterious effects than hitherto believed. Further, the disease environment is likely to have shifted in an unfavorable direction.[49]

Urbanization, too, may have played an important role. The share of population living in areas of 2,500 persons and more grew from 11% in 1840 to 20% in 1860 (see Table 8.1). There was reasonably accurate registration of deaths in several large American cities (New York City, Boston, Philadelphia, Baltimore, New Orleans) from the early nineteenth century. Time series of crude death rates for these cities indicate either deteriorating mortality (as in New York, Philadelphia, New Orleans) or no improvement in the antebellum period. The period from 1800 to 1860 has been characterized as the time of the "transportation revolution" in the United States. Increased internal movement of people and goods, accompanied by growth in migration from abroad, greater commercialization, and urbanization, all served to break down barriers to disease transmission. The disease environment was becoming national and international in scope. Local rural isolation offered less protection than before. As an example, the cholera epidemics of 1832/33 and 1849/50 spread rapidly

---

[49] Thompson and Whelpton, *Population Trends in the United States*, p. 230; Taeuber and Taeuber, *Changing Population of the United States*, p. 269; Coale and Zelnik, *New Estimates of Fertility and Population*; Jacobson, "An Estimate of the Expectation of Life in the United States in 1850"; Easterlin, "Population Issues in American Economic History"; Vinovskis, "Mortality Rates and Trends in Massachusetts before 1860"; Fogel, "Nutrition and the Decline in Mortality since 1700: Some Preliminary Findings," pp. 439–555, esp. Figure 9.1; Fogel, "Nutrition and the Decline in Mortality since 1700: Some Additional Preliminary Findings," Pope, "Adult Mortality in America before 1900."

from Europe to the United States and then from American cities to the countryside.[50]

The new disease environment may well have had an impact on human stature in the United States in the nineteenth century. Research shows, for example, that Union Army recruits and West Point Cadets born after the 1820s began to get shorter. This trend continued until the late nineteenth century and is confirmed by data for a variety of other populations (e.g., free blacks in Maryland, Georgia convicts, students at Amherst College, Pennsylvania soldiers, and Ohio National Guardsmen). Final adult heights depend, in significant part, on net nutritional status, which is, in turn, dependent on the frequency of illness. A population may have reasonable levels of food intake, but a virulent disease environment will impair net nutritional status, meaning the amount of nutrients available for replacement and augmentation of tissue. Repeated bouts of infectious disease, especially gastrointestinal infections, impair the body's ability to absorb nutrients and divert calories, proteins, vitamins, and minerals in the diet to fighting the infection rather than to tissue construction or reconstruction. The downturn in heights dating from those born about 1830 also coincides with the rise in mortality seen in the genealogical data in the 1840s and 1850s, the period of child and adolescent growth of these age cohorts. There is some evidence that food availability or distribution (by region or socioeconomic status) deteriorated in the 1820s and 1830s, and possibly later. But it is far from clear that it was a sole cause. More likely, nutrition was interacting with a changing disease environment, which was, in turn, affected by urbanization, rapid population turnover, the settling of new areas, migration waves from abroad, and the apparent spread of malaria, fevers, and gastrointestinal disease. Something close to modern stature had been achieved in the United States by the late eighteenth century, but these new factors, the reduced food availability, and the worsening disease environment led both mortality and stature to deteriorate in the mid–nineteenth century, before recovering after the Civil War Such evidence of declining heights is thus consistent with a worsening disease environment.

John Komlos has looked at the possible implication of diet, notably a reduction in both protein and calorie intake. Interestingly, the United States was experiencing relatively rapid growth in real output per capita

[50] Taylor, *The Transportation Revolution 1815–1860*; Haines, "Health, Height, Nutrition, and Mortality"; Craig and Weiss, "Nutritional Status and Agricultural Surpluses"; Rosenberg, *The Cholera Years*.

from at least the 1830s – about 1.5% per annum growth in real GDP per capita over the period 1840 to 1860. The agricultural sector was also expanding quite rapidly during this period, although the growth of output per worker may have slowed in the 1840s before accelerating again in the 1850s. This anomaly has become known as the "antebellum puzzle." Multivariate analysis of county-level data provides evidence that counties with higher death rates and greater proportions urban had shorter recruits during the American Civil War. However, there is also some support for the dietary hypothesis, mainly for the postbellum period.[51]

Higgs has argued, partly on the basis of the death rate data from Kuznets presented in Table 8.3, that rural mortality began its decline in the 1870s and that this occurred mostly because of improvements in diet, nutrition, housing, and other aspects of the standard of living. He saw little role for public health before the twentieth century, at least for rural areas. As for urban mortality, Meeker finds little improvement prior to about 1880, but thereafter urban public health measures, especially the construction of pure central water distribution systems and sanitary sewers, were important. According to Condran and Crimmins-Gardner, census mortality data for larger American cities in 1890 and 1900 suggests that mortality was improving, in part because of public health measures, although the precise relationships were difficult to measure. After about 1900, there is no doubt that mortality improved dramatically in both rural and urban areas and across groups.[52]

Table 8.2 provides data on the expectation of life at birth and the infant mortality rate (deaths in the first year of life per thousand live births) for the white population in the United States from 1850 onward. No comprehensive, comparable, and reliable mortality estimates are available prior to 1850. The mortality estimates in Table 8.2 for the 1850–90 period are based on a collection of actual nineteenth- and early twentieth-century American life tables (for various states and cities, as well as for the Death Registration Area), which I used to construct a model American life table system. Census mortality data for older children and young adults were

---

[51] Haines, "Health, Height, Nutrition, and Mortality"; Craig and Weiss, "Nutritional Status and Agricultural Surpluses"; Steckel, "Stature and Living Standards"; Komlos, "The Height and Weight of West Point Cadets"; Komlos. "Anomalies in Economic History."

[52] Higgs, "Mortality in Rural America"; Meeker, "The Improving Health of the United States"; Condran and Crimmins-Gardner, "Public Health Measures and Mortality." The census mortality data for many cities at the end of the nineteenth century were rather reasonable for the reason that they often reported registered vital statistics. For an overview, see Preston and Haines, *Fatal Years*, chaps. 1 and 2.

fitted to this model system to produce the estimates presented here. The figures for 1900 are indirect estimates of national mortality based on data from the 1900 census manuscripts. My indirect estimates of child mortality, calculated from the data on children ever born and children surviving from the public use sample of the 1900 census, accord quite well with the Death Registration Area data and therefore indicate that the various biases were offset. For 1910 and thereafter, official Death Registration Area data are used. After 1900 the Death Registration Area grew rapidly and became representative by 1920 (and complete by 1933).[53]

The evidence in Table 8.2 is consistent with the interpretations given here. Both the expectation of life at birth and the infant mortality rate (and the crude death rate estimates in Table 8.3) show sustained improvement in mortality (i.e., rising expectation of life or falling infant mortality or crude death rates) only from about the 1870s onward. It does not appear that the 1880 census year (June 1879 to May 1880) was especially unusual in terms of high mortality, but the 1850 census year was marked by a cholera epidemic. What is apparent is that serious fluctuations in mortality were less likely after the 1870s and that this change was an integral part of the mortality transition. This pattern also confirms one unusual aspect of the American demographic transition, namely, that fertility began its decline well before mortality did. Although levels of mortality in the United States in the mid–nineteenth century were comparable to those in western and northern Europe, significant mortality fluctuations were still occurring right up to the twentieth century. Consistent control of mortality, in terms of a sustained decline and a dampening of mortality peaks, only comes after the 1870s. This was also true in England and Wales.[54] New findings of rising mortality in the 1840s and 1850s further indicate that mortality in the United States was not substantially under control until after the Civil War.

What were the causes of the "epidemiologic transition" in the United States? A variety of ecobiological, public health, medical, and socioeconomic factors came into play. These categories are not mutually exclusive, since economic growth, for instance, can make resources available for public health projects, and advances in medical science can inform the effectiveness of public health. In all likelihood, the ecobiological factors were not too significant. Although there may have been favorable changes

[53] Haines, "The Use of Model Life Tables to Estimate Mortality"; Preston and Haines, *Fatal Years*, chap. 2; Haines, "Estimated Life Tables for the United States."

[54] Mitchell, *European Historical Statistics*, Table B6.

in the etiology of a few specific diseases or conditions in the nineteenth century (notably scarlet fever and possibly diphtheria), reduced disease virulence or changes in transmission mechanisms were not apparent.[55]

The remaining (socioeconomic, medical, and public health) factors are often difficult to disentangle. For example, if the germ theory of disease (a medical/scientific advance of the later nineteenth century) contributed to better techniques of water filtration and purification in public health projects, then how should the contribution of medicine versus public health be apportioned? Thomas McKeown has proposed that, prior to the twentieth century, medical science did little to reduce mortality in Europe and elsewhere.[56] He arrived at this conclusion by eliminating the alternatives: if ecobiological and medical factors are eliminated, the mortality decline before the early twentieth century must have been due to socioeconomic factors, especially better diet and nutrition, as well as improved clothing and shelter (i.e., a better standard of living). In fact, the trend in the standard of living itself is subject to considerable debate. Some room was left for public health, albeit a rather empirical (as opposed to scientific) one. These general results were based particularly on the experience of England and Wales, where much of the mortality decline between the 1840s and the 1930s was due to reductions in deaths from respiratory tuberculosis, other respiratory infections (e.g., bronchitis), and nonspecific gastrointestinal diseases (e.g., diarrhea, gastroenteritis). No effective medical therapies were available for these infections until well into the twentieth century.

It is true that medical science did have a rather limited direct role before the twentieth century. In terms of specific therapies, smallpox vaccination was known by the late eighteenth century and diphtheria and tetanus antitoxin and rabies therapy by the 1890s. Many other treatments were symptomatic. The germ theory of disease, advanced by Pasteur in the 1860s and by the work of Koch and others in the 1870s and 1880s, was only slowly accepted by what was a very conservative medical profession. Even after Robert Koch conclusively identified the tuberculosis bacillus and the cholera vibrio in 1882 and 1883, various miasma anticontagionist theories were common among physicians in the United States and elsewhere. Hospitals, having originated as pest houses and alms houses, were (correctly) perceived as generally unhealthy places to be. In 1894 in Milwaukee, an

---

[55] The term "epidemiologic transition" and a similar causal categorization were advanced by Omran in "The Epidemiologic Transition."
[56] McKeown, *The Modern Rise of Population.*

angry crowd prevented the removal of a child to a hospital during a small-pox outbreak on the grounds that the child would die there (as another child had previously). Surgery was also a dangerous undertaking before the advances of William Halsted at Johns Hopkins in the 1880s and 1890s. Major thoracic surgery was rarely risked and, if attempted, patients had a high probability of dying from infection or shock, or both. The best practice in amputations was to do them quickly to minimize risks. Although anesthesia had been introduced in America in the 1840s and the use of antisepsis in the operating theater had been advocated by the British surgeon Joseph Lister in the 1860s, surgery was not considered even reasonably safe until the twentieth century.[57]

Although medicine had little direct impact on mortality in the United States over this period, it did play an indirect role, through the advances in public health. After John Snow identified polluted water as the source of a cholera outbreak on London in 1854, pure water and sewage disposal became important issues for municipal authorities. New York City constructed its 40-mile-long Croton Aqueduct in 1844, and Boston was also tapping various outside water sources by aqueduct before the Civil War. Chicago, which drew on Lake Michigan for its water, also had to cope with sewage disposal directly into its water supply from the Chicago River. Water intakes were moved further offshore in the 1860s, requiring tunnels several miles long driven through solid rock. But this was only a temporary solution. Finally, the city had to reverse the flow of the Chicago River, using locks and the Illinois Sanitary and Ship Canal, and send the effluent down to the Illinois River. The project took eight years (1892–1900) and was called one of the "engineering wonders of the modern world." The bond issue to fund it and create the Chicago Sanitary District was overwhelmingly approved in 1889 by a vote of 70,958 to 242. This does not take into account that, at an early date, the entire downtown area had to be raised by one story to facilitate the gravity flow of sewage.[58]

In the late nineteenth century, massive public works projects took shape in larger metropolitan areas to provide clean water and proper sewage disposal. But progress was uneven. Baltimore and New Orleans, for example, were rather late in constructing adequate sanitary sewage systems. As time passed, filtration and chlorination were added to remove or neutralize particulate matter and microorganisms, in response to the findings of

[57] Duffy, *The Healers*, chaps. 10, 16–17; Starr, *The Social Transformation of American Medicine*, chaps. 4–5; Leavitt, "Politics and Public Health."
[58] Cain, "An Economic History of Urban Location and Sanitation"; Galishoff, "Triumph and Failure."

the new science of bacteriology. According to Charles Chapin in his compendious 1901 study of urban sanitation in the United States, public health officials were often much more cognizant of the need to pay attention to bacteriology than were physicians, who sometimes saw public health officials as a professional threat. Another contentious issue was how to marshal resources to pay for these public works and public health projects. Such projects were in large part locally funded and hence moved at an uneven pace toward constructing water and sewer systems, establishing public health departments, and the like. Indeed, one reason for the better mortality showing of the 10 largest cities in 1900 as compared with remaining cities of 25,000 or more was the capacity of the largest cities to secure the necessary resources for public health reform and improvement.[59]

By 1900, public water supplies were available to 42% of the American population and sewers to 29%, although many households were not connected to the pipes running under the streets and roads in front of their houses. It took longer for filtered water to reach many families. In 1870, almost no water was filtered in the United States. By 1880, about 30,000 persons in urban areas (defined as places with 2,500 persons or more) were receiving it. The number grew to 1.86 million in 1900, 10.8 million in 1910, and over 20 million in 1920; this last figure represented about 37% of the whole urban population and a much higher proportion of those living in large cities. In a study of the mortality decline in Philadelphia between 1870 and 1930, Condran and Cheney showed the drastic reduction in typhoid mortality on a ward-by-ward basis once water filtration was progressively introduced after the turn of the century.[60]

Water and sewer systems were not the sole seasons for advances in public health, though they were among the most effective weapons in the fight to prolong and enhance human life. Simply by reducing the incidence and exposure to disease in any way, communities were able to improve overall health, net nutritional status, and resistance to disease. Other areas of public health activity from the late nineteenth century onward included vaccination against smallpox; the use of diphtheria and tetanus antitoxins (from the 1890s); more extensive use of quarantine (as

---

[59] Chapin, *Municipal Sanitation*; Cain, "An Economic History of Urban Sanitation and Location"; Duffy, *The Sanitarians*, chaps. 12–16; Preston and Haines, *Fatal Years*, chap. 3.

[60] Abbott, *Past and Present*; Whipple, "Fifty Years of Water Purification"; Condran and Cheney, "Mortality Trends in Philadelphia."

more diseases were identified as contagious); the cleaning of urban streets and public areas to reduce disease foci; physical examinations for school children; health education; improved child labor and workplace health and safety laws; legislation and enforcement efforts to reduce food adulteration and especially to obtain pure milk; measures to eliminate ineffective or dangerous medications (e.g., the Pure Food and Drug Act of 1906); increased knowledge of and education about nutrition; stricter licensing of physicians, nurses, and midwives; more rigorous medical education; building codes to improve heating, plumbing, and ventilation systems in housing; measures to alleviate air pollution in urban settings; and the creation of state and local boards of health to oversee and administer these programs.

Public health proceeded on a broad front, but not without delays and considerable unevenness in enforcement and effectiveness. In the case of pure milk, it became apparent that pasteurization (heating the milk to a temperature below boiling for a period of time), known since the 1860s, was the only effective means of ensuring a bacteria-free product. Certification or inspection of dairy herds was insufficient. Pasteurization was resisted by milk sellers, however, and it only came into practice quite late. In 1911, only 15% of the milk in New York City, one of the more advanced urban areas in public health, was pasteurized. In 1908 only 20% of Chicago's milk was so treated. Pasteurization did not become compulsory in Chicago until 1908, and in New York City until 1912. Boston began required medical examinations of school children in 1894, and New York made the vaccination of school children mandatory in 1897. The federal government instituted the Children's Bureau in 1912 and in 1914 issued a pamphlet on infant care that became the best-selling publication ever issued by the Government Printing Office. Other examples of this rather uneven progress can easily be found.[61]

Public health can thus be seen as having played a significant part in the mortality transition, although it was tied, to some extent, to the reduced incidence of infectious and parasitic disease and improvements in general health. An indicator of health status, final adult stature (discussed above), began to show secular improvements by the late nineteenth century. Early in the twentieth century, medical science began to make a major contribution via direct therapies, drugs, and surgical interventions.

---

[61] Duffy, *The Sanitarians*, chaps. 12–16; Preston and Haines, *Fatal Years*, chap. 1.

CAUSE OF DEATH

By the late nineteenth century, we begin to have reasonable data on the causes of death. Much of the mortality decline since the Civil War was due to reductions in death from infectious and parasitic diseases, both of the respiratory (usually airborne) and gastrointestinal (usually waterborne) types. In a study of Philadelphia over the period 1870–1930, about two-thirds of the drop in age-standardized death rates came from lower mortality for various infectious diseases, including a 22% decline for death from respiratory tuberculosis alone. Among children (who accounted for much of the decline), significant contributions were made by reductions in mortality from diphtheria and croup, scarlet fever, smallpox, and respiratory tuberculosis. Diphtheria antitoxin, water filtration, and quarantine helped, but an improved standard of living was also important, especially for tuberculosis. Over half of the mortality decline for those aged 20–39 came in the area of respiratory tuberculosis, for which no specific therapy was available until the 1940s.[62]

Reliable cause-of-death information for larger areas of the nation become available in 1900 with the initiation of the Death Registration Area. The crude death rate for the Death Registration Area, at least, declined by 25% between 1900 and 1920. Of this decline, 70% was accounted for by the drop in all infectious and parasitic diseases. And 24% of that reduction was due to lower mortality from respiratory tuberculosis. Over the longer period, 1900–60, the crude death rate declined by 45%, while mortality from all infectious and parasitic diseases was reduced by 90%. The decline in mortality from infectious disease actually exceeded that from all causes combined because mortality from chronic, degenerative diseases (cancer, cardiovascular disease) increased.[63]

One of the great events in human history has been the prolongation of life and reduction in mortality in the modern era, chiefly due to the great declines in death from epidemic and endemic infectious disease. Americans and most in the developed world no longer live with the kind of fear and fatalism that characterized a world in which sudden and pervasive death from disease was a fact of life. For the United States, most of this improvement took place since the late nineteenth century.

[62] Condran and Cheney, "Mortality Trends in Philadelphia."
[63] Preston, Keyfitz, and Schoen, *Causes of Death.*

MORTALITY DIFFERENTIALS

During our period, both prior to and during the mortality transition commencing in the 1870s, significant differentials in mortality existed – by sex, rural-urban residence, race, region, nativity (native- versus foreign-born), and socioeconomic status.[64] Male mortality usually exceeds female mortality at all ages. This was generally true in the United States in the nineteenth century. The relative differences were often smaller than in the mid- to late twentieth century, as a consequence of the hazards of childbearing and pervasive exposure to disease-causing organisms.[65]

It is clear that, before about 1920, urban mortality was much in excess of rural mortality. In general, the larger the city, the higher the death rate. A variety of circumstances contributed to the excess mortality of cities: greater density and crowding, which led to the more rapid spread of infection; a higher degree of contaminated water and food; garbage and carrion in the streets and elsewhere not properly disposed of; larger inflows of foreign migrants, which gave rise to new foci of infection as well as new victims; and also migrants from the countryside who had not been exposed to the harsher urban disease environment. Writing at the turn of the century, Adna Ferrin Weber noted the positive relationship between city size and mortality levels, both in the United States and Europe:

It is almost everywhere true that people die more rapidly in cities than in rural districts . . . . There is no inherent or eternal reason why men should die faster in large communities than in small hamlets. . . . Leaving aside accidental causes, it may be affirmed that the excessive urban mortality is due to lack of pure air, water and sunlight, together with uncleanly habits of life induced thereby. Part cause, part effect, poverty, overcrowding, high rates of mortality, are found together in city tenements.[66]

According to the Death Registration Area life tables for 1900/1902, the expectation of life at birth was 48.2 years for white males overall – 44 years in urban areas and 54 years in rural places. The figures for females were similar (51.1 years overall, 48 years urban, 55 years rural). For the seven states with reasonable registration data in both 1890 and 1900, the ratio

---

[64] For information on black mortality, see chapter 10 in this volume. In general, mortality was considerably higher for blacks than that for whites, especially in urban areas. This was a reflection of the disadvantaged socioeconomic status of the black population.

[65] Pope, "Adult Mortality in America before 1900," notes that adult female mortality often did exceed adult male mortality between the ages of 20 and 50, but this was associated with the hazards of childbearing, frontier life, and migration.

[66] Weber, *The Growth of Cities in the 19th Century*, pp. 343, 348.

of urban-to-rural crude death rates was 1.27 in 1890, and 1.18 in 1900. For young children (aged 1–4) the ratios were much higher, with urban mortality being 107% higher in 1890 and 97% higher in 1900. For infants, the excess urban mortality was 63% in 1890 and 49% in 1900. Residence in cities – with poorer water quality, lack of refrigeration to keep food and milk fresh, and close proximity to a variety of pathogens – was very hazardous to the youngest inhabitants. The rural-urban differential seems to have been true earlier as well. For seven New York counties in 1865, the probability of dying before reaching age five was .229 in urban areas but .192 in rural locations. A study of Massachusetts by Vinovskis found a roughly direct relationship between city size and mortality for 1859–61, but he suspected that the differences had been larger in the seventeenth and eighteenth centuries.[67]

The excess urban mortality began diminishing from the late nineteenth century onward, especially as public health measures and improved diet, shelter, and general living standards took effect. The excess in expectation of life at birth for rural white males over those in urban areas was 10 years in 1900. This fell to 7.7 years in 1910, 5.4 years in 1930, and 2.6 years by 1940. The original cause of the rural advantage was likely not a superior knowledge of disease, hygiene, and prevention in rural areas, since farmers were not known to be particularly careful about disease and cleanliness: "There are few occupations [other than farming] in which hygiene is more neglected."[68] The rural advantage seems to have existed simply because rural residents lived far apart, and this reduced the chances of contagion and of contaminating the water supplies. Rural-urban mortality differentials likely played a role in the deterioration of mortality in the middle of the nineteenth century, as the population shifted to cities and towns. Also, the twentieth-century mortality decline was partly propelled by the elimination of excess urban deaths.[69]

Information on mortality differences between the native- and the foreign-born populations is ambiguous. In Massachusetts, for example, the crude death rate for the native population was higher (20.4 per thousand population) than that for the foreign-born (17.4) for the period 1888 to 1895.[70] This difference disappears, however, once the results are adjusted

---

[67] Preston and Haines, *Fatal Years*, pp. 36–39; Vinovskis, *Fertility in Massachusetts*, chap. 2; Condran and Crimmins, "Mortality Differentials between Rural and Urban Areas."

[68] Abbott, *Past and Present*, p. 71.

[69] Preston and Haines, *Fatal Years*, pp. 36–39; Taeuber and Taeuber, *Changing Population of the United States*, pp. 274–5.

[70] Abbott, "Vital Statistics of Massachusetts, Table 35.

for the younger age structure of the immigrant population. Using census samples to estimate the mortality of children of native- and foreign-born parents reveals the opposite: for seven New York counties in 1865, the probability of dying before age 5 was .189 for children of native-born parents, but it was .234 for children of foreign-born parents. The same calculation using the national sample of the 1900 census gives a probability of death before 5 of .166 when both parents were native-born and .217 when both parents were immigrants. For the Death Registration Area life tables of 1900/1902, life expectancies at age 10 were rather similar by nativity: 51.6 years for native white males and 49.1 years for foreign white males. The results for 1919/11 were 51.9 and 50.3 years respectively. Differentials by nativity were converging and had largely disappeared by the 1930s, since the higher mortality of the foreign-born was largely due to lower socioeconomic status and a greater proportion in large cities. As socioeconomic attainment narrowed between the groups and as the rural-urban mortality difference disappeared, the mortality penalty paid by the foreign-born also diminished. In the late nineteenth century there had been an effect on mortality cycles in large cities which coincided with waves of immigrants. Surges in immigration produced increased death rates. They were likely affected by changes in disease environments for both the immigrants and the natives. These cycles, too, had largely disappeared in the early twentieth century.[71]

Regional differences in mortality before the twentieth century are rather difficult to establish because of the incompleteness of geographic coverage of both vital statistics and of local studies. In colonial times, New England was the area of lowest mortality, whereas the region from the Chesapeake to the south had higher mortality. This pattern continued into the first half of the nineteenth century, as is confirmed by estimates of adult mortality from genealogies for cohorts born in the late eighteenth and early nineteenth centuries. The Midwest also appears to have been a relatively healthy region. For cohorts born in the middle of the century, however, these regional differences dissipated. Indeed, the highest life expectation at age 20 for white females born in the 1850s and 1860s was in the South Atlantic states. Regional differences, such as they were, converged into the twentieth century, but as late at 1950 the region of lowest mortality was still the western Midwest, whereas the highest death rates were found

---

[71] Preston and Haines, *Fatal Years*, chaps. 2 & 3; Haines, "Mortality in Nineteenth Century America"; Glover, *United States Life Tables*; Higgs, "Cycles and Trends of Mortality."

in the Mountain states. Regional areas of poverty (e.g., West Virginia, New Mexico) have led to significant variation across states.[72]

Differences in survival probabilities also existed across socioeconomic groups, although here, too, the information is sketchy. Using census mortality data for adult males reported by occupation in 1890 and 1900 and vital registration for 1908/1910, Paul Uselding found a rough gradient, with the lowest death rates among proprietors, clerical, and other white-collar workers and the highest death rates among laborers and servants. Interestingly, professionals did only about average. Farmers and clerks did well, as, surprisingly, did workers in forestry and fisheries. The more rural environment for those in agriculture and extractive industries undoubtedly helped.[73]

These results are echoed in estimates of child mortality according to occupation of father from the 1900 census sample. Children of white-collar workers, professionals, proprietors, and farmers did better than average, whereas children of laborers (including agricultural laborers) had worse than average survival chances. Again, the advantage to professionals, such as physicians, teachers, clergy, was not great. These results stand in contrast to similar calculations from published data from the 1911 Census of Marriage and Fertility of England and Wales. In England, the differences in child mortality across socioeconomic group lines were steep. There was a strong, consistent gradient from low mortality among professional, proprietary, and white-collar groups, through moderate mortality among skilled and semiskilled manual workers, to the highest mortality among the children of unskilled manual workers. Social class clearly had much more salience in the sense of an outcome (child mortality in this case) in England in 1911 than in the United States in 1900. Social class did not have as fundamental an importance in this sense in the United States as in Britain. Greater geographic and possibly socioeconomic mobility likely played a role in the smaller American socioeconomic differences. Also, the 11-year difference in census dates may well have been important, since this was the period in which public health advances were having a growing impact. In the United States at the turn of the century, rural-urban residence was more important than father's occupation (or estimated father's income) for child survival. An exception was race, in that the black population was at a disadvantage both within occupations and within rural-urban categories.

---

[72] Preston and Haines, *Fatal Years*, chaps. 3 and 4; Pope, Adult Mortality before 1900," pp. 284–90; Taeuber and Taeuber, *Changing Population of the United States*, pp. 282–86.

[73] Uselding, "In Dispraise of Muckrakers."

Indeed, it is important to note that race in the United States took the place of class in Britain in terms of differential child mortality.[74]

There is some evidence from earlier in the nineteenth century that socioeconomic variables, such as wealth or income, occupation, and literacy, were less important in predicting mortality differentials. For the 1850s, for instance, survival probabilities differed little between the children of the poor and the wealthy. Rural-urban residence and region made more difference.[75]

This pattern began to change in the early twentieth century, however. Analysis of the 1910 census public use sample and published vital statistics from the Birth Registration Area in the 1920s has revealed, however, that the socioeconomic differentials widened in the United States as the new century progressed. Groups with a higher income and better education more easily assimilated advice and improvements in child care, hygiene, and health practices and so were "leaders" in the mortality decline of the early twentieth century, much as the groups in Britain with higher socioeconomic status had been. Public health improvements led to a reduction in the *level* of mortality but not in relative differentials across class and occupation groups. Rural-urban differences did converge in the early twentieth century, but both relative and absolute mortality differences by race did not. The role of personal and household health behavior has been inadequately emphasized in the debate on the origins of the mortality transition. It was very likely a central role, although the precise contribution to differential child mortality is not easy to assess. For adults, the mortality gradient observed at the turn of the century – from high mortality among laborers to intermediate levels among skilled manual workers to the most favorable mortality among white-collar workers – persisted up to the middle of the twentieth century.[76]

Overall, the mortality transition in the United States was a delayed event. Instead of a decline in death rates across the nineteenth century, in parallel with the decline in birth rates, mortality exhibited an increase prior to the Civil War. On a national level, the sustained decline only began in the 1870s. Year-to-year mortality fluctuations also became less marked after midcentury. In the nineteenth century, cities were definitely less healthy environments – the larger the city, the higher the mortality

[74] Preston and Haines, *Fatal Years*, chap. 5.
[75] Steckel, "Health and Mortality of Women and Children."
[76] Ewbank and Preston, "Personal Health Behavior"; Antonovsky, "Social Class, Life Expectancy and Overall Mortality."

risk. The rural advantage was slowly eroded from late in the century, particularly because of the advances in urban public health, broadly defined. The mortality disadvantage of the black population persisted throughout the period considered here, although mortality levels improved for both whites and blacks. It is not easy to assign credit to various causal factors in the mortality transition, but the principal proximate cause was the control of both epidemic and endemic infectious diseases. By the later nineteenth century, public health certainly contributed a great deal, as did improvements in diet, housing, and the standard of living. The direct role of medical intervention was rather limited before the twentieth century but then increased as the germ theory of disease was accepted and better diagnosis and effective therapies were developed. Though difficult to assess, changes in personal health behavior must be assigned importance, particularly after the turn of the twentieth century.

MIGRATION: SOURCES

The United States was, and to a great extent remains, a nation of migrants. As seen in Table 8.3, a large share of total population growth (approximately 25%) of total population growth over the period 1790–1920 was due to migration from abroad. Between 1819 and 1920, according to official statistics, over 33.7 million migrants entered the United States from abroad. But, once here, both immigrants and the native-born continued to move – westward to the frontier, from rural to urban areas, and, more recently, to suburbia and to the Sun Belt.

Sources of quantitative information on international migration include ship manifests after 1819. They recorded landing in major ports, though omitting first-class passengers. Entrance at other points, especially land borders with Canada, were not recorded. Efforts to remedy these deficiencies were made intermittently after 1855, but coverage was not complete on this until 1908. Similarly, return migration was not counted until 1907 (and discontinued in 1957). In addition to the border counts, the federal census, of course, asked each individual to specify place of birth from 1850 onward and to identify the nativity of the respondent's parents from 1870 onward. Between 1890 and 1930 immigrants were asked to indicate their duration of residence in the United States or year of immigration.[77] Some

[77] U.S. Bureau of the Census, *Historical Statistics of the United States*, pp. 97–98.

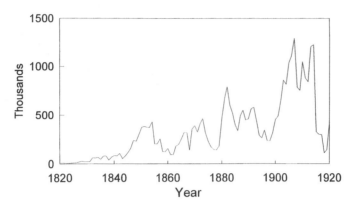

Figure 8.1. Immigrants to the United States, 1820–1920

of the basic official international migration statistics by country of origin are reported in Table 8.5. The overall trend and cycles in migration from 1820 to 1920 are depicted in Figure 8.1.

For internal migration, one must rely on census data by place of birth and current residence (which begins in 1850), "surviving" age cohorts forward or backward from census to census, direct linkage of individuals from census to census, and the census questions on residence at a previous date. Some additional data can be found in genealogical material and such things as military pension records. The census-survival technique requires estimates of mortality (and sometime fertility), which, as is apparent, are not available at the state or local level for many places in the nineteenth and early twentieth centuries. The question on residence five years prior to the census was not instituted until 1940, though the New York State census of 1855 asked a similar question.

INTERNAL MIGRATION

Table 8.4 provides a glimpse of regional population growth at the time of selected censuses between 1790 and 1920. Not surprisingly, the demographic "center" of the nation was moving from the Atlantic coastal states to the Midwest and western South. By 1920, the Mountain and Pacific states were still relatively small demographically: they constituted less than 10% of the total population (as opposed to 21% in 1990). Two migrations

Table 8.5. *Recorded immigration to the United States by origin, 1819–1920 (immigration in thousands)*

Period	Total	Origins: total Europe	North and West	East and Central	South	Other	America	Asia	Australia New Zealand	Pacific Islands	Africa
1819–20	8	8	8	—	—	—	—	—	—	—	—
1821–30	143	99	96	—	3	—	12	—	—	—	—
1831–40	599	496	490	—	5	—	33	—	—	—	—
1841–50	1,713	1,598	1,592	1	5	—	62	—	—	—	—
1851–60	2,598	2,453	2,431	2	20	—	75	41	—	—	—
1861–70	2,315	2,065	2,032	12	21	1	167	65	—	—	1
1871–80	2,812	2,272	2,070	126	75	1	404	124	10	1	—
1881–90	5,247	4,737	3,779	627	331	1	427	68	7	6	—
1891–1900	3,688	3,559	1,643	1,211	704	—	39	71	3	1	—
1901–10	8,795	8,136	1,910	3,915	2,310	1	362	244	12	1	7
1911–20	5,736	4,377	998	1,918	1,452	8	1,144	193	12	1	8

Percentage Shares

Period	Total	Origins: total Europe	North and West	East and Central	South	Other	America	Asia	Australia New Zealand	Pacific Islands	Africa
1819–20	100.0	100.0	100.0	—	—	—	—	—	—	—	—
1821–30	100.0	69.2	67.1	—	2.1	—	8.4	—	—	—	—
1831–40	100.0	82.8	81.8	—	0.8	—	5.5	—	—	—	—
1841–50	100.0	93.3	92.9	0.1	0.3	—	3.6	—	—	—	—
1851–60	100.0	94.4	93.6	0.1	0.8	—	2.9	1.6	—	—	—
1861–70	100.0	89.2	87.8	0.5	0.9	0.0	7.2	2.8	—	—	0.0
1871–80	100.0	80.8	73.6	4.5	2.7	0.0	14.4	4.4	0.4	0.0	—
1881–90	100.0	90.3	72.0	11.9	6.3	0.0	8.1	1.3	0.1	0.1	—
1891–1900	100.0	96.5	44.5	32.8	19.1	—	1.1	1.9	0.1	0.0	—
1901–10	100.0	92.5	21.7	44.5	26.3	0.0	4.1	2.8	0.1	0.0	0.1
1911–20	100.0	76.3	17.4	33.4	25.3	0.1	19.9	3.4	0.2	0.0	0.1

Source: Taeuber and Taeuber, *Changing Population of the United States,* pp. 53, 57. Prior to 1871, totals are not always for calendar years.

account for the numbers in Table 8.4: the movement from east to west and the movement from rural to urban areas. As Table 8.1 demonstrates, the urban population grew from about 5% of the total population in 1790 to 51% in 1920. Its average annual growth rate was 4.3%, in contrast to only 2.0% per annum for rural dwellers. Since there is every indication that the birth rates were lower and death rates higher in urban than in rural areas, the more rapid growth of urban areas was due to population redistribution and not to differences in natural increase. This rural-to-urban shift reflects, of course, labor market conditions as the economy changed its structure of opportunities from a rural, smallholder agriculture to an urban, industrial, and service-based economy made up predominantly of employees. This is certainly exemplified by the increase in the nonfarm share of the labor force, from 25.6% in 1800 to 44.2% in 1860 to 74.1% in 1920.[78] A primary motive for migration in ordinary times is to take advantage of wage and income differences across space, which substitutes factor mobility for interregional trade in goods and services.

Urbanization did spread across regions, albeit unevenly. The Northeast was the urban-industrial center of the nation in the nineteenth century. By 1860, New England and the Middle Atlantic regions had 61% of the nation's urban inhabitants but only 33% of the overall population. Conversely, the South had 17% of the urban population but 36% of the overall total. Even in 1920, the Northeast still had 41% of urban dwellers, with the Midwest close behind at 33%. The South still had but 17%.

From 1850 onward, we are able to examine migration by place of birth and current residence. The proportion of the native-born population residing outside the state of birth ("lifetime" migrants) was relatively stable from the middle of the nineteenth century: 23.3% of the white population in 1850, 23.5% in 1890, and 23.9% in 1920. The nonwhite population had lower rates of lifetime mobility in this period, about 15–20% until after 1920.[79] Much of this interstate movement was on an east-west axis until the closing of the frontier at the end of the nineteenth century. For instance, in 1850, of those born in Pennsylvania but residing elsewhere, 67% could be found in Ohio, Indiana, or Illinois, whereas 77% of those born in South Carolina but residing outside that state were in Georgia,

[78] Weiss, "U.S. Labor Force Estimates and Economic Growth," p. 117.
[79] U.S. Bureau of the Census, *Historical Statistics of the United States*, Series C1–3.

Alabama, Mississippi, and Tennessee. A variety of explanations has been advanced for the migration along latitudes, but recently it has been shown that real and human capital invested in seed, livestock, implements, and farming techniques made movement along climatic bands much more rational. This also provides a partial explanation for the greater preference of the bulk of the nineteenth-century immigrants from northern and western Europe for the Northeast and the Midwest – their human capital matched that climatic band better.[80] That was true for those going to rural areas, at least. The remainder of the explanation was largely the greater opportunities in the more rapidly urbanizing and industrializing North, as well as the tendency of migration streams, once established, to grow along familiar paths.

Agrarian motives for migration diminished as the frontier closed in the late nineteenth century and as rural population growth slowed dramatically (to only 0.8% per year over the period 1890 to 1920). For most of the nineteenth century, migration flows westward were consistent with the land availability hypothesis discussed in connection with the fertility transition. Rural migrants moved west to secure cheaper, good-quality land. Frederick Jackson Turner's thesis that the frontier was a demographic "safety valve" in nineteenth-century America remains a durable view. Nevertheless, by late in the century, the rural-to-urban flow assumed the dominant role. But much of the rural-urban migration was within regions or along an east-west axis, since the bulk of urban and industrial growth from the Civil War to 1920 was in the Northeast or Midwest. Notably, the South failed to increase its share of urban population over this period. The major shift to a south-to-north movement only began on a large scale with the radical shifts in demand for labor accompanying World War I and the restriction, after 1921, of cheap immigrant labor. The shift to the Sun Belt came even later, mainly after World War II. Changes in transportation technology, particularly the electric streetcar and underground railways, and later the automobile and motorized bus, led to a movement out of central cities and into suburban communities. This process was under way in parts of the Northeast by the end of the nineteenth century but really accelerated after World War I, and again after 1945. So, for instance, during the 1920s the rural part of metropolitan districts (as defined by the Bureau of the Census) increased by 55%, faster than any part of the

[80] Steckel, "Economic Foundations of East-West Migration." This does not explain *why* the antebellum South failed to urbanize and industrialize more rapidly. See Bateman and Weiss, *A Deplorable Scarcity.*

metropolitan population except for small cities. This development was suburbanization.[81]

The urbanization process was accompanied by a filling out of the city's size hierarchy. Large cities did tend to grow most rapidly. In 1810 there were only two cities with a population of more than 50,000 (New York and Philadelphia), and together they made up 29% of the total urban population. By 1860, there were 16 places with a population of 50,000 or more, and they held 50% of the nation's urban inhabitants. In 1920, the first census in which more than half of the American population was urban, 144 cities had 50,000 persons or more (25 had 250,000 or more), and they now accounted for 60% of city dwellers. The three largest cities of over one million each (New York, Chicago, and Philadelphia) alone had 19% of America's urbanites. But the urban size hierarchy did not become distorted, as it has in some developing nations. That is, large cities did not grow to such an extent that medium and smaller urban places became unimportant. In 1860 there were 213 places with a population of 5,000 to 50,000, and they held 41% of the urban inhabitants. In 1920, there were 1,323 such places, with 32% of the urban population.[82]

This urban growth had powerful economic linkages. Considerable industrial output of the period 1865–1920 was devoted to providing infrastructure and materials to house, transport, and deliver public services for the population making this massive shift to towns and cities. Iron and steel for sewer and water pipe, bridges, rails, structural pieces, and nails; concrete, stone, brick, and asphalt for roads and structures; cut timber; transport equipment; glass; and many other materials – all were demanded in huge quantities to build the cities.

Migration patterns, both internal and international, did affect regional population growth rates and shares. In 1790, the North and South each had about 50% of the total population. But differential migration and not differential natural increase began to drive the share in the North upward, as slower population growth in New England was balanced by more rapid growth in New York, Pennsylvania, and later the Midwest. The Northeast and Midwest together accounted for 56% of the nation's inhabitants in 1830 and 62% in 1860, compared with 35% for the South at the latter date. This demographic shift alone was instrumental in the political crisis

[81] Schapiro, *Filling Up America*; Turner, "Significance of the Frontier in American History"; Stilgoe, *Borderland*.
[82] U.S. Bureau of the Census, *Historical Statistics of the United States*, Series A 43–72.

leading up to the Civil War, as southern representation in the Congress slowly ebbed.[83]

The regional preference of migrants from abroad, once they landed in the United States, was strongly in favor of the Northeast and Midwest, and not the South. In 1860, for instance, a mere 5.6% of the South's white population was foreign-born, whereas the proportion was 19.3% in the Northeast and 17.4% in the Midwest. For 1910, the proportion of foreign-born living in the Northeast had risen to 26.2%. It had fallen to 3.5% in the South and held at 17.4% in the Midwest. Further, at the latter date, only 6.1% of Southern whites had a foreign-born parent or parents, whereas 30.1% of white residents of the Northeast were first-generation native-born. This had profound political implications in terms of regional growth both before and after the Civil War. Not only did it change the congressional balance of power, but it limited the supply of labor for industrial and agricultural development in the South throughout the nineteenth and early twentieth centuries.[84] The southern share slipped even further, to 31% in 1920, whereas the Northeast and Midwest held about steady at 60%. These population realignments were both the cause and effect of rapid industrial growth in the postbellum era, as many of the rural migrants and most of the later immigrants were destined for northern cities.

INTERNATIONAL MIGRATION

In discussions of migration to the United States over the long nineteenth century, the flood of immigrants from Europe usually takes center stage. It was dramatic and colorful, as new arrivals added an ethnic flavor which pervades our culture today.[85] Like internal migrants, the immigrants were most often motivated by economic concerns. Labor market models of migration provide sufficient explanations of the phenomenon in circumstances other than war or serious political or environmental upheaval. Individuals and

---

[83] The relative decline of the South took place despite the high natural increase of the black population, which raised the share of blacks from 35% of the population in 1790 to 37% in 1860. Legal importation of slaves was permitted up to 1808, but the real factor in black population growth was excess of births over deaths.

[84] U.S. Bureau of the Census, *Historical Statistics of the United States*, Series A 172–94.

[85] Bodnar, *The Transplanted*; Jones, *American Immigration*; Gould, "European Inter-Continental Emigration, 1815–1914"; "European Inter-Continental Emigration: The Road Home"; "European Inter-Continental Emigration: The Role of 'Diffusion' and 'Feedback.'"

families move to maximize the present discounted net benefits of shifting to a location with better wages, incomes, and opportunities. They must factor in the costs, including direct transportation and moving expenses, as well as lost earnings and psychological costs. Comparisons of these factors help explain why migration is selective: movers tend to be younger and single and have less wealth than nonmovers.[86]

The selectivity of migration is partly the cause of the phenomenon seen in the last column of Table 8.1. The sex ratio of the population (males per hundred females) was well above 100 in 1790 and increased in decades of highest immigration (the 1840s, 1850s, 1880s, and 1900s). Migration was selective of males in this case, as they arrived first to seek the opportunities. The sex ratio of the foreign-born white population in 1850 was 124. It was 129 in 1910. They clearly were raising the national average.[87] The general decline of the sex ratio over time was, however, due to the aging of the population. In a normal closed population, the sex ratio at birth is about 105 male births per hundred female births. Higher male than female mortality (at most, if not all, ages) then leads to a slow decline in the ratio to below 100 for older age groups. Early in the nineteenth century, the sex ratio was well above 100 since a young population (median age 16) was weighted toward groups with higher sex ratios. With an aging population caused by declining fertility, the overall sex ratio would fall as the population was weighted toward older age groups with lower sex ratios. This process was offset to a degree by inflows of migrants heavily selective of males (with the exception of the years of the Great Depression, the 1930s).

Push and pull factors operate in the migration arena, although it is often difficult to disentangle the simultaneous effects of push and pull.[88] From this perspective, one could ask whether it was poor conditions in nineteenth-century Europe or the expanding opportunities in the United States that propelled millions of souls to make the long and difficult journey. A clue lies in the waves of migration which characterized the period. Though not easily apparent from Table 8.5, there were decades in which migration surged: the 1840s, 1850s, 1880s, and the period 1900–14. These surges can be seen clearly in Figure 8.1, which plots the annual numbers of

---

[86] Sjaastad, "The Costs and Returns of Human Migration."

[87] One exception was the 1930s, when the Great Depression reduced demand for labor and, consequently, reduced the flow of migrants from abroad. The sex ratio changed in favor of females in that decade as opportunities for new employment for males fell drastically.

[88] Gould, "European Inter-Continental Emigration, 1815–1914."

officially recorded migrants from 1820 to 1940. Upswings in in-migration
corresponded to periods of relative prosperity in the American economy:
the boom beginning in 1843 and lasting until the panic of 1857; the
post–Civil War economic upsurge (1865–73); the economic peaks of the
1880s; and the prolonged prosperity from the end of the 1890s until the end
of World War I. The falloff in the 1920s reflected the new restrictive legislation. Similarly, migration troughs corresponded to the panics of 1837,
1857, 1873, and the sustained economic dislocations of the 1890s. It is not
surprising that the uncertain prospects of the American Civil War should
have led to a decline in migration, though the flows picked up again before
the end of the war. In sum, waves of immigration were roughly synchronous with long swings in economic activity in the United States. It is also
important to consider migration to the United States as one part of a global
labor market which emerged in the second half of the nineteenth century.[89]

Long swings (of about 15 to 25 years' duration) were historically associated with construction cycles and need to be distinguished from the shorter
business cycle (of about 8 to 10 years' duration) or even shorter inventory
cycles. The roughly synchronous cyclical movements in the economies of
the United States and the European countries of migrant origin point to
the dominance of pull factors in the United States rather than push factors
from Europe, since favorable conditions generally existed on both sides of
the Atlantic during upswings in migrant flows to the United States. If, in
times of relative prosperity in Europe, migrants left in increased numbers,
then American labor market conditions were the dominant factor. An
important exception was the great potato famine of the later 1840s. It was
not just confined to Ireland but also affected the continent of Europe, particularly Germany, Scandinavia, and the Netherlands, where the potato had
become an important part of the diet. Here, push factors were more clearly
at work. Analysis of the cycles in migration to the United States in the nineteenth century suggests a close correlation between migration and such sensitive cyclical indicators as miles of railroad constructed in the United States
and railroad rails consumed.[90] There is also evidence, albeit more sketchy,
that long swings in economic activity and demand for labor also affected
interstate migration flows.

---

[89] See, for example, Hatton and Williamson, "What Drove the Mass Migrations from Europe in the
Late Nineteenth Century?"

[90] Easterlin, "Influences in European Overseas Emigration before World War I": "Typically, the swings
in migration were a response to corresponding swings in the demand for labor in the United States."
Easterlin, *Population, Labor Force, and Long Swings in Economic Growth*, pp. 30–31 and chap. 2;
Neal, "Cross-Spectral Analysis of Long Swings in Atlantic Migration"; Gould, "European Inter-
Continental Emigration, 1815–1914."

Figure 8.1 also points to a long-term upward trend in gross migration across the Atlantic. Average migration increased from about 14,000 persons per year in the 1820s to almost 260,000 per year in the 1850s, to approximately 1 million annually in the peak years 1911–14, an average growth of 4.9% per annum between the 1820s and 1911–14 – very rapid indeed. More than 1 million migrants entered the United States in 6 of the 14 years before the First World War erupted in Europe in 1914. These magnitudes have not been exceeded for recorded legal migration until very recently.

This substantial secular increase was assisted by technological improvements in transportation. In the early to mid–nineteenth century, the trans-Atlantic passage on sailing vessels could take up to several weeks and cost a substantial fraction of the annual income of a peasant or manual worker. When wooden square-riggers were replaced by larger iron- or steel-hulled vessels with steam power and screw propellers, passage time dropped to about 10 days in the 1870s and about a week in 1900. Trans-Atlantic passenger fares became cheaper over the century, as did those on railroads and vessels on the inland waterways of both the United States and Europe.

This reduction in the barriers of time and cost also led to increases in return migration. For the five-year period 1908–12, when information about return migration first became available, there were 4.75 alien arrivals and 2.36 million departures of noncitizens, giving a return rate of about 50%. This is a somewhat neglected feature of immigration history, but it was quite important. For Italy, one of the best-documented and quantitatively significant cases, over 43% of all migrants who left for the United States in the 1880s returned to Italy. This "repatriation ratio" rose to 53% in the first decade of the twentieth century and to 63% during 1910–20. Overall, it seems that, by the late nineteenth century, one Italian migrant returned home for every two who left for the United States. This proportion was even higher for non-Jewish migrants from Greece, Hungary, Russia, and the Balkans. Jewish migrants tended to stay, largely because the United States offered greater freedom and less persecution. The reasons for return were varied. A large number of migrants planned to return after having earned a "nest egg." Others became dissatisfied with their lot in the New World or longed for friends, family, and familiar landscapes.[91]

---

[91] Gould, "European Inter-Continental Emigration: The Road Home"; "European Inter-Continental Emigration: The Role of 'Diffusion' and 'Feedback.'"

Another salient feature of immigration to America apparent in Table 8.5 is the changing composition of the flows across the long nineteenth century. For the decades between 1821 and 1890, 82% of all immigrants originated in northern and western Europe and only 8% in central, eastern, and southern Europe.[92] For the three decades 1891 to 1920, the situation had altered dramatically: only 25% of the migrants came from northern and western Europe and 64% from central, eastern, and southern Europe. Contemporaries described this as the shift from the "old" to the "new" immigration. This shift in composition, along with the strong upward trend in migration, spurred the government to form the U.S. Immigration Commission of 1907–10 and probably to restrict immigration. Thompson and Whelpton estimate that, at the time of the first federal census in 1790, 90% of the white population was ultimately of northern and western European origin, with 77% from Great Britain and Ireland alone. Their definition of northern and western Europe excluded Germany, which was the origin of 7.4% of the 1790 population. By 1920, northern and western Europe (excluding Germany) was the origin of only about 63% of the American population (41% from Britain and Northern Ireland) with 27% having their ancestry in central and eastern Europe (16.3% from Germany) and 4.5% in southern Europe.[93]

Why did this shift to the "new" immigration occur? As modern economic growth progressed in many of the original sending nations of northern and western Europe, growth in the demand for labor in their domestic economies improved and absorbed many of those who would have migrated abroad. The decline in the size and share of the agrarian sectors in these economies also contributed, since many of the migrants came from rural areas. Germany is an excellent case in point. In the 1880s, 1,342,000 Germans emigrated. This number dropped to 527,000 in the 1890s and to 274,000 in the 1900s.[94] The decline coincided with Germany's rapid emergence as an urbanized industrial power. The increase in outflows from central, eastern, and southern Europe began as these nations (Austria-Hungary, Russia, the Balkan states, Italy) began to experience the dislocations associated with modern economic growth and structural change.

---

[92] Northern and western Europe are defined here as Great Britain (England, Wales, Scotland); Ireland; the German states and, after 1871, the German Empire; Sweden; Norway; Denmark; Belgium; the Netherlands; France; and Switzerland. Central, eastern, and southern Europe would include Austria-Hungary, Russia, Italy, Greece, the Balkan states, European parts of the Ottoman Empire, Spain, and Portugal.

[93] Thompson and Whelpton, *Population Trends in the United States*, p. 91.

[94] Mitchell, *European Historical Statistics*, Table B8.

There is, however, also the persuasive argument that only late in the nineteenth century did the feedback of information about migration opportunities diffuse widely in southern and eastern Europe. This, combined with cheaper fares and shorter and less hazardous journeys by railway and steamship, led to an upsurge in "migration fever." Legal and institutional barriers to out-migration were also reduced or eliminated in many of these nations from the late nineteenth century onward.[95]

There was considerable nativist opposition to these migrants. The "Know Nothing" or American Party, which flourished in the 1840s and 1850s, proposed anti-alien and anti-Catholic legislation, particularly directed at the Irish. Similar groups arose in the 1870s and 1880s, particularly in California, where hostility to Chinese immigration was strong. As the labor movement grew, there were calls for immigration restriction from that quarter, which is understandable, since the more rapid expansion in the supply of labor provided by immigrants restricted the growth of real wages, raised unemployment, and made labor organizing more difficult. The short-lived National Labor Union (1866–72) advocated limits to immigration as well as repeal of the Contract Labor Law (1864). The latter allowed employers to advance the costs of passage to prospective immigrant workers. The American Federation of Labor (founded 1886) long campaigned for quotas on immigration. Nonetheless, between the Alien Act of 1798 (only briefly in force) and the Immigration Act of 1917, which imposed a literacy test, virtually nothing was done to restrict European immigration to the United States. Although migrants had to register with ships' masters (after 1819) and had to be screened for diseases, criminal records, or the possibility of becoming a public charge (after 1891), there was basically an "open door." A notable exception was the Chinese Exclusion Act of 1882 (renewed in 1892 and made indefinite in 1902), directly aimed at cutting off the flow of East Asian migrants to the West Coast. The literacy test imposed in 1917 over Woodrow Wilson's veto was merely a forerunner of the much more restrictive Emergency Immigration Act of 1921, which imposed quotas based on national origins. Immigration was limited annually to 3% of each nation's share of the American population in 1910. An even narrower law was enacted in 1924 which reduced the annual quota per country to 2% of a nation's share of the U.S. population in 1890, clearly favoring the nations of northern and western Europe at the expense of the areas of the "new" immigration. All

[95] Gould, "European Inter-Continental Emigration: The Role of 'Diffusion' and 'Feedback.'"

immigration from East Asia was terminated. In 1929, the quotas were ultimately to be based on the census of 1920, but for a total not to exceed 150,000 per year, in contrast to the levels in excess of a million a year in the years just prior to World War I.[96]

It is interesting to speculate why, after such a long period of open immigration and of strong business and employer opposition to immigration restriction, that there would have been such a rapid change in direction around 1920. The cumulative reaction to the new immigration and the increase in immigration flows since 1900 likely played a role. Labor unions were gaining some legislative influence, as the instance of the Clayton Act of 1914 (exempting the unions from the Sherman Antitrust Act) shows. But union influence waned after the war, as the failure of the large steel strike of 1919 and the decline in union membership in the 1920s attest. More important, the war itself, the postwar "red scare," and especially the discovery by employers that they had a large pool of lower-skilled workers in the rural South were more significant. Further, the rationalization of manufacturing production was under way, reducing the need for additional labor as organizational change, further mechanization, and other technological change greatly improved productivity. For example, manufacturing output grew by 53% between 1919 and 1929, whereas the manufacturing labor force was virtually stationary over the same period.[97]

It is true that immigrants did tend to be disproportionately in the occupational groups with lower skills. In 1910, the foreign-born white population was 21% of the labor force, but they were 37% of all laborers. Only 20% of them were white-collar workers, as opposed to 41% of the native whites of native parentage. Relatively few of them were proprietors, especially since only a small number went into agriculture. But the foreign-born and their second-generation offspring did make up 44% of all white-collar workers and 54% of all craftsmen and operatives.[98] Even though they did occupy a disproportionate share of the less privileged positions in terms of skill and status, they made possible, in some sense, the better-paid, higher-status occupations of the native white population.

Things did improve as the foreign-born white population and their children assimilated to the patterns of labor force activity, occupations, and

---

[96] Hutchinson, *Legislative History of American Immigration Policy.*

[97] U.S. Bureau of the Census, *Historical Statistics of the United States*, Series D130 (employees on manufacturing payrolls) and P13 (the Federal Reserve Board index of manufacturing production).

[98] Easterlin, "The American Population," Tables 5.7 and 5.8.

residence of the native whites of native parentage. A series of studies conducted since the 1960s has shed considerable light on the geographic and occupation mobility of Americans. Beginning with the pioneering work of Thernstrom on Newburyport and Boston, Massachusetts, these mobility studies have used a variety of nominal record sources (census manuscripts, city directories, voter lists, tax and property rolls) to link individual records. Although fraught with difficulties, such studies have found a high degree of geographic mobility, particularly for urban areas, in the nineteenth and early twentieth centuries. For Newburyport, almost the entire population of 1850 had disappeared by 1880, both through natural attrition and through migration (as well as linkage failure). For Boston in the period 1880–1920, net migration made up two-thirds of the population growth. There was less occupational mobility, both within the lifetimes of individuals and also across generations, but the results have indicated significant rates of upward occupational mobility, both among the native- and the foreign-born. Overall, about 10–30% of sons of working-class fathers were able to advance to higher-income and/or higher-status positions over the period 1830–1920. Over time, this would have a telling effect, and the foreign-born, even the relatively unskilled, did have some real prospects of upward socioeconomic progress. More recent studies, using censuses, immigrant ship lists, property rolls, pension records, and genealogies, are exploring mobility further. A national mobility study has linked about 40% of approximately 10,000 men from the 1880 to the 1900 manuscript censuses. Considerable geographic mobility was confirmed, and the rate of occupational mobility among the nonfarm population was considerable, not differing greatly from the rates in the middle of the twentieth century.[99]

SUMMARY AND CONCLUSIONS

This essay has focused on the evolution of the American white population over the "long" nineteenth century, 1790–1920. The discussion has perforce

[99] A summary of these mobility studies (up to 1977) may be found in Kaelble, *Historical Research on Social Mobility*. The results for Massachusetts refer to Thernstrom, *Poverty and Progress* and *The Other Bostonians*. For a recent study using genealogies, see Adams and Kasakoff, "Migration and the Family in Colonial New England." For more recent census linkage studies, see Steckel, "Household Migration and Rural Settlement"; and Galenson and Pope, "Economic and Geographic Mobility on the Farming Frontier"; and "Precedence and Wealth." The 1880–1900 national panel study is discussed in Guest, "Notes from the National Panel Study"; and Guest, Landale, and McCann, "Intergenerational Occupational Mobility." A recent important work on both geographic and social mobility is Ferrie, *Yankeys Now*.

covered fertility, marriage, mortality, and both internal and international migration. The relatively rapid population growth over this period (averaging 2.5% per year) was driven largely by high (though declining) birth rates and moderate levels of mortality, but immigration was also significant. About three-quarters of the growth was due to natural increase and about a quarter to net in-migration. More than 34 million persons entered the United States between the 1790s and the end of World War I.

Family sizes were large in the early days of the Republic, being about seven children per woman for the white population. There was a sustained decline in white birth rates from at least 1800. The fertility decline proceeded in both rural and urban areas. Conventional explanations for the fertility transition have involved such factors as the rising cost of children because of urbanization, growth of incomes and nonagricultural employment, increased value of education, rising female employment, child labor laws and compulsory education, and declining infant and child mortality. In addition, changing attitudes toward large families and toward contraception, as well as better contraceptive technologies, are also cited. Such structural explanations do well for the American experience since the late nineteenth century, but they are less appropriate for the fertility decline in rural, agrarian areas prior to about 1870. The increased scarcity and higher cost of good agricultural land has been proposed as a prime factor, although this explanation remains controversial. The standard explanations also fail fully to explain the post–World War II "baby boom" and subsequent "baby bust." One fruitful alternative has been to examine the increase of nonagricultural opportunities in farming areas, and the effect of these opportunities on parent–child bargaining over bequests and old age support for the parents.

Mortality did not begin its *sustained* decline until the 1870s. Prior to that, death rates fluctuated in response to periodic epidemics and changes in the disease environment. There is even evidence of rising death rates during the 1840s and 1850s. Expectation of life at age 20 may have fallen by 10% between the 1830s and the 1850s.[100] The demographic transition in the United States was thus characterized by the fertility decline prior to the mortality decline, which is unlike the pattern proposed by the standard model. The mortality decline since the late nineteenth century was particularly promoted by improvements in public health and sanitation, especially better water supplies and sewage disposal. The improving diet,

---

[100] Pope, "Adult Mortality in America before 1990," Table 9.4.

clothing, and shelter of the American population over the period since about 1870 also played a role. Specific medical interventions beyond more general environmental public health were not as important until well into the twentieth century. Although it is difficult to disentangle the precise effects of these different causal factors, much of the mortality decline was due to rapid reductions in specific infectious and parasitic diseases, including tuberculosis, pneumonia, bronchitis, and gastrointestinal infections, as well as in such well-known conditions as cholera, smallpox, diphtheria, and typhoid fever. In the nineteenth century, urban areas were unhealthy places, especially the largest cities. Rural areas and small towns had the most salubrious environment. These circumstances began to change by about the 1890s, when the largest cities instituted effective large public works sanitation projects and public health administration. The largest cities then experienced the most rapid improvements in death rates. Rural-urban mortality differentials converged and largely disappeared, unlike those between whites and blacks.

Migration has been a fact of life for Americans. Within the nation's boundaries, there has been significant movement east to west, following the frontier (until the late nineteenth century); from rural to urban areas; and, later, from central cities to suburbs, from South to North, and ultimately to the Sun Belt. These developments have been responsible for changing the United States from a rural to an urban nation: from only 5% urban in 1790 to over half urban in 1920 and over three-quarters urban today. The population shifted from the original areas of settlement on the Atlantic coast to the center of the nation and later to the Pacific and Mountain states. Migration from abroad, first from western and northern Europe and then, after about 1890, from central, eastern, and southern Europe, came in waves in response to upswings in business cycles and the expansion of economic opportunities in the United States. This flood of immigrants directly augmented population growth rates and indirectly acted to raise birth rates, before it was severely restricted in the 1920s by legislation and subsequently by the Great Depression. But it left an indelible stamp on the American economy, society, and culture.

BIBLIOGRAPHIC ESSAY

There exist a number of comprehensive monographs and papers on the American population. Among the classic works, see Warren S. Thompson and P. K. Whelpton, *Population Trends in the United States* (New York: McGraw-Hill, 1933); Conrad Taeuber and Irene B. Taeuber, *The Changing Population of the United States* (New York: Wiley, 1958); and Wilson H. Grabill, Clyde Kiser, and Pascal K. Whelpton, *The Fertility of American Women* (New York: Wiley, 1958). Among more recent works, the reader is directed to Richard A. Easterlin, "The American Population," in Lance Davis et al. eds., *American Economic Growth: An Economist's History of the United States*, pp. 121–83 (New York: Harper & Row, 1972), and "Population Issues in American Economic History: A Survey and Critique," in Robert Gallman, ed., *Recent Developments in the Study of Business and Economic History: Essays in Honor of Herman E. Krooss*, pp. 131–58 (Greenwich, Conn.: JAI Press, 1977); and Robert V. Wells, *Uncle Sam's Family: Issues in and Perspectives on American Demographic History* (Albany: State University of New York Press, 1985), and *Revolutions in American's Lives: A Demographic Perspective on the History of Americans, Their Families, and Their Society* (Westport, Conn.: Greenwood Press, 1982). An overview of more recent population information is found in Donald J. Bogue, *The Population of the United States: Historical Trends and Future Projections* (New York: The Free Press, 1985). An excellent collection of articles up to the late 1970s is furnished in Maris A. Vinovskis, ed., *Studies in American Historical Demography* (New York: Academic Press, 1979). The best compilation of statistical information remains U.S. Bureau of the Census, *Historical Statistics of the United States from Colonial Times to 1970* (Washington D.C.: Government Printing Office, 1975), chapters A–D. The best straightforward coverage of demographic methods with a good discussion of the statistics of the United States is Henry S. Shryock, Jacob S. Siegel, and associates, *The Methods and Materials of Demography* (Washington, D.C.: Government Printing Office, 1971). The published federal census volumes have now been reprinted up through 1880, and the published state and territorial censuses have been reprinted in a microfiche collection. An up-to-date discussion of mortality in nineteenth-century America may be found in Samuel H. Preston and Michael R. Haines, *Fatal Years: Child Mortality in Late Nineteenth Century America* (Princeton, N.J.: Princeton University Press, 1991). A recent synthetic work on immigration is John Bodnar, *The Transplanted: A History of Immigrants in Urban America* (Bloomington: Indiana University Press, 1985). For an overview of demographic history in general, see Massimo Livi-Bacci, *A Concise History of World Population*, translated by Carl Ipsen (Cambridge, Mass.: Blackwell, 1992).

REFERENCES

Abbott, Samuel W. 1897. "The Vital Statistics of Massachusetts: A Forty Years' Summary, 1856–1895." Massachusetts, State Board of Health. *Twenty-Eighth Annual Report of the Massachusetts State Board of Health*. Public Document no. 34. Boston.

————. 1900. *The Past and Present Condition of Public Hygiene and State Medicine in the United States*. Boston: Wright & Potter.

Adams, John W., and Alice Bee Kasakoff. 1984. "Migration and the Family in Colonial New England: The View from Genealogies." *Journal of Family History*, vol. 9, no. 1 (Spring), pp. 24–42.

Alter, George. 1992. "Theories of Fertility Decline: A Non-Specialist's Guide to the Current Debate on European Fertility Decline." In John R. Gillis, Louise A. Tilly, and David Levine, eds., *The European Experience of Declining Fertility, 1850–1970*, pp. 13–27. Oxford: Blackwell.

Anderson, Margo J. 1988. *The American Census: A Social History*. New Haven, Conn.: Yale University Press.

Antonovsky, Aaron. 1967. "Social Class, Life Expectancy and Overall Mortality." *Milbank Memorial Fund Quarterly*, vol. 45, no. 2, pt. 1, pp. 31–73.

Atack, Jeremy. 1977. "Returns to Scale in Antebellum United States Manufacturing." *Explorations in Economic History*, vol. 14, pp. 337–59.

Atack, Jeremy, and Fred Bateman. 1987. *To Their Own Soil: Agriculture in the Antebellum North*. Ames: Iowa State University Press.

Bateman, Fred, and Jeremy Atack. 1992. "Did the United States Industrialize Too Slowly?" Paper presented at meetings of the Development of the American Economy Program, National Bureau of Economic Research, Cambridge, Mass. (March).

Bateman, Fred, and Thomas Weiss. 1981. *A Deplorable Scarcity: The Failure of Industrialization in the Slave Economy*. Chapel Hill: University of North Carolina Press.

Bean, Lee L., Geraldine P. Mineau, and Douglas Anderton. 1990. *Fertility Change on the American Frontier: Adaptation and Innovation*. Berkeley: University of California Press.

Bodnar, John. 1985. *The Transplanted: A History of Immigrants in Urban America*. Bloomington: Indiana University Press.

Cain, Louis P. 1977. "An Economic History of Urban Location and Sanitation." *Research in Economic History*, vol. 2, pp. 337–89.

Caldwell, John C. 1982. *Theory of Fertility Decline*. New York: Academic Press.

Carr, Lois Green. 1992. "Emigration and the Standard of Living: The Seventeenth Century Chesapeake." *Journal of Economic History*, vol. 52, no. 2 (June), pp. 271–91.

Chapin, Charles V. 1901. *Municipal Sanitation in the United States*. Providence, R.I.: Snow and Farnham.

Coale, Ansley J. 1974. "The Demographic Transition." International Union for the Scientific Study of Population. In *International Population Conference: Liege, 1973*. vol. 1, pp. 53–72. Liege: IUSSP.

Coale, Ansley J., and Susan Cotts Watkins, eds. 1986. *The Decline of Fertility in Europe*. Princeton, N.J.: Princeton University Press.

Coale, Ansley J., and Melvin Zelnik. 1963. *New Estimates of Fertility and Population in the*

United States: A Study of Annual White Births from 1855 to 1960 and of Completeness of Enumeration in the Censuses from 1880 to 1960. Princeton, N.J.: Princeton University Press.

Condran, Gretchen A., and Rose A. Cheney. 1982. "Mortality Trends in Philadelphia: Age- and Cause-Specific Death Rates, 1870–1930." *Demography*, vol. 19, no. 1 (February), pp. 97–123.

Condran, Gretchen, and Eileen Crimmins-Gardner. 1978. "Public Health Measures and Mortality in U.S. Cities in the Late Nineteenth Century." *Human Ecology*, vol. 6, no. 1 (March), pp. 27–54.

Condran, Gretchen A., and Eileen Crimmins. 1979. "A Description and Evaluation of Mortality Data in the Federal Census: 1850–1900." *Historical Methods*, vol. 12, no. 1 (Winter), pp. 1–23.

―――. 1980. "Mortality Differentials between Rural and Urban Areas of States in the Northeastern United States, 1890–1900." *Journal of Historical Geography*, vol. 6, no. 2, pp. 179–202.

Craig, Lee A., and Thomas Weiss. 1998. "Nutritional Status and Agricultural Surpluses in the Antebellum United States." In John Komlos and Joerg Baten, eds., *The Biological Standard of Living in Comparative Perspective*, pp. 190–207. Stuttgart: Franz Steiner Verlag.

Crimmins, Eileen M. 1980. "The Completeness of 1900 Mortality Data Collected by Registration and Enumeration for Rural and Urban Parts of States: Estimates Using the Chandra Sekar-Deming Technique." *Historical Methods*, vol. 13, no. 3 (Summer), pp. 163–9.

David, Paul, and Warren Sanderson. 1986. "Rudimentary Contraceptive Methods and the American Transition to Marital Fertility Control, 1855–1915." In Stanley L. Engerman and Robert E. Gallman, eds., *Long-Term Factors in American Economic Growth*, pp. 307–79. Chicago: University of Chicago Press.

―――. 1987. "The Emergence of a Two-Child Norm among American Birth Controllers." *Population and Development Review*, vol. 13, no. 1 (March), pp. 1–41.

Dubester, Henry J. 1948. *State Censuses: An Annotated Bibliography of Censuses of Population Taken after the Year 1790 by States and Territories of the United States.* (Washington, D.C.: Government Printing Office).

Duffy, John. 1976. *The Healers: A History of American Medicine.* Urbana: University of Illinois Press.

―――. 1990. *The Sanitarians: A History of American Public Health.* Urbana: University of Illinois Press.

Easterlin, Richard A. 1961. "Influences in European Overseas Emigration before World War I." *Economic Development and Cultural Change*, vol. 9 (April), pp. 331–53.

―――. 1968. *Population, Labor Force, and Long Swings in Economic Growth: The American Experience.* Cambridge, Mass.: National Bureau of Economic Research.

―――. 1972. "The American Population." In Lance Davis et al., eds., *American Economic Growth: An Economist's History of the United States.* New York: Harper & Row.

―――. 1976. "Population Change and Farm Settlement in the Northern United States." *Journal of Economic History*, vol. 36, no. 1 (March), pp. 45–75.

―――. 1977. "Population Issues in American Economic History: A Survey and Critique."

In Robert Gallman, ed., *Recent Developments in the Study of Business and Economic History: Essays in Honor of Herman E. Krooss*, pp. 131–58. Greenwich, Conn.: JAI Press.

———. 1996. "The Nature and Causes of Mortality Revolution." In *Growth Triumphant: The Twenty-first Century in Historical Perspective*. Ann Arbor, Mich.: University of Michigan Press.

Easterlin, Richard A., George Alter, and Gretchen Condran. 1978. "Farms and Farm Families in Old and New Areas: The Northern States in 1860." In Tamara K. Hareven and Maris A. Vinovskis, eds., *Family and Population in Nineteenth-Century America*, pp. 22–84. Princeton, N.J.: Princeton University Press.

Ewbank, Douglas C., and Samuel H. Preston. 1990. "Personal Health Behavior and the Decline of Infant and Child Mortality: The United States, 1900–1930." In John Caldwell, et al., ed., *What We Know about Health Transition: The Cultural, Social and Behavioral Determinants of Health*. vol. 1. pp. 116–49. Canberra: Health Transition Centre, Australian National University.

Joseph P. Ferrie. 1999. *Yankeys Now: Immigrants in the Antebellum United States, 1840–1860*, New York: Oxford University Press.

Fogel, Robert W. 1986a. "Nutrition and the Decline in Mortality since 1700: Some Preliminary Findings." In Stanley L. Engerman and Robert E. Gallman, eds., *Long-Term Factors in American Economic Growth*, pp. 439–555. Chicago: University of Chicago Press.

———. 1986b. "Nutrition and the Decline in Mortality since 1700: Some Additional Preliminary Findings." National Bureau of Economic Research, Working Paper No. 1802, (January).

Forster, Colin, and G. S. L. Tucker. 1972. *Economic Opportunity and Whiter American Fertility Ratios, 1800–1860*. New Haven, Conn.: Yale University Press.

Galenson, David W., and Clayne L. Pope. 1989. "Economic and Geographic Mobility on the Farming Frontier: Evidence from Appanoose County, Iowa, 1850–1870." *Journal of Economic History*, vol. 49, no. 3 (September), pp. 635–56.

———. 1992. "Precedence and Wealth: Evidence from Nineteenth-Century Utah." In Claudia Goldin and Hugh Rockoff, eds., *Strategic Factors in Nineteenth Century American Economic History: A Volume to Honor Robert W. Fogel*, pp. 225–42. Chicago: University of Chicago Press.

Galishoff, Stuart. 1980. "Triumph and Failure: The American Response to the Urban Water Supply Problem, 1860–1923." In Martin V. Melosi, ed., *Pollution and Reform in American Cities, 1870–1930*, pp. 35–57. Austin: University of Texas Press.

Gemery, Henry A. 1984. "European Emigration to North America, 1700–1820: Numbers and Quasi-Numbers." *Perspectives in American History*, n.s. I, pp. 283–342. New York: Cambridge University Press.

Glover, James W. 1921. *United States Life Tables, 1890, 1901, 1910, and 1901–1910*. Washington, D.C.: Government Printing Office.

Gould, J. D. 1979. "European Inter-Continental Emigration, 1815–1914: Patterns and Causes." *Journal of European Economic History*, vol. 8, no. 3 (Winter), pp. 593–679.

———. 1980. "European Inter-Continental Emigration. The Road Home: Return Migration from the U.S.A." *Journal of European Economic History*, vol. 9, no. 1 (Spring), pp. 41–112.

————. 1980. "European Inter-Continental Emigration: The Role of 'Diffusion' and 'Feedback.'" *Journal of European Economic History*, vol. 9, no. 2 (Fall), pp. 267–315.

Grabill, Wilson H., Clyde Kiser, and Pascal K. Whelpton. 1958. *The Fertility of American Women*. New York: Wiley.

Guest, Avery M. 1981. "Social Structure and U.S. Inter-state Fertility Differentials in 1900." *Demography*, vol. 18, no. 4 (November), pp. 465–86.

————. 1987. "Notes from the National Panel Study: Linkage and Migration in the Late Nineteenth Century." *Historical Methods*, vol. 20, no. 2 (Spring), pp. 63–77.

Guest, Avery M., Nancy S. Landale, and James McCann. 1992. "Intergenerational Occupational Mobility in the Late Nineteenth Century United States." Unpublished paper.

Haines, Michael R. 1977. "Mortality in Nineteenth-Century America: Estimates from New York and Pennsylvania Census Data, 1865 and 1900." *Demography*, vol. 14, no. 3 (August), pp. 311–31.

————. 1979. *Fertility and Occupation: Population Patterns in Industrialization*. New York: Academic Press.

————. 1979. "The Use of Model Life Tables to Estimate Mortality for the United States in the Late Nineteenth Century." *Demography*, vol. 16, no. 2 (May), pp. 289–312.

————. 1987. "Economic History and Historical Demography." In Alexander J. Field, ed., *The Future of Economic History*, pp. 185–253. Boston: Kluwer-Nijhoff.

————. 1989. "American Fertility in Transition: New Estimates of Birth Rates in the United States, 1900–1910." *Demography*, vol. 26, no. 1 (February), pp. 137–48.

————. 1990. "Western Fertility in Mid-Transition: A Comparison of the United States and Selected Nations at the Turn of the Century." *Journal of Family History*, vol. 15, no. 1 (March), pp. 21–46.

————. 1992. "Occupation and Social Class during Fertility Decline: Historical Perspectives." In John R. Gillis, Louise A. Tilly, and David Levine, eds., *The European Experience of Declining Fertility: 1850–1970*, pp. 193–226. Oxford: Blackwell.

————. 1996. "Long Term Marriage Patterns in the United States from Colonial Times to the Present." *The History of the Family: An International Quarterly*, vol. 1, no. 1, pp. 15–39.

————. 1998. "Health, Height, Nutrition, and Mortality: Evidence on the 'Antebellum Puzzle' from Union Army Recruits for New York State and the United States." In John Komlos and Joerg Baten, eds., *The Biological Standard of Living in Comparative Perspective*, pp. 155–80. Stuttgart: Franz Steiner Verlag.

————. 1998. "Estimated Life Tables for the United States, 1850–1910." *Historical Methods*, vol. 31, no. 4 (Fall), pp. 149–69.

Haines, Michael R., and Barbara A. Anderson. 1988. "New Demographic History of the Late 19th-Century United States." *Explorations in Economic History*, vol. 25, no. 4 (October), pp. 341–65.

Hareven, Tamara K., and Maris A. Vinovskis. 1975. "Marital Fertility, Ethnicity, and Occupation in Urban Families: An Analysis of South Boston and the South End in 1880." *Journal of Social History*, vol. 8, pp. 69–93.

Hatton, Timothy J., and Jeffrey J. Williamson. 1992. "What Drove the Mass Migrations from Europe in the Late Nineteenth Century?" Working Paper Series on Historical

Factors in Long Run Growth, no. 43. Cambridge, Mass.: National Bureau of Economic Research (November).

Higgs, Robert. 1973. "Mortality in Rural America, 1870–1920: Estimates and Conjectures." *Explorations in Economic History*, vol. 10, no. 2 (Winter), pp. 177–95.

————. 1979. "Cycles and Trends of Mortality in 18 Large American Cities, 1871–1900." *Explorations in Economic History*, vol. 16, no. 4 (October), pp. 381–408.

Hutchinson, E. P. 1981. *Legislative History of American Immigration Policy, 1798–1965.* Philadelphia: University of Pennsylvania Press.

Jacobson, Paul H. 1957. "An Estimate of the Expectation of Life in the United States in 1850." *Milbank Memorial Fund Quarterly*, vol. 35, no. 2 (April), pp. 197–201.

Jones, Malwyn Allen. 1992. *American Immigration.* 2d ed. Chicago: University of Chicago Press.

Kaelble, Hartmut. 1981. *Historical Research on Social Mobility: Western Europe and the USA in the Nineteenth and Twentieth Centuries.* New York: Columbia University Press.

Knodel, John E. 1974. *The Decline of Fertility in Germany, 1871–1939.* Princeton, N.J.: Princeton University Press.

Komlos, John. 1987. "The Height and Weight of West Point Cadets: Dietary Change in Antebellum America." *Journal of Economic History*, vol. 47, no. 4 (December), pp. 897–927.

————. 1996. "Anomalies in Economic History: Toward a Resolution of the 'Antebellum Puzzle.'" *Journal of Economic History*, vol. 56, no. 1 (March), pp. 202–14.

Kuznets, Simon. 1958. "Long Swings in the Growth of Population and in Related Economic Variables." *Proceedings of the American Philosophical Society*, vol. 102, pp. 25–52.

Leavitt, Judith W. 1979. "Politics and Public Health: Smallpox in Milwaukee, 1894–95." In Susan Reverby and David Rosner, eds., *Health Care in America: Essays in Social History*, pp. 84–101. Philadelphia: Temple University Press.

Lebergott, Stanley. 1966. "Labor Force and Employment, 1800–1960." In *Output, Employment, and Productivity in the United States after 1800*, National Bureau of Economic Research, Studies in Income and Wealth, vol. 30, pp. 117–204. New York: Columbia University Press.

Leet, Donald R. 1976. "The Determinants of Fertility Transition in Antebellum Ohio." *Journal of Economic History*, vol. 36, no. 2 (June), pp. 359–78.

Lockridge, Kenneth. 1966. "The Population of Dedham, Massachusetts, 1636–1736." *Economic History Review*, vol. 19, 2d ser. (August), pp. 324–39.

McClelland, Peter D., and Richard J. Zeckhauser. 1982. *Demographic Dimensions of the New Republic: American Interregional Migration, Vital Statistics, and Manumissions, 1800–1860.* New York: Cambridge University Press.

McCusker, John J., and Russell R. Menard. 1985. *The Economy of British America: 1607–1789.* (Chapel Hill: University of North Carolina Press.

McInnis, Marvin. 1977. "Childbearing and hard Availability: Some Evidence from Individual Household Data." In Ronald Demos Lee, ed., *Population Patterns in the Past*, pp. 201–22. New York: Academic Press.

McKeown, Thomas. 1976. *The Modern Rise of Population.* New York: Academic Press.

Malthus, Thomas Robert. 1798. *An Essay on the Principle of Population.* Edited with and introduction by Antony Flew. Baltimore, Md.: Penguin Books, 1970.

Meeker, Edward. 1972. "The Improving Health of the United States, 1850–1915." *Explorations in Economic History*, vol. 9, no. 4 (Summer). pp. 353–73.

Mitchell, B. R. 1981. *European Historical Statistics, 1750–1975*. 2d rev. ed. New York: Facts on File.

————. 1983. *International Historical Statistics: The Americas and Australasia*. Detroit: Gale Research.

Neal, Larry. 1976. "Cross-spectral Analysis of Long Swings in Atlantic Migration." *Research in Economic History*, vol. 1, pp. 260–97.

Notestein, Frank W. 1953. "The Economics of Population and Food Supplies. I. The Economic Problems of Population Change." In *Proceedings of the Eighth International Conference of Agricultural Economists*. London: Oxford University Press.

Okun, Bernard. 1958. *Trends in Birth Rates in the United States since 1870*. Baltimore: Johns Hopkins University Press.

Omran, Abdel. 1971. "The Epidemiologic Transition: A Theory of the Epidemiology of Population Change." *Milbank Memorial Fund Quarterly*, vol. 49, pt. 1, pp. 509–38.

Osterud, Nancy, and John Fulton. 1976. "Family Limitation and Age at Marriage: Fertility Decline in Sturbridge, Massachusetts, 1730–1850." *Population Studies*, vol. 30, no. 3 (November), pp. 481–94.

Parker, William N., and Robert E. Gallman. 1992. "Southern Farms Study, 1860." In *Guide to Resources and Services, 1992–1993*, p. 116. Ann Arbor, Mich.: Inter-University Consortium for Political and Social Research.

Parkerson, Donald H. 1991. "Comments on the Underenumeration of the U.S. Census, 1850–1880." *Social Science History*, vol. 15, no. 4 (Winter), pp. 509–15.

Pope, Clayne L. 1992. "Adult Mortality in America before 1900: A View from Family Histories." In Claudia Goldin and Hugh Rockoff, eds., *Strategic Factors in Nineteenth Century American Economic History: A Volume to Honor Robert W. Fogel*, pp. 267–96. Chicago: University of Chicago Press.

Preston, Samuel H., and Michael R. Haines. 1991. *Fatal Years: Child Mortality in Late Nineteenth Century America*. Princeton, N.J.: Princeton University Press.

Preston, Samuel H., Nathan Keyfitz, and Robert Schoen. 1972. *Causes of Death: Life Tables for National Populations*. New York: Seminar Press.

Ransom, Roger L., and Richard Sutch. 1989. "Two Strategies for a More Secure Old Age: Life-cycle Saving by Late-Nineteenth Century American Workers." Paper presented at the National Bureau of Economic Research Summer Institute on the Development of the American Economy, Cambridge, Mass. (July).

Rosenberg, Charles E. 1962. *The Cholera Years: The United States in 1832, 1849, and 1866*. Chicago: University of Chicago Press.

Sanderson, Warren C. 1979. "Quantitative Aspects of Marriage, Fertility and Family Limitation in Nineteenth Century America: Another Application of the Coale Specifications." *Demography*, vol. 16, no. 3 (May), pp. 339–58.

Schapiro, Morton Owen. 1986. *Filling Up America: An Economic-Demographic Model of Population Growth and Distribution in the Nineteenth-Century United States*. Greenwich, Conn.: JAI Press.

Shryock, Henry S., Jacob S. Siegel, and Associates. 1971. *The Methods and Materials of Demography*. Washington, D.C.: Government Printing Office.

Sjaastad, Larry. 1962. "The Costs and Returns of Human Migration." *Journal of Political Economy*, vol. 70, no. 5, pt. 2 (October), Supplement, pp. 80–93.

Smith, Adam. 1776. *An Enquiry into the Nature and Causes of the Wealth of Nations*. Edited by Edwin Cannan. New York: Modern Library, 1937.

Social Science History. 1991. vol. 15, no. 4 (Winter).

Spengler, J. J. 1930. "The Fecundity of Native and Foreign-Born Women in New England." *Brookings Institution Pamphlet Series*, no. 2 (1). Washington, D.C.

Starr, Paul. 1982. *The Social Transformation of American Medicine*. New York: Basic Books.

Steckel, Richard. 1982. "The Fertility of American Slaves." *Research in Economic History*, vol. 7, pp. 239–86.

————. 1983. "The Economic Foundations of East-West Migration during the 19th Century." *Explorations in Economic History*, vol. 20, no. 1 (January), pp. 14–36.

————. 1986. "A Dreadful Childhood: Excess Mortality of American Slaves." *Social Science History*, vol. 10, no. 4 (Winter), pp. 427–65.

————. 1986. "A Peculiar Population: The Nutrition, Health, and Mortality of American Slaves from Childhood to Maturity." *Journal of Economic History*, vol. 46, no. 3 (September), pp. 721–41.

————. 1988. "The Health and Mortality of Women and Children, 1850–1860." *Journal of Economic History*, vol. 48, no. 2 (June), pp. 333–45.

————. 1989. "Household Migration and Rural Settlement in the United States, 1850–1860." *Explorations in Economic History*, vol. 26, no. 2 (April), pp. 190–218.

————. 1991. "The Quality of Census Data for Historical Inquiry: A Research Agenda." *Social Science History*, vol. 15, no. 4 (Winter), pp. 579–99.

————. 1992. "The Fertility Transition in the United States: Tests of Alternative Hypotheses." In Claudia Goldin and Hugh Rockoff, eds., *Strategic Factors in Nineteenth Century American Economic History*, pp. 351–75. Chicago: University of Chicago Press.

————. 1992. "Stature and Living Standards in the United States." In Robert E. Gallman and John Joseph Wallis, eds., *American Economic Growth and Standards of Living before the Civil War*, pp. 265–308. Chicago: University of Chicago Press.

Stilgoe, John R. 1988. *Borderland: Origins of the American Suburb, 1820–1939*. New Haven, Conn.: Yale University Press.

Sundstrom, William A., and Paul A. David. 1988. "Old-Age Security Motives, Labor Markets, and Farm Family Fertility in Antebellum America." *Explorations in Economic History*, vol. 25, no. 2 (April), pp. 164–97.

Taeuber, Conrad, and Irene B. Taeuber. 1958. *The Changing Population of the United States*. New York: Wiley.

Taylor, George Rogers. 1961. *The Transportation Revolution 1815–1860*. New York: Holt, Rinehart and Winston.

Teitelbaum, Michael S. 1984. *The British Fertility Decline: Demographic Transition in the Crucible of the Industrial Revolution*. Princeton, N.J.: Princeton University Press.

Temkin-Greener, H., and A. C. Swedlund. 1978. "Fertility Transition in the Connecticut Valley: 1740–1850." *Population Studies*, vol. 32 no. 1 (March), pp. 27–41.

Thernstrom, Stephen. 1964. *Poverty and Progress: Social Mobility in a Nineteenth Century City*. Cambridge, Mass.: Harvard University Press.

————. 1973. *The Other Bostonians: Poverty and Progress in the American Metropolis, 1880–1970.* Cambridge, Mass.: Harvard University Press.

Thompson, Warren S., and P. K. Whelpton. 1933. *Population Trends in the United States.* New York: McGraw-Hill.

Turner, Frederick Jackson. 1893. "The Significance of the Frontier in American History." Paper read at the meeting of the American Historical Association, Chicago (July 12).

U.S. Bureau of the Census. 1972. *U.S. Census of Population, 1970.* vol. 1, pt. 1. Washington, D.C.: Government Printing Office.

————. 1975. *Historical Statistics of the United States from Colonial Times to 1970.* Washington, D.C.: Government Printing Office.

————. 1992. *Statistical Abstract of the United States, 1992.* Washington, D.C.: Government Printing Office.

Uselding, Paul. 1976. "In Dispraise of Muckrakers: United States Occupational Mortality, 1890–1910." *Research in Economic History*, vol. 1, pp. 334–71.

Vinovskis, Maris A. 1972. "Mortality Rates and Trends in Massachusetts before 1860." *Journal of Economic History*, vol. 32, no. 1 (March), pp. 184–213.

————. 1976. "Socioeconomic Determinants of Interstate Fertility Differentials in the United States in 1850 and 1860." *Journal of Interdisciplinary History*, vol. 6, no. 3 (Winter), pp. 375–96.

————. 1978. "The Jacobson Life Table of 1850: A Critical Reexamination from a Massachusetts Perspective." *Journal of Interdisciplinary History*, vol. 8, no. 4 (Spring), pp. 703–24.

————. 1979. "Recent Trends in American Historical Demography." In Maris A. Vinovskis, ed., *Studies in American Historical Demography*, pp. 1–25. New York: Academic Press.

————, ed. 1979. *Studies in American Historical Demography.* New York: Academic Press.

————. 1981. *Fertility in Massachusetts from the Revolution to the Civil War.* New York: Academic Press.

Wahl, Jenny Bourne. 1986. "New Results on the Decline in Household Fertility in the United States from 1750 to 1900." In Stanley Engerman and Robert Gallman, eds., *Long Term Factors in American Economic Growth*, pp. 391–425. Chicago: University of Chicago Press.

————. 1992. "Trading Quantity for Quality: Explaining the Decline in American Fertility in the Nineteenth Century." In Claudia Goldin and Hugh Rockoff, eds., *Strategic Factors in Nineteenth Century American Economic History*, pp. 375–97. Chicago: University of Chicago Press.

Weber, Adna F. 1899. *The Growth of Cities in the 19th Century: A Study in Statistics.* New York: Macmillan.

Weiss, Thomas. 1992. "U.S. Labor Force Estimates and Economic Growth, 1800–1860." In Robert E. Gallman and John Joseph Wallis, eds., *American Economic Growth and Standards of Living before the Civil War*, pp. 19–75. Chicago: University of Chicago Press.

Wells, Robert V. 1971. "Family Size and Fertility Control in Eighteenth-Century America: A Study of Quaker Families." *Population Studies*, vol. 25, no. 1 (March), pp. 73–82.

————. 1975. *The Population of the British Colonies in America before 1776.* Princeton, N.J.: Princeton University Press.

————. 1985. *Uncle Sam's Family: Issues in and Perspectives on American Demographic History*. Albany, N.Y.: State University of New York Press.

Whipple, George E. 1921. "Fifty Years of Water Purification." In M. P. Ravenel, ed., *A Half Century of Public Health*, pp. 161–80. New York: American Public Health Association.

Willigan, J. Dennis, and Katherine A. Lynch. 1982. *Sources and Methods of Historical Demography*. New York: Academic Press.

Yasuba, Yasukichi. 1962. *Birth Rates of the White Population of the United States, 1800–1860: An Economic Analysis*. Baltimore: Johns Hopkins University Press.

9

THE POPULATION OF CANADA IN THE NINETEENTH CENTURY

MARVIN MCINNIS

THE BROAD CONTOURS OF CANADIAN POPULATION HISTORY

To appreciate the main outlines of growth and change in Canada's population over the course of the nineteenth century it is necessary to go back almost to the middle of the preceding century, to 1761. That marks the transition from French to British rule in Quebec and the beginning of a complex of important changes. The formal recognition of British rule came with the Peace of Paris in 1763. The fortress of Louisburg had fallen in 1758 and Quebec the following year. By 1761 what was to become Canada was in British hands, and in 1762 the new regime took a census as a sort of inventory of what it had acquired. The year 1761 ties in well with the later practice of taking censuses every decade, on years ending in one, so it makes a reasonable starting date. Long before that, of course, the British had taken possession of the colony of Nova Scotia, but 1761 marked a time of important demographic change there as well. Newfoundland was the oldest British colony in America but became a part of Canada only in the twentieth century. Hence it is left out of this account of nineteenth-century Canada.

The 140 years of population change examined in this chapter encompass a very long nineteenth century that falls into three broad periods. From 1761 to the war of 1812–14 the population of the British North American colonies was augmented largely by immigration, initial settlements in many areas, coupled with an exceptionally high rate of natural increase. The immigrants were mainly from other parts of North America, although in the later years of the period the beginnings were made in the influx from Britain. Hostilities with the United States brought about a rupture in the ongoing migration from that country to Canada. With the resumption of peace in 1815, both on the North American continent and in Europe, where Britain's long war with France finally came to an end, a period of heavy migration from Britain to Canada ensued. This reached its peak in the 1830s and 1840s but continued into the early 1850s. In this period immigration was again the dominant force shaping the Canadian population, but its source was different from that of the preceding period, and it was "high-powered immigration," in the sense that people were moving from Britain into a Canadian setting where the rate of natural increase of population was exceptionally high. The earliest groups of immigrants multiplied rapidly. A question of particular interest would be whether there is any indication of a fall in the rate of natural increase before about 1861. It is a question that cannot yet be answered. In the last decades of the nineteenth century, after 1861, the situation changed dramatically, and Canada became a country of massive emigration. In that same period the fertility transition got well under way. The one feature of population change in nineteenth-century Canada about which little can be said is the course of mortality. Until the very end of the century the evidence on death rates is very sketchy.

Table 9.1 presents an initial overview of Canada's population over the whole period. Details of sources and reliability are discussed in the next section. For the present, it should merely be noted that these are estimates of the European population of Canada at the dates shown. The enumerated aboriginal population has been removed from census figures, and no attempt has been made to estimate its totals at the various dates. Groupings of colonies are shown for convenience at this juncture. Individual colonial and provincial figures are given in later tables. The totals shown here differ from those in other sources for two reasons. One is that for the years prior to the first general census in 1851 the figures are estimates, often based on censuses or other enumerations but not necessarily for the precise years shown, and these are fresh estimates made for this study. The figures for some of the earliest years differ from other widely cited estimates. The focus on the European population, with no attempt to include estimates of the numbers of the aboriginal population, is the main source of differences in later decades. The conventionally used census totals for the late nineteenth century include discontinuous jumps from one decade to the next as new regions were added to the country and ambiguously estimated, but they incorporated only small numbers of aboriginal peoples. In the

Table 9.1. *Population of Canada and its regions, 1761–1901,*
European population only (thousands)

Year	Total	Maritimes	Ontario And Quebec[a]	West[b]
1761	75.9	11.2	64.7	—
1771	102.4	20.5	81.9	—
1781	133.7	23.7	110.0	—
1791	216.5	51.5	165.0	—
1801	332.5	86.5	246.0	—
1811	511.2	135.2	376.0	—
1821	722.0	183.0	537.0	2.0
1831	1,076.4	262.0	812.0	2.4
1841	1,629.8	423.0	1,202.0	4.8
1851	2,367.0	533.0	1,829.0	5.0
1861	3,175.0	660.5	2,495.0	19.5
1871	3,583.8	764.0	2,792.0	27.8
1881	4,216.0	867.0	3,263.0	86.0
1891	4,740.0	878.0	3,583.0	279.0
1901	5,278.0	891.0	3,803.0	584.0

[a] "Ontario and Quebec" refers to the old colony of Canada prior to 1867.
[b] West is initially only the Red River colony in Manitoba but from 1861 onward includes all of the Northwest Territories and British Columbia.

first period to be examined, 1761 to 1811, the population of what eventually would become Canada grew at an average annual rate of 3.9%. Immigration continued at a high level in the subsequent period, 1811 to 1861, when the average annual rate of growth was 3.7%. In the final 40 years of the nineteenth century, a period of emigration and falling birth rates, the rate of growth dropped to a low average of 1.3% per annum.

POPULATION IN THE FOUNDATION PERIOD: 1761–1811

When Britain assumed control over the French colony of Quebec, it acquired a French-speaking, Roman Catholic population that in 1761 amounted to about 65,000. This was a small colony in comparison with the British North American colonies to the south. The difference in size of population had been established very early. The British colonies of

Massachusetts and Virginia had received a large influx of population shortly after they had been established. Quebec, which had been established at the same time, had fewer than 1,000 people in 1650. It was still little more than a trading post. Over the whole of the French regime hardly any more than 10,000 people came from France to settle permanently in Quebec. Those few people multiplied at a legendarily high rate, yet their number amounted to only about 65,000 in 1761.

At the time they acquired Quebec, the British already controlled Nova Scotia. That colony also included a small French population – the Acadians. In the middle of the eighteenth century the British took steps to settle Nova Scotia in a way that would provide a counterbalance to the Acadians. The port city of Halifax was established, and a group of German Protestants was installed further south along the Atlantic shore at Lunenburg. In the years just before 1761, with the outbreak of hostilities with France, the British authorities rounded up and shipped out the Acadians. That was done between 1755 and 1760, so estimates of the population in 1761 are highly variable, depending upon just what account is taken of the Acadians. Some evaded the British authorities, mainly by fleeing to areas that would later become New Brunswick and Prince Edward Island. As early as 1761 some others had made their way back to Nova Scotia. The count of the Acadians is the most indeterminate element of the 1761 population estimate. The decade following 1761 was one of sharp change in the population of the Maritime area. Immediately upon the evacuation of good farmland by the Acadians, several thousand immigrants from the New England colonies arrived, augmented by a smaller number from England and Ireland. Acadians continued to find their way back to the area, if not to the actual lands from which they had been forcibly removed. This set a pattern of population change in the region that would be dominated by migratory movements over the next few decades.

In the Quebec colony, the "Canada" of the time, the population continued to grow at a high rate of natural increase, but for the first couple of decades after 1761 migration into and out of the colony was numerically not very important. Only a small number of French returned to their motherland with the assumption of rule by the British, and little more than a handful of British moved in. The latter included a few merchants and some soldiers from disbanded regiments. Probably the largest group of immigrants at this time comprised refugee Acadians.

The really momentous change came with the American War of Independence. Both regions of Canada became home to refugees loyal to the British crown. About 40,000 Loyalists sought refuge in Canada, mainly in 1784 and immediately thereafter. About three-quarters of the Loyalists settled in Nova Scotia, almost ten thousand of those on the western side of the Bay of Fundy, along Passamaquoddy Bay, and in the valley of the Saint John River. This area was quickly organized as a separate colony under the name of New Brunswick. Virtually no Loyalists settled on Prince Edward Island. It had been made into a separate colony in 1767 and the whole of the land granted out to a small number of British absentee landowners. The occupants of the island were the Acadians who had fled there at the time of the expulsion, at least those who had not later been rounded up and shipped out. The largest number of Loyalists, however, settled in Nova Scotia itself. Among them was a small black population that would later be augmented by Maroons from Jamaica, former slaves who had carried on a guerrilla war against the British, and Potomac plantation slaves liberated in the War of 1812. The numbers of blacks were thinned by emigration to west Africa, but enough remained to establish a black community that gave distinction to Nova Scotia as the one district of Canada with a black population of long standing. The loyalist influx more than doubled the population of Nova Scotia besides providing a founding population for New Brunswick to augment greatly the French Acadians and the small number of New Englanders who had made up the 1781 population of that region.

The number of Loyalists who made their way to the Quebec colony was considerably smaller. Most settled, or one should perhaps say were settled by design, in the region to the west of the seigneuries of Quebec. The bulk of this population was located along the north bank of the St. Lawrence River, from its origin in Lake Ontario to the seigneuries just upstream from Montreal. A few had settled prior to 1784 along the Niagara frontier, and an even smaller number ended up in the far west, where they augmented the only preexisting European population in the area that would eventually become Ontario, the small French settlement of Detroit. The inflow of population continued from the newly independent United States for many years. Some of the people involved were of Loyalist sympathy or relatives of earlier Loyalist settlers, but many were merely attracted by the availability of good agricultural land on favorable terms. On the one hand, the British authorities were eager to place settlers on the land and in many cases offered free grants of land; on the other hand, until Jay's Treaty of 1794, it was not entirely clear where the border was going to be placed so that some of the movement might be looked upon as simply Americans going west. By 1791 the population to the west of Quebec was large enough, and certainly differentiated enough, to succeed in making the case for the establishment of a separate colony. It was designated Upper Canada, and the older colony downstream was renamed Lower Canada. The best available evidence indicates that the 1791 population of Upper Canada consisted of a mere 14,000 English-speaking individuals, almost all originating in what had come to be designated the United States. Lower Canada, with about 150,000 people, was by far the larger colony. Despite the arrival of a small number of Loyalists and a few land-seekers from the United States, its French-speaking, Roman Catholic population remained essentially undiluted.[1]

A brief account should be taken of the aboriginal population. Only a small number resided in the settled area of Lower Canada. Most of these were Indians converted to Christianity who had moved into a few locations that were essentially church missions. To the north was an indeterminate smattering of aboriginal people in a land that supported only a very few in a traditional way of life. Upper Canada had a small aboriginal population, partly as a consequence of earlier wars among the Indian tribes that had left the area to a considerable extent depopulated. After 1784 the Indian population was more than doubled by the arrival of tribes loyal to Britain in the American Revolution, predominantly Mohawks, who were settled as refugees on generous land grants. One reason Upper Canada attracted American settlers at this time was that "the Indian problem" had been resolved there. People could settle on land that had been acquired through treaty by the British Crown, and there was essentially no danger of violent conflict with an indigenous Indian population.

From the time of the initial influx of the Loyalists through a period of continued in-migration from the United States up until the outbreak of hostilities between the United States and Britain in 1812, population growth in Upper Canada was to a great extent a matter of immigration. By 1811 the population of Upper Canada had reached about 60,000, and settlement stretched in a thin band almost continuously from the eastern border with Lower Canada, along the St. Lawrence River and the shores

---

[1] The details of early settlement, both of the Loyalists and those who followed shortly behind, have been extensively written about in the Canadian historical literature. A good compendium of much of that detail is Macdonald, *Canada, 1763–1841, Immigration and Settlement*.

of lakes Ontario and Erie, to the St. Clair River, which formed the boundary with the United States on the west. There had in this time been almost no immigration from Great Britain. One exception was the small group of Scottish Highlanders who arrived in 1804 to settle Glengarry County, the easternmost district of Upper Canada, on the boundary with Lower Canada.

A much smaller number of Loyalists and other settlers from the United States had moved into Lower Canada. Districts immediately adjoining the United States along the Richelieu River and further east, in what would become Brome and Stanstead Counties, attracted Anglophone Americans. Those areas, Stanstead especially, would evolve almost as outposts of New England. The urban centers – Quebec, which was the international seaport of the country, and Montreal, which was rising as a commercial center – attracted most of the relatively small number of immigrants from Britain who came at this time.

Further east, in the Maritime colonies, the situation was quite different. Immigration was the dominant element in population growth; but, after the initial influx of Loyalists, there was little further inflow from the United States. There, immigration from Britain became important before it had any impact on the colony of Canada. Both Nova Scotia and Prince Edward Island were greatly affected by the outpouring of population from the Scottish Highlands that got under way in the late years of the eighteenth century. An early beginning, prior to the arrival of the Loyalists, had come in 1774 with the arrival of a shipload of Scottish Highlanders at Pictou, Nova Scotia. The big influx from Scotland, however, got under way in the 1790s. A rough calculation suggests that between 1791 and 1811, as many as 16,000 to 18,000 immigrants may have arrived in Nova Scotia in this period, mostly Scottish Highlanders. In the same period, but primarily in the earlier part of it, probably an additional two and a half thousand arrived in Prince Edward Island.

The New Brunswick colony received little immigration in the 1790s, but in the following decade circumstances changed markedly. British policy directed that its imports of squared pine timber come from its colonies in North America rather than its traditional area of supply in the Baltic. New Brunswick, with abundant resources of pine forest, was the first to feel the impact of this policy-induced change. People quickly followed the lumbering activity; and in the first decade of the nineteenth century, but especially after 1808, immigrants from Britain flocked in to exploit the forest resource. This was the second discontinuous boost to New Brunswick's population, the first being the arrival of the Loyalists.

Migration to Canada, and especially the movement of settlers from the United States, was abruptly halted by the outbreak of war between the United States and Britain in 1812 and the invasion of Canada by the United States. That event marked an important redirection of Canadian population development.

IMMIGRATION, NATURAL INCREASE, AND THE DYNAMICS OF CANADIAN POPULATION CHANGE, 1815–1861

With the end of hostilities between the United States and British North America in 1815, population growth in Canada continued to be augmented greatly by immigration but from a different source. In the 1784–1815 period reviewed in the previous section the main source of immigrants to Canada had been other regions of North America. Admittedly, that had been supplemented in the Maritime colonies by a rising influx from Britain. In the old colony of Canada, however, the main source of immigrants at the beginning of the nineteenth century had been the United States, but after a war during which Canada was invaded by the United States and there was great concern on the part of the British authorities for the loyalty of settlers in Canada, that was to be no more. A small number of Americans continued to move into the colony but, officially, they were not welcome. Rapid settlement by loyal British subjects was a primary aim of the ruling authorities. Fortunately, a new supply of emigrants from Britain was found.

In Britain, the immediate aftermath of the cessation of war with France was depressed economic conditions and widespread unemployment. At least some Britons sought to emigrate, and the North American colonies, with large areas of unsettled land, were the most obvious destinations. For the next 40 years Britain would be the source of immigrants to Canada. Canada's population would continue to grow largely through immigration, but from a new direction.

The inflow began slowly in 1816 and 1817, then rose to a peak of more than 20,000 in 1819. Thereafter it fluctuated greatly over the 40-year period. A few immigrants continued to come from the United States, but their numbers are hardly discernible. The main story is the influx from Britain. All histories of Canada give a prominent place to this great inflow, which had much to do with establishing the essential character of Canada and its population. Certainly it is a story worth telling, but we should guard against overemphasizing immigration as an element of Canada's demographic evolution. Natural increase was proceeding at a high rate. We can only guess how high, but if the rate of natural increase averaged 3% per annum, which would be commensurate with a birth rate of about 50 and a death rate of about 20, the 511,000 people estimated to be living in Canada in 1811 would have increased through natural increase alone to 2,241,000 in 1861. That is 84% of the 3,175,000 enumerated in the census of that year. By inference, rapid natural increase, of the sort emphasized by Benjamin Franklin, had to be the really predominant source of Canadian population growth.

There is relatively little hard evidence on Canada's population growth over the period from 1815, at the end of the War of 1812–14, to 1861, on the eve of Canadian Confederation. Population totals are conjectural and not based on reasonably firm census enumerations until the end of the period. As for the rate of natural increase, best it might be assumed that such increase was taking place at the same rate as inferred below for the decade of the 1850s, keeping in mind that even that is based on rather conjectural evidence. Broadly, however, it might be hypothesized that prior to 1860 any decline that might have occurred in the birth rate would have been offset by an increase in the death rate as the influx of immigrants brought episodes of disease – cholera and emigrant fever.

Although there are some data on immigration, even they are rather suspect and for the most part overstated. They include a statistical series for emigration from the United Kingdom with British North America as the declared destination from 1815 onward. In 1828 the British government appointed an immigration agent for the port of Quebec, where the great majority of migrants to Canada would arrive, and from 1829 his annual reports were published. These two series have been widely referred to in past studies and are most conveniently assembled in the monograph by Helen Cowan and are reproduced here as columns 1 and 2 of Table 9.2.[2] The series of arrivals at Quebec has been reduced by the small number of immigrants to Quebec originating in the Maritime colonies. Left out of the count are immigrants who landed at ports in the Maritime colonies,

---

[2] Cowan, *British Immigration to British North America.*

Table 9.2. *Emigration from the United Kingdom to Canada and immigration to Canada, 1815–1860*

Year	Emigration, United Kingdom to Canada[a]	Immigrant arrivals at Quebec[b]	Revised, retained immigrants[c]
1815	680	n.a.	n.a.
1816	3,370		
1817	9,979		
1818	15,136		
1819	23,534		
1820	17,921		
1821	12,995		
1822	16,018		
1823	11,355		
1824	8,774		
1825	8,741		
1826	12,818		
1827	12,648		
1828	12,084		
1829	13,307	15,822	15,822
1830	30,574	27,549	24,189
1831	58,067	49,830	43,226
1832	66,339	51,200	44,654[d]
1833	28,808	21,407	19,776
1834	40,060	30,596	28,311[d]
1835	15,573	12,302	11,905
1836	34,226	27,487	25,499
1837	29,884	21,627	18,342
1838	4,577	2,993	2,993
1839	12,658	7,184	5,389
1840	32,293	22,002	18,482
1841	38,164	27,846	22,846
1842	54,123	43,818	37,903
1843	23,518	21,233	19,233
1844	22,924	19,925	17,925
1845	31,803	25,215	21,181
1846	43,439	32,753	25,153
1847	109,860	89,562[e]	54,562[f]
1848	31,065	27,097	19,742
1849	41,367	37,526	28,749
1850	32,961	31,591	18,224
1851	42,605	39,970	21,409
1852	32,873	37,992	24,695
1853	34,522	36,203	23,532
1854	43,761	52,326	32,442

Table 9.2. *(cont.)*

Year	Emigration, United Kingdom to Canada[a]	Immigrant arrivals at Quebec[b]	Revised, retained immigrants[c]
1855	17,966	20,583	15,083
1856	16,378	22,178	12,826
1857	21,001	32,073	22,748
1858	9,704	12,596	11,371
1859	6,689	8,778	4,643
1860	9,786	6,276	6,276

n.a. Cannot be calculated.

[a] Emigrant embarkations destined for British North America from U.K. ports (Cowan, *British Immigration to North America*).

[b] Immigrant arrivals at Quebec, net of arrivals from the Maritime colonies (Cowan, *British Immigration to North America*).

[c] Revised series of immigrant arrivals in Canada, net of immigration agent Buchanan's estimate of immediate departures to the United States, prepared for this chapter.

[d] Also net of Buchanan's estimate of cholera deaths.

[e] Arrivals in 1847 were not reported by Buchanan since he was incapacitated with emigrant fever. Cowan substituted data from the U.K. records relating to departures.

[f] Cowan's arrival estimate net of subagent Hawke's estimate of the number of immigrants going directly on to the United States and also net of 16,000 deaths at the ports from emigrant fever.

especially Saint John in New Brunswick.[3] It is widely recognized, however, that many immigrants to Canada quickly moved on to the United States. The "immigrant arrivals" series therefore overstates actual immigration to Canada.[4] Buchanan, the agent at Quebec, provided an estimate in almost

---

[3] These would be included in the number of emigrants departing from Britain for the North American colonies, which is the only available series for years prior to 1829. Direct migration to the Maritime colonies was most important in that early period. After 1830 Quebec greatly predominated as a destination. Saint John was by far the most important of the Maritime colony destinations. Surprisingly small numbers appear to have arrived at Halifax, and even smaller numbers came into Prince Edward Island and the Miramichi ports of New Brunswick. By the 1830s and later, the commentaries usually indicate that a high fraction of immigrants arriving at the Maritime ports, especially Saint John, were believed to have moved on to the United States. Two points of detail should be added here. One is that the arrivals series is stated to be a count of steerage passengers only, in common with immigration data for the United States. In fact, that definition was not consistently followed. A reexamination of the original reports shows that in some years cabin passengers are included in the reported figure. A more thorough housekeeping of this data source is needed. A second point is that the internal evidence of the immigration agent's reports makes clear that the arrivals from the Maritime colonies that have been deducted are indeed persons born in those colonies and not simply immigrants transshipping from Halifax and Saint John.

[4] By the late 1850s, when the railway through to the western United States from Quebec had been completed, many immigrants arriving at Quebec were known to be ticketed to U.S. destina-

every one of his annual reports of the numbers moving on to the United States. He makes clear that these are fairly crude estimates, although they are not simply a constant adjustment factor. The proportion of arrivals that he claims went on to the United States varies widely from year to year. Buchanan was well informed, on the scene, and continuously observing the situation.[5] It makes good sense to take his estimates at face value and reduce the immigration numbers accordingly, especially since what is left is almost certainly still an overstatement. Some portion of the immigrants initially taking employment or settling on land in Canada would have moved on shortly to the United States as well. The immigration numbers should also be reduced by the number of deaths at the port of arrival in those few years when that number was large. One final point should be made about the considerable upward bias in the commonly used series of arrivals at Quebec. In the year of peak immigration, the famine migration year 1847, there was no count of arrivals at Quebec. Buchanan, the agent at Quebec, had fallen prey to the emigrant fever, and the data collection system broke down. Cowan substitutes a number based on British departure data, but that is inconsistent with the rest of the series. At that time the emigrants bound for British North America counted on the British side of the Atlantic, always outnumbered the arrivals counted at Quebec, often by a considerable margin, as can be seen by comparing columns 1 and 2 of Table 9.2. At the very least, one should deduct the estimated 16,000 stated to have died on the voyage. A revised series of immigration, net of deaths en route and, primarily, of departures to the United States, but augmented by immigrant arrivals at ports in the Maritime colonies, is presented in column 3 of Table 9.2.

Until 1829 the only statistics available about the movement of people to Canada are the British data on emigration. That is probably not too serious a problem since in those years migration was still at a fairly low level, and the British colonies in North America were the preferred destination of British emigrants. Canada was receiving more immigrants than the United States. Transatlantic migrants came almost entirely from Britain and to some degree loyalty to the British Crown still counted. The main reason, though, is that in these early years many of the migrants came as organized groups, sponsored and subsidized by the British government. Government-planned and financed emigration schemes were

tions. These arrivals, identified as "passengers," were counted in a separate series and not included in the conventional Canadian immigration series. It is only by 1860 that this separation is clearly made in the annual reports on immigration.

[5] The details of his weekly reports indicate that Buchanan questioned newcomers ship by ship about their destination intentions and that his annual reports were aggregated from these weekly notes.

looked upon partly as a way of relieving the economic distress that followed the end of the Napoleonic Wars, but they were also intended deliberately to place settlers on the land in Canada so as to preempt a takeover by the United States. These government-planned settlements were discontinued in 1825. Throughout this early period, however, many emigrants were sponsored by local associations and in some cases the large landowners. No careful estimate has been made of the total of sponsored emigration, so it is not possible to say what proportion of this early surge of immigration was of that sort. In the peak years of 1818 to 1820 there were certainly many immigrants who came on their own accord. It was not all a matter of subsidized migration.[6]

After the peak in 1819, the inflow of immigrants declined to a low level in the middle of the decade. Economic conditions had improved in Britain, and farming in Canada was looking less promising. Emigrants from Britain came to Canada essentially to acquire land and to farm. There were few other economic attractions. A question of some importance concerns what made farming in Canada an attractive proposition. Canadian economic historians have made much use of a "staples" framework in which wheat produced for export to Britain acted as an engine of growth in the economy.[7] The implication is that farming in Canada was attractive because wheat could be grown for export to Britain, but the importance of the wheat staple has recently been disputed.[8] The alternative view is that the largely self-sufficient, mixed farming in Canada offered a higher level of income than many people could expect to earn in Britain. That would be true, of course, only after a period of eking out a living on a forested frontier while investing in the clearing and development of a farm. Canadians had exported wheat and wheat flour to Britain in the years of high prices during the Napoleonic Wars. The wheat staple continued to give promise in the years immediately following; and in 1818 exports were large and the price of wheat in Canada was profitably high. A case can be made that the upsurge in immigration was a response to the promise of a staple export in wheat. There was pull on the Canadian side as well as push from the British side in those years. But conditions changed rapidly. The price of wheat fell sharply in both Britain and Canada in 1819, and

---

[6] One of the largest groups, 2,000 Irish in a movement directed under government auspices by Peter Robinson, came in 1825 when emigration had dropped to a low level. That particular group comprised a little more than one-fifth of the total immigration of that year.

[7] Classic statements of this interpretation are to be found in Innis, "An Introduction to the Economic History of Ontario"; Mackintosh, "Economic Factors in Canadian History"; and, more recently, McCallum, *Unequal Beginnings*.

[8] See, in particular, McInnis, "The Early Ontario Wheat Staple Reconsidered"; and McCalla, *Planting the Province*, chap. 5.

exports from Canada ceased to be profitable. By 1822 the exclusionary provision of the British Corn Law had been invoked, and no grain could be imported to Britain. For three years, from 1822 through 1824, Canadian exports were barred from the British market. By the mid-1820s farming in Canada to produce wheat for export to Britain no longer appeared to be an attractive proposition. Immigration fell to a low level. The profitability of the wheat staple was reestablished by 1830, at a time when Britain again was experiencing rural distress.

Immigration to Canada turned up sharply again in 1830. That was too early to have been a response to improved agricultural conditions in Canada and was more likely the outcome of push factors on the British side. Immigration to Canada soared. This second great wave of immigration brought much larger numbers of settlers than the earlier peak. It also brought an epidemic of cholera and the specter of immigrants dying at the ports and along the route inland in large numbers. Nevertheless, the immigrant surge of the early 1830s was especially significant in providing the population essential to fill out the settlement of Canada. The flow of migrants dropped precipitously in the middle of the decade. The sharp drop in 1835 is especially puzzling because, although it is so dramatic, almost none of the historians of immigration, or contemporary observers for that matter, offer any explanation for it.[9] The deep trough in 1838 is well recognized to be a response to the armed rebellions in both Upper and Lower Canada in the previous year. Agricultural conditions were also quite unfavorable in Canada in the second half of the 1830s. Rural distress was also widespread in Ireland and in the Scottish highlands at that time. With the return of more prosperous conditions in the Canadian economy, immigration again soared in the early 1840s, reaching a peak in 1842. There was only a brief lull before the potato famine struck Ireland and the west of Scotland, propelling vast numbers of desperate migrants to North America. In the 1830s Canada and the United States were receiving about the same absolute number of immigrants annually, despite the fact that Canada was a much smaller country. That had changed by the early 1840s, when the balance tipped heavily toward the United States. With the famine migration of 1847, the shift in destination was massive. Henceforth the United States would be the destination of most migrants to North

[9] Hansen, *The Mingling of the Canadian and American Peoples*, is about the only writer to feel compelled to offer an explanation. He notes (p. 127) that cholera had broken out again in 1834, but a more important factor was probably the bad publicity of an unusually large number of shipwrecks in that year.

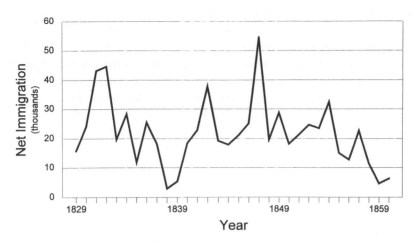

Figure 9.1. Immigration to British North America, 1829–1860

America, and Canada would be a decidedly lesser attraction. The proportion of immigrants arriving at Quebec and moving directly onward to the United States rose sharply with the famine migration and continued thereafter to be much higher than before. Even so, in terms of the absolute number of settlers, Canada continued to receive large numbers of immigrants into the first half of the 1850s. That marked the last phase of rural settlement in the old colony of Canada. By the mid-1850s almost all of the reasonably good land had been taken up. In the late years of the decade immigration dropped quite sharply. A new phase of Canadian demographic evolution had begun. The great immigration era was over.

The fluctuations in immigration shown in Table 9.2 and described in the previous paragraphs are more directly revealed in Figure 9.1, which shows only the revised net series of Table 9.2. The three series given in that table track fairly closely and together produce a cluttered graph. As Figure 9.1 shows, fluctuations in the revised series are not as pronounced as in the U.K. emigration and Quebec arrivals series. It was in years of especially large influx to Canada that the proportion of arrivals moving on directly to the United States was greater. In years when immigration was low, most stayed in Canada.

Immigration from Great Britain was made up of three ethnic streams: English, Scottish, and Irish. Every indication is that the Irish were the predominant group in the movement to Canada. Compared with their population in their homeland, Scots also came in disproportionate numbers. It is not possible, however, to do a precise accounting of the three ethnic groups separately.[10] Careful records of departures from Irish, Scottish, and English ports were kept, but those figures do not align with the ethnic composition. Many of the Scottish and Irish departed from English ports, especially Liverpool. An attempt was made to separate the three groups in the count of arrivals at Quebec, but again there was considerable confusion. Northern Irish Protestants and Scots were often not easily distinguishable. Second-generation Irish and Scottish residents of England also made up part of the flow. Ethnic composition has been a topic of great interest to historians of the Canadian immigration experience, but one has largely to despair of sorting out the numbers in this period.

An impression emerging from the foregoing discussion of the history of immigration to Canada in the first 60 years of the nineteenth century is that the available evidence is questionable and of doubtful reliability. There is some truth to that notion, but the negative side should not be overstressed. It is not clear that the recording of immigration was any more deficient than in later years for which scholars have accepted the record pretty much at face value. The main contours of Canadian demographic development seem to be evident enough. With that in mind, an accounting of Canadian population change is offered in Table 9.3 that is entirely conjectural but nevertheless probably a fair representation of what occurred. The main purpose of this exercise is to suggest that, even with little firm information, a plausible account of Canadian population development may be traced out. Two different approaches to the decomposition of decadal population change are taken in Table 9.3. The top panel is constructed on the assumption of a constant 3% per annum rate of natural increase. That is consistent with a crude birth rate of 50 per thousand and a crude death rate of 20 per thousand population, roughly in line with the facts of the 1850s and 1860s. The population projected at that rate of natural increase always falls short of the population at the end of each decade, implying some amount of immigration to make up the difference. Comparing the implied or required immigration with the measured immigration (the revised "net" series from Table 9.2), permits a calculation by inference of the fraction of the immigration that would have had to remain in Canada to balance the account. On the whole, the inferred proportions work out to plausible figures. In the first two decades

---

[10] It seems that few Welsh came to Canada. Emigrants from that part of Britain were much more likely to go to the United States.

Table 9.3. *A conjectural accounting of Canada's
population change, 1821–1861*

	1821–31	1831–41	1841–52[a]	1852–61
Assuming natural increase				
Initial population (thousands)	722	1,076	1,630	2,367
Natural increase at .030	248	370	626	722
Projected population[b]	970	1,446	2,256	3,089
Actual population	1,076	1,630	2,367	3,175
Implied immigration	106	184	111	86
Measured immigration[c]	147	211	242	154
Implied retention (%)	72	85	46	56
Assuming immigrant retention				
Initial population	722	1,976	1,630	2,367
Measured immigration	147	211	242	154
Retention assumed (%)	85	85	67	50
Terminal population less retained immigrants	950	1,451	2,205	3,098
Implied annual rate of natural increase	.0278	.0304	.0278	.0304

[a] What is commonly referred to as the census of 1851 was actually enumerated in early 1852.
[b] The population that would have resulted from natural increase only at an average annual rate of 3%.
[c] Measured immigration as the net arrivals figures reported in Table 9.2.

the retained proportion would be reasonably high, much lower in the next two decades. The 85 percent retention implied in the 1831–41 decade might seem high, but to lower it one would have to argue for a higher rate of natural increase in a decade which saw the first appearance of major disease epidemics.[11]

A somewhat different approach is adopted in the bottom panel of Table 9.3. There the key assumptions are that the proportion of immigrants retained as settlers in Canada is relatively high in the first two decades and is followed by a falling rate over the last two decades. These assumptions are inferred from commentaries of earlier writers. Again the measured immigration is the revised "net" series of Table 9.2. The assumed amount of retained immigration is deducted from the end-of-decade population,

[11] Could one argue that the birth rate in the 1830s was raised to unusually high levels by the arrival of larger numbers of immigrants moving onto frontier farms? It is not an entirely implausible argument, but one still has to wonder why the rate of natural increase should then have risen from the 1820s to the 1830s.

and a calculation made of the average annual rate of natural increase of population needed to generate that number. Once again, a reasonably plausible scenario emerges. One might wonder whether natural increase would have been quite as low as 2.78% in the 1820s. From the bottom panel it can be seen that it would be necessary to lower the rate of immigrant retention to only 72% to raise the implied rate of natural increase to 3% per annum. These exercises in Table 9.3 are entirely conjectural, but they suggest that a credible story can be told without having to resort to wildly unreasonable assumptions. That story emphasizes that even in the era of very large immigration the rapid growth of Canada's population was primarily a result of natural increase, including of course the high rates of reproduction adopted by the immigrant population after settling in Canada. It is not until around midcentury that we are able to learn much about the high birth rate in Canada.

NATURAL INCREASE OF THE POPULATION: CANADIAN FERTILITY AROUND MIDCENTURY

Immigration on a large scale was not the only reason for the rapid growth of the population of British North America. As has been pointed out, natural increase was also at a very high level. The people who moved into what is now Canada multiplied with great abundance. Precise information about the nineteenth-century Canadian rate of natural increase, and especially the rate of mortality is not available, but every indication is that mortality was rather low and fertility very high by world standards. At about the middle of the nineteenth century Canadian fertility was almost certainly higher on average than the level in the United States. The demographic literature on nineteenth-century Canada is especially thin, so there is relatively little in the way of established results upon which to base an account. What follows is drawn largely from my own research, much of it not previously published.

It is regrettable that historical demographers have paid so little attention to nineteenth-century Canada, since this country makes an intriguing population laboratory. It displays a wide variety of experience in a setting that makes for effective testing of some prominent hypotheses about the determinants of fertility. Some widely accepted presumptions about historical fertility behavior are called into question. And this is in a situation in which, on the whole, statistical data are quite good. Ironically, the data are thinnest for the basic demographic processes of fertility and mortality, which may be why the study of Canadian historical population has been so neglected. Comprehensive registration of vital statistics was not well established in Canada until the beginning of the twentieth century.[12] From 1851 onward, though, there are regular decennial censuses, and these provide an abundance of evidence if the data are used with caution and some ingenuity. The discussion that follows is based largely on the censuses. Only toward the end of the century can census data on deaths be used, in combination with death registration data, to examine patterns of mortality. Births are inferred from census counts of the stock of children. That requires assumptions about the survival of young children. It is possible reasonably to work out patterns of infant mortality in 1891 and 1901. There is little indication that infant mortality changed before 1891, so as a first approximation the infant survival patterns of 1891 are used to make estimates of fertility for earlier census years. The main body of evidence considered consists of cross sections of about 120 counties and cities of the old colony of Canada (Ontario and Quebec) for 1851, 1861, and 1891; some rougher estimates of provincial average fertility for all provinces for census years from 1851 to 1901; and data for 1861 Ontario from a sample of individual farm families drawn from the census manuscripts of that year. Primary attention is directed to the 1861 and 1891 county cross sections.

The data relating to fertility are reported in the form of the indexes developed by the Princeton European Fertility Project.[13] These have become a familiar way of looking at historical fertility and permit the Canadian evidence to be placed directly in the context of the much more thoroughly studied European experience. The index of overall fertility I_f is the product of separate indexes of marital fertility, I_g, and nuptiality, I_m. The I_f measure is a pure index, and no meaningful interpretation can be given to its absolute value. By contrast, I_g can be interpreted as the actual

---

[12] It is well known that the French Roman Catholic population of Quebec had long been well served by the registration of baptisms and burials. For the seventeenth and eighteenth centuries those data have been the basis of a major project in historical demography at the University of Montreal that has been under way for many years. By the middle of the nineteenth century, however, the church records as a source of data had weakened and were covering a smaller fraction of the total population. Both the data and their analysis in demographic studies fall away just as the issues become really interesting. Kuczynski, *Birth Registration and Birth Statistics in Canada*, provides a thorough review of historical birth registration in Canada.

[13] These are explained and extensively used in the comprehensive report on that project by Coale and Watkins, *The Decline of Fertility in Europe*.

marital fertility rate of a population expressed as a fraction of a maximum attainable level.[14] It allows us to focus on marital fertility in a situation where the fertility transition is often considered to be essentially the grand decline in marital fertility. Overall fertility is also affected by the age structure of the population of women of fecund age and by nuptiality, the proportion of women who are in fact married. These indexes provide some degree of control of age structure.[15] They also permit a direct look at the role of variations in nuptiality in populations where proportions married varied considerably and often in a way that was intended to affect the level of overall fertility.[16] Two further points should be made in relation to my use of the Princeton indexes in the Canadian case. One is that, whereas I_f is defined here simply as I_g multiplied by I_m, the full Princeton specification provides for extramarital fertility as well. There is little information on illegitimate fertility in nineteenth-century Canada, but the fertility index used here counts all children, attributing them, in effect, to married women. That imparts a slight upward bias to the measures of I_g for Canada, something to be kept in mind when comparisons are made with the European data, but the levels of overall fertility, I_m, would be unaffected. A second point is that because the marital fertility ratios used here are based on the stock of children and some widows might have young children, the Canadian estimates count widows along with married women. The probability that widows would have young children is surely lower than for married women, so that imparts a downward bias to the levels of I_g calculated for Canada.[17]

[14] Maximum attainable marital fertility is defined as the fertility ratio of the married women in any population, given their age distribution, that would result if those women had the age-specific fertility rates of Hutterite women. Details of the rationale and the calculation of these indexes is given in a chapter by Coale and Treadway in the aforementioned volume by Coale and Watkins.

[15] Marital fertility, I_g, is the ratio of actual births per married woman to the potential births per married woman if those women were bearing children at Hutterite rates. The age structure of the women being studied is the same in both the numerator and the denominator of that ratio. The potential fertility ratio, which might be designated the Standard Fertility Ratio, can be viewed, in effect, as an indicator of the influence of age structure on marital fertility. It varies from district to district only to the extent of variations in the age structure. That is a feature of some considerable interest in the case of a population like that of Canada, which is undergoing rapid change in its demographic processes and which is largely affected by migration flows that may be selective of women of particular ages.

[16] It should be pointed out that the index of nuptiality, I_m, is not simply the proportion of all adult women who are married but weights the proportions at each age by the Hutterite standard fertility rate for that age. In the context of nineteenth-century Canada, this means that I_m is usually somewhat higher than the simple proportion married.

[17] This bias should be of little consequence for national or provincial aggregates, but for individual counties or cities it may make a perceptible difference. Widows were more likely to reside in towns and cities; hence some part of the lower fertility ratios for urban areas may simply reflect the greater numbers of widows there.

The following examination of fertility in Canada in 1861 is based largely on a geographic cross section of estimates of fertility indexes for eight cities and 110 rural districts in the provinces of Canada West and Canada East, which will be referred to hereafter as Ontario and Quebec, the provinces they were to become after Canadian Confederation in 1867. The reproduction rates under consideration apply just about the time that the settlement process in the old colony of Canada was reaching completion and large-scale immigration was coming to an end. After 1861 Canada became a country of net emigration. At this time, though, Canada was a country with high fertility. The crude birth rate for 1861 is estimated at about 41 per thousand population.[18] That agrees almost exactly with the estimated birth rate of the white population of the United States at that time, which should not be entirely surprising. Fertility in both North American countries, however, was well above what was typical of Europe in the middle of the nineteenth century.

The Princeton fertility indexes have been reported for nine European nations for 1860 or a year close to that.[19] The indexes of overall fertility, shown in Figure 9.2, where the countries are arranged in ascending order of their indexes of marital fertility, ranged from an exceptionally low .275 for France to .399 for Italy. An I_f value of about .350 seems to have been typical. Ontario at .450 and Quebec at .464 were far above the European levels. The larger part of the difference was in nuptiality. Proportions of women of childbearing age who were married were much higher in Canada than in Europe, and that accounts for more of the difference in overall fertility than does the difference in rates of marital fertility. Typical I_m in Europe was .475, compared with .532 in Quebec and .578 in Ontario. For Ontario, that difference in nuptiality would account for twice as much of the difference from Europe in overall fertility as would Ontario's higher level of I_g. The indexes of marital fertility are also shown in Figure 9.2, where it is evident that I_g in Quebec, at .872, was well above that of any European country, while Belgium (.828) and the Netherlands (.816) had rates of marital fertility above the average estimated for Ontario.

One might say, then, that marital fertility in 1861 Canada was high but,

[18] This is somewhat lower than the widely cited estimate of an average of 45 over the 1856–66 decade reported by Henripin, *Trends and Factors of Fertility in Canada*. The difference lies almost entirely in Henripin's higher figure for Ontario. There is close agreement on the crude birth rate for Quebec at that time.

[19] These are Belgium (1856 and 1866 averaged), Denmark (1860), England and Wales (1861), France (1861), Italy (1864), the Netherlands (1859), Portugal (1864), Scotland (1861), and Switzerland (1860). The comparison group could be extended to include Germany in 1867 and Ireland in 1871.

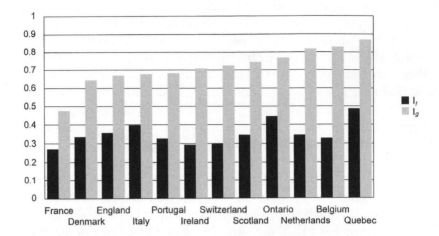

Figure 9.2. Indices of fertility, Canada and Europe, ca. 1861

on average, not so distinctly above levels to be found in Europe. Nuptiality, however, was much higher than in Europe; and it was that, more than anything else, that made the birth rate in Canada so high. This was still a time when variations in marriage proportions played the predominant role in variations in human reproduction. That was true in both Europe and Canada. Except in France, the great downward movement in marital fertility had not got under way.[20] People were adapting their childbearing mainly in the strictly Malthusian manner by delaying or even ultimately forgoing marriage.

It would have been even more instructive to graph the full distribution of all Canadian and European districts, although that could not be done in a way suitable for inclusion in this volume. It would have shown that the variation in I_f across Canadian districts in 1861 was as wide as that to

[20] Except for France, European levels of I_g that in 1861 ranged from .828 in Belgium to as low as .670 in England and .645 in Denmark, have been interpreted as reflecting essentially uncontrolled or "natural" marital fertility. Comparison with the Canadian evidence might call that into question. In Ontario, a population which had largely migrated from Britain only a short time before displayed a range of marital fertility rates that went well above the Belgian levels in some districts, while being about as low as the English in others. There is a strong implication that I_g levels of .700 or lower, found in the earlier settled districts of Ontario, while culturally similar populations in the more recently and sparsely settled districts had I_g above .900, represented deliberate adjustment of marital fertility to local circumstances. If so, the many districts of England, and other parts of Europe, with I_g in the .600–.700 range suggest that there had been a downward movement of marital fertility some time prior to the middle of the nineteenth century. The question is whether that may have come in the early nineteenth century, paralleling the well-recognized decline in France, or at some much earlier time.

be found across the provinces of nine countries of Europe (Ireland excluded), although the mean level in Canada was of course considerably higher.[21] A comparison of the detailed distribution of I_g is even more interesting. The European distribution is bimodal, with I_g in French departments well below the distribution for the rest of Europe. Overall, the interquartile range of I_g for Canada (.162) is somewhat greater than for Europe (.151), but the contrast would be much greater if France were set aside from the European observations.[22] The point to emphasize is the considerable variation in the Canadian case, more so than within most European nations. Marital fertility in Canada ranged from levels that were higher than any to be found in the European provinces (several districts, mostly in Quebec, with $I_g = 1.000$) down to levels that were as low as any to be found outside France.

Turning to the factors associated with variations in fertility in Canada, it should come as no surprise that the predominantly French province of Quebec would have fertility rates above those of English-speaking Ontario. What is more interesting is that the difference in overall fertility between the two provinces should have been as small as it was. I_f in Quebec (.487) was less than 10% above the Ontario average (.446). French Canadian marital fertility was indeed high, a point to return to shortly, but that was offset by a lower nuptiality rate. I_m averaged .583 in Ontario but only .561 in Quebec. Furthermore, substitutability between marital fertility and nuptiality was evidently a means of controlling overall fertility, as discussed next. The evidence strongly hints at a hypothesis that adaptation of fertility rates began with changing marriage patterns but that as time went on it came increasingly to be reflected in rates of marital fertility. If so, changing nuptiality and shifts in marital fertility should be thought of as integral parts of a more or less continuous process.

The factors associated with variations in fertility differ considerably within the two provinces of Ontario and Quebec so it is necessary to examine each province separately. The evidence for both provinces is summarized in Table 9.4. A detailed listing of all the counties of the two provinces would be tedious and for most readers not readily interpretable so what hopefully are meaningful groupings are given. Within Quebec, as between that province and Ontario, the main story is cultural. Looking

---

[21] The interquartile range of I_f is .082 for Canada and .084 for the nine European countries.

[22] If one were to treat the French case as unique, it might be more instructive to make the comparison with the French observations removed. Another reason for doing that is that there are a large number of observations for France, where the departments were small and numerous.

Table 9.4. *Indexes of fertility, British North America, 1861*

Geographic category	I_f	I_g	I_m
Ontario			
Provincial aggregate	.446	.765	.583
Rural districts	.453	.774	.585
Cities	.382	.679	.562
Towns and villages in rural districts			
Large towns (>4,000)	.410	.699	.587
Smaller towns (2,000–4,000)	.431	.714	.604
Larger villages (1,000–1,900)	.447	.736	.607
Small villages (<1,000)	.448	.751	.596
Settlement periods			
Earliest (before 1790)	.404	.728	.555
Early (1790–1815)	.441	.739	.597
Later (1815–30)	.459	.785	.585
Latest (after 1830)	.514	.811	.634
Quebec			
Provincial aggregate	.487	.868	.561
Rural districts	.479	.875	.547
Cities	.479	.828	.578
Predominantly anglophone districts			
(>70% anglo)	.413	.758	.547
Mixed districts (30–70%)	.487	.852	.551
Wholly francophone districts	.489	.916	.536
Heartland	.487	.945	.515
Lower St. Lawrence	.492	.870	.569
Nova Scotia	.403	.765	.527
New Brunswick	.488	.866	.564

first at I_g, the lowest levels in Quebec in 1861 were in counties that had almost wholly anglophone populations.[23] In the few predominantly anglophone districts (defined as 70% or more non-French), the index of marital

[23] The terms "francophone" and "anglophone" are used here in preference to French and English since the anglophone population, while English speaking, was more Irish and Scottish than English. One might equally refer to the cultural groups as French and British, although there are cultural differences of interest within the latter group. Evidence on the ethnic origins of people derives from the Canadian census practice of asking a question on "origin." Actually, that question was universally asked only beginning in 1871. In 1861 the census asked about country of birth, but the Canadian-born were also asked to group themselves as French, Indian, colored, and other. The "other" category would have been mainly English, Irish, or Scottish, although some of the Loyalist settlers from the United States would have had German or Dutch backgrounds.

fertility averaged .758, just about the same as the Ontario provincial figure. In culturally mixed districts, I_g was higher again, at .852,[24] and in the wholly francophone districts it averaged .916. That certainly reinforces the long-held perception of exceptionally high marital fertility among French Canadians. It would nevertheless be unwarranted to jump too hastily to a simplistic conclusion. First, a few anglophone districts in Ontario could be found with marital fertility rates every bit as high as those in French Canada. Second, in the francophone districts, I_g was not uniformly at the upper bound. In six counties, I_g was above .975, virtually at the Hutterite level, while two francophone counties had estimated values of I_g below .800, but that may just indicate errors in the underlying data. Neither of those counties had fertility rates as low in the preceding or the succeeding decade. There was, however, a sizable district in the lower St. Lawrence region, a relatively remote district, where I_g averaged well below that typical of the rest of francophone Canada. This is the rationale for singling out two groups of francophone counties of Quebec in Table 9.4. One is referred to as the "heartland" district and consists of counties near Montreal, mostly on the north shore of the St. Lawrence River. The other is the lower St. Lawrence district referred to previously. One can only speculate as to why marital fertility should have been lower there. There are hints that breast feeding may have been more common in the more remote districts of Quebec.[25] Infant mortality seems to have been lower, and it would be quite consistent to see lower marital fertility as well.

Urban fertility in Quebec is represented by only three cities. These had lower levels of marital fertility than the province as a whole, and yet the levels were still fairly high (.828).[26] In 1861 the two largest cities, Montreal and Quebec, had substantial anglophone populations, so it is rather surprising that the estimated marital fertility rates there should come out so

[24] It is natural to ask whether ethnic mix alone might account for the observed levels of marital fertility in the mixed districts. If one were to attribute to the anglophone population of such districts about the lowest value of I_g exhibited by anglophones in Canada (.680) and to francophones the level of wholly French districts (.916), a synthetic rate of marital fertility can be constructed. For two prominent mixed districts the results look as follows: Ottawa county, .804, whereas the actual 1861 value was .812; Shefford County, .842, with an actual value of .816. That looks promising, but two qualifications must be added. One is that this simple weighted averaging approach does not work out so closely in all mixed districts. The second is that French Canadian marital fertility was not universally above .900.

[25] This speculation is based largely on evidence for 1891, when fertility was still somewhat lower in that district, and for which there is evidence of lower infant mortality there as well. It may seem a bit odd to refer to I_g levels of .850 as "low," but when nearby districts have values close to unity there would seem to be something of substance to explain.

[26] One must wonder about a possible upward bias to these estimates, although the calculation has been carefully checked. Estimates for 1851 and 1871 both point to distinctly lower levels for those cities.

high. Trois-Rivières, a much smaller city and almost entirely francophone, had the lowest estimated I_g (.809). If the 1861 estimates can be accepted at face value, a point that has already been questioned, the Quebec cities had fertility levels well above those of Ontario and as high as the ethnically mixed rural districts.

Nuptiality also had an important role to play in determining variations in overall fertility within Quebec. For example, I_f was the same in rural districts as it was in the three cities because in the rural districts a lower proportion of women were married. Overall fertility was no lower in the ethnically mixed districts than in the wholly francophone districts, again because the lower I_m of the latter substituted for the higher levels of marital fertility. The lower marital fertility in the lower St. Lawrence district did not result in reduced overall fertility there because a higher proportion of women was married. French Canadians may not have moved to less than natural levels of marital fertility, but that does not mean that they were not adaptive to local circumstances. They appear to have followed the standard European approach of the time of modifying nuptiality. In that way, despite exceptionally high marital fertility rates, they were able to keep their crude birth rate down to the level of Ontario.

In Ontario, culture, or strictly speaking ethnic mix, played a much less important role in the variations in fertility. In that province only 3 out of 52 counties had high concentrations of French Canadians. All 3 had levels of marital fertility that were above average. Other than that, however, culture does not seem to have been an important factor in 1861 Ontario fertility variation. Two sources of variation deserve closer examination because they relate directly to prominent hypotheses about the reasons for fertility decline. A long-standing structural argument has emphasized urbanization. Lower fertility, so this argument goes, was characteristic of urban life, where children were more costly, they were less able to contribute to family income, and parents were more closely tied in to changing ideas of family planning and limitation. Had lower urban fertility already made its appearance in mid-nineteenth-century Ontario? It has already been noted that there is little support for that notion in the three cities of Quebec. In what follows it will be shown that in 1861 Ontario fertility was indeed lower in urban centers. One of the leading alternative lines of argument concerning nineteenth-century fertility in America is that birth rates were inversely related to the abundant availability of agricultural land. One simple way of gauging that is to look at the relationship between fertility and date of settlement. The earliest and longest settled districts would be expected to have the lowest fertility. The evidence for mid-nineteenth-century Ontario offers an excellent opportunity to assess both of these hypotheses.

The fertility indexes shown in Table 9.4 can be drawn upon as evidence. Consider first the data relating to rural/urban differentials. I_g in the five cities of Ontario was 12% below the average of the rural counties, although those counties included varying but sometimes significant proportions of population in smaller towns and villages. These latter were too small to sustain reliable estimation of fertility indexes on an individual basis but can be grouped by size and estimates made for four categories: larger towns, smaller towns, larger villages, and small villages. It is striking that all categories of town and village had lower rates of marital fertility than the strictly rural areas, and that I_g rose consistently as size of place diminished. That lends support to those who have argued that urbanization played an important role in the decline of marital fertility. On the other hand, the gradient of fertility by size of place is not very steep and small towns of two to four thousand people had rates of marital fertility almost as low as large cities. In the traditional treatment of the role of urbanization, the implication has been that it was the big city that made the difference. The Canadian evidence points more to the importance of being just off the farm. In any nonfarm setting fertility may have been significantly lower. That imparts a somewhat different twist to the urbanization argument.[27]

Another hypothesis is that fertility was highest in new areas of settlement, where land was abundant, and that it declined as the density of settlement increased, unoccupied land disappeared, and settlements aged. Just why such a relationship should have held is a matter of some controversy, but there is less debate that the relationship in fact existed. At least that is what the evidence for the United States clearly indicates. One of the attractions of Ontario as a region of study is that in general it was in so many ways like the northern United States. However one wishes to measure it, the relationship holds in nineteenth-century Ontario as well. One of the most direct ways of capturing the relationship is to look at duration of settlement. Fertility might be expected to be lowest in the

---

[27] This result also has a bearing on the land-density or duration-of-settlement argument. The contrast has usually been made between urbanization in the sense of large cities and the density of rural settlement. Both rural population densities and the duration of settlement, however, would be associated with larger proportions of population in towns and villages. The nineteenth-century Ontario data permit a more intensive investigation of this matter.

earliest settled districts and to rise with recency of settlement.[28] In Table 9.4 the rural counties of Ontario are grouped by four periods of settlement. The first group includes only those settled initially with the first waves of Loyalist immigrants (before 1790). The second group includes all the other districts in which settlement was well under way before 1815, when immigration was redirected.[29] The third group consists of those districts which were settled primarily when the first great waves of British immigrants arrived. The latest settled group is dated from after 1830.[30]

The relationship of marital fertility rates to duration of settlement has several notable features. The first, and most prominent, is that I_g rises consistently with recency of settlement. Marital fertility in the most recently settled districts was, on average, more than 10% higher than the earliest settled group. As in the case of town size, the consistency of the relationship is most striking. On the other hand, once again the gradient is not steep. That might be interpreted in one of two ways. It could be that neither urbanization nor recency of settlement made a great deal of difference. Alternatively, fertility seems to have been subtly and quite sensitively related to both size of urban center and recency of settlement.[31] The

---

[28] Even this becomes complicated. Should one group districts by period of initial settlement or according to the main period of early settlement? Some districts had a few early settlers but did not have much land taken up until several decades later. An outstanding case is Essex County in Ontario, which from a very early date, had a French Canadian population that was left over from the old Detroit settlement. Otherwise, Essex County was relatively late in having its land taken up. It was rather remote from the main centers of Ontario, and much of its land required heavy investment in drainage. One could place Essex County in the earliest settlement group or say that it was mainly settled after 1815. Actually, the greater part of settlement came even later than that. Fertility was on the high side in Essex ($I_g = .820$), but one could debate whether that reflected late settlement or a high proportion of French. Given both of those influences, one might wonder that I_g for Essex was as low as it was.

[29] One implication of this is that groups 1 and 2 were those counties which were initially settled by Americans. That might be regarded as lending a cultural dimension to the classification as well. After 1815 immigrants came almost wholly from Britain and the counties of settlement-groups 3 and 4 had larger Irish and Scottish populations. The original American settlers were mobile, however, and they and their descendants moved on to later-settled areas. Nevertheless, one outstanding feature of some of the earliest settled counties – such as Frontenac, Lennox, Niagara, and Prince Edward, which also had the lowest levels of marital fertility – is that they had the largest proportions of old American stock and probably also more continued interaction with people in the northeastern United States.

[30] It might be attractive to date that a little later, from the mid-1830s, but putting the date any later reduces sharply the number of counties in the group. A reasonable compromise is struck by the 1830 date.

[31] Timing of settlement is only imprecisely related to the land availability hypothesis. Districts that were initially settled at the same time differed considerably in how rapidly land was taken up, so that by 1861 they might show a quite different pattern of land availability. For example, Halton County, just west of Toronto, was opened to settlement rather late because the land had not been acquired from the aboriginal inhabitants. Yet, being in such an advantageous location, it filled up quickly. By contrast, Glengarry County, the easternmost in Ontario, was in the first round of initial settlement but was much slower to be fully settled.

common pattern of rural settlement was for the population of a district to reach a maximum, where it would remain for several decades, and then for its absolute number to decline fairly sharply. Eighteen of 51 counties reached their peak rural population in 1861 or a decade earlier. For many districts, then, the period subsequent to the initial date being examined was one in which population was no longer growing, despite the very high rates of natural increase.

If the main influence on fertility variations is thought to be land availability strictly speaking rather than a combination of things related to both it and the duration of settlement, one might attempt to measure it directly. There are several possible ways of approaching this, but a relatively straightforward one is to approximate the extent of cultivable land by the maximum area ever cultivated, at whatever date that may have occurred.[32] The area of land under cultivation in 1861 is then compared with the eventual maximum, and "land availability" is measured as the still-to-be-cultivated land as a percentage of the maximum. In 1861 that measure varied greatly, from a low of less than 20% in York county (adjacent to Toronto) to as high as 84% and 87% in Bruce and Russell counties, respectively. Regression analysis can then be used to evaluate the relationship between fertility and land availability. The results of such an exercise are not reported here in any detail. From that analysis, however, it emerges that marital fertility, I_g, was related to land availability in a way that was statistically significant, but it was not a strong relationship and accounted for only a modest fraction of overall variability. There was no statistically discernible relationship between nuptiality and land availability. Interestingly enough, the strongest relationship was found with overall fertility, I_f.[33] That might be interpreted as reinforcing the conclusion that in 1861 marital fertility and nuptiality were to some extent substitute ways of controlling fertility.

[32] In the great majority of counties that point was reached by the early twentieth century, before the technology of agriculture had been substantially changed by motorization. Indeed, several counties attained their maximum acreage under cultivation as early as 1881.

[33] The estimated regression equation is $I_f = 0.384 + .031LA$, where the coefficient on land availability is statistically significant, with $t = 4.53$ and $R^2 = 0.30$. That would predict an I_f value of .400 for a district with half its land yet to be brought under cultivation – only 3.5% above that for a district with 90% of its land under cultivation. That is not a remarkably strong result but for a cross section of 50 observations it should be taken as indicative of a relationship worth probing more deeply. The addition of a second explanatory variable reflecting the extent of town and village development adds nothing to the relationship. An alternative way of approaching land availability might be simply to measure the density of the rural population (exclusive of towns and villages) in relation to the maximum cultivable land. Density and land availability are, not surprisingly, quite highly correlated. Density as an explanatory variable gives a similar but not quite as strong a result as land availability.

The relationship of fertility to low-level urbanization (the extent of town and village development) might also be assessed by regressing the fertility indexes on the proportion of a county's population that resided in towns and villages. The relationship is weaker than with land availability. Interestingly, urbanization provides essentially no explanation of variations in I_f but does show a weak yet statistically significant relationship with I_g. This hints at a separate influence, urbanization, but that possibility is not easily teased out of the data at hand.

The data for Ontario provide further evidence that fertility in North America was related to the availability of agricultural land. Our understanding of just how that worked is not greatly enhanced by the evidence we have been able to review here. There are some indications that more than land availability per se may have been involved. In an earlier study, I used individual household data from the manuscript census of 1861 to show that the relationship of fertility to land availability was not just a phenomenon in the aggregate but could be established at the level of individual families.[34] That study reported results consistent with those given here – that is to say, the relationship is statistically significant but is not very strong. The picture is actually more complex, and other factors must have been at work. The challenge is to disentangle more effectively the explanation of variations in fertility.

Writing specifically of the circumstances of nineteenth-century Canada, Lorne Tepperman has pressed the case that religious and cultural factors should be given greater emphasis.[35] Little has been done to generate support for this line of argument. Analysis of county cross sections is not a very effective approach. Only a few ethnic or religious concentrations are evident at the county level. Concentrations of those sorts could be identified for smaller communities, but then one faces less reliability and considerably more random variability in the fertility measures. No really thorough study of cultural and religious influences on Canadian fertility has been carried out. As already noted, I used individual household data from the manuscript census of 1861 to carry out a preliminary investigation, but the results were impaired by weaknesses in the fertility measures employed. That study did point to a significant role of ethnicity and religion, but it was not the relationships that many might have presumed, nor was it the same pattern stressed by Tepperman. Neither Irish nor

---

[34] McInnis, "Childbearing and Land Availability."
[35] Tepperman, "Ethnic Variations in Marriage and Fertility."

Roman Catholics in general had significantly larger families in 1861 Ontario. It was the Scottish-born who had higher fertility, while those born in the United States had substantially lower fertility. At the same time, it might seem anomalous that lower fertility was associated with being Presbyterian in religion.[36]

To summarize, consider the characteristics of the counties with the lowest and with the highest levels of fertility. In Ontario the lowest levels of overall fertility were found in the cities, other than Ottawa, and in the earliest settled rural districts on the north shore of Lake Ontario. The lowest value of I_f was in the city of Toronto, but the rural county of Lennox was just about as low. Low urban fertility was a consequence of low marital fertility. Except in Toronto, nuptiality was not particularly low in the cities. Much the same can be said of the rural districts of Ontario. Five of the six counties with lowest I_f also ranked lowest in I_g. In Quebec, on the other hand, considerably lower rates of nuptiality played a much more important role in determining realtively low levels of overall fertility. The lowest levels of marital fertility in rural Canada were found in those earliest settled districts with relatively little uncultivated land remaining.[37] Four of those form a contiguous area at the east end of Lake Ontario. They, along with Lincoln County in the Niagara peninsula, were the earliest regions of settlement and furthermore were closest to the United States. Moreover, they were populated to a considerable extent with people born in the United States or their descendants. On the other hand, two of these counties, Frontenac and South Hastings, had relatively large concentrations of Catholic Irish. Two of the counties, Lincoln and South Hastings, had among the highest proportions of town and village populations of any counties in the province, and Frontenac County was adjacent to the city of Kingston. Lennox and Prince Edward Counties, however, had little urban development. Three counties of Quebec had

---

[36] The anomaly is clarified in part when one realizes that the predominant immigrant ethnic group in Ontario was Protestant Northern Irish who tended to be Anglican or Presbyterian. Just being Irish by birth does not capture this, but the religious groups were also quite mixed. In general one needs a finer mesh to sift out culture. One group that does stand out and warrants further study in detail is the highland Scottish Catholics who appear to have combined maximally high marital fertility with outstandingly low nuptiality. The only concentration of such people that stands out at the county level is seen in Glengarry County, Ontario. Later in the century it is found that a similar population in Antigonish County, Nova Scotia, displays the same pattern.

[37] The six counties with the lowest values of I_g were, in order, and with their rates in parentheses: Prince Edward (.625), Lennox (.652), Lincoln (.660), South Hastings (.675), Kent (.677), and Frontenac (.678).

rates of marital fertility as low as the lowest in Ontario.[38] They were anglo-phone counties on the southern border with the United States, settled largely by early immigrants from the United States. They had almost no urban development. Particularly significant is the fact that some rural districts in 1861 Canada had rates of marital fertility every bit as low as those of the largest cities. At the same time, it must be kept in mind that low fertility in the mid-nineteenth-century Canadian context means rates about the same as median rates then prevailing in England and other parts of Western Europe.

THE TRANSITION IN FERTILITY TO 1891: A VARIEGATED PATTERN

Throughout much of Canada, fertility fell substantially between 1861 and the end of the century. There were districts, however, mostly in French Canada, where it did not decline at all. The pattern of decline is based largely on a detailed examination of the geographic pattern of fertility in 1891 and a comparison with the pattern for 1861, already described. Similar spatial estimates for 1901 are not as reliable, but the main features do not appear to differ. The same Princeton indices of marital and overall fertility and of nuptiality are used. The estimating procedure is essentially the same as described for 1861.[39] It is possible to extend the county level estimates for Ontario and Quebec across the nation to major cities and the rest of the provinces.

Estimates of infant survival are needed to make the fertility calculations used in this study. Only at the end of the century are there enough reliable data to make reasonably firm estimates of infant and child mortality. Even then the data are complicated enough that they require intensive manipulation before they can be put to use. Nevertheless, since they offer the first look at any indicator of mortality that can be constructed for nineteenth-century Canada, they are worth some attention. A summary of estimated infant survival rates for 1891 is given in Table 9.5. This table

[38] These were Brome (.676), Mississquoi (.687), and Stanstead (.712). These were the most thoroughly anglophone counties of Quebec.

[39] The 1891 estimates are probably more accurate and, in a sense, anchor the examination of the whole of nineteenth-century fertility in Canada. They are based on the most thoroughly researched and firmly established estimates of infant survival. Indeed, the figures used in the 1861 calculation are just an assumed extension of these. The procedure is still to use survival ratios to estimate births from only those children enumerated in the age bracket of 2–4 years.

Table 9.5. *Infant mortality in Canadian cities, provinces, and counties, 1891*

Location	Infant deaths per thousand births
Montreal (Que.)	285
Quebec City (Que.)	275
Toronto (Ont.)	199
Ottawa (Ont.)	185
Halifax (N.S.)	180
Saint John (N.B.)	180
Rest of Quebec province	173
Kingston (Ont.)	168
Hamilton (Ont.)	155
London (Ont.)	150
Rest of New Brunswick province	132
Vancouver (B.C.)	122
Rest of British Columbia province	122
Winnipeg (Man.)	121
Rest of Nova Scotia province	120
Prince Edward Island	116
Rest of Manitoba province	115
Northwest Territories	112
Rest of Ontario province	105

Quebec counties		Ontario counties	
Five highest		Prescott	151
Quebec county	225	Russell	151
Portneuf	220	Nipissing	150
Deux-Montages	218	Algoma	141
L'Assomption	216	Essex	120
Montmorency	216	Grenville South	79
Five lowest		Dundas	84
Brome	90	Durham	84
Mississquoi	92	Lennox	85
Pontiac	93	Oxford	87
Stanstead	95		
Huntingdon	99		

attempts to capture the sort of variation discussed later in the chapter by reporting rates of deaths in the first year of life, per thousand births, for the 11 largest cities across the country, for the residuals of each province, and then, within the provinces of Ontario and Quebec for which the estimates were made in greater detail, the 5 highest-ranking and the 5 lowest-ranking counties of each province. Before proceeding to a consideration of infant mortality in Canada, an abbreviated account of how the estimates were derived seems in order. By the very late years of the century civil registration of deaths had developed far enough in Ontario and Quebec that reasonably reliable data were being generated.[40] Infant mortality rates centered on 1901 were used as a benchmark and then projected backward to 1891 on the basis of a combination of registration statistics, census reports of deaths in the first year of life, and census reports of deaths from causes that affected primarily infant mortality. For the cities and provinces outside Ontario and Quebec, just the relative levels in census mortality reports were used.[41]

The most prominent features of Canadian infant mortality in 1891 are its variability, the strong urban/rural differential, and the notable gap between francophone and anglophone Canada. It would be misleading to look at a Canadian average because late-nineteenth-century infant mortality appears to have had two regimes. Francophone Canada's rates of infant mortality were much higher than these of anglophone Canada. The rate for the entire province of Quebec (190) would place it among the high infant mortality group of countries, higher than France and about comparable with Italy and Germany. In striking contrast, the Ontario average (115) would place it at the low end of international experience of the time, at about the same level as Australia, Sweden, and the white population of the United States (as implied by the recent estimate by Michael Haines and Samuel Preston).[42] The infant mortality rate for Ontario was lower than that in England and Wales but by no more than might be

---

[40] Important improvements occurred in the decade of the 1890s, so that by 1900 the registration of infant deaths was notably more reliable than in 1891. The 1891 estimates here are developed by working back from those better figures for 1901. That complicates the estimating procedure. The registration data for three years centered on both census years were carefully edited. Shortfalls were notable in a few districts, especially in 1891. The reporting system had not been fully perfected. Provincial averages were computed excluding those districts. District deviations from the provincial average were calculated directly from the registration data for 1901 and then adjusted for consistency with cause of death data. The provincial average for 1891 was adjusted to district levels by projecting backward the 1901 district deviations in relation to census enumerations of total infant deaths and deaths by cause for four categories of mortality that show close relationship to infant mortality (particularly deaths from gastroenteritis).

[41] The Canadian censuses had collected mortality data from 1851 onward, but those statistics were widely regarded as incomplete and inadequate. Continuing efforts were made to improve them, especially since the country lacked an effective registration system. One of the most serious problems with census reports of deaths was the undercount of deaths of older people who left no one behind to report their passing. Infant mortality was more fully and accurately reported. By 1891 the numbers of infant deaths reported in the census in many districts exceeded those recorded in the civil registers, and in some of those districts the rates were so high that one could hardly believe they could be seriously understated. In 1901 the census office devoted a great deal of attention to special investigations of the mortality statistics.

[42] Haines and Preston, *Fatal Years*.

implied by Ontario's lesser extent of urbanization. The rate for Quebec, though, is two-thirds higher than that of Ontario and exceeds the rates for black Americans that Haines and Preston derive with the surviving-children method. Although the most remarkable feature of Canadian infant mortality is the much higher rate of francophones than of anglophones, the strong differential between the cities and the countryside also merits attention. It was much more hazardous to be born in the city. Infant mortality in Montreal and Quebec City was dramatically high by world standards. No other cities in North America came close. There may have been an ethnic component to that, but it should not be overemphasized. Montreal's population at the time was about evenly divided between French and English; certainly it was not a wholly francophone city. Toronto was still a considerably smaller city than Montreal. Nevertheless it had quite a high rate of infant mortality. In the western regions of Canada the rural/urban differential was much smaller, and the city of Vancouver had an infant mortality rate no higher than the remainder of the province of British Columbia. Low rates of infant mortality were found on the frontier of settlement in western Canada and in wholly rural Prince Edward Island, but the most favored districts were in rural Ontario. The counties of Ontario with the lowest rates of infant mortality, such as Grenville South (79) and neighboring Dundas (84), ranked quite low by international standards. In at least some parts of Canada, then, people were able to hold infant mortality down to levels as low as could be found anywhere else in the world. By contrast, in some districts of francophone Canada infant mortality was remarkably high. In the five highest counties of rural Quebec infant mortality was up almost to city levels. Three of those counties surrounded the city of Quebec and two were adjacent to Montreal, but they were still well removed from the city and, except for Quebec County, had essentially no urban development. These were quite strictly rural districts with exceptionally high infant mortality. It should be added that another six or seven rural counties came close behind, so the ones pointed out here do not stand apart.

There was an extensive region of Quebec in which rural infant mortality was especially high. The districts involved were all relatively close to the two main cities of the province.[43] A simple cultural explanation of the pattern of variation in infant mortality should not be overemphasized, however, because another region comprising several wholly francophone

---

[43] This may appear to suggest a wet-nursing industry in the countryside adjacent to Montreal and Quebec. That cannot be entirely ruled out, but a thorough investigation turned up no clear evidence to support such a hypothesis.

counties had considerably lower rates of infant deaths. In the rural districts of the lower Saint Lawrence (e.g., Charlevoix, Bellechasse, Kamouraska, Rimouski, and Temiscouata Counties), the rate of infant mortality averaged 140–50. Although still somewhat on the high side, it was well below that of districts closer to the large cities.

Statistics derived from the Canadian census of 1891 permit some further testing of suggestions in the literature about causal factors relating to infant mortality. Two that have been emphasized are illiteracy and crowded housing conditions. The former gets some weak support from the Canadian evidence but not the latter. High infant mortality is also said to be a sensitive indicator of low income. That is not borne out at all by the Canadian data. When compared with estimates of farm net income for counties of Ontario and Quebec, infant mortality was in fact lower, not higher, in the low-income counties. Since both income and infant mortality would have been higher in the cities than in the countryside, incorporating urban centers into the analysis would accentuate the inverse relationship between infant mortality and income in late-nineteenth-century Canada.[44]

Earlier it was pointed out that generally useable mortality data become available for Canada only at the beginning of the twentieth century, so it is not possible to say anything about the trend of mortality except for that in the late nineteenth century. Although synthetic life tables have been constructed for Canada as a whole and for the province of Quebec, it has to be emphasized that these are based not on actual Canadian evidence, but on the collective experience of other countries.[45] They can be used for some types of survival calculations but are not reliable for infant mor-

---

[44] A statistical analysis of all districts of Ontario and Quebec together is completely dominated by the ethnic variable representing the proportion of French. We learn nothing new from it. Regression analysis can be used to look at influences on infant mortality rates within each province. There is not enough variation within Ontario to obtain significant results. For Quebec counties, the following equation is estimated:

$$IMR = -22.5 + 53.8URB + 0.52FR + 65.2LIT + 24.5HOU + 1.59DG,$$
$$(3.8) \quad (2.4) \quad (0.9) \quad (1.0) \quad (6.6)$$

where URB is the percentage of the population living in urban centers, FR is the percentage French Canadian, LIT is the proportion unable to read or write, HOU is the the number of persons per room (an indicator of crowded housing conditions), and DG is the death rate from diarrhea and gastroenteritis. The t statistics are given in parentheses. Adjusted R^2 is 0.68. It is interesting that the FR variable is statistically significant even when the DG measure is included. The constant term is not statistically significant; and if the equation is reestimated with the constant term constrained to be zero, the coefficients of all variables remain virtually the same, with the exception of illiteracy (LIT), for which the value of the coefficient drops to 45.3, but its variance also declines so that, with a t value of 2.5, it becomes statistically significant.

[45] Bourbeau and Légaré, *Évolution de la mortalité*.

Table 9.6. *Fertility and change in fertility, Canadian cities and provinces, 1861–1891*

City and province	Indexes of fertility, 1891			Change, 1861–91 (%)		
	I_f	I_g	I_m	I_f	I_g	I_m
Cities						
Halifax	.267	.565	.473	n.a.	n.a.	n.a.
Saint John	.253	.557	.455	n.a.	n.a.	n.a.
Quebec	.359	.783	.459	−8.9	−5.8	−3.2
Trois-Rivières	.404	.793	.509	−5.4	−2.0	−3.4
Montreal	.337	.669	.504	−28.6	−19.0	−11.7
Ottawa	.285	.591	.483	−34.6	−15.1	−22.8
Kingston	.286	.612	.467	−27.6	−14.6	−15.2
Toronto	.260	.525	.495	−25.7	−22.0	−4.8
Hamilton	.267	.521	.512	−33.2	−16.5	−21.5
London	.232	.509	.455	−36.6	−23.3	−17.4
Winnipeg	.299	.542	.551	n.a.	n.a.	n.a.
Vancouver	.343	.464	.728	n.a.	n.a.	n.a.
Provinces						
Prince Edward Island	.357	.835	.427	n.a.	n.a.	n.a.
Nova Scotia	.340	.674	.505	−15.6	−11.9	−4.2
New Brunswick	.366	.706	.518	−25.0	−18.5	−8.2
Quebec (ex cities)	.458	.815	.562	−4.4	−6.9	+2.7
Ontario (ex cities)	.305	.579	.526	−32.7	−25.2	−10.1
Manitoba (ex Winnipeg)	.474	.716	.662	n.a.	n.a.	n.a.
Northwest Territories	.442	.647	.683	n.a.	n.a.	n.a.
British Columbia (ex city)	.344	.464	.741	n.a.	n.a.	n.a.

n.a. Cannot be calculated; no 1861 base.

tality, where, as already pointed out, the Canadian picture is quite compli-cated. At present, however, the levels of adult mortality portrayed by the tables in Bourbeau and Légaré probably give the best available indication of what nineteenth-century mortality might have looked like in Canada.

The estimated fertility indexes for Canada in 1891 are displayed in Table 9.6. There the more firmly based figures for Ontario and Quebec are com-bined with somewhat rougher estimates for four of the largest cities outside those provinces and for the residual parts of the provinces and the Northwest Territories. Table 9.7 presents a selection of the county data for Ontario and Quebec to exemplify points brought up in the following

Table 9.7. *Fertility and change in fertility, selected counties of Quebec and Ontario, 1861–1891*

County	Indexes of fertility, 1891			Change, 1861–91 (%)		
	I_f	I_g	I_m	I_f	I_g	I_m
Quebec						
Highest fertility counties[a]						
Deux-Montagnes	.518	1.021	.508	+1.4	+4.4	+2.9
Terrebonne	.562	1.021	.550	+11.1	+15.5	−4.0
Rimouski	.561	1.010	.555	+10.9	+16.9	−5.3
Montmorency	.496	.991	.501	+13.5	+3.7	+9.6
L'Islet	.525	.982	.535	+5.8	+2.6	+3.3
Champlain	.539	.962	.560	+13.7	+2.8	+10.7
Chicoutimi[b]	.565	.849	.666	+0.5	+2.8	−2.1
Beauce	.549	.917	.599	+2.4	−4.3	+7.0
Lowest fertility counties[c]						
Brome	.345	.523	.659	−12.2	−22.6	+13.2
Stanstead	.328	.537	.611	−9.9	−24.6	+19.6
Sherbrooke	.385	.591	.652	−10.9	−28.0	+23.7
Mississquoi	.381	.618	.617	−8.4	−10.0	+1.8
Compton	.409	.689	.594	+0.5	−12.6	+15.1
Huntingdon	.348	.723	.481	−12.9	−3.9	−7.9
St. Jean	.372	.704	.528	−22.8	−10.3	−13.9
Other counties with large declines						
Laprairie	.445	.731	.609	+3.7	−21.6	+32.4
Iberville	.445	.800	.556	−11.2	−16.8	+6.9
Ontario						
Highest fertility counties[d]						
Prescott	.477	.891	.535	−2.7	+3.0	−5.5
Glengarry	.368	.837	.440	−8.2	−19.9	+14.6
Russell	.456	.830	.550	−5.4	−17.0	+14.1
Renfrew	.405	.795	.510	−17.5	+2.2	−19.2
Nipissing	.491	.710	.693			
Algoma	.445	.709	.627			
Muskoka	.464	.644	.721			
Lowest fertility counties[e]						
Prince Edward	.205	.345	.589	−44.9	−44.3	−1.0
Lennox	.232	.430	.539	−34.6	−34.0	+1.0
Brant	.231	.450	.513	−53.2	−37.8	−24.8
Elgin	.251	.459	.547	−37.9	−35.8	−3.2
Norfolk	.268	.466	.575	−39.5	−34.6	−7.6
Wellington South	.245	.526	.466	−41.4	−29.1	−17.4

Table 9.7. *(cont.)*

County	Indexes of fertility, 1891			Change, 1861–91 (%)		
	I_f	I_g	I_m	I_f	I_g	I_m
Grenville South	.249	.489	.509	−21.2	−38.4	−12.2
Lincoln	.251	.496	.507	−32.5	−24.8	−9.9
Other counties with large declines						
Perth	.282	.585	.482	−47.3	−31.9	−22.6
Huron	.271	.591	.458	−46.3	−24.3	−29.2

[a] Five counties with highest I_g, plus three counties with highest I_f that also had high values of marital fertility.
[b] Includes Lac St. Jean and Saguenay.
[c] Five counties with lowest I_g, plus two low I_g counties that ranked lowest in I_f.
[d] Four counties with highest I_g, plus three high I_g counties with highest-ranking I.
[e] Five lowest-ranking counties by I_g, plus three low I_g counties that ranked lowest in I_f.

discussion. Note that by 1891 Canada had become a relatively low fertility part of the world. More precisely, it was anglophone Canada that had made that transition; French Canada continued to display very high fertility. More than ever, the figures for 1891 emphasize that Canada was a nation of two fertility cultures. A national average rate of marital fertility of .669 can be reported, as can an average I_f value of .338; but those figures are misleading. It is more revealing to continue to treat Quebec and Ontario separately. That is made clear in Figure 9.3, where the fertility rates for Ontario, Quebec, and the Canadian national average are depicted along with a set of European countries. The countries are ordered by their I_g values. Ontario, on the far left of the diagram, is second lowest after France. Quebec, on the far right, ranks higher than any of the European countries. In Ontario much of the fertility transition had been accomplished by 1891, a date at which it was just getting under way in many parts of Europe. The prominent features of that development are pursued first, before turning to the equally interesting case of Quebec, which remained, for the most part, resistant to a decline in fertility.

In Europe, only France had a lower rate of marital fertility than the Canadian province of Ontario, while Hungary, with I_g = .580, was not much above Ontario. Although higher proportions of women were married in Canada than in Europe, because of low marital fertility, I_f in Ontario had dropped to a typically European level. More important,

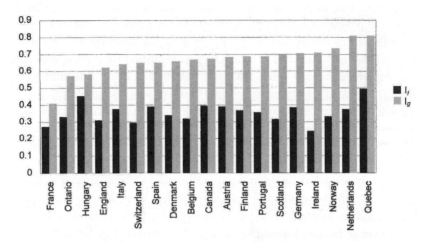

Figure 9.3. Indices of fertility, Canada and Europe, ca. 1891

Ontario still had some districts with very high fertility, but the rates of marital fertility in its low-fertility counties had fallen well below typical European levels. Fertility rates in the rural districts of Ontario were also far below those of the largest European cities. The situation in other anglophone provinces is also of interest.

Across the nation fertility had dropped to low levels in the cities. That was especially the case for overall fertility, partly because of the low rates of marital fertility but also because nuptiality in the cities tended to be lower than in the countryside. An exception was the recently founded city of Vancouver, where a remarkably high proportion of women were married. Elsewhere in anglophone Canada, low nuptiality was mainly to be found in the cities. It would probably be mistake to interpret this as some form of demographic adaptation. Rather, it reflects the fact that the cities had become places of employment opportunity for young unmarried women. In 1861 the cities, except for Toronto, had been places with relatively high rates of nuptiality. Married women moved there with their husbands. Toronto, though, had already begun to look "modern." By 1891 the cities had become places to which young women migrated because that was where the jobs were.[46] The consequent decline in the nuptiality

---

[46] It should be pointed out that this was not primarily a reflection of a congregation of immigrant women in the cities, as was seen at this time in the United States. As will be discussed in a later section, Canada was at this time a nation of large-scale emigration. Immigrants were indeed coming, including single women, but their numbers were more than offset by the massive emigration.

rate contributed importantly to the fall in overall fertility in the cities. In Ottawa and Hamilton, for example, the larger part of the drop in I_f can be attributed to the decline in I_m. By contrast, in Toronto, where the fall in nuptiality had already been largely accomplished by 1861, the decline in I_f depended mainly on a fall in I_g that was scarcely outstanding by Ontario standards. In general, marital fertility was not strikingly low in Ontario cities. By 1891 many rural districts had an I_g as low or lower. In the eastern Maritime region, city rates of marital fertility were as low as in the Ontario cities. There, however, the gap between the cities and the rural districts was much larger. In the west the city of Winnipeg had similarly low marital fertility that again reflected a sharp contrast with the rural part of the province of Manitoba. Further west, however, the situation was quite different. The newly emergent city of Vancouver had the lowest marital fertility rate in the nation.[47] Vancouver's low I_g was no lower, however, than that of the remainder of the province.[48]

The small and almost entirely rural province of Prince Edward Island reveals an outstanding picture of exceptionally high marital fertility, about as high as that of francophone Quebec, coupled with the lowest rate of nuptiality in the nation. The upshot is that overall fertility was not remarkably high. Here is seen, in accentuated form, the old European, or what is perhaps better described as Malthusian, pattern. Rural Nova Scotia and New Brunswick had lower rates of marital fertility than Prince Edward Island, but the rates were still fairly high, almost reminiscent of Ontario's rates of 30 years earlier. On the western plains, in the area of new settlement, marital fertility was also high, although not as high, perhaps, as many observers might have expected.[49] Further west, British Columbia had strikingly low marital fertility but exceptionally high nuptiality.

County data for Ontario, being more firmly based and geographically more finely differentiated, provide better clues to the processes involved in determining the pattern of fertility variation. The 1891 pattern displays a complex web of situations and processes. Marital fertility ranged from very low to very high levels by international standards. Table 9.7

---

[47] Readers might be reassured to know that this relationship holds up in subsequent years as well. It is not just a quirk of the data.

[48] In fairness, it should be pointed out that not much of that remainder could be called truly rural. It included the capital city of Victoria and several large mining towns. This was not a rural, agricultural residual of the usual sort.

[49] It is worth remembering that in 1891 the settlers of the Canadian plains were still predominantly from Ontario. It was Manitoba, rather than the Territories, that had the more prominent ethnic immigrant population with Icelandic and Russian Mennonite settlers. Manitoba did have the higher rate of marital fertility.

summarises county data relevant to this discussion, singles out the highest- and lowest-fertility counties, and emphasizes marital fertility. The highest fertility group consists of the four counties with highest I_g plus three counties not thereby included that had the highest I_f. Of course, some of the counties with the highest I_g also would be included in the list of counties with highest I_f. The main point is that these were high-fertility districts by almost any standard. Table 9.7 treats the lowest-fertility counties in similar fashion, listing the five counties with lowest I_g plus three additional counties with low I_f that are included by virtue of their low I_f values. Overall fertility is very low for all of these counties, ranging from .205 in Prince Edward to .268 in Norfolk. The five selected on the basis of low I_g also have strikingly low marital fertility. Furthermore, most of these were predominantly rural counties; yet their rates of marital fertility were well below those of the largest cities in Canada, or of anywhere else in the world, for that matter. An especially interesting feature of the Canadian fertility transition is that it was not primarily an urban phenomenon but occurred most dramatically in the countryside.

In addition, the largest declines in marital fertility came not in the lagging, high-fertility counties, but in those districts that already were in the vanguard by 1861. Lennox and Prince Edward counties had the lowest I_g in 1861 Ontario and not only were again the lowest in 1891 but had among the largest percentage declines over the period. The five lowest-fertility counties in 1891, as judged by I_g, experienced declines of more than one-third over the years since 1861. Only four other counties had larger declines, and they were all early settled, lakefront counties that also had relatively low fertility in 1861. A process that had been under way prior to 1861 continued vigorously over the succeeding three decades.

The overall fertility situation is a bit more mixed. Although the largest declines in overall fertility were in those counties that experienced the greatest declines in marital fertility, two additional counties were at the top of the list. Brant's I_f dropped by more than one-half, and the third largest drop was in South Wellington. Brant was also notable for a very large decline in I_g, whereas South Wellington was more average in that regard. These two counties included important, rapidly growing urban centers. Brantford, in the county of Brant, and Guelph, in South Wellington, held a large fraction of the population of their respective counties and were rapidly developing industrial towns.

The role of urbanization in the decline of fertility in Ontario remains unclear. By 1891 urban areas had low marital fertility, but low I_g was not the sole domain of urban areas. Indeed, as already pointed out, many rural districts had marital fertility every bit as low, and the lowest I_g values of all were to be found in rural districts. The rural counties with low I_g tended to be the ones settled earlier and had already reached their peak densities of population. A positive influence of land availability can still be seen in the 1891 figures. The counties settled late still had higher-than-average fertility, although marital fertility had fallen in almost all of them. Some of the counties settled late, such as Huron and Perth, were among those with the largest declines in overall fertility. That is because significant drops in marital fertility (25% or more) were accompanied by large declines in I_m. That again reinforces the point that, as land is increasingly taken up in the areas of new settlement, the proportion of women married declines, and then, with a lag, marital fertility begins to decline. The initial drop in I_m is partly a reflection of the selectivity of frontier settlement in favor of married women, making the early levels of I_m unusually high there, but it is not only that. An adaptation appears to be going on as nuptiality falls below the provincial average. The steep declines in marital fertility rates that come later are commonly accompanied by increases in nuptiality.

In 1891 some districts of Ontario still had very high marital fertility. They comprised, first, those few districts with large francophone populations (Prescott, Russell, and Glengarry),[50] and, second, those rececntly settled, especially on the northern forest frontier. Algoma, Nipissing, and Muskoka Counties had both high marital fertility and high nuptiality; hence their rates of overall fertility were especially high. Other northern frontier counties also ranked toward the upper end of fertility rates. Of the strictly agricultural counties, the most recently settled already had little unoccupied land remaining and by 1891 had rates of marital fertility below .600. That is, they had already fallen to levels that were low by European standards. We see this in Perth and Huron counties, listed in Table 9.7, and also in Grey and North Wellington (not shown), among the last counties to be settled, where I_g was .607 and .604 respectively.

Little else can be said about the process of fertility decline in Ontario from the evidence at hand, especially since there have been few comple-

---

[50] The francophone populations of these counties were not only just high but rising, as migrants came in from Quebec. Other pockets of francophone population, such as in Essex County, also show up with relatively high fertility. The ethnic factor is not solely a matter of French Canadian culture, however, as Glengarry County shows. Its Roman Catholic Highland Scottish population had given it the highest I_g of any Ontario county in 1861. That population was being augmented by French Canadian immigrants and the rate of marital fertility continued to be near the top.

mentary, detailed studies.[51] Some of the more obvious variables, such as literacy, do not display enough geographic variability to generate explanatory power. Income change per se reveals no association. The geographic patterns in the aggregate data examined here show interesting systematic patterns, but they do not offer explanations. The investigation of the intriguing and precocious case of fertility decline in Ontario has scarcely begun.

Quebec, which for the most part remained a bastion of high fertility, nevertheless poses some interesting questions. Of course, the overriding feature of fertility in Quebec was that, in the francophone districts that made up most of the province, marital fertility remained at extremely high levels right up to 1891. In many districts, measured levels of I_g actually rose, but given the margins of error in the data and in the estimation procedure, that should not be taken too seriously. Most observed changes were within the range of possible measurement error. French Canadian fertility seems to have remained by and large impervious to any sort of influence. Levels of I_g in most wholly francophone counties were above .900, and in at least a half-dozen districts I_g was indistinguishable from unity. This was in a setting where land was all taken up, urbanization was increasing, and income was relatively high and growing.[52] The Quebec picture, however, was not one of uniform ultra-high fertility.

As one might suppose, the three main cities of Quebec had lower fertility rates than the rural districts. The level of I_g in Montreal, with a mixed francophone-anglophone population, was only a bit above that of such European cities as Copenhagen and Edinburgh. Quebec City was more preponderantly French and had higher marital fertility, yet even there the I_g rate (.783) was almost 20% below that of the rural districts. Nuptiality was quite low in Quebec City, so overall fertility was not out of line with European standards of the time, despite the high rate of marital fertility. French Canadian fertility may have been high, but in the cities French Canadians were evidently beginning to lower their rates of reproduction. The lowest fertility in Quebec was in the predominantly anglophone districts such as Brome, Mississquoi, and Stanstead. These counties look very

---

[51] Of the more thorough investigations, Gaffield's, "Children, Schooling and Family Reproduction" focuses, unfortunately for present purposes, on Prescott County, the highest fertility district of Ontario and one in which marital fertility was especially slow to come down. Moore, "Fertility Decline in Three Ontario Cities," has looked at the larger cities and emphasizes religious and cultural variables but gives little indication of how those would have produced a change in fertility.

[52] In Canadian historical writing, Quebec is usually depicted as a lagging region with lower income and retarded industrialization. That has to be seen in relation to other parts of Canada that were progressing rapidly. By international standards, late-nineteenth-century Quebec looks prosperous and advancing economically.

much like comparable areas of Ontario. They were almost wholly rural areas, long settled, and with no land left to be taken up. By 1891 French Canadians were just beginning to move into those counties. The French Canadian presence was already somewhat greater in other low-fertility counties such as Compton, Huntingdon, and St. Jean. Sherbrooke and St. Jean also had proportionally large urban populations. Marital fertility was falling in anglophone Quebec, although not as dramatically as in Ontario. The fall was offset to a considerable degree by rising nuptiality, however, so that the declines in overall fertility were generally quite modest.

One of the most interesting features of the fertility situation in late-nineteenth-century Quebec is that marital fertility had already declined in a few wholly francophone districts. The counties of Laprairie and Iberville stand out, with I_g having dropped by more than 15% between 1861 and 1891. These were rural districts south of Montreal and were surrounded by other counties where a decline in I_g was evident, even if not as large. It appears, then, that at least in one district of francophone Quebec the fertility transition was under way by 1891, which was at least as early as in most of Europe. Why those districts might have led the way must remain a topic for future research.

What has been shown, then, is that over the late decades of the nineteenth century Canada displayed a sharply differentiated pattern of fertility change. It ranged all the way from no perceptible decline from maximal rates of reproduction to very large reductions in marital fertility. At least in much of the country the fertility transition was not only well under way but to a large extent accomplished. Elsewhere, however, reproduction remained at essentially natural rates. Canada still encompassed regions of abundant land where new settlers could continue to reproduce at high rates. It also encompassed regions such as those on the Pacific coast where marital fertility was remarkably low by the world standards of the time. Canada presents a highly variegated picture, indeed.

IMMIGRATION, EMIGRATION, AND CANADIAN POPULATION GROWTH IN THE LATTER HALF OF THE NINETEENTH CENTURY

Until the late 1850s Canada's population had grown rapidly through a combination of large-scale immigration and very high rates of natural increase. Over the years from 1861 until the end of the century that situation changed markedly. The rate of growth of the population slowed considerably, although it still remained relatively high by international standards. As the preceding section has shown, the birth rate declined substantially over the last four decades of the century, although not uniformly across the country. The other major change was that Canada switched from being a country of immigration to being one of emigration. Over the last four decades of the nineteenth century, Canada lost large numbers of people through emigration to the United States. Immigrants still arrived in Canada, in some years in quite large numbers, but many of them moved on to the United States as well. The rate of emigration from Canada was higher, as much as double, that of any European nation. Ireland and Norway are usually singled out as the nations of heaviest emigration in the late nineteenth century, but Canada was actually the outstanding country of emigration.

In the 1860s the present nation of Canada was formed out of several British North American colonies. Confederation in 1867 with the two Maritime colonies of Nova Scotia and New Brunswick ushered in a new era of great optimism and a great thirst for growth. The new nation encompassed a huge area but had a small population. With a mere three and a half million people, it was in a category with the small nations of the world: Belgium, the Netherlands, Sweden, and Switzerland. It had approximately one-tenth the population of its neighbor to the south, a ratio that had been established toward the end of the seventeenth century.[53] The British North American colonies that formed Canada had just about run out of unoccupied land fit for agricultural settlement. One of the first actions the new nation took was vastly to extend its territory. It purchased a great part of the land mass of present-day Canada from the Hudson's Bay Company and shortly thereafter induced the British colonies on the Pacific coast to join Confederation as the province of British Columbia. By 1871, then, this new Canadian nation had a huge amount of land but still very few people. The other Maritime colonies of Newfoundland and Prince Edward Island had declined to join the feder-

---

[53] The very first permanent European settlements in Canada and what was to become the United States were made at just about the same time, in the opening years of the seventeenth century. The Virginia and Massachusetts Bay colonies received large numbers of new settlers in the 1630s and 1640s, whereas New France remained nothing more than an outpost. By about 1680 a more sizable settlement had been established, and by then, or a little before, the long-term ratio of 1 to 10 had been set. Over the long haul the rates of population growth of Canada and the United States were about the same, but the size differential had been established within a few decades of the beginning of settlement.

ation, although the people of the latter soon changed their minds and entered Confederation as a separate province in 1873.

One of the priorities of the newly federated Canada was to attract immigrants and to induce settlers to its new western territory. Until the end of the century, however, western settlement proceeded slowly. Immigrants came, but in much smaller numbers than had been hoped. Most disappointingly, Canadians themselves left their homeland in vast numbers to settle in the United States. Indeed, the emigrant outflow reached the dimensions of a veritable hemorrhage and was viewed as such by many Canadians. The new nation could hardly be said to be a success when so many wanted to leave.

In nineteenth-century Canada, immigrants meant people from Britain. Apart from the French Canadians, the country was overwhelmingly British in its ethnic makeup. The early movement from the United States had brought a few people of Dutch and German stock, including Mennonites from Pennsylvania, and in the 1850s there was a small influx of Germans. Immigrants to Canada, though, were essentially British.[54] For the most part, that would continue to be the case. Canada sought immigrants to settle its western lands. British immigrants continued to arrive in Canada, but almost all of the them settled in Ontario.[55] Ever hopeful Canadian authorities assiduously sought agricultural settlers wherever they might find them. In the 1870s two non-British "ethnic" groups were brought to Canada: Icelanders fleeing disease and starvation in their homeland, and ethnically German Mennonites from Russia. Both groups made successful settlements in Manitoba, but the numbers were not large.[56] In the following decade Chinese laborers were brought to the Pacific coast to work on the construction of the Canadian Pacific Railway. Immigration of Ukrainians began in the early 1890s.[57] There were a few

---

[54] They should not be thought of as primarily English. The largest single element was Irish, and there were about as many Scots as English. Until the famine migration of the late 1840s, the Irish tended to be largely northern and Protestant. The ethnic character of anglophone Canada was, more than anything, Ulster Irish.

[55] In the report on immigration for 1869, published by the Department of Agriculture, it was estimated (p. 3) that 18,630 of the 74,365 persons who arrived at ports of entry intended to settle in Canada, 17,202 of them in Ontario. The same report says of the estimate of persons arriving who were judged to be intending to settle, "Little reliance can be placed on these figures; the data upon which they are based are imperfect, and, in some instances, conjectural." That has not deterred scholars from using them.

[56] About 6,200 Mennonites and possibly twice that number of Icelanders had been added to Manitoba's poulation by 1896.

[57] These arrived from the Austrian Empire and from Russia under the designations of Ruthenians, Galicians, and Bukovinians. The 1901 census of Canada lists only 5,682 persons of Ukrainian origin but another 10,947 Austrian and 19,825 Russian. The preponderant part of these would have come in the five years preceding the census.

hints, then, of the changing ethnic mix that would be seen in the early twentieth century; but, at least prior to 1896, the numbers were sufficiently small that the impact was negligible. Right up to nearly the end of the nineteenth century immigrants to Canada were British.[58]

Another interesting dimension of Canadian population change in this late-nineteenth-century period was a notable degree of urban growth. In 1861 Canada was an overwhelmingly rural nation. By the modern American definition of urban (i.e., having a population of more than 2,500), only 13.2% of Canada's population fell in this category. That may be a rather restrictive view of urbanization, but including smaller towns would not raise the fraction much at all. Canada had only five cities with more than 25,000 people, and one of those, Halifax, made the cutoff by a mere 26 people. There was no city with a population of more than 100,000. Montreal, the largest city (with 90,000), was not quite double the size of the next leading contender, Quebec City. Toronto, today the largest city in Canada, was third in rank, with just 45,000. Until the 1850s Quebec had been the foremost transatlantic port, but the dredging of the St. Lawrence River up to Montreal in that decade allowed Montreal to take over that function. The division of commercial activity between the two port cities on the St. Lawrence probably forestalled the emergence of a primate city in Canada. By 1861 Montreal had established ascendancy over Quebec City, but thereafter Toronto developed as a serious rival. Toronto was the commercial hub of the more economically vibrant economy of Ontario. Montreal remained the predominant banking center and the eastern terminus of the Canadian Pacific Railway, so it played an important role in the development of the Canadian west, in addition to being the leading Atlantic port.

Some might be tempted to describe the state of urbanization in Canada as rudimentary. Not only were its leading cities small, but it also had few smaller cities and towns. Canada East (Quebec Province), with the 2 largest cities and 15.7% of its population living in centers of more than 2,500, was the most urbanized part of the country, yet that was entirely a consequence of its having the 2 largest cities. Beyond that, Quebec was stunted. There were only 8 other places with more than 2,500 people, and they contained a mere 2.9% of the province's population. By contrast,

---

[58] Canada did not share in the "new" immigration that was sweeping into the United States. Very few Poles or Hungarians, only a trickle of Italians, and almost no Spanish came to Canada. Scandinavians were to migrate to Canada in the twentieth century, but, other than Icelanders, almost none came before the turn of the century, and even after that many of the Scandinavians resettled from the United States.

Canada West (Ontario) was only 13% urbanized and its metropolitan center, Toronto, had just 45,000 people, but it had already developed a structure of smaller urban places. It had 4 cities with more than 10,000 people each, and another 8 nascent cities with 5,000 to 10,000. In addition, it had a dozen smaller towns of more than 2,500 in population. In this respect, Ontario looked a lot more like the neighboring area to the south of the Great Lakes. With 24 urban places containing 9.8% of the province's population, Ontario had the greater part of its urban population outside of its largest city. To some extent Toronto was smaller than Montreal because it had to share urban function with many additional towns and cities, a situation quite different from that found in Quebec. In the Maritime colonies there were only 3 urban places separately identified in the censuses of 1861.

Nova Scotia had its capital city of Halifax but no other urban places that were separately counted. The same was true of Prince Edward Island, where the capital city of Charlottetown was the only separately identified urban place. It accourted for 8.3% of the population of Prince Edward Island, and in Nova Scotia the population of Halifax made up only 7.6% of the provincial total. New Brunswick had the small capital city of Fredericton in addition to the port city of Saint John, which in 1861 was still somewhat more populous than Halifax. With 13% of its population in centers of more than 2,500, New Brunswick was as "urbanized" as Ontario.

From this rudimentary level in 1861 Canada urbanized substantially by the end of the century. The urban proportion of the population more than doubled. Nevertheless, with only 28.7% of its population in centers of more than 2,500 in 1901, Canada was still not a very urbanized country. Large cities had become more prominent, however, and by 1901 cities of more than 25,000 population made up 21.1% of the national total. There were 11 such cities, the largest of which had grown especially rapidly. Montreal had quadrupled in size to 368,000 and Toronto had increased by a factor of five. Quebec City was left behind and only doubled in size. New cities of substantial size had emerged, notably Vancouver and Winnipeg in the West, but also the Ontario cities of Ottawa, Hamilton, London, and Saint Catharines. Urbanization in Quebec Province, however, continued to be focused largely on the two major cities of Montreal and Quebec. The province had only 14 places with more than 2,500 people, and those contained just 4% of the total population. By contrast, Ontario had 50 such places with 12% of the province's population. A well-developed structure of urban places had emerged in Ontario. On a lower absolute scale, much the same had happened in the Atlantic provinces, especially in Nova Scotia. Halifax had barely doubled in size to 51,000, but an array of smaller centers – Amherst, New Glasgow, Truro, and Yarmouth – also grew. The three Atlantic provinces had, besides Halifax and Saint John, 19 towns and cities with more than 2,500 people – more than the larger province of Quebec – and had an overall urban proportion of 21.0%, the same as the national average. An urban structure was just beginning to emerge in the Prairie provinces where only 15.2% of the population lived in urban places. British Columbia, on the other hand, was 40% urban. It was dominated by Vancouver, had a smaller capital city in Victoria, boasted several good-sized mining towns, but had very little in the way of agricultural hinterland.

By international standards, Canada in 1901 was still not a very urbanized country, but it had made substantial advances from the situation in 1861. Except in Quebec a structured urban hierarchy had developed. In that province, urbanization outside of the two main cities would have to wait until the twentieth century, which would also see a vigorous rivalry between Montreal and Toronto for preeminence. In 1901, however, Montreal still ruled supreme as the metropolis of Canada. Toronto's more rapid growth over the latter half of the nineteenth century was indicative of what was to come later.

Canada's cities and some of its agricultural districts attracted immigrants from Europe, yet the outstanding feature of the last four decades of the nineteenth century was massive emigration to the United States. Canadians left the countryside for the growing cities of the nation, but many more deserted the country to pursue opportunities south of the border. With a high, but declining, rate of natural increase, the population continued to grow, but the net impact of migration was negative, and substantially so. In a seminal article published 45 years ago, Nathan Keyfitz provided a decade-by-decade accounting of population change in Canada.[59] Using life table survival ratios, he made residual estimates of net migration and then, by adding to them the recorded immigration flows over the decade, calculated a residual estimate of gross emigration. What the balance sheets of population change over the decade showed in a dramatic way was what had long been perceived – that Canada had experienced massive emigration over the last four decades of the nineteenth century. It was the magnitude of the implied emigration that was shocking. Between 1881 and 1891, at a time when Canada's total population was

[59] Keyfitz, "The Growth of Canadian Population."

just a little over 4 million, Keyfitz estimated that 1.1 million had left for the United States. One is compelled to doubt that in just one decade one out of every four Canadians – man, woman, and child – could have departed for the United States.

Indeed, Keyfitz's estimates quickly came under critical fire, for two principal reasons. One concerned his choice of survival ratios, the other the validity of the immigration series. To start with the latter, it was pointed out that in the peak decade of emigration, the 1880s, immigration was running at the high level of 900,000 people, when net migration was estimated at 205,000. That made for an emigration of 1,100,000. Duncan McDougall, in particular, emphasized that large numbers of migrants to the United States were merely passing through Canada and may have stayed briefly before moving on.[60] It was misleading, he argued, to count this as immigration and then emigration. It should simply be netted out. As for the choice of survival ratios, there were no usable Canadian life tables for the nineteenth century, and, with so much emigration, census survival ratios were not an option. Keyfitz used a slightly adjusted version of the life table for England and Wales to obtain the needed survival ratios. Those, representing a more highly urbanized country, were probably not a very accurate reflection of the situation in Canada. Despite these criticisms Keyfitz's accounting of Canadian population change has come to be the widely accepted version and appears in almost all recent historical works that deal with the topic. An arguably more reliable alternative, however, is presented in Table 9.8. Details of this new accounting, which are, along with the previously discussed fertility estimates, a novel element of this chapter, are given in the appendix to this chapter.

To beginning with, it can be noted that the calculations are not very sensitive to the selection of survival rates. Census enumeration error is considerably more important but attracted little attention in the earlier criticisms of Keyfitz.[61] The net migration estimates presented here are built on the migration of adults, aged 15 to 44 years, when migration rates are highest; this approach gets around the most serious problems of enumeration error in the young and the elderly. For those middle ages, survival rates based on the model life tables of Bourbeau and Légaré are adequate. The net migration of adults aged 15 to 44 is then augmented by an estimate of the migration of children that is based upon the ratio of children to adult female net migration. The largest revision, however, comes from

---

[60] McDougall, "Immigration into Canada."
[61] He was himself sensitive to this problem and drew attention to it.

Table 9.8. *Accounting for Canadian population change, intercensal decades, 1861–1891 (thousands of people)*

Population	1861–71	1871–81	1881–91	1891–1901
Direct calculation				
Initial population	3,230[a]	3,689[a]	4,325	4,833
Estimated natural increase	688	860	771	821
Predicted population	3,918	4,549	5,096	5,654
End-of-decade population	3,689	4,325	4,833	5,371
Estimated net migration	−229	−224	−263	−283
Measured immigration	150	154	296	292
Implied emigration	379	378	559	575
Rate of emigration (%)	109.5	94.3	122.1	112.7
Canadian and foreign-born emigration calculated separately				
Canadian-born				
Initial population	2,547	3,105.1	3,715	4,186
Estimated natural increase	863	1,020	1,000	1,040
Predicted population	3,410	4,125	4,715	5,226
Actual end-of-decade population	3,105	3,715	4,186	4,672
Estimated emigration	305	410	529	554
Foreign-born				
Initial population	683	625	603	647
Predicted survivors	492	465	374	428
Actual end-of-decade population	625	603	647	699
Net Change	133	137	273	271
Measured immigration	150	154	296	292
Implied emigration of foreign-born[b]	17	17	23	21
Emigration of Canadian and foreign-				
born Combined	322	427	552	575

[a] Population in 1861 and 1871 includes Prince Edward Island and western regions that later became part of Canada.
[b] Net of immigration and departure within the decade.

a major alteration in the count of immigrants. Upon close examination, it turns out that the commonly used immigration series is greatly in error. Elsewhere I have shown that the commonly used, "official" immigration series contains a substantial overcount, partly because of some double-counting, most strikingly for the problematic 1880s.[62] The new immigration series revises downward the number of arrivals from 903,000 to only 296,000. That is bound to make a large difference in the accounting of

[62] McInnis, "Immigration and Emigration."

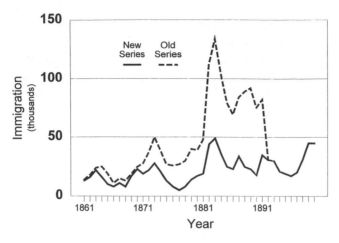

Figure 9.4. Immigration to Canada, overseas arrivals less departures to the United States, 1861–1900

population change. For the decade of the 1870s, the number of immigrants is cut in half, but for the 1860s and 1890s there is not much change. When the revised and the "official" immigration series are compared over the 1861–1901 period (see Figure 9.4), is quite evident that the major differences occur in the 1870s and 1880s. The revised series substantially downplays the idea that Canada was, like the United States, primarily a nation of immigration. Certainly there was some immigration, but considerably less than has usually been supposed. Incorporation of the revised immigration series into the accounting of population change produces, not surprisingly, a substantially altered picture of Canadian population development over the last four decades of the nineteenth century.

The highlights of the revised calculation are as follows. For all decades, the negative net migration is larger than previously presumed.[63] Then, because the revised immigration figures are lower than those used by Keyfitz, in some decades quite a bit lower, the residual emigration implied by the calculation is lower than in the Keyfitz accounting in all decades but the first. Even so, the implied numbers of emigrants are still very large for a country with as small a population as Canada has.

---

[63] That is primarily a consequence of dropping a small amount of positive net migration at older ages and reversing the fairly large positive net migration (that Keyfitz had shown for children) to a quite large negative figure, one that is more commensurate with the out-migration of middle-aged women.

Actually, it turns out that in the first decade under consideration, 1861–71, the estimated emigration is about the same as in the earlier accounting. In the revision, a larger negative net migration is coupled with a lower level of immigration so that the residual estimate of emigration from Canada is almost identical (379,000 compared with Keyfitz's estimate of 376,000). In the next two decades, however, the two sets of estimates diverge much more. In the 1870s the new figures posit a net out-migration that is twice as large and immigration of only half as much. This puts emigration from Canada in the 1870s at 308,000, in contrast to Keyfitz's figure of 438,000. In the following decade the difference is even greater. The revised estimate of net migration is not all that different from Keyfitz's, but the immigration figure is much lower. The net result is a figure of 559,000, which is only about half of his estimate of 1,108,000. Still, my revised figure represents a huge emigration from a country of barely 4.5 million people.[64] In the final decade of the nineteenth century the two sets of estimates again converge. The revised estimate of net migration is outward by a somewhat larger amount, but the figure for immigration is slightly lower, the net result being about half a million people in both series. An interesting feature of the revised series, however, is that the peak decade of emigration from Canada is the last decade of the century, not the 1880s, as has long been widely presumed.

The revised accounting offered here of population change in Canada may imply less emigration than previously thought to be the case. Nevertheless, it does not contradict the long-held view that, in the late nineteenth century, Canada was a nation characterized by massive emigration. The revised accounting does contribute to the resolution of a long-standing puzzle – how Canada should at one and the same time have been a country of immigration and of emigration on a large scale. It is now evident that Canada of that period could more accurately be described simply as a nation of emigration.[65]

What has not yet been explained is why Canada should have lost so many people to the United States. Was the economy of the newly formed Canadian Confederation a failure? A long-standing tradition in Canadian history has been to emphasize the slow growth and depressed condition of the Canadian economy over the whole period from 1873 to 1896 – as

[64] The rate of emigration per thousand mid-decade population, 122, is second in late-nineteenth/early-twentieth-century experience only to Ireland's rate of 142 per thousand in the 1870s.

[65] The evidence confirms that the situation was not just a matter of many immigrants coming first to Canada and then moving on to the United States. The emigration was more largely of persons born in Canada.

the often refered to "Long Depression." Viewed in that tradition, Canada's staple exports faltered in their expansion; the country failed to industrialize successfully; above all, its people voted with their feet in a massive emigration to the United States. In more recent times, that characterization of the late-nineteenth-century Canadian economy has been called into question and a more optimistic interpretation has emerged. By this newer account, Canada's real per capita income grew at a reasonably rapid pace over the whole period; and, at least over part of the period, industrialization proceeded quite rapidly. That interpretation might be reinforced by adding that by 1890 Canada's per capita output of manufactured goods was exceeded by only three nations in the world: the United Kingdom, the United States, and Belgium. Why, then, did so many Canadians want to emigrate?

Part of the answer lies in the demographic conditions of the early and mid–nineteenth century. As already noted, Canada was then a country with exceptionally high rates of natural increase. Birth rates were maximal in the frontier districts. Of course, the situation was not much different from that in the United States; but, in contrast to the United States, Canada had much less land suitable for cultivation onto which a growing population could expand. By shortly after midcentury, all of the potentially usable land in the Canada of the time had been taken up. In the United States, by contrast, settlement continued to push westward. In Canada, westward expansion was barred by a thousand miles of rock and bush. A vast area of land in the west was acquired at the time of Confederation, but that did not provide a solution right away. Only a few Canadians were willing to move there. The area was far from the developed part of Canada, or the relevant "rest of the world," for that matter, and it lacked effective transport connections. At the outset, it was not even known whether the Canadian segment of the North American Great Plains could be successfully farmed.[66] Eventually, the region would come to attract not only the people of central Canada but many from Europe and the United States. That, however, is a story of the twentieth century.

Over the last four decades of the nineteenth century, Canada lacked agricultural land to absorb the increase of its population. That increase

---

[66] In 1870, settlement in the United States had still not moved out onto the semiarid plains, with the exception perhaps of the Mormon settlement in Utah. Americans were still settling the more humid regions of eastern Kansas and Minnesota. The American push into the Red River Valley of the north came after 1870.

continued at a high, even if falling rate, while fertility adjusted downward. The quite rapid decline in fertility rates discussed in the previous section was not enough to keep population in line with the limited land available. The generally instructive point coming out of Canadian population history at this time is that the country that had one of the earliest and largest declines of fertility prior to 1890 was unable to adjust its population growth quickly enough to avoid massive emigration. The question might well be asked why additional population should have to be absorbed by extensive agricultural settlement. Why not expand employment in manufacturing industry or, for that matter, pursue more labor-intensive agriculture? The latter would require a shift in the mix of output to commodities with considerably more elastic demand. For a small country, the easiest way to do that is to seek out world markets. Indeed, to some extent, that is what Canadians did. Most notably, they created from the ground up a cheese industry that exported more than 90% of its output to Britain. As transatlantic transport costs fell, Canadians were also able to export live cattle and cured pork. Just by shifting from cereal crops to livestock products, though, it was probably not possible to raise the labor intensity of agriculture enough to provide employment for all of the increase in population.[67] The most obvious possibility would have been for Canada to turn to manufacturing goods for export. Most Canadian historians have been skeptical about the likelihood of that and instead have assumed that, for some reasons, Canadians were just not able to become competitive manufacturers. In a closed economy, wages and prices might be expected to adjust in such a way as to absorb all the labor in the economy. An open economy, from which the factors of production move and goods can be traded, offers a wider range of possible adjustments. The question of interest is why in the Canadian case the emigration option took precedence over other possibilities. Two considerations are important. One is that for Canada to expand exports of manufactured goods, Canadian prices, including wages, would have to drop commensurately. The U.S. border was completely open to Canadians, and a fall in wages in Canada simply increased the inducement to emigrate. In an era of unregulated international migration, wages in Canada could not deviate very far from those

---

[67] It should be acknowledged that increments to primary employment would have a multiplier effect. Each additional job in agriculture or manufacturing might be expected to be associated with two to two and one half jobs in service and commercial activities and in manufacturing directed to naturally protected local markets.

in the United States.[68] With better wage opportunities in the United States, Canadians would migrate there before other forms of adjustment could take effect.

A second consideration, which has received little attention in the literature, is that just as the problem of accommodating its increased population was first arising in Canada, and manufacturing industries to produce exports might have begun to develop, the United States sharply increased its tariffs. The tariff that was imposed during the Civil War and never removed during the remainder of the century was not only especially high but was structured in a manner that bore most heavily on nascent Canadian industries. By the early 1860s Canada had developed successful footwear and woolen cloth manufacturing industries. Shoes sold in Canada for about 25% less than in the United States. Shoes and woolens received about the highest protection offered by the Civil War tariff. With capital and labor both mobile, the erection of a tariff barrier had the predictable effect of inducing mobile factors of production to shift to the protected side of the boundary. This may not be the whole story, but when combined with the serious challenge raised by the high rate of natural increase and the lack of land for agricultural expansion, it may go some distance toward explaining why so many Canadians emigrated.[69]

Whatever the full complex of reasons, the outstanding feature of Canadian population development in the latter half of the nineteenth century was large-scale emigration, despite the substantial fall in fertility. Both forces operated to slow the growth of Canadian population at a time when the great influx of immigrants was keeping the growth rate of the

[68] What remains unknown is how much wages actually differed between Canada and the United States and how sensitive migration may have been to the wage differential. If Canada's per capita national income remained at about three-quarters the level of the United States as long as it appears to have done, that would seem to imply significantly lower wages in Canada. Why should that not have been sufficient to make Canadian manufactured exports to the United States profitable? In a similar vein, it has long been thought that the persistence of regional income differences within Canada reflected a low mobility of labor. If so, it would be difficult to maintain that Canadian labor readily moved to the United States in an elastic fashion. We are a long way from being provided with a consistent story of the economic development of the Canadian segment of North America.

[69] An added factor to mention is the geographic configuration of Canada, strung out thinly on a long border with the United States. When labor had to move, it was often just as cheap and easy to move to the United States as to another part of Canada. In the late nineteenth century the newly federated provinces, with independent histories and traditions, were not at all economically integrated. To a very large extent labor redistribution in Canada continued to be brought about by regionally differential exchanges with the United States and other countries until about the middle of the twentieth century.

population of the United States high. Between 1861 and 1901 the average annual rate of growth of Canada's population was 1.3% per annum, whereas that of the United States was 2.2%. By the end of the century Canada's population had fallen from its traditional position of 10% of that of the United States to a low point of just 7%. The century ended, however, on a more optimistic note. After 1896 the settlement of Canada's western plains got under way in dramatic fashion. The country's industries and its cities began to grow more rapidly. Immigrants began to arrive in much larger numbers, not only from overseas but from the United States. In the words of the prime minister of the day, "Canada's hour had struck."

APPENDIX: A REVISED ACCOUNTING FOR POPULATION CHANGE, 1861–1901

The revised accounting of population change presented in Table 9.8 consists of three steps. First, and most important, it employs a substantially revised immigration series. Second, it carries out the net migration calculation in a different manner. Third, it addresses the question of selecting appropriate survival ratios, an issue that was one of the foremost topics of criticism directed at Keyfitz's contribution. The survival ratio issue can be disposed of fairly easily. It hardly matters which of any more or less plausible estimates of late-nineteenth-century Canadian survival is selected. The estimates are not very sensitive to the choice of survival ratios. Here, for adult ages (over 15 years) the model life tables of Bourbeau and Légaré are adopted. Actually, the choice matters little; the results all come out to within the same numbers rounded to thousands of persons. Of much greater importance is the probable effect of census enumeration error. A striking feature of Keyfitz's net migration estimates is that, although they were strongly negative for the central, 15–44 year ages, the direction of movement invariably reversed for younger and older ages. If this result were to be taken literally, it would imply that, while many thousands of persons aged 15–44 emigrated, there was a sizable net immigration of persons 10–14. At the ages above 45, the net migration estimates typically were positive as well. The plausibility of this should have been questioned long ago. Keyfitz himself drew attention to it as an obvious problem, but the issue has not been taken up seriously. What is most likely appearing at the younger age group is the effect of the well-documented tendency to underenumerate young children. At the older ages, the problem might be either one of enumeration error, perhaps a systematic tendency of older persons to be reported as older than they actually are, or else a general deficiency of English- or any European-based life tables applied to the survival of older persons in Canada. The likely sources of the problem can be understood; the question is what to do about it. The approach followed here is to evaluate net migration only in terms of what was happening at the central, mobile ages. The first step is to estimate aggregate net migration as the net migration of persons 15–49 years of age. It is then assumed that there was essentially a zero balance for the older ages. A plausible case could be made for either some out-migration or some in-migration of older people, but the numbers would surely be so small as not to have any serious effect on the aggregate. Our best course at this stage is to ignore migration above some cutoff age, most plausibly 49. The migration of children cannot be ignored. The demography literature tends to downplay migration of children, but there is ample evidence that emigration from Canada was family migration, and some parts of the stream may in fact have been positively selective of married couples with children.[70] What is completely implausible, however, is that the migration of children would be substantially in the opposite direction to the migration of adults. Here the migration of children is estimated as a ratio to the movement of women in their middle ages. That is probably the best that can be done at present.[71]

The other major alteration made here concerns the record of immigration. Keyfitz (and, with the exception of McDougall, almost all subsequent writers) accepted without question the aggregate number of immigrant "settlers" reported annually by the immigration commissioner of the government of Canada.[72] This number was evaluated at the port of Quebec and

---

[70] French Canadians were highly concentrated in their destinations, moving overwhelmingly to the mill towns of southern New England. Unlike so many other migration movements, this one was not dominated by young, single people, especially males. The French Canadians moved in families for the most part. What New England had to offer was work for children in the textile mills. By putting their children to work in the mills, French Canadians were able substantially to augment family incomes. It seems that the wage available to adult male laborers in Massachusetts was barely 10 to 15% above that paid in Montreal. Canada had a shortage of textile mills or other industries that commonly employed large numbers of children. English Canadian emigrants to the United States from Ontario went preponderantly to Michigan. They were less likely to move as families, although many went to farm cutover land in central Michigan.

[71] Leaving aside any migration of children and simply taking the net migration of 15 to 49 year adults to reflect the aggregate would provide a lower-bound estimate of emigration. In each decade that would still imply a larger net emigration figure than the previously accepted estimates. Any amount of assumed child migration would raise the emigration estimates further.

[72] These were originally published in the annual reports of the Canadian Department of Agriculture up until 1891 and thereafter by the Department of the Interior. After the formation of the

at several inland ports of entry. Almost all of the overseas immigrants landed at Quebec. The problem was that many arrivals at Quebec were not immigrants to Canada but were headed to the United States. Passage to Quebec was usually the cheapest that European emigrants to North America could obtain; hence Quebec was an especially popular port of disembarkation.[73] The Canadian authorities were sensitive to this problem with the numbers, and they made a concerted effort to sort out those who intended to settle in Canada from those who were just passing through. The total number of arrivals at Quebec was divided into "passengers" ticketed to the United States and "immigrant arrivals intending to settle in Canada." The former usually outnumbered the latter by a considerable margin. A similar sort of categorization was made by the agents at each of the inland ports. Each year they reported total arrivals and estimated the number intending to settle in Canada. The national aggregate is the sum of those reports. The main difficulty with this is that Americans arriving for the most part at Niagara were all reported as "intended settlers." The numbers are large and should never have been accepted as part of the "true" immigrant inflow. The rail route through Canada was the shortest between New York and the American middle west, and it was heavily used by Americans. The numbers may even include some Americans who just came over to see Niagara Falls (or maybe even to honeymoon).

A further problem with the commonly used immigration series is that, beginning in 1873, it includes large numbers of arrivals reported by customs agents in addition to those counted by the immigration inspectors. Most of these additional arrivals were reported at inland ports of entry. They would almost all have come from the United States. Internal evidence indicates that many of them were returning Canadians, and most others were Americans. A few genuine immigrants may have been included, but the vast majority could in no sense have been immigrants. In some years the arrivals reported by customs exceeded the numbers counted by the immigration inspectors. It is best simply to leave the entire category out of the count of immigrants. That is, in fact, what the Canadian authorities did after 1891. The revised immigration series reported here is the same as the "official" series from 1892 onward. One must keep in mind that it still has some upward bias and that it still may contain some of the "flow-through" of immigrants really destined for the

Dominion Bureau of Statistics, they were presented as a sort of official series. Keyfitz gave as his source a table in *Canada Year Book* for 1942, but the same table has been published in many other places.

[73] It was also the case that in their eagerness to attract immigrants Canadian governments offered subsidized passages. Migrants had to remain in Canada long enough to collect rebates.

United States. For the purposes at hand, immigration is reestimated as *overseas* arrivals "intended to settle." The inflow of Americans is deducted entirely. The errors introduced by this procedure are partly offsetting. It leaves out genuine settlers arriving from the United States, but it leaves in overseas arrivals who falsely declared that they intended to settle in Canada. The latter number would have been much larger than the former, so the numbers used here should be thought of as still an upwardly biased measure of immigration. Furthermore, the count of arrivals reported by customs agents is dropped entirely. From 1867 to 1891 the revised series is considerably below the widely used "official" series of immigration.

With that explanation of how the data were handled, it is now possible to turn to Table 9.8. Net migration there is estimated as the net migration of persons 15–49 years of age at the beginning of the decade. Net migration of persons over age 45 is ignored on the grounds that the numbers most likely were trivial. An estimated number of child migrants is then added.[74] The new net migration estimate is then offset by the revised immigration figures to arrive at an estimate of gross emigration over the decade.

In a second panel of Table 9.8, separate calculations are made of the emigration of the Canadian- and foreign-born populations. For the former, the residual difference between predicted and actual end-of-decade populations is the change in population due to emigration. For the foreign-born, the change due to emigration over the course of the entire decade is the difference between immigration and the predicted change in numbers. All the numbers involved are subject to errors in enumeration, and there were probably differences between native- and foreign-born in actual survival as well. It is encouraging, therefore, that the emigration estimates of the two panels agree as closely as they do. The largest difference comes in the 1861–71 decade, which would have been affected by, among other things, casualties among the many Canadians who took up arms in the Civil War.

REFERENCES

Bourbeau, Robert, and Jacques Légaré. *Évolution de la mortalité au Canada et au Québec 1831–1931.* Montreal: Les Presses de l'Université de Montréal, 1982.

[74] Child migration is estimated in the following way. The estimated net number of female emigrants 15 to 49 years of age was multiplied by the proportion of married females in those age groups and then by the number of children per married woman recorded in the census. This affords an easy approximation but should hardly be taken as definitive. It requires further, more careful research to be fully justified.

Canada, Department of Agriculture. *Report of the Commissioner of Immigration, 1869.* Ottawa: Queen's Printer, 1871.

Coale, Ansley, and Susan Cotts Watkins. *The Decline of Fertility in Europe.* Princeton, N.J.: Princeton University Press, 1986.

Cowan, Helen I. *British Immigration to British North America: The First Hundred Years.* Rev. ed. Toronto: University of Toronto Press, 1961.

Gaffield, Chad. "Children, Schooling, and Family Reproduction in Nineteenth-Century Ontario." *Canadian Historical Review* 72 (1991): 157–91.

Hansen, Marcus Lee. *The Mingling of the Canadian and American Peoples.* New Haven: Yale University Press, 1940.

Henripin, Jacques. *Trends and Factors of Fertility in Canada.* Ottawa: Statistics Canada, 1972.

Innis, Harold A. "An Introduction to the Economic History of Ontario from Outpost to Empire." *Papers and Records of the Ontario Historical Society* 30 (1934): 111–23.

Keyfitz, Nathan. "The Growth of Canadian Population." *Population Studies* 4 (1950): 47–63.

Kuczynski, R. R. *Birth Registration and Birth Statistics in Canada.* Washington, D.C.: Brookings Institution, 1930.

McCalla, Douglas. *Planting the Province: The Economic History of Upper Canada.* Toronto: University of Toronto Press, 1993.

McCallum, John. *Unequal Beginnings: Agriculture and Economic Development in Quebec and Ontario until 1870.* Toronto: University of Toronto Press, 1980.

Macdonald, Norman. *Canada, 1763–1841, Immigration and Settlement.* London: Longmans, 1939.

McDougall, Duncan M. "Immigration into Canada, 1851–1920." *Canadian Journal of Economics and Political Science* 27 (1961): 162–76.

Mackintosh, W. A. "Economic Factors in Canadian History." *Canadian Historical Review* 4 (1923): 12–25.

McInnis, R. M. "Childbearing and Land Availability: Some Evidence from Individual Household Data." In *Population Patterns in the Past,* edited by R. D. Lee, 201–28. New York: Academic Press, 1977.

———. "The Early Ontario Wheat Staple Reconsidered." *Canadian Papers in Rural History* 8 (1992): 17–48.

———. "Immigration and Emigration: Canada in the Late Nineteenth Century." In *Migration and the International Labor Market, 1850–1939* edited by Timothy J. Hatton and Jeffrey G. Williamson, 139–55. London: Routledge, 1994.

Moore, Eric G. "Fertility Decline in Three Ontario Cities: 1861–1881." *Canadian Studies in Population* 17 (1990): 25–47.

Preston, Samuel H., and Michael R. Haines. *Fatal Years: Child Mortality in Late Nineteenth-Century America.* Princeton, N.J.: Princeton University Press, 1991.

Tepperman, Lorne. "Ethnic Variations in Marriage and Fertility: Canada 1871." *Canadian Review of Sociology and Anthropology* 11 (1974): 324–43.

10

THE AFRICAN AMERICAN POPULATION OF THE UNITED STATES, 1790–1920

RICHARD H. STECKEL

This chapter discusses the demographic history of the U.S. black population up to 1920, which differed in many ways from the experiences of other populations in the Western Hemisphere. Like the slave societies in South America and in the Caribbean, U.S. blacks originated overwhelmingly in western Africa. Prior to 1840 the number of imports was so large that the Western Hemisphere as a whole was more a demographic outpost of Africa than of Europe. British North America imported few Africans, yet natural increase was sufficient to establish the hemisphere's largest slave population in the United States by 1825.

Although both European Americans and African Americans were well established in North America by the late 1600s, their demographic history was substantially different. By the end of the colonial period blacks lived largely in the southern colonies and worked overwhelmingly as slaves, whereas whites were widely distributed geographically and were employed primarily as independent farmers, unpaid family workers, free laborers, small proprietors, or indentured servants. Contrasting mortality risks by region for blacks and whites may have influenced these geographic living patterns. Slavery was abolished in 1865, but blacks continued to live mainly in the South and largely in rural areas, a pattern that began to change only with substantial migration to northern cities around the time of World War I.

Rates of natural increase were very high by worldwide historical standards for both blacks and whites during the nineteenth century, and

The author has benefited from the comments of or discussions with Michael Haines, Susan Klepp, Daniel Scott Smith, and Stuart Tolnay, and he thanks William White for excellent research assistance.

both populations had a youthful age structure while birth rates were high. The abundant land and other resources available in the United States in the early 1800s led Malthus and his intellectual followers to expect very high birth rates to endure. Yet birth rates for both groups declined throughout the nineteenth century. Prior to the abolition of slavery, mortality rates of American blacks exceeded those of whites but were below those of slave populations elsewhere in the hemisphere. Although slaves gained freedom after the Civil War, the black population continued to face poor health.

Since the topic of specific interest here is long-term trends and geographic patterns in fertility, health, and migration, the history of this population is compared with that of American whites and of blacks in other parts of the hemisphere. The discussion begins with an overview of black population growth from 1790 to 1920. Thereafter, I examine migration, fertility, and mortality in the periods of slavery (1790–1860) and freedom (1870–1920). Although slaves have been the major object of study within the black population prior to the Civil War, some results for free blacks are available in the period from 1790 to 1860.

OVERVIEW OF POPULATION GROWTH

Table 10.1 shows that the black population of the United States grew from slightly more than 750,000 in 1790 to 10.5 million in 1920, nearly a 14-fold increase. A majority of the absolute gain occurred after 1860 (from 4.4 million to 10.5 million), but growth rates were highest in the antebellum period, especially the years prior to 1830. Between 1790 and 1810, for example, the average annual growth rate was 3.1%, which amounted to a doubling every 22.4 years. Although some of this increase was fueled by slave imports (which were outlawed after 1807), most of the antebellum growth resulted from a high rate of natural increase.[1] The shrinking growth rate was caused primarily by a decline in fertility, which more than offset a decline in mortality over the entire period.

The highly variable growth rates calculated for the late nineteenth century point to a complicating factor in the study of black population

---

[1] Because evidence is scanty, the estimates range widely. In *Time on the Cross*, p. 25, Fogel and Engerman suggest that roughly 190,000 slaves were imported to the United States from 1790 to 1809, whereas Tadman argues in *Speculators and Slaves*, p. 226, that the figure was approximately 93,000. More recently, Fogel and Engerman revised their estimate upward, to 214,000 ("The Slave Breeding Thesis", p. 55). For additional discussion, see Curtin, *The Atlantic Slave Trade*.

Table 10.1. *Growth of the black population in the United States, 1790–1920*

Year	Slave	Free black	Total black population	10-year growth (%)	Annual growth (%)	Black as percentage of total
1790	697,897	59,466	757,363			19.27
1800	893,041	108,395	1,001,436	27.75	2.79	18.87
1810	1,191,364	186,446	1,377,810	31.64	3.19	19.03
1820	1,538,038	233,524	1,771,562	25.01	2.51	18.38
1830	2,009,043	319,599	2,328,642	27.17	2.73	18.10
1840	2,487,455	386,303	2,873,758	20.96	2.10	16.84
1850	3,204,313	434,495	3,638,808	23.49	2.36	15.69
1860	3,953,760	488,070	4,441,830	19.88	1.99	14.13
1870			4,880,003	9.40	0.94	13.66
1880			6,580,793	29.68	2.99	13.12
1890			7,488,676	12.91	1.29	11.90
1900			8,833,994	16.48	1.65	11.62
1910			9,827,763	10.65	1.07	10.69
1920			10,463,131	6.26	0.63	9.90

Sources: Totals for 1790–1860 slaves and free blacks from U.S. Census Office, Population of the United States in 1860; for 1870–1920 population data from U.S. Bureau of the Census, Fourteenth Census, vol. I. All other columns calculated from census data.

history: the quality of data for study. It is clear that the growth rates based on the 1870 census were an anomaly. The remarkably low rate from 1860 to 1870 (9.4%), and the remarkably high rate from 1870 to 1880 (29.68%) are attributable to considerable underreporting in the 1870 census, which was pronounced for southern blacks. Underenumeration was also somewhat high in the censuses of 1890 and 1920. Thus, researchers should be aware of the limitations of the raw data, a point that applies not only to census data, but to information collected during the early years of vital registration.[2]

Although free blacks lived in North America since the early colonial period, their numbers did not become substantial until after

[2] For general discussions of enumeration problems and some proposed solutions see U.S. Bureau of the Census, *Negro Population, 1790–1915*, pp. 26–28; Farley, *Growth of the Black Population*, pp. 23–26; and Coale and Rives, "A Statistical Reconstruction of the Black Population." Proposed solutions generally address broad aggregates rather than state or county totals, breakdowns by age and gender, and the like. Obviously, these adjustments are incapable of correcting errors in the manuscript schedules of the census.

the American Revolution, when court decisions and gradual emancipation laws took effect. As a result of these actions, and to a lesser extent
voluntary emancipations by slaveowners, the proportion of the total
black population composed of free blacks grew steadily, from 7.9% in
1790 to 13.7% in 1830. Although gradual emancipation was debated in all
southern state legislatures in the early nineteenth century, no southern
states passed the idea as law. Indeed, impediments to voluntary emancipation imposed by southern states in the 1830s slowed the growth of this
group. In addition, birth rates were also lower for free blacks compared
with slaves.

Even though the black population of the nineteenth century had a rate
of natural increase that was remarkably high by worldwide historical standards, Table 10.1 shows that the share of blacks in the total U.S. population declined more or less continuously from 1790 to 1920. Nearly 1 person
in 5 was black at the beginning of the period and by the end it was less
than 1 in 10. The answer to this apparent puzzle lies in differential rates
of immigration to the United States. Although a few slaves were smug-
gled into the United States after 1807 and some Caribbean islands sent
migrants to the United States, primarily to eastern cities, these inflows
were trivial compared with the mass immigration from Ireland, Germany,
Scandinavia, Italy, and other parts of the Continent. In the century after
1820, the United States received 33.6 million individuals, 88.6% of whom
were from Europe.[3] In contrast, less than 360,000 people (many of whom
were not black) arrived from the West Indies, and voluntary inflows from
Africa were under 20,000 during this 100-year period.

THE ANTEBELLUM PERIOD, 1790–1860

Far more has been written about the demographic situation of slaves than
of free blacks. In an attempt to understand the course of American history
in general, and the origins of the Civil War and its aftermath in particular, historians have focused on the rise, operation, and decline of the
slave system. Free blacks have not been entirely neglected; but, even when
the subject of research, their lives are often studied primarily in comparison with slaves. In fairness, it should be observed that more historical
records are available for slaves from sources such as plantation documents

[3] U.S. Bureau of the Census, *Historical Statistics*, pt. 1, ser. C 89–119.

and probate inventories. However, many sources such as the manuscript schedules of the federal censuses have been given scant attention, and thus many research opportunities remain to tell the history of free blacks in the United States.

SLAVES

Geographic Location. Westward migration was the most far-reaching of the demographic changes in the antebellum period. In 1790 virtually all of the population resided east of the Appalachian mountains, principally near the eastern seaboard or along rivers that flowed into it, and yet by 1860 agricultural settlement had reached the eastern edge of the Great Plains. In places such as Oregon and California the population had leapfrogged the plains and the mountains to the west coast. Slaves participated heavily in this westward movement, but were essentially confined to the South for reasons of climate, soil, and the politics of admitting slave states to the Union. The geographic dispersion of slaves was also affected by the demise of the peculiar institution in the North.

The outlines of slave migration and the results of actions against slavery in the North can be told with the help of Table 10.2, which shows the population of slaves in each state in the federal censuses from 1790 to 1860. Although slavery was legal in most northern states in the late 1700s, the region had few slaves and their numbers declined dramatically after the turn of the century.[4] Most slaves who lived in the North resided in the lower half of that region, particularly in New Jersey, Pennsylvania, and the area of the lower Hudson Valley, the city of New York, and Long Island.[5]

Some historians have explained the lack of slaves in the North by climate, suggesting that the peculiar institution flourished only where staples such as tobacco, cotton, sugar, or rice could be grown. Such crops and related farm maintenance, it was argued, occupied slaves in year-

---

[4] For a discussion of the legal status of slavery and its decline in the North, see Arthur Zilversmit, *The First Emancipation.*

[5] The distribution of blacks and whites by county in 1790 makes clear that geographic location was a function of more than a simple north-south gradient. The density of blacks in the North also depended upon local economic ties with the Caribbean, religion, and ethnicity. Cities active in the Caribbean trade were more likely to have larger black populations within the urban area and its hinterland. In addition, German Lutherans, Scots-Irish Presbyterians, and Anglicans were more accepting of slavery compared with Puritans, German Reformed, Quakers, and Methodists. See Cappon, *Atlas of Early American History,* p. 67; and Wacker, *Land and People.*

Table 10.2. *Slave population by state, 1790–1860*

State	1790	1800	1810	1820	1830	1840	1850	1860
North	40,370	35,946	27,510	19,108	3,568	1,113	236	18
Connecticut	2,759	951	310	97	25	17		
New York	21,324	20,343	15,017	10,088	75	4		
New Jersey	11,423	12,422	10,851	7,557	2,254	674	236	18
Pennsylvania	3,737	1,706	795	211	403	64		
Other North	1,127	524	537	1,155	811	354		
Southeast	642,280	799,679	983,999	1,156,582	1,360,695	1,399,922	1,624,087	1,778,700
Delaware	8,887	6,153	4,177	4,509	3,292	2,605	2,290	1,798
Maryland	103,036	105,635	111,502	107,397	102,994	89,737	90,368	87,189
District of Columbia		3,244	5,395	6,377	6,119	4,694	3,687	3,185
Virginia	293,427	345,796	392,518	425,153	469,757	449,087	472,528	490,865
North Carolina	100,572	133,296	168,824	205,017	245,601	245,817	288,548	331,059
South Carolina	107,094	146,151	196,365	258,475	315,401	327,038	384,984	402,406
Georgia	29,264	59,404	105,218	149,654	217,531	280,944	381,682	462,198
Southwest	15,247	57,416	179,855	362,435	644,780	1,086,404	1,579,964	2,174,996
Kentucky	11,830	40,343	80,561	126,732	165,213	182,258	210,981	225,483
Tennessee	3,417	13,584	44,535	80,107	141,603	183,059	239,459	275,719
Missouri			3,011	10,222	25,091	58,240	87,422	114,931
Florida					15,501	25,717	39,310	61,745
Alabama				41,879	117,549	253,532	342,844	435,080

Mississippi	3,489	17,088	32,814	65,659	195,211	309,878	436,631
Arkansas			1,617	4,576	19,935	47,100	111,115
Louisiana		34,660	69,064	109,588	168,452	244,809	331,726
Texas						58,161	182,566
West					16	26	46
Total U.S.	697,897	1,191,364	1,538,125	2,009,043	2,487,455	3,204,313	3,953,760
Percentage urban							
Total U.S.	5.1	7.3	7.2	8.8	10.8	15.3	19.8
Slaves	n.a.	n.a.	n.a.	n.a.	3.8	4.1	3.5

n.a. Not available.

Notes: Other North includes Maine, Vermont, New Hampshire, Massachusetts, Rhode Island, Ohio, Indiana, Illinois, Michigan, and Wisconsin (from 1840). West includes Iowa (from 1840), Minnesota, New Mexico, Utah, California, Oregon (from 1850), Nebraska, Kansas, Dakota, Colorado, Nevada, and Washington (in 1860).

Sources: Population figures from U. S. Census Office, *Population of the United States in 1860.* Urban figures for total United States from U. S. Bureau of the Census, *Historical Statistics . . . to 1970*, pt. 1, ser. A 57–72, p. 12. Urban estimates for slaves calculated from sum of slaves in all southern cities with 4,000 people or more. City populations were listed separately within each state's section of the census reports of 1840, 1850, and 1860 (as Table II or III, depending on the year).

round activities, whereas northern agriculture based on small grains had distinct seasonal peaks that left slaves idle part of the year. Philip Coelho and Robert McGuire and Christian Warren have drawn attention to regional differences in mortality by ethnicity as a factor in the regional success of slavery and in the location of blacks following emancipation.[6] Blacks in American cities died at markedly higher rates than whites in the North, often from respiratory diseases. If these regional urban patterns also applied to the rural population (a suggestion awaiting systematic study), then high rates of illness and death among blacks may have discouraged slavery in the North. Whatever the explanation, however, we know that judicial interpretations of state constitutions and gradual emancipation laws enacted from 1780 to 1804 led to the disappearance of slavery in the North.

The dimensions of the westward movement within the South are clear from the numbers of slaves living in the eastern seaboard states (Old South) compared with states further west (New South). In 1790 nearly 98% of all southern slaves lived in the coastal states of the East, but by 1860 the western states held a clear majority. Attracted by high cotton prices and by western lands that were cheap and fertile, thousands of farmers moved to Mississippi, Alabama, and Louisiana to create large cotton plantations in the 1810s and 1820s. During the 1830s the westward movement became a tide; from 1790 to 1860 perhaps 835,000 slaves moved west, 26.7% of them in the 1830s alone.[7]

This westward movement did not drain eastern states of their populations, but the growth rates were clearly attenuated. The slave population peaked at 111,502 in 1810 in Maryland and at 4,509 in 1820 in Delaware, but in these cases the declines were assisted by manumissions. Despite all the outmigration, in 1860 Virginia and Georgia remained the two most populous slave states with over 490,000 and 460,000 bondsmen, respectively.

Like most large-scale migrations, the westward movement was selective by age, gender, and family status. In the late antebellum period, a majority of slave migrants were males (51.7%) and 59.2% were between the ages of 15 and 39 in 1860.[8] Although all historians recognize that this

---

[6] Coelho and McGuire, "African and European Bound Labor," pp. 83–115; Warren "Northern Chills, Southern Fevers," pp. 23–57.

[7] Fogel and Engerman, *Time on the Cross*, p. 46. Tadman, in *Speculators and Slaves*, p. 12, places the total at 1.1 million, of whom 25.8% moved in the 1830s.

[8] Tadman, *Speculators and Slaves*, Table A3.2. The corresponding figures obtained from Sutch, "The Breeding of Slaves," using a slightly different methodology, are 51.5% and 60.2%, respectively.

movement was stressful for slave families, no consensus on its magnitude has emerged. Robert William Fogel and Stanley Engerman maintained that 84% of the interregional slave migrants moved with their owners and that only 2% of the marriages of slaves involved in interregional movement were destroyed.[9] On the other hand, Michael Tadman attributed 60 to 70% of the interregional movement to the slave trade and argued that 20% of marriages in the Upper South were broken by the trade.[10] More recently, Fogel suggested that 15% of slave marriages may have been broken by the slave trade and that the dispute over the share of interregional migration conducted by traders remains unresolved.[11]

Although the westward movement was the most profound geographic aspect of antebellum demographic life, urbanization deserves some mention. Southern slaves lived overwhelmingly in rural areas, whereas free blacks, and to a lesser extent northern slaves, resided disproportionately in cities and towns in companion with whites.[12] By the middle of the nineteenth century the urban slave population was in decline. Richard Wade attributes the shift to the disintegration of the institution in urban areas, but Claudia Goldin argues that rising slave prices and a high elasticity of demand for slaves in urban areas provoked the decline of urban slavery.[13]

Fertility. The study of fertility and mortality during the nineteenth and early twentieth centuries is heavily constrained by data resources. Although Massachusetts passed a vital registration law in 1842, records were incomplete until 1865, and as late as 1900 only 10 states (all in the North) and the District of Columbia were included in the death registration area.[14] The birth registration area was created in 1915, but only 16 states systematically recorded births by 1900. To study long-term trends, scholars therefore use indirect measures of fertility such as the child/woman ratio, which can be tabulated from the age and gender information reported by the census. The numerator of the ratio is based on surviving children and may be biased by differential infant and child mortality rates, and migration may distort both the numerator

[9] Fogel and Engerman, *Time on the Cross*, pp. 48–49.

[10] Tadman, *Speculators and Slaves*, pp. 31, 174.

[11] Fogel, *Without Consent or Contract*, p. 448, fn. 80. See also Friedman and Galatine, "Regional Markets for Slaves," pp. 196.

[12] Wilkie, "Urbanization and De-urbanization of the Black Population."

[13] Wade, *Slavery in the Cities*; and Goldin, *Urban Slavery in the American South*.

[14] Shryock and Siegel, *The Methods and Materials of Demography*, vol. 1, pp. 27–31.

Table 10.3. *Child/woman ratios for slaves and whites, 1820–1860*

Region	1820	1830	1840	1850	1860
Slaves					
North	717	305	563	—	—
Southeast	1,490	1,499	1,434	1,396	1,369
Southwest	1,457	1,460	1,370	1,314	1,282
Total U.S.	1,395	1,516	1,435	1,354	1,320
Whites					
Total U.S.	1,593	1,413	1,348	1,186	1,164
Southern	1,635	1,571	1,556	1,353	1,303

Notes: Calculated as children under age 10 per thousand women aged 15–49; gradual emancipation in the North distorts the numbers from 1820 to 1840.
Sources: Figures for slaves in Old and New South and for southern whites are from Steckel, *The Economics*, Table 1. Figures for the North, total slaves, and total whites were calculated in similar fashion, using data from U. S. Census Office, *Census for 1820; Abstract of the Returns of the fifth Census*, pp. 48–51; *Compendium . . . from the Sixth Census*, pp. 474–75; *The Seventh Census*, Tables XXI, XXII, and XXIII; and *Population of the United States in 1860*, pp. 594–95. Prior to the 1850, census age groupings do not permit direct calculations of child/woman ratios. For these years, the desired data were estimated from the actual census age reports, using the 1850 Census Public Use Sample to estimate proportions of women aged 15 to 49.

and denominator. Nevertheless, several studies report high correlations between this ratio and direct measures such as total fertility.[15] Thus, small differences in the ratios may not reflect genuine differences in fertility behavior.

Table 10.3 presents the number of children under 10 per thousand women aged 15 to 49 in the North, the East, and the West beginning in 1820, the first year in which the census collected age data for slaves. The information for the North reflects the effects of gradual emancipation on the numbers and age composition of the population. The laws rapidly reduced the number of slaves in the early nineteenth century, and by 1850 so few slaves lived in the North that the ratio is not useful or meaningful. Though the causes of the low child/woman ratio in the North await careful study, it seems plausible that some slaves in that region delayed family formation to avoid the experience of gradual emancipation for their children. Under these laws, slaves were emancipated at ages 18 to 28,

[15] See, for example, Bogue and Palmore, "Some Empirical and Analytic Relations," pp. 316–38.

depending upon the state. If avoidance was the motive, age-specific fertility rates should have risen to much higher levels for women above the ages of emancipation.[16] By the 1820s the slave population was composed increasingly of older, less fertile women who were born before the laws became effective. The time pattern in the North also depicts the changing composition of the population across states. Pennsylvania enacted the first gradual emancipation law in 1780, and New Jersey enacted the last in 1804.

Within the South, where the vast majority of slaves lived, the child/woman ratio declined by 11% from 1820 to 1860.[17] In contrast to the ratio for whites, that for blacks was higher in the East. Initially the regional differences were small (about 2%) but widened to 7% by 1860. Early in the period the ratio for southern whites exceeded that for slaves by nearly 10%, but by the late antebellum period the ratios were nearly identical because the decline was more rapid among southern whites.

Historians, sociologists, and economists have speculated extensively about the basic environment in which slave fertility decisions were made. On the one hand, researchers have combined the aggregate fertility patterns with knowledge that plantation owners had extensive legal control over the lives of slaves to suggest that very high fertility, if not a biological maximum, was a goal of owners. Other scholars have argued that slaves exercised some important autonomy in their lives, including the sphere of marriage and the family. Only recently have household-level data been assembled to confront these ideas.

Given that the federal censuses did not collect household demographic information on slaves, probate records have proven to be the most useful source for analyzing the time trends and regional differences in slave fertility. In probate court deliberations, slaves were considered personal property that was appraised and often arranged in families. Thousands of southern estates that went through probate court are available for investigation. The data discussed below are drawn from 540 plantations in 40 counties of Virginia, Georgia, and Louisiana that were enumerated between 1801 and 1865.[18]

Differences and trends in the child/woman ratio can be explored with an analytical device called a *synthetic total fertility rate*. A total fertility rate, *R*, is defined by the following equation:

---

[16] To my knowledge, this aspect of black fertility has not been systematically studied.

[17] This discussion of slave fertility relies heavily on Steckel, "The Fertility of American Slaves," pp. 239–86, and *The Economics*.

[18] Steckel, *The Economics*, chap. 2.

Table 10.4. *Demographic characteristics by plantation size*

Symbol	Size 1–24			Size 25–74			Size >75		
	Value	N	S.D.	Value	N	S.D.	Value	N	S.D.
L	41.2	34	4.73	40.6	30	4.74	39.9	23	7.49
F	19.8			20.8			21.6		
S	2.82	1,106	1.69	2.91	1,066	1.72	3.06	702	1.82
β	0.886	114		0.868	129		0.818	110	
R	7.61			6.77			5.71		

Note: Number of slaves.
Sources: Probate records as reported in Steckel, *The Economics*, p. 104; "The Fertility of American Slaves," p. 248.

$$R = [((L - F) / S) + 1]\beta$$

where L is average age at last birth, F is average age at first birth, S is the average child-spacing interval, and β is the proportion of women who eventually have children.[19] The expression in parentheses is the total fertility rate for women who had at least one child. Multiplication by β converts the measure to the total fertility rate for the entire cohort.

The meaning of R depends on the method of estimating the variables on the right-hand side of the equation. To obtain a true total fertility rate one needs the values of L, F, S, and β in the fertility schedule pertaining to a particular time period. Unfortunately, these measures can only be estimated approximately. Because of the nature of the available data, the calculated R is biased downward in relation to the true total fertility rates. Nevertheless, R is highly correlated with the child/woman ratio at the county level in 1860, which suggests that it is a useful concept for understanding variation in that ratio.[20]

By arranging the probate data by plantation size (number of slaves), one finds that the components of R were synchronized in their effects: all acted to reduce fertility as plantation size increased. Table 10.4 shows that F and S increased and that L and β decreased as plantation size grew from under 25 slaves to 75 or more slaves. The calculated value of R was 7.41 on small

---

[19] For additional discussion, see Steckel, "The Fertility of American Slaves," pp. 245–50, or *The Economics*, chap. 3.
[20] Steckel, *The Economics*, p. 100.

farms and 5.12 on large farms, a difference of 37%. By manipulating the equation defining R, one can determine that much of the difference (37%) in the calculated values of R between the smallest and the largest category of farms was due to differences in L. Also having hefty contributions were F (23%), S (19%), and β (22%). Therefore, larger plantation sizes in the western states and a general increase in plantation size over time may have been linked with regional differences and the downward time trend in child/woman ratios.[21]

Because most of the difference in R by plantation size is explained by when and whether women married or remarried (L, F, and β), it is important to consider the environment in which slaves found partners and formed families.[22] Nineteenth-century defenders of slavery and abolitionists often took extreme positions on this issue, debating, for example, whether owners practiced systematic slave breeding. Scholarly discussions have usually been couched in terms of the role of the family. With the exception of U. B. Phillips, most scholars writing prior to the 1970s maintained that the number of important decisions made within the family were quite limited.[23] Since the 1970s, research emphasizes the autonomy of slaves and their efforts at forming an independent culture, even though marriages and families were not recognized under state law. Seasonal patterns of marriage and first birth tend to confirm the importance of marriage to many slaves.[24] Civil War pension records indicate that marriages were highly concentrated in times of slack labor demand, such as Christmas or lay-by periods, and plantation records reveal that the monthly pattern of first births was significantly different from non–first births. This and the fact that most slave women realized their first conception at least two or three years after their age of reproductive capability suggest that many slave couples anticipated marriage as a significant event.[25] Plantation lists of births reporting the name of the father show that little switching of partners occurred, especially after the

[21] Differences in R by plantation size indicate that maximum reproductive potential was not achieved in general and was therefore unlikely to have been a widespread goal. Even on small farms, the age at first birth, which was 19.8 years, could have been at least two to three years lower given what is known about age at menarche as inferred from the timing of the adolescent growth spurt.

[22] The importance of marriage or remarriage behavior by plantation size is confirmed in regression analysis on the components of R. Holding other things constant such as age, main crop, region, and time period, the probability that a woman had a child declined from 71% on farms with fewer than 25 slaves to 58% on farms with 100 or more slaves. See Steckel, "The Fertility of American Slaves," p. 262.

[23] Phillips, *American Negro Slavery*.

[24] Steckel, *The Economics*, chap. 5, and "Slave Marriage and the Family," pp. 406–21.

[25] Trussell and Steckel, "The Age of Slaves at Menarche," pp. 477–505.

first child was born.[26] Although it is conceivable that owners who gave this much support to slave families could have selected mates, the possible financial advantages were small, and it is likely that very few forced pairings took place.[27]

If slaves searched for partners, constraints on the availability of potential mates would have been important for fertility. The decline in β and a rise in L and in F with plantation size suggests that selection difficulties grew with the number of slaves on the farm, which seems counterintuitive without knowledge of plantation marriage rules and other constraints. Owners generally approved all marriages, and matches with close kin such as first cousins were not permitted. On small units (having less than 20 slaves), these restrictions usually left unattached individuals of marriageable age with few if any eligible partners on the farm. In this situation, owners usually permitted marriages to slaves owned by someone else, especially in communities of small farms where other units were located nearby. In these "abroad" marriages the man usually commuted, as little as once or twice a week if the distance was large. On large farms, however, plantation rules were institutionalized and commuting distances were greater, which resulted in a marked decline in the frequency of these marriages.[28] Because of restrictions on search, it is quite likely that the choices for potential mates actually diminished as the number of slaves on the farm increased.[29] Thus, difficulties in finding suitable partners, which free individuals did not face, was a factor reducing slave fertility below what it otherwise would have been.

Steckel explored further the relationships among fertility, main crop, and farm or plantation size (number of slaves) with a sample of 57 counties drawn from southern states in the 1860 published census.[30] In these

---

[26] Steckel, "Slave Marriage and the family."

[27] Claims and denials of slave breeding were part of the abolitionist debate, but most historians believe the practice either did not exist or was rare. For a statement of the affirmative point of view, see Sutch, in "The Breeding of Slaves"; and Gutman and Sutch, "Victorians All?" pp. 134–62. For a rebuttal, see Fogel and Engerman, *Without Consent or Contract: Conditions of Slave Life*.

[28] The incidence of marriages by slaves having different owners declined from 69% to 8% as median plantation size in the county of residence increased from less than 25 to 75 or more slaves. See Steckel, *The Economics*, p. 227.

[29] As size increased to very high levels, the number of potential mates would eventually have grown to equal or exceed that on small farms. Yet very few slaves lived on farms with as many as 100 or more individuals. Moreover, some of the benefits of growth in size, if through natural increase, would have been offset by an increase in the number of ineligible, close relatives.

[30] Steckel, "Slave Marriage," p. 267–70, and *The Economics*, pp. 219–24. Technically, the figures on plantation size refer to slaves per owner within a county. Very large slaveowners might have had slaves on more than one plantation, and in more than one county.

data the child/woman ratio declined systematically and nonlinearly as median plantation size increased. Among the staple crops, only tobacco had a systematic (positive) effect on the child/woman ratio, which may reflect lower child mortality rates and out-migration of young, unmarried women to expanding areas of the antebellum southern economy.[31] In 1860 the median size of slaveholding was 23.4 in the East and 25.2 in the West, and from the estimated regression equation it appears that size alone explains about 22% and cropping patterns 36% of the regional difference in the child/woman ratio. Details of the course of median plantation size over time are not known, but it was 17.6 slaves in 1790 and 26.7 slaves in 1860. If all of the increase occurred after 1830, then about one-half of the decline in the child/woman ratio shown in Table 10.3 was attributable to the rise of larger farms.

Comparisons of slaves and southern whites shed additional light on possible influences on fertility behavior.[32] The child/woman ratios of slaves and southern whites were poorly correlated at the county level in the sample of 57 counties discussed above ($R^2 = 0.02$). Moreover, adding region of residence as a regressor, using the knowledge that the child/woman ratio of migrants was lower for slaves than for whites, increases the R^2 to only 0.09. Therefore factors external to the plantation or to the family but associated with the county of residence had quite different effects on slave and white behavior.

Although the child/woman ratios of slaves and southern whites were

[31] In "The Breeding of Slaves for Sale," Richard Sutch makes a case for breeding using circumstantial evidence. He notes that the child/woman ratio was higher in the older slave states of the East than in those of the West, and, consistent with the breeding thesis, large numbers of slaves were shipped from east to west. Slavery was less profitable on the older, exhausted soils of the East, which might have created an incentive for owners to engage in breeding and selling surplus labor. In addition, the slave population in the United States grew at rates that were remarkably high by worldwide, historical standards. Sutch identifies a number of farms with large numbers of children and few adult men in eastern states as possible breeding operations. This circumstantial evidence alone does not make a good case, particularly when it is placed in perspective. The American white population also grew at a similarly high rate, and both were significantly below a biological maximum, as revealed by age at menarche and micro-level study of evidence on age at first birth, child-spacing patterns, age at last birth, and the proportions of women who ever had children. Contradicting a breeding model, slave birth rates declined while prices roughly doubled from 1840 to 1860. Also, many slaves would have objected to forced mating, expressing their discontent in costly ways such as shirking field labor. In addition, proponents have yet to find historical records such as stud books or diaries that document breeding practices. The adult men apparently missing from the farms identified by Richard Sutch could easily have lived on nearby farms. Scholars generally agree that owners indirectly encouraged childbearing because a spouse and children promoted social stability. Owners established separate living quarters for families and following births may have given them clothing or household items. However, fertility on plantations was reduced by other aspects of management, such as discouraging marriage to slaves who lived off the farm.

[32] Steckel, "Slave Marriage," p. 273–80, and *The Economics*, chap. 7.

similar, as shown in Table 10.3, the demographic components of their behavior were different.[33] Age at first birth, for example, was 2.1 years to 1.3 years lower among slaves than among whites, depending upon the data source used for comparisons.[34] Among southern whites, family wealth had a large, positive effect on whether women had children. Wealth, or access to resources, enabled couples to support children, which was an important consideration in a noncontraceptive society.[35] In contrast, owners provided food, clothing, and shelter, which alleviated a wealth requirement for family formation among slaves. In the absence of parental help, whites had to save income prior to marriage, which delayed family formation. Thus, family formation was subsidized for slaves in companion with whites, but slaves faced constraints on partner selection that tended to offset this contribution to fertility.

Because saving to support a family was unimportant for slaves, one may ask why age at first birth was not even lower. At first glance, very early marriage may appear to have been advantageous to both slaves and masters. Slaves might have been lured into early unions by the opportunity of separate housing, and owners would have benefited from higher fertility. An opposing consideration relevant for both masters and slaves was high infant and maternal mortality rates for very young mothers. In addition, both slaves and masters wanted to avoid precarious unions, which were more likely to follow when partner choices were made at very young ages. Unstable relationships led to discontent and costly reductions in output. Thus, owners and slaves may have desired ages at marriage above those allowed by biology.

Health. Mortality rates and other ways of measuring health are widely regarded as sensitive indices of living standards. The debate over slave health has a long tradition that dates from the abolitionist movement, and by the middle of the twentieth century historians and demographers addressed the subject in empirical studies. Early work in this era by William Postell placed the infant mortality rate at 152.6 per thousand, but later papers depicted a grimmer scenario.[36] Using census data and indirect

---

[33] Steckel, *The Economics.*

[34] Ages at marriage were several years higher in Europe their in the United States among both slaves and whites. See Hajnal, "European Marriage Patterns in Perspective."

[35] Contrary to the typical pattern for the region, genealogical evidence suggests that some gentry families in Virginia may have practiced family limitation in the late antebellum period. See Lewis and Lockridge, "'Sally Has Been Sick.'"

[36] Postell, *The Health of Slaves.*

estimation techniques, authors produced estimates which climbed from 182.7 per thousand, proposed by Robert Evans, Jr., to 274–302 per thousand and 246–75 per thousand, calculated by Reynolds Farley, and Jack Eblen, respectively.[37]

The most comprehensive investigation of diet, work, and health was made by Fogel and Engerman in *Time on the Cross*, and by others in its aftermath.[38] Participants in this debate agreed that although instances of malnutrition occurred, slaves were reasonably well fed as a group and discussion focused instead on variety in the diet and vitamin and mineral deficiencies. Fogel and Engerman placed slave mortality rates near those of the free population.

The most recent work establishes the diversity of conditions among slaves. Children's health was comparable to that in the poorest populations ever studied, whereas working-age slaves were remarkably well-off. These conclusions rest on plantation records of births and deaths, measurements of stature recorded on manifests of slaves shipped in the coastwise trade, and an approach that combines these data through the concept of net nutrition.[39] The study of human growth and development makes clear that diet, disease, and work cannot be evaluated in isolation.[40] Instead, these factors interact to determine a person's level of net nutrition (or nutritional status). Work, disease, and body maintenance place claims on the diet, and the net result influences growth and stature. Thus instances of growth retardation and illness and mortality tend to occur together.

Recognizing that decisions were made in an environment of poor medical knowledge and that many deaths would have occurred despite the best intentions and the best care that was available, explanations have been sought for the excess mortality of slaves.[41] Plantation records that were adjusted for underenumeration of deaths occurring soon after birth indicate that slave mortality rates were approximately 350 per thousand among infants and 200 per thousand at ages 1 to 4. These childhood rates were roughly double those of the entire free population in the United States, but the rates of slave and free adults were approximately equal.

---

[37] The relevant works are Evans, "The Economics of American Negro Slavery," pp. 185–243; Farley, *Growth of the Black Population*, p. 33; Eblen, "Growth of the Black Population in Antebellum America," pp. 273–89; and Eblen, "New Estimates," pp. 301–19.

[38] See, for example, Sutch, "The Care and Feeding of Slaves."

[39] Steckel, "Slave Height Profiles," pp. 363–80; "Birth Weights and Infant Mortality," pp. 173–98; "A Peculiar Population," pp. 721–41; "A Dreadful Childhood," pp. 427–65; "Growth Depression and Recovery," pp. 111–32.

[40] See, for example, Tanner, *Fetus into Man.*   [41] Steckel, "A Dreadful Childhood."

The average slave child fell below the 0.5 percentile of modern National Center for Health Statistics height standards that characterize Europeans, Americans of European descent, and African Americans who are well nourished, but the average slave adult attained the 17th (male) to the 20th (female) percentile.[42] Comparisons of average heights in studies of growth from childhood to maturity show that slave children were among the smallest ever measured, but that growth recovery during and after adolescence was remarkable if not unprecedented.

Study of plantation records suggests that prenatal conditions were poor. A majority of slave newborns probably weighed less than 2,500 grams (5.5 pounds), and perhaps two-thirds of the infant losses occurred within the first month of birth.[43] Poor prenatal health probably elevated the incidence of sudden infant death among slaves.[44] Seasonal patterns of mortality help to identify possible causes of the poor health of newborns. About three-quarters of the neonatal losses took place during the six months of February to April and September to November, and stillbirths were concentrated in the late autumn and to a lesser extent in February to April. Nutritional deprivation in the first trimester elevates stillbirths, whereas neonatal deaths are caused largely by deprivation in the first or the third trimesters. The high incidence of stillbirths during the late autumn and the concentration of neonatal deaths in February to April are consistent with acute nutritional deprivation during the late winter and early spring.

Although diet, disease, and work are ingredients in net nutrition, disease is an unlikely cause for the concentration of losses because the sickly season occurred during the late summer and early autumn. Similarly, the nutritional value of the diet was probably at a minimum during the late spring, which is inconsistent with the lack of stillbirths beginning in January and the lack of neonatal deaths during May and June. The implausibility of disease and diet as causes points to hard work as a major source of excess losses before the end of the first month. This hypothesis is supported by the fact that the plowing and planting season of late winter and early spring was particularly strenuous for adults. Evidence from plantation work records and instructions to overseers also indicate that

---

[42] The typical slave adult was 5 to 8 centimeters taller than average European adults of the era. For comparative data, see Steckel and Floud, *Health and Welfare during Industrialization*.

[43] Steckel, "Birth Weights and Infant Mortality," and "A Dreadful Childhood."

[44] Savitt, *Medicine and Slavery*; Johnson, "Smothered Slave Infants," pp. 493–520.

pregnant women had little relief from work during peak seasons in the demand for labor.[45]

Although poor prenatal care and low birth weights contributed to high mortality rates beyond the first month, a poor diet and infections then entered the picture. The meager evidence available on feeding practices suggests that slave infants may have received breast milk for nine months to one year, whereas whites probably continued for more than one year.[46] Slave women usually resumed work within three to five weeks after delivery; and while the mothers were in the fields, the young children remained in the nursery, at least on the larger plantations, under the care of older women assisted by older children. Initially the new mothers returned to the nursery two to three times per day for breast feeding, but within three months after delivery, their productivity, as measured by the number of pounds of cotton picked per day, reached normal levels. At this time one or more of the daytime breast feedings may have been eliminated, and infants probably received starchy paps and gruels, often contaminated or fed using contaminated utensils. Owners who recorded births and deaths and who noted causes of infant death frequently mentioned diarrhea or "cholera infantum," as it was called in the medical literature of the era.

Young children who survived the hazardous period of infancy encountered a poor diet and diseases that were often related to poor nutrition.[47] The child's diet emphasized hominy and fat, and owners and medical practitioners often cited whooping cough, diarrhea, measles, worms, and pneumonia as causes of death.

By ages 8 to 12 work entered the equation of slave health. Other things being equal, work would have placed a claim on the diet that retarded growth. Yet it was at the ages that work usually began, initially as a light activity, that some catch-up growth occurred.[48] Improving health accompanied the growth recovery, and mortality rates declined after early childhood, reaching 54 per thousand at ages 5 to 10, 37 per thousand at ages 10 to 14, and 35 per thousand at ages 15 to 19. Other things must not have been equal. As workers, slaves received regular allocations of meat (about one-half pound of pork per day) and other foods. Slaves may have supplemented the allocations by raising garden produce, pigs, and fowl, and by fishing and hunting. In addition, slaves may have become more

[45] Campbell, "Work, Pregnancy, and Infant Mortality," pp. 793–812.
[46] Steckel, "A Dreadful Childhood."   [47] Kiple and Kiple, "Slave Child Mortality," pp. 284–309.
[48] Steckel, "A Peculiar Population."

efficient at their work through experience, thereby leaving more nutrition from a given food supply for growth. The strong growth recovery of teenagers and workers reinforces the view that their diet was at least adequate, if not exceptional, for the disease load and the tasks they performed. Adolescents may have encountered nutritional deficiencies, but the deficiencies were not widespread or severe enough to impair the substantial recovery of average growth.

The peculiar pattern of food allocation by age may have been achieved partly at the expense of the slave family. Workers ate breakfast and lunch in the fields, and children were often fed earlier and separate from adults in the evening. Therefore parents may have had little time to spend with their children on a regular basis. After emancipation, former slaves who gravitated toward nuclear family norms may have been disadvantaged, through lack of experience, in training young children.

The decision by slaveowners to exclude or reduce meat from the diets of children can be viewed as an investment decision.[49] A better diet during childhood would have produced slaves who were bigger and more productive when they entered the labor force, but the extra rations were costly. Reasonable estimates of the costs of the rations and the benefits of the extra labor suggest that it was unprofitable for slaveowners to feed meat to children.

Although the health of slave children was poor by standards of the nineteenth century, one must distinguish effects specific to the region versus the institution of slavery. It has been argued, for example, that a relatively harsh disease environment in the South was more likely to have exposed residents to diseases, such as malaria and gastrointestinal infections that caused high death rates. How much of the excess mortality of slave children could be attributed to factors that were special to the South? In a review of evidence, primarily from genealogies, Clayne Pope notes that large north-south differences existed in the seventeenth and eighteenth centuries, but they diminished from the late eighteenth century onward and were nearly absent by the middle of the nineteenth century.[50]

Some additional information on this question is available from a national sample of nearly 1,600 families matched from the 1860 to the 1850 census manuscript schedules of population.[51] Although family members could have left the household for reasons other than death, the

---

[49] Steckel, "A Peculiar Population."   [50] Clayne Pope, "Adult Mortality in America."
[51] Steckel, "The Health and Mortality," pp. 333–45.

presence or absence in 1860 of young children and the wife who were recorded in these families in 1850 can be studied as an approximate guide to mortality conditions. Regressions of dichotomous variables representing failure to survive to 1860 on age, wealth, literacy, ethnicity, regions, and number of children show that losses were systematically higher for southern women and may have been higher for some southern children. Women's loss rates were 16.3% in the South ($t = 2.51$) compared with 10.0% in the Northeast. Among children aged 1 to 4, the expected losses were 16.3% in the South and 13.3% in the Northeast, but the difference was not statistically significant ($t = 1.26$). If the South is divided into two regions, expected losses were higher in the coastal states (18.7%; $t = 1.94$) but not the remaining states of the South compared with the Northeast.[52] Because the estimated mortality rates of slave children were approximately double those for the entire free population, the household data suggest that a modest portion of the excess mortality of slave children could be attributed to regional factors such as the disease environment.

The matched sample of households also indicates that the number of young siblings had a significant and powerful adverse effect on the survival of children aged 1 to 4. The expected loss rate of children aged 1 to 4 increased from 10.3% to 17.4% if the number of children below age 10 in the family increased from 1 to 4.[53] One could argue that additional children helped replenish the reservoir of childhood diseases, thereby increasing the chances of exposure. If this hypothesis is correct, then concentrations of children in the care facilities of plantations probably contributed to the excess mortality of slave children.

FREE BLACKS

Geographic Location. The vast westward migration that profoundly affected the lives of whites and slaves was much less important for free blacks. Table 10.5 shows that the number of free blacks in the Midwest and in the Southwest remained small or modest up to the Civil War. By 1860 only 23% of the entire free black population, in contrast with 49.2% for whites, resided

---

[52] The regions are coastal states from North Carolina to Louisiana, and the remaining states (except Texas, which was placed in the frontier).

[53] It is possible that parents who had several children sent some of them away to work or to live elsewhere. This response to crowding is an unlikely explanation for the adverse effect of the number of children on losses of those aged 1 to 4 because the number of children under age 10 had no systematic effect on the survival of those aged 5 to 7.

Table 10.5. *Free black population by state, 1790–1860*

State	1790	1800	1810	1820	1830	1840	1850	1860
North	27,109	47,154	78,181	99,281	137,529	170,556	194,721	219,682
Maine	538	818	969	929	1,190	1,355	1,356	1,327
New Hampshire	630	856	970	786	604	537	520	494
Vermont	255	557	750	903	881	730	718	709
Massachusetts	5,463	6,452	6,737	6,740	7,048	8,669	9,064	9,602
Rhode Island	3,469	3,304	3,609	3,554	3,561	3,238	3,670	3,952
Connecticut	2,801	5,330	6,453	7,844	8,047	8,105	7,693	8,627
New York	4,654	10,374	25,333	29,279	44,870	50,027	49,069	49,005
New Jersey	2,762	4,402	7,843	12,460	18,303	21,044	23,810	25,318
Pennsylvania	6,537	14,561	22,492	30,202	37,930	47,854	53,626	56,949
Ohio		337	1,899	4,723	9,568	17,342	25,279	36,673
Indiana		163	393	1,230	3,629	7,165	11,262	11,428
Illinois			613	457	1,637	3,598	5,436	7,628
Michigan			120	174	261	707	2,583	6,799
Wisconsin						185	635	1,171
Southeast	31,882	60,009	96,803	116,826	152,243	170,971	196,542	216,821
Delaware	3,899	8,268	13,136	12,958	15,855	16,919	18,073	19,829
Maryland	8,043	19,587	33,927	39,730	52,938	62,078	74,723	83,942
Dist. of Columbia		783	2,549	4,048	6,152	8,361	10,059	11,131
Virginia	12,766	20,124	30,570	36,889	47,348	49,852	54,333	58,042
North Carolina	4,975	7,043	10,266	14,612	19,543	22,732	27,463	30,463
South Carolina	1,801	3,185	4,554	6,826	7,921	8,276	8,960	9,914
Georgia	398	1,019	1,801	1,763	2,486	2,753	2,931	3,500
Southwest	475	1,232	11,462	17,397	29,827	44,604	41,645	45,097

Kentucky	114	741	1,713	2,759	4,917	7,317	10,011	10,684
Tennessee	361	309	1,317	2,727	4,555	5,524	6,422	7,300
Missouri			607	347	569	1,574	2,618	3,572
Florida					844	817	932	932
Alabama		182	240	571	1,572	2,039	2,265	2,690
Mississippi				458	519	1,366	930	773
Arkansas				59	141	465	608	144
Louisiana			7,585	10,476	16,710	25,502	17,462	18,647
Texas							397	355
West						172	1,587	6,470
Total U. S.	59,466	108,395	186,446	233,504	319,599	386,303	434,495	488,070
Percentage urban								
Total U.S.	5.1	6.1	7.3	7.2	8.8	10.8	15.3	19.8
Free blacks	n.a.	13.6	15.2	18.2	19.5	28.6	30.9	33.1

n.a. Not available.

Note: West includes Iowa (from 1840); Minnesota, New Mexico, Utah, California, and Oregon (from 1850); Nebraska, Kansas, Dakota, Colorado, Nevada, and Washington (in 1860).

Sources: Population figures from U. S. Census Office, *Population of the United States in 1860*. Percentage urban figures for total U.S. from U. S. Bureau of the Census, *Historical Statistics . . . to 1970*, pt. 1, ser. A 57–72, p. 12. Percentage urban estimates for Free blacks in 1800–30 derived from Curry, *The Free Black in Urban America*; estimates for 1840–60 calculated from sum of free black populations in large cities (over 8,000 people in the North; over 4,000 in the South). City populations were listed separately within each state's section of the census reports of 1840, 1850, and 1860 (as Table II or III, depending on the year).

west of the Appalachians, and only two states in this region, Ohio and Louisiana, accumulated populations in excess of 25,000 individuals. Indeed, a large majority of free blacks lived in the swath of seaboard states (including the District of Columbia) from New York to North Carolina throughout the antebellum period. These states were home to 78% of all free blacks in 1810 and 69% in 1860, and from 1810 onward the state roughly in the geographic middle of this area (Maryland) had more free blacks than any other state. However, the largest proportional concentration of blacks who were free lived in Delaware. As early as 1820, 74% of Delaware's blacks were free, and by 1860 almost 92% had escaped slavery.[54] During the period 1830 to 1850, more than 20% of Delaware's *total* population were free blacks, a figure that dwarfs all other states.[55]

To my knowledge, no large-scale, empirical study of regional geographic location decisions has been completed for antebellum free blacks, and this remains a promising area for research. I suspect that such a study would report that the West had little appeal because established community ties were very important to free blacks. In a world often indifferent, if not hostile to the welfare of free blacks, networks of other blacks and caring whites were essential to survival, and such communities were hard to establish anew following migration. The links in chain migration, which were quite important for whites, were difficult to forge for free blacks. Certainly the rural Southwest, where an unknown black person was usually presumed to be a slave, was dangerous territory. The avoidance of the Midwest may seem more difficult to explain on these grounds until it is recalled that several midwestern state legislatures debated the legality of slavery in the early nineteenth century, and Illinois actually conducted a statewide vote on the question in 1824. Though slavery was never legalized in any midwestern state, various social and economic restrictions made life difficult for free blacks. Moreover, the disease environment in the North was relatively inhospitable to blacks.[56]

Lack of capital was also relevant in the decision to stay or move west. In the antebellum period, the western states specialized overwhelmingly in agriculture. To become an independent farmer required investments in land and, increasingly after 1840, in equipment and tools. Blacks recently emancipated often lacked the financial means to compete economically in this environment.

In both the North and South, free blacks lived predominantly in rural

---

[54] Berlin, *Slaves without Masters.*   [55] DeBow, *Statistical View of the United States.*
[56] Warren, "Northern Chills, Southern Fevers."

Table 10.6. *Child/woman ratios: Free blacks by region, 1820–1860*

Region	1820	1830	1840	1850	1860
North	1,075	1,016	958	955	896
Southeast	1,284	1,323	1,244	1,134	1,072
Southwest	1,229	1,252	1,228	1,043	987
West	—	—	764	985	883
U.S. total	1,187	1,179	1,110	1,043	981
U.S. Whites	1,593	1,413	1,348	1,186	1,164

Note: Calculated as children under age 10 per thousand women aged 15–49.
Source: See Table 10.3.

areas throughout the antebellum period, although they tended to be more urbanized than their white or slave counterparts.[57] The bottom row of Table 10.5 shows that the share of free blacks living in urban areas was 13.6% in 1800, more than twice the national average for the entire population, and by 1860 one in three free blacks lived in a city or town. The appeal of urban areas was partly social: newcomers were prevalent in the cities, life was more fluid, and there was greater tolerance of diversity. Thus, free blacks blended into the rapidly changing urban landscape. Moreover, jobs that required little capital or training were available to blacks in the service or craft industries of the city.

Owing to the early start of abolition, Philadelphia began the nineteenth century with the largest free black population (4,200 individuals). By 1820, both New York and Baltimore had passed Philadelphia in total numbers. With a free black population of 25,200 in 1850, Baltimore was clearly the most important city for freedmen in the country. It should be noted, however, that the data for Philadelphia include only the city proper; if several nearby towns within Philadelphia county are included, the 1850 total jumps to 20,000, surpassing New York in size.

Fertility. The fertility rates of whites, slaves, and free blacks declined by varying amounts during the antebellum period. Calculations from data in Table 10.6 indicate that the ratio for free blacks fell by 17% from 1820 to 1860, and as in the case of southern whites and slaves, most of the decline occurred after 1840. Ignoring the West, which had very few free blacks, those who resided in the North consistently had the lowest ratio, which was

[57] The discussion of free black population relies on Curry, *The Free Black in Urban America.*

on average 10.8% below the national average over the period 1820 to 1860. Like the ratio for slaves but unlike that for whites, the ratio for free blacks was higher in the eastern states of the South. However, the regional difference was small, averaging 5.5% over the period 1820 to 1860, which roughly equaled the regional difference for slaves. In contrast, the regional difference for southern whites averaged 17.4% over the same period.[58]

The regional patterns of fertility have inspired hypotheses of systematic breeding of slaves. The fact that slave birth rates were higher in the eastern states, in contrast to the pattern found for whites, has led some researchers to suggest that slaveowners manipulated fertility to high levels, thereby significantly raising farm income through exports of older children or young adults.[59] The finding that free black child/woman ratios had the same regional contrast as those for slaves casts some doubt on the breeding thesis. The example of free blacks shows that high fertility was attained in the eastern states without manipulation. It is conceivable that patterns established under slavery could have persisted, but most free blacks alive in the late antebellum period were born free or had not been slaves for many years, and manipulation would not have survived slavery. Instead, I find appealing the possibility that marriage opportunities were more limited for free blacks. In the Southwest, free blacks seldom lived in communities where numerous potential partner choices were available. Although it remains to be established whether marriage opportunities were more constrained in the Southwest, overall population density was markedly lower there for free blacks. Moreover, hazards of travel for free blacks living in the region may have discouraged courtship. Those investigators who pursue the topic should also recognize that an important share (41% in 1860) of free blacks living in the western states of the South resided in Louisiana, many in New Orleans. Because birth rates are generally lower in cities compared with rural areas, the regional contrast may be partly an artifact of sample composition. These ideas and other possible explanations could be explored using household data.

---

[58] One might speculate that gradual emancipation laws affected the child/woman ratio for free blacks by increasing the concentration of older women still of childbearing age. Although we lack child/woman ratios by age of the mother to make precise simulations, this effect was no doubt minor. In 1850, for example, the share of free black women aged 40 to 49 within the age group 15 to 49 was 17.3%, compared with 14.7% for slaves and 15.8% for whites. Yet the percentages in the high fertility age groups (20 to 39) were nearly identical: 61.1% for whites, 61.2% for slaves, and 62.1% for free blacks. The argument had slightly more force in 1820 when the age group 26–44 as a share of those aged 15–49 (estimated) was 42.9% for slaves, 44.7% for whites, and 46.4% for free blacks.

[59] Gutman and Sutch, "Victorians All."

Daniel Scott Smith recently examined child/woman ratios of whites, slaves, and free blacks using the available data for all southern counties reported in the 1850 and 1860 published censuses.[60] Though this is a preliminary report and focuses on whites and slaves, some intriguing results emerge for free blacks. Among the numerous social and economic characteristics of the county, only the sex ratio of free blacks, the importance of manufacturing, and the child/woman ratio of slaves were systematically related (at 0.05 level of significance) to the child/woman ratio of free blacks in regressions for both census years. The child/woman ratio was lower in areas where manufacturing was important, higher in counties with an excess of men, and higher in places where the slave ratio was high. Main crop, farm value, religion, incidence of foreign birth, plantation size, and other variables did not systematically affect the child/woman ratio in both regressions.

The direct connection between the sex ratio and fertility is expected, and manufacturing activity or other measures of economic development are often negatively related to fertility. At this point one can only speculate about the possible mechanisms that might have linked slave and free black fertility. It would be fruitful to pursue these topics and the finding that free black fertility was lower in the North using household data from the public use samples.

Health. There is little doubt that mortality in antebellum America was high by modern standards. Although a nationwide vital registration system was lacking until the twentieth century, some scattered sources are available for study. Beginning in 1850, the U.S. Census Bureau began asking respondents about deaths in the household within the year prior to the enumeration. Numerous authors have found, however, that the data thus collected were heavily underenumerated and often bear little resemblance to actual experience of the population in cities that had death recording systems, such as Boston, Philadelphia, and Baltimore.[61] Because the black population was essentially closed after 1807, model life tables and stable populations have been used to infer various demographic rates, but this technique is of no use for free blacks alone.[62] Their experience is difficult to determine by these methods, as their population growth was affected

[60] Smith, "Demographic Worlds Made."
[61] For a discussion of this data source, see Condran and Crimmins, "A Description and Evaluation," pp. 1–23.
[62] Farley, *Growth of the Black Population*; and Eblen, "New Estimates."

by manumissions and emancipation, which were not systematically regis-tered at the state level, as well as by births and deaths.

The only reasonably abundant source of mortality data on free blacks was collected by the death registration systems used in many cities as early as the eighteenth century. Though primitive by modern standards owing to their likely underenumeration and frequent lack of informa-tion on cause of death, age, and other characteristics of the deceased, it is possible to calculate crude death rates when combining deaths so recorded with estimates of population size obtained from various censuses. The most extensive scholarly work on urban living conditions, health, and mortality has been done for Philadelphia. The context of this mortality experience is reasonably well understood from a tradition of study that began in the nine-teenth century and continued with the Philadelphia Social History Project, which collected and analyzed numerous social, economic, and demographic data.[63] Gary Nash indicates that food, clothing, and shelter for Philadel-phia slaves compared favorably with those living in the South, which suggests that mortality rates may have been lower as well.[64]

Susan E. Klepp approaches health more directly by using the bills of mortality to study time trends, causes of death, and black-white differ-ences. Like Kenneth F. Kiple's extensive studies of black health in the Western Hemisphere, she connects biological adaptation and mortality, but she also reserves an important role for socioeconomic circumstances.[65] Both blacks and whites survived in greater numbers in years with moder-ate winters, but blacks did much better than whites under these circum-stances. Moreover, fall and winter were the most deadly periods for blacks, who often died from respiratory diseases, while Euro-Americans who were unaccustomed to the warm summers of Philadelphia, often succumbed in these months to fevers and diarrheal diseases. Black crude deaths rose sharply in the early 1820s, fell, and then peaked again in the late 1840s, phenomena Klepp links with changing economic conditions, migration, and with the evolution of a public water system.

Christian Warren has studied the bills of mortality for a number of cities with a view to understanding black-white mortality as a function of latitude.[66] He reports that northern cities were particularly harsh for blacks,

---

[63] See, for example, DuBois, *The Philadelphia Negro*. The Philadelphia Social History Project is described in Hershberg, *Philadelphia*.

[64] Nash, *Forging Freedom*. Nash and Soderlund, in *Freedom by Degrees*, are more pessimistic about the condition of Pennsylvania blacks.

[65] Klepp, "Black Mortality in Early Philadelphia"; Klepp, "Seasoning and Society," pp. 473–506; and Kiple, *The Caribbean Slave*.

[66] Warren, "Northern Chills, Southern Fevers."

who frequently died during the winter months from respiratory infections, while southern cities were inhospitable to whites, who often died from fevers in the summer months. In antebellum cities of the deep South, the black-white crude death rate ratio was as low as 0.55 (New Orleans) and 0.64 (Mobile) whereas in the northern cities the ratio was as high as 1.88 (Philadelphia) and 1.84 (Providence). The highest ratio (2.37) prevailed in Boston for the period 1765–74. Although these figures are for urban areas alone, many free blacks lived in cities. Moreover, the major mechanism suggested – maladaptation to cold and little inherited immunity to respiratory infections such as pneumonia and tuberculosis – would apply to free blacks living in rural areas. Because most free blacks lived in states where the ratio exceeded 1.0 by a substantial margin, it is reasonable to believe that free black mortality exceeded that for whites living under similar circumstances.[67] The urban data show black crude death rates fluctuating but gradually trending downward from the 1820s to the Civil War in three cities, and one wonders how changing economic conditions, biological adaptation, or an improving disease environment were involved.

THE POSTBELLUM PERIOD, 1870–1920

The Civil War and the Thirteenth Amendment to the Constitution began a new political and economic era for former slaves. Although the political changes provided more freedom and opportunities for new patterns of decision making, demographic patterns tended to persist. Birth rates continued their downward trend, though likely for different reasons than prevailed in the slave era, and many African Americans continued to reside in the same state until the Great Migration to the North unfolded early in the twentieth century. Of all demographic phenomena in this period, the least is known about southern health and mortality. Plantation owners no longer kept lists of births, and deaths and with the end of slavery, heights were no longer recorded in the coastwise trade. Vital registration was just getting under way in the late nineteenth century and many southern states lagged in this effort until the 1920s.

Geographic Location. Table 10.7 gives the absolute numbers of the black population living in various states and regions from 1870 to 1920. Because black emigration and immigration were virtually nil in this era, the

---

[67] The black/white mortality ratio was 1.33 in Baltimore in the years 1817–65 and 1.40 in New York from 1820 to 1865.

Table 10.7. *Black population by state and percentage urban, 1870–1920*

State	1870	1880	1890	1900	1910	1920
North	310,235	412,715	476,929	642,862	785,012	1,193,788
New England	31,705	39,925	44,580	59,099	66,306	79,051
New York	52,081	65,104	70,092	99,232	134,191	198,483
New Jersey	30,658	38,853	47,638	69,844	89,760	117,132
Pennsylvania	65,294	85,535	107,596	156,845	193,919	284,568
Ohio	63,213	79,900	87,113	96,901	111,452	186,187
Indiana	24,560	39,228	45,215	57,505	60,320	80,810
Illinois	28,762	46,368	57,028	85,078	109,049	182,274
Michigan	11,849	15,100	15,223	15,816	17,115	60,082
Wisconsin	2,113	2,702	2,444	2,542	2,900	5,201
Southeast	2,216,705	2,941,202	3,262,690	3,729,007	4,112,488	4,325,120
Delaware	22,794	26,442	28,386	30,697	31,181	30,335
Maryland	175,391	210,230	215,657	235,064	232,250	244,479
Dist. of Columbia	43,404	59,596	75,572	86,702	94,446	109,966
Virginia	512,841	631,616	635,438	660,722	671,096	690,017
West Virginia	17,980	25,886	32,690	43,499	64,173	86,345
North Carolina	391,650	531,277	561,018	624,469	697,843	763,407
South Carolina	415,814	604,332	688,934	782,321	835,843	864,719
Georgia	545,142	725,133	858,815	1,034,813	1,176,987	1,206,365
Florida	91,689	126,690	166,180	230,720	308,669	329,487
Southwest	2,322,177	3,158,051	3,648,071	4,355,186	4,794,391	4,765,352
Kentucky	222,210	271,451	268,071	284,706	261,656	235,938

Tennessee	322,331	403,151	430,678	480,243	473,088	451,758
Missouri	118,071	145,350	150,184	161,234	157,452	178,241
Alabama	475,510	600,103	678,489	827,307	908,282	900,652
Mississippi	444,201	650,291	742,559	907,630	1,009,487	935,184
Arkansas	122,169	210,666	309,117	366,856	442,891	472,220
Louisiana	364,210	483,655	559,193	650,804	713,874	700,257
Texas	253,475	393,384	488,171	620,722	690,049	741,694
Oklahoma			21,609	55,684	137,612	149,408
West	30,886	68,825	100,986	106,929	135,872	178,871
Kansas	17,108	43,107	49,710	52,003	54,030	57,925
California	4,272	6,018	11,322	11,045	21,645	38,763
Other West	9,506	19,700	39,954	43,881	60,197	82,183
Total U.S.	4,880,003	6,580,793	7,488,676	8,840,378	9,827,763	10,463,131
Percentage urban						
Total Population	25.7	28.2	32.9	37.3	45.8	51.4
Blacks	11.8	12.9	17.6	20.5	27.4	34.0

Sources: Population figures from U. S. Bureau of the Census, *Fourteenth Census*, vol. I. Percentage urban data from U. S. Bureau of the Census, *Historical Statistics . . . to 1970*, pt. I, ser. A 73–81, pp. 12–13, except for estimate of urban blacks in 1870, which is calculated from the sum of black populations in large cities (over 8,000 people in the North, over 4,000 in the South). City populations are listed separately in each state's section in U. S. Census Office, *Population . . . 1870.*

numbers tell the story of interstate net migration under the assumption that rates of natural increase were the same across states. Because these assumptions may not hold precisely for every state, small percentage changes may not signify actual net migration.

The patterns are readily apparent from the data on percentage distribution of the population given in Table 10.8. The North gained few black residents, in relation to the national average, until the turn of the century. From 1900 onward, however, the black population in the North grew rapidly with the most explosive increase occurring from 1910 to 1920 when the share living in the North rose from just under 8% to 11.41%. New York, Pennsylvania, Ohio, Illinois, and Michigan gained the lion's share, while a population shift to New England was barely noticeable. The newcomers often arrived in the large cities of the Midwest from Alabama, Mississippi, Louisiana, and Tennessee. The Southeast continuously lost in the population standings, mainly through outflows from Maryland, Virginia, and North Carolina. Those who left these states for the North often went to New York, Philadelphia, or other large cities in New York and Pennsylvania. The Southwest eventually lost in the relative rankings by 1920, but actually gained up to 1900, largely in the states of Arkansas and Texas. The lure of the West, though never as great as for whites, is apparent from the small gains registered in California and other western states.

Following the Civil War, blacks moved in substantial numbers, but usually over short distances in search of relatives, to exercise their new freedom, or to probe employment opportunities.[68] As former slaves, they lacked the resources and the knowledge of distant labor markets to undertake interstate moves. Although legal and political restrictions may have impeded the extent of mobility, a significant number of black workers did relocate, sometimes beyond a neighboring county.[69] In South Carolina, for example, blacks were attracted to the southern counties of Beaufort and Colleton by the favorable political environment, opportunities to acquire land, and employment in the phosphate industry.

Cities and towns were popular destinations, as evident in a near doubling of the share of blacks living in urban areas (from 6.7 to 11.8%) between 1860 and 1870. The offices of the Freedmen's Bureau, which helped to solve problems for blacks, was one of its attractions, while others may have been drawn by jobs in unskilled and semiskilled occupations

---

[68] Litwack, *Been in the Storm Too Long*; Devlin, *South Carolina and Black Migration*; Wright, *Old South, New South*.
[69] Cohen, *At Freedom's Edge*.

Table 10.8. *Percentage black population by state, 1870–1920*

State	1870	1880	1890	1900	1910	1920
North	6.36	6.27	6.37	7.27	7.99	11.41
New England	0.65	0.61	0.60	0.67	0.67	0.76
New York	1.07	0.99	0.94	1.12	1.37	1.90
New Jersey	0.63	0.59	0.64	0.79	0.91	1.12
Pennsylvania	1.34	1.30	1.44	1.77	1.97	2.72
Ohio	1.30	1.21	1.16	1.10	1.13	1.78
Indiana	0.50	0.60	0.60	0.65	0.61	0.77
Illinois	0.59	0.70	0.76	0.96	1.11	1.74
Michigan	0.24	0.23	0.20	0.18	0.17	0.57
Wisconsin	0.04	0.04	0.03	0.03	0.03	0.05
Southeast	45.42	44.69	43.57	42.18	41.85	41.34
Delaware	0.47	0.40	0.38	0.35	0.32	0.29
Maryland	3.59	3.19	2.88	2.66	2.36	2.34
Dist. Of Columbia	0.89	0.91	1.01	0.98	0.96	1.05
Virginia	10.51	9.60	8.49	7.47	6.83	6.59
West Virginia	0.37	0.39	0.44	0.49	0.65	0.83
North Carolina	8.03	8.07	7.49	7.06	7.10	7.30
South Carolina	8.52	9.18	9.20	8.85	8.50	8.26
Georgia	11.17	11.02	11.47	11.71	11.98	11.53
Florida	1.88	1.93	2.22	2.61	3.14	3.15
Southwest	47.59	47.99	48.71	49.26	48.78	45.54
Kentucky	4.55	4.12	3.58	3.22	2.66	2.25
Tennessee	6.61	6.13	5.75	5.43	4.81	4.32
Missouri	2.42	2.21	2.01	1.82	1.60	1.70
Alabama	9.74	9.12	9.06	9.36	9.24	8.61
Mississippi	9.10	9.88	9.92	10.27	10.27	8.94
Arkansas	2.50	3.20	4.13	4.15	4.51	4.51
Louisiana	7.46	7.35	7.47	7.36	7.26	6.69
Texas	5.19	5.98	6.52	7.02	7.02	7.09
Oklahoma			0.29	0.63	1.40	1.43
West	0.63	1.05	1.35	1.21	1.38	1.71
Kansas	0.35	0.66	0.66	0.59	0.55	0.55
California	0.09	0.09	0.15	0.12	0.22	0.37
Other West	0.19	0.30	0.53	0.50	0.61	0.79
Total U.S.	100.00	100.00	100.00	100.00	100.00	100.00

Source: Calculated from Table 10.7.

and by a more fluid social climate and the social life of churches and clubs. Whatever the appeal of the cities, it was durable; between 1870 and 1910 the share of blacks living in urban areas rose by 132%, whereas it increased only 78% for the population as a whole.

Urban areas became even more important in the lives of blacks around the time of World War I, when there was a significant increase in movement to northern cities.[70] For more than two centuries the vast majority of Americans had moved along east-west lines, and this Great Migration was the first major departure from the traditional pattern.[71] Between 1910 and 1920 the cotton-belt states lost more than 500,000 blacks, and the rate of outflow increased to 800,000 in the 1920s.[72] The magnitude and geographic direction of departure from long-established migration patterns is a watershed in American history.

A combination of events brought forth the large outflow that began in 1916. Foremost among the immediate triggers was the growth in demand for labor surrounding World War I. Immigration from Europe, which had for decades been a source of labor supply for northern industries, diminished to a trickle after the war began. To meet the growing need for war-related products, industry turned to the potential labor supply in the South. The area was ripe for the export of workers in part because blacks had chafed for years under Jim Crow laws and other forms of social and economic repression. The deteriorating state of the cotton economy added to the discontent. Beginning with Texas in the late nineteenth century, the boll weevil swept eastward across the South in three decades, devastating an agricultural economy heavily anchored to cotton, while various storms or natural disasters exacerbated the economic misery. This, combined with the lure of northern wages, which were twice or more those in the South, made the North irresistible to some blacks. Indeed, one may ask why Southerners did not move earlier, much the way Europeans had found jobs in the North for decades. The answer may lie in lack of knowledge of distant labor markets, and in low levels of education and skills preferred by an industrial economy, and discrimination against black workers in the North.[73] Nevertheless, with the help of networks of family and friends, labor recruiting agents, and northern newspapers such as

---

[70] Numerous publications discuss the Great Migration. For examples of recent, well-done scholarly works, see Grossman *Land of Hope*; and Gottlieb, *Making Their Own Way*.
[71] Steckel, "The Economic Foundations of East-West Migration," pp. 14–36.
[72] Higgs, "The Boll Weevil," pp. 335–50.
[73] For a discussion of education among blacks in the South, see Margo, *Race and Schooling*.

Table 10.9. *Child/woman ratios: Blacks by region, 1870–1920*

Region	1870	1880	1890	1900	1910	1920
North	812	848	687	552	490	482
New England	582	696	593	528	532	586
Mid-Atlantic	705	728	601	510	467	477
East North Central	1,019	1,025	813	621	517	473
Old South	1,205	1,405	1,216	1,153	1,057	958
New South	1,219	1,422	1,226	1,119	980	839
East South Central						
(+Missouri)	1,229	1,394	1,188	1,084	960	842
West South Central	1,199	1,478	1,292	1,175	1,009	834
West	1,062	962	844	653	520	505
U.S. Total	1,183	1,362	1,173	1,077	958	834
U.S. Whites	1,325	1,268	1,134	1,099	1,005	992

Notes: Child/woman ratios calculated as children under age 10 per thousand women aged 15–49. Regional definitions are those used by the U.S. Census Bureau, except for Missouri, which is included in the New South, to aid comparison with the antebellum period. Censuses of 1880 and 1890 reported age data for the "Colored" population, defined as Negroes, Chinese, Japanese, and Civilized Indians. Including the last three groups does not materially affect ratios reported here.

Sources: Calculated from U.S. Census Office, *Vital Statistics . . . Ninth Census*, 1870, Table XXVII, pp. 624–30, and Table XXIX, pp. 650–54; *Statistics . . . at the Tenth Census, 1880*, Table XX, pp. 548–49, and Table XXI, pp. 552–645; *Report . . . at Eleventh Census: 1890*, Table 1, pp. 2–3, and Table 2, pp. 6–103; *Twelfth Census*, Table 1, pp. 2–3, and Table 2, pp. 6–109. Also U.S. Bureau of the Census, *Thirteenth Census*, Table 19, p. 303, and Table 43, pp. 352–60 and 384; *Fourteenth Census*, vol. 2, Table 3, p. 156, and Table 13, pp. 171–87 and 235.

Chicago's *Defender*, large numbers of southern blacks eventually made the geographic moves that began their transitions to an urban-industrial way of life.

Fertility. Table 10.9 depicts the broad outlines of fertility change that are visible from child/woman ratios.[74] Because of the low quality of the 1870

---

[74] The general trends noted in child/woman ratios are observed in other measures of fertility such as the gross reproduction rate (the number of daughters a woman would have if she lived to the end of her childbearing span) and total fertility. Farley, *Growth of the Black Population*, pp. 53–58 and Coale and Rives, "A Statistical Reconstruction of the Black Population," pp. 3–36.

census, particularly the underenumeration of southern blacks, one may question the accuracy of the child/woman ratios for that year. There is some doubt as to when the late-nineteenth-century fertility decline actually began, but it was clearly under way after 1880. Between 1880 and 1920 the ratio fell by 39% – nearly twice the rate for whites. Once the fertility transition was well under way among blacks, the experience was more intense than for whites.[75] As a result of rapid decline, the child/woman ratio for blacks was below that for whites by 1900. Initially 7% above the ratio for whites, the child/woman ratio for blacks was only 84% of that for whites by 1920.[76] The pace of change was somewhat greater in the North, where the ratio fell by 43% from 1880 to 1920, compared with 25% in the Southeast, 31% in the Southwest, and 30% in the West. Table 10.9 also makes clear that the transition got under way earlier in the North and in the West, where the ratio in 1880 was only 62% and 71%, respectively, of the national average.

The fertility decline occurred despite a slight increase in nuptiality.[77] Between 1890 and 1920 the age at first marriage for black women declined slightly, and the proportion of women aged 15 and older who were married rose from 57% to 59%. Therefore, causes of the overall fertility decline cannot be found in changing marriage patterns.

The search for explanations must consider the context of the fertility decline and the regional patterns. The traditional framework of demographic transition emphasizes education, modernization, urbanization, and lower child mortality rates as dynamic factors that led to reductions in the number of births. This approach has limits when applied to postbellum blacks: education levels were low, considerable decline in births occurred in rural areas, and mortality rates may have improved little (or indeed worsened) among blacks in the late nineteenth century.[78] By traditional demographic transition criteria, postbellum blacks seem unlikely

[75] We should not ignore the possible role of increasing mortality among children, as discussed below.

[76] The child/woman ratio (CW) and the net reproduction rate (NRR) tell somewhat different stories of white and black fertility. The NRR is the number of daughters a cohort of 1,000 female infants beginning life together would have during the course of their lives if the cohort were subject to both the birth and death rates at each age level which prevailed at the time of a census or survey. In 1905–10 the black NRR was 99% of that for whites, but the black CW was only 95% of the white in 1910. These differences are consistent with relatively higher child mortality among blacks, discussed later in the chapter. For data on the NRR, see the 1944 report by U.S. Bureau of the Census, *Sixteenth Census . . . Standardized Fertility Rates*, Tables 7 and 11.

[77] Farley, *Growth of the Black Population*, chap. 6.

[78] Although black education levels were low, they were rising, and it is possible that the acquisition of basic literacy had a significant impact on fertility. To my knowledge, this line of thought has not been systematically investigated in relation to postbellum black fertility.

to have been poised for substantial fertility reductions. It should be noted, however, that many black women were household heads and many worked outside the home, and both characteristics could have been factors reducing fertility.[79]

The apparent conflict of the black experience with the framework of the demographic transition has led researchers to consider factors outside this framework. Several investigators have suggested that deteriorating health may have impaired black fecundity (i.e., reduced the biological chances of conception), a line of thought supported by a dramatic rise in childlessness among black women to approximately 25% among women born in the late nineteenth century.[80] This rate of childlessness is far above the 5 to 7% sterility rate expected in healthy populations. Among the possible causes, Farley emphasizes venereal disease and mentions pellagra, while others support post-partum infections and rickets, or a variety of diseases.[81] Among these biological explanations, venereal disease has attracted the most research interest.[82] Stewart Tolnay measures its importance compared with other hypotheses by studying county-level data in six southern states in the 1940.[83] Using regressions of child/woman ratios on the incidence of venereal disease and other factors such as infant mortality rates, the share of employment in agriculture, and illiteracy rates, he concludes that venereal disease may have explained 28% of the fertility decline from 1880 to 1940. The actual incidence of venereal disease is open to doubt, but Jerome Rose's examination of skeletal lesions from a turn-of-the-century cemetery of blacks in Arkansas indicates that congenital syphilis was prevalent among children, which supports the claim that venereal disease reduced fertility.[84] Consistent with the idea that deteriorating health of black women may have impaired fecundity, Lee Meadows Jantz's survey of skeletal evidence indicates that black women, in contrast to black men and to whites of both sexes, showed a slight loss in stature from Reconstruction through the early twentieth century.[85]

---

[79] For a discussion of labor force participation, see Goldin, *Understanding the Gender Gap.* For the connection with fertility, see Van Horn, *Women, Work, and Fertility.*

[80] Farley, *Growth of the Black Population,* p. 57; and Morgan, "Late Nineteenth- and Early Twentieth-Century Childlessness," pp. 779–807.

[81] Farley, *Growth of the Black Population,* pp. 11–12 and pp. 222–26; Cutright and Shorter, "The Effects of Health," pp. 191–217; McFalls and McFalls, *Disease and Fertility.*

[82] See, for example, McFalls, "Impact of VD," pp. 2–19; and Wright, "An Examination of Factors," pp. 213–39.

[83] Tolnay, "A New Look," pp. 679–90.

[84] Rose, "Biological Consequences of Segregation and Economic Deprivation," pp. 351–60.

[85] Jantz, *Secular Change and Allometry.*

The fact that health and venereal disease may explain only a moderate portion of the fertility decline implies that ample reason exists to consider voluntary factors. The various temporal patterns by region and occupation suggest a complex process rather than a simple, single fertility transition. Birth rates declined earlier in northern than in southern states and in urban as opposed to rural areas.[86] Moreover, when declines in average family did reach the countryside, the changes were pronounced among nonfarmers.[87] Although urban fertility was relatively low among blacks relative to whites, the shift of black population from the rural south to the urban north prior to 1920 was too small to account for much of the overall fertility decline.

Several social or economic factors appear to be relevant for changes in black fertility. Edward Meeker developed and tested an economic model that points to urbanization and greater literacy as dynamic ingredients increasing the costs of black children to their parents, thereby lowering desired family size.[88] Considerable research has established a connection between family structure, particularly the absence of a husband, and fertility. Thus, the decline in black marital fertility might have been driven by rising rates of female-headed households near the turn of the century.[89] Another line of argument stresses the importance of occupational structure. Herman Lantz and Lewellyn Hendrix use data published by the 1910 census to observe that the persistence of high fertility among southern blacks as late as the early twentieth century may have been related to their concentration in farm-related occupations.[90]

Ultimately, family limitation played an important role in the black fertility transition, but there is debate over its importance during the late nineteenth and early twentieth centuries. Farley suggests that as few as 10 or 15% of black married women had ever used contraceptives as late as the 1930s.[91] On the other hand, Joseph McFalls and George Masnick suggest that a large fraction of blacks may have used birth control as early as the late nineteenth century, but observers differ in their views on its effectiveness and its impact on fertility.[92] Stewart Tolnay pursues these questions by examining age-specific marital fertility rates tabulated in

[86] Engerman, "Black Fertility and Family Structure," pp. 117–38; Tolnay, "Black Fertility in Decline," pp. 249–60; Tolnay, "Trends in Total and Marital Fertility," pp. 443–63.

[87] Tolnay, "The Decline of Black Marital Fertility," pp. 211–17.

[88] Meeker, "Freedom, Economic Opportunity, and Fertility," pp. 397–412.

[89] Engerman, "Black Fertility"; Tolnay, "The Black Fertility Transition," pp. 2–7; and Morgan et al., "Racial Differences," pp. 798–828.

[90] Lantz and Hendrix, "Black Fertility and the Black Family," pp. 251–61.

[91] Farley, *Growth of the Black Population*.

[92] McFalls and Masnick, "Birth Control," pp. 89–106.

Census Bureau reports on the fertility of American women in 1910 and 1940.[93] With these data he employs the Coale-Trussell method to measure the degree to which the age-specific rates departed from a natural (uncontrolled) standard. He reports at best weak evidence for control among rural farm women surveyed in 1910, whereas rural nonfarm women imposed modest limits on family size.

Health. Black health from Reconstruction through the early twentieth century is poorly documented when compared with other demographic phenomena, and thus we know little about trends and differentials in mortality. As late as 1900 only 4.4% of all blacks lived in the nascent death registration area, largely comprised of northeastern states, and 82% of those who lived within the registration area resided in death-prone cities or towns.[94] Other sources and methods provide useful information, but have some drawbacks. The fact that the black population was essentially closed to migration during this period makes model life table approaches and census survival analysis look promising, but the uneven quality of the census over the period and unusual age patterns of black mortality cast some doubt on the results. Several large cities had some form of death registration, but as late as 1920 nearly two-thirds of all blacks lived in rural areas. The censuses of 1900 and 1910 asked women the number of children born and the number surviving, but their evidence on health pertains only to children.

Discussions of social, economic, and medical conditions suggest a wide range of possibilities for the health of blacks. The Civil War era brought hardship, migration, and turmoil that likely had unfavorable consequences for health. In the longer term, emancipation gave blacks the freedom to allocate the labor and material resources of the family, which may have improved health for children, but Jim Crow laws and other instruments of repression that followed Reconstruction might have had a negative effect on health.[95] Eventually knowledge of the germ theory of disease, public health, personal hygiene, and new methods of infant care and feeding had a significant beneficial impact on health, but such improvements were slow to spread through the South during the late nineteenth and early twentieth centuries.[96] On the other hand, the disease environ-

---

[93] Tolnay, "The Decline of Black Marital Fertility."   [94] Preston and Haines, *Fatal Years*, p. 50.

[95] Higgs, "Mortality in Rural America," pp. 177–96; Higgs, *Competition and Coercion*; Ransom and Sutch, *One Kind of Freedom*.

[96] See Rosenberg, "The Therapeutic Revolution," pp. 3–25; Chapin, *Municipal Sanitation*; and Preston and Haines, *Fatal Years*.

ment of Southerners benefited from low population density, little urbanization, and few immigrants.

The birth and survival responses in the censuses of 1900 and 1910, though restricted to children, are perhaps the most informative single source yet studied on black health during this period. Although census officials never published the child-survival data, this evidence has proved valuable through public use of the population manuscripts, combined with newly developed demographic methods that furnish mortality estimates. In the most extensive use of this approach, Samuel Preston and Michael Haines confirm some widely held notions, but also challenge or overturn aspects of conventional wisdom about health in general and that of blacks in particular.[97] They conclude that the probability of death before age 5 was higher for blacks compared with whites (25.5% vs. 16.1%), but the difference was less than thought from death registration data (33.8% for blacks, 17.9% for whites). Thus, mortality rates were lower for blacks living in the South compared with those who resided in the death registration area, a finding consistent with the north-south gradient of relative mortality noted for cities.[98] After controlling for other influences on mortality, race remained the most important variable affecting health. In a multivariate statistical analysis that included places of residence, employment, literacy, and other variables, the probability of death was 30% higher for black children. Moreover, the disadvantage of race was more than twice as great in urban as in rural areas, and hence the death registration area presented a distorted picture of overall health conditions for blacks.

In the absence of a biological predisposition to higher black mortality in America, which has been argued by Kenneth Kiple, the mortality risks for blacks and whites should have been similar after controlling for all relevant socioeconomic variables.[99] Thus, some of the relevant variables may have been omitted from the analysis, or it is possible that variables included were mismeasured or otherwise had a different meaning for whites than for blacks. For example, occupation may have been a poor proxy for income, particularly for blacks, or blacks who lived in cities may have resided outside the reach of beneficial water and sewer services.

It is hazardous to estimate trends in black mortality from the available evidence, and for this reason it is not surprising that authors have ven-

---

[97] Preston and Haines, *Fatal Years*, chap. 4.
[98] Preston and Haines, "The Use of the Census," confirm that the pattern also appeared in data from the public use samples of 1900 and 1910.
[99] Kiple, "Survey of Recent Literature," pp. 343–67.

tured diverse conclusions. Viewing the wide range of previous estimates and the data complications, Michael Haines eschews estimates based on census survival and model life tables for blacks prior to 1900.[100] That said, census-survival methods applied by Farley suggest a mild deterioration in life expectation at birth from the middle of the nineteenth to the early twentieth century.[101] He reports that life expectation for black females fell from 27.8 years to 25.0 years between 1850–60 and 1910–20. Using a combination of census-survival and model life table approaches, Meeker argues that the health of blacks deteriorated in the three decades following the Civil War but by 1900 had improved to the levels of the late antebellum period.[102] He suggests that life expectation at birth was approximately 32 years in the 1850s but fell to 26.5 years in 1880 and then rose to slightly more than 31 years by 1900–10. By applying the age pattern of mortality in the U.N. Far East model, Douglas Ewbank maintains that life expectation at age 10 was about 39 years from 1880 to 1900 but increased to 45 years in 1920.[103] By examining the survival of children born in different years, Preston and Haines find no improvement in black child mortality in the last two decades of the nineteenth century.[104]

Whatever the overall trend in black health, it is likely that the age pattern of mortality changed substantially from slavery to freedom. Under slavery, young children had remarkably high mortality compared with adults, whereas in the late nineteenth century the mortality of children was much lower. Nearly one-half of the slave births did not survive to age 5, compared with a mortality rate of 4% for adults aged 20 to 24, and the ratio of mortality from birth to age 5 to that from age 20 to 24 was approximately 12.0.[105] In 1900 the corresponding mortality rates were 26.7% and 4.1%, and the ratio was approximately 6.5.[106] Thus, the mortality rates of black adults may have changed little in the half century following the end of slavery, and even though the public health revolution was slow in penetrating the South, the health of black children improved considerably after the Civil War.

[100] Haines, "Estimated Life Tables." Disputes over the age pattern of black mortality complicate the interpretation of model life tables. Zelnik, in "Age Patterns of Mortality," pp. 433–51, argues that the Model West table is not good. Ewbank ("History of Black Mortality," pp. 100–28) prefers the U.N. Far East Model, and Condran ("An Evaluation of Estimates," pp. 53–69) likes the Model South.

[101] Farley, *Growth of the Black Population*.

[102] Meeker, "Mortality Trends of Southern Blacks," pp. 13–42.

[103] Ewbank, "History of Black Mortality."   [104] Preston and Haines, *Fatal Years*, chap. 3.

[105] Steckel, "A Dreadful Childhood," Table 1.

[106] Calculated from Haines, "Estimated Life Tables."

CONCLUDING REMARKS

Like other Western Hemisphere populations, the black population of the United States experienced major changes from 1790 to 1920. Over these 130 years the number of individuals grew nearly 27-fold, and there were vast changes in social and economic conditions. In response, the black population relocated to the West and to urban areas, birth rates declined substantially, and health eventually improved significantly, especially for children.

Much remains to be learned about the details of these demographic changes, and even more about the social and economic events that created them. But this should not be cause for pessimism, especially if one views the glass as half full rather than half empty. Given the unexploited sources available for study, declining costs for collecting data, and new methods of analysis, it is clear that many promising research opportunities remain. Thus, I hope this review stimulates others to pursue this fascinating area of inquiry.

At the same time, researchers have acquired considerable evidence on the broad patterns of black demographic history. One of the remaining challenge is to blend this evidence with history. Scholars must remember that demographic and socioeconomic time series or collections of data by regions, states, and counties are not substitutes for direct information about agents or decision makers. Ultimately, historical demographers must ponder the agency of people – individuals, couples, families, and households who participated and shaped the process of change. Curious readers would like to know, for example, more about the discussions that prospective parents must have had regarding family limitation and the planning strategies they pursued. Many would like to know how they viewed rearing children versus work outside the home, how their personal lives adapted to changing knowledge of public health and personal hygiene, and what tactics individuals and families used to plan and to cope with long-distance migration. In many ways, the explication of the demographic past has just begun.

BIBLIOGRAPHIC ESSAY

Reynolds Farley's *Growth of the Black Population* (Chicago, 1970) is the only reasonably comprehensive work on the history of the black population in the United States. The book is written with a demographer's focus, but the author interacts with the historical and sociological literature. The volume discusses all aspects of population growth, including fertility, mortality or health, and immigration, whereas population distribution and migration are discussed only incidentally. Published over 25 years ago, the book is now somewhat dated, but it continues to provide valuable background information and discussies issues that are topics of current research and debate.

Readers who wish to pursue the literature published since Farley's book appeared have to contend with numerous, more specialized books and papers. The literature on slavery is abundant. The foremost recent work on slave fertility is Richard H. Steckel's *The Economics of U.S. Slave and Southern White Fertility* (New York, 1985). An informative survey of the literature on black health can be found in Kenneth Kiple, "Survey of Recent Literature on the Biological Past of the Black," *Social Science History* 10 (1986), 343–67. For detailed discussions of slave health, see Richard H. Steckel, "A Peculiar Population: The Nutrition, Health, and Mortality of American Slaves from Childhood to Maturity," *Journal of Economic History* 46 (1986), 721–41; and Richard H. Steckel, "A Dreadful Childhood: The Excess Mortality of American Slaves," *Social Science History* 10 (1986), 427–65. In *Speculators and Slaves* (Madison, Wisc., 1989), Michael Tadman provides the most extensive, recent discussion of the interregional slave trade. Various demographic topics are discussed in Robert William Fogel and Stanley L. Engerman (eds.), *Without Consent or Contract: Conditions of Slave Life and the Transition to Freedom*, Technical Papers, volume 2 (New York, 1992).

The demography of free blacks has been lightly studied, despite the considerable potential of data from manuscript schedules of the census and various county-level registrations of free Negroes. Informed discussions of free black history, which tend to emphasize the urban environment but include some material on demography, can be found in Ira Berlin, *Slaves without Masters* (New York, 1974); Gary B. Nash, *Forging Freedom: The Formation of Philadelphia's Black Community, 1720–1840* (Cambridge, Mass., 1988); and Leonard Curry, *The Free Black in Urban America 1800–1850* (Chicago, 1981).

The demographic experience from the end of the Civil War to 1920 is not well documented or has been modestly researched. No recent book-length effort has been undertaken on fertility during this period. Readers who would like to engage the literature should consult recent articles and the references therein, such as Stewart E. Tolnay, "Family Economy and the Black American Fertility Transition," *Journal of Family History* 11 (1986), 268–83; and Stewart E. Tolnay, "The Decline of Black Marital Fertility in the Rural South," *American Sociological Review* 52 (1987), 211–17. The most extensive work on mortality during the period is Sam Preston and Michael Haines, *Fatal Years: Child Mortality in late Nineteenth-Century American* (Princeton, 1991). Several books have been written on black migration to northern cities, and among the recent ones I recommend James R. Grossman, *Land of Hope: Chicago, Black Southerners, and the Great Migration* (Chicago, 1989); and Peter Gottlieb, *Making Their Own Way: Southern Blacks' Migration to Pittsburgh, 1916–1930* (Urbana, 1987).

REFERENCES

Berlin, Ira. 1974. *Slaves without Masters*. New York: Pantheon.

Bogue, Donald J., and Palmore, James A. 1964. "Some Empirical and Analytic Relations among Demographic Fertility Measures, with Regression Models for Fertility Estimation." *Demography* 1, 316–38.

Campbell, John. 1984. "Work, Pregnancy, and Infant Mortality among Southern Slaves." *Journal of Interdisciplinary History* 14, 793–812.

Cappon, Lester J. 1976. *Atlas of Early American History: The Revolutionary Era, 1760–1790.* Princeton, N.J.: Princeton University Press.

Chapin, Charles V. 1901. *Municipal Sanitation in the United States*. Providence, R.I.: Snow and Farnhum.

Coale, Ansley, and Rives, N. W. 1973. "A Statistical Reconstruction of the Black Population of the United States, 1880–1970: Estimates of True Numbers by Age and Sex, Birth Rates, and Total Fertility." *Population Index* 39, 3–36.

Coelho, Philip R., and McGuire, Robert A. 1997. "African and European Bound Labor in the British New World: The Biological Consequences of Economic Choices." *Journal of Economic History* 57, 83–115.

Cohen, William. 1991. *At Freedom's Edge: Black Mobility and the Southern White Quest for Racial Control, 1861–1915*. Baton Rouge: Louisiana State University Press.

Condran, Gretchen A. 1984. "An Evaluation of Estimates of Underenumeration in the Census and the Age Pattern of Mortality, Philadelphia, 1880." *Demography* 21, 53–69.

Condran, Gretchen A., and Crimmins, Eileen. 1979. "A Description and Evaluation of Mortality Data in the Federal Census: 1850–1900." *Historical Methods* 12, 1–23.

Curry, Leonard. 1981. *The Free Black in Urban America 1800–1850*. Chicago: University of Chicago Press.

Curtin, Philip D. 1969. *The Atlantic Slave Trade*. Madison: University of Wisconsin Press.

Cutright, P., and Shorter, Edward. 1979. "The Effects of Health on the Completed

Fertility of Nonwhite and White U.S. Women Born between 1867 and 1935." *Journal of Social History* 13, 191–217.

DeBow, J. D. B. 1854. *Statistical View of the United States*. Washington, D.C.: Superintendent of the U.S. Census.

Devlin, George A. 1989. *South Carolina and Black Migration, 1865–1940*. New York: Garland.

DuBois, W. E. B. 1899. *The Philadelphia Negro: A Social Study*. Philadelphia: University of Pennsylvania Press.

Eblen, Jack E. 1972. "Growth of the Black Population in Antebellum America, 1820–1860." *Population Studies* 26, 273–89.

———. 1974. "New Estimates of the Vital Rates of the United States Black Population during the Nineteenth Century." *Demography* 11, 301–19.

Engerman, Stanley L. 1977. "Black Fertility and Family Structure in the U.S., 1880–1940." *Journal of Family History* 2, 117–38.

Evans, Robert, Jr. 1962. "The Economics of American Negro Slavery." In Universities-National Bureau Committee for Economic Research, *Aspects of Labor Economics*. Princeton: Princeton University Press. pp. 185–243.

Ewbank, Douglas C. 1987. "History of Black Mortality and Health before 1940." *Milbank Quarterly* 65 (Suppl. 1), 100–28.

Farley, Reynolds. 1970. *Growth of the Black Population*. Chicago: Markham.

Fogel, Robert William. 1989. *Without Consent or Contract*. New York: W. W. Norton.

Fogel, Robert William, and Engerman, Stanley L. 1974. *Time on the Cross: The Economics of American Negro Slavery*. Boston: Little, Brown.

———. 1992. "The Slave Breeding Thesis." In Robert William Fogel and Stanley L. Engerman, eds., *Without Consent or Contract: Conditions of Slave Life and The Transition to Freedom*. New York: W. W. Norton.

Fogel, Robert William, Galantine, Ralph A., and Manning, Richard L. 1992. *Without Consent or Contract: Evidence and Methods*. New York: W. W. Norton.

Friedman, Gerald, and Galantine, Ralph A. 1992. "Regional Markets for Slaves and the Interregional Slave Trade." In Robert William Fogel, Ralph A. Galantine, and Richard L. Manning, eds., *Without Consent or Contract: Evidence and Methods*, pp. 195–99. New York: W. W. Norton.

Goldin, Claudia Dale. 1976. *Urban Slavery in the American South, 1820–1860: A Quantitative History*. Chicago: University of Chicago Press.

———. 1990. *Understanding the Gender Gap: An Economic History of American Women*. New York: Oxford University Press.

Gottlieb, Peter. 1987. *Making Their Own Way: Southern Blacks' Migration to Pittsburgh, 1916–1930*. Urbana: University of Illinois Press.

Grossman, James R. 1989. *Land of Hope: Chicago, Black Southerners, and the Great Migration*. Chicago: University of Chicago Press.

Gutman, Herbert G., and Sutch, Richard. 1976. "Victorians All? Sexual Mores and Conduct of Slaves and Their Masters." In Paul A. David, Herbert G. Gutman, Richard Sutch, Peter Temin, and Gavin Wright, eds., *Reckoning with Slavery*, pp. 134–62. Oxford: Oxford University Press.

Haines, Michael R. 1994. "Estimated Life Tables for the United States, 1850–1900." Working Paper Series on Historical Factors in Long Run Growth No. 59. Cambridge, Mass.: National Bureau of Economic Research.

Hajnal, J. 1965. "European Marriage Patterns in Perspective." In D. V. Glass and D. E. C. Eversley, eds., *Population in History*, pp. 101–43. London: Edward Arnold.

Hershberg, Theodore. 1981. *Philadelphia: Work, Space, Family, and Group Experience in the 19th Century.* New York: Oxford University Press.

Higgs, Robert. 1973. "Mortality in Rural America: Estimates and Conjectures." *Explorations in Economic History* 10, 177–96.

———. 1976. "The Boll Weevil, the Cotton Economy, and Black Migration: 1910–1930." *Agricultural History* 50, 335–50.

———. 1977. *Competition and Coercion.* Cambridge: Cambridge University Press.

Jantz, Lee Meadows 1996. "Secular Change and Allometry in the Long Limb Bones of Americans from the Mid 1700s through the 1970s." Ph.D. diss., University of Tennessee, Knoxville.

Johnson, Michael P. 1981. "Smothered Slave Infants: Were Slave Mothers at Fault?" *Journal of Southern History* 47, 493–520.

Kiple, Kenneth F. 1984. *The Caribbean Slave: A Biological History.* New York: Cambridge University Press.

———. 1986. "Survey of Recent Literature on the Biological Past of the Black." *Social Science History* 10, 343–67.

Kiple, Kenneth F., and Kiple, Virginia H. 1977. "Slave Child Mortality: Some Nutritional Answers to a Perennial Puzzle." *Journal of Social History* 10, 284–309.

Klepp, Susan E. 1988. "Black Mortality in Early Philadelphia, 1722–1859." Paper given at the Social Science History Association meetings in Chicago.

———. 1994. "Seasoning and Society: Racial Differences in Mortality in Eighteenth-Century Philadelphia." *William and Mary Quarterly* 51, 473–506.

Lantz, Herman, and Hendrix, Lewellyn. 1978. "Black Fertility and the Black Family in the Nineteenth Century: A Re-Examination of the Past." *Journal of Family History* 3, 251–61.

Lewis, Jan, and Lockridge, Kenneth A. 1988. " 'Sally Has Been Sick': Pregnancy and Family Limitation among Virginia Gentry Women, 1780–1830." *Journal of Social History* 22, 5–19.

Litwack, Leon F. (1979). *Been in the Storm Too Long: The Aftermath of Slavery.* New York: Knopf.

McFalls, Joseph A., Jr. 1973. "Impact of VD on the Fertility of the U.S. Black Population, 1880–1950." *Social Biology* 20, 2–19.

McFalls, Joseph A., Jr., and McFalls, Marguerite Harvey. 1984. *Disease and Fertility.* Orlando: Academic Press.

McFalls, Joseph A., Jr., and Masnick, George S. 1981. "Birth Control and the Fertility of the U.S. Black Population, 1880 to 1980." *Journal of Family History* 6, 89–106.

Margo, Robert A. 1990. *Race and Schooling in the South: An Economic History.* Chicago: University of Chicago Press.

Meeker, Edward, 1976. "Mortality Trends of Southern Blacks, 1850–1910: Some Preliminary Findings." *Explorations in Economic History* 13, 13–42.

———. 1977. "Freedom, Economic Opportunity, and Fertility: Black Americans, 1860–1910." *Economic Inquiry* 15, 397–412.

Morgan, S. Philip. 1991. "Late Nineteenth- and Early Twentieth-Century Childlessness." *American Journal of Sociology* 97, 779–807.

Morgan, S. Philip, McDaniel, Antonio, Miller, Andrew T., and Preston, Samuel H. 1993. "Racial Differences in Household and Family Structure at the Turn of the Century." *American Journal of Sociology* 4, 798–828.

Nash, Gary B. 1988. *Forging Freedom: The Formation of Philadelphia's Black Community, 1720–1840.* Cambridge Mass.: Harvard University Press.

Nash, Gary B., and Soderlund, Jean R. 1991. *Freedom by Degrees: Emancipation in Pennsylvania and Its Aftermath.* New York: Oxford University Press.

Phillips, Ulrich Bonnell. 1918. *American Negro Slavery.* New York: D. Appleton.

Pope, Clayne. 1992. "Adult Mortality in America before 1900: A View from Family Histories." In Claudia Goldin and Hugh Rockoff, eds., *Strategic Factors in Nineteenth Century American Economic History: A Volume to Honor Robert W. Fogel,* pp. 267–96. Chicago: University of Chicago Press.

Postell, William Dosite. 1951. *The Health of Slaves on Southern Plantations.* Baton Rouge: Louisiana State University Press.

Preston, Samuel H., and Haines, Michael R. 1991, *Fatal Years: Child Mortality in Late Nineteenth-Century America.* Princeton N.J.: Princeton University Press.

———. 1997. "The Use of the Census to Estimate Childhood Mortality: Comparisons from the 1900 and 1910 United States Census Public Use Samples." *Historical Methods* 30, 77–96.

Ransom, Roger L., and Sutch, Richard. 1977. *One Kind of Freedom: The Economic Consequences of Emancipation.* New York: Cambridge University Press.

Rose, Jerome C. 1989. "Biological Consequences of Segregation and Economic Deprivation: A Post-Slavery Population from Southwest Arkansas." *Journal of Economic History* 49, 351–60.

Rosenberg, Charles E. 1979. "The Therapeutic Revolution: Medicine, Meaning, and Social Change in Nineteenth-Century America." In Morris J. Vogel and Charles E. Rosenberg, eds., *The Therapeutic Revolution: Essays in the Social History of American Medicine,* pp. 3–25. Philadelphia: Univesity of Pennsylvania Press.

Savitt, Todd L. 1978. *Medicine and Slavery.* Urbana: University of Illinois Press.

Shryock, Henry S., and Siegel, Jacob S. 1975. *The Methods and Materials of Demography.* Vol. I. Washington, D.C.: Government Printing Office.

Smith, Daniel Scott. 1994. "Demographic Worlds Made, Imposed, and Shared: An Examination of Fertility among Whites, Slaves, and Free Blacks in the American South in 1850 and 1860." Paper given at the Social Science History Association meetings in Atlanta.

Steckel, Richard H. 1979. "Slave Height Profiles from Coastwise Manifests." *Explorations in Economic History* 16: 363–80.

———. 1980. "Slave Marriage and the Family." *Journal of Family History* 5, 406–21.

———. 1982. "The Fertility of American Slaves." *Research in Economic History* 7, 239–86.

———. 1983. "The Economic Foundations of East-West Migration during the Nineteenth Century." *Explorations in Economic History* 20, 14–36.

———. 1985. *The Economics of U.S. Slave and Southern White Fertility.* New York: Garland.

———. 1986. "Birth Weights and Infant Mortality among American Slaves." *Explorations in Economic History* 23: 173–98.

———. 1986. "A Peculiar Population: The Nutrition, Health, and Mortality of American Slaves from Childhood to Maturity." *Journal of Economic History* 46: 721–41.

————. 1986. "A Dreadful Childhood: The Excess Mortality of American Slaves." *Social Science History* 10: 427–65.

————. 1987. "Growth Depression and Recovery: The Remarkable Case of American Slaves." *Annals of Human Biology* 14: 111–32.

————. 1988. "The Health and Mortality of Women and Children, 1850–1860." *Journal of Economic History* 48: 333–45.

Steckel, Richard H., and Floud, Roderick, eds. 1997. *Health and Welfare during Industrialization*. Chicago: University of Chicago Press.

Sutch, Richard. 1975. "The Breeding of Slaves for Sale and the Westward Expansion of Slavery, 1850–1860." In Stanley L. Engerman and Eugene D. Genovese, eds., *Race and Slavery in the Western Hemisphere*, pp. 173–210. Princeton, N.J.: Princeton University Press.

————. 1976. "The Care and Feeding of Slaves." In Paul A. David, Herbert G. Gutman, Richard Sutch, Peter Temin, and Gavin Wright, eds., *Reckoning with Slavery*, pp. 231–301. New York: Oxford University Press.

Tadman, Michael. 1989. *Speculators and Slaves: Masters, Traders and Slaves in the Old South*. Madison: University of Wisconsin Press.

Tanner, James M. 1978. *Fetus into Man: Physical Growth from Conception to Maturity*. Cambridge, Mass.: Harvard University Press.

Tolnay, Stewart E. 1980. "Black Fertility in Decline: Urban Differentials in 1900." *Social Biology* 27, 249–60.

————. 1981. "Trends in Total and Marital Fertility for Black Americans, 1886–1899." *Demography* 18, 443–63.

————. 1985. "The Black Fertility Transition, 1880–1940." *Sociology and Social Research* 70, 2–7.

————. 1986. "Family Economy and the Black American Fertility Transition." *Journal of Family History* 11, 268–83.

————. 1987. "The Decline of Black Marital Fertility in the Rural South: 1910–1940." *American Sociological Review* 52, 211–17.

————. 1989. "A New Look at the Effect of Venereal Disease on Black Fertility: The Deep South in 1940." *Demography* 26, 679–90.

Trussell, James, and Steckel, Richard H. 1978. "The Age of Slaves at Menarche and Their First Birth." *Journal of Interdisciplinary History* 8, 477–505.

U.S. Census Office. 1821. *Census for 1820; 4th Census of the United States*. Washington, D.C.: Gales & Seaton.

————. 1832. *Abstract of the Returns of the Fifth Census*. Washington, D.C.: Duff Green, pp. 48–51.

————. 1841. *Compendium of the Enumeration of the Inhabitants and Statistics of the United States of America, as Obtained from the Sixth Census*. Washington, D.C.: Thomas Allen, pp. 5–103.

————. 1841. *Statistics of the United States of America; 6th Census, 1840*. Washington, D.C.: Blair and Rives, pp. 474–5.

————. 1853. *The Seventh Census of the United States, 1850*. Washington, D.C.: Robert Armstrong.

————. 1864. *Population of the United States in 1860: Eighth Census*. Washington, D.C.: Government Printing Office.

————. 1872. *The Population of the United States: Ninth Census, 1870.* (Vol 1). Washington, D.C.: Government Printing Office.

————. 1872. *The Vital Statistics of the United States: Ninth Census, 1870.* (Vol 2). Washington, D.C.: Government Printing Office, pp. 624–54.

————. 1883. *Statistics of the Population of the United States at the Tenth Census, 1880.* Washington, D.C.: Government Printing Office, pp. 548–645.

————. 1897. *Report on Population of the United States at the Eleventh Census: 1890, Part II.* Washington, D.C.: Government Printing Office, pp. 2–103.

————. 1902. *Twelfth Census of the United States: Population, Part II.* Washington, D.C.: Government Printing Office, pp. 2–109.

U.S. Bureau of the Census. 1913. *Thirteenth Census of the United States.* Vol. 1: *Population.* Washington, D.C.: Government Printing Office, pp. 303, 352–60, 384.

————. 1918. *Negro Population, 1790–1915.* Washington, D.C.: Government Printing Office.

————. 1922. *Fourteenth Census of the United States.* Vol 1. Washington, D.C.: Government Printing Office.

————. 1922. *Fourteenth Census of the United States.* Vol. 2: *Population.* Washington, D.C.: Government Printing Office, pp. 156, 171–87, 235.

————. 1944. *Sixteenth Census of the United States: 1940, Population, Differential Fertility 1940 and 1910, Standardized Fertility Rates and Reproduction Rates, A Supplement to the Report Designated "Fertility for States and Large Cities."* Washington, D.C.: Goverment Printing Office.

————. 1976. *Historical Statistics of the United States, Colonial Times to 1970.* Washington, D.C.: Government Printing Office.

Van Horn, Susan Householder. 1988. *Women, Work, and Fertility, 1900–1986.* New York: New York University Press.

Wacker, Peter O. 1975. *Land and People: A Cultural Geography of Preindustrial New Jersey, Origins and Settlement Patterns.* New Brunswick, N.J.: Rutgers University Press.

Wade, Richard C. 1964. *Slavery in the Cities: The South, 1820–1860.* New York: Oxford University Press.

Warren, Christian 1997. "Northern Chills, Southern Fevers: Race-Specific Mortality in American Cities, 1730–1900." *Journal of Southern History* 63, 23–57.

Wilkie, Jane Riblett. 1976. "Urbanization and De-urbanization of the Black Population before the Civil War." *Demography* 13, 311–28.

Wright, Gavin. 1986. *Old South, New South.* New York: Basic Books.

Wright, Paul 1989. "An Examination of Factors Influencing Black Fertility Decline in the Mississippi Delta, 1880–1930." *Social Biology* 36, 213–39.

Zelnik, Melvin. 1969. "Age Patterns of Mortality of American Negroes: 1900–02 to 1959–61." *Journal of the American Statistical Association* 64, 433–51.

Zilversmit, Arthur. 1967. *The First Emancipation: the Abolition of Slavery in the North.* Chicago: University of Chicago Press.

11

A POPULATION HISTORY OF THE CARIBBEAN

STANLEY L. ENGERMAN

I

The Caribbean region of North America consists of a large number of islands of varying sizes located in the Caribbean Sea, which is bordered on the east by the Atlantic Ocean, on the west by the Gulf of Mexico, on the north by the United States, and on the south by South America (see Map 11.1). With the exception of parts of the Bahamas, these islands, also known as the West Indies, fall between the Tropic of Cancer and the equator. Initially settled by Native Americans Indians (Amerindians) arriving from the mainland of South America, they were the first part of the New World reached by Columbus and the first of the American areas to be settled by Europeans. For the next several centuries they were the scene of intermittent conflict among European powers, leading to periodic changes in ownership of some of the islands.[1]

The West Indies comprise the four large islands of the Greater Antilles – Cuba, Hispaniola (Haiti and the Dominican Republic), Jamaica, and Puerto Rico – and many more smaller ones, which make up the Lesser Antilles. It also includes several small islands off the South American coast,

I wish to thank David Eltis, Barry Higman, David Hancock, and the participants at the Economic History Workshop at Harvard University for comments and suggestions on this topic. Parts of this essay draw on joint work with Higman for volume 3 of the United Nations Educational, Scientific, and Cultural Organization's *General History of the Caribbean.*

[1] Basic historical information on the development of the Caribbean, with some demographic analysis and data, can be found in Richardson, *Caribbean*; Knight, *Caribbean*; and Watts, *West Indies.* Demographic details for the Caribbean as part of Latin America are in Sanchez-Albornez, *Population of Latin America*, and as part of British North America, in McCusker, *The Rum Trade.* Information on the various censuses of colonial British North America prior to 1776 are in Wells, *Population of the British Colonies.*

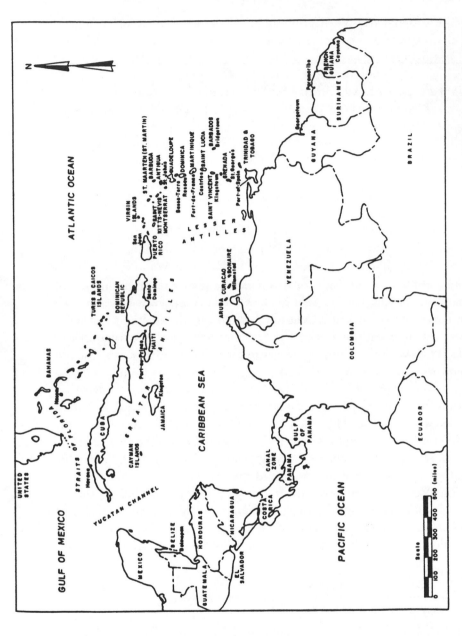

Map 11.1. The Caribbean region (*Source:* Bonham C. Richardson, *The Caribbean in the Wider World, 1492–1992* [Cambridge University Press, 1992]. Used by permission.)

in the western part of the Caribbean Sea. Cuba is the largest of the islands, with over 44,000 square miles, while many of the Lesser Antilles have areas of less than 100 square miles. In 1990 these Caribbean islands accounted for 7.9% of the population of North America (including also Canada, the United States, Mexico, and Central America), down from over 10% in 1800. In addition to the West Indies proper, former colonies of Western European nations bordering on the Caribbean, which were demographically and economically similar to the Caribbean island colonies, are often included as part of the region. These are Belize (British Honduras), Guyana (British Guiana), Surinam (Dutch Guiana), and Cayenne (French Guiana), the latter three being part of South America, and the first located in Central America.

Most of these islands are now politically independent, though the timing of independence as well as the present political status of the others varies. At no time after European settlement did any island remain in the sole possession of the Native Americans who predated the European. All islands were considered possessions of the various European settling nations – Britain, France, Spain, the Netherlands, Denmark, and Sweden – or were independent, with political power belonging to resident blacks or whites. The first colony to achieve political independence was Haiti, in 1804, but the remaining French possessions are still officially overseas departments of France. Most British colonies achieved independence with the decolonization movement after World War II. The Spanish areas of Cuba and the Dominican Republic achieved independence at different times in the nineteenth century, the former at the end and the latter before the middle of the century, while Puerto Rico was transferred to the United States in the aftermath of the Spanish-American War. Surinam became independent of the Netherlands in 1975, although the Netherlands Antilles, including the small islands off the coast of South America, remain Dutch colonies. The Swedish presence ended with the return of St. Bartholomew to the French in the 1870s, while the Danish removed themselves from the Caribbean with the sale of their Virgin Islands to the United States in 1917.

Most of these islands have tropical climates, as well as diverse patterns of vegetation and topography. Many have excellent soil for the production of sugar and other crops, and it was primarily for agricultural production, often for export to Europe, that they were settled and developed. Given the diversity in size, dates and pace of settlement, nature of crops grown, and policies of colonizing nations, many demographic and economic patterns developed, and it is, at times, difficult to present simple, overriding general summaries. Nevertheless, some general patterns can be examined.

II

The precise size of the Native American population prior to European contact remains a source of scholarly debate and disagreement, as does the size of the Native American population elsewhere in the Americas. Scholarly estimates, based on different procedures, vary between about 500,000 and about 10,000,000 but in general lean toward the lower end of this range.[2] Also still uncertain are the dates of arrival of the three groups of Native Americans in the Caribbean – the Ciboney, the Arawak (Taino), and the Carib – and the nature of their societies. It is generally believed that the Caribs were the latest to arrive, and that by the time of Columbus they had come to dominate the eastern Caribbean, although the larger islands still belonged to the Arawaks. The Ciboney had been earliest to arrive, but were more primitive than the others and were limited in numbers by the time of European contact. A reasonable estimate of the overall Native American population in the Caribbean prior to the arrival of Columbus is 750,000; almost all of this population lived on the larger islands.[3] Hispaniola had a population of about 500,000, Cuba 50,000, Puerto Rico 45,000, and Jamaica 20,000. Other islands in the Lesser Antilles were settled, but with smaller numbers, while several of the smaller islands, including Barbados and Antigua, were probably unsettled at the end of the sixteenth century.

As was the case with Native Americans on the mainland, the arrival of European soldiers and sailors led to a dramatic decline in the population of Caribbean Indians. Some of this decline was the result of military conflicts, but, as on the mainland, it was due in large part to the diseases brought to the New World by the Spanish and then by other Europeans.

---

[2] The most intense debate on the pre-Columbian Caribbean concerns Hispaniola's population. The discussion of the population in Hispaniola and elsewhere in the Spanish Americas, and its moral implications, begins with the early-sixteenth-century Spanish cleric Bartolomé de Las Casas. Currently, estimates range from less than 100,000 to more than 10 million. See Rosenblat, "Population of Hispaniola"; Cook and Borah, *Population History*; and Henige, "Contact Population of Hispaniola."

[3] The estimates used in the text are drawn from Knight, *Caribbean*. For an earlier discussion, see Steward, *Handbook*, and for a brief summary of the range of estimates, see the "Introduction" to Denevan, *Native Population*.

Information on the size of the Native American populations in subsequent years is limited. Few settling nations were concerned with their numbers, which were no doubt quite small. There were several thousand on Trinidad and Puerto Rico at the end of the eighteenth century, and somewhat larger numbers in the various Guianas.[4] In addition, St. Vincent and Dominica had several thousand black Caribs, escaped black slaves who had mingled with the Carib Indians. In the early nineteenth century several thousand Native Americans were moved to Belize and elsewhere in Central America, where their descendents still remain.[5] Native Americans are few in number today. After the start of European settlement, it took only about two centuries to equal the pre-Columbian population through the migration of white Europeans (free and under indenture contracts), white convict labor, and African slaves.

III

The first Europeans to arrive and settle in the Caribbean were the Spanish, whose settlements included Cuba, Puerto Rico, and Santo Domingo (now the Dominican Republic). The western end of Hispaniola (Haiti) was occupied by the French by the end of the seventeenth century. Although the Spanish maintained settlements on the biggest islands, their major colonial interests were in Mexico and in South America, particularly Peru. Most of the Spanish settlers and slaves went to these mainland regions in subsequent years. By the middle of the seventeenth century, settlers from England, France, and the Netherlands began crossing the Atlantic. For the largest of these groups, the British, the first half century of arrival saw more whites coming to the Caribbean than to their mainland North American colonies, but the pattern of white settlement soon shifted in favor of their continental colonies. Portuguese migration to the New World, the largest in relation to domestic population of the various European movements, was limited primarily to Brazil, since Portugal had no Caribbean presence as a settler nation. The migration from France, in its earlier stages, saw a greater movement to the West Indies, but in later periods larger numbers settled in French Canada. The Dutch migration

---

[4] Estimates of the Native American population after 1700 are discussed in Engerman and Higman, "Demographic Structure."

[5] The evolution of the black Caribs and their current status are described in Gonzalez, *Sojourners.* See also Craton, "Re-evaluation of the Black Caribs."

to the West Indies as well as to mainland North America was small in absolute numbers and represented only a fraction of the number migrating to the Dutch East Indies colonies. Similarly, the Danish and Swedish migrations were small, and although other parts of Europe made occasional forays into the New World, there was little immigration to the West Indies from these parts of Europe prior to the nineteenth century.[6]

Early in the settlement process, Spain settled on the largest islands, bypassing the many smaller islands to the east. The British and French, on the other hand, first settled in the Lesser Antilles, generally locating on the easternmost islands initially.[7] The first major British settlement was on Barbados, and that island plus the settlements in the Lesser Antilles were economically and demographically most significant prior to the expansion of the largest British island, Jamaica, which was captured from the Spanish in 1655. The British and French islands soon became specialized in the production of export crops, at first generally tobacco, with white labor, but ultimately sugar, with black labor. Because of imperial regulations, as well as the focus on Mexico and Peru, however, the Spanish colonies of Cuba and Santo Domingo were more important for trading and military purposes than for their export production. All of the European nations that had taken over the West Indian islands practiced some variant of mercantilism in setting the relations between the colonies and the metropolis. None of the colonies were free from imperial trading and taxing regulations, although no other country imposed the high cost on its West Indian colonies that Spain did. The British and French islands were settled primarily by whites coming from the metropolis (often under indenture contracts) to grow tobacco and other export crops, but this pattern shifted dramatically in the second half of the seventeenth century with the rise of the sugar economy.

The expansion of sugar production created a demand for a new and different labor force, one that could be coerced to work in the gangs that the large-scale sugar plantations required to be effective. Within Africa, a slave trade to the north and to the Middle East, as well as an internal trade in slaves, had developed centuries earlier. In the fourteenth and fifteenth centuries, African slaves were sent to southern Europe, as well as to São

---

[6] Discussions and estimates of European migration to the Caribbean are in Altman and Horn, "*To Make America*"; Canny, *Europeans*; Eltis, "Free and Coerced"; and Emmer, "Immigration." For details of the estimated migration from Britain to the Caribbean, see Gemery, "Emigration"; and Galenson, *White Servitude*. See also Karras, *Sojourners*; Games, "Opportunity"; and Choquette, "Frenchmen."

[7] This point is discussed by Engerman in "Europe." See also Watts, *West Indies*.

Table 11.1. *Estimated net slave imports by Caribbean areas
of settlement, 1500–1800*

Caribbean area	To 1700	1700–60	1761–1810	1811–70	Total
Spanish	—	20	230	692	942
British	264	626	930	—	1,820
French	156	365	650	95	1,266
Dutch	40	239	138	—	417
Danish	4	25	32	—	61
Total	464	1,275	1,980	787	4,506

Source: Curtin, *The Atlantic Slave Trade*; and Engerman and Higman, "The Demographic Structure of the Caribbean Slave Societies." The estimates for the British and French are low, according to Emmer, "Immigration into the Caribbean," but the basic contours of the trade will not differ dramatically.

Tomé and other islands off the Atlantic coast of Africa. The sixteenth century saw the development of the transatlantic slave trade to Spanish America (including the West Indies) and to Brazil. With the arrival of the British and French, the numbers of black slaves in relation to free whites rose within about a half century after settlement, and most sugar islands approached what would become the long-time ratio: more than 90% black (almost all enslaved) and less than 10% white. Those islands that for reasons of geography, economics, or policy (as in the Spanish case) did not grow sugar for export in this stage of settlement tended to have comparatively more whites, fewer black slaves, and more free blacks.

The slave trade from Africa to the Caribbean continued for about two centuries, then came to a close, the last shipments being made to Cuba in the 1860s (see Table 11.1). Overall it is estimated that the Caribbean received more than two-fifths of the approximately 10 million slaves who arrived in the New World during the period of the slave trade. Approximately 60% of that number went to the four islands making up the Greater Antilles.[8] The British islands received about 40% of the slaves imported into the Caribbean, and the French about 30%, with limited numbers going to the Dutch (even including Surinam) and the Danish colonies. The Spanish Caribbean received about 20% of the slaves

[8] Data on the slave populations of the Caribbean are given in McCusker, *Rum Trade*; Moreau de Jonnes, *Recherches Statistiques*; and Patterson, *Slavery*. Data on the slave trade, including estimates of the trade to the Caribbean, are in Curtin, *Atlantic Slave Trade*; and in Eltis, *Economic Growth*. See also the notes to Table 11.3 for other sources.

imported, mainly after the late eighteenth century, with the emergence of Cuba as a major sugar producer. In general, the numbers of slaves imported rose over time, the peaks for the French and the British arriving in the last quarter of the eighteenth century. Cuban slave imports were highest in the 1830s but were also high in the 1850s, after all of the other New World regions except for Brazil had ended their transatlantic slave trades.[9]

Slaves arrived from many regions of West Africa, even within any one importing area. The age and sex breakdown of slaves coming to the West Indies resembled that of the overall transatlantic slave trade; fewer children arrived than were present in the home populations, and about three-fifths of the slaves arriving were male.[10] These ratios varied somewhat by African region and by time period, depending in large measure upon the political and economic circumstances within Africa. Over the period of the slave trade, the mortality in the Middle Passage fell from about 20% of slaves carried in the seventeenth century to below 10% at the end of the eighteenth century, rising slightly at the end of the period owing to complications caused by Britain's decision to make the transatlantic slave trade illegal.[11] The precise extent of mortality within Africa, on the post-capture march to the coast and while waiting at the coast for shipment to the Americas, remains a source of considerable controversy, as does the magnitude of deaths attributable to the nature of the initial capture and the holding of those who became enslaved.

Clearly, the number of Africans imported into the West Indies greatly exceeded the number of whites who migrated to the islands. The ratio of black to white migrants in the Caribbean rose over time, and it greatly exceeded that for other parts of the Americas. And, as discussed later in the chapter, the numbers of slaves imported overall exceeded the total slave (and free black) populations of the West Indies at the end of the slave trade. This high (greater than one) ratio of slaves imported to slaves surviving was noted by contemporaries, as it differed dramatically from the case in the colonies that became the United States, where the slave population came to greatly exceed the numbers of slaves imported.[12]

The records that can be used for estimating the numbers and patterns

[9] Eltis, *Economic Growth*, p. 245.
[10] These general findings are presented in Eltis and Engerman, "Fluctuations."
[11] Data on slave trade mortality are in Curtin, *Atlantic Slave Trade*; Klein, *Middle Passage*; and Eltis, *Economic Growth*.
[12] For the highlighting of this problem, see Curtin, *Atlantic Slave Trade*. Also the subsequent calculations by Eltis, "Free and Coerced"; and Emmer, "Immigration."

Table 11.2. *Estimated migration of Europeans to the Caribbean, by European nation of origin, 1500–1800*

Caribbean area	Number
British	300,000
French	150,000
Spanish	40,000
Dutch and Danish	100,000
Total	590,000

Source: Emmer, "Immigration into the Caribbean."

of white migrants to the Caribbean are neither as detailed nor as accurate as those available for slaves. Detailed shipping records were often prepared for slave voyages, but the less dramatic movement of whites from Europe were not as systematically recorded. Nevertheless, some estimates of white migration can be derived from available colonial population estimates, and estimated birth and death rates can be used to calculate natural increase and then compare that with the net population changes between terminal years, although such measures have been applied mainly to the British colonies (see Table 11.2).[13] Data on departures from Spain suggest that Spanish migration to Cuba was relatively high before 1650 and then again after 1850.[14] Migration from Spain was high initially, in the sixteenth century, but then plateaued over the next three centuries. British migration began in the seventeenth century, as did the French, but the British migration was higher, to the Americas overall and to the West Indies. Both of these nations used systems of indentured labor to transport migrants to the colonies, many of whom then became permanent settlers of the New World. The numbers of British laborers and of all migrants were considerably higher than for the French. The sex ratio for white indentured workers in the seventeenth century was about 90% male, and thus it is

[13] See Gemery, "Emigration"; and Galenson, *White Servitude*.

[14] For a discussion of Spanish migration and the sources of data, see the essays by Ida Altman and Auke Preter Jacobs in Altman and Horn, "*To Make America*." The reason that the Spanish had some data on departures was that immigrants were required to obtain a royal license to emigrate. For most nations, counts of emigrants and immigrants began only in the nineteenth century. Most of the estimates of migration for earlier periods therefore are based upon demographic calculations resting on population totals at different dates and the crude birth and death rates during the interval.

probable that the overall share of males in white migration exceeded that for blacks.[15]

Over time, with the expansion of the Caribbean sugar economy, the migration of whites, though it increased absolutely, declined in comparison with the numbers of slaves brought from Africa. Up to about 1830, many more blacks than whites arrived in the Caribbean. And, as with the blacks, the total number of white migrants substantially exceeded the white population at the end of the era of the slave trade. The mortality of whites in the Caribbean was high, not only among settlers, but also among the British and French troops who were stationed there.[16] Military and other death rates fell sharply over the course of the nineteenth century, but remained two to three times the mortality rates of troops in Europe and mainland North America into the twentieth century. Although there had been some return flow of migrants to Europe, as well as some out-migration of whites – particularly from Barbados to South Carolina in the seventeenth century, and from Saint Domingue (now Haiti) to the United States, mostly to Louisiana, at the end of the eighteenth century – it was probably the measured excess of deaths over births that explains the basic pattern for whites. This experience contrasts with the major regions of white migration into the New World: Spanish areas of Mexico, Central America, and South America, and British mainland North America. These areas not only received more whites than did the Caribbean, but, unlike the West Indies, had quite substantial rates of natural increase among the white migrant population.

IV

In the Caribbean, the years between 1700 and 1900 were marked first by the importance of slavery and then by the adjustments to its aftermath. Persons purchased on the African coast were transported for sale to the Americas, where they were to be used as labor for others. Slaves were property that could be bought and sold by the free individuals in the population, and the working locations and working and living conditions of the enslaved were controlled by their owners. Although slavery existed throughout the Americas, and indeed all over the world, it was most important in those areas producing sugar for export to European markets.

[15] For a detailed study of the characteristics of indentured servants, see Galenson, *White Servitude*.
[16] See the valuable presentation and analysis of data by Curtin, *Death*.

After the westward expansion of sugar production in the Mediterranean to the Atlantic islands off the coast of Africa, basic characteristics of production and of the labor force were carried across the Atlantic to the Caribbean. Thus it was the Caribbean in which the ratio of slave to free population was highest, reflecting the efficiency of large-scale plantations in the production of sugar, and the unwillingness of free labor to work on these plantations when it could be avoided.[17]

During these two centuries, the population of the Caribbean increased at a rate about 1.6% per annum, the net outcome of immigration and natural increase (or decrease). The rates were approximately 2.0% per annum in the eighteenth century, being most rapid in the first 40 years and then falling off to 1.2% in the nineteenth as the number of slaves arriving from Africa decreased. In the eighteenth century, before the Haitian revolution, the growth of the slave population was more rapid than that of free whites, averaging about 2.3% per annum (see Figure 11.1). In this period, the Spanish colonies experienced the most rapid growth, increasing their share of the total Caribbean population from about one-quarter in 1750 to nearly 45% by 1880 (See Tables 11.3, 11.4, and 11.5). There were sharp declines in the population shares of the Dutch and Danish colonies, and smaller declines in the British (particularly after the closing of its slave trade in 1808) and the French (including Haiti) shares (see Table 11.6).

Shifts occurred among the British and French sugar-producing colonies, generally in a westward direction, to newer areas which experienced more rapid increases in sugar production. Thus, for the British, Barbados was at first the most heavily settled island and the largest producer of sugar. Its role was taken next by the other islands of the Lesser Antilles, and, finally, in the late eighteenth century by Jamaica. This movement of sugar production continued after the start of the nineteenth century, with the expansion of sugar production and slave populations in Trinidad and in British Guiana. Similarly, for the French, there was a mid-eighteenth-century expansion of Saint Domingue, with a shift of population and production from the earlier settled islands of Martinique and Guadeloupe.

This pattern of movement of sugar production, and of slave labor, had a significant impact on Caribbean demography. Rates of natural population decrease were highest in the earliest stage of settlement and of

---

[17] Useful information on the spread of the sugar economy into the Caribbean and its operations there are provided by Deerr, *History of Sugar*; Watts, *West Indies*; and Sheridan, *Sugar and Slavery*.

Table 11.3. *Caribbean populations, 1750*

Area	White	Slave	Free persons of color	Total
British[a]				
Barbados	16,772	63,410	235	80,417
St. Kitts	2,783	21,782	109	24,674
Nevis	1,118	8,299	81	9,498
Antigua	3,435	31,123	305	34,863
Montserrat	1,430	8,767	86	10,283
Virgin Islands	1,184	6,062	59	7,305
	26,722	139,443	875	167,040
Jamaica	12,000	127,881	2,119	142,000
Dominica	1,718	5,769	300	7,787
St. Lucia	2,524	9,764	506	12,794
St. Vincent	2,104	7,184	230	9,518
Grenada	1,285	12,000	455	13,740
Tobago	238	3,082	82	3,402
Trinidad[b]	126	310	295	731
Demerara and Essequibo	380	4,185	34	4,599
Berbice[c]	346	3,802	31	4,179
	8,721	46,096	1,933	56,750
British Honduras	50	114	6	170
Cayman Island	70	100	—	170
Bahamas	1,268	1,145	76	2,486
Anguilla	350	1,962	38	2,350
Barbuda	40	150	—	190
	1,775	3,471	120	5,366
	49,218	316,891	5,047	371,156
French				
Martinique	12,068	65,905	1,413	79,386
Guadeloupe[d]	8,848	45,238	1,036	55,122
St. Domingue	12,799	164,859	4,732	182,390
French Guiana	706	5,471	71	6,248
St. Martin	102	185	—	287
	34,523	281,658	7,252	323,433
Dutch				
Surinam	2,133	51,096	598	53,827
Curaçao	3,964	12,804	2,776	19,544
St. Eustatius	420	1,200	—	1,620
Saba	155	130	—	285
St. Martin	639	3,518	—	4,157
	7,311	68,748	3,374	79,433
Danish				
St. Croix	1,323	8,897	—	10,220
St. John	212	2,031	—	2,243

Table 11.3. (cont.)

Area	White	Slave	Free persons of color	Total
St. Thomas	315	3,949	138	4,402
	1,850	14,877	138	16,865
Spanish				
Puerto Rico[e]	17,572	5,037	22,274	44,883
Cuba[e]	116,947	28,760	24,293	170,000
Santo Domingo[f]	30,863	8,900	30,862	70,625
	165,382	42,697	77,429	285,508
Swedish				
St. Bartholomew	170	54	—	224
Total	258,454	724,925	93,240	1,076,619

Note: The specific years are generally those closest to 1750, but there is a spread of about 30 years in these entries. Thus the totals and broad patterns are useful for suggestive purposes only and do not represent the totals at any specific time period. For consistency of comparison over time, the placements by nationality reflect the ownership for the greatest part of the period, not necessarily the ownership at the date to which the table applies. For a discussion of the changes in ownership among nations, see the text. There are numerous estimates for many areas, often drawn from the same source with modifications and errors in transcription. Secondary sources which examined the primary materials are cited for ease in location of data. Although these estimates are to be regarded only as approximations, in very few cases would alternative choices influence basic patterns.

[a] For several of the British islands, the census closest to 1750 listed only blacks, with no breakdown between slaves and free persons of color. Various procedures were used to estimate this division, either interpolation between years for each such ratio were given, use of the ratio for the closest year known, or extrapolation on the basis of other islands or other years. If no allocations were made, and all blacks were treated as slaves, the total slave population of the British Caribbean would be increased by only 1.3 percent.

[b] Plus 2,082 Amerindians. Between 1782 and 1784 the non-Amerindian population of Trinidad increased from 731 to 5,012. There is a 1777 population estimate of 3,432, which includes the Amerindian population.

[c] Plus 244 Amerindian slaves.

[d] Includes Marie-Galante. The estimated number of free persons of color is based upon the ratio of free persons of color to the total nonslave population on Martinique.

[e] The breakdown of the free population into free persons of color and whites is based upon the first available census with such data.

[f] Free population allocated according to that given for 1766. See McCusker, *The Rum Trade*, and the sources cited there.

Sources: Engerman and Higman, "Demographic Structure of the Caribbean Slave Societies." For the British area, see McCusker, *The Rum Trade*; Wells, *The Population of the British Colonies in America before 1776*; John, *The Plantation Slaves of Trinidad, 1783–1816*; Thompson, *Colonialism and Underdevelopment in Guyana*; Sheridan, *The Development of the Plantations to 1750*; Goveia, *Slave Societies in the British Leeward Islands*. For the French, see McCusker, *The Rum Trade*; Cardoso, *Economia e Sociedade em Areas Colonies Periforieas*. For the Danish, see McCusker, *The Rum Trade*. For the Spanish, see Dietz, *Economic History of Puerto Rico*; Diáz Soler, *Historia de la Esclavitud Negra en Puerto Rico*; Kiple, *Blacks in Colonial Cuba*; Moya Rons, "Nuevas Consideracienes sobre la Historia de la Poblacion Dominicana." For the Dutch, see McCusker, *The Rum Trade*; Postma, *The Dutch in the Atlantic Slave Trade*; Goslinga, *The Dutch in the Caribbean and in the Guianas*; Patterson, *Slavery and Social Death*. For the Swedish, see McCusker, *The Rum Trade*.

Table 11.4. *Caribbean populations, 1830*

Area	White	Slave	Free persons of color	Total
British				
Barbados	14,812	82,026	5,312	102,150
St. Kitts	1,498	19,094	2,808	23,400
Nevis	453	9,194	1,403	11,050
Antigua	1,187	29,600	5,513	37,000
Montserrat	353	6,300	848	7,500
Virgin Islands	603	5,148	1,699	7,450
	19,606	151,362	17,583	188,550
Jamaica	18,903	319,074	40,073	378,050
Dominica	703	14,706	3,591	19,000
St. Lucia	1,012	13,395	3,993	18,400
St. Vincent	1,400	23,100	3,500	28,000
Grenada	710	23,884	3,806	28,400
Tobago	453	12,551	1,146	14,150
Trinidad	3,323	22,757	15,985	42,065
Demerara and Essequibo	3,100	67,968	6,433	77,500
Berbice	601	20,698	1,802	23,100
	11,302	199,059	40,256	250,615
British Honduras	302	1,898	1,999	4,200
Cayman Island	350	1,000	150	1,500
Bahamas	5,007	9,503	2,520	17,030
Anguilla	300	2,600	399	3,300
Barbuda	3	500	—	503
	5,962	15,501	5,068	26,533
	55,773	684,996	102,980	843,748
French				
Martinique[a]	9,362	86,499	14,055	109,916
Guadeloupe[b]	10,900	97,339	11,424	119,663
French Guiana	1,381	19,102	3,379	22,862
	21,643	202,940	27,858	252,441
Haiti[c]			627,761	627,761
	21,643	202,940	655,619	880,202
Dutch				
Surinam	2,029	48,784	5,041	55,854
Curaçao	2,602	5,894	6,531	15,027
St. Eustatius	132	1,614	527	2,273
Saba	?	?	?	?
St. Martin[d]	500	4,000	1,500	6,000
Aruba	465	393	1,888	2,746

Table 11.4. *(cont.)*

Area	White	Slave	Free persons of color	Total
Bonaire	90	547	839	1,476
	5,818	61,232	16,326	83,376
Danish				
St. Croix	1,892	19,876	4,913	26,681
St. John	208	1,971	202	2,381
St. Thomas	1,977	5,032	5,204	12,213
	4,077	26,879	10,319	41,275
Spanish				
Puerto Rico	162,311	34,240	127,287	323,838
Cuba	332,352	310,218	113,125	755,695
Santo Domingo[e]	38,272	15,000	38,272	91,544
	532,935	359,458	278,684	1,171,077
Swedish				
St. Bartholomew	1,723	1,387	906	4,016
Total	621,969	1,336,892	1,064,834	3,023,694

Note: For consistency of comparison over time, the placements by nationality reflect the ownership for the greatest part of the period, not necessarily the ownership at the date to which the table applies. For a discussion of the changes in ownership among nations, see the text.

[a] Between 1831 and 1835 the numbers of free persons of color doubled on Martinique and possibly on Guadeloupe.

[b] Includes dependencies: Marie-Galante, La Desirade, Les Saintes, and Saint Martin. It is assumed that the white population changed at the same rate between 1826 and 1831 as it did on Martinique.

[c] Interpolated between estimates for 1805 and 1850.

[d] Moreau de Jonnes's estimate may be too high. According to the *Encyclopedia van neder-landsch West-Indie* (see Patterson, *Slavery and Social Death*), the 1816 population was 3,559, of which 72 percent were slaves. If we apply the ratio of overstatement for Saint Bartholomew, the population of St. Martin would be only about 2,500.

[e] Nonslave population allocated one-half white and one-half free persons of color.

Sources: Engerman and Higman, "Demographic Structure of the Caribbean Slave Societies." For the British area, see Higman, *Slave Populations of the British Caribbean*. For the French, see Moreau de Jonnes, *Recherches statistiques sur l'esclavage colonial*; Leyburn, *The Haitian People*. For the Swedish, see Hyrenius, *Royal Swedish Slaves*. For the Danish, see Hall, "The 1816 Freedman Petition in the Danish West Indies"; Green-Pedersen, "Slave demography in the Danish West Indies." For the Spanish, see Moreau de Jonnes, *Recherches statistiques*; Diáz Soler, *Historia de la Esclavitud Negra*; Kiple, *Blacks in Colonial Cuba*; Esteban Deive, *La Esclavitude del Negro en Santo Domingo*. For the Dutch, see Moreau de Jonnes, *Recherches statistiques*; Hoetink, "Surinam and Curaçao"; Patterson, *Slavery and Social Death*; Hartog, *Aruba: Past and Present*.

Table 11.5. *Caribbean populations, 1880*

Area	White	Asian	Slave	Free persons of color	Total
British					
Barbados	16,054			155,806	171,860
St. Kitts	2,199			26,938	29,137
Nevis	209			11,655	11,864
Antigua[a]	1791			32,530	34,964
Montserrat	241			9,842	10,083
Virgin Islands	52			5,235	5,287
	20,596			242,006	263,195
Jamaica	14,432	11,115		555,257	580,804
Dominica[b]	361			27,850	28,520
St. Lucia	911	1,652		35,988	38,551
St. Vincent[c]	2,693	2,190		35,473	40,548
Grenada	835	1,572		41,568	43,975
Tobago	?			15,072+	18,051
Trinidad	?	48,820		?	153,128
British Guiana[d]	13,543	85,163		145,772	252,186
					574,958
British Honduras[e]	375			?	27,452
Cayman Island	864			2,202	3,066
Bahamas[f]	?			?	43,521
Anguilla	202			3,017	3,219
Barbuda	4			639	643
					77,901
					1,496,858
French					
Martinique					166,100
Guadeloupe[g]					192,735
French Guiana[h]					27,333
					386,168
Haiti[i]					1,272,788
					1,658,956
Dutch					
Surinam[j]					49,309
Curaçao					25,015
St. Eustatius					1,890
Saba					1,832
St. Martin					2,853
Aruba					3,792
Bonaire					4,986
					89,677

Table 11.5. *(cont.)*

Area	White	Asian	Slave	Free persons of color	Total
Danish					
St. Croix					18,430
St. John					944
St. Thomas					14,389
					33,763
Spanish					
Puerto Rico	411,712			319,936	731,648
Cuba	980,096	43,298	199,094	272,478	1,494,966
Santo Domingo					382,312
					2,608,926
Swedish					
St. Bartholomew[k]					(2,390)
Total					5,888,180

Note: For consistency of comparison over time, the placements by nationality reflect the ownership for the greatest part of the period, not necessarily the ownership at the date to which the table applies. For a discussion of the changes in ownership among nations, see the text.

[a] The census total differs by 643 from the total implied by the ethnic breakdown.

[b] Includes 309 Caribs.

[c] Includes 192 Caribs.

[d] Includes 7,708 Amerindians.

[e] Includes 2,037 Caribs.

[f] In 1851 whites constitued 20% of the population of the Bahamas.

[g] Includes as dependencies: St. Martin, Les Saintes, La Desirade, Marie-Galante, and (after 1878) St. Bartholomew. This includes about 19,985 East Indians among 23,675 immigrants. There was also a "population flottante" of 9,171. In 1889 the population of Guadeloupe was 122,885 and that of its dependencies 35,775 (*Annuaire de la Guadeloupe*, 1893).

[h] Includes 1,972 Amerindians and 5,024 immigrant colonists.

[i] Interpolated between estimates for 1850 and 1900.

[j] Population excludes Bush Negroes and Amerindians.

[k] By 1880 St. Bartholomew again belonged to France and was included as a dependency of Guadeloupe. Its 1872 its population was 2,390. Hyrenius, *Royal Swedish Slaves*.

Sources: Engerman and Higman, "Demographic Structure of the Caribbean Slave Societies." For the British area, see the Blue Books for various colonies. For the French, see Statistique Generale de la France, *Annuaire Statistique*; Hyrenius, *Royal Swedish Slaves*; Sanchez-Albornez, *The Population of Latin America*. For the Danish, see Westergaard, *The Danish West Indies under Company Rule*. For the Spanish, see U.S. War Department, *Report on the Census of Puerto Rico*; Kiple, *Blacks in Colonial Cuba*; Moya Pons, "Nuevas consideraciones." For the Dutch, see Van Lier, *Frontier Society*; Platt et al., *The European Possessions in the Caribbean Area*; Klomp, *Politics on Bonaire*; Hartog, *Curaçao*.

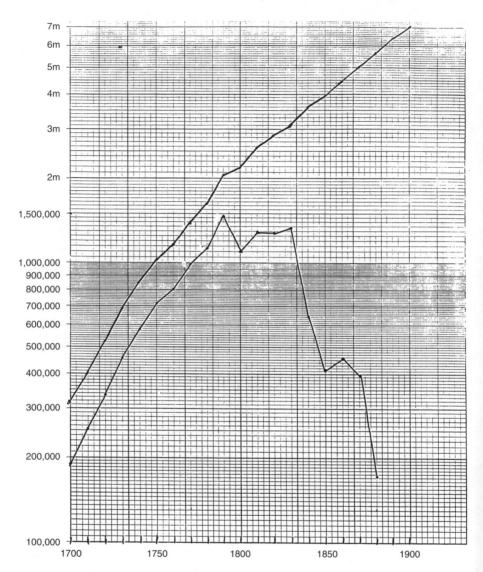

Figure 11.1. Caribbean populations, 1700–1900: Total and slave (*Source*: Worksheets underlying Engerman and Higman, "Demographic Structure of the Caribbean Slave Societies," Table 1; see Tables 11.3–11.5 above.)

Table 11.6. *Shares of Caribbean populations, by European settling area, 1750, 1880, 1990 (percentages)*

European area	1750		1880, all	1990, all
	All	Slave		
British	34.5	43.7	25.4	16.0
French	30.0	38.9	28.2	21.0
Dutch	7.4	9.5	1.5	1.7
Danish	1.6	2.1	0.6	0.3
Spanish	26.5	5.9	44.3	61.0
Swedish	—	—	—	—

Source: Engerman and Higman, "The Demographic Structure of the Caribbean Slave Societies"; United Nations, *World Population Prospects*.

expanding sugar production, a time of relatively high imports of slaves from Africa (the interisland trade in slaves being rather limited).[18] After a period of adjustment, the rate of natural decrease slowed, and, in the case of Barbados, a small natural increase became possible even before slave emancipation. Most of the relocation of the slave population occurred by changing the islands of arrival when the slave trade was open, so that when the trade ended (particularly when the British imposed controls on the extent of the interisland movement of slaves), the rate of population shifts among islands slowed down.

Some important changes in population patterns during the nineteenth century were due to the expansion of indentured labor, primarily from Asia (see Table 11.7).[19] Nearly 125,000 laborers moved from China to Cuba, for example, even while slavery and the transatlantic slave trade to Cuba persisted. Indentured labor was, however, more extensive in the aftermath of the abolition of slavery in the British, French, and Dutch areas of the Caribbean. Most of this labor came from India, but there were also streams

[18] For this point, see Higman, *Slave Populations*; and John, *Plantation Slaves*.
[19] For discussions of the migration of indentured labor to the Caribbean, see Laurence, *Question of Labour*; Laurence, *Immigration*; and Emmer, "Immigration." Data on this movement for the British islands, are in Roberts and Byrne, "Summary Statistics"; and, more generally, in Engerman, "Servants." For discussions of interisland migration, see Richardson, *Caribbean Migrants*; Roberts, *Population of Jamaica*; and Roberts, "Emigration."

Table 11.7. *Estimates of flows of contract labor to the Caribbean and return flow, nineteenth and twentieth centuries*

Flow	Years	Numbers (thousands)	Return (thousands)
From India			
British Guiana	1838–1918	238.9	78.5
Trinidad	1838–1918	143.9	33.3
Other British Caribbean	1838–1915	46.8	ca. 15.7
French Caribbean	1835–85	ca. 79.7	ca. 13.0
Surinam	1873–1916	34.0	11.6
St. Croix	1862	0.4	—
From China			
British Guiana	1852–79	13.5	—
Trinidad	1852–65	2.6	—
Other British Caribbean	1852–84	1.7	—
Cuba	1848–74	124.8	—
From Java			
Surinam	1890–1939	33.0	8.7
From Portuguese Islands			
British Guiana	1835–81	32.2	—
Other British Caribbean	1835–70	8.8	—
From Africa			
British Guiana	1834–67	14.1	—
Jamaica	1834–67	11.4	—
Trinidad	1834–67	8.9	—
Other British Caribbean	1834–67	5.0	—
French Caribbean	1854–62	5.0	—
From Yucatan			
Cuba	1849–71	ca. 2.0	—

Source: Engerman, "Servants to Slaves to Servants"; Roberts and Byrne, "Summary Statistics on Indenture and Associated Migration"; Laurence, *Immigration into the West Indies*.

of migrants from China, Java, Madeira, and Africa, among areas in the less developed world. These movements continued from India until World War I, mainly to British Guiana and Trinidad, and provided most of the labor for sugar plantations in these areas. The movement from Java to Surinam continued somewhat longer, into the 1930s. Many of the Asian indentured workers did return home when their periods of work ended, whereas very few from the black population ever returned to Africa. Enough indentured workers remained to provide relatively large shares of the population in some areas and thus were to pose ethnic difficulties between the Indians and the blacks in the twentieth century, particularly in Trinidad, British Guiana, and Surinam.

Although population continued to flow into the Caribbean, outflows were quite limited throughout the eighteenth and nineteenth centuries. There was some movement of whites, often with slaves, to Louisiana during the Haitian revolution, with the result that the postrevolution population of Haiti was entirely black.[20] Toward the end of the nineteenth century, with the beginning of the construction of the Panama Canal, temporary migrations to Panama from Jamaica and Barbados became important.[21] And at the very end of the century, emigrants mainly from Barbados, who previously had only gone elsewhere in the Caribbean region, began to move to the northern United States, particularly New York City, and to Canada.[22] This flow increased in the twentieth century, as did the numbers of people from other islands who migrated to the United States, as well as to Great Britain and elsewhere in Europe, generally to the country which had owned the colony of outflow.

V

Developments in the legal attitudes toward the slave trade and slavery had significant effects on population patterns in the West Indies. Given the failure of the slave population to reproduce itself in most areas, the end of the slave trade meant, in the absence of great successes for policies of amelioration, that those areas most dependent on the inflows of new slaves to maintain their population would suffer absolute, as well as relative, declines.[23] Thus the endings of the British, Danish, and Dutch slave trades in the first decade of the nineteenth century and the ending of the French slave trade in the next decade help to explain the fall in their share of the West Indian population. The fact that the Spanish slave trade to Cuba (as well as to Puerto Rico) continued into the 1860s, and was large after all

---

[20] On the migration from Haiti to Louisiana, see Lachance, "The 1809 Immigration." For a more general discussion of Haiti, see Leyburn, *Haitian People.*

[21] On this migration, see Newton, *Silver Men*; and Richardson, *Panama Money.*

[22] For a discussion of black migration to the United States in this period, see Reid, *Negro Immigrant.*

[23] On the British attempts at slave amelioration in the late eighteenth century, see Ward, *British West Indian Slavery.*

other regions had ended the transatlantic slave trade, helps to explain the major growth in the numbers and the share of the Cuban population in the nineteenth-century Caribbean, as does the higher percentage of white population in Cuba than in other areas of the Caribbean, the renewal of Spanish immigration, and the by then lower mortality of the slaves, and thus the lower rates of net population decrease in the Spanish islands.[24]

The ending of slavery meant dramatic changes in economic and demographic patterns. In most areas, there was a transition from large-scale production of sugar to smaller farms producing foodstuffs and related crops by the ex-slaves. The initial, and most dramatic, ending of slavery took place in the French colony of Saint Domingue, as a result of a slave uprising after 1791. Despite some early attempts to reintroduce a plantation system, the independent colony ultimately became a land of small farms. There are no reliable census population estimates for more than one century after independence, but it is generally believed that the former slave population grew rapidly after the initial declines of the revolutionary period, which were due to deaths and out-migration. The first of the West Indian legislated emancipations, with compensation and/or a period of apprenticeship, was that of the British in 1834, followed by the Swedish in 1847, the French and Danish in 1848, the Dutch in 1863, and last, the Spanish colonies of Puerto Rico in 1873 and Cuba in 1886. Given the changes in the technology of sugar production over the century, and variations in the metropolitan and the consuming nation's import duties for sugar and other colonial products, the specifics of the economic adjustments to the ending of slavery varied, but, in general, emancipation was accompanied by a natural increase in the black population in the West Indies.[25]

As already described, it was the continued in-migration of slaves that had permitted Caribbean population growth through the mid–nineteenth century. The total numbers of slaves imported exceeded the ultimate total of black population at the end of the slave period. Although such differences between number of migrants and size of population often occurred

---

[24] For a discussion of Cuban slave society, see Knight, *Slave Society*; and on Puerto Rico, see Scarano, *Sugar and Slavery*. For population distributions for Cuba through the end of the nineteenth century, see Kiple, *Blacks*.

[25] For an examination of demographic patterns in Jamaica and elsewhere in the British Caribbean after emancipation, see Roberts, *Population of Jamaica*.

initially in periods of large-scale immigration, in many cases they were reversed after a generation, when a positive natural increase began. What is unusual about the West Indian pattern is that the period with a natural rate of decline was so prolonged. The West Indian slave demographic performance was quite different from that of the slave population of the United States.[26] This has generated much debate about the causes of such differentials and their implications for comparative material treatment, working arrangements, cultural patterns, and the effects of climate and disease environments.

A major difference between the islands and the mainland was in the principal crops grown: sugar in the West Indies, and cotton in the United States in the nineteenth century, tobacco and rice earlier. Because of the nature of crop production, the producing units were larger in the West Indies. Moreover, the total population of the mainland southern states had a smaller share of slaves, about 40%, than did almost all of the islands of the West Indies. Overall, the West Indies were about three-quarters black, even higher if we restrict ourselves to the sugar-producing islands other than Cuba. And, because of the initial demographic differences in the rate of increase, the U.S. slave population had a considerably higher proportion of native-born slaves than did the West Indies, a difference with significant implications regarding disease immunities as well as cultural patterns. More important, perhaps, were the climatic and topographical conditions required by the different crops. Sugar required a tropical climate and a rather unhealthy, damp, lowland soil. With its exhausting work routines, it was considerably less healthy than the cooler, upland areas in which tobacco and cotton could be grown in the U.S. South. Even the coffee plantations of the West Indies had lower mortality rates than did the sugar plantations. Rice was the U.S. crop most similar in production requirements to the West Indies. Located in the coastal area of South Carolina and Georgia, rice plantations had a significantly poorer demographic experience than those specializing in cotton and tobacco. Given these differences in labor regimes and in geographic conditions, it is not surprising that mortality rates for slaves were higher in the West Indies than in the United States, but, as I later suggest, the differences in fertility between the regions also explain much of the differential in the natural movements of the populations.

[26] Basic material on this comparison is presented in Fogel, *Without Consent*. See also the discussion in Klein and Engerman, "Fertility Differentials."

Table 11.8. *Slave birth rates and death rates by British West Indian colony, ca. 1820s*

Colony	Period	Births (per thousand)	Deaths (per thousand)
Barbados	1826–29	58.2	52.7
St. Kitts	1825–28	41.3	36.7
Nevis	1825–28	34.7	32.6
Antigua	1824–28	32.5	31.3
Montserrat	1824–28	30.3	26.4
Virgin Islands	1825–28	43.5	24.5
Jamaica	1826–29	27.4	31.4
Dominica	1826–29	35.3	34.0
St. Lucia	1825–28	50.6	31.0
St. Vincent	1825–28	32.5	33.0
Grenada	1825–28	29.7	31.1
Tobago	1825–28	32.1	44.4
Trinidad	1825–28	33.7	34.1
Demerera–Essequibo	1823–26	28.0	47.2
Berbice	1822–25	28.7	43.3
Bahamas	1825–28	56.2	39.4
Barbuda	1825–28	47.5	26.3

Source: Higman, *Slave Populations of the British Caribbean*, pp. 308–10 (adjusted estimates). There are some minor differences in patterns if other periods are chosen.

VI

Although the variations across islands and over time, as well as the general absence of reliable censuses for most of the period, make it difficult to provide fully convincing explanations, various estimates based on plantation records, tax lists, and other sources permit some discussion of West Indian slave demographic patterns (see Table 11.8). Unfortunately, data are weakest for two of the largest areas in the region, Haiti and the Dominican Republic.[27] In the former, the absence of slavery, and in the latter, its relative unimportance, seem to have precluded national population counts. For most of the other areas, however, somewhat more is known about the demographic patterns of slaves, certainly more than those of

[27] For works on the Dominican Republic dealing, in part, with demographic issues, see Moya Pons, *Dominican Republic*; and Hoetink, *Dominican People*. On Haiti, see Leyburn, *Haitian People*; and Nicholls, *Dessalines*.

either free persons of color or whites. The birth and the survival of slaves were of great concern to their owners, as well as to those antislavery critics of the system who often used demographic data as part of their arguments, particularly the failure of the slave population to reproduce itself.[28] There are some complications in the count of slave populations because of the presence of runaways and of Maroons (whose numbers were large only in Jamaica and Surinam), as well as of individual manumissions, but these were generally limited in number so the basic conclusions would not be distorted.

The difference in demographic performance between the United States and the West Indies depended upon a number of key factors, including climate, work routines, and nutritional status. The levels of nutrition apparently differed, as indicated by direct estimates of food consumption and by the differences in heights achieved by slave populations. It is clear that the nutrition achieved by slaves in the Caribbean was lower than in the United States, and this had significant implications for fertility and mortality differences.[29]

When adjusted for estimated infant mortality, estimates of slave fertility, based on plantation records, probate records, population registers, and other sources, indicate that West Indian slave fertility was only about 60% that of that of slaves in the United States.[30] The fertility of U.S. slaves was among the highest of any society for which we have data, about as high as that of southern whites. However, the West Indian level of fertility was not low by world standards, being roughly equal to the rates in Europe at that time. West Indian fertility did differ from the European in its ages of childbearing over time, reflecting, in part, the different means of handling the burden of child support under slavery as compared with the patterns in Europe and elsewhere. West Indian slaves generally began childbearing at younger ages than did the females in Europe; had longer spacing intervals between children, because of their longer lactation period or else a combination of poorer diet and more intensive work routine; and probably terminated childbearing earlier, owing to nutritional and work factors.[31] Compared with U.S. slaves, on the other hand, West Indian slaves tended to begin childbearing later and had longer spacing between

---

[28] Such issues were frequently raised in parliamentary debates and in the pamphlet literature on slavery. For a discussion of this aspect, see Higman, "Slavery."

[29] See Higman, *Slave Populations*, pp. 280–92; and Fogel, *Without Consent*, pp. 132–47.

[30] See the data presented in Fogel, *Without Consent*; and in Fogel et al., *Without Consent or Contract*.

[31] The basic starting point for issues related to British West Indian demography, with implications for other parts of the Caribbean as well, is Higman, *Slave Populations*.

Table 11.9. *Estimates of crude birth and death rates in Trinidad, Jamaica, and the United States*

Region, date, and variable	Crude rate (per thousand)
Trinidad, 1813–15	
Birth	34.3
Death	47.8
Jamaica, 1817–20	
Birth	33.6
Death	37.2
United States, 1820–50	
Birth	61.8
Death	37.5

Source: Fogel et al., *Without Consent or Contract*, vol. 2, p. 287, col. 3.

births, while probably a smaller of percentage of women bore children than in the United States (see Tables 11.9 and 11.10).[32] The explanatory factors for such differences include African customs and patterns regarding marriage, lactation, and sexual activity; the effects of unbalanced sex ratios; work characteristics; nutritional intake; and the disease environment, which had both a direct and indirect (via the effect on the link between foodstuffs consumed and net nutrition) impact on fertility. Although the contributions of each of these factors remains uncertain, it is quite clear that the West Indian slaves had a significantly lower level of fertility on most islands, except perhaps on Barbados, than did those enslaved African who went to the United States, although it is less clear how that level compared with that in Africa.

In regard to mortality, any comparisons among or within regions is rather more difficult. First, allowance must be made for the high frequency of deaths in the period of the initial arrival by new settlers in the islands, known euphemistically as seasoning, during which time it has been estimated that between 20 and 30% of arrivals died. Second, estimates of infant and child mortality are often difficult to derive, given the various omissions, including births and infant deaths, in the records, because of

---

[32] These issues are discussed in Fogel, *Without Consent*; and in Klein and Engerman, "Fertility Differentials."

Table 11.10. *Total fertility rates of slaves in the United States (ca. 1830) and in Trinidad (ca. 1813), with an explanation for the difference in these rates*

Variable	United States	Trinidad	Difference in the fertility rates explained by each variable (%)
Total fertility rate (average number of children born to a woman living to age 49)	9.24	4.44	—
Average childbearing span (average number of years between first and last births)	20.1	14.5	39
Average birth interval (average number of years between successive births)	2.06	2.67	31
Proportion of women ever bearing a child	0.86	0.69	30

Source: Fogel, *Without Consent*, p. 149 (series after correcting the undercount in Trinidad Registrations).

social customs regarding such cataloging, and other reasons. Third, a basic issue in the contemporary debate – namely, the effect of work done by slaves on their health and mortality – requires comparisons of only those adults who worked, which means the analysis is restricted to those slaves who survived childhood. Both child and adult mortality were probably higher in the Caribbean than in the United States and in western Europe at that time, but the differences in mortality with respect to the U.S. slave population were somewhat less than those in fertility. Differences in mortality and fertility are not independent of each other, since variations in mortality influenced the duration of slave marriages and the availability of marriage partners among the slave population.

The impact of different disease environments at the time of settlement, their influence upon settlement patterns, and their continued effects over time have been studied in recent years.[33] Whites, it has been found, suf-

[33] Important examinations of the patterns of disease in the Caribbean in this period are Kiple, *Caribbean Slave*; and Sheridan, *Doctors and Slaves*. For a comparative overview of the Americas, see Kunitz, "Diseases."

fered large demographic declines in the West Indian islands, but, being free to move and choose production regimes, they adjusted by locating in large numbers on the mainland, leaving slaves to be disproportionately located in the Caribbean. Thus, even if the mortality and fertility rates of whites and blacks did not differ dramatically in any one particular location, the ability to avoid the region with the less favorable demographic experience meant that the number of whites in the New World increased dramatically in comparison with the number of slaves. It is also probable that the rate of mortality declined over time with the length of settlement of an area, as the slaves and whites became more acclimatized to the area and some of the causes of disease were reduced or eliminated. Thus the rapid pace of settlement and the movement into new areas of sugar production did have a significant effect in keeping the region-wide mortality rate high.

Other factors influenced the demography of the eighteenth- and nineteenth-century West Indies as well.[34] One was the extent of sugar production and its effect on the numbers of free and slave settlers. Spanish policy, effectively limiting sugar production in the West Indies before the 1760s, served to reduce the numbers of slaves imported into Cuba, Puerto Rico, and Santo Domingo. When the sugar boom began in Cuba at the end of the eighteenth century, the island already had a pre-dominantly white population, and the Spanish areas had generally the lowest ratios of blacks to whites in the Caribbean. As described earlier, the ending of the slave trade had a significant impact on the growth of slave populations. Although the ending of slavery had important economic and demographic implications, in that it led to imports of Asian indentured workers, as well as a large-scale white immigration from Spain to Cuba, other islands were not expanding at the end of the slave era and received few white or black immigrants.[35] Thus migration still depended on the productivity of the sugar economy, even after the ending of slavery.

---

[34] Demographic issues are, of course, covered in most of the works on slavery. Of particular use for the problems relating to the British islands are Higman, *Slave Populations*; Higman, *Slave Population*; Dunn, *Sugar and Slaves*; Handler and Lange, *Plantation Slavery*; Craton, *Searching*; Roberts, *Population of Jamaica*; John, *Plantation Slaves*; and Friedman, "Heights." See also Hall, *Slave Society*, on the Danish West Indies; Scarano, *Sugar and Slavery*, on Puerto Rico; Lamur, *Production of Sugar*, and Van Lier, *Frontier Society*, on Surinam; Debien, *Les esclaves*, on the French Islands; and Mandle, *Plantation Economy*, on British Guiana. On Latin American slavery more generally, see Klein, *African Slavery*.

[35] On migration to Cuba, see Corbitt, "Immigration"; and Knight, *Slave Society*.

VII

For the twentieth century, it is easier to determine the basic demographic patterns since most areas have had periodic censuses, which include considerable detail on population structure and movements.[36] In addition, governmental and international collections of data on population and vital statistics are greater than for any previous period.[37]

During the twentieth century most Caribbean islands have had relatively high rates of population increase (see Table 11.11). This has been due primarily to the excess of births over deaths (see Table 11.12; see also Figure 11.2). Unlike the eighteenth and nineteenth centuries, however, the twentieth century saw little immigration from overseas except to Cuba. The Caribbean region's population grew less rapidly than the population of Central and South America, and also less rapidly than that of Africa and Asia. Twentieth-century growth rates (1900–90) were highest for the Dominican Republic (2.6%) and Cuba (2.19%), whereas the French islands of Guadeloupe and Martinique had particularly low rates (0.7%). Those areas affiliated with the British Commonwealth grew at an average rate of about 1.2% per annum, the highest rate being 1.7% in Trinidad and Tobago, aided in the first two decades by the continued in-migration of East Indian contract labor. Jamaica, the largest of the British islands, grew at about 1.3% per annum, with some slowing down late in the period due to an expanding out-migration to the United States and Canada and, in the 1950s to Britain. Haiti, after apparent slow population growth in the second half of the nineteenth century, had an increasing growth rate in the twentieth century, averaging overall 1.8% per annum. Thus, with a few small exceptions, all areas of the Caribbean experienced rapid population growth in the twentieth century, even with extensive populations shifts from rural to urban areas.[38] Also in the twentieth century, the West Indian population became increasingly concentrated. Hence the popula-

---

[36] Basic information about governmental censuses are in Goyer and Domschke, *Handbook*; and in Travis, *Guide*. Official data and their sources are discussed in Mitchell, *International Historical Statistics*.

[37] See U.N. Department for Economic and Social Information and Policy Analysis, *World Population Prospects*. The World Bank also is a major source of relevant information.

[38] The most studied island for this period is Jamaica. See Roberts, *Population of Jamaica*; and Lobdell, *Economic Structure*. For fertility comparisons between Jamaica and other islands of the British West Indies, see Roberts, *Fertility*; and Byrne, *Levels of Fertility*. For data on Cuban birth rates, see Collver, *Birth Rates*.

Table 11.11. *Caribbean populations, 1900, 1950, 1990 (thousands)*

	1900	1950	1990
Anguilla	5	5	7
Antigua and Barbuda	35	46	65
Aruba	10	57	61
Bahamas	54	79	255
Barbados	196	211	257
British Virgin Islands	5	6	16
Cayman Islands	5	6	27
Cuba	1,575	5,850	10,608
Dominica	29	51	72
Dominican Republic	700	2,353	7,170
Grenada	63	76	91
Guadeloupe	182	210	390
Haiti	1,270	3,261	6,486
Jamaica	756	1,403	2,420
Martinique	208	222	360
Montserrat	12	14	11
Netherlands Antilles	50	116	175
Puerto Rico	953	2,219	3,530
St. Kitts and Nevis	46	44	42
St. Lucia	50	79	133
St. Vincent and the Grenadines	48	67	107
Trinidad and Tobago	274	636	1,236
Turks and Caicos Islands	5	5	12
U.S. Virgin Islands	31	27	107
All Caribbean islands	6,562	17,045	33,640
Belize	37	67	189
Guyana	287	423	796
Surinam	69	215	422
Cayenne	22	25	98

Sources: United Nations, *World Population Prospects*, pp. 156–7; Mitchell, *International Historical Statistics*; Engerman and Higman, "The Demographic Structure of the Caribbean Slave Societies."

tion on the five countries of the Greater Antilles came to represent more than 85% of the total Caribbean population (see Table 11.13).

Given the limited in-migration of population throughout most of the twentieth century and the increased out-migration from many parts of the Caribbean in the second half, the high rate of natural increase clearly

Table 11.12. *Crude birth and death rates, Caribbean, 1900, 1950, 1990*

Area	1900	1950	1990
Crude birth rate			
Bahamas	—	34.7	20.7
Barbados	37.2 (1916)	32.8	15.6
Cuba	44.6 (1900–1904)	29.7	17.5
Dominican Republic	46.4 (1945–50)	50.5	31.3
Guadeloupe	—	39.0	19.8
Haiti	33.4 (1932–50)	43.5	36.2
Jamaica	35.7 (1900)	34.8	23.7
Martinique	—	39.5	18.3
Puerto Rico	33.6 (1900)	36.6	19.3
Trinidad and Tobago	36.6 (1900)	38.2	26.0
All islands	—	37.5	25.2
Guyana	36.7 (1906)	43.0	27.0
Surinam	39.0 (1901–5)	43.8	28.1
Crude death rate			
Bahamas	—	11.2	5.3
Barbados	25.5	13.2	8.7
Cuba	23.7	11.1	6.5
Dominican Republic	22.6	20.3	6.8
Guadeloupe	—	13.1	6.9
Haiti	21.2	27.5	13.2
Jamaica	21.6	11.5	6.6
Martinique	—	12.9	6.4
Puerto Rico	23.8	9.0	6.8
Trinidad and Tobago	25.0	11.3	6.6
All islands	—	15.5	7.9
Guyana	25.1	17.7	7.8
Surinam	23.3	12.6	6.2

Source: United Nations, *World Population Prospects*, pp. 196, 197, 208–9; Mitchell, *International Historical Statistics*. According to Roberts, *Fertility*, the crude birth rate for St. Vincent was 38.7 in 1909–13, 40.0 in 1950, and 41.2 in 1965, and this rate fell to about 25 in the mid-1980s.

explains the population increase. The timing and pattern of changes in population growth provides an excellent example of the "demographic transition," first applied to nineteenth-century Europe. The crude birth rates (per thousand) maintained their levels, averaging in the high 30s, or, in several cases, rose, particularly after World War II, until about 1970,

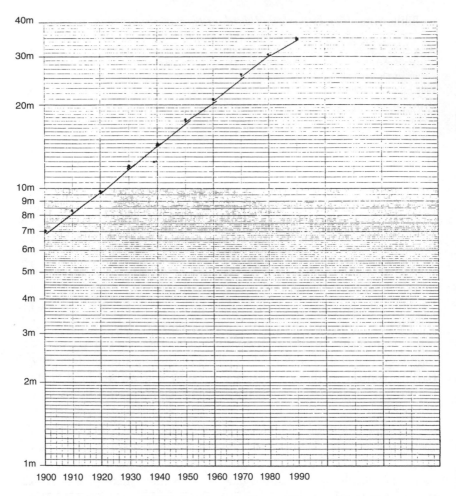

Figure 11.2. Caribbean populations, 1900–1990 (*Sources*: Computed from Engerman and Higman, "Demographic Structure of the Caribbean Slave Societies"; United Nations, *World Population Prospects*; Mitchell, *International Historical Statistics*)

when sharp declines occurred in almost all areas, lowering the average birth rate in the Caribbean in the 1980s to about 25. In several regions, the 1985–90 birth rate was approximately one-half of what it had been three decades earlier. These include Barbados, Guadeloupe, Martinique, and Puerto Rico. The Cuban birth rate fell by about 40% after midcentury, much of the sharp decline occurring after 1975. Cuba had also expe-

Table 11.13. *Five largest areas based on population, Caribbean, selected years (thousands)*

1750		1830		1900		1990	
Area	Number	Area	Number	Area	Number	Area	Number
St. Domingue	182.4	Cuba	755.7	Cuba	1,575	Cuba	10,608
Cuba	170.0	Haiti	627.8	Haiti	1,270	Dominican	
Jamaica	142.0	Jamaica	378.1	Puerto Rico	953	Republic	7,170
Barbados	80.4	Puerto Rico	323.8	Jamaica	756	Haiti	6,486
Martinique	79.0	Guadeloupe	119.7	Dominican		Puerto Rico	3,530
Percentage				Republic	700	Jamaica	2,420
of all							
Caribbean	60.7		72.9		75.3		86.0

Source: Tables 11.3, 11.4, 11.5, and 11.11.

rienced an earlier decline, between the end of World War I and the start of the depression. Fertility also declined in Haiti and the Dominican Republic, the two areas with the highest birth rate throughout. Even with the declines, however, their birth rates fell only to levels that resembled those of the other islands at midcentury. The role of the impact of economic change and of new public policies, including the introduction of fertility control methods, remains uncertain, and no doubt differs by region, but fertility reduction had by then become a frequently advocated policy.

The explanation for the increases in population growth over the century therefore lies in the declines in death rates. These declines generally began in the 1930s and led to crude death rates of about 8 per thousand in the 1980s. The death rate in many regions was less than one-half of the levels before the declines began. This differential between the onset of the decline in the death rate and the decline in the birth rate of three decades permitted West Indian populations to surge. The death rate continued to decline through the 1980s, and several parts of the Caribbean now have lower death rates than do nations in Western Europe. Even those regions with the highest death rates, Haiti and the Dominican Republic, have experienced dramatic declines, although Haiti probably still has the highest crude death rate in the Western Hemisphere, comparable to rates in the less developed nations of Africa and Asia. This West Indian decline in mortality affected most age groups, infant mortality falling more than 50% overall between the early 1950s and the early 1980s, although it did remain considerably above the levels of infant mortality in Western Europe and mainland North America. Rates of infant mortality were quite varied, but the overall Caribbean rate was pushed up considerably by the still high rates in Haiti and the Dominican Republic. Overall, life expectancy increased in the Caribbean, rising in Jamaica from about 39 in 1910 to 57 in 1950 to 71 in the 1980s, the overall regional life expectancy in the 1980s being about 67. Most other parts of the Caribbean had similar increases in the period, although Haiti's life expectation remains at least 10 years below that of the other islands.

The causes of these mortality declines no doubt include higher incomes, better nutrition, increased public health measures (such as improvements in sanitation, nutritional levels, and health education), and a reduced dependence on sugar production. Even in those areas still producing sugar, there have been sharp declines in death rates, while the changes in the patterns of disease further suggest significant changes in the demographic environment. Given that sharp mortality declines were worldwide, however, perhaps we should not look too much for location-specific factors. In some cases, such as Cuba and Puerto Rico, the introduction of public health measures by the United States early in the century may have had a long-term impact.[39]

As noted, migration accounts for the significant differences between the eighteenth and nineteenth centuries and the twentieth century. Whereas in the earlier centuries there was in-migration of black slaves, European whites, and, after the middle of the nineteenth century, East Indians, Chinese, and other indentured laborers, by the start of the twentieth century the immigrant streams were basically limited to Spaniards, going to Cuba, and East Indians, who went mainly to British Guiana and Trinidad. These were movements of contract labor that soon ended.[40] However, the earlier outflow from some of the British West Indies to Panama continued. Also, at this time immigrants began moving from Barbados and elsewhere in the British West Indies to the United States, a movement slowed by the U.S. legislation of the 1920s. The outflow from

---

[39] The causes of subsequent mortality declines in Cuba remain a source of continued controversy. Cuba had low mortality rates prior to the revolution, so that with the continued improvement after 1959, Cuba has had levels of mortality more similar to the developed nations than to the undeveloped. Measured by crude death rates, about two-thirds of the Cuban mortality decline after 1900 had occurred by 1950. By 1990 the Cuban crude death rate was comparable to that in many of the other islands of the Caribbean, with the critical exception of Haiti. See Diáz-Briquets, *Health Revolution.*

[40] On migration patterns for the West Indies, see Laurence, *Question of Labour*; Corbitt, "Immigration"; Marshall, "History"; and the other essays in Levine, *Caribbean Exodus.*

Table 11.14. *Caribbean immigrants (legal) into United States by country of birth, 1951–1990 (thousands)*

Country	1951–60	1961–70	1971–80	1981–90
Barbados	1.6	9.4	20.9	17.4
Cuba	78.3	256.8	276.8	159.2
Dominican Republic	9.8	94.1	148.0	251.8
Haiti	4.0	37.5	58.7	140.2
Jamaica	8.7	71.0	142.0	213.8
Trinidad and Tobago	1.6	24.6	61.8	39.5
Other Caribbean	18.8	26.1	51.6	70.8
All Caribbean islands (except Puerto Rico)	132.8	519.5	759.8	892.7
Puerto Rico[a]	480.0	222.0	44.0	—
Belize	—	—	—	18.1
Guyana	1.0	7.1	47.5	95.4

[a] Puerto Rico, being part of the United States, does not have separate legal counts of immigrants, and the numbers must be estimated. The periods here differ slightly from other parts of the Caribbean, covering 1950–59, 1960–69, and 1970–79. I do not yet have any estimate for the 1980s.

Source: U.S. Department of Commerce, *Statistical Abstract*, 1992, p. 11; *Statistical Abstract*, 1979, p. 90; and Bean and Tienda, *Hispanic Population of the United States*, p. 105.

the Caribbean and elsewhere did not reach a large scale until the end of World War II. In some cases, the primary factor behind migration was a political one, as in the case of the political instability and repressions in Haiti, and the Cuban revolution of 1959, but much of the flow, particularly from the Dominican Republic and Jamaica, reflected economic circumstances in the different areas. Among those heading north, British West Indians migrated both to the United States and to Canada, while Cubans, Dominicans, Haitians, and Puerto Ricans went to the United States. Within the Commonwealth, British West Indians migrated to Great Britain, but this pattern ended with the restrictive legislation of 1962 (see Table 11.14).[41]

[41] For details on the migration to the United States, see U.S. Census, *Statistical Abstract*; and the information on the specific areas of exit in Thernstrom, *Harvard Encyclopedia*. For a recent analysis, see Borjas, *Friends or Strangers*. There are interesting discussions of the political nature of migrations from Cuba and Haiti by Bach and by Stepid, in Levine, *Caribbean Exodus*. Details on the migration from the British West Indies to Great Britain are presented in Peach, *West Indian Migration*. See also Layton-Henry, "Great Britain." Information on overall Caribbean emigration pat-

Starting in the 1960s, there was large-scale migration from the French islands to France, as well as increasing numbers of migrants from Surinam to the Netherlands, peaking at the time of Surinam's independence in 1975.[42] Although the numbers of such migrants have been relatively low compared with the populations of the receiving areas, the migrants' concentration in terms of residence and of occupation has made these groups rather conspicuous in their areas of arrival. In the United States, many Caribbean migrants have located in New York City, although the recent Cuban inflow has been located primarily within Florida. The black populations of Britain and the Netherlands were small when the post–World War II migrations began, but the inflow did lead to numerous social problems in the two countries. In the United States, black West Indians represented only a small fraction of all American blacks. Nevertheless, the early twentieth-century immigrants from the West Indies were generally more skilled, more upwardly mobile, and did better economically than did U.S. blacks.[43] Attempts to limit U.S. immigration in the future would no doubt mean a significant lowering of the numbers coming from the Caribbean, who accounted for over 12% of U.S. immigrants in the 1980s and almost 17% in the 1970s.

In addition to this migration to and from the Caribbean, there was some substantial movement within the region, both in the short term and long term. Of particular importance were the long, or permanent, movements of Haitians and Jamaicans to Cuba in the second and third decades of the twentieth century, and, after some initial use of laborers from the British Lesser Antilles, the annual, seasonal movement of sugar workers from Haiti to the Dominican Republic, under governmental supervision, but with some extreme political difficulties at various times.

terns from 1950 to 1972, with particular attention to the British areas, is in Segal, *Population Policies*. Since Puerto Ricans have been U.S. citizens since 1917, movement from the island is not recorded in the immigration statistics, and that and the magnitude of the return migration make estimates of this flow difficult. Puerto Rican migration to the United States was highest in the 1950s, declining to about one-tenth of that level in the 1970s. See Bean and Tienda, *Hispanic Population*; and Friedlander, *Labor Migration*.

[42] For immigration from Surinam to the Netherlands, see Lamur, *Demographic Evolution*; and the essay by Bovenkerk in Levine, *Caribbean Exodus*. See also Entzinger, "The Netherlands." Outflows from the French areas are discussed in Burton and Reno, *French and West Indian*. See also the article by Freeman in Levine, *Caribbean Exodus*.

[43] For an early presentation of this argument, see Reid, *Negro Immigrant*. For a later examination of this question, see Sowell, "Three Black Histories."

VIII

The Caribbean has experienced three very different demographic regimes. The first was in the years of slavery, when immigration and mortality were high, and the population became predominantly black. The second was in the nineteenth century after slavery ended and there was considerable immigration of contract laborers and limited out-migration. The third came in the twentieth century, when the Caribbean experienced a "demographic transition," with mortality declining before fertility. This was similar to the transition that has taken place elsewhere in the developing world, even though most of the West Indians areas, with the exception of Haiti, had higher levels of per capita income and educational attainment than did the underdeveloped nations of Asia and Africa. After World War II there was extensive out-migration to mainland North America and Western Europe.

Few of the descendants of the pre-1492 population are still present in the Caribbean, and (except for the Spanish areas) only limited numbers of the descendants of white Europeans are in the region. The population there today consists primarily of the descendents of migrants from Africa who were brought over involuntarily as slaves but who were unable or unwilling to return after the ending of enslavement. Thus the post-Columbian period has seen an almost complete change in the ethnic composition of the West Indies. This pattern of transition has resembled that seen elsewhere in the Americas, but it has been less complete there than on the islands of the Caribbean.

BIBLIOGRAPHIC ESSAY

Given the nature of the settlement process of the Caribbean, there are relevant writings in at least four languages – English, Spanish, French, and Dutch – although the literature in English covers most issues. Extensive details are available on the censuses and the birth and death registrations in the British West Indian colonies, mainly between 1921 and 1946, in R. R. Kuczynski, *Demographic Survey of the British Colonial Empire*, volume 3, *West Indian and American Territories* (London, 1953). Useful topical essays providing bibliographic information on the Caribbean, as well as descriptions of archives and resource depositories concerning the region, can be found in Kenneth J. Grieb, ed., *Research Guide to Central America and the Caribbean* (Madison, 1985). For a bibliography on writings on population in Latin America and the Caribbean, see Barry Edmonston, *Population Research in Latin America and the Caribbean: A Reference Bibliography* (Ann Arbor, 1979). Rosemary Brana-Shute has edited a bibliography on post–slave trade migration to, from, and in the Caribbean, *A Bibliography of Caribbean Migration and Caribbean Immigrant Communities* (Gainesville, 1983).

Because of political concern with the colonies and widespread interest in the role and nature of slavery when it was legal, extensive estimates of population totals were made for political and economic purposes in the precensus era. However, many such estimates lack appropriate age breakdowns and do not provide systematic information on the vital statistics. By the twentieth century almost all of the islands had detailed censuses of population, Haiti and the Dominican Republic being among the last, and all provided vital statistics registrations. Thus more detailed examinations of demographic trends are possible for that period, although underreporting is a problem here and there. Since there are many islands in the Caribbean, it is impossible to be precise without consulting the sources on specific areas.

There is, as yet, no one work dealing with the demography of the entire Caribbean for the full post-Columbian period. Useful demographic materials are available in several one-volume histories of the Caribbean: David Watts, *The West Indies: Patterns of Development, Culture and Environmental Change since 1492* (Cambridge, 1987); Franklin W. Knight, *The Caribbean: The Genesis of a Fragmented Nationalism* (New York, 1990); and Bonham C. Richardson, *The Caribbean in the Wider World, 1492–1992: A Regional Geography* (Cambridge, 1992). Some information on the Caribbean region is found in overall histories of Latin America, particularly in the work of Nicholas Sanchez-Albornez, *The Population of Latin America: A History* (Berkeley, 1974), and his chapters in volumes 2 and 4 of the *Cambridge History of Latin America*; and in Robert V. Wells, *The Population of the British Colonies in America before 1776: A Survey of Census Data* (Princeton, 1975). Much relevant information for the pre-1776 period is presented in John J. McCusker, *The Rum Trade and the Balance of Payments of the Thirteen Continental Colonies, 1650–1775* (New York, 1988). An excellent demographic study of one island, from settlement to the time of its publication, is G. W. Roberts, *The Population of Jamaica* (Cambridge, 1957).

Since there is some debate but little evidence concerning the pre-Columbian population of the Caribbean, the best approach would be to read the relevant chapters in the general histories. The slave period is by far the most thoroughly covered aspect of Caribbean history, since there are considerable data on the slave trade and the numbers of slaves drawn from a variety of contemporary sources. An overview of this period, with many references to the literature, is the essay by Stanley L. Engerman and B. W. Higman, "The Demographic Structure of the Caribbean Slave Societies in the Eighteenth and Nineteenth Centuries," in *General History of the Caribbean*, volume 3, edited by Franklin W. Knight (London, 1947). Among studies of specific colonial powers, the most significant work is the magisterial contribution of B. W. Higman, *Slave Populations of the British Caribbean, 1807–1834* (Baltimore, 1984), which draws upon the slave registrations that began in the second decade of the nineteenth century and ended with slave emancipation in 1834. His earlier book on Jamaica, *Slave Population and Economy in Jamaica, 1807–1834* (Cambridge, 1976), was also a highly original contribution to the study of Caribbean demography. Other useful studies include A. Meredith John, *The Plantation Slaves of Trinidad: A Mathematical and Demographic Inquiry* (Cambridge, 1988); Michael Craton, *Searching for the Invisible Man: Slaves and Plantation Life in Jamaica* (Cambridge, Mass., 1978); and J. R. Ward, *British West Indian Slavery, 1750–1834: The Process of Amelioration* (Oxford, 1988), also on Jamaica; and Kenneth F. Kiple, *Blacks in Colonial Cuba, 1774–1899* (Gainesville, 1976); and Manuel Moreno Fraginals, "Africa in Cuba: A Quantitative Analysis of the African Population in the Island of Cuba," in *Comparative Perspectives on Slavery in New World Plantation Societies*, edited by Vera Rubin and Arthur Tuden (New York, 1977), pp. 187–201. Important studies of the slave trade that include information on the Caribbean are Philip D. Curtin, *The Atlantic Slave Trade: A Census* (Madison, 1969); David Eltis, *Economic Growth and the Ending of the Transatlantic Slave Trade* (New York, 1987); and Herbert S. Klein, *The Middle Passage: Comparative Studies in the Atlantic Slave Trade* (Princeton, 1978). For estimates of the white migration, see the chapters in *"To Make America": European Emigration in the Early Modern Period*, edited by Ida Altman and James Horn (Berkeley, 1991); David Galenson's *White Servitude in Colonial America: An Economic Analysis* (Cambridge, 1981), for the British Caribbean, provide a useful starting point. An important source for immigration into the Caribbean is K. O. Laurence, *Immigration into the West Indies in the 19th Century* (Barbados, 1971). His recently published book, *A Question of Labour: Indentured Immigration into Trinidad and British Guiana, 1875–1917* (Kingston, 1994), provides considerable detail on the nature of indentured labor in British Guiana and Trinidad. On Latin American slavery in general, with some discussion of the Caribbean, see Herbert S. Klein, *African Slavery in Latin America and the Caribbean* (New York, 1986).

Few works dealing with the twentieth century cover the overall demography of the Caribbean. For post–World War II, there are several publications with relevant data, by the United Nations and by the World Bank. Data based upon official government censuses are contained in B. R. Mitchell, *International Historical Statistics: The Americas, 1750–1988* (New York, 1993), which details the sources from which the material is drawn. Useful demographic studies include G. W. Roberts, *Fertility and Mating in Four West Indian Populations: Trinidad and Tobago, Barbados, St. Vincent, Jamaica* (Mona, 1975); G. W. Roberts, *The Population of Jamaica* (Cambridge, 1957); H. E. Lamur, *The Demographic Evolution of Surinam 1920–1970: A Socio-Demographic Analysis* (The Hague, 1973); and Jay R. Mandle, *The Plantation Economy: Population and Economic Growth in Guyana, 1838–1960* (Philadelphia, 1973). The nature and magnitude of out-migration from the Caribbean is described in Ceri Peach, *West Indian Migration to Britain: A Social Geography* (London, 1968); and in essays contained in *The Caribbean Exodus*, edited by Barry Levine (New York, 1987).

REFERENCES

Altman, Ida, and James Horn, eds. *"To Make America": European Emigration in the Early Modern Period.* Berkeley: University of California Press, 1991.

Bean, Frank D., and Marta Tienda. *The Hispanic Population of the United States.* New York: Russell Sage Foundation, 1987.

J. Borjas, George. *Friends or Strangers: The Impact of Immigrants on the U.S. Economy.* New York: Basic Books, 1990.

Burton, Richard D. E., and Fred Reno, eds. *French and West Indian: Martinique, Guadeloupe, and French Guiana Today.* Charlottesville: University Press of Virginia, 1995.

Byrne, Joycelin. *Levels of Fertility in Commonwealth Caribbean, 1921–1965.* Mona: Institute of Social and Economic Research, University of the West Indies, 1972.

Canny, Nicholas, ed. *Europeans on the Move: Studies on European Migration, 1500–1800.* Oxford: Clarendon Press, 1994.

Cardoso, Ciro Falmarion S. *Economia e Sociedade em Areas Colonias Periforieas: Guiana Francesca e Para, 1750–1817.* Rio de Janeiro: Ediçao Graal, 1984.

Choquette, Leslie. "Frenchmen into Peasants; Modernity and Tradition in the Peopling of French North America." *Proceedings of the American Antiquarian Society* 104 (1994): 27–49.

Collver, O. Andrew. *Birth Rates in Latin America: New Estimates of Historical Trends and Fluctuations.* Institute of International Studies Research Series no. 7. Berkeley: University of California, 1965.

Cook, Sherburne F., and Woodrow Borah. *Essays in Population History: Mexico and the Caribbean I.* Berkeley: University of California Press, 1971.

Corbitt, Duvon C. "Immigration into Cuba." *Hispanic American Historical Review* 22 (1942): 280–308.

Craton, Michael. *Searching for the Invisible Man: Slaves and Plantation Life in Jamaica.* Cambridge, Mass.: Harvard University Press, 1978.

———. "A Re-evaluation of the Black Caribs of St. Vincent: An Exercise in Historical Triangulation." In *The Lesser Antilles in the Age of European Expansion,* edited by Robert L. Paquette and Stanley L. Engerman, 71–85. Gainesville: University Press of Florida, 1996.

Curtin, Philip D. *The Atlantic Slave Trade: A Census.* Madison: University of Wisconsin Press, 1969.

———. *Death by Migration: Europe's Encounter with the Tropical World in the Nineteenth Century.* Cambridge: Cambridge University Press, 1989.

Debien, Gabriel. *Les esclaves aux Antilles françaises, XVIIe–XVIIIe siècles.* Basse-Terre: Société d'histoire de la Guadeloupe, 1974.

Deerr, Noel. *A History of Sugar.* London: Chapman and Hall, 1949, 1950.

Deneven, William M., ed. *The Native Population of the Americas in 1492.* Madison: University of Wisconsin Press, 1976.

Diáz-Briquets, Sergio. *The Health Revolution in Cuba.* Austin: University of Texas Press, 1983.

Diáz Soler, E. Luis M. *Historia de la Esclavitud Negra en Puerto Rico.* Rio Piedras, Editorial Universitaria, Universidad de Puerto Rico, 1965.

Dietz, James L. *Economic History of Puerto Rico: Institutional Change and Capitalist Development.* Princeton, N.J.: Princeton University Press, 1986.

Dunn, Richard S. *Sugar and Slaves: The Rise of the Planter Class in the English West Indies, 1624–1713.* Chapel Hill: University of North Carolina Press, 1972.

Eltis, David. "Free and Coerced Transatlantic Migrations: Some Comparisons." *American Historical Review* 88 (1983): 251–80.

———. *Economic Growth and the Ending of the Transatlantic Slave Trade.* New York: Oxford University Press, 1987.

Eltis, David, and Stanley L. Engerman, "Fluctuations in Sex and Age Ratios in the Transatlantic Slave Trade, 1663–1864." *Economic History Review* 46 (1993): 308–23.

Emmer, P. C. "Immigration into the Caribbean: The Introduction of Chinese and East Indian Indentured Laborers between 1839 and 1917." In *European Expansion and Migration: Essays on the Intercontinental Migration from Africa, Asia, and Europe,* edited by P. C. Emmer and M. Mörner, 245–76. New York: Berg, 1992.

Engerman, Stanley L. "Servants to Slaves to Servants: Contract Labour and European Expansion." In *Colonialism and Migration: Indentured Labour before and after Slavery,* edited by P. C. Emmer, 263–94. Dordrecht: Martinus Nijhoff, 1986.

————. "Europe, the Lesser Antilles, and Economic Expansion, 1600–1800." In *The Lesser Antilles in the Age of European Expansion,* edited by Robert L. Paquette and Stanley L. Engerman, 147–64. Gainesville: University Press of Florida, 1996.

Engerman, Stanley L., and B. W. Higman. "The Demographic Structure of the Caribbean Slave Societies in the Eighteenth and Nineteenth Centuries." In *General History of the Caribbean,* vol. 3, edited by Franklin W. Knight, 45–104. London: UNESCO, 1997.

Entzinger, Han B. "The Netherlands." In *European Immigration Policy: A Comparative Study*, edited by Tomas Hammar, 50–88. Cambridge: Cambridge University Press, 1985.

Esteban Deive, Carlos. *La Esclavitud del Negro en Santo Domingo, 1492–1844.* Santo Domingo: Museo del Hombre Dominicana, 1980.

Fogel, Robert W. *Without Consent or Contract: The Rise and Fall of American Slavery.* New York: W. W. Norton, 1989.

Fogel, Robert W. et al., eds. *Without Consent or Contract: Evidence and Methods.* New York: W. W. Norton, 1992.

Friedlander, Stanley. *Labor Migration and Economic Growth: A Case Study of Puerto Rico.* Cambridge, Mass.: MIT Press, 1965.

Friedman, Gerald C. "The Heights of Slaves in Trinidad." *Social Science History* 6 (1982): 482–515.

Galenson, David W. *White Servitude in Colonial America: An Economic Analysis.* Cambridge: Cambridge University Press, 1981.

Games, Alison F. "Opportunity and Mobility in Early Barbados." In *The Lesser Antilles in the Age of European Expansion*, edited by Robert L. Paquette and Stanley L. Engerman, 165–81. Gainesville: University Press of Florida, 1996.

Gemery, Henry A. "Emigration from the British Isles to the New World, 1630–1700: Inferences from Colonial Populations." *Research in Economic History* 5 (1980): 179–231.

Gonzalez, Nancie L. *Sojourners of the Caribbean: Ethnogenesis and Ethnohistory of the Garifuna.* Urbana: University of Illinois Press, 1988.

Goslinga, Cornelis Ch. *The Dutch in the Caribbean and in the Guianas, 1680–1791.* Assen/Maastricht: Van Gorcum, 1985.

Goveia, Elsa V. *Slaves in the British Leeward Islands at the End of the Eighteenth Century.* New Haven, Conn.: Yale University Press, 1956.

Goyer, Doreen S., and Eliane Domschke. *The Handbook of National Population Censuses: Latin America and the Caribbean, North America, and Oceania.* Westport, Conn.: Greenwood Press, 1983.

Green-Pedersen, Svend E. "Slave Demography in the Danish West Indies and the Abolition of the Slave Trade. In *The Abolition of the Atlantic Slave Trade: Origins and Effects in Europe, Africa and the Americas*, edited by David Eltis and James Walvin, pp. 231–57. Madison: University of Wisconsin Press, 1981.

Hall, Neville A. T. "The 1816 Freedman Petition in the Danish West Indies: Its Background and Consequences." *Boletin Latinoamericanos y del Caribe* 29 (December 1981): 55–73.

————. *Slave Society in the Danish West Indies: St. Thomas, St. John and St. Croix.* Mona: University of the West Indies Press, 1992.

Handler, Jerome S., and Frederick W. Lange. *Plantation Slavery in Barbados: An Archeological and Historical Investigation.* Cambridge, Mass.: Harvard University Press, 1978.

Hartog, Johan. Aruba: *Past and Present, From the Times of the Indians until Today.* Oranjestal: D. J. DeWit, 1961.

————. Curaçao: *From Colonial Dependence to Autonomy.* Aruba: D. J. DeWit, 1968.

Henige, David. "On the Contact Population of Hispaniola: History as Higher Mathematics." *Hispanic American Historical Review* 58 (1978): 217–37.

Higman, B. W. *Slave Population and Economy in Jamaica, 1807–1834.* Cambridge: Cambridge University Press, 1976.

————. "Slavery and the Development of Demographic Theory in the Age of the Industrial Revolution." In *Slavery and British Society, 1776–1846,* edited by James Walvin, 164–94. Baton Rouge: Louisiana State University Press, 1982.

————. *Slave Populations of the British Caribbean, 1807–1834.* Baltimore, Md.: Johns Hopkins University Press, 1984.

Hoetnik, H. "Surinam and Curaçao." In *Neither Slave nor Free: The Freedmen of African Descent in the Slave Societies of the New World,* edited by David W. Cohen and Jack P. Greene, pp. 59–83. Baltimore, Md.: Johns Hopkins University Press, 1972.

————. *The Dominican People, 1850–1900: Notes for a Historical Sociology.* Baltimore, Md.: Johns Hopkins University Press, 1982.

Hyrenius, Hannes. *Royal Swedish Slaves.* Demographic Research Institute Report no. 15. Gothenburg: University of Gothenburg, 1977.

John, A. Meredith. *The Plantation Slaves of Trinidad: A Mathematical and Demographic Inquiry.* Cambridge: Cambridge University Press, 1988.

Karras, Alan L. *Sojourners in the Sun: Scottish Migrants in Jamaica and the Chesapeake, 1740–1800.* Ithaca, N.Y.: Cornell University Press, 1992.

Kiple, Kenneth F. *Blacks in Colonial Cuba, 1774–1899.* Gainesville: University Presses of Florida, 1976.

————. *The Caribbean Slave: A Biological History.* Cambridge: Cambridge University Press, 1984.

Klein, Herbert S. *The Middle Passage: Comparative Studies in the Atlantic Slave Trade.* Princeton, N.J.: Princeton University Press, 1978.

————. *African Slavery in Latin America and the Caribbean.* New York: Oxford University Press, 1986.

Klein, Herbert S., and Stanley L. Engerman. "Fertility Differentials between Slaves in the United States and the British West Indies: A Note on Lactation Practices and Their Possible Implications." *William and Mary Quarterly* 35 (1978): 357–74.

Klomp, Ank. *Politics on Bonaire: An Anthropological Study.* Assen/Maastricht: Van Gorcum, 1986.

Knight, Franklin W. *Slave Society in Cuba during the Nineteenth Century.* Madison: University of Wisconsin Press, 1970.

————. *The Caribbean: The Genesis of a Fragmented Nationalism.* New York: Oxford University Press, 1990.

Kunitz, Stephen J. "Diseases and Mortality in the Americas since 1700." In *The Cambridge World History of Human Disease,* edited by Kenneth F. Kiple, 328–34. Cambridge: Cambridge University Press, 1993.

Lachance, Paul L. "The 1809 Immigration of Saint-Domingue Refugees to New Orleans: Reception, Integration and Impact." *Louisiana History* 29 (1988): 109–41.

Lamur, Humphrey E. *The Demographic Evolution of Surinam 1920–1970: A Socio-Demographic Analysis.* The Hague: Martinus Nijhoff, 1973.

————. *The Production of Sugar and the Reproduction of Slaves at Vossenburg, Suriname 1705–1863*. Amsterdam: Amsterdam Center for Caribbean Studies, 1987.

Laurence, K. O. *Immigration into the West Indies in the 19th Century*. Barbados: Caribbean Universities Press, 1971.

————. *A Question of Labour: Indentured Immigration into Trinidad and British Guiana, 1875–1917*. Kingston: Ian Randle, 1994.

Layton-Henry, Zig. "Great Britain." In *European Immigration Policy: A Comparative Study*, edited by Tomas Hammar, 89–126. Cambridge: Cambridge University Press, 1985.

Levine, Barry B., ed. *The Caribbean Exodus*. New York: Praeger, 1987.

Leyburn, James G. *The Haitian People*. New Haven, Conn.: Yale University Press, 1941.

Lobdell, Richard A. *Economic Structure and Demographic Performance in Jamaica, 1891–1935*. New York: Garland, 1987.

McCusker, John J. *The Rum Trade and the Balance of Payments of the Thirteen Continental Colonies, 1650–1775*. New York: Garland, 1988.

Mandle, Jay R. *The Plantation Economy: Population and Economic Growth in Guyana, 1838–1960*. Philadelphia: Temple University Press, 1973.

Marshall, Dawn. "A History of West India Migrations: Overseas Opportunities and 'Safety-Valve' Policies." In *The Caribbean Exodus*, edited by Barry B. Levine, 15–31. New York: Praeger, 1987.

Mitchell, B. R. *International Historical Statistics: The Americas, 1750–1988*, 2d ed. New York: Stockton Press, 1993.

Moreau de Jonnes, Alex. *Recherches Statistiques sur l'esclavage Colonial*. Paris: Bourgogne et Martinet, 1842.

Moya Pons, Frank. "Nuevas Consideracienes sobre la Historia de la Poblacion Dominicana." *Eme Eme: Estudios Dominicanos* 3 (November–December 1974): 3–28.

————. *The Dominican Republic: A National History*. New Rochelle: Hispaniola Books, 1995.

Newton, Velma. *The Silver Men: West Indian Labour Migration to Panama, 1850–1914*. Mona: Institute of Social and Economic Research, University of the West Indies, 1984.

Nicholls, David. *From Dessalines to Duvalier: Race, Colour and National Independence in Haiti*. Cambridge: Cambridge University Press, 1979.

Patterson, Orlando. *Slavery and Social Death: A Comparative Study*. Cambridge, Mass.: Harvard University Press, 1982.

Peach, Ceri. *West Indian Migration to Britain: A Social Geography*. London: Oxford University Press, 1968.

Platt, Raye R., et al. *The European Possessions in the Caribbean Area: A Compilation of Facts . . .* New York: American Geographical Society, 1941.

Potsma, Johannes Menne. *The Dutch in the Atlantic Slave Trade, 1600–1815*. Cambridge: Cambridge University Press, 1990.

Reid, Ira De A. *The Negro Immigrant: His Background, Characteristics and Social Adjustment, 1899–1937*. New York: Columbia University Press, 1939.

Richardson, Bonham C. *Caribbean Migrants: Environment and Human Survival on St. Kitts and Nevis*. Knoxville: University of Tennessee Press, 1983.

————. *Panama Money in Barbados, 1900–1920*. Knoxville: University of Tennessee Press, 1985.

————. *The Caribbean in the Wider World, 1492–1992: A Regional Geography*. Cambridge: Cambridge University Press, 1992.

Roberts, G. W. "Emigration from the Island of Barbados." *Social and Economic Studies* 4 (1955): 245–88.

————. *The Population of Jamaica*. Cambridge: Cambridge University Press, 1957.

————. *Fertility and Mating in Four West Indian Populations: Trinidad and Tobago, Barbados, St. Vincent, Jamaica*. Mona: Institute of Social and Economic Research, University of the West Indies, 1975.

Roberts, G. W., and J. Byrne. "Summary Statistics on Indenture and Associated Migration Affecting the West Indies, 1834–1918." *Population Studies* 20 (1966): 125–34.

Rosenblat, Ángel. "The Population of Hispaniola at the Time of Columbus." In *The Native Population of the Americas in 1492*, edited by William M. Denevan, 43–66. Madison: University of Wisconsin Press, 1976.

Sanchez-Albornez, Nicholas. *The Population of Latin America: A History*. Berkeley: University of California Press, 1974.

Scarano, Francisco A. *Sugar and Slavery in Puerto Rico: The Plantation Economy of Ponce, 1800–1850*. Madison: University of Wisconsin Press, 1984.

Segal, Aaron Lee, ed. *Population Policies in the Caribbean*. Lexington, Mass.: D. C. Heath, 1975.

Sheridan, Richard B. *The Development of Plantations to 1750*. Barbados: Caribbean University Press, 1970.

————. *Sugar and Slavery: An Economic History of the British West Indies, 1623–1775*. Baltimore, Md.: Johns Hopkins University Press, 1973.

————. *Doctors and Slaves: A Medical and Demographic History of Slavery in the British West Indies, 1680–1834*. Cambridge: Cambridge University Press, 1985.

Sowell, Thomas. "Three Black Histories." In *Essays and Data on American Ethnic Groups*, edited by Thomas Sowell, 7–64. Washington, D.C.: Urban Institute, 1978.

Steward Julian H., ed. *Handbook of South American Indians*. Vol. 4: *The Circum-Caribbean Tribes*. Washington, D.C.: Smithsonian Institution, Bureau of American Ethnology, 1948.

Thernstrom, Stephan, ed. *Harvard Encyclopedia of American Ethnic Groups*. Cambridge, Mass.: Harvard University Press, 1980.

Thompson, Alvin D. *Colonialism and Underdevelopment in Guyana, 1580–1803*. Bridgetown: Carib Research, 1987.

Travis, Carol, ed. *A Guide to Latin American and Caribbean Census Material: A Bibliography and Union List*. Boston: G. K. Hall, 1990.

U.N. Department for Economic and Social Information and Policy Analysis. *World Population Prospects: The 1992 Revision*. New York: United Nations, 1993.

U.S. Bureau of the Census. *Statistical Abstract of the United States, 1979*. Washington, D.C.: Government Printing Office, 1979.

U.S. Bureau of the Census. *Statistical Abstract of the United States, 1992*. Washington, D.C.: Government Printing Office, 1992.

U.S. War Department. *Report on the Census of Puerto Rico, 1899*. Washington, D.C.: Government Printing Office, 1900.

Van Lier, R. A. J. *Frontier Society: A Social Analysis of the History of Surinam*. The Hague: Martinus Nijhoff, 1971.

Ward, J. R. *British West Indian Slavery, 1750–1834: The Process of Amelioration.* Oxford: Oxford University Press, 1988.

Watts, David. *The West Indies: Patterns of Development, Culture and Environmental Change since 1492.* Cambridge: Cambridge University Press, 1987.

Well, Robert V. *The Population of the British Colonies in America before 1776: A Survey of Census Data.* Princeton, N.J.: Princeton University Press, 1975.

Westergaard, Waldemer. *The Danish West Indies under Company Rule, 1671–1754.* New York: Macmillan, 1917.

12

CANADA'S POPULATION IN THE TWENTIETH CENTURY

MARVIN MCINNIS

INTRODUCTION

Over the first nine decades of the twentieth century Canada's population increased more than fivefold. That is a remarkable development, especially for one of the high-income countries of the industrialized developed world. This record of population growth is shown in Table 12.1, which presents population totals at decennial census dates and the average annual growth rates over the intercensal periods. Between 1901 and 1991 (the date of the most recent decennial census), Canada's population grew at an average annual rate of 1.82%. The province of Newfoundland was added to Canada in 1949. Excluding the addition of Newfoundland, the average rate of growth would still have been 1.72% per annum. The most rapid growth occurred in the first decade of the century; indeed, it extended over the whole period leading up to the outbreak of World War I in 1914. The second most rapid growth occurred in the decade of the 1950s, which, at 2.67% per annum, was almost as high as the 2.98% attained in the first decade of the century. Removing the discontinuous jump brought by the addition of Newfoundland, the Canadian population still grew at 2.47% per annum in the 1950s. The slowest growth was in the 1930s, although it was only slightly above the rate of growth in the last decade of the nineteenth century, the period just preceding the 90 years under review here. Over this period, variations in the rate of growth of Canada's population have largely reflected fluctuations in immigration. Rapid population growth in the twentieth century marked a turnaround for Canada, for the growth of population had slowed in the late decades of the nineteenth century. A falling birth rate combined with heavy emigration brought the

Table 12.1. *Canada's population at census dates
and intercensal growth rate*

Year	Population (thousands)	Average annual rate of growth, preceding decade
1901	5,371	1.06
1911	7,207	2.98
1921	8,788	2.00
1931	10,377	1.68
1941	11,507	1.04
1951	14,009	1.99
1961	18,238	2.67
1971	21,568	1.69
1981	24,343	1.22
1991	27,297	1.15

Source: Statistics Canada, decennial censuses of Canada.

rate of increase over the last decade of the nineteenth century down to a modest 1.06% per annum. In 1901 Canada was, in terms of population, one of the small nations of the world. With only 5.4 million people, it was about the same size as Sweden (5.1) and the Netherlands (5.1), smaller than Belgium (6.7) but larger than Australia (3.8). Canada's population was just 7% of that of the United States. By 1981 it had grown to 10.7% of the number of people in the United States, owing in large part to a higher rate of immigration.

The dramatic turnabout in the demographic situation in Canada came with a great reversal in the tide of international migration. Around the beginning of the new century, Canada was suddenly transformed from a nation of heavy emigration over several decades into one of the leading destinations of international migrants. Immigration to Canada continued at a relatively high rate in the years after World War I, right up to the beginning of the Great Depression. In this chapter the first three decades of the century are considered as a piece, followed by a two-decade inter-regnum marked by depression and war. A final period also treated as essentially one piece is the 30 years between 1951 and 1981. It might have been preferable to make the break in 1946, at the end of World War II, but the exigency of using decennial census data makes it necessary to move the time division forward to 1951. It took two or three years after the end of World War II for the main features of the postwar demographic regime to become established, so the difference between 1946 and 1951 is not really consequential. The period from 1951 to 1981 was another era of immigration, but it encompassed both a rise and a fall in fertility. This account ends with evidence from the census of 1981. Because most features of Canada's demographic development have stabilized over the subsequent period, that terminal date, while convenient, does not leave much untold. A table of basic population numbers for Canada and the main regions of the country, along with numerous other demographic measures, is provided in the appendix to this chapter (Table 12A.1).

Since the most dramatic episode of change was the era of mass immigration at the beginning of the century, it makes an appropriate starting place for an examination of the development of Canada's population in the twentieth century. There is a bit of a problem with demarcating appropriate periods. The first two decades of the century were characterized by heavy immigration, even though World War I intervened to cut back the flow. Canada did not immediately follow the United States with restrictive policies in the 1920s and therefore experienced continued large-scale immigration during that decade. The net effect was not so great since emigration picked up again in the 1920s. It seems most convenient, however, to treat the entire period from 1901 to 1931 as one dominated by immigration to Canada. The magnitude, nature, and implications of that movement are the first concern of this chapter.

Over that same period, the birth rate in Canada continued the decline that had begun several decades previously in the nineteenth century.[1] It bottomed out in the 1930s, but by far the greater part of the fall had been accomplished by the 1931 census date, so it seems appropriate to consider the continuation, or perhaps more accurately the completion, of the fertility transition in Canada in the 1901–31 period. Thereafter, the most interesting changes in Canada's demographic situation occur in the period following World War II. That leaves the 1931–41 decade as an anomaly. Not much attention need be directed to it because not much was happening. Nevertheless, a short section focusing on that decade is included just to give the story continuity and completeness of coverage.

During the twentieth century Canada saw a great decline in mortality, much as the United States did. Because that experience is not so easy to divide into periods, it is discussed as a unit here. In the earlier half of that period, the years from 1901 to 1941, Canada made its largest gains in the reduction of mortality in the infant and early childhood years. After 1941,

---

[1] The nineteenth-century Canadian experience is reviewed in Chapter 9 of this volume.

with the introduction of antibiotic medicines and safer surgical procedures, the length of adult life was extended. There is not a great deal here
that is distinctively Canadian, and the patterns of change quite closely
mirror those in the United States. For that reason the discussion of mortality change is compressed into one section that covers the entire 1901–91
period.

The period from the end of World War II up to the present can be
treated in much the same way as the 1901–31 period, except that the order
of the topics is reversed. The first noteworthy feature was the much publicized swing in the birth rate, the baby boom and the baby bust, which
Canada shared with the United States. That deserves a full section. The
period coincides with one in which immigration once again emerged to
play a leading role in the development of Canada's population. In relation
to the size of population, immigration was especially large in the 1950s,
raising that decade's growth almost to the level attained in 1901 to 1911.
The first great postwar wave of immigration coincided with the baby
boom. Thereafter immigration continued at a high, if fluctuating, level,
but the base population had increased, so the relative impact of the immigrant inflow was not so great. After the fall in the birth rate in the 1960s,
a large, and in more recent times augmented, level of immigration again
became the dominant element in Canada's population growth. Immigration since 1961 has also changed the ethnic composition of the population, especially in the regions of greatest attraction to the "new"
immigration. The story is brought to a close in the early 1980s, largely
because the most interesting features of change are over by then and the
most recent Canadian demographic situation appears to have stabilized,
with low, beneath replacement levels of fertility, coupled with relatively
high but rather widely fluctuating levels of immigration. That is to say,
the circumstances of the 1960s and 1970s seem to have continued onward
into later years with no fundamental change.

THE ERA OF MASS IMMIGRATION,
1901–1931

In the late decades of the nineteenth century, Canada was a country of
mass emigration.[2] Right around the turn of the century the situation

---

[2] Again, this is discussed in Chapter 9 of this volume; see especially Table 9.1.

changed dramatically. From 1901 up until the outbreak of World War I in 1914, a massive flow of immigrants poured into Canada, and the population became strikingly transformed. It was much larger, its regional distribution was greatly altered, and its ethnic composition changed. This development had largely to do with the rapid settlement of western Canada. Following the confederation of British North American colonies in 1867, the new nation had greatly increased in size by adding two small colonies in the west – the Red River colony, renamed Manitoba, and British Columbia on the Pacific coast – and by acquiring from the Hudson's Bay Company the vast territory in between that comprised mainly the Canadian segment of the Great Plains of North America. The intention was to create an agricultural frontier of settlement in imitation of the United States. The problem was that over the last three decades of the nineteenth century few people wanted to settle in the Canadian west. In 1891, only 350,000 people lived in western Canada – just 7.2% of the national population. Just before the turn of the century the situation changed, and people began to pour into western Canada to take up free homesteads. In addition to farms, commercial centers and transport facilities were established – all the accoutrements of a modern economy. The effects of this especially dramatic boom spilled over into the rest of the country. The lumber industry of British Columbia expanded to supply the construction boom in the Prairie region. In eastern Canada manufacturing and commercial activity boomed as well. This was the episode that transformed Canada into a fully continental economy. By 1931 the Prairie region had 2.4 million people, or 23% of the national total, and British Columbia, with 698,000, accounted for 6.7% of the nation. By contrast, the Atlantic provinces, which had to a large extent been left out of the great boom, had their share of the national population drop from 16.6% at the turn of the century to a little less than 10% in 1931.

The great influx of population into the Canadian Prairies was made up of three groups of roughly equal size: migrants from eastern Canada, almost all from Ontario; immigrants from the United States; and immigrants from Europe. The immigrants substantially outnumbered the Canadians who settled in the Prairie provinces. This great upsurge in immigration is shown in Figure 12.1. By the turn of the century, immigration to Canada had already risen to about 50,000 per year. That added about 1% per annum to the growth of Canada's population. By 1903 the inflow had tripled, and it rose to a peak of 400,000 in 1913. That was at a time when Canada's population was about 6 million, so the huge

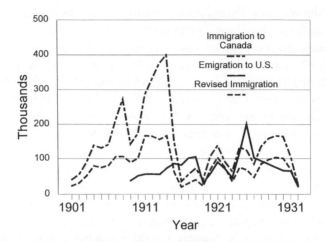

Figure 12.1. Immigration to Canada and emigration to the United States, 1900–1931

immigration added almost 7% in a single year. Between 1901 and 1911, the rate of immigration was 2.8% of the average population, a rate almost triple that of the United States, which was also at that time experiencing one of its peak periods of immigration. The great migration to Canada in this period was one of the most pronounced episodes experienced by any nation in recorded world history.

Not surprisingly, the influx of people dropped sharply with the outbreak of World War I, yet even through the war years it continued at a level of 50,000 per year or more, and with the end of the war immigration rose again. In the years around 1920, Canada continued to be a large recipient of immigrants. Simply cumulating the annual flow of immigrants, the addition to the population of Canada would have been 1,782,000 and 1,592,000, respectively, in the first two decades of the century. In the 1920s an additional 1,144,000 immigrants were recorded as entering the country. The net contribution of immigration to Canada's population growth, however, was considerably less. Many immigrants returned to their country of origin; others moved on to the United States. It is also quite likely that many immigrants were counted more than once, as they often went back to their home country, then entered Canada again.[3] People born in Canada continued to emigrate to the United States.

---

[3] My maternal grandfather, for example, came to Canada in 1903 as a member of a large organized settlement. A few years later he returned to Scotland to court a woman he had known there and then returned to Canada, again to take up a homestead to which his fiancée came to be married. Such stories abound.

One known element of this offset, immigration into the United States from Canada, is also shown in Figure 12.1. There were two periods in which American immigration from Canada was larger than total immigration to Canada: in the early years of World War I, when Canada was at war but the United States was not; and in the middle of the following decade. In the late 1920s, though, Canada was still admitting large numbers of immigrants, whereas the United States was tightly restricting entry from the Eastern Hemisphere.

Accounting for the components of change in the Canadian population has been an issue of considerable controversy. Two elements are in dispute. First, there is the matter of deriving a residual estimate of net migration after accounting for natural increase. Second, there has been controversy over the selection of an appropriate measure of immigration. In a seminal paper published in 1950, Nathan Keyfitz provided a decade-by-decade accounting for the growth of Canada's population.[4] He first estimated the net migration of the population 10 years of age and older at the end of each decade by using life table survival rates. In the absence of reliable Canadian life tables for years prior to 1921, Keyfitz used tables for England and Wales, adjusted by the ratio of Canadian to English survival values in 1931 and 1941. With the addition of estimates of intercensal births and deaths of children born within the decade, Keyfitz was able to provide a "reconstruction of Canada's population record"[5] (his Table 11). He took as immigration the cumulated officially recorded inflow, then derived a residual estimate of emigration. It should be emphasized that Keyfitz put forward his estimates in a highly tentative way, scrupulously drawing attention to anomalies and likely sources of error.

Subsequent writers have challenged Keyfitz's selection of survival rates and questioned the use of the officially recorded inflow of immigrants. The strongest challenge came from Duncan McDougall, who substituted the Glover life table of 1901/10 for the United States as a basis for adjusting later Canadian life tables.[6] The resulting survival ratios are slightly lower than those employed by Keyfitz; hence McDougall's estimates of positive net migration are larger. The debate on this issue came at a time when only limited information was available on historical survival rates. Subsequently, Australian and Danish life tables became available that might give better representations of Canadian historical experience, and model life tables have also entered into routine use. Thanks to Robert

---

[4] Keyfitz, "The Growth of the Canadian Population."
[5] Keyfitz, "Growth of the Canadian Population," Table 11.
[6] McDougall, "Immigration into Canada."

Bourbeau and Jacques Légaré, we now have, a series of historical survival rates for Canada based on model life tables.[7] The main point, however, is that all the concern over which set of survival rates to select was probably misplaced, at least for decades such as 1901 to 1911 when net migration was very large. Other sources of error had potentially much larger effects. Keyfitz's reconstruction also relied on an estimate of births over the course of each decade, and that was probably open to greater error than the calculation of deaths. Furthermore, both Keyfitz and McDougall implicitly assumed that there were no immigrants under the age of 10. The published tables of the 1911 census of Canada do not give the age distribution of the native- and foreign-born, but an unpublished tabulation exists. From it one can establish that 7.4% of the population born outside of Canada was under the age of 10. This provides a lower-bound estimate of child immigration.[8] Of the 1,782,000 immigrants recorded as entering Canada in the 1901–11 decade, at least 120,000 would have been children younger than 10 years of age in 1911. Properly accounting for that segment of the immigrant population would entail a larger adjustment than any likely modification of the survival rates.

The more serious issue raised by McDougall was the overstatement of immigration implied by Keyfitz's use of the cumulated annual inflow of recorded immigrants. For reasons pointed out above, that is almost certainly an overstatement, and using it leads to residual estimates of emigration that look astonishingly high. McDougall substituted figures derived from European emigration statistics augmented by a crudely derived figure for migration from the United States to Canada. For the decades 1901 to 1911 and 1911 to 1921, his immigration numbers are only 67% and 80%, respectively, of the numbers used by Keyfitz. The other main contribution to this debate came from Zenon Sametz, who had long been wrestling with the issue and devoted a short section to it in a general textbook on economic geography.[9] His abbreviated treatment is not easy to follow precisely, but it seems to side with Keyfitz on the matter of survival rates. It has net migration figures that are almost identical to those of Keyfitz but offers a blend of McDougall and "official" immigration figures. More recent writers have either relied on Sametz or presented the wide range of possibilities encompassed by the Keyfitz and McDougall

---

[7] Bourbeau and Légaré, *Evolution de la mortalité*.
[8] Some immigrant children would have left before the end of the decade, and some would have died. We can use the survival ratio of children 5–9 years of age to estimate the latter.
[9] Camu, Weeks, and Sametz, *Economic Geography of Canada*, pp. 56–64.

alternatives. This section of the chapter presents a new and different accounting of Canadian population change in the early decades of the twentieth century. Before turning to that, however, it may be helpful to look to a more straightforward, if seldom-used, quantitative solution to gauging the magnitude and impact of immigration.

A more parsimonious figure for immigration to Canada can be derived from the tabulation at each census date of the immigrant population by period of arrival. This excludes immigrants who returned or moved on to the United States and also the small number who died between their time of arrival and the date of the census. The stock of the immigrant population at the end of each decade, however, represents what we really would like to know – the amount by which the enumerated population has increased through immigration. It is a meaningful and interpretable number, more so perhaps than the annually recorded inflow, and rather surprisingly it has not received much attention in the literature on immigration to Canada. The immigrant population measured in the census has the added virtue of being cross-tabulated with several other variables. Its geographic distribution is known, down to a fairly detailed level, as is its occupational distribution and its distribution by country of origin. We can gain a considerable depth of understanding from this source; hence what follows concentrates on it in and in that way seeks to bypass what has been the most contentious issue of previous studies of immigration to Canada.

Although the stock of immigrant population is most commonly examined in census date cross sections, its tabulation by period of arrival permits a retrospective reconstruction of the time pattern of immigration, as depicted in Figure 12.1 in comparison with the annual flow of recorded immigration. In each year the information is taken from the immediately subsequent census, but an annual figure can be determined only for some years; for other years the annual average over a block of several years is shown. Hence the stock-based figures are not only lower but also smooth out the extreme annual fluctuations. The temporal and regional patterns of immigration, as given by this source, are summarized in Table 12.2. The immigrant population from the most recent decennial census is shown for each of seven time periods for Canada and five regions of the country.

The years prior to World War I are divided into three sub-periods, which reveal a mounting intensity of immigration. Canada gained an immigrant population of 1.325 million in the nine years from 1906 to 1914. That would have been a little more than 20% of the population in 1906.

Table 12.2. *Immigrant population at census dates by period of arrival,*
Canada and regions, 1911–1931 (thousands)

Period	Canada	Atlantic provinces	Quebec	Ontario	Prairie provinces	British Columbia
1901–5	385.0	6.9	34.7	54.7	247.9	40.8
1906–11	828.0	15.7	63.8	163.9	457.1	127.5
1911–14	524.0	13.9	48.8	179.0	215.8	66.0
1915–18	116.0	7.0	13.0	30.7	51.3	14.1
1919–21	215.0	10.2	20.7	86.1	70.9	27.4
1921–25	280.0	8.0	33.9	120.1	82.9	35.3
1926–31	468.0	17.5	64.8	177.9	164.4	43.5

Few countries have ever experienced such an influx. The war interrupted the transatlantic flow of people, but immigration resumed at quite a high level immediately after the war. This was not a movement of displaced persons, as was seen after World War II, but mainly immigration from traditional sources, Britain and the United States.[10] The Canadian economy recovered only slowly from the severe setback it received in World War I, and that may account for the rather modest level of immigration in the early 1920s. After 1925 immigration picked up again and continued at a remarkably high pace until the onset of the Great Depression in 1930.

The "great immigration" to Canada was unquestionably related to the settlement of the western plains and the transformation of Canada into the world's leading exporter of wheat. That said, many writers have been at pains to show that immigration did not flow exclusively to the western agricultural region. Industrial development in central Canada, to whatever extent it may or may not have been indirectly associated with the Wheat Boom, also attracted many immigrants. Most striking is the fact that hardly any immigrants went to the Atlantic provinces. In the earliest sub-period, the first five years of the century, the Prairie region drew two-thirds of the immigrants. Only a decade earlier, central Canada had been an area of surplus population that was losing large numbers of emigrants to the United States. In the first stages of the boom, central Canada could readily meet increased demand for labor without having to draw heavily

[10] Part of the postwar inflow was a planned migration of demobilized servicemen from Britain whose reward for their military service was a small farm in one of the less desirable locations in Canada.

on Europe. As the boom continued, an increasing proportion of immigrants remained in Ontario. By the last period of the boom, 1911 to 1914, Ontario was absorbing almost as many immigrants as the Prairie region. The province of Quebec retained only a small share of national immigration, but about two-thirds of the immigrant population of Quebec was in the city of Montreal itself.[11] In the years following World War I immigration concentrated to a much greater extent in central Canada, mainly Ontario. By the 1920s Ontario was receiving more immigrants than the Prairie provinces. What is perhaps surprising, though, is the large number of immigrants that continued to settle in the Prairie region in the latter half of the 1920s, well after agricultural settlement had been largely completed and after there had been a substantial retreat from farming in the first half of the decade.

The most important consequence of the "great immigration" was the filling out of settlement in Canada, from coast to coast. The modern Canadian nation had begun with a small population in what is now southern Ontario and Quebec, and an even smaller population on the Atlantic coast. The greater part of the huge land mass of the nation had been added to that but at the turn of the century still had very few people. In the first two decades of the twentieth century, aided to a great extent by immigration, the completion of Canadian settlement was essentially accomplished. In 1901 fully 88% of Canada's population resided in the older regions that originally formed the country. By 1921 that had dropped to 72% and the western regions of British Columbia and the Prairie provinces accounted for more than one-quarter of the national population. That distribution is just about the same as it is today.[12]

Although there is little question that the settlement of a large tract of previously unoccupied land was at the heart of the rapid expansion of population in Canada in the early years of the twentieth century, the literature has long raised questions about how much emphasis should be placed on the rural economy per se as an attraction to immigrants. At the heart of the issue is the question: what was the distribution of immigrants between agriculture and industry and between rural and urban places? Of the immigrant population of Canada in 1921, only 43.5% were rural residents, by a definition that was closer to being the strictly farm population, at a time when 52.6% of the total population was rural. It may be

---

[11] If the greater Montreal district could be taken into account, it would encompass by far the greater part of Quebec Province's immigrants.

[12] In 1981 the western regions had 29% of the national population (see Table 12A.1).

correct in that sense to state that the immigrants were disproportionally urban, but such a statement requires two important qualifications. One is that the Canadian census definition of urban included all incorporated places of one thousand persons or more, carrying the concept of urban right down to modest villages in the countryside. The second is that the still largely rural population of eastern Canada was overwhelmingly native-born. Viewed in that light, it might be thought surprising that the proportion of immigrants that did in fact go to the rural areas was so high. Furthermore, the immigrants came not only to farm but also to fulfill the range of other activities needed to create a basically rural economy – to build and operate the transport system and the system of urban service centers. Furthermore, we should keep in mind that the new economy of western Canada also included British Columbia, where immigrants were also miners, loggers and fishermen, commonly residing in small urban centers.

The 1921 immigrant population was tabulated in the census for the 15 largest cities of Canada, cities with populations of 30,000 or more. The 649,000 immigrants in those cities accounted for 41% of Canada's immigrant population. In over half of those cities immigrants accounted for one-third or more of the total population. These were immigrant cities to an extent not seen in the United States at this time. The 15 Canadian cities and their immigrant populations are shown in Table 12.3. On the west coast, the cities of Vancouver and Victoria were more than one-half immigrant, and the cities in the Prairie provinces had proportions almost as high. In Ontario, the city of Toronto was 38% immigrant, as was the smaller industrial city of Hamilton. Clearly, then, immigration to Canada was not just a matter of agricultural settlement.

Urbanization in Canada is discussed further in a subsequent section of this chapter, but it should already be evident that the great immigration of the early years of the century substantially augmented the urban population. In 1901 only about one-third of Canada's population lived in incorporated places with more than 1,000 people; by 1931 that fraction had risen to a little more than one-half. Proportionally, the biggest increase came in the first decade of the century. One might also look at the population living in larger cities, those above 30,000 in population. That number rose by almost two and half times, from 878,000 in 1901 to 3 million in 1931. The 800,000 immigrants living in those cities in 1931 contributed a substantial fraction of that growth. If one were to add the natural increase of immigrants, it might be said that roughly one-half of the growth could be attributed to immigration.

Table 12.3. *Total and immigrant populations of larger Canadian cities, 1921*

City	Total population	Immigrant population	Percentage immigrant
Montreal	618,506	115,582	18.7
Toronto	521,893	197,125	37.8
Winnipeg	179,087	85,233	47.6
Vancouver	117,217	59,957	51.1
Hamilton	114,151	44,346	38.9
Quebec	95,193	1,846	1.9
Ottawa	107,843	18,095	16.8
Calgary	63,305	30,208	47.8
London	60,959	16,701	27.4
Edmonton	58,821	26,129	44.5
Halifax	58,372	8,996	15.5
Victoria	38,727	20,752	53.6
Windsor	38,591	10,967	28.4
Saint John	47,166	3,374	7.2
Brantford	29,440	9,312	31.7

The division between rural agricultural and urban elements in the contribution of immigrants can also be assessed through occupations. Since occupational data in the Canadian census were not cross-tabulated by period of immigration, information only on the foreign-born of all periods is available for particular occupations. However, by far the greater proportion of the foreign-born arrived between 1901 and 1921, and therefore the total of foreign-born workers is a fair indication of immigrants in that period. A selection of prominent occupations with large foreign-born representation is shown in Table 12.4. Interestingly, in 1921 almost 30% of all agricultural workers in Canada were lifetime immigrants. For farm operators, the proportion was 32%, and for farm laborers, 38%. Immigration undisputably contributed in a large way to Canada's agricultural workforce. Nevertheless, numerous nonfarm occupations had even higher foreign-born representation. Only a selection of larger occupations is presented. These are given in descending order of immigrant proportion.

In North America, janitors, miners, and railway sectionmen were occupations that traditionally drew large numbers of immigrants so it is not surprising to see them high on the list. In early-twentieth-century Canada, though, skilled occupations such as machinists, bricklayers, and painters were also heavily dependent upon immigrants. What is perhaps more sur-

Table 12.4. *Foreign-born workers in major occupations, Canada, 1921*

Occupation	Total workers	Foreign-born	Percentage foreign-born
All agricultural	1,041,618	307,632	29.5
Farmers	646,288	205,513	31.8
Agricultural laborers	170,328	64,476	37.9
Nonagricultural			
Janitors	8,619	5,252	60.9
Coal miners	22,829	13,624	59.7
Laborers in mines	9,713	5,252	54.1
Railway section and trackmen	15,760	8,226	52.2
Bricklayers and masons	8,052	3,926	48.8
Machinists	28,713	12,698	44.2
Painters	20,506	8,542	41.7
Railway office employees	17,641	6,878	39.0
Locomotive firemen	6,035	2,129	35.3
Carpenters	51,256	16,535	32.3
Loggers	32,379	9,528	29.4
Government clerks	34,613	9,814	28.4

prising is that nonproduction occupations such as office employees and government clerks also has high proportions of immigrants. The strong role of immigration in supplying labor throughout the Canadian economy is perhaps most strikingly indicated by the fact that 28% of government clerks were foreign-born. In general, the occupation data further underscore the fact that the mass immigration to Canada was more than just a matter of agricultural settlement.

The sources of Canada's immigrants in the nineteenth century were preponderantly Britain and Ireland. In the twentieth century, the mass immigration drew on new sources. Eastern Europe was the most notable. People who today are referred to as Ukrainians came both from Russia and from the Austrian Empire. They came as Galicians, Bukovinians, and Ruthenians. There were also Doukhobour, Jewish, and Orthodox Russians, some Hungarians, Rumanians, and a few Serbs. The identities changed from census to census, and it is difficult to sort out the various strands of these immigrant streams. Together they comprised the largest non-Anglo-Saxon group. They are grouped here as immigrants from Slavic Europe. Other prominent groups in the "new immigration" were

Scandinavians, many of whom moved to Canada after some years in the United States; Italians, although they made up a far smaller part of the immigration to Canada than to the United States at the time; Chinese, who concentrated initially in British Columbia; and a small number from Germany, although a larger number of German-speaking immigrants came from Austria but cannot easily be separated from the various Slavic groups.[13]

The new, nontraditional immigrants, for all the attention they have received in Canadian historical writing, were in reality the smaller part of the overall picture. About 30% of the immigrants who arrived in Canada in the period before World War I were from nontraditional sources. By far the largest number of immigrants were born in Britain, Ireland, and the United States. One of the most interesting features of the immigration to Canada in this period was the large influx from the United States. It made up one-fifth of the total flow, but one should add to the numbers of American-born some unknown number of others who had previously moved to the United States and then migrated to Canada. In the late eighteenth and early nineteenth centuries the United States had been the principal source of immigrants to Canada. In the latter half of the nineteenth century the situation was reversed. Few Americans migrated to Canada, while large numbers of Canadians emigrated to the United States. Around the turn of the twentieth century, the tide turned again. The annual inflow indicated an even larger component of American immigration, but it is believed that a large fraction returned to the United States. It is also interesting that immigration from the United States continued at a relatively high level into the years of World War I and those immediately following.

Table 12.5 shows the distribution of the 1921 and 1931 immigrant populations by period of arrival for several categories of birthplace. Only during the 1915–18 war years were fewer than half of all immigrants from Britain and Ireland. Slavic Europe provided the largest number from nontraditional sources. Immigrants from there were proportionally most numerous in the first decade of the century. In later periods the traditional sources rose in importance. Unlike the situation in the United States, where there was widespread concern about an increasing proportion of immigrants coming from nontraditional sources, the "new immigration"

---

[13] Immigrants who gave their country of origin as just Austria are grouped with the "all other" category in Tables 12.5 and 12.6.

Table 12.5. *Canadian immigrant population by country of birth and period of arrival (thousands)*

Origin	1900–10	1911–14	1915–18	1919–21	1921–31
All immigrants	742	523	116	215	749
Traditional	512	367	92	180	403
Britain and Ireland	372	283	36	130	308
United States	134	80	53	47	87
Newfoundland	6	4	3	3	8
Nontraditional	230	156	24	35	346
Slavic Europe	119	83	5	8	201
Scandinavia	28	15	4	4	56
Italy	13	12	2	6	14
Germany	8	5	—	—	19
China	13	11	4	3	4
All others	49	31	9	14	52
Nontraditional as percentage of total	31.0	29.9	20.5	16.2	46.2

to Canada was more of a passing phenomenon and did not represent a rising trend. Besides a large number of Austrians, the "all other" category included a scattering of immigrants from Belgium, the Netherlands, France, and Greece, as well as some Japanese and East Indians.

Table 12.6 presents the 1921 immigrant population by region of residence for the main regions of immigrant destination. Few immigrants moved to the Atlantic provinces and a large proportion of those who did were Newfoundlanders who mainly moved to Nova Scotia. Two-thirds of all the Newfoundland-born population in Canada were in the Atlantic provinces, and Newfoundlanders accounted for one-third of the immigrant population of the Atlantic provinces. If one abstracts from Newfoundlanders as being only "quasi immigrants," the Atlantic region appears even more bereft of an immigrant population. That region, and Quebec as well, is simply left off the table to avoid having many virtually empty cells. Attention is concentrated on the three regions that received most of the immigrants. The Prairie provinces gained the largest numbers from Slavic Europe. The prairies received two-thirds of Canada's immigrants from that region, but even then that group made up only 19% of total immigration. The Prairies got an even larger fraction of Scandinavian immigrants. The Prairie region was also the destination of

Table 12.6. *Canada's immigrants by region of residence and area of origin, 1900–1921 (thousands)*

Origin	Ontario	Prairies	British Columbia	Canada total
All immigrants	496	692	210	1,597
Traditional	396	460	154	1,152
Britain and Ireland	343	265	126	821
United States	50	194	27	314
Newfoundland	3	1	1	17
Nontraditional				
Slavic Europe	47	134	7	215
Scandinavia	5	35	8	50
Italy	17	6	4	32
Germany	2	11	1	15
China	5	7	17	30
All others	26	40	18	102

the largest number of immigrants born in the United States. Not surprisingly, British Columbia on the Pacific coast was the main recipient of immigrants from China and also from other Asian countries. Four-fifths of Ontario's immigrant population in 1921 was from traditional source countries.

FERTILITY IN CANADA, 1901–1931

By the end of the nineteenth century Canada was already well into its fertility transition. In some parts of the country marital fertility had been falling for almost half a century. That decline continued into the twentieth century, and by the early 1930s the transition had largely been accomplished. The fertility transition in Canada has not been extensively documented or explained, in part because the requisite data have not been readily at hand. At the turn of the century the collection of vital statistics in Canada was still in its rudimentary stages, so there are no reliable national records of the annual flow of births and infant deaths. By 1921, however, the collection of vital statistics under the auspices of the newly established Dominion Bureau of Statistics was well under way. By 1931 a reliable and consistent national system was fully in place. This discussion spans not just the fertility transition but a statistical transition. The main problem to be faced is that before at least the mid-1920s statistics of births and birth rates were not well established or carefully evaluated, and thus do not provide a strong base from which to construct an account of demographic change.

For decennial census years or decades centered on them, several alternative estimates of births and birth rates have been offered, notably by Nathan Keyfitz, Jacques Henripin, and Ellen Gee.[14] All three estimate only crude birth rates, but they are in some conflict over just what was the pattern of change. The earliest estimate, that of Keyfitz, depicts a birth rate that remains level from 1901 to 1921 before dropping in the 1920s. Henripin has the birth rate continuously declining, but at higher levels throughout. Gee strikes an intermediate level but follows Keyfitz in showing a flat birth rate over the first two decades of the century. All agree, and the vital statistics are adequate to support the view, that the Canadian birth rate was declining in the 1920s. There is an unresolved dispute here that it would be helpful to sort out, if that can be done. An attempt at least will be made here.

In Chapter 9 I reported estimates of fertility for Canada and several regions of the country for the census year 1891. A procedure comparable to the one used there can be followed to estimate births in the census years of the early twentieth century, and those estimates can be linked with estimates based on vital statistics for at least some provinces in 1911 and 1921. Unfortunately, one important piece of information is missing for the 1901 census year. That is the one census in which the marital status of women was not cross-tabulated by age, thus preventing a separate examination of marital and overall fertility. It limits the prospect of probing beneath the aggregate crude birth rate. Since the birth rate did not change much from 1891 to 1901, the period from 1891 to 1931 as a whole is examined here, rather than 1901 to 1931, to allow a more thorough look at the elements of change. For 1901 and 1911 estimates of births are made by applying reverse survival rates to the numbers of children enumerated in the census. That requires an assumption about the rate of infant and child survival.

Since the survival rates used for the 1891 estimates were developed from a projection of more carefully measured 1901 rates, the assumptions made for the latter year are probably quite well grounded. There was very little change in infant survival between 1891 and 1901. The survival ratios used for 1911 are more in the nature of crude interpolations. For 1921, two

---

[14] Keyfitz, "The Growth of the Canadian Population"; Henripin, *Trends and Factors*; Gee, "Early Canadian Fertility Transition."

Table 12.7. *Estimated fertility rates, Canada, 1891–1931*

| | | Fertility rate | | |
Census year	Crude birth rate	General	Marital	Percentage married
1891	32.6	134	253	53.1
1901	29.8	121	na	na
1911	30.0	125	215	58.2
1921	29.3	121	195	61.8
1931	23.2	94	159	58.7

Sources: For 1891–1911, estimated as explained in text. For 1921 and 1931, births from Statistics Canada, *Vital Statistics*; women, total, and married, 15–49 years, from decennial censuses of Canada.

estimates of the number of births can be made, one derived from the census stock of young children, using a first set of reasonably well-founded Canadian life tables to adjust them for survival, the other based on the rudimentary and probably underregistered vital statistics. These two sources are in close enough agreement that the currently "official" crude birth rate regularly cited by Statistics Canada, of 29.3 births per thousand population, can be accepted as about as the most accurate figure likely to be obtained. For all the census years except 1901, the number of births can be related to the number of married women in the reproductive ages, as well as to all women in those ages. The results of these calculations are displayed in Table 12.7.

The crude birth rate in Canada was level at about 30 per thousand population from the beginning of the century until 1921. It then dropped by 20% over the following decade. That pattern is repeated in the general fertility rate, the ratio of births to women aged 15 to 49. By contrast, the marital fertility rate, the ratio of births to married women 15 to 49 years old, shows a continuous decline. Viewed as a fall in marital fertility, then, the fertility transition in Canada continued apace. A substantial rise over the first two decades of the twentieth century in the proportion of women married arrested the fall in the crude birth rate. That appears to be in contrast to the United States, where the crude birth rate of the white population fell continuously, although the rate of decline was somewhat assuaged in the first decade of the century.[15] In Canada, the proportion

[15] At least that is the pattern given by Coale and Zelnik, *New Estimates of Fetility*.

of women 15–49 years of age who were married, widowed, or divorced, and therefore much more likely to bear children, rose from 53% in 1891 to almost 62% in 1921. It declined somewhat thereafter.

The interruption in the fall in the Canadian birth rate has been noted by previous writers but has been interpreted mainly as a break in the fertility transition.[16] That is partly because attention has been directed solely to the crude birth rate. Looking at marital fertility, there is no interruption in the decline. The explanation offered in the past has tied the flattening out of the birth rate to the great influx of immigration in the first two decades of the century. That is not, in principle, very persuasive since most of the immigrants were from Britain and the United States and would not obviously have had higher fertility than the Canadian-born population. A more probable explanation would relate the change to settlement on the western agricultural frontier and would emphasize the role of the frontier in fostering earlier marriage. While plausible, even that explanation may be weak since there are indications that nuptiality rose in the older, settled regions of the country, especially in the cities. The increase in proportions married was apparently a pervasive phenomenon of this period but one that has not been analysed and accounted for.[17]

A more detailed picture of the changing pattern of fertility in Canada in the early years of the twentieth century can be obtained from an examination of Table 12.8. It substitutes fertility rates for 1891 in place of those that cannot all be calculated for the 1901 census date and compares them with 1921 and 1931. The pattern of change over the entire period 1891 to 1931 gives a close approximation to change in the first three decades of the century, since 1901 fertility would have been only a little below that shown for 1891. Table 12.8 allows us to capture some of the effect of the difference between rural and urban residence and the difference between the areas of new settlement in the west and the older settled eastern regions. It also sheds some light on the cultural difference between francophone and anglophone populations of the country, especially the way it affected the heart of the fertility transition, the fall in marital fertility. In

[16] Besides the recent work of Gee, see the earlier studies of Tracey, "Fertility of the Population"; and Hurd, "The Decline in the Canadian Birth-Rate."

[17] In an earlier paper, I argued that the desire, especially of young adult women, to marry at earlier ages and to form households of their own, in an age when marriage was delayed as a means of controlling fertility, may have accelerated the acceptance in Canada of control of fertility within marriage. With widespread acceptance of control of fertility within marriage, couples could more readily undertake marriages at an earlier age. See McInnis, "Women, Work and Childbearing."

Table 12.8. *Indexes of fertility and nuptiality, Canadian cities and provinces, 1891, 1921, 1931*

City or province	General fertility rate			Percentage married			Marital fertility rate		
	1891	1921	1931	1891	1921	1931	1891	1921	1931
Montreal	119	103	85	.50	.56	.54	236	183	160
Toronto	99	70	60	.50	.58	.56	200	120	107
Winnipeg	120	84	53	.55	.62	.55	217	135	96
Vancouver	129	63	50	.71	.65	.61	181	97	82
Hamilton	100	81	78	.51	.63	.69	194	128	113
Ottawa	108	77	65	.48	.51	.49	223	151	133
Quebec City	133	121	116	.46	.46	.43	291	261	270
London	84	63	57	.46	.58	.57	185	110	100
Calgary	—	88	65	—	.67	.58	—	131	112
Edmonton	—	94	71	—	.67	.56	—	140	127
Halifax	98	82	83	.47	.53	.53	208	153	157
Saint John	92	77	80	.46	.54	.53	201	142	151
Kingston	101	—	73	.47	—	.55	217	—	132
Trois-Rivières	149	—	137	.51	—	.50	293	—	272
Prince Edward Island	128	116	98	.43	.54	.56	300	216	176
Residual Nova Scotia	125	121	99	.51	.58	.58	247	206	171
Residual New Brunswick	153	139	119	.52	.60	.58	291	231	204
Residual Quebec	177	161	132	.56	.57	.52	315	284	251
Residual Ontario	113	104	86	.52	.63	.63	216	166	137
Residual Manitoba	188	148	96	.66	.67	.61	284	220	157
Saskatchewan	176	132	100	.68	.76	.64	258	175	156
Residual Alberta	176	156	111	.68	.74	.68	258	213	163
Residual British Columbia	132	99	70	.74	.72	.66	178	138	106
Canada, national	134	121	94	.53	.62	.59	253	195	106

— Cannot be calculated.

anglophone Canada, that decline was very pronounced between 1891 and 1931; and, although the steepest rate of decline within the period came in the 1920s, the larger part of the overall fall had been accomplished by 1921. For Canada as a whole, and for the province of Ontario, outside of the large cities, the marital fertility rate declined 37% between 1891 and 1931. By 1931 the fertility transition had essentially been completed. A little more than 60% of the fall had occurred by 1921. In the large cities of the nation, the fertility decline was somewhat greater. In Toronto, for example, the overall decline was 47% and in Vancouver 55%. Marital fertility decline was certainly a characteristic of the cities, as we have long been led to believe, but it was not exclusively to be found there. The residual areas of provinces, apart from the larger cities, had almost as great a decline. The most rural provinces, Prince Edward Island in the east and Saskatchewan in the west, both had declines in marital fertility of 40%. Again, quite generally, the decline did not come entirely in the decade of the 1920s but earlier as well. The major exception to this general and pervasive fall in marital fertility was in the francophone areas of the country. Montreal was only about one-half francophone, but that fact largely accounts for why the drop in marital fertility was less there than in the other large cities of the nation. Quebec City and Trois-Rivières were almost wholly francophone. In both there was only the most modest downward movement of marital fertility, and the rates in 1931 remained at levels characteristic of the nineteenth century. The province of Quebec, outside of the three separately identified cities, also experienced only a small decline in marital fertility. Residual Quebec included some anglophone districts such as suburbs of Montreal and the upper Ottawa Valley and Eastern Township districts. Those regions would have accounted for a large part of the 20% fall in the marital fertility rate in residual Quebec, although there were a few francophone districts in which the fertility transition was under way by the early twentieth century.[18] In the greater part of French Canada, however, fertility remained largely undiminished. In the early years of the twentieth century the contrast in fertility between English and French Canada was probably at its peak.

The literature on the fertility transition in Canada has been mainly descriptive and has made little attempt to analyze or to provide explanations. The usual presumption is that Canadians followed patterns set in the rest of the European world and for most of the same reasons. That notion undoubtedly contains a grain of truth; nevertheless the Canadian experience offers some challenges to conventional explanations. Rural Canada seems to be surprisingly in line with the urban experience. Land-abundant, agricultural regions such as the prairie provinces had the high levels of marital fertility at the end of the nineteenth century that one might expect, but over the early years of the twentieth century they pulled sharply into line with the rest of the country. In addition, the effects of urbanization are seen in relatively small cities in Canada. With respect to fertility, the most avant-garde city in Canada was not Montreal, the country's largest city (albeit one with a large francophone population) or

---

[18] Most of these were in the Richelieu Valley, just to the east of Montreal.

Toronto, the second largest city, but the smaller western Ontario city of London. A more detailed examination of the evidence than is provided here would show that rural counties around London were also notable for low fertility and early fertility decline. There are hints of something like a western Ontario "culture" of early fertility decline. That was a region of relatively prosperous agriculture and a well-developed structure of small manufacturing cities and towns. Its population was well educated and mobile – quick to respond to economic opportunities elsewhere. The resistance of French Canada to fertility decline is better known and is certainly a prominent feature of the Canadian fertility experience. The point of interest here is that the cultural influence pervaded urban as well as rural French Canada. Again, however, a more detailed examination would turn up exceptional areas that deserve closer attention. We can say in general that French Canadian "culture" accounts for the great lag in the decline of fertility in the francophone parts of the country, but no thoroughgoing explanation has been given of just which aspects of that culture were most important.

It has already been noted that while the marital fertility rate was falling in Canada the decline in the crude birth rate was arrested in the first two decades of the twentieth century. That was almost true of the general fertility rate as well. Nationally, it dropped less than 10% between 1891 and 1921, and it is most likely that all of that decline occurred before 1901. At the same time there was a pronounced rise in nuptiality that served largely to offset the decline in marital fertility. In the city of Toronto, for example, the proportion of 15- to 49-year-old women who were ever married rose from 50% in 1891 to 58% in 1921; in Hamilton it rose from 51% to 63%. In the latter part of the nineteenth century the cities of Canada had become magnets for young, single women. If women did not marry, there was little economic opportunity for them in the countryside. Nonagricultural employment for young women was found mainly in the cities. In the early twentieth century the imbalance in economic opportunity was partly rectified while the earlier influx of young women to the cities had been absorbed into marriage and family formation. In part, then, the rise in the proportion married in the cities represented something of the completion of a transition and the resumption of a more normal relationship, but that can only have been part of the story. Nuptiality was rising in rural regions as well. In Ontario, outside the larger cities, the percentage of those married rose from 52 in 1891 to 63 in 1921 – or just about as much as in the cities. In the wholly rural province of Prince Edward Island, the proportion married had been at the remarkably low level of 43% in 1891 and rose to 54% in 1921. The fact that rising nuptiality was an integral part of change in rural Canada in the early twentieth century is a particularly interesting development and one that has gone largely unrecognized and undiscussed. A tentative interpretation is that control of fertility within marriage, which had begun early in Canada by international standards and had already become fairly widespread by the late nineteenth century, had proceeded far enough to permit some degree of abandonment of the delayed marriage practices of the nineteenth century that had been adopted largely in face of the absence of control of marital fertility.[19] Once a sufficient number of couples had learned to control fertility within marriage and had acted on their resolve to do so, it became possible for many more women to attain the socially and economically desired married state at an earlier age. Eventually, alternatives to marriage in the form of careers for women would emerge, but that is largely a development of the later years of the twentieth century. In the first two decades of the century, marital fertility was controlled to a sufficient degree to permit a reversion to earlier and more universal marriage.

By the 1920s the statistical foundation for the study of fertility in Canada had improved, and an interpretative literature based on that began to appear, most notably authored by Burton Hurd, W. R. Tracey, Robert Renee Kuczynski, and Enid Charles.[20] That literature focused mainly on cross-sectional differentials in fertility and made only a limited contribution to our understanding of the fertility transition. The most thoroughgoing study was the 1941 census monograph by Charles. The fact that it was a very complex analysis for its time and wartime delays meant that it appeared only in 1948, by which time the postwar baby boom was under way and the study seemed to be dated. Consequently, this great pioneering effort by Charles never received the attention it deserved.

Charles exploited the data of the 1941 census of Canada that asked, for the first time, the number of children ever born, and she cross-tabulated them with numerous variables. Charles made extensive use of complex cross-tabulation and also an early application of factor analysis. Unfortunately for the purposes at hand, she did not attempt to exploit the implicit time dimension but concentrated on a single cohort – married women who were 45 to 54 years of age in 1941 and would have completed their

---

[19] That is the gist of the argument developed by McInnis in "Women, Work and Childbearing."
[20] Hurd, "The Decline in the Canadian Birth Rate"; Tracey, "Fertility of the Population"; Kuczynski, *Birth Registration and Birth Statistics in Canada*; Charles, *Changing Size of the Family in Canada*.

childbearing. Those women would have been at the peak of their fertility in the 1916–26 period. They offer a good look at Canadian fertility at a time of rapid change, at a time when there were exceptionally wide differentials in fertility. Great care has to be taken in attempting to link those differentials to the causes of the ongoing decline in fertility. Nevertheless, coming as they do in the very middle of the period under consideration here, they warrant closer attention.

Charles emphasized a sociological or cultural explanation of fertility differentials. Some of the flavor of her findings can be gained from the first section of Table 12.9, drawn from her complex cross-tabulations. All of the characteristics pertain to 45- to 54-year-old married women. The group averages of children ever born ranged from 8.33 for Canadian-born, French mother tongue, Roman Catholic, rural, farm-born residents with only elementary education, down to 1.85 for Canadian-born, English mother tongue, Protestant, non-farm-born, city residents with postsecondary education, and 1.70 for their otherwise similar counterparts whose mother tongue was another European language.

Religion evidently played an important role independent of ethnicity; city dwellers had lower fertility than rural residents; there was a gradient with educational attainment as well, but it was more pronounced for French than for English. Most notable, however, are the interesting relationships in the interaction terms. Charles's results provide considerable support for the cultural or sociological explanation offered by early transition theorists, a view that has recently come back into vogue. That interpretation, however, is limited by design to variables of a cultural sort. Charles's exploration of more economic variables emphasized occupation, although she also looked at earnings, but was carried out as a parallel investigation without full cross-tabulation by cultural variables. Some glimmerings of her results may be gained from the second part of Table 12.9.

It is evident from this table that ethnicity remains a dominant influence on fertility patterns, but urban residence, advanced education, and high income can go a long way toward narrowing the differential. For French Canadians, the lowest family size was to be found among urban, well-educated, and better-off families with an average of 3.86 children. That is still almost double the family size of ethnically British women who matched in all other attributes. French women with similar characteristics but with income in the $950 to $2,950 class averaged 4.34 children. With similar income but less education, they averaged 6.28. Higher-educated,

Table 12.9. *Average number of children ever born to Canadian-born*
45- to 54-year-old women

Mother tongue	Religion	Residency	Area born	Years of schooling	Number
French	Roman Catholic	Rural	Farm	0–8	8.33
Other	Roman Catholic	Rural	Farm	0–8	6.45
English	Roman Catholic	Rural	Farm	0–8	5.68
French	Roman Catholic	City	Nonfarm	0–8	5.46
English	Protestant	Rural	Farm	0–8	3.97
English	Protestant	City	Nonfarm	0–8	2.85
English	Protestant	City	Nonfarm	9–12	2.14
English	Protestant	City	Nonfarm	>13	1.85
European	Protestant	City	Nonfarm	>13	1.70
English	Roman Catholic	City	Nonfarm	>13	2.57
English	Protestant	Rural	Farm	>13	2.70
English	Roman Catholic	City	Nonfarm	9–12	2.99
French	Roman Catholic	City	Nonfarm	>13	3.62

Ethnic background	Residency	Years of schooling	Annual income	Number
French	Rural	0–8	<$950	7.47
French	Urban	0–8	<$950	6.44
French	Rural	0–8	>$2,950	6.21
French	Rural	13+	>$2,950	4.84
French	Urban	13+	>$2,950	3.86
British	Urban	0–8	<$950	3.74
British	Urban	13+	<$950	2.54
British	Urban	13+	>$2,950	2.10
British	Rural	0–8	>$2,950	3.21
British	Urban	0–8	<$950	3.74
British	Rural	0–8	<$950	4.50
European	Rural	0–8	<$950	5.04

Source: Charles, *Changing Size of the Family in Canada*.

prosperous, British ethnic urban dwellers had by about 1920 evidently completed the fertility transition and were bearing children at the replacement level. Less education, lower income, and rural residence all restrained fertility from falling so low. That was the case for French Canadians as well, but with them culture was another important factor. For every matching category, the French ethnic group had two and a half to three more children than the British ethnic group. Charles's study provides ample identification of factors associated with lower-than-natural fertility, but a well-grounded explanation of what brought fertility down in the first place remains an issue for future research.

ACCOUNTING FOR POPULATION CHANGE, 1901–1931

It should be said at the outset that there is no unique, "correct" way to factor population change into its component elements. The main difficulty with previously published endeavors has been the ambiguity over the immigration record. The estimates of emigration are residual calculations. Inflated numbers of immigrants based on counts of those who entered the country more than once, who returned shortly to their country of origin, or who passed on quickly to the United States, have resulted in implausibly high numbers of emigrants. Keyfitz, for example, estimates that in the decade 1911–21, 1.48 million emigrants left Canada. That would amount to 18.5% of the mid-decade population, man, woman, and child. Especially in a population with one-third of its members under 15 years of age, that seems hardly plausible. Furthermore, this was from an economy that had just experienced one of the most spectacular economic booms ever seen in any country. Other problems with previous attempts at accounting for population change have included uncertainty about the course of the birth rate and the lack of a reliable life table from which to calculate mortality. None of the problems has yet been wholly solved, and more research needs to be done. That said, an alternative and in many ways more plausible accounting can be offered. It draws upon the fertility record as reported in the preceding section. It again takes a rather extreme position on the immigration record by using the stock of the immigrant population as reported in each decennial census. That number entirely nets out immigrants who entered and then left the country in the course of the decade, the issue emphasized by McDougall. This treatment is consistent with a decade-by-decade accounting. It also measures immigrants net of mortality in the course of the decade after arriving in Canada. That number would be small and furthermore is left out of the conventional life table survival calculations that operate on the initial census population. The estimates reported here are aggregate calculations that use crude death rates based on extensive experimentation with possible mor-

Table 12.10. *Components of Canada's population*
growth, intercensal decades, 1901–1931
(thousands of persons)

Component	1901–11	1911–21	1921–31
Initial population	5,371	7,207	8,788
Actual growth	1,836	1,581	1,589
Natural increase	1,232	1,298	1,391
Net migration	604	283	198
Immigration	1,214	855	748
Emigration	610	572	550

tality patterns. The crude death rate is computed from an estimate of total deaths derived from a backward projection of a 1931 Canadian life table on the basis of several alternative trends. The result is a life table for adult ages that is very close to the model life table reported by Bourbeau and Légaré.[21] Note, however, that the least sensitive element of the estimation process is the mortality assumption. All of the life tables explored in doing these calculations generate quite similar results. For 1921–31, the estimated number of deaths is almost the same as that reported by the Dominion Bureau of Statistics.[22] For the preceding decade, Keyfitz's adjustment of total deaths to account for deaths in World War I and in the influenza epidemic of 1918 is used.[23] The resulting calculations are reported in Table 12.10. The main difference from earlier studies lies in the generally lower number of immigrants and, hence, the lower level of emigration.

What stands out from this calculation is that even with more conservative figures for immigration the residual calculation of emigration remains at a very high level. The rates of emigration implied here – more than 75 per thousand population, even in Canada's period of great immigration – were exceeded only by those of Ireland, Norway, and Italy in their peak decades of emigration.[24] One might wonder whether even the estimates of Table 12.11 (see p. 570) are on the high side, yet they are well

[21] Bourbeau and Légaré, *Evolution de la mortalité*. For ages under five, the model life tables of Borbeau and Légaré do not adequately take into account the differences between Quebec and the rest of Canada.

[22] In *Vital Statistics*, annually. (As in *1961*, table D1.)

[23] Keyfitz, "The Growth of the Canadian Population," Table 4, puts the figure at 120,000.

[24] Hatton and Williamson, "International Migration," Table 1.1.

below those reported by earlier writers.[25] It is also clear that it is only in the period prior to World War I, indicated essentially by the 1901–11 estimate, that Canada had a substantial gain from immigration. In the following two decades *net* in-migration was considerably lower. It contributed only 18% of overall population growth in 1911 to 1921 and 12% in the following decade. Despite the very heavy immigration, then, the Canadian population grew mainly through natural increase.

A decade-by-decade calculation is not the only way to determine how much immigration contributed to Canada's population growth. One might also wish to make a cumulative statement to show how much it contributed over the entire 1901–31 period. This is to recognize that immigrants add not only directly to the nation's population but also through their natural increase. Over a longer span of time, then, their cumulative effect may be greater. A crude calculation can be made by applying the rate of natural increase used in the earlier reported estimate to the 1901 population of Canada and asking how that compared with the actual 1931 population. Total growth was actually 5 million; natural increase of the initial population might have generated an increase of 3.2 million. By that calculation, immigrants and their children would have contributed 36% of the growth of the Canadian population. That is high in comparison with other countries, but it still leaves the natural increase of the initial population as the larger element in total growth. Alternatively, one could add to the 2.052 million Canadians of 1931 who had immigrated since 1901 an estimate of the children they might have had if their fertility rates were the same as the national average. That would add an almost equivalent number and make the immigrant contribution 39% of total population growth over the period. A difficulty with this sort of calculation is that it takes no account of emigration from Canada. One can hardly assume that Canadians of 1901 would not have emigrated and added their own natural increase to the population of the United States rather than Canada. That would increase the quantitative importance of immigration to Canada. What, however, should be assumed about emigration? Was it entirely independent of immigration? Canadian writers in the earlier years of this century, most notably Arthur Lower, espoused a displacement

---

[25] The present estimates are not easily reconciled with intercensal changes in the number of Canadian-born residing in the United States. The latter are well below what is implied. The large number of Canadians residing in the United States in 1900 would have been subject to high mortality because of their older ages, but that still might not be enough to effect a reconciliation.

thesis.[26] They argued that in the absence of large-scale immigration many fewer Canadians would have left for the United States. That argument has since been discredited to a considerable extent. It was thought to have too much of a flavor of nativist, anti-immigrant sentiment. It has never been subjected to a really thorough assessment, although one careful study found that for the 1901–11 decade there was substantial support for the displacement idea, although only for the skilled segment of the Canadian labor force, not for the more numerous unskilled workers. This is a point that still needs to be sorted out. If one were to accept the rather rough estimates made previously – that, including the natural increase of immigrants, somewhat more than one-third of Canada's population growth between 1901 and 1931 could be attributed to immigration – and to make a crude judgmental allowance for the fact that some amount of immigration would have been needed to replace Canadians who would have emigrated regardless of the actual immigration, it might not be too far off the mark to conclude that almost one-half of Canada's population growth over the first three decades of the century could be attributed to immigration. That is partly because the greatest inflow came early in the century, giving the longest period of time for immigrants to contribute to population growth through their own natural increase.

URBANIZATION IN THE GREAT IMMIGRATION PERIOD, 1901–1931

Over the course of the twentieth century, Canada has been transformed from a largely rural to a largely urban nation, much as the United States has. A large part of that change had been accomplished by 1931, the end of the period under consideration here. Indeed, the very first decade of the century witnessed the greatest shift of all from rural to urban population, at a time when masses of immigrants were moving to rural Canada. The nation had only a few cities at the beginning of the century, but those cities grew rapidly and the number of cities also increased substantially. By 1931 the composition of today's Canadian urban system had been established.

For the purposes of this discussion the urban population of Canada is treated in three categories: "metropolitan Canada," defined as the Census

---

[26] Lower, "The Case Against Immigration."

Metropolitan Areas of 1981 so long as they had at least 25,000 people in the year considered; "major urban," defined as all centers of 25,000 or more, including the CMAs; and "broad urbanization," defined here to match the American census definition of urban as population in places of 2,500 or more. The standard Canadian definition includes persons in incorporated places of 1,000 or more. A case might be made that in the smaller Canadian economy and society towns of less than 2,500 might still be urban in the sense that the American definition attempts to convey. It is a qualification that cannot be pursued here, and the American definition is adopted for the sake of convenience. Numerically it makes little difference, and urban populations by either definition track each other quite closely. The driving element in growth is the large cities, metropolitan Canada. The urban population of Canada and its composition in terms of these three components is shown for four pivotal census dates in Table 12A.2. Of the 23 metropolitan districts resent in 1981, only 11 had passed the 25,000 mark in population by 1901. Those 11 housed one-fifth of the nation's population. There were no other cities with more than 25,000 population. The United States in 1900 had 160 such cities, containing 26% of the national population. In terms of "major urbanization," then, Canada lagged behind the United States but not by much. By 1931 all but one of the late-twentieth-century metropolitan districts of Canada had passed the 25,000 mark, and the metropolitan population was 38.7% of the national total.[27] In 1931 Canada had four additional cities with more than 25,000 people so the measure of "major urbanization" was 40.2%. That brought Canada abreast of the United States, which in 1930 had 40.0% of its population living in cities of more than 25,000 people.

Returning to the situation in Canada at the beginning of the century, it may be stretching a bit to think of even one-fifth of the population as residing in metropolitan districts. Strictly speaking, they were more "metropolitan-to-be." The metropolitan description certainly fit Montreal and Quebec City. Although the latter had barely 100,000 people, it did have a considerable suburban buildup beyond the central city. Toronto had no more than 10% of its population outside the city itself. London and Hamilton were limited almost entirely to their central cities. Halifax and Saint John did have outlying, ex-urban communities, largely by virtue of their harbor locations, but those cities were small, with only 51,000 and 49,000 people, respectively. New Westminster has been grouped here with

---

[27] The exception was Sudbury, the mining and smelting center in northern Ontario, which still had only 22,000 people.

Vancouver in 1901, even though it was still a distinctly separate and relatively distant town. In a sense, then, the numerical statistic probably overstates the metropolitan extent of Canada in 1901.

The 40% "major urban" statistic for Canada in 1931 more realistically reflects the state of affairs at that time. The 22 metropolitan districts made up 38.7 points of that figure and, even if some of them were still fairly small, they had more of the sense of metropolitan places. Toronto had developed an extensive suburban structure, as had Vancouver and Winnipeg. Ottawa included a sizable area across the river in the province of Quebec. Kitchener and St. Catharines made it onto the list only by virtue of being composites of several cities and towns. By 1931, there were 26 cities in Canada with a population more than 25,000, up from 11 in 1901. The population of those cities had increased by 178% over the three decades. Three-quarters of that growth came in the 11 original metropolitan areas which doubled their population. The most interesting point is that by the measure of "major urbanization" (population in cities of 25,000 or more) Canada had become as urbanized as the United States. Admittedly, even its largest cities were still smaller than those of the United States, but then the nation's population was less than 10% of that of its neighbor to the south (8.4%, to be precise).

Unlike many countries, Canada has not had a single dominant metropolis. The two largest centers, Montreal and Toronto, have been of almost comparable size. Toronto has grown more rapidly over the course of this century. Starting at only 70% the size of Montreal, the Toronto Metropolitan Area today exceeds that of Montreal in population, but not greatly. Toronto grew more rapidly than Montreal between 1901 and 1931 and by the latter date had reached 80% of Montreal's population. Canada's major cities have essentially been ports. As an inland port, on the same lake and river system as Montreal, Toronto in the nineteenth century started out being subsidiary to Montreal. The latter was the leading commercial center of the nation until some time in the twentieth century. In addition, in the latter half of the nineteenth century Montreal reinforced its position as the predominant Atlantic port of the nation even though it was more than a thousand miles from the ocean. Prior to the middle of the nineteenth century, Quebec City had been the principal Atlantic port, but Montreal assumed that role after the river channel was dredged to allow ocean ships to reach it. Had Montreal been the leading port from the outset and not had to share economic function with Quebec City, it might have established a position of dominance early on. Quebec languished for almost one hundred years after Montreal usurped its seaport function and, economically, Quebec became decidedly subsidiary to Montreal.

Canada's eastern cities lined up at increasing distances from the ocean. That was in contrast to the United States, which had an array of port cities up and down the coast. Halifax and Saint John were the small port cities of the small economies of the Atlantic provinces, a region that came to be integrated only slowly into the rest of the Canadian economy, and that only in the twentieth century. The main body of the Canadian economy was served by Montreal. However, its competitor, Toronto, was the leading urban center of the more vibrant region of the Canadian economy and eventually came to be the metropolitan focus of industrial Canada. Winnipeg was, in effect, the eastern port of the Prairie "island," although it was connected to the actual maritime port at Thunder Bay by 400 miles of rail line. The port function on the western frontier of the Prairie "island" was shared between Calgary and Edmonton largely because there were two rail lines through two mountain passes. Vancouver differed from the American Pacific ports in having almost no immediate hinterland. Although Canada's Pacific economic relations remained fairly limited, Vancouver was perhaps less a port city than a commercial center for the lumber industry of British Columbia. With the opening of the Panama Canal, however, Vancouver's position as Canada's western port was greatly enhanced, and it continued to be the only major city on Canada's Pacific coast. Victoria attained city status by virtue of being the provincial capital, but its island location prevented it from ever being a real contender with Vancouver for major metropolitan status. Functionally, the Canadian metropolitan system consisted of nodes on an essentially linear economy, with a few offshoot manufacturing cities in Ontario. Only in the sparsely settled Prairie region was there much of a north-south dimension. Overall, the Canadian urban system divided economic function in a way that precluded the emergence of a single dominant metropolis.

By the broadest measure of urbanization – population in centers of 2,500 or more – Canada still lagged behind the United States. At the beginning of the century, 28.7% of Canada's population was urban by that definition. By 1931 the proportion had risen to 49.7%, but the United States in 1930 had 56.0% of its population in centers of 2,500 or more. The growth in Canada was especially pronounced in the 5,000 to 25,000 category. Many smaller towns stagnated or even declined in population. That was especially the case in the province of Ontario, which at the turn of the century had the most extensive structure of smaller towns.

An interesting feature of urban structure in Canada was the paucity of smaller urban places (less than 25,000) in the province of Quebec. It had only 14 such centers in 1901, with a combined population of 66,000 – only 4% of the province's population. By contrast, Ontario had 50 such centers with 257,000 people, making up 12% of the province's total population. In addition, more of Ontario's towns were in the 5,000 to 25,000 range. Ontario had developed an array of smaller urban manufacturing centers of a sort that was notably lacking in Quebec. Urbanization in Quebec meant essentially Montreal and Quebec City. By North American standards, that was a truncated and underdeveloped urban system. It underscores just how very rural Quebec society was outside of the metropolitan area of Montreal.

Western Canada had just begun to be settled and still had only nascent urban places. The Atlantic provinces did not have large cities, but they had a fairly well developed urban structure. With only half the population of Quebec, the region had a larger absolute number of people living in towns and cities of 2,500 to 25,000 population than did Quebec. The proportion of population in the Atlantic provinces in urban centers of that size was almost as high as in Ontario.

Over the 1901–1931 period Quebec was catching up with the rest of Canada in smaller-level urbanization. The population in that category grew by two and one-half times, and its proportion of the provincial total doubled. This development had two components. In the long-settled agricultural districts, service centers and small manufacturing towns emerged – places such as Joliette, St. Jerome, Drummondville, and East Angus. Industrial towns also emerged on the natural resource frontier – LaTuque, Shawinigan Falls, Thetford Mines. The upshot was that by 1931 Quebec had acquired a more substantial network of smaller urban centers. In Ontario, the 1901–31 period saw a polarization within the established system. Some of the older towns, especially the larger ones, grew quite rapidly: for example, Sarnia increased by 118%, Guelph by 83%, and Stratford by 78%. On the other hand, many of the smaller established urban places stagnated or even declined. Those that experienced an absolute decline included Almonte, Arnprior, Prescott, and Picton. Other well-established towns remained stagnant over the three decades – places such as Strathroy, Lindsay, Goderich, and Carleton Place. Like Quebec, Ontario saw substantial communities arise on the natural resource frontier: Cobalt, Timmins, Fort Francis, Sturgeon Falls, and, most notable of all, the great nickel mining and smelting center of Sudbury, which would eventually attain the status of a metropolitan area.

Apart from the places that would eventually grow into metropolitan areas, very few of those in Western Canada had even reached the 2,500 level in 1901 – in Manitoba, the market towns of Brandon and Portage la Prairie; and in British Columbia, the mining towns of Nanaimo, Nelson, and Rossland. There were as yet no centers even of that size in the great agricultural region that was to become the provinces of Alberta and Saskatchewan. Between 1901 and 1931, a system of smaller urban places came into being in the prairie region alongside the leading cities. They were mostly rural service and railway marshaling centers: Dauphin, Weyburn, Moose Jaw, and Lethbridge.

All the standard sources on this period note that the largest recorded increase in the urban proportion of Canada's population occurred between 1901 and 1911.[28] By the broad definition used here, the urban share of the population rose from 28.7% to 37.2%. That happened in a decade when the rural population posted a large increase as well, as the process of settlement of the Canadian west was at its peak. That process created a whole new economy in the Canadian west, from the ground up as it were, along with its appropriate structure of urban places. Winnipeg and Vancouver had already come into being and by 1901 were cities of considerable size. Other cities just coming into existence would eventually become the metropolitan areas of the region – Calgary, Edmonton, Regina, and Saskatoon – but there was a network of smaller cities as well, although only a portion of those had reached a threshold size by 1911. Then there was a myriad of new smaller towns, such as Russell, Manitoba; Camrose, Alberta; and Biggar, Saskatchewan (which proudly declared at the entrance to town, "New York may be big but this is Biggar").

This new urban structure in the west was far from the whole story. The large cities of central Canada were growing rapidly as well. Even the otherwise lagging Atlantic region experienced rapid urban growth, slightly more rapid, in fact, than the rate in central Canada. Of the total increase in urban population, 60% came in the 11 metropolitan regions already established in 1901; their population increased by 59%. The total number of cities larger than 25,000 rose to 19. The 8 nonmetropolitan centers had an increase in population of 185% over the decade and accounted for 15% of total urban growth. Most of those, however, were the new cities of the

---

[28] See, for example, Stone, *Urban Development in Canada*; or McVey and Kalbach, *Canadian Population*, chap. 6.

west. The smaller urban centers, those in the 2,500 to 25,000 class, had a lower rate of population increase in this decade, but it was still a healthy 49% and the growth of this group accounted for one-quarter of all the urban population growth between 1901 and 1911.

THE INTERLUDE OF THE 1930s

By 1930 the era of mass immigration to Canada had come to an end. Canada, like the United States, had fallen into a deep economic depression – the worst ever experienced. Immigration dropped precipitously, from a little over 100,000 in 1930 to 27,500 in the following year, and from there on down to a low of just over 11,000 in 1935. Economically depressed, Canada had ceased to be an attractive destination for migrants. At the same time, emigration from Canada to the United States, which had been running at 75,000 to 80,000 per year in the late 1920s, also dropped to next to nothing. Judged in terms of unemployment, the depression was even more severe in the United States, so there was little to attract Canadians south of the border. International migration ceased to be a significant factor in Canadian demographic development.

By the 1930s the birth rate in Canada had also fallen to a low level. With the crude birth rate down to barely 20 per thousand over most of the decade, the fertility transition was seemingly over. There were still a few pockets of high fertility in various parts of the country, but numerically they were not important. The crude birth rate dropped from 23.2 in 1931 to 21 in 1933, and it remained low until the outbreak of World War II at the end of the decade. The death rate settled at a low, fairly stable level of 10 per thousand. As the next section explains, little happened to bring about further reductions in mortality until after 1940. In general, the 1930s were noted for their demographic quiescence. Over the decade the total population of the nation grew by only 10.9%, the lowest growth of any decade in the twentieth century.

Although the birth rate was low, and remained low, one might wonder whether conditions of economic depression were pushing it any lower. The answer is yes, but in an interesting way. One might have thought that the depressed economy would have deterred marriages and that fertility might have fallen because of the postponement of marriage. That does not appear to have been the case. The crude rate of marriages per thousand

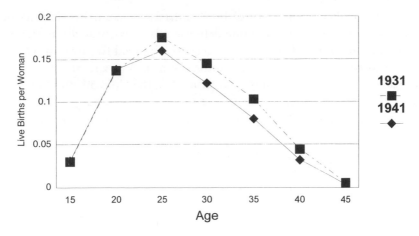

Figure 12.2. Age-specific fertility rates, Canada, 1931 and 1941

population was already low at 6.4 by 1931 and fell to just 5.9 in 1932. Thereafter it drifted upward, reaching 7.9 in 1938, and it shot up to 10.8 in 1940 (but that involves World War II and is another story). Canadians evidently were taking the advice of a popular American song of the time.[29] At the same time, the total fertility rate continued to fall, from 3,200 in 1931 to a low of 2,646 in 1937. That drop of 17% is hardly trivial. The important point is that Canadians in the depressed 1930s were adjusting their birth rates by controlling fertility within marriage – a good indication that this had become a thoroughgoing contracepting society by the time. This was well before the era of modern, highly efficient contraceptives. It had become widely the case that even under conditions of severe economic depression Canadians were able and willing to continue marrying yet control their fertility within marriage.[30] The age-specific patterns of fertility in Canada in 1931 and 1941 are compared in Figure 12.2. What is portrayed there to some extent minimizes the change, since fertility had already begun to swing upward by the time of the census of 1941. Nevertheless, it shows that there was virtually no change in fertility at the youngest ages. The big drop occurred in the rates for women over 30 years of age. Again, that reinforces the conclusion that the main downward adjustment in fertility was coming within marriages. Canada went to war

---

[29] "Potatoes are cheaper, tomatoes are cheaper; now's the time to fall in love."

[30] This is stated, perhaps with some reflective bias, by an author who in 1938 was the first-born of a marital union formed in 1933.

in 1939, two years in advance of the United States, and the outbreak of war not only ended the economic depression but also brought a surge in marriages and births. The crude marriage rate jumped from 7.9 in 1938 to 10.8 in 1940; the birth rate rose from 20.6 in 1939 to 24.2 in 1943. That Canada mobilized and went to war earlier than the United States provides an opportunity to examine whether it was war or the end of the depression that most affected the demographic situation, a point pursued later in this chapter.

As with the United States, Canada had in the 1930s both an industrial depression and a crisis in its agricultural economy. The latter faced both depressed prices and dust-bowl conditions in the Plains region. The agricultural crisis in Canada was both more important and longer lasting than in the United States. The worst dust-bowl conditions in the Canadian prairie region came in 1937, late in the depression years. On the other hand, the industrial regions of Canada, while hard hit, probably did not suffer quite as severely as those of the United States, where unemployment soared to even higher levels. An important point to remember, especially when tracing demographic implications, is that many of those who continued to be employed through the depression did not experience declines in real incomes. Prices fell as fast as or faster than wages. Young people who had recently moved into the industrial cities were able to seek refuge with their families in rural areas. There, at least, they could find housing, food crops, fish, and firewood. What this meant demographically is that there was also a quiescence of internal migration. City growth slowed notably. The Atlantic region, which had been an area of heavy emigration in the 1920s, ceased to lose people but thereby stored up an adjustment problem for future years. Quebec cities barely retained their natural increase, which was admittedly higher than in the rest of the country. Toronto, Hamilton, and London – the major cities in Ontario – probably did not even retain their natural increase. Winnipeg's population remained constant, and even Vancouver grew by barely 10%. Rural-to-urban migration had essentially ground to a halt. Similarly, interregional migration dropped to a low level. In the Prairie region, people were driven off their drought-besieged farms, but they had nowhere promising to go. Only British Columbia, which began to give indications of its future as the destination of many economic refugees from the Prairie provinces, grew substantially more than would have resulted from its natural increase. With the lowest birth and death rates in the nation, British Columbia's population increased by almost 18% over the decade.

MORTALITY DECLINE IN CANADA, 1901–1981

There is no natural break in Canadian mortality history, so the entire 80 years under examination in this chapter are considered here apiece. Broadly speaking, the record is one of generally falling mortality throughout the entire period. The reasons for and the immediate source of the mortality decline varied over time, however, and that is the main concern here. It should also be pointed out that prior to the establishment of reliable national collection of vital statistics in the years following World War I, Canadian mortality records are of dubious quality and not much explored. The lack of readily available, reliable statistics of mortality at the beginning of the twentieth century has diverted attention from this feature of Canadian demographic development.

The Canadian census of 1901 collected an abundance of information on mortality, with all the limitations of that kind of source, although it is probably about as good as that sort of mortality data can be. Nevertheless, deaths would have been undercounted for well-known reasons, especially for young, single adults and for the elderly. With care and some adjustment and integration with such vital registration data as existed at the time, the census data contribute to synthetic estimates of rates of infant mortality. The same data also give an indication of the relative importance of some of the prominent and better-diagnosed causes of death. By the turn of the century several provinces had systems of death registration in place, enforced by legal requirements of permits for burials. These systems were still developing, however, and had not been perfected. What is most noticeable is that a few districts, often in the more remote, outlying areas, had manifestly defective returns. The more serious difficulty lies in obtaining population counts by age for the set of districts with reasonably reliable reporting of deaths so that rates of mortality can be calculated. Until much more careful research is undertaken, we can say very little about Canadian mortality at the outset of the twentieth century. Table 12A.1 gives estimates of several measures for 1901: an infant mortality rate, a crude death rate, and the expectation of life at three key ages. However, these estimates should be regarded, as little more than a rough indication of mortality at the time.

For what they may be worth, these estimates point to a crude death rate in Canada in 1901 of 14.4. That number is probably a lower bound of the range of possibilities, but it fits consistently with other calculations made in this chapter. It would imply a lower death rate in Canada than in the United States at the time, which might be consistent with the more rural nature of the Canadian population and the smaller sizes of the main cities. The cooler Canadian climate may also have freed the country from some of the diseases prevalent in the American South. On the other hand, two important sources of mortality point toward higher death rates in Canada. One is infant mortality, the other tuberculosis. Although a definite comparison cannot be made, it appears that Canada had a higher death rate from tuberculosis than the United States, at a time when that disease was one of the foremost causes of death. The estimate given here of the Canadian average rate of infant mortality in 1901 – 139 deaths per thousand live births – is above the rate for the white population of the United States in 1900. Francophone Canadians, about one-quarter of the nation's population, had notably high infant mortality. In the cities of Quebec and Montreal, one infant in four did not reach its first birthday. As one observer dramatized it, the rate of infant mortality in Canada's largest city, Montreal, was about comparable to that in Calcutta. Shocking though that may be, large cities around the world had high rates of infant mortality. What is even more intriguing, however, is that rural areas of the province of Quebec also had high rates of infant deaths. In some purely rural counties the rate may have reached 200 or more. Rates of infant mortality for anglophone Canadians, by contrast, appear to have been commensurate with those of adjacent areas of the United States. For the province of Ontario, the 1901 rate of infant mortality was an estimated 117; for Quebec 186. For the nation as a whole, on a somewhat shakier basis, the rate is placed at 139 per thousand births.

What we do know is that the high rates of infant mortality in French Canada reflected in particular the large number of deaths in the summer months from diarrhea and enteritis – which are indicative of unsanitary feeding of babies. It appears that French Canadians were not breast feeders and that their infants suffered accordingly. In 1901 infectious diseases still took a large toll on infants and young children. Immunization programs lagged, particularly in Quebec, and in 1900 there was great concern over an outbreak of smallpox. By the second decade of the twentieth century, rates of infant mortality in Canada had begun to come down rapidly, very much in line with the experience of the United States and ostensibly for much the same reasons. Water and milk supplies, especially in the cities, were made safer, and cleanliness in the handling of babies was promoted through education. What is most interesting, though, is that infant mortality rates were also falling in rural areas. For example, between 1901 and 1931 the rate of infant mortality fell by 35% and 40%, respectively, in the Ontario counties of Grey and Prince Edward. These were both very largely rural counties that already had relatively low rates of infant mortality at the turn of the century. Researchers have some idea of why infant mortality fell in the cities, but there is much yet to be learned about the course of events in the rural districts. In the city of Toronto the timing of the decline in infant mortality was closely associated with two developments, the chlorination of the water supply and the requirement that milk sold in the city be pasteurized. Since these changes occurred close together, it is difficult to sort out the separate effects, but there are indications that chlorination may have played a larger role than pasteurization. It is also important to note that infant mortality continued to decline through the 1920s. By 1931 the rate of infant mortality in a by then well-monitored Canada from the point of view of vital statistics stood at 86 per thousand births. That remained well above the 60 per thousand for the white population of the United States, but the rate of infant mortality in the Canadian province of Quebec was, as late as 1931, still above 100. The story in brief, then, is that infant mortality was falling in the early twentieth century in Canada, as it was in the United States, but that the higher level of infant mortality among French Canadians kept Canada at a higher level than the United States. After 1931 Canada caught up with the United States. The rate of infant mortality in Canada was cut in half between 1931 and 1951, and the decline continued thereafter. By 1981, with an infant mortality rate of less than 10 per thousand births, Canada had one of the lowest rates in the world.

The progress of mortality decline over the course of the century can be summarized by estimates of the increase of expectation of life. Table 12A.1 shows three values for the life expectancy of females at each of four census dates. In addition to the commonly observed expectation of life at birth, values are given at ages 10 and 40. The objective is to abstract from the effects of infant and early childhood deaths and then to focus on mortality reduction at older ages. As has been observed for many other countries in the twentieth century, the overall gain in life expectancy has been greater at birth than at older ages, and proportionally the greatest gain came in the early twentieth century when infant mortality was declining from high levels. Interestingly, the expectation of life at age 40 rose by more than one-third over the 80-year period, from 29.9 to 40.7. More-

Table 12.11. *Comparative cause-specific death rates,*
Canada, 1901–1981 (per 100,000 population)

Cause	1901	1931	1951	1981
Tuberculosis	178.0	73.4	24.2	0.8
Influenza and pneumonia	190.5	49.6	38.9	18.9
Diabetes	46.9	12.3	11.3	12.1
Violent death	60.7	69.1	48.5	63.8

Sources: For 1901, Census of Canada, 1901. For 1931, 1951, 1981,
Statistics Canada, *Vital Statistics*.

over, the gain was continuous over all the periods. It was not concentrated
in the years since 1951, when medical advances have been so prominent.
The pattern may be a reminder of the importance of the decline in deaths
from tuberculosis in a society in which that disease was a leading cause of
death. It would be interesting to give greater attention to changes in deaths
from individual causes. There are severe limits to what can be done along
that line because of changes over time in the reporting and classification
of deaths. Table 12.11 shows cause-specific rates of death per hundred thousand population for four causes that can be tracked with reasonable confidence over the entire 80-year period. These are tuberculosis, diabetes,
influenza, and pneumonia; violent deaths are also included. Tuberculosis
ranked just below influenza and pneumonia as a leading cause of death in
the 1901 census tables, although one has to wonder whether some deaths
from lung conditions may have been mistakenly identified as tuberculosis. An overstatement of deaths from that cause might explain why deaths
from tuberculosis appear to have declined so drastically between 1901 and
1931. By contrast, it seems surprising that over the period 1931 to 1951,
encompassing the introduction of antibiotics, the mortality rate declined
so little. Medical advance is more clearly seen in the 1951–81 period when
the death rate from influenza and pneumonia was cut about in half. The
death rate from diabetes, though much lower than that from the two foregoing diseases, declined fairly sharply in the first period, as might have
been expected when insulin treatment was introduced. Since 1931 the
death rate from diabetes has remained about the same. It is notable that
there has been no long-term reduction in the rate of violent deaths. Accidental deaths were quite prevalent in early-twentieth-century Canada. It

appears that some progress was made toward the middle of the century, but that has been reversed in the years since 1951, mainly because of the increased incidence of death from automobile accidents.

THE FERTILITY SWING IN POST–WORLD WAR II CANADA

At first glance, the pattern of Canadian fertility in the years since 1940 looks much like that of the United States. It has been common to link the baby boom and baby bust experiences of the two countries. Closer examination, however, will reveal some interesting differences in the experiences of Canada and the United States. As Figure 12.3 shows, the falling total fertility rate that reached a low point in both countries in the mid-1930s reversed at the end of that decade and moved sharply upward during the war years. Immediately after the end of the war, both countries recorded an especially sharp spike in the total fertility rate – the first indication of a postwar baby boom – although in 1948 the rate settled at a plateau that was just a little above the level attained before the Great Depression of the 1930s. In 1951 the total fertility rate again began to climb, marking the onset of the classic baby boom about which so much has been written. The peak was reached in the United States in 1957; in Canada the absolute maximum was reached in 1959, but the 1957 value of the total fertility rate was so close to the 1959 figure that it is accurate enough to say that both countries reached peak fertility at the same time. The peak in Canada was at a higher level than in the United States, but Canadian fertility had historically been above the American level and the differential in 1957 was narrower than it had previously ever been. From the peak in 1957 the drop in fertility gained pace, and by 1962 the total fertility rate was plummeting in both countries. The fall in Canada was even more precipitous than in the United States, and by 1968 fertility in Canada had fallen below the rate in the United States. The Canadian rate has continued to be lower right up to the present. By 1981 the total fertility rate in Canada stood at only 1.70, compared with 1.82 in the United States, and far below the 3.20 of 1931 or the 3.50 of 1951. Over a few short years there had been a veritable revolution in fertility. Since the mid-1970s reproduction in Canada has been continuously below what is regarded as the replacement level.

The close correspondence of timing of fertility change in the two

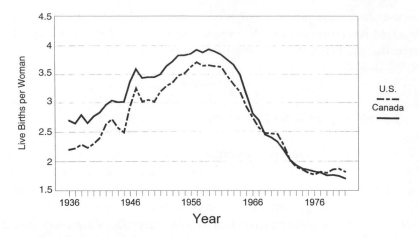

Figure 12.3. Total fertility rates, Canada and the United States, 1936–1981

countries and the fact that the dimensions of the change were broadly similar have given strength to a presumption that Canada and the United States shared a basically similar social phenomenon. The general impression given by most writing on the topic is that the baby boom was a ubiquitous development throughout northern America. That in turn has given impetus to a search for common causes. The same can be said for the drastic fall in fertility after 1960. The more intensive look at Canadian fertility history that follows raises some doubts about that portrayal. One cannot at this juncture substantiate a claim that the fertility experience of Canada in the period since 1940 differed fundamentally from that of the United States. There are nevertheless points of difference that deserve emphasis. Unfortunately, the literature on fertility patterns in Canada is much thinner than that for the United States, both analytically and even descriptively, and that limits any ability to reach firmly supported conclusions.

In 1957, at the peak of the baby boom in Canada, the total fertility rate was 48% higher than what it had been 20 years earlier at the depth of the Great Depression, when fertility was at its low point. That was a smaller rise than the 68% recorded in the United States. It should be emphasized that the larger part of the increase in Canada had been accomplished by 1946. The total fertility rate (TFR) rose 27.5% between 1937 and 1946; in the United States that gain was also somewhat larger, at 33%. After the temporary spike in 1947, fertility in both countries sat at a plateau until

1951, when, once again, it began to rise. Annual data on Canadian fertility and related measures for the years 1946 through 1981 are provided in Table 12.A.3. The fertility rise of the 1950s in Canada was only a further 13.6% above the 1946 base. This baby boom, upon which so much attention has been showered, measured comprehensively by a period rate, seems hardly to have been such a profound change. In the United States, the 1950–57 increase in the total fertility rate was somewhat greater, at 22.8%. Furthermore, the "boom" that everyone talks about was of merely seven years' duration. Two observations seem to be worth emphasizing: the rise in fertility came in two phases, one before 1946 and one after 1950, separated by several years of stability; and the first of those phases involved the greater increase in fertility. The latter point requires some elaboration. It would be widely acknowledged that at least part of the earlier phase of fertility increase should be attributed to recovery from an unusually low situation, brought about by the severely depressed economy. Recovery to the predepression level would take account of the greater part of the increase in fertility that occurred during World War II. However, fertility had been on a long downward trend prior to 1931, so in the absence of depression in the economy one still might have expected fertility to have continued to fall. What should be taken as the appropriate base against which to measure the baby boom?

It may be pure coincidence but is nevertheless intriguing that a projection of the downward linear trend of the total fertility rate in Canada between 1901 and 1931 gives an estimated figure for 1981 that is almost identical to what was actually recorded. Indeed, although fertility rose well above that trend line and then fell sharply back toward it, by 1971 fertility in Canada resumed the same downward trend it had been on in the first three decades of the century and steadily followed that trend, at just a slightly lower level, until the end of our period (see Figure 12.4). Nothing too profound should be read into this, and there are good reasons for not believing that it provides a representation of some deep, underlying trend in Canadian fertility. For one thing, no one expects fertility to decrease linearly forever. The usual presumption, surely, is that it would flatten out at some post-transition equilibrium level. Indeed, that is closer to what has happened in Canada in the years since 1981. That level has been well below the replacement level of fertility. In 1931 the most that people might have expected would be that fertility might continue to decline to about the replacement level and that the total fertility rate might flatten out at approximately 2.0. That sort of alternative depiction of the trend of fer-

Figure 12.4. Actual and trend total fertility rates, Canada, 1901–1981

tility can be drawn but, at the scale permitted here, cannot clearly be distinguished from the linear trend shown in Figure 12.4. Neither conception of the trend should be taken too seriously, but either one might give some indication of an immediate post-depression, expected level of fertility. In fact, it does not matter which of the trends one selects. Both would imply that Canada's TFR reattained its trend level in 1942. By that standard, the slightly more than 10% increase in fertility between 1937 and 1942 would be the "recovery" from depression, and the overall dimension of the baby boom, in terms of TFR, would be a rise of one-third (32.8% between 1942 and 1957). That is a substantial enough increase to reestablish the fertility rise as a social event of considerable importance. It remains the case, however, that almost half of the upsurge occurred before 1946, during the war rather than afterward. Between 1942 and 1946 the total fertility rate rose by 13.9%; between 1946 and 1957 it rose 16.6%. Recalling that the two phases were separated by a period of several years of stability, one might think the search for causes should also be separated into two phases.

One small point that might be raised about the beginning of the upsurge (or "recovery") is whether it had to do with war and mobilization or with the upturn in the economy. In the United States the most pronounced jump in fertility came between 1941 and 1942, after that country had declared war. In Canada that, too, was the largest rise in any year of the period, but Canada had gone to war in 1939. In Canada there was a perceptible increase in fertility between 1939 and 1940 but, following the pattern of the United States, the larger rise came when the United States went to war after 1941, and presumably the whole North American economy shifted gears.

People should have been surprised at the thought that Canada would have followed the United States all that closely in the baby boom. A substantial part of the Canadian population – French Canada, or at least the rural segment of it – probably did not have a baby boom at all. As late as 1930 the fertility of the French Canadian population remained high by North American standards. About all that happened in rural French Canada is that the fall in fertility might have been arrested for a few years. The French comprised a numerically significant part of the Canadian population so the foregoing points to at least one reason why Canada should have had a less pronounced baby boom than did the United States. More generally, though, the geography of the baby boom has received little attention. To look at it in any detail requires statistical data that are not usually available. A serious limitation to the use of detailed geographic data on fertility in Canada is that prior to the end of World War II Canadian birth registrations were tabulated according to where births occurred, rather than according to the place of residence of parents. Even at the provincial level, that raised some complications, but it seriously contaminated data for more geographically detailed districts. For her 1941 census monograph, Enid Charles had a special tabulation made of 1940–42 births by place of residence of parents, and it provides the basis for reported gross reproduction rates (GRRs) by city and county across Canada for 1941.[31] These can be compared with estimates prepared for this chapter[32] for comparable districts for 1961 – shortly after the absolute peak of fertility but before the big decline. These data afford a unique look at the geography of the baby boom. It has not previously been examined in Canada, and there seem to be no comparable studies for the United States. The great difficulty lies with summarizing such data in a reasonable and effective way. They can be mapped, but that is not easily

---

[31] Charles, *Changing Size of the Family in Canada*. See especially Table 11.
[32] McInnis, "Geographic Dimensions of the Baby Boom."

Table 12.12. *Variations in 1941–1961 change in gross reproduction
rates by geographic districts*

Change	Number of districts	Percentage of women 15–49 years of age
Extreme increase, >75%	18	16.5
Large increase, 50–75%	28	20.4
Above-average increase, 35–50%	39	31.5
Average increase, 25–35%	31	11.3
Below-average increase, 15–25%	33	8.3
Increase, but less than 15%	31	6.9
Fall in GRR	16	5.1
Total	196	100.0

interpretable by readers unfamiliar with the geography of Canada. What is presented here is a brief summary in Table 12.12 that attempts to capture the main picture these data portray.

The gross reproduction rate is used here as the measure of fertility because that is the only rate provided by Charles for 1941, and she does not supply the underlying data needed to calculate alternative measures. It was necessary, then, to match estimated GRRs, using decennial census data on numbers of women in conjunction with vital registrations, to the GRRs provided for 1941. This is done for 196 larger cities and counties that include both lesser urban and rural populations. This evidence reveals wide variation in fertility experience during a period when the GRR rose substantially on average, from 1.42 to 1.87. That increase of 31.7% is closely in line with the one-third rise in the total fertility rate referred to previously. Changes in individual cities and counties ranged from very large increases, in a few places even doubling, to no change at all, or even a continued decline in fertility. That hardly corresponds to the common perception of a ubiquitous, pervasive rise in fertility. There were even declines in GRR in 16 districts that comprised 5.1% of women of child-bearing age, and the rise was minimal, less than 15%, in another 31 districts comprising 6.9% of women. These were almost exclusively districts with predominantly French Canadian populations, mainly in rural Quebec. The nickel mining and smelting city of Sudbury in northern Ontario had a decline in GRR, and there was very little increase in the cities of Cornwall, Ontario, and Hull, Quebec (the latter just across the river from Ottawa). These cities that missed out on the baby boom had large French Canadian populations. At the other extreme, the most extreme increases in GRR were in the cities, especially but not exclusively those of western Canada. In Winnipeg, Saskatoon, and Regina, the GRR doubled. All of the large cities of western Canada are in the "extreme increase" group, as are also Toronto and Ottawa, and Moncton and Charlottetown in the Maritime provinces. Increases of more than 75% were not confined to the larger cities and suburban areas adjacent to them (such as Carleton County, Ontario, which includes suburbs of Ottawa). Large increases also occurred in several rural counties of Nova Scotia: Antigonish, Lunenburg, and Victoria. The next group, with almost as large increases, encompasses a wider range of places: again cities, such as Hamilton, Kitchener, and Victoria, British Columbia, and suburban areas close to large cities (Peel and York counties in Ontario, containing suburbs of Toronto, and Montreal Island outside of the city itself, in Quebec), but also a group of rural counties in eastern Ontario (Leeds, Grenville, Stormont, and Renfrew).

Unqualified generalizations cannot readily be extracted from this complex picture. It has already been pointed out that French Canadians did not generally participate in the baby boom, but GRR increases in the largest French cities, Montreal and Quebec, and their nearby suburbs were greater than average. A few other counties of French Canada (St. Hyacinthe, Charlevoix, Nicolet, and Rivière-du-Loup) also had above-average increases in fertility. Most prominently, the baby boom was a phenomenon of western Canada, especially in the cities. Outside the cities of the prairie provinces, the increase in GRR was notably lower, but still above average. In British Columbia the increase in fertility outside the two main cities was lower still, a little below the national average. An extensive area of western Ontario (including Essex, Kent, Lambton, and Norfolk counties) had very modest increases in fertility. The cities of Brantford, Sarnia, and St. Catharines in western Ontario also had below-average increases. Whatever was motivating people to have increased numbers of children was generating quite widely varying outcomes across the country.

Studies of the baby boom in Canada, the United States, and other countries have emphasized a separation of change in completed family size – cohort fertility – from the effects of the timing of childbearing. This is most directly done by comparing the period measure, the TFR, with an estimate of completed family size. Such estimates for Canada have been made by demographers at Statistics Canada for cohorts whose childbearing is centered on current years from 1946 onward.[33] These are reproduced in Table 12A.3 and are depicted along with TFR for 1936–81 in Figure 12.6 (p. 581). There is a degree of imprecision in estimating cohort fertility for recent cohorts that may not have fully completed their childbearing and also in aligning in time the cohort with the period measure. The former problem is considerably eased by the compression of fertility into younger ages in the more recent years shown in Table 12A.3. The main point to emphasize is that completed family size changed much less in the baby boom period than current or period measures of fertility such as the total fertility rate. It has already been noted that in Canada the rise in the total fertility rate was not as great as the often-stated impression of the baby boom might imply. The cohort measure of completed family size points to an even milder rise. From 1946 to 1957, the peak of the baby boom, the cohort fertility rate increased only 6.6%. Over the same period the total fertility rate went up 16.3%. The implication is that shifts in the timing of fertility were more important than the more fundamental change in completed family size. That is essentially the conclusion of writers such as Lionel Needleman, who have examined the fertility change in Canada and is substantially in line with the most widely accepted account of the experience of the United States as well. The increase in cohort fertility in Canada, however, was even smaller than in the United States. In Canada the baby boom was to an even greater extent a matter of altered timing of fertility than it was south of the border. That reinforces the case made here that in comparison with the United States, Canada had a less profound baby boom and less discontinuous change than has popularly been believed.

The explanation for the rise in fertility in the 1950s is to be found largely in a shift in the age pattern of childbearing. It all came about as a consequence of relatively modest changes in underlying reproductive behavior. Marriage and the initiation of childbearing are closely interrelated. The median age of marriage is not a very sensitive statistic, but it dropped by about a year, from 22.5 in 1946 to 21.5 in 1957. This does not look like an enormous rush to marry at earlier ages, but then we are seeking to explain only a modest rise of 16 percent in the total fertility rate. To explain the change in fertility by stating that women married earlier tells us little, since one of the leading reasons to marry was to begin raising a family. Mar-

---

[33] These are conveniently reported by Romaniuc, *Fertility in Canada*.

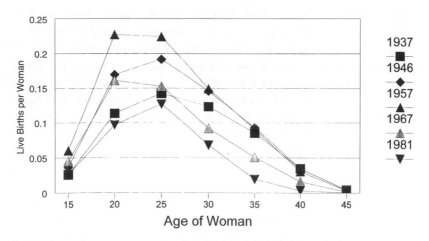

Figure 12.5. Age-specific birth rates, Canada, 1936–1981

riage and the initiation of childbearing are interlinked decisions. At any rate, what happened in Canada, as in the United States, is that those joint decisions were moved downward in age to some degree. Not surprisingly, the median age at first birth move downward by about the same amount as the median age at marriage. The average age at which women bore children did not change over the 1946–57 period of rising fertility because reductions in fertility at older ages were offsetting the increased fertility at younger ages. Women had gained more deliberate control of fertility and were shifting childbearing to younger ages. The pattern is depicted in Figure 12.5, which compares age-specific fertility rates for selected years from the low level of 1937 to the peak level of 1957 and on through the lower fertility years of 1967 and 1981. This figure shows that the early stage of fertility increase, from 1937 to 1946, was associated primarily with a general upward shift in the age distribution of fertility rates. Over the course of the postwar rise in fertility, the age pattern of childbearing shifted, so that in 1957 the highest rate occurred in the 20- to 24-year group rather than for women 25–29, as had previously been the case.

The rise in fertility in Canada represented by the baby boom may not have been very large, but it was sustained for several years and added to the growth of the country's population. A very rough calculation might put that in perspective. Narrowly conceived, the classic baby boom of the 1950s meant that the crude birth rate was about one point per thousand higher on average over a period of 14 years (from 1950 to 1964, by which time fertility was back down to the 1950 level). That would have added a little more than 200,000 to Canada's population, approximately equivalent to the number of immigrants arriving in the peak year of that period, or to a couple of year's average immigration. A more comprehensive view would take into account the entire period of above-trend fertility, keeping in mind all the difficulties of specifying a long-term trend. As mentioned earlier, Canadian fertility probably pushed above its long-run twentieth-century trend in 1942 and was back down to trend level by 1971 or 1972. Cumulating the excess fertility resulting from the fertility rate being above a crudely estimated trend level suggests that by 1971 Canada's population would have been about 3.2 million larger than had fertility followed its long-term trend. That is almost 15% of the 1971 population but should be thought of as an upper-bound estimate of the contribution of the baby boom. In effect, it assumes that all of the immigrants who came to Canada over that period fully participated in the high level of fertility, and it is based on about the most extreme assumption of the trend rate of decline.

More dramatic than the baby boom was the decline in fertility that followed it. TFR began to slide downward after 1959, and from 1964 until 1971 it dropped precipitously. As can be seen in Figure 12.6, the cohort fertility rate was falling as well. Since about 1967 the period and cohort measures have moved in unison. This marked a fundamental change in reproductive behavior, not just another shift in the timing of childbearing. The median age of marriage did not rise over the entire period of rapid decline in fertility. It was only after the mid-1970s, when fertility continued to drift downward, that the median age of marriage of single women rose again. By 1981 it was back to where it stood in 1946. During the fertility fall, women were not postponing marriage, but they were shifting to somewhat later childbearing. The median age at first birth reached a low of 22.88 in 1965, just as the fertility decline gained momentum, and by a decade later it had risen above 24. The age pattern of fertility rates, seen in Figure 12.6, indicates a general downward movement of fertility rates between the peak in 1957 and 1967, by which time the TFR had fallen by one-third, but not much alteration of the shape of the pattern. Between 1967 and 1981, however, the shape of the distribution changed as well. The greatest fall came in the 20- to 24-year age group and the highest rates of fertility are now for women 25 to 29 years, as was the case back in 1937, before the episode of increased fertility got under way. Childbearing has come to be concentrated in a much narrower span of ages, which of course

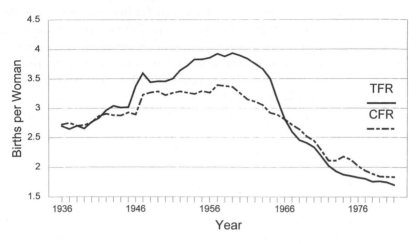

Figure 12.6. Total period and cohort fertility rates, Canada, 1936–1981

is much easier to do when women, on average, have fewer than two children. Childlessness has reemerged as an important contributor to low fertility. During the high-fertility period of the 1950s fewer than 10% of married women in Canada had no children at all; by 1981 the proportion was approaching 20%.

Fertility fell throughout the country, whereas the earlier rise in fertility had not occurred everywhere. Now all regions were affected, and almost all subgroups of society acted quite similarly. The Roman Catholic French Canadians of Quebec had long been characterized by high fertility and in rural Quebec had not really participated in the baby boom. When fertility declined after the early 1960s, it fell rapidly in Quebec as well. By 1981 fertility rates in Quebec were lower than elsewhere in the country. The 1981 census tabulations of childbearing record a rural/urban differential, but the rural farm population has only slightly higher fertility than the people of the metropolitan centers. Except for a few numerically small groups such as Mormons, Mennonites, and Hutterites, religious differentials have almost vanished. The immigrant population has no different fertility than the native-born. Over a wide selection of cultural, geographic, and other groupings, the range of variation in fertility measures has narrowed to about 25%. What has emerged as the most substantial differential in fertility is associated with education. Fertility rates for women with university education are only one-half those of women with the lowest level of educational attainment.

The most salient feature of the decline in fertility in Canada in the late twentieth century has been its association with educational advance. In that respect, Canada has shared in a worldwide phenomenon. It would be of considerable interest to examine whether the educational advance of women and the association of that with falling fertility have been more pronounced in Canada than in the United States and other prosperous industrial countries, but the difficulties of data comparability impede that. The extension of women's education beyond secondary school has a dual impact on fertility, in the first place occupying women with something other than family formation in their early adult years, then raising the opportunity cost of women's time and extending the range of their possible activities. This may account for the complexity of the relationship between fertility and the participation of women in the labor force. The labor force participation of Canadian women over the age of 25, to focus primarily on women who might be married, is given in Table 12A.3. The participation rate remained fairly stable through the period of rising fertility in the 1950s and began its upward climb only in 1956, just before the baby boom reached its peak. Since then it has risen steadily, with the increase accelerating somewhat in the 1970s. The full and complex interaction between increased education of women, their greater participation in the labor market, and the management of reproduction has yet to be satisfactorily worked out. Explanations that have been offered for the United States may well apply in much the same way to Canada, but we do not yet have the research to confirm that.

IMMIGRATION TO CANADA SINCE 1945

Immigration to Canada resumed in a large way in the years following the end of World War II and since then has continued to be an especially prominent feature of Canada's demographic development. Mainly because of the nature of the statistical information on which it is based, this section looks at the period between 1945 and 1981. By the latter date the main features of Canada's current demographic situation had stabilized. There has been little change in recent years that would modify the account given here. The annual flow of immigrant arrivals for the years between 1945 and 1981 is shown in Figure 12.7. Following a short upsurge immediately after the war, Canada experienced three main

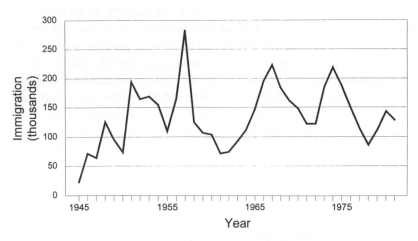

Figure 12.7. Immigration to Canada, 1945–1981

waves of immigration, with peaks in 1957, 1967, and 1974. It is convenient, and reasonably accurate, to think of these as decadal swings, so one can speak of the immigration of the 1950s or the 1960s. These waves of immigration had rather different characteristics and are best considered individually.

At the conclusion of World War II, Canadian policy looked favorably upon immigration as a source of population and economic growth, harkening back to the glory days prior to 1914. At the same time there was a strong preference for British and northern European people. Canada recognized, however, the need to contribute to resolving the plight of many Europeans whose lives had been disrupted by the war, so it was prepared to accommodate what were commonly referred to as DP's (displaced persons) especially if they committed themselves to work on farms or on the natural resource frontier. There was a notable surge in immigration in 1948. Then, after a brief tapering off, the inflow resumed in a large way, and throughout the 1950s immigration to Canada continued at a rate in excess of one-half of 1% of the Canadian population per year, and in some years well above that. By the end of the decade immigration was falling, and it dropped to quite low levels at the beginning of the 1960s. One phase of the postwar immigration experience had been completed. The prospering and rapidly growing Canadian economy attracted another wave of immigrants in the 1960s, auspiciously reaching a peak in Canada's centennial year, 1967. The influx once again faltered somewhat at the start of the new decade, but immigration levels did not fall to the low levels of 1961 and 1962. The pace picked up again, moving to another peak in 1974.

Besides the large contribution made to the growth of the nation's population over the years since 1945, the outstanding feature of Canada's immigration experience has been the shift in the origins of immigrants. British and other northern Europeans gave way to immigrants from Mediterranean Europe, and then non-European immigrants from Third World countries came to dominate. The increasing ethnic and cultural diversity that had begun in the early years of the twentieth century was accentuated in the years after World War II. Picking up notably in the late 1960s, nonwhite, non-European immigration rose to become the most prominent feature of recent Canadian immigration patterns. By 1980 immigrants born in Europe and the United States had dropped to only one-quarter of the total inflow.

The detailed configuration of immigrant birth places is best seen in the tabulation of the immigrant population in the 1981 census of Canada. A summary is given here as Table 12.13. It shows that in 1981 immigrants who had arrived since 1945 made up 13.5 percent of Canada's population. That is well below the 22.5% recorded in 1921. Those who had arrived in Canada within the decade prior to the census made up 38% of the whole immigrant population. The census tabulation categorizes four periods of immigration: 1945–54, 1955–69, 1970–77, and 1978–81. The proportions of the entire stock of post-1945 immigrant population arriving in each of those periods were, respectively, 20.5, 41.2, 28.0, and 10.3%. The periods are of unequal length, however, and on a per annum basis the largest inflow was in the eight-year period 1970–77. Except for the earliest period, though, the annual averages do not differ much. The total immigrant population arriving since 1945 (as distinguished from the somewhat larger total number of foreign-born) was only 68% of the cumulated annual inflow of immigrants from 1945 up to 1981. Some immigrants would have returned to their country of origin, others would have moved on to other destinations, and a few would have died. For immigrants of the most recent period, 1978–81, the number is 83% of the cumulated annual inflow. The literature on Canadian immigration has directed attention entirely to the annual inflow data, but the census stock of immigrant population gives a more direct appraisal of the contribution of immigration to the growth of Canada's population and at the same time provides considerably more detail about the characteristics of the immigrant population. The following examination of the Canadian immigrant experience focuses on the immigrant population in 1981, as summarized in Table 12.13.

Table 12.13. *Summary of 1981 immigrant population by period of arrival (numbers in thousands, column percentages in parentheses)*

Region of origin (birth)	All periods	1945–54	1955–69	1970–77	1978–81
All Origins	3,287.1	672.6	1,355.6	920.5	338.4
United States and Europe	2,282.4	634.9	1,123.6	438.4	85.5
(total)	(69.4)	(94.4)	(82.9)	(47.6)	(25.3)
United States	200.8	18.8	72.7	82.6	26.7
	(6.1)	(2.8)	(5.4)	(9.0)	(7.9)
United Kingdom	654.8	174.7	305.7	132.5	41.9
	(19.9)	(26.0)	(22.6)	(14.4)	(12.4)
Other northern Europe	507.1	201.6	232.2	56.3	16.9
	(15.4)	(30.0)	(17.1)	(6.1)	(5.0)
Southern Europe	588.6	92.7	371.4	117.7	17.8
	(18.2)	(13.8)	(27.4)	(12.8)	(5.3)
Eastern Europe	366.5	147.1	141.5	45.7	16.1
	(11.1)	(21.9)	(10.4)	(5.0)	(4.8)
Caribbean	209.4	4.3	55.0	121.3	28.8
	(6.4)	(0.6)	(3.7)	(13.2)	(8.5)
South Asia	163.1	2.4	30.8	101.8	28.1
	(5.0)	(0.4)	(2.3)	(11.1)	(8.3)
East Asia	341.6	12.5	66.5	148.6	114.0
	(10.4)	(1.9)	(4.8)	(16.1)	(33.7)
Other	290.6	18.5	79.7	110.4	82.0
	(8.8)	(2.8)	(5.9)	(11.3)	(24.2)

The origins of immigrants are given in terms of areas of birth. It is worth noting that, overall, the largest single group was from Britain, although Mediterranean Europe was a close second. Since immigrants from individual Third World sources have arrived in more recent years, they account for much smaller fractions of the total immigrant population. That picture changes when the numbers of immigrants are separated by period of arrival. The United States is not commonly thought of as an important source of immigration to Canada, yet, over the whole period, more immigrants were born in the United States than in South Asia and almost as many as in the Caribbean region. Guyana is grouped here with the Caribbean, rather than with South America, because its people share characteristics with Trinidad, Jamaica, and other British Caribbean countries that were the source of most immigrants to Canada from that part of the world. A few came from Haiti, but almost none from Spanish America. One of the more interesting features of Canadian immigration, and perhaps a tribute to the great strength of intervening opportunities, is the exceedingly small number of Mexicans in Canada's immigrant population. In the years since 1981, the inflow from Central America has picked up somewhat, but the numbers are still quite small, and Mexico still contributes very few immigrants to Canada. Prior to 1981 immigrants to Canada from East Africa consisted almost wholly of ethnic East Indians and are grouped here with South Asia. That may give a bit of upward bias to the numbers from South Asia. Fewer than 10% of that number were Pakistanis – a point of some interest in light of a common practice in Canada of associating South Asian immigrants with Pakistan.

The category of immigrants shown as arriving in the years 1945–54 represents the early postwar influx. About 94% of them came from Europe as a whole and the United States. Great Britain contributed more than one-quarter, and other northern European countries – Germany, the Netherlands, and Scandinavia – made up an even larger number.[34] Mediterranean Europe was beginning to make its presence felt as Italy contributed the largest number of any single country other than the United Kingdom. The leading contributor in the northern European group was the Netherlands. An organized, government-sponsored movement from that country to Canada was a well-publicized part of the picture. Eastern Europe, Poland and the former Soviet Union, in particular, along with Germany, were prominent origins as Canada absorbed large numbers of Europe's "displaced persons." Canadian policy still favored northern Europeans, and, except for a few Chinese, mainly with family ties, nonwhites were effectively barred from entry.

The 1955–69 period was one of increased migration but still very largely from Europe. The Canadian economy was growing vigorously while Europe was still struggling to recover from the ravages of war. The natural resource frontier of Canada – base metals, petroleum, and wood pulp for paper – was driving the economy forward, accompanied by unusually rapid urbanization in the nation's heartland. Both areas of development brought a burgeoning demand for labor. Immigrants were attracted and readily accommodated. The composition of immigration from Europe shifted, though, as Portuguese and Greeks joined with Italians to make Mediterranean Europe the foremost source. That region

---

[34] The experience of the Dutch immigration to Canada in the years immediately after World War II is ably discussed by Petersen, in *Planned Migration*. That work contains much useful commentary on wider aspects of Canada's immigration history.

would appear larger still as a source if Yugoslavians were included, instead of being grouped with Eastern Europe. The British still outnumbered immigrants from any other single country. Immigration from Germany increased from the previous period, and large numbers were still coming from the Netherlands. The peak inflow of the entire 1945–81 period came in 1957, when refugees from the Hungarian uprising added to an unusually large number of immigrants from Britain who came in the wake of the Suez Crisis. At the end of the period, another refugee group, Czechs this time, was accommodated.

Toward the end of the 1955–69 period, the influx from Third World countries got under way. Canada enacted a major shift in immigration policy in 1966, endeavoring to remove overt racial bias by introducing an explicit point system in evaluation immigrant applications. This was to usher in a regime of controlled immigration whereby the skill needs of the labor market were to guide selection. Large numbers of immigrants were still desired, and Canada declared itself to be a country open to immigration, even if in a somewhat controlled way. This change in policy came just as Europeans were losing interest in Canada as a country of settlement. Italian, German, even Yugoslavian immigration was falling sharply. Only the Portuguese and the British continued to come from Europe. If Canada were to continue to be a country of large-scale immigration, it would have to be willing to admit people from the Third World. A selection policy declared to be racially unbiased came just in time. The pattern of things to come is seen in the substantial increase in immigration from non-European sources in the 1955–69 period, even though most of that inflow would have come in just the last few years of the period. East Asia, with Taiwan and Mainland China contributing about equally and each more than Hong Kong, made up almost 5% of the immigrants of the period. The movement into Canada from Jamaica and Trinidad noticeably got under way at this time as well.

The 1970s witnessed the great shift in origins of immigrants to Canada. Table 12.13 divides it into two parts, with the last three years (1978 to mid-1981) tabulated separately. Between 1970 and 1977, immigration from the United States and Europe fell to a little less than half of the total. Another way of looking at it, though, is to emphasize that it still amounted to almost one-half of a large number of immigrants. It is also of interest that immigration from the United States picked up sharply in this period. Almost 10% of Canada's immigrants were born in the United States. The big story, however, was the shift to Third World sources. East Asia led with 16% of all immigrants. It now included large numbers of Filipinos as well as Chinese, and the Chinese came more predominantly from Hong Kong. Almost as many immigrants came from the Caribbean region, with Guyanians and francophone Haitians adding to the earlier established flow from Trinidad and Jamaica. South Asians tripled in numbers from the previous period as immigrants from India were augmented by ethnically Indian refugees from East Africa. Real cultural diversity had arrived on the Canadian scene.

The pattern that has prevailed up to the present is best revealed by the last column of Table 12.13. One-third of immigrants were from East Asia. The continuing inflow from China and the Philippines was augmented by 43,000 Vietnamese. Immigration from Korea, however, which had never been large, fell to almost nothing. A notable contrast between Canada and the United States is the lack of attraction to Canada of Koreans who were moving in quite large numbers to the United States. Immigration from South Asia and the Caribbean declined relatively, although both regions still contributed 8% to 9% of the total. A wider assortment of "other sources" rose to almost one-quarter of all immigration. Continental Europe had ceased to be a large contributor of migrants to Canada, but Britain and the United States continued to contribute substantial numbers. Even in this most recent period, 1978–81, Britain provided a larger number of Canada's immigrants than any other single country. Even if we add together the Chinese from Hong Kong, Taiwan, and the mainland, they still did not outnumber the British born in that period.

The common perception of a great dominance of Third World immigrants and striking ethnic diversity in Canada is reinforced by the concentration of immigrants in general, and Third World immigrants especially, in a few large cities. Much of the country has been only mildly affected by the changes of the past three decades. Toronto and Vancouver, and to a lesser extent Edmonton and Calgary, have become ethnically diverse immigrant cities. Much of the rest of Canada sees and hears more of immigrants and racial diversity on the national news than it experiences firsthand. More generally, the large-scale immigration to Canada since 1945 has served substantially to alter the geographic distribution of the population of the country. This is the case in two important ways. First there has been a substantial redistribution of the population by provinces and regions. That has had significant political as well as economic implications. Second, the rural/urban distribution of the population, and especially its increased concentration in the largest cities, has been substantially affected by immigration. At the same time, those have been affected greatly by internal redistribution of the native-born population as well. Immigration and internal migration have been acting in concert. Immigrants have been attracted to the same areas of growth as have internal migrants. Nevertheless, there is an unresolved question of whether immigration may have been to a considerable extent a substitute for internal migration in Canada. This is an issue that is almost never addressed in Canadian policy discussions. It is at least possible that internal migration might have been even greater in Canada had immigration not been so heavy. One might wonder whether more people might have moved from depressed regions such as northeast New Brunswick to Toronto had so many immigrants not settled in Toronto. Internal migration in Canada has tended to be at lower rates than in the United States. On the other hand, in relation to population, immigration has been higher into Canada than into the United States. Could it be that in Canada immigration has to some degree been substituting for internal migration to a greater extent than in the United States? In terms of direction, internal migration and immigration in Canada appear to have been complements, but overall they may have been substitutes as well.

The regional redistribution can be described quite succinctly. In relative terms, Canada east of Ontario has lost population in comparison with the provinces from Ontario west. In 1951 the Atlantic provinces (augmented by the recent addition of Newfoundland to Canada) and Quebec together accounted for 40.6% of the nation's population. By 1981 that had shrunk to 35.6%. Both regions lost native-born internal migrants to the rest of Canada. Metropolitan Montreal attracted immigrants, especially in the years before 1970, but they often became westward internal migrants at a later date. The rest of Quebec province attracted few immigrants. The Atlantic provinces have not been entirely bereft of immigrants, but compared with other parts of anglophone Canada they have not been a great attraction. At the same time, there has been an outpouring of population westward from Atlantic Canada.

It has really been only in the years since World War II that Canada has developed a nationally integrated labor market and a truly national system of internal migration. Prior to that time regional redistribution of population in Canada was largely accomplished through individual regional exchanges with the rest of the world. Before 1940 few people moved from Quebec and the Atlantic provinces to western Canada. Emigration from Atlantic Canada went overwhelmingly to the United States. That was largely true of Quebec in the nineteenth century as well, but in the twentieth century out-migration from Quebec declined substantially, and an internal frontier was opened in the northern mining and forest region. Western Canada was settled more by immigrants than by migrants from the older regions of Canada. Ontarians, however, did play an important role in settling the Canadian west, contributing about one-third of the migrants to the region. Drought and agricultural depression in the 1930s had precipitated an out-migration of population from the prairie provinces, and that continued in the early postwar years. By the 1950s, however, there had emerged something more of a national system of internal population redistribution, qualified only by the substantially reduced inclination of francophone Quebecers to leave their native province. People from the Atlantic provinces moved in large numbers to Ontario, and there was a more general tendency for people to relocate throughout the entire country. What is especially interesting is that it took so long for that to happen.

The declining fraction of the national population residing in Quebec and the Atlantic provinces was offset about equally by increases in Ontario and in Canada west of Ontario. In 1951 Ontario had 32.8% of the nation's population. That rose to 35.4% in 1981. The west gained almost as much, increasing from 26.6% of the national total in 1951 to 29.0% in 1981. Although these are substantial redistributions, it is somewhat surprising that they are not even greater. Thirty years of vigorous development brought a population gain of only 2.6 percentage points, or merely 8.0%, to the relative size of Ontario. The picture is a bit more vivid when one subdivides the west. The part of the country west of Ontario saw its share of the national population increase by 9.0% over the same 30 years, but within the western region there was also an east/west division. The westernmost provinces of Alberta and British Columbia grew rapidly, their share of the national population rising from 15.0% in 1951 to 20.4% in 1981. Manitoba and Saskatchewan declined in relative share over the same period, from 11.5 to 8.2%. It might be added that their decline had already begun a decade earlier, and by 1951 they were down from their all-time high. Immigrants concentrated heavily in Ontario, British Columbia, and

Alberta. Those same provinces were the leading destinations of internal migrants as well.

While the regional and provincial distribution of population was undergoing substantial change, the other notable development was the greatly increased proportion of the population residing in metropolitan cities. The period from 1951 to 1981 was one of rapid urbanization, with a particular emphasis on larger centers. Details are given in Table 12A.2, but by the broadest definition of urban, the proportion rose from 55.2% to 68.9%. The percentage of the population in cities of more than 25,000 went up from 44.4 to 64.9 and the number of such cities rose from 36 to 68. The number of census metropolitan areas (CMAs) remained unchanged at 24, but the proportion of the national population residing in those centers rose from 41.8% to 56.1%. The proportion of the total urban population found in CMAs went up as well. The most rapidly growing CMAs over the 1951–81 period were Kitchener/Waterloo, followed closely by Calgary. Only two CMAs grew less rapidly than the national population. Those were Windsor, which had early been established as an automobile manufacturing center but had seen the industry shift to other locations, and Winnipeg, whose slow growth reflected the reorientation of western Canada away from the east toward the further west.

Immigrants were attracted to urban places and to the largest cities, especially. That has been even more the case in the most recent times. The European immigrants who came to Canada in the years right after World War II dispersed fairly widely across the country, at least from Montreal westward. Many found initial employment on the natural resource frontier, in mines, in the forest industry, and in the company towns built around pulp mills. A considerable number even started their Canadian work in agriculture. Many of the "displaced persons" were accepted by Canada on condition that they work on farms, and many of those involved in the planned migration from the Netherlands settled in farming communities in several locations across the country. Construction work was a favored initial occupation of many immigrants, and that, too, was quite widely dispersed, although some large metropolitan projects, such as the Toronto subway built in the 1950s, absorbed many immigrant workers. The immigrants who arrived in later periods, and especially those of Third World origins, were much more inclined to settle in the largest metropolitan areas, particularly in Toronto. That was partly because of the occupational selectivity of the post-1966 immigration policy. Third World

Table 12.14. *Migrant population of selected metropolitan areas as a percentage of total population, 1976–1981 migrants and total post-1945 immigrants*

CMA	Net migration balance	All in-migrants	From same province	From other provinces	From other countries	Post-1945 immigrants
Calgary	+12.3	35.0	5.8	24.0	5.6	21.1
Edmonton	+5.8	27.6	6.7	16.3	4.6	19.7
Winnipeg	−4.3	20.7	10.7	6.4	3.6	19.2
Vancouver	+1.6	17.6	4.5	8.0	5.2	29.6
Halifax	−1.9	17.2	5.2	10.5	1.5	6.1
Ottawa/Hull	−1.2	16.0	7.0	6.2	2.8	13.8
Toronto	−0.7	13.8	4.9	3.4	5.5	38.0
St. Catharines	−1.9	10.4	6.8	2.0	1.6	22.0
Quebec City	−0.2	9.4	8.5	0.1	0.8	2.2
Montreal	−4.0	8.0	4.3	1.2	2.5	16.1

immigrants often had to have technical or professional qualifications. Then, the movement from the West Indies and the Philippines frequently started with women coming to Canada under special provisions for domestic workers. They also concentrated in the largest cities. Hence it was not just the nature of economic change but also the structure of Canadian immigration policy that drew so many newcomers to the largest cities. Family members, more distant relatives and friends who came later, added to the established concentrations. In 1981, post-1945 immigrants accounted for 38.0% of the population of the Toronto CMA. Vancouver was 29.6% immigrant and Hamilton 26.0%. By contrast, Quebec City was only 2.2% immigrant. Montreal's 16.1%, while relatively high by American standards, was low for Canada. These figures are shown in Table 12.14 along with comparable data for several other CMAs. That table also shows the pattern of migration as a component of metropolitan area population growth as measured by the migration flows and migration balance of the five years leading up to the 1981 census.

Table 12.14 reveals a highly varied role of immigration and internal migration in the growth of metropolitan area populations. A selection of

CMAs is listed in order of the proportion of total population that had migrated into each area in the 1976–81 period. The origins of these migrants are shown in three categories: migrants from within the same province as the CMA, migrants from other provinces, and immigrants from other countries. The first column also shows a net balance of migration, although it is rather tricky to interpret. It nets out not only migrants from the CMA to other areas in Canada but also net emigration from the country, and it is rather sensitive to variations in the extent to which CMAs were redefined extensively enough to capture ex-urban spillover (more on that in a few particular cases). The proportion of the 1981 population that had immigrated to Canada since 1945 is also shown in the last column. This indicates that Canada's leading concentration of immigration – Toronto, where 38.0% of the population had arrived in the country since 1945 – was well down the list in the proportion of overall in-migrants to the city. It nevertheless ran a close second to Calgary and just outdistanced Vancouver, with 5.5% of its population having arrived from other countries within the preceding five years. Toronto's small negative net balance through migration is simply an indication that the overall urban area of Toronto was extending faster than the census bureau was redefining the metropolitan area. It might also indicate that native-born persons rather than immigrants were those moving to the furthest suburbs. Calgary and Vancouver were about as prominent locations for recent immigrants as was Toronto. Vancouver gets lots of public attention in that regard; Calgary much less so. That might perhaps be because in Calgary the immigrants were swamped by the numbers of internal migrants. Calgary led all Canadian CMAs, with Edmonton not too far behind, as a magnet for migration of all sorts. In Calgary of 1981, 35.0% of the population had moved into the CMA in the preceding five years. That included immigrants to a somewhat greater degree than any other Canadian city, but it also included a whopping 24.0% from other provinces. Edmonton, the other Alberta CMA, also had a large proportion (16.3%) from other provinces. By contrast, Toronto's leading source of in-migrants was immigrants from other countries, followed closely by in-migrants from elsewhere in Ontario. Other provinces were the least important source of population gain for Canada's largest CMA. Vancouver has often been noted to be a city of immigrants, but it had twice as many in-migrants from the rest of Canada as immigrants. The small net migration balance of Vancouver is another case of the CMA definition not keeping up with urban sprawl. Montreal and Quebec City had the lowest proportions of in-migrants of the major CMAs, and in the case of Montreal net migration was outward to the extent of 4.0% of the population. Montreal was still gaining immigrants (2.5% of population) and was indeed more of a magnet for immigrants than Quebec City, Halifax, or, for that matter, even St. Catharines in Ontario. Montreal, and to an even greater extent Quebec City, drew migrants mainly from the province of Quebec. Halifax represents another sort of migration pattern. Halifax, like the Atlantic region in general, attracted few immigrants, and its net migration balance was negative. Nevertheless, Halifax drew large numbers of people from other provinces. In 1981 more than 10% of its population had moved in from other provinces within the previous five years.

Between 1951 and 1981 urbanization in Canada was especially vigorous, and the large metropolitan areas grew much more rapidly than the remainder of the country. That immigration to Canada was so voluminous played an important role in that development, especially in the latter half of the period. Recent immigrants to Canada have been strongly attracted to the largest cities. Immigration has been far from the whole story; internal migration has also played a large role. It was previously noted that Calgary, one of the most rapidly growing CMAs, although attracting immigrants as strongly as any other city, grew much more through in-migration from other provinces. Quebec City has grown quite rapidly but almost entirely on the basis of migration of Quebecers from within the province.

It is appropriate to bring this discussion of immigration to Canada in recent decades to a close with a review of the composition of Canada's population growth. Just how much has immigration contributed to overall change? That is summed up in Table 12.15. With highly reliable vital statistics, the calculation is straightforward. Except for the figures in the final column, these are data routinely provided by the government of Canada. Immigration is still counted as the cumulated annual inflow over the course of the intercensal decade. The implied emigration is simply a residual. Throughout the whole period immigration contributed a large part of population growth, and the proportion has increased with each decade. That is in large part because of the declining contribution of births, especially in the most recent decade. Emigration continues to be quite large, partly through the return of immigrants to their

Table 12.15. *Components of decadal population change,
Canada, 1951–1981 (thousands of persons)*

	1951–61	1961–71	1971–1981[a]	1971–81[b]
Total growth	4,228	3,330	2,712	2,712
Births	4,468	4,105	3,578	3,578
Deaths	1,320	1,497	1,665	1,665
Natural increase	3,148	2,608	1,913	1,913
Immigration	1,543	1,429	1,429	1,259
Implied emigration	463	707	630	460
Immigration as percentage of total growth	36.5	42.9	52.7	46.4
Net growth due to migration (%)	25.5	21.7	29.5	29.5

[a] Cumulated annual inflow of immigrants.
[b] 1981 census stock of immigrants.

home countries, but more because of continuing emigration to the United States. Given that, Canada has had to maintain a relatively large flow of immigration just to maintain a positive balance – another respect in which Canada's demographic situation differs from that of the United States. The standard approach to this calculation of the composition of population growth biases upwardly the contribution of immigration by using the cumulated annual flow. The other extreme version of the calculation can be appraised by using the end-of-decade stock of immigrants who arrived over the course of the decade. For the 1971–81 decade, that is reported in the last column of Table 12.15. It does not affect the net migration balance but lowers the gross contribution of immigration, for the 1971–81 decade, from 52.7% to 46.4%. The usual way in which the calculation is done in Canada tends to some degree to inflate the importance of immigration. At various junctures in the foregoing discussion it has been indicated that there is a tendency to overstate the role of migration in Canada in other ways as well. That said, even allowing for those sorts of biases, Canada has been a major destination of immigration in recent decades. Immigration has been a central feature of Canadian population change and has contributed more to Canadian population growth than is the case for most countries of the world.

Table 12A.1. *Principal indicators of Canada's demographic record*

Year	1901	1931	1951	1981
Total population (000s)	5,371	10,377	14,009	24,343
Population as percentage of				
U.S. population	7.1	8.4	9.2	10.7
Regional distribution				
Atlantic	894	1,007	1,618	2,234
Quebec	1,649	2,875	4,055	6,439
Ontario	2,183	3,432	4,598	8,625
Prairie provinces (includes				
NWT)	440	2,363	2,564	4,277
British Columbia (includes				
Yukon)	205	698	1,174	2,768
Rural	3,832	5,222	6,280	7,575
Urban	1,539	5,155	7,729	16,768
Percentage urban	28.7	49.7	55.2	68.9
Canadian-born	4,672	8,069	11,950	20,500
Foreign-born	700	2,308	2,059	3,843
Percentage foreign-born	13.0	22.2	14.7	15.8
Average annual immigration over five years				
Centered on census date				
(thousands)	74.2	66.5	139.4	118.8
As percentage of census				
population	1.38	0.64	0.99	0.49
Population by mother tongue				
English	n.a.	4,772	8,281	14,750
French	n.a.	2,087	4,069	6,176
Other	n.a.	3,518	1,659	3,157
Crude birth rate	29.8	23.2	27.2	15.3
Total fertility rate	4.009	3.200	3.503	1.704
Marital fertility rate	212	161	159	84
Crude death rate	14.4	10.5	10.1	7.0
Expectation of life				
At age 0	50.2	62.1	70.8	79.0
At age 10	52.9	58.7	64.0	69.9
At age 40	29.9	33.0	35.6	40.7
Infant mortality rate	139	86	39	9

Table 12A.2. *Urban and metropolitan Canada*

Area	1901	1931	1951	1981
Urban broadly defined[a]				
Population (thousands)	1,539	5,155	7,729	16,768
Percentage of total population	28.7	49.7	55.2	68.9
Major urban[b]				
Number of places	11	26	36	68
Population (thousands)	1,134	4,197	6,227	15,762
Percentage of total population	21.1	40.4	44.4	64.7
Metropolitan[c]				
Number of places	11	23	24	24
Population (thousands)	1,134	4,042	5,853	13,659
Percentage of total population	21.1	39.0	41.8	56.1
Toronto	240	828	1,117	2,999
Montreal	368	1,040	1,395	2,828
Vancouver	33	333	531	1,268
Ottawa/Hull	98	188	282	718
Edmonton	#	84	173	657
Calgary	#	84	139	593
Winnipeg	48	289	354	585
Quebec	104	188	275	576
Hamilton	68	175	260	542
St. Catharines	35	100	162	304
Kitchener/Waterloo	#	53	63	288
London	43	78	122	284
Halifax	51	79	134	278
Windsor	#	115	158	246
Victoria	#	61	104	233
Regina	#	57	71	164
St. John's (Newfoundland)	—	—	68	155
Oshawa	#	34	52	154
Saskatoon	#	44	55	154
Sudbury	#	25	71	150
Chicoutimi	#	31	56	135
Thunder Bay	#	46	66	121
Saint John	#	50	78	114
Trois-Rivières	#	50	68	111

[a] Metropolitan population plus all others residing in places 2,500+.

[b] Metropolitan plus other cities 25,000+.

[c] 1981 CMAs having at least 25,000 population at census date.

less than 25,000 population.

Table 12A.3. *Canadian fertility rates and related measures, 1946–1981*

Year	Total fertility rate	Cohort fertility rate	Median age of mother At childbirth	Median age of mother At first birth	Median age at marriage, single brides	Labor force participation, women 25–64
1946	3.37	3.18	27.52	24.24	22.5	18.0
1947	3.60	3.19	27.17	24.07	22.4	17.9
1948	3.44	3.22	27.32	23.87	22.3	18.2
1949	3.46	3.23	27.41	23.75	22.2	17.7
1950	3.46	3.25	27.50	23.66	22.1	17.0
1951	3.50	3.26	27.5	23.52	22.0	18.6
1952	3.64	3.29	27.48	23.43	22.0	18.8
1953	3.72	3.27	27.52	23.38	21.9	18.5
1954	3.83	3.24	27.52	23.32	21.9	18.9
1955	3.83	3.29	27.5	23.30	21.8	19.4
1956	3.86	3.27	27.39	23.25	21.6	20.4
1957	3.92	3.39	27.31	23.14	21.5	21.8
1958	3.88	3.38	27.26	23.12	21.4	22.5
1959	3.94	3.36	27.20	23.04	21.3	23.2
1960	3.90	3.26	27.11	22.99	21.2	24.5
1961	3.84	3.15	27.01	22.96	21.1	25.5
1962	3.76	3.11	26.61	22.93	21.1	26.0
1963	3.67	3.06	26.32	22.90	21.2	26.8
1964	3.50	2.92	26.43	22.94	21.2	27.8
1965	3.15	2.89	26.66	22.88	21.2	28.6
1966	2.81	2.81	25.02	22.89	21.2	29.8
1967	2.60	2.72	25.35	22.98	21.2	30.9
1968	2.45	2.64	25.50	23.07	21.3	31.4
1969	2.40	2.52	25.51	23.17	21.4	32.3
1970	2.33	2.44	25.62	23.21	21.4	32.9
1971	2.19	2.28	25.37	23.39	21.3	33.7
1972	2.02	2.11	25.55	23.54	21.2	34.3
1973	1.93	2.11	25.48	23.60	21.2	35.7
1974	1.88	2.28	25.35	23.87	21.3	36.5
1975	1.85	2.12	25.30	23.88	21.5	40.0
1976	1.82	2.02	25.21	24.00	21.6	41.1
1977	1.81	1.94	25.86	24.19	21.7	42.1
1978	1.76	1.89	26.00	24.37	21.9	44.5
1979	1.76	1.84	26.13	24.54	22.1	45.5
1980	1.75	1.84	26.23	24.62	22.3	46.8
1981	1.70	1.83	26.38	24.71	22.5	48.5

Romaniuc, *Fertility in Canada*; Statistics Canada, *Vital Statistics* (annual).

REFERENCES

Bourbeau, Robert, and Jacques Légaré. *Evolution de la mortalité au Canada et au Québec, 1831–1931.* Montreal: Presses de l'Université de Montréal, 1982.

Camu, Pierre, E. P. Weeks, and Z. W. Sametz. *Economic Geography of Canada.* Toronto: Macmillan of Canada, 1964.

Charles, Enid. *The Changing Size of the Family in Canada.* Census Monograph no. 1, Eighth Census of Canada, 1941. Ottawa: King's Printer, 1948.

Coale, Ansley, and Melvin Zelnik. *New Estimates of Fertility and Population in the United States.* Princeton, N.J.: Princeton University Press, 1963.

Gee, Ellen M. Thomas. "Fertility and Marriage Patterns in Canada: 1851–1971." Unpublished Ph.D. diss., University of British Columbia, 1978.

———. "Early Canadian Fertility Transition: A Components Analysis of Census Data." *Canadian Studies in Population* 6 (1979): 23–32.

Hatton, Timothy J., and Jeffrey G. Williamson. "International Migration 1850–1939." In *Migration and the International Labor Market, 1850–1939*, editor by Hatton and Williamson. London: Routledge, 1994.

Henripin, Jacques. *Trends and Factors of Fertility in Canada.* Ottawa: Statistics Canada, 1972.

Hurd, W. Burton. "The Decline in the Canadian Birth Rate." *Canadian Journal of Economics and Political Science* 3 (1937): 40–57.

Keyfitz, Nathan. "The Growth of Canadian Population." *Population Studies* 4 (1950): 47–63.

Kuczynski, Robert Rene. *Birth Registration and Birth Statistics in Canada.* Washington, D.C.: Brookings Institution, 1930.

Lower, A. R. M. "The Case against Immigration." *Queen's Quarterly* 37 (1930): 557–74.

McDougall, Duncan M. "Immigration into Canada, 1851–1920." *Canadian Journal of Economics and Political Science* 27 (1961): 162–76.

McInnis, R. M. "Geographic Dimensions of the Baby Boom in Canada." Unpublished memorandum for *Historical Atlas of Canada Project*, February 1988. Summary mapping of this shown on Plate 59 of *Historical Atlas of Canada*, vol. 3. Toronto: University of Toronto Press, 1990.

———. "Women, Work and Childbearing: Ontario in the Second Half of the Nineteenth Century." *Histoire sociale/Social History* 24 (1991): 237–62.

McVey, Wayne W., and Warren E. Kalbach. *Canadian Population.* Toronto: Nelson Canada, 1995.

Needleman, Lionel. "Canadian Fertility Trends in Perspective." *Journal of Biosocial Science* 18 (1986): 43–56.

Petersen, William. *Planned Migration: The Social Determinants of the Dutch-Canadian Movement.* Berkeley: University of California Press, 1955.

Romaniuc, Anatole. *Fertility in Canada: From Baby-boom to Baby-bust.* Ottawa: Statistics Canada, Demography Division, 1984.

Stone, Leroy O. *Urban Development in Canada.* Ottawa: Statistics Canada, 1968.

Tracey, W. R. "Fertility of the Population of Canada." *Eighth Census of Canada, 1931.* Vol. 12: *Monographs*, 99– . Ottawa: King's Printer, 1942.

13

MEXICO'S DEMOGRAPHIC TRANSFORMATION: FROM 1900 TO 1990

ZADIA M. FELICIANO

INTRODUCTION

During most of the nineteenth century Mexico experienced slow population growth, but during the twentieth century its population grew rapidly. For the years 1810–70 its population growth averaged only 0.5% per year, which implied a doubling of the population every 144 years (McCaa, 1993). During the twentieth century, after the Mexican revolution, its population grew dramatically, with the growth rate peaking from 1950 to 1970 at an average annual rate of 3.3% per year. This implied a doubling of the population in 21 years. This demographic transformation was due in large part to a substantial decline in the mortality rate and to an increase in fertility rates from mid-1930s until 1970. Unlike the large flows experienced by the United States and Canada, immigration to Mexico was negligible and thus had little impact on population growth.

During the twentieth century, Mexico's population urbanized and concentrated around cities. In 1900 only 28.3% of the Mexican population lived in urban areas, but by 1990 71.3% of the Mexican population was urban. Mexico City's population grew at a very fast rate, rising from fewer than half a million residents in 1910 to 13 million by 1980, making it one of the largest cities in the world, with approximately 20% of the Mexican population.[1] The growth of Mexico City slowed during the 1980s, and the

---

This chapter has benefited from helpful comments and suggestions by Robert E. McCaa and Michael R. Haines. Thanks to Galit Hershco, Eric Kamau, Andrew Ostrowsky, and Leonard Usvyat for their research assistance.
[1] Statistics are based on Census of Population data reported in Estadisticas Historicas de Mexico (1994). The population of Mexico City in 1900 refers to the oldest jurisdiction used in census documents. It comprises four delegations: M. Hidalgo, Cuauhtémoc, B. Juárez, and V. Carranza. The

percentage of the population residing in the metropolitan area dropped to 18%. Out-migration to the United States became such an important demographic phenomenon that by 1990 it involved more than 2% of the Mexican population. The number of Mexicans living in the United States increased from approximately 103,000 in 1900 to more than 4 million in 1990.

This chapter summarizes Mexico's demographic transformation from 1900 to 1990. It describes trends in population growth, mortality, and fertility at the national and regional levels and presents descriptive and quantitative evidence on the factors that may be responsible for the decline in mortality rates and fluctuations in fertility. Attention is also given to urbanization, the growth of Mexico City, and the migration of Mexicans to the United States.

POPULATION GROWTH

During most of the nineteenth century, Mexico's population grew at a slow pace, averaging 0.5% per year between 1810 and 1870. This slow growth may be attributed to epidemics, political insurrection, and the war with the United States in the years 1846–48 (McCaa, 1993). Under the leadership of Porfirio Díaz (1877–1911), however, the country entered a period of political stability and economic growth. For more than 30 years, it was free of wars, and from 1900 to 1909 the gross domestic product increased by an average annual rate of 3.6%. In addition, transportation between regions of the country was greatly improved with the construction of railroad lines.[2] These factors contributed to a substantial increase in population growth during the Díaz regime, averaging between 1 and 1.5% per year (Alba, 1993a).

However, some have claimed that the overall population did not share in the prosperity of the Díaz years. Researchers point to statistics showing that although agricultural production as a whole increased by 21.3% between 1877 and 1907, corn production, the main food staple of Mexicans, increased by only 0.8% (Ordorica and Lezama, 1993). Others (Coatsworth 1990) maintain that the production of corn and other food

population of Mexico City in 1980 and 1990 refers to the metropolitan area of Mexico, which includes the 4 delegations of Mexico City, the 12 delegations of the Federal District, and several contiguous urban areas in the state of Mexico.

[2] The lines expanded from the existing 684 kilometers in 1877 to approximately 19,205 kilometers in 1910 (Coatsworth, 1981).

products grew at the same rate as the population. In addition, real wages increased from 1885 to 1907. These statistics suggest that the standard of living in Mexico increased during most of the Díaz regime.

The government of Díaz was overthrown at the onset of the Mexican revolution, which lasted from 1910 to 1920. The armed conflict, which began its violent phase in 1913, produced many casualties and also a sharp decline in real wages combined with an increase in food prices such as corn, beans, and rice. In addition, many Mexicans fled to western parts of the United States (Ordorica and Lezama, 1993).[3] All of these factors contributed to a decline in population growth.

It is difficult to analyze the demographic impact of the war because there are no records of vital statistics for this period. Most of the research on demographic changes during the revolution is based on the Mexican censuses of population for 1910 and 1921. The reliability of the 1921 census is questionable. About 60% of the municipalities of the country did not complete the work required to process and tabulate the census results. Furthermore, census personnel adjusted some of the statistics because they questioned the credibility of data coming from local authorities (Ordorica and Lezama, 1993).

Calculations of population growth rates using census data show an average annual population growth of 1.1% between 1900 and 1910, but −0.5% from 1910 to 1921 (see Table 13.1, Panel A). According to Collver (1965), this implies 2.2 million more deaths from 1910 to 1919 than during the previous decade. Collver suggests that these figures exaggerate the number of casualties and proposes a more conservative estimate of 723,000 more deaths from 1910 to 1919 than from 1900 to 1909. Manuel Gamio estimates that 1.3 million individuals disappeared from the records between 1910 and 1921.[4] He classifies them as those who emigrated to other countries (700,000), those who died in battle (300,000), and those who died in the epidemic of the Spanish influenza between 1918 and 1919 (300,000).

Between 1921 and 1970 Mexico experienced a demographic transformation. Population growth increased dramatically, from an annual rate of 1.7% during the 1920s to 3.3% during the 1960s (see Table 13.1, Panel

---

[3] Part of this emigration was economic since the western states of the U.S. were experiencing a large economic boom at the time and demand for labor was growing.

[4] See Ordorica and Lezama (1993) for a summary of the literature on population growth during the Revolution. Gamio's estimates are in an unpublished mimeo (not dated) by Moises Gonzalez Navarro, El Colegio de Mexico.

Table 13.1. *Basic demographic indicators for Mexico, 1900–1990*

A. Population

Year	Population	Annual rate of change (%)[a]
1900	13,556,206	1.1
1910	15,109,738	−0.5
1920	14,365,689	1.7
1930	16,593,839	1.8
1940	19,845,290	2.6
1950	25,854,814	3.0
1960	35,011,982	3.3
1970	48,986,990	3.1
1980	66,957,839	2.0
1990	81,699,869	

B. Birth and mortality, average annual crude rates

Period	Birth rate per thousand[b] (official)	Birth rate per thousand (Collver)[c]	Mortality rate per thousand[b] (official)	Mortality rate per thousand (Collver)[c]	Infant mortality per thousand[b] (official)	Infant mortality (Collver and Aguirre/ Camposortega)[d]
1900–9	33.8	46.3	32.9	34.1	296.9	220.0
1910–19		41.9		37.5		221.5
1920–29	32.5	44.8	25.2	29.9	205.2	165.5
1930–39	43.9	43.8	24.4	25.1	131.2	135.5
1940–49	43.9	44.2	19.8	19.8	111.0	134.6
1950–59	45.0	45.4	13.8	14.0	84.2	95.1
1960–69	45.0		10.2		66.2	77.0
1970–79	41.8		8.0		51.5	70.5
1980–89	35.0		5.7		28.3	
1990	33.5		5.2		23.9	

[a] Computed from Censo General de la Población, 1900–90. Official rates for 1900–9 refer to the years 1900–7 and rates for 1920–29 refer to the years 1922–29.

[b] Computed using vital statistics data from Anuario Estadistico de los Estados Unidos Mexicanos, 1900–90.

[c] Estimates Collver (1965). Alternative estimates are 44.6 births per thousand for 1900–10, 38.9 for 1910–19, and 44.3 for 1921–29. Alternative mortality measures are 34.1 deaths per thousand for 1900–10, 37.5 for 1910–19 and 29.9 for 1921–29.

[d] Estimates by Collver (1965) for years 1900–39 and estimates by Aguirre and Camposortega (1981) for years after 1939. The period 1940–49 refers to the average for 1947–51, 1950–59 refers to the average for 1957–61, 1960–69 refers to average for 1967–71, and 1970–79 refers to average for 1972–75.

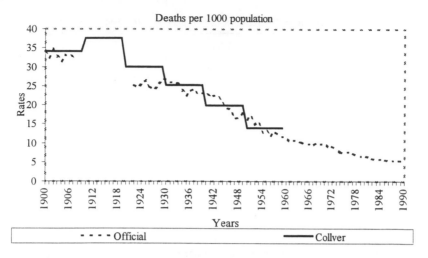

Figure 13.1. Crude mortality rate in Mexico, 1900–1990 (*Sources*: Official: calculated using vital statistics data from Anuario Estadistico de los Estados Unidos Mexicanos, 1900–90; Collver: estimates by Collver, 1965)

A). Mexico had one of the fastest-growing populations in the world during the 1960s, almost three times the annual growth rate (1.2%) of the United States and almost two times the annual growth rate of Canada (1.8%).[5] Mexico's population increased from 14 million in 1921 to 48 million in 1970. Population growth slowed to 3.1% per year during the 1970s and 2.0% per year during the 1980s. The 1990 census shows a population count of 81 million.

Most of the increase in population growth from 1921 to 1970 was due to a large decrease in mortality rates (see Figure 13.1). Official vital statistics indicate that, the crude death rate was 32.9 per thousand between 1900 and 1909, 24.4 per thousand between 1930 and 1939, 13.8 per thousand between 1950 and 1959, and only 5.2 per thousand in 1990 (see Table 13.1, Panel B).[6] Reductions in infant mortality greatly contributed to the decline in mortality rates (see Figure 13.2). There were 297 deaths of infants per thousand births from 1900 to 1909, 131 from 1930 to 1939,

---

[5] *World Development Report 1967.*
[6] According to Collver (1965), death registration was complete from 1895 to 1910. When the register opened in 1922, the coverage was not complete but gradually improved until it was nearly complete by 1940. For this reason the large decline in mortality rates from 32.9% between 1900 and 1909 to 25.2% between 1922 and 1929 may overstate the actual decline in mortality rates during this period.

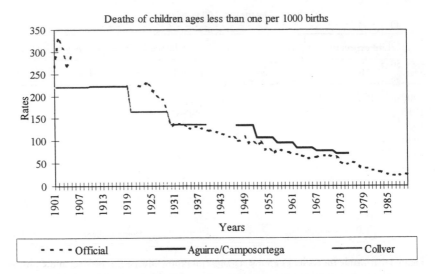

Deaths of children ages less than one per 1000 births

Figure 13.2. Infant mortality rate in Mexico, 1901–1990 (*Sources*: Official: calculated using vital statistics data from Anuario Estadistico de los Estados Unidos Mexicanos, 1901–90; Aguirre & Camposortega: estimates by Aguirre & Camposortega, 1981; Collver: estimates by Collver, 1965)

84 from 1950 to 1959, and 24 in 1990 (see Table 13.1, Panel B). This implies a 92% decline in infant mortality rates from the beginning of the century to 1990, and a 61% decline from the 1920s to 1990.

Unfortunately, the official statistics on mortality are not accurate. Collver (1965) estimates that the mortality rate from 1900 to 1959 was actually higher than the official rate. The undercounting of deaths is largest from 1920 to 1929. (Although the civilian register reopened in 1922, the coverage was incomplete.) Thus, the decline in mortality rates from the period 1900–9 to 1920–29 based on official statistics is sharper than was actually observed at the time (see Table 13.1, Panel B).

Official infant mortality rates are even more problematic. Before 1930, official rates may overestimate actual infant mortality because births were seriously underreported. Although changes in government regulations in 1929 facilitated and encouraged birth registration (Cook and Borah, 1974) and thereby improved statistics on births, the deaths of infants remained underreported. As a result, most researchers have found that after 1930 official statistics underestimate infant mortality rates (Camposortega, 1988).

Rabell and Mier y Terán (1986) explain that conservative estimates of

Table 13.2. *Life expectancy, 1900–1990*

	Life expectancy at birth				Change in life expectancy at birth		
Year	All	Males	Females	Period	All	Males	Females
1900	25.3	25.0	25.6				
1910	27.6	27.3	27.9	1900–10	2.3	2.3	2.3
1921							
1930	36.8	36.1	37.5				
1940	39.8	38.1	41.4	1930–40	3.0	2.0	4.0
1950	48.5	46.5	50.4	1940–50	8.7	8.4	9.0
1960	57.6	55.7	59.6	1950–60	9.2	9.2	9.2
1970	61.1	59.0	63.2	1960–70	3.5	3.3	3.6
1980	64.8	61.6	68.1	1970–80	3.7	2.6	4.8
1990	71.0	68.0	74.2	1980–90	6.2	6.4	6.1

Sources: Estimates for 1900–10 are by Arriaga (1968); for 1930, from Benitez and Cabrear (1967); for 1940–80 from Camposortega (1988); and for 1990 from Consejo Nacional de Población, printed in González García de Alba y Monterrubio Gómez (1993).

infant mortality for 1940 place the number of infant deaths between 170 and 230, whereas the official count was 122. According to these estimates, in 1970 there were between 65 and 95 infant deaths per thousand births compared with the official estimate of 69 (Rabell and Mier y Terán, 1986). Nevertheless, even these estimates support the notion that infant mortality rates declined dramatically during the century.

As mortality rates declined, life expectancy in Mexico for both sexes increased, moving from 25.3 years in 1900 to 71.0 years in 1990 (see Table 13.2). This represents an increase of 45.7 years during the century. The largest gains in life expectancy occurred between 1940 and 1960, an increase from 39.8 years to 57.6 years. This amounts to a gain of 17.9 years of life expectancy in 20 years. The growth in life expectancy slowed down between 1960 and 1980, when gains were limited to approximately 3.6 years per decade. Between 1980 and 1990, life expectancy increased more rapidly, for a gain of approximately 6 years. Improvements in life expectancy have been greater for females, who achieved a life expectancy of 74.2 years in 1990, compared with a life expectancy of 68.0 years for males.

Changes in the causes of death provide some information on the possible reasons for the large decrease in mortality rates between 1920 and 1990. According to official statistics, 47% of all deaths were due to infectious and

Table 13.3. *Percentage of deaths by cause, 1930–1990*

	Infectious diseases and parasites	Circulatory system	Respiratory system	Digestive system	Cancer	Accidents and violence	Other
1930	47.0	1.9	16.0	4.0	0.7	4.1	26.3
1940	43.1	3.7	20.0	4.7	1.2	5.1	22.2
1950	34.6	6.2	20.7	5.1	2.0	5.9	25.5
1960	25.6	8.5	19.3	5.3	3.4	6.5	31.4
1970	23.1	10.5	21.8	5.6	4.0	7.2	27.8
1980	13.7	16.4	13.5	7.1	6.5	15.5	27.3
1990	9.7	19.8	10.5	7.9	10.1	13.9	28.1

Source: Estadisticas Historicas de Mexico, Instituto Nacional de Estadistica e Informatica, 1994.

parasitic diseases in 1930, but only 25.6% of all deaths in 1960 (see Table 13.3).[7] This represents a 45% decrease in the proportion of deaths due to infectious diseases. By 1990 less than 10% of deaths were attributed to these causes. Improvements in housing, availability of potable drinking water, and increases in vaccination contributed to the decline (Perez, 1988).

Deaths due to problems in the circulatory system (primarily heart disease) grew in importance, accounting for 1.9% of deaths in 1930, 8.5% of deaths in 1960, and 19.8% of deaths in 1990. Deaths due to accidents and violence also increased in importance, accounting for 4.1% of deaths in 1930, 6.5% of deaths in 1960, and 13.9% of deaths in 1990. This increase is due in part to a rise in the number of car accidents.

Although mortality rates declined dramatically since the beginning of the century, fertility rates fluctuated. As would be expected, births decreased during the revolution years, 1910–20. During the 1920s, immediately after the revolution, birth rates increased but stayed relatively constant between the 1930s and the mid-1950s, when fertility increased again until the late 1960s. Fertility rates have been in transition since the early 1970s, when women began to reduce the number of births. Fertility rates declined rapidly during the 1980s and have continued to decline during the 1990s.

---

[7] Camposortega (1989) explains that these statistics may not be accurate since a large proportion of deaths was not certified by a physician. It is estimated that 45.6% of deaths were not certified by a physician in 1940, 37.3% in 1960, and 22.8% in 1975.

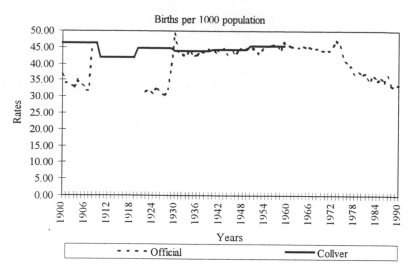

Figure 13.3. Crude birth rate in Mexico, 1900–1990. The sudden increase in fertility rates in 1929 is due to new government regulations that facilitated and encouraged birth registration (Cook and Borah, 1974). (*Sources*: Official: calculated using data from Anuario Estadistico de los Estados Unidos Mexicanos, 1900–90; Collver: estimates by Collver, 1965)

Because of the questions surrounding the accuracy of official statistics, demographers disagree on the birth rates and fertility rates calculated for Mexico in the early part of the century. The underregistration of births and their gradual improvement over time may have artificially created an upward trend in fertility rates. According to Collver (1965), 27% of births were not registered between 1895 and 1909, 3% were not registered during the late 1920s, and a negligible number were not registered during the 1940s. Others claim that underregistration was as high as 19% in 1930 but consider it negligible by the 1960s.[8]

In Collver's estimation, crude birth rates were 46.3 per thousand between 1900 and 1909, declined to 41.9 during the revolution, and increased to 44.8 during the 1920s, staying close to this level until the late 1950s. This suggests a relatively constant fertility rate from 1900 until the 1950s, which was affected only by the revolution (see Table 13.1, Panel A and Figure 13.3). Mier y Terán (1989) calculates that birth rates between 1900 and 1909 were substantially higher than Collver's, at 50–54 per

---

[8] See Mier y Terán (1989) for a review of this literature.

thousand. She suggests that fertility rates declined from the early part of the century to the 1920–29 period. Official birth rates show a decline in fertility after the early 1970s.

Although the crude birth rate indicates that fertility rates were constant from 1930 to 1960, the general fertility rate and the total fertility rate show that births increased during the 1950s and 1960s (see Table 13.4, Panel A).[9] The crude birth rate is less reliable than the general fertility rate and the total fertility rate because it is affected by changes in age structure. Estimates by Mier y Terán show general fertility rates of 207 births per thousand women aged 15–44 for the years 1930–39. The rate was stable until the 1950s, when it rose to 214, and it continued to increase until the 1960s, when it reached 222. Total fertility rates also show an increase from the 1940s to the 1960s, from 6.0 to 6.7 children per woman. As in the case of other fertility measures, the total fertility rate declines after 1970, reaching 3.4 children per woman in 1990.

Alternative measures of fertility can be calculated from census data. The Mexican population censuses from 1950 to 1990 tabulate the number of live births for women of different age groups. The average number of children born to women aged 15–49 increased from 2.6 in 1950 to 3.1 in 1970, but then declined to 2.9 and 2.4, respectively, in 1980 and 1990 (see Table 13.4, Panel B). The increase in number of children ever born from 1950 to 1970 and subsequent decline is observed in every age group: 15–19, 20–24, 25–29, 30–34, 35–39, and 40–49. These census statistics support the evidence that fertility rates increased during the 1950s and 1960s and declined after 1970.

The decline in fertility rates in Mexico is an important development since the rapid population growth could have limited the economic development of the country. Changes in fertility have been the result of socioeconomic conditions rather than government intervention. Fertility has declined mainly as a result of a decrease in age of the mother at the birth of the last child. The largest declines in births have occurred among women aged 30–39 and 40–49 (González García and Monterrubio Gómez, 1993). Increases in literacy rates, schooling, female labor force participation, and use of family planing methods may have contributed to the transition from high to moderate fertility rates.

A demographic balancing equation illustrates the factors contributing to population growth in Mexico during the century (see Table 13.5). The

---

[9] The general fertility rate is defined at the number of births per thousand women of childbearing age. The total fertility rate is defined as the number of births women would have if they experienced a given set of age-specific birth rates throughout their reproductive span.

Table 13.4. *Fertility statistics, 1900–1990*

A. General and total fertility

	General Fertility Rate		Total Fertility Rate	
Period	Vital statistics[a]	Estimates (Mier y Teran)[b]	Estimates (Mier y Teran)[c]	Estimates (CNP)[d]
1900–9	125			
1921–29	122			
1930–39	170	207		
1940–49	177	205	6.04	
1950–59	190	214	6.26	
1960–69	200	222	6.65	
1970–79	182			6.37
1980–89	142			4.31
1990	130			3.39

B. Average number of children ever born by age group of women[e]

Age of women	1950	1960	1970	1980	1990
15–19	0.19	0.21	0.24	0.19	0.17
20–24	1.21	1.29	1.39	1.44	0.99
25–29	2.50	2.65	3.05	2.75	2.11
30–34	3.52	3.84	4.52	4.07	3.13
35–39	4.45	4.74	5.65	5.38	4.05
40–49	4.94	5.01	6.14	6.40	5.19
15–49	2.55	2.63	3.05	2.94	2.36

[a] Calculated using vital statistics data from Anuario Estadistico de los Estados Unidos Mexicanos, 1900–90. Refers to women aged 15–49.
[b] Mier y Teran (1989). Refers to women aged 15–44.
[c] Mier y Teran (1989). Refers to women aged 15–49.
[d] Estimated by Consejo Nacional de Población, printed in González García de Alba y Monterrubio Gómez (1993). Refers to women aged 15–49.
[e] Calculated from data in Censo de la Población, 1950–90.

number of deaths has declined since 1900, even though the population has increased substantially. Births more than tripled from 1900 to 1990. Net migration, individuals arriving in Mexico minus those leaving Mexico, has only become important in the last two decades and has not played a large role in the demographic transformation of the country. Figure 13.4 combines estimates of crude birth and death rates in Mexico during the twentieth century. It shows how population growth resulted

Table 13.5. *Demographic balancing equation, 1900–1990*

Period	Net population change[a]	Births[b]	Deaths[c]	Net migration (A + B)	Net migration of Mexicans[d] (arriving-leaving) (A)	Net migration of foreigners[e] (B)	Error
1900–10	1,553,532	6,586,460	4,906,096	−59,088	−118,522	59,434	−67,744
1910–20	−744,049	6,195,658	5,471,808	−280,757	−264,503	−16,254	−1,187,142
1920–30	2,228,150	6,993,361	4,626,712	−96,022	−155,044	59,022	−42,477
1930–40	3,251,451	7,952,600	4,371,678	281,528	264,029	17,499	−610,998
1940–50	6,009,524	9,978,100	4,406,639	−72,016	−76,984	4,968	510,079
1950–60	9,157,168	13,549,496	4,103,312	−80,360	−121,485	41,125	−208,655
1960–70	13,975,008	18,555,589	4,163,956	−216,093	−183,809	−32,284	−200,532
1970–80	17,970,849	23,783,991	4,502,371	−1,361,794	−1,439,510	77,716	51,023
1980–90	14,742,030	25,831,116	4,169,956	−1,581,376	−1,653,300	71,924	−5,337,754

[a] Population count based on Censo General de la Población.
[b] Births computed using birth rate estimates by Collver (1965) for years 1900–29 and official birth rates for years 1930–90.
[c] Deaths computed using mortality rate estimates by Collver (1965) for years 1900–29 and official mortality rates for years 1930–90.
[d] Estimates of Mexicans moving to Mexico from the United States minus those leaving Mexico to the United States. Based on U.S. census statistics.
[e] Estimates from Mexican census.

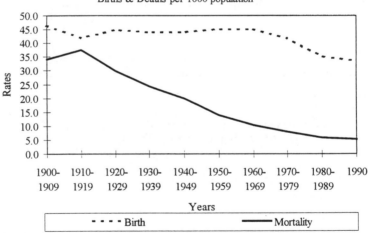

Births & Deaths per 1000 population

Figure 13.4. Crude birth and mortality rates in Mexico, 1900–1990 (*Sources*: Years 1900–29 are estimates from Collver, 1965; years 1930–90 computed using vital statistics data from Anuario Estadistico de los Estados Unidos Mexicanos, 1900–90)

Table 13.6. *Socioeconomic indicators, 1900–1990*

Year	Literacy of population aged 12 and up (%)	Health expenditure as a percentage of GDP[a]	Number of vaccines[b] as a percentage of population	Average	GDP growth (%)
1900	22.3		3.6	1900–9	3.59
1910	27.7	0.1	2.5[d]	1910–19	
1920	33.9	0.1[c]		1920–29	1.03
1930	38.5	0.2	3.7	1930–39	2.59
1940	46.0	0.5	21.1	1940–49	5.14
1950	56.8	0.3	16.9	1950–59	6.31
1960	66.5	0.4	8.5	1960–69	7.15
1970	76.3	3.5	32.9	1970–79	6.48
1980	83.0	4.3	34.3	1980–89	2.12
1990	87.4	3.0	51.7	1990	4.46

Note: Calculated using data from Estadisticas Historicas de Mexico, Instituto Nacional de Estadistica e Informatica, 1994.
[a] Expenditures by main agencies in the health care sector.
[b] Refers to 1925.
[c] Vaccines administered by the Secretaria de Salubridad y Assistencia.
[d] Refers to 1917.

mainly from the large decline in mortality rates and the high fertility rate, which began its decline only after 1970.

ACCOUNTING FOR CHANGES IN MORTALITY AND FERTILITY

Although Mexican researchers have written extensively on national demographic trends, their causes have not always received close attention. Some of the trends therefore remain puzzling. Why, for example, do mortality rates show a decrease after the Mexican revolution (1920–29) compared with the last decade of the Díaz regime (1900–9)? At the aggregate level, this is hard to understand since the gross domestic product grew at an annual rate of 3.6% between 1900 and 1909 but only at 1.0% between 1921 and 1929 (see Table 13.6). Underregistration during the 1920s may be partly responsible for these trends.

According to Camposortega (1989) mortality data show a clear pattern of increasing life expectancy since the 1920s. This coincides with a period of gradual improvements in the living conditions of Mexicans. One indicator of improving socio-economic conditions is the literacy rate, which increased from 33.9% in 1921 to 38.5% in 1930 and 46.0% in 1940 (see Table 13.6). Macroeconomic data support Camposortega's claim, since GDP grew more rapidly during the 1930s (2.6% per year) than during the 1920s (1.0% per year).

The large decline in official crude mortality rates, from 23.1 deaths per thousand in 1940 to 11.5 deaths per thousand in 1960, has been attributed to both health care policies and economic conditions. National vaccination campaigns were conducted during the 1940s. According to Camposortega (1989), vaccination campaigns were responsible for the eradication of typhus and smallpox in 1952, and for a large decrease in deaths due to malaria and its eventual eradication in 1970. Vaccination campaigns also brought a large reduction in deaths due to measles. With the eradication of smallpox, mortality rates responsible for 10.5 deaths per 10,000 in 1930 began their decline. In the case of malaria, which had been responsible for more than 11.9 deaths per 10,000 in 1940, the figure was only 2 per 10,000 in 1960. And measles, which was responsible for 8.9 deaths per 10,000 in 1940, caused only 1.7 deaths per 10,000 in 1960.

During this period, the government created new health care and social security institutions such as the Mexican Institute for Social Security (Instituto Mexicano del Seguro Social), established in 1944. Individual well-being and economic conditions significantly improved between 1940 and 1960. The literacy rate increased from 46.0% in 1940 to 66.5% in 1960. GDP grew at an average annual rate of 5.1% during the 1940s and 6.3% during the 1950s (see Table 13.6).

After 1960, mortality rates continued to decline but at a slower rate. Access to health care continued to improve. For example, the population covered by medical insurance increased from 25.3% in 1970 to 39.9% in 1978 (Camposortega, 1989). Literacy rates increased from 66.5% in 1960 to 83.0% in 1980. Aggregate economic well-being improved during the 1960s and 1970s when GDP was growing at an average annual rate of 7.2% and 6.5%, respectively. However, economic conditions worsened in the country during the 1980s, and in that period GDP grew at only 2.1% per year. Surprisingly, the economic crisis did not stop the downward trend in mortality rates.

Table 13.7 shows ordinary least-squares regression estimates of the

Table 13.7. *Regression of crude death rate on socioeconomic conditions*
(dependent variable: log (deaths per thousand))

Variable	1900–90[a]	1930–90[b]	1930–90[c]
Log (GDP per Capita)[d]	−1.11**	−1.48**	−1.36**
	(.02)	(.15)	(.19)
Log (Vaccines per Capita)		−0.07	−0.05
		(.05)	(.07)
Log (Expenditures on		0.15**	0.12
Health Care per capita)		(.05)	(.07)
R-squared	0.97	0.97	0.98
Observations	77	25	12

[a] Includes all years 1900–90, except 1908–21.
[b] Selected years based on availability of data on vaccines and health expenditures. The years included are 1930, 1935, 1940, 1945, 1950, 1955, 1960, 1965, 1970, 1975, and all years between 1976 and 1990.
[c] Selected years based on availability of data on vaccines and health expenditures. The years included are on a five-year basis begining in 1930 until 1990.
[d] In 1970 pesos.
** .05 significance level.

relationship between mortality rates (deaths per thousand), GDP per capita, number of vaccines per capita administered by the Mexican health department, and expenditures on health care per capita.[10] The elasticity of GDP per capita on mortality rates is estimated to be between −1.0 and −1.5. The results suggest that most of the decline in mortality rates can be explained by improvements in income per capita. As Mexicans' income increased, they were able to buy more food, better housing and more health care. In the regressions, the number of vaccinations administered by the Secretaría de Salubridad y Asistencia is not significantly related to mortality rates. The results may simply indicate that number of vaccines is not a good measure of access to basic health care. Expenditures on health care per capita appear to be positively related to mortality rates. The results are puzzling since one would expect expenditures on health care to improve health. They reflect the fact that large increases in health care expenditures did not occur until the 1970s, when the decline in mortality rates was slower.

[10] Vaccines were administered by the Secretaría de Salubridad y Asistencia. Regression estimates are based on selected years, depending on availability of data on vaccines and health care expenditures.

Trends in fertility rates are more complex than trends in mortality. As previously discussed, fertility rates declined during the Mexican revolution, increased during the 1920s, but stayed constant from the 1930s until the 1950s, when fertility rates increased again, and then began to decline during the 1970s. The decline in births during the revolution is not surprising. As a result of the conflict, couples were more likely to be separated, and the number of marriages declined (Ordorica and Lezama, 1993). Lack of political and economic stability, may have also contributed to the decline in fertility. After the revolution, as the country began to stabilize politically and economically, fertility rates increased. But why did fertility rates increase during the 1950s and 1960s? The average annual growth rate of GDP increased from 1.0% during the 1920s to 6% and 7% during the 1950s and 1960s. If the number of desired children increased with income (i.e., children were not inferior goods), then this simple fact could explain the trend. It is clear, however, that mortality rates were declining during this period. If the goal was to have a given number of surviving children, fertility rates should have stabilized or even declined.

The increase in fertility rates during the 1950s and 1960s may have resulted from sociopolitical attitudes. For many years the Mexican government encouraged increasing fertility rates as a way to populate the country. Porfirio Díaz had attempted to increase the population of Mexico by attracting European immigrants but had failed. After the revolution, Mexican authorities continued to promote increasing fertility rates as a way to achieve the population growth that was believed necessary for Mexico to progress as a nation (Alba, 1993b).

Juárez, Quilodrán, and Zavala de Cosio (1989) argue that the increase in fertility rates is due to the decline in mortality rates. If no effective contraceptives are used, and mortality rates decline, the reproductive lifetime of the couple increases and therefore births per couple increase. Moreover, as nutrition improves and access to health care increases, the number of pregnancies that end with a live birth also increases.

The transition to lower fertility rates occurred just when Mexico was experiencing economic prosperity. GDP was growing at the rate of 6.5% per year during the 1970s. Female literacy, which had been increasing since the 1920s, reached 73.1% in 1970 and 84.8% in 1990. The proportion of females completing elementary school also grew rapidly, from 18 percent among women born between 1927 and 1931 (who were aged 15 and older in 1946) to 73 percent among women born between 1962 and 1966 (who were aged 15 and older in 1981) (Mier y Terán, 1993).

The increase in educational levels is closely related to the decrease in fertility. More educated women have lower fertility rates. Moreover, even though all groups of women have experienced a reduction in fertility, the largest decline occurred among more educated women. The total fertility rate for women who did not attend school was 8.1 children from 1972 to 1976, but it declined to 6.3 children 10 years later (a reduction of 22%). The total fertility rate for women with more than 6 years of schooling was 3.7 children from 1972 to 1976, but it dropped to 2.5 children 10 years later (a 32% reduction) (Mier y Terán, 1993).

Fertility declined mostly because of an increase in the use of contraceptives. In 1976, 30.2% of women who had sexual partners stated that they had used contraceptives such as the pill, diaphragm, sterilization, or abstention. The most frequently used contraceptive was the pill. Contraceptives became more common in subsequent years. By 1987, 52.7% of women with partners used one of these contraceptives, and the most frequently used contraceptive then was sterilization (González García de Alba and Monterrubio Gómez, 1993). Another factor that may have contributed to the decline in fertility rates is the rise in age at first sexual union. In cases when no contraceptives are used, this shortens the period in which a fertile woman is exposed to having children.

REGIONAL DIFFERENCES IN MORTALITY AND FERTILITY

Regional differences in levels and trends of mortality and fertility rates may help explain national changes in mortality and fertility during the twentieth century. Mexico has 32 states. I have chosen to divide the country into five regions: North Border, North, Center, South, and Mexico City.[11] There are significant differences in the mortality rates of these regions. Between 1930 and 1939 mortality rates were lower in the North Border and North regions, with 20.1 and 22.4 deaths per thousand, respectively (see Table 13.8 and Figure 13.5). The Center, South, and Mexico City regions had similar mortality rates, close to 25 per thousand.

[11] The North Border is composed of states along the U.S.-Mexico border: Baja California, Baja California Sur, Coahuila, Chihuahua, Nuevo Leon, Sonora, and Tamaulipas. The North Region includes Durango, Nayarit, San Luis Potosi, Sinaloa, and Zacatecas. The Center region includes Aguascalientes, Colima, Guanajuato, Guerrero, Hidalgo, Jalisco, Mexico, Michoacan, Morelos, Puebla, Queretaro, Tlaxcala, and Veracruz. The South region includes Campeche, Chiapas, Oaxaca, Quintana Roo, Tabasco, and Yucatan. The Mexico City region includes only the Distrito Federal.

Table 13.8. *Mortality and fertility by region, 1930–1990*

Rate	Years	Total	North Border	North	Center	South	Mexico City (D.F.)
Crude	1930–39	24.37	20.13	22.40	25.85	24.14	25.01
death	1960–69	10.18	8.44	9.24	10.82	12.09	9.26
	1990	5.18	4.95	4.51	5.23	5.36	5.44
General	1930	187.43	166.70	219.40	198.87	165.33	149.73
fertility	1960	201.52	206.43	236.49	206.22	191.83	171.15
	1990	130.28	108.46	133.81	135.52	181.35	96.76

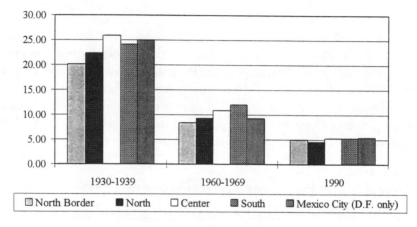

Figure 13.5. Mortality rate by region, 1930–1990 (*Source*: Estimated using data from Anuario Estadistico de los Estados Unidos Mexicanos)

During the 1960s, mortality rates continued to be lower in the North Border and North region, at 8.4 and 9.2 deaths per thousand, respectively. Mexico City had achieved mortality rates similar to these regions. The Center and South had the highest mortality rates, over 10 per thousand. By 1990, differences in mortality rates had mostly disappeared.[12]

Table 13.9 shows regressions of mortality rates on state socioeconomic conditions during the 1930s and in 1990. Between 1930 and 1939, states with higher wages had lower mortality rates. The coefficient on average

---

[12] According Rabell and Mier y Terán (1986), official data underestimate regional differences in mortality rates since regions with higher mortality rates are more likely to have underregistration of deaths, especially in the case of infant deaths.

Table 13.9. *Regressions of mortality rate and general fertility rate on socioeconomic conditions*

Dependent variable	Average mortality, 1930–39	Mortality, 1990	Change in mortality, 1930–39 to 1990	Average GFR, 1930–39[a]	GFR, 1990	Change in GFR, 1930–39 to 1990
Average salary[b]	−5.26**	0.00		53.79**	−0.01	
	(2.17)	(.00)		(20.90)	(.00)	
% Literate	0.00	0.03		−1.35**	−3.41**	
	(.07)	(.03)		(.65)	(.62)	
% Indian[c]	0.12	0.10**		−1.56	2.21*	
	(0.16)	(.04)		(1.65)	(1.16)	
Change in Average salary, 1935–80[d]			0.00			0.00
			(.00)			(.00)
Change in literacy, 1930–90			−0.15**			0.65
			(.06)			(.93)
Change in indigenous population, 1930–90			0.70*			9.64*
			(.36)			(5.28)
Adjusted R^2	0.23	0.11	0.24	0.12	0.60	0.02
Observations	32	32	32	32	32	32

[a] GFR is general fertility rate. In all GFR regressions, literacy refers to female literacy.

[b] In regressions for years 1930–39, average salary is wage per day in 1935 for agricultural workers. These data come from the Anuario Estadistico 1938. In regressions for 1990, average salary is average monthly income in 1980, from Censo General de la Población, 1980. No information on overall income by state was available in 1990.

[c] Percentage of the population that speaks an indigenous language.

[d] The 1935 daily salary was converted to a monthly salary by assuming individuals worked for 6 days a week and a month has 4.3 weeks. The 1935 pesos were converted to 1978 pesos using an index of wholesale prices for Mexico City. This is one of the few price indexes that exist from 1930 to 1978. Source is Estadisticas Historicas de Mexico, Instituto Nacional de Estadistica e Informatica, 1994.

* .10 significance level. ** .05 significance level.

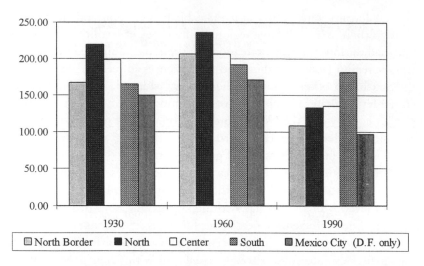

Figure 13.6. General fertility rate by region, 1930–1990 (*Source*: Estimated using data from Anuario Estadistico de los Estados Unidos Mexicanos)

salary is significant at the 5% level. By 1990, however, average salary was no longer as important in explaining mortality rates. States with a larger percentage of indigenous population (those who speak an indigenous language) had higher mortality rates in 1990. Regressions also show that changes in mortality rates between the 1930s and 1990 can be explained by the increase in literacy rates and the decrease in the percentage of the population that is of indigenous origin.

The strong relationship between income and mortality rates is consistent with time-series regressions of mortality rates on income per capita. Increases in income or wages are associated with a decrease in mortality rates because higher incomes imply better nutrition, housing facilities, and access to health care. Higher levels of literacy may be associated with better socioeconomic conditions in a state and therefore lower mortality rates. The positive and significant relationship between the proportion of the population that is indigenous and mortality rates suggests that the indigenous population is at a greater health disadvantage in Mexico.

Regional differences in fertility rates are larger than regional differences in mortality. Between 1930 and 1939, Mexico City had the lowest general fertility rate (150 births per thousand women aged 15–49), followed by the North Border and the South regions (165 births per thousand women) (see Table 13.8 and Figure 13.6). The North and Center regions had the highest general fertility rates, 219.4 and 198.9 births per thousand, respectively. In 1990 there were still large regional differences in fertility rates. Mexico City had the lowest fertility rate (96.8 per thousand), followed by the North Border region (108.5 per thousand). Differences in fertility rates between the South and other regions of the country widened. The South had the largest fertility rate (181.4 per thousand), almost two times higher than that of Mexico City and the North Border region. Not all of these changes are real, since underregistration of births during the 1930s varied by region.

Table 13.9 shows regressions of general fertility rates on socioeconomic conditions at the state level. States with higher wages had higher fertility rates from 1930 to 1939. The coefficient on average salary is significant at the 5% level. Moreover, states with higher literacy rates had lower fertility rates. The coefficient on percentage literate is significant at the 5% level. In 1990, average salary did not seem to affect general fertility rates, but higher literacy rates were strongly associated with lower general fertility rates. The coefficient on literacy rate is significant at the 5% level. The change in the general fertility rate from the 1930s to 1990 was not significantly affected by changes in average wages or literacy. Instead, states that experienced lower reductions in the proportion of indigenous people experienced lower reductions in fertility rates.

Both the 1930s regression and the 1990 regression suggest that states with higher literacy rates had lower fertility rates. This implies that women with more education are more likely to control their fertility, either because of their greater access to information and resources or because they choose to have fewer children. Changes in the general fertility rate within states from the 1930s to 1990 are not well explained by income or literacy. Regressions suggest that states with a lower reduction in the proportion of indigenous population had lower reductions in their fertility rates. One explanation for this result is that Mexican-Indian females do not have the information or resources they need to make use of effective contraceptives. Alternatively, they may be choosing to have more children.

Regression results show that regions with a large proportion of Indians have higher mortality and fertility rates. A large proportion of the Mexican population is of Indian ancestry. The 1921 census classified the population by race: 29.2% Indian, 59.3% mixed white and Indian race, and 10% white. The Mexican census has collected information on the proportion of the population that speaks an Indian language from the beginning of the century. According to these data, 12.9% of the population spoke an Indian language in 1910, 13.4% in 1930, and 6.5% in 1990. The Indian

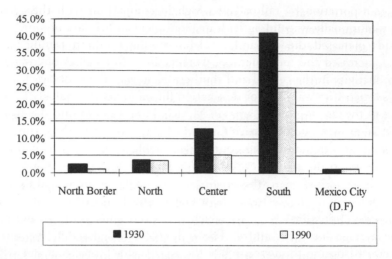

Figure 13.7. Percentage of the population that speaks an Indian language, 1930 and 1990 (*Source*: Estimated using data from Censo General de la Población)

population is highly concentrated by region. In the south of Mexico, over 40% of the population spoke an Indian language in 1930. Even though the proportion speaking an Indian language in the South decreased to 25% in 1990 (see Figure 13.7), it is still a large group in the area.

REGIONAL MIGRATION AND URBANIZATION

In addition to the large changes in mortality and fertility, Mexico experienced substantial regional and international migration between 1900 and 1990. Before the construction of the Mexican railroad at the end of the nineteenth century, the mobility of the population was constrained by the high cost of transportation, since it took a long time to reach distant destinations. Coatsworth (1981) has calculated that the cost of the average railroad journey in 1910 (67 kilometers) was 1.63 pesos by rail compared with 2.41 pesos by foot. This implies that the construction of the railroad reduced traveling costs for workers by 32.4%.[13] Although the cost

---

[13] Costs include travel expenses such as railroad tickets and forgone earnings during the time spent on the trip.

of transportation by railroad was high in comparison with the average minimum daily wage in agriculture, equivalent to 6.3 days of work, railroads increased the demand for labor in the northern mining states and increased the movement of workers away from areas of low labor productivity in the central and southern regions of the country.

Mexico City was a major destination for migrants and quickly became one of the fastest-growing areas in Mexico. From 1900 to 1910 the average annual growth rate of Mexico City was 3.7%, more than three times the average growth rate in the country (see Table 13.10).[14] Since it offered relative safety during the revolution, Mexico City grew at at 2.8% per year between 1910 and 1921, while the national population decreased by 0.5% per year. From 1921 to 1970, the average annual growth rate of Mexico City was approximately 7.0%, which was two to three times greater than the average for the country. The influx of immigrants to the region decreased during the 1970s, when the city grew at 5.0%, one and a half times the average growth rate in the country. From 1980 to 1990, Mexico City grew at 1.3% annually, a slower rate than the 2.0% average growth rate of the country. Mexico City had become less attractive as a destination compared with the more economically vibrant states of the northern border region.

Since 1910, when Mexico City was but a fraction of the Distrito Federal, its area has expanded to cover the Distrito Federal and 27 municipalities of the state of Mexico. The city's population increased from half a million in 1910 to 15 million in 1990 (see Table 13.10). Whereas 3.1% of the population lived in Mexico City in 1910, by 1940 this had increased to 9.2%, and 20.0% in 1980. By 1990 the level of concentration in Mexico City had decreased, with 18.5% of the population now living in the metropolitan area.

The decline of agriculture and the growth of manufacturing and service sectors drew rural populations to cities and promoted the growth of the urban population in Mexico. Close to 70% of workers were employed in agriculture, forestry, and fishing in 1910; these figures declined to 58% in 1950 and 23% in 1990.[15] The decline in agriculture was more pronounced from 1940 to 1980, a period of accelerated urban growth. The urban population grew at an annual rate of only 2.8% during the 1920s, but moved close to 6.0% from 1940 to 1980, then declined to 3.2% during the 1980s (see Table 13.10). The percentage of the Mexican population that is urban

---

[14] Data come from Estadísticas Históricas de Mexico.   [15] Ibid.

Table 13.10. *Urbanization and the growth of Mexico City, 1900–1990*

Year	Urban population	Percentage urban population	Mexico City population[a]	Percentage of population in Mexico City	Period	Average annual Growth rate, urban (%)	Average Annual growth rate, Mexico City (%)
1900	3,849,489	28.3	344,721	2.5	1900–10	1.3	3.7
1910	4,351,172	28.7	471,066	3.1	1910–21	0.2	2.8
1921	4,465,504	31.2	615,367	4.3	1921–30	2.8	7.9
1930	5,540,631	33.5	1,029,068	6.2	1930–40	2.5	7.7
1940	6,896,111	35.1	1,802,679[b]	9.2	1940–50	5.8	7.2
1950	10,983,483	42.6	3,137,599[b]	12.2	1950–60	6.1	6.7
1960	17,705,118	50.7	5,251,755[b]	15.0	1960–70	5.6	7.0
1970	27,308,556	57.8	8,799,937[b]	18.2	1970–80	6.0	5.0
1980	44,299,729	66.3	13,354,271[c]	20.0	1980–90	3.2	1.3
1990	57,959,721	71.3	15,047,685[d]	18.5			

[a] Computed from Census of Population, 1900–90.
[b] Metropolitan area of Mexico.
[c] The following municipalities from the state of Mexico are included: Chimalhuacan, Ecatepec Naucalpan de Jarez, La paz, Tultitlan, Atzapan de Zaragoza, Nezahualcoyotl, Coacalco, Huixquilucan, Cuautitlan, Cuautitlan Izcalli y Tlalnepantla.
[d] The following municipalities from the state of Mexico are included: Acolman, Atenco, Atizapan de Zaragoza, Coacalco, Cuautitlan, Chalco, Chicoloapan, Chimalhuacan, Ecatepec, Huixquilucan, Ixtapaluuca, Jaltenco, Melchor Ocampo, Naucalpan, Nezahulcoyotl, Nextalpan Nicolas Romero, La paz, Tecamac, Teoloyucan, Tepotzotlan, Texcoco, Tlalnepantla, Tultepec, Tultitlan, Zumpango, Cuautitlan Izcalli.

Source: Estadisticas Historicas de Mexico, Instituto Nacional de Estadistica e Informatica, 1994.

increased from 28.7% in 1910, to 35.1% in 1940, 66.3% in 1980, and 71.3% in 1990.

INTERNATIONAL MIGRATION

The United States has become an increasingly important destination for Mexican migrants. From U.S. census data, it appears that 103,000 Mexicans lived in the United States in 1900. That number increased to 4.3 million in 1990. Historical accounts (Corwin, 1973; Cardoso, 1980; Fogel, 1982) suggest that Mexicans began migrating to the United States in large numbers after 1895, when the main lines of the Mexican railroad system were constructed. At the time, American and Mexican railroads were already connected. The new lines enabled American railroads to reach the most populated areas of Mexico.[16]

Between 1890 and 1900, the net number of Mexicans migrating to the United States was approximately 26,000. This increased to 119,000 between 1900 and 1910, and 265,000 between 1910 and 1920 (see Table 13.11). This represents an increase in the average annual growth rate of Mexicans migrating to the United States, from 3.3 percent during the 1890s to approximately 12% between 1900 and 1921.

Economic conditions appear to be the most important factor contributing to the increase in migration, despite the fact that many Mexicans went to the United States during the revolution looking for safety. Railroads connected the booming American Southwest with rural Mexico. At the beginning of the century, according to Cardoso (1980), a peon in the central states of Mexico rarely earned 15¢ a day but could earn 50¢ a day working in railroad construction in the southwestern United States.

At the end of the 1920s, Mexican migration to the United States decreased substantially, and during the 1930s many migrants returned to Mexico. As a result of the economic hardships created by the Great Depression, public hostility rose against foreign labor, and unemployed U.S. workers eagerly took many jobs previously held only by Mexicans. Between 1931 and 1934, more than 350,000 Mexicans who had been living

---

[16] One of the main lines connecting the north and south of Mexico, the Mexican Central Railroad, opened passenger service from Mexico City to Ciudad Porfirio Díaz in Coahuila (U.S.-Mexico border state) in 1884. By 1894, the Mexican Central Railroad lines had reached the most populous states of Mexico in the central plateau.

Table 13.11. *Emigration from Mexico to the United States, 1890–1990*

	Mexicans living in the United States	Migrants as a percentage of Mexican population	Period	Net migrating during decade	Average annual growth of migrants (%)
1890	77,853	0.2	1890–90	25,540	3.3
1900	103,393	0.9	1900–10	118,522	11.5
1910	221,915	1.7	1910–20	264,503	11.9
1921	486,418	1.1	1920–30	155,044	3.2
1930	641,462	−1.6	1930–40	−264,029	−4.1
1940	377,433	0.4	1940–50	76,984	2.0
1950	454,417	0.5	1950–60	121,485	2.7
1960	575,902	0.5	1960–70	183,809	3.2
1970	759,711	3.0	1970–80	1,439,510	18.9
1980	2,199,221	2.5	1980–90	1,653,300	7.5
1990	4,298,014				

Sources: U.S. Census of Population, 1890–1990, and Censo General de la Población, 1900–90.

in the United States returned to Mexico (Corwin, 1973). Much of the return migration was voluntary, in response to the economic distress in the U.S., but some was coerced by local authorities.

During World War II, the number of Mexicans migrating to the United States increased; net migrants grew at 2.0% per year. In 1942 Mexico and the United States signed an agreement on large-scale recruitment and contract of Mexicans to work in certain agricultural areas of the United States. The agreement, the Bracero Program, was initially an emergency program to satisfy perceived labor shortages created in agriculture by World War II. However, the program lasted until 1964, many years after the war had ended. Under the program, 4.5 million temporary workers were admitted to the United States.[17] Large-scale illegal migration of Mexicans to the United States appears to have originated with this program. Employers encouraged Braceros whose contracts had ended to return illegally to bypass U.S. and Mexican regulations. Mexicans also had an incentive to come illegally, since they could avoid contract denial.

---

[17] Some Braceros were recontracted several times, but possibly 1.5 million of the total admitted were distinct persons who for the most part had never been in the United States. (Corwin, 1973).

Census statistics from 1970 to 1980 show a dramatic increase in Mexican migration to the United States (see Table 13.11). The average annual growth rate of net migrants (those arriving in the United States minus those returning to Mexico) was 18.9% during the 1970s. Some of this increase is due to efforts by the U.S. Census Bureau to count illegal immigrants. Nevertheless, the statistics suggest Mexican migration has substantially increased since 1970. This is supported by the fact that the average annual growth rate of Mexicans migrating to the United States was 7.5% from 1980 to 1990.

CONCLUSION

Mexico's demographic history during the twentieth century is strikingly different from that of the United States and Canada. Mexico did not attract many European immigrants, and for this reason its population growth depended entirely on natural increase, growth of births, and deaths in the country. Even without a large influx of immigrants, the population grew at a fast pace by world standards, especially between 1950 and 1970, when it grew by more than 3.0% per year.

The twentieth century has been a period of demographic transformation in Mexico. The country experienced a transition from high mortality rates at the beginning of the century (34 deaths per thousand) to low mortality rates in 1990 (5 deaths per thousand). Most of the decline can be attributed to an increase in economic growth, in association with improvements in food intake, the availability of potable drinking water, and housing. Increases in vaccination rates may also have contributed to a large decline in deaths due to infectious diseases.

Fertility rates were high at the beginning of the century, declined during the revolution, but increased after the war. Fertility stayed constant during the 1930s and 1940s, increased during the 1950s and 1960s, and began its transition to lower rates during the early 1970s. The total fertility rate decreased from 6.7 children in 1970 to 3.4 in 1990. This rapid decline in fertility is one of the most important developments in the demographic history of the country. It can be attributed to higher levels of literacy and schooling, increases in the labor force participation of women, and the use of effective contraceptives.

During the century, Mexico City grew rapidly, becoming one of the largest cities in the world. Its growth did not slow until the 1980s. Two and a half percent of the population lived in the city in 1900, 20.0% in 1980, and 18.5% in 1990. As the agricultural sector declined, migration from rural to urban areas increased and the rate of urbanization rose. The proportion of the population living in urban areas grew from 28% in 1900 to 71% in 1990.

The number of Mexicans migrating to the United States grew rapidly from 1900 to 1920, when the western states of the United States were experiencing an economic boom. During the Great Depression migration came to a halt and many Mexicans returned home. Large-scale migration did not resume until the early 1970s. The number of Mexicans living in the United States increased from 103,000 in 1900 to 4.3 million in 1990 and has continued to grow rapidly during the 1990s. Despite this large growth, outward migration did not play an important role in the demographic transformation of the country.

BIBLIOGRAPHIC ESSAY

There is an extensive literature on demographic trends in Mexico. Most of the articles in journals and books cover a few decades and are written in Spanish. One of the most informative summary books is *El Poblamiento de Mexico: Una Visión Histórico Demográfica* published by the Secretaría de Gobernación and the Consejo Nacional de Población (1993). It consists of four volumes with detailed articles that include summary demographic data accompanied by a thorough analysis of events and factors that contributed to the demographic transformation of Mexico. Each article covers a few decades, starting with colonial times. Most of the articles, however, cover the twentieth century because a data are scarce before this time period. Another useful book that compiles articles on the demographic history of Mexico is *La Población En El Desarrollo Contemporaneo de México*, by Francisco Alba and Gustavo Cabrera (1994).

Andrew Collver's *Birth Rates in Lain America* provides useful estimates of crude birth rates and death rates in Mexico from the beginning of the century until the 1950s. Sergio Camposterga Cruz's article "El Nivel y la Estructura de la Mortalidad en México, 1940–1980" provides estimates on life expectancy, and important discussions on the factors that contributed to the decline in mortality rates. Both articles provide useful discussions on the accuracy of the Mexican vital statistics data. They both agree that birth rates and death rates calculated from government statistics are not reliable before 1940.

There are three main sources of demographic statistics for Mexico: the censuses, the Anuario Estadístico, and Estadísticas Históricas de México. The decennial censuses cover 1900 to 1990. They have population counts by state, age, and gender. From 1950 to 1990 the censuses include information on children ever born to women by age of female. All censuses contain information on number of individuals that speak an American Indian language and literacy of the population. Most of the censuses are reliable except for the 1921 census, taken immediately after the Mexican Revolution. The Anuario Estadístico is an annual government publication available since the beginning of the century, which contains vital statistics such as births and deaths, and immigration data. The Estadísticas Históricas de México is a two-volume book containing the most important statistics available for Mexico from colonial times to 1990. It summarizes information from all decennial censuses and the Anuario Estadístico. It also contains data from other sources. It is a valuable source of data for any one interested in doing research on Mexico.

REFERENCES

Aguirre, A., and Sergio Camposortega. "Evaluación de la Información Basica Sobre Mortalidad Infantil en México." *Demografia y Economia* 14, no. 4 (1980): 447–66.

Alba, Francisco. "Cambios demográficos y el fin del Porfiriato." In *El Poblamiento de México: Una Visión Histórico Demográfica.* Vol. 3, 148–65. Mexico, D.F.: Secretaría de Gobernación y Consejo Nacional de Población, 1993a.

———. "Crecimiento Demográfico y Transformación Económica, 1930–1970." In *El Poblamiento de México: Una Visión Histórico Demográfica.* Vol. 4, 75–95. Mexico, D.F.: Secretaría de Gobernación y Consejo Nacional de Población, 1993b.

Alba, Francisco, and Gustavo Cabrera. *La Población en el Desarrollo Contemporaneo de México.* Mexico, D.F.: El Colegio de Mexico, 1994.

Arriaga, E. *New Life Tables for Latin American Populations in the Nineteenth and Twentieth Centuries.* Berkeley: University of California Press, 1968.

Benítez, Raúl, and Cabrear, Gustavo. *Tablas Abreviadas de Mortalidad de la Población de México 1930, 1940, 1950, 1960.* Mexico, D.F.: El Colegio de Mexico, 1967.

Camposortega Cruz, Sergio. "El Nivel y la Estructura de la Mortalidad en México, 1940–1980." In *La Mortalidad en México: Niveles, Tendencias y Determinantes*, edited by Mario Bronfman and José Gómez de León, 205–71. Mexico, D.F.: Centro de Estudios Demográficos y de Desarrollo Urbano, El Colegio de México, 1988.

———. "La Evolución de la Mortalidad en México, 1940–1980," *Estudios Demográficos y Urbanos* 4, no. 1 (1989): 229–64.

Cardoso, Lawrence A. *Mexican Emigration to the United States 1897–1931.* Tucson, Ariz.: University of Arizona Press, 1980.

Coatsworth, John H. *Growth against Development.* De Kalb, Ill.: Northern Illinois University Press, 1981.

———. *Los Orígenes del Atraso.* Mexico, D.F.: Alianza Editorial Mexicana, 1990.

Collver, O. Andrew. *Birth Rates in Latin America.* Institute of International Studies Research Series No. 7. Berkeley: University of California, 1965.

Cook, Sherburne F., and Borah Woodrow. *Essays in Population History: Mexico and the Caribbean.* Los Angeles: University of California Press, 1974.

Corwin, Arthur F. "Causes of Mexican Emigration to the United States: A Summary View." *Perspectives in American History* 7 (1973): 101–20.

Fogel, Walter. "Twentieth-century Mexican Migration to the United States." In *The Gateway: U.S. Immigration Issues and Policies*, edited by Barry R. Chiswick, 193–221. Washington, D.C.: American Enterprise Institute, 1982.

González García de Alba, Ligia, and María Isabel Monterrubio Gómez. "Tendencias en la Dinámica y Distribución de la Población, 1970–1992." In *El Poblamiento de México: Una Visión Histórico Demográfica.* Vol. 4, 155–87. Mexico, D.F.: Secretaría de Gobernación y Consejo Nacional de Población, 1993.

Instituto Nacional de Estadística, Geografía e Informática. *Estadísticas Históricas de México.* Mexico, D.F.: 1994.

Juárez, Fátima, Julieta Quilodrán, and María Zavala de Cosío. "De una Fecundidad Natural a una Controlada: México 1950–1980." *Estudios Demográficos y Urbanos* 4 (1989): 4–51.

McCaa, Robert. "The Peopling of Nineteenth-Century Mexico: Critical Scrutiny of a Censured Century." In *Statistical Abstract of Latin America* 30, pt. 1, edited by James W. Wilkie, Carlos Alberto Contreras, and Christof Anders Weber, 603–33. Los Angeles: University of California, 1993.

Mier y Terán, Marta . "La Fecundidad en México: 1940–1980. Estimaciones Derivadas de la Información del Registro Civil y de los Censos." In *La Fecundidad en México: Cambios y Perspectivas*, edited by Beatriz Figueroa Campos, 19–62. Mexico D.F.: Centro de Estudios demográficos y de Desarrollo Urbano, El Colegio de México, 1989.

———. *Fertility Transition and Women's Life Course in Mexico.* New York: United Nations, 1993.

Ordorica, Manuel, and José Luis Lezama. "Consecuencias Demográficas de la Revolución Mexicana." In *El Poblamiento de México: Una Visión Histórico Demográfica.* Vol. 4, 33–53. Mexico, D.F.: Secretaría de Gobernación y Consejo Nacional de Población, 1993.

Pérez Astorga, Javier. " Mortalidad por Causas en México 1950–1980." In *La Mortalidad en México: Niveles, Tendencias y Determinantes*, edited by Mario Bronfman and José Gómez de León, 307–29. Mexico D.F.: Centro de Estudios Demográficos y de Desarrollo Urbano, El Colegio de Mexico, 1988.

Rabell, Cecilia Andrea, and Marta Mier y Terán Rocha. "El Descenso de la Mortalidad en México de 1940 a 1980." *Estudios Demográficos y Urbanos* 1, no. 1 (1986): 39–64.

World Bank. *World Development Report 1967.* New York: Oxford University Press.

14

GROWTH AND COMPOSITION OF THE AMERICAN POPULATION IN THE TWENTIETH CENTURY

RICHARD A. EASTERLIN

The population of the United States is the product of the nation's changing economic, social, and political environment. The United States has always been a land of economic opportunity, but the nature of those opportunities changed greatly over the long term, with important consequences for population. Stretching from colonial times to the end of the nineteenth century, the vast agricultural opportunities of the new lands appropriated from Native Americans significantly affected population growth and distribution. The onset of the first industrial revolution in the nineteenth century brought with it new economic opportunities, centered especially in cities and towns, that additionally influenced population. In the twentieth century, a second, and then a third industrial revolution have further altered the economic environment shaping population growth and distribution. The long-term boom-and-bust pattern of economic growth over the past two centuries is reflected in similar population swings.

Each of the "industrial revolutions" that has played such an important role in U.S. population history signifies the gradual introduction and diffusion throughout the economy of a new general-purpose technology in methods of production. But population history has also been shaped by technological revolutions in social conditions – in methods of prolonging life and limiting reproduction. The most important are those with regard to health and mortality, a succession again of three revolutions, in this case, in methods of controlling disease: the first in the latter part of the nineteenth century, the second in the 1930s and 1940s, and the third, beginning in the late 1960s. The 1960s also saw the introduction of new contraceptive techniques for limiting family size, as well as a liberalization of laws relating to contraception and induced abortion, and the resurgence of a strong feminist movement. Another important social development influencing population patterns in the twentieth century has been the rapid expansion of secondary schooling, which took place largely in the period from 1910 to 1950.

On the political side, shifting public policies, especially with regard to immigration, have significantly influenced U.S. population. An era of unrestricted immigration throughout much of the nineteenth century was brought to a close by exclusionary public action, first, against Chinese and Japanese in the 1880s and 1890s, and, then, against immigrants from southern and eastern Europe in the 1920s. In the mid-1960s, new immigration legislation, shaped by family and humanitarian considerations and labor needs of the American economy, replaced the 1920s system of national quotas, with important consequences for the volume and origins of the immigrant flow. The macroeconomic policies initiated by the Employment Act of 1946 and their variable implementation over the last four decades have also had a major impact on population.

Much of the U.S. population record reflects economic and social processes shared in common with the American population's primary area of origin, northern and western Europe, especially Great Britain. But the U.S. population experience differs from that in Europe in two important respects, agricultural settlement and immigration. In northern and western Europe the settlement of new lands had been completed well before the onset of industrialization. Partly as a result, northern and western Europe became a source of immigrants to America.

The following starts with an overview of America's population on the eve of World War I. Taken up next is the record of change through the mid–twentieth century, and the changes in population composition and distribution that resulted. Then demographic developments from midcentury down to the present are examined, followed by a summary of the current status of the population. Finally, the outlook for future population change is briefly discussed in the light of experience in the twentieth century.

THE UNITED STATES ON THE EVE OF WORLD WAR I

POPULATION COMPOSITION

The American population on the eve of World War I may be divided into three large groups that had participated in different ways in nineteenth-

Table 14.1. *Race-nativity distribution of U.S. population,*
1900 and 1950 (percentages)

Population	1900	1950
Total	100.0	100.0
White	87.9	89.5
Native stock*ᵃ*	54.0	67.1
Foreign stock	33.9	22.4
Foreign-born	13.4	6.7
Native-born of foreign or mixed parentage	20.6	15.7
Nonwhite	12.1	10.5
Black	11.6	10.0
Other	0.5	0.5

*ᵃ*Native white of native parentage.
Source: Taeuber and Taeuber (1958), pp. 72, 83.

century economic development: the native white stock (54%), the foreign white stock (34%), and nonwhites (12%; see Table 14.1). The foreign white stock includes immigrants plus the first generation of their descendants.[1] The native white stock is defined as native-born whites both of whose parents were born in the United States, that is, native whites of native parentage. It thus includes all of the descendants of earlier generations of white immigrants.

In 1900, almost all of the nonwhite population were blacks (96 percent), descended almost entirely from the black population at the start of the nineteenth century. (Also included were a small number of black immigrants, chiefly from the West Indies, and their descendants, plus the descendants of an unknown but probably small number of slaves illegally imported in the nineteenth century.) The remainder of the nonwhite population were mostly Chinese, Japanese, and Native Americans, most of the last having been herded onto reservations. In the following discussion, when nonwhites are considered, the focus will be on blacks, because of their numerical preponderance.

---

[1] In census terminology, the latter group is labeled native-born whites of foreign or mixed parentage, that is, those born in the United States whose parents included at least one immigrant.

Table 14.2. *Occupational distribution of native white stock,
foreign white stock, and nonwhites, 1910 (percentages)*

Occupation	Native white stock	Foreign white stock			
		Total	Native white of foreign or mixed parentage	Foreign-born white	Non-white
All	100	100	100	100	100
Farm	49	16	19	13	46
Nonfarm	51	84	81	87	54
All nonfarm	100	100	100	100	100
White-collar	41	28	38	20	2
Craftsman and operatives	36	43	41	43	22
Unskilled laborers	13	18	11	24	30
Domestic servants	4	5	4	6	32
Other service workers	5	6	6	7	14

Source: Kaplan and Casey (1958); Hutchinson (1956), underlying worksheets.

ECONOMIC ACTIVITY

The occupational distribution of the three principal population groups on the eve of World War I reveals their differing participation in the economic processes dominating nineteenth-century American development. For much of the native white stock, agricultural settlement had been the principal focus. It was the native white stock that disproportionately dominated the westward movement, north and south, and, consequently, the growth of America's farms and small towns. In 1910, half of the native white stock was still occupied in farming, compared with only about one-sixth of the foreign white stock (Table 14.2). The foreign white stock's labor supply was directed principally toward meeting the labor demands of industrialization in the larger towns and cities, particularly the requirements for manual labor. The native white stock, too, participated in industrialization, but more in the higher-echelon white-collar and craft occupations. The native white stock also dominated business and craft occupations in the smaller towns and villages.

The black population, as slaves, had been a major source of farm labor in much of Southern agriculture prior to the Civil War. Before World

Table 14.3. *Urban-rural distribution of native white stock,*
foreign white stock, and nonwhites, 1910 (percentages)

Population	Native white stock	Foreign white stock		Foreign-born white	Non-white
		Total	Native white of foreign or mixed parentage		
Total	100.0	100.0	100.0	100.0	100.0
Urban	35.6	67.5	64.7	71.4	27.3
>500,000	5.9	25.3	22.7	29.0	4.0
25,000–500,000	14.5	26.4	26.1	27.0	12.4
2,500–24,999	15.1	15.8	16.0	15.5	10.7
Rural	64.4	32.5	35.3	28.6	72.7

Source: Thompson and Whelpton (1933), pp. 47, 48, 70, 77.

War I, to the extent that blacks participated at all in the new economic opportunities, it was almost entirely in the South – in further settlement of the West South Central region and the gradual expansion of cities. Blacks remained largely concentrated in the lowest rungs of the occupational ladder, as farm and nonfarm laborers, and domestic servants (Table 14.2).

GEOGRAPHIC DISTRIBUTION

Because of the differing participation of the three population groups in nineteenth-century economic opportunities, their geographic distribution on the eve of World War I differed greatly. The native white stock, the leading group in agricultural settlement, was widely distributed, with four persons out of five on farms, in small villages, or in towns with a population of less than 25,000 (Table 14.3). Among the foreign white stock – the group that supplied much of the manual labor demands of industrialization – over one-half were in communities with a population of more than 25,000 persons, and, of these, half again were in cities of a half million or more. In large cities outside of the South, the foreign white stock made up close to three-fourths of the population. The black population, whose participation in both agricultural settlement and industrialization had been so limited, remained almost wholly concentrated in the South – nine out of ten were there, the vast majority on rural farms.

STRATIFICATION, ASSIMILATION, AND INTEGRATION

Nineteenth-century America was a land of exceptional economic opportunity. No other nation in the history of the world has accepted such an enormous influx of immigrants – a net flow of close to 24 million persons between 1840 and 1910. Nevertheless, the United States remained highly stratified in terms of occupation and geographic location. This is clear even from the simple tripartite division of the population considered here. The native white stock dominated proprietor, craft, and business occupations in the countryside, towns, and villages, as well as professional, business, and craft jobs in the cities. Immigrants chiefly supplied the manual labor for industrialization, and blacks remained largely in the South in the lowest-status occupations.

American schooling was an important factor working to increase occupational mobility. The children of immigrants benefited from the availability of free education in urban areas and achieved a level of education close to that of the native white stock, with a literacy rate of about 95%. Because of this, they were better able to compete with the native stock in the nonfarm sector and find fairly similar jobs (Table 14.2). But blacks, most of whom were raised in the rural South, suffered from a severe schooling deficit, even in comparison with new immigrants. In 1900, over half of adult blacks were illiterate, compared with about one-fourth of immigrants.

To some extent, stratification moderated problems of assimilation and integration in nineteenth-century America, because different population groups were largely in different occupational and geographic labor markets and only in limited contact with each other. However, as settlement opportunities receded in the latter part of the nineteenth century, and the native white stock increasingly turned toward cities for employment, competition and friction between the native and foreign white stock grew. This was exacerbated by the shift in immigrant origins from northern and western Europe to southern and eastern Europe – what was called at the time, the "new immigration." This shift in immigrant origins fostered the view among those of native white stock that immigrants were different from themselves. Increasing competition with these "new" immigrants led to a growing outcry for immigration curtailment and eventually resulted in severely restrictive legislation in the 1920s. Because blacks remained so poorly educated and so largely concentrated in the South, the United States on the eve of World War I had hardly begun seriously to face the problem of racial integration.

The issue of economic equality between the sexes also remained largely in the background. Most women were married, and their primary work, both in rural and urban areas, was in the home. This included not only childbearing and childrearing, but many household tasks that had only been taken over in part by factory production, such as baking and sewing. Many women living on farms participated in agricultural activity as unpaid family laborers, but they were not consistently counted as gainful workers by census enumerators, who focused on "principal activity" as the basis for labor force classification. In the nonfarm sector, where women accounted for about one-fourth of the labor force, most women were not permanently in the labor market – the great majority were unmarried and usually left the labor force when they married. Women workers were confined largely to so-called female occupations and thus were not usually in competition with men. Nearly half of women in the labor force were in unskilled jobs, as domestic servants, farm laborers, service workers, or the like, work done largely by black or immigrant women (Table 14.4). About one-fourth were semiskilled machine operators, most of them in the textile, apparel, and footwear industries, which had a long history of employing young, single women. Of the remainder, who were chiefly in white-collar jobs, most were teachers or held newly emerging clerical or sales jobs.

MORTALITY

On the eve of World War I, the growth and composition of the U.S. population was being shaped not only by the economic environment, but by a new social revolution. Just as the development of scientific methodology had given birth at the beginning of the nineteenth century to an explosion of new knowledge in methods of production – the first industrial revolution – so, too, in the last half of the nineteenth century there was a revolution in knowledge of methods of disease control. The critical breakthrough was the validation of the germ theory of disease and establishment of the science of bacteriology. A public health movement to clean up the large northern and midwestern cities had been under way for some time before this advance in knowledge. But the scientific breakthrough

Table 14.4. *Occupational distribution of females and males, 1900 and 1950*

	Female		Male	
Occupation	1900	1950	1900	1950
All	100.0	100.0	100.0	100.0
White-collar	17.8	52.5	17.6	30.5
Professional, technical	8.2	12.2	3.4	7.2
Managers, officials, proprietors[a]	1.4	4.3	6.8	10.5
Clerical	4.0	27.4	2.8	6.4
Sales	4.3	8.6	4.6	6.4
Manual	27.8	22.4	37.6	48.4
Craftsmen, foremen	1.4	1.5	12.6	19.0
Operatives	23.8	20.0	10.4	20.5
Unskilled laborers[a]	2.6	0.8	14.7	8.8
Service	35.4	21.5	3.1	6.2
Domestic	28.7	8.9	0.2	0.2
Other	6.8	12.6	2.9	6.0
Farm	18.9	3.7	41.7	14.9
Farmers and farm managers	5.9	0.7	23.0	10.0
Farm laborers and foremen	13.1	2.9	18.7	4.9

[a] Excluding farm.
Source: Kaplan and Casey (1958), p. 7.

provided new justification and impetus for a number of public health measures: effective sewage disposal, purification of water supply, paved streets, safer food supplies, swamp drainage, rodent control, isolation and quarantine of disease victims, and education in personal hygiene and the care of infants.

Before this revolution in methods of infectious disease control, mortality had been much higher in urban than rural areas. An estimate for a group of northern states around 1900 – several decades after urban mortality had begun to decline – put expectation of life at birth in urban areas at almost nine years less than that in rural areas, 46 versus 55 years (Thompson and Whelpton, 1933, p. 242). Although economic advance had improved resistance to disease and in this way made for lower mortality, it had also increased exposure to disease by increasingly concentrating population in high-density urban centers, thereby tending to raise mortality. Only in the last quarter of the nineteenth century, with the revolution in knowledge of methods of controlling disease and improving health ushered in by the germ theory of disease, was the adverse effect of economic growth on life expectancy due to urbanization gradually removed (Table A.2 in the book appendix; see also Mokyr and Stein, 1997).

Because of their differing locations and participation in economic opportunities, mortality differed noticeably among the three principal population groups. The native white stock had the lowest mortality. This was partly due to its leading role in agricultural settlement and resulting rural residence. Even in urban areas, however, the native white stock fared best, probably because its higher economic status enabled it largely to avoid living in the high-density central city slums, with their high levels of exposure to disease. At the other extreme of the mortality spectrum were the blacks. Although residing in rural areas, their virtual exclusion from the benefits of education and economic growth resulted in malnutrition, inadequate shelter, and extremely high mortality. Blacks in urban areas, north and south, fared even worse than their rural counterparts; the combination of low income, poor education, and high population density resulted in their having the highest mortality of any population group, urban or rural (Table A.2).

The mortality of the foreign white stock fell between that of the native white stock and blacks, but was closer to the former. The foreign white stock were, on the one hand, beneficiaries of the income opportunities opened up by economic growth in urban areas; on the other, they were disproportionately exposed to the adverse living conditions of large cities. A rough order-of-magnitude estimate of life expectancy at birth around 1900 for each of the three groups, urban and rural combined, would be native white stock, about 52 years or more; foreign white stock, around 49 years; and black, 40 years or less (Preston and Haines, 1991, pp. 100, 228).

FERTILITY

At the start of the twentieth century, rates of childbearing in the United States were high compared with those in northern and western Europe. This was due chiefly to three factors. One was the high rate of childbearing of new immigrants from southern and eastern Europe, reflecting the high fertility levels of their countries of origin. A second was the relatively high fertility rate of the native white stock participating in the settlement of new agricultural areas. The third was the high fertility rate of the black population, the highest of all three population groups.

But rates of childbearing were not uniformly high. In urban areas the native white stock already had a fertility rate considerably below that of its rural counterpart. Moreover, within the rural sector, fertility of the native white stock in the older settled areas east of the Mississippi had been falling for a long time and was considerably below that in the areas of recent settlement. Within the population of foreign white stock, the fertility of the offspring of immigrants was much less than that of the immigrants themselves, a pattern widely observed as an immigrant population assimilates to the domestic population. Within the black population, those in urban areas had substantially lower fertility than those in rural areas.

A rough idea of the magnitude of the differences in childbearing is given by the average number of children born to women aged 45–49 in 1910, those who had recently completed their childbearing (Grabill, Kiser, and Whelpton, 1958, pp. 22–23, 46, 106-7). The highest rate by far was that of black women on southern farms, who averaged close to eight births per woman. This rate is similar to that found in developing countries in which fertility is not intentionally controlled, and to that of the white population of the United States around 1800. Below this, with five to six births per woman, were the first generation of immigrant women and the native white stock in areas of recent agricultural settlement. The lowest childbearing rates, on the order of three to four children per woman, prevailed among the native white stock in urban areas and in long-settled rural areas, among the offspring of recent immigrants (the second generation), and among blacks in the urban North.

These patterns reflected the play of different factors on the various population groups. The very high fertility of rural blacks was in part due to their adverse mortality conditions. With child mortality about two-thirds higher than that of rural native whites, the prospect of offspring surviving to adulthood was not bright, and the need for limiting family size small. The high fertility of immigrant women was, in part, an echo of the high fertility in their areas of origin. High immigrant fertility was also due to a special demographic feature of the immigrant population, a high proportion of males to females in the marriageable ages. This resulted in an unusually high proportion of women being married and thus bearing children. In areas of recent agricultural settlement, high fertility of the native white stock was similarly influenced by a high ratio of males to females of marriageable age, as well as the relatively low costs and high returns of children. Relatively low rates of childbearing in urban areas arose from the opposite situation with regard to costs and returns. In contrast to children on farms, those in urban areas were costly to raise and their income-earning opportunities minimal. Among urban black women, marital separation and unusually high rates of childlessness, perhaps due to sterility problems, appear to have been important sources of low fertility.

THE U.S. POPULATION TO 1950

The economic environment of the U.S. population in the first half of the twentieth century was strikingly different from that in the nineteenth century. Agricultural opportunities had by and large come to an end, aside from wartime booms, and the year 1910 marked the incipient decline of the farm population. Industrial growth continued to generate growing labor demands in urban areas and thus further geographic concentration of population. But the underlying technology gradually shifted from the coal-steam-iron complex of the first industrial revolution to that of the second industrial revolution, based on electricity, the internal combustion engine, petroleum, nonferrous metals, and chemicals, with new and less rigid implications for the composition and location of labor demands. The conditions of labor supply were also drastically altered, first by World War I, which cut off the flow of persons from Europe, and then by legislation passed in 1921 and 1924 that capped the total flow and shifted the sources of immigration back toward northern and western Europe. The historic long-term boom-and-bust pattern of economic growth continued, with vigorous expansions during World Wars I and II and most of the 1920s, and the longest and deepest depression on record in the 1930s.

On the social side, the public health movement continued to grow and diffuse, punctuated by the worldwide influenza epidemic of 1918. In the 1930s and 1940s, a new breakthrough in control of communicable disease occurred with the development of effective therapy for infectious diseases, based on the discovery of antibiotics and sulfa drugs. Also, schooling took a new leap forward. Among whites, back in the third quarter of the mid–nineteenth century, the average level of schooling had reached an elementary education, and very little change occurred for several decades thereafter. Starting around 1910, however, high school education began to expand rapidly, and by 1950 a high school diploma was becoming the norm.

In the period from World War I to 1950, the white population became much more ethnically homogeneous, and the native- and foreign-born stocks more similar in location and economic activity. The isolation of blacks in the rural South also diminished markedly. However, the occupational segregation of both blacks and females, though lessening somewhat, remained high.

In the five years preceding World War I, the rate of net immigration per year to the United States averaged more than 5 persons per thousand population, about the same level as the average rate that had prevailed since 1870. There was a temporary immigration upsurge after World War I, but then severe restrictions were imposed by congressional legislative acts in 1921 and 1924. The 1924 legislation set an upper limit on immigration considerably below the pre–World War I volume and established a system of immigrant quotas from each country that particularly favored immigrants from northern and western Europe. The 1930s depression further discouraged immigration. The average rate of net immigration per year for the entire period 1915 to 1950 ended up at about one-fifth of the prior rate, little more than one person per thousand population.

In the nineteenth century, immigrants and blacks had both been sources of less-skilled labor, but they supplied demands in different regions of the country – immigrants, the industrial demands of the urban North; blacks, the agricultural demands and, then, the gradually expanding urban demands of the South. There was little immigration to the South and fairly little black migration to the North, even after the abolition of slavery.

The sharp curtailment of immigration starting with World War I changed all this, opening up a number of less-skilled jobs for blacks in the North. The result was a sharp upsurge in black out-migration from the rural South, especially to industrial centers in the Northeast and Midwest, along with the continued migration of rural blacks to southern cities. This flow was moderated but not eliminated by the Great Depression. It resumed in even greater force in the 1940s with the economic boom of the war and postwar period, expanding to include the West as a destination for blacks, along with the North. By 1950 almost one-third of blacks lived in the North or West, almost all in urban areas, and another third were in urban areas in the South. Only about one in five remained on southern farms.

In the twentieth century, with the disappearance of agricultural opportunities, the native white stock, too, turned increasingly to urban areas for employment. Whereas in 1900, about two thirds of the native white stock lived in rural areas, by 1950 close to two-thirds were in urban areas. Although the foreign white stock remained most concentrated in urban areas – more than 4 out of 5 – the geographic distribution of the three population groups was much more similar by 1950 than it had been on the eve of World War I.

The white population was becoming more homogeneous, not only in location, but also in composition. The sharp curtailment of immigration reduced noticeably the proportion of foreign-born in the white population, to about 1 person in 13 by 1950 (Table 14.1). A corresponding decline occurred in this period in the share in the white population of those of foreign white stock, to one-fourth in 1950.

The racial makeup of the population as a whole in 1950 was just about the same as in 1910, with nonwhites accounting for a little over one-tenth of the total (Table 14.1). Within the nonwhite population, the share of blacks continued to be about 95 percent.

ECONOMIC ACTIVITY AT MIDCENTURY

The first half of the twentieth century saw the disappearance of farming as the principal occupation of male workers: in 1900, 42% had been engaged in farming; by 1950, this figure was down to 15% (Table 14.4). A substantial decline occurred among all three groups in the population, and by 1950, nonfarm work occupied 4 out of 5 blacks, 5 out of 6 of the native white stock, and over 9 out of 10 of the foreign white stock (Table 14.5; Hutchinson 1956, Tables A-2a, A-2b; U.S. Bureau of the Census, 1953, pp. 276 ff.).

Within the nonfarm sector, the trend toward greater homogeneity within the white population was again marked. Among white males, the broad occupational distribution of second-generation immigrants was virtually identical to that of the native stock; of nine major categories of occupations, there was not one in which the share of second-generation immigrants differed from that of the native white stock by much more than one percentage point. In contrast, black males remained concentrated

Table 14.5. *Occupational distribution of whites and blacks, 1950 (percentages)*

Occupation	White	Black
All	100.0	100.0
Farm	11.3	18.8
Nonfarm	88.7	81.2
All nonfarm	100.0	100.0
White-collar	45.0	11.9
Professional, technical	10.5	4.1
Managers, officials, proprietors[a]	11.3	2.2
Clerical	14.6	4.2
Sales	8.7	1.5
Manual	46.2	52.1
Craftsmen, foremen	17.4	7.0
Operatives	22.8	24.0
Unskilled laborers[a]	5.9	21.2
Service	8.8	35.9
Domestic servants	1.2	17.1
Other	7.6	18.9

[a] Excluding farm.
Source: U.S. Bureau of the Census (1953), II, Part I, pp. 1–276 to 1–279.

in the lowest-status occupations – over three-fourths were operatives, nonfarm laborers, or service workers, which was more than twice the proportion for the native white stock. The occupational distribution of male immigrants fell between that for the native white stock and blacks, but was considerably closer to the former.

These disparities in occupational status corresponded rather closely to those in schooling. In 1950 the educational attainment of second-generation immigrants was identical with that of the native white stock, 9.8 years of school completed among males 25 years of age and older. The corresponding figure for blacks was 6.4 years, while that for foreign-born whites was 8.2 years (U.S. Bureau of the Census, 1954, p. 57).

STRATIFICATION, ASSIMILATION, AND INTEGRATION

The first half of the twentieth century thus saw the progressive assimilation of the population of foreign white stock, which had come almost wholly from Europe. Assimilation was partly a result of the 1920s legislation first described that reduced the size of the foreign white stock by severely curtailing its principal source, immigration, while substantially increasing the English-speaking component of the flow. Partly it was the result of the growing education in urban areas of immigrants' children. This schooling reduced or eliminated language and other differences from the native white stock and made it possible for immigrants' children to move up the occupational ladder more easily than the immigrants themselves.

But progress with regard to social and economic integration of blacks remained slow. As has been noted, the period from 1910 on did see an enormous exodus of the black population from farms in the rural South. But blacks in urban areas were, like earlier generations of new immigrants, highly concentrated in central cities and in the lowest-skilled jobs, and handicapped by inadequate schooling. The rapid expansion of secondary schooling had hardly touched the black population, many of whom had been educated in the South, the most laggard region with regard to the establishment of secondary education. Even among younger men – those aged 25 to 29 – the educational gap between blacks and whites in 1950 was very great, virtually the difference between a high school and elementary school education (Folger and Nam, 1967).

Women continued to be highly concentrated in women's work (Table 14.4). Although the share of women in the total nonfarm labor force increased from 24% in 1900 to 30% in 1950, the great bulk of this increased share was due to the disproportionate expansion of female jobs. Most important by far was the enormous growth of clerical jobs. While total nonfarm jobs – male plus female – about tripled between 1900 and 1950, clerical jobs grew more than eightfold and came to account for nearly three-tenths of the nonfarm work of women. This expansion of clerical work reflected especially the burgeoning administrative and office requirements of firms, as their size grew with the second industrial revolution. With regard to professional job opportunities, women benefited especially from the increased demand for teachers owing to the expansion of secondary education, and for professional nurses, as the new technology of disease control was implemented. About one woman worker in eight held a low-skilled service job outside the home (such as waitress, fountain worker, cook, beautician, cleaning woman), jobs that had expanded along with the growth of cities. The proportion of women in domestic service fell to less than 1 in 10, partly because of the expansion of the relative demand for service workers outside the household, and partly the sharp curtailment of immigration from southern and eastern Europe.

During World War II there was a substantial surge in employment of women as machine operators in a number of industries outside the traditional textile-apparel-footwear sector, but after the war these jobs reverted largely to men. Taking the period 1900 to 1950 as a whole, occupational segregation by gender diminished mildly, but it was still very high at midcentury.

Up until World War II, the increased demand for women workers was filled largely by single women or those in marriages broken by death or divorce (Goldin, 1990, pp. 17, 26; Long, 1958, Table A-6). There was also a modest growth in labor force participation of married women in intact marriages, but in 1940 less than one wife in seven was in the labor force. The decade 1940 to 1950 saw an abrupt break in this pattern, a shift to married women, especially older married women, to fill the expanding demand for women workers. This shift in the sources of female labor supply was due to new demand and supply conditions in the women's labor market that developed during and after World War II.

The growing employment of women before World War II is attributable largely to the rapidly expanding demand for female labor, especially clerical workers, and the increasing supply of young women with the appropriate educational qualifications as secondary education expanded. The importance of unmarried young women in filling the growing demand raises doubt about two other factors often cited as "freeing" women for labor market activity: reduced childbearing, and increased availability of household appliances. These explanations would apply primarily to women who were married and homemakers. Most young unmarried women lived at home with their parents and were childless.

MORTALITY, 1900–1950

The great breakthrough in the control of communicable disease that had started with the public health movement in the latter part of the nineteenth century accelerated in the late 1930s with the advent of effective therapy against infectious disease through the use of antibiotics and sulfa drugs. By 1950 the average expectation of life at birth in the United States had soared to 68 years, a nationwide level unheard of only a half century before, and totally unanticipated at that time. Expectation of life improved markedly in both urban and rural areas, but most markedly in urban. By 1950 the vast nineteenth-century excess of urban over rural mortality had disappeared.

Although difficult to measure precisely, the disappearance of mortality differentials by place of residence was probably accompanied by a widening of mortality differentials by socioeconomic status, that is, by education, income, and occupation (Preston and Haines, 1991). At the beginning of the twentieth century medical care and hygienic practices were, by today's standards, rudimentary. Because of the lack of knowledge about health, more money or education did not do much to bring better health and longer life expectancy. Such advantages as accrued arose largely from the ability to escape living in urban slums. As medical and hygienic knowledge increased, differences among households in material resources and level of education could more readily be translated into corresponding differences in health and life expectancy. Thus, with the development of sound scientific knowledge of disease, mortality differences in the population became less a matter of environmental conditions – whether one lived in city centers, their peripheries, or rural places – and more a matter of behavioral decisions dependent on income and education.

The reduction of mortality reflected largely a sharp decrease in mortality due to infectious diseases, such as influenza, pneumonia, tuberculosis, typhoid, and gastrointestinal disease. Among the various age groups in the population, the young, especially infants and children, who had suffered the highest fatality rates from many of these diseases, were the principal beneficiaries of the sharp reduction in their incidence. By contrast, the reduction in mortality was fairly small among the oldest segment of the population, where the principal killers were the degenerative diseases of old age, primarily heart disease, stroke, and cancer. Females benefited more than males from the advance in life expectancy. The modest advantage that females had enjoyed at the turn of the century in life expectancy at birth – perhaps two years – rose by 1950 to more than five. One contributor to this was the sharp decline in maternal mortality, as deaths from infection during pregnancy and childbirth were brought under control.

Among the principal population groups, blacks, who in 1900 were worst off by far, enjoyed the greatest improvement. By 1950 black life expectancy at birth was almost 61 years (Table A.2). However, blacks still lagged behind whites by about eight years. Within the white population, there was probably little difference in 1950 in mortality of the foreign and native stocks, because of the elimination of urban-rural mortality differences.

FERTILITY, 1900–1950

The great reduction in infant and child mortality, coupled with growing education, the shifting nature of labor demands, and immigration restriction, had a major impact on rates of childbearing. Fertility is strongly affected by child mortality – a decline in child mortality inducing lower rates of childbearing. Between 1900 and 1950 the likelihood of a white infant dying by age five fell from 1 in 6 to 1 in 33; of a black infant, from more than 1 in 4 to less than 1 in 16. For both population groups, then, uncontrolled fertility would result in more surviving children than were wanted. Declining infant and child mortality thus created a pervasive pressure to limit family size. The principal techniques of this kind were to defer marriage, and, for those married, to use what are today called "traditional" methods of contraception: withdrawal, rhythm, and to use condoms. Induced abortion was probably used too, but its numerical prevalence is uncertain.

The end of agricultural settlement and the growing urbanization of both the native white stock and blacks in the first half of the twentieth century meant a growing concentration of these population groups in a city environment making for relatively low fertility. In addition, in rural areas pressure for lower fertility was aggravated by a severe agricultural recession starting in the 1920s. This pressure expanded to the whole population with the general economic collapse of the 1930s. Special factors operating to lower the fertility of immigrants also arose from the restrictive legislation of the 1920s, which had an adverse impact on women's marriage by reducing the proportion of males to females. This legislation also shifted the origins of European immigrants from high- to low-fertility countries.

The growth of female education is sometimes said to have reduced childbearing by opening up new job opportunities for women in urban areas, especially in the rapidly expanding clerical sector, and thus increasing the attractiveness of the labor market in comparison with childbearing. However, the quantitative impact of this factor is uncertain, because it relates primarily to a choice confronting married women, and before World War II most married women did not work. Conceivably this factor may have encouraged later marriage of single women, and, in this way, reduced childbearing. Growing education may also have lowered female fertility by helping to spread knowledge of contraception, as well as reduce inhibitions against its use, and by fostering more materially centered life styles that conflicted with traditional family-centered ways of living.

By 1950 childbearing behavior within the United States population, like mortality and the rural-urban distribution of population, was much more uniform than in 1900. In the white population, fertility differences between the native and foreign stock had largely disappeared. Although blacks continued to have higher fertility than whites, owing to their higher fertility in rural areas, the excess had been sharply reduced. In 1950, among white women aged 45–49, the average number of children ever born had fallen to 2.3; among blacks, to 2.7.

Declining fertility, coupled with immigration restriction, brought down sharply the rate of growth of the U.S. population in the first half of the twentieth century, more than offsetting the stimulus to population growth from declining mortality. The rate of population growth fell from its twentieth-century high of close to 2% a year in 1905–10 to its all-time low in the 1930s of about 0.7%.

THE U.S. POPULATION, 1950 TO THE PRESENT

In the period after World War II, unprecedented labor market developments had an enormous impact on the U.S. population. Up to the early 1970s, there prevailed the strongest labor market in the history of the American economy – the unemployment rate from 1946 through 1973 averaged 4.7%, much better than the 6% or more taken as the full employment standard in the 1990s. This exceptionally strong labor market was due to both demand and supply factors. The growth of aggregate demand was stimulated, first, by the backlog of consumer and investment demand that had accumulated at home and abroad during the Great Depression and World War II, and, then, by the demands generated by the Korean and Vietnam wars. The growth of aggregate demand was also promoted by deliberate measures of federal fiscal and monetary policy. These measures reflected advancing knowledge of how to control the level of economic activity – a technological revolution in social science – that had led to the passage of the Employment Act of 1946 committing the federal government to promoting high levels of employment. A tight labor market was also promoted by labor supply conditions after World War II. Not only was immigration restricted, but rates of labor market entry from the domestic population fell to an all-time low, echoing the very low birth rates of the 1920s and 1930s.

A number of new developments starting in the 1970s led to a marked weakening of the labor market. Total labor demand grew more slowly, as inflation fears led to a retreat from the use of fiscal and monetary policy to pursue full employment. Also, labor supply grew more rapidly. One important reason was new immigration legislation that increased substantially the inflow of foreign workers. Another was the upsurge in labor force growth caused by the entry into the labor market of the post–World War II baby boom generation.

The composition of both labor demand and labor supply also shifted significantly. The composition of labor demand was newly influenced by the rise of foreign competition, a new computer-based industrial revolution, and by antidiscriminatory legislation that opened up new opportunities for women and blacks. The composition of labor supply was altered by growing college enrollments, which partly reflected the growing proportion of high school graduates, and partly new federal policies. These policies provided veterans of military service with college tuition and stipends, and also established new college loan programs. Also contributing to higher college enrollments was a great expansion of state university and college systems with low tuition rates.

Starting in the late 1960s, there was a new breakthrough in the control of disease, the first major advance in reducing mortality from the degenerative diseases of old age, in this case, heart disease and stroke. With regard to childbearing, a number of new techniques of limiting family size were introduced in the 1960s, most notably the oral pill and intrauterine device, and anti-abortion laws were liberalized. The 1960s also saw the reemergence of a strong feminist movement.

These varied developments – economic, social, and political – produced a number of dramatic changes in the American population – changes unforeseen at the end of World War II. An unprecedented boom in childbearing occurred from the end of the war through the early 1960s, followed by an equally severe baby bust. Mortality reduction at older ages accelerated sharply, and population aging came to the fore as an issue. A "new" new immigration developed with a pronounced shift to areas of origin other than Europe. The roles and status of blacks and women in the economy grew. There was also a southern and westward shift of population, and a new geographic form of cities emerged, with suburbanization and the rise of polycentric cities.

IMMIGRATION, 1950–1990

From the end of World War II to the mid-1960s, the flow of immigrants to the United States remained fairly small and came largely from Europe. Starting in 1965, a series of changes in immigration legislation altered dramatically the immigration picture in the United States. The 1965 Amendments to the 1952 Immigration and Nationality Act shifted the basis of American immigration policy from a quota allocation based on national origins to one based principally on three considerations: reuniting families, needed labor skills, and providing asylum for political refugees. (Some of these changes had been foreshadowed in the 1952 legislation.) Additional legislation in 1980 and 1990 sought to clarify and modify the new eligibility criteria relating to kinship, skills, and refugee status, and a 1986 act sought to reduce the growing stream of illegal immigrants by imposing penalties on the employers of such immigrants.

The results of the new rules governing immigration were substantial and largely unforeseen. The net number of new immigrants, which from 1945 to 1965 had averaged around 3 million persons per decade, rose noticeably, reaching more than 7 million in the 1980s. This was the highest decade total since the 8 million plus recorded in the first decade of the twentieth century. In comparison with the size of the American population as a whole, however, the volume of immigration was smaller than before World War I. In the 1980s the average annual rate of immigration – 3.2 immigrants per thousand population – was less than one-third the rate of 1901–10.

Even more startling is the change in origins of immigration brought about by the new legislation – what might be called the "new" new immigration came into being. In the 1950s, about 70% of immigrants had come from Europe, Canada, and Oceania. By the 1980s, this proportion had fallen to a mere 13 percent, while Latin America accounted for half of the migration stream (with Mexico responsible for half of the Latin American total), and Asia, more than a third. In 1990 the seven leading countries of origin of immigrants were, in descending order, Mexico, the Philippines, Vietnam, the Dominican Republic, Korea, China, and India.

The new legislation altered noticeably not only the volume and national origins of immigrants but also a number of other characteristics. Compared with the period of free immigration before World War I, the proportion of females and of married persons rose considerably, reflecting the priority given to reuniting families and the importance of refugee or quasi-refugee movements. Also, the occupational composition of immigration shifted sharply in the direction of higher skill. For example, in the 1960s the proportion of legal immigrants who in their native country had been in professional occupations was close to one-fourth, compared with a mere 1% in 1901–10; the proportion that had been laborers and domestic servants was around 20%, compared with over 70% in 1901–10.

Much more publicized in the popular press has been illegal immigration. Unlawful entry into the United States is not a new phenomenon. So-called wetbacks – Mexicans illegally crossing the Rio Grande River into the United States – were a prominent concern in the 1950s. But illegal immigration, like legal immigration, has been increasing, although illegal immigrants, in contrast to legal, are by and large unskilled.

The principal countries of origin of illegal immigrants are much the same as for legal immigration. For example, Mexico, the leading source of legal immigration, is estimated to account for over 30% of illegal immigrants. There is a considerable two-way movement across the U.S.-Mexico border, indicating that a significant share of migration is temporary, although the net flow is to the United States. The best estimate of the total of net illegal immigration from all countries put it at about 200,000 per year in the early 1980s, compared with about 700,000 per year for legal immigrants.

Though fairly small in relation to the population as a whole, immigration is making a sizable contribution to population *growth*. Of the nation's estimated population increase of over 20 million between 1980 and 1990, net legal immigration accounted for about one-third. In contrast, in the 1950s legal immigration accounted for little more than one-tenth of population growth. The increased importance of immigration as a source of population growth is partly due to the increased inflow of immigrants, but chiefly to the "baby bust," the drop in fertility since the early 1960s of the resident American population.

These developments – new immigration and lower fertility of the domestic population – raised the share of the foreign-born in the total population from its historic low of 4.7% in 1970 to 8.0% by 1990. The 1990 figure, however, is still far short of the twentieth-century high for the foreign-born of almost 15%, posted in 1910.

As has been seen, new government policies are responsible for the emergence of the "new" new immigration. But it is important to recognize that other factors have been at work. Illegal immigration and most legal immigration today is stimulated by the opportunities for employment at comparatively attractive wages offered in the United States, as was true also of immigration in the past. Without this labor demand, immigration would not have increased. Also, conditions in the country of origin have been important in influencing the size of the flow. The "new immigration" before World War I was partly a result of an upsurge in population growth in central, southern, and eastern Europe as the mortality revolution spread to those areas. The current "new" new immigration is a continuation of this historical pattern, as the mortality revolution and associated higher population growth extend to Latin America and Asia. That this type of "push" factor is important is shown by the low level of immigration from Mexico before World War II. At that time there were no legal restrictions, but population growth in Mexico was much less than recently, and, as a result, Mexican immigration to the United States was quite low.

It seems likely that the current high population growth in Latin America and Asia, creating a push for emigration from those areas, will not continue at its present rate. Fertility rates in these areas of origin of immigration are now trending downward, and as this reduces population growth, it is likely that immigration from these areas to the United States will also gradually subside.

The effect of immigration on the economy is a much-debated subject. The evidence that has been assembled appears to indicate that immigration has only a minor impact on the employment opportunities of the native labor force, reducing slightly the job possibilities of low-skill native workers. Several reasons are given for the small impact of immigration on employment of native workers. For one thing, immigration itself creates new employment opportunities. This is because immigration encourages the retention of industries that would otherwise have moved abroad, raises the aggregate demand for goods by increasing the number of new households, and adds new entrepreneurs to the economy. In addition, those new immigrants who have deficiencies in language, education, and prior work experience are in low-skill labor markets, where they compete only to a small extent with native workers. The evidence indicates too that immigration has little impact on general wage levels, and that immigrants, including illegal aliens, rather than being a burden to the American taxpayer, are a net benefit – they pay more in taxes than they receive in the form of government benefits (Fix and Passel, 1994). However, some groups within the population do appear to suffer adverse effects. Thus, in areas where the local economy is weak and already contains a high proportion of immigrants, the wages of low-skilled workers appear to be adversely affected by immigration. Also, immigration is typically concentrated in the younger working ages, and rapid immigration may create competition with inexperienced native workers newly entering the labor market.

MORTALITY IN THE SECOND HALF OF THE CENTURY

The period from 1936 to 1954 witnessed the highest rate of decline in mortality in U.S. history, as the second mortality revolution, based on effective therapy with antibiotics and sulfa drugs, led to the near elimination of many infectious diseases. With mortality from these diseases reduced to very low rates, analysts in the 1960s foresaw further advances foundering on the hard rock of the degenerative diseases of old age – heart disease, stroke, and cancer. A 1964 publication of the National Center for Health Statistics warned that the death rate for the United States had reached a point where further declines like those in the past were unlikely (U.S. Department of Health, Education, and Welfare, 1964). As reasonable as this view seemed at the time, it was very shortly undercut by events. From 1968 to 1982, a new decline in mortality set in at a rate not much lower than that from 1936 to 1954. Since 1982, mortality has continued to decline, but the rate of improvement has fallen back to about that of 1900–36, when the first mortality revolution was diffusing throughout the population.

By 1992 life expectancy at birth in the population as a whole had risen to 76 years, an 8-year improvement over the midcentury value. Blacks continued to gain on whites through 1982, although the decade since then has seen a mild reversal. In 1992 the life expectancy deficit of blacks compared with whites stood at 6.7 years versus the 8 years of 1950. With regard to differences by gender, in 1992 life expectancy of females was 79 years, compared with a little over 72 for males. Over the period since 1950, female life expectancy improved more than that of males, but the gain was concentrated in the period through 1968, by which time females had a 7.5-year advantage. As of 1992, the advantage of females had shrunk slightly to 6.7 years.

In the first two mortality revolutions, from the late nineteenth century through 1954, reductions in mortality occurred at every age, but they were especially concentrated in the younger ages. Indeed, even in the period of virtual stagnation in overall mortality, from 1954 to 1968, substantial improvement continued at ages under 15, as it has since. Beginning around 1968, however, there developed a noticeable break with the historic age pattern of mortality reduction at ages 15 and over. Those aged 15 to 44 have had noticeably lower rates of mortality decline than they did before 1954, and those aged 45 and over have had higher rates of decline. This shift in age pattern partly reflects the impact of AIDS in retarding mortality decline among those in the younger adult ages, and partly the effect on mortality at older adult ages of advances in the prevention and treatment of heart disease and stroke. Since 1968, mortality decline at ages 65 and over has been more rapid than ever before. This development has led forecasters to raise their projections of the future size and proportion of the older population.

The recent decline in mortality at older ages can be viewed as the start of a third mortality revolution. As infectious disease has come under control, medical research has shifted toward diseases of older age and led to new understanding of these diseases. Although the specific determinants of the decline in mortality due to heart disease have yet to be firmly established, two broad sets of causes have been suggested: lifestyle and medical factors. Lifestyle changes encompass reduced cigarette smoking, improved diet, and greater exercise. Major new medical care developments are advances in identifying high risk cases of cardiovascular disease and the use of drugs to treat hypertension. It is likely, too, that public Medicare and Medicaid programs have contributed to old age mortality decline by extending these advances throughout the population. Both lifestyle and medical advances largely reflect the impact of new knowledge and research. These developments may signal broader advances in the attack on degenerative disease in the future.

FERTILITY AND FAMILY FORMATION SINCE 1950

Fifty years ago, at the end of World War II, experts were confidently predicting continued low rates of childbearing that would, within a few decades, result in cessation of population growth. What followed, however, was an abrupt reversal of prior patterns of fertility and family formation. Young adults began marrying earlier, and the proportion marrying rose. Married women started having children at a younger age, and the proportion who remained childless diminished. Family size, in consequence, began to grow. Divorce rates leveled off and fell sharply below values based on extrapolation of the prior uptrend. The rate of out-of-wedlock births declined, and the prevalence of single-parent female-headed households leveled off. Fewer young adults lived "doubled-up" in their parents' homes.

In the labor market, the number and proportion of women working continued to rise, though they continued to be mostly employed in women's jobs. But associated with the shift in childbearing patterns, there was a dramatic change in the age and marital composition of women workers. Among women under 35, labor force participation, which had been rising steadily for at least a half century before 1940, leveled off abruptly for two decades. At the same time, labor force participation of women aged 45 to 64 rose much more rapidly than had been true before 1940. Because most older women were married, this shift in age pattern brought with it a corresponding shift from single to married women as the principal source of growth in the female labor supply.

It is probably safe to say that never in U.S. history had there occurred such an abrupt reversal in prior trends across such a broad spectrum of behavior. Yet, just as the experts were adjusting to the new conditions – and forecasting their likely persistence – a new turnaround began, extending from the 1960s to the late 1980s. Age at marriage increased, and the proportions marrying fell. Part of this new marriage pattern was due to the emergence of new living arrangements that lowered the frequency of marriage – cohabitation of young, unmarried adults of the opposite sex. Even if one adds these unmarried-couple unions to married-couple unions, however, it remains true that the average age at which unions were formed increased, and the proportion of young adults in unions declined.

Other family formation patterns reversed as well. Among those in unions, there was an increase after 1960 in the average age of mothers at first birth and in the proportion who had no children at all, and a sizable downturn in completed family size. Divorce rates turned sharply upward. Childbearing outside of marital unions rose, as did the prevalence of households headed by single women. The proportion of younger adults

living doubled up with their parents also increased. Labor force participation of women under age 35 once again turned sharply upward, while
that of older women grew much more slowly than in the period from
1940 to 1960. As these developments occurred, national attention turned
to problems of broken marriages, children born out of wedlock, and
families headed by single mothers – the "breakdown" of the traditional
family.

The young adults of the 1940s and 1950s reversed the family formation
patterns of their parents, only to see their own offspring, in turn, reverse
family patterns again. Why should such a remarkable turnaround
occur over a mere three generations? The answer lies chiefly in two reasons
– the nature of the labor market for young men, and the material standard of living to which young adults aspire. Together, these conditions
govern the ability of young men to support on the basis of their own earnings the standard of living that they and their partners desire. In a situation where men are viewed as the primary breadwinners, as was true in
the past, this relationship is a crucial determinant of family-forming
behavior.

In the boom conditions in the decade and a half after World War II, it
was easy for young men to find jobs, their earnings were good and grew
rapidly, and opportunities for advancement were abundant. Moreover, the
material aspirations of young men and women were modest. In a nor-
mally expanding economy, each generation is born into a more affluent
environment, and, being raised in such conditions, comes to take its more
abundant material environment as the norm – as a measure of its baseline needs on reaching adulthood. The post–World War II generation
of young adults, however, had been raised in an abnormally depressed
economy. The Great Depression of the 1930s brought a halt to the normal
advance of living standards. Then, in World War II, although jobs were
plentiful for those not in the armed forces, potential advances in consumption levels, especially in consumer durables, were sacrificed in order
to arm the military forces of the United States and its allies. As a result,
the normal advance from one generation to the next in the level of consumption, and thus in the material aspirations of young adults, ceased
from the late 1920s through mid-1940s. Those reaching adulthood after
World War II thus had deflated material aspirations – deflated by virtue
of growing up in the unusually depressed consumption environment
of the Great Depression and World War II. Because of this, when the
American economy embarked on its great growth surge after World War

II, young men found it easy to support from their own earnings the modest material aspirations of themselves and their partners.

This sharp improvement in young men's *relative* income – the earnings needed to support the material aspirations that they and their partners had formed during their upbringing – was the principal force driving the turnaround in young adults' demographic behavior in the period after World War II. But it was reinforced by government policies that provided special benefits for war veterans. Veterans of military service who would not otherwise have gone to college benefited from the educational provisions of the G. I. Bill, and college enrollments surged sharply upward. As a result, young men gained an unusual educational advantage over older men in the labor market. The G. I. Bill also made it possible to purchase a home with a mortgage obtained at below market rates, and thus made it easier for those planning families to find appropriate housing. But a strong labor market was of fundamental importance in increasing home ownership, because it ensured sufficient income to meet the carrying charges on a home mortgage. Taken altogether, these various circumstances meant that pressures to live at home with one's parents diminished sharply, while the opportunity for earlier marriage and family formation increased greatly.

Some have claimed that the rise in young women's childbearing in the baby boom period was due to a poor labor market for young women, which led them to turn to family pursuits. But, in fact, the women's labor market, as well as the men's, was strong during the postwar boom, as is shown by the continued growth in the share of women in the total labor force, from 24 to 32% between 1940 and 1960. It is true that young unmarried women, who in prior times would have been the main source of additions to the female labor force, dropped out of the labor market to marry and raise families. But the diminution in the supply of young women was not because of insufficient demand. Faced with this reduction in their normal supply of women workers, employers, who had previously insisted as a job qualification on a woman being single, scrapped this restriction and began hiring married women. Some of those that they hired were young wives, and even young mothers, whose labor force participation rates rose somewhat. But most were older women, especially women over age 45, whose labor force participation increased at rates never before seen. To social commentators of the 1950s, the cause of this abrupt increase in labor force participation of older women was a matter for much speculation. But its roots lay in straightforward changes in supply and demand:

continued growth of women's jobs, coupled with a leveling off in the labor supply of younger women, that together created new opportunities for older women.

In this new economic and family environment, divorce rates ceased their previous climb. In part this was because the strong labor market for males – who were viewed traditionally as the primary breadwinners – reduced domestic frictions due to economic needs of the family. In part it was because the bond that children provide to keep marriages intact was much stronger and more widespread, owing to the increase in both the proportion of families with children and the number of children per family.

The exceptional labor market for young men after World War II was the result of the unusually rapid growth of aggregate demand combined with a sharply decreased supply and improved relative education of young male workers. The growth of aggregate demand was spurred by the enormous backlog of demand that had accumulated at home and abroad for a decade and a half during the Great Depression and World War II. It was supported by governmental monetary and fiscal policies oriented toward the full employment objective of the Employment Act of 1946. On the labor supply side, a surge of immigration like that that had occurred in economic booms of the past was prevented by the restrictive legislation of the 1920s'. There was a modest increase in the inflow, including an inflow of illegal immigrants crossing the Rio Grande River from Mexico, but it was a small fraction of prior immigration. Moreover, the entry of new workers into the labor market as a result of the growth of the native population fell to an all-time low, a lagged effect of the low birth rates of the 1920s and 1930s. Also, the educational advantage of younger over older workers increased greatly, partly because of the expansion of secondary schooling that had been going on since 1910, and partly because of growing college enrollments due both to the increased flow of high school graduates and federal and state policies lowering the cost of college attendance.

Gradually, however, the aggregate supply and demand forces supporting a tight labor market for young men began to weaken and thus to lay the basis for another turnaround in family-forming behavior. The labor market for young men started to deteriorate in the 1960s, with the entrance of the vanguard of the baby boom generation into the labor market. The result of the greatly increased numbers of new entrants and resulting adverse pressures on wages and employment was a mild decline in the rate of marriage and childbearing through 1967. The increasing involvement of the United States in the Vietnam War in the late 1960s, however, significantly moderated the impact of the growing supply of young men on the labor market, because the armed forces absorbed an increasing proportion of young men and this decreased their civilian labor supply. Also, in order to avoid conscription for an unpopular war, some young men took advantage of legislation that for a time led to draft deferment because of marital status and parenthood. These circumstances brought about a small upturn in marriage and childbearing in the late 1960s.

But the gradual deterioration in the labor market for young men that began in the 1960s accelerated in the 1970s and early 1980s. Inflationary pressures, which had grown as a result of war demands in the late 1960s, were sharply aggravated in the 1970s by new supply-side influences, especially several sharp increases in the international price of oil. As fear of rapid inflation grew, there occurred a progressive retreat by the federal government from the use of monetary and fiscal policies to promote full employment. Economic recession was increasingly seen by the monetary authorities as a way of halting mounting inflationary expectations. Restrictive monetary policies were consequently adopted that culminated in the severest recession since the end of World War II, with the unemployment rate rising to near 10% in 1982–83.

Young male workers are hardest hit by a weak labor market, because many of them are new workers with little experience. But the labor market difficulties of young men after 1980 were compounded by adverse changes in the composition of labor demand. This was due to the growth of foreign competition in the goods markets and to the impact of the new computer-based third industrial revolution. Foreign competition reduced especially the demand for American manufactures and thus for manufacturing labor, which requires a relatively large proportion of younger males. Foreign competition also encouraged the adoption by American firms of the new computer technology, which was seen by businessmen as a way of cutting costs and increasing American competitiveness. This had a detrimental effect on the demand for less-skilled labor, aggravating the worsening demand for young male workers. In addition, new antidiscrimination legislation led to increased competition from women for jobs traditionally held by men, especially white-collar jobs. Reinforcing the growing entry of women into career-type jobs were two other factors. The weak labor market for young men led to worsening marriage opportunities and a feeling among many women that they should be prepared to support themselves independently. Also, the growth of a feminist movement advocating equal opportunity in the labor market led young women to give increasing attention to the possibility of a working career.

Labor supply conditions, as well as demand conditions, had adverse effects on the wages and employment of young men. The impact of the baby boom on the labor market continued through the 1970s and carried over into the first half of the 1980s, with continued high rates of labor market entry. In addition, the upswing in immigration after 1965 led to a noticeable growth in the supply of foreign workers and increased somewhat competition with younger native workers.

The result of the deteriorating labor market for young men was a growing shortfall in their ability to support on the basis of their own earnings a couple's material aspirations. In turn, this brought on the sweeping demographic turnaround of the 1960s through 1980s. Marriage rates and childbearing turned down, and childlessness increased. Completed family size, which had risen to over three children per woman among the parents of the baby boom generation fell to less than two per woman among the baby boomers themselves. There was an increase in broken marriages and births outside of marriage, and a resulting rise in the proportion of households headed by single mothers. The proportion of young adults living doubled up with their parents also rose.

Similar changes in family patterns had occurred in the 1930s when there was a dramatic worsening in the labor market for young men owing to the collapse of aggregate demand in the Great Depression. A new demographic development after 1960, however, was the emergence and growth of cohabitation of unmarried young adults of the opposite sex. This development was due in substantial part to developments in the 1960s that reduced the likelihood that sexual intercourse would lead to pregnancy and childbearing. New techniques of contraception – the oral pill and intrauterine device – were introduced. Abortion laws were liberalized, making access to legal induced abortion more readily available. The resurgent women's movement fostered attitudinal changes that encouraged women to take advantage of these developments. Under these conditions, cohabitation could be seen as having certain advantages previously found in marital unions – "safe sex" and economies of scale in the household – without the long-term commitments that went with marriage and family. In addition, for the growing number of single mothers, cohabitation offered a way of increasing the economic resources available for support of one's children.

Virtually all segments of the population – black and white, more and less educated, higher- and lower-income – participated in the great swing in demographic behavior from the end of World War II to the late 1980s (see, for example, the fertility rates in Table A.2, for blacks and whites). This widespread impact arose because everyone in the population was affected by changing economic conditions in similar ways. Many long-standing differences in childbearing persisted, however. Black fertility remained somewhat higher than white, though converging, while persons of higher economic status had somewhat lower fertility than those of lower status.

POPULATION COMPOSITION AND ECONOMIC ACTIVITY IN 1990

As has been seen, the makeup of the population of the United States has always been significantly affected by the volume and origins of its immigrants. The white population at the birth of the nation was almost wholly of northern and western European origin. In the latter part of the nineteenth century and beginning of the twentieth century, immigration from southern and eastern Europe broadened considerably the national origins of the white population. Then, with the restrictive legislation of the 1920s, the white population became increasingly homogeneous. But the 1965 Immigration Act, which removed national origins criteria for admission, set in motion a new trend in population composition, as inflows from Latin America and Asia surged to the fore. By 1990, the Hispanic share of the total population, less than 3% in 1950, was approaching that of blacks – 9% compared with 12% – and the share of those of Asian ethnicity had risen to 3% (Table 14.6). Problems of assimilation of immigrants resurfaced, compounded, in the case of Asians, by differences in race.

In the past, differences in education have contributed significantly to differences in the jobs held by different population groups, and this continues to be true down to the present. But immigrants since 1965 have been much more varied in their educational qualifications than the immigrant flow at the beginning of the century. Among the foreign-born aged 25–64, those from Asia (and also the small proportion from Africa) have schooling levels as good as or better than the native white population –

Table 14.6. *Race-ethnicity distribution of U.S.*
population, 1970 and 1990

Ethnicity	1970	1990
Total	100.0	100.0
White	83.5	75.7
Black	10.9	11.8
Hispanic	4.6	8.8
Asian	0.6	2.9
American Indian	0.4	0.8

Source: Harrison and Bennett (1995), pp. 142, 202–3.

an average of 13 years of school completed (Chiswick and Sullivan, 1995). At the other extreme, those born in Mexico average little more than 7 years of schooling. Immigrants from other parts of Latin America (chiefly El Salvador, the Dominican Republic, Colombia, Guatemala, Jamaica, and Cuba) fall in between, averaging slightly over 11 years of school completed.

These differences in education are reflected in differences in occupational status. The occupational distribution of Asians born abroad looks much like that of non-Hispanic whites, with over 6 out of 10 in managerial, professional, technical, sales, and administrative support jobs (ibid., pp. 247–48). In contrast, 2 out of 3 workers from Mexico hold the lowest-status jobs of operative/laborer, service worker, or farm worker. The occupational distribution of immigrants from other parts of Latin America falls between these two, in keeping with their intermediate level of education. Taken all together, the foreign-born today supply a somewhat larger share of the workers in the less-skilled jobs than in the labor force as a whole, and conversely for the higher skilled jobs, but the difference of the foreign born from the average occupational distribution is not great.

Although Mexican immigrants are disproportionately concentrated in the less-skilled jobs, this is less true of their children, especially those raised in the United States. School enrollment of immigrants' children in the United States today is not much below that of the native-born population. As with children of immigrants in the past, the better education and English fluency of the children of immigrants enable them to move up the job ladder and assimilate to the rest of the native-born

Table 14.7. *Occupational distribution of race-ethnicity groups by sex, 1990*

Ethnicity	All occupations	Managerial and professional	Technical, sales, administrative support	Service	Precision production, craft, and repair	Operators, fabricators, and laborers	Farming, forestry, and fishing
Males							
White	100.0	26.7	22.1	8.6	19.8	19.2	3.7
Black	100.0	13.5	18.5	19.3	14.5	31.3	2.9
Hispanic	100.0	11.4	16.4	16.1	19.8	28.7	7.6
Asian	100.0	32.5	27.3	13.6	11.3	13.4	1.9
American Indian	100.0	14.2	14.7	14.3	23.2	27.9	5.7
Females							
White	100.0	29.1	44.9	15.4	2.2	7.6	0.8
Black	100.0	20.1	38.9	25.6	2.4	12.7	0.3
Hispanic	100.0	16.1	38.5	23.6	3.5	16.1	2.1
Asian	100.0	27.8	39.8	16.3	4.2	11.2	0.7
American Indian	100.0	20.7	38.9	24.4	3.2	11.6	1.2

Source: Harrison and Bennett (1995), p. 177.

population.[2] The assimilation of Hispanics is probably helped too by the fact that most of them are whites.

The share of blacks in the total population edged up slightly between 1950 and 1990, from 10 to 12%. Over this period, differences between blacks and whites in occupational status have diminished (Table 14.7). These gains by blacks partly reflect the reduction of racial discrimination by employers as the labor shortages of the World War II and postwar economic boom forced employers to turn to black workers. The gains are also due to the passage of equal employment opportunities legislation. They reflect, too, a reduction in the schooling gap between blacks and whites. In 1990, for example, the proportion of blacks aged 25–34 who were high school graduates was 77%. The corresponding figure for non-Hispanic whites was 89%, making a 12-point black-white difference. In 1970 this gap had stood at 22 percentage points.

ASSIMILATION, INTEGRATION, AND
ECONOMIC EQUALITY

Discrimination by race continues to exist in the United States. Yet the lesson of American history is that education is an important factor

---

[2] Note that in Table 14.7, the occupational distribution of all Hispanics, which includes those born in the United States, is considerably closer to non-Hispanic whites than that for Mexican immigrants cited in the text.

enabling the disadvantaged to move up the economic ladder, and this is evidenced in the recent occupational data for both blacks and Asian immigrants. Similarly, the assimilation of Hispanic immigrants is being fostered by the education of their children in the United States, in much the same way as was true of immigrants in the past. It is also clear that race and other barriers are more likely to break down when the labor market is exceptionally strong. This suggests that macroeconomic policy is a form of social policy as well, because a strong labor market promotes assimilation and integration. As educational, language, and economic differences diminish, tolerance of those of different origins grows.

The second half of the twentieth century has seen the first major breakthrough toward equal economic opportunity for women. As has been noted, equal employment opportunity legislation dating from the 1960s stimulated employers to drop discriminatory policies in hiring women. Encouraged by this development and by the feminist movement, women became more willing to apply for what had previously been "men's jobs." In addition, the worsening marriage market and growth of single-mother families fostered concerns among many women that they needed to be ready to support themselves independently.

These developments led women to prepare themselves better for the labor market through increased schooling. In recent decades the level of education of young women has surged ahead of that of young men. Perhaps most noteworthy is the increased share of women obtaining professional degrees. Between 1970 and 1990, the proportion of professional degrees accounted for by women increased in law from 5 to 41%; in medicine, from 8 to 33%; in dentistry, from 1 to 26%; and in business (MBA degree), from 5 to 37% (Bianchi 1995, p. 115).

Because of developments such as these, there was a major increase in the proportion of women in white-collar jobs previously held very largely by men. Between 1970 and 1990, as the proportion of women in the labor force as a whole rose from 38 to 46%, the proportion of women who were managers or executives increased from 19 to 42%; in professional specialties, from 44 to 54%, and in technicians' jobs, from 34 to 46% (Bianchi 1995, p. 125). The overall gap between the occupational distribution of men and women narrowed considerably, especially at the younger ages. Nevertheless, occupational segregation remained high. Women made few gains in blue-collar and protective service jobs traditionally held by men, and there was little desegregation of the leading women's jobs – secretaries, typists, receptionists, preschool teachers, registered and practical nurses, dental hygienists and assistants, housekeepers, and childcare workers.

RECENT TRENDS IN GEOGRAPHIC DISTRIBUTION

Most Americans today live with a sense of spatial congestion, and for good reason: economic growth has continued to concentrate population in urban areas. In 1990 close to four out of five persons lived in "metropolitan areas" (a Census Bureau concept that is a modern version of the older "urban area"). What few Americans realize, however, is that there are vast tracts of the country that are losing population. In the period 1940–60 more than half of the 3,100 counties of the United States experienced an *absolute* decrease in total population, most of them rural counties. Since then rural depopulation has moderated somewhat, but between 1980 and 1988 4 counties out of 10 still lost population.

Although urbanization continues to rise, the motor vehicle, which came in with the second industrial revolution, has somewhat relaxed the trend toward geographic concentration of the population. This moderation has come about through two decentralizing developments in the structure of urban areas: suburbanization, and the emergence of polycentric cities. These developments surfaced before 1950, but they have become most important quantitatively since then, as automobile ownership has become well-nigh universal.

Before the automobile, most people, of necessity, lived in close proximity to their place of work. The automobile vastly increased the potential range of commuting, and thus led to greatly increased residential settlement of rural areas adjacent to central cities. By 1970 the suburban population of the nation exceeded the central city population. Although the growth of suburbs had been foreshadowed by locational shifts associated with the introduction of horse-drawn trolleys and electric streetcars, the present massive magnitude of suburbanization is based on widespread personal ownership of automobiles.

The development of motor vehicle transportation also played a key role in the emergence of polycentric cities. Nineteenth-century cities, such as those in the Northeast and Midwest, had a very high concentration of population at one node and a considerably lower-density surrounding population – a monocentric structure owing especially to the key role in their growth played by the railroad. Large cities whose growth has occurred chiefly in the twentieth century, most of which are located in the Southwest and West, have a polycentric structure. These cities have a complex of scattered high-density centers (though their highest-density centers are not nearly as dense as in large nineteenth-century cities), with each center usually surrounded by a lower-density residential periphery. Because of this scattered structure, twentieth-century cities tend to spread out into former rural areas more than the older nineteenth-century cities. But the older cities, too, have moved toward a polycentric structure in the twentieth century, with industrial parks and central offices locating near beltways and in suburban rings. These developments have given rise to what are sometimes called "edge cities," although "suburban cities" would seem a better name. Because of the new polycentric form of cities, today in metropolitan areas throughout the country suburb-to-suburb commuters typically outnumber suburb-to-central-city commuters by at least three to one or more.

Just as rural depopulation is the counterpart of urbanization, so, too, the spread of urban areas through suburbanization and the formation of polycentric nodes has started to take its toll on the old central city cores. Even by 1940–50, 1 out of 20 central cities was experiencing a decline in total population; by 1980–88, however, this proportion was approaching one in two. Hardest hit have been the older central cities of the Northeast, over two-thirds of which experienced declines between 1984 and 1988. But even in the west, one out of six central cities saw its population decline in the late 1980s.

The second industrial revolution, which lowered cost differences among different locations and widened possible sources of energy through electrification and the exploitation of petroleum resources, has altered the regional distribution of population, toward what might loosely be called the Sun Belt. Despite the nineteenth-century westward movement of population, over six-tenths of the population in 1900 was still located in the Northeast and Midwest regions. Starting most noticeably after World War II, a major shift set in toward the far West and South, and today these Sun Belt regions are themselves approaching a six-tenths share of the population. This movement has moderated the nineteenth-century trend toward population concentration in the cities of the Northeast and Midwest and has contributed to a wider dispersal of the population throughout the nation, much of it in newer urban centers and adjacent rural areas. The states that have benefited most from this shift are California, Arizona, Texas, and Florida – hence the term Sun Belt. The westward component of the shift has been the most sizable. Indeed, by 1990, the total population of the Mountain and Pacific states exceeded that of the New England and Middle Atlantic states.

As has been seen, in the first half of the twentieth century the spatial distribution of population became more similar among population groups. Since 1950 the combination of major new regional shifts of population, suburban movements, and the increased importance of immigration in population growth, has led to the emergence of growing disparities in the overall spatial distribution of different racial and ethnic groups. At the same time, there are signs of a breakdown in some of the traditional spatial barriers, partly because of equal housing laws, and partly because of reduced disparities in economic and educational status.

The rise of Hispanics and Asians as minority groups has increased regional disparities in population distribution. Recent immigrants and their native-born offspring are more likely than are non-Hispanic whites to settle in or near west coast or southwest port-of-entry areas, and thus to increase regional disparities in population distribution. Moreover, the post–World War II economic resurgence of the South has led to greater retention of blacks in the South and even to some black in-migration to the South. This reversal of the trends of the first half of this century has renewed, to some degree, the concentration of blacks in the South. Similarly, there has been increased disparity in the distribution between metropolitan and nonmetropolitan areas of Hispanics and Asians, on the one hand, and non-Hispanic whites, on the other, because immigrants are highly concentrated in larger metropolitan areas. Poorer blacks, too, remain concentrated in central cities.

But if one shifts from broad geographic aggregates to the neighborhood level, and considers blacks as a whole, including the rising proportion of middle-class blacks, there has been a recent reduction in segregation in most major metropolitan areas. Among Hispanics and Asians, segregation at the neighborhood level has increased, but this is because of the high level of immigration and the tendency of immigrants to pile up in immigrant enclaves. If one were to distinguish the second generation from the immigrants themselves, it is likely that the movement toward reduced segregation would again be evident.

THE FUTURE

The virtually unanimous consensus among forecasters today is that American childbearing rates will remain low in the future or decline even further, that total population will eventually stabilize and perhaps turn down, and that the proportion of the older population will rise markedly.

These projections, although dressed with frequent cautions that they are not predictions, have so captured the minds of the public, media, and policy makers that they are taken as virtual fact. Although they may prove to be correct, it is useful to recall that at the end of World War II, demographic forecasters were confidently projecting exactly the same outlook. In the event, these forecasts proved totally wrong. There is little in the record of official projections since then to give one greater confidence in today's projections, because these projections simply extrapolate past conditions into the future. Thus, as fertility rose after World War II, fertility and population growth projections were similarly increased. Then, when it became clear that a baby bust was under way, the projections were correspondingly reduced. Put simply, population projections have followed, rather than forecast, population growth.

As we have seen, the growth and composition of the American population in the twentieth century has been shaped by a variety of economic, political, and social conditions. The difficulty of foreseeing future population change stems from the difficulty of anticipating such conditions over the next century. An increasingly critical determinant of future change that is especially difficult to foresee is public policy. The advance of medical knowledge, so important for mortality reduction, is dependent, in substantial part, on continued governmental support for basic health research – the recent advances in mapping genetic disorders are largely a product of such funding. Immigration has moved to center stage in political debate, with many concerns echoing those of the 1920s. New immigration policies that are likely to result will – if the past is any guide – have unforeseen effects. Perhaps less well recognized is that public policy is also important in shaping future childbearing behavior. This is because the outlook for fertility depends especially on the role of domestic and international economic policy in shaping the growth of aggregate demand. If economic policy were to return seriously to a full employment objective, then the next decade or two might replicate conditions similar to those after World War II, when a vigorous economic boom occurred as a baby bust generation passed through the family forming ages. A shortage of younger workers in the coming years is likely because a new baby bust generation is now entering the labor market, although high immigration could moderate the shortage. But if aggregate demand were strong and immigration limited, the resulting relative affluence of the young might engender a sizable fertility upturn. If, however, inflation fears lead to continued braking of economic growth by public policy, then the outlook for a significant fertility upswing is less likely. All of this serves only to underscore the difficulty of foreseeing the American population of the future.

BIBLIOGRAPHIC ESSAY

The data underlying this chapter are from many sources. The chief primary source is the decennial census of population of the United States, particularly the U.S. summary volumes. Also used extensively are the publications of the U.S. National Center for Health Statistics (previously the National Office of Vital Statistics), which compiles the basic data on births, deaths, marriages, and divorce. A valuable reference that assembles some historical data from these two primary sources is Bureau of the Census, *Historical Statistics of the United States* (Washington, D.C., 1975). Some of the data in this publication are updated in Bureau of the Census, *Statistical Abstract of the United States* (Washington, D.C., issued annually). These two works also include references to other major sources of demographic information.

The chapter draws too on a number of analytical studies that build on these and other data. Of particular value are the census monographs, a number of which are cited below. Two invaluable studies of American population in the first part of the twentieth century are Warren S. Thompson and P. K. Whelpton, *Population Trends in the United States* (New York, 1933), and the census monograph by Conrad Taeuber and Irene B. Taeuber, *The Changing Population of the United States* (New York, 1958). There are no comparable comprehensive analytical studies for the second half of the twentieth century. Useful compilations of historical data through 1980 on many topics appear in Donald J. Bogue, *The Population of the United States: Historical Trends and Future Projections* (New York, 1985). An excellent publication in the census monograph tradition presenting findings from the 1990 census, often in historical perspective, is the multiauthored volume edited by Reynolds Farley, *State of the Union: America in the 1990s*, 2 vols. (New York, 1995). The present chapter also draws on prior work by the present author, *Population, Labor Force, and Long Swings in Economic Growth: The American Experience* (New York, 1968); "The American Population" in Lance E. Davis, Richard A. Easterlin, and William N. Parker, eds., *American Economic Growth: An Economist's History of the United States* (New York, 1972); *Birth and Fortune*, 2d ed. (Chicago, 1987); and Richard A. Easterlin, D. Ward, W. S. Bernard, and R. Ueda, *Immigration* (Cambridge, 1982).

On mortality, an excellent study of American conditions around the beginning of the twentieth century is Samuel H. Preston and Michael R. Haines, *Fatal Years: Child Mortality in Late Nineteenth Century America* (Princeton, 1991). The National Center for Health Statistics provides frequent analyses of mortality. See, for example, U.S. Department of Health, Education, and Welfare, National Center for Health Statistics, *The Change in Mortality Trend in the United States*, 3:1 (Washington, D.C., 1964); and U.S. Department of Health, Education and Welfare, "Final Mortality Statistics, 1977," *Monthly Vital Statistics Report* 28:1 (supplement), May 11, 1–35 (Hyattsville, Md., 1979). A pioneering analysis of the recent decline in mortality is Eileen M. Crimmins, "The Changing Pattern of American Mortality Decline, 1940–1977 and Its Implications for the Future," *Population and Development* 7:2 (1981), 229–54. A recent update appears in Eileen M. Crimmins, Mark D. Hayward, and Yasuhiko Saito, "Changing Mortality and Morbidity Rates and the health Status and Life Expectancy of the Older Population," *Demography* 31:1 (1994), 159–75.

The most comprehensive study of fertility up to 1950 is the census monograph by W. H. Grabill, C. V. Kiser, and P. K. Whelpton, *The Fertility of American Women* (New York, 1958). Recent developments are examined in Easterlin, *Birth and Fortune* (1987); Diane Macunovich, "Relative Income and Price of Time" (1996). A good analysis of historical change in marriage and divorce is Andrew J. Cherlin, *Marriage, Divorce, Remarriage* (Cambridge, Mass., revised and enlarged edition, 1992). For recent developments, see Sara McLanahan and Lynne Casper, "Growing Diversity and Inequality in the American Family" (1998). The pioneering census monograph on family structure is Paul C. Glick, *American Families* (New York, 1957). Two valuable historical studies that bring the analysis of family change up to the present are James A. Sweet and Larry L. Bumpass, *American Families and Households* (New York, 1987); and Donald J. Hernandez, *America's Children: Resources from Family, Government, and the Economy* (New York, 1993).

The pioneering work on historical trends in education is John K. Folger and Charles B. Nam, *Education of the American Population* (Washington, 1967). A good overview of recent developments is Robert D. Mare, "Changes in Educational Attainment and School Enrollment," in Reynolds Farley, ed., *State of the Union*.

There are a number of excellent historical studies on economic activity of the population that are surprisingly little used these days – the census monograph by Gertrude Bancroft, *The American Labor Force: Its Growth and Changing Composition* (New York, 1958); John D. Durand, *The Labor Force in the United States, 1890–1960* (New York, 1948); and Clarence D. Long, *The Labor Force Under Changing Income and Employment* (Princeton, N.J., 1958). Valuable compilations of occupational data are given in Alba M. Edwards, *Sixteenth Census of the United States: 1940. Population: Comparative Occupation Statistics for the United States, 1870 to 1940* (Washington, 1943); this is updated to 1950 in David L. Kaplan and M. Claire Casey, *Occupational Trends in the United States, 1900 to 1950*, Bureau of the Census Working Paper no. 5 (Washington, 1958). Recent developments are examined in James R. Wetzel, "Labor Force, Unemployment, and Earnings"; and John D. Kasarda, "Industrial Restructuring and the Changing Location of Jobs," both in Reynolds Farley, ed., *State of the Union*.

On the subject of spatial distribution of population, a major statistical compilation on American internal migration through 1950 is Simon Kuznets and Dorothy S. Thomas, eds., *Population Redistribution and Economic Growth*, 3 vols. (Philadelphia, 1957, 1960, 1964). The early growth of suburbanization is recorded in Donald J. Bogue, *The Population of the United States* (Glencoe, Ill., 1959). Accounts of recent developments are in Easterlin, forthcoming, Kasarda, and William H. Frey, "The New Geography of Population Shifts," both in Reynolds Farley, ed., *State of the Union*.

The economic activity of the foreign white stock through 1950 is the subject of a census monograph by Edward P. Hutchinson, *Immigrants and their Children, 1850–1950* (New York, 1956). Excellent recent overviews of U.S. immigration are Michael Fix and Jeffrey S. Passel, *Immigration and Immigrants: Setting the Record Straight* (Washington, D.C., 1994) and Barry R. Chiswick and Teresa A. Sullivan, "The New Immigrants," in Reynolds Farley, ed., *State of the Union*.

Recent studies of minority populations are Reynolds Farley, *Blacks and Whites: Narrowing the Gap?* (Cambridge, Mass., 1984); Frank D. Bean and Marta Tienda, *The Hispanic Population of the United States* (New York, 1989); and Roderick J. Harrison and Claudette E. Bennett, "Racial and Ethnic Diversity" in Reynolds Farley, ed., *State of the Union*. A basic historical study of women is Claudia Goldin, *Understanding the Gender Gap: An Economic History of American Women* (New York, 1990). Recent developments are excellently analyzed in Suzanne Bianchi, "Changing Economic Roles of Women and Men," in Reynolds Farley, ed., *State of the Union.*

REFERENCES

Bancroft, Gertrude. *The American Labor Force: Its Growth and Changing Composition.* New York, 1958.

Bean, Frank D., and Marta Tienda. *The Hispanic Population of the United States.* New York, 1989.

Bianchi, Suzanne. "Changing Economic Roles of Women and Men." In Reynolds Farley, ed., *State of the Union, America in the 1990s: Volume One: Economic Trends*, pp. 107–54. New York, 1995.

Bogue, Donald J. *The Population of the United States.* Glencoe, Ill., 1959.

———. *The Population of the United States: Historical Trends and Future Projections.* New York, 1985.

Cherlin, Andrew J. *Marriage, Divorce, Remarriage.* Rev. and enlarged. Cambridge, Mass., 1992.

Chiswick, Barry R., and Teresa A. Sullivan, "The New Immigrants." In Reynolds Farley, ed., *State of the Union, America in the 1990s.* Vol. 2: *Social Trends*, pp. 211–70. New York, 1995.

Crimmins, Eileen M. "The Changing Pattern of American Mortality Decline, 1940–1977 and Its Implications for the Future." *Population and Development Review* 7:2 (1981), pp. 229–54.

Crimmins, Eileen M., Mark D. Hayward, and Yasuhiko Saito. "Changing Mortality and Morbidity Rates and the Health Status and Life Expectancy of the Older Population." *Demography* 31:1 (1994), pp. 159–75.

Durand, John D. *The Labor Force in the United States, 1890–1960.* New York, 1948.

Easterlin, Richard A. *Population, Labor Force, and Long Swings in Economic Growth: The American Experience.* New York, 1968.

———. "The American Population." In Lance E. Davis, Richard A. Easterlin, and William N. Parker, eds., *American Economic Growth: An Economist's History of the United States.* New York, 1972.

———. *Birth and Fortune.* 2d ed. Chicago, 1987.

———. "Twentieth Century American Population Growth." In Stanley Engerman and Robert E. Gallman, eds., *The Cambridge Economic History of the United States.* Vol. 3: *The Twentieth Century.* Forthcoming.

Easterlin, Richard A., D. Ward, W. S. Bernard, and R. Ueda. *Immigration.* Cambridge, 1982.

Edwards, Alba M. *Sixteenth Census of the United States: 1940 Population: Comparative Occupation Statistics for the United States, 1870 to 1940.* Washington, D.C., 1943.

Farley, Reynolds. *Blacks and Whites: Narrowing the Gap?* Cambridge, Mass., 1984.

Fix, Michael, and Jeffrey S. Passel. *Immigration and Immigrants: Setting the Record Straight.* Washington, D.C., 1994.

Folger, John K., and Charles B. Nam. *Education of the American Population.* Washington, D.C., 1967.

Frey, William H. "The New Geography of Population Shifts." In Reynolds Farley, ed., *State of the Union, America in the 1990s.* Vol. 2: *Social Trends*, pp. 271–336. New York, 1995.

Glick, Paul C. *American Families.* New York, 1957.

Goldin, Claudia. *Understanding the Gender Gap: An Economic History of American Women.* New York, 1990.

Grabill, W. H., C. V. Kiser, and P. K. Whelpton. *The Fertility of American Women.* New York, 1958.

Harrison, Roderick J., and Claudette E. Bennett. "Racial and Ethnic Diversity." In Reynolds Farley, ed., *State of the Union, America in the 1990s.* Vol. 2: *Social Trends*, pp. 141–210. New York, 1995.

Hernandez, Donald J. *America's Children: Resources from Family, Government, and the Economy.* New York, 1993.

Hutchinson, Edward P. *Immigrants and Their Children, 1850–1950.* New York, 1956.

Kaplan, David L., and M. Claire Casey. *Occupational Trends in the United States, 1900 to 1950.* Bureau of the Census Working Paper No. 5. Washington, D.C., 1958.

Kasarda, John D. "Industrial Restructuring and the Changing Location of Jobs." In Reynolds Farley, ed., *State of the Union, America in the 1990s.* Vol. 1: *Economic Trends*, pp. 215–67. New York, 1995.

Kuznets, Simon, and Dorothy S. Thomas, eds. *Population Redistribution and Economic Growth.* 3 vols. Philadelphia, 1957, 1960, 1964.

Long, Clarence D. *The Labor Force under Changing Income and Employment.* Princeton, N.J., 1958.

McLanahan, Sara, and Lynne Casper. "Growing Diversity and Inequality in the American Family." In Reynolds Farley, ed., *State of the Union, America in the 1990s.* Vol. 2: *Social Trends*, pp. 1–45. New York, 1995.

Macunovich, Diane. "Relative Income and Price of Time: Exploring Their Effects on U.S. Fertility and Female Labor Force Participation, 1963–93." In *Fertility in the United States: New Patterns, New Theories, Population and Development Review.* Supplement to vol. 22 (1996), pp. 223–57.

Mare, Robert D. "Changes in Educational Attainment and School Enrollment." In Reynolds Farley, ed., *State of the Union, America in the 1990s.* Vol. 1: *Economic Trends*, pp. 155–213. New York, 1995.

Mokyr, Joel, and Rebecca Stein. "Science, Health, and Household Technology: The Effect of the Pasteur Revolution on Consumer Demand." In Timothy F. Bresnahan and Robert J. Gordon, eds., *The Economics of New Goods*, pp. 143–200. Chicago, 1997.

Preston, Samuel H., and Michael R. Haines. *Fatal Years: Child Mortality in Late Nineteenth Century America.* Princeton, N.J., 1991.

Sweet, James A., and Larry L. Bumpass. *American Families and Households.* New York, 1987.

Taeuber, Conrad, and Irene B. Taeuber. *The Changing Population of the United States.* New York, 1958.

Thompson, Warren S., and P. K. Whelpton. *Population Trends in the United States.* New York, 1933.

U.S. Bureau of the Census, *United States Census of Population: 1950.* Vol. 2: *Characteristics of the Population, Part 1, U.S. Summary.* Washington, D.C., 1953.

―――. *United States Census of Population: 1950, Nativity and Parentage.* Washington, D.C., 1954.

―――. *Historical Statistics of the United States.* 2 vols. Washington, D.C., 1975.

―――. *Statistical Abstract of the United States.* Washington, D.C., annual.

U.S. Department of Health, Education, and Welfare, National Center for Health Statistics. *The Change in Mortality Trend in the United States,* 3:1. Washington, D.C., 1964.

Wetzel, James R. "Labor Force, Unemployment, and Earnings." In Reynolds Farley, ed., *State of the Union, America in the 1990s.* Vol. 1: *Economic Trends,* pp. 59–105. New York, 1995.

15

CONCLUDING REMARKS

MICHAEL R. HAINES AND RICHARD H. STECKEL

The population of a nation constitutes its most valuable resource. The study of how that population grows or declines over time via the vital processes of fertility and mortality, as well as the process of international migration, is fundamental to our understanding of that society. Also, how the population redistributes itself between regions and between rural and urban (and suburban) residence, how the age and sex structure is reshaped, and how the racial and ethnic composition changes are crucial questions. All "modern" societies have undergone the demographic transition from high to low levels of fertility and mortality. The chapters in this volume deal with several of these issues.

A number of them concentrate on pretransition populations (those in colonial British North America, New France, and Mexico prior to 1900, and the Amerindian population); but several treat populations which have undergone the demographic transition, at least in part (those in the United States and Canada in the nineteenth and twentieth centuries, Mexico and the Caribbean in the twentieth century). The demographic transition in North America has by no means been "standard." The ideal type of demographic transition model has four stages. During the first stage, fertility is high and fairly stable, kept there by social and economic forces raising the value of children and by values which reinforce large family goals. Mortality is also high but variable, marked by epidemics and crisis mortality. Population growth is rather slow and uneven. The second stage consists of the mortality transition, which is marked by a reduction in baseline mortality and lower mortality peaks and variability, the latter the consequence of greater control of the disease environment and of such events as famine and war. The cause of the mortality transition is usually assumed to be human intervention in the mortality process via public health and medical science. Fertility remains high because it is affected by more fundamental socioeconomic factors, and thus population growth rates rise significantly. This is then followed by the third stage, that of the fertility transition. As economic development and modernization change the value of children to families, parents begin taking deliberate control of numbers and spacing of births, both via control of marriage and control of fertility within conjugal unions. In the fourth and terminal stage, society becomes demographically mature, with low birth and death rates and moderate to low rates of population growth.

This simplified picture of the demographic transition poses some problems. It lacks predictive power in a number of cases, such as the United States and anglophone Canada. It fits the historical experience of many other nations rather poorly. There is no role for migration, either international or internal. For many developing nations in the twentieth century, on the other hand, it furnishes a reasonable description. It would include Mexico and much of the Caribbean, but is rather wide of the mark for the United States and Canada, at least for the anglophone population of the latter. For both those populations, fertility started its decline (from very high levels) well in advance of the mortality transition. And in both populations, migration from abroad was an extremely important component of population growth (see Table B.3).

In the United States white fertility was declining from at least 1800, and the fertility of the black population showed signs of a downtrend even late in the era of slavery (the 1830s). But the sustained transition in mortality did not commence until the 1870s. In addition, net foreign in-migration was an important source of overall population growth. This included substantial importation of black slaves before 1808. A similar story of the timing of the fertility and mortality transitions can be told for Canada, although with some difference for the francophone population.

In the United States the rate of population growth was rapid, increasing from 2.41% per annum over the period 1650 to 1700 to about 3% per annum between 1700 and 1850. This was caused largely by high (though declining) birth rates and moderate levels of mortality, but immigration was also important. Between 1790 and 1990, about three-quarters of the growth was due to natural increase and about a quarter to net in-migration. More than 34 million persons entered the United States between the 1790s and the end of World War I, and Canada had perhaps 5 million enter over the same period. In contrast, Mexico and the Caribbean experienced almost all their modern population growth though natural increase. Indeed, both were areas of net out-migration in the twentieth century.

The fertility of American families was high in colonial times and in the early nineteenth century. Family sizes averaged about seven children per woman for the white population around 1800 and between seven and eight children per black slave mother in the 1850s. There was a continuing decline in white birth rates from at least 1800 and for black birth rates from at least midcentury. The fertility decline took place in both rural and urban areas. The standard explanations for the fertility transition cite factors such as the rising cost of children because of urbanization, the growth of incomes and nonagricultural employment, increased value of education, rising female employment, child labor laws and compulsory education, and declining infant and child mortality. Changing attitudes toward large families and toward contraception, as well as better contraceptive technologies, are also mentioned. Such structural explanations do well for North America since the late nineteenth century, but they are less appropriate for the fertility decline in rural, agrarian areas in the United States and anglophone Canada prior to about 1870. The increased scarcity and higher cost of good agricultural land and bequest motives have been proposed as central factors, although the explanation remains controversial. An alternative has been to examine the increase in nonagricultural opportunities in farming areas, and the effect of these opportunities on parent–child bargaining over bequests and old age support for the parents. Similar conclusions apply to Canada, with the caveat that fertility decline in francophone areas lagged significantly behind those in anglophone areas. The standard structural explanations also fail to account for the post–World War II "baby boom" and subsequent "baby bust" which took place in the United States and Canada but not in Mexico or the Caribbean.

In contrast to fertility in the United States and Canada, fertility in Mexico and much of the Caribbean remained high until well into the twentieth century. Crude birth rates in the range of 42 to 46 per thousand were characteristic of Mexico between 1900 and 1960. Similarly, crude birth rates varied from about 30 to about 50 in the Caribbean circa 1950, while sustained declines had not really appeared. More recently, however, birth rates have begun their transition in many areas of the Caribbean and also in Mexico, where the crude birth rate declined from 45 per thousand in the 1950s to 33.5 per thousand in 1990.

Mortality did not begin its *sustained* decline in the United States until the 1870s. Prior to that, death rates fluctuated in response to periodic epidemics and changes in the disease environment. There is even evidence of rising death rates during the 1840s and 1850s, particularly from vital statistics for several cities and genealogical investigations. Expectation of life at age 20 may have fallen by 10% between the 1830s and the 1850s. Military recruits were becoming shorter in the immediate antebellum period in the United States, consistent with a deteriorating disease environment. Thus in the United States the fertility decline preceded the mortality decline, in contrast to the standard model of demographic transition. The mortality decline since the late nineteenth century has been greatly influenced by improvements in public health and sanitation, especially better water supplies and sewage disposal. The improving diet, clothing, and shelter of the American population over the period since about 1870 has also played a role. Specific medical interventions beyond more general environmental public health were not as important until well into the twentieth century. Although it is difficult to disentangle the precise effects of these different causal factors, much of the mortality decline was due to rapid reductions in infectious and parasitic diseases, including tuberculosis, pneumonia, bronchitis, and gastrointestinal infections, as well as such well-known conditions as cholera, smallpox, diphtheria, and typhoid fever. In the nineteenth century, urban areas were unhealthy places, especially the largest cities. Rural areas and small towns had the most salubrious environment. These circumstances began to change by about the 1890s, when the largest cities instituted large and effective public works sanitation projects and public health administration. The largest cities then experienced the most rapid improvements in death rates. Rural-urban mortality differentials have converged and largely disappeared, unlike those between whites and blacks.

The mortality situation in nineteenth-century Canada has been less well documented, but mortality levels were likely moderate in the anglophone areas and somewhat higher in francophone regions. Variability was much more substantial before late in the nineteenth century. Death rates had already reached quite moderate levels by the turn of the century (14–15 per thousand by 1901). Although the mortality environment was more benign than in tropical and semitropical areas, it seems that the mortality transition was under way by then.

In both Mexico and the Caribbean, the mortality transition indeed preceded the fertility transition. Deaths were in decline in Mexico from the 1930s at the latest and in the Caribbean by World War II (and earlier in some cases). These areas thus conformed more closely to the conventional picture of the timing of the demographic transition.

Migration has been a fact of life for the peoples of North America. Within the United States, there has been significant movement east to west, following the frontier (until the late nineteenth century); from rural to urban areas; and, later, from central cities to suburbs, from South to North, and ultimately to the Sun Belt. These developments have been responsible for changing the United States from a rural to an urban nation: from only 5% urban in 1790 to over half urban in 1920 and over-three quarters urban today. Canada followed a similar course, moving from about 20% urban in 1871 to 76% in 1991. Mexico has exhibited a strong acceleration in urbanization since 1940. The society was 28% urban in 1900 and 35% urban by 1940. But thereafter the growth of cities, particularly spurred by an outflow from rural areas, took off: to 51% of the population by 1960 and 71% by 1990 — not too different from levels in the United States and Canada. Today, the Federal District (greater Mexico City) is home to almost 20% of the entire population of the nation. This rapid urbanization and the accompanying rural exodus has posed significant social and economic issues. Large numbers of Mexicans have also migrated to the United States to find work. An estimated 18 million persons of Mexican origin now reside in the United States. At the time of the 1990 census, there were 4.3 million Mexican-born enumerated in the United States, which translates to 5.3% of the total population of Mexico at that date. And this was likely an undercount. There has been a similar outflow from the Caribbean to the United States and elsewhere, particularly Great Britain. Between 1950 and 1990, 2.5 million Caribbean residents legally emigrated to the United States, and three-quarters of a million left Puerto Rico between 1950 and 1980. In the 1990 U.S. Census, 1.9 million Caribbean-born were enumerated.

The population of the United States shifted from the original areas of settlement on the Atlantic coast to the center of the nation and later to the Pacific and mountain states. Canada experienced a similar movement westward, but the original areas of settlement, Ontario and Quebec, still make up about two-thirds of Canada's population. Migration from abroad, first from western and northern Europe and then, after about 1890, from central, eastern, and southern Europe, came in waves in response to upswings in business cycles and the expansion of economic opportunities in the both Canada and the United States. This flood of immigrants directly augmented population growth rates and indirectly acted to raise birth rates, before it was severely restricted in the 1920s by legislation and subsequently by the Great Depression. But it left an indelible stamp on the economy, society, and culture. The timing was different between the two nations, however. Canada had a negative net migration balance up to about 1900, losing most of those migrants to the United States, but with some returning abroad. Thereafter, Canada had a strong positive net migration flow (except in the 1930s). In Mexico, migrants have left rural areas and the south for the large cities of the center and north (Mexico City and the Federal District, Monterrey, Guadalajara. Puebla, Leon), as well as moving to the United States. Population redistribution in the Caribbean has been mainly outward, although capital cities have grown rapidly.

ISSUES AND QUESTIONS
FOR RESEARCH

Researchers continue to pore over a number of questions about the historical demography of North America, many of a quantitative nature. (1) We need estimates, or better estimates, of fertility and mortality for the populations of European and African origins and the indigenous populations before the early twentieth century, especially for the early nineteenth century and the colonial period in the United States, for the nineteenth century as a whole in Canada, and prior to 1900 in Mexico. Work on the parish registers of French Canada before 1800 has produced a strong database which can tell us much for the period roughly 1660 to 1800. Similar work seems possible for Mexico. (2) We need better information on the cause of death (as well as basic information on deaths by age and sex) before the early twentieth century. (3) Improved estimates of migrant flows, both gross and net, will be of great value, particularly for the period before the early nineteenth century. (4) Ultimately, we will require more information on differentials in fertility and mortality by race, gender, ethnic/linguistic group, socioeconomic status, regions, and rural-urban residence. Census samples should be of assistance here. The Integrated Public Use Micro Sample (IPUMS) project on the United States conducted by Steven Ruggles is a model in this respect. Such projects should be possible for Canada since 1851 and for Mexcio and the Caribbean in the twentieth century. (5) Recent investigations in historical anthropometry and health have opened avenues of research which show great potential. Many nations have such data, including those in Latin America. (6) The demography of the Amerindian population from contact onward needs further exploration, especially in the area of population size and distribution, as well as vital processes.

Numerous socioeconomic questions also merit attention. (1) When and why did socioeconomic factors such as education and income become important for the mortality transition and for mortality fluctuations and differentials? (2) Can we formulate a replacement for conventional demographic transition theory? Do the studies in this volume suggest any alternative answers to one of society's most important questions? (3) The analysis of fertility is complex. For the study of mortality, in contrast, we can usually assume that people want better health and longer lives for themselves and their families. But the motives for childbearing are diverse and complex. We need to ask whether we will ever develop a comprehensive theory of fertility which will apply broadly across time and space. Do the studies here help to simplify our understanding of the determinants of reproductive behavior, or do they only add more complexity? (4) Demographically "mature" nations such as the United States and Canada now face an important new set of problems. As fertility declines, as population growth slows, and as the population ages, how will they finance social security systems and health care for older citizens and for society as a whole? For example, the median age of the population of the United States has risen from about 16 years in 1800 to almost 33 years in 1990. Although these issues are less pressing for many developing nations where fertility is still relatively high and where the population is still relatively young, they will ultimately have to be faced. (5) What will be the future of migration to, from, and within the North American region? Will the North American Free Trade Agreement (NAFTA) reduce the flow of labor from Mexico to the United States by enhancing the flow of capital? Will the Caribbean basin become an even more important supplier of immigrant labor to the United States (and elsewhere)? Will the income inequalities which drive this migration persist? (6) What are the future challenges, especially for the United States and Canada, as racial and ethnic diversity grow through immigration and differential natural increase? (7) Will political concerns impede the collection of demographic data and possibly have an impact on their reliablity? Will the movement toward a smaller role for government and increased pressure on budgets number among its casualties one of the premier public goods, namely socioeconomic and demographic data collection? (8) What will happen to city growth and the structure of urban areas? Will central cities continue to deteriorate in the United States? Will the suburbanization characteristic of the United States and Canada spread to other areas? What does the future hold for the very large metropolis (e.g., Mexico City)? (9) What will regional patterns of population redistribution look like and what social and economic consequences will they have?

Historical data and historical studies can shed light on these types of issues. We have seen episodes of xenophobia before in the United States, namely in the 1840s and 1850s with the large influx of Irish and German immigrants, and again in the period 1900 to 1914 as huge numbers of migrants from southern and eastern Europe entered the country. Recent efforts to restrict immigration seem to mirror these occurrences. Data collection has been a political issue before. As an instance, the U.S. Congress was not reapportioned in the 1920s – the only decade in which that happened – because the census of 1920 showed that the urban population outnumbered the rural population for the first time in American history. Past trends in urbanization, suburbanization, and regional population redistribution provide clues to the present situation and enable us to forecast future scenarios. Examples of the value of historical information and analysis can be multiplied. The contributions to this volume not only summarize many of the recent advances in the population history of North America, but they also point out the areas and issues in need of research.

APPENDIX

MEASUREMENT AND ESTIMATION

Demography, the study of human populations, depends heavily on various measurement and estimation techniques. Most of the results presented in this volume are simple tabulations or standard demographic rates. But a number of the newer findings arise from rather sophisticated techniques.[1] Estimation of better demographic information is of importance for research in a variety of fields. Basic demographic structures and events, reflected in birth and death rates, population size and structure, growth rates, the composition and growth of the labor force, marriage rates and patterns, household composition, the levels and nature of migration flows, causes of death, urbanization and spatial population distribution, and other such factors, determine the human capital of society as producers and consumers and also the ways in which that human capital reproduces, relocates, and depreciates. Demographic events are important both as indicators of social and economic change and as integral components of modern economic growth.

Most of the measures presented here are relatively straightforward, such as crude birth and death rates, rates of total and natural increase, and rates

---

[1] An introduction to demographic measurement may be found in Henry S. Shryock, Henry S., Jacob S. Siegel, and associates, *The Methods and Materials of Demography* (Washington, D.C.: government Printing Office, 1971). See also Michael R. Haines, "Economic History and Historical Demography," in Alexander J. Field, ed., *The Future of Economic History* (Boston: Kluwer-Nijhoff, 1987), pp. 185–253; Michael R. Haines and Barbara A. Anderson, "New Demographic History of the Late 19th-Century United States," *Explorations in Economic History*, vol. 25, no. 4 (October 1988), pp. 341–65; J. Dennis Willigan and Katherine A. Lynch, *Sources and Methods of Historical Demography* (New York: Academic Press, 1982).

of net migration. These are presented in Tables A.1 and A.3 of the end of this appendix and are given as rates per thousand midperiod population per year. So, the crude birth rate (CBR) is births per thousand population per year. The crude death rate (CDR) is total deaths per thousand population per year. For both these rates, births and deaths are often taken as an average for a series of years around a central date in order to smooth out annual fluctuations in vital events. The rate of natural increase (RNI) is equal to the crude birth rate minus the crude death rate. The rate of total increase (RTI) in the rate of overall population growth expressed per thousand instead of the usual percent. The rate of net migration (RNM) is equal to the rate of total increase minus the rate of natural increase. It is a residual (i.e., not measured directly) and describes a net flow (i.e., the difference between in-migration and out-migration). Examples of gross migration flows are seen in Table 8.5. Table A.3 uses these measures in the form of the demographic balancing equation (RTI = CBR − CDR + RNM) to look at the components of population growth.

In addition, however, some of the results discussed in this volume arise (at least in theory) from age-specific measures, but such data must usually be summarized to be useful and intuitively interpretable. One technique used to summarize them is the life table. It takes age-specific death rates either for cross sections of a population at various ages at a point in time, which generates period life tables, or for an actual group of people born in the same time period (a cohort), which provides cohort life tables, and converts them into other measures. These other measures would include the expectation of life at any age: that is, the average number of years of life remaining if that group experienced the age-specific mortality rates embodied in the life table. Table A.2 presents the expectation of life at birth ($\mathring{e}_0$) for the white population from 1850 onward. Another life table measure is the probability of an infant surviving from birth to the first birthday (exact age 1), which is presented here as the infant mortality rate (infant deaths per thousand live births per annum).

Age-specific fertility rates can be summarized in similar fashion. One instance provided in Table A.2 is the total fertility rate (TFR), which is the sum of age-specific births for all women aged 15 to 49.[2] This can be interpreted as the average number of births a woman would have if she

---

[2] In fact, the total fertility rates before 1940 in Table A.2 were estimated indirectly without first obtaining the age-specific rates, though estimates of age-specific overall and marital fertility rates now exist for the period back to the later nineteenth century. See Michael R. Haines, "American Fertility in Transition: New Estimates of Birth Rates in the United States, 1900–1910," *Demography*, vol. 26, no. 1 (February 1989), pp. 137–48.

survived her whole reproductive life and if she experienced rates of child-bearing given by the age-specific data. It is akin to completed family size for all women of childbearing age (not just married women). This is calculated here for cross-sectional (or period) data and would apply to a synthetic cohort. It can be estimated for true cohorts, however.[3]

Table A.2 also provides a measure of fertility known as the child/woman ratio, which is the number of surviving children aged 0–4 per thousand women aged 20–44. It is a wholly census-based fertility rate, requiring no vital statistics. It is, in fact, the main direct source of information on fertility in the United States in the nineteenth century and is the basis for the early estimates of the crude birth rate and the total fertility rate also given in Table A.2. The child/woman ratio does have some serious drawbacks, since it deals with surviving children at the census and not actual births in the preceding five years. It also suffers from relative differences in underenumeration of young children and adult women.[4]

These measures, some additional rates, and the life table are explained in technical terms in the following pages.

BASIC DEMOGRAPHIC MEASURES

I. Crude Rates

(1)   Crude birth rate = CBR $= \dfrac{B_t}{P_t} * k$

>   where B_t = live births in time period t
> P_t = midperiod population of time period t
>   (an approximation for person years lived during time period t)
>
> k = a constant, usually 1,000

(2)   Crude death rate = CDR $= \dfrac{D_t}{P_t} * k$

>   where D_t = deaths in time period t
> P_t = midperiod population of time period t

---

[3] For an example, see Lee L. Bean, Geraldine P. Mineau, and Douglas Anderton, *Fertility Change on the American Frontier: Adaptation and Innovation* (Berkeley: University of California Press, 1900), chap. 4.

[4] Alternative measures of fertility, mortality, marriage, and migration, in addition to estimation procedures, are discussed in Shryock and Siegel, *The Methods and Materials of Demography*; and Haines, "Economic History and Historical Demography."

(an approximation for person years lived during time period *t*)

k = a constant, usually 1,000

(3) Rate of natural increase = RNI = CBR − CDR

(4) Rate of total increase = RTI (during time period *t* to *t* + *n*)

(a) exponential RTI = $r_e = [\ln(P_{t+n}/P_t)/n] * k$

(b) compound interest RTI = $r_c = [(P_{t+n}/P_t)^{1/n}] * k$

(c) linear RTI = $r_e = [(P_{t+n} - P_t) / (n * .5 * \{P_{t+n} + P_t\})] * k$

where P_t = population at time t

P_{t+n} = population at time t + n

n = duration of time period

ln = natural logarithm

k = a constant, may be 1,000 or 100 or 1

(5) Rate of residual net migration = RRNM = RTI − RNI

where k = 1,000 for both RTI & RNI

II. More Refined Rates: Fertility

(1) General fertility ratio = GFR = $\dfrac{B_t}{(P^F_{15-49})_t} * k$

where $(P^F_{15-49})_t$ = midperiod female population aged 15–49 in time period *t* (an approximation to person years lived during time period *t*)

(2) Age-specific fertility rate = $(b_i)_t = \dfrac{(B_i)_t}{(P^F_i)_t} * k$

where $(b_i)_t$ = age-specific fertility rate for the ith age group in period *t*

$(B_i)_t$ = live births to mothers in the ith age group during period *t*

$(P^F_i)_t$ = midperiod female population i^{th} age group period *t* (an approximation for person years lived)

k = a constant, often 1 but may be 1,000

(3) Total fertility rate = TFR = $\displaystyle\sum_{i=15}^{49}(b_i)_t * k$

where k = a constant (1 or 1,000)

(4) Gross reproduction rate = GRR = $\displaystyle\sum_{i=15}^{49}(b_i^F)_t * k$

where $(b_i)_t$ = age-specific fertility rate for female births only in period *t*

(5) Net reproduction rate $= \text{NRR} = \sum_{i=15}^{49} (b_i^{F})_t * (L_i / l_o) * k$

where $(L_i/l_0) =$ probability of a woman of surviving from birth to age i (from an appropriate life table)

$k =$ a constant (1 or 1,000)

(6) Child/woman ratio $= (P_{0-4})_t / (P^{F}_{15-49})_t * k$

where $(P_{0-4})_t =$ population aged 0–4 at time t

$k =$ a constant (1 or 1,000)

(7) COALE'S INDICES OF FERTILITY AND NUPTIALITY[5]

Standard schedule:	Age groups (i)	Births per married Hutterite woman, 1921–1930 (F_i)
	15–19	.300
	20–24	.550
	25–29	.502
	30–34	.447
	35–39	.406
	40–44	.222
	45–49	.061

$I_f =$ index of overall fertility

$= \dfrac{B_t}{\sum F_i w_i}$

$I_h =$ index of illegitimate fertility

$= \dfrac{B_t^{I}}{\sum F_i u_i}$

$I_g =$ index of marital fertility

$= \dfrac{B_t^{L}}{\sum F_i m_i}$

$I_m =$ index of proportions married

$= \dfrac{\sum F_i m_i}{\sum F_i w_i}$

where $I_f = I_g * I_m + I_h * (1 - I_m)$

$B_t =$ total births at time t in the population studied

$B_t^{L} =$ legitimate births at time t in the population studied

$B_t^{I} =$ illegitimate births at time t in the population studied

$w_i =$ total women in the ith age group in the population studied (using five year age groupings)

$m_i =$ total married women in the ith age group in the population studied (using five year age groupings)

$u_i =$ total unmarried women in the ith age groups in the population studied (using five year age groupings)

[5] Ansley J. Coale, "Factors Associated with the Development of low Fertility: An Historic Summary," United Nations, World Population Conference, 1965, vol. 2 (New York: United Nations, 1967), pp. 205–9.

F_i = births per woman in the "standard" population in the ith age interval

III. More Refined Rates: Mortality

(1)   Age-specific mortality rate = $(d_i)_t^j = \dfrac{(D_i)_t^j}{(P_i)_t^j} * k$

where $(d_i)_t^j$ = age-specific mortality rate for the ith age group in period t for sex j (male, female, both sexes)

$(D_i)_t^j$ = deaths to persons in the ith age group during period t for sex j

$(P_j)_t^j$ = midperiod population i^{th} age group in period t for sex j (an approximation for person years lived)

k = a constant, often 1 but may be 1,000

(2)   Infant mortality rate = $IMR_t = \dfrac{(D_o)_t}{(B)_t} * k$

where IMR_t = the infant mortality rate for period t

$(D_o)_t$ = deaths in the first year of life during period t

$(B)_t$ = live births in period t

k = a constant, often 1,000

(3)   The life table

   (i)   Central death rates (used to calculate the life table and usually based on published vital statistics and census population data):
$$_nM_x = (_nD_x \,/\, _nP_x)$$
   where $_nM_x$ = the central death rate over the age interval x to $x + n$

   $_nD_x$ = deaths for the same age interval

   $_nP_x$ = average person years lived in the interval, approximated by the midperiod population for the age interval

   (ii)   Probability of dying between exact age x and exact age $x + n$:
$$_nq_x = (2 * n *_n M_x) / (2 + n *_n M_x)$$
   where n is the size of the age interval in years

   (iii) Persons remaining alive out of 100,000:
$$l_x = l_{x-n} * (1 - {_nq_x})$$

(iv)   The radix of the life table:

$$l_0 = 100,000$$

(v)   Deaths in the age interval x to $x + n$:

$$D_x = l_x - l_{x-n}$$

(vi)   Person years lived in the age interval:

$$L_x = n * (f_1 * l_x + f_2 * l_{x-n})$$

where $f_1 = f_2 = .5$ and $f_1 + f_2 = 1.0$, except for the age intervals below age 5. In that case, different separation factors need to be used. For example,

age (x)	f_1	f_2	
0	.33	.67	for males
0	.35	.65	for females
1	.41	.59	
2	.47	.53	
3, 4	.48	.52	

(vii) $P(x) = (L_x / L_{x+n})$

(viii) $T_x = \sum\limits_{i=x}^{\infty} L_i$

(ix) $T_\infty = \mathring{e}_\infty / l_x$

(x) $\mathring{e}_x = T_x / l_x$

(xi)   The life table needs to be "closed"; that is, the final expectation of life needs to be determined. For example,

$$\mathring{e}_\infty = 3.725 + .0000625 * l_\infty$$

(xii) $$m(x) = D_x / L_x$$

Here is an example of a historical life table (Haines, 1998):

United States, total population, both sexes, 1850

Age (x)	$q(x)$	$l(x)$	$D(x)$	$L(x)$	$P(x)$	$T(x)$	$\mathring{e}(x)$	$m(x)$
0	0.228727	100,000	22,873	84,904	0.87877	3,833,886	38.34	0.26940
1	0.055301	77,127	4,265	74,611	0.96347	3,748,982	48.61	0.05717
2	0.025287	72,862	1,842	71,886	0.97963	3,674,372	50.43	0.02563
3	0.016207	71,020	1,151	70,421	0.98579	3,602,486	50.73	0.01634
4	0.012331	69,869	862	69,421	0.97752	3,532,065	50.55	0.01241
5–9	0.033241	69,007	2,294	339,301	0.97286	3,462,644	50.18	0.00676

10–14	0.020820	66,713	1,389	330,094	0.97322	3,123,344	46.82	0.00421
15–19	0.032862	65,324	2,147	321,254	0.96019	2,793,250	42.76	0.00668
20–24	0.046985	63,178	2,968	308,467	0.95054	2,471,996	39.13	0.00962
25–29	0.052057	60,209	3,134	293,210	0.94548	2,163,529	35.93	0.01069
30–34	0.057127	57,075	3,261	277,223	0.94043	1,870,319	32.77	0.01176
35–39	0.062158	53,814	3,345	260,709	0.93476	1,593,096	29.60	0.01283
40–44	0.068531	50,469	3,459	243,700	0.92609	1,332,387	26.40	0.01419
45–49	0.079687	47,011	3,746	225,688	0.91161	1,088,687	23.16	0.01660
50–54	0.097841	43,264	4,233	205,740	0.88709	863,000	19.95	0.02057
55–59	0.129621	39,031	5,59	182,509	0.85332	657,260	16.84	0.02772
60–64	0.166283	33,972	5,649	155,738	0.80689	474,751	13,97	0.03627
65–69	0.225295	28,323	6,381	125,663	0.74182	319,013	11.26	0.05078
70–74	0.300630	21,942	6,596	93,219	0.65539	193,350	8.81	0.07076
75–79	0.407498	15,346	6,253	61,095	0.63894	100,131	6.53	0.10235
80+	1.000000	9,092	9,092	39,036	0.00000	39,036	4.29	0.23292

BASIC DATA

Table A.I. *Estimated population of North America, 1650–1990 (population in thousands)*

Date	United States[a] Total	White	Black	Other	Canada[b] Total	Mexico	Caribbean	Amerindian United States[a]	Amerindian Canada	Implied Total
1650	75	72	3	n.a.				1,152		1,227
1700	251	223	28	n.a.	17[c]			987		1,255
1750	1,171	935	236	n.a.	71[d]			780		2,022
1800	5,308	4,306	1,002	n.a.	362[c]	5,100	1,077	600		12,447
1850	23,192	19,553	3,639	n.a.	2,546	7,600	3,024[g]	370	125	36,732
1900	76,057	66,839	8,834	384	5,592	13,566	6,977[h]	250	128	102,442
1950	150,826	135,035	15,042	749	14,009	25,855	17,775[h]	357	166	208,822
1980	226,546	194,713	26,683	5,150	24,343	66,958		1,367	491	319,214
1990	248,719	208,710	30,486	9,523	27,297	81,700	35,145[h]	2,065	395	394,926
Implied annual growth rates (%)										
1650/1700	2.42	2.26	4.47					−0.31		0.05
1700/1750	3.08	2.87	4.26		2.86			−0.47		0.95
1750/1800	3.02	3.05	2.89		3.26			−0.52		3.63
1800/1850	2.95	3.03	2.58		3.90	0.80	3.44	−0.97		2.16
1850/1900	2.38	2.46	1.77		1.57	1.16	1.19	−0.78	0.05	2.05
1900/1950	1.37	1.41	1.06	2.23	1.84	1.29	1.87	0.71	0.52	1.42
1950/1990	1.25	1.09	1.77	6.36[d]	1.67	2.88	1.70	4.39[f]	2.17	1.59

[a] Includes Alaska from 1900.
[b] Includes Newfoundland from 1850 and Labrador from 1900. Canadian censuses were taken in years ending in "1" (i.e., 1851, 1901, 1951, 1981, 1991).
[c] 1700/10.
[d] 1750/60.

^{e} 1800/1810.

^{f} The extraordinary growth rate of the "other" population from 1950 to 1990 is largely due to reidentification of individuals to the Amerindian population.

^{g} 1830.

^{h} Includes Belize, Guyana, Surinam, and Cayene.

Source: U.S. Bureau of the Census, *Historical Statistics of the United States* (Washington, D.C.: Government Printing Office, 1975); U.S. Bureau of the Census, *Statistical Abstract of the United States, 1993* (Washington, D.C.: Government Printing Office, 1993); Statistics Canada, *Historical Statistics of Canada*, 2d ed. (Ottawa: Statistics Canada, 1983); B. R. Mitchell, *International Historical Statistics: The Americas and Australasia* (Detroit, Mich.: Gale Research, 1983); C. Matthew Snipp, *American Indians: The First of this Land* (New York: Russell Sage, 1989); Russell Thornton, *American Indian Holocaust and Survival: A Population History since 1492* (Norman: University of Oklahoma Press, 1987); Russell Thornton and Joan Marsh-Thornton, "Estimating Prehistoric American Indian Population Size for United States Area: Implications for the Nineteenth Century Population Decline and Nadir," *American Journal of Physical Anthropology*, vol. 55 (1981), pp. 47–53; United Nations, *Demographic Yearbook: 1993* (New York: United Nations, 1995); Robert McCaa, "The Peopling of Nineteenth-Century Mexico," in James W. Wilkie, Carlos Alberto Contreras, and Christof Anders Weber, eds., *Statistical Abstract of Latin America*, pp. 603–33 (Los Angeles: University of California, Latin American Studies Center, 1993). Also Chapter 13 in this volume, Table 13.1; and Chapter 11, Tables 11.3 and 11.9.

Table A.2. *Fertility and mortality in North America, 1800–1991*

| | United States | | | | | | | | | |
| Approximate date | Birth rate[a] | | Child/woman ratio[b] | | Total fertility rate[c] | | Expectation of life[d] | | Infant mortality rate[e] | |
	White	Black[f]	White	Black	White	Black[f]	White	Black[f]	White	Black[f]
1800	55.0		1,342		7.04					
1810	54.3		1,358		6.92					
1820	52.8		1,295	1,191	6.73					
1830	51.4		1,145	1,220	6.55					
1840	48.3		1,085	1,154	6.14					
1850	43.3	58.6[g]	892	1,087	5.42	7.90[g]	39.5	23.0	216.8	340.0
1860	41.4	55.0[h]	905	1,072	5.21	7.58[h]	43.6		181.3	
1870	38.3	55.4[i]	814	997	4.55	7.69[i]	45.2		175.5	
1880	35.2	51.9[j]	780	1,090	4.24	7.26[i]	40.5		214.8	
1890	31.5	48.1	685	930	3.87	6.56	46.8		150.7	
1900	30.1	44.4	666	845	3.56	5.61	51.8[k]	41.8[k]	110.8[k]	170.3[k]
1910	29.2	38.5	631	736	3.42	4.61	54.6[l]	46.8[l]	96.5[l]	142.6[l]
1920	26.9	35.0	604	608	3.17	3.64	57.4	47.0	82.1	131.7
1930	20.6	27.5	506	554	2.45	2.98	60.8	48.5	60.1	99.9
1940	18.6	26.7	419	513	2.22	2.87	64.9	53.9	43.2	73.8
1950	23.0	33.3	580	663	2.98	3.93	69.0	60.7	26.8	44.5
1960	22.7	32.1	717	895	3.53	4.52	70.7	63.9	22.9	43.2
1970	17.4	25.1	507	689	2.39	3.07	71.6	64.1	17.8	30.9
1980	15.1	20.9	300	367	1.77	2.18	74.5	68.5	10.9	22.2
1990	15.8	21.5	298	359	2.01	2.48	76.1	69.1	7.6	18.0

Canada

Approximate date	Birth rate[a]			Child/woman ratio[b]			Total fertility rate[c]			Expectation of life[d]		Infant mortality rate[e]	
	Total	Quebec	Rest of Canada	Total	Quebec	Rest of Canada	Total	Quebec	Rest of Canada	Total	Quebec	Total	Quebec
1851	43.6	45.0	42.8	874						41.1	40.9	175.3	179.8
1861	41.2	43.1	40.2	776						41.6	41.6	178.1	179.0
1871	35.8	43.2	32.3	666						42.6	42.1	165.0	178.3
1881	34.0	42.0	30.3	613	626	535				44.7	42.9	154.1	162.9
1891	32.6	39.8	29.4	556	611	463		5.69	4.05	45.2	44.2	155.0	154.0
1901	29.8	37.7	26.3	532	602	438		4.90	3.92	48.6	46.3	154.0	144.8
1911	30.0	37.6	27.0	565	615	477		4.84	4.01	52.5	49.4	138.0	120.5
1921	29.3	37.6	26.2	545	554	473	3.36[m]	4.84	3.92	56.7	53.2	118.0	100.5
1931	23.2	29.1	21.8	466	490	390	3.20	4.00	2.89	61.0	57.0	84.0	77.5
1941	22.4	26.8	21.4	397	404	335	2.83	3.39	2.60	64.6	61.6	58.0	64.0
1951	27.2	29.8	26.1	555	525	477	3.50	3.78	3.38	68.5	66.5	39.7	54.6
1961	26.0	26.1	26.1	606	531	529	3.84	3.70	3.90	71.2	70.0	27.3	30.2
1971	16.8	14.8	17.6	390	311	357	2.19	1.90	2.29	72.8	71.7	18.0	22.1
1981	15.3	15.5	15.2	303	264	277	1.67	1.61	1.73	75.3		9.6	
1991	14.6	12.7	14.8	301			1.83	1.72	1.85	78.0		6.8	

697

Table A.2. (cont.)

Mexico

Approximate date	Birth rate [a,n]	Child/woman ratio [b]	Total fertility rate [c,n]	Expectation of life [d]	Infant mortality rate [e,n]
1900	46.3	729		25.3	220.0
1910	41.9	750		27.6	221.5
1920	44.8				165.5
1930	43.8			36.8	135.5
1940	44.2	630	6.04	39.8	
1950	45.4	684	6.26	48.5	134.6[o]
1960	45.0	787	6.65	57.6	95.1[p]
1970	41.8	860	6.37	61.1	77.0[q]
1980	35.0		4.31	64.8	28.3
1990	33.5	528	3.39	71.0	23.9

[a] Births per thousand population per annum.
[b] Children aged 0-4 per thousand women aged 15-44. Taken from U.S. Bureau of the Census, *Historical Statistics of the United States* (Washington D.C.: Government Printing Office, 1975), Series 67-68 for 1800-1970. For the black population, 1820-1840, W. S. Thompson and P. K. Whelpton, *Population Trends in the United States* (New York: McGraw-Hill, 1933), Table 74, adjusted upward 47% for relative underenumeration of black children aged 0-4 for the censuses of 1820-1840. For Canada, data from *Historical Statistics of Canada* and United Nations, *Demographic Yearbook*.
[c] Total number of births per woman if she experienced the current period age-specific fertility rates throughout her life.
[d] Expectation of life at birth for both sexes combined.
[e] Infant deaths per thousand live births per annum.
[f] Black and other population.
[g] Average for 1850-59.

[b] Average for 1860–69.

[i] Average for 1870–79.

[j] Average for 1880–84.

[k] Approximately 1895.

[l] Approximately 1903.

[m] For 1926.

[n] Average for the decade beginning with the date, e.g., 1900–9, 1910–19, etc., except for 1990.

[o] Average for 1947–51.

[p] Average for 1957–61.

[q] Average for 1967–71.

Source: U.S. Bureau of the Census, *Historical Statistics of the United States* (Washington, D.C.: GPO, 1975); U.S. Bureau of the Census, *Statistical Abstract of the United States, 1986* (Washington, D.C.: GPO, 1985); and *Statistical Abstract of the United States, 1997* (Washington, D.C.: GPO, 1997); Ansley J. Coale and Melvin Zelnik, *New Estimates of Fertility and Population in the United States* (Princeton, N.J.: Princeton University Press, 1963). Ansley J. Coale and Norfleet W. Rives, "A Statistical Reconstruction of the Black Population of the United States, 1880–1970: Estimates of True Numbers by Age and Sex, Birth Rates, and Total Fertility," *Population Index*, vol. 39, no. 1 (January 1973), pp. 3–36; Michael R. Haines, "Estimated Life Tables for the United States, 1850–1900," *Historical Methods*, vol. 31, no. 4 (Fall, 1998), pp. 149–69; Samuel H. Preston and Michael R. Haines, *Fatal Years: Child Mortality in Late Nineteenth Century America* (Princeton, N.J.: Princeton University Press, 1991), Table 2.5; Richard H. Steckel, "A Dreadful Childhood: The Excess Mortality of American Salves," *Social Science History* (Winter 1986), pp. 427–65; Marvin McInnis, personal communication; Statistics Canada, *Historical Statistics of Canada*, 2d ed. (Ottawa: Statistics Canada, 1983); B. R. Mitchell, *International Historical Statistics: The Americas and Australasia* (Detroit: Gale Research, 1983); United Nations, Demographic Yearbook; Robert Bourbeau and Jacques Legare, *Evolution de la Mortalite au Canada et au Quebec 1831–1931* (Motreal: Le Presses de l'Université de Montréal, 1982). See also Chapter 13 in this volume, Tables 13.1 and 13.2.

Table A.3. *Components of population growth, United States (1800–1990), Canada (1851–1991), and Mexico, (1900–1990) (rates per thousand midperiod population per year)*

Period	Average population (thousands)	RTI	CBR	CDR	RNI[a]	RNM[a]	RNM as % of RTI
United States							
1790–1800	4,520	30.08			26.49	3.59	11.9
1800–10	6,132	31.04			26.85	4.19	13.5
1810–20	8,276	28.62			24.70	3.92	13.7
1820–30	11,031	28.88			26.93	1.95	6.8
1830–40	14,685	28.27			23.67	4.60	16.3
1840–50	19,686	30.65			22.88	7.77	25.3
1850–60	26,721	30.44			20.35	10.09	33.2
1860–70	35,156	23.62			17.64	5.98	25.3
1870–80	44,414	23.08	41.16	23.66	17.50	5.58	24.2
1880–90	55,853	22.72	37.03	21.34	15.69	7.03	30.9
1890–1900	68,876	18.83	32.22	19.44	12.78	6.06	32.2
1900–10	83,245	19.08	30.10	17.27	12.83	6.25	32.8
1910–20	98,807	14.86	27.15	15.70	11.45	3.41	23.0
1920–30	114,184	14.01	23.40	11.08	12.32	1.68	12.0
1930–40	127,058	7.01	18.39	11.18	7.21	−0.20	−2.9
1940–50	140,555	13.50	22.48	10.39	12.09	1.41	10.4
1950–60	164,011	17.67	24.81	9.47	15.34	2.33	13.2
1960–70	190,857	12.27	20.26	9.55	10.71	1.56	12.7
1970–80	214,306	10.83	15.49	9.00	6.49	4.34	40.1
1980–90	238,466	9.34	15.91	8.70	7.21	2.13	22.8
Canada							
1851–61	2,833	28.21	45.22	23.65	21.57	6.65	23.6
1861–71	3,460	13.29	39.60	21.97	17.63	−4.35	−32.7
1871–81	4,007	15.91	36.94	19.72	17.22	−1.31	−8.3
1881–91	4,579	11.11	33.28	19.00	14.28	−3.18	−28.6
1891–01	5,102	10.55	30.34	17.25	13.09	−2.54	−24.0
1901–11	6,289	29.40	30.61	14.31	16.30	13.11	44.6
1911–21	7,998	19.83	29.26	13.38	15.88	3.95	19.9
1921–31	9,583	16.62	25.20	11.01	14.19	2.43	14.6
1931–41	10,942	10.34	20.97	9.80	11.17	−0.83	−8.0
1941–51	12,913	17.06	24.67	9.40	15.27	1.79	10.5
1951–61	16,124	28.99	27.71	8.19	19.52	9.47	32.7
1961–71	19,903	16.77	20.63	7.52	13.10	3.67	21.9
1971–81	22,956	14.37	15.57	7.26	8.31	6.05	42.1
1981–91	25,820	12.13	14.74	7.09	7.65	4.48	37.0
Mexico							
1900–10	14,333	10.85	46.30	34.10	12.20	−1.35	−12.4
1910–20	14,738	−5.05	41.90	37.50	4.40	−9.45	187.1

Table A.3. *(cont.)*

Period	Average population (thousands)	RTI	CBR	CDR	RNI[a]	RNM[a]	RNM as % of RTI
1920–30	15,480	14.42	44.80	29.90	14.90	−0.48	−3.3
1930–40	18,220	17.89	43.80	25.10	18.70	−0.81	−4.5
1940–50	22,850	26.46	44.20	19.80	24.40	2.06	7.8
1950–60	30,434	30.32	45.40	14.00	31.40	−1.08	−3.6
1960–70	42,000	33.59	45.00	10.20	34.80	−1.21	−3.6
1970–80	57,973	31.25	41.80	8.00	33.80	−2.55	−8.2
1980–90	74,329	19.90	35.00	5.70	29.30	−9.40	−47.2

Note: RTI = rate of total increase; CBR = crude birth rate (live births per one thousand population per year; CDR = crude death rate (deaths per one thousand population per year); RNI = rate of natural increase (= CBR − CDR); RNM = rate of net inernational migration.

[a] For the United States, rate of net migration calculated directly from net migrants 1790–1860. Gross migrants used for 1860–70. For 1870–1980, RNM = RTI − RNI and thus is a residual. Prior to 1870, RNI is calculated as a residual (= RTI − RNM). For Canada for 1861–1981, RNM = RTI − RNI.

Sources: (1) Unadjusted populations. United States: U.S. Bureau of the Census, *Historical Statistics of the United States* (Washington, D.C.: Government Printing Office, 1975); U.S. Bureau of the Census, *Statistical Abstract of the United States, 1990* (Washington, D.C.: Government Printing Office, 1990). Canada: Statistics Canada, *Historical Statistics of Canada*, 2d ed. (Ottawa: Statistics Canada, 1983); United Nations, *Demographic Yearbook*, 1986, 1995. "Population and Growth Compnents" Statistics Canada, Demography Division (1998) (available from http://WWW.StatCan.CA/english/Pgdg/People/Population/demo03.htm) (visited on 8/15/98). Mexico: See Chapter 13 in this volume, Table 13.1.

(2) Births and deaths. United States: 1870–1940: Simon Kuznets, "Long Swings in the Growth of Population and Related Economic Variables," *Proceedings of the American Philosophical Society*, vol. 102, no. 1 (February 1958), pp. 25–52. 1940–90: Same as in (1). Canada: 1921–1981: *Historical Statistics of Canada*, 1900–1920: B. R. Mitchell, *International Historical Statistics: The Americas and Australasia* (Detroit, Mich.: Gale Research, 1983). United Nations, *Demographic Yearbook*, 1985, 1986, 1992. "Population and Growth Compnents" Statistics Canada, Demography Division (1998) (available from http://WWW.StatCan.CA/english/Pgdg/People/Population/demo03.htm) (visited on 8/15/98). Mexico: Birth and death rates, Chapter 13 in this volume, Table 13.2.

(3) Net migrants. United States: 1790–1820: Henry A. Gemery, "European Emigration to North America: Numbers and Quasi-Nubers," *Perspectives in American History*, N.S. 1 (1984), supplemented by estimates of slave imports from Philip Curtin, *The Atlantic Slave Trade: A Census* (Madison: University of Wisconsisn Press, 1969.) 1820–1860: Peter D. McClelland and Richard J. Zeckhauser, *Demographic Dimensions of the New republic: American Interregional Migration, Vital Statistics and Manumissions, 1800–1860* (New York: Cambridge University Press, 1982), and also supplemented by estimates of slave imports from Curtin.

Table A.4. *Population by race, residence, nativity, age, and sex, United States (1800–1990),*
Canada (1851–1991), and Mexico (1900–1990)
(population in thousands)

United States

Census date	Total	Growth (% p.a.)	White	Black	Other	Urban	%	Foreign-born	%	Median age	Sex ratio[a]
1790	3,929	—	3,172	757	n.a.	202	5.1	n.a.	—	(NA)	103.8
1800	5,308	3.01	4,306	1,002	n.a.	322	6.1	n.a.	—	16.0[b]	104.0
1810	7,240	3.10	5,862	1,378	n.a.	525	7.3	n.a.	—	16.0[b]	104.0
1820	9,639	2.86	7,867	1,772	n.a.	693	7.2	n.a.	—	16.7	103.3
1830	12,866	2.89	10,537	2,329	n.a.	1,127	8.8	n.a.	—	17.2	103.1
1840	17,070	2.83	14,196	2,874	n.a.	1,845	10.8	n.a.	—	17.8	103.7
1850	23,192	3.06	19,553	3,639	n.a.	3,544	15.3	2,245	9.7	18.9	104.3
1860	31,443	3.04	26,923	4,442	79	6,217	19.8	4,104	13.1	19.4	104.7
1870	39,819	2.36	33,589	4,880	89	9,902	24.9	5,567	14.0	20.2	102.2
1880	50,156	2.31	43,403	6,581	172	14,130	28.2	6,680	13.3	20.9	103.6
1890	62,948	2.27	55,101	7,489	358	22,106	35.1	9,250	14.7	22.0	105.0
1900	75,994	1.88	66,809	8,834	351	30,160	39.7	10,341	13.6	22.9	104.4
1910	91,972	1.91	81,732	9,828	413	41,999	45.7	13,516	14.7	24.1	106.0
1920	106,711	1.49	94,821	10,463	427	54,158	50.8	14,020	13.1	25.3	104.0
1930	122,755	1.40	110,287	11,891	597	68,955	56.2	14,283	11.6	26.5	102.5
1940	131,669	0.70	118,215	12,866	589	74,424	56.5	11,657	8.9	29.0	100.7
1950	150,697	1.35	134,942	15,042	713	96,468	64.0	10,431	6.9	30.2	98.6
1960	179,823	1.77	158,832	18,872	1,620	125,269	69.7	9,738	5.4	29.5	97.1
1970	203,302	1.23	178,098	22,580	2,883	149,325	73.4	9,619	4.7	28.1	94.8

| | 1980 | 226,546 | 1.08 | 194,713 | 26,683 | 5,150 | 167,051 | 73.7 | 14,080 | 6.2 | 30.0 | 94.5 |
| | 1990 | 248,710 | 0.93 | 208,704 | 30,483 | 9,523 | 187,053 | 75.2 | 21,632 | 8.7 | 32.8 | 95.1 |

Canada

Census date	Total	Growth % p.a.	British origin	French origin	Amer-Indian	Urban	%	Foreign-born	%	Median age	Sex ratio
1851	2,436	—								17.2	105.4
1861	3,230	2.82								18.2	105.7
1871	3,689	1.33	2,110	1,083	23	722	19.6	594	16.1	18.8	102.7
1881	4,325	1.59	2,548	1,299	109	1,110	25.7	603	13.9	20.1	102.5
1891	4,833	1.11	—	—	—	1,537	31.8	644	13.3	21.4	103.7
1901	5,371	1.06	3,063	1,649	128	2,014	37.5	700	13.0	22.7	105.0
1911	7,207	2.94	3,999	2,062	106	3,273	45.4	1,586	22.0	23.8	112.9
1921	8,788	1.98	4,869	2,453	114	4,352	49.5	1,956	22.3	23.9	106.4
1931	10,377	1.66	5,381	2,928	129	5,572	53.7	2,308	22.2	24.7	107.4
1941	11,507	1.03	5,716	3,483	126	6,252	54.3	2,018	17.5	27.0	105.3
1951	14,009	1.97	6,710	4,319	166	7,941	56.7	2,060	14.7	27.8	102.4
1961	18,238	2.64	7,997	5,540	220	11,069	60.7	2,845	15.6	26.5	102.2
1971	21,568	1.68	9,324	6,180	313	14,115	65.4	3,296	15.3	26.4	100.2
1981	24,343	1.21	9,674	6,439	491	18,436	75.7	3,867	15.9	29.6	98.3
1991	27,297	1.15	8,083	6,593	395	20,907	76.6	4,941	18.1	33.5	97.2

Table A.4. (cont.)

Mexico

Census date	Total	Growth % p.a.	Urban	%	Foreign-born	%	Mexican in U.S.	% OF Mexican Population	Median age Group	Sex ratio
1900	13,556	—	3,850	28.40			103	0.76	15–19	98.5
1910	15,110	1.09	4,351	28.80			222	1.47	15–19	98.0
1921	14,366	-0.46	4,466	31.09	101	0.70	486	3.38	20–24	95.5
1930	16,594	1.60	5,541	33.39	160	0.96	642	3.87	20–24	96.3
1940	19,845	1.79	6,896	34.75	177	0.89	377	1.90	15–19	97.4
1950	25,855	2.65	10,983	42.48	182	0.70	454	1.76	15–19	97.0
1960	35,012	3.03	17,705	50.57	224	0.64	576	1.65	15–19	99.5
1970	48,987	3.36	27,309	55.75	191	0.39	760	1.55	15–19	99.6
1980	66,958	3.13	44,300	66.16	269	0.40	2,199	3.28	15–19	97.7
1990	81,700	1.99	57,960	70.94	341	0.42	4,298	5.26	15–19	96.6

[a] Males per 100 females.
[b] White population.

Source: U.S. Bureau of the Census, Historical Statistics of the United States (Washington, D.C.: Government Printing Office, 1975); U.S. Bureau of the Census, Statistical Abstract of the United States, 1992 (Washington, D.C.: Government Printing Office, 1992); Statistics Canada, Historical Statistics of Canada (Ottawa: Statistics Canada, 1983); United Nations, Demographic Yearbook. See also Chapter 13 in this volume, Table 13.1 and 13.7.

abolition, 448, 457
aboriginal population, 1, 12–14; Canada, 372, 376
abortion, 631, 648, 650, 661
Acadians, 108, 374, 375
Acatzingo, 257, 272
accidents, deaths due to: Canada, twentieth century, 570–1; Mexico, 1900–1990, 608
accounting for changes: Canadian population, 1901–1931, 555–8; mortality and fertility: Mexico, 1900–1990, 613–17
Actopan (town), 264
adaptation: demographic, 410, 413; in family limitation, 326–7; Native Americans, 30–40
adults living doubled-up in parents' homes, 656–7, 661
Africa, 502, 519; death rate, 515; immigration from, 1; population growth, 511; slave trade in, 488–9; smallpox mortality, 260
African American demography, colonial, 4–5
African American population, 6–7; colonial U.S., 191–240; postbellum period, 1870–1920, 461–73; in 1790, 220t; 1790–1920, 433–81; *see also* black population (U.S.)
African Americans, 31; percentage in population of British colonies, 193t; *see also* blacks
Africans: in black population, colonial U.S., 219–21; in colonial Mexico, 262, 264, 265, 266
Afro-mestizos, 263
Afro-Mexicans, 266, 284
age: factor in marriage, 115–16, 117
age at death: African American population, colonial U.S., 217; early North American populations, 79; estimates of, 52; seasonality of deaths according to: St. Lawrence Valley, 127f
age at first birth (U.S.), 448, 656

age at first conception: African American women, 202–4, 203t
age at first marriage: black population: U.S. postbellum period, 1870–1920, 468; and fertility: white population, colonial U.S., 152, 153–4t, 179; St. Lawrence Valley, 113–14, 114f; white population, U.S., 1790–1920, 317–19, 320
age at marriage: in Mesoamerica, 250–1; Mexico, 270, 271–3, 272f, 292
age distributions, slaves, 207–8
age pattern(s) of mortality (U.S.), 473, 655
age structure: African American population, colonial U.S., 208; Mesoamerica, 250; white population, colonial U.S., 146, 155; white population, U.S., 1790–1920, 323; white population of New York, 155, 155t
agency of people: in demographic change, 474
aging of population(s), 323, 351, 651, 655, 683
agricultural revolution: Mesoamerica, 242, 244, 255
agricultural settlement, U.S., 437, 634, 635, 639, 640–1, 648
agriculture: ancient Mesoamerica, 241–2, 247, 251–2; Canada, 100, 566; dietary shift accompanying, 80–1, 83; immigrants in: Canada, twentieth century, 539, 541; Mexico, 1900–1990, 623, 628; St. Lawrence Valley, 109, 110; U.S., 307, 317, 332
Aguascalientes, 281, 283
Aguirre-Beltrán, Gonzalo, 257, 262, 264, 265
AIDs, 655
Alabama, 60, 440, 464
Alarcón, Hernando de, 26
Alaska, 13, 35
Alaska Native Village Areas, 33
Alberta, 563, 590, 591
Albuquerque, 38

Aleuts, 9, 32, 34, 67
Algeria, 11
Algoma County (Canada), 413
Alien Act of 1798 (U.S.), 355
Allen, Wilma H., 67–8
Allison, Marvin J., 59
Almonte, Ontario, 562
Alta California, 26, 27
Amatenango, Chiapas, 250, 270
American Bottom, Illinois, 65
American Federation of Labor, 355
American Indian Holocaust and Survival
  (Thornton), 11
American Indian population, 677; California,
  24–30, 25t; in Caribbean, 7; demography of,
  683; 1800–1890, 24t
American Indian tribes, 33–5, 40; blood
  quantum requirement, 33–4, 34t
American Indians/Amerindians, 9; differential
  survival of, 30; impact of disease on, 54;
  Mesoamerica, 242; population decline, 54;
  tuberculosis among, 58; *see also* Native
  Americans
American life tables, 332–3
*American Population before the Federal Census of
  1790* (Greene and Harrington), 145
American Revolution, 175, 214; and black
  migration, 211; colony persistence and out-
  migration, 174t
American War of Independence, 374–5, 376
Amherst, Nova Scotia, 420
Anasazi, 83
Anawalt, Patricia, 271
Anchorage, 38
ancient epoch (Mexico), 241–52, 294
Ancient Greeks, 79
ancient Mesoamerican, 241–52
Andalucía, 273
Anderson, T. L., 156, 167
Anderton, Douglas, 326
Andover, 159t
Andover, Greven, 156
anemia, 66, 246
anesthesia, 335
Angel, J. L., 56
anglophone Canada, 589, 678, 679, 680; ethnic
  character of, 417n54; fertility, nineteenth
  century, 394–5, 402, 409, 410, 414–15;
  fertility, twentieth century, 548–50; infant
  mortality, nineteenth century, 404–5;
  mortality, twentieth century, 568
ankylosing spondylitis, 76
antebellum period (U.S.), 1790–1860: black
  population, 436–61
"antebellum puzzle," 332
Antelope House, 72–3

anthropology, 221–2
anthropometric measures: African American
  population, colonial U.S., 212–19; *see also*
  height; stature
antibiotics, 532, 570, 641, 647, 654
Antigonish County, Nova Scotia, 401n36, 577
Antigua, 486
Antilles, 106
Apache Indians, 33
Appalachians, 173
Arawak (Taino), 7, 486
archaeology/archaeological sources: African
  American population, colonial U.S., 212–19,
  221–2; population estimates, 51, 52
Archaic period, 68, 75, 77, 81, 83
Archaic populations, 59
Arikara (people), 78
Arizona, 60, 68, 294, 667; Native American
  population, 35
Arkansas, 60, 464, 469
Armelagos, G. J., 63
Arnprior, Ontario, 562
Arroyo Hondo Pueblo, 79
arthritis, 76, 81, 83
Asia, 519; death rate, 515; immigration from, 1;
  immigration from, to Canada, 545;
  immigration from, to U.S., 662–3, 665, 668;
  indentured labor from, in Canada, 501–3,
  510; population growth, 511, 653; smallpox
  mortality, 260
assimilation, 356–7, 662, 663–4; Native
  Americans, 23; U.S. population, twentieth
  century, 636–7, 645–6, 664–5
Atlantic crossing: passage mortality, 168
Atlantic provinces (Canada): immigrants to,
  538, 544; population redistribution, 589, 590;
  population size, 533; port cities, 561; urban
  structure, 562; urbanization: nineteenth
  century, 420
Atlantic region (Canada), 566
Aunis, 109
Australia: infant mortality, 404; life tables, 535;
  population size, 530
Australian Aborigines, 11
Austria: immigration from, to Canada, 543, 544
Austria-Hungary, 354
automobile, 666
Averbuch site, 66, 79
Aztecs, 250, 271, 283; life expectancy, 247–8

baby boom, 679; Canada, 7–8, 532, 552, 571,
  572–3, 574, 575, 577–8, 579–80, 581, 582;
  U.S., 8, 151, 316, 319, 358, 650, 658, 661
baby boom generation, 659, 661
baby bust, 579; Canada, 532, 571; U.S., 8, 358,
  651, 652, 669

bacteriology, 336
Bahamas, 211, 483
Bahm site, 68
Bailyn, Bernard, 147
Bajío, 292
Baker, B. J., 63
Balkans, 353, 354
Baltimore, 459; death rates, 330; free blacks in, 457; sewage system, 335; vital registration, 311
baptismal series: colonial Mexico, 266, 269, 279
Barbados, 198, 486, 488, 492, 501, 508, 516; birth rate, 514; emigrants from, 503; sugar production, 493
Basketmaker people, 72–3
bastards: colonial Mexico, 272–3
Bay of Fundy, 375
Bean, Lee L., 326
Beaufort County, South Carolina, 464
behavior (U.S., twentieth century) and fertility, 656; and mortality, 647
Belgium, 392n20, 416, 425; immigration from, to Canada, 544; population size, 530
Belize (British Honduras), 485; Native American population, 487
Bellechasse County (Canada), 406
Berdan, Frances, 271
Beringa, 9, 14, 55
Berkeley, Sir William, 169, 170
Berry, David R., 79
Berryman, Hugh E., 79
Biggar, Saskatchewan, 563
bills of mortality, 158n30, 329
bioarcheological evidence, 2, 250
biological adaptation: and mortality, 460, 461
biological predisposition to higher mortality: blacks, 472
biomedical studies: African American population, colonial U.S., 212–19
birth control, 294; Mexico, 271; St. Lawrence Valley, 119, 121n8; *see also* contraception/contraceptives
birth intervals: African American women, 205; Mesoamerica, 250; Mexico, 270; St. Lawrence Valley, 119n5, 121; West Indian slaves, 507–8
birth rates: Caribbean, 513–15; in demographic transition, 678, 679; immigrants and, 682; and land availability, 396–7; Mexico, 8, 291–2, 293, 294–5, 608, 609; Native Americans, 27; and population decline, 22; St. Lawrence Valley, 117, 131; slaves: British West Indies, 506; *see also* crude birth rates
birth rates, Canada, 6, 373, 388; age-specific, 1936–1981, 579f; 1815–1861, 379; French Canada, 105–6; nineteenth century, 392, 416, 425; twentieth century, 529–30, 531, 532,

546–8, 555, 564–5, 566
birth rates, U.S.: black population, 1790–1920, 436, 458, 461, 474; blacks: postbellum period, 1870–1920, 470; 1800s, 434; regional differentials: white population, 1790–1920, 322–3; twentieth century, 650; white population, colonial U.S., 145–6; white population, 1720–1920, 320, 321, 358
Birth Registration Area (U.S.), 311, 312, 343, 441
birth spacing: white population, U.S., 1790–1920, 322
births: monthly variations of: St. Lawrence Valley, 118; seasonal pattern in: African American women, 205–6
Black, Thomas K., III, 71
black Caribs, 487
Black Death plague, 19
Black Legend, 257
Black Mesa, 65, 70, 72, 78, 247
black population: Britain and Netherlands, 518; Canada, 375; Caribbean, 519
black population, U.S., 146, 309; antebellum period, 1790–1860, 436–61; fertility, 678; infant mortality, 405; in-migration, 316; mortality, 339n64, 344; population growth: 1790–1920, 434–6, 435t; by state, 1870–1920, 465t; by state and percentage urban, 1870–1920, 462–3; underenumeration of, 312; *see also* African American population
Blackfeet Reservation, 34
blacks in U.S. population, twentieth century, 633; assimilation, integration, and economic equality, 1950 to present, 664–5; economic activity, mid-twentieth century, 643–4; fertility, 639–41; fertility, 1900–1950, 648–9; fertility and family formation, 1950 to present, 655–62; geographic distribution, 635–6; geographic distribution, recent, 666–8; mortality, 637–9, 640; mortality, 1900–1950, 646–8; mortality: 1950 to present, 654–5; 1950 to present, 649–68; occupational distribution, 634–5, 636, 643–4; population composition and distribution, 1900–1950, 642–3; population composition and economic activity in 1990, 662–4; stratification, assimilation, integration, 636–7; stratification, assimilation, integration: 1900–1950, 645–6
Blakely, Robert L., 79
Blasky Mound site, 68
Bledsoe, Anthony J., 28
Blood (Indians), 35
Board of Trade, 143
Bogdan, Georgieann, 62–3
bone size and strength: early North American population, 80–1

Borah, Woodrow, 254–6, 257, 270, 292
Boston, 337, 459; black-white crude death rate ratio, 461; blacks in, 208; crude death rate, 165; death rates, 330; mobility studies, 357; pure water supply, 335
bound labor: colonial U.S., 192–3
Bourbeau, Robert, 407, 421, 428, 535–6, 556
Bovee, Dana L., 69
Bracero Program, 626
Brain, Jeffrey P., 30
Brandon, Manitoba, 563
Brant, 412
Brantford, Ontario, 577
Brazil, 487, 489, 490
breastfeeding, 66, 119, 204, 205, 395, 451, 568
Bridges, Patricia S., 67
British colonies: percentage of African Americans in, 193t, 198; white population growth in, 178t; white population of, 149, 150t
British Columbia, 416, 539, 540, 561; added to Canada, 533; Asian immigrants to, 545; Chinese immigrants in, 543; cities and towns, 563; fertility, 411, 577; Native American population, 38; population growth, 566, 590–1; urbanization, 420
British Corn Law, 384
British forces: slaves joining, 211
British Guiana, 493, 502, 503, 516; *see also* Guyana
British North America, 373–4, 382, 492, 677; fertility and family size in, 305; fertility indices, 1861, 394t; immigration to, 379, 385f; population of, 309; slave population, 195, 433
British North American colonies: Canada formed out of, 416; confederation of, 533; population of, 371
British Privy Council, 143
British rule in Quebec, 371, 373, 374
British West Indies, 198, 516; out-migration, 517; slave birth and death rates, 506t
Brome County (Canada), 377, 414–15
bronchitis, 359, 680
Bruce county (Canada), 399
bubonic plague, 14
Buchanan (agent), 381–2
Bucks County, 165
Buikstra, Jane E., 58, 59, 82
Bukovinians, 542
Bullen, Adelaide K., 62
burial series: Mexico, 266–8, 269, 274, 279, 286–7, 291

Cabrera y Quintero, Cayetano, 259–60
Cabrillo, Juan Rodriguez, 26
Cahokia site, 62

calcium pyrophosphate deposition disease, 76
Caldwell, John C., 327
Calgary, 561, 563, 591; immigrants in, 588, 593; population redistribution, 594
California, 280, 294, 437, 667; disease in, 71, 72, 81; Native American population, 24–30, 35; population recovery of Native Americans, 39–40, 39t
California Native American Heritage Commission, 39–40
Calusa (people), 17
Calvo, Thomas, 257, 270, 271
Campeche, 281, 285
Camposortega Cruz, Sergio, 614
Camrose, Alberta, 563
Canada, 6, 7–8, 324, 485; aboriginal population, 13; accounting for population change, 1901–1931, 555–8; colony, 99–101; components of decadal population change, 1951–1981, 595t; demographic transition, 677, 678, 679, 680, 681–2; Dominion Bureau of Statistics, 545, 556; era of mass immigration, 1901–1931, 532–45; European population of, 1761–1901, 373t; evidence of tuberculosis in, 60; fertility, 1901–1931, 545–55; fertility, post-World War II, 371–82; fertility rates and related measures, 598t; geographic configuration of, 427n69; immigrants from U.S. to, 372, 375–6, 377, 378–9, 398n29, 533, 538, 543, 545, 548, 584, 585, 587–8; immigrants to U.S. from, 416, 420–8, 534–5, 595, 651; immigration since 1945, 582–95, 583f; immigration to, from West Indies, 503, 517; lacked dominant metropolis, 560, 561; mortality decline, 1901–1981, 567–71; Native American population, 23, 31, 33, 38; new problems in, 683–4; 1930s, 564–6; population, foundation period, 1761–1811, 373–78; population, nineteenth century, 371–432; population, twentieth century, 529–99, 530t; population history, 371–3; port cities, 560–1; status/nonstatus Indians, 35; urban and metropolitan, 597t; urbanization: 1901–1931, 558–64
Canada East (Quebec Province), 391, 418; *see also* Quebec
Canada West (Ontario), 391, 419; *see also* Ontario
Canadian Confederation, 391, 416–17, 425; economy of, 424–7
Canadian Pacific Railway, 417, 418
cancer, 647, 654
Capac, Huayna, 259
Cardoso, Lawrence A., 625
Carib, 7, 486, 487
Caribbean, 15, 437n5, 683; demographic

transition, 7, 677, 678–9, 680–1, 682; five
largest areas based on population, 515t;
immigration from, to Canada: twentieth
century, 585, 588; population history of,
483–528; region, 484f

Caribbean populations, 1700–1900, 500f; 1750,
494–5t; 1830, 496–7t; 1880, 498–9t; 1900,
1950, 1990, 512t; 1900–1950, 514f; shares of,
by European settling area, 501t

Caribbean Sea, 485

Carleton County, Ontario, 577

Carleton Place, Ontario, 562

Carolinas, 173

Carr-Saunders, A. M., 10–11

Cassidy, Claire Monod, 71, 81–2

castas, 273

catastrophists, 252, 254–6, 257, 259

Catawba, 31

cause(s) of death, 682; African American
population, colonial U.S., 208–9; Canada,
twentieth century, 567, 570–1; Mexico,
287–8, 607–8, 608t; St. Lawrence Valley,
127–8; slave children, 451; white population,
U.S. 1790–1920, 338

Cayenne (French Guiana), 485

cemetery demography, 217

census(es), 4, 682; Caribbean, 511; Mexico, 254,
263–5, 269, 603, 610, 627

census(es), Canada: enumeration error in
population change, nineteenth century,
421–2, 429; nineteenth century, 371, 372, 389,
404, 406; twentieth century, 529, 530, 531,
536, 537, 540, 546, 552, 555, 559, 567, 576,
584; Quebec, 102

census(es), U.S., 5–6, 309, 320–11, 312, 317, 321,
328, 344, 345, 471, 472; colony, 4, 143; 192;
first, 354; information on black population,
435, 443, 446, 448–9, 452; manuscript
schedules, 2, 437; mortality data, 332–3, 342;
self-identification of race in, 32, 35, 40, 41;
white population, colonial U.S., 145, 146

Census Metropolitan Areas (CMAs), (Canada),
558–9, 591, 592, 593–4

Census of Marriage and Fertility of England
and Wales, 342

census survival method, 345, 471, 472, 473

Center region (Mexico), 617–18, 620–1

Central America, 15, 485, 492; Native American
population, 487; population growth, 511

Central Mexican Basin, 5; population in,
244–6, 245f, 251

Central Mexican Symbiotic Region, 257

Central Ohio River Valley, 81–2

chain migration (U.S.), 456

Champlain, Samuel de, 99

Chapin, Charles, 336

Charbonneau, Hubert, 4, 99–142

Charcas, 266

Charentes region, 109

Charles, Enid, 552–5, 575, 576

Charles County, Maryland, 162, 165

Charles IV, king of Spain, 260

Charles Parish, Virginia, 161, 162–4

Charlevoix County (Canada), 406, 577

Charlottetown, Prince Edward Island, 419, 577

Cheney, 336

Cherokee Indians, 19, 33, 35, 40; "Trail of
Tears," 22

Cherokee Nation of Oklahoma, 35

Chesapeake, 329; African American population,
200, 204, 205, 206, 207, 208–9, 211, 217, 219;
demographic transition in, 198; malaria in,
213; local records in, 146; mortality, 161, 310,
341; slaves, 214

Chiapas, 266, 277, 281, 283, 285, 287

Chicago, 335, 337, 349

Chicago River, 335

Chicago Sanitary District, 335

Chichén Itzá, 242, 246

Chihuahua, 266, 285, 287

child-bequest hypothesis, 324, 325, 358, 679

child care, 21, 328

child costs and benefits, 324, 327, 328, 358, 470,
641, 679

child labor laws (U.S.), 327, 328, 337, 358, 679

child marriage: ancient Mexico, 250

child mortality, 2–3; African Americans, 209,
213; blacks: U.S. postbellum period, 1870–
1920, 468n75, 473; blacks: U.S. twentieth
century, 640; Canada, 402, 513; colonial
Mexico, 269; St. Lawrence Valley, 124, 125,
130, 132; slaves: West Indies, 508–9; U.S., 161,
647, 648, 679; white population, colonial
U.S., 161; white population, U.S.,
1790–1920, 328, 333, 341, 342–3, 358

child/woman ratio, 441–2, 469, 687; African
American population, colonial U.S., 201–2;
blacks by region, 1870–1920, 467–8, 467t;
colonial Mexico, 270; free blacks: U.S.
antebellum period, 1790–1860, 457t, 458,
459; population density and, 324; slaves: U.S.
antebellum period, 1790–1920, 442–5, 447–8;
slaves and whites: U.S., 1820–1860, 442t;
white colonial population, 144, 146; white
population, U.S. 1794–1920, 322, 325

childbearing: adapting in Malthusian manner,
392; African American population, colonial
U.S., 199, 202–6, 219; age pattern of:
Canada, twentieth century, 578–9, 580–1; in
Mesoamerica, 250; motives for, 683; public
policy and: U.S., 669; timing of: Canada,
twentieth century, 577–8; U.S., twentieth

childbearing (*cont.*)
century, 639–40, 641, 646, 648–9, 650–1, 655–6, 658, 660, 661, 668; West Indian slaves, 507–8
childbirth, deaths from, 207, 647
childhood stress, 70
childlessness: black women, 469; Canada, twentieth century, 581; U.S. population, twentieth century, 641, 656, 661, 662; white population, U.S. 1790–1920, 321
children: causes of deaths in: white population, U.S. 1790–1920, 338; human capital, 326; immigrants, 110, 536, 429
children, slave, 202n30, 210, 212; health of, in U.S., 449, 450, 451, 452; mortality: U.S. antebellum period, 1790–1860, 452, 453; in West Indies, 490
children ever born, 2–3; Canada, twentieth century, 552–5, 554t; white population, U.S. 1790–1920, 320–1
children surviving, 2–3
Children's Bureau (U.S.), 337
childspacing: African American women, 204–5
Chile, 60
China: immigration from, to Canada, 543, 545, 587, 588; immigration from, to U.S., 652; indentured labor from, to Caribbean, 501, 502
Chinese: in Canada, 417; hostility to, in U.S., 355; immigration restrictions on: U.S., 632; in U.S., twentieth century, 633
Chinese Exclusion Act of 1882 (U.S.), 355
Chippewa (Ojibwa) Indians, 33
Chiribaya culture, 58–9
Choctaw Indians, 33
cholera, 14, 22, 27, 176, 290–1, 359, 379, 680; epidemics, 330–1, 333, 384; polluted water and, 335
cholera infantum, 451
Cholula, 247, 258, 268
church (the): in Quebec, 101; in St. Lawrence Valley, 112–13, 117
Ciboney, 7, 486
cities, 684; death registration systems, 471; migration of Indians to, 38
cities, Canada: fertility, nineteenth century, 410–11, 414; immigrants, twentieth century, 540, 541t, 588, 589, 591–2, 594; infant mortality, twentieth century, 569; marital fertility, twentieth century, 549–50; nineteenth century, 418–20; population growth, 317; twentieth century, 557, 559–61, 562–4, 566, 568, 576–7; young, single women in, 551
cities, U.S.: blacks in, 194, 211, 464–6; free

blacks in: antebellum period, 457, 461; migration from, white population, colonial U.S., 173–4; mortality in, 1790–1920, 339, 340, 343–4; polycentric, 651, 666–7; population growth, 317; population in, twentieth century, 635; public health, 359; size hierarchy, 349
Civil War (U.S.), 332, 350, 352, 427, 431, 434, 461, 471
civil war, Mexico, 277, 290, 293
civilizations, ancient: disappearance of, 246
Clayton Act of 1914 (U.S.), 356
climate: and crops, 505; effect on slaves, 507; and mortality, 160, 208–9, 568
Coahuila, 281, 283
Coale, Ansley, 248, 326–7, 329
Coale-Trussell method, 471
Coalescent Tradition, 78
Coatsworth, John H., 288, 622
Cobalt, Ontario, 562
Cockburn, T. Aiden, 80
Codex Mendoza, 250, 271
Coelho, Philip, 440
coffee plantations, 505
cohabitation of unmarried young adults, 656, 661–2
cohort fertility: Canada, twentieth century, 577, 578, 580
Colbert, Jean-Baptiste, 100
"cold filter" hypothesis, 55
Cole, Harold N., 62
Colima, 281, 283
Colleton County, South Carolina, 464
Collver, O. Andrew, 603, 606, 609
Colombia, 663
colonial epoch (Mexico), 241, 252–76
colonial U.S.: African American population, 191–240; mortality, 329; socioeconomic dimensions of demographic experience, 174–6; vital registration, 311; white population, 143–90
colonialism: disease and, 21; and Native American population decline, 22–3, 24
colony censuses, 4, 143, 192
Colorado, 75, 294
Columbus, Christopher, 7, 9–10, 483, 486
Compton (county, Canada), 415
compulsory education, 327, 328, 679
computer resources, 3
conception: seasonal patterns in: African American women, 205–6
Conde de Revillagigedo, Viceroy, 264
Condran, Gretchen, 332, 336
congenital disorders, 76–7
congenital syphilis, 60, 61
Congress (U.S.), 350

Connecticut, 156, 173
Constitution (U.S.): Thirteenth Amendment,
461
contraception/contraceptives, 321, 358, 470, 616,
679; in Canada, 564; in Mexico, 617, 627;
twentieth-century U.S., 631, 648, 649, 650,
661
contract labor: to Caribbean, 502t, 511, 516,
519
Contract Labor Law, 355
Cook, Della C., 59, 71, 82
Cook, Sherburne F., 25, 28, 254–6, 257, 270,
292
Copán, 247
Copenhagen, 414
coprolites, 72–5
Cornwall, Ontario, 576
Cortes, Hernán, 250, 258
cotton, 440, 505
Council Bluffs Ossuary, 62
coureurs de bois, 100
Coutume de Paris, 100
Covelo Indian Community of Confederated
Tribes, 31
Cowan, Helen, 379, 382
cranial lesions, 246
Creek Indians, 33
cribra orbitalia, 246
Crimmins-Gardner, Eileen, 332
Croton Aqueduct, 335
Crow Creek site, 66, 68, 78
crude birth, death, marriage rates: French
Canada, 105, 105f
crude birth rate (CBR), 685–6; Caribbean,
1900, 1950, 1990, 513–15, 513t; in
demographic transition, 679; Mesoamerica,
248; Mexico, 270, 292, 609–10, 609f, 611–12,
612f; Trinidad, Jamaica, U.S., 508t
crude birth rate, Canada: nineteenth century,
391, 396; twentieth century, 546–8, 551, 555–6,
564, 579–80
crude birth rate, U.S., 309; white population,
colonial U.S., 144, 155–8, 157t; white
population, 1790–1920, 314; and natural
increase: white population, colonial U.S.,
167, 167t
crude death rate (CDR), 685–6; Canada, 386,
567–8; Caribbean, 1900, 1950, 1990, 513t,
515–16; Mexico, 1900–1990, 611–13, 612f;
Trinidad, Jamaica, U.S., 508t
crude death rates, U.S.: African American
population, colonial U.S., 208; Andover,
Boston, Philadelphia, 159t; free blacks: U.S.
antebellum period, 1790–1860, 460, 461; and
natural increase: white population, colonial
U.S., 167, 167t; white population, colonial

U.S., 144, 158, 162–5, 163–4t; white
population, U.S. 1790–1920, 310, 314, 330,
338
crude mortality rate, 52; Mexico, 1900–1990,
605, 605f, 614–15, 615t
Cuba, 483, 487, 488, 504; birth rate, 514–15;
immigrants to U.S., 663; independence, 485;
Native American population, 486; out-
migration, 517, 518; population growth, 511;
public health measures, 516; slave trade to,
489, 490, 501, 503, 510; Spanish migration to,
491; white population in, 504
Cuicuilco, 242
Cuitlahuatzin (emperor), 258
cultural change, 222
cultural factors in disease, 70, 71
culture and fertility in Canada: nineteenth
century, 393–5, 396, 400–1; twentieth
century, 548, 551, 553, 554–5
Curtin, Philip, 4–5, 146, 195, 213
curvature (kyphosis) of the spine, 57
Cybulski, Jerome S., 60, 66
Czechs, 587

Danger cave, 73
Danish life tables, 535
Darwinian evolutionism, 260
data, 2; imperfect, 4; *see also* sources
data collection, 684
Dauphin, 563
David, Paul A., 325–6
death rate: Canada, 1815–1861, 379; Caribbean,
515–16; cause-specific: Canada, 1901–1981,
570–1, 570t; in demographic transition,
678, 680; early North American
populations, 80; immigrants in passage,
111; Mexico, 284, 294; slaves: British
West Indies, 506t; white population,
colonial U.S., 145–6; white population,
U.S., 358; *see also* crude death rates;
mortality rates
death registration area, 311, 312, 329, 332, 333,
338, 339, 341, 441, 471, 472
death registration systems: Canada, 567; U.S.,
459, 460, 471
deaths in passage, 148
De la Rosa, Don Luis, 288
Deerfield, Massachusetts, 155
degenerative diseases, 338, 650, 654
degenerative joint disease: early North
American populations, 76, 80, 81
Delaware, 194; free blacks in, 456; slave
population, 440
Demeny, Paul, 248
demographic balancing equation, 314; Mexico,
1900–1990, 610–13, 612t

demographic change: black population, U.S. 1790–1920, 474; Caribbean, 7; Mexico, 278–81, 601–30
demographic conditions: Canada, nineteenth century, 425
demographic determinism, 295
demographic disaster: Mexico, 5, 241, 251, 252–8, 253t, 264, 290, 293–4; disease as cause of, 258–62
demographic dynamics of Mexico: in collapse of cultural centers, 242; epochs of, 241; late colonial, 268–76
demographic experience: of African Americans, 191–2, 221, 222; white population, colonial U.S., 174–6, 177
demographic history: Mexico, twentieth century, 627–8; U.S. black population to 1920, 433–4; patterns of, 196–7
demographic measures, basic, 687–92
demographic patterns: African American population, postbellum period, 1870–1920, 461; Caribbean, twentieth century, 511–18; slaves: West Indies, 506–10
demographic record (Canada): principal indicators of, 596t
demographic recovery; *see* population recovery
demographic regimes: Caribbean, 519; early American 221; Native Americans, 21, 23
demographic revolution: Mesoamerica, 245; Mexico, 276, 279, 293–4; St. Lawrence Valley: at time of British conquest, 131; slaves (U.S.): antebellum period, 1790–1860, 436, 437–53
demographic system: reproduction and: St. Lawrence Valley, 128–30
demographic systems, high-pressure, 269, 270, 276; Mesoamerica, 250–2; Mexico, 294
demographic transition, 677–82; African American population, colonial U.S., 197–8; in Caribbean, 513–18, 519; elements in, 468–9; U.S., 307, 311, 313–16, 323–4, 333, 358–9; theory, 323–8, 683
demographic turnaround: U.S., 1960s–1980s, 661–2
demographically mature nations, 683–4
demography: measurement and estimation in, 685–92; reconstruction from human skeletal remains, 77–80
Denis, Hubert, 99–142
Denmark, 392n20; slave trade, 503; in West Indies, 485, 488, 489, 493, 504
dental alterations/attrition, 61, 65, 246, 247
dental caries, 64, 65, 81, 82, 83
dental hypoplasia, 70–1, 72, 81, 82
depopulation: Native Americans, 13, 15–18, 21, 24, 30–1

depopulation ratios, 12; colonial Mexico, 255
Desjardins, Bertrand, 4, 99–142
Detroit (French settlement), 375
diagnosis, paleopathological, 57–60
diaphyseal osteomyelitis, 61
diarrhea, 66, 176, 209, 247; cause of infant mortality, 451, 568
Díaz, Melchor, 26
Díaz, Porfirio, 602–3, 613, 616
Dickel, David N., 71
Dickson Mound, Illinois, 62, 71, 79, 82
diet: African American population, colonial U.S., 214–17, 218, 219; and dental disease, 64, 65; early North American populations, 80–1, 83; Mesoamerica, 247; slaves: U.S. antebellum period, 1790–1860, 449, 450, 451–2; white population, colonial U.S., 175; white population, U.S. 1790–1920, 331–2, 334, 340, 344, 358
Diez de la Calle, Juan, 262
differential mortality: male/female: African Americans, 217; West Indies/West Africa, 213
differential reproduction: Quebec, 129–30
diphtheria, 14, 27, 334, 338, 359, 680; antitoxin, 334, 336, 338
diphyllobothriasis, 73
disasters: and population growth: Mexico City, 287, 287f
disease, 214, 449; analysis of, 56–7; on boats in passage, 111; brought to Canada by immigrants, 379; as cause of demographic disaster in colonial Mexico, 258–62; effect on Native Americans, 1, 14–15, 17–18, 19–23, 24, 26, 27, 29–30; with European contact, 15, 20, 54, 83, 486–7; immunities: slaves, 505; indirect effects of, 21; and infant mortality: slaves in antebellum U.S., 450–51; lack of, in North America, 54–5; in Mesoamerica, 247; in Mexico, 285–91; nutritional status and (U.S.), 176; pathogens, 52, 55, 213; patterns of, in early North American populations, 51–97; in pre-Coluumbian America, 3–4, 56–7, 63–4; precontact, 55, 58, 60, 63; St. Lawrence Valley, 127, 128, 132; in South (U.S.), 176; and sterility, 469–70; susceptibility to, 213; *see also* epidemic disease/epidemics
disease control: revolution in methods of, 637–8, 639; U.S., twentieth century, 631, 641, 646–7, 650, 654
disease environment, 461, 680; acclimation to new, 206; Caribbean, 509–10; colonial U.S., 151, 161; and fertility, 508; Native Americans, 23; New World, 5; North (U.S.), 456; slaves in, 197, 198, 208, 210; South (U.S.), 160, 165,

169, 452, 453, 471–2; and stature, 331; U.S.,
1790–1920, 330–1, 341, 358
displaced persons (DPs), 538, 583, 586, 591
displacement thesis, 557–8
District of Columbia, 311, 329, 441, 456
Distrito Federal (Mexico); *see* Federal District
divorce rates: U.S., twentieth century, 656, 659
DNA technology, 57, 59
Dobyns, Henry, 11, 12, 15–17, 23–4, 53–5
Dominica, 487
Dominican Republic, 483, 487, 506; birth
rate, 515; death rate, 515; immigrants to U.S.,
652, 663; independence, 485; infant
mortality, 516; migration within Caribbean,
518; out-migration, 517; population growth,
511
Downshire Papers, 156
Drake, Sir Francis, 26
Drummondville (Quebec), 562
Duffy, John, 19
Dundas (county, Canada), 405
Durango, 283
duration-of-settlement argument, 397–9
Dutch: slave trade, 503; in West Indies, 501,
504; *see also* Netherlands
Dutch East Indies, 488
dysentery, 15, 27, 66, 289

East (U.S.): slaves in, 442, 443
East Africa, 586, 588
East Angus (Quebec), 562
East Asia: immigration from, 355, 356, 587, 588
East Indians: in Caribbean, 516; immigration to
Canada, 544, 586, 588
east-west movement (U.S.), 347, 348, 359
Easterlin, Richard, 2, 8, 329–30, 631–75
Eastern Band of Cherokee Indians, 35
Eastern Europe: immigrants from, to Canada,
542, 586, 587
Eastern Township, 550
Eblen, Jack, 449
ecobiological factors: in U.S., 333–4
economic activity (U.S.), mid-twentieth
century, 643–4; in 1990, 662–4; twentieth
century, 634–5, 650
economic change (U.S.), 631, 632
economic conditions: and emigration: England,
378, 383; and migration of blacks to North
(U.S.), 466–7
economic equality: U.S., 1950 to present, 664–5
economic growth: Mexico, 8; U.S., 631
economic opportunity: U.S., twentieth century,
636, 639
economic policy (U.S.), 669
economic well-being: Mexico, 1900–1990, 614
economy: Canada, nineteenth century, 424–7;

and immigration: Canada, 384; Canada,
twentieth century, 533, 538, 555, 561, 563,
564–6, 573, 583, 586; and fertility: Canada,
twentieth century, 574, 575; Mexico, 258,
602, 627
economy (U.S.): change from agriculture to
industry, 347; effect of immigration on:
twentieth century, 653–4; and migration, 352,
359; twentieth century, 641, 657–8, 660; and
urban growth, 349
edge cities, 667
Edinburgh, 414
Edmonton, 38, 561, 563; immigrants in, 588, 593
education: Mexico, 277; value of, 358, 679
education and fertility: Canada, twentieth
century, 553–4, 574, 575, 581–2; Mexico,
1900–1990, 616–17, 621
education (U.S.), 324, 326, 327, 328; blacks in,
468, 664; and economic mobility, twentieth
century, 664–5; female, twentieth century,
648–9; of immigrants, 662–3; twentieth
century, 632, 636, 641–2, 645, 648; of
workers, twentieth century, 650, 659
education, higher (U.S., twentieth century),
650, 658; of women, 665
Egypt, 11
El Cedral, 242
El-Najjar, Mahmoud Y., 60, 63
El Salvador, 663
El Tajín, 242
elite, St. Lawrence Valley: differential fertility
of, 121–2; emigration, 131; nuptiality, 113,
116–17; reproduction, 130
Elting, James J., 62
emancipation, 219, 460, 471; West Indies, 504;
see also gradual emancipation (U.S.)
Emergency Immigration Act of 1921 (U.S.), 355
emigrant fever, 379, 382
emigration: British, 382–3; Canada, 6, 7, 372,
373; Canada, nineteenth century, 391,
410n46, 415–28; Canada, twentieth century,
529–30, 531, 532, 534f, 538, 543, 555–8, 564,
590, 595; Mexico, 8; Mexico to U.S., 280–1
293, 294, 603, 626t; in population change:
Canada, 1901–1930, 555–8; Quebec, 3;
registers, 4, 146–7; St. Lawrence Valley, 104
employment, 591, 636, 643; *see also*
occupational distribution
Employment Act of 1946 (U.S.), 632, 650, 659
employment opportunities (U.S.): and black
migration, 464–6; immigration and, 653–4
Engerman, Stanley L., 7, 160, 195, 441, 449,
483–528
England, 79; age at first marriage, 319; child
mortality, 342; death rate, 276; family size,
155; infant mortality, 404; life tables for, 421,

England (*cont.*)
535; marital fertility, 392n20; mortality, 333, 334; population growth, 149; rate of natural increase, 179; in West Indies, 487
English Canada: fertility, twentieth century, 550
Enriquez, Martin, 250
enteritis, 568
environment: and fertility: St. Lawrence Valley, 117, 119–20; and mortality: Canada, 122–3, 128, 132; *see also* disease environment
epidemic disease/epidemics, 680; Canada, 1815–1861, 387; cause of population decline, 257; colonial Mexico, 258, 259–60, 261–2, 276; colonial Mexico: region and race in, 267f 268; French Canada, 106; independent Mexico, 285–91; myth, and reasons for population decline: Native Americans, 19–23; Native Americans, 12, 15–18, 27, 29–30, 53–4; U.S., 358
epidemiologic transition: U.S., 333–4
epidemiological approach, 56–7
epidemiological environment: morbidity/mortality effect from contact with, 148
epidemiology: and slave trade, 213
equal employment opportunity legislation (U.S.), 664
Eskimo, 67
españoles, 273, 274
Esper, Johann Friedrich, 56
Essay on the Principle of Population (Malthus), 305
Essex County, Ontario, 413n50, 577
estimation, 685–92; indirect, 448–9; white population, colonial U.S., 144–8
ethnic composition: Canada, nineteenth century, 417–18; Canada, twentieth century, 532, 533; West Indies, 519
ethnic diversity, 588, 683
ethnicity: in colonial Mexico, 262–8; and fertility: Canada, twentieth century, 553–5; regional differences in mortality by: U.S., 440; and slavery, 437n5
ethnohistorical sources, 52, 53, 55, 58, 246, 250
ethno-races of New Spain, 263f
ethno-racial groups: colonial Mexico, 262–3, 264, 274, 284
Etowah, Georgia, 79
Euro-Americans: health, 460; and Indians, 27–8, 31
Euromestizos, 262–3, 264
Europe: class and height differences in, 175–6; conquests, 255; demographic revolution, 276; epidemics in, 19; fertility indices, 391, 392–3, 392f; fertility rates, 507; immigrants to U.S. from, 354, 355, 359, 636, 641, 648, 651, 662;

immigration from, 1; immigration from, to Canada, twentieth century, 533, 584, 586–7, 588, 591; marital fertility, 409–10; mortality revolution, 653; potato famine in, 352; smallpox mortality, 260, 261; U.S. immigration policy and, 632
European colonialism, 10–11; and Native American population decline, 21, 22–3
European contact, 52; different responses to, 30; disease introduced by, 15, 20, 54, 83, 486–7; effect on Native Americans: Caribbean, 486–7; Mesoamerica, 242; and population decline: Native Americans, 24, 25–6
Europeans: in Mexico, 251–2, 262, 263, 265; migration to Caribbean, 491t; in West Indies, 483, 485, 487–8
Evans, Robert, Jr., 449
Ewbank, Douglas, 473
excess of births over deaths: Caribbean, 511; French Canada, 104; St. Lawrence Valley, 117; white population: U.S., 1790–1920, 316
excess of deaths over births: African American population, colonial U.S., 197; West Indies, 492
expectation-of-life data: white colonial population, 144
extinction: paleopopulations, 251
extramarital fertility: Canada, nineteenth century, 390

Fairgrieve, Scott I., 60, 66
families: distribution of, in New France, 120f
family formation: African American population, colonial U.S., 199, 200, 202; mortality rates and, 222; slaves: U.S. antebellum period, 445–6, 448; U.S. population: 1950 to present, 655–62
family immigration: St. Lawrence Valley, 109, 110
family limitation, 474; in black fertility transition, 470–1; Canada, nineteenth century, 396; preconditions for, 326–7; U.S., twentieth century, 648, 650; white population, U.S. 1790–1920, 321
family migration: Canada, nineteenth century, 429
family reconstitution, 192; colonial Mexico, 269–70; white population, U.S., 309, 329
family size: African American population, colonial U.S., 204; blacks, 320; Canada, twentieth century, 577–8; U.S., 648, 650, 661, 679; white population, colonial U.S., 152–5, 153–4t, 156–7, 179; white population, U.S., 1790–1920, 307, 358
family status: slaves in Westward movement:

U.S., 440–1
family structure: and fertility, 470
famine, 15; in Mesoamerica, 247; in Mexico, 259, 265, 268, 287, 288, 289, 293; and migration, 384–5, 417n54
Farley, Reynolds, 449, 469, 470, 473
farming: Canada, 1815–1861, 383–4; U.S., twentieth century, 634, 643
fatalism, 260, 338
Faulhaber, Johanna, 248n17
Fay Tolton site, 68–9
fecundity, 118, 469
Federal District (Mexico), 257, 281, 283, 623, 681, 682
Feliciano, Zadia M., 8, 601–30
female-headed households: black, 469, 470
female occupations, 637
feminist movement: U.S., twentieth century, 631, 650, 661, 665
Ferdinand Maximilian, Archduke, 281
fertility, 1; accounting for changes in: Mexico, 1900–1990, 613–17; African American population, colonial U.S., 197, 199–206; analysis of, 683; black population: U.S. postbellum period, 1870–1920, 467–71; black population, U.S., 1790–1920, 434; Canada, 1861–1891, 407t; Canada, mid-nineteenth century, 388–402; Canada, 1901–1931, 545–5; Canada, nineteenth century, 412, 413, 426, 427–8; Canada, post-World War II, 571–82; Canada, twentieth century, 531, 551–2, 565–6, 565f; in Caribbean, twentieth century, 515; decreased postepidemic, 21; in demographic transition, 577, 578, 579; free blacks: U.S. antebellum period, 1790–1860, 457–9; Mexico, 270–1, 273, 291–3; Mexico, 1900–1990, 608–10, 613; Native Americans, 22, 23, 54; North America, 1800–1991, 695–8t; public policy and: U.S., 669–70; regional differences: Mexico, 1900–1990, 617–22, 618t, 620f; slave population, U.S., antebellum period, 1790–1860, 441–8; slaves: West Indies, 505, 507–8, 509, 510; U.S. population, 1900–1950, 648–9; U.S. population, 1950 to present, 655–62; U.S. population, twentieth century, 8, 639–41, 652–3, 669; white population, colonial U.S., 151–8, 179–80; white population, U.S., 1790–1920, 305, 307, 309, 317–23, 358; white population, U.S. 1800–1990, 308t; *see also* marital fertility
fertility control, 678; Canada, nineteenth century, 399; Canada, twentieth century, 548n17, 552; Caribbean, 515; within marriage: Canada, twentieth century, 564–5

fertility decline (U.S.), theories of, 323–8
fertility estimates, 682
fertility indices: British North America, 1861, 394t; Canada, 1891, 407; Canada, nineteenth century, 397; Canada and Europe, 391, 392–3, 392f
fertility measures, 2
fertility rates: adaptation of, 393, 396; age pattern of: Canada, twentieth century, 580; age-specific, 686–7; age-specific, by social class: St. Lawrence Valley, 122f; Canada, 6; Canada, 1901–1981, 574f; Canada/U.S., 571–3, 572f, 575; colonial African Americans, 5; estimated, 1891–1931, 547t; increase in: Native Americans, 31; in Mesoamerica, 248–50, 251; Mexico, 1900–1990, 601, 602, 616–17, 627; St. Lawrence Valley, 119f; of slaves: U.S. and Trinidad, 509t; total period and cohort fertility: Canada, 1936–1921, 581f; white colonial population, 144, 146
fertility statistics: Mexico, 1900–1990, 611t
fertility transition, 678, 679; Canada, 6, 7, 372; Canada, nineteenth century, 390, 402–15, 407t, 408–9t; Canada, twentieth century, 531, 545, 547, 548–9, 550–1, 552, 554, 564; U.S., 6; U.S. postbellum period, 1870–1920, 468; white population: U.S., 307; white population: U.S., 1790–1920, 320, 322, 324, 325, 326–8, 348, 358
fictive widows, 273
Filles du Roi, 107, 109, 110
financial intermediaries, 326
first births: St. Lawrence Valley, 118, 121
first industrial revolution, 631, 637, 641
fiscal policy (U.S.), 650, 659, 660
five-year death probabilities, ratio of: St. Lawrence Valley, 125f
Florescano, Enrique, 276
Florida, 17, 18, 62, 667; Cuban migrants to, 518
Fogel, Robert W., 147, 159, 160–1, 165, 166, 168–9, 170, 172, 195, 330, 441, 449
food production, Mexico, 288–9, 602–3; and population growth, 241
forced relocation: colonial Mexico, 258
foreign-born: share of population: U.S., twentieth century, 653
foreign white stock (U.S., twentieth century), 633; assimilation, integration, and economic equality, 1950 to present, 664–5; economic activity, mid-twentieth century, 643–4; fertility, 639–41; fertility, 1900–1950, 648–9; fertility and family formation, 1950 to present, 655–62; geographic distribution, 635; geographic distribution, recent, 666–8; mortality, 637–9; mortality, 1900–1950,

foreign white stock (*cont.*)
646–8; mortality, 1950-present, 654–5; 1950
to present, 649–68; occupational
distribution, 634, 636, 643–4; population
composition and distribution, 1900–1950,
642–3; population composition and
economic activity in 1990, 662–4;
stratification, assimilation, integration,
636–7; stratification, assimilation,
integration, 1900–1950, 645–6
Formosa, 11
Forster, Colin, 324
Fort Ancient, 59, 82
Fort Apache Reservation, 34
Fort Center, Florida, 60, 62, 66
Fort Francis, Ontario, 562
fractures, 67, 68, 81, 246
France, 290, 307, 328; fertility in, 118, 119, 120,
322; immigrants from, to St. Lawrence
Valley, 106–7, 108–9, 110, 111; immigration
from, to Canada, 128, 544; infant mortality,
404; marital fertility, 391, 392, 393, 409;
marriage rate, 132; migration to, from West
Indies, 491, 518; mortality, 124–5; in North
America, 99–101, 131; slave trade, 503; war(s)
with Britain, 372, 378; in West Indies, 485,
487, 488, 489, 490, 493, 501, 504
francophone Canada, 679, 680; fertility,
nineteenth century, 395, 396, 414, 415;
fertility, twentieth century, 548–50; infant
mortality, nineteenth century, 404–6; marital
fertility, nineteenth century, 413; mortality,
twentieth century, 568
Franklin, Benjamin, 144, 152, 179, 305, 379
Fredericton, New Brunswick, 419
free blacks, 5, 6; demographic behavior of, 7; in
Mexico, 266; in West Indies, 490
free blacks (U.S.), 194, 211, 219, 435–6;
antebellum period, 436–7, 441, 453–61; diets
of, 216–17; by state, 1790–1860, 454–5t
Freedmen's Bureau, 464
French Canada, 487; family size, 553; fertility,
nineteenth century, 409, 414; fertility,
twentieth century, 550, 551, 575, 576, 577, 581;
fertility transition, 402; infant mortality, 568,
569; parish registers, 682
French Canadians, 128, 417; marital fertility,
395, 396
French regime: immigrants of, 131; mortality in,
125; nuptiality in, 114, 115
French rule in Quebec, 371, 374
French-speaking population: Canada, 373, 376;
St. Lawrence Valley, 129, 129f; *see also*
francophone Canada
Frontenac (county, Canada), 398n29, 401
frontier, Canada, 413, 548

frontier, U.S., 359, 681; closing of, 347, 348; sex-
selective migration, 325
Fulton County, Illinois, 77
fungi, diseases caused by, 58
fur trade, 99–100, 103, 109, 110

G. I. Bill, 658
Galacians, 542
Galenson, David, 146
Gallina site, 68
Gálvez, José, 26
Gamio, Manuel, 603
gastrointestinal diseases, 209, 331, 334, 359, 647,
680; cause of death: white population, U.S.
1790–1920, 338; slave deaths, U.S. South, 452
Gee, Ellen, 546
Gemery, Henry A., 4, 143–90, 147–8, 166
genealogical data, 2, 103; white population,
colonial U.S., 146; white population, U.S.,
1790–1920, 309, 313, 329, 345; white
population, U.S. 1920–1970, 331
gender: slaves in westward movement: U.S.,
440; *see also* sex ratios
general fertility rate: Mexico, 1900–1990, 610
genetic homogeneity: and disease, 14–15
genetic resistance: to smallpox, 260–1
genocide: Native Americans, 22, 23, 27, 30
geographic distribution: Canada, twentieth
century, 588–91; colonial African Americans,
5; U.S. population, recent, 666–8; U.S.
population, twentieth century, 635–6
geographic location: black population: U.S.
postbellum period, 461–7; free blacks: U.S.,
antebellum period, 453–7; slaves: U.S.
antebellum period, 437–41
geographic mobility, 3
geographic patterns, 6; blacks in U.S., 433, 434
Georgia, 18, 60, 443; coast, 70, 71, 80; rice
plantations, 505; slave population, 210–12,
440
Gerhard, Peter, 255, 260
germ theory of disease, 334, 344, 471, 637, 639
German immigrants (U.S.), 314, 684
Germany, 352; age at first marriage, 319;
immigration from, to Canada, 417, 543, 586,
587; immigration from, to U.S., 354, 436;
infant mortality, 404
Gibson, Charles, 255
Gila River Reservation, 34
Gilbert, William Harlen, Jr., 31
girl/woman ratio: African American population,
colonial U.S., 201, 202
Glen Williams site, 60
Glengarry County, Ontario, 377, 401n36, 413
Glover life table, 535
Goderich, Ontario, 562

gold rush, 27, 28
Goldin, Claudia, 441
Goodman, Alan H., 71, 82
gradual emancipation (U.S.), 436, 442; laws, 440, 442–3, 458n58
Gragg, Larry Dale, 156
Grasshopper Pueblo, Arizona, 79
Great Basin, 71
Great Britain, 503; black population, 518; conquest of St. Lawrence Valley, 131; controls on slave trade in Caribbean, 501; emancipation of slaves, West Indies, 504; emigration schemes, 382–3; immigrants from, 354, 632; immigrants from, to Canada, 372, 374, 377, 378–9, 380–1t, 382–3, 385–6, 398, 417, 418, 538, 542, 543, 548, 584, 585, 586, 587, 588; immigration from, to West Indies, 491, 517; slave trade, 503; in West Indies, 485, 487, 488, 489, 490, 493, 501, 511; *see also* England
Great Depression, 7, 316, 351, 359, 530, 538, 571, 572, 625, 628, 642, 649, 657, 659, 661, 682
Great Immigration: Canada, twentieth century: urbanization in, 558–64
"great migration" (Canada), 538, 539
Great Migration, 461, 466–7
Great Plains of North America, 533
Greater Antilles, 483, 512; slaves in, 489
Greece, 353, 544
Greene, Evarts B., 145, 172
Greenland, 13, 33
Gregg, John B., 59, 62
Gregg, Pauline S., 59, 62
Grenville County, Ontario, 577
Grenville South (county, Canada), 405
Grey County, Ontario, 413, 569
"Grito," 277, 281
gross domestic producet (GDP): Mexico, 613, 614, 615, 616; U.S., 332
gross reproduction rates (GRRs): Canada, twentieth century, 575–7, 576t
Grubb, Farley, 146, 168, 169–70
Guadalajara, 264, 270, 271, 272, 291, 682; population of, 283–4
Guadeloupe, 493; birth rate, 514; population growth, 511
Guanajuato, 261, 281
Guatemala, 663
Guelph, Ontario, 412, 562
Guerrero, 283, 285
Guyana, 106, 485, 584, 588; *see also* British Guiana

Haines, Michael R., 1–8, 177–9, 305–69, 404, 405, 472, 473, 677–84
Haiti, 483, 487, 506, 519; birth rate, 515; death rate, 515; immigrants to Canada, 585, 587;

independence, 485; infant mortality, 516; migration within Caribbean, 518; out-migration, 517; population growth, 511; revolution, 493, 503
Halifax, Nova Scotia, 374, 381n3, 419, 559; population redistribution, 594; population size, nineteenth century, 418, 420, port city, 561
Halsted, William, 335
Hamilton, Ontario, 411, 419, 577; immigrant population, 540, 592; nuptiality, 551; population size, 566
Hardin site, 62
Harrington, Virginia D., 145, 172
Harris lines, 72, 81
Hartney, Patrick C., 60
Haven site, 62
Hawaiians, 11
headright records, 146, 147
health, 6; black population, 1790–1920, 474; black population: postbellum period, 469–70, 471–3; free blacks: antebellum period, 459–61; Native Americans, 3, 55; research, 669; slaves, 7; slaves: antebellum period, 448–53; twentieth century, 631; white population, 1790–1920, 337
Health and Nutrition in the Americas database, 246
health behavior, 343, 344
health care: Mexico, 8, 614, 615, 616
heart disease, 8, 647, 650, 654, 655
Heerwald site, 69
height: as data source, 2; slaves, 450, 507; *see also* stature
Heiple, Kingsburg G., 67
helminths, 75
Hendrix, Lewellyn, 470
Henripin, Jacques, 546
Henry, Louis, 161
herpes, 176
Hesquiat Harbour, British Columbia, 60
Hidalgo, Father, 277
Hidalgo del Parral, 291
Higgs, Robert, 156, 332
Hingham, Mass., 156
Hispanics in U.S., 665, 668; assimilation of, 664
Hispaniola, 483, 487; Native American population, 486; population of, 486n2
historical anthropometry, 682–3
historical demography, 2
Historical Statistics of the United States, Colonial Times to 1970, 145
Hogup cave, 73
Hollimon, Sandra E., 68–9
Hong Kong, 587, 588

Hooton, F. A., 56
Hopi Pueblo and trust lands, 34
Horn, James, 146, 172
hospitals, 334–5; registers, 103
housing, 344, 406; Mexico, 608, 627
Hrdlička, Aleš, 56, 58
Hudson Valley: slaves in, 437
Hudson's Bay Company, 416, 533
Huitzillan, 250, 271
Hull, Quebec, 576–7
human capital, 326, 348, 685; across
    generations, 327, 328
human remains: analysis of, 52, 68, 72, 76, 208,
    217–19; demographic reconstruction from,
    77–80; study of, 55–7
humans, first: in America, 241, 242
Humboldt, Alexander von, 264, 265, 278, 280
Hungarian uprising, 587
Hungary, 353, 409, 542
hunger: Mexico, 287–8
"Hungry Forties," 314
Huntingdon (county, Canada), 415
Hurd, Burton, 552
Huron County (Canada), 413
Hurons, 100
Hutchinson, Dale L., 71
Hutchinson's teeth, 61
Hutterite level, 390n14, 395
Hutterites, 581
hygiene, personal, 471, 474, 638

Iberville (county, Canada), 415
Icelandic immigrants: Canada, nineteenth
    century, 411n49, 417
Ile-de-France, 109
illegal immigrants (U.S.), 626, 627, 651, 652,
    653, 654, 659
illegitimacy: colonial Mexico, 271; St. Lawrence
    Valley, 120–1
Illinois, 60, 65, 68, 456, 464
Illinois Sanitary and Ship Canal, 335
Illinois Valley, 71, 72
illiteracy: and infant mortality: Canada,
    nineteenth century, 406; *see also* literacy
immigration/immigrants, 1, 682; to British
    North America, 385f; Caribbean, 7, 493, 511,
    512, 516, 519, 557; to colonies, 166; Mexico, 8,
    277, 601, 616, 627
immigration/immigrants, Canada, 4, 6, 7, 8,
    100, 371–2, 423f; accounting of, twentieth
    century, 535–8; and birth rate, twentieth
    century, 548; cities, twentieth century, 540,
    541t, 591–2; by country of birth and period
    of arrival, twentieth century, 543–4, 544t;
    1811–1861, 373; 1815–1861, 378–8, 380–11t;
    fertility, twentieth century, 581; foundation

period, 374–8; metropolitan areas, twentieth
    century, 592t; mass, 1907–1931, 532–45, 564;
    moved on to U.S., 381, 382, 385, 421, 430–1,
    534, 555; since 1945, 582–95, 583f; nineteenth
    century, 391, 398, 415–28; nineteenth century:
    revised series, 421–8; population change/
    growth through: twentieth century, 537–8,
    555–8, 594–5; by region of residence,
    twentieth century, 544–5, 545t; retained,
    1815–1861, 386–8; sources of, twentieth
    century, 542–5, 584–9, 585t; temporal and
    regional patterns of, twentieth century,
    537–9, 538t; twentieth century, 529, 530, 531,
    532, 534f, 537–9, 538t, 540, 542–3, 564, 580,
    584–9, 590–1, 592–5; from U.S., 372, 375–6,
    377, 378–9, 398n29, 533, 538, 543, 545, 548,
    584, 585, 587–8
immigration/immigrants, St. Lawrence Valley,
    102, 104, 105, 106–11, 107f, 108f, 128, 131;
    according to category and period of arrival,
    110t; effect on marriage market, 111–12;
    fertility, 119–20; health of, 128; importance of
    first, 128–9; mortality, 125–6
immigration/immigrants, U.S., 341, 356, 384–5,
    534; African American population, colonial
    U.S., 195–8; from Canada, 416, 420–8, 534–5,
    595, 651; to Canada, 372, 375–6, 377, 378–9,
    398n29, 533, 538, 543, 545, 584, 585, 587–8;
    composition of, 8, 354–5; differential rates of,
    436; 1820–1920, 345f; from Europe, 466;
    fertility, twentieth century, 639; impact on
    labor market, 661; 1950–1990, 651–4; 1990,
    662–4; opposition to, 355–7; population
    growth from, 143, 144, 146–8, 151, 179, 668,
    678; sources of, 346t, 636–7, 651–2;
    twentieth century, 639, 642, 659; white
    population, colonial U.S., 146; white
    population, 1790–1920, 305–7, 314, 330, 331,
    352, 358
Immigration Act (1965, U.S.), 662
Immigration Act of 1917 (U.S.), 355
Immigration and Nationality Act (U.S.), 651
immigration policy: Canada, 587, 591–2; U.S.,
    632, 651, 669
immigration restriction: Canada, 531; U.S.,
    316–17, 348, 352, 354, 355–6, 518, 535, 636–7,
    641, 642, 643, 645, 648, 649, 650, 662, 682,
    684
immunity (to disease), 14, 18; acquired, white
    population, colonial U.S., 176; Africans, 213;
    smallpox: Mexico, 259, 260
incest taboos, 200
income: and fertility: Mexico, 1900–1990, 621;
    and infant mortality: Canada, nineteenth
    century, 406; and mortality, 330; and
    mortality: Mexico, 1900–1990, 615, 620; and

mortality decline: Caribbean, twentieth century, 516
indentured labor/servitude, 192; Caribbean, 501–3; colonial U.S., 146, 149, 151, 155, 157, 169, 176; diet, 214–15; Native Americans, 29, 29t; St. Lawrence Valley, 110; seasoning mortality, 169; in West Indies, 491–2, 510, 516
independence: Mexico, 241, 275–6, 277–93, 294; West Indies, 485
India, 11, 652; indentured labor from, to Caribbean, 501–2, 503
Indian Act of Canada, 35
Indian Knoll, 77, 79
Indian language(s), 41
Indian language speakers: persistence of, in independent Mexico, 281–5, 286f; and mortality/fertility: Mexico, 1900–1990, 621–2, 622f
Indian Wars of the Northwest (Bledsoe), 28
Indians: Canada, 376; of colonial Mexico, 262, 263, 264, 265, 266, 268, 274; of independent Mexico, 284–5; Quebec, 102; St. Lawrence Valley, 111, 128; *see also* American Indians/ Amerindians; Native Americans
indigenous population, 10–11; Mexico, 620, 621–2
indios/indias, 273, 274
Indo-mestizos, 263
industrial revolutions, 631, 637; computer-based, 650, 660; U.S., twentieth century, 641
industrialization: Canada, 425, 426, 427, 538; U.S., 317, 324, 325, 350, 634, 635, 636
industry: immigrants in: Canada, twentieth century, 539, 541
infant care and feeding, 471, 568–9, 638
infant mortality, 213, 679; Canada, nineteenth century, 389, 395, 402–7, 403t; Canada, twentieth century, 531, 567, 568–9; Caribbean, twentieth century, 515–16; early Native American populations, 77–8, 79, 81, 83; Mexico, 269, 605–7, 606f; reduction in: U.S, twentieth century, 647, 648; St. Lawrence Valley, 121, 124, 125, 127, 128–9; slaves: U.S. antebellum period, 1790–1860, 448, 449, 450, 451; slaves: West Indies, 508–9; white population, colonial U.S., 160, 161; white population, U.S., 332, 333, 358; white population, U.S., 1790–1920, 310, 328, 340
infant survival: Canada, 402, 405, 546–7
infanticide, 27
infection: in Mesoamerica, 246; nonspecific evidence of, 69–70
infectious diseases: control of: U.S., 344, 359, 680; deaths due to: Mexico, 1900–1990, 607–8; deaths due to: U.S., 1790–1920, 338;

decrease in mortality due to: U.S., twentieth century, 647, 654, 655; early North American population, 81; *see also* disease; disease environment
influenza, 15, 19, 27, 647; deaths from: Canada, twentieth century, 570; epidemic of 1918, 556, 603, 641; in Mexico, 259, 293, 603
Initial Coalescent period, 68
Initial Middle Missouri period, 68–9
Integrated Public Use Micro Sample (IPUMS), 682
integration (U.S. population): 1900–1950, 645–6; 1950 to present, 664–5; twentieth century, 636–7
intergenerational wealth transfer, 324, 327
intermarriage: Native Americans and, 40–1
internal migration: African American population, colonial U.S., 210–12, 214, 221; blacks: U.S., twentieth century, 642–3, 645; Canada, twentieth century, 566, 589, 590, 591, 592–3, 594; white population, colonial U.S., 146, 149, 166–74; white population, U.S. 1790–1920, 312, 330, 345–50, 358
intestinal parasites, 55, 72–5, 83, 176; identified from North American archaeological contexts, 74–5t
Inuit (Eskimo), 9, 32, 34, 38
Ireland, 352; emigration, 416, 556; immigrants from, to Canada, 374, 385–6, 400–1, 417n54, 542, 543; immigrants from, to U.S., 314, 354, 355, 436, 684; potato famine, 384
Irene Mound site, 60, 62
Iroquois Indians, 17, 30, 33, 128
Iroquoian ossuaries, 66
Işcan, Mehmet Yaşar, 60, 62
Ishi (Indian), 28
Italy, 353, 354, 556; immigration from, to Canada, 543, 586, 587; immigration from, to U.S., 436; infant mortality, 404; marital fertility, 391

Jacobson, Paul H., 329
Jaffe, A. J., 80
Jaina, 247
Jalisco, 281, 291
Jamaica, 198, 211, 483, 488, 503, 507; immigrants to Canada, 585, 587, 588; immigrants to U.S., 663; life expectancy, 516; migration within Caribbean, 518; Native American population, 486; population growth, 511; sugar production, 493
Jamestown Mounds, 68
Jantz, Lee Meadows, 469
Japanese: immigrants to Canada, 544; immigration restrictions on: U.S., 632; in U.S., twentieth century, 633

Java, 11, 502
Jay's Treaty of 1794, 376
Jewish migrants, 353
Jim Crow laws, 466, 471
Johansson, S. Ryan, 19
Johns Hopkins, 335
Jones, Alice Hanson, 176n76
Jones, Joseph, 56
Joliette (Quebec), 562
Juárez, Fátima, 616
judicial archives (Quebec), 103

Kahnawake (Indians), 35
Kamouraska County (Canada), 406
Katzenberg, M. Anne, 59
Kent County, Ontario, 577
Kentucky, 173, 212
Keyfitz, Nathan, 420–1, 423, 424, 428, 429, 535, 536–7, 546, 555, 556
kidney and bladder stone disease, 77
King, Virginia Himmelsteib, 213
Kingston, Canada, 401
Kiple, Kenneth F., 213, 460, 472
Kitchener, 560, 577, 591
Klein, Herbert, 270
Klepp, Susan E., 213, 460
"Know Nothing" (American) party, 355
Koch, Robert, 334
Komlos, John, 331–2
Korea, 588, 652
Korean War, 649
Kroeber, Alfred L., 11, 12, 25, 52–3, 54
Kroeber, Theodora, 28
Kubler, George, 255
Kuczynski, Robert Renee, 552
Kuznets, Simon, 314, 332

La Venta, 242
labor demand: Canada, twentieth century, 538–9; composition of: U.S., twentieth century, 660–1; female labor: U.S., twentieth century, 646; and illegal immigration: U.S., 653; immigrants and: Canada, twentieth century, 542, 586, 587; immigrants and: U.S., 316, 354; industrialization: U.S., 634, 635, 636; and slavery, 211–12; U.S., twentieth century, 641, 642–3, 648, 650, 653
labor force: composition of, 325; structure of, and fertility transition: U.S., 326; in sugar production, 488–90, 493
labor force participation of women: black, 469; Canada, twentieth century, 582; Mexico, 1900–1990, 627; U.S., 324, 327, 358, 637, 655–6, 657, 656, 658–9, 660–1, 665, 679
labor market: in assimilation and integration: U.S., 665; and black migration to North:

U.S., 466–7; and fertility: white population, U.S., 1790–1920, 325–6; global, 352; and immigration: U.S., 352, 355, 356; and internal migration: U.S., 347, 348; models of migration, 350–1; national: Canada, twentieth century, 589; U.S., 1950 to present, 649–50
labor market for young men: and change in family patterns: U.S., twentieth century, 657–62
labor requirements: colonial U.S., 192–4, 197, 205
labor unions (U.S.): and immigration restriction, 355, 356
lactation, 507, 508
Lake Patzcuaro, 251
Lallo, John W., 71, 79, 82
Lambert, Patricia, 62, 71, 81
Lambston County, Ontario, 577
land: scarcity and cost of (U.S.), 358
land availability: Canada, nineteenth century, 396–7, 416; U.S., 152, 305, 434; and fertility: Canada, nineteenth century, 399, 400, 413, 415, 425, 426; and fertility: U.S., 152; hypothesis, 324, 325, 326, 327, 328, 348, 679
land-density argument, 397–8
Lantz, Herman, 470
Laprairie (county, Canada), 415
Larsen, Clark Spencer, 22, 60, 62, 70, 71, 80
Late Archaic, 62
Late Woodland, 77, 79, 82
Latin America, 683; immigrants from, to U.S., 651–2, 662, 663; population growth, 653
latitude: and health: free blacks: U.S. antebellum period, 1790–1860, 460–1; migration along, 348
LaTuque (Quebec), 562
Laurentian Valley; *see* St. Lawrence Valley
Leeds County, Ontario, 577
Légaré, Jacques, 4, 99–142, 407, 421, 428, 536, 556
Lennox (county, Canada), 398n29, 401, 412
Leon, Mexico, 266, 682
leprosy, 176
Lesser Antilles, 483, 485, 493, 518; Native American population, 486; settlement of, 488
Lethbridge, 563
Levy, Daniel S., 165
Lewis, Barbara, 62
Libben Late Woodland site, 67, 70
life changes: African American population, colonial U.S., 207, 208, 209, 214; Mexico, 286, 291
life conditions: Mesoamerica, 246–50
life cycle model, 325–6, 327
life expectancy: African American population,

colonial U.S., 197, 206, 207–8; American
mainland populations, 163–4t, 165; blacks:
U.S., twentieth century, 648; Canada,
twentieth century, 569–70; Caribbean,
twentieth century, 516; early North American
populations, 77–8, 79, 81; Mesoamerica,
247–8, 250; Mexico, colonial, 274–5, 275t;
Mexico, independent, 285–91, 285t, 291;
Mexico, 1900–1990, 607, 607t, 614; Native
Americans, 3, 15; St. Lawrence Valley, 125;
U.S., 680; tables: white population, colonial
U.S., 161–2, 165; U.S. population, twentieth
century, 638, 647, 639, 654–5; white
population, U.S., 1790–1920, 310, 330
life expectancy at birth, 1; blacks: U.S.
postbellum period, 473; early North
American populations, 79; U.S. population,
1950 to present, 654–5; white population,
colonial U.S., 161, 162, 165; white
population, U.S., 332, 333, 339, 340
life experiences: African American population,
colonial U.S., 221
life span: precontact North America, 80
life stresses of slavery, 217–18
life table reconstruction, 79
life table survival rates, 420, 421, 535–6
life tables, 332–3, 686; Canadian, 406, 547, 555,
556; *see also* model life tables
Lincoln County (Canada), 401
Lindsay, Ontario, 562
lines of increased density, 72, 82
Lister, Joseph, 335
literacy/literacy rate: black population: U.S.
postbellum period, 1870–1920, 470; and
fertility: Canada, nineteenth century, 414;
and fertility: Mexico, 1900–1990, 621, 627;
Mexico, 277, 614, 616; and mortality:
Mexico, 1900–1990, 620; U.S., 324, 325, 327,
636
Liverpool, 386
local records: U.S., 146, 309
London: cholera, 335; smallpox deaths, 260–1
London, Ontario, 419, 559; fertility, 551;
population size, 566
"Long Depression," 425
Long Island: slaves in, 437
"long" nineteenth century (1790–1920), 307–9;
immigration flows across, 354; U.S.
population increase in, 314–16; periods of, in
Canadian population history, 371–2; white
population, U.S., 357–8
López de Velasco, Juan, 256
Los Angeles, 38
Louis XIV, king of France, 100
Louisburg, fortress of, 371
Louisiana, 440, 443, 464, 492, 503; free blacks

in, 458; population size, 456; slaves in, 195
Lovejoy, C. Owen, 67
Lower, Arthur, 557–8
Lower Canada, 376, 377; armed rebellion in, 384
Lower Illinois Valley, 82
Lower Mississippi Valley, 82–3
Lower South: African American population,
194, 219, 220; exodus of slaves from, 211–12;
slave diet in, 215; slaves in, 200, 205, 211
Loyalists, 172, 211; refuge in Canada, 375, 376,
377, 398
Lumbee Indians, 31, 33
Lunenburg, 374
Lunenburg County, Nova Scotia, 577

McCaa, Robert, 5, 241–304
McClary, Andrew, 73
McCusker, John J., 145, 177, 222
McCutchan-McLaughlin site, 65
McDougall, Duncan, 421, 429, 535, 536–7, 555
McFalls, Joseph, 470
McGuire, Robert, 440
McInnis, Marvin, 6, 7–8, 371–432, 529–99
McKeown, Thomas, 334
McNeill, William, 19
macroeconomic policy, 665
Madeira, 502
Madero, Francisco, 290
Madura, 11
major urban Canada, 559, 560, 561
malaria, 14, 27, 207, 109, 213, 452; in Mexico,
614; white population, colonial U.S., 165,
169, 176
male bias: African American population,
colonial U.S., 218–19
male-female ratio: St. Lawrence Valley, 112, 114,
115, 117; *see also* sex ratios
malnutrition, 66; African Americans, 213, 214,
217, 218; blacks: U.S., twentieth century, 639;
in Mesoamerica, 246, 247; Native Americans,
22; slaves, 449
Malthus, Thomas, 144, 149, 276, 305, 434
Malthusian threat, 54, 251, 273, 295, 411
Malthusianists, 276
Manitoba, 411, 417; added to Canada, 533; cities
and towns, 563; Native American population,
38; population decline, 590
manumissions, 194, 440, 460, 507
manuscript schedules of population, 2, 3
Maori, 11
Marfil, 266
Marion County, Indiana, 77
marital fertility: Canada, nineteenth century,
389, 390, 391–3, 394–6, 397, 398–9, 401–2,
409–12, 413, 414, 415; Canada, twentieth
century, 545, 546, 547, 548–50, 551, 552

marital status: white population, U.S., 1790–1920, 319
Maritime colonies (Canada), 378; confederation with Canada, 416–17; immigrants arriving at, 377, 379–81; urbanization, 419
Maritime provinces (Canada): fertility, 577
Maritime region (Canada), 374; fertility, 411
Maroons, 375, 507
Márquez Morfín, Lourdes, 260
marriage, 21; African American population, colonial U.S., 199–200; age of: Canada, twentieth century, 578–9, 580; Canada, twentieth century, 564–5, 566; contracts (Quebec), 103; control of, 678; controlling fertility within: Canada, twentieth century, 565–6; delaying/forgoing, 292, 294–5, 392, 552, 648, 649; factors affecting, 222; fertility within: white population, U.S. 1790–1920, 320, 321, 326, 358; independent Mexico, 292–3; slave, 198, 199–200, 441, 445–6, 509; U.S., twentieth century, 656, 660, 661, 665
marriage market: Mexico, 271–2, 293, 295; St. Lawrence Valley, 109, 111–17, 131–2
marriage opportunities: free blacks: U.S. antebellum period, 1790–1860, 458; for women: U.S., twentieth century, 660–1
marriage rate: French Canada, 105; St. Lawrence Valley, 131, 132
marriageways: Mexico, 271, 291–3, 294
Martin, Debra L., 62, 68, 70, 71, 72, 78
Martinique, 493, 511, 514
Maryland, 168n48, 464; free blacks in, 456; life expectancy, 310; out-migration, 173; slave population, 201, 205, 217, 440; white population, colonial U.S., 152, 155–6, 158, 164–5, 169
Masnick, George, 470
Massachusetts, 374; census of 1885, 320; mortality information, 328, 329, 330, 340; out-migration, 173; vital registration, 311, 441; white population, colonial U.S., 156, 158–60
Massachusetts Bay colony, 416n53
Massachusetts-Maryland life table for 1850, 329
maternal mortality: St. Lawrence Valley, 121, 127; slaves: U.S. antebellum period, 1790–1860, 448
Matlazahuatl, 261–2
mean age at death: Mesoamerican precontact populations, 249t
measles, 14, 19, 27, 176, 451; in Mexico, 259, 289, 290, 614
measurement, 685–92; indirect, 147; white population, colonial U.S., 144–8
medicine: and decline in death rate: Canada, twentieth century, 570; in epidemiologic transition, U.S., 333, 334–5, 337, 344, 359;

and mortality: U.S., 647, 655, 669, 678, 680
Mediterranean Europe: immigration from, to Canada, twentieth century, 584, 585, 586–7
Meeker, Edward, 470, 473
Meister, Cary W., 22
men: immigrants, St. Lawrence Valley, 109–10
Menard, Russell R., 145, 165, 169, 177, 222
Mendizábal, Miguel Othón de, 255
Mendoza, Daniel, 59
Mennonites, 411n49, 417, 581
Mensforth, Robert P., 70
Merbs, Charles F., 14, 62, 63, 64, 67, 79, 83
mercantilism, 488
Merriam, C. Hart, 25
Mesoamerica, 5, 12, 15; ancient, 241–52; demographic transformation in, 294; political cataclysms, 295; subregions of, 255
mestizaje, 284
mestizos: colonial Mexico, 265, 273
Métis, 31, 33, 35
metropolitan Canada, 558–60
Mexican Institute for Social Security, 614
Mexican revolution, 283, 603, 608, 613, 616
Mexico, 2, 5, 8, 15, 485, 488, 492; ancient, 243f; demographic indicators, 604t; demographic transformation, 1900–1990, 601–30; demographic transition, 677, 678–9, 680–1, 682; immigration to U.S., 651–2, 653, 659, 663, 681; international migration, 586, 625–7; mortality and fertility by region, 618t; peopling of, 241–304; population, 1790–1920, 280f; population estimates, 1790–1910, 279t; regional differences in mortality and fertility, 617–22; regional migration and urbanization, 622–5; Secretaría de Salubridad y Asistencia, 615; states and territories of, 282f
Mexico City, 8, 257, 262, 268, 273, 281, 291, 682, 684; Euromestizo elite of, 250; migrants in, 283, 623; population growth, 287, 287f, 290, 601–2, 623, 627–8; smallpox epidemic in, 289; urbanization and growth of, 624t
Mexico City region, 617, 618, 620, 621
miasma anticontagionist theories, 334
Michigan, 35, 464
Michoacán, 265, 266
Middle Archaic period, 82
Middle Atlantic: benign mortality conditions, 305; emancipation in, 194; population of, 667; urban inhabitants, 347; vital registration, 311; white population, colonial U.S.: fertility, 156–7, 158; white population, 1790–1920, 317, 323
middle colonies (U.S.), African American population, colonial U.S., 193, 194, 219; crude birth rates: white population, 155, 156; migration: white population, 173; mortality:

white population, 159, 165; seasoning mortality: white population, 169–70; white population, 149, 151, 166–7, 170, 177, 179
Middle East, 260
Middle Effigy Mound phase, 60
Middle Mississippian, 79, 82
Middle Missouri sites, 68
Middle Passage, 195, 490
Midwest (U.S.), 294, 345, 667; black population in, 464; free blacks in, 453, 456; immigrants in, 348, 350; mortality, 341; population growth, 349; urban inhabitants, 347; white population, 1790–1920, 320, 322–3, 324
Mier y Terán, Marta, 606–7, 609–10
migrants, 168n49; dying in passage or seasoning, 148, 166
migration, 6, 681; African American population, colonial U.S., 4–5, 210–12, 221; blacks: U.S. postbellum period, 1870–1920, 464–7; in Caribbean, 516–18; and delayed marriage: colonial Mexico, 273; future of, 683; international, 530–1; Mexico, 281–5, 622, 625–7; Native Americans, 3, 9; push and pull factors in, 351–2; into/out of Quebec, 374; Mexicans to U.S., 625–7, 628; paleopopulations, 251; patterns: and regional population growth rates and shares (U.S.), 349–50; regional: Mexico, 1900–1990, 622–5; selectivity of, 351; series, 147, 148; slave, U.S., 437; statistics (U.S.), 311–12; streams, 348; swings in U.S., 352–3; from West Indies, 503; white population, colonial U.S., 166–74, 171t; white population, U.S. 1790–1920, 314–16, 344–5, 356–7, 358, 359; *see also* emigration; immigration/immigrants; internal migration
Milanich, Jerald T., 17
military immigrants: St. Lawrence Valley, 107–8, 110, 111
milk, pasteurization of, 337, 569
Miller, Robert J., 76
Miller-Shavitz, Patricia, 60, 62
Milner, George R., 60, 62, 68
Milwaukee, 334–5
Mineau, Geraldine P., 326
Minneapolis-St. Paul, 38
minimalists, 252–3, 256, 267
"Mission Indians," 26–7
mission system, 26–7, 30
Mississippi, 440, 464
Mississippi Valley, 18, 30, 66, 101
Mississippian Acculturated Late Woodland, 79
Mississippian period, 59, 71, 79, 81, 82
Mississquoi (county, Canada), 414–15
Missouri Valley, 18

Mixteca Alta, 292
Mixtón War, 258
Mobile (Alabama), 461
mobility, geographic and occupational (U.S.), 357
model life tables, 3, 22, 248, 274, 421, 428, 259, 471, 473, 536
moderates, 252, 256, 257
modern epoch (Mexico), 241
Mohawks, 376
Moncton, 577
monetary policy (U.S.), 650, 659
Monterey, California, 26
Monterrey, Mexico, 283, 680
Montreal, 104, 131, 562; as commercial center, 377; dominant metropolis, 418, 420, 560–1; fertility, 414, 577; immigrants in, 539, 589, 592; infant mortality, 405, 568; marital fertility, 395–6, 550; Native American population, 38; population size, 418, 419, 559, 560, 594
Montreal Island, 577
Moodie, R. L., 56, 63
Mooney, James, 12, 13, 25, 31, 52–3, 54
Moose Jaw, 563
morbidity: in pre-European-contact North America, 55, 69–70, 71, 72, 76–7, 80, 81, 83
Morelos, 271, 283
Morgan, Philip David, 220–1
Mormon Historical Demography Project, 322, 326, 327, 330
Mormons, 581
Morse, Dan, 62
mortality, 1; accounting for changes in: Mexico, 1900–1990, 613–17; African American population, colonial U.S., 5, 195, 197, 206–9, 217; and aging of population, 323; analysis of, 683; blacks in American cities, 440; Canada, 372; Canada, nineteenth century, 388, 389, 407; Canada, twentieth century, 531–2, 556, 564, 567–71; Caribbean, 492, 519; control of, U.S., 333; in demographic transition, 680; early North American populations, 54, 77, 78, 79, 80, 83; estimates, 682; free blacks: U.S. antebellum period, 1790–1860, 460–1; gap: white population, colonial U.S., 160–1; geographic patterns and: U.S., 433; increased postepidemic, 21, 26; in Mesoamerica, 248, 251; Mexico, independent, 286–91; Native Americans, 22, 23; North American, 1800–1991, 695–8t; in passage/on arrival in destination, 148, 166; post-1492, 51; regional differences: Mexico, 1900–1990, 617–22, 618t, 618f; in revolution in Mexico, 293; St. Lawrence Valley, 122–8, 130, 131, 132; slaves: West Indies, 505, 507, 508–9, 510; in

mortality (*cont.*)
transatlantic slave trade, 490; U.S.
antebellum period, 1790–1860, 459; U.S.
population, 1900–1950, 646–8; U.S.
population, 1950 to present, 654–5; U.S.
population, twentieth century, 8, 637–9, 640,
651; white population, colonial U.S., 146, 151,
158–65, 166, 170, 180; white population,
U.S., 1790–1920, 307, 310, 328–37; white
population, U.S. 1800–1990, 308t, 316,
358–9; whites in Caribbean, 492; *see also*
childhood mortality; infant mortality
mortality differentials: social classes: St.
Lawrence Valley, 125–6; by socioeconomic
status: U.S., twentieth century, 647; white
population, U.S. 1790–1920, 339–44, 359
mortality rates: black population, U.S., 434;
blacks: U.S. postbellum period, 1870–1920,
468, 471, 472–3; Canada, 6; and family
formation, 222; French Canada, 106; Mexico,
5, 8, 601, 602, 605–7, 608, 613, 614–15, 616,
627; Native Americans, 31; and population
decline, 22; slaves: U.S. antebellum period,
1790–1860, 448–9, 451, 452–3, *see also* death
rate
mortality revolutions, 653, 655; second, 654
mortality transition, 677–8, 680–1, 683; white
population, U.S., 1790–1920, 328, 333, 337,
343, 344
Mosher, Clelia, 321
Motolinía, Fray Toribio de Benavente, 258
Moundville, Alabama, 60, 62, 66
Mountain states (U.S.), 342, 345, 359, 667
mulberry molars, 61
Muskoka County (Canada), 413
Mycobacterium tuberculosis, 57, 59

Na-Dine, 9
nadir, 54; Native American population, 13–14,
21, 23; population of Central Mexican Basin,
244; population of colonial Mexico, 257, 262
Nahua (Aztec), 248, 250–1; civilization, 251
Nahuatl language, 248, 251, 258, 274
Nanaimo, British Columbia, 563
Nantucket, Massachusetts, 155
Napoleon III, 277
Napoleonic Wars, 383
Nash, Gary, 460
Natchez Indians, 30
National Center for Health Statistics, 450, 654
National Labor Union, 355
National Statistical Institute (INEGI, Mexico),
279–80
Native American societies/cultures: change in,
22, 23; differences in, and differential impact
of disease, 21, 30; and population decline, 24

Native Americans, 1, 3, 631; care for smallpox
victims, 261; and disease, 14–15, 52;
indentured, 29, 29t; issues in twenty-first
century, 40–1; new groups of, 31, 41;
population history of, 9–50; population size,
12–14; redistribution and urbanization, 35–9;
survival, adaptation, and population
recovery, 30–40; at time of European
contact, 10f; U.S., twentieth century, 633; in
West Indies, 483, 485, 486–7; *see also*
American Indians/Amerindians
native white stock (U.S., twentieth century),
633; assimilation, integration, and economic
equality, 1950 to present, 664–5; economic
activity, mid-twentieth century, 643–4;
fertility, 639–41; fertility, 1900–1950, 648–9;
fertility and family formation, 1950 to
present, 655–62; geographic distribution, 635;
geographic distribution, recent, 666–8;
homogeneity, 643; mortality, 637–9;
mortality, 1900–1950, 646–8; mortality, 1950
to present, 654–5; 1950 to present, 649–68;
occupational distribution, 634, 636, 643–4;
population composition and distribution,
1900–1950, 642–3; population composition
and economic activity in 1990, 662–4;
stratification, assimilation, integration,
636–7; stratification, assimilation,
integration, 1900–1950, 645–6
nativism, 355, 558
nativity: fertility differentials by: white
population, U.S., 1790–1920, 320–1;
mortality differences: white population, U.S.,
1790–1920, 339, 340–1, 344
natural decrease: West Indies, 493, 501, 505
natural fertility: colonial Mexico, 271; St.
Lawrence Valley, 119, 122, 131
natural fertility populations, 250
natural increase, 505, 678; African Americans:
colonial U.S., 193, 197, 198, 201; black
population: U.S., 1790–1920, 433–4, 436,
464; Canada, 100, 104, 106, 371, 372;
Canada, 1761–1811, 374; Canada, 1815–1861,
378–88; Canada, mid-nineteenth century,
388–402; Canada, nineteenth century,
415–16, 420, 425; Canada, twentieth century,
557, 558, 566; in Caribbean, 493, 511–12; and
implicit crude birth and death rates: white
population, colonial U.S., 167t; Mexico, 627;
population growth from: colonial U.S., 143,
144, 149, 151, 177–9, 180; slave population,
West Indies, 501; and urban population
growth: white population, U.S., 1790–1920,
347, 349; white migrants to West Indies, 491;
white population, colonial U.S., 166–8, 170;
white population: U.S., 1790–1920, 316, 358

natural resource frontier (Canada), 562, 591
natural selection, 260
Navajo Indians, 33
Navajo Nation, 35
Navajo Reservation and trust lands, 34
naval office records, 195, 196
Navarro y Noriega, Francisco, 264, 265, 278
Nayarit, 281, 285
Nazca culture, 59
Needleman, Lionel, 578
Nelson, British Columbia, 563
net migrant flow, 147
net migration: Canada, twentieth century, 535,
536; Mexico, 1900–1990, 611
net nutrition (concept), 449, 450
net reproduction rate (NRR), 468n76
Netherlands, 352, 416; immigration from, to
Canada, 544, 586, 487, 591; migration to,
from West Indies, 518; population size, 530;
in West Indies, 485, 487–8, 489, 493
Netherlands Antilles, 485
Netherlands Indies, 11
Nevada Great Basin, 66
never-married: St. Lawrence Valley, 113; white
population, U.S., 1790–1920, 317–19
New Brunswick, 374, 375, 381n3, 589;
immigrants, 377–8; joined Canada, 416;
marital fertility, 411; urbanization, 419
New England, 101, 106, 131, 132, 324, 667;
benign mortality conditions, 305; blacks in,
193–4, 219, 464; crude birth rates: white
population, colonial U.S., 155, 156, 157, 158;
immigrants from, to Canada, 374, 375; life
expectancy, 329; local records, in, 146;
mortality, 159, 161, 162, 165, 341; population
growth, 349; slave marriages, 199n17; slaves
in, 437, 443; urban inhabitants, 347; vital
registration, 311; white population, colonial
U.S., 149, 151, 159, 161, 162, 165, 166–7, 170,
172, 173, 177, 179; white population
1790–1920, 317, 323
New France, 99, 107, 416n53, 677; British
conquest of, 101; distribution of families,
120f; family size, 156
New Glasgow, Nova Scotia, 420
"new" immigration: Canada, 532, 542–4; U.S.,
354, 355, 356, 418n58, 636–7, 643
New Jersey, 155, 156, 310
New Mexico, 35, 60, 281, 342
"new" new immigration, 651, 653
New Orleans, 461; blacks in, 217; death rates,
330; free blacks in, 458; sewage system, 335;
vital registration, 311
New South, slaves in, 440
New Spain, 261, 283; bastardy rates, 273;
censuses, 264; epidemics, 268; life expectancy

in, 274–5; marriage and remarriage in, 274;
regulating fertility and reproduction in, 271;
vaccination in, 289
New Westminster, 559–60
New World, 221, 483, 487; black population of,
198; British leadership in populating, 149;
disease in, 5, 14; indentured laborers in,
491–2; slaves in, 489, 490, 510; white
migration to, 492, 510
New York City, 211; black population, 201, 464;
Caribbean migrants in, 503, 518; death rates,
330; free blacks in, 457; Native American
population, 38; pasteurized milk in, 337;
population size, 349; slaves in, 437; vital
registration, 311; water purification, 335
New York State, 18, 60, 172; age structure of
white population, 155, 155t; black population
in, 464; in-migration, 173; mortality, 340,
341; Native American population, 35;
population growth, 349; white population:
U.S., 1790–1920, 317–19
Newburyport, Massachusetts, 357
Newfoundland, 371, 416–17, 544; added to
Canada, 529, 589
Niagara, 430
Niagara (county, Canada), 398n29
Niagara frontier, 375
Nicolet County, 577
Nipissing County (Canada), 413
nonvenereal syphilis (bejel), 60, 61
nonwhites (U.S., twentieth century), 633;
assimilation, integration, and economic
equality, 1950 to present, 664–5; economic
activity, mid-twentieth century, 643–4;
fertility, 639–41; fertility, 1900–1950, 648–9;
fertility and family formation, 1950 to
present, 655–62; geographic distribution,
635–6; geographic distribution, recent,
666–8; mortality, 637–9; mortality,
1900–1950, 646–8; mortality, 1950 to present,
654–5; 1950 to present, 649–68; occupational
distribution, 634–5, 636; population
composition and distribution, 1900–1950,
642–3; population composition and
economic activity in 1990, 662–4;
stratification, assimilation, integration,
636–7; stratification, assimilation,
integration, 1900–1950, 645–6
Norfolk, 412
Norfolk county, Ontario, 577
Normandy, 109
Norsemen, 9
North (U.S.): black population in, 464, 643;
free blacks in, 456–7, 459–60; life
expectancy, white population, 1790–1920,
310; population size, 349; slavery in, 437–40,

North (U.S.) (*cont.*)
442–3; white population, colonial U.S., 160–1

North America, 485, 488; aboriginal population size, 12–14; demographic transition, 677–82; estimated population, 1650–1990, 693–4t; fertility and mortality, 1800–1991, 695–8t; historical demography research issues and questions, 682–4; infant mortality, 516; migration from Carribbean to, 519

North American Free Trade Agreement (NAFTA), 683

North American Indians: estimates of aboriginal population, 13t

North American populations, early: patterns of disease in, 51–97

North Border region (Mexico), 617, 618, 620, 621

North Carolina, 464; blacks in, 204, 205; Native American population, 35

North region (Mexico), 617, 618, 620–1

North Wellington County (Canada), 413

Northampton, Massachusetts, 155

Northeast (U.S.): cities of, 667; immigrants in, 348, 350; population growth, 349; urban-industrial center, 347; white population, 1790–1920, 320, 322, 325

Northern California Indians, 23

Northern Mexico, 72

Northern Plains, 68

northern/western Europe: immigrants to U.S. from, 354, 359, 642, 662

Northwest Coast, 66

Northwest Territories, 407

Norway: emigration, 416, 556

Notestein, Frank, 324

Nova Scotia, 371, 544; blacks in, 211; fertility, 577; immigrants to, 377; joined Canada, 416; Loyalists in, 375; marital fertility, 411; settlement of, 374; urbanization, 419, 420

Nubia, Egypt, 79

Nuevo León, 283

nuptiality: African American population, colonial U.S., 199–206; black population: U.S. postbellum period, 1870–1920, 468; Canada, nineteenth century, 389, 390, 391, 392, 393, 396, 399, 401, 402, 410–11, 413, 414; Canada, twentieth century, 548, 551–2; St. Lawrence Valley, 109, 111–17, 128; summary of, 116t; white population, colonial U.S., 151–8; white population: U.S., 1790–1920, 317–23

nutrition, 175, 176: African Americans, 213, 217, 218; and disease, 15, 176; and fertility, 508; inadequate: Native Americans, 15, 27; and mortality decline, 334, 516; slaves, 450, 507;

and stature, 213, 214, 331; white population, U.S., 1790–1920, 331, 332

Nuvakwewtaqa (Chavez Pass), Arizona, 76

Oak Creek Pueblo, Arizona, 65, 79

Oaxaca, 245, 270, 272, 281, 283, 285, 287, 291, 292

occupational distribution: blacks in U.S., twentieth century, 664; immigrants to U.S., twentieth century, 652, 663; race-ethnicity groups by sex: U.S., 1990, 664t; U.S. population, twentieth century, 634, 634t, 635, 636, 642, 643–4, 644t, 645; U.S. population, twentieth century: females and males, 638t, 665

occupational selectivity of immigration policy: Canada, twentieth century, 591–2

occupational structure: and fertility, 470

occupations: immigrants: Canada, twentieth century, 541–2, 542t

Oceania, 255, 651

Ocozocuautla, 268

Ohio, 456, 464

Ohio River Valley, 66, 70, 71, 72, 82

Oklahoma: Native American population, 35, 39

Oklahoma City, 38

Old South, slaves in, 440

Oñate, Juan de, 26

Ontario, 6, 60, 375, 533, 681; cities and towns, 561, 562–3; data from, 389; fertilty, 391, 393–5, 396–8, 400, 401, 402, 551, 577; fertility transition, 407–14, 408–9t; immigrant population, 539, 540, 545; infant mortality, 403–5, 406, 568, 569; marital fertility, 549; Native American population, 38; nuptiality, 551; population redistribution, 590–1; Toronto commercial hub of, 418; urbanization, 419

Oregon, 437

Ortiz de Montellano, B. R., 247–8

osteoarthritis, 246

osteochondritis, 61

osteomas, 77

osteomyelitis, 57

osteophytosis, 246

osteoporosis, 67

Ottawa, Ontario, 401, 411, 419, 560, 577

Ottawa Valley, 550

out-migration: from Caribbean/West Indies, 7, 492, 511, 512, 516–17, 519; Mexico to U.S., 1900–1990, 602; white population, colonial U.S., 172; *see also* migration

out-of-wedlock births: U.S., twentieth century, 656, 657, 661

own-children methods, 2

Owsley, Douglas W., 68–9, 78

Pacific coast region (Canada): fertility, nineteenth century, 415
Pacific states, 345, 359, 667
Pakistanis: in Canada, 586
Palatine Bridge site, 62
Palenque, 242
paleodemography: Mesoamerica, 246–50
Paleo-Indians, 9
paleopathology, 55–7, 58–9, 62, 247
paleopopulations, 251
Palkovich, Ann M., 59
Panama, 503, 516
Panama Canal, 503, 561
pandemics, 17, 259
panics of 1837, 1857, 1873, 352
Papago Reservation, 34
parasitic diseases/parasitism, 15, 66, 338, 359, 680; deaths due to: Mexico, 1900–1990, 608; in Mesoamerica, 246
Paris, 109
parish records/registers, 2, 146; Quebec, 103; U.S., 309, 311, 313
passage mortality: white population, colonial U.S., 166, 168–9, 179
Passamaquoddy Bay, 375
Pasteur, Louis, 334
pasteurization, 337
Patzcuaro, 245
Peace of Paris, 371
Peel County, Ontario, 577
pellagra, 15, 469
peninsulares, 273
Pennsylvania, 149, 168; black population in, 211, 464; out-migration, 173; population growth, 349; slaves in, 437, 443
Perche, 109
periodontal disease, 65, 217, 218
periostitis/periosteal lesions, 61, 69–70, 81, 82, 83
Perquimans County, North Carolina, 165
Perth County (Canada), 413
Peru, 60, 488
Perzigian, Anthony J., 59, 70, 82
Pezzia, Alejandro, 59
Pfeiffer, Susan, 60, 66
Philadelphia, 165, 170, 459, 461; blacks in, 200–1, 202, 211, 213, 217, 464; cause of deaths in, 338; death rates, 330; differential mortality in, 208, 209; free blacks in, 457; mortality decline in, 336; population size, 349; vital registration, 311
Philadelphia Social History Project, 460
Philippines, 11, 260, 652; immigration from, to Canada, 588, 592
Phillips, U. B., 445
Phoenix, 38

Picton, Ontario, 562
Pictou, Nova Scotia, 377
Pine Ridge Reservation and trust lands, 34
Piñeyro, Salvadro, 277–8
pinta, 60, 61, 63
pioneers (St. Lawrence Valley), 129; contribution to genetic endowment of French-speaking population of Quebec, 129f; distribution of, 129, 130f
Plains Crow Creek site, 62
Plains Indians, 22–3
Plains Village site, 68–9
Plains population: mortality among, 78, 81
plantation colonies, 196, 197
plantation records, 6, 199, 201, 436, 449, 450–1, 506, 507
plantation size: demographic characteristics by, 444–5, 444t; and slave fertility: U.S. antebellum period, 1790–1860, 444–5, 446–7
Plymouth colony: life expectancy, 162
pneumonia, 14, 27, 359, 451, 461, 647, 680; deaths from: Canada, twentieth century, 570
Poitou region, 109
Poland, 586
political change (U.S.), 631, 632
Pooler site, 62
Pope, Clayne L., 330, 452
population by race, residence, nativity, age, sex: U.S., Canada, Mexico, 701–3t
population change, 1; Canada, 1820–1861, 387t; Canada, 1901–1931: accounting for, 555–8; Canada, nineteenth century: accounting for, 420–31, 422t; dynamics: Canada, 1815–1861, 378–88; colonial Mexico, 266–8
population composition (U.S.): eve of World War I, 632–3; 1900–1950, 642–3; in 1990, 662–4; twentieth century, 631–75
population decline: epidemic disease as cause of, 257; epidemic disease myth and: Native Americans, 19–23; Mexico, origins to revolution, 244, 252; Native Americans, 12, 15–30, 54
population density: African American population, colonial U.S., 5, 199, 200, 201, 222; and child/woman ratios, 324; colonial Mexico, 257; and disease, 14, 71; early North American populations, 80, 81, 82, 83; Mesoamerica, 242–4; Mexico, 1790–1910, 278–80, 279t; and mortality: U.S., twentieth century, 638, 639; St. Lawrence Valley, 132
population distribution: African Americans, colonial U.S., 192–4; Canada, twentieth century, 588–91; colonial U.S., 149; U.S., 1900–1950, 642–3

population estimates: for 1492, 51–5; Native Americans, 22t, 23–4; prior to European contact, 53t

population growth, 1; African Americans, colonial U.S., 192–4; black population, U.S., 1790–1920, 434–6, 435t; Caribbean, 504–5, 511–14, 515; components of, 699–700t; before 1492, 51; in demographic transition, 677, 678–9; immigrants in, 537–8, 557–8, 584, 652–3, 682; Mexico, 1900–1990, 601, 602–13, 627; Mexico, origins to revolution, 241, 244, 245, 250, 251, 265, 266, 268, 276, 277–80; Native Americans, 3; and political catastrophe, 295; St. Lawrence Valley, 111, 131–2

population growth, Canada, 100; 1761–1811, 373; 1815–1861, 378, 379; 1901–1931, 556t; French Canada, 104, 106; immigration in, 377; nineteenth century, 415–28; twentieth century, 529–30, 532, 533, 557, 558, 590; twentieth century: composition of, 594–5; twentieth century: fertility in, 580; twentieth century: immigration's contribution to, 537–8, 557–8, 584

population growth, U.S., 6; colonial United States, 143, 144; components of, 1790–1990, 315t; free blacks: antebellum period, 1790–1860, 459–60; twentieth century, 631–75; twentieth century: immigration in, 652–3; white population, colonial U.S., 149–51, 177–80, 178t; white population, 1790–1920, 305–7, 312, 313–17, 344, 345, 349, 358, 359

population history, 221, 222; Canada, 371–3; Caribbean, 483–528; U.S., 631–2

population patterns: Caribbean, nineteenth century, 501–3

population proxies, 144–5

population recovery: aboriginals, 11; Mexico, 244, 260–2, 265, 266, 294; Native Americans, 11, 30–40, 32t; Native Americans in California, 39–40, 39t

population redistribution, 1, 7; Native Americans, 35–9; prairie provinces, 590

population size: Canada, twentieth century, 530; Caribbean, 493; Central Mexican Basin, 244–6; Mexico, 1900–1990, 605; Native Americans, 4, 21–2, 22t; North America, 51; number of migrants and, 504–5; U.S., 309; white population, colonial U.S., 144–5

porotic hyperostosis, 65–6, 82, 83, 246

Portage la Prairie, Manitoba, 563

Portolá, Gaspar de, 26, 27

Portugal, 487

Portuguese: immigration to Canada, 586, 587

postbellum period (U.S.), 1870–1920: African American population, 461–73

Postell, William, 448

potato famine, 314, 352, 384

Potter, J., 156, 167, 168n49

Pott's disease, 57, 59

poverty, 260, 342

Powell, Mary Lucas, 60, 62, 63, 66

Powers, Stephen, 24–5

Prairie "island" (Canada): port cities, 561

Prairie provinces, 550; economic refugees from, 566; fertility, 577; immigration to, 538, 539, 540, 544–5; population redistribution, 590; population size, 533–4; urbanization, 420

pre-Columbian America, 304

Prem, Hans, 259

premarital conceptions: St. Lawrence Valley, 120–1, 122

prenatal condition: slaves: U.S. antebellum period, 1790–1860, 450–1

Prescott (district, Canada), 413

Prescott, Ontario, 562

Preston, Samuel, 404, 405, 472, 473

Prince Edward County, Ontario, 398n29, 401, 569; fertility, 411, 412

Prince Edward Island, 374, 375, 381n3, 416–17; immigrants, 377; infant mortality, 405; marital fertility, 411, 550; nuptiality, 551–2; urbanization, 419

Princeton European Fertility Project, 389–90, 391, 402

Princeton Model West life tables, 161–2

probate inventories/records; 6, 196, 199, 201, 207, 309, 313, 437, 443, 507

Providence, 461

pseudopathology, 57

public health, 471, 474; and epidemiologic transition in U.S., 333, 334, 335–7; Mexico, 289–90; and mortality, 330, 343, 344, 678; and mortality decline: Caribbean, twentieth century, 516; movement: U.S., twentieth century, 637–8, 641, 646–7; and population growth: Mexico, 241; U.S., 336–7, 340, 680; and white population, U.S., 1790–1920, 332, 358, 359

public policy: and fertility: Caribbean, 515; U.S., 632, 669–70

Puebla, 262, 272, 283, 285, 682

Pueblo Indians, 33, 72–3

Puerto Rico, 483, 487, 503, 504; birth rate, 514; Native American population, 486, 487; out-migration, 517, 681; public health measures, 516; slave imports, 510; transfered to U.S., 485

pulque, 260, 289

Pure Food and Drug Act (U.S.), 337

Quakers, 156–7, 165
quarantine, 260, 261, 336–7, 338, 638
Quauhchichinollan, 250, 271
Quebec, 4, 6, 128, 544, 681; computerized
    population register, 103–4; county rates of
    marital fertility, 401–2; early settlers in,
    104–6; fertility, nineteenth century, 391,
    393–6, 402; fertility, twentieth century, 576,
    577, 581; fertility transition, 407–9, 408–9t,
    411, 414–15; immigrants arriving at, 379–82,
    385, 386, 429–30, 539; infant mortality,
    nineteenth century, 403–4, 405–6; infant
    mortality, twentieth century, 568, 569;
    Loyalists in, 375; marital fertility, nineteenth
    century, 395–6; marital fertility, twentieth
    century, 550; parish records, 2; population
    growth, 374; population redistribution, 589,
    590; population size, 374; premarital
    conceptions and illegitimate births, 120–1; as
    seaport, 377; settlement at, 99; smaller urban
    places in, 562, 566; sources in, 101–4, 389;
    territorial organization of, 100–1; transition
    from French to British rule, 371, 373;
    urbanization, 418, 419, 420, 562
Quebec City, 104, 130, 131, 562, 594; censuses
    for, 102; fertility, 414; immigrant population,
    592; infant mortality, 405; marital fertility,
    550; population size, 418, 419, 559, 560;
    principal Atlantic port, 560–1
Quebecers, 129, 590, 594
Querétaro, 281
Quilodrán, Julieta, 616

Rabell, Cecilia, 266, 269, 606–7
rabies therapy, 334
race: in colonial Mexico, 262–8; and health,
    472; mortality differentials: white
    population, U.S, 1790–1920, 339, 342–3,
    344
race-ethnicity distribution: U.S. population,
    1970 and 1990, 663t
race-nativity distribution: U.S. population,
    1900 and 1950, 633t
railroads, 666; Mexico, 602, 622–3, 625
Raisbeck Mounds, 60
Ramenofsky, Ann F., 17–18
Ransom, Roger L., 326
rate of natural increase (RNI), 685–6; white
    population, U.S., 1790–1920, 314
rate of net migration (RNM), 686; white
    colonial population, 144; white population,
    U.S., 1790–1920, 314
rate of total increase (RTI), 685–6; white
    colonial population, 144
Red River colony (Canada), 533
Reff, Daniel, 259

refugees, 651, 652
Regina, 38, 563, 577
regional change: independent Mexico, 281–5
regional differences: birth rates: white
    population, U.S., 1790–1920, 322–3, 325; in
    mortality and fertility: Mexico, 1900–1990,
    617–22, 618t, 618f, 620f; mortality
    differentials: white population, U.S.,
    1790–1920, 339, 341–2, 343; population
    growth: white population, U.S., 1790–1920,
    317, 320
regional distribution of population: Canada,
    twentieth century, 533, 588–91
regional growth (U.S.): migration patterns and,
    347, 349–50
regional migration: Mexico, 1900–1990, 622–5
regional population distribution, 684
registers: birth, marriage, burial, baptisms:
    Quebec, 102, 103, 127; Mexico, 254, 266,
    269, 271, 286, 291–2
registration statistics (Canada), 404
Registre de la Population du Québec Ancien
    (RPQA), 102, 103
Reichs, Kathleen J., 62
Reinhard, Karl J., 66, 72–5, 83
religion: and fertility: Canada, 400–1, 553; and
    slavery, 437n5
religious orders, 113, 117
remarriage: in colonial Mexico, 270, 273–4; St.
    Lawrence Valley, 114–16, 115f, 117, 121
removals/relocations: Native Americans, 3
Renfrew County, Ontario, 577
repatriation ratio, 353
reproduction: African Americans, 197, 198; of
    blacks in North America, 222; and
    demographic system: St. Lawrence Valley,
    128–30; factors affecting, 222; limiting, 631;
    in Mesoamerica, 251; white population,
    colonial U.S., 166
Republic of Mexico, 241
research on population change, 2–3; issues and
    questions for, 682–4
reservations, 3, 28, 31, 34, 35, 36–7f
residential units, size of slave, 199–200, 201,
    202, 222
respiratory diseases/infections, 176, 334;
    affecting blacks: U.S., 440, 460, 461; cause
    of death: white population, U.S., 1790–1920,
    338; susceptibility: African American
    population, colonial U.S., 206, 208, 209
return migration: indentured laborers, 502–3;
    from Canada, 534, 584, 594–5; Mexicans
    from U.S., 625–6, 628; from U.S., 344, 353;
    from West Indies, 492
revolution (Mexico), 280–1, 293–4
rice, 505

Index

Richelieu River, 377
Rimouski County (Canada), 406
Rivière-du-Loup County, 577
Roman Catholic population (Canada), 373,
    376, 389n12, 401, 413n50
Rose, Jerome C., 71, 82–3, 469
Rosebud Reservation and trust lands, 34
Rosenblat, Angel, 252, 256–7, 262
Rossiter, W. S., 143
Rossland, British Columbia, 563
Rothschild, Bruce M., 76
Round Valley Indian Reservation, 31
Royal African Company, 195
Ruggles, Steven, 682
Rumanians, 542
rural districts: Canada, twentieth century, 550,
    563, 569
rural to urban movement, 8, 347, 348, 359, 558,
    681
rural/urban differentials: fertility: Canada,
    nineteenth century, 396, 401–2, 410, 411, 412,
    413, 414, 415; fertility: U.S., twentieth
    century, 640; fertility: white population,
    U.S., 1790–1920, 322, 326; infant mortality:
    Canada, nineteenth century, 404–6;
    mortality: U.S., 680; mortality: white
    population, U.S., 1790–1920, 339–40, 342,
    343, 344
rural/urban population distribution: Canada:
    twentieth century, 589; immigrants, 539–40,
    541; U.S. population, twentieth century,
    635–6, 635t, 643
Russell, Manitoba, 563
Russell County (Canada), 399, 413
Russia, 353, 354
Russians: immigration to Canada, 411n49, 542
Ruthenians, 542
Rutman, Anita H., 213
Rutman, Darrett B., 213

Sahagún, Bernardino de, 259
St. Bartholomew, 485
Saint Catharines, Ontario, 419, 560, 577, 594
St. Clair River, 377
Saint Domingue, 492, 493, 503
St. Hyancinthe County, 577
St. Jean (county, Canada), 415
St. Jerome (Quebec), 562
Saint John, New Brunswick, 381, 419, 420, 559,
    561
Saint John River, 375
St. Lawrence River, 99, 100, 104, 131, 375, 376,
    395, 418
St. Lawrence Valley: European presence in,
    104–6; high fertility regime, 117–22;
    immigration to, 106–11, 107f, 108f;

population of, 1608–1760, 99–142
St. Vincent, 487
Salem, Massachusetts, 162, 310
Sametz, Zenon, 536
San Carlos Reservation, 34
San Diego de Alcala, 26
San Francisco Solano, 26
San José de Parral, 268
San Luis de la Paz, 266, 271, 273, 275
San Luis Potosí, 242, 281, 283, 285
Sanders, William T., 244, 255
sanitation, 80, 332, 358, 680
Santa Barbara Channel Islands, 81
Santa Clara, California, 27
Santo Domingo, 487, 488, 510
São Tomé, 488–9
Sarnia, Ontario, 562, 577
Saskatchewan, 563; marital fertility, 550;
    population decline, 590; Native American
    population, 38
Saskatoon, 563, 577
Saul, Frank, 246
scalping, 67–8
Scandinavia, 352; immigration from, to
    Canada, 418n58, 543, 544, 586; immigration
    from, to U.S., 436
scarlet fever, 14, 27, 289, 334, 338
Schapiro, Morton, 157
Schermer, S. J., 62
schooling; *see* education
Schultz site, 73
scientific methodology, 637–8
Scotland, 384; highlands, 384; immigrants from,
    to Canada, 385–6, 401
Scottish Highlanders: in Canada, 377, 401n36,
    413n50
seasonality: conception and birth: African
    American women, 205–6; conception
    according to birth order: St. Lawrence Valley,
    118f; deaths: St. Lawrence Valley, 127f; first
    marriages, 112f; infant mortality among
    slaves: U.S. antebellum period, 1790–1860,
    450–1; marriages: St. Lawrence Valley, 112,
    117, 118
seasoning: to disease environment, 160
seasoning mortality: slaves, 206–7; West Indies,
    508; white population, colonial U.S., 147,
    151, 164, 166, 167, 168–70, 176, 180
second industrial revolution, 641, 666, 667
sedentism, 80, 81, 82, 247
Serbs, 542
Serra, Fray Junípero, 26
settlement growth rates: Canada, twentieth
    century, 539–40; colonial U.S., 149–51, 177,
    179
settlement patterns: colonial Mexico, 254; in

demographic transition, 681–2; and disease, 18, 71; and fertility: Canada, nineteenth century, 397–9
Seven Years' War, 108
sewage disposal, 332, 335–6, 358, 638, 680
sex: mortality differences: white population, U.S., 1790–1920, 339
sex ratios: African American population, colonial U.S., 197, 199, 200, 201–2, 204, 210, 222; and fertility: free blacks, 459; indentured workers, 491–2; St. Lawrence Valley, 112, 121; slaves, 196; slaves to West Indies, 490; unbalanced, 508; U.S. population, twentieth century, 641; white population: colonial U.S., 146, 151, 152, 155, 156, 157–8; white population: U.S., 1790–1920, 325, 351
sexual dimorphism, 82, 83
Shadomy, H. Jean, 58
Shawinigan (Quebec), 562
Shenandoah Valley, 210
Sherbrooke (county, Canada), 415
Sherman Antitrust Act (U.S.), 356
ship passenger lists/manifests, 146, 147, 344
shocks, 19–20, 30
single, those remaining: St. Lawrence Valley, 113, 116–17
single-parent female-headed households, 273, 656, 657, 661–2, 665
Sioux Indians, 33
Six Nations of the Grand River, 35
skeletal age, 52
skeletal biology, 55; analysis of: Mesoamerica, 246–7; demographic reconstruction from, 77–80; evidence of disease, 67, 68, 69–70, 72, 76, 80; treponemal disease, 61–2
skeletal tuberculosis, 57–8, 59–60
slave imports: Caribbean/West Indies, 489t, 490–92; U.S., 1790–1920, 434
slave labor: colonial U.S., 192–4
slave marriages, 198, 199–200, 441, 445–6, 509
slave population: U.S.: fertility, 320; U.S.: by state, 1790–1860, 438–9; West Indies, 506
slave raids, 15, 27
slave trade, 191, 195, 211–12, 214, 220, 441; Caribbean, 488–90, 491, 501; data set, 196; ending of, 501, 510; epidemiology and, 213; legal attitudes toward, 503–4
slaveowners, 199, 208, 212, 218–19, 448; Loyalist, 211; and slave diet, 216, 452; and slave fertility, 443, 446, 447n31, 458; and slave marriage, 198, 200
slavery, 191, 209; abolition of, 433, 434, 501; Caribbean, 492–501, 510, 519; ending of, in West Indies, 504; legal attitudes toward, 503–4; in Mexico, 266; Midwest and, 456; of Native Americans, 29; in population growth:

Caribbean, 504–5, 516; resistance or accommodation to, 221
slaves, 5, 192, 219; breeding of, 447n31, 458; demographic behavior of, 6–7; demographic situation of, U.S., antebellum period, 436, 437–53; male, 197; runaway, 211, 507; in South, 194; West Indies, 506–10; women, 197
Slavic Europe: immigration from, to Canada, 542, 543, 544
smallpox, 176, 338, 359, 680; age-specific case-fatality rates of, in unvaccinated populations, 20t; epidemics, 19–20, 106, 125, 127; Mexico, 258–9, 260, 262, 286–7, 289–90, 614; mortality, 260–1; Native Americans, 14, 18, 27; vaccination, 260, 261, 289, 290, 334, 336, 614; victims, care for, 261
Smith, A. E., 146, 168
Smith, Billy G., 165
Smith, Daniel Blake, 161
Smith, Daniel Scott, 156, 459
Smith, Marvin T., 17
Snow, Dean, 17
Snow, John, 335
social classes: and mortality: St. Lawrence Valley, 125–6
social organization, 21, 31
social revolution: U.S., twentieth century, 637–9
social security: Mexico, 1901–1990, 614
social transformation: in colonial Mexico, 262–8
socioeconomic and cultural structural adjustment hypothesis, 326–7
socioeconomic conditions/factors, 683–4; black population: U.S., 1790–1920, 474; in black fertility: U.S. postbellum period, 1870–1920, 470; colonial demographic experience, 174–6; in epidemiologic transition: U.S., 333, 334; and fertility: Mexico, 1900–1990, 610, 613t, 616–17, 621; Mexico, 1900–1990, 614; and mortality, 460, 461; and mortality: Mexico, 1900–1990, 618–20, 619t
socioeconomic status: fertility: white population, U.S., 1790–1920, 323; mortality differences by: U.S., twentieth century, 647; mortality differentials: white population, U.S., 1790–1920, 339, 341, 342–3
Sokoloff, K. L., 173–4
Sonoma, California, 26
Sonota Complex, 78
Souden, David, 146
sources: African American immigration, 195–6, 199; African Americans, 192; Canadian population: nineteenth century, 389–91; migration, 1790–1920, 344–5; population estimates, 51–5; population of Mexico,

sources (*cont.*)
  origins to revolution, 254; Quebec, 101–4; reliability of: Canadian immigration, 386; slaves: U.S., 436–7, 441; West Indian slave demographic patterns, 506, 507; white population, colonial U.S., 143–8, 151, 155–6, 157; white population, U.S., 1790–1920, 309–13
South (U.S.), 345; African American population, colonial U.S., 194; black-white crude death rate ratio, 461; blacks in, 433, 643, 668; free blacks in, 456–7; immigrants in, 350; mortality: white population, 1790–1920, 310; population shift to, 667; slaves in, 437, 443; urban inhabitants, 347, 348; westward movement in, 437, 440; white population, colonial U.S., 159–61, 162–3, 165, 167–8, 169, 170, 176, 177, 179; white population, 1790–1920, 317, 320, 322–3; white population growth, 149; white population migration, 173
South America, 15, 483, 485, 492, 511
South Asia: immigration from, to Canada, 585, 586
South Atlantic: white population, U.S., 1790–1920, 325, 341
South Carolina, 492; black population, 194, 464; blacks/slaves, 201, 202, 203–4, 205–6, 210–12, 213, 221; demographic transition in, 198; rice plantations, 505
South Central (U.S.): white population, U.S., 1790–1920, 325
South Dakota, 66
South Hastings (county, Canada), 401
South region (Mexico), 617–18, 620, 621
south-to-north migration, 348, 359
South Wellington, 412
Southeast, 30; blacks in: postbellum period, 1870–1920, 464; epidemics in, 17–18; evidence of disease in, 62–3, 66; temporal trends, 80–1
Southern California Indians, 23, 24–30
southern and eastern Europe: immigrants from, 354, 355, 359, 639, 662, 684
southern colonies (U.S.): white population, 149, 151, 157–8
Southern Sinagua, 65; population, 79
Southwest, 30; black population in, postbellum period, 1870–1920, 464; disease in, 62, 65, 66, 68, 70, 72, 83; epidemics in, 17, 18; free blacks in, 453, 456, 458; mortality, 78–9; tuberculosis in, 59
Soviet Union: immigration to Canada, 586
Spain: immigration from, to Cuba, 491, 510; in New World, 492; slave trade, 503–4; in West Indies, 485, 487, 488, 493, 504, 510

Spanish America, 585; slave trade to, 489; vaccination campaign in, 260
Spanish-American War, 485
Spanish Caribbean: slaves in, 489–90
Spanish conquest/colonization: Mexico, 5, 252–8, 294
Spanish Louisiana, 212
spondyloarthropathy, 76
spondylolysis, 67
spouses, age gap between: colonial Mexico, 273; St. Lawrence Valley, 113–14, 117
stable population theory, 19–20
Stafford County, Virginia, 206–7
standard of living: and fertility: U.S., twentieth century, 657–62; Mexico, 1900–1990, 603; and mortality decline: U.S., 334; and mortality decline: white population, U.S., 1790–1920, 338, 340, 344; white population, U.S., 1790–1920, 332
Stanstead County (Canada), 377, 414–15
staple crops, 197; and slave fertility: U.S. antebelllum period, 1790–1860, 447; and slavery: U.S., 437–40
"staples" framework, 383–4
Starna, William A., 62
starvation: in colonial Mexico, 276; among Native Americans, 22, 28, 30
states (U.S.): vital registration, 311
statistical series: immigrants to Canada, 379–82, 385
Statistics Canada, 547, 578
stature: African Americans, 213–14, 217, 218; black women, 469; early North American populations, 81, 82; in Mesoamerica, 247; white population: colonial U.S., 175–6; white population: U.S., 1790–1920, 331, 337
Steckel, Richard H., 1–8, 326, 433–81, 677–84
Steinbock, R. Ted, 60–1, 77
sterility, 251; black women, 469–70; St. Lawrence Valley, 119, 120, 121
Stettler, H. L., 156
Stewart, T. D., 55, 61–2
Stiles, Ezra, 144
Stodder, Ann L. W., 62, 68
Storey, Rebecca, 250
Stormont County, Ontario, 577
Stratford, Ontario, 562
Strathroy, Ontario, 562
stratification: U.S. population, 1900–1950, 645–6; U.S population, twentieth century, 636–7
stress, 70, 71; in Mesoamerica, 246–50; work-related, 218
stroke, 647, 650, 654, 655
Sturgeon Falls, Ontario, 562
subsistence: and disease, 71; early North

American population, 80–1
suburbanization/suburbs, 348, 359, 684; U.S., 349, 651, 666, 667
Sudbury, Ontario, 559n27, 563, 576
Suez Crisis, 587
sugar economy, 488–9, 492–501, 504, 505, 510, 516
sugar islands: black/white ratios, 489
sulfa drugs, 641, 647, 654
Sullivan, Norman C., 60
Sun Belt, 348, 359, 667, 681
Sundown site, 65
Sundstrom, William A., 325–6
superfecundity thesis, 144
surgery, 335, 532
Surinam, 485, 489, 502, 503, 507; independence, 485, 518; out-migration, 518
surname analysis, 147
survival: Native Americans, 30–40
surviving-child method, 405
Sutch, Richard, 215, 326, 447n31
Sutherland, Stella H., 145, 169, 172
Swanton, John R., 52–3
Sweden, 416; infant mortality, 404; population size, 530; in West Indies, 485, 488, 504
Switzerland, 416
synthetic total fertility rate, 443–5
syphilis, 27, 30, 60–2, 63, 289, 469; evidence for, 56; in Mesoamerica, 246

Tabasco, 281
Tacuba, 271
Tadman, Michael, 441
Taeuber, Conrad, 329
Taeuber, Irene B., 329
Taiwan, 587, 588
Tamaulipas, 283
Tarascan-speaking peoples, 259
Tasmania, 11
tax records, 4, 313, 506; colonial Mexico, 254, 257
Taylor, Mark G., 79
Tchefuncte burial, 62
technological revolutions, 631
Tehuacán, 245
Tehuacán Valley, 242, 244
Temiscouata County (Canada), 406
temporal trends, 72, 80–3
Tennessee, 60, 173, 464; slaves in, 212
Tenochtitlan, 254, 258
Teopisca, 268
Teotihuacán, 242, 245, 247, 250, 251, 274–5
Teotihuacán Valley, 245–6
Tepperman, Lorne, 400
tetanus antitoxin, 334, 336
Texas, 30, 277, 280, 281, 294, 464, 466, 667;

Native American population, 35, 79
Thernstrom, Stephen, 357
Thetford Mines (Quebec), 562
third industrial revolution, 660
Third World, 8, 71; immigration from, to Canada, twentieth century, 584, 585, 587, 588–9, 591–2
Thomas, R., 156, 167
Thompson, Warren S., 329, 354
Thornton, Russell, 3, 9–50
Thunder Bay, 561
Time on the Cross (Fogel and Engerman), 449
Timmins, Ontario, 562
Timucuan-speaking population, 17
Tlapacoya, 242
Tlatilco, 247
Tlaxcala, 258
tobacco, 210, 488, 505
Tobago, 511
Tolnay, Stewart, 469, 470–1
Tolowa Indians, 30–1
tooth decay, 217, 218
Toronto, 410, 411, 420; dominant metropolis, 560, 561; fertility, 401, 549, 577; immigrants in, 540, 588, 589, 591, 592, 593; infant mortality, 405; Native American population, 38; nuptiality, 551; population size, 418, 419, 566; suburban structure, 559, 560
total fertility rate (TFR), 686–7; Canada, twentieth century, 572–3, 574, 576, 577, 578, 580; Mexico, 1900–1990, 610; women's educational level and: Mexico, 1900–1990, 617
Tracey, W. R., 552
trade routes, 16f
trans-Atlantic passage: improvement of transportation technology, 353
trans-Atlantic slave trade, 195, 196, 197, 490; to Cuba, 501; end of, 504; to Spanish America, 489
transportation costs: Mexico, 622–3
transportation revolution, 330
transportation technology, 348, 353, 355
trauma, 57, 66–9; evidence for, 63; in pre-Columbian times, 56, 82, 83
Treatise on the Cultivation of Maize in Mexico, A (de la Rosa), 288
Treaty of Versailles, 101
Treponema pallidum, 61
treponemal disease/infections, 15, 55, 60–3; early North American populations, 83; Mesoamerica, 246
tribal affiliation/enrollment (Native Americans), 33–5, 41
Trinidad, 493, 503, 516; immigrants to Canada, 585, 587, 588; indentured labor, 502; Native

Trinidad (*cont.*)
    American population, 487; population
    growth, 511
triumphalists, 265
Trois-Rivières, 99, 104, 396, 550
Truro, Nova Scotia, 420
trust lands, 34
tuberculosis, 15, 27, 57–60, 63, 461, 680; cause
    of death: white population, U.S. 1790–1920,
    338; deaths from: Canada, twentieth century,
    568, 570; early North American populations,
    82, 83; Mesoamerica, 246; U.S., 176, 334, 359,
    647
Tucker, G. S. L., 324
Tula, 242
Tulsa, 38
Turner, Frederick Jackson, 348
Tuscarora, 30
two-child norm, 321
typhoid, 14, 336, 359, 647, 680; epidemic, 106,
    127
typhus, 19, 27; Mesoamerica, 247; Mexico, 259,
    261–2, 286–7, 614

Ubelaker, Douglas H., 3–4, 14, 23, 24, 51–97,
    79
Ukrainians: immigration to Canada, 417, 542
U.N. Far East model, 473
United Keetoowah Band of Cherokee Indians,
    35
United Kingdom, 425
United States, 8, 485; aboriginal population, 13;
    African American population, 1790–1920,
    433–81; baby boom/baby bust, 571–2, 577–8;
    border with Canada, 426; Canadian
    emigration to, 416, 420–8, 534–5, 595; cities,
    560, 561; crude birth rate: white population,
    547; death rate, twentieth century, 568;
    demographic center of, 345; as demographic
    laboratory, 307; demographic transition,
    677–82; European settlement in, 416n53; eve
    of World War I, 632–41; fertility, nineteenth
    century, 391; fertility rate, twentieth century,
    571–3, 575; future population, 668–70;
    immigrants from, to Canada, nineteenth
    century, 372, 375–6, 377, 378–9, 398n29;
    immigrants from, to Canada, twentieth
    century, 533, 538, 543, 545, 548, 584, 585,
    587–8; immigrants to Canada: moved on to,
    381, 382, 385, 421, 430–1; immigration, 384–5,
    534; immigration from West Indies to, 503,
    516, 517, 518; immigration restrictions,
    316–17, 348, 352, 354, 355–6, 518, 531, 535,
    636–7, 641, 642, 643, 645, 648, 649, 650,
    662, 682, 684; infant mortality, 569; invasion
    of Mexico, 290; Mexicans in, 280–1, 294,

602, 603, 625–7, 628; Native American
    population, 31–3; new problems in, 683–4;
    population, 1800–1990, 306t; population,
    1900–1950, 641–9; population, 1950 to
    present, 649–68; population growth,
    nineteenth century, 428; population growth
    and composition, twentieth century, 631–75;
    slave population of, 490, 505, 507, 508, 509;
    tariffs, 427; urban population, 561; white
    population of, colonial U.S., 143–90; white
    population of, 1790–1920, 305–69
U.S. Bureau of Indian Affairs, 33, 38
U.S. Caucasian, 79
U.S. Census Bureau, 280, 348, 459, 471, 627
U.S. House of Representatives, 310
U.S. Immigration Commission, 354
University of Montreal, 4, 103
Upham, Steadman, 18
Upper California, 281
Upper Canada, 376, 377, 384
Upper South: blacks in, 194, 200, 211, 219, 441
urban fertility: Canada, nineteenth century,
    395–6
urban growth: Mesoamerica, 251
urban mortality: U.S., twentieth century, 638–9
urban population: Canada, twentieth century,
    561–4; immigrants: Canada, twentieth
    century, 539–40, 541; Mexico, 1900–1990,
    623–5, 628; U.S., 347; white population,
    U.S., 1790–1920, 317
urban/rural differences; *see* rural/urban
    differentials
urban sanitation, 336, 337
urban structure: Canada, 420, 562–4
urbanization, 684; blacks: U.S. postbellum
    period, 1870–1920, 464–6, 470; Canada,
    1901–1931, 558–64; Canada, nineteenth
    century, 418–20; Canada, twentieth century,
    540, 586, 591, 594; effect of economic growth
    on life expectancy due to, 639; and fertility:
    Canada, 396–7, 398, 400, 412–13, 414, 550;
    free blacks: antebellum period, 1790–1860,
    457; and growth of Mexico City, 624t;
    Mexico, 8, 281–5, 601–2, 622–5, 628, 681;
    and mortality, 330, 331; Native Americans, 3,
    35–9, 38t, 40, 41; slaves and: U.S. antebellum
    period, 1790–1860, 441; U.S., 324, 325, 326,
    347, 349, 358, 359, 679; U.S., twentieth
    century, 648, 666, 667; white population,
    U.S., 1790–1920, 307, 330–1
Uselding, Paul, 342
Utah, 326, 327

vaccination, 261, 334, 336; Mexico, 8, 289, 290,
    608
vaccination campaigns: Mexico, 614, 615, 627;

Spanish possessions, 260

Valladolid, 266

Valley of Mexico, 244, 255

Valsequillo, 242

Van Blerkom, Linda Miller, 55

Vancouver, British Columbia, 410, 419, 420, 563; fertility, 549; immigrant population, 540, 588, 592, 593–4; infant mortality, 405; marital fertility, 411; Native American population, 38; population size, 566; as port, 561; suburban structure, 560

Vasconcelos, José, 284

venereal diseases: Native Americans, 14, 30; and sterility, 469–70; syphilis, 60–1

Veracruz, 281

verruga, 55

Victoria, British Columbia, 520, 540, 561, 577

Victoria County, Nova Scotia, 577

Vietnam, 588, 652

Vietnam War, 649, 666

Villaflor, G. C., 173–4

Villaseñor y Sánchez, José Antonio, 263–4

Vinovskis, Maris A., 158–9, 162, 325, 330, 340

violence: deaths from: Canada, twentieth century, 570–1; deaths from: Mexico, 1900–1990, 608; early North American populations, 81, 82; evidence of, 67–9

Virgin Islands, 485

virgin soil epidemics, 15, 18; Mexico, 258, 260, 290–1

Virginia, 168n48, 374, 443, 464; life expectancy, 310; out-migration, 173; piedmont: slaves in, 201–2, 210; population, 143; slave population, 202, 205, 206–7, 212, 440

Virginia colony, 416n53

vital data: deficiencies in collection of (U.S.), 313

vital rates: African American population, colonial U.S., 195; millennial model of, 294; U.S., 309–10; white population, colonial U.S, 145–6

vital registration system: Canada, 389; U.S., 6, 311, 459, 461

vital statistics: Canada, 545–46, 547, 567; Caribbean, 511; Mexico, 603

Vizcaino, Sebastian, 26

Wade, Richard, 441

Wahl, Jenny Bourne, 326

Wales, 79; child mortality, 342; infant mortality, 404; life tables for, 421, 535; mortality, 333, 334

Walker, Phillip L., 62, 67, 71, 81

Walker River Paiute, 33

Walsh, Lorena S., 4–5, 165, 191–240

War of 1812, 375, 378

warfare, 1, 68, 69; demographic costs of: Mexico, 258, 290; early North American populations, 22, 28, 80; and life expectancies: Native Americans, 15

Warren, Christian, 440, 460–1

Washington: Native American population, 35

water filtration/purification (U.S.), 334, 335–6, 337, 338, 358, 638

water supplies: and infant mortality: Canada, twentieth century, 568, 569; Mexico, 1900–1990, 608, 627; U.S., 332, 680

Waterloo, 591

wealth: and childbearing: U.S. antebellum period, 1790–1860, 448

wealthholding patterns: colonial U.S., 176n76

weaning, 250

Weaver, David S., 63

Weber, Adna Ferrin, 339

Wells, Robert V., 161–2, 165

West (U.S.): black population, 1790–1920, 474; black population: postbellum period, 1870–1920, 464; black population, twentieth century, 642–3; free blacks in, 456, 457; population shift to, 667; white population, 1790–1920, 322

West Africa, 211, 213, 214, 490

West Indies, 7, 168, 194, 198, 204, 211, 483–6, 489, 503–4; crops grown in, 505; ethnic composition of, 519; immigration from, to U.S., 436, 633; immigration to Canada, 592; morbidity/mortality, 213; population concentration in, 511–12; settlement of, 487–8; slave demographic patterns, 506–10; slave imports, 490–2; slave mortality, 206

West South Central region (U.S.), 635

West Virginia, 342

western Canada, 591; fertility, twentieth century, 577; infant mortality, 405; settlement of, 7, 533, 590; urban places, 562, 563

Western Europe: infant mortality, 516; migration from Caribbean to, 519

Western Hemisphere: Native American populations, 10, 11; slaves transported to, 195

Western Jalisco, 258

western settlement: Canada, 416–17, 425, 428, 538–9, 548

westward migration/movement (U.S.), 1, 437, 634, 681; free blacks in, 453–6; nineteenth century, 425, 667; selectivity, 440–41; 1790–1920, 317; in South, 440

wet nursing, 121, 122, 125–6, 405n43

wetbacks, 652

Weyburn, 563

Wheat Boom (Canada), 538

wheat staple, 383–4

Whelpton, P. K., 329, 354

white population of U.S., 5–6, 391, 433–4, 662; child/woman ratio: antebellum period, 1790–1860, 447–8; colonial U.S., 4, 143–90; foreign-born, 316; infant mortality, 404; in mainland British colonies and early Republic, 150t; 1790–1920, 305–69; 1790–1920, by region, 318t; *see also* native white stock (U.S.)

whites: and disease environment in West Indians, 509–10; migrating to West Indies, 490–2; movement of, from Caribbean to Louisiana, 503

Whitmore, Thomas, 255, 257

whooping cough, 14, 176, 451

Widmer, Lee, 59

widows/widowhood: Canada, nineteenth century, 390; Mexico, 270, 273–4, 295; St. Lawrence Valley, 114–16, 117, 121

Wigglesworth, Edward, 144

Wilcox, Walter F., 166

Willey, P., 68

Williams, H. U., 56

Williams, John A., 59, 68, 73

wills (U.S.), 309, 313

Wilson, Woodrow, 355

Windsor, 591

Winnipeg, 38, 411, 419, 560, 563, 591; fertility, 577; population size, 566; as port city, 561

women: economic equality for: U.S., twentieth century, 637, 665; employment: Canada, twentieth century, 551, 552; employment opportunities: Canada, nineteenth century, 410; immigrants: St. Lawrence Valley, 107, 109, 110; job opportunities: U.S., twentieth century, 648–9; labor force participation: Canada, twentieth century, 582; new role of, 1; status of, U.S., twentieth century, 651

women married: U.S., twentieth century, 640; Canada, nineteenth century, 413

women's jobs, 656, 659, 665

women's work: U.S., twentieth century, 637, 645–6

Wood, Peter, 213

Woodland period, 68

Woodland population, 59, 62, 81, 82

work: and fertility, 508; and slave health, 213, 218, 219, 449, 451–2, 507, 509

work-related stress: African American population, colonial U.S., 218

World War I, 348, 353, 466, 529, 641; deaths n, 556; and immigration to Canada, 531, 534, 535, 538, 543; U.S. on eve of, 632–41

World War II, 530, 564, 565, 641, 649, 669; Canada in, 565–6; and fertility: Canada, 573, 575; labor shortages, 663; and living standards: U.S., 657–8, 659; Mexican migration to U.S. in, 626; women workers in, 646

Xavier de Balmis, Francisco, 260

xenophobia, 684

Yahi Yana Indians, 28

Yarmouth, Nova Scotia, 420

Yasuba, Yasukichi, 157, 324, 325

yaws, 60, 61, 246

yellow fever, 14, 165, 176

York County, Ontario, 399, 577

Yucatán, 281, 283, 285

Yugoslavia, 587

Yuki Indians, 30–1

Zacatecas, 281

Zambardino, Rudolph, 256

Zapata, Emiliano, 283

Zavala de Cosío, Maria, 616

Zelnik, Melvin, 329

Zuni Pueblo, 34